The Routledge Handbook of Corpus Linguistics

The Routledge Handbook of Corpus Linguistics 2e provides an updated overview of a dynamic and rapidly growing area with a widely applied methodology. Over a decade on from the first edition of the *Handbook*, this collection of 47 chapters from experts in key areas offers a comprehensive introduction to both the development and use of corpora as well as their ever-evolving applications to other areas, such as digital humanities, sociolinguistics, stylistics, translation studies, materials design, language teaching and teacher development, media discourse, discourse analysis, forensic linguistics, second language acquisition and testing.

The new edition updates all core chapters and includes new chapters on corpus linguistics and statistics, digital humanities, translation, phonetics and phonology, second language acquisition, social media and theoretical perspectives. Chapters provide annotated further reading lists and step-by-step guides as well as detailed overviews across a wide range of themes. The *Handbook* also includes a wealth of case studies that draw on some of the many new corpora and corpus tools that have emerged in the last decade.

Organised across four themes, moving from the basic start-up topics such as corpus building and design to analysis, application and reflection, this second edition remains a crucial point of reference for advanced undergraduates, postgraduates and scholars in applied linguistics.

Anne O'Keeffe is senior lecturer at MIC, University of Limerick, Ireland. Her publications include the titles *From Corpus to Classroom* (2007), *English Grammar Today* (2011), *Introducing Pragmatics in Use* (2nd edition 2020) and, as co-editor, *The Routledge Handbook of Corpus Linguistics* (1st edition 2010). With Geraldine Mark, she was co-Principal Investigator of the English Grammar Profile. She is co-editor, with Michael J. McCarthy, of two book series: *The Routledge Corpus Linguistics Guides* and *The Routledge Applied Corpus Linguistics.*

Michael J. McCarthy is emeritus professor of applied linguistics, University of Nottingham. He is (co)author/(co)editor of 57 books, including *Touchstone, Viewpoint, The Cambridge Grammar of English, English Grammar Today, From Corpus to Classroom, Innovations and Challenge in Grammar* and titles in the *English Vocabulary in Use* series. He is author/co-author of 120 academic papers. He was co-founder of the CANCODE and CANBEC spoken English corpora projects. His recent research has focused on spoken grammar. He has taught in the UK, Europe and Asia and has been involved in language teaching and applied linguistics for 56 years.

Routledge Handbooks in Applied Linguistics

Routledge Handbooks in Applied Linguistics provide comprehensive overviews of the key topics in applied linguistics. All entries for the handbooks are specially commissioned and written by leading scholars in the field. Clear, accessible and carefully edited *Routledge Handbooks in Applied Linguistics* are the ideal resource for both advanced undergraduates and postgraduate students.

The Routledge Handbook of Corpus Approaches to Discourse Analysis
Edited by Eric Friginal and Jack A. Hardy

The Routledge Handbook of World Englishes
Second Edition
Edited by Andy Kirkpatrick

The Routledge Handbook of Language, Gender and Sexuality
Edited by Jo Angouri and Judith Baxter

The Routledge Handbook of Plurilingual Language Education
Edited by Enrica Piccardo, Aline Germain-Rutherford and Geoff Lawrence

The Routledge Handbook of the Psychology of Language Learning and Teaching
Edited by Tammy Gregersen and Sarah Mercer

The Routledge Handbook of Language Testing
Second Edition
Edited by Glenn Fulcher and Luke Harding

The Routledge Handbook of Corpus Linguistics
Second Edition
Edited by Anne O'Keeffe and Michael J. McCarthy

For a full list of titles in this series, please visit www.routledge.com/series/RHAL

The Routledge Handbook of Corpus Linguistics

Second edition

Edited by Anne O'Keeffe and Michael J. McCarthy

LONDON AND NEW YORK

Cover image credit: © Getty Images

Second edition published 2022
by Routledge
2 Park Square, Milton Park, Abingdon, Oxon, OX14 4RN

and by Routledge
605 Third Avenue, New York, NY 10158

Routledge is an imprint of the Taylor & Francis Group, an informa business

First edition published by Routledge 2010

British Library Cataloguing-in-Publication Data
A catalogue record for this book is available from the British Library

Library of Congress Cataloging-in-Publication Data
Names: O'Keeffe, Anne, editor. | McCarthy, Michael, 1947-editor.
Title: The Routledge handbook of corpus linguistics / edited by Anne O'Keeffe, Michael J. McCarthy.
Other titles: Handbook of corpus linguistics
Description: Second edition. | Abingdon, Oxon ; New York, NY : Routledge, 2021. | Series: Routledge handbooks in applied linguistics | Includes bibliographical references and index.
Identifiers: LCCN 2021030156 | ISBN 9780367076382 (hardback) | ISBN 9781032145921 (paperback) | ISBN 9780367076399 (ebook)
Subjects: LCSH: Corpora (Linguistics)--Handbooks, manuals, etc. | Discourse analysis--Handbooks, manuals, etc.
Classification: LCC P128.C68 R68 2021 | DDC 410.1/88--dc23
LC record available at https://lccn.loc.gov/2021030156

ISBN: 978-0-367-07638-2 (hbk)
ISBN: 978-1-032-14592-1 (pbk)
ISBN: 978-0-367-07639-9 (ebk)

DOI: 10.4324/9780367076399

Typeset in Times New Roman
by MPS Limited, Dehradun

For Ron Carter, whose insight, humour and friendship we will forever miss.

Contents

PART III
Corpora, language pedagogy and language acquisition 297

Illustrations

Figures

Tables

Contributors

Svenja Adolphs is a professor of English language and linguistics at the University of Nottingham, UK. Her research interests are in multimodal spoken corpus linguistics, corpus-based pragmatics and discourse analysis. Along with Dawn Knight, Adolphs recently edited *The Routledge Handbook of English Language and Digital Humanities* (2020).

Carolina P. Amador-Moreno is a professor of English linguistics at the University of Bergen. Her research interests centre on the English spoken in Ireland and include stylistics, discourse analysis, corpus linguistics, sociolinguistics and pragmatics. She is the author, among others, of *Orality in Written Texts: Using Historical Corpora to Investigate Irish English (1700–1900),* Routledge (2019); *An Introduction to Irish English,* Equinox (2010); the co-edited volumes *Irish Identities: Sociolinguistic Perspectives,* Mouton de Gruyter (2020); *Voice and Discourse in the Irish Context,* Palgrave-Macmillan (2017); *Pragmatic Markers in Irish English* (2015), John Benjamins; and *Fictionalising Orality,* a special issue of the journal *Sociolinguistic Studies* (2011).

Laurence Anthony is a professor of applied linguistics at the Faculty of Science and Engineering, Waseda University, Japan, where he is also the Director of the Center for English Language Education (CELESE). He has a BSc degree (mathematical physics) from the University of Manchester, UK, and MA (TESL/TEFL) and PhD (applied linguistics) degrees from the University of Birmingham, UK. His main research interests are in corpus linguistics, educational technology and English for specific purposes (ESP). He received the National Prize of the Japan Association for English Corpus Studies (JAECS) in 2012 for his work in corpus software design.

Sarah Atkins is a research fellow at the Aston Institute for Forensic Linguistics, Aston University, where she leads on a number of external projects and partnerships. She also holds a visiting research fellowship at the Centre for Sustainable Working Life, Birkbeck, University of London. She has conducted research in a range of professional settings, most notably in health care, with an emphasis on applying findings to practice. Her work on communication skills training in medical education, which combines corpus linguistic and micro-analytic approaches to spoken interaction, has resulted in a range of policy applications and award-winning workshops for health care professionals.

Paul Baker is a professor of English language at Lancaster University. He has written 20 books on various aspects of language, identity, discourse and corpus linguistics.

These include *Sociolinguistics and Corpus Linguistics* and *Using Corpora to Analyse Gender*. He is commissioning editor of the journal *Corpora* and a fellow of the Royal Society of Arts. His latest book, *Fabulosa: The Story of Polari, Britain's Secret Gay Language,* was a *Times Literary Supplement* Book of the Year in 2019.

Oliver Ballance is a lecture in Applied Linguistics and English for Academic Purposes in the School of Humanities, Media and Creative Communication at Massey University, New Zealand. Oliver teaches courses on EAP and curriculum design and supervises postgraduate research projects. His own research interests are focused upon the interface between corpus linguistics and language for specific purposes.

Silvia Bernardini is a professor of English linguistics at the Department of Interpreting and Translation of the University of Bologna, Italy, where she teaches translation from English into Italian and corpus linguistics. She has published widely on corpus use in translator education and for translation practice and research. Her research interests include the investigation of the points of contact between translation and interpreting and translation and non-native writing, seen as instances of bilingual language use.

Gavin Brookes is research fellow in the Department of Linguistics and English Language at Lancaster University. He is Associate Editor of the *International Journal of Corpus Linguistics* (John Benjamins) and Co-Editor of the *Corpus and Discourse* book series (Bloomsbury). Gavin has published widely on corpus linguistics, (critical) discourse studies and health communication, and is the author of *Corpus, Discourse and Mental Health* (with Daniel Hunt, Bloomsbury, 2020) and *Obesity in the News: Language and Representation in the Press* (with Paul Baker, Routledge, 2021).

Graham Burton is a researcher and lecturer at the Faculty of Education, Free University of Bozen-Bolzano and has written coursebooks and other teaching materials for a number of publishers. His PhD focused on how the consensus on pedagogical grammar for ELT evolved, how it is sustained and how it compares to empirical data on learner language.

Angela Chambers is a professor emerita of applied languages at the University of Limerick. She has taught in universities in France, the United Kingdom and Ireland. Her research interests focus on the use of corpora in language learning. She has published extensively in this area, including articles in journals such as *Language Learning & Technology*, *ReCALL*, the *International Journal of Corpus Linguistics*, the *Revue Française de Linguistique Appliquée* and *Language Teaching*. In 2007 she was guest editor for a special issue of *ReCALL* on corpora in language learning. She currently teaches academic writing at the postgraduate and postdoctoral level.

Winnie Cheng is former professor and former Director of the Research Centre for Professional Communication in English (RCPCE) of the Department of English at The Hong Kong Polytechnic University. Her research interests include corpus linguistics, conversation analysis, critical discourse analysis, discourse intonation, EAP, ESP, intercultural communication, pragmatics and writing across the curriculum.

Brian Clancy is currently a lecturer in applied linguistics at Mary Immaculate College, Ireland. His research work focusses on the blend of a corpus linguistic methodology with the discourse analytic approaches of pragmatics and sociolinguistics. His primary methodological interests relate to the use of corpora in the study of language varieties and the construction and analysis of small corpora. His published work explores language use in intimate settings, such as between family and close friends, and the language variety Irish English. He is the author of *Investigating Intimate Discourse: Exploring the Spoken Interaction of Families, Couples and Close Friends* (Routledge, 2016) and co-authored *Introducing Pragmatics in Use* (Routledge, 2011 and 2020).

Susan Conrad is a professor of applied linguistics at Portland State University, Portland, Oregon, USA. She has used corpus linguistics to study English grammar in a variety of contexts, from general conversation to engineering. Her publications include the *Grammar of Spoken and Written English, The Cambridge Introduction to Applied Linguistics, Real Grammar* and *Register, Genre, and Style*. She coordinates the Civil Engineering Writing Project, in which corpus linguists and engineers collaborate to improve students' writing skills. Her teaching experiences in southern Africa, South Korea and the United States convinced her corpus techniques were useful long before they were well known.

Averil Coxhead is a professor at Te Herenga Waka/Victoria University of Wellington, Aotearoa/New Zealand where she teaches undergraduate and postgraduate courses in applied linguistics and TESOL. Averil is the author of *Vocabulary and English for Specific Purposes Research* (Routledge, 2018) and co-author of *English for Vocational Purposes* (Routledge, 2020) and a textbook series with Professor Paul Nation entitled *Reading for the Academic World* (Seed Learning, 2018). Her current research includes technical multiword units in trades education, vocabulary in hip hop (with Friederike Tegge) and wordlists in trades such as carpentry and plumbing in English and their translation into Tongan with Falakiko Tu'amoheloa.

Sara T. Cushing is a professor of applied linguistics at Georgia State University. She received her PhD in applied linguistics from UCLA. She has published research in the areas of assessment, second language writing and teacher education. She has been invited to speak and conduct workshops on second language writing assessment throughout the world, most recently in Vietnam, Colombia, Thailand and Norway. Her current research focuses on assessing integrated skills, the use of automated scoring for second language writing and applications of corpus linguistics to assessment.

Philip Durrant is an associate professor in language education at the University of Exeter. He has been a language teacher and researcher for over 20 years, working at schools and universities in the UK and Turkey. He has published widely on corpus linguistics, vocabulary learning and academic writing.

Fiona Farr is an associate professor of applied linguistics and TESOL at the University of Limerick. She is the Director of CALS (Centre for Applied Language Studies) and Research Director in MLAL. Her research interests include teacher education and professional development, applied corpus linguistics; and language learning and technology. She is the author of *Teaching Practice Feedback: An Investigation of Spoken and Written Modes* (2011), *Practice in TESOL* (2015) and *Social Interaction in Language Teacher Education* (2019, with Farrell and Riordan). She is the co-editor of the *EUP Textbooks in TESOL* series and of the *Routledge Handbook of Language Learning and Technology* (2016).

Lynne Flowerdew is currently a visiting research fellow in the Department of Applied Linguistics and Communication, Birkbeck, University of London. Her main research and teaching interests include corpus linguistics, discourse analysis, EAP/ESP and disciplinary writing. She has published widely in these areas in international journals and prestigious edited collections and has also authored and co-edited several books.

Jamie Garner is a lecturer in the Department of Linguistics at the University of Florida, where she also serves as the coordinator of the undergraduate Linguistics and undergraduate Teaching English as a Second Language (TESL) programs. Her current research interests include learner corpus research, phraseology and second language acquisition. Her research has been published in the *International Journal of Learner Corpus Research, System, The Modern Language Journal, System* and *International Review of Applied Linguistics in Language Teaching.*

Mathew Gillings is an assistant professor at the Vienna University of Economics and Business. He completed his PhD at the ESRC Centre for Corpus Approaches to Social Science at Lancaster University, where he explored verbal cues to deception through the use of corpus-based methods. His research interests are in various aspects of corpus linguistics, but most recently he has applied the method to the study of deception, politeness and Shakespeare's language.

Gaëtanelle Gilquin is a professor of English language and linguistics at the University of Louvain. She is the coordinator of LINDSEI (Louvain International Database of Spoken English Interlanguage) and PROCEED (PROcess Corpus of English in EDucation) and one of the editors of the *Cambridge Handbook of Learner Corpus Research.* Her research interests include the use of native and learner corpora for the description and teaching of language, the analysis of the writing process through screencasting and keylogging and the comparison of learner Englishes and world Englishes.

Sylviane Granger is an emerita professor of English language and linguistics at the University of Louvain. In 1990 she launched the first large-scale learner corpus project, the *International Corpus of Learner English,* and since then has played a key role in defining the different facets of the field of learner corpus research. Her current research interests focus on the analysis of phraseology in native and learner language and its integration into reference and instructional materials. One of her latest publications is *Perspectives on the L2 Phrasicon: The View from Learner Corpora* (2021).

Bethany Gray is an associate professor of English (Applied Linguistics and Technology program) at Iowa State University. Her research investigates phraseological, grammatical and lexico-grammatical variation across registers of English, with a particular focus on disciplinary variation in academic writing and the development of grammatical complexity in novice and L2 writers. She is a co-founding editor of *Register Studies*

(John Benjamins), and her work appears in journals such as *Applied Linguistics, TESOL Quarterly, Journal of English for Academic Purposes, Corpora* and *International Journal of Corpus Linguistics.* Her books include *Linguistic Variation in Research Articles* (John Benjamins) and *Grammatical Complexity in Academic English* (Cambridge University Press, co-authored with Douglas Biber).

Chris Greaves was a senior research fellow in the English Department of the Hong Kong Polytechnic University until his retirement in 2012. He is well-known for his ground-breaking corpus linguistics software such as ConcApp, iConc and ConcGram and his research in the areas of corpus linguistics and phraseological variation. Sadly, Chris passed away in December 2020 before this volume went into production.

Sarah Grech holds a PhD in linguistics from the University of Malta. She is a senior lecturer with the Institute of Linguistics and Language Technology, University of Malta. Her research interests are in sociophonetics and language variation and change. She is currently leading or co-coordinating projects on Maltese English, as well as learner English in Malta, in order to identify key features of this variety of English within Malta's multilingual context.

Stefan Th. Gries is a professor of linguistics in the Department of Linguistics at the University of California, Santa Barbara (UCSB) and Chair of English Linguistics (corpus linguistics with a focus on quantitative methods, 25 per cent) at the Justus-Liebig-Universität Giessen. He was a Visiting Chair (2013–17) of the Centre for Corpus Approaches to Social Science at Lancaster University, visiting professor at five LSA Linguistic Institutes between 2007 and 2019 and the Leibniz Professor (spring semester 2017) at the Research Academy Leipzig of the University of Leipzig.

Michael Handford is a professor of applied linguistics at Cardiff University, where he is Director of internationalisation for the School of English, Communication and Philosophy. His research interests include discourse in professional settings, cultural identities at work, the application of corpus tools in discourse analysis, using corpora for the analysis of intercultural communication, essentialism and stereotyping, engineering education and communication, diversity and education and internationalisation in higher education. He is the author of *The Language of Business Meetings*, published by Cambridge University Press, and co-editor with J.P. Gee of the *Routledge Handbook of Discourse Analysis.*

Kevin Harvey is an associate professor in sociolinguistics in the School of English at the University of Nottingham. His principal research interests lie in the field of applied discourse analysis, multi-modal discourse analysis and corpus linguistics. Broadly, he is interested in interdisciplinary approaches to professional communication, with a special emphasis on health communication. He is editor of the dementia blog, *Dementia Day-to-Day*, and currently runs a series of dementia reading groups in care homes and local hospitals. His books include *Investigating Adolescent Health Communication: A Corpus Linguistics Approach* (Bloomsbury, 2013) and *Exploring Health Communication: Language in Action* (with Nelya Koteyko, Routledge, 2013).

Frazer Heritage holds a PhD in linguistics from Lancaster University and is currently an assistant lecturer in the Department of Psychology at Birmingham City University. His research focuses on corpus approaches to both critical discourse analysis and critical sociolinguistics. Frazer is interested in the linguistic construction and representation of gender, sexuality, and identity in different corpora, particularly in corpora of videogames and of language from social media. He is the author of the monograph *Language, Gender and Videogames: Using Corpora to Analyse the Representation of Gender in Fantasy Videogames* (Palgrave Macmillan, 2021).

Susan Hunston is a professor of English language at the University of Birmingham, where she has worked since 1996. Her research focuses on corpus linguistics, especially the lexis–grammar interface, and on discourse analysis, especially evaluative language and academic discourse. She has written several books, most recently *Interdisciplinary Research Discourse* (2019, Routledge) with Paul Thompson, and numerous articles. Susan has held lectureships at Mindanao State University, the National University of Singapore and the University of Surrey and has also worked as a grammarian on the *COBUILD* project.

Christian Jones is a senior lecturer in TESOL and applied linguistics at the University of Liverpool. His main research interests are connected to spoken language, and he has published research related to spoken corpora, lexis, lexico-grammar and instructed second language acquisition. He is the co-author (with Daniel Waller) of *Corpus Linguistics for Grammar: A Guide for Research* (Routledge, 2015), *Successful Spoken English: Findings from Learner Corpora* (with Shelley Byrne and Nicola Halenko) (Routledge, 2017) and editor of *Literature, Spoken Language and Speaking Skills in Second Language Learning*, a collection of research on this area (Cambridge University Press, 2019).

Martha Jones is an assistant professor in the School of Education at the University of Nottingham. She is the MA Teaching English for Academic Purposes (web-based) course leader and teaches on the face-to-face and web-based MA Teaching English to Speakers of Other Languages programme. Martha's publications have focused on the development and exploitation of corpora for teaching and research purposes, the acquisition of academic and disciplinary vocabulary, the use of ePortfolios in teacher education and the development of e-resources, including an open educational resource. She has also conducted research using combined corpus and genre-based approaches focusing on disciplinary written discourse.

Dawn Knight, Cardiff University, has expertise in corpus linguistics, discourse analysis, digital interaction and non-verbal communication. She was Principal Investigator on the £1.8m ESRC/AHRC-funded National Corpus of Contemporary Welsh (CorCenCC) and Welsh government–funded Cross-lingual Word-Embeddings projects. Knight has experience constructing and utilising corpora using traditional and innovative crowdsourcing methods and in co-designing corpus applications (including the Digital Replay System [DRS]).

Almut Koester is a full professor of English business communication at Vienna University of Economics and Business (WU) and, before that, was a senior lecturer in English language at the University of Birmingham in England. She is the author of *The Language of Work* (2004), *Investigating Workplace Discourse* (2006) and *Workplace Discourse* (2010). Her research focuses on spoken workplace discourse and business corpora, and her publications have examined genre, modality, relational language, vague language, idioms and conflict talk. She is currently exploring the areas of language awareness and creativity and is interested in applying research findings to teaching business English.

Phoenix Lam is an assistant professor in the Department of English at The Hong Kong Polytechnic University. She is also a member of the Department's Research Centre for Professional Communication in English (RCPCE). Her research areas are in corpus linguistics, discourse analysis and intercultural and professional communication. Her publications appear in *Discourse Studies, English for Specific Purposes, Journal of Pragmatics* and *Journal of Sociolinguistics*. Her latest research focuses on the discursive construction of online place branding through a corpus-assisted discourse analytic approach.

Xiaofei Lu is a professor of applied linguistics and Asian studies at Pennsylvania State University. His research interests are primarily in corpus linguistics, computer-assisted language learning, English for Academic Purposes, second language writing and second language acquisition. He is the author of *Computational Methods for Corpus Annotation and Analysis* and lead co-editor of *Computational and Corpus Approaches to Chinese Language Learning.* His work appears in *Applied Linguistics*, *International Journal of Corpus Linguistics*, *Journal of English for Academic Purposes*, *Journal of Second Language Writing*, *Language Learning & Technology*, *Language Teaching Research*, *ReCALL*, *System*, *TESOL Quarterly* and *The Modern Language Journal,* among others.

Michaela Mahlberg is a professor of corpus linguistics at the University of Birmingham, UK, where she is also the Director of the Centre for Corpus Research. Her publications include *Corpus Stylistics and Dickens's Fiction* (Routledge, 2013), *English General Nouns: A Corpus Theoretical Approach* (John Benjamins, 2005) and *Text, Discourse and Corpora. Theory and Analysis* (Continuum, 2007, with M. Hoey, M. Stubbs and W. Teubert). She is the editor of the *International Journal of Corpus Linguistics* (John Benjamins) and together with Gavin Brookes she edits the book series *Corpus and Discourse* (Bloomsbury). As Principal Investigator of the AHRC-funded *CLiC Dickens* project, Michaela led the development of the CLiC web app.

Anna Marchi is a senior assistant professor of English language and linguistics at Bologna University's Department of Interpreting and Translation. Her research interests include corpus-assisted research methods, news discourse and journalism studies. Recently she has published *Self-reflexive Journalism: A Corpus Study of Journalistic Culture and Community in the Guardian* (Routledge 2019) and co-edited *Corpus Approaches to Discourse: A Critical Review* (Routledge 2018). She earned a PhD at Lancaster University and has worked in the area of corpus linguistics and corpus-assisted discourse studies since 2005 (collaborating with the Universities of Siena, Cardiff, Swansea and Lancaster).

Geraldine Mark is a research associate at Cardiff University and PhD student at Mary Immaculate College, Limerick. Her main research interests are in L2 language development, L1 and L2 spoken language, and the use of corpora in informing language teaching and learning. She is co-author of *English Grammar Today* (2011,

Cambridge University Press) and co-Principal Investigator (with Anne O'Keeffe) of the English Grammar Profile, an online resource profiling L2 grammar development.

Gerlinde Mautner is a professor of English business communication at *Wirtschafts-universität Wien* (Vienna University of Economics and Business), visiting professor at Durham Business School, UK, and Vice-President for humanities and social sciences of Austria's largest research funding organisation (FWF). She pursues research interests located at the interface of language, society, business and the law. Since the mid-1990s, her work has also had a strong methodological focus, concerned in particular with the relationship between corpus linguistics and discourse studies.

Jeanne McCarten taught English in Sweden, France, Malaysia and the UK before starting a publishing career with Cambridge University Press. As a publisher, she had many years' experience of commissioning and developing ELT materials and was involved in the development of the spoken English sections of the Cambridge International Corpus, including CANCODE. Currently a freelance ELT materials writer, corpus researcher and occasional teacher, her ongoing professional interests lie in successfully applying corpus insights to learning materials. She is co-author of the corpus-informed print, online and blended courses *Touchstone* and *Viewpoint*, and *Grammar for Business,* published by Cambridge University Press.

Michael J. McCarthy is emeritus professor of applied linguistics, University of Nottingham. He is (co)author/(co)editor of 57 books, including *Touchstone, Viewpoint, The Cambridge Grammar of English, English Grammar Today, From Corpus to Classroom, Innovations and Challenge in Grammar* and titles in the *English Vocabulary in Use* series. He is author/co-author of 120 academic papers. He was co-founder of the CANCODE and CANBEC spoken English corpora projects. His recent research has focused on spoken grammar. He has taught in the UK, Europe and Asia and has been involved in language teaching and applied linguistics for 56 years.

Tony McEnery is distinguished professor in the Department of English Language and Linguistics at Lancaster University and Changjiang Chair at Xi'an Jiaotong University. He is General Editor of the journal *Corpora* (Edinburgh University Press) and was founding director of the ESRC-funded Centre for Corpus Approaches to Social Science (CASS) at Lancaster. He has published widely on corpus linguistics and is the author of *Corpus Linguistics: Method, Theory and Practice* (with Andrew Hardie, Cambridge University Press, 2011) and *The Language of Violent Jihad* (with Paul Baker and Rachelle Vessey, Cambridge University Press, 2021).

Dan McIntyre is a professor of English language and linguistics at the University of Huddersfield, where he teaches corpus linguistics, stylistics and the history of the English language. His major publications include *Corpus Stylistics: Theory and Practice* (Edinburgh University Press, 2019; with Brian Walker), *Applying Linguistics: Language and the Impact Agenda* (Routledge, 2018; co-edited with Hazel Price) and *Stylistics* (Cambridge University Press, 2010; with Lesley Jeffries). He also wrote *History of English: A Resource Book for Students* (Routledge, second edition 2020). He co-founded *Babel: The Language Magazine* and is co-author of *The Babel Lexicon of Language* (Cambridge University Press, 2022).

David Oakey is a lecturer in TESOL and applied linguistics in the Department of English at the University of Liverpool, UK. His research interest is in the description, acquisition, teaching and learning of lexis, formulaic language and phraseology, particularly in interdisciplinary discourse situations where users encounter unfamiliar meanings of familiar words. He uses corpus linguistics and usage-based approaches to look at the behaviours of forms, meanings and patterns and has published on various aspects of this work. He has taught undergraduate and graduate classes in English lexis and corpus linguistics at universities in China, Turkey, the UK, and the United States.

Kieran O'Halloran is a reader in applied linguistics at King's College, University of London. He is an educationalist who researches and teaches creative thinking and critical thinking using digital technologies. He draws on posthumanist theory for these ends, intersecting his interest in critical thinking with critical discourse studies and an interest in creative thinking with literary stylistics. Publications include *Posthumanism and Deconstructing Arguments: Corpora and Digitally-Driven Critical Analysis* (Routledge 2017) and *Digital Literary Studies: Corpus Approaches to Poetry, Prose, and Drama* (with David Hoover and Jonathan Culpeper, Routledge 2014).

Anne O'Keeffe is senior lecturer at MIC, University of Limerick, Ireland. Her publications include the titles *From Corpus to Classroom* (2007), *English Grammar Today* (2011), *Introducing Pragmatics in Use* (2nd edition 2020) and as co-editor *The Routledge Handbook of Corpus Linguistics* (1st edition 2010). With Geraldine Mark, she was co-Principal Investigator of the English Grammar Profile. She is co-editor, with Michael J. McCarthy, of two book series: *The Routledge Corpus Linguistics Guides* and *The Routledge Applied Corpus Linguistics*.

Maria Pavesi is a professor of English language and linguistics at the University of Pavia, where she was Director of the University Language Centre and coordinator of the Foreign Language Teachers' Education programme. Her research has addressed several topics in English applied linguistics, focussing on informal second language acquisition, the sociolinguistics of dubbing and film dialogue and corpus-based audiovisual translation studies. Her most recent publications include 'Corpus-Based Audiovisual Translation Studies: Ample Room for Development' (Routledge 2019) and '"I Shouldn't Have Let This Happen": Demonstratives in Film Dialogue and Film Representation' (Bloomsbury 2020). In 2019, she also co-edited the *Multilingua* special issue on *Audiovisual Translation as Intercultural Mediation*. Since 2005, she has coordinated the development of the *Pavia Corpus of Film Dialogue*, a parallel and comparable corpus of English and Italian film transcriptions.

Pascual Pérez-Paredes is a professor of applied linguistics and linguistics, University of Murcia. His main research interests are language variation, the use of corpora in language education and corpus-assisted discourse analysis. He has published research in journals such as *CALL, Discourse & Society, English for Specific Purposes, Journal of Pragmatics, Language, Learning & Technology, System* and the *International Journal of Corpus Linguistics.* He is assistant editor of Cambridge University Press (CUP) *ReCALL* and author of *Corpus Linguistics for Education. A Guide for Research,* in the Routledge Corpus Linguistics Guides series.

Geraint Rees is tenure-track lecturer and Serra Húnter Fellow at Universitat Rovira i Virgili, Tarragona. His research interests include corpus linguistics, lexicography, vocabulary acquisition and learning technologies. His PhD research, undertaken at Universitat Pompeu Fabra, Barcelona, deals with the selection and presentation of vocabulary in EAP course materials and dictionaries. His current focus is on the integration of lexicographic resources with other technologies. He has worked on ColloCaid, a project developing an integrated text editor and lexicographic resource to help academic writers with English collocations. He is reviews editor for the *International Journal of Lexicography*.

Randi Reppen is a professor of applied linguistics and TESL at Northern Arizona University (NAU) where she teaches in the MA and PhD programmes. She has extensive experience in building corpora and using corpora for linguistic research. She is the author of *Using Corpora in the Language Classroom* (2010), co-editor with Doug Biber of *Cambridge Handbook of Corpus Linguistics* (2015) and the lead author of two corpus-informed grammar series, *Grammar and Beyond* 2nd edn with *Academic Writing 1–4* (2021) and the *Grammar and Beyond Essentials* 1–4 (2019). Her research has also appeared in academic journals, including *International Journal of Corpus Linguistics, Journal of Second Language Writing, TESOL Quarterly, IJLCR, Discourse and Communication* and *the Modern Language Journal.*

Ute Römer is an associate professor in the Department of Applied Linguistics and ESL at Georgia State University. Her research interests include phraseology, second language acquisition and using corpora in language learning and teaching. She serves on a range of editorial boards of professional journals and is General Editor of the book series *Studies in Corpus Linguistics* (John Benjamins). Her research has been published in a range of applied, corpus and cognitive linguistics journals, including *Language Learning, The Modern Language Journal, Studies in Second Language Acquisition, Annual Review of Applied Linguistics, International Journal of Corpus Linguistics, Corpora* and *Cognitive Linguistics.*

Christoph Rühlemann is a researcher at the University of Freiburg. Besides journal articles on conversational language, storytelling and conversational structure, he has published monographs including *Visual linguistics with R* (2020) published with Benjamins, *Corpus Linguistics for Pragmatics* (2018) published with Routledge, *Narrative in English Conversation: A Corpus Analysis of Storytelling* (2013) published with Cambridge University Press and *Conversation in Context. A Corpus-Driven Approach* (2007) with Continuum, and is the co-editor of *Corpus Pragmatics. A Handbook* (2015; with Karin Aijmer) published with Cambridge University Press. He is currently Project Director of a DFG-funded research project on "Multimodal Storytelling Interaction" at Albrechts-University Freiburg.

Tony Berber Sardinha is a professor with the Applied Linguistics Graduate Program, Pontifical Catholic University, Sao Paulo, Brazil. His interests include corpus linguistics, register variation, forensic linguistics, metaphor analysis and applied linguistics. His latest publications include *Multi-Dimensional Analysis: Research Methods and Current Issues* (Bloomsbury), *Multi-Dimensional Analysis: 25 Years On* (Benjamins), *Metaphor in Specialist Discourse* (Benjamins) and *Working with Portuguese Corpora* (Bloomsbury). He is the Corpus Linguistics editor for the new edition of the *Encyclopedia of Applied Linguistics* (ed. Carol Chapelle). He serves on the editorial board of major journals in the field such as the *International Journal of Corpus Linguistics, Corpora, Register Studies* and *Applied Corpus Linguistics*.

Charlotte Taylor is a senior lecturer in English language and linguistics at the University of Sussex. She is co-editor of the *CADAAD Journal*. Her current interests lie in the intersection of language and conflict in two contexts: investigating mock politeness and the representation of migration. She also has a keen interest in methodological issues in corpus and discourse work. Her book-length publications include *Corpus Approaches to Discourse* (with Anna Marchi), *Exploring Absence and Silence in Discourse* (with Melani Schroeter), *Patterns and Meanings in Discourse* (with Alan Partington & Alison Duguid) and *Mock Politeness in English and Italian*.

Ana Maria Terrazas-Calero is currently a lecturer in English studies at the University of Extremadura (Spain), where she teaches English sociolinguistics, variations of the English language, early modern English and medieval English history. She is also a doctoral student at Mary Immaculate College, University of Limerick (Ireland). She has created the Corpus of Contemporary Fictionalized Irish English as part of her thesis, which investigates the portrayal of this variety in contemporary fiction. Her research and publications focus on pragmalinguistic elements of Irish English, examining their use, pragmatic functions and indexical value regarding contemporary Irish identity as represented in fictional dialogue.

Paul Thompson is a reader in applied corpus linguistics at the University of Birmingham, UK. He is currently Acting Director of the Centre for Corpus Research. He is also the founding co-editor of the *Applied Corpus Linguistics* journal (Elsevier). He was a member of the research team on the British Academic Written English (BAWE) and British Academic Spoken English (BASE) corpus projects. His most recent publication is *Interdisciplinary Research Discourse: Corpus Investigations into Environment Journals* (2019, Routledge) co-authored with Susan Hunston.

Elaine Vaughan lectures in applied linguistics and TESOL at the University of Limerick, Ireland. She has published on teacher discourse in workplace meetings; communities of practice; the pragmatics of Irish English; humour and laughter; the use of corpora and corpus-based approaches for intra-varietal, pragmatic and sociolinguistic research; corpus-based critical discourse analysis; and media representations of Irish English. She is co-editor, with Carolina Amador-Moreno and Kevin McCafferty, of *Pragmatic Markers in Irish English* (2015, John Benjamins); and with Raymond Hickey of the special issue of the journal *World Englishes* on Irish English (2017).

Alexandra Vella holds a PhD in linguistics from the University of Edinburgh. She is an associate professor with the Institute of Linguistics and Language Technology, University of Malta. Her area of expertise is phonetics and phonology, with a focus on prosody. She continues to work on describing the intonational phonology of Maltese and its dialects, also looking to extending insights gained to modelling the intonation of Maltese English, the variety of English of speakers of Maltese. She is the lead researcher on projects involving the compilation and annotation of spoken data of the languages and language varieties of Malta.

Brian Walker is a visiting researcher in the Department of Linguistics and Modern Languages at the University of Huddersfield. His research focusses on the stylistic analysis of texts, including political speeches and print news report, using corpus methods and tools. His recent publications include *Keywords in the Press* (Bloomsbury, 2018; with Lesley Jeffries) and *Corpus Stylistics: Theory and Practice* (Edinburgh University Press, 2019; with Dan McIntyre).

Martin Warren was a professor of English language studies in the English Department of the Hong Kong Polytechnic University and a member of its Research Centre for Professional Communication in English until his retirement in 2018. He taught and researched in the areas of corpus linguistics, discourse analysis, intercultural communication, lexical semantics, phraseological variation, pragmatics and professional communication.

Martin Weisser received his PhD from Lancaster University in 2001 and his professorial qualification (Habilitation) from Bayreuth University in 2011. He is currently an adjunct professor at the University of Bayreuth, specialising in general corpus linguistics, corpus pragmatics and the creation of corpus analysis tools, such as the Dialogue Annotation and Research Tool (DART) and the Simple Corpus Tool. He is the author of *How to Do Corpus Pragmatics on Pragmatically Annotated Data: Speech Acts and Beyond* (Benjamins 2018) and *Practical Corpus Linguistics* (Wiley-Blackwell 2016).

Viola Wiegand is a lecturer at the University of Birmingham. She has contributed to the development of the CLiC web app and research on body language and character speech in nineteenth-century fiction. Her research interests span corpus linguistics and stylistics, the use of corpora in language learning and teaching, discourse analysis, and digital humanities. Viola's PhD thesis focused on contemporary surveillance discourse in a range of domains. She is assistant editor of the *International Journal of Corpus Linguistics* (John Benjamins) and has co-edited *Corpus Linguistics, Context and Culture* with Michaela Mahlberg (De Gruyter, 2019).

Acknowledgements

Bringing together this volume for a second time was both an exciting and a challenging endeavour. It would not have been possible without the generosity of the contributors. The compilation of the volume coincided with the COVID-19 global pandemic. This adversely affected society in so many ways. Within the academic community, in addition to personal challenges, various lockdowns brought many practical and logistical difficulties. As we slowly emerge from the gloom of this time, this Handbook, in its small way, is a testament to our collective resilience. To all contributors, including those who had to pull out due to the challenges of this difficult period, we thank you sincerely.

To colleagues and friends in the academic community, we also owe our gratitude. These include, *inter alia*, those who generously acted as reviewers, advisers and conveyers of support and encouragement: Svenja Adolphs, Carolina Amador-Moreno, Laurence Anthony, Tony Berber Sardinha, Gavin Brookes, Graham Burton, Niall Curry, Averil Coxhead, Fiona Farr, Brian Clancy, John Kirk, Dawn Knight, Mike Handford, Michaela Mahlberg, Geraldine Mark, Jeanne McCarten, Tony McEnery, Kieran O'Halloran, Joan O'Sullivan, Pascual Pérez-Paredes, Ute Römer, Christoph Rühlemann, Ana Mª Terrazas-Calero, Paul Thompson, Elaine Vaughan, Martin Warren, Viola Wiegand and Martin Weisser. Sadly, during the writing of this volume, Chris Greaves, one of our contributors, passed away.

We also thank our editorial assistant Eleni Steck for her calm help and advice. To Louisa Semlyen, Senior Publisher at Taylor & Francis Group, we thank you for inviting us to edit this volume a second time. We extend a special expression of gratitude to the following doctoral students who provided crucial editorial assistance in this project. Their insights and perspectives were invaluable: Shane Barry, Giana Hennigan, Gerard O'Hanlon, Rose O'Loughlin and Deborah Tobin. Finally, to our partners and family, Ger, Jack and Jeanne, as ever, we thank you sincerely.

Chapter 14 makes use of the *English Vocabulary Profile* and Chapter 22 uses examples from the *English Grammar Profile*. These resources are based on extensive research using the *Cambridge Learner Corpus* and are part of the *English Profile* programme, which aims to provide evidence about language use that helps to produce better language teaching materials. See http://www.englishprofile.org for more information.

In Chapter 38, we acknowledge the use of data from films in the *Pavia Corpus of Film Dialogue* (PCFD) in adherence with copyright clearance for use in research publications.

Chapter 47 acknowledges the use of a screenshot from the 'IBM immersive insights' *YouTube* video (Figure 47.1). In the use of Figures 47.4 and 47.5, we acknowledge the permission to use a text from the *US Food and Drug Administration* website text on animal testing. Additionally, Chapter 47 wishes to acknowledge the permission of Oxford University Press to reuse material from O'Halloran (2020).

1

'Of what is past, or passing, or to come[1]': corpus linguistics, changes and challenges

Anne O'Keeffe and Michael J. McCarthy

1 Corpus linguistics: a decade on

This new edition of the *Routledge Handbook of Corpus Linguistics* gives us an opportunity to reflect on where the discipline was ten years ago, where it is now and where it might be heading. These three perspectives involve reflection not only on technological advances but also on methodological progress and on the academic and social impact of corpus linguistics (CL).

There can be no doubt that CL has benefited from technological progress in the last decade. Computers work faster; software has, in the main, become more intuitively usable by scholars and others who are non-specialists in computer science; and the mathematical processes which yield results that linguists can interpret have become more sophisticated, and indeed CL has led many of these changes (see Chapters 9 and 13, this volume). The enhanced access to corpora via online interfaces has generally enabled a far broader population to explore data from a greater range of languages than was the case just ten years ago. For example, at the time of writing, the *Sketch Engine* corpus interface is a repository of over 500 corpora across 95 languages (Kilgarriff *et al.* 2014). Within this, a user can access the *TenTen Corpus Family* (so called because their target is to accrue 10 billion or 10^{10} words for each language), a suite of comparable corpora comprising collections of web-based texts from over 35 languages. The *English-Corpora.org* site (curated by Mark Davies and formerly known as *BYU Corpora*) provides access to multi-million- and multi-billion-word corpora of contemporary and historical English, as well as specialised collections such as *The TV Corpus* (325 million words), *The Movie Corpus* (200 million words) and *the Corpus of American Soap Operas* (100 million words). Clearly in the last decade, the limitations on corpus size have been obviated by the capacity to store vast amounts of data in the cloud but it has also seen the honing of artificial intelligence tools to automatically gather data according to defined curation parameters, thus leading to big data collections that can be rapidly assembled and grown over time.

DOI: 10.4324/9780367076399-1

2 Big data, rapid data, critical perspectives

It is striking, in the last decade, how corpus interfaces can respond rapidly to contemporary themes in society and can curate collections that allow researchers to examine how a phenomenon is both being constructed linguistically and is impacting society. More and more, this is fostering the critical corpus voice and the potential for activism, as evidenced in many works in the last decade, *inter alia*, Grant (2013), Brindle (2018), Dance (2019), Larner (2019), Cunningham and Egbert (2020), Clarke (2019) and Baker *et al.* (2021) (see also Chapters 40–44 and 46–47, this volume).

It has become the norm that major political and societal events come under the corpus linguist's research gaze. The 2016 Referendum in the UK, for instance, which led to the withdrawal from the European Union (EU) (referred to as Brexit) can be investigated using the *Brexit Corpus* in *Sketch Engine*. This 100-million-word corpus comprises mostly tweets relating to the referendum, plus news, comments and blogs. A corpus such as this becomes a repository for patterns of and influences on thought: because texts were written before the referendum, researchers can trace opinions and track trends and coinage in language use (see also Islentyeva 2020 on attitudes in the British press to migration amid Brexit).

A more global example of corpus development in rapid response to a major societal event relates to the 2020 COVID-19 global pandemic. At the time of writing (and still amid this pandemic), the *Covid-19 Corpus*, available on *Sketch Engine,* comprises over 224 million words of texts released as part of the *COVID-19 Open Research Dataset* (CORD-19). Meanwhile on *English-Corpora.org,* the *Coronavirus Corpus* makes available over 1 billion words (Davies 2021). The latter corpus was designed to be a record of the social, cultural and economic impact of COVID-19 (Davies 2021). The data give us an insight into shifts in thought about the pandemic. For example, Davies (2021) notes evidence of relative naiveté in March 2020 in the early stages of the virus's spread where it was viewed as a short-term problem, with the word *re-opening* (of schools and businesses) being noted. One month later, from April 2020 onwards, the corpus shows a shift to a realisation of the longer-term nature of the virus, reflected in the prominence of words and collocates such as *ban + gatherings; travel; sale; entry; mask + wear; wearing; face; required; wore; wears.*

Hyland and Jiang (2021) look at the most highly cited SCI articles on COVID-19 published in the first seven months of 2020 to explore scientists' use of hyperbolic and promotional language to boost aspects of their research in a quest to ascertain whether this enthusiasm influenced the rhetorical presentation of research and encouraged scientists to "sell" their studies. Their results illustrate a significant increase in hype to stress certainty, contribution, novelty and potential, especially regarding research methods, outcomes and primacy. Hyland and Jiang's (2021) work sheds light on scientific persuasion at a time of intense social anxiety, and it is a marker of the important role that the linguist fulfils when armed with convincing empirical evidence.

These kinds of large rapid-response corpora, such as the *Brexit Corpus,* the *Covid-19 Corpus* and the *Coronavirus Corpus,* offer an interesting insight into the processes of modern-day corpus-building and neatly illustrate the development since the publication of the first edition of this Handbook one decade ago. For instance, the *Coronavirus Corpus* grows on a daily basis. As Davies (2021) details, new articles come from links harvested from hourly searches of *Bing News* (as well as over 1,000 websites) to locate articles that have appeared in the previous 24 hours. These are then downloaded, cleaned of boilerplate material, tagged and lemmatised before being added to the existing corpus. To find articles for the corpus, automatic searches using the search *items coronavirus, COVID or COVID-19* are used, plus a list of other words and strings used to search titles, such as *at-risk; self-isolat*; lock-down, stockpile*; testing; vaccine; ventilator* (see Davies 2021 for a full list). This kind of corpus curation automaticity means we can assume that, as major themes emerge in contemporary society, we are guaranteed to have a corpus with "fresh" data to analyse, and we are much indebted to such endeavours.

Corpora can be a repository of human thought for future analysis. However, there is a need to stop and think about this and to query whether this rapid curation is a "re-fraction" of our shared reality. Now more than ever, such reflection on the creation of big data corpora is crucial because the principles of curation determine how we as corpus creators and analysts represent social reality. O'Halloran in Chapter 47, this volume, brings a very timely and important philosophical perspective to this. O'Halloran's chapter offers a coda to the Handbook, and it also marks the major change in terms of the proliferation and treatment of data in the last decade (see also O'Halloran 2017).

Another facet of the revolution in mass corpus data gathering has been the use of crowdsourcing. A decade ago, though smart phones were available, one could not assume their widespread use. In recent years, personal mobile devices are at the core of large spoken corpus data-gathering exercises, for example, *The National Corpus of Contemporary Welsh* (Knight *et al.* 2021) and *The Spoken British National Corpus* 2014 (Love *et al.* 2017). Devices allow for high-quality audio and/or video recordings to be made and easily uploaded, along with consent and user-information documentation. This type of crowdsourcing revolutionises spoken data gathering, but it has implications for the way we design corpora and their sample frames (this is discussed in relation to the *British National Corpus* 1994 and 2014 in Love *et al.* 2017 and Love 2020).

3 Many text types, many modes

What is considered corpus data is also changing. Corpus content used to be heavily focused on breadth of representation of scanned written texts, e.g. the 100-million-word written text component of the *British National Corpus* (BNC1994). As discussed, the use of personal devices and automated tools to harvest data means that a corpus can now be whipped up in short order. Anyone interested in building a corpus on a particular topic can do so much more quickly than a decade ago and can access a far wider range of text types.

Early corpora were slow and considered enterprises. Design matrices were refined as sampling frames (see Crowdy 1993; McCarthy 1998). Now, with so many data types available in electronic form, the capacity to automatically find, harvest and store these has never been easier. However, there is still a need to keep in mind the original principles of careful corpus curation and design. Documenting design decisions and rationales remains crucial, and work such as Love (2020), which gives insights into the design decisions and rationales of the Spoken BNC 2014, is essential if we are to offset the risk of taking our eye off long-held principles. Amid so much change in terms of what constitutes "data", have we as a community brought up to date what it means to create a representative corpus in terms of text types? Are binary terms like "spoken" and "written" corpora any longer fit for purpose? The proliferation of new media since the publication of the first volume of this Handbook causes us to reflect on these questions.

At the time of its publication in 2010, *Facebook, Twitter* and online content streaming platforms such as *YouTube* were all in their start-up phase. *Netflix* had just begun its streaming enterprise, and virtual communication via computer-mediated communication tools such as *Skype* was not widely adopted. *Whatsapp, Facetime, Instagram, Zoom* and *TikTok* (originally *Musical.ly*) did not launch until 2009, 2010, 2010, 2013 and 2014, respectively, and did not become widely used until much later as mobile personal devices, especially smart phones, became more popular. From a corpus linguistics perspective, all of these applications and platforms have already had an impact on the creation, definition and processing of data. These data are easy pickings for corpus builders because they are very "captureable", but, we ask, do we have the capacity to treat these data for what they are: multi-modal? Chapters 40 and 46 on corpora of news and social media are new chapters in this edition of the Handbook, and they bring a timely perspective to this issue, as does Chapter 7.

In the introductory chapter to the first edition of this Handbook in 2010, we expressed our excitement about being at the point where technology allowed for 'the creation of multi-modal corpora, in which various communicative modes (e.g. speech, body-language, writing) could all be part of the corpus, all linked by simple technologies such as time-stamping and all accessible at one go' (McCarthy and O'Keeffe 2010: 6). We proclaimed that those interested in the study of spoken language using corpus linguistics would no longer 'have to rely only on the transcript of a speech event' because we are now at a point where video and audio stream can be tied to the transcript, thus 'offering invaluable contextual and para-linguistic and extra-linguistic support to the analysis' (2010: 6) (see also Knight and Adolphs 2020). Alas, while we were factually accurate, we were very premature in our excitement. A decade on, we are still working with impoverished representations of spoken language. What is more acute now, however, as mentioned, is that we have never before had so much multi-modal content, from online streaming to social media. Closed-caption facilities available on many content sharing and communication platforms are of a relatively high standard and thus lessen the chore of transcription, or at least give the researcher a major head start. However, while we are surrounded by multi-modal data, we are still working with a text-based paradigm for their investigation. Our default setting is to reduce all data to a text-based representation of discourse, regardless of the richness of its provenance. This is a pressing issue for the study of social media content where so often intertextuality is central to the message. Our systems and protocols are still not ready for these new data, and we need to find ways to capture and process multi-modal features (e.g. how can we best incorporate emojis; gifs; or the combination of audio, video, emoji, text and filters in a *TikTok?*).

Treating rich multi-modal data as a reduced one-dimensional written transcript devoid of accompanying sound, image, gesture, gaze, head nods, etc., means, as Rühlemann (2019) notes, we are observing only the transcribed speech of a given communicative event rather than the unified whole. The technical, financial and temporal challenges of transcribing and capturing the entire multi-modal "bundle" (Crystal 1969) means that researchers continue to make do with impoverished orthographic transcription of *what* has been said at the expense of *how* it has been communicated. We would argue that, as a research community, the lack of widespread advances in multi-modal transcription has caused a stagnation and has meant that we are largely ignoring both the richness of the data and the affordances of the digital technology that are currently available to us. In this edition of the Handbook, we make no predictions about what will happen in the next decade in this respect, but we do note our desire for change.

4 The impact of learner corpus research

Learner corpora were traditionally designed, built and analysed by researchers as sources of information on areas such as contrastive error analysis (L1 versus L2 interference). Many studies led to better understandings of learner language as a system (see Granger *et al.* 2015). Interestingly in the last decade, the contrastive focus is shifting. More and more, we are learning about what learners of a language *can do.* We are seeing a *profiling turn* where, very much influenced by calibrated proficiency scales like the *Common European Framework of Reference for Languages* (CEFR, Council of Europe 2001), there is a need to empirically test these competency profiles (e.g. Thewissen 2013; O'Keeffe and Mark 2017; McEnery *et al.* 2019; see also Chapters 22 and 23 this volume). Using corpora to test intuitively derived competence descriptors and scales for what constitutes a given level of competence in a language is an area ripe for further development. Profiling learner competence has also been moving apace in machine learning. More and more learner data are fed to machines as training data. The learner data thus become fodder for the machine, which is being trained to process learner performances in terms of group or individual profiling for purposes of adaptive feedback or automated assessment. The Institute for Automated Language Teaching and Assessment (ALTA) at the University of Cambridge, for example, develops methods for operations such as automatic speech recognition, learner profiling, automated essay grading and automated feedback systems based around learner corpora, applying novel techniques of language modelling to the data (for example, Felice *et al.* 2014). Such approaches include three-dimensional data cubing, where learners occupy one dimension, their disciplines the second and change over time the third, on the basis of which individuals and groups can be "modelled" for machines to take over the work of analysis and feedback. Similarly at ALTA, the development of a chatroom corpus of teacher–learner interactions is targeted at creating a chatbot to give adaptive feedback independently, but closely aligned with, typical teacher–student feedback.

Notable also in the last decade, and reflected in Chapters 22 and 23, among others, in this volume, is the move towards the use of CL in pursuit of second language acquisition (SLA) research questions. This is long overdue, as noted by Johansson (2009); De Knop and Meunier (2015); Flowerdew (2015); McEnery *et al.* (2019) and O'Keeffe (2021), among others. Corpus-based work on usage-based perspectives on SLA is growing rapidly, building on seminal work such as Ellis *et al.* (2015). However, as Römer and Garner note (Chapter 23, this volume), echoing Mackey (2014), partnerships between experts on SLA and CL need to be fostered if the benefits of longitudinal learner corpora are to be fully reaped. O'Keeffe (2021) also notes the need for reaching out to SLA for an enhanced understanding of and rationale for data-driven learning (DDL) (see also Chapters 21 to 33, this volume).

5 Our history and our future

In our introduction to the first edition of this Handbook, we said that CL was perhaps most readily associated in the minds of linguists with searching through screen after screen of concordance lines and wordlists in an attempt to make sense of phenomena in texts. We noted that this method of exegesis can be traced back to the thirteenth century, when biblical scholars and their teams of minions pored over the Christian Bible and manually indexed its words, line by line, page by page. Concordancing arose out of a practical need to specify for other biblical scholars, in alphabetical arrangement, the words contained in the Bible, along with citations of where and in what passages they occurred. In 2021, concordancing programmes can replicate the work of 500 monks in nanoseconds. Though concordances go back centuries as a laborious practice, they represent a significant link to past scholarship, and their spirit remains at the heart of the discipline for any linguist hoping to go beyond the number crunching of frequency lists, keyword lists, cluster lists and so on. We are still, in the final analysis, practitioners of rhetoric. The persuasiveness of our arguments about language depends on the plausible and robust interpretation of the principled empirical evidence which the data throw up. Grammatical description is a case in point, and Halliday's position rings as true today as a quarter of a century ago:

> ... the corpus does not write the grammar for us. Descriptive categories do not emerge out of the data. Description is a theoretical activity; and ... a theory is a designed semiotic system, designed so that we can explain the processes being observed.
>
> *(Halliday 1996: 24)*

Our debt to the past goes beyond an acknowledgement of the laborious process of manual concordancing of sacred texts and can be extended to the work of lexicographers and that of pre-Chomskyan structural linguists. In both cases, collecting reliable data was essential to their work. Dr Samuel Johnson's first comprehensive dictionary of English, published in 1755, was the result of many years of working with a corpus of endless slips of paper, logging samples of usage from the period 1560 to 1660. And perhaps the most famous example of the 'corpus on slips of paper' were the more than 3 million slips attesting word usage that the Oxford English Dictionary (OED) project had amassed by the 1880s, stored in what nowadays might serve as a garden shed. These millions of bits of paper were, quite literally, pigeon-holed in an attempt to organise them into a meaningful body of text from which the world-famous dictionary could be compiled.

The first computer-generated concordances had appeared in the late 1950s, using punched-card technology for storage (see Parrish 1962 for an early discussion of the issues). At that time, the processing of some 60,000 words took more than 24 hours. However, considerable improvements came about in the 1970s. Meanwhile, from as early as 1970, library and information scientists had developed a keen interest in Key Word In Context (KWIC) concordances as a way of replacing catalogue indexing cards and of automating subject analysis (Hines *et al.* 1970), and many well-known bibliographies and citation source works benefitted from advances in computer technology. Before it found its way into the linguistic terminology, the term *corpus* had long been in use to refer to a collection or binding together of written works of a similar nature. The OED attests its use in this meaning in the eighteenth century, such that scholars might refer to a 'corpus of the Latin poets' or a 'corpus of the law'. The OED's first citation of the word *corpus* in the linguistic literature is dated at 1956, in an article by W. S. Allen in the *Transactions of the Philological Society*, where it is used in the more familiar meaning of 'the body of written or spoken material upon which a linguistic analysis is based' (OED online, 2021). McEnery *et al.* (2006) note that the more specific term *corpus linguistics* did not come into common usage until the early 1980s; Aarts and Meijs's work (1984) is seen as the defining publication with regard to coinage of the term.

As editors, we have had the privilege of bringing this volume together for a second time. Like a time capsule, it may be opened in ten years' time, and a decade may again show stunning changes and it may still point to a lack of progress in other respects. This has clearly been a decade of immense growth for corpora. We have such a richness of ever-growing data and ever-advancing tools. In summary, there is little to limit the timeliness and the bigness of corpora now, but with this comes both a risk and a responsibility to safeguard the tenets of principled sampling, corpus design and representativeness. We hope this *Handbook* can play a role in this process.

We have structured the 46 main chapters of the volume under four themes:

- Building and designing a corpus: the basics;
- Using a corpus to investigate language;
- Corpora, language pedagogy and language acquisition;
- Corpora and applied research.

Any one of these themes could have filled an entire handbook in its own right, but we hope that the selection of chapters that we bring together continues in the spirit of the first *Routledge Handbook of Corpus Linguistics* to enthuse anyone wishing to get started with building and analysing a corpus. We hope it will inspire readers to continue to build more corpora (big and small), to use corpora more to enhance language learning and to mine more corpora in the pursuit of robust critical perspectives on the use of language and discourse in the construction of our shared reality.

Note

1 From *Sailing to Byzantium*, a poem by William Butler Yeats, first published in 1928.

References

Aarts, J. and Meijs, W. (1984) *Corpus Linguistics: Recent Developments in the Use of Computer Corpora in English language Research*, Amsterdam: Rodopi.

Baker, P. Vessey, R. and McEnery, T. (2021) *The Language of Violent Jihad*, Cambridge: Cambridge University Press.

Brindle, A. (2018) *The Language of Hate: A Corpus Linguistic Analysis of White Supremacist Language*, London: Routledge.

Clarke, I. (2019) 'Stylistic Variation on the Donald Trump Twitter Account: A Linguistic Analysis of Tweets Posted Between 2009 and 2018', *PLoS ONE* 14(9): e0222062. 10.1371/journal.pone.0222062

Council of Europe (2001) *Common European Framework of Reference for Languages: Learning, Teaching, Assessment*, Cambridge: Cambridge University Press

Crowdy, S. (1993) 'Spoken Corpus Design', *Literary and Linguistic Computing* 8(4): 259–65.

Crystal, D. (1969) *Prosodic Systems and Intonation in English*, Cambridge: Cambridge University Press.

Cunningham, C. D. and Egbert, J. (2020) 'Using Empirical Data to Investigate the Original Meaning of "Emolument" in the Constitution', *Georgia State University Law Review* 36(5): 465–89.

Dance, W. (2019) 'Disinformation Online: Social Media User's Motivations for Sharing "Fake News"', *Science in Parliament* 75(3): 20–22.

Davies, M. (2021) 'The Coronavirus Corpus. Design, Construction, and Use', *International Journal of Corpus Linguistics*, Published online: 3rd May 2021. 10.1075/ijcl.21044.dav

De Knop, S. and Meunier, F. (2015) 'The "Learner Corpus Research, Cognitive Linguistics and Second Language Acquisition" Nexus: A SWOT Analysis', *Corpus Linguistics and Linguistic Theory* 11(1): 1–18.

Ellis, N. C., O'Donnell, M. and Römer, U. (2015) 'Usage-Based Language Learning', in B. MacWhinney and W. O'Grady (eds) *The Handbook of Language Emergence*, Hoboken, NJ: John Wiley & Sons, pp. 163–80.

Felice, M., Yuan, Z., Andersen, O. E., Yannakoudakis, H. and Kochmar, E. (2014) 'Grammatical Error Correction Using Hybrid Systems and Type Filtering', in *Proceedings of the Eighteenth Conference on Computational Natural Language Learning (CoNLL 2014): Shared Task*, Baltimore, MD: Association for Computational Linguistics, pp. 15–24,

Flowerdew, L. (2015) 'Data-Driven Learning and Language Learning Theories: Whither the Twain Shall Meet', in A. Leńko-Szymańska and A. Boulton (eds) *Multiple Affordances of Language Corpora for Data-Driven Learning*, Amsterdam: John Benjamins, pp. 15–36.

Granger, S., Gilquin, G. and Meunier, F. (eds) (2015) *The Cambridge Handbook of Learner Corpus Research*, Cambridge: Cambridge University Press.

Grant, T. (2013) 'Txt 4N6: Method, Consistency and Distinctiveness in the Analysis of SMS Text Messages', *Journal of Law and Policy* 21(2): 467–94.

Halliday, M. A. K. (1996) 'On Grammar and Grammatics', in R. Hasan, C. Cloran and D. G. Butt (eds) *Functional Descriptions: Theory in Practice*, Amsterdam: John Benjamins, pp. 1–38.

Hines, T. C., Harris, J. L. and Levy, C. L. (1970) 'An Experimental Concordance Program', *Computers and the Humanities* 4(3): 161–71.

Hyland, K. and Jiang, K. F. (2021) 'The Covid Infodemic: Competition and the Hyping of Virus Research' *International Journal of Corpus Linguistics*. 10.1075/ijcl.20160.hyl

Islentyeva, A. (2020) *Corpus-Based Analysis of Ideological Bias. Migration in the British Press*, London: Routledge.

Johansson, S. (2009). 'Some Thoughts on Corpora and Second-language Acquisition', in K. Aijmer (ed.) *Corpora and Language Teaching*, Amsterdam: John Benjamins, pp. 33–44.

Kilgarriff, A., Baisa V., Bušta J., Jakubíček M., Kovář V., Michelfeit J., Rychlý P. and Suchomel V. (2014) 'The Sketch Engine: Ten Years On', *Lexicography* 1(1): 7–36.

Knight, D. and Adolphs, S. (2020) 'Multimodal Corpora', in M. Paquot and St. Th. Gries (eds) *A Practical Handbook of Corpus Linguistics*, New York: Springer International Publishing, pp. 351–69.

Knight, D., Morris, S. and Fitzpatrick, T. (2021) *Corpus Design and Construction in Minoritised Language Contexts: The National Corpus of Contemporary Welsh*, London: Palgrave Macmillan.

Larner, S. D. (2019) 'Formulaic Sequences as a Potential Marker of Deception: A Preliminary Investigation', in T. Docan-Morgan (ed.) *The Palgrave Handbook of Deceptive Communication*, London: Palgrave Macmillan, pp. 327–46.

Love, R. (2020) *Overcoming Challenges in Corpus Construction: The Spoken British National Corpus 2014*, London: Routledge.

Love, R., Dembry, C., Hardie, A., Brezina, V. and McEnery, T. (2017) 'The Spoken BNC2014: Designing and Building a Spoken Corpus of Everyday Conversations', *International Journal of Corpus Linguistics* 22: 319–44.

Mackey, A. (2014) 'Practice and Progression in Second Language Research Methods', *AILA Review* 27: 80–97.

McCarthy, M. J. (1998) *Spoken Language and Applied Linguistics*, Cambridge: Cambridge University Press.

McCarthy, M. J. and O'Keeffe, A. (2010) 'Historical Perspective: What Are Corpora and How Have They Evolved?', in A. O'Keeffe and M. J. McCarthy (eds) *The Routledge Handbook of Corpus Linguistics*, London: Routledge, pp. 3–13.

McEnery, T., Xiao, R. and Tono, Y. (2006) *Corpus-Based Language Studies. An Advanced Resource Book*, London: Routledge

McEnery, A., Brezina, V., Gablasova, D., Banerjee, J. V. (2019) 'Corpus Linguistics, Learner Corpora and SLA: Employing Technology to Analyze Language Use', *Annual Review of Applied Linguistics* 39: 74–92.

OED Online. (2021) Oxford University Press. www.oed.com/view/Entry/41873. [Accessed 25 August 2021].

O'Halloran, K. A. (2017) *Posthumanism and Deconstructing Arguments: Corpora and Digitally-Driven Critical Analysis*, London: Routledge.

O'Keeffe, A. (2021) 'Data-Driven Learning – A Call for a Broader Research Gaze', *Language Learning* 54: 259–72.

O'Keeffe, A. and Mark, G. (2017) 'The English Grammar Profile of Learner Competence: Methodology and Key Findings', *International Journal of Corpus Linguistics* 22(4): 457–89.

Parrish, S. M. (1962) 'Problems in the Making of Computer Concordances', *Studies in Bibliography* 15: 1–14.

Rühlemann, C. (2019) *Corpus Linguistics for Pragmatics: Guide for Research*, London: Routledge.

Thewissen, J. (2013) 'Capturing L2 Accuracy Developmental Patterns: Insights from an Error Tagged Learner Corpus', *The Modern Language Journal* 97(S1), 77–101.

Part I

Building and designing a corpus: the basics

2

Building a corpus: what are key considerations?

Randi Reppen

1 Building a corpus: what are the basics?

As can be seen from this volume, a corpus can serve as a useful tool for discovering many aspects of language use that otherwise may go unnoticed. Unlike straightforward grammaticality judgments, when asked to reflect on language use, our recall and intuitions about our language use often are not accurate (Svartvik and Quirk 1983). Therefore, a corpus is essential when exploring issues or questions related to language use. The wide range of questions related to language use that can be addressed through a corpus is a strength of this approach. Questions that range from the level of words and intonation to how constellations of linguistic features work together in discourse can all be explored through corpus linguistic methods and tools. Questions related to aspects of how language use varies by situation or over time are also ideal areas to explore through corpus research.

Each year, the number of corpora that are available for researchers to use is increasing. So, before tackling the task of building a corpus, be sure that there is not an existing corpus that meets your research needs. Each day, more and more corpora of different languages are becoming available on the Web. However, you might be interested in exploring types of language that are not adequately represented by existing corpora. In this case you will need to build a corpus. Depending on the types of research questions being addressed, the task of constructing a corpus can be a reasonably efficient and constrained task, or it can be quite a time-consuming task. Having a clearly articulated research question is an essential first step in corpus construction, since this will guide the design of the corpus. The corpus must be representative of the language being investigated. If the goal is to describe the language of newspaper editorials, collecting personal letters would not be representative of the language of newspaper editorials; neither would collecting entire newspapers be representative of the language found in the editorial section. There must be a match between the language being examined and the type of material being collected (Biber 1993). Representativeness is closely linked to size, which is addressed in the next section (see also Chapters 4, 5 and 6, this volume).

DOI: 10.4324/9780367076399-2

2 What kind of data do I use and how much?

The question of corpus size is a difficult one. There is not a specific number of words that answers this question. Corpus size is certainly not a case of one size fits all (Carter and McCarthy 2001). For explorations that are designed to capture all the senses of a particular word or set of words, as in building a dictionary, the corpus needs to be large, very large – tens or hundreds of millions of words. However, for most questions that are pursued by corpus researchers, the question of size is resolved by two factors: representativeness (Have I collected enough texts [words] to accurately represent the type of language under investigation?) and practicality (time constraints). In some cases, it is possible to completely represent the language being studied. For example, it is possible to capture all the works of a particular author, or historical texts from a certain period or texts from a particular event (e.g. a radio or TV series, political speeches). In these cases, complete representation of the language can be achieved. An example of this is the 604,767-word corpus of nine seasons of the popular television sitcom *Friends* (Quaglio 2009). However, in most cases it is not possible to achieve complete representation, and in these cases corpus size is determined by capturing enough of the language for accurate representation. For example, Vaughan (2008) examined the role of humour in English-language teacher faculty meetings at two institutions. Since this was a specific question in a specific context, a relatively small corpus (40,000 words) was adequate to explore the role of humour in these two settings (see Chapter 33, this volume, for more on this corpus).

Smaller, specialized corpora, such as the examples noted earlier, can be very useful for exploring grammatical and discourse features, but for studies of low-frequency grammatical features or lexical studies such as compiling a dictionary, millions of words are needed to ensure that all the senses of a word are captured (Biber 1990), thus reinforcing the interrelationship of research question, representativeness, corpus design and size.

3 How do I collect texts?

Once a research question is articulated, corpus construction can begin. The next task is identifying the texts and developing a plan for text collection. In all cases, before collecting texts, it is important to have permission to collect them. When collecting texts from people or institutions, it is essential to get consent from the parties involved. The rules that apply vary by country, institution and setting, so be sure to check before beginning collection. There are texts that are considered public domain. These texts are available for research, and permission is not needed. Public domain texts are also available for free, as opposed to copyrighted material, which in addition to requiring permission prior to use may have fees associated with it. Even when using texts for private research, it is important to respect copyright laws. This includes material that is available online (see Chapters 3 and 7, this volume, for more on ethical considerations when building a corpus).

When creating a corpus, certain procedures are followed, regardless of whether the corpus is representing spoken or written language. Some issues that are best addressed prior to corpus construction include: What constitutes a text? How will the files be named? What information will be included in each file? How will the texts be stored (file format)?

In many cases, what constitutes a text is predetermined. When collecting a corpus of in-class writing, a text could be defined as all the essays written in the class on a particular day, or a text could be each student's essay. The latter is the best option. It is always best to create files at the smallest "unit", since it is easier to combine files in analysis rather than to have to open a file, split it into two texts or more and then resave the files with new names prior to being able to begin any type of analysis. So, even if you are creating a corpus of in-class writing with the goal of comparing across different classes, having the essays stored as individual files rather than as a whole class will allow the most options for analysis. When considering spoken language, the question of what constitutes a text is a bit messier. Is a spoken text the entire conversation, including all the topic shifts that might occur? Or is a spoken text a portion of a conversation that addresses a particular topic or tells a story? The answers to these questions are, once again, directly shaped by the research questions being explored (Biber *et al.* in press).

Before saving a text, file naming conventions need to be established. File names that clearly relate to the content of the file allow users to sort and group files into sub-categories or to create subcorpora more easily. Creating file names that include aspects of the texts that are relevant for analysis is helpful. For example, if the research involved building a corpus of *Letters to the Editor* from newspapers that represented two different demographic areas (e.g. urban vs. rural) and included questions related to the gender of the letter writer, then this information could be included in the file name. In this case, abbreviating the newspaper name, including the writer's gender, and also including the date of publication would result in a file name that is reasonably transparent and also a reasonable length. For example, a letter written by a woman in a city in Arizona printed in October 2008 could have a file name of azcf108. It is ideal if file names are about seven to eight characters. If additional space is needed, a dot (.) followed by three additional characters can be used. File names of this length will not cause problems across different analytical tools or software backup tools. Using backup software and keeping copies of the corpus in multiple locations can avoid the anguish of losing the corpus due to computer malfunction, fire or theft. Secure storage of data is also a key concern in terms of data protection (see Chapter 3, this volume).

In many cases a *header,* or *metadata* (information about the data), is included at the beginning of each corpus file or is linked to each file (see Chapter 3, this volume). The information is in the header (included at the beginning of the file), while metadata is typically kept in a separate document linked to the file. The information in a header or metadata might include demographic information about the writer or speaker, or it could include contextual information about the text, such as when and where it was collected and under what conditions. The use of a metadata file instead of a header is preferable to add a layer of data security. A metadata file also provides an easier means to search for specific characteristics (e.g. texts with particular attributes such as first language or different language events) in large corpora.

If a header is used, it is important that the format of the header is consistent across all files in the corpus. Since creating a corpus is a huge time investment, it is a good idea to include any information in the header that might be relevant in future analysis. Headers often have some type of formatting that helps to set them apart from the text. The header information might be placed inside angle brackets (< >) or have a marking to indicate the end of the header and the beginning of the text. This formatting can be used to keep information in the header from being included in the analysis of the text, avoiding inflating frequency counts and counting information in the header as part of the text. Following is an example of a header from a conversation file.

Example header:

<Begin header>
<File name – spknnov06.mf>
<Setting = two friends chatting at a coffee shop>
<Speaker 1 = Male 22 years old>
<Speaker 2 = Female 33 years old>
<Recorded = November 2006>
<Transcribed = Mary Jones December 2006>
<Notes: Occasional background traffic noise makes parts unintelligible>
<End of header>

Determining the file format for storing texts may seem inconsequential; however, saving files in a format that is not compatible with the tools that will be used for analysis will result in many extra hours of work. Most corpus analysis tools function well with the file format *plain text* or *UTF8*. When scanning written texts, downloading texts from the internet, or entering texts (keyboarding), you are always given an option as to how to save the file. From the drop-down "*Save as*" menu, choose the option *plain text*. If the text is already in electronic format and has been saved by a word processing program, use the "*Save as*" option and select *plain text*, or add the file extension (the part after the dot [.] in the file name) *txt*.

Whether creating a corpus of spoken or written texts, some decisions are best made during the design phase. Creating a corpus of written texts is an easier task than building a corpus of spoken texts, but both have challenges associated with them. Often, written texts are already in electronic format; however, if the texts are not in electronic format, they will need to be entered in electronic form. If the texts represent learner language, novice writing or children's writing, it is important to preserve the non-standard spelling and grammar structures. These may be of keen interest. In this case, it is often best to create an original version, preserving all idiosyncrasies, and a "clean" version that has standardised spelling used for more conventional analyses. Decisions about how to treat any art or non-orthographic markings will also need to be made. These challenges pale in comparison to the many decisions that need to be made when collecting a spoken corpus. First of all, a spoken corpus obviously does not exist in written form, but will need to be recorded and then transcribed in order to be analysed using available corpus tools. Digital recording devices have made the collection of spoken texts more straightforward. Phones, tablets and other devices can provide high-quality sound recordings which can be easily transferred to a computer, etc. (see Chapter 3, this volume, for more on recording options).

Once the files have been recorded, it is necessary to transcribe the spoken recordings into an electronic format. Unfortunately, current speech recognition software is not able to accurately convert the spoken files into text files, so this is accomplished by individuals listening to the recordings and transcribing, or keying them, into the computer. Transcribing a spoken text into a written format is a very time-consuming and tedious process. Depending on the quality of the recording and the level of detail included in the transcription (marking prosody, marking intonation, timing pauses, etc.), it can take 10 to 15 hours to transcribe an hour of spoken language (see Chapter 3, for more on transcription).

Transcription freeware applications are available that make the process of transcribing a bit easier. These have settings that allow the rate of speech to be slowed without distorting the sound quality, and they can be set to repeat set intervals of speech so as to save the transcriber from having to manually stop and rewind recordings.

Before beginning to transcribe audio files, several decisions must be made. Some of the more common questions that need to be addressed prior to transcription include: How will reduced forms be transcribed? If the speaker says *wanna* or *gonna* for *want to* or *going to*, will what the speaker actually said be transcribed, or will the complete form be transcribed, or will both forms (double coding) be transcribed (e.g. *wanna/want to*), allowing maximum flexibility for analysis? Many times it is difficult to hear or understand what was said; this can be due to background noises or the speaker not being near the recording device. What will be transcribed in these instances? The transcriber can make a best guess and indicate that with a (@@) after the guessed word or syllables. Or the transcriber might simply write *unclear* and the number of syllables (e.g. *unclear – two syllables*) after the utterance. Overlapping speech is another challenge in transcribing natural speech events. Speakers often talk at the same time or complete each other's turns. Often listeners will use conversational facilitators or minimal responses (e.g. *uh huh, mmm, hum*, etc.) to show that they are listening and attentive to what the speaker is saying. These overlaps and insertions are a challenge for transcribers. It is a good idea to standardise the spelling of these conversational facilitators. For example, it might be that *mmm* is always spelled with three *M*s, or that the reduced form of *because* is always represented as *cuz*. How laughter will be transcribed is another decision. Making these decisions ahead of time will save many hours of anguish as you search files for particular features, only to realize that you need to spend time standardising these forms (see Chapter 33, this volume, where different transcription approaches to laughter are exemplified). Repetitions and pauses are also features of spoken language that require transcribing decisions. Will pauses be timed? Or will the transcription conventions simply guide the transcriber to note short pauses (maybe two to five seconds in length) and long pauses (maybe those longer than six seconds) through the use of … for short pauses and ……. for long pauses? Again, this decision will be informed by the research goals of the corpus. Some corpora are carefully transcribed and include detailed prosodic information (Svartvik and Quirk 1983; Cheng *et al.* 2008; Staples 2015). This type of transcription is very time consuming but allows researchers to capture many of the aspects of spoken language that are typically lost through the transcription process. Creating a prosodically transcribed corpus is often done in two stages: first, just creating a transcription and then going back and adding the prosodic markings. In some cases, the corpus can be set up to have multiple layers of annotations. These multiple layers of annotation can greatly enhance the types of analysis that can be performed, but they also need to be governed by practical considerations (Cook 1990). For more on transcribing, coding and marking up of spoken corpora, see Chapter 3, this volume. This chapter will also guide you through the considerations involved in building a multi-modal spoken corpus, where the transcription aims to capture and align the spoken word (written down) with the prosodic and visual components (hand gestures, head nods, gaze, etc.).

4 How much mark-up do I need?

The term *mark-up* refers to adding information to a corpus file. Not all corpora contain mark-ups; however, certain types of mark-ups can facilitate corpus analysis. Mark-ups can be divided into two types: document mark-up and annotations. Document mark-up refers to markings much like Hypertext Markup Language (HTML) codes that are used to indicate document features such as paragraphs, fonts, sentences (including sentence numbers), speaker identification and marking the end of the text (see Chapters 3 and 4, this volume, for more on mark-up). At a basic level the header can be considered a type of mark-up, since it provides additional information about the text. The prosodic markings of a spoken corpus, mentioned in the previous section, are a form of mark-up. Annotations cover a wide range of possibilities. The most common form of corpus annotation involves including parts of speech (POS) tags, which label each word in a corpus as to its grammatical category (e.g. noun, adjective, adverb, etc.). These tags can be very useful for addressing a number of questions and help to resolve many of the issues related to simply searching for a particular word. Many words are polysemous, yet when a word's part of speech is known, much is accomplished to disambiguate and focus search results. For example, a POS tagged corpus makes a search of the modal verb *can* much more efficient by not including instances of *can* as a noun, or the very common word *that,* which has many different grammatical functions (see Chapter 9, this volume, for an example of how POS tagging can be used).

By using a template for corpus mark-up, it is possible for corpus texts to have multiple annotations. For example, a text could be viewed as just a plain text, or it could also be viewed with the POS tags, or possibly the POS and prosodic annotations. This is a useful way of annotating a corpus and providing users with access to the versions that meet their needs.

5 Looking to the future

Given the enormous and ongoing changes in the world of technology, it is difficult to imagine the scope of changes that might take place in the area of corpus construction and tools. However, making a wish list for the future is always a delightful task. One of the changes that we hopefully will see in the near future is greater availability of spoken corpora. This could be a result of two factors. First, researchers may be more able and willing to share the spoken corpora that they have assembled. Second, creating spoken corpora will likely benefit from technological advances in speech recognition, thus making the task of transcribing spoken language to electronic form a much more efficient process and a more automated task. Perhaps digital sound files will be fed through a conversion programme and then the researcher can go through to edit any areas that are problematic. Currently, exploratory work is being done using crowdsourcing as a means for increasing the efficiency and accuracy of spoken transcription and prosodic coding (see Chapter 3, this volume). This could be a tremendous boost to spoken language researchers.

The development and use of video and multi-modal corpora is another area that will probably change dramatically in the next decade. Much research is already being done in this area (Carter and Adolphs 2008; Knight and Adolphs 2008; Dahlmann and Adolphs 2009; Adolphs and Carter 2013; and Chapter 7, this volume), and given how quickly technology can advance, this seems to be the next area that can provide new levels of corpus building and analysis, allowing us to ask and answer questions that are not even imagined at this point in time.

Further reading

Biber, D. and Reppen, R. (2015) *The Cambridge Handbook of English Corpus Linguistics*, Cambridge: Cambridge University Press. (This edited volume covers methodological considerations of corpus compilation and analyses and applications of corpus analysis. Each chapter includes a survey of the field followed by a detailed case study.)

Biber, D., Conrad, S. and Reppen, R. (1998) *Corpus Linguistics: Exploring Language Structure and Use*, Cambridge: Cambridge University Press. (This book provides an overview of corpus linguistics and its many applications, including discovering patterns of language use to researching language change over time. The chapters build from the lexical to the discourse level, each with detailed examples of studies related to the topic being covered in the chapter. The book ends with a series of methodology boxes that provide readers with answers to many of the methodological processes related to using corpora for research.)

Love, R., Dembry, C., Hardie, A., Brezina, V. and McEnery, T. (2017) 'The Spoken BNC2014: Designing and Building a Spoken Corpus of Everyday Conversations', *International Journal of Corpus Linguistics* 22(3): 319–44. (This article provides a thorough description of the decisions involved in the creation of the spoken portion of BNC2014, including the challenges faced in collecting, compiling and annotating a representative and publicly available corpus of English conversation.)

O'Keeffe, A., McCarthy, M. J. and Carter, R. A. (2007) *From Corpus to Classroom: Language Use and Language Teaching*, Cambridge: Cambridge University Press. (The authors have done extensive research on language and patterns of use. This information is the foundation for the practical applications of corpus research that is presented to English-language teachers. In addition to English-language teachers, language researchers will see this book as a wonderful resource on many aspects of language, especially spoken language).

Reppen, R. and Simpson-Vlach, R. (2020) 'Corpus Linguistics' , in N. Schmitt and M. Rodgers (eds) *An Introduction to Applied Linguistics*, London: Arnold, pp. 91–108. (This chapter presents an overview of corpus linguistics and highlights how the methodology of corpus linguistics can be used to explore many areas of interest in the area of applied linguistics.)

Useful web links

Laurence Anthony's homepage https://www.laurenceanthony.net/ (This has links to a variety of resources for both analysing and building corpora. In addition to the well-known *AntConc* concordancing software, there is *AntCoreGen* (2019) that allows users to build discipline-specific corpora. This site also includes tools for converting files, analysing vocabulary, annotating texts for part of speech (PoS) and analysing n-grams).

CROW (Corpus repository of writing) writecrow.org (This site has extensive resources that include a web interface with a corpus of university student writing in English and the assignments used to generate the writing. It also has links and free resources to help researchers create and analyse corpora.)

References

Adolphs, S. and Carter, R. A. (2013) *Spoken Corpus Linguistics: From Monomodal to Multimodal*, London: Routledge.

Biber, D. (1990) 'Methodological Issues Regarding Corpus-Based Analysis of Linguistic Variation', *Literary and Linguistic Computing* 5(4): 257–69.

Biber, D. (1993) 'Representativeness in Corpus Design', *Literary and Linguistic Computing* 8(4): 243–57.

Biber, D., Egbert, J., Keller, D. and Wizner, S. (in press) 'Describing Registers in a Continuous Situational Space: Case Studies from The Web and Natural Conversation', in E. Seoane and D. Biber (eds) *Corpus-based Approaches to Register Variation*, Amsterdam: John Benjamins.

Carter, R. A. and Adolphs, S. (2008) 'Linking the Verbal and Visual: New Directions for Corpus Linguistics', *Language and Computers special issue 'Language, People, Numbers'* 64: 275–91.

Carter, R. A. and McCarthy, M. J. (2001) 'Size Isn't Everything: Spoken English, Corpus and the Classroom', *TESOL Quarterly* 35(2): 337–40.

Cheng, W., Greaves, C. and Warren, M. (2008) *A Corpus-Driven Study of Discourse Intonation*, Amsterdam: John Benjamins.

Cook, G. (1990) 'Transcribing Infinity: Problems of Context Presentation', *Journal of Pragmatics* 14: 1–24.

Dahlmann, I. and Adolphs, S. (2009) 'Spoken Corpus Analysis: Multimodal Approaches to Language Description', in P. Baker (ed.) *Contemporary Approaches to Corpus Linguistics*, London: Continuum Press, pp. 125–39.

Knight, D. and Adolphs, S. (2008) 'Multi-Modal Corpus Pragmatics: The Case of Active Listenership', in J. Romeo (ed.) *Corpus and Pragmatics*, Berlin: Mouton de Gruyter, pp. 175–90.

Quaglio, P. (2009) *Television Dialogue: The Sitcom Friends vs. Natural Conversation*, Amsterdam: John Benjamins.

Staples, S. (2015) *The Discourse of Nurse-Patient Interactions: Contrasting Communicative Styles of US and Internationals Nurses*, Amsterdam: John Benjamins.

Svartvik, J. and Quirk, R. (eds) (1983) *A Corpus of English Conversation*, Lund, Sweden: Lund Studies in English.

Vaughan, E. (2008) '"Got a Date or Something?": An Analysis of the Role of Humour and Laughter in the Workplace Meetings of English Language Teachers', in A. Ädel and R. Reppen (eds) *Corpora and Discourse: The Challenges of Different Settings*, Amsterdam: John Benjamins, pp. 95–115.

3

Building a spoken corpus: what are the basics?

Dawn Knight and Svenja Adolphs

1 Overview of spoken corpora

Throughout the development of corpus linguistics there has been a noticeable focus on analysing written language and, at the time of writing, written corpora run close to the 20-billion-word mark (e.g. the *EnTenTen* suite; Jakubíček *et al.* 2013). Using these corpora, the possibilities for generating new insights into the ways in which language is structured and used are both exciting and unprecedented. Spoken corpora, on the other hand, tend to be much smaller in size than their written counterparts.

A chapter in the first edition of this Handbook featured a 'wish-list for future corpora' which included a hope that 'creating spoken corpora will benefit from technological advances in speech recognition, thus making the task of transcribing spoken language to text files a much more efficient process and more automated task' (Reppen 2010: 36). Despite the passing of a decade and the ever-increasing sophistication of speech-to-text technologies, a fully accurate and sophisticated automated approach to spoken corpus construction has still not been developed. The collection and processing of spoken corpora remains largely manually driven and is typically costlier and more time-consuming to undertake than the construction of written corpora. This has resulted in the comparative lag in the development of spoken datasets versus their written counterparts and an on-going 'written-biased view' in corpus linguistic research (Lüdeling and Kytö 2008: vi).

Despite these challenges, there remains a growing interest in developing spoken corpora; this is a testament to the value they provide to a diverse number of research communities. Following on from the early developments of relatively small spoken corpora in the 1960s, such as the 500,000-word *London-Lund Corpus* (Svartvik 1990), the past five decades have seen major advances in the collection and development of spoken corpora, particularly in the English language, but not exclusively. Examples of English spoken corpora include the 5-million-word *Cambridge and Nottingham Corpus of Discourse in English* (CANCODE; McCarthy 1998), the 1-million-word *Limerick Corpus of Irish English* (LCIE; Farr *et al.* 2004), the 1-million-word *Hong Kong Corpus of*

DOI: 10.4324/9780367076399-3

Spoken English (HKCSE; Cheng and Warren 2002) and the recently released 11.5-million-word *Spoken British National Corpus 2014* (Spoken BNC 2014; Love *et al.* 2017).

In addition, there is a growing interest in the development of specialist spoken corpora, including corpora of learner language (e.g. *Trinity Lancaster Corpus*, Gablasova *et al.* 2019) and business and academic discourse (e.g. CANBEC, Handford 2007 and BASE, Thompson and Nesi 2001). Similarly, there has also been a growing interest in spoken corpora in other languages, including the Welsh-language Siarad corpus (Deuchar *et al.* 2018), the 2.8-million-word ORAL2013 balanced corpus of informal spoken Czech (Komrsková *et al.* 2017) and the 2.3-million-word *Forschungs- und Lehrkorpus gesprochenes Deutsch* (Schmidt 2016). Each of these corpora provides researchers with rich samples of spoken language in use, which form the basis of new and emerging descriptions of naturally occurring discourse.

In recognition of the fact that spoken discourse is multi-modal in nature, a number of spoken corpora align audio and/or visual data streams with the transcripts of conversations. Examples include the *Nottingham Multi-Modal Corpus* (NMMC: a 250,000-word corpus of videoed single-speaker and dyadic discourse, Knight *et al.* 2006); the *Augmented Multi-Party Interaction Corpus* (AMI: a 100-hour meeting room video corpus, McCowan *et al.* 2005); and the SCOTS Corpus (a corpus of Scottish texts and speech comprising audio files with aligned transcriptions, Anderson *et al.* 2007).

Research outputs based on the analysis of spoken corpora are wide-ranging and include, for example, descriptions of lexis and grammar (e.g. Biber *et al.* 1999; Carter and McCarthy 2006), discourse particles (Aijmer 2002), courtroom talk (Coulthard 2013), media discourse (O'Keeffe 2006) and health care communication (Hunt and Harvey 2015). This research covers phenomena at the utterance level, as well as at the level of discourse. A number of studies start with the exploration of concordance outputs and frequency information as a point of entry into the data and carry out subsequent analyses at the level of discourse (e.g. McCarthy 1998). Others start with a discourse analytical approach followed by subsequent analyses of concordance data.

2 Corpus design

While some forms of specialist literary corpora, such as the *CliC Dickens* corpus (see Mahlberg *et al.* 2016 and Chapters 36 and 37, this volume) fully represent the complete works of a given author, it is near impossible for the majority of corpora to capture or contain *all* examples of language that they seek to represent. The parameters of language from a given population or context are often indeterminable, so many unknowns are involved in this process. Corpora are thus best understood as 'a category organised around a prototype' (Gries and Newman 2014: 259), a model, a snapshot of language, one which should, as far as possible, accurately represent the language variet(ies) and/or register(s) that it is sampled from.

Although it would be useful to have prescribed and agreed-upon standards in corpus design and construction, 'it is difficult to unify an activity which has to satisfy very divergent and often conflicting research goals' (Corrigan and Mearns 2016: 4 – see also Chapter 20, this volume, for further discussion on corpus design). Design principles used in the development of corpora are, instead, often locally determined and require considerable attention *a priori* to data collection. Despite this lack of "standards", in 2005 Sinclair offered some basic principles that are still often used as a useful starting point for designing both spoken and written corpora (for similar guidelines see Reppen and

Simpson 2002: 93, Wynne 2005 and Chapter 4 of this volume). These follow (Sinclair 2005):

1. The contents of a corpus should be selected without regard to the language they contain, but according to their communicative function in the community in which they arise.
2. Corpus builders should strive to make their corpus as representative as possible of the language from which it is chosen.
3. Only those components of corpora which have been designed to be independently contrastive should be contrasted.
4. Criteria for determining the structure of a corpus should be small in number, clearly separate from each other and efficient as a group in delineating a corpus that is representative of the language or variety under examination.
5. Any information about a text other than the alphanumeric string of its words and punctuation should be stored separately from the plain text and merged when required in applications.
6. Samples of language for a corpus should, wherever possible, consist of entire documents or transcriptions of complete speech events, or should get as close to this target as possible. This means that samples will differ substantially in size.
7. The design and composition of a corpus should be documented fully with information about the contents and arguments in justification of the decisions taken.
8. The corpus builder should retain as target notions representativeness and balance. While these are not precisely definable and attainable goals, they must be used to guide the design of a corpus and the selection of its components.
9. Any control of subject matter in a corpus should be imposed by the use of external, not internal, criteria.
10. A corpus should aim for homogeneity in its components while maintaining adequate coverage, and rogue texts should be avoided.

These guidelines are necessarily idealistic, and the extent to which a resultant corpus is considered to be representative, balanced and/or homogeneous (if at all) will be relative to the decisions made in the design process, that is, the specific aims of the research and/or project.

With regard to these guidelines, there are a number of issues that pertain specifically to the construction of spoken corpora, best described in relation to the basic stages of construction:

- Recording;
- Transcribing, coding and mark-up;
- Management and analysis.

These stages interact, with each stage influencing the next. The stage of recording data is determined by the type of analysis planned, which in turn determines the granularity and detail of transcription, coding and mark-up and the participants and/or contexts in which recordings take place. It is therefore important to plan the development of a corpus carefully and to consider all practical and ethical issues that may arise. The approach that emerges during the process of construction is be reconsidered and modified throughout (i.e. it is iterative).

Planning necessarily leads to an informed selection of discourse events to be recorded for the corpus. It is impossible to create a "complete picture" of discourse in corpora (Thompson 2005), so it is the responsibility of the corpus constructor(s) to limit the potential detrimental effect that the selection may have on the representativeness, homogeneity and balance of the corpus.

Recording

The recording stage is the data collection phase. As with other stages of corpus compilation, there is no agreed-upon best and/or standard approach to data collection. The specific aims of a research project and the questions that will be asked of the dataset determine what approach is used. There is, however, a general consensus that data collection should be principled.

It is important that all recordings are both suitable and rich enough in the information required for in-depth linguistic enquiry, as well as being of a high enough quality to be used and re-used in a corpus database (Knight *et al.* 2006). It is therefore advisable to strive to collect data which is as accurate and exhaustive as possible, capturing as much information from the discursive environment as possible. This involves documenting information about the participants, location and overall context in which the event takes place, as well as the type of recording equipment being used and the technical and physical specifications applied to the recording itself. The loss or omission of data cannot be easily rectified at a later date, since real-life communication cannot be authentically rehearsed and replicated (see Chapter 4, this volume, for more detailed discussions on authenticity in corpus design and construction).

You will also need to consider how and where you will recruit contributors from. When developing the spoken component of CorCenCC (*Corpws Cenedlaethol Cymraeg Cyfoes – The National Corpus of Contemporary Welsh*, Knight *et al.* 2021) and the Spoken BNC2014, participant recruitment methods included the use of extensive social and print media campaigns, email and newsletter advertisements and national TV and radio interviews. In the case of the Spoken BNC2014, participants were also paid for their contributions, something which obviously would not be possible for a lone researcher without sufficient funding.

With regard to recording equipment, there are a number of voice recorders, phones, tablets and other mobile devices which support high-quality recording of spoken interaction. Recordings made on these devices are born digital and can be easily transferred to a PC or other device. Video recordings of spoken interactions are an invaluable alternative to pure sound recordings, as the resulting data offer further scope for analysis. The availability of very small and unobtrusive and mobile video recording equipment also means that recording can be carried out a variety of different contexts "in the wild".

Crowdsourcing methods are also becoming increasingly popular in the creation of spoken corpora. Crowdsourcing involves the outsourcing, typically via online or app-based means, of specific forms of tasks or activities via open calls to a large (potentially global) network of unknown labourers (i.e. the *crowd*). It focuses on the power of people volunteering information about what they think and do. Crowdsourcing approaches are widely used across a range of different public-facing online and app-based platforms as a means of completing numerous different tasks and activities (e.g. fundraising or supporting business start-ups).

The application of crowdsourcing methods in linguistics is still at a relatively early stage of development, but crowdsourcing methods have been used extensively in other fields such as computer science and are increasingly being applied in the arts, humanities and social sciences (see Weinberger 2020 for an example). In the applied linguistic context, crowdsourcing methods have been used in the translation and/or transcription of speech, to annotate datasets and to collect dialectic data (see Adolphs *et al.* 2020 for an example). A community-driven, crowdsourcing approach was also used to complement the use of more traditional approaches in the collection of spoken Welsh-language data in CorCenCC. In this example, crowdsourcing was facilitated either live, via a mobile app or by uploading pre-recorded files via an interactive website. This approach enabled users to collect and upload data; accurately and appropriately tag and annotate in terms of the source, type, topic, date of collection and other relevant metadata categories; and attribute full permission forms.

A similar approach was used by the developers of the Spoken BNC2014 who embarked on a 'national participation campaign' (Love *et al.* 2017: 320) based on a 'Public Participation in Scientific Research' approach (PPSR, Shirk *et al.* 2012). Here, anyone interested in participating signed up via the project website and then were asked to record their own conversations using audio recorders on their mobiles, submitting recordings along with relevant permission forms and metadata information.

A recent study by Adolphs *et al.* has also examined the potential for developing a new type of spoken corpus, crowdsourcing language as it is received rather than produced. Participants were asked to input, via an app, the language they hear around them, 'to investigate the level of precision and recall of the "crowd" when it comes to reporting language they have heard in real certain contexts' (Adolphs *et al.* 2020). This approach has yet to be tested on a more extensive scale, however.

While crowdsourcing methods have the potential to upscale the collection of a volume of data, it is not possible to carefully sample contextual variables when crowdsourcing approaches are used, as it is not possible to predetermine which contexts speakers will record their interactions in. Crowdsourcing is also technologically driven and so relies on contributors' access to relevant technological resources for it to be implementable. These factors need to be considered when designing a corpus, with more traditional, targeted and laborious methods considered to complement and support any crowdsourcing approaches used.

Since the construction of spoken corpora is quite expensive, the issue of cost-effectiveness requires consideration, in particular, weighing up the advantages between capturing large amounts of data (in terms of time, number of encounters or discourse contexts), the amount of detail added in transcriptions and annotations and the nature of analyses that the data may support relative to the cost of carrying out these tasks. In terms of the number of hours of recording needed to achieve a particular word count, in the development of previous spoken corpora, such as CANCODE, one hour of recorded casual conversation accounted for approximately 10,000 words of transcribed data. This is only a very broad estimate, as the number of words per hour of recording depends on a range of different factors, including, amongst others, the discourse context and the rate of speech of the participants.

This discussion leads to the wider question of *how much data is enough?* At the heart of this question is the variable under investigation and a key 'factor that affects how many different encounters you may have to record is how frequently the variable you are interested in occurs in talk' (Cameron 2001: 28). Thus, the amount of data we need to record to analyse words or phrases that occur quite frequently is less than we would need to study less frequent items. The study of minimal response tokens in discourse, such as *yeah, mmhm*, etc., which are frequent in certain types of interactions, therefore requires less data to be collected than the study of more lexicalised patterns which function as response tokens and which may be less frequent, such as *that's great* or *brilliant*. For further discussions on what kinds of data to collect and how much, see Chapter 2, this volume.

3 Metadata

Aside from recording the actual interaction between participants engaging in conversation, it is also important to collect and document information about the event itself. Metadata, or "data about data", is the conventional method used to do this. Love *et al.* provide a useful distinction between the different "types" of corpus metadata: 'at the level of the text (i.e. situational variables representing features of the recording as a whole) and at the sub-text level (i.e. social variables at the level of the speaker)' (Love *et al.* 2019: 300). These levels are further divided into more specific groupings, with, for example, categorical and non-categorical types of metadata as forms of text-level descriptors (Love *et al.* 2019: 300).

Metadata can be kept in a separate database or included as a "header" at the start of each document (usually encoded though mark-up language). A separate database with this information makes it easier to compare different types of texts in a corpus and has the distinct advantage that it can be further extended by other users of the same dataset, whilst also enabling such users to critically evaluate the quality of the dataset.

One example of descriptive metadata commonly collected is the demographic information relating to the individual participants. This may include details such as the age, accent/dialect, occupation (often classified according to the National Statistics Socio-economic classification, NS-SeC: Rose *et al.* 2005), birthplace, mother tongue and education level – details that are often included in speaker information forms. In addition, information concerning the number of speakers in a recording, recording location and, sometimes, conversation topics are often documented. The detail and range of this information will impact on the sorts of queries that can be carried out using the corpus. For a more detailed discussion of the different forms of corpus metadata, see Chapter 4, this volume.

Permission and ethics

Within a British and/or European context, it is important that the processes involved in the production, analysis, publication and sharing of data are compliant with the requirements of the General Data Protection Regulations (GDPR, for details see Tikkinen-Piri *et al.* 2017, although note that these requirements are subject to change as a consequence of Brexit).

Typical practice in addressing ethics on a professional or institutional level suggests that corpus developers should ensure that formal written consent is received from all participants involved *a priori* to carrying out the recording. Conventionally, this consent stipulates how recordings are to take place and how data are presented and outlines how recordings will subsequently be used. Whilst a participant's consent to record may be relatively easy to obtain and commonly involves a signature on a consent form, it is important to ensure that this consent holds true at every stage of the corpus compilation process. If a corpus is to be made publicly or widely available, participants need to provide *consent to distribute* recorded material and be provided with information about how recorded data are to be accessed, stored and distributed and by whom. Once data are distributed, it can be difficult or impossible to deal with requests for retraction of consent at a later stage.

A further issue to tackle is the notion of anonymity and the process that is applied to the data to ensure that anonymity can be maintained. Traditional approaches to corpus development emphasise the importance of striving for anonymity when developing records of discourse situations to protect the identities of those involved. To achieve this, the names of participants and third parties are often manually modified or completely omitted, along with any other details that may make the identity of referents obvious (a process also known as 'de-identification' by McEnery *et al.* 2017). This can include but is not restricted to people's names, email and Internet Protocol (IP) addresses, phone numbers and home addresses. The quest for anonymity can also extend to the use of specific words or phrases used, as well as potentially sensitive and/or controversial topics of discussion or particular opinions.

Issues of anonymity are more easily addressed when constructing text-based corpora. If the data used are already in the public domain and freely available, no alterations to the texts included are usually required. Otherwise, permission needs to be obtained from the relevant authors or publishers of texts (copyright holders), and specific guidelines concerning anonymity can subsequently be discussed and addressed with the authors and alterations to the data made as necessary. Similar procedures are involved if constructing spoken corpora based solely on transcripts of recorded events. Modifications in relation to names, places and other identifiers can be made at the transcription stage or as a next step following the initial transcription of data.

Anonymity is more problematic when it comes to audio or video records of conversations in corpora. Audio data is "raw", existing as an "audio fingerprint" of vocalisations that are specific to an individual. This makes it relatively easy to identify participants when audio files are replayed. Alteration of vocal output for the purpose of anonymisation can make it difficult for the recording to be used for further phonetic and prosodic analysis and is thus generally not advisable. A similar problem arises with the use of video data. Although it is possible to shadow, blur or pixelate video data in order to conceal the identity of speakers, these measures can be difficult to apply in practice (especially with large datasets). In addition, such measures obscure facial features of the individual, blurring distinctions between gestures and language forms. As a result, datasets may become unusable for certain lines of linguistic enquiry.

Considering the difficulties involved in the anonymisation of audio-visual data, it is important to discuss these issues fully with the participants prior to the recording and to ensure that participants understand the nature of the recording and the format of distribution and access. And while those who agree for their day-to-day activities to be recorded for research purposes may not be concerned about anonymity, the issue of protecting the identity of third parties remains an ethical challenge with such data, as does the issue of reusing and sharing contextually sensitive data recorded as part of multi-modal corpora.

This situation then raises a challenge that is central to the development of any corpus, namely, how can multi-site, multi-user, multi-source, multi-media datasets protect the rights of study participants as an integral part of the way in which they are constructed and used? Reconciling the desire for the traceability and probity of corpus data with the need for confidentiality and data protection requires serious consideration and should be addressed at the outset of any corpus development project. For further discussions of the ethics and copyright in corpus design and construction, see Chapter 4, this volume.

4 How do I transcribe spoken data?

One of the biggest challenges in corpus linguistic research is probably the representation of spoken data. There is no doubt that the collection of spoken language is far more laborious than the collection of written samples, but the richness of this type of data can make the extra effort worthwhile. Unscripted, naturally occurring conversations can be particularly interesting for the study of spoken grammar and lexis and for the analysis of the construction of meaning in interaction (for examples see Carter 2004; McCarthy 1998). However, the representation of spoken data is a major issue in this context, as the recorded conversations have to undergo a transition from the spoken mode to the written before they can be included in a corpus. In transcribing spoken discourse, we have to make various choices as to the amount of detail we wish to include in the written record (see Chapter 2, this volume, for further discussions on this matter). Since there are so many layers of detail that carry meaning in spoken interaction, this task can easily become a black hole (McCarthy 1998: 13) with a potentially infinite amount of contextual information to record (Cook 1990). The reason for this is that spoken interaction is essentially multi-modal in nature, featuring a careful interplay between textual, prosodic, gestural and environmental elements in the construction of meaning (see Adolphs and Carter 2013).

In terms of individual research projects, it is therefore important to decide exactly on the purpose of the study, to determine what type of transcription is needed. It is advisable to identify the spoken features of interest at the outset and to tailor the focus of the transcription accordingly. For example, a study of discourse structure might require the transcription to include overlaps but not detailed prosodic information.

At the same time there is a need to follow certain guidelines in the transcription in order to make them reusable by the research community. This, in turn, would allow both the size and quality of corpus data available for linguistic research to be enhanced, without individuals or teams of researchers expending large amounts of time and resources to start from scratch each time a spoken corpus is required.

A number of different types of transcription conventions are available, including those adopted by the Network of European Reference Corpora (NERC), which was used for the spoken component of the COBUILD project (Sinclair 1987). This transcription system contains four layers, ranging from basic orthographic representation to very detailed transcription, including information about prosody. Another set of guidelines for transcribing spoken data has been recommended by the Text Encoding Initiative (TEI) and has been applied, for example, to the original *British National Corpus* (BNC – see Sperberg-McQueen and Burnard 1993). These guidelines include the representation of structural, contextual, prosodic, temporal and kinesic elements of spoken interactions and provide a useful resource for the transcription of different levels of detail required to meet particular research goals.

Wray and Bloomer provide a useful rubric for some of the more universally used notations for orthographic transcription, which mark, for example, who is speaking; where interruptions, overlaps, backchannels and laughter occur in the discourse; and some basic distinct pronunciation variations (Wray and Bloomer 2013: 195–204).

Variations of basic orthographic transcription conventions are used in, for example, the Spoken BNC2014 and CANCODE.

Basic textual transcription can be extended through the use of phonemic and phonetic transcription. Phonemic transcription is used to represent pronunciation. Phonetic transcriptions, on the other hand, use the International Phonetic Alphabet (IPA) and indicate how specific successive sounds are used in a specific stretch of discourse. Similarly, in multi-modal corpora, there is a potential to enhance transcriptions with the mark-up of sequences of gesture in talk. The amount of information that can be included within a phonetic and multi-modal transcript is substantial and, for example, if video recordings are to support the audio recordings, the time for transcription can be increased by 'an hour to annotate the intonation and rhythm patterns in a single minute of speech' and 'a further hour to conduct a detailed annotation for one minute of a video' (Lin and Chen 2020: 72). Again, it therefore pays to be selective and to concentrate on marking only those features relevant to a specific research question or project.

The sharing and reuse of datasets increase the amount of information that could potentially be included in a transcript, with researchers adding more detail over time. The *SCOTS Corpus* is a good example of this. While the corpus developers used a basic orthographic approach to transcription, by making the original audio clips available online, other researchers are able to make their own additional transcriptions (and other layers of information), helping to extend and repurpose the data for their own studies to, for example, better support phonetic analysis (Anderson *et al.* 2007).

Layout of the transcript

Once decisions have been taken as to the features that are to be transcribed and the level of granularity and detail of the information to be included, the next step is to decide on an appropriate layout of the transcription. There are many different possibilities for laying out a transcript, but it is important to balance the level of detail to be included in the transcript and its readability.

The most commonly used format is a linear representation of turns with varying degrees of detail in terms of overlapping speech, prosody and extra-linguistic information. The following example is taken from a sub-component of the NMMC. While this corpus is fully aligned with audio and video streams, the basic transcriptions are formatted as follows:

In this figure, speakers are denoted by <$1> and <$2> tags, false starts are framed by <$=> and <\$=> and interruptions are indicated by the presence of the + tag.

Figure 3.1 presents the data linearly, ordering the conversation in a temporal way, rather like a conventional drama script. When using a linear format of transcription, it is particularly difficult to show speaker overlap, and for this reason some prefer to use different columns and thus separate transcripts according to who is speaking, as depicted in Figure 3.2 (see Thompson 2005 for further discussion on column transcripts). As speech is rarely "orderly" in the sense that one speaker speaks at a time, linear transcription may be seen as a misrepresentation of discourse structure (Graddol *et al.* 1994: 182). This criticism is particularly resonant if, for example, four or five speakers are present in a conversation and where there is a high level of simultaneous speech. The use of column transcripts therefore allows for a better representation of overlapping speech, presenting contributions from each speaker on the same line rather than with one positioned after the other.

A final, alternative method of representing speech is as a form of time-series data, with the talk of each speaker arranged on an individual line (or track), aligned with the audio

<$2> <$=> Oh well I <\$=> I'm just reading things at the moment and just+
<$1> Right.
<$2> +kind of vague+
<$1> So what given the amount of stuff of metaphor is huge?
<$2> Yeah well I've been looking through some of the stuff on scientific metaphors and+
<$1> Uh-huh.
<$2> +er particularly how they're used for educational purposes in+
<$1> Right.
<$2> +explaining concepts erm +
<$1> Yeah.

Figure 3.1 An example of transcribed speech, taken from the NMMC

<$1>	**<$2>**
	<$=> Oh well I <\$=> I'm just reading things at the moment and just+
Right.	
	+kind of vague+
So what given the amount of stuff of metaphor is huge?	
	Yeah well I've been looking through some of the stuff on scientific metaphors and+
Uh-huh.	
	+er particularly how they're used for educational purposes in+
Right.	
	+explaining concepts erm +
Yeah.	

Figure 3.2 A column-based transcript

output from the recording. This method is commonly used in transcription and coding software such as Anvil (Kipp 2001) and ELAN (Wittenburg *et al.* 2006), both of which also support video and other forms of time-series data, as seen in Figure 3.3 (taken from ELAN).

Speech is arranged according to the time at which it occurred. Overlapping contributions are indicated (as with Figure 3.2) as text which is positioned at the same point along the score, the timeline, across each individual speaker track. The contributions of multiple speakers can be represented using this method of transcription.

Ongoing advancements in the representation and alignment of different data streams have started to provide possibilities for studying spoken discourse in an integrated framework, including textual, prosodic and video data. The alignment of the different elements and the software needed to analyse such a multi-modal resource are still in the early stages of development, and at the present time it is probably beyond the scope of the majority of individual corpus projects to develop a searchable resource that includes the kind of dynamic representation that would address the need for a less linear layout of transcription.

Coding spoken data

The coding stage refers to 'the assignment of events to stipulated symbolic categories' (Bird and Liberman 2000: 26). This is the stage where qualitative records of events start to become

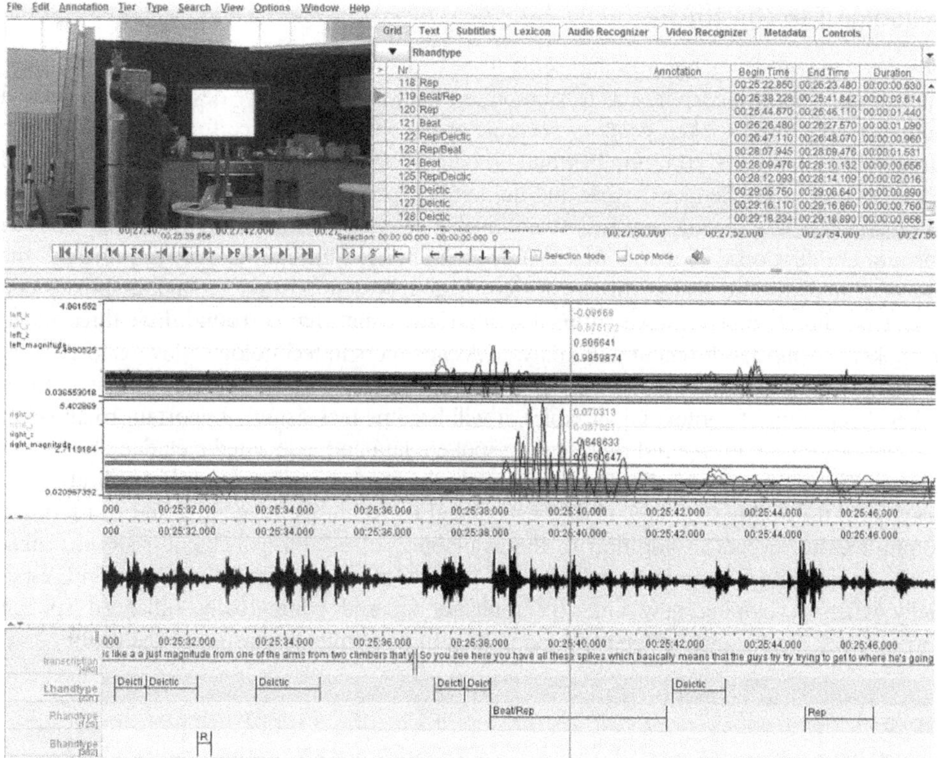

Figure 3.3 Time-based tracks in ELAN[1]

quantifiable as specific items that are relevant to the variables under consideration are marked up for future analyses (Scholfield 1995: 46). The coding stage is essentially a development of the transcription stage, but operating at a higher level of abstraction. Coding provides further detail to the basic systems of annotation and mark-up applied through the use of transcription notation and may include, amongst others, annotation of grammatical, semantic, pragmatic or discoursal features or categories. The majority of corpora include some type of annotation, as they allow corpora to be navigated in an automated way.

Early standards for the mark-up of corpora, known as the Standard Generalised Mark-up Language (SGML, which has been succeeded by Extensible Markup Language [XML]), were developed in the 1980s (see Chapter 4, this volume). SGML was traditionally used for marking up features such as line breaks and paragraph boundaries and typeface and page layout, providing standards for structuring both transcription and annotation. SGML is used in the BNC1994 corpus (see Aston and Burnard 1997). With modern advances in technology and associated advances in the sophistication of corpora and corpora tools, movements towards a redefinition of SGML have been promoted, although the majority of corpora today still use modified versions of the SGML or adopt their own conventions (mainly based on XML, as used in the Spoken BNC2014, which has a certain level of compatibility with TEI; Love *et al.* 2017). See Chapter 2, this volume, for discussions relating to how much mark-up is needed in a corpus.

5 Looking to the future

The development of techniques and tools to record, store and analyse naturally occurring interaction in spoken corpora has revolutionised the way in which we describe language and human interaction. Spoken corpora serve as an invaluable resource for the research of a large range of diverse communities and disciplines, including computer scientists, social scientists and researchers in the arts and humanities, policy makers and publishers. In order to be able to share resources across these diverse communities, it is important that spoken corpora are developed in a way that enables reusability. This can be achieved through the use of guidelines and frameworks for recording, representing and replaying spoken discourse. In this chapter we have outlined some of the issues that surround these three stages of spoken corpus development and analysis. As advances in technology allow us to develop new kinds of spoken corpora, which include audio-visual data-streams, as well as a much richer description of contextual variables, it will become increasingly important to agree on conventions for recording and representing spoken data and associated metadata. Similarly, advances in voice-to-text software may ease the burden of transcription but will also rely heavily on the ability to follow clearly articulated conventions for coding and transcribing communicative events in addition to the availability of established discourse-level frameworks (which are yet to exist). Adherence to agreed-upon conventions of this kind, especially when developing new kinds of multi-modal and contextually enhanced spoken corpora, will significantly extend the scope of spoken corpus linguistics in the future.

Note

1 Screenshot of ELAN software in use. At the time of writing, ELAN is freely available to download via The Language Archive website: https://archive.mpi.nl/tla/elan

Further reading

Adolphs, S. and Carter, R. A. (2013). *Spoken Corpus Linguistics: From Monomodal to Multimodal*, New York: Routledge. (This book examines the challenges faced in designing, building and utilising spoken corpora. It focuses both on approaches to traditional, mono-modal datasets, as well as moving into the multi-modal domain.)

Love, R. (2020).*Overcoming Challenges in Corpus Construction*, New York: Routledge. (This book provides a detailed overview of the design, construction and potential applications of the *Spoken British National Corpus 2014*).

Wynne, M. (ed.) (2005). *Developing Linguistic Corpora: A Guide to Good Practice*, Oxford: Oxbow Books. (This book provides an overview of some of the key issues and challenges faced in the construction of corpora, from collection to coding and tagging, to analysis.)

References

Adolphs, S. and Carter, R. A. (2013) *Spoken Corpus Linguistics: From Monomodal to Multimodal*, New York: Routledge.

Adolphs, S., Knight, D., Smith, C. and Price, D. (2020) 'Crowdsourcing Formulaic Phrases: Towards a New Type of Spoken Corpus', *Corpora* 15(1): 141–68.

Aijmer, K. (2002) *English Discourse Particles: Evidence from a Corpus*, Amsterdam: John Benjamins.

Anderson, J., Beavan, D. and Kay, C. (2007) 'SCOTS: Scottish Corpus of Texts and Speech', in J. Beal, K. Corrigan and H. Moisl (eds) *Creating and Digitizing Language Corpora: Volume 1: Synchronic Databases*, London: Palgrave Macmillan, pp. 17–34.

Aston, G. and Burnard, L. (1997) *The BNC Handbook: Exploring the British National Corpus with SARA*, Edinburgh: Edinburgh University Press.
Biber, D., Johansson, S., Leech, G., Conrad, S. and Finegan, E. (1999) *Longman Grammar of Spoken and Written English*, Harlow: Pearson Education Limited.
Bird, S. and Liberman, M. (2000) 'A Formal Framework for Linguistic Annotation', *Speech Communication* 33: 23–60.
Cameron, D. (2001) *Working With Spoken Discourse*, London: SAGE Publications Ltd.
Carter, R. A. (2004) *Language and Creativity: The Art of Common Talk*, London: Routledge.
Carter, R. A. and McCarthy, M. J. (2006) *Cambridge Grammar of English: A Comprehensive Guide*, Cambridge: Cambridge University Press.
Cheng, W. and Warren, M. (2002) 'The Intonation of Declarative-Mood Questions in a Corpus of Hong Kong English: // ↘↗ beef ball // → you like', *Teanga: Journal of the Irish Association of Applied Linguistics* 21: 151–65.
Cook, G. (1990) 'Transcribing Infinity: Problems of Context Presentation', *Journal of Pragmatics* 14: 1–24.
Corrigan, K. P. and Mearns, A. (2016) *Creating and Digitizing Language Corpora: Volume 3: Databases for Public Engagement*, London: Palgrave Macmillan.
Coulthard, M. (2013) 'On the Use of Corpora in the Analysis of Forensic Texts', *International Journal of Speech Language and the Law* 1: 27–43.
Deuchar, M., Webb-Davies, P. and Donnelly, K. (2018) *Building and Using the Siarad Corpus*, Amsterdam: John Benjamins.
Farr, F., Murphy, B. and O'Keeffe, A. (2004) 'The Limerick Corpus of Irish English: Design, Description and Application', *Teanga* 21: 5–29.
Gablasova, D., Brezina, V. and McEnery, T. (2019) 'The Trinity Lancaster Corpus: Development, Description and Application', *International Journal of Learner Corpus Research* 5(2): 126–58.
Graddol, D., Cheshire, J. and Swann, J. (1994) *Describing Language*, Buckingham: Open University Press.
Gries, S. T. and Newman, J. (2014) 'Creating and Using Corpora', in D. Sharma and J. Podesva (eds) *Research Methods in Linguistics*, Cambridge: Cambridge University Press, pp. 257–87.
Handford, M. (2007) *The Genre of the Business Meeting: A Corpus-Based Study*, unpublished PhD Thesis, University of Nottingham.
Hunt, D. and Harvey, K. (2015) 'Health Communication and Corpus Linguistics: Using Corpus Tools to Analyse Eating Disorder Discourse Online', in P. Baker and T. McEnery (eds) *Corpora and Discourse Studies: Integrating Discourse and Corpora*, London: Palgrave Macmillan, pp. 134–54.
Jakubíček, M., Kilgarriff, A., Kovář, V., Rychlý, P. and Suchomel, V. (2013) 'The TenTen Corpus Family', Paper presented at the *7th International Corpus Linguistics Conference*, Lancaster, UK: Lancaster University.
Kipp, M. (2001) *ANVIL - A Generic Annotation Tool for Multimodal Dialogue [Computer Software]*, Retrieved from: https://www.anvil-software.org [Accessed 31 March 2021].
Knight, D., Bayoumi, S., Mills, S., Crabtree, A., Adolphs, S., Pridmore, T. and Carter, R. A. (2006) 'Beyond the Text: Construction and Analysis of Multi-Modal Linguistic Corpora', Paper presented at *2nd International Conference on e-Social Science*, Manchester.
Knight, D., Morris, S. and Fitzpatrick, T. (2021) *Corpus Design and Construction in Minoritised Language Contexts: The National Corpus of Contemporary Welsh*, London: Palgrave Macmillan.
Komrskova, Z., Kopřivova, M., Lukes, D., Poukarová, P. and Goláňová, H. (2017) 'New spoken corpora of Czech: ORTOFON and DIALEKT', *Journal of Linguistics/Jazykovedný Casopis* 68: 219–28.
Lin, P. and Chen, Y. (2020) 'Multimodality 1: Speech, Prosody and Gestures', in S. Adolphs and D. Knight (eds) *Routledge Handbook of English Language and Digital Humanities*, London: Routledge, pp. 66–84.
Love, R., Brezina, V., McEnery, A., Hawtin, A., Hardie, A. and Dembry, C. (2019) 'Functional Variation in the Spoken BNC2014 and the Potential for Register Analysis', *Register Studies* 1(2): 296–317.
Love, R., Dembry, C., Hardie, A., Brezina, V. and McEnery, T. (2017) 'The Spoken BNC2014: Designing and Building a Spoken Corpus of Everyday Conversations', *International Journal of Corpus Linguistics* 22: 319–44.

Lüdeling, A. and Kytö, M. (2008) 'Introduction', in A. Lüdeling and M. Kytö (eds) *Corpus Linguistics: An International Handbook*, Berlin: Walter de Gruyter, pp. 1–12.

Mahlberg, M., Stockwell, P., de Joode, J., Smith, C. and O'Donnell, M. B. (2016) 'CLiC Dickens: Novel Uses of Concordances for the Integration of Corpus Stylistics and Cognitive Poetics', *Corpora* 11(3): 433–63.

McCarthy, M. J. (1998) *Spoken Language and Applied Linguistics*, Cambridge: Cambridge University Press.

McCowan, I., Carletta, J., Kraaij, W., Ashby, S., Bourban, S., Flynn, M., Guillemot, M., Hain, T., Kadlec, J., Karaiskos, V., Kronenthal, M., Lathoud, G., Lincoln, M., Lisowska Masson, A., Post, W., Reidsma, D. and Wellner, P. (2005) 'The AMI Meeting Corpus', in Proceedings of the *5th International Conference on Methods and Techniques in Behavioral Research*, Wageningen: Noldus Information Technology, pp. 137–40.

McEnery, T., Love, R. and Brezina, V. (2017) 'Compiling and Analysing the Spoken British National Corpus 2014', *International Journal of Corpus Linguistics* 22(3): 311–8.

O'Keeffe, A. (2006) *Investigating Media Discourse*, London: Routledge.

Reppen, R. (2010) 'Building a Corpus', in A. O'Keeffe and M. J. McCarthy (eds) *The Routledge Handbook of Corpus Linguistics*, London: Routledge, pp. 31–7.

Reppen, R. and Simpson, R. (2002) 'Corpus Linguistics', in N. Schmitt (ed.) *An Introduction to Applied Linguistics*, London: Arnold, pp. 92–111.

Rose, D., Pevalin, D. and O'Reilly, K. (2005) *The National Statistics Socio-Economic Classification: Origins, Development and Use [Online]*, Retrieved from: https://www.ons.gov.uk/methodology/classificationsandstandards/otherclassifications/thenationalstatisticssocioeconomicclassificationnssecrebasedonsoc2010 [Accessed 31 March 2021].

Schmidt, T. (2016) 'Good Practices in the Compilation of FOLK, the Research and Teaching Corpus of Spoken German', *International Journal of Corpus Linguistics* 21(3): 396–418.

Scholfield, P. (1995) *Quantifying Language*, Clevedon: Multilingual Matters Ltd.

Shirk, J., Ballard, H., Wilderman, C., Phillips, T., Wiggins, A., Jordan, R., McCallie, E., Minarchek, M., Lewenstein, B., Krasny, M. and Bonney, R. (2012) 'Public Participation in Scientific Research: A Framework for Deliberate Design', *Ecology and Society* 17: 29–48.

Sinclair, J. (1987) 'Collocation: A Progress Report', in R. Steele and T. Threadgold (eds) *Language Topics: Essays in Honour of Michael Halliday*, Amsterdam: John Benjamins, pp. 319–31.

Sinclair, J. (2005) 'Corpus and Text - Basic Principles', in M. Wynne (ed.) *Developing Linguistic Corpora: A Guide to Good Practice*, Oxford: Oxbow Books, pp. 1–16.

Sperberg-McQueen, C. and Burnard, L. (1993) *Guidelines for Electronic Text Encoding and Interchange (TEI P3) [Online]*, Retrieved from: https://tei-c.org/Vault/GL/p4beta.pdf [Accessed 31 March 2021].

Svartvik, J. (1990) *The London-Lund Corpus of Spoken English. Description and Research*, Lund: Lund University Press.

Thompson, P. (2005) 'Spoken Language Corpora', in M. Wynne (ed.) *Developing Linguistic Corpora: A Guide to Good Practice*, Oxford: Oxbow Books, pp. 59–70.

Thompson, P. and Nesi, H. (2001) 'The British Academic Spoken English (BASE) Corpus Project', *Language Teaching Research* 5: 263–4.

Tikkinen-Piri, C., Rohunen, A. and Markkula, J. (2017) 'EU General Data Protection Regulation: Changes and implications for personal data collecting companies', *Computer Law and Security Review* 34(1): 134–53.

Weinberger, S. H. (2020). *The Speech Accent Archive [Computer Software]*, Retrieved from http://accent.gmu.edu/ [Accessed 31 March 2021].

Wittenburg, P., Brugman, H., Russel, A., Klassmann, A. and Sloetjes, H. (2006) 'ELAN: A professional framework for multimodality research, in *Proceedings of the Fifth International Conference on Language Resources and Evaluation (LREC 2006)*.

Wray, A. and Bloomer, A. (2013) *Projects in Linguistics and Language Studies*, 3rd edn, London: Routledge.

Wynne, M. (ed.) (2005) *Developing Linguistic Corpora: A Guide to Good Practice*, Oxford: Oxbow Books.

4

Building a written corpus: what are the basics?

Tony McEnery and Gavin Brookes

1 Written corpora: an introduction

Despite the expansion in the range of modern-day corpora, the field of corpus linguistics continues to privilege the study of written language over other modes. This is because constructing corpora of written texts tends to be considerably easier, cheaper and quicker than constructing corpora of other modes such as speech. Indeed, the ready availability of machine-readable language in an increasing range of written genres means that it has never been easier to build corpora of written language. As well as outnumbering corpora representing other modes, written corpora tend to be much larger than their counterparts. For example, both the original and updated versions of the *British National Corpus* (BNC) contain around 90 per cent writing and 10 per cent speech (Aston and Burnard 1998; Love *et al.* 2017; Hawtin 2018).

All this does not mean to say, however, that the task of building a written corpus is necessarily easy or without complication. This chapter explores the main considerations involved in building a written corpus and addresses some of the challenges that the builders of such corpora typically face. The distinction between writing, speech and other modes is, at best, blurry. For the purposes of this chapter, we adopt a broad view of "written" language, taking it to include texts containing language that has been handwritten or typed, including using a computer or other digital device, but also texts that represent speech but which have not been transcribed for the express purpose of linguistic research, such as those found in the Old Bailey corpus of trial discourse dating from 1674 to 1913 (Huber *et al.* 2016). For corpora that represent spoken language in some form, like the Old Bailey example, we will focus on the design and construction of corpora using the written forms of such texts, rather than the collection and transcription of original spoken discourse (see Chapter 3, this volume). While we pay special attention in this chapter to issues of particular relevance to the construction of written corpora, many of the points raised will be applicable to the construction of other types of corpora, too.

DOI: 10.4324/9780367076399-4

2 Design

Being as clear as possible on what we want to do with our corpus prior to designing it is important, as not only will this factor into our decision-making throughout the corpus-building process, but it might also be the case that an existing, publicly available corpus is sufficient for our requirements. Once we are clear about our purpose in using a corpus, the distinction between specialised and general corpora becomes relevant. Specialised corpora are designed to represent a particular genre or variety of language, usually within a specified context and/or time frame (e.g. Brookes and Baker's [2021] corpus of newspaper articles mentioning *obesity*). General corpora, meanwhile, represent language use on a broader scale, often whole languages (e.g. the BNC), and tend to be much larger than specialised corpora. If we are interested in studying the use of a particular linguistic item or feature on a broad scale, then it is likely that an existing general-language corpus will meet our needs. However, if we are interested in a particular variety or genre, or language around a particular topic or within a particular (recent) time period, then it is likely that we will have to build our own corpus.

Should we need to build our own written corpus, the decision regarding which texts to include in it can be quite straightforward and may be determined by our research question (e.g. with so-called "closed" or "finite" text types, such as the known literary works of a deceased author). However, in many cases it is not possible to include all relevant texts in a corpus. This is because corpus builders tend not to have access to, or even knowledge of, the full extent of the texts that could be deemed relevant to their research purposes, however well-defined these are. Most corpora therefore constitute *samples* of all possible candidate texts. Designing a corpus essentially involves deciding on which texts will be included in this sample and whether we will include these texts in their entirety or sample material from them. These considerations touch upon the related considerations of authenticity and representativeness.

Authenticity

The concept of *authenticity* in corpus linguistics research denotes a quality of language being "naturally occurring" or as existing in the "real life" (McEnery and Wilson 2001). Anything which involves the linguist beyond the minimum disruption required to acquire the data is reason for declaring our collection to be a special corpus, built with a looser interpretation of the criterion of authenticity. This opens up the possibility of special corpora composed of language that is semi-elicited by researchers through, for example, surveys or questionnaires, or that which is produced as part of a psycholinguistic experiment. In most cases, though, when designing a written corpus, we usually want to include in it texts that can be judged as being as "authentic" as possible, with minimal interference from the researcher. The task of capturing and including authentic language in a corpus tends to pose much less of an obstacle for the collection of written texts than it does for spoken texts (see Chapter 3, this volume).

Even so, researchers such as Mishan (2004: 219) question the capacity of corpora to represent "authentic" language at all, claiming that the process of transposing texts into corpora 'forfeit[s] a crucial criterion for authenticity, namely context' (see also: Widdowson 2000). However, as technology develops, some of this context-stripping is more a question of choice than necessity – to an extent, the use of annotation (discussed later) along with recent advances in the development of multi-modal corpora and methods of multi-modal corpus linguistic analysis represent means of recontextualising the texts in a corpus, at least to an extent (see Chapters 3 and 7, this volume, for more on multi-modal corpora).

Some issues surrounding authenticity are particularly pronounced in, and in some cases unique to, written corpora. One such issue relates to orthographic representation. Many types of written texts contain nonstandard spellings of words. Typical examples include texts that have not been professionally edited, for example student essays; casually produced texts such as those found on social media sites; and other types of user-generated web content like blogs, wikis and personal websites. The issue of nonstandard representation is also relevant to the collection of historical texts which, however carefully produced, are likely to have been written using now-outdated spelling conventions. Texts such as these are not problematic in themselves but can present an issue for the purposes of producing automated frequency counts. We can address this issue, however, by standardising the spellings in our corpus – yet unless this is done with due regard for authenticity, we may compromise any claims regarding the authenticity of our corpus. We will return to consider this issue in Section 3.

Another issue pertaining to authenticity in the compilation of written corpora concerns the volume of online language that is produced by so-called social media "bots". Bots can automatically generate large volumes of social media content very quickly. Such content can also be difficult for the untrained eye to distinguish from content that is produced by humans. A 2018 study of 1.2 million tweets containing hyperlinks to external websites reported that 66 per cent of the tweeted links in the sample were shared by suspected bots (Wojcik *et al.* 2018). Although bots are trained on natural language, the texts they produce clearly cannot be considered to constitute "authentic" instances of language use, and so will have to be accounted for and preferably removed if we are building a corpus of social media posts such as tweets, unless, of course, our goal is to generate a special corpus of bot tweets.

Representativeness: balance and size

Once we have decided on the written language or variety we want to investigate, we must decide on which texts to include in our corpus. Unless we are building a very specialised corpus, we are unlikely to be able to include all texts belonging to the language or variety we are interested in. In this case, a general corpus will necessarily represent a sample of the totality of the language or variety that we are interested in studying. When deciding on which texts to include in our sample, we want to ensure that it results in a corpus that is representative of our given language or variety of interest. A widely accepted definition of "representativeness" in the context of corpus linguistics is provided by Biber (1993: 244), who describes it as 'the extent to which a sample includes the full range of variability in a population'. Here, "population" refers to the 'notional space within which language is being sampled' (McEnery and Hardie 2012: 8).

For the design of some corpora, such as those comprising texts that are not so easily accessed, for example because they are written in a minority language (see McEnery and Ostler 2000 for a discussion) or to which we have been granted privileged access, the issue of representativeness is less pressing, as we may want to employ a more opportunistic approach and collect as many texts as we can. However, for the majority of corpora, representativeness is a central consideration and informs how many texts we want to include and in what proportions.

Biber (1993) suggests that in corpus design, 'variability can be considered from situational and from linguistic perspectives, and both of these are important in determining representativeness. Thus, a corpus design can be evaluated for the extent to which it includes: 1) the range of text types in a language, and 2) the range of linguistic distributions in a language' (*ibid.*). A corpus can therefore be considered representative if it matches the situational and linguistic variability of the population under study (see also Chapters 1, 5 and 6, this volume, on representativeness). These issues can be viewed as aligning to two further features of representativeness: *balance* and *size*.

Balance

The concept of *balance* refers to the internal consistency of a corpus in terms of the proportions that are contributed by each variable (situational and linguistic). To maximise representativeness, the balance of these variables should reflect both qualitatively and quantitatively the situational and linguistic variables that constitute our target population. The ideal of a balanced corpus that matches the make-up of our target population is, however, usually not met because our ability to judge the representativeness of our corpus depends on a clear definition of the "population" under study. Yet establishing such a definition can be extremely difficult, or even arbitrary, in practice. The main reason for this is that we are usually not aware of the full extent of the population that we are studying, let alone how variables distribute across it. For example, assembling a balanced corpus of written British English would require knowledge of all written British English throughout the course of history and how this writing distributes in terms of, amongst other things, the demographics of writers, the genres and purposes of different types of writing and the times and places in which that writing took place. A related issue here is that even if we have a rough idea of the breakdown of writing with respect to these variables, we ideally also need to know how widely the texts have been received. Another challenge to balancing our corpus to match the distribution of the authentic language it is designed to represent is that there are particular contexts or types of language to which we, as (corpus) linguists, have limited or no access, e.g. texts produced in private domains.

Data availability can present a particular challenge for designing representative corpora of historical written texts. One issue is that the archives from which the texts for such corpora are sourced can be incomplete. Another more general issue relating to the compilation of historical corpora is that it can be difficult, and in many cases impossible, to identify the socio-demographic backgrounds of those who authored the texts we are sampling, particularly when those authors are anonymous. The anonymity of texts' authors is not a challenge that is particular to historical texts, though, as the anonymous nature of much online interaction, including social media texts, presents difficulties for demographically balancing any corpus containing such texts.

In view of these challenges, it is not surprising that most corpora (written or otherwise) are not balanced in a way that perfectly represents the distributions of their target populations. Balanced, representative corpora are best viewed as a theoretical ideal rather than as being necessarily achievable in practice, resulting in two broad approaches to text selection in corpus design: "balanced" and monitor corpora. The "balanced" corpus approach uses a sampling frame which ensures equal representation of a particular set of variables by dictating which types of language or texts should be included in a corpus and in what proportions. Such corpora are balanced in the sense that they provide an equal representation of a set of variables. They do not necessarily reflect the actual distribution of those variables in the target population that the corpus is designed to represent. The Brown family of corpora, based on the sampling frame established by Kučera and Francis (1967), is a good example of this. The sampling frame produces corpora which contain approximately 1 million words of written English prose in samples of approximately 2,000 words taken from 500 different text sources from 4 categories of writing (press, general prose, learned writing and fiction), which are further split into 15 subcategories or genres. Corpora such as the LOB (Johansson *et al.* 1978), the Freiburg-Brown corpus of American English (Frown; Hundt *et al.* 1999) and the Freiburg-LOB Corpus of British English (FLOB; Hundt *et al.* 1998) and the AmE06 and BE06 corpora (Baker 2009) followed that basic sampling frame. The benefits of building a corpus according to a sampling frame is that it can then be compared more systematically against other corpora which were designed using that same sampling frame, and so contain identical proportions of texts belonging to each category and subcategory. Yet the balance they such strive for is not necessarily representative of the proportions with which the variables in question occur in the real-world populations they nominally represent.

Monitor corpora continue to grow over time, but not according to the variables which produce "balanced" corpora. Instead, size and currency are given precedence over balance. Perhaps the best-known example of a monitor corpus is the Bank of English (see McEnery and Hardie 2012: 80). The texts in this corpus began to be collected during the 1980s and now constitute part of a larger monitor corpus, the 4.5 billion-word Collins Corpus. While it could be argued that monitor corpora produce an imbalanced view of the languages or situations under study (explored more in the next section), it might also be argued that any imbalance self-corrects over time due to the sheer size of the corpus and the fact that the skew in the texts included is not consistent. The concept of the 'Web as Corpus' (Gatto 2014) is, in many ways, comparable to the use of monitor corpora, as it takes as its starting point a massive collection of texts that continues to grow. In the case of Web as Corpus, this growth occurs independently of the researcher's efforts, as more and more user-generated content is added every second, potentially offering the largest and most up-to-date view on (most) languages that is possible at any given time.

The use of the Web as a Corpus, or at the very least the use of the Web for obtaining material to put into a corpus, seems to overcome many of the practical limitations that attend to the construction of corpora of written language derived from other domains. As Collins (2019: 32) points out, the Web is 'freely available, encompasses a breadth of texts from around the world and is of unimaginable size. Texts are already in a computer-readable format, so researchers do not need (on the whole) to undergo tasks of digitisation (as with written texts) or transcribing spoken data'. Indeed, because of the relative ease with which they can be collected and the minimal amount of processing they require for corpus analysis, corpora of Web texts are often very large in size. An example of this is the *TenTen* family of corpora (Jakubíček *et al.* 2013), which represent online texts written in a variety of languages. At the time of writing, the *Sketch Engine* tool (Kilgarriff *et al.* 2014) hosts 38 corpora from the *TenTen* family.[1] The latest (2015) edition of the English-language version, *EnTenTen*, contains 15 billion words of online written English. Unlike most corpora, the Web consists of a mixture of texts that have been carefully prepared and edited, along with what McEnery and Hardie (2012: 7) describe as more 'casually prepared' material, and the propensity for the latterl to contain non-standard orthographic representations can prove problematic when searching for online uses of a word or phrase of interest. Furthermore, the Web is not clearly divided by genre, with the texts returned by a search engine query, for example constituting an undifferentiated mass of language data that is likely to require a significant amount of processing and grouping prior to analysis. Recent research indicates that organising online language in this way, for example, according to register, may be challenging (Biber and Egbert 2018). The ever-changing nature of the Web can also make reproducing analyses impossible, as the results of a Web search can change along with the addition and removal of online material, though downloading and archiving data can help here, particularly in cases where that data can then be shared and made available to other researchers in the future.

Of course, not all corpora fit neatly into the distinction between balanced and monitor corpora, and it is even possible to combine approaches. For example, the *Corpus of Contemporary American English* (COCA; Davies 2009) can be described as a monitor corpus in the sense that texts are continually added to it, yet these additions are subject to a stringent sampling frame which ensures that the corpus is balanced in terms of the text varieties it contains.

Size

One of the most common questions that arises during corpus design is: How big does the corpus need to be? If we are following a strict sampling frame, such as that of the Brown corpus, then the size of our corpus can be determined for us from the outset. However, such cases aside, as in other aspects of corpus design there is no one-size-fits-all approach to how large a corpus should be. While corpora tend to be so large that their size would defy any plausible attempt at analysis by hand and eye alone (McEnery and Hardie 2012), there is little principled reasoning behind how large a corpus should be.

One school of thought is that the corpus should be as large as possible, with computational capacity and software speed being the only limits on the number of texts we collect (Sinclair 1991). Biber (1993), on the other hand, suggests that a corpus of 1 million words should be sufficient for undertaking grammatical studies, while Leech (2003) suggests that a similar number of words is sufficient for carrying out comparative work between language varieties. These are very general guidelines, though, and there is no consensus on ideal or adequate corpus size. Debate on this issue continues, and "big" has not always been assumed to be "beautiful"; one clear advantage of building a smaller corpus is that the human analyst is likely to be able to account for a larger proportion of the uses of even the most frequent words and, in some cases, to account for every use of a word of interest. Additionally, a more manageable amount of data makes it easier for researchers to investigate the contexts in which the texts in the corpus were produced, as well as to link these insights to analytical findings (Baker 2006) (see also Chapters 5 and 6).

Determining how large our corpus should be is, however, a luxury that we are not always afforded. As noted in the previous section, in some cases it can be beneficial to adopt an "opportunistic" approach to corpus design by collecting all texts that are available to us. The design of such corpora does not seek to address issues relating to balance or skew, but rather represent 'nothing more nor less than the data that it was possible to gather for a specific task' (McEnery and Hardie 2012: 11). For example, considering extinct languages for which a body of literature survives, such as Classical Latin, may allow us some degree of choice in corpus design. However, for other languages, such as Eteocypriot, the surviving texts are much fewer in number and our understanding of them is limited, meaning that our choice in corpus building is limited and a corpus approach to the language is neither necessary nor, perhaps, credible.

In summary, the size of the corpus we build is likely to depend, on the one hand, on the type of analysis that we want to carry out on it and, on the other, on practical considerations and limitations regarding what is possible. Whatever the size of our corpus, it is important that we engage critically with what insight it does and does not have the capacity to afford.

3 Ethics and copyright

Ethical standards and principles in corpus building are, as in other areas of linguistics, widely debated, and there is no "gold standard" for corpus builders to follow. Some researchers argue that for ethical purposes we should draw a distinction between texts that exist within public and private domains, with texts existing within private domains which are thus likely intended for private audiences, requiring informed consent from their authors before they can be collected and studied.

Beyond the public–private distinction, we should also consider the potential risk of the research we are carrying out to do harm to those whose texts we are collecting and analysing, weighing up the benefits of the research against the potential for harm. Such decisions are, of course, not straightforward, and nor are they to be taken lightly. In any case, when collecting texts which do not exist in the public domain, it is good practice to anonymise those texts by removing mentions of details by which the authors could be identified in so far as that is possible. For more detailed discussions of ethical considerations in the design of written corpora, see McEnery and Hardie (2012: Chapter 3), Collins (2019: 34–7) and Hunt and Brookes (2020: 77–81).

In addition to ethical considerations, we have to be mindful of copyright restrictions that might prohibit distribution of the texts we want to include in our corpus. It is illegal, for example, to download an entire text and then redistribute it without the permission of the copyright holder. This clearly presents a problem if we intend to make our corpus available to others at any point. McEnery and Hardie (2012: 59) discuss some of the ways in which we can address copyright issues when building a written corpus. The first is to contact the copyright holder to request permission to reproduce the text(s) in question under the terms of some specified licence. This is most feasible if one or a small number of texts are to be sampled. Alternatively, we could focus our data collection only on those texts whose owners have explicitly permitted their public redistribution, for example a website which declares its content to be in public domain or which is available under a licence permitting copying and redistribution. Restricting a corpus to such texts would, however, almost inevitably lead to a skew in the types of texts our corpus then represents. Thirdly, if we collect data without permissions necessary for redistribution, we can nevertheless share our corpus with others by hosting it on a tool which allows other researchers to run concordance queries but shows only a very limited amount of text in the output. Since it is impossible to reconstruct the original texts from the tiny snippets that such a concordance would provide, which are small enough to count as "fair use", this "redistribution" is unlikely to constitute a dangerous copyright violation.

Finding legal ways of sharing our corpus is useful not only to those who set out to provide a public resource, but this can also help with research ethics, as it helps to ensure the replicability of our research. Such concerns may lead us, where for legal reasons we cannot distribute a corpus, to provide a clear set of instructions for recompiling a corpus, legally, for the purposes of replication. For example, if a corpus has been created from a news consolidation service which prohibits text sharing, then researchers may publish the parameters and query used to gather data from that service so that other users with access to it can effectively re-recreate the corpus for themselves. A final point on copyright which is important to bear in mind is that, when collecting online texts, it is important to be sensitive to potential differences in copyright and fair dealing laws across the various geographical zones represented by our data. What is legal in one jurisdiction may be illegal in another, and corpus builders should be aware of that.

4 Text gathering and processing

In this section, we will consider text collection, after which we will consider two processes commonly undertaken on texts collected for inclusion in a corpus: cleaning and annotation.

Text collection

The internet has undoubtedly transformed the process of corpus building, as it grants instant access to an unimaginable number of downloadable texts that already exist in an electronic format. These texts do not just constitute e-language, as many texts that were originally written in the more traditional sense are now available on websites or online archives, with such resources providing much more convenient means for corpus building than their original paper forms. For example, websites like *LexisNexis* can be used to download the text from large numbers of news articles according to user-determined criteria, while *Project Gutenberg* allows one to download copies of literary texts which can then be stored and analysed as corpora. If we decide to download texts from online sources such as these, we may have to convert them into a format that is suitable for the tool we are using. This may mean that we need to convert some texts from one format to another, e.g. from a PDF into plain UTF8 text.

If we want to collect data from a lot of websites or from websites that have a large number of pages, it can be helpful to use a website copier like *HTTrack* or *BootCat* (Baroni and Bernardini 2004), which can scrape all text, and in the former case images and hyperlinks, from user-determined webpages with impressive efficiency. Online texts can also be retrieved in a less structured manner using *BootCat*, which can compile a relatively unstructured corpus of texts in terms of registers by trawling the Web using search terms specified by the user.

If the texts we want to include in our corpus are not readily available in electronic form or do exist electronically but in the form of graphics files not amenable to corpus processing, then they will either have to be keyed in by hand or, if the print quality is sufficient, scanned in using Optical Character Recognition (OCR) software. In most cases, scanning texts is more efficient than keying them in, which can be extremely time consuming. However, scanning also presents issues, as OCR can struggle with texts whose pages are structured into columns. OCR is also prone to error, especially if texts are damaged or of low quality. This is a particular issue when compiling corpora of historical written texts, where the results will usually have to be corrected by hand. This task generally becomes more painstaking the larger our corpus is and the older the texts in it are. This process brings us to the next step in written corpus construction: cleaning.

Cleaning

The texts we collect for a corpus may need to be processed further before we can start analysing them, as some of their features may adversely affect the accuracy of the analytical procedures we intend to carry out, as well as impinging on the corpus's representativeness in a more general sense.

The first cause for concern in this regard is the presence of so-called "boilerplate" text. This is language that occurs within the texts we have collected but which is likely to constitute "noise" in the context of our corpus and which get in the way of our analysis. For example, if we download news articles from *LexisNexis*, the text files given will include labels which denote what is the "headline", "byline" and "author". Found in every text, the occurrences of these elements can accumulate quickly and thus become a problem for frequency-based corpus measures. Tools can help with this – for example, *WordSmith Tools* (Version 7 on; Scott 2016) now includes a "Boilerplate removal" function. Rather than simply removing such elements, we may wish to use them as a form of metadata, in which case they can provide the basis for corpus annotation, discussed later. Deciding on what counts as "boilerplate" material, however, is a subjective judgment and may depend on our research aims (Collins 2019: 40).

Another issue that can arise during the collection of online written material is the presence of duplicate texts. For example, *LexisNexis* can store multiple versions of the same news text, such as online and print versions of the same article, as separate downloadable files. Again, tools can help – version 7 of *WordSmith Tools* includes a "duplicate text" function which ranks texts by similarity, allowing the corpus builder to check high-similarity results and, if they wish, remove duplicate texts from their corpus. Like the identification of boilerplate material, though, deciding on what counts as duplicate texts will depend on the aims of our research – some research, for example, may wish to explore small differences between online and print versions of a newspaper text.

Another consideration that arises during corpus cleaning relates to the presence of nonstandard orthography. Inconsistent orthographic representation is a characteristic feature of much user-generated online content, which can contain typos, abbreviations and spelling mistakes, while texts sampled from different geographical locations and historical periods can exhibit distinct spelling conventions even within the same language. For this reason, corpus builders who do not wish to study such variation as a linguistic phenomenon may choose to standardise the spelling in their corpora so that they can improve the accuracy of their frequency counts. Tools like *VARD* (Baron 2011) are useful for this purpose, as they can quickly scan for instances of non-standard orthography and present these to the user, at which point the user can make a decision to either standardise spelling variants or retain them in their current form. Where standardisation occurs, the original spellings are typically retained as a matter of best practice, with corpus mark-up used to differentiate the standardised and original forms.

Text encoding

To help analyse our data, there are three types of information that we may wish to encode in our corpus: metadata, textual markup and linguistic annotation. Metadata is information about the text itself. For a written text, this may include information about its author, language and date of publication. The second type of text encoding, textual mark-up, typically represents paralinguistic features of the texts in the corpus, for example denoting where italicisation might start and end in a stretch of writing, or telling us where an image occurs within a text. Finally, linguistic annotation can mark linguistic features we believe to be implicit in our texts, e.g. we can linguistically annotate our corpus with information about parts of speech, lemmas, grammatical structures and semantic categories, *inter alia*. Whether or not we annotate our corpus and with what types of information will depend, again, upon the kinds of analysis we want to carry out, as well as the resources we have available. Resources for annotating corpora are ever more widely available. As well as online systems which provide such features as part of speech and semantic annotation, tools such as *#LancsBox* (Brezina *et al.* 2015) and *Sketch Engine* provide annotation for parts of speech in a range of languages. For example, *#LancsBox* provides part-of-speech annotation for over 20 languages and lemmatisation for a subset of these. *Sketch Engine* also provides part-of-speech tagging and lemmatisation for a wide range of languages.

Metadata, textual markup and linguistic annotation are all usually encoded in corpora using *eXtensible Markup Language* (XML). The use of XML is standard not only in the annotation of corpora but also, for example, the reliable transfer of webpages and word-processor documents from one machine to another. Using XML, tags are contained within angular brackets (<tag>), which makes the tags searchable but also allows the words within the brackets (i.e. the tags themselves) to be excluded from corpus analytical procedures.

Linguistic annotation may be introduced into a corpus automatically, semi-automatically or manually. Automatic annotation is, naturally, appealing and for some tasks it can be carried out with a high degree of accuracy. For example, the CLAWS tagger (Garside *et al.* 1987) annotates texts for parts of speech with around 97 per cent accuracy. Similarly, VARD (Baron 2011) can generally successfully link words in irregular spelling in a corpus to their standard form, with the standard form introduced as a linguistic annotation encoded in a suitable markup language, e.g. XML. Yet some types of written texts are particularly likely to pose challenges to automated taggers. For example, orthographic and grammatical variation in historical texts can pose processing issues to taggers trained on contemporary and standard forms, as can texts that have the propensity to be grammatically unpredictable, like learner language and unedited and user-generated e-language. Automated taggers are also likely to struggle with texts containing more than one language, while the "patchiness" (McEnery and Hardie 2012: 31) of taggers for languages other than English remains a challenge to the field. Regardless of the type of text we are analysing, it is advisable to manually check automatic tags to correct errors. One approach to this is to create a small, "gold standard" subset of your corpus which can be manually checked to measure tagger performance (McEnery and Hardie 2012: 31).

Whichever approach to annotation we choose, Leech (1993) proposed a number of maxims which should be followed as closely as possible: 1) it should be possible to remove the annotations and revert back to the raw corpus; 2) it should be possible to extract the annotations themselves from the texts for storage elsewhere; 3) the annotation scheme should be based on guidelines that are available to the end user of the corpus; 4) it should be made clear how and by whom the annotation was carried out; 5) the end user should be made aware that the annotations are not infallible; 6) annotations should be based, as far as possible, on widely agreed upon and theory-neutral principles; and 7) no annotation scheme has the *a priori* right to be considered as a standard; standards, where they exist, emerge through practical consensus (see also: McEnery and Wilson 2001: 33–4).

Annotation can add value to a corpus, making it easier to search in a linguistically meaningful way, and so we would encourage corpus builders to annotate their written corpora if they can envisage ways in which the resultant tags could enrich their analyses. However, annotation is not essential for corpus analysis, and since it can be a time-consuming and resource-draining process, we would caution against annotation for annotation's sake.

5 Challenges and future directions

The structure of Sections 2 through 4 reflects the order in which much corpus construction occurs. However, this is not hard and fast, and it is quite normal for corpus construction to be iterative, e.g. corpus annotations may be added after a first version of a corpus is complete. We must also note that there are some potentially important aspects of corpus construction that we have not explored in much detail here, such as ways of sharing corpus data and evaluating representativeness following construction (for a discussion, see Love 2020).

Throughout, however, corpus builders should always be guided in their choices by the purposes that they intend for the corpus they are building. Importantly, those choices and the rationale behind them must be documented in a detailed and comprehensive manner in order for others to evaluate, replicate and potentially use our corpus in the future.

Our exploration of the considerations underlying corpus design in this chapter has highlighted a number of challenges that persist with regard to the capacity of written corpora to represent the texts on which they are based. For texts derived from contexts that are characteristically multi-modal in their design, such as news articles and online texts employing memes and emojis we anticipate development in the capacity of corpora to represent visual elements in ever more sophisticated ways. Research in this area is ongoing and promising. For historical texts, there is an urgent need for ever more sophisticated means of gathering and accurately formatting historical documents for corpus analysis. Development in this area could lead to the construction of larger corpora which reach ever further into the past without users becoming concerned about their accuracy. Finally, the development of written corpora perhaps more than any other type brings to the fore issues relating to "aboutness" in corpus design. Many written corpora, especially those containing news texts, are designed to represent texts "about" particular topics. The concept of "aboutness" in the context of corpus linguistics is rather vague yet seems to underpin, both explicitly and implicitly, much written corpus design, being employed in seemingly inconsistent ways. Designers of written corpora, and corpus linguistics in general, would thus benefit from greater theoretical and empirical engagement with the concept of aboutness and its consequences for corpus design in the future.

Note

1 For a list of the *TenTen* corpora (and others) hosted on *Sketch Engine*, see: https://www.sketchengine.eu/documentation/tenten-corpora/#:~:text=The%20TenTen%20Corpus%20Family%20%28TenTen%20corpora%29%20is%20a,specialized%20in%20collecting%20only%20linguistically%20valuable%20web%20content.

Further reading

Collins, L. (2019) *Corpus Linguistics for Online Communication: A Guide for Research*, London: Routledge. (This book introduces the construction and analysis of online corpora, including discussing ethical considerations of online text collection.)

Love, R. (2020) *Overcoming Challenges in Corpus Construction: The Spoken British National Corpus 2014*, London: Routledge. (This book provides a refreshingly candid account of the challenges associated with corpus design and how these can be overcome.)

References

Aston, G. and Burnard, L. (1998) *The BNC Handbook: Exploring the British National Corpus with SARA*, Edinburgh: Edinburgh University Press.

Baker, P. (2006) *Using Corpora in Discourse Analysis*, London: Continuum.

Baker, P. (2009) 'The BE06 Corpus of British English and Recent Language Change', *International Journal of Corpus Linguistics* 14(3): 312–37.

Biber, D. and Egbert, J. (2018) *Register Variation Online*, Cambridge: Cambridge University Press.

Baron, A. (2011) *Dealing with Spelling Variation in Early Modern English Texts*, unpublished PhD thesis, Lancaster University.

Baroni, M. and Bernardini, S. (2004) 'BootCaT: Bootstrapping Corpora and Terms from the Web', *Proceedings of LREC 2004*. http://www.lrec-conf.org/proceedings/lrec2004/pdf/509.pdf.

Biber, D. (1993) 'Representativeness in Corpus Design', *Literary and Linguistic Computing* 8(4): 243–57.

Brezina, V., McEnery, T. and Wattam, S. (2015) 'Collocations in Context: A New Perspective on Collocational Networks', *International Journal of Corpus Linguistics* 20(2): 139–73.

Brookes, G. and Baker, P. (2021) *Obesity in the News: Language and Representation in the Press*, Cambridge: Cambridge University Press.

Collins, L. C. (2019) *Corpus Linguistics for Online Communication: A Guide for Research*, London: Routledge.

Davies, M. (2009) 'The 385+ Million Word Corpus of Contemporary American English (1990-present)', *International Journal of Corpus Linguistics* 14(2): 159–90.

Garside, R., Leech, G. and Sampson, G. (eds) (1987) *The Computational Analysis of English: A Corpus-based Approach*, London: Longman.

Gatto, M. (2014) *Web As Corpus: Theory and Practice*, London: Bloomsbury.

Hawtin, A. (2018) *The Written British National Corpus 2014: Design, Compilation and Analysis*, unpublished PhD thesis, Lancaster University.

Hundt, M., Sand, A. and Siemund, R. (1998) 'Manual of Information to Accompany the Freiburg-LOB Corpus of British English ("FLOB")', [online], Available at: www.hit.uib.no/icame/flob/index.htm.

Hundt, M., Sand, A. and Skandera, P. (1999) 'Manual of Information to Accompany the Freiburg Brown Corpus of American English ("Frown")', [online], Available at: http://khnt.hit.uib.no/icame/manuals/frown/INDEX.HTM.

Hunt, D. and Brookes, G. (2020) *Corpus, Discourse and Mental Health*, London: Bloomsbury.

Huber, M., Nissel, M. and Puga, K. (2016) *Old Bailey Corpus 2.0*, [Website], URL: http://fedora.clarin-d.uni-saarland.de/oldbailey/index.html.

Jakubíček, M., Kilgarriff, A., Kovář, V., Rychlý, P. and Suchomel, V. (2013) 'The TenTen Corpus Family', *7th International Corpus Linguistics Conference*, pp. 125–7.

Johansson, S., Leech, G. and Goodluck, H. (1978) *Manual of Information to Accompany the LancasterOslo/Bergen Corpus of British English, for Use with Digital Computers*, Oslo: University of Oslo.

Kilgarriff, A., Baisa, V., Bušta, J., Jakubíček, M., Kovář, V., Michelfeit, J., Rychlý, P. and Suchomel, V. (2014) 'The Sketch Engine: Ten Years On', *Lexicography* 1: 7–36.

Kučera, H. and Francis, W. N. (1967) *Computational Analysis of Present-Day American English*, Providence: Brown University Press.

Leech, G. (1993) 'Corpus Annotation Schemes', *Literary and Linguistic Computing* 8(4): 275–81.

Leech, G. (2003) 'Modality on the Move: The English Modal Auxiliaries 1961-1992', in R.

Facchinetti, M. Krug and F. Palmer (eds) *Modality in Contemporary English*, Berlin and New York: Mouton de Gruyter, pp. 223–40.
Love, R. (2020) *Overcoming Challenges in Corpus Construction: The Spoken British National Corpus 2014*, London: Routledge.
Love, R., Dembry, C., Hardie, A., Brezina, V. and McEnery, T. (2017) 'The Spoken BNC2014: Designing and Building a Spoken Corpus of Everyday Conversations', *International Journal of Corpus Linguistics* 22(3): 319–44.
McEnery, T. and Hardie, A. (2012) *Corpus Linguistics: Method, Theory and Practice*, Cambridge: Cambridge University Press.
McEnery, T. and Ostler, N. (2000) 'A New Agenda for Corpus Linguistics – Working with All of the World's Languages', *Literary and Linguistic Computing* 15(4): 403–20.
McEnery, T. and Wilson, A. (2001) *Corpus Linguistics: An Introduction*, 2nd edn, Edinburgh: Edinburgh University Press.
Mishan, F. (2004) 'Authenticating Corpora for Language Learning: A Problem and its Resolution', *ETL Journal* 58(3): 219–27.
Scott, M. (2016) *WordSmith Tools version 7*, Stroud: Lexical Analysis Software.
Sinclair, J. (1991) *Corpus, Concordance, Collocation*, Oxford: Oxford University Press.
Widdowson, H. G. (2000) 'On the Limitations of Linguistics Applied', *Applied Linguistics* 21(1): 3–25.
Wojcik, S., Messing, S., Smith, A., Rainie, L. and Hitlin, P. (2018) *Bots in the Twittersphere: An Estimated Two-Thirds of Tweeted Links to Popular Websites are Posted by Automated Accounts not Human Beings* Pew Research Center. https://www.pewresearch.org/internet/2018/04/09/bots-in-the-twittersphere/.

5

Building small specialised corpora

Almut Koester

1 What's the point of a small corpus?

Over the years there have been two opposing trends in the compilation of corpora. On the one hand, corpora are getting ever larger, with "mega-corpora", such as the Bank of English, the Cambridge International Corpus (CIC) and the Corpus of Contemporary American English (COCA) having millions or billions of words. On the other hand, smaller, more specialised corpora are being compiled, focusing on specific registers and genres.

But what is the point of a small corpus? Surely, the point of a computer-based corpus is to allow the electronic storage and machine analysis of huge amounts of text which could not be handled manually. According to John Sinclair (2004), the "father" of corpus linguistics, 'small is not beautiful; it is simply a limitation' (p. 189). While he concedes that it may be possible to get valid results from a small corpus, he argues that these results will be limited. In a large corpus, on the other hand, 'underlying regularities have a better chance of showing through the superficial variations' (ibid.:189). To illustrate this, Sinclair looked for the phrase *fit into place* in a 2-million, 20-million and 200-million-word corpus and did not find any examples until he searched the largest 200-million-word corpus, and even then only half a dozen.

This anecdote illustrates the fact that small corpora are not suitable for certain types of analysis, particularly lexis and phraseology, but others have argued that a smaller corpus may be perfectly adequate for some purposes. Lexical items, except for the most common words, are relatively infrequent, and therefore a large corpus is necessary to carry out lexicographical research (see Chapter 27, this volume). However, grammatical items, such as pronouns, prepositions and auxiliary and modal verbs, are very frequent and can therefore be reliably studied using a relatively small corpus (Carter and McCarthy 1995). There may even be some disadvantages to working with a very large corpus. The sheer volume of data for high-frequency items may become unmanageable and result in analysts having to work with a smaller sub-sample (ibid.: 143). In a small corpus, on the other hand, *all* occurrences, and not just a random sample of high-frequency items, can be examined. Furthermore, in working with very large corpora,

DOI: 10.4324/9780367076399-5

where the samples examined come from many vastly different contexts, it is difficult, if not impossible, to say anything about the original context of use of the utterances (Flowerdew 2004). See also Sections 2 and 3 later and Chapter 4, this volume.

Smaller, more specialised corpora have a distinct advantage when it comes to contextual information: They allow a much closer link between the corpus and the contexts in which the texts in the corpus were produced. Where large corpora, through their de-contextualisation, give insights into lexico-grammatical patterns in the language as a whole, smaller, specialised corpora give insights into patterns of language use in particular settings. With a small corpus, the corpus compiler is often also the analyst and therefore usually has a high degree of familiarity with the context. This means the quantitative findings revealed by corpus analysis can be balanced and complemented with qualitative results (Flowerdew 2004). As we shall see, specialised corpora are also usually carefully targeted and set up to reflect contextual features, such as information about the setting, the participants and the purpose of communication. Therefore, analysis of such corpora can reveal connections between linguistic patterning and contexts of use.

This link between the corpus and the contexts of use is particularly relevant in the fields of English for Specific Purposes (ESP) and English for Academic Purposes (EAP), where small, specialised corpora have been compiled to inform pedagogy (see Chapter 28, this volume). Tribble (2002) argues that large corpora do not meet the needs of teachers and learners in ESP/EAP, as they provide 'either too much data across too large a spectrum, or too little focused data, to be directly helpful to learners with specific learning purposes' (p. 132). Smaller, more focused corpora, which have been set up for a specific research or pedagogical purpose, are much more likely to yield insights that are directly relevant for teaching and learning for specific purposes (ibid.).

Furthermore, from a practical point of view, any corpus an individual researcher or practitioner, such as an ESP/EAP teacher, can construct will necessarily be small, due to the limitation of collecting, and for a spoken corpus, transcribing the data. The aim of this chapter is therefore to provide some guidelines for building a small, specialised corpus and to discuss, with concrete examples, what can be learnt from such a corpus.

2 How small and how specialised?

But just how small and how specialised can a corpus be? The answer to this question depends crucially on what the corpus will be used for, that is the purpose of the research. But let's first define what we mean by a "small" corpus. Opinions diverge regarding what is considered "large" or "small" when it comes to corpora. First, it depends on whether the corpus is written or spoken. As it takes a long time to compile a spoken corpus (see Chapter 3, this volume), spoken corpora tend to be smaller than written ones. According to O'Keeffe *et al.* (2007: 4), spoken corpora containing over a million words of speech are considered large, whereas with written corpora, anything under 5 million words of text is quite small. But many small corpora, even written ones, are a great deal smaller than that, and Flowerdew (2004: 19) notes that there is general agreement that small corpora contain up to 250,000 words.

As already noted, when analysing high-frequency items, a relatively modest corpus may still yield robust and powerful findings, for example, the European Corpus of Academic Talk (EuroCoAT), a corpus of office hour consultations with just under 60,000 words (MacArthur *et al.* 2014), and Koester's (2006, 2010) 34,000-word Corpus of American and British Office Talk (ABOT). What is more important than the actual size of the corpus is how well it is designed and that it is "representative". There is no ideal size for a corpus; it all depends on what the corpus contains and what is being investigated (Flowerdew 2004). Nevertheless, it is possible to give some general guidelines regarding minimal sample size. These issues will be discussed in Section 3.

With regard to the degree of specialisation, a corpus may be more or less specialised, and it may be specialised in different ways, depending, again, on the purpose of the research (see also Hunston 2002: 14). Flowerdew (2004: 21) lists a number of parameters according to which a corpus can be specialised:

- Specific purpose for compilation, e.g. to investigate a particular grammatical or lexical item;
- Contextualisation: particular setting, participants and communicative purpose;
- Genre, e.g. promotional (grant proposals, sales letters);
- Type of text/discourse, e.g. biology textbooks, casual conversation;
- Subject matter/topic, e.g. economics;
- Variety of English, e.g. Learner English.

Many specialised corpora have been compiled to study a particular language variety, for example, the Limerick Corpus of Irish English (Farr *et al.* 2004) or the International Corpus of Learner English (ICLE website). Since the early 2000s, interest in *English as a lingua franca* (ELF) has led to the compilation of a number of ELF corpora, including the Vienna-Oxford International Corpus (VOICE 2013), the spoken academic English as a lingua franca (ELFA 2008) corpus and the Written ELF in Academic Settings (WrELFA 2015) corpus. Other corpora focus on specific academic or professional genres; for example, the Michigan Corpus of Spoken Academic English (MICASE, see Simpson *et al.* 2002) and the British Academic Spoken English (BASE) corpus both consist of spoken academic genres, primarily lectures and seminars. Examples of professional genre corpora (see also Cheng 2014) are the Cambridge and Nottingham Business English Corpus (CANBEC, see Handford 2010), a corpus of business meetings, the Enron email corpus (Kessler 2010) and the NHS Feedback Corpus (NHSFC), consisting of online patient comments and provider responses (Baker *et al.* 2019). The Construction Industry Corpus (CONIC) is an example of a corpus that is specialised both in terms of professional genre and variety (ELF) (Handford and Koester 2019). Specialised corpora can vary considerably in size, ranging from those with fewer than 100,000, such as EuroCoAT with 58,834 words (MacArthur *et al.* 2014), to a corpus like NHSFC, which contains approximately 40 million words (Baker *et al.* 2019).

The degree of specialisation also varies, for example, corpora representing a language variety such as Irish English are quite general in terms of the genres they comprise (see Chapter 6, this volume). However, such corpora can be set up to include more specialised sub-corpora, for example, the Hong Kong Corpus of Spoken English (HKCSE) has four sub-corpora: conversation, business discourse, academic discourse and public discourse (Warren 2004). Many ESP/EAP corpora are very specialised indeed, as they have been compiled for specific research or pedagogical purposes, for example, the 250,000-word Corpus of Environmental Impact Assessment (EIA) consisting of 60 summary reports commissioned by the Hong Kong Environmental Protection Department (Flowerdew 2008). An example of a corpus designed for a specific pedagogical purpose is the Indianapolis Business Learner Corpus (IBLC), which consists of 200 letters of application (Connor *et al.* 1997; Upton and Connor 2001). The letters were written by business communication students from three different countries as part of an international business writing course (see Section 3). Specialised corpora like these are designed to provide insights into the genres investigated, such as specific types of scientific (e.g. environmental impact statements) or academic genres (e.g. letters of application). They will obviously not be useful for predicting language patterns in other registers and genres or, for example, for teaching English for general purposes.

While specialised corpora may vary in size, an important point is that such corpora do not need to be as large as more general corpora to yield reliable results. The reason for this is that as specialised corpora are carefully targeted, they are more likely to reliably represent a register or genre than general corpora. Even with relatively small amounts of data, 'specialised lexis and structures are likely to occur with more regular patterning and distribution' than in a large, general corpus (O'Keeffe *et al.* 2007: 198).

The next two sections will provide practical guidelines for building a small, specialised corpus, but see also Chapter 2 for general guidelines for corpus design, Chapter 3 for compiling spoken corpora and Chapter 4 for written corpora.

3 Important considerations in the design of a small, specialised corpus

As with any corpus, the most important consideration in designing a small, specialised corpus is that it should be representative (see Chapters 2, 3, 4 and 6, this volume, for more on representativeness). Biber (1993: 243) defines representativeness as 'the extent to which a sample includes the full range of variability in a population'. Biber (ibid.) identifies two types of variability: *situational* and *linguistic*. Situational variability refers to the range of registers and genres in the target "population", i.e. in the text types or speech situation to be included in the corpus. Linguistic variability refers to the range of linguistic distributions found in the population.

If a very specific type of genre is being investigated, then it may be straightforward to establish situational representativeness, as all the samples collected will accurately represent that genre. However, in most cases, there is some degree of variability even within a given genre, and it is therefore important to ensure that the corpus is "balanced" so that the corpus reflects the full range of variability found in the genre (see Chapter 6, this volume). For example, there may be different sub-genres, or perhaps the genre is used in different types of organisations or by different people. If all the samples come from just one organisation, then the corpus will be representative of the genre as used in that organisation, but not of the genre as a whole. Of course, the aim of the research may simply be to study the genre in that particular organisation, but generally the purpose of a corpus is to yield insights not only into itself but also into typical language use in the genre, register or variety from which it was taken (Tognini-Bonelli 2001: 53–4). The NHS Feedback Corpus (NHSFC), for example, comprises a complete set of genre exemplars within an organisation in a given time period, as it includes all patient comments and provider replies over two and a half years (Baker *et al.* 2019). While this genre set comes from just one organisation, the findings and implications are potentially far-reaching, as the NHS is such a large organisation with a unique position in the UK.

Good sampling is therefore essential for designing a representative corpus, but there are, of course, practical limitations to sampling. It will never be possible, particularly for a small corpus, to collect samples from *all* the situations in which a fairly widespread genre is used. What is important is to ensure that the samples are collected from a range of typical situations. For example, data for the ABOT Corpus, which was designed to investigate the most frequently occurring genres in spontaneous face-to-face office interactions, were collected from offices in a range of organisations and business sectors (Koester 2006). Only those genres which occurred across various office settings were selected for inclusion in the corpus, thereby ensuring that the corpus was not biased towards any one setting.

For specialised corpora, linguistic representativeness (at least at the lexical level) can be measured by the degree of "closure" or "saturation" (see McEnery and Wilson 2001: 148–67; McEnery *et al.* 2006: 15–16). A corpus is considered to be saturated when the addition of new data (i.e. word tokens) does not yield new lexical items (i.e. word types). Moreover, linguistic representativeness also depends on the number of words per text sample and number of samples per register or genre included in the corpus. According to Biber (1993), the most common linguistic features (e.g. personal pronouns, contractions, past and present tense and prepositions) are relatively stable in their occurrence across 1,000-word samples. To adequately represent a register or a genre in a corpus, Biber (1990) found that the linguistic tendencies are quite stable, with ten (and to some extent even five) text samples per genre or register.

Biber's studies indicate that it is not necessary to have millions of words or a huge number of texts in a corpus to get reliable results (at least for high-frequency items). But even these relatively modest criteria cannot always be met, for example, having text samples that contain at least 1,000 words. This is especially the case for a spoken corpus, as many spoken interactions (for example, service encounters) are relatively short and do not amount to 1,000 words; and even some written texts, especially in workplace contexts (e.g. emails), may contain fewer than 1,000 words. It is more important to collect complete texts or interactions, rather than artificially controlled samples of a certain length, to adequately represent the genre or text type (Flowerdew 2004). One can still try to ensure that any sub-corpus within the corpus (for example, a particular genre or sub-genre) is represented by at least 1,000 words (even if these are spread across different texts or conversations) and that every sub-corpus contains at least five, if possible ten, different samples.

The ABOT Corpus will again be used to illustrate how a small corpus can be designed, as well as to indicate some of the problems and pitfalls. A 'corpus-driven' approach (Tognini-Bonelli 2001: 84) was used to establish the genres in the ABOT Corpus; this meant that it was not possible from the outset to gather a minimum number of exemplars per genre. Some genres, such as decision-making, were much more frequent than others, such as reporting, which meant that some sub-corpora contain more generic episodes or "texts" than others. About half of the sub-corpora contain between seven and eleven text samples, but others contain fewer than five. Clearly for those genres represented by fewer than five exemplars, the results of corpus analysis will be less reliable than for the genres with more text samples. But again, this reflects the reality of the target situation in that certain genres are typically more frequent in office interactions than others. To ensure that results from analysing the ABOT Corpus were reliable, comparisons were often made between "macro-genres" (similar genres grouped together), rather than between individual genres.

It was not possible to achieve lexical saturation or closure for the ABOT Corpus, as adding data from a different workplace setting would most likely have resulted in the addition of new lexical items. However, as the aim was to study generic features rather than lexical items, this limitation was acceptable. A related issue is that of 'local densities' (Moon 1998: 68): With genres that are under-represented, certain items may appear to be frequent in a genre simply because they occur frequently in one particular encounter. However, such local densities are usually easy to spot (e.g. if most examples of a lexical item come from one encounter), and this should be taken into account when interpreting the results.

Another challenge to representativity can arise with historical corpora, such as the Bolton/Worktown Corpus (BWC) compiled from manually recorded conversations of working-class people in Bolton (1937–40) totalling approximately 80,000 words (Timmis 2018). As Timmis points out, historical corpora can only include those documents that happen to have survived. To increase the representativeness of a corpus faced with the problem of data scarcity, researchers should try to include data from multiple sources in the corpus (ibid.).

These examples regarding the compilation of relatively small spoken corpora illustrate how the principles of corpus design interact with practical considerations relating to the nature of the data collected and how limitations regarding sampling can be dealt with. While every effort should be made to make the corpus as representative as possible, optimum representative sampling may not always be possible, particularly when compiling a spoken corpus, due to restrictions in relation to access and obtaining permissions, or simply limitations on the researcher-cum-corpus compiler's time (particularly as transcription is time consuming).

The most important consideration regarding corpus design is that the corpus should be set up in a way that is suitable for the purpose of the research. While many larger corpora were compiled for research into general linguistic phenomena, specialised corpora are often designed to answer specific research questions. For example, the aim of the IBLC was 'to study language use, accommodation across cultures, and genre acquisition of native and non-native speaking students in an undergraduate business communication class' (Upton and Connor 2001: 316). The data collected for the corpus consisted of letters of application written by business communication students in institutions in different countries as part of a writing project. The project involved students at each university reading and evaluating letters of students from other countries (see Connor *et al.* 1997). The corpus thus included data from both native and non-native students, had a cross-cultural element and involved a specific genre (letters of application) and could therefore be said to be well-designed to answer the research question.

4 Compiling and transcribing a small, specialised spoken corpus

Many of the limitations of a small corpus can be counterbalanced by reference to the context. Indeed, for specialised corpora, gathering contextual data about the setting from which the texts or discourses were collected can be essential, as it is often not possible to make sense of such specialised discourse without some background knowledge. For the 500,000-word sub-corpus of business discourse collected as part of the HKCSE, data collection was preceded by a period of observation in the organisations, which enabled the research assistant to choose sites for recording that would reflect a cross-section of the organisations' functions (Warren 2004). Warren notes that this period of observation and orientation was found to be essential at a later stage to interpret the data.

Although methods of ethnographic observation, note-taking and interview are not usually associated with corpus studies, there is no reason these methods cannot also inform and complement corpus analysis (ibid.: 137). In the case of small, specialised corpora, such contextual information is extremely valuable: It is often essential for interpreting the data, and it can be drawn on in qualitatively analysing the corpus results. For example, Harrington (2018) used both ethnographic and corpus linguistic methods in a study of interactions in an asylum reception centre. In addition to field notes and interview data, untranscribed data, which is not part of the corpus, can also inform the analysis in various ways. In some cases, it may be necessary to consult discourse participants or other representatives of the organisation to aid with transcription or corpus compilation. Warren (2004) gives the example of an encounter which the compilers of the business sub-corpus of HKCSE were not able to assign to any of the team's list of genres. After consulting an employee of the organisation, a new genre category was created for the sub-corpus.

Background information is useful not only in interpreting the data but can also be an integral part of corpus design. Having detailed information about the speakers or writers, the goals of the interactions or texts and the setting in which they were produced as part of the corpus database means that linguistic practices can easily be linked to specific contextual variables. This can be done by having each contributor complete a speaker/writer information sheet and obtaining as much information as possible about the text samples (e.g. through participant observation and interviews with people in the organisation). This information can be included as a header at the top of each text file or transcript and/or stored in a database, which can be drawn on in carrying out the analysis. Speaker information collected for HKCSE includes place of birth, gender, occupation, educational background, time spent living or studying abroad and mother tongue (Warren 2004). In designing the Cambridge and Nottingham Business English Corpus (CANBEC), a spoken meetings corpus of 1 million words, Handford (2010) collected information in the following main categories:

1. Relationship between the speakers, e.g. peer, manager-subordinate, colleagues from the same or different departments;
2. Topic, e.g. sales, marketing, production;
3. Purpose of the meeting, e.g. internal/external, reviewing, planning;
4. Speaker information, e.g. age, title, department, level in the company;
5. Company type and size.

In Section 5, we will see how this information was used in the corpus analysis.

Data collected for a spoken corpus will need to be transcribed and decisions made as to how detailed or "close" the transcription should be. If the corpus is quite small, it may be possible to transcribe the recording in more detail than for a large corpus, where there may be so much data to transcribe that time-consuming close transcription is not possible. As with decisions about corpus size and sampling, the level of detail required for the transcription depends on the aim of the project (see Chapters 2 and 3, this volume). For example, there is no need to transcribe prosodic features (intonation) if these features will not be analysed. However, it is worth remembering that the more detailed the transcription is, the more faithfully it represents the original interaction and the more features are available for later analysis. The transcription conventions used also need to be computer-readable, and as most corpus software requires texts to be stored as plain text files, any codes used should be available in plain text format.

Small, spoken corpora are often used to examine interactive features, and for such analysis, pauses, overlaps, interruptions and unfinished words or utterances, as well as non-linguistic features of interaction, such as laughter, should be indicated. An even closer transcription would also code for certain features of intonation, showing, for example, any syllables that are emphasised or whether an utterance ends in a rising or falling tone, as is done for the VOICE corpus of spoken ELF interactions (see VOICE Project). A very detailed prosodic transcription was pioneered with an early general corpus, the Survey of English Usage corpus (Svartvik and Quirk 1980), part of the London-Lund Corpus of Spoken English. An example of a specialised corpus showing detailed prosodic information is the HKCSE, which uses Brazil's (1997) discourse intonation system, where the utterances are transcribed as tone units and prominence, tone and key (pitch) are shown (see Cheng *et al.* 2008).

5 What can be learnt from a small, specialised corpus?

Having covered the issues involved in designing and compiling a small, specialised corpus, this section will discuss the advantages of small corpora in terms of what can be learnt from them. As already mentioned at the beginning of this chapter, one of the main advantages of a small, specialised corpus is that, unlike with a large corpus, the language is far less de-contextualised. Indeed, as Handford (2010: 7) points out, such contextual information may be essential in interpreting the data.

According to Flowerdew (2008), context is relevant for corpus analysis in two ways:

1. The context can inform the corpus-based analysis, for example, when the compiler-cum-analyst of a small, specialised corpus has access to background information to aid in the interpretation of the data;
2. The linguistic patterns identified through corpus analysis can tell us something about the social and cultural context from which the data were taken.

For both types of contextual links between corpus and context, small, specialised corpora have a clear advantage over large corpora. The first type was discussed in Section 4 on corpus compilation; here we will examine the second more closely.

Corpus analysis using word or keyword lists and concordances (see Chapter 9, this volume) can reveal insights into contexts of use. Patterns identified can be linked to specific contexts, for instance, showing in which genre(s) certain words or expressions occur and who uses them most. For example, a study of hotel interactions from the business sub-corpus of HKCSE (Cheng 2004) showed that the word "minibar" occurred in all checking-out interactions and was used exclusively by hotel staff, not by guests. Further investigation of frequent or key words and phrases may lead to the discovery of pragmatically specialised uses within a professional context. A good example of this is from a study of a 60,000-word corpus of telephone calls to NHS Direct (Adolphs *et al.* 2004). Starting with a keyword list and following up with a qualitative examination of these words revealed that many of the words and expressions performed interpersonal functions aimed at eliciting symptoms from callers. One such key expression is the vague category marker "or anything", which health advisors frequently used in eliciting symptoms from callers, for example:

(1)
N: 'And so there's no swelling anywhere to your face or anything?'
(Adolphs et al. 2004: 19)

The use of this vague expression invites callers to add their own description to the proposed symptoms, and thus performs a pragmatically specialised function within this professional genre.

Finally, let's consider some specific examples of how factors, such as genre, topic or the relationship between the participants, can influence local contexts of use. As shown in Section 4, CANBEC was designed to enable searches according to topic and purpose of the meetings and relationship between the speakers. Quantitative findings, such as frequency counts, can therefore be linked to such factors. The use of the lexical items *issue* and *problem* in CANBEC provides an interesting illustration of the role such factors can play in local contexts. These words appear to be synonyms, and basic corpus searches do indeed reveal similar patterns: They both have a high frequency and enter into similar collocations. However, the frequency of these two lexical items varies considerably when looking at the topics discussed in the meetings and the relationship between the speakers (Handford 2010: 188–95). *Issue*, for example, is more frequent in human resources and marketing meetings, whereas *problem* occurs most in procedural and technical meetings. In terms of speaker relationships, *issue* occurs more in interactions between managers and subordinates, whereas *problem* is used more in peer discussions. The following example from a meeting between peers, in which both *issue* and *problem* are used, illustrates how these two words in fact perform slightly different functions:

(2)
Well I- I thi- think that's another **issue**. And the other the and and another **issue** which comes on- onto that is that erm I'm still waiting ... apparently one of the **problems** with getting some of the information off the computer is ...
(adapted from Handford 2010: 193)

Handford (ibid.) notes that, while both words have the 'prosody of difficulty', *problem* seems to indicate more of a concrete obstacle, something that should be solved, whereas *issue* is somewhat more nebulous, and perhaps indicates that further discussion is needed. This fits with the nature of the meeting topics, where each of these words occurs most frequently: In technical and procedural meetings, more concrete *problems* are raised, whereas in human resources and marketing meetings, wider discussions "around" *issues* seem to be required. Considering speaker relationship, Handford argues that *problem* comes across as more categorical and could therefore potentially be face-threatening. This explains its higher frequency in peer meetings, where threats to face are less likely, thanks to the equal relationship between participants. In meetings between unequal participants (managers and subordinates), *issue* may be a useful euphemistic alternative to *problem*, serving to mitigate a potentially face-threatening act (ibid.: 192–4).

In the ABOT Corpus of workplace interactions (see Section 3), we can also observe the influence of local contexts on the frequency and use of various words and patterns. Both CANBEC and ABOT show that modals of obligation (*have to*, *need to*, *should*) are very frequent in workplace interactions (Koester 2006, 2010; Handford 2010). However, in both corpora, these modals, as well as their collocational patterns, are differentially distributed according to local contexts, such as genre and speaker relationship. The

Table 5.1 Total number of occurrences of modals of obligation in each macro-genre (per thousand words)

	Collaborative		*Unidirectional*	
	Raw freq.	*Density PTW*	*Raw freq.*	*Density PTW*
have (got) to	64	4.4	42	2.9
need (to)	32	2.2	22	1.5
should	28	1.9	22	1.5

genres in ABOT are grouped into two "macro-genres": unidirectional and collaborative (Koester 2010: 24–5). In unidirectional genres, one of the speakers clearly plays a dominant role by imparting information or giving instructions. In collaborative genres, such as decision-making and planning, participants contribute more or less equally towards accomplishing the goal of the encounter. In the ABOT Corpus, all the modals of obligation are more frequent in collaborative genres than in unidirectional genres, as shown in Table 5.1 (Koester 2006: 85–8).

Table 5.1, which shows both raw frequency and frequency per thousand words (or "density"), also shows that the difference in frequency is greater the stronger the modal: i.e. *have to*, which is the most forceful, occurs much more frequently, whereas *should*, the least forceful, is only marginally more frequent in collaborative genres.

Moreover, collocational patterns of modals and pronoun combinations also vary systematically with genre. Thus, in collaborative genres, *we* and *you* are the most frequent pronouns used with the modals noted earlier, whereas in unidirectional genres, *I* occurs most frequently in combination with all three modals. In unidirectional genres, *you have to* does not occur at all: there is just one example of *you'll have to* and a few instances of *you don't have to*.

Both the lower frequency of the more forceful modals and the infrequent use of the pronoun *you* in combination with all three modals of obligation can be linked to the feature that all unidirectional genres have in common, namely the fact that one speaker plays a dominant role. This imbalance in the speakers' roles generally means more care is taken to avoid face-threatening acts, even if the actual social or institutional relationship between the speakers varies. This results in more indirect and hedged language, as illustrated in the following example, where a speaker makes a request using *I need you to* instead of *you need to*:

(3)
I need you to sign off on this pack too.

[Author's data]

Another reason for the frequency of the first-person pronoun *I* is that in procedural discourse or instruction-giving (the most frequent unidirectional genre), the person receiving instructions frequently "invites" directives by saying *should I*, e.g.:

(4)
What should I do. Just - get the estimate...

[Author's data]

In collaborative genres, on the other hand, participants play a more equal role, and therefore more direct forms, such as *you have to* or *you should* are unproblematic, e.g.:

(5)
You have to make sure you can get access to that.

[Author's data]

Also, most collaborative genres are action-orientated, meaning people are trying to get things done (decisions, plans, arrangements), which results in the frequent use of modals of obligation with the first-person pronoun *we*, e.g.:

(6)
We need to get it moving.

[Author's data]

Corpus analysis can also reveal specific pragmatic meanings of collocational patterns, so-called "semantic prosodies" (see Chapter 27, this volume), within a specialised genre. Flowerdew (2008) found that the collocation *associated with* was very frequent in a corpus of environmental reports. Not only did it occur 139 times in the 250,000-word corpus, but it was found across all 23 companies from which the reports were drawn, indicating that this is a typical phrase for the genre and not a result of "local prosody" (see Section 3). In 135 of these instances, the phrase seemed to have a negative semantic prosody, for example:

(7)
difficulties associated with hydraulic dredging

(Flowerdew 2008: 121)

Flowerdew (2008: 121) concludes that this phrase is 'most likely an attenuated form of "caused by"' which is used by scientists to 'avoid claiming a direct causal effect, thereby forestalling any challenges from their peers', and therefore forms part of the discourse practices of the genre of environmental reports. In order to determine whether this finding is generalisable to other types of scientific writing, Flowerdew searched for the phrase *associated with* in the much larger 7-million-word Applied Science domain of the British National Corpus (BNC) and found that in 40 per cent of the samples examined, the phrase also has a negative semantic prosody. Such comparisons with a larger corpus, covering a similar variety or genre as the smaller, specialised corpus, are useful in testing the validity of findings from a smaller corpus and reinforcing the robustness of any generalisations made (see also Flowerdew 2003). By comparing a small corpus against a larger "benchmark" corpus, "keywords" can also be identified (e.g. using Wordsmith Tools [Scott 2019], Antconc or other applications, as described in Chapter 9, this volume): These are words that are unusually frequent in the small corpus compared to their normal frequency in the language (see Chapters 9 and 10, this volume).

This chapter has shown that while small corpora are not suitable for all types of analysis, a small, specialised corpus can nevertheless provide valuable insights into specific areas of language use and can even have certain advantages over large corpora. The main advantage is in the close link that exists between language patterns and contexts of use, as illustrated throughout this chapter from corpus design, through compilation and transcription to corpus analysis and findings. This interplay of language and context in corpus studies can be followed up in other chapters in this volume which deal with special areas of language use. Chapter 6 (this volume) looks at building a corpus to represent a language variety, and Chapter 7 at building a specialised audio-visual corpus. Other chapters focus on specific registers and genres; for example, Chapter 28 examines English for Academic Purposes, Chapter 41 looks at forensic linguistics and Chapter 43 explores health communication.

Transcription conventions used in data extracts:

.	falling intonation at end of tone unit
...	ellipted utterance
-	sound abruptly cut off, e.g. false start

Further reading

Flowerdew, L. (2004) 'The Argument for Using English Specialized Corpora to Understand Academic and Professional Settings', in U. Connor and T. Upton (eds) *Discourse in the Professions*, Amsterdam: John Benjamins, pp. 11–33. (This chapter is useful for anyone wanting to build a specialised corpus. As well as presenting a rationale for using specialised corpora, it provides useful guidelines for defining a specialised corpus and for corpus design.)

Handford, M. (2010) *The Language of Business Meetings*, Cambridge: Cambridge University Press. (This book provides a complete description of all the steps involved in building and exploiting a corpus of one professional genre (the business meeting) from data collection and corpus compilation to corpus analysis and interpretation.)

Harrington, K. (2018) *The Role of Corpus Linguistics in the Ethnography of a Closed Community*, London: Routledge. (This book provides a good representative study of a small, specialised corpus which focuses on the spoken interaction of a specific community: the residents of an asylum reception centre. It shows how corpus linguistics can be combined with other methods, in this case ethnography and conversation analysis.)

O'Keeffe, A., McCarthy, M. J. and Carter, R. A. (2007) *From Corpus to Classroom: Language Use and Language Teaching*, Cambridge: Cambridge University Press. (This book provides an accessible introduction to the most important topics in corpus research. The role of qualitative as well as quantitative analysis is a theme throughout the book, and many chapters address the topic of what can be learned from small, specialised corpora, in particular Chapters 8 and 10.)

References

Adolphs, S., Brown, B., Carter, R., Crawford, C. and Sahota, O. (2004) 'Applying Corpus Linguistics in a Health Care Context', *Journal of Applied Linguistics* 1(1): 9–28.

Baker, P., Brookes, G. and Evans, C. (2019) *The Language of Patient Feedback*, London: Routledge.

BASE (*British Academic Spoken English*) and BASE Plus Collections, https://warwick.ac.uk/fac/soc/al/research/collections/base/ [Accessed 9 August 2020].

Biber, D. (1990) 'Methodological Issues Regarding Corpus-Based Analyses of Linguistic Variation', *Literary and Linguistic Computing* 5(4): 257–69.

Biber, D. (1993) 'Representativeness in Corpus Design', *Literary and Linguistic Computing* 8(4): 243–57.

Brazil, D. (1997) *The Communicative Role of Intonation in English*, Cambridge: Cambridge University Press.

Carter, R. A. and McCarthy, M. J. (1995) 'Grammar and the Spoken Language', *Applied Linguistics* 16 (2): 141–58.
Cheng, W. (2004) '//→ did you TOOK// ↗ from the miniBAR//: What is the Practical Relevance of a Corpus-driven Language Study to Practitioners in Hong Kong's Hotel Industry?', in U. Connor and T. A. Upton (eds) *Discourse in the Professions*, Amsterdam: John Benjamins, pp. 141–66.
Cheng, W. (2014) 'Corpus Analyses of Professional Discourse', in V. Bhatia and S. Bremner (eds) *The Routledge Handbook of Language and Professional Communication*, London: Routledge, pp. 13–25.
Cheng, W., Greaves, C. and Warren, M. (2008) *A Corpus-Driven Study of Discourse Intonation*, Amsterdam/Philadelphia: John Benjamins.
Connor, U., Davis, K., De Rycker, T., Phillips, E. M. and Verckens, J. P. (1997) 'An International Course in International Business Writing: Belgium, Finland, the United States', *Business Communication Quarterly* 60(4): 63–74.
ELFA (2008) *The Corpus of English as a Lingua Franca in Academic Settings*, Director: Anna Mauranen, http://www.helsinki.fi/elfa [Accessed 4 August 2020].
Farr, F., Murphy, B. and O'Keeffe, A. (2004) 'The Limerick Corpus of Irish English: Design, Description and Application', *Teanga: The Irish Yearbook of Applied Linguistics* 21: 5–29.
Flowerdew, L. (2003) 'A Combined Corpus and Systemic-Functional Analysis of the Problem-Solution Pattern in a Student and Professional Corpus of Technical Writing', *TESOL Quarterly* 37(3): 489–511.
Flowerdew, L. (2004) 'The Argument for Using English Specialized Corpora to Understand Academic and Professional Settings', in U. Connor and T. A. Upton (eds) *Discourse in the Professions*, Amsterdam: John Benjamins, pp. 11–33.
Flowerdew, L. (2008) 'Corpora and Context in Professional Writing', in V. K. Bhatia, J. Flowerdew and R. H. Jones (eds) *Advances in Discourse Studies*, London: Routledge, pp. 115–31.
Handford, M. (2010) *The Language of Business Meetings*, Cambridge: Cambridge University Press.
Handford, M. and Koester, A. (2019) 'The Construction of Conflict Talk across Workplace Contexts: Towards a Theory of Conflictual Compact', *Language Awareness* 28(2):186–206.
Harrington, K. (2018) *The Role of Corpus Linguistics in the Ethnography of a Closed Community*, London: Routledge.
Hunston, S. (2002) *Corpora in Applied Linguistics*, Cambridge: Cambridge University Press.
ICLE website, https://uclouvain.be/en/research-institutes/ilc/cecl/icle.html [Accessed 4 August 2020].
Kessler, G. (2010) 'Virtual Business: An Enron Email Corpus Study', *Journal of Pragmatics* 42(1): 262–70.
Koester, A. (2006) *Investigating Workplace Discourse*, London: Routledge.
Koester, A. (2010) *Workplace Discourse*, London: Continuum.
MacArthur, F., Alejo, R., Piquer-Piriz, A., Amador-Moreno, C., Littlemore, J., Ädel, A., Krennmayr, T. and Vaughn, E. (2014) *EuroCoAT, The European Corpus of Academic Talk*, http://www.eurocoat.es.
McEnery, T. and Wilson, A. (2001) *Corpus Linguistics*, Edinburgh: Edinburgh University Press.
McEnery, T., Xiao, R. and Tono, Y. (2006) *Corpus-Based Language Studies*, London: Routledge.
Moon, R. (1998) *Fixed Expressions and Idioms in English: A Corpus-based Approach*, Oxford: Clarendon Press.
O'Keeffe, A., McCarthy, M. J. and Carter, R. A. (2007) *From Corpus to Classroom: Language Use and Language Teaching*, Cambridge: Cambridge University Press.
Scott, M. (2019) *Wordsmith Tools, Version 7 (corpus analytical software suite)*, Oxford: Oxford University Press.
Simpson, R. C., Briggs, S. L., Ovens, J. and Swales, J. M. (2002) 'The Michigan Corpus of Academic Spoken English', Ann Arbor, MI: The Regents of the University of Michigan, https://lsa.umich.edu/eli/language-resources/micase-micusp.html [Accessed 7 August 2020].
Sinclair, J. (2004) 'Trust the Text: Language', *Corpus and Discourse*, London: Routledge.
Svartvik, J. and Quirk, R. (1980) *A Corpus of English Conversation*, Lund: Liberläromodel.
Timmis, I. (2018) *Historical Spoken Language Research*, London: Routledge.
Tognini-Bonelli, E. (2001) *Corpus Linguistics at Work*, Amsterdam: John Benjamins.

Tribble, C. (2002) 'Corpora and Corpus Analysis: New Windows on Academic Writing', in J. Flowerdew (ed.) *Academic Discourse*, London: Longman, pp. 131–49.
Upton, T. A. and Connor, U. (2001) 'Using Computerized Corpus Analysis to Investigate the Textlinguistic Discourse Moves of a Genre', *English for Specific Purposes* 20: 313–29.
VOICE. (2013) *The Vienna-Oxford International Corpus of English* (version 2.0 online).
VOICE. (2007) VOICE Transcription Conventions [2.1], available at http://www.univie.ac.at/voice/voice.php?page=transcription_general_information [Accessed 5 March 2020].
Warren, M. (2004) '//so what have YOU been WORKing on REcently//: Compiling a Specialised Corpus of Spoken Business English', in U. Connor and T. A. Upton (eds) *Discourse in the Professions*, Amsterdam: John Benjamins, pp. 115–40.
WrELFA. (2015) *The Corpus of Written English as a Lingua Franca in Academic Settings*, Director: Anna Mauranen, Compilation manager: Ray Carey, http://www.helsinki.fi/elfa [Accessed 8 October 2021].

6

Building a corpus to represent a variety of a language

Brian Clancy

1 What is a variety of a language?

In the literature, a *variety* of a language is, to say the least, broadly defined. Crystal (2001: 6–7) maintains that in its most general sense, the notion of a variety includes 'speech and writing, regional and class dialects, occupational genres (such as legal and scientific language), creative linguistic expression (as in literature), and a wide range of other styles of expression'. Similarly, McEnery *et al.* (2006: 90) suggest that varieties of a language are equally expansive, covering, for example, 'the standard language (standardised for the purposes of education and public performance), dialects (geographically defined), sociolects (socially defined), idiolects (unique to individual speakers) and jargons (particular to specific domains)'. These approaches to the definition of the term are in themselves problematic, especially for the corpus builder(s). However, it does appear that a language variety is, in principle, systematic, coherent and predictable. Therefore, it is possible to say with some degree of certainty in a given language how people from a particular region will speak (for example, "British English" or "Liverpool English"), how lawyers will write ("legal French") or how television commentators will present a type of sport ("sports commentary").

Quirk (1995) refers to the confusion that this slew of language varieties can cause. He cites the example of the word *English* preceded by a specific adjective or noun to designate a specific variety. This list of varieties of English includes but is certainly not limited to varieties such as "American English", "legal English", "BBC English", "working-class English" or "Chicano English". Although each is referred to as a variety, they are all formed on 'desperately different taxonomic bases' (ibid.: 22). For example, academic discourse (spoken and/or written) is a variety that may be used equally by speakers of both American English and British English and speakers of other languages such as Spanish. This, in turn, raises the question of whether or not there exists a variety of American Academic English as opposed to one of British Academic English as opposed to Spanish Academic English. The answer to this question can be found in the distinction between register and dialect. In corpus linguistics, registers are delimited in non-linguistic terms, defined by Biber *et al.* (1999) as situational characteristics such as

DOI: 10.4324/9780367076399-6

mode, interactiveness, domain, communicative purpose or topic (cf. Halliday 1978). This results in varieties such as legal English and academic discourse, but also varieties such as political discourse, workplace discourse, classroom discourse, crime fiction, etc.; in other words, these varieties are use-related. Dialect, on the other hand, has been defined as a variety associated with different groups of individuals, identifiable through pronunciation, lexical and grammatical variation (Biber *et al.* 1999). This variation is often attributed to social characteristics such as gender, age, social class, ethnicity or religion and therefore accounts for national varieties but also those such as BBC English, working-class English or Chicano English. These varieties are user-related.

Accordingly, the starting point for the building of a corpus for a variety of a language could usefully be based on a fundamental decision: Is the proposed corpus being built to represent a *Variety* of a language, such as American English or British English, or is it representing a *variety* of a language such as legal English or academic English? A Variety is defined geographically and is user-related, where an individual is in a sense "tied" to and identified by it (Quirk 1995). Therefore, Irish people speak Irish English, and this includes its corresponding dialects. On the other hand, a variety is defined situationally and is use-related; therefore, it involves the discourse activity the individual is involved in or the purpose for which they are using language. For example, a conversation between two academics could feature two language Varieties, say American English and British English, but one language variety, academic English. Indeed, many corpora constructed to represent a Variety of a language are built using a range of varieties of that language (see, for example, the Cambridge and Nottingham Corpus of Discourse in English (CANCODE) or the first British National Corpus (BNC1994) (see Chapters 3 and 4, this volume). The decision made to choose between Variety or variety will be largely based on the research questions the corpus is expected to answer. This fundamental choice also has defining repercussions in relation to issues of corpus design such as the construction of the corpus sampling frame, which in turn has implications on *size*, *diversity of texts* and *representativeness and balance* (see Chapters 2, 3 and 4, this volume).

2 Issues of corpus design for a variety of a language

Building a corpus for a variety of a language involves building something that is representative of a whole; therefore, the design of the corpus is of particular importance. Many of the decisions made by the corpus builder(s) in the design stage are based on the proposed uses of the corpus and on the research questions that these entail (see Chapters 2, 3 and 4, this volume). However, as McEnery *et al.* (2006: 73) caution, 'corpus building is of necessity a marriage of perfection and pragmatism'. Although corpus builder(s) should always strive to build the perfectly representative corpus, issues such as corpus size, text diversity and number and length of texts, as outlined in this section, may result in decisions based on factors outside of the control of corpus designers.

Issue 1: address corpus size

In general, the primary issue connected to corpus size is that of resources, and it is here that the corpus builder(s) may have to "cut their coat according to their cloth". In the design stage, a number of fundamental decisions must be made. A key decision is whether the corpus will consist of written texts, spoken texts, computer-mediated texts or a combination of some or all of these. The timeframe for collection, computerisation, annotation and, if required, tagging and parsing has to be considered. Spoken corpora are generally smaller in size than written corpora, primarily due to the transcription process. Chafe *et al.* (1991) observe that it takes six person-hours to transcribe one minute of speech for the Santa Barbara Corpus. McCarthy (1998) notes that it takes, on average, 20 hours to transcribe 1 hour of recorded spoken data. Estimates for the American component of the International Corpus of English (ICE-USA) range from 10 hours to transcribe a 2,000-word carefully prepared monologue to 20 hours for a dialogue containing numerous speaker overlaps (Meyer 2002). For this reason, spoken corpora such as CANCODE, the spoken component of BNC1994 and the Spoken British National Corpus 2014 (Spoken BNC2014) have required considerable funding both from universities and major publishing houses. Written texts can also prove problematic when building a corpus, especially when issues of copyright are considered (see Atkins *et al.* 1992: 4; McEnery *et al.* 2006: 77–9; see also Chapter 4, this volume).

The corpora for the study of geographical, user-related language varieties differ in size, largely dependent upon the nature of the texts which they contain. These include but are not limited to the following corpora:

- The Global Web-based English Corpus (GloWbE), a 1.9-billion-word corpus of web-based materials (blogs, newspapers, company websites, etc.) from 20 countries;
- The Corpus of Contemporary American English (COCA), a corpus of 560 million words (to date), evenly divided between the years 1990 and 2017 (20 million words per year);
- The BNC1994, a 100-million-word corpus designed to be representative of both written and spoken British English, and the companion Spoken BNC2014, an 11.5-million-word spoken corpus;
- The International Corpus of English (ICE) project, with 14 one-million-word corpora, each representing a different variety of English;
- CANCODE, a 5-million-word corpus of spoken British (and some Irish) English;
- The Limerick Corpus of Irish English (LCIE), a 1-million-word corpus designed to be representative of spoken Irish English.

It should be pointed out that there are also a range of non–English-language corpora designed to represent a number of different languages. For example, there are a number of languages, amongst them Czech, Hungarian, German, Polish, Russian and Welsh, that have embraced the *national corpus* concept. In addition, the TenTen Corpus Family, available through Sketch Engine, is composed of comparable 10-billion-word, web-based corpora. These corpora are currently available in 30+ different languages.

There are also a number of corpora that have been designed to facilitate the examination of situational, use-related varieties. For example, COCA is divided into a number of component parts – spoken language, fiction, magazines, newspapers and academic texts. Similarly, CANCODE is subdivided into spoken texts from intimate, pedagogical, professional, socialising and transactional settings (McCarthy 1998). There are also a number of corpora specifically designed to represent use-related varieties. Examples of these include written academic corpora such as the British Academic

Written English Corpus (BAWE), a 6.5-million-word corpus of undergraduate and postgraduate written assessments; spoken academic corpora such as the 1.8-million-word Michigan Corpus of Spoken Academic English (MICASE); computer-mediated communication corpora such as the Birmingham Blog Corpus, a 628.5-million-word corpus; or formal workplace corpora, such as the 1-million-word Business Letter Corpus. These corpora, amongst others, are available online through a range of search interfaces.

When considering corpus size, the purpose of the corpus should also be addressed. A comprehensive examination of the variation between lexical features or less frequent grammatical features generally requires a larger corpus, for example, GloWbE or the BNC. In contrast, Vaughan and Clancy (2013) point out that use-related corpora in the 20,000 to 200,000-word range are more than adequate for the investigation of high-frequency pragmatic variation in spoken language. However, ultimately, the size of a corpus might be better determined 'not by focusing too intently on the overall length of the corpus but by focusing more on the internal structure of the corpus' (Meyer 2002: 34). The internal structure of a corpus refers to matters such as diversity of texts and length and number of texts to include, and it is to these matters that attention now turns.

Issue 2: consider the diversity of texts to include

Many corpora designed to be representative of a language variety are, in essence, multi-purpose. They can be used, for example, to describe lexico-grammatical features, to study differences between different national varieties or to study variation within the different registers that comprise the corpus. Therefore, a corpus of this type necessarily requires a wide range of texts, which can be selected according to a range of different criteria. The Brown Corpus used a sampling frame derived from the collection of books and periodicals in the Brown University Library and Providence Athenaeum in 1961. The Lancaster-Oslo-Bergen (LOB) corpus also chose two sampling frames; for books, the publications listed for 1961 in *The British National Bibliographic Cumulated Subject Index, 1960–1964,* and for periodicals and newspapers, those listed in *Willing's Press Guide* (1961) (see Johansson *et al.* 1978). The BNC1994 collected written texts under three criteria: domain, time and medium. Domain refers to the context type of the text (nine different context types – for example, leisure, applied science and world affairs – were identified); time refers to when the texts were produced (texts were sampled in the period 1960–93); and medium refers to the type of text publication (book, journal, newspaper, etc.). In relation to the spoken component of the BNC1994, 4.2 million words of the corpus were collected by a process of demographic sampling. Recordings were collected from individuals, and demographic information such as name, age, occupation, gender and social class was noted (Crowdy 1993). This was further subdivided into region and interaction type (monologue or dialogue). The demographically sampled spoken corpus was complemented by texts collected on context-governed criteria. These texts related to more formal speech contexts, such as those encountered in educational or business settings (see Aston and Burnard 1998 for a full description of the design).

In their initial corpus design phase, the CANCODE team developed a set of spoken text types to correspond to existing text typologies for the written language. McCarthy (1998) describes the corpus design as a 'genre-based' approach where not only is a population of speakers targeted but the context and environment in which the speech is produced are also taken into consideration. The framework used for CANCODE sought to combine the nature of speaker relationship with goal types prevalent in everyday, spoken interaction. The nature of the speaker relationship was divided into five broad contexts: transactional, professional, pedagogical, socialising and intimate. For each of these contexts, three goal types were identified: information provision, collaborative task and collaborative idea (see McCarthy 1998: 9–10 for a definition of the terms). Therefore, for example, a university lecture is defined as a pedagogical context with an information provision goal type, whereas a family cooking together would be an example of an intimate collaborative task. This, according to McCarthy (ibid.: 9), 'offers the possibility of linking their [the data] contextual and social features directly with the lexico-grammatical "nuts and bolts" of their step-by-step creation'. This design matrix was, in turn, adopted by LCIE, which allows for a direct comparison between these two corpora (Clancy 2016).

The ICE suite of corpora also contains a range of spoken and written texts collected according to specifically delineated criteria (see Greenbaum 1991; Nelson 1996; Meyer 2002). The written component contains both printed and non-printed (for example, student essays, social letters) material, although the printed material accounts for 75 per cent of the written corpus. From a spoken viewpoint, ICE contains 60 per cent dialogic material and 40 per cent monologic; again, the criteria for the inclusion of this material are thoroughly specified, with dialogues divided into public and private and monologues into scripted and unscripted. In the ICE corpora, the speakers chosen were adults of 18 years of age or older who had received a formal education through the medium of English to at least secondary school level (however, this design proved to be flexible in the case of well-known, established political leaders and radio or television broadcasters whose public status made their inclusion appropriate). Information was also recorded about gender, ethnic group, region, occupation and status in occupation and role in relation to other participants. MICASE also employed context-governed criteria in collecting the data. The corpus contains speech events across the major academic disciplines in a university, for example, biological and health sciences, physical sciences and engineering and humanities and the arts. However, the professional disciplines of law, medicine and dentistry were excluded. Demographic information such as age, gender, academic role and first language were recorded.

Issue 3: address text length and number

In determining how "long" a text should be in order to warrant inclusion in the corpus, the issue of corpus size must be returned to. Both spoken and written texts range dramatically in size from a few words (for example, a quick note to a friend) to millions of words (for example, a long novel) (see Chapters 2, 3 and 4, this volume). It is important to remember that the results generated from a small corpus of texts can be skewed by one relatively long text. Traditionally, the best solution to this dilemma is to build a corpus large enough to dilute even the lengthiest text. In other words, the bigger the corpus, the better. However, Biber (1990) maintains that the underlying parameters of linguistic variation can be replicated in a relatively small corpus if that corpus represents the full range of variation. In contrast, larger corpora are not adequate for overall analyses of textual variation if they fail to represent the range of variation. Biber (1993) examines statistical formulae for determining sample size based on a normal distribution of grammatical features. He found that for nouns, a sample of 59.8 × 2,000-word texts (approximately 120,000 words) is required for representativeness; for less common grammatical features such as conditional clauses, a sample of 1,190 × 2,000-word texts (approximately 2.4 million words) is required. In the ICE suite of corpora, each text contains approximately 2,000 words, with the ending occurring at a suitable discourse break (Greenbaum 1991). These 2,000-word samples are problematic, however, because if the text is longer than 2,000 words, then the question arises as to what part of the text should be omitted. In selecting samples to be included in a corpus, attention must also be paid to ensure that text initial, middle and end samples are balanced (McEnery *et al.* 2006).

In terms of the number of texts to be included, corpora differ greatly in their approach. The ICE compilers decided that each regional corpus would be 1 million words. They also decided on ten texts (20,000 words) as the minimum for each text category. Texts in the Brown and LOB corpora are also 2,000 words long, and therefore each corpus contains 500 texts. The demographically sampled component of the Spoken BNC1994 consists of 153 texts and approximately 4.2 million words, giving an average text length of approximately 27,500 words. In contrast, the 11.5-million-word Spoken BNC2014 contains 1,251 texts, resulting in an average text length of over 9,000 words. The CANCODE matrix of speech genres yields 15 cells, and the initial target was to gather approximately 65,000 words per cell. MICASE contains a total of 152 speech events ranging in type from lectures, to meetings, to dissertation defences, to service encounters and therefore seeks to cover all speech which occurs in an academic setting. These speech events range in length from 19 to 178 minutes and in word count from 2,805 to 30,328 words (see Simpson-Vlach and Leicher 2006). The 2.6-million-word Michigan Corpus of Upper-Level Student Papers (MICUSP) contains 829 different types of undergraduate and postgraduate written assignments (research report, research proposal, argumentative essay, etc.) across 16 academic disciplines. What is obvious here, and is indeed a theme running throughout the chapter, is that there is no "one size fits all" approach to corpus design and therefore it is important that corpora are transparent in their design decisions in order that any results generated can be critically assessed.

3 Assessing the representativeness and balance of a corpus

Although a "Hail Mary" might be a more apt metaphor in this instance, representativeness is referred to as a "Holy Grail" of the corpus linguistic enterprise (see Chapters 2, 3 and 4, this volume). For specific-purpose corpora, it can be a relatively straightforward matter – a corpus of the writing of Jane Austen is representative of her work if it contains all of her published novels, for example. However, for corpora for general use, this goal is obviously more difficult to achieve, given the range of texts that might be required in order to represent said variety. According to Leech (1991: 27), a corpus is representative if 'findings based on its contents can be generalised to a larger hypothetical corpus', which, although helpful from a theoretical viewpoint, is rather vague when it comes to the practicalities of corpus design and compilation. Sinclair (2005) outlines six practical steps towards achieving as representative a corpus as possible (see Chapter 3, this volume). Biber's (1993) seminal article outlines in detail how to construct a statistically representative corpus; however, it appears that for designers of general-purpose corpora, in most cases, a compromise is reached regarding representativeness. Recent corpora designed for the study of a language variety such as the Spoken BNC2014 have used an opportunistic approach to data collection (see Love *et al.* 2017), where participants are invited to contribute to the corpus using their own digital audio recorders and are responsible for obtaining consent and providing the required metadata. This approach facilitates the collection of large amounts of data in relatively short periods of time for a relatively low cost. The corpus designers, freed from the onerous responsibilities of, for example, actively seeking out participants, providing audio equipment, furnishing and completing consent forms and recording metadata, are instead able to concentrate on issues of representativeness and balance.

A balanced corpus relies heavily on intuition and best estimates (Atkins *et al.* 1992; Sinclair 2005; McEnery *et al.* 2006). Therefore, balance, in common with representativeness, is also a rather vague, but important, notion. In relation to corpora built to represent a language variety, when assessing the balance of a corpus, it is useful to examine other corpora, and it is becoming increasingly popular, 'for good or ill' (McEnery *et al.* 2006: 17), to adopt an existing corpus model and, in doing so, to assume that issues of balance have been addressed. Written corpora like the Brown Corpus and the LOB are generally accepted as balanced corpora. The spoken component of the BNC1994 sought balance through a design that combined both demographic and context-governed data. The Spoken BNC2014 has a "core" of data with evenly balanced demographic categories (gender, age, accent/dialect and socio-economic status) surrounded by a large "mantle" of additional data (see Love *et al.* 2017). When building a corpus that represents both spoken and written language, it is important to consider the balance between the two. The BNC1994 has a 90:10 per cent split between written and spoken texts, respectively. In contrast, the ICE suite of corpora opted for a 60:40 per cent split in favour of spoken language. Neither of these are likely to sufficiently capture the everyday linguistic experience of most people, who experience more speech than writing in their day-to-day lives. The Longman Spoken and Written English (LSWE) corpus contains four core registers (or varieties): conversation, newspaper language, fiction and academic prose. According to Biber *et al.* (1999: 25), these four were selected on the basis of balance in that they cover 'much of the range of variation in English'. For example, conversation is the register most commonly encountered by native speakers, whereas academic prose is a highly specialised register that native speakers encounter infrequently. Between these two extremes are the popular registers of newspapers and fiction. The corpus was designed to contain 5,000,000 words per register. In all of these corpora, balance has been associated with proportionality; however, an effort should be made to ensure that this proportionality represents the variety's 'textual universe as a whole' (Leech 2007: 136).

CANCODE, whose genre-based design was successfully adapted in the creation of LCIE, is also considered a balanced corpus; however, this notion of balance was arrived at in a slightly different way from corpora such as the BNC. The initial target for the CANCODE team was a figure of 65,000 words per cell. It was found that certain data – for example, intimate conversations and business meetings – were more difficult to collect than other types because of their sensitive nature. At an early stage in the construction of the corpus, some cells were found to contain more data than others. The progress from the initial 1 million words to the final target of 5 million addressed these imbalances and attempted, where possible, to equally cover all the context types in the corpus. McCarthy (1998) maintains that a fluid corpus design is more important than a rigid adherence to numerical targets within a fixed sample frame. This notion of corpus design as fluid, organic and cyclical in order to maintain balance is referred to by Biber (1993: 255) as the 'bottom-line' in corpus design. Returning to an earlier point, Hunston

(2002) stresses that it is key to consider balance when interpreting data from a corpus. Many corpora built to represent a variety of a language are, by nature, multi-purpose; therefore, the builder(s) cannot predict all the queries that may be made of it. Thus, it is necessary to document all decisions made in regard to the design criteria. Researchers who access the corpus can then check this documentation to ensure that it is suitable for the proposed purpose. In this way, the responsibility for the integrity of corpus literacy is shared and should be guided by Hunston's (ibid.: 23) principle that 'a statement about evidence in a corpus is a statement about that corpus, not about the language or register of which the corpus is a sample'.

4 What can a corpus tell us about a language Variety? Irish English

Although long recognised as a variety of English in its own right, as illustrated by studies such as Joyce (1910) and Bliss (1979), the description of Irish English (IrE) has benefitted considerably from the study of a number of language corpora. There is a range of corpora of both written and spoken IrE available to researchers interested in studying the variety (for more on these corpora, see Vaughan and Clancy 2016). Two of the more commonly consulted corpora are LCIE and the Ireland component of ICE, ICE-Ireland. LCIE is a 1-million-word corpus of naturally occurring spoken IrE, whereas ICE-Ireland, in keeping with the ICE project, represents both spoken (600,000 words) and written (400,000 words) IrE. The corpora allow the description of IrE as a variety in itself rather than how it is similar to or different from other varieties of English such as British English (BrE). Both contain detailed demographic information such as age and gender and also information about where the speakers were born and where they lived at the time of recording (geographical information) and level of education. ICE-Ireland also details the religious background of the participants in the corpus, which is relevant, as the corpus contains speech from both the Republic of Ireland and Northern Ireland. LCIE, on the other hand, was collected exclusively in the Republic. The spoken component of ICE-Ireland has also been both prosodically and pragmatically tagged and made available as SPICE-Ireland (see Kirk 2016).

The size of both LCIE and ICE-Ireland, in addition to the emergence of SPICE-Ireland, has resulted in a primary focus on the realm of linguistic pragmatics, given that it is possible to examine patterns of linguistic form and function in light of their interactional and situational contexts of occurrence. This has allowed researchers to provide some insightful findings in relation to linguistic representations of socio-cultural norms in Irish society. Some of these studies are presented here for illustrative purposes. In common with the growth of corpus pragmatic studies more generally, many of these studies have focussed on the use of pragmatic markers (PMs). Although *like* is by no means unique to IrE (see, for example, Andersen 2001; Tagliamonte 2005), it can be considered a relatively new development in IrE (Amador-Moreno 2010). The marker has emerged from corpus studies as a prominent item in the socio-pragmatic system of Irish English (see O'Keeffe *et al.* 2020). Kallen (2013) and Schweinberger (2015) demonstrate how clause- or sentence-final *like* is more frequent in ICE-Ireland than in ICE-Great Britain. The marker *now* has also been identified as a key item in IrE. Clancy and Vaughan (2012) have shown that *now* is more frequent in the spoken IrE represented in LCIE than in other corpora, such as the spoken component of the BNC (1994) or the Scottish Corpus of Texts and Speech (SCOTS). In IrE, *now* has emerged as highly polysemous, functioning as a temporal adverb, a discourse marker, a pragmatic marker and a deictic presentative. The socio-pragmatic function of both *like* and *now* is pivotal in understanding the behaviour of these PMs. In IrE, *like* and *now* frequently occupy the final position in an utterance to soften or mitigate face-threatening behaviour such as disagreement, challenge or evaluation, a function that is less frequent in corpora of British English (see also Vaughan *et al.* 2017).

Corpus studies in IrE have also strived for a better understanding of pragmatic phenomena beyond the sphere of pragmatic markers. One of these areas is the link between grammar and pragmatics. O'Keeffe and Amador-Moreno (2009) and Filppula (2012) have examined the frequency of occurrence of aspectual forms in IrE through a focus on the structures *be after* + *V-ing* and MODAL + *be V-ing,* respectively. Both of these forms are more frequent in IrE than in British English (see also Kirk 2017). The *be after* + *V-ing* structure was shown to have important politeness functions in IrE, whereas more frequent use of MODAL + *be V-ing* has been tentatively associated with a predisposition toward high levels of personal commitment in IrE. Thus, these pragmatic functions of the progressive are indicative of membership of the IrE-speaking community. Another area that has received some attention in IrE corpus research is the turn-taking system. O'Keeffe and Adolphs (2008) and McCarthy (2015) focus primarily on non-minimal lexical items at turn-initial position and their distribution in IrE and BrE. While there is an overlap between the form and function of these items across the two varieties, each has its own distinct core of adjectives, adverbs and intensifiers at turn opening that are used with greater frequency and convey different shades of meaning. IrE shows a greater preference for items that convey intensification and informality in turn-initial position, which could help define the variety.

These corpus studies of IrE are essential to our understanding of socio-pragmatic competence in the variety. They are illustrative of a wider corpus linguistic bent to the study of IrE, which is fast amounting to a considerable body of research. In addition to corpora such as LCIE and ICE-Ireland, emerging corpora of IrE such as CORIECOR (see Amador-Moreno and McCafferty 2012), Millar's (2015) blog corpus and Vaughan and Moriarty's array of corpora of performed discourses (see, for example, Vaughan and Moriarty 2018) are making important contributions to the description of the variety.

5 What can a corpus tell us about a language variety? The case of Irish intimate discourse in LCIE

LCIE was designed to parallel the CANCODE corpus and therefore adopted a framework that, in terms of data collection, features a number of cells, for example, intimate collaborative idea or pedagogical information provision, that serve as a guide for achieving representativeness and balance. In common with many spoken corpora, LCIE also adopted an opportunistic approach to data collection which, given that the corpus design team were housed in a university setting, resulted in much of the data collection in the more informal context types such as intimate and socialising, at least, being undertaken by university students. In terms of the distribution of data in LCIE, 56 per cent of the data collected for the corpus is from an intimate context (see Clancy 2016). In this sense, LCIE cannot be considered a balanced corpus; however, given that balance in a spoken corpus designed to represent a variety of a language can be difficult to achieve, this is not necessarily problematic. In fact, the data collected in the intimate context type might be considered representative of a particular demographic – university students in their early to mid-twenties and their families and close friends (also predominantly university students). This context type, in essence, forms the core of the LCIE corpus.

In keeping with studies that have used LCIE more generally, research on the intimate sub-corpus of LCIE has also seen a focus on the understanding of pragmatic phenomena such as reference, turn taking, (im)politeness and pragmatic markers. For example, the PMs *kind/sort of* and *I think* have been shown to occur with less frequency in intimate discourse than in other varieties such as radio phone-in or spoken academic discourse (Clancy 2005; Clancy 2016). The function of *kind/sort of* has been linked to the reduction of social distance between speakers and the creation of a relaxed relationship between conversational participants (Holmes 1993), functions that are arguably unnecessary in the intimate sphere. Other items that are associated with the creation of group solidarity, such as the pronoun *we*, have also been shown to occur with a lower frequency in intimate discourse than in other spoken contexts such as the workplace or media discourse (Clancy 2016). Intimates use *we* less frequently due to a pre-existing, well-established group identity that may need less maintenance than in other groups (see also Clancy 2020). Similarly, *I think*, amongst other functions, has been shown to preface, and thereby mitigate, disagreement sequences (see, for example, Muntigl and Turnbull 1998). However, a feature of IrE as a variety seems to be that mitigation occurs in towards the closing of a speaker turn, and this has also been shown to be true of intimate discourse, specifically family discourse. Disagreement sequences in IrE family discourse are characterised by low levels of mitigators such as *I think* in preface position, as family members can become quickly involved in disagreements, frequently using a *yeah but* turn preface, safe in the knowledge that mitigation can be performed later in the speaker turn by PMs such as *like* or *you know* (Clancy 2018). Similarly, Vaughan *et al.* (2017) found that Irish intimates, in comparison to their British counterparts, perform mitigation in the form of indirectness and imprecision in different ways, frequently through a clustering of vague category markers such as *or something like that* with traditional PMs such as *you know*.

This is not to suggest that the pragmatic features of Irish intimate discourse is fundamentally distinct from families and friendship groups in other cultures. Clancy and McCarthy (2015) have explored the phenomenon of turn co-construction in the intimate and socialising context types in IrE and BrE and found that 10 per cent of *when* clauses at the turn-initial position were second-speaker completions in both corpora and, in the case of turn-initial *if* clauses, the figure for the co-construction rose to 19 per cent in LCIE and 22 per cent in CANCODE. Co-construction has a pragmatic function in that speakers, in addition to viewing syntax as a shared interactional resource (see Rühlemann 2007), co-construct utterances through a process of comment, qualification or evaluation. This process demonstrates that for intimates in both IrE and BrE, the concept of meaning is also viewed as a shared resource between speakers, where utterance meaning can be negotiated and modified unproblematically. This study – and, indeed, all of the studies outlined in these sections – represents the opportunities offered by corpora for the description of both user- and use-related linguistic varieties.

Further reading

Biber, D. (1993) 'Representativeness in Corpus Design', *Literary and Linguistic Computing* 8(4): 243–57. (In this article, Biber outlines how to construct a statistically representative corpus. In common with many seminal texts, this work has proven to be both inspirational and contentious.)

Douglas, F. (2003) 'The Scottish Corpus of Texts and Speech: Problems of Corpus Design', *Literary and Linguistic Computing* 18(1): 23–37.

Kučera, K. (2002) 'The Czech National Corpus: Principles, Design, and Results', *Literary and Linguistic Computing* 17(2): 245–57. (Both of these articles explore, and discuss practical solutions to, the problems encountered during the design and construction of large, non-English language corpora representative of language varieties.)

Meyer, C. (2002) *English Corpus Linguistics: An Introduction*, Cambridge: Cambridge University Press. (This book provides an accessible introduction to corpus linguistics in addition to a step-by-step guide to corpus design, construction and analysis. Meyer draws heavily on corpora such as the BNC and ICE in order to illustrate each stage.)

References

Amador-Moreno, C. (2010) *An Introduction to Irish English*, London: Equinox.

Amador-Moreno, C. and McCafferty, K. (2012) 'A Corpus of Irish English Correspondence (CORIECOR): A Tool for Studying the History and Evolution of Irish English', in B. Migge and M. Ní Chiosáin (eds) *New Perspectives on Irish English*, Amsterdam: John Benjamins, pp. 265–88.

Andersen, G. (2001) *Pragmatic Markers and Sociolinguistic Variation: A Relevance-Theoretic Approach to the Language of Adolescents*, Amsterdam: John Benjamins.

Aston, G. and Burnard, L. (1998) *The BNC Handbook: Exploring the British National Corpus with SARA*, Edinburgh: Edinburgh University Press.

Atkins, S., Clear, J. and Ostler, N. (1992) 'Corpus Design Criteria', *Literary and Linguistic Computing* 7(1): 1–16.

Biber, D. (1990) 'Methodological Issues Regarding Corpus-based Analyses of Linguistic Variation', *Literary and Linguistic Computing* 5(4): 257–69.

Biber, D. (1993) 'Representativeness in Corpus Design', *Literary and Linguistic Computing* 8(4): 243–57.

Biber, D., Johansson, S., Leech, G., Conrad, S. and Finnegan, E. (1999) *The Longman Grammar of Spoken and Written English*, London: Longman.

Bliss, A. (1979) *Spoken English in Ireland 1600-1740*, Dublin: Dolmen Press.

Chafe, W., Du Bois, J. and Thompson, S. (1991) 'Towards a New Corpus of American English', in K. Aijmer and B. Altenberg (eds) *English Corpus Linguistics*, London: Longman, pp. 64–82.

Clancy, B. (2005) '"You're fat. You'll eat them all": Politeness Strategies in Family Discourse', in A. Barron and K. Schneider (eds) *The Pragmatics of Irish English*, Berlin: Mouton de Gruyter, pp. 177–99.

Clancy, B. (2016) *Investigating Intimate Discourse: Exploring the Spoken Interaction of Families, Couples and Close Friends*, London: Routledge.

Clancy, B. (2018) 'Conflict in Corpora: Investigating Family Conflict Sequences Using a Corpus Pragmatic Approach', *Journal of Language Aggression and Conflict* 6(2): 228–47.

Clancy, B. (2020) 'Intimacy and Identity in Irish English: A Corpus Pragmatic Approach to the Study of Personal Pronouns', in R. Hickey and C. Amador-Moreno (eds) *Irish Identities: Sociolinguistic Perspectives*, Berlin: Walter De Gruyter, pp. 153–72.

Clancy, B. and McCarthy, M. J. (2015) 'Co-Constructed Turn-Taking', in K. Aijmer and C. Rühlemann (eds) *Corpus Pragmatics: A Handbook*, Cambridge: Cambridge University Press, pp. 430–53.

Clancy, B. and Vaughan, E. (2012) '"It's Lunacy Now": A Corpus-Based Pragmatic Analysis of the Use of 'Now' in Contemporary Irish English', in B. Migge and M. Ní Chiosáin (eds) *New Perspectives on Irish English*, Amsterdam: John Benjamins, pp. 225–46.

Crowdy, S. (1993) 'Spoken Corpus Design', *Literary and Linguistic Computing* 8(4): 259–65.

Crystal, D. (2001) *Language and the Internet*, Cambridge: Cambridge University Press.

Filppula, M. (2012) 'Exploring Grammatical Differences between Irish and British English', in B.

Migge and M. Ní Chiosáin (eds) *New Perspectives on Irish English*, Amsterdam: John Benjamins, pp. 85–100.
Greenbaum, S. (1991) 'The Development of the International Corpus of English', in K. Aijmer and B. Altenberg (eds) *English Corpus Linguistics*, London: Longman, pp. 83–91.
Halliday, M. A. K. (1978) *Language as a Social Semiotic: The Social Interpretation of Language and Meaning*, London: Edward Arnold.
Holmes, J. (1993) '"New Zealand Women are Good to Talk to": An Analysis of Politeness Strategies in Interaction', *Journal of Pragmatics* 20: 91–116.
Hunston, S. (2002) *Corpora in Applied Linguistics*, Cambridge: Cambridge University Press.
Joyce, P. W. (1910) *English as We Speak it in Ireland*, Dublin: M.H. Gill.
Johansson, S., Leech, G. and Goodluck, H. (1978) *Manual of Information to Accompany the Lancaster/Oslo-Bergen Corpus of British English, for Use with Digital Computers*, Oslo: Department of English, University of Oslo.
Kallen, J. (2013) *Irish English Volume 2: The Republic of Ireland*, Berlin: Walter De Gruyter.
Kirk, J. (2016) 'The Pragmatic Annotation Scheme of the SPICE-Ireland Corpus', *International Journal of Corpus Linguistics* 21(3): 299–322.
Kirk, J. (2017) 'The Present Perfect in Irish English', *World Englishes* 36(2): 239–53.
Leech, G. (1991) 'The State of the Art in Corpus Linguistics', in K. Aijmer and B. Altenberg (eds) *English Corpus Linguistics*, London: Longman, pp. 8–30.
Leech, G. (2007) 'New Resources, or Just Better Old Ones? The Holy Grail of Representativeness', in M. Hundt, N. Nesselhauf and C. Biewer (eds) *Corpus Linguistics and the Web*, Amsterdam: Rodopi, pp. 133–49.
Love, R., Dembry, C., Hardie, A., Brezina V. and McEnery, T. (2017) 'The Spoken BNC2014: Designing and Building a Spoken Corpus of Everyday Conversations', *International Journal of Corpus Linguistics* 22(3): 319–344.
McCarthy, M. J. (1998) *Spoken Language and Applied Linguistics*, Cambridge: Cambridge University Press.
McCarthy, M. J. (2015) '"Tis Mad, Yeah": Turn openers in Irish and British English', in C. Amador-Moreno, K. McCafferty, and E. Vaughan (eds) *Pragmatic Markers in Irish English*, Amsterdam: John Benjamins, pp. 156–75.
McEnery, T., Xiao, R. and Tono, Y. (2006) *Corpus-based Language Studies: An Advanced Resource Book*, London: Routledge.
Meyer, C. (2002) *English Corpus Linguistics: An Introduction*, Cambridge: Cambridge University Press.
Millar, S. (2015) 'Blathering Beauties: The Use of Pragmatic Markers in an Irish Beauty Blog', in C. Amador-Moreno, K. McCafferty and E. Vaughan (eds) *Pragmatic Markers in Irish English*, Amsterdam: John Benjamins, pp. 292–317.
Muntigl, P. and Turnbull, W. (1998) 'Conversational Structure and Facework in Arguing', *Journal of Pragmatics* 29(3): 225–56.
Nelson, G. (1996) 'The Design of the Corpus', in S. Greenbaum (ed.) *Comparing English Worldwide: The International Corpus of English*, Oxford: Oxford University Press, pp. 27–36.
O'Keeffe, A. and Adolphs, S. (2008) 'Response Tokens in British and Irish Discourse: Corpus, Context and Variational Pragmatics', in K. Schneider and A. Barron (eds) *Variational Pragmatics: A Focus on Regional Varieties in Pluricentric Languages*, Amsterdam: John Benjamins, pp. 69–98.
O'Keeffe, A. and Amador-Moreno, C. (2009) 'The Pragmatics of the *be + after + V-ing* Construction in Irish English', *Intercultural Pragmatics* 6(4): 517–34.
O'Keeffe, A., Clancy, B. and Adolphs, S. (2020) *Introducing Pragmatics in Use*, 2nd edn, London: Routledge.
Quirk, R. (1995) *Grammatical and Lexical Variance in English*, London: Longman.
Rühlemann, C. (2007) *Conversation in Context*, London: Continuum.
Schweinberger, M. (2015) 'A Comparative Study of the Pragmatic Marker *Like* in Irish English and in South-Eastern Varieties of British English', in C. Amador-Moreno, K. McCafferty and E. Vaughan (eds) *Pragmatic Markers in Irish English*, Amsterdam: John Benjamins, pp. 114–34.
Simpson-Vlach, R. and Leicher, S. 2006. *The MICASE Handbook: A Resource for Users of the Michigan Corpus of Academic Spoken English*, Ann Arbor, MI: Michigan University Press.

Sinclair, J. (2005) 'Corpus and Text – Basic Principles', in M. Wynne (ed.) *Developing Linguistic Corpora: A Guide to Good Practice*, Oxford: Oxbow Books, pp. 1–16.

Tagliamonte, S. (2005) '*So* who? *Like* how? *Just* what? Discourse Markers in the Conversation of Young Canadians', *Journal of Pragmatics* 37: 1896–915.

Vaughan, E. and Clancy, B. (2013) 'Small Corpora and Pragmatics', *Yearbook of Corpus Linguistics and Pragmatics* 1: 53–73.

Vaughan, E. and Clancy, B. (2016) 'Sociolinguistic Information and Irish English Corpora', in R. Hickey (ed.) *Sociolinguistics in Ireland*, London: Palgrave, pp. 365–88.

Vaughan, E. and Moriarty, M. (2018) 'Voicing the "Knacker": Analysing the Comedy of the Rubberbandits', in D. Villabuena-Romero, C. Amador-Moreno and M. Sánchez-García (eds) *Voice and Discourse in the Irish Context*, London: Palgrave, pp. 13–45.

Vaughan, E., Clancy, B. and McCarthy, M. J. (2017) 'Vague Category Markers as Turn-Final Items in Irish English', *World Englishes* 36(2): 208–23.

7

Building a specialised audiovisual corpus

Paul Thompson

1 What are audiovisual corpora and what are they used for?

In broad terms, an audiovisual corpus is a corpus that consists of orthographic transcripts of spoken-language communication events and the audio and video recordings of those events. This type of corpus is also called a "multi-modal corpus", but in this chapter the term "audiovisual corpus" is used, as it precisely describes corpora which combine audio and visual data, while "multi-modal" can also include collections of annotated digital images of texts, for example, which are beyond our concern here.

An audiovisual corpus is likely to contain timestamps in the transcripts, which makes it possible to locate the relevant parts of the audio and/or visual files, so that the transcribed text can be listened to and/or viewed. At their most basic, the links consist of indexical information included with the transcripts, which allows the researcher to find the section of the recording manually (for example, simply logging the beginning timepoint of each speaker's turn within the related video file), but in a more sophisticated form the annotation, included in an electronic document, allows the user to click on a button or activate a timestamp link within the electronic version of the transcript, which opens the audio or video file at the exact point in a media player. Audiovisual corpora are usually additionally annotated with non-lexical information, such as speaker gestures, laughter, gaze or prosodic features. As audiovisual corpora are fundamentally spoken-language corpora, and as spoken language is temporal in nature, these annotations are usually tied to timestamps, which allow the analyst to see which events and features occur co-temporaneously with which words, for how long and in which order.

Audiovisual corpora can be categorised by the types of data that they contain. The data can be (1) existing audiovisual texts, such as films, or television advertisements, or (2) they can be data collected especially for the corpus project. In the latter case, there is a cline between (2A) data that are produced under tightly controlled experimental conditions and (2B) data that have been recorded with an aim to capture "authentic language use" as closely as possible. An example of (1) is Poignant *et al.* (2015) testing a new method for automatically identifying speakers in TV broadcasts, using three hours of annotated extant TV video recordings from the REPERE corpus. For (2A), an

DOI: 10.4324/9780367076399-7

example is a study by Foster and Oberlander (2007) who constructed a corpus of recordings of an actor reading 444 sentences (for the purposes of the research alone), which they then annotated in order to determine relationships between prosodically accented words and head and eyebrow movement. The motivation for this research was to develop an embodied conversational agent (a computer interface) that looks and behaves like a human. An illustration of (2B) is the Corpus of Academic Spoken English (CASE; Brunner *et al.* 2017), which is a collection of Skype conversations between speakers of English as a lingua franca, in which each conversation is between 30 and 200 minutes in duration; this duration was preferred because it was hypothesised that it would reduce the participants' sense of being recorded and consequently result in more "natural" data. The contrast between (2A) and (2B), then, is between language use under tightly controlled conditions and language use in natural settings.

Audiovisual corpora can be developed or used for a variety of purposes. Broadly speaking, these can be divided into four categories, which are not discrete (in that one corpus might be used for a variety of purposes or a project might create a corpus for blended purposes):

- Creating a conventional language corpus;
- Analysis of language (and language-related) behaviour;
- A resource for learning;
- Language documentation.

Creating a conventional language corpus

The British Academic Spoken English corpus (Thompson and Nesi 2001) is an example of a corpus that is fundamentally a collection of transcripts of lectures and seminars that has been annotated for speaker turns, pauses, kinesic and other related events and which can be investigated using conventional corpus analysis tools (concordancing, wordlist generation, collocation information and so on). The data corpus files were derived from the audio and video files which were used in the development of the annotated transcripts that make up the final corpus. These media files are available to researchers for separate investigation, and the video files were also used in a separate language teaching materials development project called EASE. The corpus can be accessed through Sketch Engine Open (https://app.sketchengine.eu/#open).

Analysis of language (and language-related) behaviour

Speech processing and human–computer interaction researchers explore the relations between different verbal and non-verbal communication behaviours. Audiovisual corpora can be used to investigate the relationship between the information that is gained from visual and auditory channels for the understanding of spoken language, for the analysis of behaviour or for the interpretation of an individual's emotional state, for example. Schuller *et al.* (2009) developed an audiovisual corpus (AVIC) of spontaneous conversational speech to test their approach to automatic processing of audiovisual (AV) information (including facial expression, eye activity and acoustic features), which could be used in technical applications such as automated customer care or tutoring systems. Another example of the use of AV corpora in the assessment of emotional state is the development of tools that can be used in the detection of psychological disorders:

Scherer *et al.* (2014) used their Distress Assessment Interview Corpus (DAIC), a collection of dyadic interactions between an interviewer and a paid participant (in either (1) an assessed condition of distress or (2) of no distress), to look at gaze and smile behaviour among others. Gaze direction (towards the interlocutor, for example, or towards the floor), smile intensity and duration were analysed, and the study found that downward eye gaze, less intense smiles and shorter smile duration were indices that could assist in automatic identification of patients with psychological disorders.

A resource for learning

Audiovisual corpora can be used for human learning purposes in diverse ways: for trainee actors, for example, for student nurses or doctors, or for language learners and teachers. Teo (2018) reports a study that explores how the Singapore Corpus of Research in Education (SCoRE) was used in professional development activities with teachers in Singapore; the transcripts were searched with concordancing software for particular words and expressions, and then portions of the classroom recordings were used as examples of particular interactions that the workshop participants could then reflect upon.

The SCoRE corpus (Hong 2005) contains transcripts and recordings of teacher and student talk in approximately 500 lessons obtained from over 100 primary (age 7 to 12 years) and secondary (age 13 to 16 years) schools in Singapore. The corpus interface allows the user to search for words or phrases in the corpus and then choose to view a video clip (if available) or listen to an audio clip. The corpus data have also been annotated on a number of levels: Searches can be made by part of speech; by semantic category; or by syntactic, pragmatic or pedagogical features. The recordings have been divided into speaker turns, and for each turn there is a sound file. The user is given the choice for any search to receive the results in turns (in other words, with each word shown within the full turn of the speaker) rather than as Key Word In Context (KWIC) concordances; if this option is chosen, the user is given the text for each turn in which the search items occur and also a link to the audio or video file. In addition to the access to the audiovisual material, the interface generates statistics on the frequency of occurrence of each feature in each file, both in raw terms and as a percentage of the entire file.

Another audiovisual resource for learning is Hasebe's (2015) interface to a corpus of TED Talks (https://yohasebe.com/tcse/), which allows the learner (typically, an intermediate/advanced English for academic purposes learner) to conduct word, lemma, n-gram and construction searches on the corpus, to view concordance lines and then to click on any line and view the video from that utterance forwards, with the full transcript showing below the video.

Language documentation

In language documentation work, the audiovisual data often accompany the transcripts and can be used for language typology work. These resources can be accessed through collections such as the Endangered Languages Archive at SOAS (https://www.soas.ac.uk/elar/). The archives are searched in the way that library catalogues are searched, but the addition of metadata allows more refined searches to be made. In the SOAS collection, several resources are downloadable as video (.mp4), audio (.wav) and ELAN files (.eaf; an explanation of ELAN will come later in this chapter), which allows researchers the opportunity to do close analysis of individual files, and it is possible to extract the text from many transcripts for frequency and pattern analysis. These collections tend to be "opportunistic" corpora (cf McEnery and Hardie 2012: 11) in that they are made up of recordings made in naturalistic settings, often with compromised audio quality and with a single camera perspective and without following a rigorous sampling frame. Mosel (2018) provides a comprehensive overview of the relationship between language documentation studies and corpus linguistics.

The range of purposes for which audiovisual corpora are developed is large and cannot be satisfactorily covered within a single chapter. There is a thriving area of translation studies, for example, called "corpus-based audio-visual translation studies", which looks at dubbing and captioning of TV and film, amongst other things (see Chapter 38, this volume). Corpora are also established to test computational treatment of video data for automated transcription in situations where acoustic quality is poor (how, and to what extent, can visual data help to improve the quality of the transcription?), or to test tools for annotation of non-verbal behaviours in video data of human interactions. Tran *et al.* (2013), for example, examine lip movements in whisper and neutral speech within a corpus of whisper speech and find that most visual features around the mouth other than lip-spreading remain relatively constant in both whispered and neutral speech, indicating that visual information about the speaker's mouth movements potentially can assist in transcription. Hart *et al.* (2016) use automatic analysis of motion in video recordings of scripted doctor–patient interactions under different conditions; they propose that their automated processes can be used in training of clinicians.

The purpose of the rest of this chapter is to give an overview of what the process of building an audiovisual corpus entails, from initial conception through project design to data collection, processing and finally the development of tools and interfaces for exploitation. Design criteria and data collection are discussed in Section 2, and transcription and annotation issues are reviewed in Section 3. Several tools are available for the development of audiovisual corpora which make the job of linking points in the transcript to points in the video and audio files much easier. Some of these tools tie the developer into a proprietary system, while others use systems which have a higher degree of potential for interchangeability. A number of these tools will be discussed in Sections 3 and 4. As technology is advancing quickly, it is unwise to provide too much information on specific tools and platforms, so the discussion that follows will not attempt to be exhaustive. The final section of this chapter looks towards the future and speculates on what advances may be made in the coming years.

2 Collecting data

Corpus design is discussed in detail elsewhere in this volume (see Chapters 2, 3, 4 and 5, this volume, among others). Audiovisual recordings carry challenges for the anonymisation of data, and care should be taken in the planning stages to ensure that appropriate ethical procedures are followed. Where the participants can clearly be identified through their physical features (on video) or acoustic features (through audio), they must be asked to provide informed consent, and the researchers need to decide in advance what the data are to be used for and to ensure that the data will be used only for the purposes stated. In some cases, the AV data will only be available to the research team, and it is therefore easier to preserve anonymity, but if the audio and video recordings are to be made public in any form (such as in conference presentations or on the internet), permission to use them for such purposes must be obtained before the data are collected. It is advisable to consult a legal expert in cases where the video recordings are to be put into the public domain. Various techniques can be used for anonymising individuals in video data, such as pixelisation, blurring, placing black patches over eyes or transforming the images to look like drawings. Anonymisation tools can be found in many image editing programmes; thought needs to be given as to whether the technique does fully preserve anonymity, and also to whether there is a danger of information loss where, for example, important information from facial expressions may be lost when blurred. Consideration should also be given to the possible uses the researchers put the data to in advance of data collection, as it is usually difficult to return to all participants to collect data further retrospectively.

Quality video recording in particular requires good lighting and camera work, as well as cameras and microphones that are fit for task. Decisions about the camera angles to take and the lighting required will depend on the purposes of the project. In the Headtalk project conducted at the University of Nottingham, UK (see Chapter 3, this volume), the focus was on the uses of head nodding and hand gestures in conversation. The team therefore developed techniques for the automatic analysis of the video data, which identified head and hand movements and tracked the movements. To make the head and hand identifiable, it was necessary to ensure that participants were seated with their face towards the camera, in a well-lit location and wearing long sleeves, so that each hand could be distinguished clearly from the rest of the arm (Knight *et al.* 2009). One of the elements to be considered in preparing for good data collection, then, may be that of visual detail — what clothes the participants should wear, what the background is, how well the speakers' features stand out against that background, whether lighting is required to improve the visibility of key features and so on.

An example of relatively complex audiovisual data collection is the AMI (Augmented Multi-party Interaction; https://groups.inf.ed.ac.uk/ami/corpus/overview.shtml) Meeting Corpus, which consists of 100 hours of recordings of meetings McCowan *et al.* (2005). The data in the corpus are drawn from video material recorded with a number of cameras in a given smart room. The cameras are arranged to capture different shots of participants and several audio captures on several microphones, which then have to be synchronised. The cameras are set to capture each participant's facial and hand gestures (most are seated around the table and can only be seen from the midriff up), and the cameras are fitted with fish-eye lenses, so that peripheral information can be gathered. For analysis purposes, three or four camera angles can be placed in a row alongside each other on the screen, so that a more comprehensive perspective of the event can be captured. In addition to the individual-view camera shots, there are cameras set to capture the whole room and output from a slide projector and an electronic whiteboard.

The quality of data collected for an audiovisual corpus will depend not only on the positioning and number of recording devices but also on the equipment used and the processes by which data are transferred, synchronised and saved, and also on the skill of those who capture the data. It is not possible to examine these points in detail here, but it should be noted that generally speaking, it is advisable to capture data at the highest resolution and then to make use of compression technologies at later stages, when smaller file sizes, and faster transfer times, are required, and keep the high-resolution recordings as archive material.

3 Preparing transcriptions and annotations

While signed language (SL) corpora are not, strictly speaking, audiovisual corpora, as they do not typically include audio data, they are an excellent source of insight into how multimodal data can be annotated on a variety of levels. Johnston (2010) describes the challenges that SL corpus developers face: SLs do not have widely accepted written forms that can be used in transcription, and yet a corpus requires a machine-readable form that is searchable. His recommendation is to place annotation rather than transcription at the heart of SL corpora and to make the data searchable by the annotations. Searching for annotated features on one or more levels ("tiers" as they are termed in the ELAN programme) can then take the analyst to the relevant section (or sections) of the video and does not privilege the word (or phrase) over the other aspects of communication.

In most audiovisual corpus projects, however, the transcription of the data does remain central to the project. One of the first decisions to be made is that of which transcription and spelling conventions to use. For many languages, it is possible to work by precedent and to find guidelines from other projects about the conventions that were used. The choice will be determined to a large extent by the nature of the research, and in cases where a corpus is being developed as a resource to be placed in the public domain, predictions of the range of potential uses for the corpus have to be made in order to provide for those users (see Chapters 2 and 3, this volume). For an extensive and detailed discussion of a particular set of transcription and annotation conventions for a spoken language corpus, in that instance, the CASE corpus, see Brunner *et al.* (2017).

Consistency is essential whatever the system chosen. The team that is responsible for making the transcription needs to set up a shared document for specifying the conventions to be used. This document sets out the agreed conventions but is subject to addition and amendment as the team encounters problematic cases of spelling or coding that have to be decided on during the course of transcription. Where the members of the team are working in geographically diverse locations, it is advisable to set up shared documents, using a cloud-based collaborative word processing facility, or to set up a discussion wiki.

Transcription and coding can be performed concurrently or sequentially; in other words, one approach is to produce an orthographic transcription (although this could also be a storyboard, a set of descriptions of the visual or locational features) quickly and then use this as the basis for one or many layers of annotation, while another approach is to create the transcription and insert the timestamps concurrently, and possibly to insert other levels of annotation as well, such as pause lengths or events in the local environment that may have an effect on the interaction. In recent years the accuracy of automatic transcription has increased greatly with the demand for online closed captioning, for example, and this is an option that is worth testing. Recordings can be sent to a professional transcription service, provided that the transcription service has experience providing transcriptions to the specifications of a linguistic research team. If working with ELAN, the tool developed at the Max Planck Institute for Psycholinguistics, Nijmegen, The Netherlands (Wittenburg *et al.* 2006), one can insert the timestamps directly into the transcripts from within the program. Alternatively, working with *Praat*, the freeware research transcription tool for the synthesis, analysis and manipulation of speech, the transcriber can work from the spectrogram to the orthographic (or other) transcription and link the two at whatever level is required (for example, phoneme, word or utterance).

When working with video data, some transcribers prefer to work with the audio input first, as they find the visual mode distracts their attention from the oral, while other transcribers have a preference for a bimodal view of the event, on the basis that paralinguistic, gestural and other features help them to make sense of the audio input.

Several transcription programmes are available for use with audio files, and the researcher's choice will be determined by considerations of operating system, range of functions in the package, file types supported and the design of the interface. Programmes such as NCH's *Express Scribe* accommodate the use of a Universal Serial Bus (USB)–connected transcriber's foot pedal so that the audio can be controlled with a foot and leave the hands free for keyboard input. Typically, transcribers will want to be able to adjust the speed of the playback (transcribers often choose to slow the audio playback), make fine-tuned movements back and forwards, adjust volume, loop sections and place markers in the file.

The video annotation and analysis tool *Anvil* (Kipp 2014) presents a multiple view of the video input in one window (or more, if there is more than one video input), the video controls in another window, a description of the gesture codes applied to the present view of the video and, below, the transcription within a multi-level representation that is similar to a musical score. As the video moves, the transcription lines move past, too, and at any point in the transcription the researcher can see the multiple levels of annotation applied. This window can also present speech waveforms and the *Praat* intensity diagrams (Anvil imports *Praat* files directly). In addition to *Praat* files, *Anvil* can import Rhetorical Structure Theory (RST) files from the RST programme made by O'Donnell (http://www.wagsoft.com) for coding clause relations. *Anvil* is an Extensible Markup Language (XML) tool, and the programme produces XML files, which gives the potential for interchangeability.

EXMARaLDA (https://exmaralda.org/en/) is an open-source toolkit which creates XML files. The EXMARaLDA project has developed a set of concepts and tools for the transcription and annotation of spoken language and for the creation and analysis of spoken language corpora. The tools are Java programmes which can be used for editing transcriptions in partitur (musical score) notation and for merging the transcriptions with their corresponding recordings into corpora and enriching them with metadata (see also Chapter 3, this volume). A demonstration of data that have been marked up using EXMARaLDA can be found on its website.

The discussion so far has concentrated on processes and technologies for annotating data without providing an example of what annotation frameworks might be used with multi-modal data. The annotation scheme for the AMI corpus (see Section 2 earlier) describes individual actions and gestures on four "layers": head gestures, hand gestures (further separated into deictic and non-deictic), leg gestures and trunk gestures. The trunk events, to take an example, are coded as one of the following: shrug, sit_upright, lean_forward, lean_backward, other_trunk, no_trunk, or off_camera. The coding is added using the Event Editor in the *NITE Toolkit* (Carletta *et al.* 2003), and it is entered into an XML file that is created purely for trunk gesture information. In other words, each layer of coding is held in a separate file.

4 The interface: assembly and analysis

Programmes like *ELAN* and *Anvil* allow the researcher both to annotate the corpus data and to search it. Some research projects upload their corpus files to archives in, for

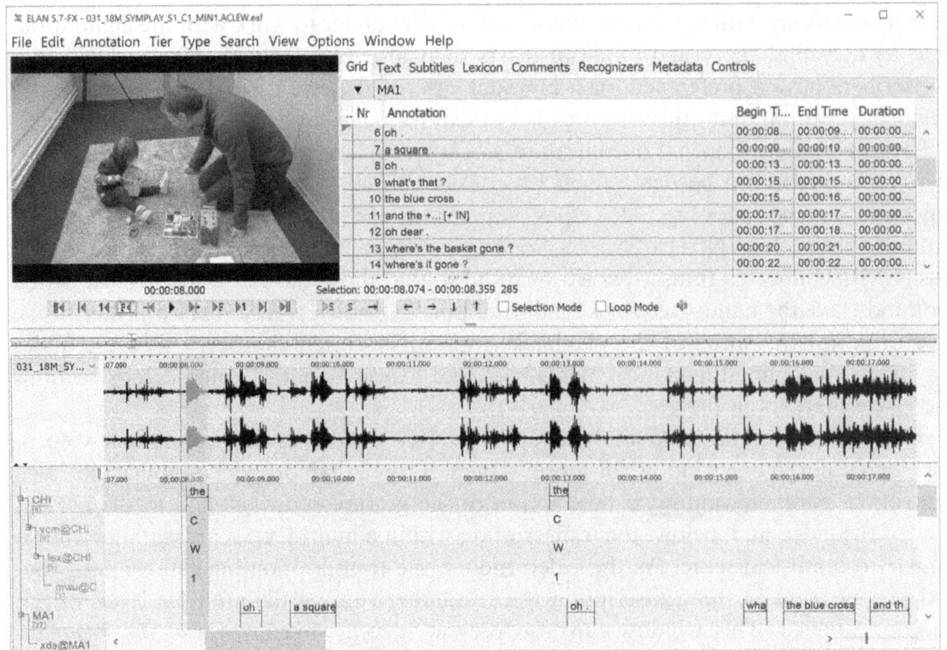

Figure 7.1 The ELAN programme interface (showing a sample from the ACLEW project, https://psyarxiv.com/bf63y/): video, annotations with timestamps and waveforms

example, the .eaf (ELAN) format, along with video and audio files (such as .mp4 and .wav files) so that other researchers can load the data into ELAN for further annotation and/or analysis (for details, see the ELAN Handbook, https://www.mpi.nl/corpus/manuals/manual-elan.pdf) (Figure 7.1).

Other projects provide web-based search interfaces. This offers a number of challenges, including the following:

- Download or streaming speeds;
- File formats;
- Provision of adequate flexibility.

The corpus builder needs to consider the limitations of access to the internet for potential users of the corpus, particularly the differing speeds of data transfer, and also the frequent congestion of the internet. When investigating an audiovisual corpus, the user does not want to wait several minutes for a video to open in the local browser, and preferably the video should open almost immediately. Clearly, there is much to be said for creating data with smaller file sizes: a 100-MB file will take much longer to send and load than a 10-MB file. One solution is to use video streaming, which is a technique for transferring compressed video data to a computer over the internet in a continuous flow so that a user can begin viewing it before the entire file has been received. One factor affecting the choice between streaming and non-streaming video is whether the corpus holder wants to prevent the video being held temporarily (at least) on the user's computer in the case of streaming video; this is prevented, but if the file is downloaded to the user's computer, it is possible that the user will save a copy locally, and this might contravene copyright or any data protection agreements which had stated that the data would not be held anywhere beyond the project's servers, for example.

The second problem is that of file formats. At the time of writing, there is a variety of video file formats such as MPEG-4 (.mp4), Shockwave (.swf), QuickTime (.mov), Audio/Video Interleaved (.avi) and Windows Media Video (.wmv). The choice of video file format will be partly determined by the quality of the picture and by the size of files produced, but it will also be affected by the currency of the player required for playback of the file. In most cases, video player plug-ins can be downloaded for popular internet browsers, but the corpus developer will probably want to choose a media player that is widely used and that is likely to have a long life (with new plug-ins regularly created for newer versions of the browsers). One example of the problem is the set of video files that formed part of the SACODEYL project. SACODEYL (see, for example, Hoffstaedter and Kohn 2009) was a consortium of researchers from across Europe that produced a corpus of videos and transcripts of teenager talk in a variety of languages which was searchable online. Unfortunately, the format of the videos, Real Video (.rv), is no longer supported and, consequently, the video files can no longer be viewed (the SMIL files for SACODEYL are, however, fully accessible through http://webapps.ael.uni-tuebingen.de/backbone-search/).

The Scottish Corpus of Texts and Speech (SCOTS; https://www.scottishcorpus.ac.uk) is an example of a website that contains video data that is accessible through a browser. The transcripts are segmented into tone units, and the user is able to click on any given point on the transcript, then select the video view icon from the bottom of the screen and activate the video at that point of the file. The video is activated by a JavaScript command that communicates with a video plug-in. The video starts playing at that point and then continues until manually stopped. The benefit of this method is that the mark-up of the document is relatively simple: A timestamp is recorded for the beginning point of each segment, and the Hypertext Markup Language (HTML) for the document has an identifier which is linked to that timestamp.

It is not necessary to add information about the closing point of each segment (although, technically, it would not be difficult to retrieve that information from the timestamp for the next segment). This is an approach taken on several corpus websites which provide access to audio or video files. If a researcher wants to take a rough-and-ready approach to combining transcript, audio and/or video files, then a simple strategy is to insert timestamps into the transcript that point to a position in a given media file, with angle brackets around the timestamp. The transcript can then be searched in a standard corpus analysis programme such as AntConc (Anthony 2019). To do this in AntConc, change the "Tag" settings to "Hide tags" so that the timestamps do not appear in the concordance views, but they can be viewed when a given concordance line is selected and then "File View" is opened – the nearest timestamp before the node word provides the information about where in the related recording the word is uttered. In the CASE corpus transcripts, for example, timestamps are added as simple time counts from the audio file, as in #00:01:01-1# (1 minute, 1 second). This is a relatively unsophisticated technique but could be useful in student research projects.

In an online corpus search facility, researchers may prefer to play only a smaller section, either because this is seen to be a more economical way to transfer data from one source to another (if the user is going to activate a video at a given point and then play the video straight through, then all of the video file has to be transmitted, potentially), or because the user is interested in working intensively with that section. Approaches that can be taken here are:

- Split the audio (or video) file into short chunks (for example, at 20-second intervals);
- Split the files at selected points, such as at turn boundaries;
- Select parts of a recording on the grounds of a query.

In the first approach, the sound files are split into equal-sized chunks (this can be done automatically using a file-splitting command), and file links are manually added to the transcript files at the break points. The audio files load quickly, and the method of aligning text to sound is efficient, but one drawback is that a 20-second extract will have arbitrary boundaries.

The SCoRE corpus (mentioned in Section 1 earlier) employed the second method: Individual sound files were created for each of the speaker turns in the original audio files. The interface employs JavaScript to activate the media player (built around the Adobe Flash player) to play the sound files. Each turn in the transcripts is coded with information about the corresponding sound file, and when a turn is retrieved and displayed in a search results page, a hyperlink to the sound file is created. It is this link which retrieves the sound file and opens the media player. Once the media player opens, it then automatically plays the file. The controls to the player allow the user to manipulate the file, with play and pause functionality.

A similar approach but with added sophistication, exemplifying the third option of selecting points of a recording through timestamp information, is taken in the design of the GLOSSA corpus query interface created at the Tekstlab at the University of Oslo. Glossa is freely available through GitHub for installation on a local server (GitHub, https://github.com, is an open-source code repository hosting service). The results are shown in a window (see Figure 7.2) with a video player, an orthographic transcript and waveform and spectrogram for close phonetic analysis.

5 Looking to the future

One prediction that can be made with confidence is that data transfer speeds and storage power will continue to increase rapidly, and this will change current concepts about the size and potential of such corpora. However, whether these changes will lead to the development of many more audiovisual corpora will depend on decisions over resource allocations, such as researcher time and budgeting for equipment, which are far greater than the costs of creating monomodal corpora. With reference to technological needs, there will be an increasing requirement to store, clean up, annotate and align data at least semi-automatically, and we can expect that the tools for doing this will become more sophisticated, and in turn will lead to faster, more efficient processing of data. An example of the increased capacity of research projects to capture and process data is the Human Speechome Project (HSP; see Roy *et al.* 2006) based at the Massachusetts Institute of Technology. This project followed the language development of a single child in the first three years of the child's life. To gather the data, cameras and microphones were set up in all rooms in the house, with these recording devices running from morning to evening every day. While the project itself was so specialised that it is unlikely to be replicated, the technologies that were developed to process the huge quantities of data suggest that automatic processing of visual data is likely to be an area of

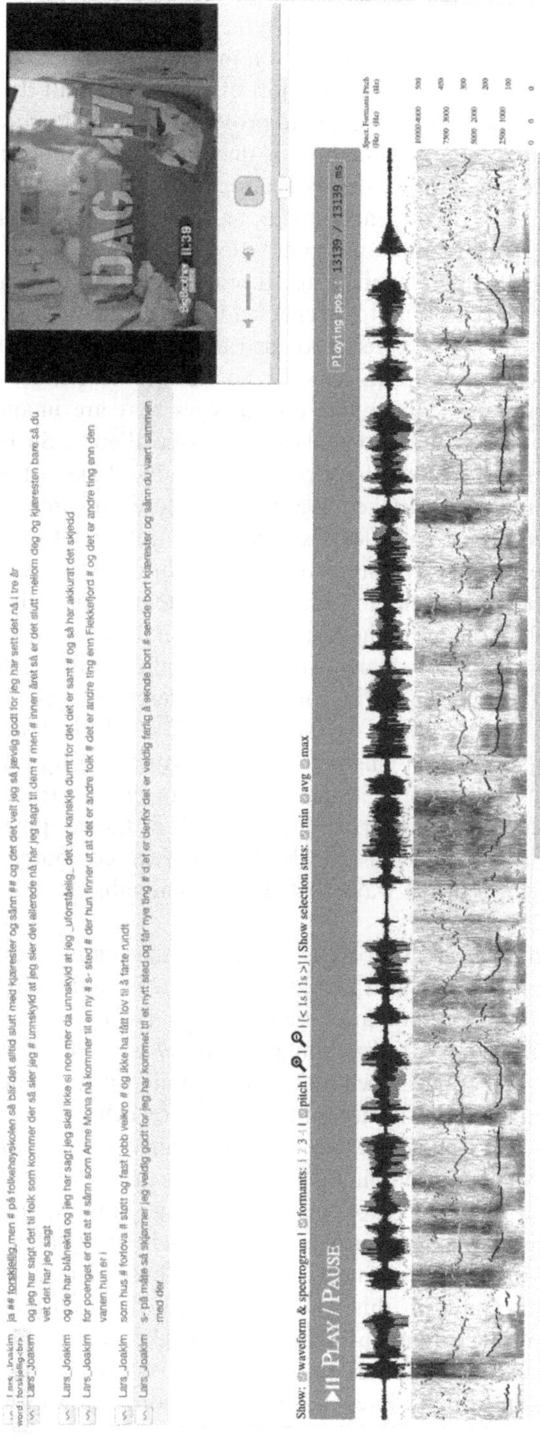

Figure 7.2 Screenshot of Glossa interface, showing results of a search on the Norwegian Big Brother corpus

major development in the creation of AV corpora. With so much video data to be examined, it was necessary to identify which parts of the data require attention, and so the HSP team created methods for automatically reading the video data and noticing which cameras were picking up movement. On the basis of this information, the human coders were then able to focus their attention on the video information that was relevant to them. Second, in order to speed up the job of transcribing all the oral interaction, speech recognition tools were used in order to provide a rough initial transcription of the speech, along with semi-automated coding of that data, and a human transcriber was then able to verify and extend the work as necessary (Kubat *et al.* 2007). Developers of audiovisual corpora are likely to contribute to, and benefit from, advances in the semi-automatic processing, transcription and annotation of data.

The HSP team observed that language use is often connected to location and activity. Certain communicative events tend to be enacted in the kitchen, for example, such as at the time that the parents make coffee. Provided that they are annotated appropriately and accurately, audiovisual corpora make it possible to search for the relationships between location, activity and language use in ways that are unique, and these observations may lead to new developments in linguistic theory. Such work may offer further confirmation for those who have previously shown links between language and physical contexts of use (e.g. Mitchell 1957). To capture information about location, participants can be equipped with devices such as wearable global positioning system (GPS) trackers, as well as audiovisual recorders (see, for example, Adolphs *et al.* 2011).

As observed earlier, one serious constraint on the creation of audiovisual corpora to be placed in the public domain is the need to obtain informed consent from all participants who are recorded, particularly where video information is captured. Projects such as the AMI corpus and the CHIL corpus have therefore worked with participants in controlled environments. At the same time, linguistic and behavioural researchers will need to gather information about language in use in natural settings. A possible solution in coming years may be the use of techniques used in motion tracking and face and gesture analysis, or the use of avatars to build models of human physical activity from video input, and then convert these models into anonymised computer-generated animated figures that behave in the ways that the original subjects did, without compromising their identity.

There is a trend towards greater collaboration and sharing in research ('shareability' as Guichon 2017 terms it), and this is already evident in audiovisual corpus development. Collaborative tools for annotation and processing of data have been created (for example, the collaborative tool *Audino,* Singh Grover *et al.* 2020). Other tools are made available and can be further developed by the community through GitHub. Corpus files have been placed in shared repositories for easy access by other research teams for some time, as, for example, the Child Language Data Exchange System (CHILDES) project, established in 1984, and now containing 130 corpora; the number of new audiovisual corpora being placed in shared repositories is growing. This expansion of pooling of resources and of tools is a highly positive movement within research.

At the time of writing, the coronavirus pandemic has led to a massive increase in online communication and with this will come a growth in corpora (like the CASE corpus) of online communications through platforms like Zoom and Microsoft Teams. Such data are easily collected and are in a sense more complete than video records of everyday interactions in offline contexts, where the record is always highly partial.

A challenge that needs to be addressed in the coming years is that of how AV corpus research is communicated to a broad audience. In the research world, the typical way to report the results of research is to publish articles or as books in modes which are based upon printed paper (even though the majority of papers now are available in PDF or HTML formats, they are principally in the form of "pages" of text – note the implications of the word "paper" itself). It can be argued that AV corpus analysis deserves to be communicated in a more multi-modal manner, with potential for delivering the report of the study through interactive videos, or by providing access to samples of the data (particular pieces to be analysed and discussed) through the internet or as downloadable appendices to the study. In the meantime, while the written text is still privileged, Guichon (2017) calls for more journals to allow researchers to publish multimodal data along with their article.

Further reading

The following provide a useful overview of audiovisual corpora and tools for annotating data:

Abuczki, A. and Ghazaleh, E. (2013) 'An Overview of Multimodal Corpora, Annotation Tools and Schemes', *Argumentum* 9: 86–98; available at https://pdfs.semanticscholar.org/42af/4a32c736fc5b7ef2f7ae2252f1c1b2a3ab76.pdf [Accessed 7 August 2020].

Allwood, J. (2008) 'Multimodal Corpora', in A. Lüdeling and M. Kytö (eds) *Corpus Linguistics. An International Handbook*, Berlin: Mouton de Gruyter, pp. 207–25.

References

Adolphs, S., Knight, D. and Carter, R. A. (2011) 'Capturing Context for Heterogeneous Corpus Analysis: Some First Steps', *International Journal of Corpus Linguistics* 16(3): 305–24.

Anthony, L. (2019) *AntConc* (Version 3.5.8) [Computer Software]. Tokyo: Waseda University. Available from https://www.laurenceanthony.net/software.

Brunner, M.-L., Diemer, S. and Schmidt, S. (2017) '"... Okay So Good Luck with that ((Laughing))?" - Managing Rich Data in a Corpus of Skype Conversations', *Studies in Variation, Contacts and Change in English*, 19.

Carletta, J., Evert, S., Heid, U., Kilgour, J., Robertson, J. and Voormann, H. (2003) 'The NITE XML Toolkit: Flexible Annotation for Multi-Modal Language Data', *Behavior Research Methods, Instruments, and Computers* 35(3): 353–63.

Foster, M. and Oberlander, J. (2007) 'Corpus-Based Generation of Head and Eyebrow Motion for an Embodied Conversational Agent', *Language Resources and Evaluation* 41(3): 305–23.

Guichon, N. (2017) 'Sharing a Multimodal Corpus to Study Webcam-Mediated Language Teaching', *Language Learning & Technology* 21(1): 56–75.

Hart, Y., Czerniak, E., Karnieli-Miller, O., Mayo, A. E., Ziv, A., Biegon, A., Citron, A. and Alon, U. (2016) 'Automated Video Analysis of Non-verbal Communication in a Medical Setting', *Frontiers in Psychology* 7: 1130.

Hasebe, Y. (2015) 'Design and Implementation of an Online Corpus of Presentation Transcripts of TED Talks', *Procedia: Social and Behavioral Sciences*198(24): 174–82.

Hoffstaedter, P. and Kohn, K. (2009) 'Real Language and Relevant Language Learning Activities: Insights from the SACODEYL Project', in A. Kirchhofer and J. Schwarzkopf (eds) *The Workings of the Anglosphere. Contributions to the Study of British and US- American Cultures*, Trier: WVT, pp. 291–303.

Hong, H. (2005) 'SCORE: A Multimodal Corpus Database of Education Discourse in Singapore Schools', *Proceedings of International Conference of Corpus Linguistics*, Birmingham, July 14–17, 2005.

Johnston, T. (2010) 'From Archive to Corpus: Transcription and Annotation in the Creation of Signed Language Corpora', *International Journal of Corpus Linguistics* 15(1): 106–31.

Kipp, M. (2014) 'ANVIL: A Universal Video Research Tool', in J. Durand, U. Gut and G. Kristofferson (eds) *Handbook of Corpus Phonology*, Oxford: Oxford University Press, pp. 420–36.

Knight, D., Evans, D., Carter, R. A. and Adolphs, S. (2009) 'HeadTalk, HandTalk and the Corpus: Towards a Framework for Multi-Modal, Multi-Media Corpus Development', *Corpora* 4(1): 1–32.

Kubat, R., DeCamp, P., Roy, B. and Roy, D. (2007) 'TotalRecall: Visualization and Semi-Automatic Annotation of Very Large Audio-Visual Corpora', *Ninth International Conference on Multimodal Interfaces* (ICMI 2007).

McCowan, I., Carletta, J., Kraaij, W., Ashby, S., Bourban, S., Flynn, M., Guillemot, M., Hain, T., Kadlec, J., Karaiskos, V. and Kronenthal, M. (2005) The AMI meeting corpus. In Proceedings of the 5th international conference on methods and techniques in behavioral research 88: 100).

McEnery, T. and Hardie, A. (2012) *Corpus Linguistics*, Cambridge: Cambridge University Press.

Mitchell, T. F. (1957) 'The Language of Buying and Selling in Cyrenaica: A Situational Statement', *Hesperis* 44: 31–71.

Mosel, U. (2018) 'Corpus Compilation and Exploitation in Language Documentation Projects', in K. Rehg and L. Campbell (eds) *The Oxford Handbook of Endangered Languages*, Oxford: Oxford University Press.

Poignant, J., Besacier, L. and Quénot, G. (2015) 'Unsupervised Speaker Identification in TV Broadcast Based on Written Names', *IEEE/ACM Transactions on Audio, Speech, and Language Processing* 23(1): 57–68.

Roy, D., Patel, R., DeCamp, P., Kubat, R., Fleischman, M., Roy, B., Mavridis, N., Tellex, S., Salata, A., Guinness, J., Levit, M. and Gorniak, P. (2006) 'The Human Speechome Project', paper presented at *28th Annual Conference of the Cognitive Science Society*; available at https://www.media.mit.edu/cogmac/publications/cogsci06.pdf [Accessed 25 October 2020].

Scherer, S., Stratou, G., Lucas, G., Mahmoud, M., Boberg, J., Gratch, J., Rizzo, A. and Morency, L-P. (2014) 'Automatic Audiovisual Behavior Descriptors for Psychological Disorder Analysis', *Image and Vision Computing* 32: 648–58.

Schuller, B., Müller, R., Eyben, F., Gast, J., Hörnler, B., Wöllmer, M., Rigoll, G., Höthker, A. and Konosu, H. (2009) 'Being Bored? Recognising Natural Interest by Extensive Audiovisual Integration for Real-Life Application', *Image and Vision Computing* 27: 1760–74.

Singh Grover, M., Bamdev, P., Kumar, Y., Hama, M. and Shah, R. (2020) 'Audino: A Modern Annotation Tool for Audio and Speech', in *Woodstock '18: ACM Symposium on Neural Gaze Detection*, June 03-05, 2018, Woodstock, NY.

Teo, P. (2018) 'Professionalising Teaching: A Corpus-Based Approach to the Professional Development of Teachers in Singapore', *Cambridge Journal of Education* 48(3): 279–300.

Thompson, P. and Nesi, H. (2001) 'The British Academic Spoken English (BASE) Corpus Project', *Language Teaching Research* 5(3): 263–4.

Tran, T., Mariooryad, S. and Busso, C. (2013) 'Audiovisual Corpus to Analyse Whisper Speech', *2013 IEEE International Conference on Acoustics, Speech and Signal Processing*, Vancouver, BC, pp. 8101–5.

Wittenburg, P., Brugman, H., Russel, A., Klassmann, A., Sloetjes, H. (2006) 'ELAN: A Professional Framework for Multimodality Research', in *Proceedings of LREC 2006, Fifth International Conference on Language Resources and Evaluation.*

8

What corpora are available?

Martin Weisser

1 Corpus formats

Before describing what types of corpora actually do exist, it is perhaps necessary to clarify the title of this chapter a little more. When taking about 'availability' here, I do not really refer to availability in the true sense as '(readily) being available for everyone's use', but in fact rather what 'is out there'.

Furthermore, while an abundance of corpora exists, many were not compiled for purposes of research into corpus linguistics proper at all, but instead to provide a basis for the production of language engineering/natural language processing (NLP) tools, where the objective is not necessarily to gain deeper insights into language itself, but to achieve particular aims, such as to build dialogue systems that can interact with human users, etc. While I shall also discuss those corpora, my main aim will be to provide you with a (non-exhaustive) list of important corpora that are predominantly useful for conducting research in corpus linguistics proper, as well as to enable you to understand what their overall characteristics, advantages and limitations are. As I am unable to give detailed references for all of the corpora listed here, please consult my web pages on corpus-based linguistics links (CBLLinks) at http://martinweisser.org/corpora_site/CBLLinks.html for further information.

Moving on to establishing a typology, it is again necessary to point out a little 'caveat' – any attempt to assign different corpora to exact categories will always be marred to some extent by the fact that they often tend to fall in between such precise categories, so that it would be better to see the elements of the proposed typology not as fixed category labels, but instead rather features or attributes (cf. Atkins *et al.* 1992) that may characterise individual corpora.

The first feature we can use to describe a corpus is its mode of production (e.g. written, spoken, multi-modal). This has very clear implications on which steps are necessary in order to prepare the data for inclusion in a corpus, the storage format, representation (see later) and annotation, as well as any potential metadata, and hence also clearly relates to the design criteria discussed further later on.

DOI: 10.4324/9780367076399-8

Single-mode corpora

In the early days of electronic corpora (see Section 3), there was no question as to how many modes of language a corpus would cover. All were invariably *single-mode*, initially *written* only, then either written or *spoken*. Examples of such early written corpora are the whole *Brown family* (see Section 2), and of spoken ones the *Lancaster/IBM Spoken English Corpus* (SEC) and the *London-Lund Corpus of Spoken English* (LLC).

However, even if this distinction appears to be relatively clear-cut, we still need to be careful in applying it, as, for example, the SEC essentially contains texts that were *written to be spoken,* and many works of fiction contain written materials that are meant to be "*speech-like*", such as conversations between characters in novels. This type of speech clearly does not reflect ordinary everyday spoken interaction, and hence technically may skew any analyses aiming at solely identifying the features of written language (for an alternative view see Chapter 36, this volume, which argues that speech representation in fiction can be used to explore orality).

While most textbooks generally only make a distinction between the written vs. spoken modes, these days, we should also add a category *multi-modal,* as more corpora are now being created that also contain video-based information, such as the *Nottingham Multimodal Corpus* (NMMC) or the *Corpus of Video-Mediated English as a Lingua Franca Conversations* (ViMELF) (see Chapters 3 and 7, this volume).

Mixed-mode corpora

Mixed corpora appeared in the early 1990s. The best known smaller type of these is probably represented by the ongoing *International Corpus of English* (ICE) initiative, started in 1988 (Greenbaum 1991: 85), and designed to capture differences between international varieties of English through comparable corpora of 1 million words each, although efforts to create mixed-mode corpora were also under way at a similar time in other countries, such as Germany, where the *Wendekorpus Mannheim* was created in order to capture the language reflecting the German reunification.

Perhaps the best example of a much larger mixed corpus is the original *British National Corpus* (henceforth referred to as BNC1994), with its overall size of approximately 100 million words, divided into 90% written and 10% spoken language. Contrasting this with the 60% spoken vs. 40% written divide of the ICE corpora, we can still see a clear emphasis towards written language in the BNC1994, although this preference is probably at least partly due to the greater effort required in handling spoken language data, especially for a corpus of this size. A similar imbalance can be found in the *Corpus of Contemporary American English* (COCA), which has an 80:20 per cent divide between written and spoken language in its currently more than 560 million words. However, as the COCA only contains 'spoken' materials from media sources such as television and radio programmes, there is at least some debate about whether these genuinely reflect everyday spoken language (see Chapter 38, this volume).

Corpus representation and annotation formats

In terms of the 'physical' form that corpora take, we can make an initial distinction between the *raw data* (also known as *primary data*) and any potential available *metadata* (i.e. information about the data, see Chapters 2, 3 and 4, this volume). Earlier corpora generally have less metadata, as awareness of the need for such information was low in the early 1960s, and understandably more emphasis had to be placed on storing the data itself, due to less advanced computer technology and severely limited computer memory. A certain degree of metadata, however, has always been available through file numbering and category labels. In earlier, smaller corpora, this was generally complemented by fairly substantial *manuals* to accompany the data, whereas larger modern corpora often do not exhibit this feature.

Concerning the actual format(s) the primary data come in, we can distinguish between two levels, those of *representation* and *annotation* (Leech *et al.* 2000: 1), where the former essentially refers to rendering the raw data in a specific *encoding* and form. Here, most corpora, even spoken ones, will be represented as text in orthographic form and very few rendered phonetically/phonemically only. Some corpora, such as the *BYU corpora* created by Mark Davies, however, are by default not directly available as text, but stored in databases only accessible through interfaces (see Section 4). Yet others, such as the BNC1994, may be available in both formats.

In addition to their representation, corpora may contain various levels of annotation. Annotations may consist purely of textual mark-up, e.g. underscores (_) to link words and part-of-speech (POS) tags, *Standard Generalised Markup Language* (SGML) or some form of pseudo-SGML for older corpora or, more recently, *Extensible Markup Language* (XML), all using mark-up *tags* in angle bracket notation (<…>) (see Chapter 3, this volume). Use of XML also has the inherent advantage in that the default encoding is assumed to be *UTF-8*, a form of *Unicode*, which already makes it possible to store characters from many different languages, thus obviating the need to use so-called *character reference entities*, e.g. é for *é*, which can still be encountered in older corpora.

For annotations, we can distinguish between *structural mark-up*, which essentially divides texts into smaller units of language, such as paragraphs, sentences or words, and *feature-level mark-up*. The latter encompasses such types of mark-up as POS tags, parsing (which blurs the distinction between structure and features somewhat), phonetic or prosodic, semantic, pragmatic, discourse and stylistic information (cf. Leech 2005: 18), as well as further, lesser used annotation levels. XML annotations may either appear *inline*, with tags directly inserted into the text, or in *standoff format*, where annotations stored in a separate file are linked to the units in the primary text, generally either at the word level or to a timestamp that points into a multimedia file. Later, I shall provide a non-exhaustive list of some of the corpora containing the different levels of feature mark-up, excluding those that are only POS tagged, because the latter is a kind of standard annotation available for many corpora. With regard to POS tagging, though, it is important to bear in mind that the granularity of the tagset has an influence on the kind of research that can be conducted using a corpus, with corpora that are annotated using a larger tagset allowing for genuine grammar-based analyses, whereas more restricted tagsets are more suited towards rough syntactic analyses (cf. Weisser 2016).

Phonetically and/or prosodically annotated corpora may contain multiple levels of annotation, minimally an orthographic representation interspersed with symbols that indicate prosodic features, such as in the LLC, the *Hong Kong Corpus of Spoken English* (HKCSE) or the *Santa Barbara Corpus of Spoken American English* (SBCSAE). More complex formats contain multiple standoff tiers, such as the *Intonational Variation in English* (IViE) corpus, which has different levels of prosodic information, or the *Learning the Prosody of a foreign language* (LeaP) corpus, which also features a tier for phonetic representation, albeit in SAMPA (Speech Assessment Methods Phonetic Alphabet; Ide *et al.* 2017: 146) transliteration.

Pragmatically annotated corpora minimally add information about the illocutionary force of an *utterance* or *functional unit* in terms of a *speech act* or *move*, thereby making it possible to relate form to function. The most extensive speech-act annotation schemes in terms of speech-act coverage to date are the Switchboard-DAMSL (SWBDD) and DART schemes. Pragmatics corpora may also comprise further information about the status of completeness of a unit, its syntax, timestamps, etc. (see Weisser 2015 and 2019 for more details). Examples of pragmatically annotated corpora are the *MapTask Corpus*, the *Switchboard Dialog Act Corpus* (SwDA), the *Trains corpora*, the *Speech Act Annotated Dialogues (*SPAADIA) Corpus and the *SPICE-Ireland*, the pragmatically enriched version of the Irish ICE sub-corpus.

Stylistically annotated corpora are rather rare, probably because they require a far higher degree of interpretation on the part of the compilers (Leech *et al.* 1997: 94–100). They essentially provide information about different levels of speech, such as direct, indirect or reported speech or narrative, as well as literary descriptions. Examples of stylistic corpora are the *Lancaster Speech, Writing and Thought Presentation Spoken Corpus* (SWandTP), which contains annotations for various types of direct/indirect speech and thought; the *Narrative Corpus*, composed of narrative passages from conversations in the BNC1994; and the *Corpus Linguistics in Cheshire* (CLiC) corpus, containing annotations that facilitate the identification of fictional speech and literary body language, i.e. the way posture and mimicry of characters are described.

Parsed corpora, or *treebanks*, offer information about the syntactic structure and constituents of the sentences in the corpus, including POS tags. They may either represent general phrase structure trees or dependency structures. Although English ones constitute the majority, treebanks are available for a variety of other languages, as the following non-exhaustive list shows:

- English: *Lancaster Parsed Corpus* (LPC), *Penn Treebank*, *Diachronic Corpus of Present-Day Spoken English* (DCPSE), ICE-GB;
- German: *Tübinger Baumbank des Deutschen/Spontansprache* (TüBa-D/S), *Tübinger Baumbank des Deutschen/Zeitungskorpus* (TüBa-D/Z), *TIGER Korpus;*
- Romance languages: *Turin University Treebank* (Italian); *UAM Spanish Treebank* (Spanish); *Projecto Floresta Sintá(c)tica* (Portuguese);
- Slavic languages: *BulTreeBank* (Bulgarian); *Prague Dependency Treebank* (Czech);
- Asian languages: *Chinese Treebank* (Chinese); *Korean Treebank* (Korean).

The two common annotation formats for such parsed corpora are labelled bracketing, using either square or round brackets, possibly combined with multiple levels of indentation, or some form of (standoff) XML, which are then usually translated into a visual representation of a tree structure via dedicated programmes (see Chapters 2, 3 and 4, this volume).

Corpora containing discourse-related information mainly encompass annotations pertaining to discourse relations. They are generally built 'on top of' treebanks, i.e. complementing these through additional information beyond syntax and argument structure. Examples are the *Penn Discourse Treebank 3* (PDTB), with mark-up for discourse relations and connectives; the *Potsdam Commentary Corpus* (PCC), which sports annotations on the levels of POS, morphology, coreference, connectives and RST structure; the *French Discourse Treebank* (FDTB) that marks up discourse connectives; and the *Prague Discourse Treebank* 2.0 (PDiT), which has annotations for discourse connectives and the units they link, together with their semantic relations, as well as coreference and bridging.

Semantically annotated corpora may cover a variety of different types of annotation, ranging from *word-sense disambiguation* (WSD), via named *entity recognition* (people, institutions or places), to semantic roles (agent, patient, etc.) or relations between entities (see Kübler and Zinsmeister 2015, Chapter 5). For instance, the *SemCor* corpus contains POS tags and sense definitions from WordNet, a lexical database that links cognitively related terms; the *PropBank* corpus argument structure with roles and modifiers, such as locations, causes, etc.; the *TimeBank* corpus markup about events, temporal linking devices and relationships; and the *Groningen Meaning Bank* (GMB) POS tags, with named entities, word senses, syntactic information, logical relations and *discourse representation structure* (DRS).

Most treebanks and corpus resources that encompass semantic or discourse annotation, however, appear to be created predominantly for NLP purposes and may either not be publicly available or can only be accessed through dedicated tools.

2 Conceptual design

To develop a better understanding of which use existing corpora may be put to, it is important to have some knowledge of the design concepts, criteria and methods that have been, or are being, applied in their compilation. As other chapters in this handbook will deal with these notions in more detail, I will only provide a broad overview here.

General and national corpora

General corpora, also sometimes referred to as *reference corpora*, are designed to reflect language use in as many facets as possible, i.e. to be *representative* of a given language in its entirety, both in terms of reception and production (cf. Atkins *et al.* 1992). This is why they require careful composition, as well as normally also being of larger size. In the 1960s, when the first electronic corpora began to be developed, the (implicit) assumption was that the most representative form of language was its written one, so that materials deemed to be 'too spoken' were explicitly excluded from the Brown Corpus (see Francis and Kucera 1979). As many of these earlier corpora are still being used today, though, especially in teaching aspects of corpus linguistics, it is important to know a little more about their composition and how this may differ from more recent general corpora.

As already pointed out, earlier written corpora like the *Lancaster-Oslo-Bergen Corpus* (LOB), the *Kolhapur Corpus of Indian English* or the *Australian Corpus of English* (ACE), along with their 'diachronic' counterparts B-BROWN, FROWN, FLOB, BE06 and AmE06, follow the original design of the Brown Corpus closely in order to ensure comparability. All of them, as well as the German LIMAS Corpus, which is loosely modelled on the Brown, consist of approximately 1 million words, divided into 500 text samples of 2,000 words in length. The English corpora are subdivided into 15 main categories, whereas the LIMAS takes a different approach, based around 33 thematic rubrics. Table 8.1 shows the composition of the *Brown Corpus*, along with the number and percentage of samples each category contains.

Table 8.1 The composition of the *Brown Corpus*

Label	*Text category/genre*	*# Samples*	*%*
A	Press: Reportage	44	8.8%
B	Press: Editorial	27	5.4%
C	Press: Reviews	17	3.4%
D	Religion	17	3.4%
E	Skills and Hobbies	36	7.2%
F	Popular Lore	48	9.6%
G	Belles Lettres, Biography, Essays	75	15.0%
H	Miscellaneous: Government Documents, Foundation Reports, Industry Reports, College Catalogue, Industry House Organ	30	6.0%
J	Learned	80	16.0%
K	General Fiction	29	5.8%
L	Mystery and Detective Fiction	24	4.8%
M	Science Fiction	6	1.2%
N	Adventure and Western Fiction	29	5.8%
P	Romance and Love Story	29	5.8%
R	Humour	9	1.8%

The minor differences between the corpora of national varieties in the Brown family are, for instance, reflected in the literary categories that mirror the cultural and local situation. Hence, in category N of the ACE, *Western Fiction* in the Brown is replaced by *Bush Fiction*, and, according to its manual, the same category in the Kolhapur corpus is wholly composed of "adventure" because Western Fiction was simply not available. An important thing to note from Table 8.1 is that the category *religion* here accounts for 3.4% of the overall corpus data, which now appears anachronistic to say the least.

Regarding the structural design of these corpora, it is also worth observing that their original versions only contain one single file for each category, thus combining multiple samples, where each sample may still contain multiple subdivisions, such as multiple articles for one edition of a newspaper. This design may work well if one wants to treat each category as one homogeneous piece of data, but makes it more difficult to investigate issues of dispersion that, amongst other things, depend on the length of the individual samples (see Chapter 13, this volume).

In terms of *metadata*, most of the little that is available generally needs to be extracted from the manuals, so that it is relatively difficult to access, at least for the original versions of the Brown family. The XML version of the Brown corpus at least contains some *metadata* in its header (within the file), from where it can easily be extracted.

More recent general corpora, such as the BNC1994 or COCA, can be seen as more representative, both regarding their size, running into hundreds of millions of words, and in that they seek to capture both written and spoken language. However, there still is an imbalance towards written language despite the fact that it clearly does not constitute the majority of language that we are exposed to in our daily lives, neither from a receptive nor a productive point of view.

The sampling of the BNC1994 nevertheless tried to strike a balance between production and reception, as well as the spread of textual categories according to both medium (books, newspapers, published, unpublished, written to be spoken, etc.) and domain (imaginative vs. informational) for the written part. The spoken part is divided into the context-governed and demographic sections, where the former comprises public monologues and dialogues from the domains of education, news, business, politics, leisure activities, etc., and the second unconstrained conversations between speakers from different educational backgrounds and ages.

In terms of metainformation for the written component of the BNC1994, there is an abundance of data related to authors, publication-related information and assumed audience, and for the spoken component, there is information about the speakers, interaction types, etc. This makes it possible to create specially designed sub-corpora from the data to investigate individual domains or compare them to one another.

At the time of writing, an updated version of the BNC, called BNC2014, is being compiled, of which so far only the spoken component is available (see Chapters 3 and 4, this volume). This component comprises 11,422,617 words, but because it only covers demographically sampled data, it is not directly comparable to the BNC1994 in all respects. In the spoken BNC1994, a total of 6.28 million is drawn from institutional contexts, while 4.3 million was recorded from private conversations. Conversely, all of the BNC2014 derives from casual conversations. Chapter 39, this volume, contains a case study where a sub-corpus of private conversations from the BNC1994 have been isolated and compared diachronically with all of the Spoken BNC2014. The written component will also contain materials from new and social media that were not available for the BNC1994.

The *(Open) American National Corpus* was originally intended to become the American counterpart of the BNC, following the same general design criteria, but with the addition of 10% written materials from modern media, such as emails, web pages, chats, etc. However, to date only a fraction of the envisaged 100 million words has been released. The COCA, which contains more than 600 million words covering the years 1990–2019, at the time of writing, follows a different design and is divided into five equally sized categories: *fiction*, *popular magazines*, *newspapers*, *academic* and *spoken*, where the latter is entirely culled from media sources, so that there is no spontaneous dialogue as in the BNC1994.

While some other national corpora, such as the Thai National Corpus or the Turkish National Corpus (TNC), are explicitly based on the original sampling design of the BNC1994, in other countries, attempts at achieving greater representativeness have resulted in the creation of what might be termed *fusion corpora*, i.e. corpora that collate existing and newly developed corpora into monitor corpora (see later) by storing them in central repositories or databases and where it is possible to either draw on the whole resulting corpus or user-defined virtual corpora to achieve the level of genericity, representativeness or balance required, rather than having one monolithic and static corpus. This is, for instance, the case in Germany, where the German Reference Corpus (*Deutsches Referenzkorpus*; DeReKo), currently comprising more than 46.9 billion words, and the German Research and Teaching Corpus of Spoken German (*Forschungs- und Lehrkorpus Gesprochenes Deutsch*; FOLK), both housed at the Institute for German Language, or for the *Australian National Corpus* (AusNC). It is particularly notable, though, that the German reference data here are deliberately split into a written and a spoken corpus. However, there is also another large reference collection available, the Digital Dictionary of the German Language (*Digitales Wörterbuch der Deutschen Sprache*; DWDS), whose sub-corpora are sampled according to more traditional criteria.

Some other well-known national corpora already in existence are the *Czech National Corpus*, the *Hellenic National Corpus* (HNC), the *Sejong 21 Corpora* (aka 'Korean National Corpus'), the *National Corpus of Polish* (NKJP) and the *Russian National Corpus*.

Specialised corpora

In contrast to the general reference or national corpora discussed earlier, most smaller corpora can be seen as specialised corpora (see Chapter 5, this volume). Such corpora usually only cover a single domain and tend to be created for highly specific research purposes, such as terminology extraction, investigating the language of a particular variety or register, etc. As they do not need to cover all aspects of a given language, they are usually also much smaller than the reference corpora, and it is easier to achieve representativeness in compiling them, even though careful selection and balance are still required. A good example of a highly specialised corpus is the *Louvain Corpus of Native English Essays* (LOCNESS), which comprises English essays written by British and American native speakers. It was collected in order to provide a basis for comparison to the materials in the *International Corpus of Learner English* (ICLE). Due to its specialised nature, it only contains 324,304 words to match the 200,000 words set as a target for the individual ICLE sub-corpora.

Comparable and translation/parallel corpora

Comparable corpora tend to be specialised corpora that are similar in their design frames, but usually do not contain multiple genres (Kenning 2010: 487–8). Hence, the LOCNESS and sub-corpora of the ICLE referred to earlier can be seen as genuine comparable corpora in the strict sense, but LOB and FLOB only in the widest sense, even if it is possible to compare them to one another, also at multiple register/genre levels.

Translation corpora, as their name indicates, consist of genuinely parallel texts that have been translated from one another into one or more target languages (see Chapter 34, this volume). A well-known example of a translation corpus is the *European Parliament Proceedings Parallel Corpus* (Europarl), which comprises translations of the parliamentary proceedings of the European Union between 1996 and 2011 in 21 European languages.

Static vs. dynamic corpora

A further distinction we can make between corpora is whether they are completely static and remain unchanged once released or grow dynamically by being added to periodically.

'Synchronic' (modern) corpora

As we saw earlier, the earliest electronic corpora were essentially conceived as being more or less completely synchronic, i.e. to reflect language at a single (contemporary) point in time. This is certainly true for the early stages of existence of the Brown family, and even still to some extent of the BNC1994, even if the earliest materials contained therein go back as far as the 1960s. It is also still true for later derivatives of the Brown family, such as FLOB and FROWN, which are supposed to reflect the language exactly 30 years after LOB and BROWN, and there was no intention initially to ever add to these corpora. As we shall see further below, though, the situation has changed somewhat since then.

Monitor corpora

Corpora that are designed to grow over time from the outset are referred to as *monitor corpora* because they are supposed to reflect a language, including any changes, across individual points in time. The best-known early monitor corpus for English is probably the *Bank of English*, a balanced part of the COLLINS Corpus, which is inaccessible to the general public. A more recent well-known monitor corpus of American English is the COCA, while the DeReKo is the best-known German one.

Historical and diachronic corpora

While the early corpora of the Brown family were essentially conceived as purely synchronic in nature, the earliest historical corpora, such as the *Helsinki Corpus* or *A Representative Corpus of Historical English Registers* (ARCHER), were designed to represent older stages of English across different time periods, ca. 750–100 for the Helsinki Corpus, and 1650–1990 for ARCHER. Something similar goes for the more recent German DWDS corpora, where e.g. the *Deutsches Textarchiv* (German Text Archive) covers data from 1473 to 1927, the *DWDS Kernkorpus* (Core Corpus) from 1900 to 1999 and the *DWDS-Kernkorpus 21* currently from 2000 to 2010, and will be expanded into a monitor corpus.

Whereas some of the historical corpora are, of course, limited with regard to their content by the very fact that there is only a finite amount of data available for the oldest time periods, the distinction between synchronic and diachronic corpora is getting more and more blurred because there is now an increasing number of 'follow-up' corpora being produced. These either pre- or post-date the initial corpora, so that we may now need to add the concept of *pseudo-diachronic corpora* to our terminology, as they provide opportunities for pseudo-longitudinal studies on the same genres. Examples of this phenomenon are the BLOB-1931–LOB–FLOB–BE06 series, or the BNC1994 and BNC2014.

Another new development here are plans for some older existing corpora to receive updates for categories that did not exist in the original designs, such as new media. This idea has already been discussed with reference to the ICE corpora.

Further coverage- or compilation-based subdivisions

In addition to the more conceptual distinctions we have explored earlier, we can make some further distinctions based on the content and coverage or compilation techniques employed in corpus creation.

National vs. international corpora

If a language is spoken in multiple countries, with distinct varieties, and especially if these are of cultural relevance to a country, then it makes sense to create separate corpora for these varieties that can be compared to one another to identify commonalities and differences. Although, in a sense, all of these corpora may be seen as national corpora, they generally do not have the scope of the large national corpora of the major varieties we discussed earlier. Compilations of such corpora can be seen as international corpora, with perhaps the best-known examples for English being the ICE initiative that covers both spoken and written language, but where many sub-corpora are already somewhat dated, and the *Global Web-Based English* (GloWbE) Corpus, which comprises 1.9 billion words of writing from 20 different countries covering materials from 2012 to 2013. An interesting recent addition to the world of international English corpora is the all-written 10-million-word *Pakistan National Corpus of English* (PNCE).

The German *Korpus C4* follows the fusion design principle in that it combines corpus materials provided by the four German-speaking areas, Germany, Austria, Southern Tyrol (Italy) and Switzerland, into a single resource that can be searched either as a whole or by individual sub-corpus.

Learner and academic corpora

Another type of specialist corpora are learner or academic corpora. Amongst the former, we have already referred to the ICLE corpus, which contains 3.7 million words produced by learners from 16 countries (see Chapter 22, this volume). The spoken counterpart to the ICLE is the *Louvain International Database of Spoken English Interlanguage* (LINDSEI), which also has a native-speaker counterpart, the *Louvain Corpus of Native English Conversation* (LOCNEC). A more recent corpus is the *Spoken Learner Corpus* (SLC; aka Trinity Lancaster Corpus) of 4 million words from spoken exams, graded on CEFR scales. An initiative focussing on Asian learners is the *International Corpus Network of Asian Learners of English* (ICNALE), comprising both spoken and written data, albeit, at 200 to 300 words per file, rather limited in length. Probably the best-known German learner corpus is the *Fehlerannotierte Lernerkorpus des Deutschen als Fremdsprache* (FALKO), which contains summaries and essays by learners and native speakers.

Academic corpora, although possibly containing (advanced) learner data, focus on speech or writing at the university level (see Chapters 28, 29 and 30, this volume). Some of the best-known examples are the *Michigan Corpus of Academic Spoken English* (MICASE) and *Michigan Corpus of Upper-level Student Papers* (MICUSP) and their British counterparts, the *British Academic Spoken English* (BASE) and *British Academic Written English* (BAWE). Academic corpora like these may be used for research into the registers of academic language, but also sometimes to create academic resources, such as textbooks or vocabulary lists (see Chapters 21–30, this volume). The most famous and frequently cited example of the latter is still the *Academic Word List* (AWL), despite the fact that the corpus underlying it is heavily skewed towards commerce and law categories, and can therefore hardly be deemed representative.

Mega-corpora and web corpora

As we saw earlier, many of the modern national/reference corpora consist of millions, if not billions, of words, and can therefore be referred to as *mega-corpora.* Although the earliest of these mega-corpora were still compiled in a more traditional way, nowadays there is a growing trend to harvest more and more corpora, such as the COCA, directly from the Web. The biggest challenges in this endeavour are to remove boilerplate text, avoid duplicate material, and collect appropriate metadata. Further well-known examples of such web corpora are the 14-billion-word *iWeb Corpus* and the *TenTen* and *COrpora from the Web (COW)* suites of corpora for different languages.

3 Historical development

The earliest pre-electronic corpora were compiled and stored on filing cards or paper-based slips of indexes, and contained attested usage samples in the form of biblical or literary concordances, or were used as the basis for descriptive grammars and dictionaries, such as the Oxford English Dictionary (Meyer 2008). Early computerised written corpora, initially stored on punch cards, only began to be produced in the United States, Britain, and Germany from the mid-1960s onwards. Interestingly, though, the foundation for the largest reference corpus in the world, the DeReko, was already laid in 1964, beginning with the compilation of the *Mannheimer Korpus.*

Although the origins of the first spoken corpus of English, the LLC, date back to the late 1950s, the corpus itself was not completed until 1980. By that time, however, already two spoken German corpora, the *Freiburger Korpus* and the *Dialogstrukturen-Korpus* (dialogue structures), had been compiled.

The beginnings of the compilation of historical corpora date back to 1985 with the completion of the *Bonner Frühneuhochdeutschkorpus* (Bonn Corpus of Early Modern High German), while the earliest diachronic corpus of English, the diachronic part of the Helsinki Corpus, was not released until 1991. The year before that also saw the inception of the ICE project, the first project to produce both mixed and varietal corpora of English. Again in 1991, the first mixed corpus of German, the *Wendekorpus Mannheim,* was published.

The first parsed corpus, the *Lancaster Parsed Corpus,* was released in 1986, but more and more treebanks, such as the Penn Treebank, began to be produced from the early 1990s onwards. More recently, many treebanks have also been enriched with other types of information, such as semantic or discourse annotations, albeit predominantly for NLP purposes. Although grammars had already been produced from corpora in the 'pre-electronic age', and some modern grammars started drawing on electronic corpus data from the 1980s, the first 'major' corpus-based grammar, the *Longman Grammar of Spoken and Written English,* was only published in 1999. The late 1990s also constitute the beginning of a trend towards pseudo-diachronic series of corpora revolving around the Brown and LOB corpora.

The release of BNC1994 represented a milestone in the development of modern mega-corpora, but their main development did not start until the first decade of the new millennium. Since then, there also has been an increasing trend towards the compilation of web-based and monitor corpora. The first decade of the new millennium brought the release of the most important and well-known learner and academic corpora.

The end of the twentieth century and first decade of the twenty-first mark the beginnings of corpus-based critical discourse analysis (CDA), while the development of corpus pragmatics as a sub-discipline of CL, despite its origins reaching back to approaches to discourse analysis from the 1970s, dates back to the previous decade (see Chapter 19, this volume).

4 Access, interfaces and usability

When discussing the accessibility of corpora, we need to distinguish between two different modes, *offline* and *online* availability, although, of course, some corpora are never made publicly accessible. Offline accessibility means that the researcher has access to the corpus on their own computer, and hence there is an optimal degree of flexibility regarding the processing, only limited by the type of software being used or the researcher's own programming skills. While initially corpora were distributed via CD ROMs, such as the ICAME CD, in basic raw text or (pseudo-)SGML formats, nowadays web downloads through repositories like the Oxford Text Archive (OTA), with data encoded in XML, are increasingly becoming the norm. For instance, the Brown and the BNC1994 are now freely available as raw text and in an XML format based on the Text Encoding Initiative (TEI) standard. To avoid copyright issues and enable researchers to at least carry out word frequency–based processing, sometimes frequency lists are also made available, for instance, for the BNC1994, Brown, BE06 and AmE06.

Online accessibility means that the user is able to run searches on the corpus, most commonly through a web interface like BNCweb, CQPweb and the BYU interfaces for English, or COSMAS for German corpora. These generally have very fast database back-ends that allow the user to carry out various types of operations, including basic and contextual searches, running queries involving POS tags or collocational analysis, as well as to store queries for re-use. Other options that are frequently available in such interfaces are the ability to select or create sub-corpora or virtual corpora by choosing texts based on metadata, or to compare data across multiple corpora.

While online interfaces generally work well for many users who only need to carry out relatively basic operations, such as concordancing, frequency analysis, etc., discourse-level analyses are usually not easily possible, either due to limitations in displaying enough context or the inability to add further levels of annotation that may be essential for advanced corpus analysis. Hence, it would be highly commendable if more options to obtain offline data were to become available.

In addition, for copyright reasons, analysis results from some online interfaces, such as the BYU ones, cannot even be downloaded directly for further processing, which may limit their usefulness to some extent. On the other hand, for the same reasons, some types of offline materials, such as the COW data, cannot ever be used for much that goes beyond basic lexical analysis, as the order of sentences in the corpora is scrambled, and therefore no analysis beyond this level is possible.

While the development of mega-corpora and the increasing availability of online data for corpus compilation have brought distinct advantages, the trend towards building larger corpora has not been without issues. Regarding web data, as pointed out earlier, the availability of metadata might be severely limited, and it may even be difficult to assign the texts to exact categories, especially if they are harvested largely automatically. However, especially when it comes to spoken data, the increasing trend towards 'economy' in corpus compilation is rather worrying. For instance, my own research using parts of the BNC1994 has revealed that up to 10% of the spoken materials may either have been mistranscribed, or large sections marked as unclear without precise indications of their length, which could affect even otherwise relatively unproblematic operations such as the generation of reliable frequency lists. This is even more problematic in trying to use the data for pragmatics-related research, as the data may simply be too incoherent to analyse at all.

Related to these content issues are issues of representation. For instance, even if standardised formats, such as the TEI format, generally help to ensure exchangeability and comparability, their usefulness is sometimes hampered through excessively detailed headers or unnecessary levels of nesting, which may cause problems of legibility if extensive reading of the data is required, as is often the case in CDA or corpus pragmatics. In addition, below the TEI u (utterance) tag, which is used to mark speaker turns, there is no provision for marking functional units within turns, so that most researchers still resort to the word as the level of analysis for most types of feature frequency counts. This, however, is inappropriate for handling especially pragmatic aspects, where something like the c-unit, a clause-like functional unit, would be more suitable. Despite recommendations to this effect already having been made in Leech *et al.* (2000), even the recently produced Trinity Lancaster Corpus still does not have such necessary functional subdivisions, and it would be better if a pragmatics-oriented annotation scheme, such as the DART scheme (Weisser 2019), would generally be adopted for spoken data.

5 Looking forward: the future of corpora

While more and more corpora are being created and used for various purposes all the time, others simply seem to disappear, as my attempts at keeping the CBLLinks web pages up to date while writing this chapter have shown. One positive step towards achieving more sustainability, however, has been the creation of additional repositories, such as the European *Common Language Resources and Technology Infrastructure* (CLARIN), where corpora and associated metadata can be stored by compilers and distributed to interested users. As more governments are beginning to realise the need for maintaining language resources, the number of such repositories is likely to increase in the foreseeable future.

Furthermore, because larger web-based interfaces, such as the BYU interface, CQPweb, or the *Sketch Engine*, keep on being developed and/or extended through additional corpora, more specialised corpora of different sizes will probably become available.

Overall, as discourse-related corpus research is becoming increasingly important, we should probably hope that the trend towards more – and often bigger – corpora will also be accompanied by an equal move towards more offline access, more facilities for adding more levels of annotation and improved structuring of data, higher quality and better access to metadata.

Further reading

Crowdy, S. (1993) 'Spoken Corpus Design', *Literary and Linguistic Computing* 8(4): 259–65.

Love, R., Dembry, C., Hardie, A., Brezina, V. and McEnery, T. (2017) 'The Spoken BNC2014: Designing and Building a Spoken Corpus of Everyday Conversations', *International Journal of*

Corpus Linguistics 22(3): 319–44. (The papers by Crowdy [1993] and Love et al. [2017] describing the collection of data for the BNC1994 and BNC2014, respectively, offer substantial insight into the challenges of spoken corpus design.)

Davies, M. (2015) 'Corpora: An Introduction', in D. Biber and R. Reppen (eds) *The Cambridge Handbook of English Corpus Linguistics*, Cambridge: Cambridge University Press. (A more concrete overview of the potential that corpora of different sizes have for investigating different linguistic phenomena, providing examples from some major corpora of English.)

Sinclair, J. (2004) 'Corpus and Text - Basic Principles', in M. Wynne (ed.) *Developing Linguistic Corpora: A Guide to Good Practice*, Oxford: Oxbow. (A concise overview of design principles, including more abstract information about corpus sizes required for different types of analysis.)

References

Atkins, S., Clear, J. and Ostler, N. (1992) 'Corpus Design Criteria', *Literary and Linguistic Computing* 7(1): 1–16

Francis, N. and Kucera, H. (1979) *Manual of Information to Accompany A Standard Corpus of Present-Day Edited American English, for Use with Digital Computers*. Revised edition. Providence: Brown University.

Greenbaum, S. (1991) 'The Development of the International Corpus of English', in K. Aijmer and B. Altenberg (eds) *English Corpus Linguistics: Studies in Honour of Jan Svartvik*, London: Longman, pp. 83–91.

Ide, N., Calzolari, N., Eckle-Kohler, J., Gibbon, D., Hellmann, S., Lee, K., Nivre, J. and Romary, L. (2017) 'Community Standards for Linguistically-Annotated Resources', in N. Ide and J. Pustejovsky (eds) *The Handbook of Linguistic Annotation*, New York: Springer, pp. 113–65.

Kenning, M.-M. (2010) 'What are Parallel and Comparable Corpora and How Can we Use them?', in A. O'Keeffe and M. McCarthy (eds) *The Routledge Handbook of Corpus Linguistics*, London: Routledge, pp. 487–500.

Kübler, S. and Zinsmeister, H. (2015) *Corpus Linguistics and Linguistically Annotated Corpora*, London: Bloomsbury.

Leech, G. (2005) 'Adding Linguistic Information', in M. Wynne (ed.) *Developing Linguistic Corpora: A Guide to Good Practice*, Oxford: Oxbow, pp. 17–29.

Leech, G., McEnery, T. and Wynne, M. (1997) 'Further Levels of Annotation', in R. Garside, G. Leech and A. McEnery (Ed). *Corpus Annotation: Linguistic Information from Computer Corpora*, London: Longman, pp. 85–101.

Leech, G., Weisser, M., Wilson, A. and Grice, M. (2000) 'Survey and Guidelines for the Representation and Annotation of Dialogue', in D. Gibbon, I. Mertins and R. Moore (eds) *Handbook of Multimodal and Spoken Language Systems*, Dordrecht: Kluwer Academic Publishers, pp. 1–101.

Meyer, C. (2008) 'Origin and History of Corpus Linguistics - Corpus Linguistics vis-à-vis other disciplines', in A. Lüdeling and M. Kyto. (eds) *Corpus Linguistics: An International Handbook*, Berlin: Walter de Gruyter, pp. 84–110.

Weisser, M. (2015) 'Speech Act Annotation', in K. Aijmer and C. Rühlemann (eds) *Corpus Pragmatics: A Handbook*, Cambridge: Cambridge University Press, pp. 84–113.

Weisser, M. (2016) *Practical Corpus Linguistics: An Introduction to Corpus-based Language Analysis*, Malden, MA and Oxford: Wiley-Blackwell.

Weisser, M. (2019) 'The DART Annotation Scheme: Form, Applicability and Application', *Studia Neophilologica* 91(2): 131–53.

9 What can corpus software do?

Laurence Anthony

1 Comparing online tools, offline tools and DIY tools

What is the difference between online, offline and DIY tools?

Corpus software comes in primarily three different forms: online tools, offline tools and DIY tools. Online tools usually exist in the "cloud", meaning that they reside on one or more remote servers and are developed, managed and updated remotely. To use these tools, you will need to have an internet connection, and you connect to them through a standard web browser, such as Chrome, Firefox, Edge or Safari (on a Macintosh computer). Some of these tools are made freely available, while others require a one-time payment or a subscription fee. Some commonly used and frequently cited online corpus tools include *CQPweb,*[1] *English-Corpora.org,*[2] and *Sketch Engine.*[3]

In contrast, offline tools need to be purchased as a standalone package or, more commonly, downloaded from a provider (for free, with a one-time payment or with a subscription fee) and then manually installed onto your local computer's hard drive. Although these tools are created by external programmers, as a user of these tools, you are generally responsible for managing where they are stored and when they are updated. To use these tools, you need to have a computer with an operating system, hard disk space, and random access memory (RAM) memory that matches the requirements of the software. Some commonly used and frequently cited offline corpus tools include *AntConc,*[4] *#LancsBox,*[5] *Wmatrix,*[6] and *WordSmith Tools.*[7]

DIY tools usually come in the form of "scripts". These are text files containing a list of commands that need to be executed by a scripting programming language, such as Python or R. These scripts may be given as a listing in a research paper or personal blog, supplied as an addendum to a book or book chapter, appear in a forum post (such as on *Stack Overflow*[8]) or sent as a personal communication through email. They may also be provided on an individual researcher's website or in a project repository hosted on sites such as *GitHub.*[9] DIY tools are often in a state of constant flux, with tools frequently created, updated, renamed, moved and deleted. Two examples of DIY corpus tool repositories that are relatively stable but sit at the opposite ends of the scale in terms of size

DOI: 10.4324/9780367076399-9

and scope are the huge library of Python scripts that form the *Natural Language Toolkit*[10] and the R scripts for the book *Quantitative Corpus Linguistics with R* (Gries 2016).[11] Of course, a researcher may also choose to write their own scripts using a knowledge of programming.

How are online, offline and DIY tools used in corpus linguistics?

Online, offline and DIY corpus software tools can play an important role at every stage of a corpus linguistics project. At the corpus design and development stage, software tools can assist in the collection of raw data that goes into the corpus. For example, there are numerous general-purpose online and offline tools as well as DIY tools that can help researchers convert raw data in the form of audio recordings, webpages, scanned books, PDF/Word files and other data formats into a form more suitable for corpus analysis. For example, many online PDF-to-text converters can be easily found through a simple Internet search. Care should be taken when using these, however, as it can be unclear if the site will store and use the data for its own purposes. They may also only convert a single file at a time, which is inappropriate for many corpus building tasks that require huge numbers of files to be converted. One alternative is *AntFileConverter,*[12] which is an offline tool that can batch-convert PDF and Word files into a text format without any restriction on the number of files being processed.

There are also online, offline and DIY tools that can automatically visit a website and automatically "scrape" the text data from each page and store the results locally. One such tool is the online *Web Scraper*[13] tool that is available for both Chrome and Firefox browsers, and a popular offline web scraping tool is *BootCat.*[14] A more advanced data collection tool for the automatic download and storage of academic research articles is *AntCorGen.*[15] This tool provides an interface to the *PLOS ONE*[16] open-access interdisciplinary journal and allows you to select not only the area of specialisation but also the sections of the article (e.g. title, abstract, introduction) that you are interested in analysing. Another advanced data collection tool was used as part of the *CorCenCC* project.[17] This was a custom-built online mobile app that recorded spoken data from participants in the project and sent the data to a server for upload into the project database. There are even tools such as *FireAnt*[18] that can access the application programming interfaces (APIs) of social media platforms and collect data in the form of posts, "tweets" and so on, as well as the associated metadata of the sender (e.g. name, location, date of post) and that of their target audience members.

Online, offline and DIY corpus software tools can also help corpus designers to clean, tag and annotate their corpora. For part-of-speech (POS) tagging (i.e. the explicit labeling of words in a corpus as nouns, verbs, adjectives and so on), a commonly used offline tool is *TagAnt.*[19] This tool provides a one-click method to POS-tag a batch of text files using the *TreeTagger* engine[20] and works with multiple Western languages, including Dutch, English, French, German, Italian and Spanish. A similar offline tool called *SegmentAnt*[21] provides one-click POS tagging of Chinese and Japanese texts. Semantic tagging of texts (i.e. the tagging or word senses, such as *emotion*, *time*, *education* and *science and technology*), can be achieved using the online *UCREL Semantic Analysis System* (*USAS*) tool,[22] which is also incorporated into the general-purpose offline corpus analysis toolkit *Wmatrix.*[23] This tool also works with multiple languages, including Chinese, Dutch, English, Italian, Portuguese and Spanish. There are also tools to assist with higher-level annotation of corpus data. For sentence parsing of texts to annotate structural features such as the subject and predicate, tools like the *Stanford Parser*[23] can be used. There are also tools such as the offline *UAM tool*[24] that can be used to apply a custom annotation scheme to texts at multiple levels (e.g. phrase, clause, sentence, paragraph, document) and also output the results in different formats for further processing and analysis.

Corpus software tools are most commonly associated with the task of analysing large amounts of corpus data. Indeed, numerous online, offline and DIY tools have been specially designed for this purpose, providing researchers with qualitative and quantitative information on a wide range of features and patterns in text-based and multimodal corpora. Tools that assist in the bottom-up analysis of corpora can provide information on the frequency of occurrence and dispersion of single words and also multiword units (MWUs), such as clusters (sometimes referred to as n-grams or lexical bundles) (see later and Chapter 15, this volume). They can also be used to identify which words commonly co-occur with other words in the same corpus (i.e. collocations, see later and Chapter 15, this volume) and which words appear unusually frequently compared to their frequency in a reference corpus (i.e. keywords, see Chapter 10, this volume). They can also be used to identify common patterns of word and phrase usage in context (i.e. concordances, see later and Chapter 10, this volume) and visualise where these word and phrase patterns occur in individual tests and/or the corpus as a whole (i.e. dispersion plots, see later). Although these same tools can be used more indirectly to identify top-down patterns of usage, there are other tools designed specifically to analyse corpus data at the top-down level. For example, there are tools that can identify prototypical texts in a corpus (e.g. *ProtAnt*[25]), as well as tools that can analyse discourse structure and rhetorical purpose (e.g. *AntMover*[26] and *AWSum*[27]). The use of corpus tools to assist in the analysis of corpora at the bottom-up and top-down level will be the focus of Sections 2 and 3 of this chapter.

One other important area that online, offline and DIY corpus software tools play an important role in is the visualisation of results from a corpus linguistics project. Most online and offline tools will produce results in a tabular form, such as concordance outputs and word frequency lists. However, some can produce more complex visualizations. For example, *AntConc*[4] and *WordSmith Tools*[7] can produce dispersion plots of word and phrase usage in the form of stacked "barcode" charts that immediately reveal where the results appear in the corpus. *#LancsBox*[5] can produce collocates in a tabular form or as a network of connected nodes, where clicking on one node (either the target word or one of its collocates) will expand the network to show further connections between that word and its related collocates. Online corpus tools and DIY tools offer even more possibilities for advanced visualisation of results using browser-based *JavaScript*[28] libraries that can generate and even animate 2D and 3D visualisations of massive amounts of data. Some of these features can be seen in the visualisations provided by the online *Michigan Corpus of Upper-Level Student Papers* (MICUSP) interface,[29] which shows results as dynamically updated bar charts and pie charts with user-initiated color highlighting of relevant columns and values. *Kaleidographic*[30] is an online tool that allows users to upload their own data and generate animated multi-layered visualisations. Even more impressive visualisations can be generated using DIY tools. These tools can utilise dedicated graphics packages and JavaScript libraries to produce complex and often striking visualisations. To see what can be achieved with these tools, one only needs to look at the visualisations produced by Jack Grieve[31,32] and Stefan

Gries,[33] among many other researchers who use them to explain a wide range of linguistic phenomena.

Which are better: online, offline or DIY tools?

It is difficult to say whether an online, offline or DIY tool is the right choice for a particular corpus linguistics project, but each has certain strengths and weaknesses that are worth considering.

Online tools have largely become the tool of choice for many projects, both inside and outside of corpus linguistics. There are numerous reasons why this is the case. First, the growth of the internet, the advance of server technology and the fall in prices and increased efficiency and capacity of memory devices has meant that online tools can be cheaply stored and quickly accessed at remote locations. Server systems can also distribute tasks across multiple computers, hugely increasing the overall speed and performance of a system. From a user's perspective, the complexity of an online tool can also be largely ignored. All a user needs to do is launch a standard internet browser, type or search for the address of the hosting server and start using the tool. Many software developers also prefer creating online tools, because they only need to develop the software to run on standard browsers instead of developing the software to run natively on multiple computer systems running different operating systems and different versions of the same operating system. Updating software is also simple when it is hosted online. The developer only needs to send the new code to the server, and it will be immediately accessible to all the users of the software around the world.

In the field of corpus linguistics, online tools offer some unique advantages over offline and DIY tools. First, they can be designed to access massive corpora that would be too large to fit on anybody's personal computer. They can also be designed to limit a user's access to the corpus data (e.g. only producing wordlists and concordances of a fixed context size), which might be important if the corpus data are copyright protected or contain sensitive information. Also, custom online corpus tools can be designed and tailored to work with a specialised corpus that might use a unique POS-tagging system or rich annotation layer. They can also be specially tailored to facilitate the types of searches and analyses that the corpus was designed for and visualise the results accordingly. There are numerous examples of such online corpus interfaces. For example, online tools designed to provide a general interface to various large-scale corpora include *CQPweb,*[1] *English-Corpora.org*[2] and *Sketch Engine,*[3] mentioned earlier. There are also tools designed specifically for a single corpus, including the *MICUSP* interface[29] mentioned earlier, the *Scottish Corpus of Texts and Speech* (SCOTS) interface,[34] *OpenSourceShakespeare*[35] and many others. To get an idea of the breadth of availability of online tools that interface to custom corpora, you can visit the *Clarin* portal, which lists a vast number of corpora resources.[36]

Although online tools have many strengths, these same strengths can also be viewed as the tools' greatest weaknesses. For example, the fact that online tools often hide the raw data of a corpus behind a web browser interface means that the researcher is essentially dealing with a "black box" technology. They may not know what data are in the corpus or how the data were collected, cleaned or processed. They may not even know which parts of the corpus are being displayed by the tool. *English-Corpora.org,*[2] for example, restricts users to only viewing a random sample of concordance lines in its output. While this may be sufficient for viewing general patterns of word usage, it is far from sufficient for discourse-level analyses. A related problem is that most online tools (with *Sketch Engine*[3] being a notable exception) do not allow the import of custom data. For researchers investigating a niche language variety or even a major language variety that happens to not have an online corpus tool available, it means that online tools can no longer be an option. Developing specialised online interfaces to different corpora also means that we get an explosion of different tools, each with its own idiosyncratic interface and results display. It should also be mentioned that the most widely used online corpus tools require registration and a subscription fee.

In today's world of the internet, you might wonder why anybody would still use an offline tool for corpus analysis. This is especially true when it is noted that the distinction between online and offline tools is becoming increasingly blurred. Through the development of technologies such as JavaScript and HTML5, online tools can now replicate many of the features of traditional offline tools, including menus, scrolling windows and animated displays. However, offline tools still have their place, especially when it comes to corpus research. First, offline tools provide the user with direct access to the data. It can be viewed in its raw form, loaded into the tool and probed in various ways. In this way, offline tools are more transparent than online tools. They can also offer users a more familiar and intuitive interface, reminiscent of other tools on their system, such as word processors. Importantly, the same interface can be used irrespective of the corpus data loaded into the tool. Offline tools also have more scope for expansion, especially if they provide third-party developers with the ability to create add-ons for the tool. The limited memory and processing power of personal computers may also not be a major concern for researchers if they are only dealing with moderately sized corpora that do not require distributed systems or advanced hardware to process. It is also important to note that offline tools are increasingly gaining features traditionally only associated with online tools, including direct access to cloud resources.

Currently, the most widely used general-purpose offline corpus analysis toolkits are *AntConc,*[4] which is a freeware tool for Windows, Macintosh and Linux computers, and *Wordsmith Tools,*[7] which is a commercial tool available for Windows (and which can also be run on other operating systems if Windows is installed as a virtual machine). Of course, there are numerous other offline tools, some designed to provide a broad range of corpus analysis functions (as discussed in Sections 2 and 3 of this chapter), and others designed for quite specific purposes, such as collecting, cleaning and tagging corpus data, or counting unique features in a corpora, as exemplified by *KfNgram*[37] and *AntGram,*[38] that are designed to identify open-slot phrases (p-frames) in a corpus.

DIY tools have a unique place in the history of corpus linguistics. In the early 1960s, the development of mainframe computers led to the birth of modern corpus linguistics. These mainframe computers are quite reminiscent of modern server computers, in the sense that they were large, powerful (for their time), externally managed machines that served entire departments or organisations. However, to use these machines, corpus researchers had to write (or use) specialised software programmes, load them into these mainframe computers (usually with punch cards) and wait sometimes days or weeks for the results to be returned. These DIY tools in many ways served as templates for the online and offline tools used today. Examples of these early programmes include *Concordance* (Dearing 1966), *Concordance Generator* (Smith 1966), *Discon* (Clark 1966) and *Drexel Concordance Program* (Price 1966). One particularly interesting example is *CLOC* (Reed 1978), which was a tool developed for the highly influential COBUILD project at the University of Birmingham, headed by John Sinclair. To create the CLOC tool, the researchers in Sinclair's team invented a new programming language called ATOL (Reed 1978; Sinclair *et al.* 2004; Moon 2007). Today, DIY tools are again gaining prominence in corpus linguistics as researchers adopt increasingly advanced statistical measures and visualisation techniques to understand their data. Many of these measures and techniques are only applicable in narrowly scoped contexts, and so are outside the realm of more general-purpose online and offline tools. Therefore, DIY tools offer a researcher the possibility to be truly innovative in their work. Of course, the downside to this approach is that they need at least some knowledge of programming to confidently use DIY tools developed by others and a much greater knowledge of programming if they hope to develop such tools on their own. To illustrate this point, a bug in the code of a well-established online or offline tool is likely to be noticed by its many users, leading to corrections and updates, especially if the code is made open source.[39] On the other hand, a bug in the code of a DIY tool that has been posted on a forum or created by the researcher themselves may go unnoticed for a long period, potentially invalidating all the research produced by the tool.

2 Finding bottom-up language patterns

Online, offline and DIY tools are primarily used in corpus linguistics research studies to identify bottom-up language patterns. To illustrate the ways in which corpus software can assist in such tasks, I will use *AntConc.*[4] However, it should be noted that alternative tools can be used for this purpose. Many operate in similar ways, with the biggest differences being the interface design and simplicity or complexity of the searches made possible. The corpus data I will use with the software is the written component of the *International Corpus Network of Asian Learners of English (ICNALE)* corpus,[40] which comprises 1.3 million words of learner English from ten countries in Asia, collected in the form of 200- to 300-word essays (Ishikawa 2013).

What are the "important" words in a corpus?: word frequency and keyword analysis

Word frequencies

Corpus software tools are extremely accurate and fast at counting and ranking the occurrences of strings of characters in text files. If these strings of characters are defined to represent word tokens, then we can use the tools to count and rank the frequencies of words in and across the texts of a corpus. This gives us a rough measure of word "importance" based on frequency. By extension, we can also obtain a measure of word "importance" based on their "range" (dispersion) values through a corpus. Figure 9.1 shows a screenshot of *AntConc* displaying frequency values for all the words in the ICNALE corpus after the files are loaded into the tool via the file menu. The figure shows that the corpus comprises a total of 1,316,265 *tokens* (individual words) from 15,355 unique word *types*. What immediately stands out is the predominance of function words (*the, to, a, and, in, of*), which certainly play an important role in language. You may also notice two nouns in the list that stand out for their content value: *time* (rank 8) and *smoking* (rank 9). The ICNALE corpus essays are controlled for content with only the following two prompts being used: (a) *It is important for college students to have a part-time job* and (b) *Smoking should be completely banned at all the restaurants in the*

File Edit Settings Help

Target Corpus
Name: ICNALE
Files: 80
Tokens: 1316265

CHN_A2_PTJ_001.txt
CHN_A2_SMK_001.txt
CHN_B2_PTJ_001.txt
CHN_B2_SMK_001.txt
CHN_B11_PTJ_001.txt
CHN_B11_SMK_001.txt
CHN_B12_PTJ_001.txt
CHN_B12_SMK_001.txt
ENS1_a_PTJ_001.txt
ENS1_a_SMK_001.txt
ENS2_a_PTJ_001.txt
ENS2_a_SMK_001.txt
HKG_A2_PTJ_001.txt
HKG_A2_SMK_001.txt
HKG_B2_PTJ_001.txt
HKG_B2_SMK_001.txt
HKG_B11_PTJ_001.txt
HKG_B11_SMK_001.txt
HKG_B12_PTJ_001.txt
HKG_B12_SMK_001.txt
IDN_A2_PTJ_001.txt
IDN_A2_SMK_001.txt
IDN_B2_PTJ_001.txt
IDN_B2_SMK_001.txt
IDN_B11_PTJ_001.txt

Progress 100%

KWIC Plot File Cluster N-Gram Collocate Word Keyword

Word Types 15355/15355 Word Tokens 1316265/1316265 Page Size 100 hits 1 to 100 of 15355 hits

	Type	Rank	Freq	Range	NormFreq	NormRange
1	the	1	54593	80	41475.691	1.0
2	to	2	43965	80	33401.329	1.0
3	a	3	31469	80	23907.8	1.0
4	and	4	28968	80	22007.726	1.0
5	is	5	28702	80	21805.639	1.0
6	in	6	28043	80	21304.98	1.0
7	of	7	24947	80	18952.87	1.0
8	time	8	22062	76	16761.063	0.95
9	smoking	9	21191	44	16099.342	0.55
10	it	10	19609	79	14897.456	0.988
11	that	11	18550	80	14092.907	1.0
12	for	12	18504	80	14057.959	1.0
13	i	13	17050	79	12953.319	0.988
14	part	14	16342	71	12415.433	0.887
15	job	15	15300	57	11623.799	0.713
16	they	16	14983	80	11382.966	1.0
17	have	17	14561	79	11062.362	0.988
18	can	18	13049	80	9913.657	1.0
19	not	19	12810	80	9732.083	1.0

Search Term Words Case Regex

Start

Sort by Frequency Invert Order

Time taken (creating word list) 0.0673 ms

Figure 9.1 Screenshot of *AntConc* displaying frequency values for all the words in the ICNALE corpus

country. It is not surprising, therefore, to see these important content words ranked so high. It should be noted that the words *part* and *job* from *part-time-job* are ranked fifteenth and fourteenth in the list.

Keywords

We can go one step further and compare the frequencies of words in the *target* corpus (i.e. the corpus which is being examined) with those in another corpus that represents some kind of language standard (i.e. a *reference* corpus). By determining which words appear unusually frequently in the target corpus compared to the reference corpus using a statistical measure such as log likelihood, we can identify so-called *keywords* (see Pojanapunya and Watson Todd 2018). We can also do something similar but using dispersion as the counting measure (see Egbert and Biber 2019). For more on the statistical underpinnings of dispersion, see Chapter 13, this volume.

Figure 9.2 shows a screenshot of *AntConc* showing a standard frequency-based keyword list for the ICNALE written corpus. In this example, only the Japanese learner essays have been loaded into the tool through the file menu and serve as the *target* corpus, whereas the complete corpus (of 1.3 million words of learner English from ten countries in Asia) has been loaded into the tool via the keyword tool preference menu to serve as the *reference* corpus. In this way, the list of keywords represents words that appear unusually frequently in Japanese learner writing compared with Asian learner writing in general. Note that the keywords here have been ranked by the log likelihood keyness measure with a cutoff at $p < 0.05$ with a Bonferroni correction (Armstrong 2014), leaving 155 keywords remaining. This is the default setting, but it can be changed in the keyword tool preferences window.

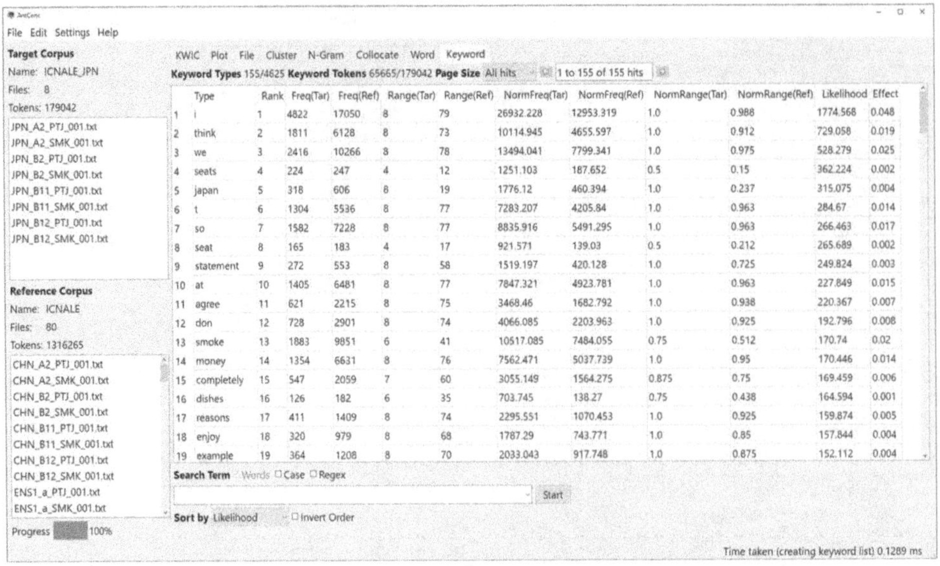

AntConc

File Edit Settings Help

Target Corpus
Name: ICNALE_JPN
Files: 8
Tokens: 179042

JPN_A2_PTJ_001.txt
JPN_A2_SMK_001.txt
JPN_B2_PTJ_001.txt
JPN_B2_SMK_001.txt
JPN_B11_PTJ_001.txt
JPN_B11_SMK_001.txt
JPN_B12_PTJ_001.txt
JPN_B12_SMK_001.txt

Reference Corpus
Name: ICNALE
Files: 80
Tokens: 1316265

CHN_A2_PTJ_001.txt
CHN_A2_SMK_001.txt
CHN_B2_PTJ_001.txt
CHN_B2_SMK_001.txt
CHN_B11_PTJ_001.txt
CHN_B11_SMK_001.txt
CHN_B12_PTJ_001.txt
CHN_B12_SMK_001.txt
ENS1_a_PTJ_001.txt
ENS1_a_SMK_001.txt

Progress 100%

KWIC Plot File Cluster N-Gram Collocate Word Keyword

Keyword Types 155/4625 **Keyword Tokens** 65665/179042 **Page Size** All hits 1 to 155 of 155 hits

	Type	Rank	Freq(Tar)	Freq(Ref)	Range(Tar)	Range(Ref)	NormFreq(Tar)	NormFreq(Ref)	NormRange(Tar)	NormRange(Ref)	Likelihood	Effect
1	i	1	4822	17050	8	79	26932.228	12953.319	1.0	0.988	1774.568	0.048
2	think	2	1811	6128	8	73	10114.945	4655.597	1.0	0.912	729.058	0.019
3	we	3	2416	10266	8	78	13494.041	7799.341	1.0	0.975	528.279	0.025
4	seats	4	224	247	4	12	1251.103	187.652	0.5	0.15	362.224	0.002
5	japan	5	318	606	8	19	1776.12	460.394	1.0	0.237	315.075	0.004
6	t	6	1304	5536	8	77	7283.207	4205.84	1.0	0.963	284.67	0.014
7	so	7	1582	7228	8	77	8835.916	5491.295	1.0	0.963	266.463	0.017
8	seat	8	165	183	4	17	921.571	139.03	0.5	0.212	265.689	0.002
9	statement	9	272	553	8	58	1519.197	420.128	1.0	0.725	249.824	0.003
10	at	10	1405	6481	8	77	7847.321	4923.781	1.0	0.963	227.849	0.015
11	agree	11	621	2215	8	75	3468.46	1682.792	1.0	0.938	220.367	0.007
12	don	12	728	2901	8	74	4066.085	2203.963	1.0	0.925	192.796	0.008
13	smoke	13	1883	9851	6	41	10517.085	7484.055	0.75	0.512	170.74	0.02
14	money	14	1354	6631	8	76	7562.471	5037.739	1.0	0.95	170.446	0.014
15	completely	15	547	2059	7	60	3055.149	1564.275	0.875	0.75	169.459	0.006
16	dishes	16	126	182	6	35	703.745	138.27	0.75	0.438	164.594	0.001
17	reasons	17	411	1409	8	74	2295.551	1070.453	1.0	0.925	159.874	0.005
18	enjoy	18	320	979	8	68	1787.29	743.771	1.0	0.85	157.844	0.004
19	example	19	364	1208	8	70	2033.043	917.748	1.0	0.875	152.112	0.004

Search Term Words ☐Case ☐Regex Start

Sort by Likelihood ☐Invert Order

Time taken (creating keyword list) 0.1289 ms

Figure 9.2 Screenshot of *AntConc* showing a standard frequency-based keyword list for the Japanese component of the ICNALE written corpus

One thing that you might immediately notice in the figure is the disappearance of function words, which dominated a standard word frequency list. This is because function words generally appear with the same frequency distribution across all corpora. You might also notice that the words in the list are presented in lowercase, which is a common practice in the field, as it conflates the same word types together, although this setting can be changed in the tool preferences. The highest ranked keywords in the list are *I* and *think*, suggesting that the Japanese learners use the expression *I think* more frequently in their writing than other Asian students. The words *seat* and *seats* are also ranked high in the list, suggesting that seating in restaurants and other places might be an important theme of the essays. Two words in the list might be confusing on first viewing: *don* and *t*. With the default settings in *AntConc*, "words" are defined as strings of letter characters based on the Unicode letter character set.[41] This means that words like *don't* will be split into two parts. Similarly, words like *I'm* will be split into *I* and *m* and words like *20th* will lose the number and appear as just *th*. Although this setting reflects the standard practice in the field, it can be changed so that such words are not split. One final note of interest in the list is the fact that not only do *don* and *t* appear with a high ranking but also *I*, *agree* and *statement*. This result suggests that a key phrase in the Japanese writing might be *I don't agree with the statement that*… This point will be explored later.

One question that many novice researchers in corpus linguistics have is where to cut off the list of keywords before the rankings become meaningless. Strictly speaking, all 155 words in the list are keywords as defined by the statistical measure. However, they are not all "important" to the same degree. Log likelihood captures the size (or effect) of difference in frequency so it can be used not only as a cutoff measure but also a ranking measure. So, you may decide to look at only the first 50 or 100 keywords, as these are the "most important". However, some researchers have argued that keyness measures should be complemented by a more robust effect size measure by which the words are ranked. Unfortunately, there is currently no established effect size measure that researchers agree on. In Figure 9.2, effect sizes for the keywords are shown based on the dice coefficient (the same measure used to rank keywords in *Sketch Engine*[3]). Although the keywords are ranked by log likelihood keyness values, this setting can also be changed in *AntConc* to order the keywords by effect size.

Word frequency, keyness and effect size measures are not the only ways to identify *important* words in a corpus. In the field of vocabulary research, one common practice is to divide up frequency and/or dispersion lists (or even lists based on other criteria such as curriculum plans or knowledge of words, see Schmitt *et al.* 2021) to create *level lists*. Then, going beyond *AntConc*, online tools such as *MultilingProfiler*[42] and *Compleat Lexical LexTutor*[43] and offline tools such as *AntWordProfiler*[44] can be used to *profile* corpus texts, highlighting words at these different levels and showing how many words the levels cover. This information can provide researchers (as well as teachers and learners) with a measure of the suitability or difficulty of texts for a particular purpose.

What are the "important" multi-word units in a corpus?: cluster, n-grams and lexical bundle analysis

The results of the keyness analysis shown in Figure 9.2 suggests that Japanese learners of English use *I think* and *I don't agree with the statement that…* in their writing relatively more frequently than other Asian students. Clearly, however, the two phrases are very different in nature. The first expression perhaps reflects a feature of the learners' writing style, whereas the second expression may reflect a particular worldview. Both aspects of language use can be explored using corpus tools.

To identify phrases or MWUs in a corpus, you can use a "cluster" tool (sometimes referred to as an "n-gram" tool or "lexical-bundle" tool depending on the researcher/developer). *AntConc*'s cluster tool allows you to search for a particular word or phrase and then displays all occurrences of that word/phrase together with a set number of words immediately preceding or following it. These results can immediately reveal frequent multi-word patterns that may have gone unnoticed using just a frequency or keyword list. Figure 9.3a shows a screenshot of *AntConc* displaying two-word clusters for the search word *I* ranked by frequency, where *I* appears on the left. (The settings can be changed to show clusters with the word appearing on the right.) You will notice, first, that the clusters appear in lowercase, as you found with the frequency and keyword tools. The highest-ranked cluster confirms the hypothesis that *I think* is prevalent in Japanese learner writing (the expression is used 1505 times across all 8 files in the corpus). You might also notice that *i agree*, *i don[t]*, and *i disagree* are all high-ranked clusters, suggesting that the worldview of the learners is more complex and diverse than that hinted at from just the keyword list results. When the tool settings are set to four-word clusters, the phraseology used by the students becomes more pronounced, with the highest-ranked clusters being *i think it is*, *i agree with the*, *i think that it* and *i agree with this* (see Figure 9.3b).

Corpus software tools can also be used to find the occurrence of every cluster in a corpus regardless of the search word, be it two words, three words, or four words long. Without additional filtering, these lists can sometimes look quite noisy, with two-word n-grams like *in the*, *it is* and *of the* ranking highly. However, by setting a minimum

(a)

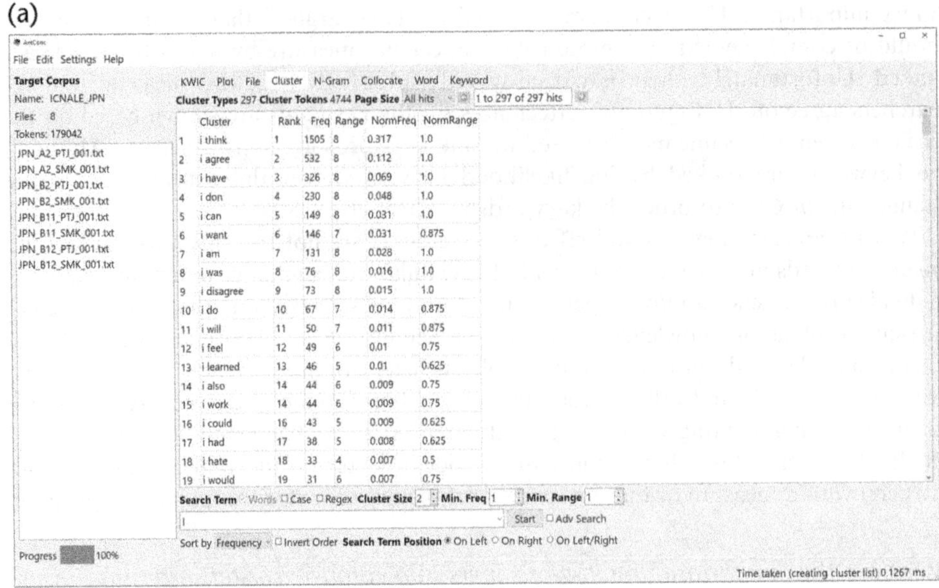

(b)

File Edit Settings Help

Target Corpus
Name: ICNALE_JPN
Files: 8
Tokens: 179042
JPN_A2_PTJ_001.txt
JPN_A2_SMK_001.txt
JPN_B2_PTJ_001.txt
JPN_B2_SMK_001.txt
JPN_B11_PTJ_001.txt
JPN_B11_SMK_001.txt
JPN_B12_PTJ_001.txt
JPN_B12_SMK_001.txt

KWIC Plot File Cluster N-Gram Collocate Word Keyword
Cluster Types 2028 Cluster Tokens 4087 Page Size All hits 1 to 2028 of 2028 hits

	Cluster	Rank	Freq	Range	NormFreq	NormRange
1	i think it is	1	198	7	0.048	0.875
2	i agree with the	2	153	8	0.037	1.0
3	i think that it	3	143	8	0.035	1.0
4	i agree with this	4	139	8	0.034	1.0
5	i think smoking should	5	71	3	0.017	0.375
6	i think that smoking	5	71	4	0.017	0.5
7	i think that we	7	43	5	0.011	0.625
8	i think that the	8	40	8	0.01	1.0
9	i have a part	9	39	5	0.01	0.625
10	i think that college	10	37	3	0.009	0.375
11	i have two reasons	11	36	8	0.009	1.0
12	i have three reasons	12	31	7	0.008	0.875
13	i think college students	13	29	4	0.007	0.5
14	i think we should	14	27	6	0.007	0.75
15	i think that they	15	24	5	0.006	0.625
16	i disagree with the	16	23	7	0.006	0.875
17	i agree this statement	17	22	8	0.005	1.0
18	i agree that smoking	18	20	3	0.005	0.375
19	i agree with that	19	19	5	0.005	0.625

Search Term Words Case Regex Cluster Size 4 Min. Freq 1 Min. Range 1
i
Start Adv Search
Sort by Frequency Invert Order Search Term Position On Left On Right On Left/Right
Progress 100%
Time taken (creating cluster list) 0.1958 ms

Figure 9.3 (a and b) Screenshots of *AntConc* displaying clusters in the ICNALE corpus

length, frequency and/or range for the n-gram (criteria that are traditionally used to define "lexical bundles"), more salient or "important" n-grams can be identified. Figure 9.4a and b, respectively, show screenshots of *AntConc* displaying all the two-word and four-word n-grams in the ICNALE corpus. As the length of the n-grams increases, you will notice phrases such as *a part time job*, *restaurants in the country* and *should be completely banned* stand out. In this way, n-gram analysis can be useful in exploratory research, revealing features of a corpus that might easily go unnoticed through a close reading of individual texts or a casual inspection of the corpus as a whole.

How are words connected to other words?: collocate analysis

Cluster tools are useful for revealing phrase and MWU patterns when the words are contiguous (appearing next to each other). However, we also know that words are connected to each other at further distances. For example, in a learner's essay on the topic of smoking, we can imagine that the word *smoking* may be linked strongly with the word *banned*, as in the phrase *smoking should be banned*, even though the words are not contiguous. Corpus software tools can quicky and accurately calculate the strength of connection between a search word and every other word in the corpus using a statistical measure, with the Mutual Information and T-Score measures being common choices (for more information see Gries 2010 and Chapter 13, this volume). The result of such an analysis is a list of so-called "collocates" of a target word, with the strength of connection (or collocation) used to rank the words.

To prevent the tool from generating spurious collocates (e.g. words with very low frequencies that just happen to appear near the target word), the tools include options and filters. For example, *AntConc* has an option to only include collocates that reach a statistical threshold level based on log likelihood. It also has options to restrict collocates to only those that appear above a minimum frequency. Figure 9.5 shows a screenshot of *AntConc* displaying the collocates of *smoking* in the ICNALE corpus that appear statistically significantly together (log likelihood; $p < 0.05$) and have a minimum frequency of ten in the corpus. The strongest collocate is *cessation*, which appears 3 times to the left and 12 times to the right of *smoking* in the corpus in phrases such as *smoking cessation leads to reduced stress*. The next highest collocate is *section*, which appears far more frequently in the corpus, but not quite at the same strength of association. One phrase in the corpus where this collocate appears is *divided in smoking and non smoking section*, revealing that perhaps this collocate reflects a common language learning error (*section* being treated as a plural noun). As expected, the word *banning* (rank 10) is also a strong collocate of *smoking*, appearing in phrases such as *banning smoking*, *banning of smoking* and *banning all smoking areas*.

Collocate analysis is an extremely powerful way to identify patterns of language usage. It is not surprising, therefore, that many online tools offer this function in different forms, including *FLAX*,[45] *Hyper Collocation*,[46] *Just* the *Word*,[47] *SkELL*,[48] *StringNet*[49] and *WriteAway*.[50] As mentioned earlier, there are also offline tools such as *#LancsBox*[5] that can present collocates of a target word in the form of a network of connected nodes, where clicking on one node will expand the network to show further connections between the collocate and its related collocates.

(a)

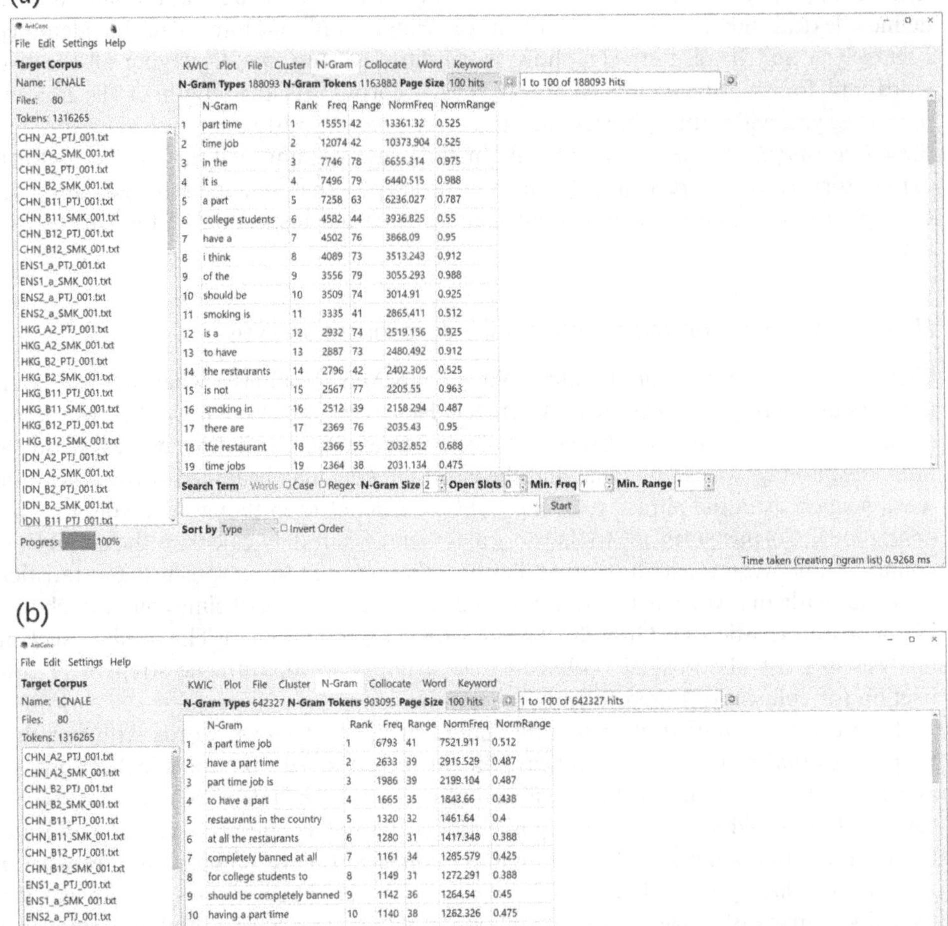

(b)

Figure 9.4 (a and b) Screenshots of *AntConc* displaying n-grams in the ICNALE corpus

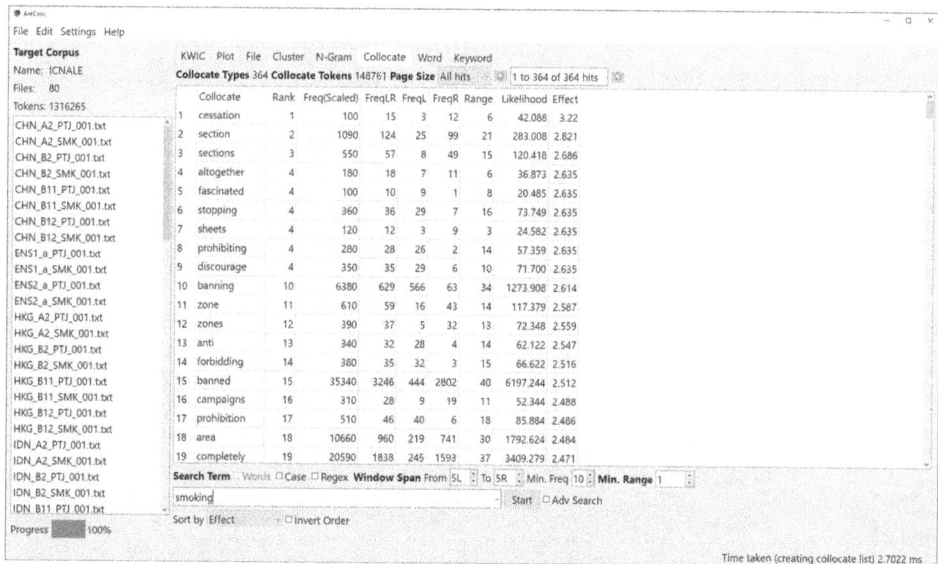

Figure 9.5 Screenshot of *AntConc* displaying the collocates of *smoking* in the ICNALE corpus

How are words used in context?: concordance analysis

Understanding why words, keywords, clusters, n-grams, lexical bundles and collocates appear at the ranks they do requires analysing the context in which they appear in a corpus. One way to do this is simply by searching for the item in an individual text and then closely reading that text to understand the context. However, when there are many tens, hundreds or thousands of texts in the corpus, this becomes a serious challenge. Also, it is virtually impossible to identify frequently occurring patterns of usage this way. Corpus linguists understood this problem from the very earliest days and developed software tools to address the problem. The result is a concordancer (sometimes referred to as Key-Word-In-Context (KWIC) concordancer).

Concordancers are designed to find all the occurrences of a search term in a corpus and display these in an ordered fashion together with the words that surround them. The display is usually referred to as a "concordance", and the analysis of concordances is often referred to as "concordancing". Figure 9.6 shows a screenshot of *AntConc* displaying the concordance for the search term (or node) *smoking* in the ICNALE corpus. You will notice many interesting features from the figure. First, the concordance lines do not correspond to sentences. Rather, they are designed to position the target word in the center of the screen surrounded by a fixed number of characters (or words) to the left and right. (Note, however, that some concordancers give the option to display concordance lines as complete sentences.) Second, the lines are ordered by the frequency of occurring patterns in the results according to the sort parameters. In Figure 9.6, these are the phrases that result from combining the first, second, and then third word to the right of the search word as indicated by the 1R, 2R, and 3R settings at the bottom of the screen. In AntConc, these are referred to as KWIC patterns. This ordering allows salient patterns to be noticed as you scroll through the concordance. For example, the ordering shown in Figure 9.6 immediately reveals that *smoking is a bad...* is the most salient smoking pattern used by the

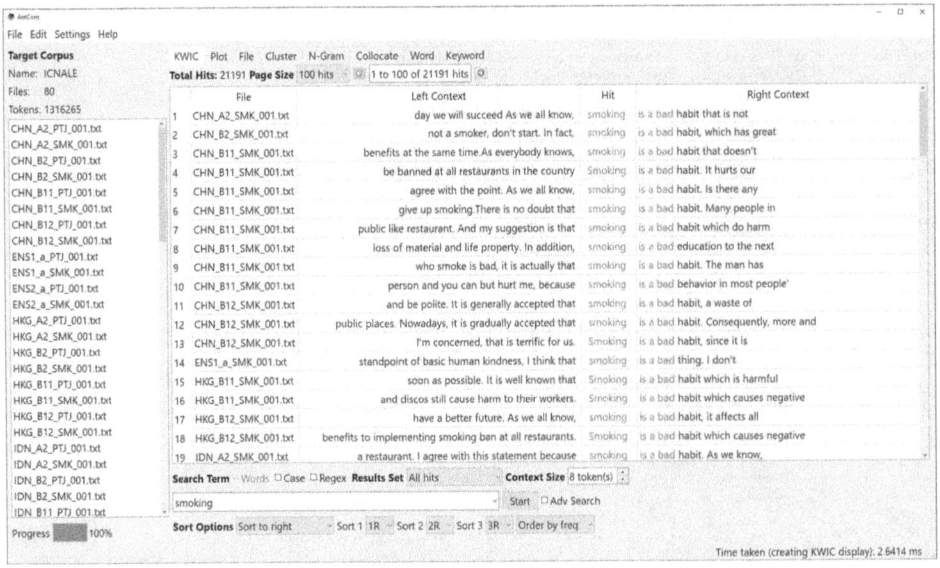

Figure 9.6 Screenshot of *AntConc* displaying the concordance for the search term *smoking* in the ICNALE corpus

learners in the corpus. Note that the ordering presented in *AntConc* is a first in the field, with other tools opting to order concordance lines alphabetically according to the sort parameters (an option also available in *AntConc*). Newcomers to the field may question why an alphabetical ordering of the lines would be used in so many tools, despite its obvious limitations. For a discussion of this intriguing, question, see Anthony (2018).

Another feature of concordancers is that they usually provide a way for the user to see the target word in a concordance line within a wider context. For example, in *AntConc*, if you click on the target word in any concordance line, the software will jump to the *File* tool and show the target word within the context of the original file. Finally, you may notice a Results Set option in the concordance display of *AntConc*. This allows a so-called "thinning" of the results to reduce the overall number of lines displayed in the concordance whilst still revealing common patterns of usage. This feature (and the equivalent "random sample" option in other tools) is particularly useful when dealing with very large corpora that might generate thousands or millions of results and thus far too many to scroll through to find all the salient patterns.

Concordancers are not the only tools that can reveal the contexts in which a word is used. One alternative tool is called a concordance plot (or dispersion plot) tool, which shows the positions of a search word or phrase in all the corpus texts, positioned relative to the start and end points of the files. Figure 9.7a and b show screenshots of *AntConc* displaying the concordance plot for the phrase *banning smoking* in the ICNALE corpus. In Figure 9.7a, the lengths of the texts are normalised, which makes it easier to compare the relative positions of the search term across texts. In Figure 9.7b, the relative lengths of the texts are maintained, highlighting the fact that some essays are a great deal longer or shorter than others. In both figures, it is clear that the phrase *banning smoking* is not dispersed through texts in the same way, with some learners using the term frequently,

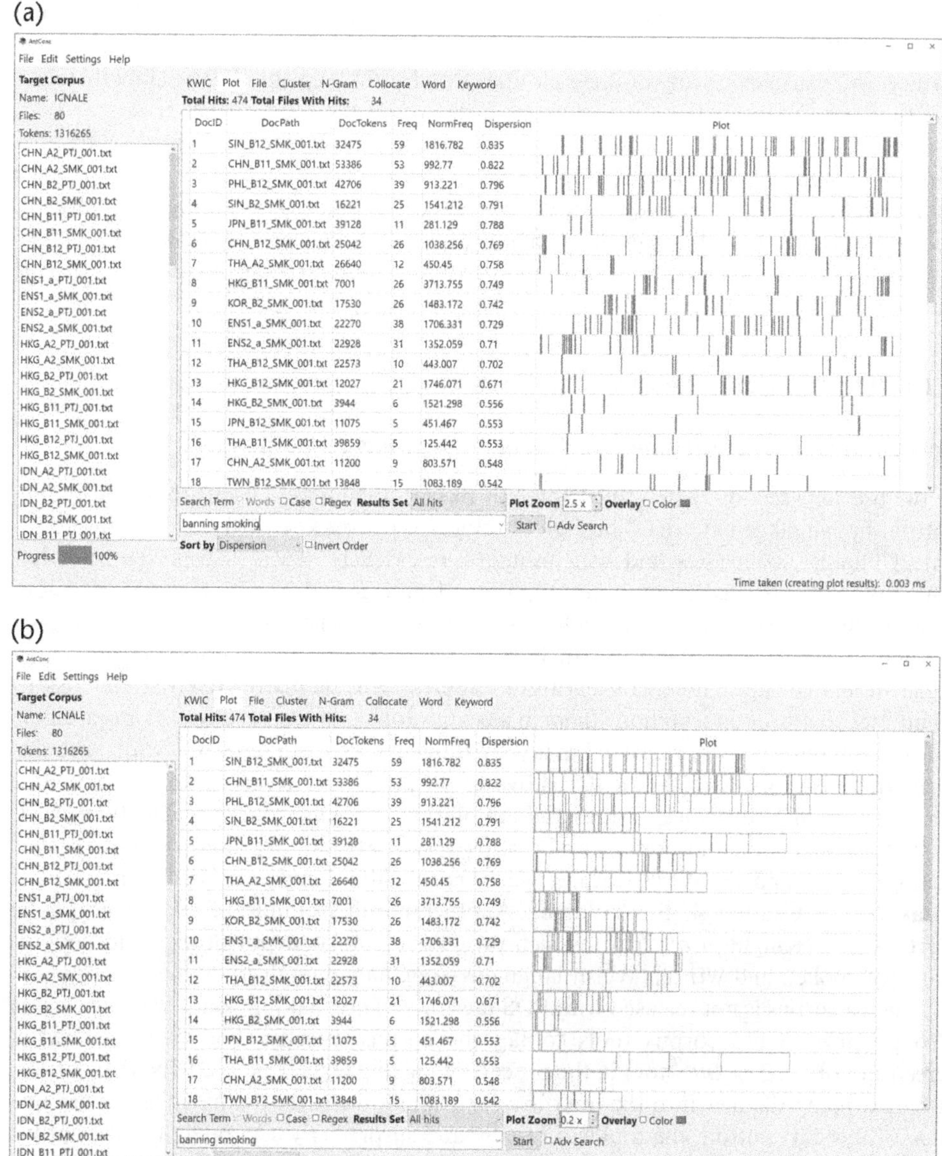

Figure 9.7 (a and b) Screenshots of *AntConc* displaying concordance plots for the phrase *banning smoking* in the ICNALE corpus

presumably arguing for or against the banning of smoking, and others rarely using the phrase at all, perhaps because they express an alternative opinion. To investigate this further, you can click on any of these plot lines, and *AntConc* will take you directly to the *File* tool and show the word in context as it does with the concordance tool.

There are also concordancers specifically designed to work with aligned or parallel corpora. Online tools such as *SketchEngine*[3] and dedicated offline tools such as *AntPConc,*[51] for example, allow you to generate concordances in a corpus of works in one language and link these results to matching lines in a corpus of translations. These tools can be invaluable for translators and others working on multi-lingual projects (see Chapter 34, this volume).

3 Finding top-down language patterns

How can corpora be searched for top-down features of languages?

In the previous section, I described some of the most common corpus tools for finding bottom-up language patterns. Through the study of words, keywords, clusters, n-grams, lexical bundles, collocates and concordances, researchers can also begin to form hypotheses and make predictions about top-down language features, such as text cohesion, register, discourse structure and pragmatic phenomenon. The first step towards this goal is often to tag the corpus texts with POS information and/or annotate the texts with higher-level markup that signals features of interest. It is then a relatively trivial task to count these features or search for them in a corpus tool as you would count or search for words and phrases. Fortunately, many existing corpora are released with such information. *The Spoken BNC2014*[52] (Love *et al.* 2017) is a recent example of such a corpus, containing a rich set of tags and annotations marking token-level features, such as POS, lemma forms, utterances and overlaps; sub-text-level features, such as speaker demographics; and text-level features, such as the situational context and number of speakers (see Chapter 4, this volume). Another recent example of such a corpus is *CorCenCC*[17] (Knight *et al.* 2020), which provides a similar depth of tags and annotations for spoken and written Welsh language (see Chapter 3, this volume).

When a corpus is not released with POS tags or you are making your own corpus, it is also possible to use corpus tools to tag the corpus directly. Figure 9.8a shows a screenshot of the *TagAnt*[19] tool in the process of tagging texts from the ICNALE corpus. After dropping the files into the interface (or loading them via the file menu), with one click of the start button, the tool can rapidly and surprisingly accurately tag the corpus with POS tags using the *TreeTagger*[20] engine. Figure 9.8b shows a screenshot of *AntConc* displaying a wordlist for the ICNALE corpus using this tagged data. The most frequent "words" are now a sentence period, a comma, and the word *the*, which is tagged as a determiner (DT). It is important to note that to use this POS data, it had to be loaded into AntConc via one of the corpus manager settings in the file menu. Other settings in the manager allow AntConc to read data with even more complex formats.

Although POS-tagging corpus data is a fast and relatively simple task, manually annotating corpora for top-down-level features of language can be a slow and error-prone activity. Therefore, several corpus software developers have strived to develop tools that can automatically annotate corpus texts with top-down features, although this is still a surprisingly underdeveloped area (see Chapter 8, this volume). One very early example is *AntMover,*[53] which aims to automatically annotate the "move" structure of

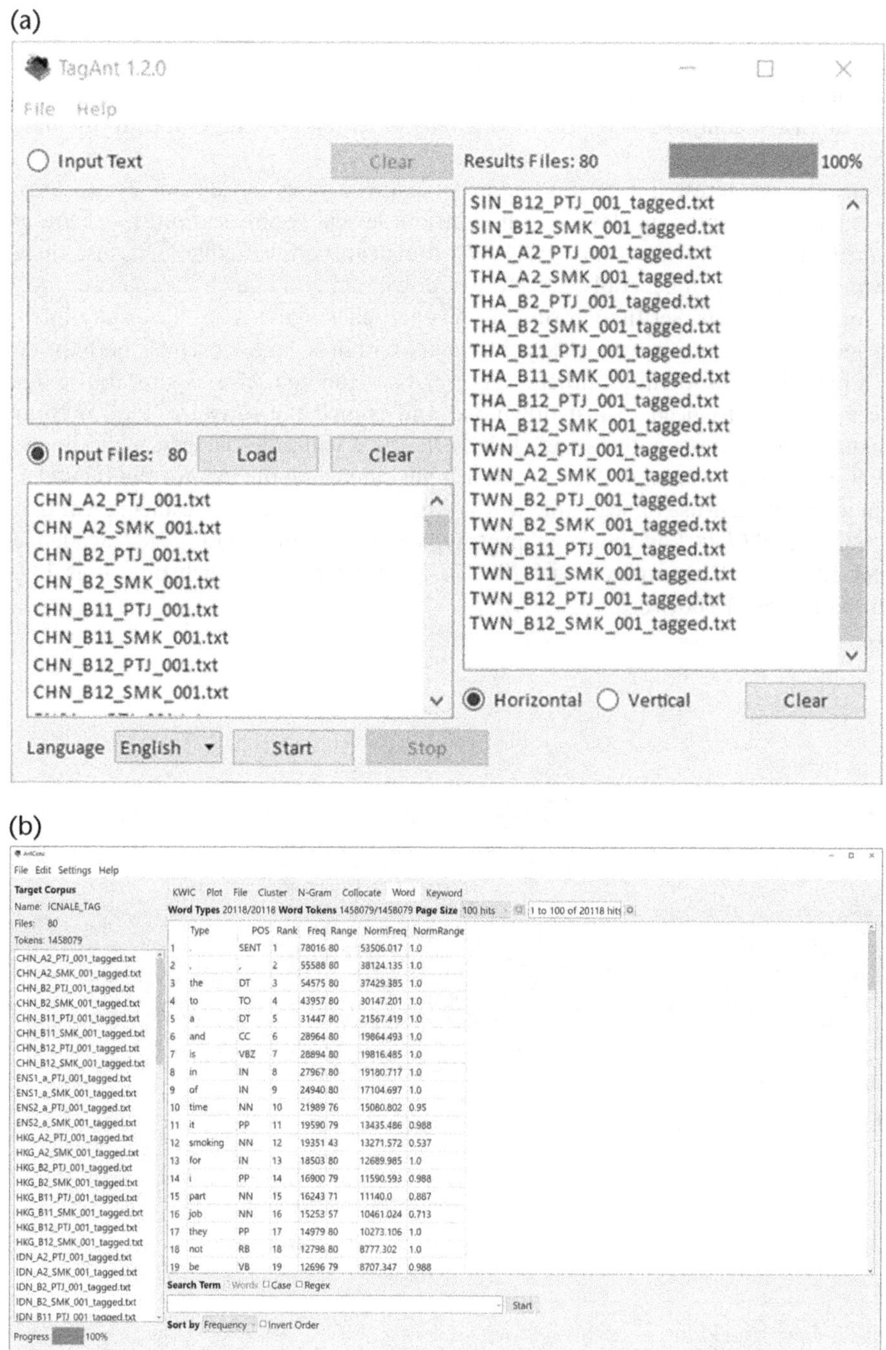

Figure 9.8 (a and b) *TagAnt* POS tagging texts and *AntConc* displaying a wordlist for the ICNALE corpus tagged by part of speech

texts in a way that is reminiscent of the work of Swales (1990) and many others. A more recent example is *AntCorGen,*[15] mentioned earlier, which collects research articles and assigns them to section categories such as *title*, *abstract* and *introduction*, allowing researchers to easily compare and contrast language features as they appear in these higher-level structural units.

For researchers interested in evaluating texts against a range of top-down measures, such as readability, sentiment, lexical cohesion and lexical sophistication, *the Suite of Automatic Linguistic Analysis Tools (SALAT)* tools can be invaluable.[54] To use these freely available tools, you generally need to just download and launch the relevant tool, load in your target texts, set the various options and click start. Also, if you are interested in identifying prototypical or atypical texts within a larger corpus, perhaps to confirm a hypothesis or identify outliers, the *ProtAnt*[25] can be useful. Again, to use this freeware tool, you just need to just download and launch the software, load in your target texts, set the various options and click start, and it will rank the texts accordingly. Figure 9.9 shows a screenshot of *ProtAnt* after it has ranked all the texts of the ICNALE corpus in terms of their use of academic words[55] (Coxhead 2000). The results reveal that the file *SIN_B2_PTJ_001* is the most prototypically academic, with 178.7 academic words per 1,000 words, compared with file *THA_B2_SMK_001*, which only uses 33.8 academic words per 1,000 words.

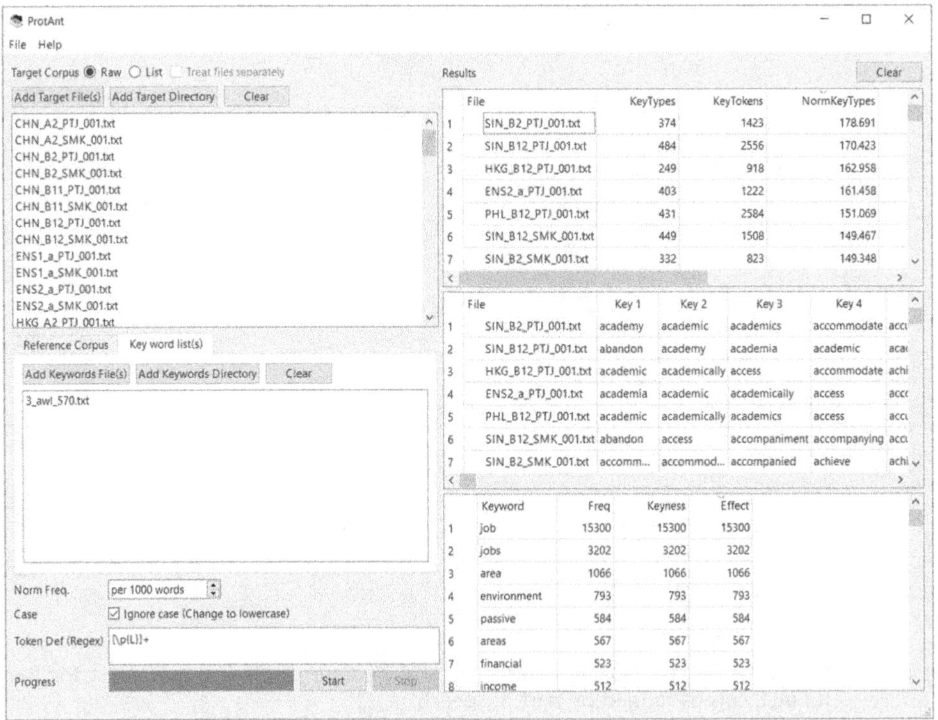

Figure 9.9 Screenshot of *ProtAnt* after ranking texts of the ICNALE corpus by their use of academic words

4 Managing data in and between corpus tools

Online, offline and DIY software tools provide corpus linguists with a huge range of options for collecting, analysing and visualizing data. However, no single tool is likely to provide the full range of features and functions necessary to complete a corpus study. For example, most data collection tools will offer few, if any, ways to analyse the data collected. General-purpose corpus toolkits like *AntConc*[4] provide many of the basic features for analysing corpora, but they do not provide advanced statistical measures and visualisation techniques that are only available in cutting-edge DIY tools. Conversely, DIY tools are unlikely to come with any data and can usually only perform a very narrow range of analyses. So, they not only need to be supplied with data, but they also need to output data in a form that can be used with other tools. These limitations of all online, offline and DIY tools highlight the importance of *data interoperability*, a term used in computer science to describe the ability of systems to share data and resources with other systems.

Anthony and Evert (2019) consider four levels of interoperability that can be adopted by different systems. One level is the adoption of a common corpus format, which allows corpus creators to build corpora with the knowledge that the data can be loaded smoothly into an existing tool for analysis. One commonly adopted format at this level is the UTF-8 encoded plain text format. Corpora saved in this format are stripped of all tags and markup, and the UTF-8 encoding ensures that all the word strings in the corpus will be interpreted and rendered correctly by the corpus analysis tool. The ICNALE corpus used in the previous section is released in such a format. Another commonly adopted format is a simple tagged corpus format, where each word in a UTF-8 encoded plain text corpus is tagged with an underscore followed by the relevant tag (e.g. *the_dt*).

A second level of interoperability is the adoption of a standardised plug-in API architecture by the host system, which allows third-party developers to add features to existing systems. While such plug-ins are commonly found in many computer applications (notably text editors such as *Notepad++*[56] and programming environments such as *Visual Studio Code*[57]), they are rarely found in current corpus analysis tools, perhaps due to the size of the community and the limited number of people in the community who could contribute such plug-ins. The third level of interoperability is a reverse of the second level, with the host system adopting a generalised platform that feeds data and results to specialised plug-in modules. Again, though, this is rarely seen in existing corpus tools.

The fourth and perhaps most promising form of interoperability described by Anthony and Evert (2019) is the adoption of a standard *data* format (as compared to a *corpus* format). Already, this form of interoperability is used to some extent by many tools. For example, tools will often output results in a UTF-8 encoded text-based, tabular format (e.g. tab-separated values [TSV]) that can be loaded directly into spreadsheet programs like Microsoft Excel for further analysis and visualisation. The tabular format can also be read by most DIY tools, offering more opportunities for analysis and visualisation. Anthony and Evert extend this idea and propose a standardised tabular data model composed of one or more tables stored as a collection of text files in a TSV format or collectively in a single *SQLite*[58] database file. The structure can capture the output of corpus tools in a standardised way and greatly simplify the sending and receiving of data between tools. *AntConc*[4] fully adopts this *multiple TSV (MTSV)* format for import and export of all data, but it has yet to be incorporated into other mainstream tools. However, the authors have received interest from many of the major corpus tool developers in the field and so there is hope that it will become more widely adopted.

5 Programming your own tools

Much of this chapter has been focused on the possibilities afforded by online, offline and DIY corpus software tools. This does not mean, however, that you should ignore the option of programming your own custom tools in a truly DIY fashion. Minimally, a basic understanding of programming will provide you with an understanding of how existing corpus tools work, raising your awareness of their limitations and the existence of possible bugs in the system. A basic knowledge of programming is also vital if you want to safely use DIY scripts provided by others. Simple mistakes in the format of input data or the commands to run these tools can often render the output completely meaningless. However, a knowledge of programming also offers far greater possibilities. During the corpus data collection stage, simple file (re)naming and cleaning scripts that run in fractions of a second can save a researcher days, weeks or even months of manual work. During the analysis stage, existing scripts can be modified or new scripts created that circumvent the need to manually edit data to suit a particular tool or constantly switch between different tools before arriving at a desired answer. In short, programming opens the possibility to create new tools that advance your research is ways that no existing tools can. In the words of Stefan Gries (2009: 12), programming puts you 'in the driver's seat'.

Fortunately, learning to program is becoming far easier than it was in the past. Firstly, modern scripting languages such as Python are designed to be easier to understand and more "human-readable" than older languages, like C. Secondly, there are now many freely available and excellently designed online courses such as those at *w3schools.com,*[59] as well as numerous online video tutorials on *YouTube* and other content creator platforms. Thirdly, languages such as Python and R have a huge community of users, who are willing to answer questions and offer advice on programming issues at sites such as *StackOverflow.*[8] This is especially true in the case of the R community within corpus linguistics, which has a strong and growing presence in the field. As an example, the *Language Technology and Data Analysis Laboratory (LADAL)*[60] run by Martin Schweinberger provides information and practical, hands-on tutorials to help researchers develop their data, text and statistical analysis skills. In short, there has never been a better time to start learning to code.

Notes

1 *CQPWeb*. Accessed at: https://cqpweb.lancs.ac.uk/
2 *English-Corpora.org*. Accessed at: https://www.english-corpora.org/corpora.asp
3 *Sketch Engine*. Accessed at: https://www.sketchengine.eu/
4 *AntConc*. Accessed at: https://www.laurenceanthony.net/software/AntConc/
5 *#LancsBox*. Accessed at: http://corpora.lancs.ac.uk/lancsbox/
6 *Wmatrix*. Accessed at: http://ucrel.lancs.ac.uk/wmatrix/
7 *WordSmith Tools*. Accessed at: https://www.lexically.net/wordsmith/
8 *Stack Overflow*. Accessed at: https://stackoverflow.com/
9 *GitHub*. Accessed at: https://github.com/
10 *NLTK*. Accessed at: https://www.nltk.org/

11 *Stefan Th. Gries companion website for QCLWR*: Accessed at: http://www.stgries.info/research/qclwr/qclwr.html
12 *AntFileConverter*. Accessed at: https://www.laurenceanthony.net/software/antfileconverter/
13 *Web Scraper*. Accessed at: https://webscraper.io/
14 *BootCaT*. Accessed at: https://bootcat.dipintra.it/
15 *AntCorGen*. Accessed at: https://www.laurenceanthony.net/software/antcorgen/
16 *PLOS ONE*. Accessed at: https://journals.plos.org/plosone/
17 *CorCenCC*. Accessed at: https://www.corcencc.org/
18 *FireAnt*. Accessed at: https://www.laurenceanthony.net/software/fireant/
19 *TagAnt*. Accessed at: https://www.laurenceanthony.net/software/TagAnt/
20 *TreeTagger*. Accessed at: https://www.cis.uni-muenchen.de/~schmid/tools/TreeTagger/
21 *SegmentAnt*. Accessed at: https://www.laurenceanthony.net/software/segmentant/
22 *UCREL Semantic Analysis System (USAS)*. Accessed at: http://ucrel.lancs.ac.uk/usas/
23 *Stanford Parser*. Accessed at: https://nlp.stanford.edu/software/lex-parser.shtml
24 *UAM CorpusTool*. Accessed at: http://www.corpustool.com/
25 *ProtAnt*. Accessed at: https://www.laurenceanthony.net/software/protant/
26 *AntMover*. Accessed at: https://www.laurenceanthony.net/software/antmover/
27 *AWSuM*. Accessed at: http://langtest.jp/awsum/
28 *What is JavaScript*? Accessed at: https://developer.mozilla.org/en-US/docs/Learn/JavaScript/First_steps/What_is_JavaScript
29 *MICUSP*. Accessed at: https://elicorpora.info/
30 *Kaleidographic*. Accessed at: http://www.kaleidographic.org/
31 *Jack Grieve's homepage*. Accessed at: https://sites.google.com/view/grievejw
32 *Jack Grieve's resources*. Accessed at: https://sites.google.com/view/grievejw/resources?authuser=
33 *Stefan Th. Gries homepage*. Accessed at: http://www.stgries.info/index.html
34 *Scottish Corpus of Texts and Speech (SCOTS) corpus*. Accessed at: https://www.scottishcorpus.ac.uk/
35 *OpenSourceShakespeare*. Accessed at: https://www.opensourceshakespeare.org/
36 *CLARIN Resource Families*. Accessed at: https://www.clarin.eu/portal
37 *KfNgram*. Accessed at: http://www.kwicfinder.com/kfNgram/kfNgramHelp.html
38 *AntGram*. Accessed at: https://www.laurenceanthony.net/software/antgram/
39 *What is open source?* Accessed at: https://opensource.com/resources/what-open-source
40 *ICNALE: The International Corpus Network of Asian Learners of English*. Accessed at: http://language.sakura.ne.jp/icnale/
41 *Programming with Unicode*. Accessed at: https://unicodebook.readthedocs.io/unicode.html
42 *MultiLingProfiler*. Accessed at: http://www.multilingprofiler.net/
43 *Compleat Lexical LexTutor*. Accessed at: https://www.lextutor.ca/
44 *AntWordProfiler*. Accessed at: https://www.laurenceanthony.net/software/antwordprofiler/
45 *FLAX*. Accessed at: http://flax.nzdl.org/
46 *Hyper Collocation*. Accessed at: https://hypcol.marutank.net/?q=highlightandd=f
47 *Just the Word*. Accessed at: http://www.just-the-word.com/
48 *SkELL*. Accessed at: https://skell.sketchengine.co.uk/
49 *String Net*. Accessed at: http://nav4.stringnet.org/ret.php
50 *WriteAway*. Accessed at: http://writeaway.nlpweb.org/
51 *AntPConc*. Accessed at: https://www.laurenceanthony.net/software/antpconc/
52 *British National Corpus 2014*. Accessed at: http://corpora.lancs.ac.uk/bnc2014/
53 *AntMover*. Accessed at: https://www.laurenceanthony.net/software/antmover/
54 Suite of Automatic Linguistic Analysis Tools (SALAT). Accessed at: https://www.linguisticanalysistools.org/
55 *The Academic Word List*. Accessed at: https://www.wgtn.ac.nz/lals/resources/academicwordlist
56 *Notepad++*. Accessed at: https://notepad-plus-plus.org/
57 *Visual Studio Code*. Accessed at: https://code.visualstudio.com/
58 *SQLite*. Accessed at: https://www.sqlite.org/
59 w3schools.com. Accessed at: https://www.w3schools.com/
60 *Language Technology and Data Analysis Laboratory*. Accessed at: https://slcladal.github.io/

Further reading

Anthony, L. (2013) 'A Critical Look at Software Tools in Corpus Linguistics', *Linguistic Research* 30(2): 141–61. (A look at the history of corpus tools development and a proposal for corpus tools development as part of a team.)

Anthony, L. (2021) 'Programming for Corpus Linguistics', in M. Paquot and St. Th. Gries (eds) *Practical Handbook of Corpus Linguistics*, Berlin and New York: Springer, pp. 181–207. (An introduction to the basic concepts of programming with step-by-step examples for writing simple corpus tools.)

McEnery, T. and Hardie, A. (2012) *Corpus Linguistics: Method, Theory and Practice*, Cambridge: Cambridge University Press. (A comprehensive review of corpus linguistics charting its history from the 1960s and earlier and explaining the most common tools, methods and practices.)

Viana, V., Zyngier, S. and Barnbrook, G. (eds) (2011) *Perspectives on Corpus Linguistics*, Amsterdam: John Benjamins Publishing. (A unique book that records interviews with leading corpus linguists of the field who express their opinions on a wide range of topics, including the importance of tools and the value of programming knowledge.)

References

Anthony, L. (2018) 'Visualization in Corpus-Based Discourse Studies', in C. Taylor and A. Marchi (eds) *Corpus Approaches to Discourse: A Critical Review*, London: Routledge, pp. 197–224.

Anthony, L. and Evert, S. (2019) 'Embracing the Concept of Data Interoperability in Corpus Tools Development', *paper presented at Corpus Linguistics 2019 (CL2019)*, 1st–3rd July 2019, Cardiff, UK.

Armstrong, R. A. (2014) 'When to Use the Bonferroni Correction', *Ophthalmic and Physiological Optics* 34(5): 502–508.

Clark, R. (1966) *Computers and the Humanities* 1(3): 39.

Coxhead, A. (2000) 'A New Academic Word List', *TESOL Quarterly* 34(2): 213–38.

Dearing, V. A. (1966) *Computers and the Humanities* 1(3): 39–40.

Egbert, J. and Biber, D. (2019) 'Incorporating Text Dispersion into Key Word Analyses', *Corpora* 14(1): 77–104.

Gries, St. Th. (2009) 'What is Corpus Linguistics?', *Language and Linguistics Compass* 3: 1–17.

Gries, St. Th. (2010) 'Useful Statistics for Corpus Linguistics', in A. Sánchez Pérez and M. Almela Sánchez (eds) *A Mosaic of Corpus Linguistics: Selected Approaches*, Frankfurt am Main: Peter Lang, pp. 269–91.

Gries, St. Th. (2016) *Quantitative Corpus Linguistics with R: A Practical Introduction*, London: Routledge.

Ishikawa, S. (2013) 'The ICNALE and Sophisticated Contrastive Interlanguage Analysis of Asian Learners of English', in S. Ishikawa (ed.) *Learner Corpus Studies in Asia and the World*, Kobe, Japan: Kobe University, pp. 91–118.

Knight, D., Morris, S., Fitzpatrick, T., Rayson, P., Spasić, I., Thomas, E-M., Lovell, A., Morris, J., Evas, J., Stonelake, M., Arman, L., Davies, J., Ezeani, I., Neale, S., Needs, J., Piao, S., Rees, M., Watkins, G., Williams, L., Muralidaran, V., Tovey-Walsh, B., Anthony, L., Cobb, T., Deuchar, M., Donnelly, K., McCarthy, M. and Scannell, K. (2020) *CorCenCC: Corpws Cenedlaethol Cymraeg Cyfoes - The National Corpus of Contemporary Welsh*, Cardiff: Cardiff University. 10.17035/d.2020.0119878310

Love, R., Dembry, C., Hardie, A., Brezina, V. and McEnery, T. (2017) 'The Spoken BNC2014: Designing and Building a Spoken Corpus of Everyday Conversations', *International Journal of Corpus Linguistics* 22(3): 319–44.

Moon, R. (2007) 'Sinclair, Lexicography, and the COBUILD Project: The Application of Theory', *International Journal of Corpus Linguistics* 12(2): 159–81.

Pojanapunya, P. and Watson Todd, R. (2018) 'Log-likelihood and Odds Ratio: Keyness Statistics for Different Purposes of Keyword Analysis', *Corpus Linguistics and Linguistic Theory* 14(1): 133–67.

Price, K. (1966) *Computers and the Humanities* 1(3): 39.

Reed, A. (1978) *CLOC [Computer Software]*, Birmingham: University of Birmingham.
Schmitt, N., Dunn, K., O'Sullivan, B., Anthony, L. and Kremmel, B. (2021) *Knowledge-Based Vocabulary Lists*, Sheffield: Equinox Publishing Ltd.
Sinclair, J., Jones, S. and Daley, R. (2004) *English Collocation Studies: The OSTI Report*, London: Continuum.
Smith, P. H. (1966) *Computers and the Humanities* 1(3): 39.
Swales, J. (1990) *Genre Analysis: English in Academic and Research Settings*, Cambridge: Cambridge University Press.

10

What are the basics of analysing a corpus?

Christian Jones

1 What are the basics?

Although corpora are not new and have been used to analyse language for many years, we are fortunate to live in an era where many are freely available and increasingly, the software we can use to analyse our own data is also free (for example, Anthony 2019; Davies 2019). However, Evison (2010) is right to suggest that on their own, corpora cannot tell us much about language (see also Chapter 2, this volume). The insights come from our own analysis of the data. In order to analyse a corpus, we need to know three main things: why we are using a corpus, what we aim to find out and what the limitations of our analysis are. I will briefly discuss each area in turn.

Why am I using a corpus?

A corpus is simply a searchable collection of texts (written or spoken) stored in an electronic form. Sinclair (1991) suggests that this collection should be principled so that it represents the types of language we wish to better understand. Corpora are often mono-modal (using one medium, normally text) but can be multi-modal (using more than one medium such as text and video). Due to costs and ethical considerations (we cannot anonymise video easily), most corpora are mono-modal, though this situation is changing and increasingly, multi-modal corpora are appearing (Adolphs and Carter 2013; Ishikawa 2019). Such corpora are particularly useful when analysing speech and sign languages (see also Chapter 7, this volume).

We can use a corpus to uncover patterns of usage and to test our intuitions about how language is used by particular groups of users, in particular texts (Jones and Waller 2015). It can tell us which form or forms occur with greater frequency, how words are used together in discourse and allow us to compare this usage across different types of data (commonly, spoken vs. written), historical periods and genres. What a corpus cannot do is tell us why certain forms are used, why speakers tend to use one item with or before another or why a certain form is rarely used. Such findings must come from our own interpretations of the data. As long as we keep this in mind, even a basic search

DOI: 10.4324/9780367076399-10

of a corpus can reveal something to us and will often provide a useful starting point for further investigations.

What am I trying to find out?

Before we start any search, it will help if the purpose is clear. This will influence how we search, what corpora we search and what kinds of analysis we undertake. Jones and Waller (2015: 158) describe a principled research cycle as one which starts from our beliefs and intuition about a language area, moves on to examining the literature to check what others have told us about this, sets clear research questions, decides on which corpora to search and then how best to analyse them. To give an example, a search can start from a question which an English as a second language (ESL) student might ask a teacher, such as "Do people say X?" We can give an intuitive answer and then check in a corpus. In this case, our "research question" is "how frequently do people say x?" As the student uses the word "say", we will want to look in a spoken corpus and preferably one which contains the kind of speech they wish to use. It will then be helpful to make comparisons between the frequency of this item in different corpora, perhaps comparing its frequency with written corpora. Finally, we may wish to undertake qualitative analysis of concordance lines to explore how speakers use this item in context. Carter (2016) is a good example regarding how quantitative and qualitative exploration can be combined to answer questions about how language is used; in this case to analyse creativity in everyday conversations.

What are the limitations of my analysis?

It is important to be aware of the limitations of any analysis. Any search will be limited by the design and size of a corpus. A spoken corpus, for example, might only contain examples of monologic talk, which will mean we cannot use it to explore how items are used in interactive dialogue. Also, there can sometimes be a tendency to think that the larger the corpus, the more authoritative it is. This is not automatically true, and even a corpus of many millions of words is still only a partial view of the language (Cook 1998). Instead, it is better to consider whether the size of the corpus allows you to make observations about language in use which match the questions you are seeking answers for.

The sections in this chapter show some basics of analysing corpora, looking at both quantitative frequency analysis and qualitative analysis of concordance lines and extended texts, often in combination. In each section, I have tried to show how we can work with open-access corpora or use freely available analysis tools to work with our own data. I have also tried to show that analysing corpus data does not need to be limited to searching for single words. For obvious reasons of space and brevity, the examples given are not accompanied by extensive explanations of the research project they could be part of and are simply included to be illustrative.

2 Exploring frequency

One of the simplest and most common means of analysing a corpus is to look at frequency. The most basic search which can be undertaken is to check on the frequency of a word or longer sequence. All freely available corpora will enable you to do this via the "search" function, and this can give you the frequency of items in one corpus or when

Table 10.1 The frequency of *I mean* per million words in informal TV shows across time using the TV corpus

1950s	*1960s*	*1970s*	*1980s*	*1990s*	*2000s*	*2010s*
339.34	379.66	701.38	756.35	713.81	761.18	803.66

comparing two corpora or sub-corpora (see Chapter 9, this volume). Increasingly, comparisons can also be made across different times to track the historical change of an item, if the corpus is large enough to do so. This is achieved by simply searching for the item you wish to check and typing it into the "search" box. The example in Table 10.1 (see later) shows the frequency of *I mean* per million words across the TV corpus (Davies 2019), a corpus of 325 million words of informal TV shows from the 1950s to the 2010s from the UK and Ireland, the United States, Australia and New Zealand. These data are produced using the "chart" button available with this corpus.

This shows a steady increase across time so that there are now more than double the number of occurrences than in the 1950s in these data. A finding such as this does not tell us a great deal about the language, but it allows us to say, as suggested by analyses of other spoken corpora (e.g. O'Keeffe *et al.* 2007), that *I mean* is very frequent in much spoken language, particularly the language of informal conversations. A simple search also enables us to compare frequency across sub-corpora. We can do this by clicking "sections" and choosing which two sub-corpora we wish to compare. For example, we may wish to check the frequency of *I mean* in the UK/Ireland shows in this corpus compared to US shows in this corpus. Selecting both tells us that the item is somewhat more frequent in the American shows (US = 822.01 per million words, UK/Ireland = 508.1 per million words). This basic information can provide a starting point for further analysis. We could, for example, look at some of the data in context and try to work out if there are any differences in the way this item functions in the US and UK/Ireland data.

Commonly, frequency is also analysed by means of producing a frequency list, which can tell us the words or larger sequences which occur most often in any given corpus. Many corpora will now produce frequency lists, and in some cases, (e.g. Spoken BNC2014, Love *et al.* 2017) several different types are available, including all word forms or only lemmas (a base form such as "run" from which all inflections such as "runs" can be derived). A list based on all word forms will provide separate frequency counts for items such as "runs", "running" and "run", while one for lemmas would give one count only for "run".

We can also use corpus analysis software to produce frequency lists from our own data. Table 10.2 gives an example of three such frequency lists, two derived from the Spoken BNC2014 (11 million words of informal conversations of British English) and one produced using data from the UCLan Speaking Test Corpus (USTC) (Jones *et al.* 2018: 46), a corpus of 91,000 words of successful (at pass level) speaking tests at Common European Framework of Referenced for Languages (CEFR) B1–C1 levels. It shows the top ten most frequent items in each corpus. The data in this example are taken from the B1 section of the USTC corpus, and the figures show the total number of occurrences in each corpus.

Table 10.2 Sample frequency lists

N	*Spoken BNC2014 (all word forms)*	*Spoken BNC2014 (lemmas)*	*USTC B1 sub-corpus (all word forms)*
1.	I (435,613)	Be (743,461)	Er (1,391)
2.	It (354,259)	I (467,272)	I (1,126)
3.	You (311,450)	It (354,267)	The (688)
4.	The (297,665)	You (311,515)	And (523)
5.	's (292,876)	The (297,666)	To (461)
6.	And (275,495)	And (275,496)	Erm (320)
7.	Yeah (260,026)	Yeah (260,026)	In (296)
8.	That (230,781)	Not (240,180)	Is (288)
9.	A (215,473)	Do (236,550)	So (288)
10.	? (213,437)	A (232,816)	A (269)

As mentioned previously, such frequency lists on their own tell us little about the language used in any given corpus, and there is obviously a need to interpret them ourselves. It is also important to remember that most frequency lists will contain a high proportion of grammatical items (such as the determiner *the*) as their most common item. Frequency lists will also be heavily influenced by the type of data in any corpus. This results here in common items, such as the contracted *s*, which reflect the general nature of unrehearsed speech. The register of each corpus also has a large influence on the most frequent item in such lists (Biber 2012). Here, the Spoken BNC2014 features conversations between native speakers on topics they have chosen, while the USTC features spoken test data. Alongside the fact that these are second-language speakers at a pre-intermediate level, the frequency of items such as *er* and *so* in the learner data reflects the register of these tests. Learners do not choose the topics, have to speak in real time and will be aware that this is a test where they may need to give extended answers and reasons. All of these factors may account for the frequent use of items such as *er* and *so* in these data.

Despite the earlier caveats, as with basic frequency searches, lists such as these give useful initial indications about corpus data and provide starting points which we can then follow up on. The frequency lists provided earlier, for example, seem to indicate some of the typical linguistic features which characterise the interactive nature of conversations: the need for speakers to express viewpoints, to address each other (*I, you*), to respond to each other (*yeah*) and to link turns and ideas together (*it, that*). We can choose areas such as these for further investigation. A closer look at the USTC data, for example (Jones *et al.* 2018: 46), shows how the use of *it's* is the eighteenth most frequent word in this corpus at the B1 level (152 occurrences). This significantly increases as levels progress from B1 to C1 (at the C1 level there are 276 occurrences), as learners become better able to link the ideas not only within their own turn but also across turns, adding to what other speakers are saying and referring back to things said by others or themselves. Jones *et al.* (2018: 119) give the following as an example of this. The students are discussing tourism as part of an interactive task.

(1)
<$2 M > I personally think the same about the location the hotel is really important.

<$1 F > Yeah.
<$2 M > I said if **it's** near to the attraction point then that's good but if **it's** far away then you know it will be costly to travel up.
<$1 F > Yeah spend more

[USTC]

Normalisation

As suggested, raw frequency is a fairly basic measure, and it is also important to note that an item may display more frequency simply because the size of the corpus is bigger. *The*, as an example, will obviously occur more times in a larger corpus than in a smaller one. For this reason, we also need to consider normalisation, which simply means how many times a word or larger pattern occurs per million words, or per thousand words in smaller corpora. Many corpora will now produce these data for you (see, for example, the data in Table 10.1), but if not, you can calculate this figure for yourself.

To take a simple example, we may wish to look at the use of the pronoun *I* from the frequency lists in Table 10.2. Such comparison is simple in the Corpus of Contemporary American English (COCA) (Davies 2008), a written and spoken corpus totalling more than a billion words. When we look at the "chart" view in search, we can see the overall frequency is a little higher overall in the spoken data (2,283,884 occurrences in 126.1 million words) compared to the fiction sub-corpus (2,191,345 occurrences in 118.3 million words), but the occurrences per million words are a little higher in the fiction corpus (18,106.58 spoken vs. 18,520.17 fiction). This simply shows us that looking only at raw frequency is not always the most helpful form of analysis.

You may also wish to calculate this with your own data and make comparisons with other smaller corpora. To produce such a figure in your own data, Evison (2010: 126) gives a simple formula. Divide the total amount of occurrences by the number of tokens in the corpus and multiply by 1,000 to get occurrences per 1,000, or 10,000 or 1 million to obtain those figures. Your choice of which calculation to use will be dictated by the size of your corpus, and it is important to be consistent in your calculations so that you compare data from different corpora in the same way. With smaller corpora, using a per 1,000 figure is generally considered to be most useful. For example, in the USTC data (Jones *et al.* 2018) at the C1 level, *yeah* occurs 442 times in this sub-corpus of 23,083 tokens (this excludes the examiner utterances), giving a normalised frequency of 19.14 occurrences per 1,000 words, while at the B1 level it occurs 250 times in 17,171 tokens (excluding the examiner utterances), giving a normalised frequency of 14.55 per 1,000 words. This shows us that the use of *yeah* increases as learners move from the B1 to C1 level, and as Jones *et al.* (2018: 127) note, is one linguistic marker which shows the increased ability to interact across turns and to co-construct conversations, which increases as levels progress.

3 Exploring keyness

Another way we can compare frequency is by looking at keyness. This allows us to look at the frequency of items in one corpus in comparison to another, normallya larger, reference corpus, and check which words occur significantly more (positive keywords) or significantly less (negative keywords) in our corpus compared to a reference corpus. The

Table 10.3 Positive keywords in USTC (B2) compared with LINDSEI as a reference corpus

N	*Keyword*	*Freq.*	*%*	*Texts*	*RC. Freq.*	*RC. %*	*Keyness*	*P-value*
1	Er	1,312	6.16	17	29,325	3.02	536.42.	p<.001
2	Culture	88	0.41	6	174	0.02	316.25	p<.001
3	Agree	55	0.26	15	61		243.59	p<.001
4	Can	204	0.96	17	2,224	0.28	204.39	p<.001
5	Technology	31	0.15	4	8		186.75	p<.001
6	You	518	2.43	17	9,842	1.24	185.92	p<.001
7	Will	137	0.64	16	1,165	0.15	184.46	p<.001
8	Preston	24	0.11	10	0		174.89	p<.001
9	UK	19	0.09	10	0		138.45	p<.001
10	Weather	42	0.2	5	101	0.01	138.28	p<.001

RC = reference corpus; % = the percentage of the total corpus which this item's total occurrences represent.

corpora must be comparable to make keyness searches worthwhile, and it is important to be clear about what we are comparing and why. For example, if we compare the USTC data with another corpus of spoken learner data, we need to ensure it contains data similar to interactive spoken exams and not monologues.

Many open-access corpora now have keyness built in as a feature. For example, the CLiC corpus (Mahlberg *et al.* 2016) features the works of Dickens and allows us to compare these with a mixed reference corpus of nineteenth-century novels using the "keywords" function. We can also calculate this with our own data. The example in Table 10.3, taken from Jones *et al.* (2018: 56), shows the positive keywords in comparison between the USTC learner spoken test data (B2 level) and the Louvain International Database of Spoken English Interlanguage (LINDSEI) (Gilquin *et al.* 2010) corpus, which has over a million words of learner speech from learner of different L1s, levels and ages, and used interview data which had clear similarities to the USTC data. For example, there were discussion tasks in both datasets. To undertake the analysis, a wordlist was made from learner turns in the LINDSEI data with the Wordlist function in WordSmith (Scott 2015) and then the keyword function was used to make comparisons with our data. Other freely available software will also calculate key words in the same way by comparing word lists (see Chapter 9, this volume).

The keyness score here is based on log likelihood, which measures the statistical significance of keywords. Significance measures help us to be sure results are important in terms of keyness, and commonly anything below 0.05 ($p < 0.05$) is considered significant; that is, there is a less than 5 per cent chance that the results are due to chance. The p-values displayed in Table 10.3 simply show that each keyword is significantly more frequent in the USTC corpus in comparison to LINDSEI.

Although some of the words here (such as *UK* and *weather*) clearly reflect the topics discussed in the USTC data, others such as *can* and *will* are of interest to us as researchers and are something we could follow up on with further study. We could examine uses of *can*, for example, by looking at this in context and deciding how form(s) and functions compare with those in the LINDSEI data (see Jones *et al.* 2018, chapter 2 for an extended discussion of keywords in USTC).

Quick and simple comparisons to determine more or less frequent use of an item in comparisons between one corpus and another can also be made using an online log-likelihood calculator (Log-Likelihood and Effect Size Calculator 2020; Rayson and Garside 2000). This calculator allows you to input the frequency of words or phrases in corpora of different sizes and make a comparison using log likelihood as a measure, determining whether each item is significantly more (+) or significantly less (-) frequent in one corpus compared with another. The calculator produces a score, and the online site provides a detailed breakdown of how different scores relate to different levels of significance. For example, if the score is 6.63, it will be significant at the level $p < 0.05$ (see also Rayson and Garside 2000 and the calculator website for more details).

An example of such a calculation can be made by looking at *think* from the Spoken BNC2014 and comparing its frequency with the spoken section of COCA (Davies 2008), which consists of 126 million words of US TV and radio show data of an unscripted nature. When inputting these data, you need the raw frequency (not the normalised frequency) of the item plus the number of tokens in each corpus. Checking this via the calculator shows that *think* is used significantly more (+4040.81, $p < 0.0001$) in the Spoken BNC2014 and indicates that it may be an item worthy of further investigation. We may wish to look at this item in context and see what forms and functions exist with it (which other words or phrases are used in conjunction with it, for example) and then try to understand what this can tell us about each set of data. One obvious comparison here might be differences in usage between UK and US English and why these might occur in each corpus.

4 Exploring larger patterns

Analysing keywords and wordlists may suggest that we can only use frequency measures to look at single words. However, in most data, it is common to look at larger patterns of language use. One simple way to do this is to search data for collocates of frequent words or keywords, an option which most open-access corpora and all commonly available software will give us. We can do this in a corpus such as the 100-million-word American soap opera corpus (Davies 2011) by clicking the "collocates" section, then inputting our search term and then choosing the span of collocates (the number of words to the left or right) which we are checking collocate with the node word (the target word). Commonly, researchers wish to look at collocates which occur up to four words before or after the target word, but it is perfectly possible to simply check what comes directly after or before a target word. In this corpus (and associated corpora available from the same site), if we click "relevance" below the search bar, we can produce a mutual information score. This shows us how high the chance of co-occurrence is in any one corpus, and the higher the score is from zero, the higher chance there is of co-occurrence, suggesting a strong association (McEnery and Wilson 2001; Oakes 2004). Note that this score does not necessarily show us the words which most frequently come before or after a target item, but those which are most likely to co-occur. To give an example, we can search for a word such as *paper* in the American soap opera corpus and look for collocates occurring up to four words after this. The data show us that the top five items (in terms of MI scores) are *clips* (11.93), *shredder* (10.67), *airplanes* (10.42), *scissors* (10.13) and *trail* (10.02), which all differ in frequency (*clips* = 24, *shredder* = 7, *airplanes* = 11, *scissors* = 38, *trail* = 112). This tells us that in these data, we are most likely to find *paper* in co-occurrence with *clips*. Such searches are useful, as they start to

Table 10.4 Four-word n-grams in the CLiC Dickens corpus

N	*Four-word n-grams*	*Frequency*
1	As if he were	405
2	As if he had	266
3	At the same time	255
4	In the course of	215
5	In the midst of	206
6	As if it were	204
7	I beg your pardon	200
8	I don't know what	200
9	On the part of	200
10	What do you mean	199
11	With an air of	197
12	It would have been	194
13	Said the old man	194
14	In a state of	192
15	For the first time	190

show how words are patterned together and can give us insights to usage in a particular corpus, which we can then compare to usage in other corpora. For more about collocates, see Chapters 9, 14 and 15, this volume.

We can also look at larger patterns of co-occurrence by searching for what are termed "n-grams", also commonly referred to as clusters, chunks or formulaic sequences in the literature, albeit with slight differences in the definitions (see Chapter 15, this volume). N-grams have been defined as 'two, three, four (or more) sequence[s] of words that combine in data' (Jones and Waller 2015: 194). Online corpora and corpus tools allow us to specify the length of n-gram we wish to search. Although longer sequences are possible, there is a large drop-off in frequency after four-word sequences (O'Keeffe *et al.* 2007), and so most searches will focus on items from two to four words in length. A search in the CLiC fiction corpus (Mahlberg *et al.* 2016) under "clusters", for example, produces the list of four-word n-grams from the whole Dickens corpus displayed in Table 10.4.

Such n-grams can be a useful basis for further investigation of corpora. We could, for example, simply click on an n-gram to see how it is used in context in sets of concordance lines and how it contributes to meaning in extended text. Extract 2 shows some samples of *with an air of* from the CliC corpus, looking at the texts from Dickens. These are displayed in a list here, but in the actual corpus, the keyword in context (in this case "with an air of") is displayed in the middle of the concordance line and will be highlighted.

(2)

1. carrying a reticule came curtsying and smiling up to us **with an air of** great ceremony. "Oh!" said she. "The wards in Jarndyce!
2. Yes." He folded his arms and sat looking at me **with an air of** the profoundest astonishment

3. friend," pursued Miss Flite, advancing her lips to my ear **with an air of** equal patronage and mystery, "I must tell you a secret
4. one knee, and gently smoothed the calves of his legs, **with an air of** humble admiration. 'That I had but eyes!' he cried
5. you see.' 'What is this!' said Gashford, turning it over **with an air of** perfectly natural surprise. 'Where did you get it from
6. replied Barnaby, finishing his task, and putting his hat on **with an air of** pride. 'I shall be there directly.' 'Say "my lord,"
7. the more impressive, Mr. Micawber drank a glass of punch **with an air of** great enjoyment
8. 'Trotwood,' said Mr. Dick, **with an air of** mystery, after imparting this confidence

(CliC [online] 2020)

We can see that in terms of form, it tends to be followed by abstract nouns such as *mystery*. In terms of function, it serves to tell us about how certain characters behave, allowing the author to build a picture of their character. It is therefore a device by which the author can speak to us about characters and help to formulate our view (the view the authors hope we will take) of them. A more detailed picture of this n-gram could be developed by looking at how it relates to particular characters in particular Dickens books. It is possible to use the "search for types" function in CLiC to produce all examples of *pride,* for example, and then look at which texts they are used in and by which characters. Such investigations allow us to interrogate the data in some depth, moving from the general to the specific and away from single words.

We can also look at n-grams within our own data and produce frequency lists, which we can normalise and also explore for keyness in some of the ways described in previous sections. In the freely available corpus analysis tool Antconc (Anthony 2019), this function is under the "clusters/n-grams" tab, and as with the CLiC corpus, you can specify the length of n-gram you wish to search for. Table 10.5 shows the top 10 four-word n-grams from the USTC data, as described in Jones et al. (2018: 67), at the B2 level. Note that in this data, a contracted form is counted as two words

When we view n-grams in this way, it gives a clearer indication about the prefabricated nature of much language use and how the most frequent items of language are often formulaic in nature, something which has been described for many years in corpus research (e.g. Sinclair 1991). As mentioned in earlier discussion of word frequency, such data also reflect the specific register of the corpus. In these USTC data, learners are answering and discussing questions and tasks set by an examiner. The nature of such questions and tasks often requires learners to express their own view and the views of their fellow test takers. This is one reason why there are several sequences with *think.* It is also notable that there are no examples of sequences many learners will be taught to express a viewpoint around words such as *opinion* or *view*. Jones *et al.* (2018) suggest that this is because learners in these data favoured items which are multi-functional, and *I think it's* can be used both to buy time and express an opinion, for example.

It is also worth noting that some n-grams may seem fragmentary (such as *They don't have* in Table 10.5) and need further investigation and interpretation in order to understand how the language is being used. These fragments can be part of larger, more meaningful frames such as e.g. *They don't have + noun* and can serve important functions in discourse.

Table 10.5 Four-word n-grams from USTC at the B2 level

N	*Four-word n-grams*	*Frequency*
1.	I agree with you	21
2.	I think it's	20
3.	A lot of time	19
4.	What do you think	16
5.	Spend a lot of	15
6.	I don't like	12
7.	I don't know	10
8.	They don't have	10
9.	Do you think about	9
10.	I don't think	9

Lexico-grammar

Investigating larger patterns of language beyond the single word can also enables us to explore lexico-grammar. Halliday and Matthiessen (2004: 45) define this term as 'patterns which lie somewhere between structures and collocations having some of the properties of both'. They give the example of *take pride/delight + in + -ing,* where we can see the collocates of *take* are also commonly associated with *in* and *ing*. In other words, words go together with other words, but are also likely to be found in the company of certain grammatical patterns. Many modern corpora make it relatively simple to search for these patterns (see Chapter 11, this volume, for more on patterns). We can start from an example such as *I think* and search for what most commonly comes after it in the COCA spoken corpus (Davies 2008), which consists of unscripted TV and radio shows. Using a wildcard search (search for *I think* *), we can see that one very common item which comes directly after it is *there's*. If we then search for *I think there's* * we see the most common pattern is *I think there's a* and what follows this is most often *lot*. We can then search the data further using the parts of speech (POS) next to the search bar or further wildcard searches to find out the most common patterns. In this case, the most common pattern is *a lot + of + noun phrase* (e.g. *people/blame/truth*). This allows us to build a picture of the lexico-grammar of *I think* in these data. We can see from this simple analysis that in this spoken section of the COCA corpus, *I think* is often patterned in a particular way, which we could describe as *I think + there's + a lot of + noun phrase* and we can also list the most frequent noun phrases. We might also wish to check the frequency of *there's* with countable nouns such as *people* in contrast to the use of *I think there are + countable noun phrase.* Viewing concordance lines also allows us to investigate how this pattern functions. Some sample concordance lines are shown in extract 3.

(3)

1. **I think there's a lot of people** that are pulling for her. Mr-JACKSON: Yeah. STORM: Yeah
2. .Well **I think there's a lot of people** who are committing on a plan that they haven't read.

3. my ideals or some of my views. But **I think there's a lot of people** similar to me who maybe don't get labeled the same way
4. like in "The Wizard of Oz," and **I think there's a lot of people** now stepping back and saying, "Oh, my God.
5. **I think there's a lot of people** that would love to attack us in the United States.
6. Well, I think there is there -- **I think there's a lot of people** who believe it was a suicide, but there's still a lot
7. **I think there's a lot of people** that have ideas against the government or against whatever philosophies or groups,
8. **I think there's a lot of - I think there's a lot of people** over there that's been around too long. But I mean…

[COCA spoken sub-corpus]

One obvious function here (due to the nature of the discourse) is to use this sequence to refer back to the topic of interest and add support to your view. Saying *a lot of people* adds authority to an opinion and, of course, means you do not need to say exactly who those people are and therefore your viewpoint is harder to challenge! It is also clear that such a sequence contributes to the cohesion of this discourse, allowing speakers to link ideas within their own turns in relation to the topic under discussion.

5 Exploring language in context

Every time we look in a corpus, we are, of course, exploring language within a context or contexts. However, it is also possible to use a corpus to explore how language forms and functions are used in extended discourse. One way we can do this is by comparing language used in different corpora to explore how lexical items are "primed" (Hoey 2005) in terms of forms and function in different types of discourse. A definition of lexical priming is as follows:

> the theory of lexical priming suggests that each time a word or phrase is heard or read, it occurs along with other words (its collocates). This leads you to expect it to appear in a similar context or with the same grammar in the future, and this "priming" influences the way you use the word or phrase in your own speech and writing.
>
> *(Macmillan Online Dictionary 2020)*

Hoey (2005) further suggests that we are also primed to expect items to occur in particular positions in a sentence or spoken turn and with particular meanings and that these will vary according to the genre of the texts we are looking at. Jones and Waller (2015:31) give the example of *married,* which they show tends to colligate (go together with a particular grammatical form) with *is* as part of a non-defining relative clause in newspaper texts and functions to add information when people are being described in news reports. For example, 'The woman, who is married and lives in Sefton, was attacked when…'. They contrast this with its use in a spoken corpus (from COCA) where it is primed to co-occur with *get* and colligate with *going to* and allows TV show guests (particularly on chat shows) to describe future or future in the past plans such as *I was going to get married.*

Table 10.6 The priming of *divorced* in academic and fictional texts

	Academic corpus	*Fictional corpus*
Words which most frequently follow *divorced*	*from* (294, 2.5), *or* (37, 0.3), *families* (12, 0.1)	*him* (67, 0.6) *when* (40, 0.3) *from* (40, 0.3).
Common patterns	X+ is divorced from reality	She divorced him / …and divorced him
Common meaning/use	Used to form part of a discursive argument Figurative meaning.	Used to form part of a narrative description. Literal meaning.
Examples	*Yet the mantra is not entirely divorced from reality*	*A few years later, when his cocaine habit had bankrupted them, she divorced him.*
Position	End of clause	Complete clause, often following the conjunction *and* at the end of sentences.

Searching the COCA corpus and starting from a word or sequence allows us to investigate language in this way. To use a similar example to *married*, we may be interested in how an item such as *divorced* is used in contrasting corpora. We can investigate this by searching for items to get an overall picture of how they are used by using the "word" function in this corpus. This gives us collocates, clusters, texts, topics associated with a word and concordance lines at one click. In this case, common collocates listed are *parent* and *get,* while *divorced mother of two* and *parents are getting divorced* are common clusters. We can then explore these patterns by searching for them in contrasting corpora and checking how they are primed in different texts. In the search section of COCA, this can be achieved by a search for *divorced* and by simply checking what comes after it with a wildcard search (*divorced* *). If we also compare usage in different datasets (in this case the academic and fiction sub-corpora), we can then examine concordance lines to see how the item is primed in these different texts. Some summative results are displayed for *divorced* in Table 10.6. The academic corpus in this case is 119.8 million words of academic texts and the fiction corpus of 118.3 million words. Frequency figures are displayed here overall in total and then per million words in brackets.

This kind of description shows how the item *divorced* is primed in different ways within different corpora and shows how we can use a corpus to explore language in context. This helps to build descriptions that take account of how different genres of texts within corpora will affect the usage and meaning of particular items. Using corpora in this way can help us to move beyond basic frequency searches and to combine both qualitative and quantitative analysis of language in context.

Further reading

Adolphs, S. and Carter, R. A. (2013) *Spoken Corpus Linguistics: From Monomodal to Multimodal*, London: Routledge. (This provides a useful description and analysis, showing some of the possibilities available when designing and working with spoken corpora.)

Collins, L.C. (2019) *Corpus Linguistics for Online Communication: A Guide for Research*, London: Routledge. (This is a useful and highly practical introduction to using corpora to investigate forms of online communication such as the use of social media.)

Hoey, M. (2005) *Lexical Priming: A New Theory of Words and Language*, London: Routledge. (This is an influential book, which shows how corpora can be used to investigate and further our understanding of language in use.)

Timmis, I. (2015) *Corpus Linguistics for ELT: Research and Practice*, London: Routledge. (Aimed at those teaching English as a second or foreign language, this is a useful and practical introduction to corpus linguistics which will benefit anybody interested in working with corpora.)

References

Adolphs, S. and Carter, R. A. (2013) *Spoken Corpus Linguistics: From Monomodal to Multimodal*, London: Routledge.

Anthony, L. (2019) *AntConc (Version 3.5.8) [Computer Software]*, Available from: https://www.laurenceanthony.net/software/antconc/ [Accessed 15 February 2020].

Biber, D. (2012) 'Register as a Prediction of Linguistics Variation', *Corpus Linguistics and Linguistics Theory* 3(2): 9–37.

Carter, R. A. (2016) *Language and Creativity: The Art of Common Talk*, 2nd edn, London: Routledge.

CLiC [Online] [1 February 2020], Available from click: http:\\lic.bham.ac.uk

Cook, G. (1998) 'The Uses of Reality: A Reply to Ronald Carter', *ELT Journal* 52(1): 57–63.

Davies, M. (2008-) *The Corpus of Contemporary American English (COCA): 600 million words, 1990-present*. [Online], [6 February 2020], Available from: https://www.english-corpora.org/coca/.

Davies, M. (2011-) *Corpus of American Soap Operas: 100 million words*. [Online], [20 February 2020]. Available from: https://www.english-corpora.org/soap/.

Davies, M. (2019-) *The TV Corpus: 325 million words, 1950-2018*. [Online], [20 February 2020] Available from: https://www.english-corpora.org/tv/.

Evison, J. M. (2010) 'What Are the Basics of Analysing a Corpus?', in A. O'Keeffe and M. J. McCarthy (eds) *The Routledge Handbook of Corpus Linguistics*, London: Routledge, pp. 122–35.

Gilquin, G., De Cock, S. and Granger, S. (2010) *LINDSEI: Louvain International Database of Spoken English Interlanguage*. [CD-ROM], Louvian: Presses Universitaires de Louvain.

Halliday, M. A. K. and Matthiessen, C. (2004) *An Introduction to Functional Grammar*, 3rd, London: Routledge.

Hoey, M. (2005) *Lexical Priming: A New Theory of Words and Language*, London: Routledge.

Ishikawa, S. (2019) 'The ICNALE Spoken Dialogue: A New Dataset for the Study of Asian Learners' Performance in L2 English Interviews', *English Teaching* (The Korea Association of Teachers of English) 74(4): 153–77.

Jones, C. and Waller, D. (2015) *Corpus Linguistics for Grammar: A Guide for Research*, London: Routledge.

Jones, C., Byrne, S. and Halenko, N. (2018) *Successful Spoken English: Findings from Learner Corpora*, London: Routledge.

Log-Likelihood and Effect Size Calculator (2020) [Online], [2 February 2020]. Available from: http://ucrel.lancs.ac.uk/llwizard.html.

Love, R., Dembry, C., Hardie, A., Brezina, V. and McEnery, T. (2017) 'The Spoken BNC2014: Designing and Building a Spoken Corpus of Everyday Conversations', *International Journal of Corpus Linguistics* 22(3): 319–44.

Macmillan Online Dictionary (2020) *Definition of lexical priming*. [Online], [5 February 2020]. Available from: https://www.macmillandictionary.com/dictionary/british/lexical-priming.

Mahlberg, M., Stockwell, P., de Joode, J., Smith, C. and O'Donnell, M. B. (2016) 'CLiC Dickens: Novel Uses of Concordances for the Integration of Corpus Stylistics and Cognitive Poetics', *Corpora* 11(3): 433–63.

McEnery, T. and Wilson, A. (2001) *Corpus Linguistics*, 2nd edn, Edinburgh: Edinburgh University Press.

Oakes, M. P. (2004) *Statistics for Corpus Linguistics*, Edinburgh: Edinburgh University Press.

O'Keeffe, A., McCarthy, M. J. and Carter, R. A. (2007) *From Corpus to Classroom: Language Use and Language Teaching*, Cambridge: Cambridge University Press.

Rayson, P. and Garside, R. (2000) 'Comparing Corpora Using Frequency Profiling', in *Proceedings of the workshop on Comparing Corpora held in conjunction with the 38th annual meeting of the Association for Computational Linguistics 1-8 October 2000*, Hong Kong, pp. 1–6.

Scott, M. (2015) *WordSmith Tools. v.6.0.0.252. [Online]*, Stroud: Lexical Analysis Software Ltd, Available from: http://lexically.net/wordsmith/ [Accessed 29 December 2015].

Sinclair, J. (1991) *Corpus, Concordance, Collocation*, Oxford: Oxford University Press.

11

How can a corpus be used to explore patterns?

Susan Hunston

1 Types of patterns

The term "pattern" is often used in corpus linguistics with a variety of meanings. Its core definition might be "an observed regularity", but the nature of that regularity is not fixed.

When considering this variation, a number of distinctions might be made. These can be summarised as:

a. The level of abstraction. "Pattern" may refer to specific words occurring together – something akin to "phraseology" – or it may refer to abstract categories such as grammatical classes or semantic categories.
b. The scale of the phenomenon. "Pattern" may be used to describe local regularity, that is, recurring sequences of words or categories, or a global regularity, that is, the greater or lesser frequency of a feature in specific populations of texts.
c. The nature of the corpus. "Pattern" may be used to describe the language in an individual text, or in the texts produced by an individual writer or in a general corpus of texts.
d. The source of the phenomenon. In those cases where a "pattern" is observed in a general corpus, it may be assumed that the pattern is the consequence of constraints imposed by the language itself (such as *start* followed by a to-infinitive verb) or that it is a consequence of people repeating the same ideas (such as *start* occurring in a clause beginning with the conjunction *before*).

These distinctions can be used to discuss a number of examples.

Repetition in the language of individual speakers may be observed without recourse to a corpus (see distinction c). Political speeches have long been known to incorporate this kind of regularity. One instance is the speeches of former US President Barack Obama, which contain many instances of patterning, such as those in examples 1 and 2.

 DOI: 10.4324/9780367076399-11

(1)
I've gone to some of the best schools in America and lived in one of the world's poorest nations.
(2)
The church contains in full the kindness and cruelty, the fierce intelligence and the shocking ignorance, the struggles and successes, the love and yes, the bitterness and bias that make up the black experience in America.

In example 1 we find repetition of the superlative and its co-text: *some of the best schools in America; one of the world's poorest nations*. In example 2 there is repetition of binomial opposites: *the kindness and cruelty; the intelligence and the ignorance; the struggles and successes; the love and the bitterness*. It is also notable that although Obama here creates patterns of repetition within his own speech, he also draws on patterns that are widely used in English, such as "quantity + *of the* + superlative adjective + plural-noun + *in* place" (*some of the best schools in America; one of the richest women in Germany*) or "*the* + group of people + *experience* (*the black experience; the visitor experience; the US experience*).

Turning to patterns identified in a corpus, the word "pattern" may be used to describe the co-occurrence of individual words (see distinction a). A researcher may talk about the patterns of usage of a word, meaning the phrases that word occurs in or the collocates it attracts. For example, the word *cake*, when it is used figuratively, might be observed to occur in the following phrases:

- *the icing on the cake;*
- *a piece of cake;*
- *have one's cake and eat it.*

These might be described as the "patterns" of the figurative word *cake*.

The word "pattern" can also refer to more abstract categories of language (see distinction a). For example, Lei and Liu (2018) use the term "collocation patterns" to refer to identified combinations of word classes. They specify 11 such patterns, including "adjective + noun" and "verb + noun". Thus there is a finite number of patterns and each one is precisely identified as a pair of word classes. Similarly, Lehmann (2018) refers to "four variant patterns" that are used with the verb *provide*. These are specified as "the *with*-pattern", "the *to*-pattern", "the *for*-pattern" and the "npnp pattern". Examples from the British National Corpus are "*providing* them with a route out of poverty", "*provide* exit visas to intellectuals", "*providing* a single nest site for a group of four birds" and "we did *provide* them facilities". In this example the "pattern" is not simply the co-occurrence of two words (such as *provide* and *with*), but the sequence of more abstract elements: verb + noun phrase + prepositional phrase.

Hanks (2013) specifies semantic categories as well as grammatical ones. For example, one of the patterns noted for the verb *agree* in the Pattern Dictionary of English Verbs (https://pdev.org.uk) is:

- [Human | Institution] **agree** to [Activity = Future | Proposition]

This notation specifies that in an example such as example 3, the subject (*he*) must be a noun phrase indicating a human being or human institution, and the to-infinitive clause (*to stand as Vice President*) necessarily indicates a future activity.

(3)
...he's agreed to stand as Vice President.

[BNC]

In the examples used so far, what has been described as a pattern might be said to be an integral part of how English works. Alternative explanations can be found for patterns, however (see distinction d). For example, the wordform *decide* is often preceded by phrases that suggest either rights and obligations (*a woman's right to decide; have the opportunity to decide; it is up to each local authority to decide; they will now have to decide; has 28 days to decide*) or possibility, ability and futurity (*a debate which could decide; they just cannot decide; the office will decide; has yet to decide; is planning to decide*). This has more to do with real-world conditions in which decisions are taken than with restrictions on the verb: we can or cannot decide, we have an obligation to decide or the right to make a decision rests with us. Hunston (2008) refers to patterns occurring as the result of what people often say as "semantic sequences".

The final example of how the word "pattern" is used takes us beyond concordance lines and refers to the distribution of a word or structure across a corpus or between corpora (see distinction b). For example, Laws and Ryder (2018) refer to 'the effect of context formality on the usage patterns of derivatives between different speech registers'. Here, 'usage patterns' means the relative frequency of a particular feature (derivatives) in sub-corpora comprising registers. In this chapter, however, it is local patterns, specifically those observed using concordance lines, that are the focus of discussion.

It is clear from this introductory discussion that the term "pattern" is a problematic one and is used in at least two senses. In a general sense it means any regularity in phrasing or in frequency that has been observed. In a technical sense a pattern can be a defined set of entities incorporating aspects of phrasing and/or frequency. This ambiguity as to whether we are looking at a general thing here or a specific one carries over into the examination of concordance lines, which is the topic of the next section.

2 Reading concordance lines

In this section we explore local patterns in a corpus, identified using the "keyword in context" (KWIC) method, otherwise known as the set of concordance lines. Essentially, concordance lines consist of a node word or phrase with a small amount of context (measured in characters) to the left and the right (see Chapters 9, 10 and 14, this volume, for more on concordances). In most concordancing programmes the amount of context can be increased on demand. Showing more context requires wrapping the lines, which gives a more "normal" reading experience but reduces the visual impact of any repetition. Most programs, too, allow the concordance lines to be manipulated in ways that make repetition visually salient. These techniques range from being able to sort lines so that the word(s) before or after the node occur in alphabetical order to using colour to identify word class.

For example, if concordance lines are obtained with the wordform *view* as the node word (the examples that follow are from the Bank of English corpus), sorting those lines so that the words immediately to the left of the node are in alphabetical order draws attention to the frequency of *from* and *of* in that position. These prepositions occur in the phrases *obscured / hidden from view* and *point of view*. Left-sorting also brings together, and so makes noticeable, those lines where *view* is preceded by *the* or *this*. *The view* focuses attention on the phrase *the view that*:

```
things that they didn't need. But the view that design is dead portrays the
  medieval scholars. Yet this was the view that all major Christian theologians
 eventually takes place. However, the view from the Moroccan side of the wall
      from the applicant. It took the view that the risk of his association
```

The frequency of *This view...* suggests that *view* is often used to refer back and to summarise a segment of the preceding discourse; this is labelled "encapsulation" in Sinclair's (1990/2004) terminology:

```
 the success of their treatment. This view of clients as experts on matters
 in Capital and Class (1986). 10 This view was expounded by RIIA prominents
biological and chemical weapons. This view was then supported by a senior
```

Sorting the lines to the right of *view* additionally draws attention to phrases where *view* is followed by *of*, and we might note that *view of* is often preceded by an adjective:

```
the success of their treatment. This view of clients as experts on matters
  Black himself did not have a clear view of the age at which a child could
  historians by and large take a dim view of my grandfather's role and
      which reflected a market-frame view of the state's responsibility to
```

Expanding the concordance lines allows ambiguities to be resolved. For example, expanding the lines where *view* is followed by *that* shows that there are two distinct patterns – *view* + appositive clause (example 4) and *view* + relative clause (example 5):

(4)
But the view that design is dead portrays the same lack of perspective for which the 1980s themselves are so famous. (Appositive clause)
(5)
Yet this was the view that all major Christian theologians insisted on – and many still do today. (Relative clause)

[BoE]

What should be obvious is that the concordancing programmes only find and organise the data. Interpretation is a human activity. We now consider what skills are needed to find patterns in concordance lines. As noted earlier, observing patterns involves identifying similarity and forming notional categories. It also involves ignoring distractors, that is, separating what might be important from what is unlikely to be so. (Note, though, that it is impossible to be precise about what is and is not patterned – what is overlooked by one observer might be noticed by another.) These points will be illustrated with a small set of concordance lines from the Bank of English obtained by searching for the lemma REACT. The result of this search gives examples of all wordforms in the lemma: *react, reacted, reacting, reacts.* Twenty random lines have been selected and then sorted so that the words following the node word are in alphabetical order.

```
1      could not believe the way Vieira reacted after he was dismissed. The
2   at all. When asked today how they'd react if the White House sent them a ne
3    step, which will enable viewers to react immediately to what they have see
4       two-thirds of the radical pairs reacting (in a field of typically only
5   any more, I don't know how he would react. Is there any point in making
6    growth because stock markets could react." Mr Visco said stock markets in
7       police officer at Selhurst Park reacted similarly to the Cantona inciden
8       mail, in New York, Adrian Clark reacted to Simon Hoggart's discussion of
9  market has come, and how people will react to it. The best seats and places
10 strength of a substance and the body reacts to fight off any diseases which
11      from the air and induce them to react to form harmless gases. Last
12           is the poster!" Herzen was reacting to a swelling trade in images. T
13     efforts you may find the magician reacting too early or late. Also bear in
14   conference was to see how he would react when asked questions by journalis
15 protect. How is management likely to react when a group threat- ens to quit?
16     twenty-year-old son felt free to react with such ferocity indicates that
17 eposition sulfur and nitrogen oxides react with atmospheric water vapor to
18 above such common tasks, refusing to react with the molecular masses. <p> Bu
19        Commentators and crowd alike reacted with astonishment when Lara
20       during the investigation. They reacted with anger and said: `The findin
```

Which of these lines might be grouped together to illustrate the "same pattern"? Looking only at what follows the node word, we might observe the following:

- a full stop (lines 5 and 6);
- the word *to* (lines 8, 9, 10, 11, 12);
- the word *when* (lines 14 and 15);
- the word *with* (lines 16, 17, 18, 19, 20).

Looking at the same evidence but in a more linguistically informed way we might express this as follows:

- REACT is followed by a subordinating conjunction (*after* in line 1, *if* in line 2 and *when* in lines 14 and 15); in each case the subordinate clause indicates an event that is the stimulus of the reaction;
- REACT is followed by a preposition (*to* in lines 8, 9 and 12, *with* in lines 16–20);
- REACT is followed by an adverb (lines 3 and 7); in each case the adverb is followed by the preposition *to*;
- REACT is followed by a to-infinitive clause (lines 10 and 11); in each case the clause indicates a reason for the reaction;
- In none of the lines is REACT followed by a noun phrase, an object. In other words, it is an intransitive verb.

A further observation might be that *react with* in lines 17 and 18 works differently from *react/reacted with* in lines 16, 19 and 20. The question that might prompt line 17 or 18 is something like "what does the object/substance (not) react with?", whereas the question prompting the other lines is something like "how did the person/people react?". Putting all this together suggests that a maximum of eight different patterns might be identified in these lines:

1. REACT followed by a subordinate clause indicating stimulus

```
1      could not believe the way Vieira reacted after he was dismissed. The
2   at all. When asked today how they'd react if the White House sent them a ne
14    conference was to see how he would react when asked questions by journalis
15 protect. How is management likely to react when a group threat- ens to quit?
```

2. REACT followed by the preposition *to*

```
8       mail, in New York, Adrian Clark reacted to Simon Hoggart's discussion of
9  market has come, and how people will react to it. The best seats and places
12            is the poster!" Herzen was reacting to a swelling trade in images. T
```

3. REACT followed by an adverb and then by the preposition *to*

```
3    step, which will enable viewers to react immediately to what they have see
7       police officer at Selhurst Park reacted similarly to the Cantona inciden
```

4. REACT followed by a to-infinitive clause indicating consequence

```
3    step, which will enable viewers to react immediately to what they have see
7       police officer at Selhurst Park reacted similarly to the Cantona inciden
```

5. REACT followed by the preposition *with* answering the question 'how?'

```
10 strength of a substance and the body reacts to fight off any diseases which
11      from the air and induce them to react to form harmless gases. Last
```

6. REACT followed by the preposition *with* answering the question 'what?'

```
16     twenty-year-old son felt free to react with such ferocity indicates that
19         Commentators and crowd alike reacted with astonishment when Lara
20      during the investigation. They reacted with anger and said: `The findin
```

7. REACT followed by a full stop

```
17 eposition sulfur and nitrogen oxides react with atmospheric water vapor to
18 above such common tasks, refusing to react with the molecular masses. <p> Bu
```

8. Other lines

```
5   any more, I don't know how he would react. Is there any point in making
6    growth because stock markets could react." Mr Visco said stock markets in
```

Some observers might wish to amalgamate some of these groups. For example, it might be argued that group 3 is simply a variant of group 2 – that the presence or absence of the adverb does not affect the pattern of "REACT + *to* + noun". It is possible, too, to join group 6 with groups 2 and 3 because in each case the prepositional phrase is obligatory. Others might argue that groups 1, 4 and 7 should be conflated because in each case REACT is the end of a clause. Still others would want to add group 5 to those because, it could be argued, in those lines the prepositional phrase beginning with *with* adds only peripheral information. Adding line 13 from group 8, this would yield only two groups:

A. REACT coming at the possible end of a clause

```
1      could not believe the way Vieira reacted after he was dismissed. The
2   at all. When asked today how they'd react if the White House sent them a ne
5   any more, I don't know how he would react. Is there any point in making
6    growth because stock markets could react." Mr Visco said stock markets in
10 strength of a substance and the body reacts to fight off any diseases which
11       from the air and induce them to react to form harmless gases. Last
13     efforts you may find the magician reacting too early or late. Also bear in
14    conference was to see how he would react when asked questions by journalis
15 protect. How is management likely to react when a group threat- ens to quit?
16       twenty-year-old son felt free to react with such ferocity indicates that
19           Commentators and crowd alike reacted with astonishment when Lara
20        during the investigation. They reacted with anger and said: `The findin
```

B. REACT followed by the preposition *to* or *with* as a necessary part of the clause

```
3    step, which will enable viewers to react immediately to what they have see
7        police officer at Selhurst Park reacted similarly to the Cantona inciden
8        mail, in New York, Adrian Clark reacted to Simon Hoggart's discussion of
9  market has come, and how people will react to it. The best seats and places
12            is the poster!" Herzen was reacting to a swelling trade in images. T
17 eposition sulfur and nitrogen oxides react with atmospheric water vapor to
18 above such common tasks, refusing to react with the molecular masses. <p> Bu
```

There are, of course, intermediate positions – it is possible to make three or four groups here as well as eight or two. The point is that no one grouping is absolutely right or wrong; all the groupings use formal information (that is, information based on the form of words) but also linguistic interpretation (distinguishing between the preposition *to* and the to-infinitive, for example, or between the two uses of *with*). A smaller number of groups tends to give a limited amount of information – the division into groups A and B, for example, tells us very little except that REACT may occur with *to* and *with* or may not. On the other hand, division in many groups runs the danger of masking genuine similarities – placing the lines with adverbs into a different group from those without tends to hide the importance of the link between REACT and *to*.

In addition, of course, quite different groups can be made if different aspects of the concordance lines are brought into account. For example, all the lines in which the subject of REACT is non-intentional (not a thinking human being or animal) can be grouped together, giving a set comprising these lines (in line 18 the subject is *Gold*):

```
4        two-thirds of the radical pairs reacting (in a field of typically only
6    growth because stock markets could react." Mr Visco said stock markets in
10 strength of a substance and the body reacts to fight off any diseases which
11       from the air and induce them to react to form harmless gases. Last
18 above such common tasks, refusing to react with the molecular masses. <p> Bu
```

It is noticeable that this set includes all the lines where REACT is followed by a to-infinitive clause and the only line where it is followed by *with* giving essential information.

To summarise: Observing patterns in concordance lines essentially involves grouping those lines together. In most examples, several alternative groupings could be proposed, each highlighting different kinds of information. There is no objectively correct grouping, although some will be more useful for particular purposes than others. Although the presence of individual words may provide help in grouping, usually a wider context and more interpretation are needed to form groups (that is, to identify patterns) that might be thought to be appropriate.

3 Grammar patterns

In this section of the chapter the discussion will be restricted to a particular kind of pattern, described by Francis (1993) and Hunston and Francis (2000) as grammar patterns. (Note that each individual pattern is referred to as a grammar pattern, while the concept is referred to as pattern grammar.) This is a technical use of the word "pattern" and describes a specific phenomenon: the restrictions on what is found to occur as the complementation of verbs, nouns and adjectives. It is sometimes referred to as an extension of Firth's (1968) notion of "colligation", or co-occurrence of grammatical categories. The concept of pattern grammar ignores lexical collocation and the kind of patterning that is the product of what speakers often say and instead describes only the co-occurrence of specific words with classes of word, phrase and clause. In an example such as *they have to decide how best to collect waste*, the repetition in the corpus of "obligation + *decide how to*" is ignored but the co-occurrence of the lemma DECIDE and a clause beginning with a question word is given the nomenclature **V wh** (verb followed by a clause beginning with a *wh-* word). In the examples where REACT is followed by a clause (*how they'd react if the White House sent them…*), the sequence "REACT + if-clause" is not treated as a pattern, whereas the sequence "REACT + *to* + noun phrase" (*he reacted to Simon Hoggart's discussion…*) is coded as the pattern **V *to* n** (verb followed by a prepositional phrase beginning with *to*). The two examples of *view* followed by the word *that* are treated differently (see examples 4 and 5 above). Where *that* introduces a relative clause, it is ignored, but where *that* introduces an appositive clause, the example is coded as the pattern **N that** (noun followed by that clause). The distinction being made here is between patterns that are used with a whole word class and those that constrain the specific words that they are used with. For example, a modal of obligation (as in *have to decide*) is used with any member of the word class "verb", but a *wh-* clause (as in *decide how best to collect waste*) complements only certain verbs. A relative clause is used with any member of the word class "noun", but appositive *that* clauses are used with only certain nouns (*announcement, claim, hint, intuition, observation, suggestion, theory, view,* etc). There is an important notion of dependency here: The *wh-* clause is dependent on the verb DECIDE and the appositive that-clause is dependent on the noun *view*. The if-clause following *react* (*how they'd react if…*), however, is not dependent on the verb REACT. Only the dependent patterns are termed grammar patterns. The number of such patterns is large but is limited by the fact that in English there are only a certain number of phrase and clause types (noun phrase, verb phrase, that-clause, to-infinitive clause, *wh-* clause, etc.) and only a certain number of prepositions (*at, in, on, with,* etc). Altogether there are about 200 grammar patterns: about 100 relating to verbs and 50 each for nouns and adjectives.

Although the range of patterns is finite, this does not mean that which word occurs in which pattern is also fixed. There is variation between varieties of English. In British

English, for example, the verb MISTAKE is used in the pattern **V n *for* n** (see example 6), whereas in other varieties it is also used in the pattern **V n *as* n** (see example 7).

(6)
...it might be possible to mistake these species for large gastropods.
[BNC]

(7)
...he might mistake a friendly comment as an invitation...
[ANC]

Words also change the patterns they occur with. Well-known examples in British English might be the verb IMPACT, which used to be used only with *on*, as in example 8, but which is now used also in the pattern **V n**, as in example 9.

(8)
The way we undertake our Census may impact on our ability to understand our future society.
[English Web 2013 sample]

(9)
This evolution ultimately will impact society in an incredibly positive way...
[English Web 2013 sample]

In spite of this variation, it might be said that most patterns remain consistent over long periods of time, making it feasible to specify both patterns and the words used with them. One attempt to do this is described in Hunston and Francis (2000); the results can be found at https://grammar.collinsdictionary.com/grammar-pattern. (This web resource incorporates an updated version of the information found in Francis *et al.* 1996, 1998). In this work, all the words occurring with a given pattern are divided into "meaning groups". For example, the entry for the pattern **ADJ that** lists 115 adjectives divided into 12 groups. Examples include *surprised that..., angry that..., glad that..., certain that..., insistent that..., lucky that...*. In the next section we consider how this information might be relevant to English language teaching and learning.

4 Grammar patterns and language education

Willis (2003: 28–47) discusses grammar patterns in terms of 'the grammar of class', which, along with 'the grammar of structure' and 'the grammar of orientation', comprises the grammar learners need to know. For example, in example 10, knowing the grammar of structure means knowing that the subject *I* precedes the verb *had forgotten* and that the indirect question is formed by the sequence "question phrase + subject + verb + object" (*how much I love this pasta*). Knowing the grammar of orientation means being able to use the past perfect (*had forgotten*) to locate the forgetting before the act of making the pasta. Knowing the grammar of class means being able to use *forget* with a *wh-* clause (*had forgotten how much*), that is, knowing the grammar patterns that are used with the verb FORGET.

(10)
I had forgotten just how much I love this pasta until I made it earlier this week.
[English Web 2013 sample]

It is apparent that some of the information covered under the topic of pattern grammar is routinely covered in any English language teaching syllabus. The use of that-clauses or to-infinitive clauses with some verbs, for example, is a familiar topic in grammar. The term "sentence pattern" is often used to distinguish SVO clauses, SVOO clauses and others, with passing mention that the pattern(s) available will depend on the choice of main verb in the clause. (The pattern grammar equivalents of these observations are the **V that** pattern, the **V to-inf** pattern, the **V n** pattern and the **V n n** pattern.) The value of a systematic listing of lexically dependent patterns, and the lexis on which they are dependent, however, is still being explored. The most obvious learner group targeted by such exploration is learners of English as a foreign language (Hunston 2002; see also Chapters 22 and 23, this volume), but there are also developments in teaching English in contexts where it is a first or additional language (McSorley and Patten 2019). Here I will mention just four aspects of this exploration: awareness, accuracy, complexity and academic English.

It has long been acknowledged that a language teaching syllabus is unlikely to contain a sequenced list of patterns in the way that many contain a sequenced list of tenses, for example. Like collocation, a confidence in using grammar patterns is likely to be fostered by raising **awareness** of patterns. Most recommended activities, then, encourage this awareness. The activities can accompany a text comprehension exercise, can involve activities such as rewriting or can emerge as one of the outcomes of hands-on corpus investigation by students (see Chapters 21, 29 and 30, this volume). But why should learners be made aware of grammar patterns? The next two aspects answer this question.

Perhaps the most obvious relevance of grammar patterns for learners is that their correct use (that is, the use that aligns with that of expert speakers of English) increases **accuracy** and reduces error. Learners sometimes over-generalise patterns, for example, using SUGGEST in the same way as RECOMMEND (e.g. "he suggested me to go") or using the verb EMPHASISE with *on* ("they emphasised on the importance…") by analogy with the noun EMPHASIS ("they place emphasis on the importance…"). Learners may sometimes simply be uncertain which preposition to use with a given noun or adjective, or may find a set of patterns difficult to manage. Examples such as "Students are easy to use on-line dictionaries" suggest a confusion between "On-line dictionaries are easy to use" and "Students find it easy to use on-line dictionaries". It should be noted, however, that pattern alone does not guarantee accuracy. Alqarni (2019) has investigated patterns in learner English and notes that examples such as that shown in example 11 are inaccurate in terms of standard English.

(11)
I agree to ban smoking in restaurants.
[ICLE-Chinese]

In this example, the pattern **V to-inf** is correct, but the meaning is not: In Hanks's (2013) terms, the implicature of *agree to ban smoking* is that the writer themselves will execute the ban, whereas the more likely intended implicature is that someone else, such as the government, will ban smoking and the writer simply agrees with this proposal. Alqarni (2019) draws on Hanks's extensive work on verb patterns to explain the inaccuracy in usage here.

Awareness of pattern does more than increase accuracy, however. It also expands language repertoire and increases the **complexity** of language use. Many grammar patterns extend a basic clause to link ideas. For example, example 12 uses the pattern ***it*** **v-link ADJ** ***of*** **n to-inf** to connect the idea "it was good of you" with the idea "you let me know".

(12)
It was good of you to let me know.

[English Web 2013 sample]

The patterns that involve prepositional phrases require an idea to be expressed as a noun phrase and can require some sophisticated manipulation of language, requiring learners to be flexible and raising awareness of what can be expressed in a noun. For example, the pattern **v-link ADJ** ***about*** **n** links adjectives that express emotion (*happy, angry, sad,* etc.) with the cause of the emotion. That cause may be a simple entity or it may be an event. Rewriting exercises can be used to practise the pattern. Table 11.1 gives some examples. The prompt column shows what is given as a prompt to learners. The response column shows what learners are expected to write. In example 1 the task is easy because the noun phrase *the terrible mess* is present in the prompt itself. Example 2 is slightly more difficult because the verb *meet* has to be changed to *meeting* in order to be used following a preposition. In example 3, the verb *were sold* is changed to the noun *sale* when the response is given. Similarly in example 4, the clause *the work was delayed* is changed to the noun phrase *a delay in the work*. In example 5 the rewriting makes use of *the fact that* to produce the noun phrase.

A question that often arises in discussions about grammar patterns is the relevance of this work to **academic English**, both in the context of teaching English for academic purposes in higher education institutions and in the context of increasing command of academic vocabulary among learners in secondary schools, whether they are monolingual or bilingual speakers of English. Grammar patterns are lexis specific rather than register

Table 11.1 Rewriting with the pattern **v-link ADJ *about* n**

Example	*Prompt*	*Response*
1	There was a terrible mess. Robin was cheerful.	Robin was cheerful about the terrible mess.
2	I wanted to meet some friends. Ann was not enthusiastic.	Ann was not enthusiastic about meeting friends.
3	Some paintings were sold. Jenny was unhappy.	Jenny was unhappy about the sale of the paintings.
4	The work was delayed. The residents were furious.	The residents were furious about a delay in the work.
5	I wanted to leave. Dave was bitter.	Dave was bitter about the fact that I wanted to leave.

specific, so there are no patterns which are exclusive to academic English. On the other hand, as the patterns associated with given vocabulary items are an important part of how those items are used, there is increasing interest in recording the patterns of key academic vocabulary. Green (2019), for example, argues for the enrichment of vocabulary lists with pattern information and has built a database of academic vocabulary patterns to support this. McSorley and Patten (2019) have worked with secondary school teachers to change the way academic vocabulary is taught to include patterns as part of that instruction (see Chapters 24 and 28, this volume, for more on vocabulary lists).

5 Grammar patterns and language theory

The concept of patterns raises questions about language theory, that is, what account of language structure best fits observed use of language, on the one hand, and empirical evidence for how language is stored in the brain, on the other. The patterning of language is a topic dealt with under a wide variety of headings – "formulaic language", "chunks", "lexical bundles", etc. – all of which make the following observations (see Chapters 15 and 17, this volume):

- Language production depends on stocks of ready-made language. From Pawley and Syder's (1983) seminal article onwards, the contribution of formulaic phrases to the ability to speak at normal speed has been noted. This may be a trivial observation that has nothing to do with the "real" structure of language and that is a consequence only of real-time memory capacity and the tendency of speakers to repeat what they have heard. It may, on the other hand, be a profound observation about the nature of language.
- Language processing (comprehension) depends on "chunking" i.e. deciding what unit of language makes the most sense. The unit may be a word ("apple") or a phrase ("apple of one"s eye") or an instantiated pattern ("divide the apple in two"). Sinclair (1991) noted that the default position is to interpret the phrase, or unit of meaning, rather than the individual words. For example, the hearer understands "apple of one"s eye" as a single unit, not as a combination of the name of a fruit and the organ of sight. Research by Mauranen (2019) seeks to establish empirically whether the chunks used by language processors (individuals hearing a spoken utterance) match intuitive sequence chunking.
- Lexis and grammar are closely interlinked. Descriptions of language need to acknowledge the dependency of one on the other. At the least, dictionaries need to record grammatical information about the words in them, and grammar reference books need to record information about the lexical restrictions on the features described.

One of the questions raised by these observations is how the apparently systematic structures of grammar arise from the patterning of individual words. Proponents of emergent grammar (e.g. Hopper 2011) see grammatical systems as constantly in flux and dependent upon an ongoing amassing of language instances. This is compatible with the proposal that pattern recognition arises from the experience of individual instances.

Another question is how language is stored in the brain, or what the learnt units of language look like. One answer is the proposal of constructions, a concept arising from cognitive linguistics (Goldberg 2006; Hoffmann and Trousdale 2013; Hilpert 2014; Patten and Perek 2019). A construction is a unit of any size which matches form and function or meaning. A construction can be a word (*apple*), a phrase (*apple of one's eye*), a structure such as the ditransitive (*give someone an apple*) or an abstraction such as subject–verb inversion that has the meaning of "interrogative" (*did you eat the apple*). Constructions, properly speaking, exist in the brain, but the term is often used for regularities observed in corpora, whether or not there is empirical evidence that speakers have them stored (see Chapters 22 and 23, this volume).

Construction grammar is appealing to corpus linguists because it is entirely compatible with, and indeed utilises, observations of patterning in language. It offers a useful vocabulary that can cut through the tangle of terminology ("formulaic language", "chunk", "pattern", etc.). Any kind of regularity in language can be labelled a construction. This is both a strength and a weakness: "Construction" is a neutral term for "observed regularity" that does not draw on any one model of grammar, but because anything can be described as a construction, the term tends to lose meaning. Because there are no unit types, there is no hierarchy of unit types. This again is both a strength and a weakness: It allows the description to move away from the restrictions of group, phrase and clause, but it means that observations of different levels of abstraction are treated alike. There is a hierarchy of constructions, but the levels in the hierarchy are not clearly described. This is where pattern grammar can be of assistance, because there are obvious similarities between one level of construction, exemplified by the ditransitive, and its "pattern" counterpart **V n n**. Hunston and Su (2019) and Hunston (2019) suggest that the most useful alignment of pattern and construction would label as a "construction" not the pattern itself, but the pattern along with a sub-set of the words occurring with it. For example, one construction might be proposed that consists of the pattern **ADJ that** where the adjective is an emotion word (*angry that*... etc.), another that consists of the same pattern but this time with adjectives associated with speaking (*insistent that*... etc.) and another where the adjective relates to a judgement of luck or correctness (*lucky that*..., *right that*... etc.). This offers the possibility of building a comprehensive "constructicon" (Perek and Patten 2019) comprising all constructions in English at a given level of abstraction based on the records of grammar patterns and their node words. This would represent a concrete example of cooperation between corpus linguistics and cognitive linguistics.

Further reading

Hunston, S. and Perek, F. (eds) (2019) *Constructions in Applied Linguistics*, special issue of the *International Journal of Corpus Linguistics* 24(3). (This journal issue explores the applicability of patterns to discourse analysis and language teaching, the development of resources such as constructicon and the connections between patterns and construction grammar. It comprises papers by U. Römer, S. Gries, N. Groom, S. Hunston and F. Perek and A. Patten.)

Hunston, S. and Francis, G. (2000) *Pattern Grammar: A Corpus-Driven Approach to the Lexical Grammar of English*, Amsterdam: Benjamins. (This book outlines the connections between Grammar Patterns, meaning, discourse, and approaches to grammar.)

McSorley, E. and Patten, A. (2019) 'Addressing the Vocabulary Gap Using the Pattern Grammar Approach', *Impact* 6xx. (This paper discusses how attention to patterns can improve the teaching of academic vocabulary.)

References

Alqarni, A. (2019) *Applying Corpus Pattern Analysis to Learner Corpora: Investigating the Pedagogical Potential of the Pattern Dictionary of English Verbs*, unpublished PhD thesis, University of Birmingham.

Firth, J. (1968) 'A Synopsis of Linguistic Theory, 1930–55', in F. R. Palmer (ed.) *Selected Papers of J. R. Firth (1952–59)*, London: Longmans, pp. 168–205.

Francis, G. (1993) 'A Corpus-Driven Approach to Grammar: Principles, Methods and Examples', in M. Baker, G. Francis and E. Tognini-Bonelli (eds) *Text and Technology: In Honour of John Sinclair*, Amsterdam: Benjamins, pp. 137–56.

Francis, G., Hunston, S. and Manning, E. (1996) *Collins Cobuild Grammar Patterns 1: Verbs*, London: HarperCollins.

Francis, G., Hunston, S. and Manning, E. (1998) *Collins Cobuild Grammar Patterns 2: Nouns and Adjectives*, London: HarperCollins.

Goldberg, A. (2006) *Constructions at Work: The Nature of Generalization in Language*, New York: Oxford University Press.

Green, C. (2019) 'Enriching the Academic Wordlist and Secondary Vocabulary Lists with Lexicogrammar: Toward a Pattern Grammar of Academic Vocabulary', *System* 87: 102158.

Hanks, P. (2013) *Lexical Analysis: Norms and Exploitations*, Cambridge: MIT Press.

Hilpert, M. (2014) *Construction Grammar and its Application to English*, Edinburgh: Edinburgh University Press.

Hoffmann, T. and Trousdale, G. (eds) (2013) *Construction Grammar Handbook*, Oxford: Oxford University Press.

Hopper, P. (2011) 'Emergent Grammar', in J. P. Gee and M. Handford (eds) *The Routledge Handbook of Discourse Analysis*, London: Routledge.

Hunston, S. (2002) *Corpora in Applied Linguistics*, Cambridge: Cambridge University Press.

Hunston, S. (2008) 'Starting with the Small Words: Patterns, Lexis and Semantic Sequences', *International Journal of Corpus Linguistics* 13(3): 271–95.

Hunston, S. (2019) 'Patterns, Constructions, and Applied Linguistics', *International Journal of Corpus Linguistics* 24(3): 324–53.

Hunston, S. and Francis, G. (2000) *Pattern Grammar: A Corpus-driven Approach to the Lexical Grammar of English*, Amsterdam: Benjamins.

Hunston, S. and Su, H. (2019) 'Pattern, Construction and Local Grammar: The Case of Evaluation', *Applied Linguistics* 40(4): 567–93.

Laws, J. and Ryder, C. (2018) 'Register Variation in Spoken British English: The Case of Verb-forming Suffixation', *International Journal of Corpus Linguistics* 23(1): 1–27.

Lehmann, H. (2018) 'Lexical Preference and Variation in the Complementation of *Provide*', *International Journal of Corpus Linguistics* 23(1): 55–84.

Lei, L. and Liu, D. (2018) 'The Academic English Collocation List: A Corpus-Driven Study', *International Journal of Corpus Linguistics* 23(2): 216–43.

Mauranen, A. (2019) 'Repeated Sequences: What Can Corpora Tell us about Units of Processing?' Paper given at the CAAD conference, Universitat Jaume 1, November 2019.

McSorley, E. and Patten, A. (2019) 'Addressing the Vocabulary Gap Using the Pattern Grammar Approach', *Impact* 6. https://impact.chartered.college/article/addressing-the-vocabulary-gap-pattern-grammar-approach/.

Patten, A. and Perek, F. (2019) 'Pedagogic Applications of the English Constructicon', in H. Boas (ed.) *Pedagogic Construction Grammar: Data, Methods and Applications*. Berlin: de Gruyter.

Pawley, A. and Syder, F. (1983) 'Two Puzzles for Linguistic Theory: Nativelike Selection and Nativelike Fluency', in J. Richards and R. Schmidt (eds) *Language and Communication*, London: Longman, pp. 191–226.

Perek, F. and Patten, A. (2019) 'Towards an English Constructicon Using Patterns and Frames', *International Journal of Corpus Linguistics* 24(3): 354–84.

Sinclair, J. (1991) *Corpus Concordance Collocation*, Oxford: Oxford University Press.

Sinclair, J. (1990/2004) 'Trust the Text', in J. Sinclair *Trust the Text: Language, Corpus and Discourse*, London: Routledge, pp. 9–23.

Willis, D. (2003) *Rules, Patterns and Words: Grammar and Lexis in English Language Teaching*, Cambridge: Cambridge University Press.

12

What can corpus software reveal about language development?

Xiaofei Lu

1 What is language development?

Language development refers to the process in which the language faculty develops in a human being. First language (L1) development is concerned with how children acquire the capability of their native language, while second language (L2) development is concerned with how children and adults acquire the capability of an L2.

Theories of L1 development generally need to address at least the following three questions: what children bring to the language learning task, what mechanisms drive language acquisition and what types of input support the language-learning system (Pence and Justice 2017). Psychologists have taken drastically different approaches to answering these questions, among which the rationalist, empiricist and pragmatist paradigms have been the most influential (Russell 2004). The rationalist approach, inspired by Chomskyan linguistics, takes the view that the language faculty does not depend on external sources for its content, but is internal to each individual. For rationalists, children are born with innate formal knowledge of a universal grammar, and they bring this domain-specific knowledge to the task of acquiring the I-language (i.e. the internal and individual language) of their native tongue. Language input is used to discover the parameters that their native language uses to satisfy the universal grammar. The empiricist approach, upheld by connectionists, believes that the content of the language faculty is not innate, but is derived from perceptual experience. For empiricists, children employ domain-general mechanisms of associative learning to acquire the rules and representations of their native language through experience with sufficient speech input. The pragmatist or socio-cognitivist approach advocates that children recruit their socio-cognitive capacity to actively construct their language faculty. Within this paradigm, language is viewed as a socio-cultural action, and the language development process is viewed as involving children constructing a series of models or working theories of their mother tongue from the evidence that is available to them.

Theories of L2 development generally seek to explain a different set of questions, including the nature of L2 knowledge, the nature of interlanguage, the contributions of

DOI: 10.4324/9780367076399-12

knowledge of the L1, the contributions of the linguistic environment and the role of instruction (Ortega 2014). A total of 14 contemporary theories of or approaches to L2 development or acquisition are presented in VanPatten and Williams (2014) and Atkinson (2011). These theories take different stances with respect to the various aspects of L2 development. For example, concerning the nature of L2 knowledge, the Chomskyan universal grammar theory, which is committed to nativism (a theoretical perspective positing that children have the innate ability to acquire language), argues that L2 learners cannot obtain knowledge of ungrammaticality and ambiguity from linguistic input, but possess pre-existing knowledge of the grammar that constrains their learning task (White 2014). Contrastively, the skill acquisition theory, which is committed to conscious processing, claims that development happens from initial representation of knowledge through proceduralisation of knowledge to eventual automatisation of knowledge (DeKeyser 2007). Still different is the Vygotskian sociocultural theory, which views L2 knowledge as socially distributed, 'places mediation, either by other or self, at the core of development and use' and understands development 'not only in terms of target-like performance but also in terms of the quality and quantity of external mediation required' (Lantolf and Thorne 2011: 24).

2 How do we measure language development?

In addition to the theoretical question of how language development takes place, another important and more practical question that is of interest to teachers, researchers, parents and/or clinicians is what stage of language development a particular child or L2 learner is in, or in other words, how much a child or L2 learner knows about the language system and its use at a particular point. Measurement of language development is especially important for children suffering any delay or disorder in their language development. There are multiple ways to answer this question, including naturalistic observation, production, comprehension and judgment tasks, formal testing and language sample analysis, among others. In this section, we focus on how language development can be measured through analysing spoken or written language samples produced by a child or L2 learner.

A number of measures of language development have been proposed and explored in the child language development literature. Some measures are based on verbal output, e.g. mean length of utterance (MLU) (Brown 1973) and number of different words (NDWs), while others are based on structural analysis, e.g. Developmental Sentence Scoring (DSS) (Lee 1974), Index of Production Syntax (IPSyn) (Scarborough 1990) and Developmental Level (D-Level) (Rosenberg and Abbeduto 1987; Covington *et al.* 2006). Both DSS and IPSyn were developed to evaluate children's grammatical development, although they work in different ways. The DSS metric assigns a score to each sentence. It considers eight different types of grammatical forms, including indefinite pronouns, personal pronouns, main verbs, secondary or embedded verbs, conjunctions, negatives and two types of questions. Variants of the same type of grammatical form are scored differently based on the order in which children develop the ability to use them. The score of a sentence is the sum of the points for each type plus one point if the sentence is fully grammatical. The average DSS of a speaker can be computed using a representative language sample. The IPSyn metric does not apply to individual sentences, but examines the number of times 56 target grammatical structures are used in a sample produced by a speaker. These include various types of noun phrases, verb phrases, questions and some specific sentence structures. Each occurrence of any of the target grammatical structures in the language sample receives one point. However, a maximum of two occurrences of each structure are counted, and the maximum score a language sample can receive is 112. The D-Level scale classifies each sentence into one of eight increasingly more complex categories (levels zero through seven), depending on the syntactic structures it contains. For example, a sentence containing a finite clause as the object of the main verb is classified as level three, and a sentence containing an embedded clause serving as the subject of the main verb is classified as level six.

In the L2 development literature, a large number of developmental index studies have attempted to identify objective measures of complexity, accuracy and fluency (CAF) of production that can be used to index the learner's level of development or overall proficiency in the target language. This is generally achieved by assessing the development of L2 learners at known proficiency levels in the target language using various measures. Developmental measures identified in such a way allow teachers and researchers to evaluate and describe the learner's developmental level in a more precise way. In addition, they can be used to examine the effect of a particular pedagogical treatment on language use. Wolfe-Quintero *et al.* (1998) provided a comprehensive review of the measures explored in 39 second and foreign language writing studies and recommended several measures that were consistently linear and significantly related to programme or school levels as the best measures of development or error. These include three measures of fluency, i.e. mean length of the T-unit, where a T-unit is a main clause plus any subordinate clauses (Hunt 1965), mean length of clause, and mean length of error-free T-unit; two measures of accuracy, i.e. error-free T-units per T-unit and errors per T-unit; two measures of grammatical complexity, i.e. clauses per T-unit and dependent clauses per clause; and two measures of lexical complexity, i.e. total number of word types divided by the square root of twice the total number of word tokens and the total number of sophisticated word types divided by the total number of word types. In terms of syntactic complexity, recent research has argued for the need to focus on more fine-grained measures (Kyle 2016), measures of phrasal complexity, as well as co-occurrence patterns of lexico-grammatical features (e.g. Biber *et al.* 2016). In a similar spirit, Hawkins and Buttery (2010) proposed and illustrated the identification of a systematic set of criteria for each proficiency level in the Common European Framework of Reference for Languages (CEFR). These features captured the emergence, frequency, accuracy and usage distribution of relevant linguistic properties (e.g. verb co-occurrence frames and relative clauses) characterising each proficiency level. They further argued for the need to consider L1-specific features, a view supported by later research demonstrating the influence of L1 on the acquisition order and/or usage of different linguistic properties (e.g. Lu and Ai 2015; Murakami and Alexopoulou 2016).

3 How can we use a corpus to find out more about first language development?

In this section, we discuss several ways in which a corpus of child language development data may be used to find out more about L1 development. Some of these will be illustrated using the following corpora and corpus analysis software: the *Child Language Data Exchange System* (CHILDES) database, the *Computerized Language Analysis* (CLAN) programme (MacWhinney 2000), Computerized Profiling (Long 2019) and D-Level Analyzer (Lu 2009). We briefly introduce each of these first.

The CHILDES database contains transcripts and media data collected from conversations between young children of different ages and their parents, playmates and caretakers. These data are contributed by researchers from many different countries, following the same data collection and transcription standards. Each file in the database contains a transcript of a conversation and includes a header that encodes information about the target child or children (e.g. age, native language, whether the child is normal in terms of language development, etc.), other participants, the location and situation of the conversation, the activities that are going on during the conversation and the researchers and coders collecting and transcribing the data. The conversation is transcribed in a one-utterance-per-line format, with the producer of each utterance clearly marked in a prefix. Each utterance is followed by another line that consists of a morphological analysis of the utterance. Any physical actions accompanying the utterance are also provided in a separate line. The CLAN programme is a collection of computational tools designed to automatically analyse data transcribed in the CHILDES format. Some of the automatic analyses that the programme can run on one or more files in the CHILDES database include word frequency, type/token ratio, a measure of vocabulary diversity called D (Durán *et al.* 2004), mean length of turn, mean length of utterance and DSS score, among others.

Computerized profiling is a set of programmes designed to analyse both written language samples and phonetically transcribed spoken language samples. Linguistic analysis at a range of different levels can be performed, including simple corpus statistics, semantics, grammar, phonology, pragmatics and narratives. For example, at the grammar level, the following four procedures can be run: IPSyn; DSS; Black English Sentence Scoring (BESS) (Nelson 1998), which is an adaptation of DSS for use with speakers of African American Vernacular English; and the Language Assessment, Remediation, and Screening Procedure (LARSP) (Crystal *et al.* 1989), a system for profiling the syntactic and discourse development of children that is related to both age and stage.

The D-Level Analyzer is a computer programme designed to automate the measurement of syntactic complexity using the revised D-Level scale (Covington *et al.* 2006). Given a raw sentence as input, the analyser assigns it to an appropriate level on the scale. The programme achieves an accuracy of 93.2 per cent on spoken child language acquisition data from the CHILDES database.

First of all, a corpus can be used to describe the characteristics of language produced by children in different age groups or different stages of development. Children may exhibit a considerable amount of variability in terms of language development. However, it is useful to understand the average capability, as well as the range of capabilities exhibited by children within the same age group. Researchers generally agree that there are certain milestones in child language development, or approximate ages at which specific language capabilities usually emerge or mature. For example, at approximately 12 months of age, words start to emerge; at approximately 24 months of age, children possess more than 50 vocabulary items and begin to spontaneously join these items into self-created two-word phrases; and at approximately 30 months of age, children produce utterances with at least two words, and many with three or even five words (Lenneberg 1967). A large corpus consisting of language samples produced by children of different age groups can be used to complement or confirm naturalistic observations for establishing or revisiting such milestones. The CHILDES database constitutes a good example of such a corpus. Given a set of data that consists of transcripts of conversations involving targeted groups of children in a particular age group, e.g. 18 months, it is possible to use CLAN, computerized profiling and D-Level Analyzer to find out the average as well as the range of different types of developmental metrics of interest exhibited by all the children in the group.

Second, a corpus can be used to investigate the sequence or order in which children acquire different aspects of the system of their native language, as well as to track the development of individual children over time. This type of investigation necessitates a corpus of longitudinal data, i.e. data collected from the same child or group of children over an extended period of time, e.g. one to five years. An early example of this type of research is Ramer (1977), who conducted a longitudinal study to investigate the developmental sequence of syntactic acquisition in seven children. Specifically, she aimed to find out whether there is 'a universal sequence of emergence of grammatical relations leading up to the production of S + V + O constructions' (p. 144). She analysed her corpus data using a hypothesised simplicity–complexity dimension based on the number of grammatical relations produced and their expansions. She reported that the sequence of acquisition specified in the hypothesised dimension was observed in the data from all seven children. Khaghaninejad *et al.* (2018) analysed a corpus in the CHILDES database containing the utterances produced by five L1 Farsi Iranian children over a year to examine the order of acquisition of Farsi consonants. Their analysis generated a "timeline" for L1 Farsi children to acquire idealised articulations of different consonants.

Third, a corpus can be used to assess the validity and adequacy of the various metrics proposed for measuring child language development. This is an important enterprise, as such measures are often used for evaluating the level of language development of children with developmental delays or disorders. One of the ways to approach this problem is closely related to the descriptive and longitudinal research discussed earlier. Since these metrics were proposed to measure language development, many of them were based on observation of child language acquisition. Given a particular measure, it is sensible to evaluate whether it reflects the developmental sequence or significantly differentiates the developmental levels of children in different age groups. An example of this type of research is Lu (2009), who analysed data from the CHILDES database using the D-Level Analyzer and reported a correlation of 0.648 ($p < .001$) between average D-Level scores and speaker age, as well as significant between-age differences in average D-level scores. A second way to approach this problem is to examine whether a proposed measure significantly differentiates between the developmental levels of children with and without developmental disorders within the same age group. A good example of this line of research is Hewitt *et al.* (2005). They compared scores of kindergarten children with a mean age of six years with and without specific language impairment (SLI) on three commonly used measures, i.e. MLU in morphemes, IPSyn and NDWs. They found that children with SLI showed significantly lower mean scores for all of the three measures, except for some sub-tests of the IPSyn. In relation to this line of research, a corpus can also be used to provide normative information for valid and adequate measures. To improve the feasibility of applying these measures in practical situations and to enable researchers and clinicians to make sense of the analytical results using these measures, it is necessary to have normative information for different age groups for benchmarking purposes. The CHILDES database could again be used for providing such normative information.

Finally, a corpus can also be used to gain in-depth understanding of language development disorders. Through comprehensive contrastive analyses, it is possible to qualitatively and quantitatively describe the developmental differences between children with and without language disorders, e.g. in terms of vocabulary size and range of syntactic structures. In addition, longitudinal data can be used to investigate the effect of a particular therapeutic intervention. Early interventions play a critical role in optimising the developmental trajectory of children with language disorders during the best window of opportunity (Pence and Justice 2017). By analysing language samples produced before and after a particular intervention, it is possible to evaluate whether targeted changes have systematically occurred in a statistically significant way.

4 How can we use a corpus to find out more about second language development?

In this section, we discuss a number of ways that a corpus of learner language can be used to find out more about L2 development. The *Longitudinal Database of Learner English* (LONGDALE) (Meunier 2016) constitutes an excellent example of such a resource. LONGDALE contains data from English learners from diverse L1 backgrounds, with all learners contributing data at least once a year for three or more years. Various types of spoken, written and experimental data are included. The database also includes comprehensive information about the learners and tasks, such as age, gender, language background, proficiency level and task type, among others. The *International Corpus of Learner English* (ICLE; Version 2) (Granger *et al.* 2009), while initially designed for comparing learner English among learners from different L1 backgrounds as well as against L1 English, has good potential for L2 development research as well. This corpus contains 3.7 million words of academic writing, mostly argumentative, by intermediate to advanced learners of English as a foreign language, mostly university students, representing 16 different mother tongue backgrounds. The following learner variables are recorded for each written text: age, learning context, proficiency level, gender, mother tongue, region, knowledge of other foreign languages and L2 exposure. These variables allow for cross-sectional or quasi-longitudinal analysis that can offer useful insight into a learner's L2 development (Meunier 2015; see also Chapters 22 and 23, this volume).

Various corpus processing tools can be used to analyse learner corpora in the different ways to be discussed next (e.g. Lu 2014, 2017). For example, Coh-Metrix (McNamara *et al.* 2014) can be used to assess the coherence and cohesion of language samples using a large set of linguistic features. The *Biber Tagger* (Biber 1988) can be used to analyse a large number of lexico-grammatical features of language samples. The *Lexical Complexity Analyzer* (LCA) (Lu 2012) and the *Tool for the Automatic Analysis of Lexical Sophistication* (TAALES) (Kyle *et al.* 2018) can be used to assess the lexical density, lexical diversity and lexical sophistication of learner texts using a large number of metrics. The *L2 Syntactic Complexity Analyzer* (L2SCA) (Lu 2010) and the *Tool for the Automatic Analysis of Syntactic Sophistication and Complexity* (TAASSC) (Kyle 2016) are both designed for L2 writing syntactic complexity analysis. In addition, computational systems for automated grammatical error detection in learner writing are emerging (Leacock *et al.* 2014), such as the *Criterion Online Writing Evaluation Service* developed by Educational Testing Service (ETS) (available at www.ets.org/criterion), Cambridge English *Write and Improve* (available at https://writeandimprove.com) and the *Grammar and Mechanics Error Tool* (GAMET) (Crossley *et al.* 2019).

The first way a corpus can be used to reveal L2 development is as a database for describing the characteristics of the inter-language of learners at known proficiency levels. To this end, it is necessary to have a learner corpus that encodes information about the learners' proficiency levels. Proficiency level can be conceptualised in a number of different ways, e.g. classroom grades, holistic ratings, programme levels, school levels and standardised test scores (Wolfe-Quintero *et al.* 1998). The CEFR has also been increasingly used as a calibration for proficiency level within learner corpora, such as the *Cambridge Learner Corpus* (CLC), which is composed of data from the Cambridge English Language Assessment (Barker *et al.* 2015), and the *EF-Cambridge Open Language Database* (EFCAMDAT), which consists of written samples from over 174,000 adult learners of English as a second language (ESL) across the world (Huang *et al.* 2018). Linking to the same framework of proficiency makes the results from different data sources more comparable. Nevertheless, it should be noted that the use of any type of calibration for proficiency, be it age, year of schooling or the CEFR, is a workaround for not being able to obtain large amounts of genuine longitudinal data (e.g. Meunier 2015), which, if available, would be the preferred data source for investigating L2 development. In terms of analysis, one may choose to focus on a particular aspect of the inter-language, for example, the degree to which informal, colloquial patterns or styles are used in formal, written language. One may also attempt to provide a comprehensive description of the lexico-grammatical system of the inter-language. For example, in the *English Grammar Profile* project, O'Keeffe and Mark (2017) examined the patterns of grammatical development across the six levels of the CEFR using the CLC. Their project resulted in a database of over 1,200 empirically derived statements that can be used to characterise the grammatical competence of English learners at different CEFR levels.

This type of descriptive study can benefit both from error analysis and from contrastive analysis of learner data and L1 speaker data. To conduct an error analysis, it is necessary to first design an error annotation scheme, which should be consistently followed in identifying and annotating errors in learner text. An early example of an error annotation scheme can be found in Granger (2003), which assigns each error first to one of the following nine major domains: form, morphology, grammar, lexis, syntax, register, style, punctuation and typo, and then to a specific category within the domain. Lüdeling and Hirschmann (2015) offer a systematic review of issues surrounding error annotation and existing error annotation systems in learner corpus research. An error-annotated learner corpus enables one to easily identify the common errors that learners at a given proficiency level tend to make.

A contrastive study of learner data and L1 speaker data helps us to look at the characteristics of the inter-language from a different perspective, in particular, how it converges with or differs from L1 speaker usage. For example, one may assess whether learners tend to overuse or underuse certain words, phrases, collocations, grammatical constructions, speech acts, etc., relative to L1 speakers (Granger 1998; De Cock 2000). It is important, however, to ensure that the learner data and the L1 speaker data are of comparable nature in terms of mode, genre, field, etc. The *Trinity Lancaster Corpus*, which contains 4.2 million words of interaction between English learners and L1 speakers (Gablasova *et al.* 2019), constitutes an excellent source of data for this purpose. Importantly, however, it should be noted that recent notions in learner corpus research are starting to move away from using L1 speaker data as a norm for comparing learner data and focus on L2 competence as an entity for analysis in its own right (e.g. Granger 2015).

Second, a corpus may be used in developmental index studies to identify objective metrics that can be used to index levels of L2 development or the learner's overall language proficiency. Earlier studies of CAF differences between different proficiency levels contained substantial variability in terms of choice and definition of measures, writing task used, sample size, corpus length, timing condition, etc., making it challenging to compare the results reported (Wolfe-Quintero *et al.* 1998), as these factors have been found to affect the CAF of learner language (e.g. Alexopoulou *et al.* 2017; Hsu 2019). To eliminate such inconsistency and variability, recent research has evaluated or compared large sets of measures on the same learner corpus or corpora. For example, Lu (2011) used L2SCA to analyse large-scale L2 writing data from the *Written English Corpus of Chinese Learners* (WECCL) (Wen *et al.* 2005). The corpus is a collection of over 3,000 essays written by English majors in nine different colleges in China. Each essay in the corpus is annotated with a header that includes the following information: mode (written or spoken), genre (argumentation, narration or exposition), school level (first, second, third or fourth year in college), year of admission (2000, 2001, 2002 or 2003), timing condition (timed with a 40-minute limit or untimed), institution (a two- to four-letter code) and length (number of words in the essay). Students in the same school level within the same institution wrote on the same topics, but topics varied from institution to institution. Given the information that is available in the corpus, proficiency level is conceptualised using school level. Through the analysis, this study provided useful insights into how different syntactic complexity measures perform as indices of college-level L2 writers' language development, how they relate to each other and how their performances are affected by external factors.

Third, a corpus can be used to examine the contributions of knowledge of the L1 as well as the effect of L1 transfer. On the one hand, knowledge of the L1 may prove helpful in learning certain aspects of the L2, and learners with different L1 backgrounds may show strengths in learning different aspects of the L2. On the other hand, the intrusion of L1 may result in difficulty in acquiring certain lexico-grammatical aspects of the L2 and prevalence of certain forms or grammatical patterns that deviate from the target language in the inter-language. Consequently, the inter-languages of learners at the same proficiency level but with a different L1 background may demonstrate some significantly different characteristics. A contrastive study of such inter-languages may provide evidence of L1 influence, either positive or negative, on learner development and output (e.g. Granger *et al.* 2015; Murakami and Alexopoulou 2016). The ICLE corpus constitutes an excellent source of data for this type of research, as students with diverse L1 backgrounds are represented. A contrastive study of a learner's L1 and inter-language will provide further evidence of the L1 influence. One example of this type of research is Lu and Ai (2015), who analysed data from the ICLE and the *Louvain Corpus of Native English Essays* (LOCNESS) (Granger 1996) with L2SCA to examine differences in the syntactic complexity in English writing among college-level writers with eight different L1 backgrounds, including seven L2 groups and one L1 group. They reported that the seven L2 groups demonstrated drastically different patterns of difference from the L1 group.

Fourth, longitudinal learner corpora can be used to examine the trajectories and patterns of learner development and to provide evidence to validate or challenge the claims and assumptions of different theories of or approaches to L2 development. For example, the complex dynamic systems approach views language development as a dynamic process characterised by changing patterns of variability and interactions among different subsystems of the language (Verspoor *et al.* 2011). Multiple longitudinal studies from this approach have reported evidence that L2 developmental trajectories, as well as the patterns of interaction among different CAF features, are highly variable and that such variability follows the principles of dynamic systems (e.g. Larsen-Freeman 2006; Caspi 2010). Usage-based approaches to L2 development take the position that L2 learning is achieved by learning constructions, understood as conventionalised form-meaning mappings at varied levels of complexity that are entrenched as language knowledge in the speaker's mind (Goldberg 1995). Research within this framework posits that language acquisition is shaped by exposure to and usage of language and has reported that a learner's repertoire of constructions starts with fixed sequences and becomes increasingly more complex and productive (Ellis *et al.* 2016). For example, Römer (2019) analysed verb–argument constructions (VACs) in a large-scale corpus of written texts produced by L2 learners at varied levels of English proficiency and found that the learners' inventory of VACs developed from fixed sequences to more diverse, productive and complex ones (see also Chapter 23, this volume).

Finally, a corpus may be used to examine the role of instruction or the effect of a particular pedagogical intervention on language development. For example, by examining corpus data of different groups of learners at the same school level or programme level that are exposed to different types of instruction method, material or linguistic environment, we may better understand whether differences in instruction result in differences in L2 development. In addition, by comparing the learner's production prior to and after a period of targeted pedagogical intervention, we may assess whether the intervention is effective in helping the learner acquire particular aspects of the L2.

5 Looking to the future

As a field, corpus-based language development research will benefit tremendously from the following future developments. First, language samples produced by children and L2 learners often contain many errors and as such present a challenge to natural language processing (NLP) technology, especially when it comes to measures that involve syntactic, semantic and discourse analysis. Therefore, continued enhancement of existing NLP technology and development of robust new NLP technology will facilitate more accurate and reliable automatic analysis of language samples using more diversified measures. A second avenue for future development in the field lies in the systematic collection and sharing of large-scale child and L2 development data that encode richer information about the children or learners producing the data. For child language development research, large-scale longitudinal data and data of children with language disorders are particularly valuable. The *Growth in Grammar Corpus* (Durrant *et al.* 2021), a large collection of texts written by school children in England as part of their school work, constitutes an excellent example of this avenue of development. For L2 development research, systematical annotation of the learner's proficiency level using as many conceptualisations as possible will prove especially useful to L2 development researchers. These include school levels, programme levels, standardised test scores, holistic ratings, classroom grades, etc. Large-scale data with richer information will make it easier to draw more reliable conclusions for many of the types of research discussed earlier. Finally, analysis of L2 development data will benefit from the development of consistent and standardised error annotation standards, as well as improved automatic error detection techniques. L2 development researchers have often devised their own annotation schemes for error analysis, which makes comparison and sharing of research results problematic. The field in general will benefit from a more consistent annotation scheme. There has also been an increasing stream of research in automatic error detection and correction (Leacock *et al.* 2014; Crossley *et al.* 2019). The maturity of such techniques will facilitate automatic error analysis of large-scale L2 development data and enable researchers to gain more reliable insights into L2 use.

Further reading

Atkinson, D. (ed.) (2011) *Alternative Approaches to Second Language Acquisition*, London: Routledge. (This edited volume presents a comprehensive introduction to and comparison of six non-cognitivist approaches to second language acquisition.)

Lu, X. (2014) *Computational Methods for Corpus Annotation and Analysis*, Singapore: Springer. (This book provides a systematic and accessible introduction to diverse types of computational tools that can be used for automatic or computer-assisted annotation and analysis of text corpora at various linguistic levels.)

MacWhinney, B. (2000) *The CHILDES Project: Tools for Analyzing Talk*, 3rd edn, Mahwah: Lawrence Erlbaum Associates. (This book provides hands-on instruction on how to transcribe naturalistic child language development data following the CHILDES format and automatically analyse such data using CLAN. Readers are introduced to a set of computational tools designed to improve the readability of transcripts, to automate the data analysis process and to facilitate the sharing of transcribed data.)

Pence, L. K. and Justice, L. M. (2017) *Language Development from Theory to Practice*, 3rd edn, New York: Pearson. (This book provides an extremely accessible introduction to the theory and practice of child language development. The material presented in the book is also highly relevant to clinical, educational and research settings.)

VanPatten, B. and Williams, J. (eds) (2014) *Theories in Second Language Acquisition: An Introduction*, 2nd edn, New York: Routledge. (This edited volume presents a comprehensive introduction to early and contemporary theories in second language acquisition. It provides an excellent overview of each of these compelling theories.)

References

Alexopoulou, T., Michel, M., Murakami, A. and Meurers, D. (2017) 'Task Effects on Linguistic Complexity and Accuracy: A Large-Scale Learner Corpus Analysis Employing Natural Language Processing Techniques', *Language Learning* 67(S1): 180–208.

Atkinson, D. (ed.) (2011) *Alternative Approaches to Second Language Acquisition*, London: Routledge.

Barker, F., Salamoura, A. and Saville, N. (2015) 'Learner Corpora and Language Testing', in G. Granger, G. Gilquin and F. Meunier (eds) *The Cambridge Handbook of Learner Corpus Research*, Cambridge: Cambridge University Press, pp. 511–33.

Biber, D. (1988) *Variation Across Speech and Writing*, Cambridge: Cambridge University Press.

Biber, D., Johansson, S., Leech, G., Conrad, S. and Finegan, E. (1999) *Longman Grammar of Spoken and Written English*, New York: Longman.

Biber, D., Gray, B. and Staples, S. (2016) 'Predicting Patterns of Grammatical Complexity Across Language Exam Task Types and Proficiency Levels', *Applied Linguistics* 37(5): 639–68.

Brown, R. (1973) *A First Language*, Cambridge: Harvard University Press.

Caspi, T. (2010) *A Dynamic Perspective on Second Language Development*, unpublished PhD dissertation, University of Groningen, Groningen, Netherlands.

Covington, M. A., He, C., Brown, C., Naçi, L. and Brown, J. (2006) *How Complex is that Sentence? A Proposed Revision of the Rosenberg and Abbeduto D-Level Scale*, Atlanta: The University of Georgia, Artificial Intelligence Center.

Crossley, S. A., Bradfield, F. and Bustamante, A. (2019) 'Using Human Judgments to Examine the Validity of Automated Grammar, Syntax, and Mechanical Errors in Writing', *Journal of Writing Research* 11(2): 251–70.

Crystal, D., Fletcher, P. and Garman, M. (1989). *Grammatical Analysis of Language Disability*, 2nd edn, London: Cole & Whurr.

De Cock, S. (2000) 'Repetitive Phrasal Chunkiness and Advanced EFL Speech and Writing', in C. Mair and M. Hundt (eds) *Corpus Linguistics and Linguistic Theory*, Amsterdam: Rodopi, pp. 51–68.

DeKeyser, R. (2007) 'Skill Acquisition Theory', in B. VanPatten and J. Williams (eds) *Theories in Second Language Acquisition: An Introduction*, Mahwah: Lawrence Erlbaum Associates, pp. 97–114.

Durán, P., Malvern, D., Richards, B. and Chipere, N. (2004) 'Developmental Trends in Lexical Diversity', *Applied Linguistics* 25(2): 220–42.

Durrant, P., Brenchley, M. and McCallum, L. (2021) *Understanding Development and Proficiency in Writing: Quantitative Corpus Linguistic Approaches*, Cambridge: Cambridge University Press.

Ellis, N. C., Römer, U. and O'Donnell, M. B. (2016) *Usage-Based Approaches to Language Acquisition and Processing: Cognitive and Corpus Investigations of Construction Grammar*, Hoboken: Wiley-Blackwell.

Gablasova, D., Brezina, V. and McEnery, T. (2019) 'The Trinity Lancaster Corpus: Development, Description and Application', International Journal of Learner Corpus Research *5*(2): 126–58.

Goldberg, A. E. (1995) *Constructions. A Construction Grammar Approach to Argument Structure*, Chicago: University of Chicago Press.

Granger, S. (1996) 'From CA to CIA and Back: An integrated approach to computerized bilingual and learner corpora', in K. Aijmer, B. Altenberg and M. Johansson (eds) *Languages in Contrast: Paper from a Symposium on Text-based Cross-linguistic Studies. Lund Studies in English*, Vol. 88, Lund: Lund University Press, pp. 37–51.

Granger, S. (ed.) (1998) *Learner English on Computer*, Boston: Addison Wesley Longman.

Granger, S. (2003) 'Error-Tagged Learner Corpora and CALL: A Promising Synergy', *CALICO Journal* 20(3): 465–80.

Granger, S. (2015) 'Contrastive Interlanguage Analysis: A Reappraisal', *International Journal of Learner Corpus Research* 1(1): 7–24.

Granger, S., Dagneaux, E., Meunier, F. and Paquot, M. (2009) *International Corpus of Learner English Version 2*, Louvain: Presses Universitaires de Louvain.

Granger, S., Gilquin, G. and Meunier, F. (eds) (2015) *The Cambridge Handbook of Learner Corpus Research*, Cambridge: Cambridge University Press.

Hawkins, J. and Buttery, P. (2010) 'Criterial Features in Learner Corpora: Theory and illustrations', *English Profile Journal* 1: 1–23.

Hewitt, L. E., Scheffner, H. C., Yont, K. M. and Tomblin, J. B. (2005) 'Language Sampling for Kindergarten Children with and without SLI: Mean Length of Utterance, IPSYN, and NDW', *Journal of Communication Disorders* 38(3): 197–213.

Hsu, H.-C. (2019) 'The Combined Effect of Task Repetition and Post-Task Transcribing on L2 Speaking Complexity, Accuracy, and Fluency', *Language Learning Journal* 47(2): 172–87.

Huang, Y., Murakami, A., Alexopoulou, T. and Korhonen, A. (2018) 'Dependency Parsing of Learner English', *International Journal of Corpus Linguistics* 23(1): 28–54.

Hunt, K. W. (1965) *Grammatical Structures Written at Three Grade Levels*, Urbana: National Council of Teachers of English.

Khaghaninejad, M. S., Moloodi, A. and Saadi, R. F. (2018) 'A Timeline for Acquisition of Farsi Consonants: A First Language Acquisition Corpus-Based Analysis', *Theory and Practice in Language Studies* 8(12): 1711–24.

Kyle, K. (2016) *Measuring Syntactic Development in L2 Writing: Fine Grained Indices of Syntactic Complexity and Usage-Based Indices of Syntactic Sophistication*, unpublished PhD dissertation, Georgia State University, Atlanta.

Kyle, K., Crossley, S. and Berger, C. (2018) 'The Tool for the Automatic Analysis of Lexical Sophistication (TAALES): Version 2.0', *Behavior Research Methods* 50(3): 1030–46.

Lantolf, J. P. and Thorne, S. L. (2011) 'The Sociocultural Approach to Second Language Acquisition', in D. Atkinson (ed.) *Alternative Approaches to Second Language Acquisition*, London: Routledge, pp. 24–47.

Larsen-Freeman, D. (2006) 'The Emergence of Complexity, Fluency, and Accuracy in the Oral and Written Production of Five Chinese Learners of English', *Applied Linguistics* 27(4): 590–619.

Leacock, C., Chodorow, M., Gamon, M. and Tetreault J. (2014) *Automated Grammatical Error Detection for Language Learners*, 2nd edn San Rafael: Morgan & Claypool Publishers.

Lee, L. (1974) *Developmental Sentence Analysis*, Chicago: Northwestern University Press.

Lenneberg, E. H. (1967) *Biological Foundations of Language*, Hoboken: John Wiley & Sons.

Long, S. H. (2019) *Computerized Profiling* (Version 10.0.0), Milwaukee: Marquette University.

Lu, X. (2009) 'Automatic Measurement of Syntactic Complexity in Child Language Acquisition', *International Journal of Corpus Linguistics* 14(1): 3–28.

Lu, X. (2010) 'Automatic Analysis of Syntactic Complexity in Second Language Writing', *International Journal of Corpus Linguistics* 15(4): 474–96.

Lu, X. (2011) 'A Corpus-Based Evaluation of Syntactic Complexity Measures as Indices of College-Level ESL Writers' Language Proficiency', *TESOL Quarterly* 45(1): 36–62.

Lu, X. (2012) 'The Relationship of Lexical Richness to the Quality of ESL Learners' Oral Narratives', *The Modern Language Journal* 96(2): 190–208.

Lu, X. (2014) *Computational Methods for Corpus Annotation and Analysis*, Dordrecht: Springer.

Lu, X. and Ai, H. (2015) 'Syntactic Complexity in College-Level English Writing: Differences among Writers with Diverse L1 Backgrounds', *Journal of Second Language Writing* 29: 16–27.

Lu, X. (2017) 'Automated Measurement of Syntactic Complexity in Corpus-Based L2 Writing Research and Implications for Writing Assessment', *Language Testing* 34(4): 493–511.

Lüdeling, A. and Hirschmann, H. (2015) 'Error Annotation Systems', in S. Granger, G. Gilquin and F. Munier (eds) *The Cambridge Handbook of Learner Corpus Research*, Cambridge: Cambridge University Press, pp. 135–57.

Meunier, F. (2015) 'Developmental Patterns in Learner Corpora', in S. Granger, G. Gilquin and F. Meunier (eds) *The Cambridge Handbook of Learner Corpus Research*, Cambridge: Cambridge University Press, pp. 379–400.

MacWhinney, B. (2000) *The CHILDES Project: Tools for Analyzing Talk*, 3rd edn, Mahwah: Lawrence Erlbaum Associates.

McNamara, D. S., Graesser, A. C., McCarthy, P. M. and Cai, Z. (2014) Automated Evaluation of Text and Discourse With Coh-Metrix, Cambridge: Cambridge University Press.

Meunier, F. (2016) 'Introduction to the LONGDALE Project', in E. Castello, K. Ackerley and F. Coccetta (eds) *Studies in Learner Corpus Linguistics. Research and Applications for Foreign Language Teaching and Assessment*, Berlin: Peter Lang, pp. 123–6.

Murakami, A. and Alexopoulou, T. (2016) 'L1 Influence on the Acquisition Order of English Grammatical Morphemes: A Learner Corpus Study', *Studies in Second Language Acquisition* 38(3): 365–401.

Nelson, N. W. (1998) *Childhood Language Disorders in Context: Infancy Through Adolescence*, 2nd edn, Boston: Allyn & Bacon.

O'Keeffe, A. and Mark, G. (2017) 'The English Grammar Profile of Learner Competence: Methodology and Key Findings', *International Journal of Corpus Linguistics* 22(4): 457–89.

Ortega, L. (2014) 'Second Language Learning Explained? SLA Across 10 Contemporary Theories', in B. VanPatten and J. Williams (eds) *Theories in Second Language Acquisition: An Introduction*, 2nd edn, New York: Routledge, pp. 245–72.

Pence, L. K. and Justice, L. M. (2017) *Language Development from Theory to Practice*, 3rd edn, New York: Pearson.

Ramer, A. L. H. (1977) 'The Development of Syntactic Complexity', *Journal of Psycholinguistic Research* 6: 145–61.

Römer, U. (2019) 'A Corpus Perspective on the Development of Verb Constructions in Second Language Learners', *International Journal of Corpus Linguistics* 24(3): 268–90.

Rosenberg, S. and Abbeduto, L. (1987) 'Indicators of Linguistic Competence in the Peer Group Conversational Behavior of Mildly Retarded Adults', *Applied Psycholinguistics* 8(1): 19–32.

Russell, J. (2004) *What is Language Development? Rationalist, Empiricist, and Pragmatist Approaches to the Acquisition of Syntax*, Oxford: Oxford University Press.

Scarborough, H. S. (1990) 'Index of Productive Syntax,' *Applied Psycholinguistics* 11: 1–22.
VanPatten, B. and Williams, J. (eds) (2014) *Theories in Second Language Acquisition: An Introduction*, 2nd edn, New York: Routledge.
Verspoor, M. H., De Bot, K. and Lowie, W. (eds) (2011) *A Dynamic Approach to Second Language Development: Methods and Techniques*, Amsterdam: John Benjamins.
Wen, Q., Wang, L. and Liang, M. (2005) *Spoken and Written English Corpus of Chinese Learners*, Beijing: Foreign Language Teaching and Research Press.
White, L. (2014) 'Linguistic Theory, Universal Grammar, and Second Language Acquisition', in B. VanPatten and J. Williams (eds) *Theories in Second Language Acquisition: An Introduction*, 2ndedn, New York: Routledge, pp. 34–53.
Wolfe-Quintero, K., Inagaki, S. and Kim, H.-Y. (1998) *Second Language Development in Writing: Measures of Fluency, Accuracy, and Complexity*, Honolulu: University of Hawai'i, Second Language Teaching and Curriculum Center.

13

How to use statistics in quantitative corpus analysis

Stefan Th. Gries

To begin with what sounds like a disappointing start for this chapter: Usually, corpora do not directly provide what most linguists are interested in, such as meaning, communicative function/intention, information structure, cognition/processing and language proficiency/dialect. Instead, a prototypical corpus provides information on the presence or absence of character strings (typically a grapheme such as any letter [in any language], a space, a number or special characters like "%", "~", "@", "™", etc.):

- In (certain parts/locations of) corpora;
- In the presence or absence of other character strings.

Note that character strings can be anything: text that was scraped from the Web, transcribed audio or video data (of spoken or signed language) with or without context and any kind of annotation that was then added to the actual text such as lexical/structural annotation (on morphemes, parts of speech, parse trees), annotation providing information about the speakers, contextual annotation providing information about the circumstances of language production, etc. That has two consequences: First, whatever a linguist using corpus data is interested in will have to be studied via (i) frequencies of occurrence of something (text or annotation) somewhere in (parts of) a corpus or via (ii) frequencies of co-occurrence of two or more things.

Second, ultimately, corpus-linguistic analysis will involve the notion of *correlation*. For instance, if one wants to study meaning, e.g. the semantics of a certain word or argument structure construction, one typically has to retrieve examples for the word/construction from one's corpus, annotate them for characteristics of interest and correlate those characteristics with each other and/or with the meanings or kinds of uses of the word/construction. Similarly, if one wants to study information structure and its role for constituent ordering, one typically has to retrieve examples of the constructions in question, annotate them for information-structural and other characteristics and correlate those with each other and the constructional choices.

Trivial as that may seem, this reliance on the notion of correlation also means that corpus linguistics has often a very close to connection to statistical analysis – because

DOI: 10.4324/9780367076399-13

statistics is how we make sense of frequencies, distributions and correlations. This chapter will discuss some of the most frequent kinds of statistical applications in corpus linguistics: I will begin with some statistics that are, in a sense at least, specific to corpus linguistics and that are ordered in terms of how much contextual information they include; I will then turn to applications of statistical methods that are very general, but are here discussed for corpus data annotated for (potentially many) contextual features/ information.

1 Frequency and dispersion

Frequency information

The most basic kind of statistic, and one that is typically completely acontextual, is *token frequency of occurrence*, i.e. the frequency with which something – a morpheme, a word, a multi-word unit, a grammatical construction, etc. – occurs in a corpus or in a part of a corpus; this would lead to statements such as "the word *x* occurs 134 times in corpus *c*". This kind of statement might be compared to another one such as "the word *y* occurs 150 times in corpus *c*", but often we also have to make comparisons between different corpora that are not equally large, in which case we often find normalisations such as "*x* occurs 55 times per million words in corpus *c*, which is more often than *y*'s occurrence of 34 times per million words in corpus *d*". And similar statements can be made for *token frequencies of co-occurrence* such as "in corpus *c*, *criticise* is used 43 times per 100 K passives, but only 13 times per 100 K actives". Such token frequencies have been important in many areas because of their correlations with many experimental tasks (word naming, picture naming, word retrieval); thus, frequency is often used as an explanatory or even just as a control variable in statistical analyses of corpora and experimental data. Also, frequency is a dimension that informs lexicographic work, curriculum/textbook design and many other applications.

Another kind of frequency information is *type frequency*, i.e. the number of types that, for instance, occur in a certain lexically or syntactically defined slot. For example, a corpus might contain 500 instances of the verb lemma *cause* followed by some nominal direct object, and these 500 tokens might instantiate 80 noun lemma types – some very frequent ones (e.g. *problems*, which might account for 120 of the 500 tokens), some intermediately frequent ones (e.g. *pain*, which might account for another 40 tokens) and some really rare ones (e.g. *cerebral palsy*, which might account for just one token). Type frequencies have been considered important for studies of productivity (see Bybee and Thompson 1997; Bybee and Hopper 2001), as when a productive morpheme attached to more types than an unproductive one, or studies of category formation, as when a lexical item becomes a grammatical item by virtue of being associated with many semantically very diverse words. In a sense, very low type frequency can also reveal phraseologisms or fixed expressions: Since the type frequency of the word immediately after the adverb *hermetically* is one in just about every corpus (because *sealed* is just about always the next word), this is a good indicator that it may be a fixed expression.

Given the relevance of frequency information, and especially the relative simplicity with which it can be obtained, frequency data are among the most widely provided corpus statistics. However, frequency is not without its problems, both conceptually and methodologically. For instance, frequency is correlated with many other aspects of language and cognition but that does not entail that it also has a causal effect on these other aspects, which is an entirely different hypothesis to (dis)prove. Statistically and methodologically, however, reporting a frequency, in particular a token frequency, on its own, is just as problematic as reporting an average (such as a mean) on its own: In fact, a frequency of, say, a word *w* in a corpus *c is* kind of a mean, namely the mean of the numbers you get when every word in *c* that is not *w* is coded as 0 and every word in *c* that is *w* is coded as 1. Therefore, the old statistical adage that one should never report an average without a measure of dispersion applies to corpus frequencies, too, and we turn to dispersion now.

Dispersion

The notion of dispersion in corpus linguistics is related to the notion of dispersion in statistics, and it refers to the evenness with which an element is distributed throughout a corpus. From that definition, it also follows that dispersion in corpus linguistics is related to the notion of recency (the effect that we remember and repeat things we have encountered recently more than things we have encountered earlier) in cognitive psychology (see Gries 2019, Chapter 4): What dispersion quantifies is the degree of regularity with which you encounter the element in question when you read the corpus from beginning to end, i.e. the variability in how recently you saw that element if you just saw it again. If a word is distributed very evenly in the corpus, you will see it in regular intervals as you go through the corpus, but if a word is distributed very clumpily (i.e. unevenly), you will not see it at all for a long (corpus) time, then you will see it very often in a very short period of time and then maybe never again.

Consider as an example the words *staining* and *enormous* in the Brown corpus, a corpus containing 500 parts with approximately 2,000 words each of written American English of the 1960s. Both words have the same frequency in the corpus – 37 – but nevertheless their distribution in the corpus could hardly be more different: All 37 occurrences of *staining* are in just 1 of the 500 corpus parts, but the 37 occurrences of *enormous* are spread out over 36 different corpus parts. Put differently, if you randomly pick 1 of the 500 corpus parts, there is only a 0.002 chance it contains *staining*, but there is a 0.072 chance it contains *enormous*. Therefore, trying to characterise both words' distribution by just providing their frequency is completely misleading (and yet still what most corpus studies do).

Of course, this was an extreme example – frequency and dispersion are usually correlated: Obviously, high-frequency function words will be the most evenly dispersed; obviously, it is hapaxes (words with a frequency of 1) that will be most unevenly dispersed. However, in spite of that general correlation, dispersion and frequency deviate from each other most in the range of intermediately frequent lexical words, which is why keeping them separate at all times is essential.

Thus, dispersion should be a central corpus statistic for any corpus-linguistic application involving acquisition/learning, language change or processing, and there are now initial results that indicate dispersion can outperform the predictive power of frequency (Adelman *et al.* 2006; Baayen 2010; Gries 2010). Basically whenever a linguist wants to measure the probability that a linguistic element is known or familiar to a speaker or the familiarity of a linguistic element to a speaker, frequency is usually the easiest statistic to obtain, but should always be augmented by a dispersion statistic; see Gries (2008) and Lijffijt and Gries (2012) for a comprehensive overview of most dispersion measures known then and Gries (2021) for an update of that discussion and an updated script to compute dispersion.

2 Association/contingency

The next kind of basic statistic involves at least a bit of contextual information, namely *co-occurrence information.* In its simplest form, such co-occurrence information may come as frequencies of co-occurrence or probabilities of co-occurrence in the form of statements such as "of the 600 instances of the ditransitive construction (V $NP_{Recipient}$ $NP_{Patient}$ as in *gave him a book*) in corpus *c*, 200 (i.e. 0.333 or 33.3 per cent) have a form of the verb lemma *give* in its verb slot". Of course, the perspective can also be reversed, as in "of the 400 instances of the verb lemma *give* in corpus *c*, 200 (i.e. 0.5 or 50 per cent) occur in the ditransitive construction". Thus, if one is concerned with the co-occurrence of two elements – *give* and the ditransitive – then their co-occurrence frequency is one number – here, 200 – but to compute a relative frequency/percentage or probability, we need to decide what to normalise it against: the frequency of the construction, i.e. computing *p*(*give*|ditransitive), or the frequency of the verb, i.e. computing *p*(ditransitive|*give*), which amounts to answering different questions. Normalising against the construction's frequency says something about how prominent a role *give* plays for the ditransitive, whereas normalising against the verb's frequency says something about how prominent a role the ditransitive plays for *give.*

However, most applications involving co-occurrence do not just settle for co-occurrence frequency, but also report an association measure, a statistic quantifying the degree of association between the two elements, which is usually computed from a 2 × 2 co-occurrence table such as shown in Table 13.1. In Table 13.1, the italicised frequencies are retrieved with, ideally, a programming language, whereas the regular frequencies are then computed via subtraction from the italicised ones; the letters in the lower-right corners of each cell indicate how these cells are usually referred to in the literature, which means that the most important cell, the one with the co-occurrence frequency, is usually designated *a*.

For such tables, the two relative frequencies mentioned are easy to compute: *p*(*give*| ditransitive) is $^{a}/_{a+c}$ whereas *p*(ditransitive|*give*) is $^{a}/_{a+b}$. However, literally dozens of association measures can be computed from such a table. Two simple ones are *MI* (for *mutual information*) and the *OR* (the *odds ratio*), which are computed as shown in (1) and (2), respectively:

1. $MI = log_2\left(a \div \frac{(a+b)\cdot(a+c)}{a+b+c+d}\right) \approx 6.381$
2. $\text{OR} = \frac{a}{b} \div \frac{c}{d} = 248$ (sometimes, *OR* is reported in its logged version)

If *MI* > 0/*OR* > 1, then the two elements under consideration occur more often together than expected by random chance (they are "attracted to each other"); if *MI* < 0 / *OR* < 1, then they occur less often together than expected by random chance (they "repel each other"); and if *MI* = 0/*OR* = 1, then they occur together at chance level. In the hypothetical examples provided earlier, therefore, *give* and the ditransitive are strongly attracted to each other. Typically, researchers would compute *MI* or *OR* for all types that might occur in a certain slot/position and then rank-order them. For instance, they

Table 13.1 A co-occurrence table based on the frequencies of co-occurrence (and assuming a corpus size of 100,000 constructions, however defined)

	Ditransitive construction	*Other constructions*	*Sum*
give	*200* *a*	200 *b*	*400* *a + b*
other verbs	400 *c*	99,200 *d*	99,600 *c + d*
Sum	*600* *a + c*	99,400 *b + d*	*100,000* *a + b + c + d*

might compute *OR* for every verb type attested in the ditransitive construction and then rank them from the highest *OR* to the lowest.

This kind of statistical method has many applications, virtually all of which are based on the so-called distributional hypothesis:

> If we consider words or morphemes A and B to be more different in meaning than A and C, then we will often find that the distributions of A and B are more different than the distributions of A and C. In other words, difference of meaning correlates with difference of distribution.
>
> *(Harris 1970: 785f)*

For our present example, this translates into the expectation that a construction such as the ditransitive will be particularly strongly attracted to verbs whose meanings/functions are compatible with, or even highly similar to, the construction's meaning function. And indeed, in a study of the ditransitive (Stefanowitsch and Gries 2003), *give* and *tell* score the highest association scores, and their semantics are indeed very closely related to the semantics of the ditransitive ("transfer"). Similar considerations apply to the co-occurrence of, for instance, near-synonymous lexical items, whose meaning differences can be so subtle as to be inaccessible even to native speakers, but which can be inferred from other lexical items they are attracted to. For instance, virtually no native speakers are able to explain the difference between *botanic* and *botanical*, yet if one uses association measures to identify the nouns these two forms prefer to modify, clear patterns emerge (see Gries 2003).

However, the range of applications goes well beyond such simple examples: Association measures can be used in, say,

- First-language acquisition contexts: Do children learn syntactic constructions on the basis of the verbs that these constructions are most associated with in their caretakers' speech? How quickly and early do children generalise the use of certain syntactic constructions? (See Pine *et al.* 2013 for a corpus-based study of determiners in English.)
- Second-/foreign-language acquisition/learning contexts: As non-native speakers of a language learn more and more words and constructions, do their preferred usage patterns resemble those of their input or that of native speakers? (See Wulff 2016 for a study of *that* complementation.)

- Diachronic linguistics: Can we quantify the degree of grammaticalisation of verbs by seeing how the degrees of associations with their preferred complements change over time (e.g. by weakening)? (See Hilpert 2006 for discussion of how to monitor linguistic change in diachronic corpus data using association measures.)
- Psycholinguistic studies of speech production: Are speakers more likely to reduce the articulation of words that are highly predictable from, say, the previous word(s)? (See Bell *et al.* 2009 for a study of word durations based using, among other things, conditional probabilities and *MI*.)

In other words, the fact that association measures essentially quantify the notion of contingency (the degree to which two stimuli are probabilistically related), a central component of theories of learning and processing (e.g. Ellis 2006), these measures are probably useful in any scenario in which some linguistic phenomenon might be conditioned or determined at least in part by some other linguistic phenomenon in its context; Evert (2009) provides a good overview of many critical issues. Current topics of discussion involve questions such as "should we use measures that quantify mutual attraction/repulsion (such as *MI*/*OR*) or ones that quantify directional association?" or "should we use measures that are less sensitive to overall frequency/corpus size?" and others, but the general utility of being able to quantify attraction/repulsion of linguistic and other units is hardly ever called into question anymore.

3 Context and concordances

The last somewhat more specifically corpus-linguistic kind of statistic is on a form of output that many corpus linguists would probably not even apply any statistics to: the concordance display, i.e. the display of the search word(s) or tag(s) in question in a central column with a typically user-defined amount of context on the left and right. This is the most informative, context-rich display, because one can see the complete co-text of the expression in question (or, with relevant annotation, the context of the expression). At the same time, it is a display that might appear to defy the very notion of statistical analysis – at least not before annotation has been added, in which case we often apply the methods to be discussed in Sections 4 and 5. However, we will briefly discuss two useful applications of statistical methods to concordances: type-token ratios and lexical gravity.

Type-token ratios

Type-token ratios (TTRs), i.e. the number of types in a certain (part of a) text divided by the number of tokens in the same corpus (part), are a measure of lexical density/richness so it might seem as if this measure could have been mentioned in Section 1. However, since TTRs are very much correlated with the size of a text or a corpus, they are not usually used for that purpose. However, TTRs *can* be more useful when applied to, say, the fixed number of words around a node word or tag of interest. For instance, if one retrieves all instances of two words in a large corpus and then, for every instance of one of the two words, also retrieves exactly 200 words of co-text – 100 before the word in question, 100 after it – then one can compute the TTR for each instance's context and compare them, because then the "text length" in the window has been held constant. What might this be good for? Szmrecsanyi (2006) computes TTRs (on 100 words of context) as a proxy for lexical density in a case study of future choice (*will* vs. *be going to*) in a part of the *British National Corpus* and finds that the TTRs enter into significant and surprising interactions with the main predictor in his study (for instance, he found that increasing TTRs increase the odds for *will*-futures in some corpora, but decrease it in others). Thus, even such a statistically simple method applied to an unlikely target – a concordance display – can yield important results.

Lexical gravity

Another interesting and underused application of statistical tools to concordances is Mason's (1999) notion of lexical gravity. For each slot around, say, a word of interest, he computed the entropy (a measure of randomness) of the frequency distribution of all words in that slot, and the lower the entropy of the slot, the more it deserves attention in the form of an analyst exploring that slot.

How does this work? The entropy H of a frequency distribution is a measure of the evenness of the frequency distribution. In other words, if one has a concordance of a word with 200 instances, then one would look at, say, all 18 slots around the word from nine words to the left (L9) to nine words to the right (R9). Then, for each of these 18 slots, one generates a frequency list of the 200 tokens in it and then computes the corresponding H-value (see Gries 2014: 40–1 for how to compute H). H will be high if the word types making up the 200 tokens are fairly evenly distributed, it will be low if a very small number of types account for most tokens and it will be 0 if a single type accounts for all 200 tokens (recall the example of *hermetically* earlier). Thus, slots for which one obtains a (very) low entropy value will be interesting because it is these slots that the node word whose concordance one is exploring has the strongest impact on. In other words, the entropies function as a pointer towards "where to look next" that is arrived at in a completely data-driven, statistically informed fashion.

4 Regression and classification approaches

The previous sections dealt with, in a sense, specifically corpus-linguistic statistics – "in a sense" because, of course, many disciplines use 2 × 2 co-occurrence tables, but arguably their particular use to compute association measures is a prominent corpus-linguistic method. This section and the next, by contrast, deal with general statistical techniques whose application to corpus data is really not all that different from their use in other areas. The first of these is concerned with regression and classification approaches, where the goal typically is to determine which of potentially very many different (predictor) variables explain speakers' behaviors such as word durations or choices of one of several alternatives, e.g. the choice of one or more functionally similar morphemes, lexical items, grammatical constructions, etc.

In such situations, a researcher's starting point is usually a concordance of a phenomenon in question (e.g. a syntactic alternation between two constructions), which is then imported into spreadsheet software so that each instance can be annotated for all the variables the researcher considers relevant – for instance, because they might be causally related to the phenomenon in question or because they might be variables that only need to be controlled for while one studies the potentially causal predictors. This process typically leads to a spreadsheet or data frame in the so-called *case-by-variable format*: Each instance of the linguistic phenomenon has its own row (i.e. the number of rows corresponds to the sample size *n*), and each variable the data are annotated for has its own column.

Such datasets are then often studied with either a regression-based approach or a tree-based approach. For either method, the researcher formulates one or more hypotheses regarding which (predictor) variables will be correlated with the (response) variable of the phenomenon in question and codifies this hypothesis in a *model*. For instance, if one studied the genitive alternation (*of*-genitive as in *the speech of Captain Picard* vs. *s*-genitive as in *Captain Picard's speech*), one might hypothesise that the choice of one genitive over the other will be related to the length of "the possessor" (*Captain Picard*), the length of the possessum (*the speech*) and the kind or degree of animacy of the possessor (*Captain Picard* is human) and would therefore minimally formulate a model such as that in (3). In this model, the tilde (~) means "as a function of"; therefore, the tilde separates the response variable on the left (the choice of genitive) and the predictors/controls on the right, and in this model the hypothesis is that genitive choices are influenced by possessor length and ("+") possessum length and ("+") possessor animacy.

3. GENITIVE ~ POSSESSORLENGTH + POSSESSUMLENGTH + POSSESSORANIMACY

Both regression and tree-based approaches usually return two types of information: First, they quantify how well the researcher's hypotheses embodied in the model fit the data; second, how much each variable on right of the "~" contributes to the hopefully good fit of the model. The former is often expressed with one of several so-called R^2-values, which range from 0 (very bad fit) to 1 (perfect fit) or other kinds of statistics such as classification or prediction accuracies (how often in a percentage does the model make the right prediction?) and related scores.

The latter, the information about the predictors, usually comes in three kinds:

- An *effect direction*, which states how certain values of the predictors/controls affect genitive choices; for instance, such a model might indicate that the probability of *s*-genitives *in*creases, rather than *de*creases, when the possessor is animate (as opposed to abstract);
- An *effect size*, which states how much certain values of the predictors/controls affect genitive choices; for instance, such a model might indicate that the length of the possessor is a better/stronger predictor of genitive choices than the length of the possessum;
- A *significance test*, which states how likely the effect of a certain predictor/control variable in one's sample would be if, in the population from which the corpus sample was drawn, there was no such effect. If that probability is very small (conventionally below 0.05 or 5 per cent) for a certain predictor, then one typically interprets this as meaning that the effect in one's data is not due to random variation.

With these kinds of information and, typically, some visualisation of the effects that were found, a researcher would then revisit the initial hypotheses: Did the model fit the data well and in a way that confirms the initial hypotheses or not and, hopefully, why is that the case?

While such a model is multifactorial – it considers the potential impact of multiple variables on the phenomenon at the same time – it might still be severely lacking in ways that are still often not understood in the field. This is because the model discussed earlier only tested the so-called *main effects* of the three predictors. For instance, it tested how much POSSESSORLENGTH contributes to genitive choices regardless of the values of the other predictors POSSESSUMLENGTH and POSSESSORANIMACY, and the same for the other predictors. Thus, the model's results for POSSESSORLENGTH assume and imply that POSSESSORLENGTH has the same effect no matter whether the possessum is short or long and/or whether the possessor is animate, inanimate/concrete or abstract. Thus, if the effect of POSSESSORLENGTH on genitive choices is different for different degrees of POSSESSORANIMACY, this model can, by definition, not reveal that because it does not contain a predictor encoding that possibility; that is, by formulating the model as we did in (3), we forced the model to assume that each predictor has the same effect everywhere.

In order to be able to analyse such questions, one's model needs to contain what is called an *interaction term*. An interaction term of predictors A and B, written as A:B, allows the effect of predictor A to vary as a function of another predictor B. To use a non-linguistic example: The effect of taking a certain medication (predictor A) may depend on whether one is taking it with a glass of water or a glass of vodka – if the medication is taken with water, it helps; if it is taken with vodka, it might make matters (much) worse.

In our genitive example, if one expected that the effect of POSSESSORLENGTH was *not* the same regardless of whether the possessor is animate or not, one would include an interaction term in the model, which is often written as in (4):

4. GENITIVE ~ POSSESSORLENGTH + POSSESSUMLENGTH + POSSESSORANIMACY + POSSESSORLENGTH:POSSESSORANIMACY

If the interaction term now returns, say, a significant result with a strong effect, then we interpret this as confirmation that the effect of POSSESSORLENGTH does indeed vary depending on POSSESSORANIMACY.

This scenario may seem useful in only a small number of circumstances – but that impression would be mistaken: The notion of interaction is one of the most frequent and important ones for such analyses. First, this is so because we already know that predictors often modify the effect of other predictors. For instance, in the case of particle placement (the alternation between *Captain Picard gave back the phaser* and *Captain Picard gave the phaser back*), there is a strong tendency for idiomatic verb phrases to prefer the particle before the direct object (DO), but when the DO is pronominal, the idiomaticity suddenly "doesn't matter" anymore, and the particle goes behind the DO goes behind the DO. In other words, IDIOMATICITY does not have the same effect everywhere: It has a strong effect when the DO is lexical but none when it is pronominal – that is an interaction.

Interactions play an even more important role in a second way. Imagine the earlier study of the genitive alternation was actually diachronic, covering three different time periods. In that case, one would have another predictor TIME with three levels. However, including TIME as a predictor as in (5) is not enough:

5. GENITIVE ~ POSSESSORLENGTH + POSSESSUMLENGTH + POSSESSORANIMACY + TIME

This is because this regression model would only indicate whether each of the three linguistic predictors has an effect regardless of what the other two linguistic predictors and TIME are doing. And from an effect of TIME, we would only learn whether *s*-genitives become more or less frequent over time, but *not* whether the effects of POSSESSORLENGTH,

POSSESSUMLENGTH or POSSESSORANIMACY changed over time – for that we would need each of these variables to interact with TIME, as in (6).

6. GENITIVE ~ POSSESSORLENGTH + POSSESSUMLENGTH + POSSESSORANIMACY + TIME + POSSESSORLENGTH:TIME + POSSESSORLENGTH:TIME + POSSESSORANIMACY:TIME

In other words, the last term, POSSESSORANIMACY:TIME, determines whether the effect of POSSESSORANIMACY has been changing over time: Maybe the effect of animate possessors was stronger 200 years ago than it is now.

The same would be true if one studied the genitive alternation in native and non-native data: To determine whether the three predictors' effects differ between native and non-native speakers, one would need to include (i) a predictor NATIVE with, say, the levels *yes* and *no* and (ii) that predictor's interactions with all other predictors. Or, if one assumed that a speaker's choices change over time in a conversation or in response to what an interlocutor just said (as in priming effects, see Szmrecsanyi 2006 or Hoey 2005), then one most likely needs an interaction of all relevant predictors with a variable that encodes when in a conversation something happened (e.g. a time index or sentence/utterance counter) or what the other speaker just did. In other words, whenever one's thinking about a phenomenon involves the question or expectation that some predictor's effect will not be the same everywhere, one needs a model with interactions of at least that predictor with other variables to do justice to the complexity of one's expectations or hypotheses. The way in which interactions are studied differs between regression models and tree-based approaches (such as classification, regression or conditional inference trees or random forests; see Levshina (2021) for discussion and exemplification), but regardless of how one studies interactions in each approach, it is definitely one of the most fundamental things to consider in one's analyses.

Another important range of issues corpus linguists using these kinds of methods need to be aware of is what one might call the potential *repeated-measurements structure* of one's data: A lot of times, our data contain more than one data point from a speaker. This is important because it means that this speaker's potentially idiosyncratic behavior is represented in the data multiple times, which means that all the data points from that speaker are related, which can heavily distort analyses. Why is that? As a somewhat unrealistic, but nonetheless instructive, example, imagine a learner corpus study of the genitive alternation. We know that the *s*-genitive is very strongly preferred when the possessor is short and animate and the possessum is long and a concrete object. Now imagine a non-native speaker who is at such an early level that they do not know yet an *s*-genitive even exists. That learner might therefore use the *of*-genitive even when everything in the context "screams" *s*-genitive. If that speaker now were to produce multiple such data points, those data points will of course go completely against the overall trend of everyone who actually knows both genitives exist and, thus, weaken the otherwise very robust correlations. Controlling for the fact that these unexpected *of*-genitives all come from the same person is one central reason for the rise of mixed-effects modeling in corpus linguistics. Once one has developed a good general understanding of regression modeling, this kind of approach should be next on one's list.

5 Exploratory analyses

While the previous section was concerned with hypothesis-testing approaches towards regression and classification, another widely used family of approaches are exploratory in nature. In other words, in this kind of work we may have a potentially quite large dataset – again typically cases described by variables in a spreadsheet – and we are interested in identifying any kind of interesting structure in the data, which are too large for "normal human eyeballing" to be successful and reliable. "Any kind of structure" is deliberately general: It can refer to finding (i) groups made up by the cases (i.e. rows) or (ii) groups made up by the variables (i.e. columns), and often the algorithms then identify these groups of cases or variables by trying to maximise within-group similarities and minimise between-group similarities. That means the goal of these algorithms is to create groups that contain members that are as similar as possible to each other while at the same are as different as possible from the members of other groups. For some of these methods, the researcher needs to provide the algorithm with a number of groups to identify; in others, the algorithm will either "propose" a number on the basis of the data that the researcher can then accept or reject, or the algorithm will represent the data in a certain fashion from which the researcher can then pick a most suitable number of groups or dimensions.

The following two sections briefly discuss the probably most frequently used methods: hierarchical cluster analysis followed by principal components analysis and correspondence analysis.

Hierarchical cluster analysis

The point of a hierarchical cluster analysis is usually to find groups among the cases. For instance, we might have different speakers or different languages for which we have numeric or categorical data, and we want them to be grouped, or clustered, on the basis of the data. Moisl (2015), a book-length treatment of cluster analysis for corpus data, gives as an example (Chapter 2, Table 2.3) the application of clustering 24 speakers on the basis of the frequencies with which the speakers used 12 different phonemes in a corpus. Looking at $24 \cdot 12 = 288$ numbers is not going to help that much, but for a hierarchical cluster analysis, this is actually a small dataset.

This kind of analysis typically proceeds in three steps. First, the analysis computes a so-called distance matrix, which states for every case how distant it is from – i.e. how dissimilar it is from – every other case. Second, the analysis then computes a cluster structure by successively amalgamating all cases into groups/clusters such that within-group/cluster similarity, or cohesion, is as high as possible. Finally, the resulting structure is represented in a tree with the cases at the bottom and, hopefully, groups/clusters emerging from the connections of the branches. Consider Figure 13.1 for the results of such a cluster analysis applied to nine Russian verbs, all meaning "to try", for which we (Divjak and Gries 2006) had frequency data regarding 87 lexical, morpho-syntactic and semantic features based on 1,585 annotated concordance lines.

Figure 13.1 is instructive in particular because it is not completely obvious how many clusters to assume, an uncertainty that is not uncommon in exploratory analyses. One's first impulse might be to go with three clusters of three verbs each, and that is the solution we adopted; however, at least considering a four-cluster solution might also be useful, namely {*silit'sja, poryvat'sja, norovit'*}$_1$, {*tuzit'sja, tscit'sja, pyzit'sja*}$_2$, {*probovat'*}$_3$ and {*pytat'sja, starat'sja*}$_4$. The results from this three-cluster solution were then interpreted in terms of a radial network of senses and its relation to the treatment of these near synonyms in traditional Russian lexicography.

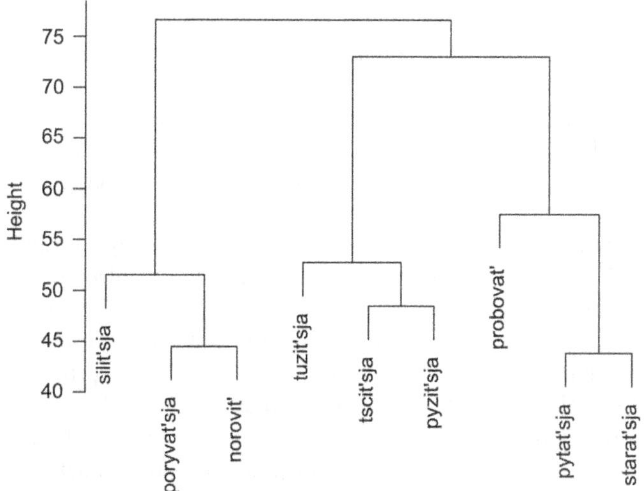

Figure 13.1 Dendrogram of the data discussed in Divjak and Gries (2006)

It needs to be highlighted here that this kind of exploratory approach is not necessarily completely objective: Not only does one have to interpret the cluster structure returned by the analysis, which can be subjective to a certain degree, the analyst also has to make and defend some choices during the process. For example, the computation of the distance matrix can be done with different distance or similarity measures that do not all return identical results; similarly, there are different ways in which the cases can be amalgamated into clusters and, again, the researcher must choose one and justify the choice. On the one hand, this may seem like a weakness of the approach because it seems to indicate a lack of "a clear answer"; on the other hand, we are talking about *exploratory* approaches, so it should not come as a surprise that different ways of exploring the same data can lead to different aspects of the data being highlighted in these different analyses. Gries (2013: Section 5.6) and Desagulier (2018: Section 10.6) are useful first sources to consult, but Moisl (2015) provides a much more comprehensive discussion.

Principal components analysis and (multiple) correspondence analysis

The two analytical methods of this section are conceptually similar. Both take as input matrices of often co-occurrence frequencies (like Table 13.1, just with many more rows and columns) and try to represent the multiple dimensions of information contained in these matrices using much fewer – often just two or three – dimensions; these dimensions are usually orthogonal (i.e. mutually independent or uncorrelated), and both analyses will also indicate how much of the information in the original matrix the now two or three dimensions still represent. Principal component analyses (PCAs) are usually done on numeric measurements, whereas (multiple) correspondence analyses ([M]CAs) are usually done on frequency data.

For instance, a PCA might indicate that a dataset with 20 columns can actually be reduced to, or compressed into, a dataset with only 4 columns (then called principal components) while still retaining 85 per cent of the information contained in the original 20 columns. The PCA would manage that by detecting correlations between the original columns – in other words, redundant information – and then "merging" multiple columns into a principal component. In a somewhat similar vein, a CA decomposes a chi-squared statistic of a co-occurrence table into orthogonal components – which means correspondence analysis uses interrelations between columns (like a PCA) but also between rows (unlike a PCA) – and then represents those in a two- or three-dimensional plot to reveal distributional patterns impossible to see just from the co-occurrence frequencies themselves.

These methods can be extremely useful both on their own for the description and exploration of multidimensional, or multivariate, corpus data, but PCA is also sometimes used to prepare data for regression modeling of the type discussed in the previous section. This is because regressions and tree-based models sometimes have a lot of difficulties dealing with predictors that are highly correlated with each other, a problem referred to as *(multi)collinearity*. This is because if multiple predictors are highly related to each other, then the regression or tree "does not know" to which of them it should attribute what the response variable is doing. If the relevant predictors are numeric, a PCA could be used to reduce the number of correlated predictors – maybe even down to one – so that the subsequent application of a hypothesis-testing model is less jeopardised. As these techniques become more popular in corpus linguistics – in particular (M)CA has become more widely used especially over the last few years – corpus linguists should become more familiar with them; Levshina (2021) and Desagulier (2018: Section 10.2, and 10.4–10.5) are good places to learn more about these methods.

Further reading

Gries, St. Th. (2013) *Statistics for Linguistics with R*, 2nd edn, Berlin and Boston: De Gruyter Mouton. (A still very useful overview of statistical methods, focusing mostly on corpus data and different kinds of regression modeling, but discussing also hierarchical cluster analysis.)

Levshina, N. (2015) *How to Do Linguistics with R: Data Exploration and Statistical Analysis*, Amsterdam: John Benjamins. (A textbook on R in linguistics in general, with many applications pertinent to the sections in this chapter.)

Paquot, M. and Gries, St. Th. (eds) (2021) *Practical Handbook of Corpus Linguistics*, Berlin and New York: Springer. (A new handbook of corpus linguistics with overview chapters on many central corpus-linguistic notions, as well as many hands-on chapters on statistical techniques applied to corpus data using R.)

References

Adelman, J. S., Brown, G. D. A. and Quesada, J. F. (2006) 'Contextual Diversity, Not Word Frequency, Determines Word-Naming and Lexical Decision Times', *Psychological Science* 17(9): 814–23.

Baayen, R. H. (2010) 'Demythologizing the Word Frequency Effect: A Discriminative Learning Perspective', *The Mental Lexicon* 5(3): 436–61.

Bell, A., Brenier, J. M., Gregory, M., Girand, C. and Jurafsky, D. (2009) 'Predictability Effects on Durations of Content and Function Words in Conversational English', *Journal of Memory and Language* 60(1): 92–111.

Bybee, J. L. and Thompson, S. A. (1997) 'Three Frequency Effects in Syntax', *Berkeley Linguistics Society* 23: 65–85.

Bybee, J. L. and Hopper, P. J. (2001) *Frequency and the Emergence of Linguistic Structure*, Amsterdam and Philadelphia: John Benjamins.

Desagulier, G. (2018) *Corpus Linguistics and Statistics with R: Introduction to Quantitative Methods in Linguistics*, Berlin and New York: Springer.

Divjak, D. S. and Gries, St. Th. (2006) 'Ways of Trying in Russian: Clustering Behavioral Profiles', *Corpus Linguistics and Linguistic Theory* 2(1): 23–60.

Ellis, N. C. (2006) 'Language Acquisition as Rational Contingency Learning', *Applied Linguistics* 27(1): 1–24.

Evert, S. (2009) 'Corpora and Collocations', in A. Lüdeling and M. Kytö (eds) *Corpus Linguistics: An International Handbook*, Vol. 2, Berlin and New York: Mouton de Gruyter, pp. 1212–48.

Gries, St. Th. (2003) 'Testing the Sub-Test: A Collocational-Overlap Analysis of English *-ic* and *-ical* Adjectives', *International Journal of Corpus Linguistics* 8(1): 31–61.

Gries, St. Th. (2008) 'Dispersions and Adjusted Frequencies in Corpora', *International Journal of Corpus Linguistics* 13(4): 403–37.

Gries, St. Th. (2010) 'Dispersions and Adjusted Frequencies in Corpora: Further Explorations', in St. Th. Gries, S. Wulff, and M. Davies (eds) *Corpus Linguistic Applications: Current Studies, New Directions*, Amsterdam: Rodopi, pp. 197–212.

Gries, St. Th. (2014) 'Quantitative Corpus Approaches to Linguistic Analysis: Seven or Eight Levels of Resolution and The Lessons They Teach Us', in I. Taavitsainen, M. Kytö, C. Claridge and J. Smith (eds) *Developments in English: Expanding Electronic Evidence*, Cambridge: Cambridge University Press, pp. 29–47.

Gries, St. Th. (2019) *Ten Lectures On Corpus-Linguistic Approaches In Cognitive Linguistics*, Leiden and Boston: Brill.

Gries, St. Th. (2021) 'Analyzing Dispersion', in M. Paquot and St. Th. Gries (eds) *Practical Handbook of Corpus Linguistics*, Berlin and New York: Springer, pp. 99–118.

Harris, Z. S. (1970) *Papers in Structural and Transformational Linguistics*, Dordrecht: Reidel.

Hilpert, M. (2006) 'Distinctive Collexeme Analysis and Diachrony', *Corpus Linguistics and Linguistic Theory* 2(2): 243–56.

Hoey, M. (2005) *Lexical Priming: A New Theory of Words and Language*, London: Routledge.

Levshina, N. (2021) 'Conditional Inference Trees and Random Forests', in M. Paquot and St. Th. Gries (eds) *Practical Handbook of Corpus Linguistics*, Berlin and New York: Springer, pp. 611–43.

Lijffijt, J. and Gries, St. Th. (2012) 'Correction to "Dispersions and Adjusted Frequencies in Corpora"', *International Journal of Corpus Linguistics* 17(1): 147–9.

Mason, O. (1999) 'Parameters of Collocation: The Word in the Centre of Gravity', in J. M. Kirk (ed.) *Corpora Galore: Analyses and Techniques in Describing English*, Amsterdam: Rodopi, pp. 267–80.

Moisl, H. (2015) *Cluster Analysis for Corpus Linguistics*, Boston and Berlin: De Gruyter.

Pine, J. M. Freudenthal, D., Krajewski, G. and Gobet. F. (2013) 'Do Young Children Have Adult-Like Syntactic Categories? Zipf's Law and the Case of the Determiner', *Cognition* 127(3): 345–60.

Stefanowitsch, A. and Gries, St. Th. (2003) 'Collostructions: Investigating the Interaction of Words and Constructions', *International Journal of Corpus Linguistics*, 8(2): 209–43.

Szmrecsanyi, B. (2006) 'Language Users as Creatures Of Habit: A Corpus-Based Analysis of Persistence in Spoken English', *Corpus Linguistics and Linguistic Theory* 1(1): 113–50.

Wulff, S. (2016) 'A Friendly Conspiracy of Input, L1, and Processing Demands: That-Variation in German and Spanish Learner Language', in L. Ortega, A. E. Tyler, H. I. Park and M. Uno (eds) *The Usage-Based Study of Language Learning and Multilingualism*, Georgetown: Georgetown University Press, pp. 115–36.

Part II

Using a corpus to investigate language

14

What can a corpus tell us about lexis?

David Oakey

1 Corpus linguistics and lexis

A corpus linguistic approach to language study naturally leads to a focus on linguistic form: Corpus analysis software first presents language as written forms to be seen by the researcher on a screen, rather than as sounds in the air to be recorded and transcribed, or as processes in the mind to be inferred through experiment. In the English language, the basic meaningful written form is the word, and the study of words, their forms and meanings, all falls within the scope of lexis. Corpus linguistics, therefore, has a lot to tell us about lexis.

Lexis is usually viewed as one side of a separation between the form of a language and its meanings, between its syntax and semantics, and between its grammatical structures and the words used in them. Many decades of analysis of ever-larger text corpora, however, have revealed patterns of language use that blur the traditional boundaries between lexis and grammar, and a common theme of corpus linguistics has been a rejection of a clear distinction between the two systems. Halliday (1991: 32), for example, developed the notion of *lexicogrammar* which views lexis and grammar as opposite ends of a single continuum, in a similar way to how waves and particles are seen as complementary aspects of light, and the use of corpus data was crucial to the development of Halliday's ideas (Halliday, 1966: 159 cited in Oakey 2020: 3). Lexis, as seen by corpus linguists, now involves not only the meaning relations between words themselves but also how meanings arise from the grammatical configurations in which words are used in the real world.

Corpus linguistics has thus had an effect on researchers' theoretical stances towards language: When electronic corpora were first collected in the 1960s, they were in direct opposition to the dominant linguistic research paradigm of the time, which focused on internal mental representations of language for which corpus evidence was irrelevant. In the opinion of a contemporary reviewer, for example, 'many linguists will be uninterested in pursuing their researches into LANGUAGE with the questionable aid of a million words of typographic USAGE' (Maverick 1969: 75) (emphasis in the original).

DOI: 10.4324/9780367076399-14

Since then, however, within theoretical linguistics more value has been placed on evidence from language use. Murphy (2010: 5), for example, has pointed out that theoretical models of the mental lexicon (language “in here” or “I-language”) need to be consistent with the observed features of usage (language “out there” or “E-language”) that are provided by reference to a corpus. Taylor (2012: 1) similarly argues that while the goal of linguistic theory should be a theory of language in the mind, it ‘must begin with a study of language as encountered’ and that I-language and E-language should be ‘aligned as closely as possible’. Taylor even goes on to liken language as represented in the brain to a corpus, and states that ‘knowledge of a language consists in knowledge of the kinds of facts that are recorded in a corpus and that can be extracted from it’ (ibid: 3). From corpus linguists there have also been proposed lexically based theories of language which are based primarily on corpus evidence: Lexical priming (Hoey, 2005) and the theory of norms and exploitations (Hanks 2013), for example, both draw on evidence from language use and prioritise the role of lexis over grammar in making meaning.

Thus the lexis described in this chapter is both similar to and different from lexis from the pre-corpus era. The following sections describe how corpus linguistics can offer the researcher lexical insights in a wide range of areas and highlight where our existing knowledge of language can be extended and where new discoveries can be made.

2 Word frequency lists

The simplest use of a corpus in relation to lexis is to show word frequency (see Chapter 10, this volume), and counting words pre-dates the invention of computers by several centuries. The earliest wordlists are in the form of concordances, or indexes, to sacred texts such as the Bible or the Koran. These concordances aim to reveal more to followers of a religion by providing an index of where each word occurs in the text, together with some of the surrounding context to show how the word is used.

The forerunners of modern corpus linguists proceeded from counting and indexing words in single texts to collecting ever-larger samples from many texts which represented the variety of language being studied. Producing concordances by hand is a labour-intensive task, and manually counting words and their meanings in these text collections was an effort that ‘still boggles the mind’ (Gilner 2011: 69). In the first half of the twentieth century, psychologist George Zipf used a corpus of 44,000 words of American newspaper English to investigate the relationship between word length, variety, and frequency (Zipf 1935: 24). In the field of English language teaching Irving Lorge and Edward Thorndike, in their *Semantic Count of English Words*, created a list of words and their different senses (Lorge and Thorndike 1938), cross-referenced with the Oxford English Dictionary, based on various corpora eventually totalling 4.5 million words. Various scholarly committees then combined several existing wordlists, culminating in West’s *General Service List of English Words* (West 1953) of 2,000 headwords and their most frequent meanings and derivations.

The introduction of computers to the study of language built on this previous work and essentially continued doing things the same way, only faster. In 1964, computer-generated English word counts were produced from the million-token Brown Corpus of American written English, based on samples of texts from different varieties of fiction and non-fiction (Francis and Kučera 1964/1979). Counting words was still an intensive use of resources, even with computerisation, and it took a million-dollar IBM 7070 mainframe computer with 50Kb of RAM '14 hours of continuous dedicated processing with the aid of six tape drives to construct the first word list' (Kučera 2002: 307). Today's researchers, by contrast, have a tremendous amount of computing power on hand, either on their desktop or in the cloud.

In the decades since the Brown Corpus, corpora have grown ever larger, from the COBUILD Bank of English (Sinclair 1987) of 18 million tokens, the British National Corpus (1994) of 100 million tokens, the Corpus of Contemporary American English (Davies 2008-) of 1 billion tokens, to corpora taken automatically from webpages such as the English Web 2020 corpus of 38 billion tokens on *Sketch Engine* (Kilgarriff *et al.* 2004, 2014). The majority of these resources are accessible to researchers online, usually by subscription, and all of the observations about lexis in this chapter can be replicated by the reader.

A wide variety of corpus-derived wordlists has since been compiled in this pre-corpus tradition, although the tendency of list makers to include the frequent senses of each word in the list in the manner of Thorndike, Lorge, and West has fallen away. It is now customary to use wordlists as a way of evaluating the words which occur in a text or texts. List makers now refer to how many of the word forms in a text or corpus are matched by the word forms in a particular wordlist, known as the "coverage" of a text by a list, with no information about the different meanings of these word forms (e.g. Nation 2013: 16). Information about word sense frequencies is now instead to be found in language learner dictionaries, which, since the introduction of the COBUILD dictionary in 1987, have used corpora as a basis for their definitions and list the different meanings of a headword in order of their frequency in the corpus (see Chapter 28, this volume).

The most frequent words in any wordlist from a corpus of written English are the "grammatical" or "function" or "closed-class" words such as *the*, *to*, and *of*. These have little meaning in themselves in a wordlist but are essential for building meaning by combination with other words. It can be seen from Table 14.1 that the top ten most frequent words in the 12 stories by Arthur Conan Doyle comprising *The Adventures of Sherlock Holmes* (Conan Doyle 1892) are grammatical words. The list was obtained from *Sketch Engine* (op. cit.) (see Chapter 9, this volume for more on software). It can be seen that, in addition to the usual common grammatical words, the wordlist contains *be* and *have*. This is because in this instance the tool has been instructed to count lemmas, and so the 4,566 occurrences for *be* also include other forms of the lemma such as *is*, *was*, *were*, *are*, *been* and *being*. Rows 211–218 from lower down the frequency list show how much less common lexical words are such as *wife* and *mind*. Indeed, word frequencies in different corpora, whatever size, display similar distributions: A very small number of words occur very frequently, a lot more words occur infrequently and around half the words occur only once.

Word frequency lists can be displayed graphically instead of as a table, and Figure 14.1 shows the full wordlist for *The Adventures of Sherlock Holmes* displayed in different visualisations. The word clouds in Figure 14.1a and b reveal how much grammatical words dominate the wordlist. Word clouds, in which the size of the word is proportional to its frequency of occurrence, can display word frequency information quickly in a small amount of space; frequent words are those which are legible, while infrequent words are displayed but are too small to be read. Figure 14.1a includes grammatical words, which are the most visible in the cloud, whereas Figure 14.1b omits

Table 14.1 Excerpts from word frequency lists for *The Adventures of Sherlock Holmes* in *Sketch Engine*

	Sketch Engine	
Rank	Word	Frequency
1	the	5601
2	be	4566
3	i	3032
4	and	3001
5	to	2681
6	of	2645
7	a	2623
8	have	2125
9	in	1757
10	that	1743
–	–	–
211	lie	61
212	mind	61
213	between	60
214	fact	60
215	run	60
216	wife	60
217	chair	59
218	course	59
219	drive	59
220	meet	59

grammatical words, and so far fewer words are immediately legible, and the differences between the size of these words and that of less frequent words is noticeably smaller.

The other way of visually displaying a wordlist is through frequency charts. Figure 14.1c shows the word frequencies in two ways: A line graph shows the cumulative percentage of the words in the corpus at each point in the frequency list. Thus *give* is the 213th word form in the list and at that point these 213 word forms – known as types – account for 67 per cent of all the words – known as tokens – in the corpus. Figure 14.1c also shows a bar chart of the word frequencies, but the precipitous fall in frequencies at the top of the list, and the very large number of words which occur only once in the corpus, means that the bars are difficult to see. Word frequencies are therefore often plotted on a log scale, shown in Figure 14.1d, which plots a word's frequency against its rank in the word list. The log scale, in this case to the power of 10, allows both large and small frequencies to be visible. The most frequent word in the list, *the*, has a rank of 1 and occurs 5,601 times, while the least frequent words in the list, each of which occurs only once, comprise 44 per cent of the list. The roughly straight line made by the points on the chart suggest a constant relationship between a word's frequency in a list and its rank in that list, a property first observed in written corpora in the pre-computer era in the study by Zipf in 1935.

Frequency lists for modern large corpora provide more information about the words in the corpus. The word frequency list for the 1-billion-token *Corpus of Contemporary American English* (COCA) in Table 14.2 shows the frequencies of words in the corpus as

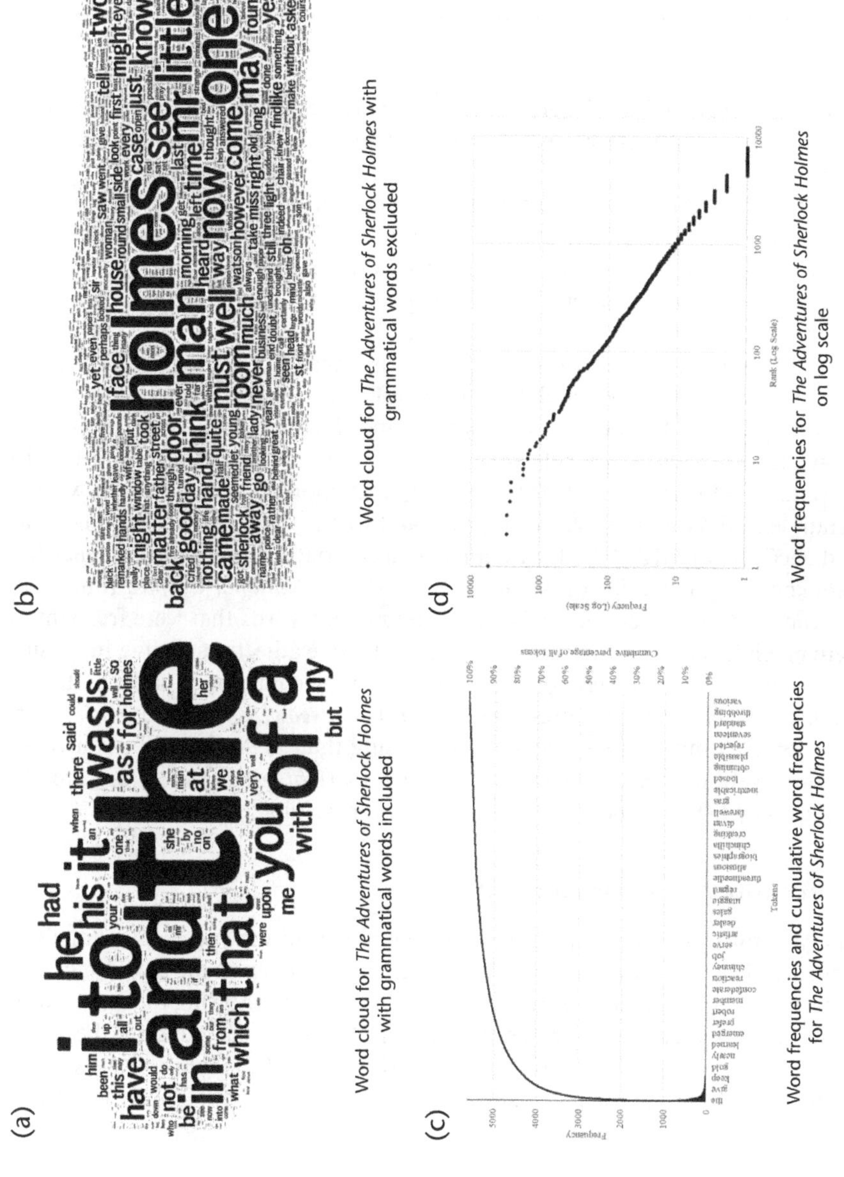

(a) Word cloud for *The Adventures of Sherlock Holmes* with grammatical words included

(b) Word cloud for *The Adventures of Sherlock Holmes* with grammatical words excluded

(c) Word frequencies and cumulative word frequencies for *The Adventures of Sherlock Holmes*

(d) Word frequencies for *The Adventures of Sherlock Holmes* on log scale

Figure 14.1 Different ways of graphically presenting a word frequency list for *The Adventures of Sherlock Holmes*

Table 14.2 Sample from the word frequency list for the *Corpus of Contemporary American English* (COCA)

Rank	*Word*	*Freq*	*#texts*	*%caps*	*Blog*	*Web*	*TVM*	*Spok*	*Fic*	*Mag*	*News*	*Acad*
2585	partners	35,578	20,671	13	4414	4790	2578	2538	1523	5919	6370	7446
2595	closely	35,323	28,239	1	3881	4767	1051	3976	3566	5285	4582	8215
2605	notion	35,179	23,089	0	4815	4811	756	3872	2258	4580	3452	10635
2615	turkey	34,960	12,175	58	3455	4613	2816	4164	1956	6206	6002	5748
2625	joint	34,802	20,524	23	2775	4531	2645	3715	2441	4900	5265	8529
2635	flowers	34,622	17,489	11	1932	2463	4747	2039	8473	9461	3660	1845
2645	refused	34,450	25,654	1	3813	4461	1703	3940	5874	4684	6288	3685
2655	figured	34,340	25,587	3	4108	3252	9668	2871	7401	3421	2751	867
2665	shots	34,212	19,679	6	4973	3679	4137	3585	3512	6471	6862	993
2675	ford	34,111	13,688	98	3203	2881	1991	5206	2559	7018	8983	2180

a whole and also in each of the different genres or varieties of English collected in the corpus: blogs, websites, TV programmes, spoken language, fiction, magazines, newspaper and academic prose.

The list shows that 58 per cent of occurrences of the word form *turkey* are capitalised and thus likely to refer to the country, while the other 42 per cent of occurrences are likely to refer to the bird. Similarly the vast majority (98 per cent) of occurrences of *ford* are capitalised and thus likely to refer to the American motor company rather than to a river crossing.

One of the strengths of COCA for the study of lexis is that it contains over 127 million tokens of unscripted speech. Spoken data is more difficult to collect than written data in terms of transcription costs and privacy concerns, and the analysis of large amounts of spoken language use in corpora is relatively recent. Studies of conversations in English corpora have revealed that certain words are used much more in speech than in writing, and important lexical differences between speech and writing have quickly become clear. Buttery and McCarthy (2012: 288), for example, in a comparison of word frequency lists from the spoken and written fiction sections of the *British National Corpus*, found that only 65 per cent of words occurred on both lists and many words that were frequent on one list were much less frequent in the other list. Evaluative adjectives ending in -y, such as *yucky*, *stroppy*, *comfy* and *grumpy*, were much more common in speech than in writing; nouns indicating facial expressions like *grimace*, *scowl*, *smirk* and *pout*, on the other hand, occurred much more frequently in writing than in speech. Words used for keeping a conversation going, response tokens such as *right*, *yeah* and so on, are also higher in frequency lists for speaking than in those for writing.

3 Words in context: concordance lines

Corpus analysis software has adapted another method from the pre-corpus linguistics era mentioned earlier, that of concordancing. Instead of an index of the location of each word in a corpus, concordancing software presents lines of text showing the search word in the centre of the screen and a pre-set number of characters surrounding the search term; these concordance lines are also known as Key Word-In-Context (KWIC) lines (see Chapter 9, this volume, for more on concordancing software). Concordance lines show a word in its immediate lexical and grammatical environment and are ideal for investigating the relations between words, their forms and meanings.

Concordance lines offer a fascinating snapshot of a word's lexical and grammatical behaviour. The software drags snippets of speech and writing into alignment, regardless of context, so that at times the researcher feels like they are performing the equivalent of eavesdropping on private conversations or rifling through private correspondence. The context on either side of the aligned search word offers clues to the situation of language use it was used in and the register or variety constituted by that situation. Whether written or spoken, fiction or real life, the word is taken by the software and impartially aligned for inspection. The juxtaposition, for example, of daytime TV chat show, impassioned movie dialogue, dull instruction booklet or parliamentary debate can be intriguing.

Figure 14.2 shows a random sample of ten concordance lines for a search for the word form *remote* in COCA. Generally the context around *remote* in these lines is enough to reveal its part of speech and its meaning. It is used as part of a compound noun *remote control,* and as an attributive adjective is used to modify nouns like *area* or *areas*, *islands* and *places*. Words immediately to the right of *remote* are sorted so that words with initial letters nearer the beginning of the alphabet are higher up the screen. This helps the corpus linguist identify words that are used repeatedly with *remote*, such as *control* and *area*.

In the Collins COBUILD dictionary, based on analysis of vastly more examples of *remote* than in these few lines, the "far away" sense of *remote* is the most frequent meaning found:

> Remote areas are far away from cities and places where most people live, and are therefore difficult to get to.
>
> *(Collins COBUILD Advanced Learner's Dictionary 2018: 1270)*

and the nouns *area* and *places* seen in the surrounding context are used in the definition itself to reinforce their importance to this meaning of *remote*. Early corpus lexicographers manually read through concordance lines like these to identify the meanings of the words from the context. This was only possible, however, because the number of occurrences of less frequent words in these early corpora was low. Moon (2007: 166), for example, described how the Collins COBUILD dictionary definition for *skate* was based on the 35 examples found in the first Bank of English corpus of 7.5 million tokens. Modern corpora are much larger and contain many, many more occurrences of even low-frequency words; *skate*, for example, occurs nearly 300,000 times in the English Web 2020 corpus. It would of course be impossible for a corpus linguist to read all the concordance lines for the word and make systematic judgements on its meaning from the surrounding context in each case, and so most concordancing software allows a limited number of randomly sampled lines to be displayed. Word profiling software which generalises patterns from concordances, such as *Sketch Engine*, is normally used for lexicographical work on dictionaries and will be discussed more in Section 4 on collocation.

When corpus linguists began to look at large numbers of concordance lines, they noticed that words were repeatedly used in certain grammatical configurations. Patterns became immediately visible from the regularities in concordance lines arising from the font in which they were presented. Figure 14.3 shows concordance lines for *want*; words immediately to the right of *want* are sorted so that words nearer the beginning of the alphabet are higher up the screen. The repeated infinitive complementation of *want* by *talk*, followed by

```
bodies of two young men were found in this remote area called the Geronimo Trail outside Douglas, A
ust pack up the ole minivan and drive into remote areas and survive off the land are living in a fa
ese. Any American who has ever commanded a remote control knows the unavoidable truth about this na
 the space with fumes. The operator uses a remote control to keep a safe distance. Happily missing
lent and yet full of dimly heard echoes, a remote disturbance of mumbling voices, swept into town p
y because their home is on one of the most remote islands in the Pacific. It is also because they h
s like this. Listen. Mark grabs the STEREO REMOTE off the kitchen counter and turns up the volume t
ve comes first, always, drives me to these remote places. She didn't have the heart for it. So tell
nd that they needed to be redistributed to remote rural areas and re-educated. Ms-UNG: Yes. SIMON:
at the further away the story is, the more remote the population, the less interest the press has.
```

Figure 14.2 Concordance lines for *remote* in COCA

```
es and a data stick. "This is what they want to stop."# "Wait, "Virginia said.
thing very bad happened to her. I don't want to surround myself with that. So you wan
ompany, but before I accept the badge I want to take a moment to think through the
  "# Angela Rogers added: "I just don't want to take a risk on Obama. We just can't take
It means, what do you have that I might want to take from you in a bet? What do I have
 impeachment proceedings in Congress. I want to take that  now to Democratic Congressman Eric
hout registering, which I really didn't want to take the time to do right now, but does what
llance and other things that he did not want to talk about, particularly because its name, Dirty
u changed your mind. You probably don't want to talk about it. You're doing the right thing.
s information is being compromised. You want to talk about the 1800s Erica, maybe you should go bac
ey. I heard about what happened. Do you want to talk about it? That's cool. Do you mind
     He's... He's not... I don't really want to talk about Glen. Okay. What about other family?
 if he did acid. Bradley said he didn't want to talk about that stuff. # Howard said he doesn't
en by your own definition of what women want to talk about, you'd pass it. According to wikipedia
     she said angrily. Versus: "I don't want to talk about it," she said and smacked her hand
```

Figure 14.3 Sample concordance lines for *want* in COCA sorted one, two and three words to the right of the search word

post-modifying prepositional phrases beginning with *about,* causes vertical white lines to be visible to the right of *want* which are not observable on the left of the word.

Patterns in concordance lines like this revealed a strong relationship between the meaning of a word and the grammatical pattern it was used in and led to the notion of pattern grammar (Hunston and Francis 2000) in which words are used in similar grammatical configurations when used with similar meanings. Generalisations from concordance lines like *want to talk* led to the formulation of grammar patterns, such as **V to-inf**, which were added to COBUILD dictionary definitions. Grammar patterns have similarities to the concept of "construction", a concept from cognitive linguistics where lexis takes on meaning by being used in a particular grammatical sequence (Hunston and Su 2017: 570), and are an example of how corpus linguistics has blurred the boundaries between traditional grammar and lexis.

4 Collocation and semantic prosody

Corpus linguistics has had a lasting effect on the study of collocation, an important area of lexis also identified in the pre-corpus linguistics era. It has long been known that particular words have a tendency to combine more often with some words rather than with others. The twentieth-century British linguist J. R. Firth's famous example was *strong tea* (Firth 1957). He pointed out that while words in theory can be combined in many different ways, allowing for grammatical constraints, language users largely prefer to use particular combinations more than others, and supposedly synonymous words can sound "odd", particularly to native speakers of the language, when combined. The word *powerful* is regarded as a synonym of *strong*, yet the collocation *powerful tea* seems at the very least to mean something different than *strong tea*. Corpus linguistics has enabled researchers to quantify these typical combinations and calculate the probability of their co-occurrences in a corpus so that the likelihood of a particular word being followed by another particular word can be predicted.

Frequent collocations of a word can easily be observed from the surrounding context in concordance lines. In Figure 14.2, as we have already seen, concordance lines show that the word form *remote* occurs with *control, area, areas, islands* and *places*. In larger corpora, word profiling software such as *Sketch Engine* summarises the many hundreds of thousands of concordance lines for occurrences of words like *remote* to produce a behavioural profile known as a "word sketch". Table 14.3 shows part of a word sketch for *remote*.

Sketch Engine lists collocations in terms of their typicality rather than their absolute frequency, here based on how often *remote* collocates with a word rather than with other words. The adjective *remote* collocates with nouns like *control, villages, locations* and *server* much more frequently than it does with other nouns.

The learning of collocations has long been seen as crucial to attaining proficiency when learning a language (Palmer 1933; Sinclair *et al.* 1970/2004; Lewis 1993; Nesselhauf 2003; Oakey 2010; Szudarski 2018). Through the *English Vocabulary Profile* site (Capel 2015) it is possible to see the collocations used by English language learners at different proficiency levels, as measured against the *Common European Framework of Reference for Languages* (CEFR) (Council of Europe 2021). The site summarises results from the Cambridge Learner Corpus, a collection of hundreds of thousands of exam papers by English learners from the lowest proficiency level, A1, to the highest, C2. In the case of *remote*, the corpus shows that learners at level B2 are able to use the word with its most frequent sense of "far away," collocating with nouns such as *area*. More proficient learners at level C2, in addition, can

Table 14.3 Excerpt from the word sketch for *remote* based on the English Web 2020 corpus in *Sketch Engine*

Modifiers of remote	*Nouns modified by remote*	*Verbs complemented by remote*
geographically	control	shake
geographically remote	*remote control*	*shake the Wii Remote*
impossibly	location	program
impossibly remote	*remote locations*	*program a firestick remote*
partially	server	use
Full-time, partially remote position	*a remote server*	*using the Wii remote*
infinitely	attacker	swing
infinitely remote	*allows remote attackers to*	*swing the Wii Remote*
however	village	grab
however remote	*remote villages*	*grabbed the TV remote*
live	monitoring	point
a live remote from	*remote monitoring*	*pointing the Wii Remote*
exceedingly	access	tilt
exceedingly remote	*remote access to*	*by tilting the Wii Remote*
extremely	island	pair
extremely remote	*a remote island*	*pair a different firestick remote*
inconceivably	viewing	programme
inconceivably remote	*remote viewing*	*programming your Harmony remote*
relatively	computer	connect
a relatively remote	*the remote computer*	*Connect Virtual Technician remote*
fairly	working	replace
a fairly remote	*remote working*	*replaces the original Wii Remote*

use *remote* with its less frequent senses of "far away in time", collocating *remote* with *past*, and "far away from reality", collocating *remote* with *possibility*.

Corpus linguistics studies language in use as a moving target. The COVID-19 pandemic offers many examples of the kind of real-world lexical shift which corpus linguists are well placed to study. In February 2020 the disease caused by the SARS-CoV-2 virus was officially named by the World Health Organization as *COVID-19* (WHO 2020). It then began to be written and spoken about in the news and on social media, and this writing and speech began to be archived in online corpora; in turn, results from corpus-informed studies into the lexis of COVID-19 in English swiftly appeared. The Oxford English Dictionary (OED 2020) provided empirical proof, from their 8-billion-token monitor corpus of web-based news which is collected almost in real time, of the vertiginous increase in use of the words *coronavirus* and *COVID-19* between December 2019 and March 2020 and listed frequent collocations such as *outbreak, infection, spread* and *fear*. Also prior to December 2019, similar to the other corpora surveyed here, the OED corpus showed that the most common collocates of *remote* were familiar nouns like *control, island* and *village*. However, restrictions on office working imposed as a result of the COVID-19 pandemic led to many employees having to work from home. The proportion of people working remotely rose from 5.7 per cent of workers in January/February 2020 to 43.1 per cent in April 2020 (Felstead and Reuschke 2020). By the end of 2020, consequently, the most frequent collocates of *remote* had suddenly become *learning, working* and *work force* (Schuessler 2020).

Evidence on collocations from corpus linguistics has blurred traditional category boundaries in lexicology. Both synonymy and antonymy are paradigmatic lexical relations between words: When synonyms are substituted, there is no change in the propositional meaning of the sentence as a whole (Carter 2012: 34), whereas when antonyms are substituted, the propositional meaning of a sentence becomes opposite. Corpus evidence, however, has shown that antonyms are actually used together in sentences rather than instead of each other; antonyms like *right and wrong* and *high and low* co-occur much more often than by chance (Jones *et al.* 2012), and evidence of such collocations shows that syntagmatic relations are also important in understanding their use.

The traditional view of synonymy has similarly been challenged by corpus linguistic work on collocations. Word processing software often has thesaurus tools which offer synonyms to help writers choose alternative words. The synonyms for *strong* listed on the software on my PC include *robust*, *sturdy* and *solid*, all of which would sound odd when used to describe tea. Use of such thesaurus synonym tools can be risky: Extensive word substitution by student writers using thesaurus suggestions has been termed *roget-ing* (Grove 2014: 7) and has been seen to result in meaningless combinations when collocational relations are unwittingly broken. Grove (ibid) gives the example of *left behind* transformed through roget-ing into *sinister buttocks* and *powerful personalised services* into *Herculean personalised liturgies*.

Liberman (2012) illustrates how unfamiliar collocations can sound "odd" using a statement by Mitt Romney, a presidential candidate in the 2012 US presidential election, who said in a speech that 'I was a severely conservative governor.' Liberman lists puzzled reactions to this statement from US political commentators and quotes Molly Ball of *The Atlantic* magazine as saying that the statement 'described conservatism as if it were a disease'. Liberman points out that reference to a corpus can help explain how the collocation "severely conservative" had such a poor reaction. The word cloud from COCA and the word sketch visualisation from the English Web 2020 in Figure 14.4 show the adjectives occurring one word to the right of *severely*; both images are very revealing about the lexical environment brought about by the use of the word.

The corpus evidence in Figure 14.4 shows the overwhelming tendency of *severely* to collocate with words with negative meanings. This is a fact about language use which is replicable: It can be observed by looking in both COCA and Sketch Engine, two independently collected corpora. This aspect of collocation has been found to be so widespread that it has been termed *semantic prosody*: 'the consistent aura of meaning with which a form is imbued by its collocates' (Louw 1993: 57). A word, like *conservative*, can take on a negative meaning purely by reason of its collocation with *severely*. The negative semantic prosody of *severely* in Liberman's example meant that Mitt Romney, while clearly intending to say something positive, instead was understood to be saying that he thought *conservative* was a negative quality.

An example of positive semantic prosody can be seen from the verb collocates of the noun *diversity,* as shown in Figure 14.5. The examples in the corpus show that diversity is seen as something to be *respected*, *promoted*, *celebrated*, *valued* and *embraced*, for example.

There may be language users for whom *diversity* has a negative semantic prosody, e.g. for ideological reasons, but they are either too few in the corpus or the users do not speak or write about it by using the word *diversity* in a way that can be picked up by corpus linguistic analysis.

Figure 14.4 Adjectives modified by *severely* in COCA and English Web 2020 on Sketch Engine

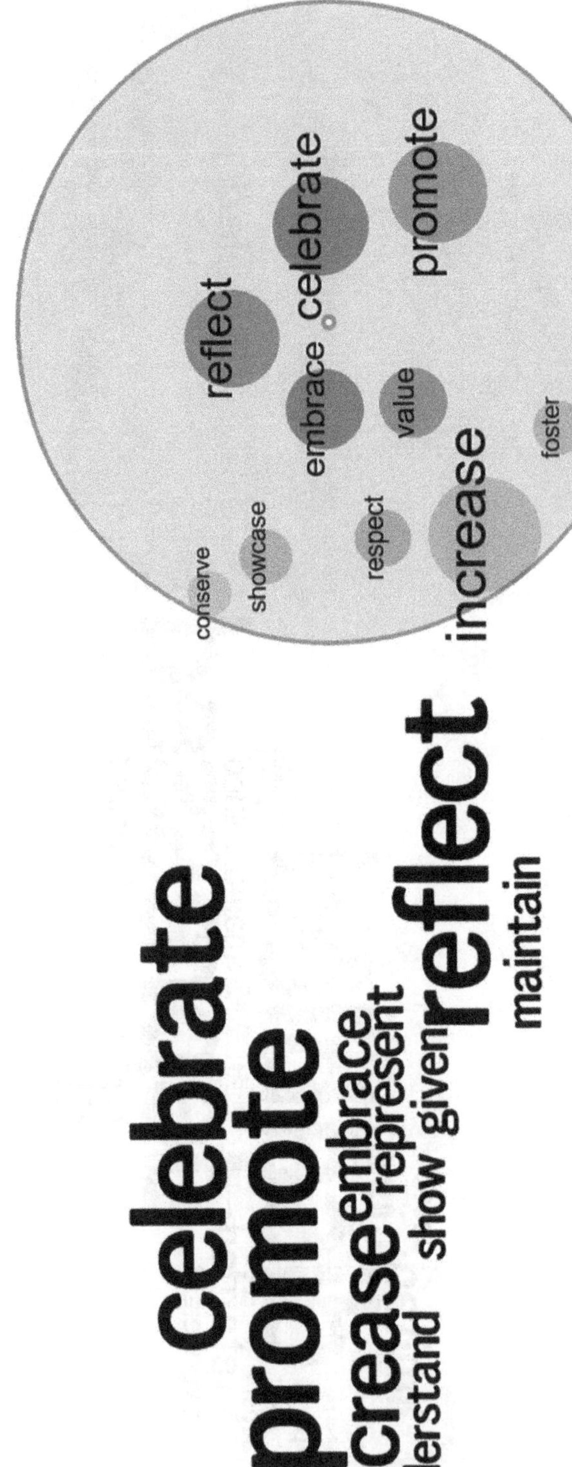

Figure 14.5 Verbs for which *diversity* is the object in COCA and English Web 2020 on Sketch Engine

The idea of semantic prosody is similar to the traditional lexical relation of connotation, which involves the positive or negative associations a word conjures up (Carter 2012: 36), but semantic prosody is less subjective, since it can be quantified through examining a word's collocations. Semantic prosody can also be criticised (Hanks 2013: 124), since it is implausible that every word can be divided semantically into objectively determined categories of positive and negative polarity. But corpus analysis shows how a word tends to be used, and the researcher can better determine the speaker's or writer's attitude to what they are talking about in specific contexts. Semantic prosody is another example of how corpus linguistics has blurred the boundaries between traditional grammar and lexis. Books on both subjects, in fact, deal with the concept in more detail: i.e. *Corpus Linguistics for Grammar* (Jones and Waller 2015) and *Corpus Linguistics for Vocabulary* (Szudarski 2018).

5 Metaphor

The patterns of lexis observed using corpus linguistics methods have been influential in revealing more about metaphor. Word meaning can be seen as literal and metaphorical, where features of one domain have been transferred to another target domain. The literal sense of the noun *crescendo*, for example, refers to sound becoming louder and more intense. The most frequent verb with *crescendo* as its object in COCA is *reach*, and Figure 14.6 shows example concordance lines for this collocation. It can be seen that only four lines (4, 5, 9 and 10) refer to uses of the word in its musical sense, in the form of *applause*, *cheering*, *music* and *musketry*.

Even then, the collocation of *crescendo* with *reach* means its original sense has changed to one of an endpoint, or climax, which is the kind of change which is resisted by some language users. The music critic Miles Hoffman (2013: 17) is adamant that 'you cannot "reach" a crescendo ... even if you make the most enormous crescendo in the world, you will not have "reached" anything until you get to the top.' He believes that musicians will never accept that 'a word that for centuries has had one and only one precise meaning will, through repeated flagrant misuse, come to mean something else' (ibid). This example shows where a corpus linguist can document the process of changing use through which a word evolves new meanings according the lexical preferences of its users. The meanings of *crescendo* in the other lines are metaphorical, transferring this new climactic aspect of the meaning of *crescendo* to other things that can grow more intense, such as *outcry, speculation, attacks, sensation, concerns* and *hostility*.

Metaphorical as opposed to literal language has traditionally been seen as belonging to the domain of literature, but more recent work has instead argued that metaphors used in language reflect the way people think and that studying related metaphors in language can reveal conceptual networks (Deignan 2005: 4). A distinction has thus arisen between linguistic and conceptual metaphors, with the former providing evidence for the existence of the latter (Deignan 2017). Corpus evidence about lexis and meaning is thus becoming more relevant to the E-language and I-language dialectic mentioned in Section 1.

An area for future corpus linguistic work on metaphor is the COVID-19 coronavirus, which has already been shown to have greatly impacted lexical behaviour. Hunston (2020), using the 10-billion-token *News on the Web* corpus (Davies 2016-), described how language users have extended the meanings of words and combinations such as *isolation*, *social distance* and *lockdown* in order to accommodate new COVID-19–related meanings

```
1.  as the outcry from animal rights activists reached a crescendo. JEFFREY-KAHN: We did acknowled
2.  e speculation gained strength all fall and reached a crescendo when Lloyd Carr made his
3.  list fervor. The attacks began in 1990 and reached a crescendo the following year in
4.  st free throw attempt missed, the applause reached a crescendo, climaxing as the second shot
5.  their way up Crescent Street. The cheering reached a crescendo. " I wouldn't ever try to do
6.  't it obvious? " The sensation in my chest reached a crescendo, and I felt sick. I leaped up
7.  n trial just before public safety concerns reached a crescendo. In June 1992, public
8.   # SOVIET HOSTILITY to the West over Dnitz reached a crescendo in the week that followed,
9.    Connie. Then you can collapse. The music reached a tumultuous crescendo, and she was off the
10. Wayne's support as the Colonials' musketry reached a crescendo. Monckton fell so close to the
```

Figure 14.6 Concordance lines for *crescendo* as the object of *reach* in COCA

and pointed out that 'our thoughts have been guided by wartime metaphors' (Hunston 2020: 1). This fact is reflected in the observable use around the term *coronavirus* of collocations like *fight, battle* and *combat,* revealing that the virus is seen as an enemy that needs to be fought. In this respect the linguistic and conceptual metaphors around the coronavirus are similar to that observed by corpus linguists in reporting of the SARS outbreak in 2003 (Wallis and Nerlich, 2005), and in public discourse in general (Flusberg *et al.* 2018). If people talk about the response to the coronavirus using militaristic linguistic metaphors, it is because they think of it in similar terms.

This chapter has given a brief overview of the wide range of areas where corpus linguistics can offer the researcher lexical insights. With access to a corpus and basic software, the reader can follow up by counting words, identifying repeated patterns and investigating the relations between words, their forms and meanings and their use.

Further reading

Deignan, A. H. (2017) 'From Linguistic to Conceptual Metaphors,' in E. Semino and Z. Demjen (eds) *The Routledge Handbook of Metaphor and Language*, London: Routledge, pp. 102–17. (This chapter is a very readable 'way in' to using corpora to study metaphor and makes a convincing case for the necessity of using corpus data to inform research into this important area of lexis at the interface of E-language and I-language.)

Flowerdew, L. (2012) *Corpora and Language Education*, New York: Palgrave Macmillan. (A wide-ranging survey of applications of corpus linguistics to language teaching and learning, this book contains insights on features blurring the boundaries between lexis and grammar and their implications for learners of English.)

Hanks, P. (2013) *Lexical Analysis*, Cambridge, MA: MIT Press. (This book propounds a lexically driven theory of language reflecting the tendency of users to choose certain ways of expressing themselves. A fascinating overview of words and meanings and how their use changes over time.)

Hasselgård, H., Ebeling, J. and Oksefjell Ebeling, S. (eds) (2013) *Corpus Perspectives on Patterns of Lexis*, Amsterdam: John Benjamins. (This collection of papers illustrates pertinent questions of lexis that can be investigated by a corpus linguistic approach.)

Murphy, M. L. (2010) *Lexical Meaning*, Cambridge: Cambridge University Press. (This book is a readable survey of traditional concerns in the study of lexis and is useful for benchmarking corpus linguistic studies.)

References

British National Corpus (Version 1.0) (1994), Oxford: Oxford University Computing Service.

Buttery, P. and McCarthy, M. J. (2012) 'Lexis in Spoken Discourse', in J. P. Gee and M. Handford (eds) *The Routledge Handbook of Discourse Analysis*, London: Routledge, pp. 285–300.

Capel, A. (2015) 'The English Vocabulary Profile', in J. Harrison and F. Barker (eds) *English Profile in Practice*, Cambridge: UCLES/Cambridge University Press, pp. 9–27.

Council of Europe (2021) *Common European Framework of Reference for Languages* (CEFR), Available online at https://www.coe.int/en/web/common-european-framework-reference-languages/level-descriptions.

Carter, R. (2012) *Vocabulary: Applied Linguistic Perspectives*, 2nd edn, London: Routledge.

Collins *COBUILD Advanced Learner's Dictionary*, 9th edn, (2018), London: Collins.

Conan Doyle, A. (1892) *The Adventures of Sherlock Holmes*, London: George Newnes.

Davies, M. (2008-) *The Corpus of Contemporary American English* (COCA), 1 Billion Words, 1990–2019. Available online at https://www.english-corpora.org/coca/.

Davies, M. (2016-) *Corpus of News on the Web* (NOW), *10 Billion Words from 20 Countries*. Available online at https://www-english-corpora.org/now/.

Deignan, A. (2005) *Metaphor and Corpus Linguistics*, Amsterdam: John Benjamins.

Deignan, A. H. (2017) 'From Linguistic to Conceptual Metaphors', in E. Semino and Z. Demjen (eds) *The Routledge Handbook of Metaphor and Language*, London: Routledge, pp. 102–17.

Felstead, A. and Reuschke, D. (2020) 'Homeworking in the UK: Before and During the 2020 Lockdown', WISERD Report, Cardiff: Wales Institute of Social and Economic Research. Accessed on 5 February 2021 from: https://wiserd.ac.uk/publications/homeworking-uk-and-during-2020-lockdown.

Firth, J. R. (1957) 'A Synopsis of Linguistic Theory 1930-1955', in J. R. Firth (ed.) *Studies in Linguistic Analysis*, Oxford: Basil Blackwell, pp. 1–32.

Flusberg, S. J., Matlock, T. and Thibodeau, P. H. (2018) 'War Metaphors in Public Discourse', *Metaphor and Symbol* 33(1): 1–18.

Francis, W. N. and Kučera, H. (1964/1979) *Manual of Information to Accompany A Standard Corpus of Present-Day Edited American English, for Use with Digital Computers*, Providence, RI: Brown University Department of Linguistics.

Gilner, L. (2011) 'A Primer on the General Service List', *Reading in a Foreign Language* 23: 65–83.

Grove, J. (2014) 'A Crafty Cheek in Sinister Buttocks', *Times Higher Education*, 7 August 2014, p. 7.

Halliday, M. A. K. (1991) 'Corpus Studies and Probabilistic Grammar', in K. Aijmer and B. Altenberg (eds) *English Corpus Linguistics,* London: Longman, pp. 30–43.

Halliday, M. A. K. (1966) 'Lexis as a Linguistic Level', in C. E. Bazell, J. C. Catford, M. A. K. Halliday and R. H. Robins (eds) *In Memory of J. R. Firth*, London: Longmans, pp. 148–62.

Hanks, P. (2013) *Lexical Analysis*, Cambridge, MA: MIT Press.

Hoey, M. (2005) *Lexical Priming: A New Theory of Words and Language*, London: Routledge.

Hoffman, M. (2013) 'A Crescendo of Errors', *New York Times*, July 29, 2013. Accessed on 23 February 2020 from: https://www.nytimes.com/2013/07/29/opinion/a-crescendo-of-errors.html.

Hunston, S. E. (2020) 'Changing Language in Unprecedented Times', *University of Birmingham, Department of English News*, 8th April 2020. Accessed on 23 April 2020 from: https://www.birmingham.ac.uk/schools/edacs/departments/englishlanguage/news/2020/changing-language.aspx.

Hunston, S. E., and Francis, G. (2000) *Pattern Grammar: A Corpus Driven Approach to the Lexical Grammar of English*, Amsterdam: Benjamins.

Hunston, S. and Su, H. (2017) 'Patterns, Constructions, and Local Grammar: A Case Study of 'Evaluation'', *Applied Linguistics* 40(4): 567–93.

Jones, S., Murphy, M. L., Paradis, C. and Willners, C. (2012) *Antonyms in English: Construals, Constructions and Canonicity*, Cambridge: Cambridge University Press.

Jones, C. and Waller, D. (2015) *Corpus Linguistics for Grammar: A Guide for Research*, London: Routledge.

Kilgarriff, A., Rychlý, P., Smrž, P. and Tugwell, D. (2004) The Sketch Engine. *Information Technology*, Available at https://www.sketchengine.eu/wp-content/uploads/The_Sketch_Engine_2004.pdf.

Kilgarriff, A., Baisa V., Bušta J., Jakubíček M., Kovář V., Michelfeit J., Rychlý P. and Suchomel V. (2014) 'The Sketch Engine: Ten Years On', *Lexicography* 1(1): 7–36.

Kučera, H. (2002) 'Obituary for W. Nelson Francis', *Journal of English Linguistics* 30: 306–9.

Lewis, M. (1993) *The Lexical Approach: The State of ELT and a Way Forward*, Hove: Language Teaching Publications.

Liberman, M. (2012) 'Severely X', University of Pennsylvania Language Log, 11th February 2012. Accessed 2 February 2020 from: http://languagelog.ldc.upenn.edu/nll/?p=3762.

Lorge, I. and Thorndike, E. L. (1938) *A Semantic Count of English Words*, New York: Institute of Educational Research, Teachers College, Columbia University.

Louw, B. (1993) 'Irony in the Text or Insincerity in the Writer? The Diagnostic Potential of Semantic Prosodies', in M. Baker, G. Francis and E. Tognini-Bonelli (eds) *Text and Technology: In Honour of John Sinclair*, Amsterdam: Benjamins, pp. 157–76.

Maverick, G. V. (1969) 'Review of "Computational Analysis of Present-Day American English" by Henry Kučera and W. Nelson Francis', *International Journal of American Linguistics* 35: 71–75.

Moon, R. (2007) 'Sinclair, Lexicography, and the COBUILD Project: The Application of Theory', *International Journal of Corpus Linguistics* 12(2): 159–81.
Murphy, M. L. (2010) *Lexical Meaning*, Cambridge: Cambridge University Press.
Nation, I. S. P. (2013) *Learning Vocabulary in Another Language*, 2nd edn, Cambridge: Cambridge University Press.
Nesselhauf, N. (2003) 'The Use of Collocations by Advanced Learners of English and Some Implications for Teaching', *Applied Linguistics* 24(2): 223–42.
Oakey, D. J. (2010) 'English Vocabulary and Collocation', in S. Hunston and D. J. Oakey (eds) *Introducing Applied Linguistics: Concepts and Skills*, London: Routledge, pp. 14–23.
Oakey, D. J. (2020) 'Phrases in EAP Academic Writing Pedagogy: Illuminating Halliday's Influence on Research and Practice', *Journal of English for Academic Purposes* 44: 1–16.
OED (2020) 'Corpus Analysis of the Language of COVID-19', *OED Blog*, 14th April 2020. Accessed on23 April 2020 from https://public.oed.com/blog/corpus-analysis-of-the-language-of-covid-19/.
Palmer, H. E. (1933) *Second Interim Report on English Collocations*: *Submitted to the Tenth Annual Conference of English Teachers*, Tokyo: The Institute for Research in English Teaching.
Schuessler, J. (2020) 'Oxford's 2020 Word of the Year? It's too Hard to Isolate', *New York Times*, 22nd November 2020. Accessed on 23 November 2020 from: https://www.nytimes.com/2020/11/22/arts/oxford-word-of-the-year-coronavirus.html.
Sinclair, J. M. (1987) *Looking Up: An Account of the COBUILD Project in Lexical Computing*, London: Collins ELT.
Sinclair, J. M., Jones, S. and Daley, R. (1970/2004) *English Collocation Studies: The OSTI Report*, London: Continuum.
Szudarski, P. (2018) *Corpus Linguistics for Vocabulary: A Guide for Research*, London: Routledge.
Taylor, J. R. (2012) *The Mental Corpus: How Language Is Represented in the Mind*, Oxford: Oxford University Press.
Wallis, P. and Nerlich, B. (2005) 'Disease Metaphors in New Epidemics: The UK Media Framing of the 2003 SARS Epidemic', *Social Science and Medicine* 60(11): 2629–39.
West, M. (1953) *A General Service List of English Words*, New York: Longmans, Green and Co.
World Health Organisation (WHO) (2020) 'Naming the Coronavirus Disease (COVID-19) and the Virus that Causes it', Accessed on 5 February 2021 from: https://www.who.int/emergencies/diseases/novel-coronavirus-2019/technical-guidance/naming-the-coronavirus-disease-(covid-2019)-and-the-virus-that-causes-it.
Zipf, G. K. (1935) *The Psycho-Biology of Language: An Introduction to Dynamic Philology*, Cambridge, MA: MIT Press.

15

What can a corpus tell us about multi-word units?

Chris Greaves and Martin Warren

1 Background

The idea that we best know the meaning of a word, not by examining it in isolation, but by the company that it keeps is usually ascribed to Firth (1957), who describes how meanings are often created by the associations of words rather than by individual words. Firth terms these associations 'meaning by "collocations"' to which, he argues, it is possible 'to apply the test of "collocability"' (1957: 194). He provides examples of meaning by collocation such as 'one of the meanings of *night* is its collocability with *dark*, and of *dark*, of course, collocation with *night*' (1957: 196). The test of collocability refers to the notion that words are collocates when they are associated with sufficient frequency to exclude the possibility that they are chance co-occurrences. Based on abundant corpus evidence, corpus linguists have concluded that words very often have a preference for what they combine with. For example, O'Keeffe *et al.* (2007: 59–60) point out that the verbs *go* and *turn* both combine with *grey*, *brown* and *white*, but they do not always both combine in the same way with other words. Thus, one can say 'people go mad, insane, bald or blind', but not 'people turn mad, insane, bald or blind' (2007: 59–60). The latter are instances of words which do not collocate and are termed 'lexical repulsion' by Renouf and Banerjee (2007: 417). In this chapter, we are concerned with word associations, although it should be noted that studying why words do not associate can also offer insights into register, style and semantics (Renouf and Banerjee 2007: 439) plus creativity.

The first computer-mediated corpus-driven study 'to test the assumption that collocation was an important part of the patterning of meaning' (Sinclair *et al.* 2004: xvii) was in 1960s. A research team, led by John McH. Sinclair, compiled a spoken corpus of 135,000 words to study English collocation (Sinclair *et al.* 1970). The final report (see Sinclair *et al.* 1970, reprinted in 2004) and Sinclair's later work contain three fundamental findings which have far-reaching consequences for corpus linguistics in general, and research into multi-word units of meaning in particular. First, the primacy of lexis over grammar in terms of meaning creation – 'on the whole grammar is not involved in the creation of meaning, but rather concerned with the management of meaning'

DOI: 10.4324/9780367076399-15

(Sinclair *et al.* 2004: xxv). Second, that meaning is created through the co-selection of words. Third, that, by virtue of the way in which meaning is created, language is phraseological in nature, which is embodied in his famous "idiom principle" (1987). It is not overstating Sinclair's role in corpus linguistics to say that he has placed the study of multi-word units of meaning at the centre of corpus linguistics through his emphasis on language study ultimately being the study of meaning creation.

What is a multi-word unit?

Despite the fact that the importance of collocation was established in the 1960s (Halliday 1966; Sinclair 1966; Sinclair *et al.* 1970), it is only relatively recently that the study of multi-word units has become more widespread. These studies have begun to explore the extent of phraseology, or to analyse the inner workings of the phraseological tendency, in the English language. For example there have been studies of extended units of meaning, pattern grammar, phraseology, n-grams (sometimes, termed lexical bundles, lexical phrases, clusters and chunks), *skipgrams* (these include a limited number of intervening words), phrase-frames and phrasal constructions (see, for example, Sinclair 1987, 1996, 2004a, 2005, 2006, 2007a, 2007b; Stubbs 1995, 2001; Partington 1998; Biber *et al.* 1999; Hunston and Francis 2000; Tognini-Bonelli 2001; Hunston 2002; Carter and McCarthy 2006; O'Keeffe *et al.* 2007; Scott and Bondi 2010; Breeze 2013; Grabawski 2015; Durant 2017; Shin *et al.* 2018). Here we do not focus on pattern grammar (see Chapter 11, this volume) because it is not concerned with the meanings of a particular unit of meaning but rather with 'words which share pattern features, but which may differ in other respects in their phraseologies' (Hunston and Francis 2000: 247–48). However, it is important to bear in mind that it has been established by pattern grammarians (see, for example Sinclair 1991; Hunston and Francis 2000) that 'it is not patterns and words that are selected, but phrases, or phraseologies, that have both a single form and meaning' (Hunston and Francis 2000: 21). More recently, research into "constructions" (see Hunston and Perek 2019) shows the links between grammar and phraseological variation.

Most of the studies of multi-word units have focused on n-grams, but it will be seen that is not the case in this chapter where collocation includes phraseological variation. Typically, n-grams are grouped together based on the number of fixed contiguous words they contain. Determining the cut-off for including n-grams in frequency lists varies, but a common cut-off remains 20 per million (see, for example, Scott and Tribble 2006). This decision is partly driven by the size of the corpus being examined, especially when researchers want to analyse larger n-grams. Interestingly, the frequency of n-grams decreases dramatically relative to their size, so that while Carter and McCarthy (2006: 503) find 45,015 two-word n-grams in their 5-million word-corpus, they find only 31 six-word n-grams with 20 instances or more. This observation has important implications because the undoubted prevalence of phraseology in the language does not mean that language use is not unique or creative.

This point has been made very convincingly by Coulthard in his role as a forensic linguist appearing as an expert witness in court cases (see, for example, Coulthard and Johnson 2007). Coulthard (2004) demonstrates that the occurrence of two instances of a nine-word n-gram, *I asked her if I could carry her bags*, in two separate disputed texts, one a statement and the other an interview record, is so improbable as to cast serious doubt on their reliability as evidence in a court case (Coulthard and Johnson 2007:

196–8). Coulthard (2004) bases his findings on a Google search conducted in 2002 in which he found 2,170,000 instances of the two-word n-gram *I asked*, 86,000 instances of the four-word n-gram *I asked if I*, four instances of the seven-word n-gram *I asked her if I could carry* and no instances of the full nine-word n-gram (2007: 197). This intriguing finding still holds true if the reader cares to conduct a Google search.

Importantly, Coulthard and Johnson draw the conclusion that 'we can assert that even a sequence as short as ten running words has a very high chance of being a unique occurrence' (2007: 198). This both confirms the phraseological tendency in language (Sinclair 1987) and its uniqueness and creativity; a fact that should not be lost sight of when we study multi-word units.

Most studies of multi-word units in the form of n-grams adopt an inclusive approach to phraseology and keep all recurring contiguous groupings of words in their lists of data as long as they meet the threshold frequency level, if any (see for example, Biber *et al.* 1999; Carter and McCarthy 2006; Shin *et al.* 2018). Some, however, have a less inclusive view, exemplified by Simpson (2004) who ignores 'strings that are incomplete or span two syntactic units' (2004: 43) and the potential consequences are discussed at length elsewhere (Gray and Biber 2015).

Restricting the size of the n-grams examined is another decision often made by researchers. It is quite common for researchers to focus on larger n-grams in their studies, and various arguments are put forward for ignoring the far more numerous two-word and three-word n-grams. Hyland (2008) states that he decided on four-word bundles instead of five-word because there are more of them and they are easier to categorise than three-word. Such a selective approach to the study of n-grams is not without its critics. Sinclair (2001), for example, is critical of those who ignore two-word n-grams, which easily outnumber all the rest of the n-grams in a corpus combined, simply for convenience. By not examining the largest group, researchers avoid the fundamental issue of 'whether a grammar based on the general assumption that each word brings along its own meaning independently of the others is ultimately relevant to the nature of language text' (2001: 353) and, in effect, misrepresent the prevalence of n-grams. Other researchers (see, for example, Carter and McCarthy 2006; Scott and Tribble 2006; O'Keeffe *et al.* 2007; Breeze 2013) do include all n-grams, irrespective of size, in their studies, and such an approach is important for a fuller understanding of their importance.

2 Why study multi-word units of meaning?

The study of multi-word units of meaning has led to many new and interesting findings which have pedagogical implications. Some of these findings are described and discussed next.

Once the n-grams have been identified, researchers have classified them in terms of their structural patterns, functions and register/genre specificity. In a study of four corpora, each representing a different register (conversation, fiction, news and academic prose), Biber *et al.* (1999: 996–7) identify the most frequent n-grams (they use the term "lexical bundles") in their data. They classify them based on the structural patterns they encompass, for example, noun phrase with post-modifier fragment, and so on, along with the grammatical category of the final word in the n-gram (1999: 996–7). Carter and McCarthy (2006: 503–4) focus on the structure of the n-grams in their corpus and most frequently find prepositions plus articles, subject plus verb, subject plus verb with complement items and noun phrases plus *of*. The identification of n-grams to distinguish between genres has also proved to be fruitful. Grabawski (2015) examines the n-grams in pharmaceutical discourse, while Breeze (2013) is able to distinguish between four legal genres by identifying their key n-grams. Such distinctions can also be useful for those engaged in teaching English for academic purposes (EAP), as Durrant (2017) illustrates in a study of how the n-grams vary in university students' writing based on their different disciplines.

Studies of n-grams have sought to determine their functions. Carter and McCarthy (2006: 505 a-f) examine the functions which n-grams perform and the list includes relations of time and space, other prepositional relations, interpersonal functions, vague language, linking functions and turn-taking. Biber *et al.* (1999) also categorise n-grams based on four discourse functions: referential bundles, text organisers, stance bundles and interactional bundles. The first two are more frequently found in academic discourse, while the others are more widespread in conversation. Referential bundles include time, place and text markers, such as *at the beginning of*, whereas text organisers express, for example, contrast (e.g. *on the other hand*), inference (e.g. *as a result of*) or focus (e.g. *it is important to*). Stance bundles convey attitudes towards some proposition, such as *I don't know why*, and interactional bundles signal, for example, politeness. Adel and Erman (2012) look at the more overarching functions of n-grams which is their contributions to fluency and idiomaticity.

Interest in register and genre-specific usage of multi-word units has been the focus of a number of studies (see, for example, Biber *et al.* 1999; Carter and McCarthy 2006; Scott and Tribble 2006; O'Keeffe *et al.* 2007; Hyland 2008). Biber *et al.* (1999, 2004), Carter and McCarthy (2006) and Hyland (2008), for example, have all found that the analysis of the n-grams in a register or genre affords an important means of differentiation. Thus the functions performed by n-grams identified by Carter and McCarthy (2006) described earlier differentiate spoken and written language (see Tables 1 to 8 in the Appendix). For example, the use of n-grams to express time and place relations, often by means of prepositional phrases, are more commonplace in written discourse (2006: 505a), for example, *she sat on the edge of the bed.* Another function more often associated with written discourse is the use of n-grams such as *of a/the* and *to the* used when describing possession, agency, purpose, goal and direction (2006: 505b). Another function more frequently found in written discourse is that of linking, for example, *at the same time* and *as a result of* (2006: 505e). Spoken discourse also has its distinctive functions typified by specific n-grams and Carter and McCarthy (2006: 505c), such as reflecting interpersonal meanings, for example, *you know* and *I think*. Being vague is also more frequently found in spoken discourse (2006: 505d), whether it is because the speaker cannot be specific or the context does not require specificity, for example, *kind of* and *sort of thing*.

Academic genres have attracted a disproportionate amount of interest compared with other genres (see, for example, Biber *et al.* 2004; Cortes 2002 and 2004; Nesi and Basturkmen 2006; Hyland 2008; Durrant 2017; Shin *et al.* 2018). These studies have all served to demonstrate how a detailed examination of n-grams can reveal genre-specific features in language use. It is now well-known that academic language contains distinctive high-frequency n-grams which characterise the conventions of academic spoken and written discourses, as well enabling us to better appreciate differences between the various disciplines. Examples of n-grams typical of academic language include *for example, the importance of* and *in the case of* (Carter and McCarthy 2006: 505g).

While studies of n-grams make up the majority of the studies of multi-word units, another form of multi-word unit is the idiom, although the borderline between n-grams and idioms is not without ambiguity. O'Keeffe *et al.* (2007: 82–3) suggest useful methodologies for extracting idioms from a corpus, given that idioms cannot be automatically identified by corpus linguistics software. They point out that certain words are "idiom-prone" (2007: 83) because they are "basic cognitive metaphors" and give the examples of parts of the body, money, and light and colour. They illustrate one method by first searching for *face* in CANCODE and then studying the 520 concordance lines which revealed 15 different idioms, for example, *let's face it* and *keep a straight face* (2007: 83). The second method is to first sample texts from the corpus in order to study them qualitatively to identify idioms. The idioms found are then searched for in the corpus as whole. This method has led to the identification of many idioms in CANCODE, and the five most frequently occurring are *fair enough*, *at the end of the day*, *there you go*, *make sense* and *turn round and say* (2007: 85). Also, idioms, like n-grams, can be described in terms of their functions and register- and genre-specificity (McCarthy 1998).

3 From n-grams to phraseological variation

The criticism from Sinclair (2001: 351–2) that the practice of only examining longer n-grams of three words or more neglects by far the largest group, i.e. two-word n-grams which, based on their prevalence, merit the most attention, has already been mentioned. However, Sinclair's (2001) criticism of n-gram studies does not end there. He raises other issues which question the extent to which the concentration on examining n-grams has led to other forms of multi-word units being overlooked. He points out that the 'classification of the bundles is by the number of words in a string, there is no recognition of variability of exponent or of position or of discontinuity' (2001: 353). He also criticises attempts to relate n-grams to 'the nearest complete grammatical structure' because 'reconciliation with established grammatical units is doomed to fail' (2001: 353). His reason for this prediction is that 'a grammar must remain aware of lexis, and that the patterns of lexis cannot be reconciled with those of a traditional grammar' (2001: 353).

It should be noted that at least some of the limitations of concentrating on the study of n-grams have not gone unnoticed by some engaged in such studies. Nesi and Basturkmen (2006), for example, point out that the identification of n-grams 'does not permit the identification of discontinuous frames (for example, *not only… but also…*)' (ibid: 285). Similarly, Biber *et al.* (2004: 401–2) state that one of their research goals 'is to extend the methods used to identify lexical bundles to allow for variations on a pattern'. However, they point out that the problem with undertaking this more comprehensive kind of study is in 'trying to identify the full range of lexical bundles across a large corpus of texts', a point which is taken up again by Gray and Biber (2015).

Sinclair's criticisms raise fundamental issues about what he terms the phraseological tendency in language (1987), and he proposes his own model for identifying and describing 'extended unit of meanings', or 'lexical items' (1996, 1998). Sinclair later expresses a preference for the term "meaning shift unit" rather than "lexical item" (Sinclair 2007a). The lexical item is taken to 'realize an element of meaning which is the function of the item in its cotext and context' (Sinclair 2004b: 121) and is 'characteristically phrasal, although it can be realized in a single word' (2004b: 122). It is made up of five categories of co-selection; namely the core, semantic prosody, semantic preference, collocation and colligation. The core and the semantic prosody are obligatory, while collocation, colligation and semantic preference are optional. The core is 'invariable, and constitutes the evidence of the occurrence of the item as a whole' (Sinclair 2004b: 141), that is the word(s) is(are) always present. Semantic prosody is the overall functional meaning of a lexical item and provides information about 'how the rest of the item is to be interpreted functionally' (2004b: 34). Collocation and colligation are related to the co-occurrences of words and grammatical choices with the core, respectively (2004b: 141). The semantic preference of a lexical item is 'the restriction of regular co-occurrence to items which share a semantic feature, e.g. about sport or suffering' (ibid: 142). These co-selections are also described in terms of the process by which they are selected. It is the selection of semantic prosody by the speaker that then leads to the selection of the core and the other co-selections of a lexical item.

Clearly, Sinclair's lexical item encompasses much more than we might find in lists of n-grams, but how do we find these co-selections in a corpus? Cheng *et al.* (2006) have developed the means to fully automatically retrieve the co-selections which comprise lexical items from a corpus. The corpus linguistics software is *ConcGram* (Greaves 2009), and the products of its searches are called concgrams (Cheng *et al.* 2006, 2009). These researchers argue that it is important to be able to identify lexical items without relying on single word frequency lists, lists of n-grams or some form of user-nominated search. The reasons for this are that single-word frequencies are not a reliable guide to frequent phraseologies in a corpus, and n-grams miss instances of multi-word units that have constituency (AB, A*B, A**B, etc.) and/or positional (AB, BA, B*A, etc.) variation (Cheng *et al.* 2006). While programmes are available which find *skipgrams* (Wilks 2005) and phrase-frames (Fletcher 2006), which both capture a limited amount of constituency variation, they still miss many instances of both constituency and positional variation (Cheng *et al.* 2006). *ConcGram* identifies all of the co-occurrences of two or more words irrespective of constituency and/or positional variation fully automatically with no prior search parameters entered, and so it supports corpus-driven research (Tognini-Bonelli 2001).

Cheng *et al.* (2009) distinguish between "co-occurring" words (i.e. concgrams) and "associated" words (i.e. phraseology) because, while *ConcGram* identifies all of the co-occurrences of words in a wide span, not all of them are necessarily meaningfully associated. In order to illustrate the difference between a typical concordance display and a *concgram* concordance, a sample of the two-word *concgram* "expenditure/reduce" is given in Figure 15.1. All of the examples of concgrams are from a 5-million word sample of the *British National Corpus* (3 million written and 2 million spoken) and generated fully automatically (i.e. with no nominated search words).

These concordance lines illustrate the benefits of uncovering the full range of phraseological variation, as the search for this particular *concgram* found 38 instances, but only 4 of the 38 are n-grams. Another interesting point is that while there are 42 instances of "expenditure/increase" in this corpus, there is only 1 instance of "decrease/expenditure", and so while *reduce* and *expenditure* are collocates, *expenditure* and *decrease* are examples of lexical repulsion (Renouf and Banerjee 2007). By not simply focusing on the node, *concgram* concordance lines highlight all of the co-occurring words and so shift the reader's focus of attention away from the node to all of the words in the concgram.

Studies of concgrams suggest that they help in the identification of three kinds of multi-word units (Warren 2009). These are collocational frameworks (Renouf and Sinclair 1991Sinclair Weigand 1998; Warren and Leung 2016), meaning shift units (also

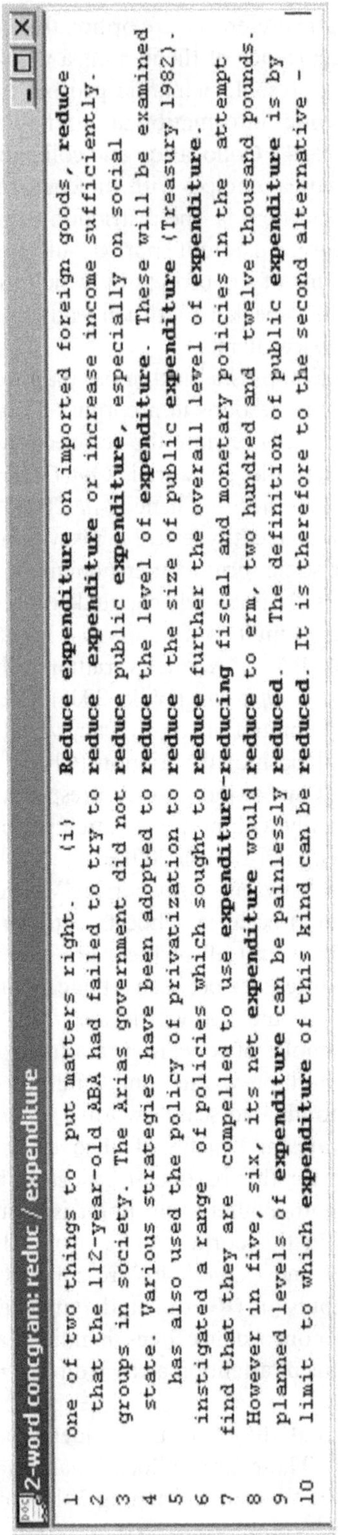

2-word concgram: reduc / expenditure

1	one of two things to put matters right. (i) **Reduce** **expenditure** on imported foreign goods, **reduce**
2	that the 112-year-old ABA had failed to try to **reduce** **expenditure** or increase income sufficiently.
3	groups in society. The Arias government did not **reduce** public **expenditure,** especially on social
4	state. Various strategies have been adopted to **reduce** the level of **expenditure**. These will be examined
5	has also used the policy of privatization to **reduce** the size of public **expenditure** (Treasury 1982).
6	instigated a range of policies which sought to **reduce** further the overall level of **expenditure**.
7	find that they are compelled to use **expenditure-reducing** fiscal and monetary policies in the attempt
8	However in five, six, its net **expenditure** would **reduce** to erm, two hundred and twelve thousand pounds.
9	planned levels of **expenditure** can be painlessly **reduced**. The definition of public **expenditure** is by
10	limit to which **expenditure** of this kind can be **reduced**. It is therefore to the second alternative –

Figure 15.1 Sample concordance lines for "expenditure/reduce"

termed "lexical items", Sinclair 1996, 1998; Warren 2010), and organisational frameworks (Warren 2015).

It is well-known that so-called "grammatical" words top single-word frequency lists, and it is therefore no surprise that these words also top *concgram* frequency lists. Renouf and Sinclair (1991) call the co-selections of these words "collocational frameworks", and even though they are very common, they are rarely studied. Initial studies of concgrams to find collocational frameworks (Greaves and Warren 2007, 2008; Li and Warren 2008) show that the five most frequent are *the….. of*, *a/an….. of*, *the….. of the*, *the….. in* and *the….. to* (Li and Warren 2008). A sample of one of the most frequent collocational frameworks is in Figure 15.2.

The widespread use of collocational frameworks suggests that they deserve greater attention from researchers, teachers and learners. As long ago as 1988, Sinclair and Renouf (1988) argued that they should be included in a lexical syllabus, but to date they remain overlooked. Newer grammars based on corpus evidence list and describe n-grams (see, for example, Biber *et al.* 1999; Carter and McCarthy 2006). Carter and McCarthy (2006: 503–5) list four-word n-grams in written texts, including *the end of the* and *the side of the*. If collocational frameworks are to be included in future grammars, these n-grams might be preceded by a description of their three-word collocational framework, *the….. of the*. Warren (2015) finds that the density of collocational frameworks in texts is a means of differentiating between texts such as informal social conversations and more formal written texts, with the former having a much lower density than the latter. In a study of the collocation frameworks *any … may* and *may …any* (Warren and Leung 2016), they are found to be 70 times more frequent in regulatory texts and are thus determining phraseologies of such texts and provide that collocational frameworks can be genre-specific.

The idea behind searching for concgrams was to be able to identify and describe meaning shift units (Sinclair 2007a). These multi-word units are important for a fuller description of phraseology, and Cheng *et al.* (2009) outline a procedure for analysing concgrams which can help to identify meaning shift units. They analyse the two-word concgram "play/role", and a sample of the concordance lines is in Figure 15.3.

In their study (Cheng *et al.* 2009), all of the concordance lines of "play/role" are studied and all the *concgram* configurations and their frequencies are described. The canonical form is identified and its meaning described. In Figure 15.3, the canonical form is exemplified in lines 1 to 3, which is the most frequent configuration. The canonical form is then used as benchmark for all the other *concgram* configurations, and the result is a ranking of the *concgram* configurations based on the extent of their adherence to the canonical form. At the end of this process, a meaning shift unit is identified and described with all its potential variations which together comprise a 'paraphrasable family with a canonical form and different patterns of co-selection' (Cheng *et al.* 2009).

One type of multi-word unit can exhibit extreme constituency variation. Hunston (2002: 75) briefly describes such multi-word units and provisionally labels them 'clause collocations'. They are the product of the tendency for particular types of clause to co-occur in discourses. She provides an example, *I wonder….. because*, where *I wonder* and *because* link clauses in the discourse (ibid: 75). Hunston points out that such collocations are difficult to find because the *I wonder* clause can contain any number of words (ibid: 75). Based on the distinction between organisation-oriented elements and message-oriented elements used in linear unit grammar, Sinclair and Mauranen (2006) and

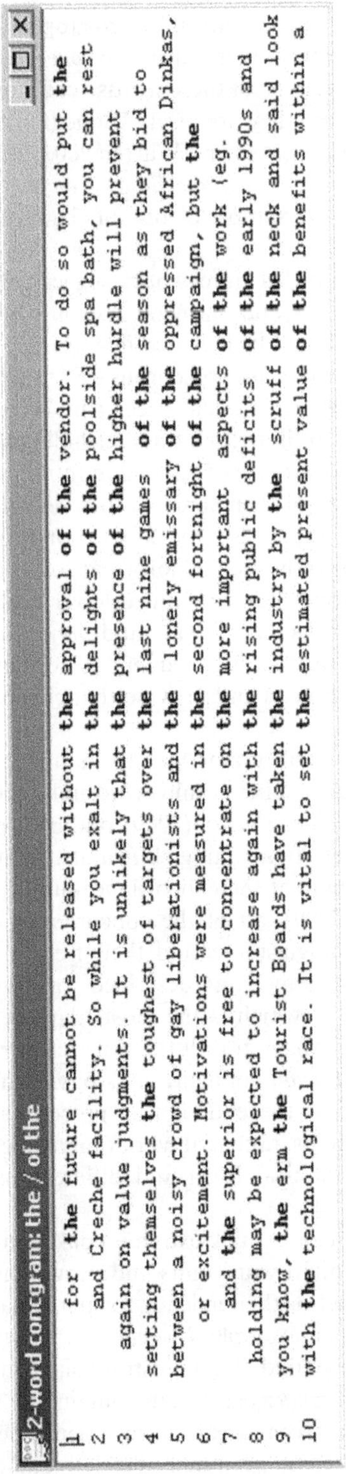

2-word concgram: the / of the

1	for **the** future cannot be released without	**the**	approval **of the**	vendor. To do so would put **the**
2	and Creche facility. So while you exalt in	**the**	delights **of the**	poolside spa bath, you can rest
3	again on value judgments. It is unlikely that	**the**	presence **of the**	higher hurdle will prevent
4	setting themselves **the** toughest of targets over	**the**	last nine games **of the**	season as they bid to
5	between a noisy crowd of gay liberationists and	**the**	lonely emissary **of the**	oppressed African Dinkas,
6	or excitement. Motivations were measured in	**the**	second fortnight **of the**	campaign, but **the**
7	and **the** superior is free to concentrate on	**the**	more important aspects **of the**	work (eg.
8	holding may be expected to increase again with	**the**	rising public deficits **of the**	early 1990s and
9	you know, **the** erm **the** Tourist Boards have taken	**the**	industry by **the** scruff **of the**	neck and said look
10	with **the** technological race. It is vital to set	**the**	estimated present value **of the**	benefits within a

Figure 15.2 Sample concordance lines for the collocational framework *the..... of the*

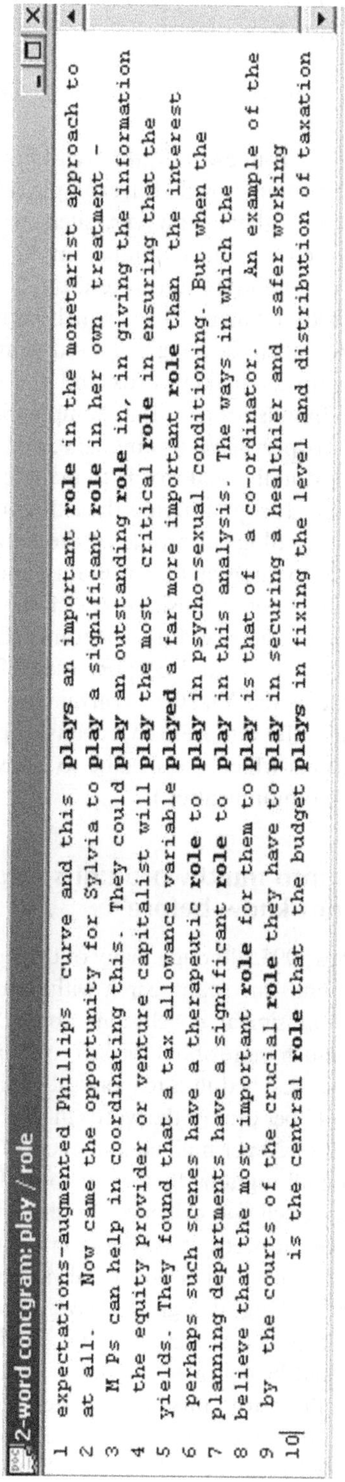

2-word concgram: play / role

1 expectations-augmented Phillips curve and this **plays** an important **role** in the monetarist approach to
2 at all. Now came the opportunity for Sylvia to **play** a significant **role** in her own treatment -
3 M Ps can help in coordinating this. They could **play** an outstanding **role** in, in giving the information
4 the equity provider or venture capitalist will **play** the most critical **role** in ensuring that the
5 yields. They found that a tax allowance variable **played** a far more important **role** than the interest
6 perhaps such scenes have a therapeutic **role** to **play** in psycho-sexual conditioning. But when the
7 planning departments have a significant **role** to **play** in this analysis. The ways in which the
8 believe that the most important **role** for them to **play** is that of a co-ordinator. An example of the
9 by the courts of the crucial **role** they have to **play** in securing a healthier and safer working
10 is the central **role** that the budget **plays** in fixing the level and distribution of taxation

Figure 15.3 Sample concordance lines for the meaning shift unit "play/role"

Warren (2015) term these multi-word units "organisational frameworks" to denote the ways in which organisational elements in the discourse, such as conjunctions, connectives and discourse particles, can be co-selected. Searches for concgrams uncover organisational frameworks because they retrieve co-occurring words across a wide span. Sample concordance lines of the organisational framework *I think…. because* are given in Figure 15.4.

Some instances of organisational frameworks are well-known and are sometimes listed in grammars as "correlative conjunctions", for example, *either…. or*, *not only….. but also* and *both….. and*. There are others, however, such as *I think…. because* and Hunston's *I wonder….. because*, which are not so familiar, and possibly others which are currently unknown, which deserve more attention. Interestingly, these phaseologies are shown to be genre-specific in a study (Warren 2015) which compares the use of organisational frameworks across different modes, registers and genres.

There has been considerable interest in keywords and the notion of keyness (see Chapter 9, this volume) in corpus linguistics (see, for example, Scott and Tribble 2006). Given that multi-word units are so pervasive in language, concgrams can be used to extend the notion of keyness beyond individual words to include the full range of multi-word units. They are a starting point for quantifying the extent of phraseology in a text or corpus and determining the phraseological profile of the language contained within them. There is plenty of evidence to suggest that n-grams, including those made up entirely of grammatical words, can be genre-sensitive, which has been described earlier, and there is evidence that this is also the case for concgrams. Early studies using concgrams to examine the aboutness of texts and corpora (see Milizia and Spinzi 2008; O'Donnell *et al.* 2012; Sui 2016; Meng and Yu 2016; Warren and Leung 2016; Hou 2017) suggest that these multi-word units offer a more comprehensive phraseological profile of texts and corpora. Word associations which are specific to a text or corpus are termed "aboutgrams" (Sinclair, personal communication).

4 What has corpus research into multi-word units told us about phraseology that we did not know before?

As observed by Stubbs (2005) Stubbs 1995, although many of the studies of n-grams, phrasal constructions and extended lexical units involve research within quite different methodological traditions, they have arrived at similar conclusions about 'how to model units of meaning' (2005: 8). We now know much more about the key role played by multi-word units in the English language, and this has resulted in a reappraisal of the status of lexis.

Biber *et al.* (1999: 995) find that 45 per cent of the words in their conversation corpus are in recurrent n-grams using a cut-off of 20 per million. Altenberg (1998) puts the percentage as high as 80 per cent by including all n-grams that occur more than once. Whatever the percentage, these findings provide conclusive evidence for the "phraseological tendency" (Sinclair 1987) in language. However, it needs to be borne in mind that both these figures exclude multi-word units with constituency and or positional variation, and we are now only just beginning to realise that only looking at n-grams leaves much of the phraseological variation in English undiscovered. If phraseological variation is added to the percentage of n-grams in a corpus, the figure would be considerably closer to 100 per cent.

The findings from studies of multi-word units have impacted lexicography along with the writing of English language grammars and English language textbooks. The reason why many of the findings have fed into the fields of EAP and English for a specific

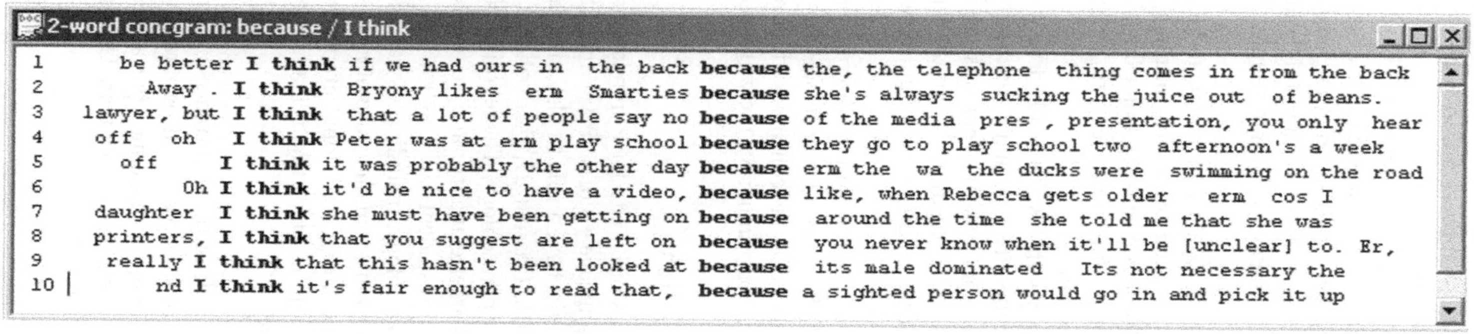

2-word concgram: because / I think

N					
1	be better	**I think**	if we had ours in the back	**because**	the, the telephone thing comes in from the back
2	Away .	**I think**	Bryony likes erm Smarties	**because**	she's always sucking the juice out of beans.
3	lawyer, but	**I think**	that a lot of people say no	**because**	of the media pres , presentation, you only hear
4	off oh	**I think**	Peter was at erm play school	**because**	they go to play school two afternoon's a week
5	off	**I think**	it was probably the other day	**because**	erm the wa the ducks were swimming on the road
6	Oh	**I think**	it'd be nice to have a video,	**because**	like, when Rebecca gets older erm cos I
7	daughter	**I think**	she must have been getting on	**because**	around the time she told me that she was
8	printers,	**I think**	that you suggest are left on	**because**	you never know when it'll be [unclear] to. Er,
9	really	**I think**	that this hasn't been looked at	**because**	its male dominated Its not necessary the
10	nd	**I think**	it's fair enough to read that,	**because**	a sighted person would go in and pick it up

Figure 15.4 Sample concordance lines for the organisational framework *I think.... because*

purpose (ESP) is that studies have also been conducted which compare the use of multi-word units by expert and novice writers and speakers. For example, in his study of four-word n-grams, Hyland (2008: 5) states that these multi-word units are 'familiar to writers and readers who regularly participate in a particular discourse, their very "naturalness" signalling competent participation in a given community'. He finds that the opposite is often true of novice members of the community, and the absence of discipline-specific n-grams might signal a lack of fluency. This means that learners need to acquire an 'appropriate disciplinary-sensitive repertoire' of n-grams (Hyland and Tse 2004) which is further supported by more recent studies (see, for example, Adel and Erman 2012; Hyland 2012; Shin *et al.* 2018).

Another indication that our understanding of language has been enhanced by research into multi-word units is the notion of "lexical priming" put forward by Hoey (2005) which builds on the five categories of co-selection (Sinclair 1996, 1998, 2004) and argues that patterns of co-selection require that speakers, writers, hearers and readers are primed for appropriate co-selections.

Hoey puts forward ten priming hypotheses (2005: 13). Every word is primed to occur with particular other words, semantic sets, pragmatic functions and grammatical positions. Words which are either co-hyponyms or synonyms differ with respect to their collocations, semantic associations and colligations, as do the senses of words which are polysemous. Words are primed for use in one or more grammatical roles and to either participate in or avoid particular types of cohesive relation in a discourse. Every word is primed to occur in particular semantic relations in the discourse and to either occur in or avoid certain positions within the discourse. These hypotheses are a result of Hoey's extensive study of lexical cohesion, and he concludes that naturalness depends on speakers and writers conforming to the primings of the words that they use (2005: 2–5).

5 Implications and future research

Findings from the study of multi-word units have implications for the learning and teaching of applied linguistics, language studies, EAP and ESP (Hassan and Wood 2015). It is clear that multi-word units have a role to play in data-driven learning (DDL) activities (Johns 1991; Warren 2016; Chapter 21, this volume) and should further advance the learning and teaching of phraseology. The learning of idiomaticity (Adel and Erman 2012) and how to signal intertextuality, and so improve coherence (Warren 2016), are important attributes for students of English and are underpinned by a knowledge and application of phraseology, including its variations.

Sinclair's claim that 'a grammar must remain aware of lexis, and that the patterns of lexis cannot be reconciled with those of a traditional grammar' (2001: 353) predicts a break with traditional grammar, and this prediction is made elsewhere by Sinclair and is summed up in the following quote:

> By far the majority of text is made of the occurrence of common words in common patterns, or in slight variants of those common patterns. Most everyday words do not have an independent meaning, or meanings, but are components of a rich repertoire of multi-word patterns that make up a text. This is totally obscured by the procedures of conventional grammar.
>
> *Sinclair (1991: 108)*

The inadequacies of conventional grammar have been addressed, at least in part, by Sinclair and Mauranen's (2006) linear unit grammar which 'avoids hierarchies, and concentrates on the combinatorial patterns of text'. Sinclair (2007b) also advocates local grammars as a better way of handling phraseological variation. Both local grammars and linear unit grammars have yet to be widely applied in studies of multi-word units, but Hunston and Sinclair (2000), for example, demonstrate the applicability of a local grammar to the concept of evaluation, and these grammars have considerable potential in furthering our descriptions and understanding of multi-word units. Similar studies describe the local grammars of movement in financial English (Sui 2016) and of disclaimers in the texts accompanying financial products (Cheng and Ching 2018). More surprisingly, perhaps, is the finding that collocational frameworks also have their local grammars (Warren and Leung 2016) which suggests there is the need for more research in this area.

Another of Sinclair's yet to be realised ambitions is the compilation of a dictionary which fully captures the phraseology of language. 'A dictionary containing all the lexical items of a language, each one in its canonical form with a list of possible variations, would be the ultimate dictionary' Sinclair *et al.* (2004: xxiv). As our knowledge of phraseology grows with the study of multi-word units, such a dictionary becomes ever more feasible.

Sinclair (2001: 357) states that for him any corpus 'signals like a flashing neon sign "Think again"'and it is Sinclair's notion of the idiom principle (1987) and his work on units of meaning which have led all of us to think again about whether meaning is in individual words or whether the source of meaning in language is through the co-selections made by speakers and writers. All of the corpus evidence confirms Sinclair's fundamental point that it is not the word that is a unit of meaning, but the co-selection of words which comprise a unit of meaning (2001: xxi). The future exploration of multi-word units in corpus linguistics promises to tell us much more about how meaning is created.

Acknowledgements

We gratefully acknowledge the support we received from Professor John McHardy Sinclair who was a member of the *concgram* team and worked with us on concgrams from the outset. His brilliant ideas led directly to many of ConcGram's functions and helped enormously in our analyses of concgrams.

The work described in this paper was substantially supported by a grant from the Research Grants Council of the Hong Kong Special Administrative Region (Project No. PolyU 5440/13 H).

Further reading

Cheng, W. (2012) *Exploring Corpus Linguistics*, London: Routledge. (This book provides a good introduction to concgramming and multi-word units.)

Gray, B. and Biber, D. (2015) 'Phraseology', in D. Biber and R. Reppen (eds) *The Cambridge Handbook of English Corpus Linguistics*, Cambridge: Cambridge University Press.

Hunston, S. and Su, H. (2019) 'Pattern, Construction and Local Grammar: The Case of Evaluation', *Applied Linguistics* 40(4): 567–93. (Both of these articles provide concise overviews of closely related current topics.)

References

Adel, A. and Erman, B. (2012) 'Recurrent Word Combinations in Academic Writing by Native and Non-Native Speakers of English: A Lexical Bundles Approach', *ESP Journal* 31(2): 81–92.

Altenberg, B. (1998) 'On the Phraseology of Spoken English: The Evidence of Recurrent Word Combinations', in A. P. Cowie (ed.) *Phraseology: Theory Analysis and Applications*, Oxford: Oxford University Press, pp. 101–22.

Biber, D., Johansson, S., Leech, G., Conrad, S. and Finegan, E. (1999) *The Longman Grammar of Spoken and Written English*, Harlow, England: Pearson Education.

Biber, D., Conrad, S. and Cortes, V. (2004) '"If You Look At…": Lexical Bundles in University Teaching and Textbooks', *Applied Linguistics* 25(3): 371–405.

Breeze, R. (2013) 'Lexical Bundles across Four Legal Genres', *International Journal of Corpus Linguistics* 18(2): 229–53.

Carter R. A. and McCarthy, M. J. (2006) *Cambridge Grammar of English*, Cambridge: Cambridge University Press.

Cheng, W. and Ching, T. (2018) '"Not a Guarantee of Future Performance": The Local Grammar of Disclaimers', *Applied Linguistics* 39(3): 263–301.

Cheng, W., Greaves, C. and Warren, M. (2006) 'From N-Gram to Skipgram to Concgram', *International Journal of Corpus Linguistics* 11(4): 411–33.

Cheng, W., Greaves, C., Sinclair, J. McH. and Warren, M. (2009) 'Uncovering the Extent of the Phraseological Tendency: Towards a Systematic Analysis of Concgrams', *Applied Linguistics* 30(2): 236–52.

Cortes, V. (2004) 'Lexical Bundles in Published and Student Disciplinary Writing: Examples from History and Biology', *English for Specific Purposes* 23(4): 397–423.

Coulthard, M. (2004) 'Author Identification, Idiolect, and Linguistic Uniqueness', *Applied Linguistics* 25(4): 431–47.

Coulthard, M. and Johnson, A. (2007) *An Introduction to Forensic Linguistics: Language in Evidence*, London: Routledge.

Durrant, R. (2017) 'Lexical Bundles and Disciplinary Variation in University Students' Writing: Mapping Territories', *Applied Linguistics* 38(2): 165–93.

Firth, J. R. (1957) *Papers in Linguistics 1934-1951*, London: Oxford University Press.

Fletcher, W. H. (2006) "Phrases in English" Home. Accessed on 5 February 2020 from: http://pie.usna.edu/.

Grabawski, L. (2015) 'Key Words and Lexical Bundles within English Pharmaceutical Discourse: A Corpus-Driven Description', *ESP Journal* 38: 23–33.

Gray, B. and Biber, D. (2015) 'Phraseology', in D. Biber and R. Reppen (eds) *The Cambridge Handbook of English Corpus Linguistics*, Cambridge: Cambridge University Press, pp. 125–45.

Greaves, C. and Warren, M. (2007) 'Concgramming: A Computer-Driven Approach to Learning the Phraseology of English', *ReCALL Journal* 17(3): 287–306.

Greaves, C. and Warren, M. (2008) 'Beyond Clusters: A New Look at Word Associations', 4th *Inter-Varietal Applied Corpus Studies Biennial International Conference*, University of Limerick, Ireland, 13–14 June, 2008.

Greaves, C. (2009) *ConcGram 1.0: A Phraseological Search Engine*, Amsterdam: John Benjamins.

Halliday, M. A. K. (1966) 'Lexis as a Linguistic Level', in C. E. Bazell, J. C. Catford, M. A. K. Halliday and R. H. Robins (eds) *In Memory of J.R. Firth*, London: Longman, pp. 148–62.

Hassan, L. and Wood, D. (2015) 'The Effectiveness of Focused Instruction of Formulaic Sequences in Augmenting L2 Learners' Academic Writing Skills: A Quantitative Research Study', *Journal of English for Academic Purposes* 17: 51–62.

Hoey, M. (2005) *Lexical Priming: A New Theory of Words and Language*, London: Routledge.

Hou, Z. (2017) 'The American Dream Revisited: A Corpus-Driven Study', *International Journal of English Linguistics* 7(3): 182–9.

Hunston, S. (2002) *Corpora in Applied Linguistics*, Cambridge: Cambridge University Press.

Hunston, S. and Francis, G. (2000) *Pattern Grammar: A Corpus-Driven Approach to the Lexical Grammar of English*, Amsterdam: John Benjamins.

Hunston, S. and Sinclair, J. McH. (2000) 'A Local Grammar of Evaluation', in S. Hunston and G. Thompson (eds) *Evaluation in Text: Authorial Stance and the Construction of Discourse*, Oxford: Oxford University Press, pp. 75–100.

Hunston, S. and Perek, F. (eds) (2019) Constructions in Applied Linguistics, *International Journal of Corpus Linguistics* 24(3): 155.

Hyland, K. (2008) ' "As Can Be Seen": Lexical Bundles and Disciplinary Variation', *English for Specific Purposes* 27(1): 4–21.

Hyland (2012) 'Bundles in Academic Discourse', *Annual Review of Applied Linguistics* 32: 150–69.

Hyland, K. and Tse, P. (2004) 'Is There an "Academic Vocabulary?"', *TESOL Quarterly* 41(2): 235–53.

Johns, T. (1991) 'Should You Be Persuaded: Two Samples of Data-Driven Learning Materials', in T. Johns and P. King (eds) *Classroom Concordancing, English Language Research*: Birmingham University, pp. 1–16.

Li, Y. and Warren, M. (2008) "in .... of: What Are Collocational Frameworks and Should We Be Teaching Them?", 4th International Conference on Teaching English at Tertiary Level, Zhejiang, China, 11-12 October, 2008.

Meng, C. and Yu, Y. (2016) ' "We should..." versus "We will..." How Do the Governments Report their Work in One Country Two Systems?: A Corpus-Driven Critical Discourse Analysis of Government', *Text & Talk* 36(2): 33–51.

McCarthy, M. J. (1998) *Spoken Language and Applied Linguistics*, Cambridge: Cambridge University Press.

Milizia, D. and Spinzi, C. (2008) 'The 'Terroridiom' Principle between Spoken and Written Discourse', *International Journal of Corpus Linguistics* 13(3): 322–350.

Nesi, H. and Basturkmen, H. (2006) 'Lexical Bundles and Discourse Signaling in Academic Lecturers', *International Journal of Corpus Linguistics*,11(3): 283–304.

O'Donnell, M. B., Scott, M., Mahlberg, M. and Hoey, M. (2012) 'Exploring Text-Initial Words, Clusters and Concgrams in a Newspaper Corpus', *Corpus Linguistics and Linguistic Theory*, 8(1): 73–101.

O'Keeffe, A., Carter, R. A. and McCarthy, M. J. (2007) *From Corpus to Classroom: Language Use and Language Teaching*, Cambridge: Cambridge University Press.

Partington, A. (1998) *Patterns and Meanings*, Amsterdam; John Benjamins.

Renouf, A. J. and Banerjee, J. (2007) 'Lexical Repulsion between Sense-Related Pairs', *International Journal of Corpus Linguistics* 12(3): 415–44.

Renouf, A. J. and Sinclair, J. McH. (1991) 'Collocational Frameworks in English', in K. Ajimer and B. Altenberg (eds) *English Corpus Linguistics*, London: Longman, pp. 128–43.

Scott, M. and Tribble, C. (2006) *Textual Patterns: Key Words and Corpus Analysis in Language Education*, Amsterdam: John Benjamins.

Scott, M. and Bondi, M. (2010) *Keyness in Texts*, Amsterdam: John Benjamins.

Shin, Y. K., Cortes, V. and Yoo, I. W. H. (2018) 'Using Lexical Bundles as a Tool to Analyse Definite Article Use in L2 Academic Writing: An Exploratory Study', *Journal of Second Language Writing* 39: 29–41.

Simpson, R. C. (2004) 'Stylistic Features of Academic Speech: The Role of Formulaic Expressions', in U. Connor and T. Upton (eds) *Discourse in the Professions: Perspectives from Corpus Linguistics*, Amsterdam: John Benjamins, pp. 37–64.

Sinclair, J. McH. (1966) 'Beginning the Study of Lexis', in C. E. Bazell, J. C. Catford, M. A. K. Halliday and R. H. Robins (eds) *In Memory of J.R. Firth*, London: Longman.

Sinclair, J. McH. (1987) 'Collocation: A Progress Report', in R. Steele and T. Threadgold (eds) *Language Topics: Essays in Honour of Michael Halliday*, Amsterdam: John Benjamins, pp. 319–31.

Sinclair, J. McH. (1991) *Corpus Concordance Collocation*, Oxford: Oxford University Press.

Sinclair, J. McH. (1996) 'The Search for Units of Meaning', *Textus* 9(1): 75–106.

Sinclair, J. McH. (1998) 'The Lexical Item', in E. Weigand (ed.) *Contrastive Lexical Semantics*, Amsterdam: John Benjamins, pp. 1–24.

Sinclair, J. McH. (2001) 'Review of The Longman Grammar of Spoken and Written English', *International Journal of Corpus Linguistics*, 6(2): 339–59.

Sinclair, J. McH. (2004a) *Trust the Text*, London: Routledge.

Sinclair, J. McH. (2004b) 'Meaning in the Framework of Corpus Linguistics', *Lexicographica* 20: 20–32.

Sinclair, J. McH. (2005) 'Document Relativity', (manuscript), Tuscan Word Centre, Italy.

Sinclair, J. McH. (2006) 'Aboutness 2', (manuscript), Tuscan Word Centre, Italy.

Sinclair, J. McH. (2007a) 'Collocation Reviewed', (manuscript), Tuscan Word Centre, Italy.
Sinclair, J. McH. (2007b) 'Defining the Definiendom - New', (manuscript), Tuscan Word Centre, Italy.
Sinclair, J. McH., Jones, S. and Daley, R. (1970) 'English Lexical Studies', Report to the Office of Scientific and Technical Information.
Sinclair, J. McH., Jones, S. and Daley, R. (2004) *English Collocation Studies: The OSTI Report*, London: Continuum.
Sinclair, J. McH. and Mauranen, A. (2006) *Linear Unit Grammar*, Amsterdam: John Benjamins.
Sinclair, J. McH. and Renouf, A. J. (1988) 'A Lexical Syllabus for Language Learning', in R. A. Carter and M. J. McCarthy (eds) *Vocabulary and Language Teaching*, London: Longman, pp. 140–60.
Stubbs, M. (1995) 'Collocations and Cultural Connotations of Common Words', *Linguistics and Education* 7(3): 379–90.
Stubbs, M. (2001) *Words and Phrases: Corpus Studies of Lexical Semantics*, Oxford: Blackwell.
Sui, X. (2016) 'Local Grammar of Movement on Financial English', unpublished PhD, the Hong Kong Polytechnic University, Hong Kong.
Tognini-Bonelli, E. (2001) *Corpus Linguistics at Work*, Amsterdam: John Benjamins.
Warren, M. (2016) 'Signalling Intertextuality in Business Emails', *English for Specific Purposes* 42: 26–37.
Warren, M. (2016) 'Introduction to Data-Driven Learning', in F. Farr and L. Murray (eds) *Routledge Handbook of Language Learning and Technology*, London: Routledge, pp. 337–47.
Warren, M. and Leung, M. (2016) 'Do Collocational Frameworks have Local Grammars?', *International Journal of Corpus Linguistics* 21(1): 1–27.
Warren, M. (2015) ' "I Mean I Only Really Wanted to Dry me Towels Because…": Organisational Frameworks across Modes, Registers, and Genres', in N. Groom, M. Charles and S. John (eds), Amsterdam: John Benjamins, pp. 181–99.
Wilks, Y. (2005) 'REVEAL: The Notion of Anomalous Texts in a Very Large Corpus', *Tuscan Word Centre International Workshop*, Tuscany, Italy: Certosa di Pontignano. 1–3 July 2005.

16

What can a corpus tell us about grammar?

Susan Conrad

1 Understanding grammar through patterns and contexts: moving from correct/incorrect to likely/unlikely

In recent years, corpus-based studies of grammar have expanded greatly; new corpora, additional tools and more sophisticated analyses have all increased our understanding of grammars in different language varieties. Nonetheless, the essential, groundbreaking contribution of corpus linguistics to the study of grammar remains the same: Corpus linguistics changes our conceptualisation of grammar from a simple correct/incorrect dichotomy to an understanding of patterns and choices, an understanding of what is likely or unlikely in particular circumstances.

In traditional descriptions of grammar and in many syntactic theories, grammar is addressed through sample sentences that are either grammatical or ungrammatical, acceptable or unacceptable, accurate or inaccurate (e.g. see discussions in Cook 1994). From this perspective, to describe the grammar of a language, researchers need only to judge grammaticality, and to teach a language, instructors need only to focus on the rules for making grammatical sentences. Proficiency is equated with structural accuracy.

This dichotomous view works well for certain grammatical features. For example, it is grammatically incorrect to have zero article before a singular count noun in English: **I saw Ø cow*. Aside from a few exceptions such as in the locative prepositional phrases *at home* or *in hospital*, this rule is absolute for most varieties of English. However, any reflective language user will realize that many other grammatical choices cannot be made on the basis of correct/incorrect. For example, in the previous sentence the *that* could have been omitted: *...will realize many other grammatical choices....* Both versions are equally grammatical.

Of course, for decades, work in sociolinguistics and from a functional perspective has emphasised language choices for different contexts. In language classes, students may have been taught a few variants for politeness (e.g. in English using *could you* for requests instead of *can you*), but descriptions of grammar remained focused on accuracy. In a 1998 address to the international TESOL convention, Larsen-Freeman sought to 'challenge the common misperception that grammar has to do solely with

DOI: 10.4324/9780367076399-16

formal accuracy', arguing instead for a 'grammar of choice' (Larsen-Freeman 2002: 104). Being able to describe the typical choices that language users make, however, requires doing large-scale empirical analyses. The analyses must be empirical – rather than introspective – since language users may not be consciously aware of their choices. The analyses must cover numerous data in order to tell which language choices are widespread, which occur predictably although under rare circumstances and which are more idiosyncratic.

The great contribution of corpus linguistics to grammar is that it increases researchers' ability to systematically study the variation in a large collection of texts – produced by far more speakers and writers in more contexts than could be analyzed by hand. Corpus linguistic techniques allow us to determine common and uncommon choices and to see the patterns that reveal what is typical or unusual in particular contexts. These patterns show the correspondence between the use of a grammatical feature and some other factor in the discourse or situational context (e.g. another grammatical feature, a social relationship, the mode of communication, etc.). Corpus linguistics therefore allows us to focus on the patterns that characterise how a large number of people use the language, rather than basing generalisations on a small set of data or anecdotal evidence, or focusing on the accurate/inaccurate dichotomy. As O'Keeffe *et al.* (2007) explain, corpus analyses lead us to describing grammar not just in structural terms but in probabilistic terms.

This chapter reviews some major aspects of this corpus-based perspective for describing grammar. Section 2 reviews the types of grammatical patterns most typically covered in corpus studies, and Section 3 then discusses the investigation of numerous contextual factors simultaneously. Descriptions of grammar in spoken discourse are covered in Section 4, including some grammatical patterns specific to speech rather than writing. Section 5 concludes the chapter by reviewing some new challenges for the coming years. Throughout, the majority of references and examples refer to English. The contributions of corpus linguistics are equally applicable to the grammar of any language, but English continues to be the most-studied language. Furthermore, although numerous studies are mentioned, it is no coincidence that the chapter repeatedly cites two reference grammars of English: the *Grammar of Spoken and Written English* (Biber *et al.* 1999, 2021) and the *Cambridge Grammar of English* (Carter and McCarthy 2006). These comprehensive grammars make extensive use of corpus analyses to describe grammar structure and use, and they are currently the single clearest manifestations of corpus linguistics' impact on the study of grammar.

As a first step, before further discussing the contribution of corpus linguistics to grammar, a brief review of some methodological principles for corpus linguistic investigations of grammar is in order.

Methodological principles in corpus-based grammar analysis

Any analysis of "typical" or "probable" choices depends on frequency analysis. The very mention of a choice being typical or unusual implies that, under given circumstances, it happens more or less often than other choices. For reliable frequency analysis, a corpus does not always have to be immense, but it must be designed to represent a variety of language (see chapters in Part 1, this volume) and as fine-grained as needed to describe the circumstances associated with grammar choices. For example, Carter and McCarthy (2006: 11) find ellipses to be rare in narratives, while they are common in many other parts of conversation. Any corpus that did not include numerous conversational genres or any analysis which neglected to differentiate among them would fail to discover this pattern.

Frequency counts are not sufficient for describing grammar, however. Instead, they point to interesting phenomena that deserve further investigation and interpretation. As Biber, Conrad and Cortes explain,

> ...we do not regard frequency data as explanatory. In fact we would argue for the opposite: frequency data identifies patterns that must be explained. The usefulness of frequency data (and corpus analysis generally) is that it identifies patterns of use that otherwise often go unnoticed by researchers.
>
> *(Biber et al. 2004: 176)*

In corpus-based grammar studies, interpretations of frequency analyses come from a variety of sources. They can be based on cognitive principles such as the principle of end weight (heavy, long constituents are harder to process than short constituents and so are placed at the ends of clauses); on aspects of linguistic theory, such as principles defined in systemic functional linguistics; on the historical development of the language; or on reasonable explanations of the functions or discourse effect of a particular linguistic choice. Interpretation always includes human judgments of the impact of the language choices and speakers/writers' (usually subconscious) motivations in making these choices. Thus, a corpus linguistic perspective on grammar has not made human judgments superfluous; it has actually expanded the judgments and interpretations that are made.

2 Types of grammatical patterns

This section describes and exemplifies four types of patterns that are most common in corpus-based grammar analyses. Grammatical choices are associated with vocabulary, grammatical co-text, discourse-level factors and the context of the situation. Some other patterns specific to spoken discourse, such as associations with intonation, are covered in Section 4.

Grammar–vocabulary associations (lexico-grammar)

Associations between grammar and vocabulary are often called "lexico-grammar" or sometimes "colligation". The connection between words and grammar was extensively studied in the Collins COBUILD project (Sinclair 1991). Although designed initially as a lexicography project, it became clear that grammar and lexis were not as distinct as traditionally presented, and the project also resulted in a number of books presenting "pattern grammar" – explanations of grammatical structures integrated with the specific lexical items most commonly used in them (see Hunston and Francis 1999 and Chapter 11, this volume). Since that time, lexico-grammatical relationships of various sorts have been a common contribution of corpus studies.

One type of lexico-grammatical relationship concerns the lexical items that tend to occur with a particular grammatical structure. This type of pattern can be illustrated with verbs that are most common with *that*-clause objects, e.g. *I guess I should go* or *The results suggest that there is no effect.* A large number of verbs are possible with this structure. However, beyond looking at what is possible, corpus-based grammar references present findings for the verbs that are actually most commonly used (Biber *et al.* 1999: 668–70; Carter and McCarthy 2006: 511). The reference grammars explain that the common verbs are related to expressing speech and thought. For example, Biber *et al.* (1999) find that *think, say* and *know* are by far the most common verbs with *that*-clauses in both British and American conversation (with the addition of *guess* in American English conversation). They also find that the structure is less common overall with any verb in academic prose, but *suggest* and *show* are most common. Rather than reporting thoughts and feelings, the verb + *that*-clause structures in academic prose are used to report previous research, often with non-human entities acting as the subject, as in *The results suggest that….*

This kind of lexico-grammatical pattern can also be approached from the perspective of the words themselves, usually for vocabulary teaching. The increasing use of computational analyses has expanded this area of work. For example, Ma and Qian (2020) use rule-based programming to find the most common grammar patterns for the most frequent verbs in academic English writing. They find, for instance, that the verb *require* is most common in a simple verb + noun pattern and second in a verb + noun + *to*-infinitive pattern.

Another type of lexico-grammatical relationship concerns the specific words that occur as a realisation of a grammatical function. A simple illustration is verb tense. Traditionally, a grammatical description would simply explain the form of tenses – for example, that simple present tense in English is uninflected except in third person singular when *-s* is added, that past tense is formed with *-ed* for regular verbs, etc. A corpus-based grammar can add information about the verbs used most commonly in the tenses. For example, in the *Longman Spoken and Written English Corpus*, the set of verbs occurring over 80 per cent of the time in present tense differs greatly from the verbs occurring over 80 per cent of the time in past tense (Biber *et al.* 1999: 25). The verbs common in present tense convey mental, emotional and logical states. Many are used in short, common expressions in conversations expressing the speaker's thoughts or feelings, such as *It doesn't matter* or *Never mind,* while others are used to describe the states of others or to make logical interpretations about what something *means* or what someone *doubts*. The verbs more strongly associated with past tense, on the other hand, convey events or activities, especially body movements and speech (e.g. *exclaimed, glanced, grinned, nodded, whispered*). Not surprisingly, those past tense verbs are especially common for describing characters and actions in fiction writing.

The associations between a grammatical structure and lexical items can also be analysed in terms of semantic characteristics, leading to an analysis of "semantic prosody" – the fact that certain structures tend to be associated with certain types of meaning, such as positive or negative circumstances (Sinclair 1991; Louw 1993). O'Keeffe *et al.* (2007: 106–14) provide an analysis of *get*-passives (e.g. *he got arrested*). They show that the *get*-passive is usually used to express unfortunate incidences, manifest in the lexico-grammatical association of verbs such as *killed, sued, beaten, arrested, burgled, intimidated, criticized* and numerous others. Stempel (2019) shows that the "into Ving causative" structure – e.g. *talked into buying, fooled into thinking* – is used to express negative attitudes towards the proposition, often with coercion or deception involved. These authors and others investigating semantic prosody note also that individual lexical items may not be negative – there is nothing inherently negative about *talked*, for example – but the discourse context makes the adverse connections clear.

O'Keeffe *et al.* (2007) also discuss the type of subjects usually found with *get*-passives (often human subjects – the people to whom the unfortunate incident happened) and the lack of adverbials in these clauses. The authors thus move into discussion of another type of pattern, the grammatical co-text.

Grammatical co-text

Corpus studies often investigate the extent to which a particular grammatical feature tends to occur with specific other grammatical features. Grammatical descriptions in traditional textbooks sometimes make claims about the grammatical co-text of features, and corpus studies can provide empirical testing of these claims. An interesting example is provided by Frazier (2003), who investigated *would*-clauses of hypothetical or counterfactual conditionals. Concerned about the way that English as second language (ESL) grammars virtually always present the *would*-clause as adjacent to an *if*-clause, he examined the extent to which this was true in a combination of spoken and written corpora.

Surprisingly, Frazier (2003) found that almost 80 per cent of the hypothetical/counterfactual *would*-clauses were not adjacent to an *if*-clause. Although there are several categories of *would*-clauses without *if*-clauses, the largest percentage were those that had implied, covert conditionals. It further turned out that these clauses tended to occur with certain other grammatical features, including infinitives and gerunds, as in these examples:

> If there is nothing evil in these things, if they get their moral complexion only from our feeling about them, why shouldn't they be greeted with a cheer? *To greet* them with repulsion *would* turn what before was neutral into something bad...
>
> *Letting* the administration take details off their hands *would* give them more time to inform themselves about education as a whole...
>
> *(Frazier 2003: 456–7)*

More recently, studies of the use of *if*-conditionals have expanded to include modality marking more generally and provide more theoretical explanations for patterns (Gabrielatos 2019).

Looking at grammatical co-occurrence patterns can also help to explain when rare constructions occur. For example, subject position *that*-clauses, as illustrated here, are very rare:

> (1)
> That there are no meteorites of any other age, regardless of when they fell to Earth suggests strongly that all meteorites originated in other bodies of the solar system that formed at the same time that the Earth did.
>
> *[Longman Spoken and Written English Corpus]*

Considering constructions with *that* and *the fact that*, subject position clauses occur about 20 to 40 times per million words in academic prose and newspapers and almost never occur in conversation, while *that*-clauses in other positions occur over 2,000 to 7,000 times per million words in the different registers (Biber *et al.* 1999: 674–6). These subject position clauses are obviously harder for listeners or readers to process, since they have a long constituent before the main verb. It is perhaps not surprising, then, that the subject position clauses tend to occur when the predicate of the sentence has another heavy, complex structure – a complicated noun phrase or prepositional phrase, or a complement clause, as in (1). In addition, these clauses tend to be used in particular discourse contexts, a topic further discussed in the next section.

Discourse-level factors

Many people's introduction to corpus linguistics is with simple concordance searches or collocate lists, and they sometimes believe that corpus linguistics has little to offer discourse-level study. However, this clearly is not the case (see Chapter 18, this volume).

Analysis of discourse-level factors affecting grammar often requires interpreting meaning, organisation and information structure in texts. Such analysis is part of the more qualitative, interpretive side of a corpus study, focusing on how a grammatical structure is used in context. In fact, several examples in the previous sections have noted associations that were found by analysing text at the discourse level rather than considering only discrete lexical or grammatical features. Determining semantic prosody, for instance, requires considering discourse context and assessing if it is negative.

The status of information is often important in grammar-discourse association patterns. Most commonly, studies find patterns related to whether information has already been mentioned in the discourse or is new. For example, the rare subject position *that*-clauses described in the previous section tend to restate information that has already been mentioned or implied in the previous discourse, so the subject clauses provide an anaphoric link. Similarly, Prado-Alonso (2019: 30) finds that subject-auxiliary inversion in declarative clauses (e.g. *Never have I*) serves a "focus management" function, working new information into the discourse.

Another perspective on grammar and discourse concerns matching grammar choices to their rhetorical functions. Williams (2010), for example, finds that first person pronouns tend to occur in English medical research articles in particular rhetorical moves, where researchers explain their choice of non-standard procedures, but in Spanish articles, first person is used in different rhetorical moves and with both non-standard and standard procedures, thereby creating empathy for the doctor–patient context. Studying social science research article introductions, Lu *et al.* (2020) analyse several measures of syntactic complexity and their associations with rhetorical moves. They find that longer sentences with higher density nominalisations and more frequent nonfinite dependent clauses are associated with the rhetorical move of announcing the present research.

Grammatical complexity in different types of discourse has also received a great deal of attention. Much of this work can be found in analyses of register (see Chapter 17, this volume). A major distinction found by studies has been the tendency for academic prose to have phrasal complexity, while conversation tends to have clausal complexity (Biber *et al.* 2011; Biber and Gray 2016). Research articles written in an English as a lingua franca context have been found to use complex nominal structures, too, though with some other syntactic complexity differences from American English research article writing (Wu *et al.* 2020).

Context of the situation

A number of factors in the context of the situation may be associated with the choice of a particular grammatical feature. Sociolinguistic studies have long considered how language use is affected by audience, purpose, participant roles, formality of the situation and numerous other social and regional characteristics, and corpus-based techniques can be applied in these areas. Thus far in studies of grammar, the most common perspective on variation has concerned registers (also called genres) – varieties associated with a particular situation of use and communicative purpose, and often identified within a culture by a specific name, such as academic prose, text messaging, conversation or newspaper writing. Comparisons of grammar in major registers such as academic writing and conversation have been included in descriptions of grammar studies in the previous sections. Other studies compare registers in more restricted domains. Grammatical features used in academic settings have received considerable attention. Numerous studies have analysed grammar features in universities – e.g. Fortanet (2004) describes details of the pronoun *we* in lectures, Louwerse *et al.* (2008) discuss the use of conditionals and Biber (2006, chapter 4) compares numerous grammatical features across ten spoken and written registers. A few studies compare academic settings to other professional settings. For example, in a study of engineering, Conrad (2018) finds a lower frequency of passives and other impersonal style features in writing by industry professionals compared to research journal articles, tying the lower frequencies to concerns with agency, conciseness and ease of reading for clients.

Whether focused on general or more specific settings, studies that make comparisons across registers all demonstrate that it is usually misleading to characterise the frequency and use of a grammatical feature in only one way. Instead, accurate grammatical descriptions require describing differences across registers (see Conrad 2000 and Chapter 17, this volume).

Traditional sociolinguistic variables having to do with social groups and regions were usually addressed in general categories in early corpus-based grammar research, with categories such as British and American English (e.g. in various comparisons throughout Biber *et al.* 1999; Carter and McCarthy 2006 appendix), varieties of world Englishes (Kachru 2008) or a general group such as London teenagers (Stenström *et al.* 2002). While these general classifications are still a popular topic (e.g. Baker 2017), more refined variables are becoming increasingly common in corpus studies. Calude (2017) includes gender, age, education and occupation as variables in investigating the use of demonstrative cleft constructions (such as *This is where I saw him*), finding the clefts are more typical of male rather than female speakers, adults in higher skilled jobs as compared to adults in semi-skilled jobs and middle-aged speakers over younger speakers. There are also increasingly specific regional dialect categories, as with Fernandez-Ordonez's (2010) study of grammar in rural Spanish dialects.

3 Investigating multiple influences on grammatical patterns

From the previous sections, it is probably already apparent that it is often difficult to focus on only one type of pattern when explaining grammatical choices. However, before computer-assisted analyses, it was unfeasible to consider multiple factors in a large number of texts simultaneously. Another contribution of corpus linguistics, then, has been to describe more about the multiple factors that simultaneously have an impact on grammatical choices. Corpus-based studies have used several approaches for examining multiple factors, depending on the goals and audience for the work.

Some studies provide a description of multiple factors without statistical analysis. For example, consider the case of omitting the optional *that* in a *that*-complement clause – e.g. *I think Ø I'll go*. Virtually any grammatical description includes the fact that the *that* is optional. Textbooks for ESL students often explain that it is especially common to delete it in speech (e.g. Azar 2002: 248), but a corpus analysis reveals that omission of *that* is actually associated with a number of factors (Biber *et al.* 1999: 681), as shown in Figure 16.1. One factor is a lexico-grammatical association: *That* is omitted more often when the verb in the main clause is *say* or *think* rather than any other verb. Two factors concern the grammatical co-text: *That* is omitted more often when (1) the main clause and complement clause have co-referential subjects rather than subjects that refer to different entities or (2) the *that*-clause has a personal pronoun subject rather than a full noun phrase. Another factor concerns the situational context: *That* is omitted more often in conversation than in newspaper writing generally, but the lexico-grammatical and grammatical co-text factors have a stronger effect in newspapers. That is, the choice of verb and subject types corresponds to a greater difference in percentage of *that* omission in newspapers than in conversation.

Other studies rely more on statistical analysis, which allows researchers to understand the relationship between factors in more detail. For example, Schilk *et al.* (2013) use multinomial logistic regression in studying the complementation patterns of the verb *give* in web-derived corpora of Indian, Pakistani and British English (e.g. *She gave the class a presentation* vs. *She gave a presentation to the class* vs. *She gave a presentation)*. They find three variables that affect the choice to differing extents: pronoun vs. noun use, distance since participants were mentioned in the discourse and the language variety. A statistical approach is becoming increasingly common in studies of grammar choices, ranging, for example, from the choice of indicative and subjunctive alternation in subordinate clauses in Spanish (Deshors and Waltermire 2019) to the choice of topic marking in spoken Shanghainese (Han *et al.* 2017).

Two other approaches are also often used for analysing multiple influences on grammatical choices. One is to consider a functional system within a language variety

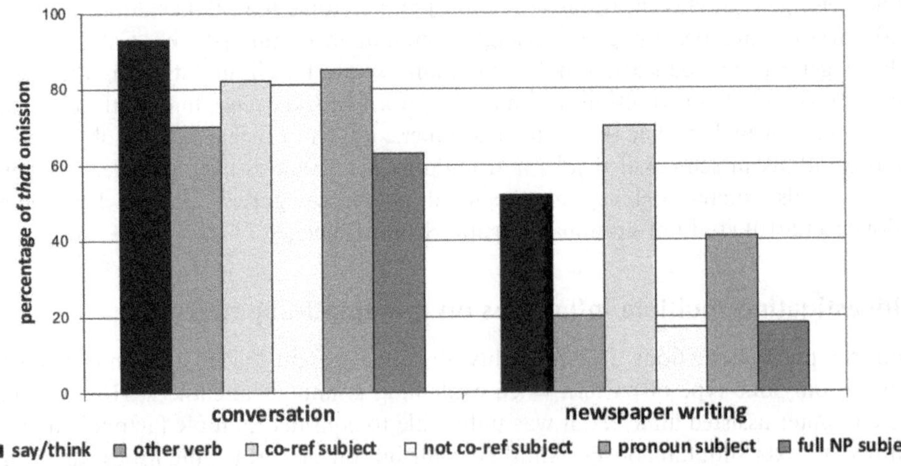

Figure 16.1 Conditions associated with omission of *that* in *that*-clauses

and describe factors that influence the grammatical features that are used to realise the system. For example, the system of metadiscourse or stance is often studied; Hyland (2017) provides a review of studies of the realisation of metadiscourse in many registers, from Twitter to research articles, most of them using a corpus-based lexico-grammatical perspective, and Gales (2015) examines the grammatical marking of stance in written threats. The other approach is to study the grammar of a variety. In this approach the focus shifts from describing grammar to describing the variety, as covered by Gray (Chapter 17, this volume).

4 Grammar and speech

The previous sections have all made mention of grammatical features in spoken discourse. Before corpus studies became popular, grammatical descriptions were based on written language (McCarthy and Carter 1995; Carter and McCarthy 2017). Unplanned spoken language was neglected or, at best, considered aberrant, with incomplete clauses, messy repairs and non-standard forms. In contrast, corpus analyses have emphasised the fact that many features of speech directly reflect the demands of social interactions. Grammar in speech, especially in conversation, has become studied as a legitimate grammar, not a lacking form of written grammar.

One factor often noted for grammatical choices in conversation concerns the need to minimise imposition and be indirect. For example, Conrad (1999) discusses the common choice of *though* rather than *however* as a contrastive connector in conversation. Placed at the end of the clause and conveying a sense of concession more than contrast, the use of *though* is a less direct way to disagree than *however*. A typical example in a conversation is as follows:

(2)

[Watching a football game, discussing a penalty call]

A:

Oh, that's outrageous.

B:

Well, he did put his foot out **though**.

[Longman Spoken and Written English Corpus]

Speaker B clearly disagrees with A's contention that the call is "outrageous", but the use of *though* (along with the discourse marker *well*) downplays the disagreement. The desire to convey indirectness can also result in the use of verb tenses or aspects not typically found in writing. For example, McCarthy and Carter (2002: 58) describe the use of present progressive with verbs of desire, as when a customer tells a travel agent that she and her husband *are wanting* to take a trip. The use of present progressive makes the desire sound more tentative and the request for help less imposing.

Other features affecting the grammatical forms that are typical of face-to-face interactions include the shared context (and in many cases shared background knowledge), the expression of emotions and evaluations and the constraints of real-time production and processing (see a further summary of factors and features in Biber *et al.* 1999 chapter 14, and Carter and McCarthy 2006: 163–75). Some of these conditions lead to common use of grammar features that are typically not even mentioned in grammars based on writing. For instance, work on discourse markers (e.g. *well, you know, I mean*) has flourished in corpus-based studies, not just of English but numerous languages, including multi-word discourse markers in Slovene (Dobrovoljc 2017) and the co-occurrence of discourse markers and disfluencies in French and English (Crible 2017).

Corpus-based studies of grammar in spoken discourse have also found associations between grammatical structures and intonation. While corpus-based work with intonation has been going on since the 1980s when the London-Lund Corpus was released with basic intonation in the transcription, the role of intonation in disambiguating the functions of features has increased in recent years. Work has included clausal structures; for example, Adolphs and Carter (2013) note that it is possible to disambiguate use of *I don't know why* as a full clause or sentence stem by considering intonation unit boundaries. Studies have also covered specific words that can realise different grammatical classes or classes that have multiple meanings. For example, Wichmann *et al.* (2010) find that *of course* is marked with prosodic prominence when it functions as an epistemic stance adverbial but not when it is a more general discourse marker. Biber and Staples (2014) find that different prosodic patterns are associated with different functions for high-frequencystance adverbials such as *actually*; when a speaker emphasises the semantic content, such as *actually* meaning "in actual fact", the adverbials are more likely to have prosodic prominence, but when the adverbials express general certainty or doubt, prosodic prominence is less likely.

In addition to intonation, many spoken interactions are distinct from writing by having a shared visual component. Exploring the patterns between grammar and nonverbals is one of the new challenges discussed in the next section.

5 New challenges with grammar and corpora

The first edition of this chapter (Conrad 2010) concluded by discussing two controversies over the value of corpus-based grammar study. The first controversy focused on teaching and learning, especially the argument that corpus investigations could be harmful because corpora would show learners unusual constructions in addition to common ones (see Owen 1996 and the response in Hunston 2002). Ten years later, this controversy has faded. Although there are many considerations for applications to language teaching, corpus linguistics has become a more firmly established way to explain grammatical choices (e.g. see Chapters 25 and 30, this volume).

A second controversy ten years ago was whether evidence from corpus studies of grammar could contribute to linguistic theory (e.g. Newmeyer 2003; Meyer and Tao 2005). Today it is clear that such evidence has a role to play. Not surprisingly, many corpus-based studies are associated with construction grammar (e.g. Gabrielatos 2019; Wible and Tsao 2020), which views multi-word patterns as building blocks of syntax, not unlike pattern grammar (Hunston 2019). Other studies contribute to the development of theories that, at first, might appear at odds with corpus techniques. Studies applying systemic functional linguistics (SFL), for instance, traditionally tended to present short text examples, but integration of SFL theory with corpus analysis is now common. Some studies focus on specific grammatical features, such as Xiang and Liu (2018)'s study of *let's* constructions, clarifying the system of MOOD in SFL. Others focus on more general constructions, such as Lee's (2016) study of South Korean newspaper reports, which expands on SFL transitivity analysis.

Today the challenges for corpus-based grammar studies hinge not so much on basic questions of whether corpus analysis is valuable, but rather on increasing the depth of analysis. As noted in the previous section, one new challenge is multi-modal analysis, investigating how patterns of grammar correspond with gestures, facial expressions and body movements (see Chapter 7, this volume). Though more work thus far has focused on words and phraseology, some includes grammar, such as identifying the grammatical categories that tend to be associated with gestures and those that do not (Kok 2017). Multi-modal analysis, however, presents several conundrums for an approach whose strengths include naturally occurring contexts and large databases of text. In addition to most people finding video recording more intrusive than audio recording, the analysis of eye gaze, facial expressions and small movements requires high-quality video. It is thus currently unfeasible to create a multi-modal corpus that includes all kinds of naturally occurring spoken interactions. In addition, analysis of non-verbals is time-consuming. Software for the coding of non-verbals is helpful (see Adolphs and Carter 2013 and Chapter 7, this volume), but analysis simply cannot cover as many speakers or as much language as in text-only analyses. The depth of analysis requires a trade-off in the breadth of texts.

The desire for more interpretive depth in corpus studies is apparent in some other developments as well. Numerous studies now investigate lexico-grammatical associations as part of critical discourse analysis (CDA), with the corpus analysis showing the systematic patterns of language use and the CDA providing more about the features' connections to groups' representations, identities and power dynamics (e.g. Wilkinson 2019 on the representation of bisexuals; Alcantud-Díaz, 2012 on the identity, social power and violence in Grimm's fairy tales; Potts *et al.* 2015 on the linguistic construction of newsworthiness for a hurricane). Nartley and Mwinlaaru (2019) provide a meta-analysis of 121 studies combining corpus linguistics and CDA. Corpus studies that cover some grammar features and lexico-grammar have also been combined with conversation analysis (Walsh 2013), so the context of the features and their use in interaction can be analysed more closely than through corpus techniques alone. Other studies advocate incorporating more input from speakers or writers represented in a corpus in order to understand the grammar patterns more fully within their contexts of use; Conrad (2021), for example, argues for the need for writing studies to combine corpus analysis and interviews of writers to understand the intentions behind their grammar choices and create targeted instructional materials. For all these approaches, balancing the strength of large-scale corpus analysis while adding more intensive analytical techniques presents a challenge that continues to be refined.

Unfortunately, a chapter of this size cannot do justice to many aspects of corpus-based grammar analysis. In fact, even traditional grammar terminology used throughout this chapter deserves interrogation, as corpus researchers highlight the gaps between traditional meta-language and features of speech and electronic communication (Carter and McCarthy 2017). Further attention is due also to diachronic studies that explain changes in grammar use over time (e.g. Biber and Gray 2016; Jenset and McGillivray 2017) and to many specific grammar features of language varieties in the world (e.g. Esimaje *et al.* 2019). Other chapters in this volume add important perspectives on methodological issues (Part I, this volume) and teaching (Part III, this volume). Nonetheless, despite its inability to do justice to all related topics, the chapter has shown that corpus linguistics has already had a profound effect on our understanding of grammar and is likely to continue to do so in the future.

Further reading

Biber, D., Johansson, S., Leech, G., Conrad, S. and Finegan, E. (2021) *Grammar of Spoken and Written English*, Amsterdam: John Benjamins. (This reference grammar covers frequency information, lexico-grammar patterns and comparisons of use in conversation, fiction writing, newspaper writing and academic prose for the major structures in English, in addition to chapters on fixed phrases, stance and conversation. It includes everything from the earlier *Longman Grammar of Spoken and Written English.*)

Carter, R. A. and McCarthy, M. J. (2006) *Cambridge Grammar of English*, Cambridge: Cambridge University Press. (This reference grammar emphasises spoken vs. written language for major grammar features of English and includes many lexico-grammatical analyses. It also covers some functional categories, such as typical grammatical realisations of speech acts and many typical ESL difficulties.)

References

Adolphs, S. and Carter, R. A. (2013) *Spoken Corpus Linguistics: From Monomodal to Multimodal*, New York: Routledge.

Alcantud-Díaz, M. (2012) 'The Sister Did Her Every Imaginable Injury: Power and Violence in Cinderella', *International Journal of English Studies* 12(2): 59–71.

Azar, B. (2002) *Understanding and Using English Grammar*, 3rd edn, White Plains, NY: Longman.

Baker, P. (2017) *American and British English: Divided by a Common Language?* Cambridge: Cambridge University Press.

Biber, D. (2006) *University Language: A Corpus-Based Study of Spoken and Written Registers*, Amsterdam: John Benjamins.

Biber, D. and Gray, B. (2016) *Grammatical Complexity in Academic English: Linguistic Change in Writing*, Cambridge: Cambridge University Press.

Biber, D. and Staples, S. (2014) 'Exploring the Prosody of Stance: Variation in the Realization of Stance Adverbials', in T. Raso and H. Mello (eds) *Spoken Corpora and Linguistic Studies*, Amsterdam: John Benjamins, pp. 271–94.

Biber, D., Conrad, S. and Cortes, V. (2004) ' "Take a Look At…": Lexical bundles in University Teaching and Textbooks', *Applied Linguistics* 25(3): 401–35.

Biber, D., Gray, B. and Poonpon, K. (2011) 'Should We Use Characteristics of Conversation to Measure Grammatical Complexity in L2 Writing Development?', *TESOL Quarterly* 45(1): 5–35.

Biber, D., Johansson, S., Leech, G., Conrad, S. and Finegan, E. (1999) *Longman Grammar of Spoken and Written English*, Harlow, England: Pearson Education.

Biber, D., Johansson, S., Leech, G., Conrad, S. and Finegan, E. (2021) *Grammar of Spoken and Written English*, Amsterdam: John Benjamins.

Calude, A. (2017) 'Sociolinguistic Variation at the Grammatical/Discourse Level: Demonstrative Clefts in Spoken British English', *International Journal of Corpus Linguistics* 22(3): 429–55.

Carter, R. A. and McCarthy, M. J. (2006) *Cambridge Grammar of English*, Cambridge: Cambridge University Press.

Carter, R. A. and McCarthy, M. J. (2017) 'Spoken Grammar: Where Are We and Where Are We Going?' *Applied Linguistics* 38(1): 1–20.

Conrad, S. (1999) 'The Importance of Corpus-Based Research for Language Teachers', *System* 27(1): 1–18.

Conrad, S. (2000) 'Will Corpus Linguistics Revolutionize Grammar Teaching in the 21st Century?' *TESOL Quarterly* 34(3): 548–60.

Conrad, S. (2010) 'What Can a Corpus Tell Us about Grammar?', in A. O'Keeffe and M. J. McCarthy (eds) *The Routledge Handbook of Corpus Linguistics*, London: Routledge, pp. 227–240.

Conrad, S. (2018) 'The Use of Passives and Impersonal Style in Civil Engineering Writing', *Journal of Business and Technical Communication* 32(1): 38–76.

Conrad, S. (2021) 'Integrating Corpus Linguistics into Writing Studies: An Example from Engineering', in K. Blewett, T. Donahue and C. Monroe (eds) *The Expanding Universe of Writing Studies: Higher Education Writing Research*, New York: Peter Lang, pp. 43–56.

Cook, V. (1994) 'Universal Grammar and the Learning and Teaching of Second Languages', in T. Odlin (ed.) *Perspectives on Pedagogical Grammar*, Cambridge: Cambridge University Press, pp. 25–48.

Crible, L. (2017) 'Discourse Markers and (Dis)fluency in English and French', *International Journal of Corpus Linguistics* 22(2): 242–69.

Deshors, S. and Waltermire, M. (2019) 'The Indicative vs. Subjunctive Alternation with Expressions of Possibility in Spanish: A Multifactorial Analysis', *International Journal of Corpus Linguistics* 24(1): 67–97.

Dobrovoljc, K. (2017) 'Multi-Word Discourse Markers and Their Corpus-Driven Identification: The Case of MWDM Extraction from the Reference Corpus of Spoken Slovene', *International Journal of Corpus Linguistics* 22(4): 551–82.

Esimaje, A., Gut, U. and Antia, B. (eds) (2019) *Corpus Linguistics and African Englishes*, Amsterdam: John Benjamins.

Fernandez-Ordonez, I. (2010) 'Investigating Spanish Dialectal Grammar with the COSER (Audio Corpus of Spoken Rural Spanish)', *Corpus* 9: 81–114.

Fortanet, I. (2004) 'The Use of "We" in University Lectures: Reference and Function', *English for Specific Purposes* 23(1): 45–66.

Frazier, S. (2003) 'A Corpus Analysis of *Would*-Clauses Without Adjacent *If*-Clauses', *TESOL Quarterly* 37(3): 443–66.

Gabrielatos, C. (2019) 'If-Conditions and Modality: Frequency Patterns and Theoretical Explanations', *Journal of English Linguistics* 47(4): 301–34.

Gales, T. (2015) 'The Stance of Stalking: A Corpus-Based Analysis of Grammatical Markers of Stance in Threatening Communications', *Corpora* 10(2): 171–200.

Han, W., Arppe, A. and Newman, J. (2017) 'Topic Marking in a Shanghainese Corpus: From Observation to Prediction', *Corpus Linguistics and Linguistic Theory* 13(2): 291–19.

Hunston, S. (2002) *Corpora in Applied Linguistics*, Cambridge: Cambridge University Press.

Hunston, S. (2019) 'Patterns, Constructions and Applied Linguistics', *International Journal of Corpus Linguistics* 24(3): 324–53.

Hunston, S. and Francis, G. (1999) *Pattern Grammar: A Corpus-Driven Approach to the Lexical Grammar of English*, Amsterdam: Benjamins.

Hyland, K. (2017) 'Metadiscourse: What Is It and Where Is It going?' *Journal of Pragmatics* 113: 16–29.

Jenset, G. and McGillivray, B. (2017) *Quantitative Historical Linguistics: A Corpus Framework*, Oxford: Oxford University Press.

Kachru, Y. (2008) 'Language Variation and Corpus Linguistics', *World Englishes* 27(1): 1–8.

Kok, K. (2017) 'Functional and Temporal Relations between Spoken and Gestured Components of Language: A Corpus-Based Inquiry', *International Journal of Corpus Linguistics* 22(1): 1–26.

Larsen-Freeman, D. (2002) 'The Grammar of Choice', in E. Hinkel and S. Fotos (eds) *New Perspectives on Grammar Teaching in Second Language Classrooms*, Mahwah, NJ: Erlbaum, pp. 103–18.

Lee, C. (2016) 'A Corpus-Based Approach to Transitivity Analysis at Grammatical and Conceptual Levels', *International Journal of Corpus Linguistics* 21(4): 465–98.

Louw, B. (1993) 'Irony in the Text or Insincerity in the Writer? The Diagnostic Potential of Semantic Prosodies', in M. Baker, G. Francis, and E. Tognini-Bonelli (eds) *Text and Technology: In Honour of John Sinclair*, Philadelphia/Amsterdam: John Benjamins, pp. 157–76.

Louwerse, M., Crossley, S. and Jeuniaux, P. (2008) 'What If? Conditionals in Educational Registers', *Linguistics and Education* 19(1): 56–69.

Lu, X., Casal, J. and Liu, Y. (2020) 'The Rhetorical Functions of Syntactically Complex Sentences in Social Science Research Article Introductions', *Journal of English for Academic Purposes* 44: 1–16.

Ma, H. and Qian, M. (2020) 'The Creation and Evaluation of a Grammar Pattern List for the Most Frequent Academic Verbs', *English for Specific Purposes* 58: 155–69.

McCarthy, M. J. and Carter, R. A. (1995) 'Spoken Grammar: What Is It and How Do We Teach It?' *ELT Journal* 49(3): 207–18.

McCarthy, M. J. and Carter, R. A. (2002) 'Ten Criteria for a Spoken Grammar', in E. Hinkel and S. Fotos (eds) *New Perspectives on Grammar Teaching in Second Language Classrooms*, Mahwah, NJ: Lawrence Erlbaum, pp. 51–75.

Meyer, C. and Tao, H. (2005) 'Response to Newmeyer's "Grammar Is Grammar and Usage Is Usage"', *Language* 81(1): 226–8.

Nartley, M. and Mwinlaaru, I. (2019) 'Towards a Decade of Synergising Corpus Linguistics and Critical Discourse Analysis: A Meta-Analysis', *Corpora* 14(2): 203–35.

Newmeyer, F. (2003) 'Grammar is Grammar and Usage is Usage', *Language* 79(4): 682–707.

O'Keeffe, A., McCarthy, M. J. and Carter, R. A. (2007) *From Corpus to Classroom: Language Use and Language Teaching*, Cambridge: Cambridge University Press.

Owen, C. (1996) 'Does a Corpus Require to Be Consulted?' *ELT Journal* 50(3): 219–24.

Potts, A., Bednarek, M. and Caples, H. (2015) 'How Can Computer-Based Methods Help Researchers to Investigate News Values in Large Datasets? A Corpus Linguistic Study of the Construction of Newsworthiness in the Reporting on Hurricane Katrina', *Discourse & Communication* 9(2): 149–72.

Prado-Alonso, C. (2019) 'A Comprehensive Corpus-Based Analysis of "X Auxiliary Subject' Constructions in Written and Spoken English', *Topics in Linguistics* 20(2): 17–32.

Schilk, M., Mukherjee, J., Nam, C., and Mukherjee, S. (2013) 'Complementation of Ditransitive Verbs in South Asian Englishes: A Multifactorial Analysis', *Corpus Linguistics and Linguistic Theory* 9(2): 187–225.

Sinclair, J. (1991) *Corpus Concordance Collocation*, Oxford: Oxford University Press.

Stempel, P. (2019) 'A Constructional Reanalysis of Semantic Prosody', unpublished Ph.D. dissertation, Rice University.

Stenström, A., Andersen, G. and Hasund, I. (2002) *Trends in Teenage Talk: Corpus Compilation, Analysis and Findings*, Amsterdam: John Benjamins.

Walsh, S. (2013) 'Corpus Linguistics and Conversation Analysis at the Interface: Theoretical Perspectives, Practical Outcomes', in J. Romero-Trillo (ed.) *Yearbook of Corpus Linguistics and Pragmatics*, Dordrecht: Springer, pp. 35–51.

Wible, D. and Tsao, N. (2020) 'Constructions and the Problem of Discovery: A Case for the Paradigmatic', *Corpus Linguistics and Linguistic Theory* 16(1): 67–93.

Wichmann, A., Simon-Vandenbergen, A. and Aijmer, K. (2010) 'How Prosody Reflects Semantic Change: A Synchronic Case Study of *Of Course*', in K. Davidse, L. Vandelanotte and H. Cuyckens (eds) *Subjectification, Intersubjectification and Grammaticalization*, Berlin: Walter De Guyter, pp. 103–54.

Wilkinson, M. (2019) '"Bisexual Oysters": A Diachronic Corpus-Based Critical Discourse Analysis of Bisexual Representation in *The Times* between 1957 and 2017', *Discourse & Communication* 13(2): 249–67.

Williams, I. (2010) 'Cultural Differences in Academic Discourse: Evidence from First-Person Verb Use in the Methods Sections of Medical Research Articles', *International Journal of Corpus Linguistic* 15(2): 214–39.

Wu, X., Mauranen, A., and Lei, L. (2020) 'Syntactic Complexity in English as a Lingua Franca Academic Writing', *Journal of English for Academic Purposes* 43: 1–13.

Xiang, D. and Liu, C. (2018) 'The Semantics of mood and the Syntax of the Let's-Construction in English: A Corpus-Based Cardiff Grammar Approach', *Australian Journal of Linguistics* 38(4): 549–85.

17

What can a corpus tell us about registers and genres?

Bethany Gray

1 Two perspectives on text varieties: register and genre

In a typical day, we encounter a range of receptive and productive language events – having conversations with our family, reading a novel, writing emails to colleagues, revising a paper for a class, reading news articles online, interacting with the server at a coffee shop…and many more. Each of these language events varies in terms of the situations in which they occur. The most obvious difference is mode (speech versus writing), but other situational differences also exist, for example:

- Purpose: e.g. news articles are informational, a novel entertains and text messages are interpersonal;
- The participants and their relationships: e.g. close personal relationships between family members, a student producing an assignment following a teacher's requirements, a knowledgeable writer of news articles writing for the general public;
- Degree of interactiveness: e.g. face-to-face service encounters and emails involve direct interaction between participants, but one occurs in real-time while the other may be asynchronous, whereas there is no direct interaction between the writer and reader of a news article.

These situational differences are associated with particular linguistic and rhetorical patterns of use. For example, novels are often written in the past tense, accompanied by many adjectives and adverbs, to narrate a story and help the reader create a mental picture of the events and characters. A service encounter at a coffee shop typically initiates with a greeting and a question from the barista asking what you'd like. In brief, we expect particular patterns of language use with each type of communicative event that we take part in.

These different types of communicative events, generally called text "categories" or "varieties", are directly relevant for corpus-based linguistics. Consider the following definition of a "corpus":

DOI: 10.4324/9780367076399-17

> a large and principled sample of texts designed to represent *a target domain of language use* (e.g. a language, dialect, or register).
>
> *(emphasis added, Egbert et al. forthcoming)*

Each of the varieties listed earlier can be considered a domain of language use. Many corpora are introduced with the phrase "a corpus of…", followed by a labeling of the domain it is intended to represent – a corpus *of business emails*, a corpus *of university lectures*, a corpus *of argumentative essays produced by L2 writers*, etc. Even general corpora are usually structured as sub-corpora of particular text categories. For example, the Corpus of Contemporary American English (COCA) is structured around sub-corpora of unscripted television/radio programs, fiction, popular magazines, newspapers and academic journals (Davies 2009), with recent additions of blogs and scripted TV/movies.

This recognition of text varieties has long been an integral component of corpus-based research; decades of empirical research has demonstrated that linguistic patterns of use are strongly mediated by text variety (Biber and Conrad 2019). Biber (2010: 243) goes so far as to claim that this research has 'shown that descriptions of grammatical variation and use are not valid for the language as a whole'. Thus, corpus-based research which fails to account for text categories in a systematic way is unlikely to produce meaningful descriptions of language use. Consider the frequency of a single part-of-speech category: nouns. Biber *et al.* (1999: 65) report that nouns occur in news writing at a rate of about 300,000 times per 1 million words. In contrast, nouns occurred in conversation just over 100,000 times per million words. Had the analysis presented a single rate of occurrence for "English" (about 200,000 times per million words if the corpora were combined), that pattern of use would fail to reflect reality. Recognising this inherent variation across text categories, corpus research has sought to uncover the typical patterns of particular domains/text categories and to map the variation that occurs across the range of domains that we encounter.

Given the integral role of text categories in corpus linguistics, it is not surprising that various terms have been used to refer to such categories, such as "register" and "genre". As Biber and Conrad (2019: 21–3) point out, some scholars use "genre" or "register" exclusively, others use the terms interchangeably and still others differentiate between the two. Of those which differentiate register and genre, readers may be most familiar with the systemic functional linguistics (SFL) approach. In SFL, "register" and "genre" exist on different semiotic planes (the "context of situation" and the "context of culture", respectively; see Halliday 1978; Hasan 1995).

However, for our purposes in relating the concept of text categories to corpus linguistics, "register" and "genre" can both be considered terms to refer to different domains of language use. Instead, the remainder of this chapter will follow Biber and Conrad (2019) in distinguishing between register and genre *approaches* to the analysis of text categories. That is, the chapter takes the position that any text category can be analysed from a register or a genre perspective.

In a register perspective, the analyst is concerned with the pervasive linguistic features that characterize the text variety and the connections that can be drawn between observed linguistic patterns of use and the non-linguistic characteristics of the variety:

> The underlying assumption of the register perspective is that core linguistic features (e.g. pronouns and verbs) serve communicative functions. As a result, some

> linguistic features are common in a register because they are functionally adapted to the communicative purposes and situational context of texts from that register.
>
> *(Biber and Conrad 2019: 2)*

Studies taking a register perspective often focus on lexical, phraseological, grammatical and lexico-grammatical features, documenting their quantitative distributions, lexical associations and discourse functions in specific registers or across registers. For example, the *Longman Grammar of Spoken and Written English* (Biber *et al.* 1999; republished as Biber *et al.* 2021) found that *wh*-clefts (e.g. *what I'd like to do is..., what this shows is...*) are more common in speech than in written registers, providing a way to manage the flow of information. Deroey (2012) then analysed the discourse functions of such clefts in academic lectures, finding that 67 per cent were used for an "informing" purpose (describing, interpreting or providing a gloss for concepts introduced in the lecture), while 15 per cent were used to organise the classroom discourse – two functions that are particularly important given the spoken mode and informational purpose of academic lectures. The register approach will be described in Sections 2 and 3.

In contrast, a genre perspective of text varieties is concerned with text structure and the conventionalised components that combine to create a text, which are typical or expected of a particular text variety (Biber and Conrad 2019: 2). For example, business emails conventionally begin with a greeting/salutation, and television game shows typically include a segment in which the players are introduced. Corpus-based research has less commonly focused on these sorts of conventionalised structures, more often addressing questions of text structure. One line of research in particular has demonstrated the contributions of the corpus-based genre perspective: rhetorical move analysis. Thus, genre-based approaches are the focus of Section 4.

2 Corpus-based register studies

Corpus-based research on the linguistic characteristics of registers has resulted in a large canon of empirical research findings. This section provides an overview of the major trends and highlights several topics that have received considerable attention (for a review of many earlier register studies, see Biber 2010). The studies discussed here share a goal of describing the quantitative distributions and functional uses of linguistic features in particular discourse contexts. However, these studies also demonstrate the breadth of corpus-based register research in terms of several parameters:

1. The scope of the registers investigated, from studies that directly compare a range of spoken and written registers, to those focusing on registers within speech or writing, to studies that offer detailed descriptions of a single register (e.g. Handford 2010 on business meetings).
2. The nature of the registers investigated, with some studies focusing on relatively general registers (e.g. conversation or academic writing) and others analysing more specialised domains (e.g. academic lectures or historical fiction novels).
3. The linguistic level of the features being analysed, including lexical, phraseological, grammatical/syntactic and lexico-grammatical features, or a constellation of features that form a functional "system" (such as stance, the expression of epistemic certainty/doubt, attitudes and evaluations).

4. The overarching goal of the research: to document the use and variability of a particular linguistic feature as mediated by register, or to describe registers with respect to particular linguistic features.

Research with a primary focus on linguistic features often accounts for register in systematic ways, recognising that linguistic patterns are variable across registers. For example, two major corpus-based research grammars have documented the variable patterns of use of grammatical features across registers in terms of quantitative distributions, their typical lexical associations and discourse functions. *The Longman Grammar of Spoken and Written English* (*LGSWE,* Biber *et al.* 1999) documents patterns of use across four general registers (conversation, fiction, news and academic writing), and the *Cambridge Grammar of English* (Carter and McCarthy 2006) accounts for spoken and written variation.

The remainder of this section is organised around the linguistic level of the analysis, focusing specifically on how these features are examined relative to register.

Phraseological patterns

Register research on phraseological patterns has revealed fundamental differences in the frequency and nature of formulaic language across registers. While Greaves and Warren (Chapter 15, this volume) provide a broader overview of different types of multi-word units, here I focus specifically on two types of phraseological patterns: lexical bundles and frames (or p-frames).

The term "lexical bundle" refers to frequent, recurrent continuous sequences identified empirically based on corpus analysis. Biber *et al.* (1999) identify major patterns of register variation, showing that the most common sequences in speech and writing differ in terms of their typical structures and functions. Biber *et al.* (2004) further develop the framework, finding that:

1. Two spoken registers (academic speech and conversation) generally contain more lexical bundles than written registers (textbooks and academic prose);
2. Bundles differ structurally and functionally across registers: written registers use informational/referential noun and prepositional phrase bundles (e.g. *as a result of*), while conversation relies primarily on dependent clauses (e.g. *you might want to*) and verb-based bundles (e.g. *take a look at*) conveying stance;
3. Classroom teaching integrated the more informational, noun/prepositional phrase bundles and discourse-organising bundles alongside the bundle types typical of speech, which they relate to the instructional/informational purpose of that register.

A common goal has been to identify the most important phraseological units in specific registers. Academic writing has received particular attention, such as Candarli and Jones (2019) on research articles in education, Cortes (2004) on student and published writing in history and biology and Hyland (2008) on bundles across disciplines. Bundle use has also been explored in spoken academic language (e.g. Nesi and Basturkmen 2006) and in a range of non-academic registers (e.g. Breeze 2013 on legal registers; Mahlberg *et al.* 2019 on nineteenth-century novels).

Frames (or p-frames) are a related phraseological feature that have shown clear register-based patterns. Frames are frequently recurring sequences of words with an internal variable "slot" that can be realised with multiple words (e.g. *the * of the* can be realised as *the end of the* and *the purpose of the*). Such sequences are seen as highly productive building blocks of discourse, and the frequency and nature of frames vary across speech and writing. Gray and Biber (2015) found a higher frequency of frames in conversation than in academic writing, with frames that were more "fixed" in nature (i.e. they had a limited number of different words occurring in the variable slots). Meanwhile, frames in academic writing were more likely to be variable (occurring with a wider range of fillers). Frames have also been investigated in specialised registers, such as book reviews (Römer 2010), pedagogical materials for engineering courses (Nekrasova-Beker 2019) and L2 English writing (Garner 2016).

Grammatical and lexico-grammatical features

At the most general level, grammatical and lexico-grammatical studies of register variation have focused on the speech–writing divide, often focusing on individual linguistic features. For example, Diani (2008) analyses emphasisers in spoken and written academic registers, while Kennedy (2002) examines the distribution of modal verbs across registers in the BNC. These features can be quite narrowly defined, such as Lindley's (2020) study of progressive aspect verb phrases occurring with *always* in six spoken and written registers, or more broadly, such as Biber's (1999) study on *that*- and *to*-complement clauses in speech and writing.

Other research has focused on spoken or written registers exclusively, such as Barbieri's (2005) comparison of quotatives across four spoken registers (conversation, service encounters, study groups and office hours) and Nesselhauf and Römer (2007) on the lexical associations of progressive aspect in speech. Within written registers, comparisons across registers are common (e.g. Zhang 2015 on extraposed clauses across academic versus popular writing; Crompton 2017 on the use of demonstrative *this* in anaphoric reference in three argumentative registers). Analyses of individual registers are also prevalent, such as Padula *et al.* (2020) on popularised engineering articles.

While this research represents a very small sample of register-based grammar research, these studies illustrate the focus on detailed analyses of particular grammatical features that consider patterns of use in specific registers – including quantitative distributions, frequent lexical associations and the discourse functions of the features within particular register contexts.

It is also possible to take a slightly different perspective, in which the focus of corpus-based register research is not on a single individual feature, but rather on a set of related features, thus enabling descriptions of registers in terms of broader linguistic patterns. One such area of research considers structural devices related to grammatical complexity. This research has documented fundamentally distinct patterns across registers, with spoken registers relying on grammatical devices that are clausal in nature (e.g. verb + *that*-complement clauses), while complexity in informational written registers is largely the result of phrasal structures (e.g. attributive adjectives, nouns as noun modifiers and prepositional phrases) (Biber 1988). Complexity has been investigated synchronically and diachronically across spoken and written registers (Biber and Gray 2016), as well as in more specialised written registers (e.g. military/navy language in Noguera-Diaz and Perez-Paredes 2019) and student writing (e.g. Staples *et al.* 2016).

Stance and evaluation

A second area of research that involves a set of related linguistic features is the expression of stance and evaluation – the speaker/writer's marking of epistemic certainty/doubt, attitudes and evaluations. Biber *et al.* (1999: Chapter 12) survey a range of lexico-grammatical markers of stance (e.g., modal verbs, stance adverbials, *that*- and *to*-complement clauses controlled by stance nouns, verbs and adjectives), showing distinctive patterns across spoken and written registers in terms of the overall marking of stance (with a higher preponderance of stance in speech), the typical stance meanings (a focus on epistemic meanings in academic writing) and the structural devices most frequently used for stance expression across registers.

Epistemic stance has been viewed as an important component of academic writing. Hyland's (1998) study of boosting (expressions of certainty) and hedging (expressions of doubt) across disciplines has been particularly influential, leading to detailed investigations of particular stance devices, such as stance noun + *that*-clauses (Charles 2007; Jiang 2017). Recent developments have focused on expanding definitions of stance to account for the more implicit marking of stance in written registers (e.g. Biber and Zhang 2018) and re-envisioning the issue of formality in stance marking across registers (Larsson 2019).

Applied register research: comparing pedagogical registers to target registers

Many of the studies in this section have clear relevance to the teaching and learning of academic registers, providing detailed descriptions of particular registers important for novice and learner language users (see also Coxhead, this volume). Noteworthy from a register perspective is research that compares domains used for language instruction with target, "real-life" registers. For example, TED talks have been used to teach academic listening and notetaking, on the assumption that they are similar to academic lectures (spoken and informational). However, TED talks are typically shorter, more scripted, lack direct interaction with the audience and are intended for entertainment as well as information. Thus, studies have investigated the extent to which TED talks and lectures share linguistic patterns of use in terms of lexical density, speech rate and academic vocabulary use (Wingrove 2017) and lexical bundles (Liu and Chen 2019). Another example of this type of comparison is Miller's (2011) analysis of reading passages from English for Academic Purposes (EAP) textbooks and university textbooks. The goal of such research is to evaluate whether registers used to simulate a target domain for pedagogical purposes are indeed linguistically similar to that target register. This research has consistently demonstrated linguistic similarities and differences between the domains being used for pedagogical input and the target registers they are intended to help students learn, to better inform how these resources are utilised in the language classroom.

Corpus-based studies of registers produced by novice language users and L2 learners are common (see Pérez-Paredes and Mark; Römer, this volume). One line of research has compared novice or L2 language production to the target registers they will need to produce. For example, Conrad (2018) analyses the use of passive voice in student writing in civil engineering with reports written by practicing engineers, finding that students used passive voice much more frequently, whereas practitioners avoided the use of passive voice.

Other research has focused directly on how register mediates novice and learner language production. For example, Staples and Reppen (2016) analyse a range of lexico-grammatical devices in two first-year composition registers (rhetorical analysis and argumentative papers) produced by L2 English writers, while Staples *et al.* (2016) analyse grammatical complexity features in university student writing across levels, disciplines and registers (essays, critiques, case studies and explanation papers). Such research has shown that register variation is systematic even in learner and novice writing, further supporting the need to account for register in learner corpus research.

3 Uncovering register variation through multi-dimensional analysis

The studies surveyed in the previous section had the goal of investigating characteristics of a particular feature (or set of related features) in a limited set of registers. In this section, we turn to research with a different goal: to model overall patterns of register variation in terms of a comprehensive set of linguistic features.

Multi-dimensional (MD) analysis was developed during the 1980s (e.g. Biber 1988) to enable comprehensive, comparative descriptions of spoken versus written registers (see Biber 2019 for a discussion of the theoretical precursors of the MD approach). The MD analysis approach involves carrying out exploratory factor analysis to identify patterns of co-occurrence between a wide range of linguistic features (e.g. semantic categories of words, grammatical features and part-of-speech classes, lexcio-grammatical combinations and syntactic features). The statistical analysis results in multiple "dimensions", or sets of co-occurring features, which can be used to quantitatively describe each text and sub-corpus. Finally, each dimension is interpreted functionally.

To illustrate, consider an example from Gray (2015), an MD analysis of quantitative, qualitative and theoretical research articles in six disciplines that revealed four dimensions of variation. Figure 17.1 shows the quantitative characterisation of each sub-corpus (i.e. its dimension score) along Dimension 2; the two sets of features that statistically co-occurred in the data on this dimension are also presented. Sub-corpora on the positive end of the dimension exhibited relatively higher frequencies of the features associated with this pole of the dimension, while sub-corpora on the negative end had higher frequencies of the complementary set of features.

Based on this distribution of the registers/disciplines, the underlying communicative functions of the co-occurring features and analyses of text excerpts, Gray (2015) interpreted the positive pole of this dimension as showing narrative description. Features such as third person pronouns, past tense and perfect aspect were especially common in qualitative research, as well as in humanities and social science disciplines, as they described the participants and events in the research – they told a story (select narrative features **bolded** or <u>underlined</u>):

(1)

Qualitative Applied Linguistics

In the HIST course I **observed**, all APs **began** with a topic **introduction**, followed by a rationale for topic choice. At this stage, **presenters** usually **included** personal anecdotes <u>that **positioned themselves** as 'licensed' to discuss their topic</u>.

[AJRC-AL-QL]

Figure 17.1 Distribution of RA types in six disciplines along Dimension 2 "Contextualized Narrative Description" vs. "Procedural Description" (adapted from Gray 2015)

In contrast, the features associated with the negative pole (which were much more common in the hard sciences) created a procedural description of previous findings and of the actions carried out in the study procedures (select procedural features **bolded**):

> (2)
> *Quantitative Physics*
> Many experimental features suggestive of the **liquid-gas phase** transition of nuclear **matter have been observed** in the Fermi **energy** regime of **nucleus-nucleus** collisions.
> [...]
> The **data have been obtained by** the Indra-Aladin Collaborations (Indra at GSI). The Indra set up **is described** in Refs. [21,22].
>
> *[AJRC-PHY-QT]*

This brief example illustrates three characteristic that distinguish MD analysis from other approaches, as identified by Biber (2019: 13). First, dimensions represent a quantitative, continuous parameter of variation, and text categories fall along this continuous range according to the extent to which they are similar and different. Second, the sets of features that represent each dimension are determined empirically (based on factor analysis). Finally, 'no single parameter or dimension is adequate in itself to capture the full range of variation among registers' (Biber 2019: 13). For example, the

MD analysis described earlier revealed three additional dimensions of variations, with each dimension revealing a different distribution of disciplines/text types along the dimension.

Originally developed to investigate the differences between spoken and written registers, Biber's (1988) dimensions have become ubiquitous in the description of a wide range of registers in English and have revealed five parameters of variation:

1. Dimension 1: Involved vs. informational production;
2. Dimension 2: Narrative discourse;
3. Dimension 3: Situation-dependent vs. elaborated reference;
4. Dimension 4: Overt expression of persuasion;
5. Dimension 5: Impersonal style.

These original 1988 dimensions have been used to explore variation in a wide range of registers, including, TV dialogue (Al-Surmi 2012; Berber Sardinha and Veirano Pinto 2017, 2019); student, academic and practitioner writing in engineering (Conrad 2018); and historical change in speech-based and written registers (Biber and Finegan 2001).

New MD models have identified dimensions of variation in specialised workplace domains (Friginal 2008 on call center discourse; Staples *et al.* 2020 on health care interactions), spoken and written academic language (Biber 2006), disciplinary writing (Thomspon *et al.* 2017), university student writing (Hardy and Friginal 2016; Gardner *et al.* 2019), L2 English assessment data (LaFlair and Staples 2017) and pop songs (Bertoli-Dutra 2014). The MD analysis approach has also been applied to languages other than English, including Brazilian Portuguese (Berber Sardinha *et al.* 2014), Spanish (Biber *et al.* 2006) and Korean (Kim and Biber 1994), among others.

4 Corpus-based genre studies

As introduced in Section 1, a genre approach to analysing text varieties focuses on conventionalised structures used to construct texts, or what Biber and Conrad (2019) call 'genre features'. Biber and Conrad (2019) identify two types of genre features: (a) features that occur one time in a conventionalised location within a text (such as the opening and closing of a business letter) and (b) the rhetorical organisation or structuring of the text. Corpus-based analyses of the first type of genre feature are relatively rare, but corpus-based studies of the rhetorical structuring of texts have been more common. Perhaps the most productive line of corpus-based genre studies has employed Swalesian rhetorical move analysis, where *moves* are 'discoursal or rhetorical units performing coherent communicative functions in texts' (Swales 2004: 228–9), such as 'introduce the cause and/or establish credentials' in fundraising letters (Upton 2002).

While early move analyses were typically carried out on individual texts or a highly restricted sample (as the analysis required manual coding of moves), studies that analyse the move structure across texts in a corpus are now common, with increasingly large corpora (e.g. Cotos *et al.*'s 2016 analysis of 900 research articles). Corpus-based move analyses typically (a) use or adapt an existing move framework or develop a move/step structure for the genre under investigation; (b) code the corpora for moves and steps; (c) quantify the analyses to identify the frequency of particular moves/steps, characterising discoursal units that are obligatory and optional; and (d) examine the typical patterning of moves (i.e. the ordering of the moves in the genre of interest).

Written academic genres and disciplinary research writing have by far received the most attention. These studies often focus on specific sections of the research article (e.g. Tseng 2018 on theoretical framework sections) and on particular disciplines (e.g. Ye 2019 on energy engineering). However, additional research on other written academic registers is becoming more prevalent, such as Cotos (2019) on grant proposals and Samar *et al.* (2014) on conference abstracts.

Corpus-based move analyses have also expanded to spoken academic genres: e.g. Lee (2016) on EAP classroom lessons and Hu and Liu (2018) on three-minute thesis presentations. Move/step schema are also being developed and applied to a range of non-academic registers, such as Zhang and Vásquez (2014) on online reviews and Groom and Grieve (2019) on British patents.

5 Emerging perspectives on register and genre

In this section, I conclude the chapter by exploring two areas of research which are picking up momentum within the field.

Juxtapositions of the register and genre approaches

One area of research that has become more common in recent years is the integration of the register and genre perspectives to language variation – that is, research which pairs analyses of rhetorical structuring and/or rhetorical conventions of texts with the pervasive linguistic characteristics of text varieties. For example, Cortes (2013) associates lexical bundles in research article introductions with three rhetorical moves, identifying bundles that seem to "trigger" particular moves. Omidian *et al.* (2018) also pair bundles with move analysis, while Yoon and Casal (2020) examine p-frames in conference abstracts.

Recent research has investigated broader sets of linguistic features, such as syntactic and lexical complexity measures (Tankó 2017) and more than 40 grammatical features (Kanoksilapatham 2007). However, these studies have been restricted in terms of the text categories and/or disciplines investigated. Most recently, Gray *et al.* (2020) have broadened the scope of this combination of genre and register approaches. Using a corpus of 900 research articles across 30 disciplines, they carry out multi-dimensional analysis on 14 moves across all sections of *Introduction-Method-Results-Discussion* (IMRD) research articles. They identify four dimensions of variation, enabling comprehensive description of the typical linguistic realisations of rhetorical moves regardless of discipline.

Expanded analyses of web registers/genres

The past decade has seen an explosion in the amount of communicative events that we experience through electronic and web-based modalities, and corpus-based register and genre research has likewise expanded to provide a fuller understanding of linguistic patterning of these electronic registers. Blogs have received considerable attention; for example, Smith (2019) investigates personal blogs for their adherence to style guide prescriptivisms compared to news writing. Herring and Paolillo (2006) examine gender and genre variation in blogs, while Zou and Hyland (2019) analyse how writers create engagement in academic blogs. Research has also focused on a number of other individual web registers, such as online question and answer forums (Baker and Egbert 2018) and online consumer reviews (Vásquez 2012).

Studies on web registers have also often relied on multi-dimensional analysis approaches, such as Liimata's (2019) MD of posts on Reddit, Ehret and Taboada's (2020) MD of online news comments (compared to conversation) and Clarke and Grieve (2017) on abusive language on Twitter. Efforts have also been undertaken to provide a fuller accounting of the range of online registers. Berber Sardinha (2018) uses MD analysis to compare blogs, webpages, Facebook posts, Twitter posts and emails. But perhaps one of the most revolutionary developments in corpus-based analyses of web registers are attempts to inductively identify the full range of public internet registers. Biber *et al.* (2015) create large random samples of texts from the searchable Web and develop a taxonomy of text categories to capture the traditional and new registers that can be found online. Biber and Egbert (2018) then provide a comprehensive linguistic analysis of four major register categories (narrative web registers, opinion/advice/persuasion registers, informational descriptions/explanations/procedures and oral registers). One of the major findings that has emerged out this research is the degree of hybridisation that occurs in online registers, where individual texts reflect characteristics of multiple registers.

Further reading

Biber, D. and Conrad, S. (2019) *Register, Genre, and Style*, 2nd edn, Cambridge: Cambridge University Press. (Part 1 of this book explores three perspectives on text varieties and introduces a practical framework for corpus-based register studies. Part II synthesises research on spoken, written, academic/professional and electronic registers. Part III introduces multi-dimensional analysis and contextualises register studies within the field of linguistics.)

Biber, D. and Reppen, R. (eds) (2015) *The Cambridge Handbook of English Corpus Linguistics*, Cambridge: Cambridge University Press. (Part III, titled "Corpus Analysis of Varieties", synthesises research on particular registers. Chapters include spoken discourse, academic writing, register variation, diachronic register description, literary registers, World Englishes, English as a lingua franca and learner language.)

Berber Sardinha, T. and Veirano Pinto, M. (eds) (2019) *Multi-Dimensional Analysis: Research Methods and Current Issumes*, London: Bloomsbury. (This book provides an up-to-date overview of the theory, methods and application of multi-dimensional analysis. It covers all stages of the research process, from the history and theory of the approach to corpus design and annotation (Part 1) and the statistical analyses and functional interpretation (Part 2). Part 3 contains three illustrations of the MD method.)

Römer, U., Cortes, V. and Friginal, E. (eds) (2020) *Advances in Corpus-Based Research on Academic Writing: Effects of Discipline, Register, and Writer Expertise*, Amsterdam: John Benjamins. (This edited volume assembles 14 corpus-based studies of a range of written academic registers (EFL student writing, first-year composition, research articles across disciplines, stand-alone-literature reviews, conference abstracts). Studies also demonstrate a range of linguistic focci: academic vocabulary, lexical bundles and p-frames, verb constructions, adjectives as nominal pre-modifiers and multi-dimensional analyses.)

Staples, S. (2015) *The Discourse of Nurse-Patient Interactions*, Amsterdam: John Benjamins. (This book presents a comprehensive analysis of a professional spoken register and interactions between US (L1 English) and international (L2 English) nurses and patients in a US context. The analyses encompass situational analyses of the register, accompanied by lexico-grammatical descriptions and the analysis of spoken features (fluency, prosody and non-verbal communication).

References

Al-Surmi, M. (2012) 'Authenticity and TV Shows: A Multidimensional Analysis Perspective', *TESOL Quarterly* 46(3): 472–95.

Baker, P. and Egbert, J. (eds) (2018) *Triangulating Methodological Approaches in Corpus Linguistic Research*, London: Routledge.

Barbieri, F. (2005) 'Quotative Use in American English: A Corpus-Based, Cross-Register Comparison', *Journal of English Linguistics* 33(3): 222–56.

Berber Sardinha, T. (2018) 'Dimensions of Variation across Internet Registers', *International Journal of Corpus Linguistics* 23(2): 125–57.

Berber Sardinha, T., Kauffmann, C. and Acunzo, C. M. (2014) 'A Multi-Dimensional Analysis of Register Variation in Brazilian Portuguese', *Corpora* 9(2): 239–71.

Berber Sardinha, T. and Veirano Pinto, M. (2017) 'American Television and Off-Screen Registers: A Corpus-Based Comparison', *Corpora* 12(1): 85–114.

Berber Sardinha, T. and Veirano Pinto, M. (2019) 'Dimensions of Variation across American Television Registers', *International Journal of Corpus Linguistics* 24(1): 3–32.

Bertoli-Dutra, P. (2014) 'Multi-Dimensional Analysis of Pop Songs', in. T. Berber Sardinha and M. Veirano Pinto (eds) *Multi-Dimensional Analysis, 25 Years On: A Tribute to Douglas Biber*, Amsterdam: John Benjamins, pp. 149–76.

Biber, D. (1988) *Variation across Speech and Writing, Cambridge: Cambridge University Press.*

Biber, D. (1999) 'A Register Perspective on Grammar and Discourse: Variability in the Form and Use of English Complement Clauses', *Discourse Studies* 1(2): 131–50.

Biber, D. (2006) *University Language: A Corpus-Based Study of Spoken and Written Language*, Amsterdam: John Benjamins.

Biber, D. (2010) 'What Can a Corpus Tell us about Registers and Genres?', in A. O'Keeffe and M. J. McCarthy (eds)*The Routledge Handbook of Corpus Linguistics*, 1st edn, London: Routledge, pp. 241–54.

Biber, D. (2019) 'Multi-Dimensional Analysis: A Historical Synopsis', in T. Berber-Sardinha and M. Veirano Pinto (eds) *Multidimensional Analysis: Research Methods and Current Issues*, London: Bloomsbury, pp. 11–26.

Biber, D. and Conrad, S. (2019) *Genre, Register, and Style*, 2nd edn, Cambridge: Cambridge University Press.

Biber, D., Conrad, S. and Cortes, V. (2004) '"*If You Look At…*": Lexical Bundles in University Teaching and Textbooks', *Applied Linguistics* 23: 371–405.

Biber, D., Davies, M., Jones, J. and Tracy-Ventura, N. (2006) 'Spoken and Written Register Variation in Spanish: A Multi-Dimensional Analysis', *Corpora* 1(1): 1–37.

Biber, D. and Egbert, J. (2018) *Register Variation Online*, Cambridge: Cambridge University Press.

Biber, D., Egbert, J. and Davies, M. (2015) 'Exploring the Composition of the Searchable Web: A Corpus-Based Taxonomy of Web Registers', *Corpora* 10(1): 11–45.

Biber, D. and Finegan, E. (2001) 'Diachronic Relations among Speech-Based and Written Registers in English', in S. Conrad and D. Biber (eds) *Variation in English: Multi-Dimensional Studies*, London: Routledge, pp. 66–83.

Biber, D. and Gray, B. (2016) *Grammatical Complexity in Academic English: Linguistic Change in Writing*, Cambridge: Cambridge University Press.

Biber, D. and Zhang, M. (2018) 'Expressing Evaluation without Grammatical Stance: Informational Persuasion on the Web', *Corpora* 13(1): 97–112.

Biber, D., Johansson, S., Leech, G, Conrad, S. and Finegan, E. (1999) *The Longman Grammar of Spoken and Written English*, London: Longman.

Biber, D., Johansson, S., Leech, G., Conrad, S. and Finegan, E. (2021) *The Grammar of Spoken and Written English*, Amsterdam: John Benjamins.

Breeze, R. (2013) 'Lexical Bundles across Four Legal Genres', *International Journal of Corpus Linguistics* 18(2): 229–53.

Candarli, D. and Jones, S. (2019) 'Paradignmatic Influences on Lexical Bundles in Research Articles in the Discipline of Education', *Corpora* 14(2): 237–63.

Carter, R. A. and McCarthy, M. J. (2006) *Cambridge Grammar of English*, Cambridge: Cambridge University Press.

Charles, M. (2007) 'Argument or Evidence? Disciplinary Variation in the Use of the Noun *that* Pattern in Stance Construction', *English for Specific Purposes* 26: 203–18.

Clarke, I. and Grieve, J. (2017) 'Dimensions of Abusive Language on Twitter', *Proceedings of the* First Workshop on Abusive Language Online, 1–10.

Conrad, S. (2018) 'The Use of Passives and Impersonal Style in Civil Engineering Writing', *Journal of Business and Technical Communication* 32(1): 38–76.

Cortes, V. (2004) 'Lexical Bundles in Published and Student Disciplinary Writing: Examples from history and biology', *English for Specific Purposes* 23: 397–423.

Cortes, V. (2013) 'The Purpose of This Study Is to: Connecting Lexical Bundles and Moves in Research Article Introductions', *Journal of English for Academic Purposes* 12: 33–43.

Cotos, E. (2019) 'Move Analysis of Broader Impact Statements in Grant Applications', *English for Specific Purposes* 54: 15–34.

Cotos, E., Link, S. and Huffman, S. (2016) 'Studying Disciplinary Corpora to Teach the Craft of Discussion', *Writing and Pedagogy* 8(1): 33–64.

Crompton, P. (2017) 'Complex Anaphora with *This:* Variation between Three Written Argumentative Genres', *Corpora* 12(1): 115–48.

Davies, M. (2009) 'The 385+ Million Word *Corpus of Contemporary American English (1990-2008+)*', *International Journal of Corpus Linguistics* 14(2): 159–90.

Deroey, K. (2012) '*What They Highlight Is*...: The Discourse Functions of Basic *wh*-Clefts in Lectures', *Journal of English for Academic Purposes* 11: 112–24.

Diani, G. (2008) 'Emphasizers in Spoken and Written Academic Discourse: The Case of Really', *International Journal of Corpus Linguistics* 13(3): 296–321.

Egbert, J., Biber, D. and Gray, B. (forthcoming) *Designing and Evaluating Language Corpora: A Practical Framework for Corpus Representativeness*, Cambridge: Cambridge University Press.

Ehret, K. and Taboada, M. (2020) 'Are Online News Comments Like Face-to-face Conversation? A Multi-Dimensional Analysis of an Emerging Register', *Register Studies* 2(1): 1–36.

Friginal, E. (2008) *The Language of Outsourced Call Centers: A Corpus-Based Study of Cross-Cultural Interaction*, Amsterdam: John Benjamins.

Gardner, S., Nesi, H. and Biber, D. (2019) 'Discipline, Level, Genre: Integrating Situational Perspectives in a New MD Analysis of University Student Writing', *Applied Linguistics* 40(4): 646–74.

Garner, J. (2016) 'A Phrase-Frame Approach to Investigating Phraseology in Learner Writing Across Proficiency Levels', *International Journal of Corpus Linguistics* 2(1): 31–68.

Gray, B. (2015) *Linguistic Variation in Research Articles: When Discipline Tells Only Part of the Story*, Amsterdam: John Benjamins.

Gray, B. and Biber, D. (2015) 'Lexical Frames in Academic Prose and Conversation', in S. Hoffmann, B. Fischer-Starcke and A. Sand (eds) *Current Issues in Phraseology*, Amsterdam: John Benjamins, pp. 109–34.

Gray, B., Cotos, E. and Smith, J. (2020) 'Combining Rhetorical Move Analysis with Multi-Dimensional Analysis: Research Writing across Disciplines', in U. Römer, V. Cortes and E. Friginal (eds) *Advances in Corpus-Based Research on Academic Writing*, Amsterdam: John Benjamins, pp. 138–68.

Groom, N. and Grieve, J. (2019) 'The Evolution of a Legal Genre: Rhetorical Moves in British Patent Specifications, 1711 to 1860', in T. Fanego and P. Rodríguez-Puente (eds) *Corpus-Based Research on Variation in English Legal Discourse*, Amsterdam: John Benjamins, pp. 201–34.

Halliday, M. A. K. (1978) *Language as a Social Semiotic: The Social Interpretation of Language and Meaning*, London: Edward Arnold.

Handford, M. (2010) *The Language of Business Meetings*, Cambridge: Cambridge University Press.

Hardy, J. and Friginal, E. (2016) 'Genre Variation in Student Writing: A Multi-Dimensional Analysis', *Journal of English for Academic Purposes* 22: 119–31.

Hasan, R. (1995) 'The Conception of Context in Text', in P. Fries and M. J. Gregory (eds) *Discourse in Society: Systemic Functional Perspectives. Meaning and Choice in Language: Studies for Michael Halliday*, Norwood, NJ: Ablex, pp. 183–283.

Herring, S. and Paolillo, J. (2006) 'Gender and Genre Variation in Weblogs', *Journal of Sociolinguistics* 10(4): 439–59.

Hu, G. and Liu, Y. (2018) 'Three Minute Thesis Presentations as an Academic Genre: A Cross-Disciplinary Study of Genre Moves', *Journal of English for Academic Purposes* 35: 16–30.
Hyland, K. (2008) 'As Can be Seen: Lexical Bundles and Disciplinary Variation', *English for Specific Purposes* 27: 4–21.
Hyland, K. (1998) 'Boosting, Hedging and the Negotiation of Academic Knowledge', *Text* 18(3): 349–83.
Jiang, F. (2017) 'Stance and Voice in Academic Writing: The "noun + that" Construction and Disciplinary Variation', *International Journal of Corpus Linguistics* 22(1): 85–106.
Kanoksilapatham, B. (2007) 'Rhetorical Moves in Biochemistry Research Articles', in D. Biber, U. Connor and T. Upton (eds) *Discourse on the Move: Using Corpus Analysis to Describe Discourse Structure*, Amsterdam: John Benjamins, pp. 73–120.
Kennedy, G. (2002) 'Variation in the Distribution of Modal Verbs in the British National Corpus', in R. Reppen, S. Fitzmaurice and D. Biber (eds) *Using Corpora to Explore Linguistic Variation*, Amsterdam: John Benjamins, pp. 73–90.
Kim, Y. J. and Biber, D. (1994) 'A Corpus-Based Analysis of Register Variation in Korean', in D. Biber and E. Finegan (eds) *Sociolinguistic Perspectives on Register*, Oxford: Oxford University Press, pp. 157–81.
LaFlair, G. and Staples, S. (2017) 'Using Corpus Linguistics to Examine the Extrapolation Inference in the Validity Argument for a High-Stakes Speaking Assessment', *Language Testing* 34(4): 451–75.
Larsson, T. (2019) 'Grammatical Stance Marking across Registers: Revisiting the Formal-Informal Dichotomy', *Register Studies* 1(2): 243–68.
Lee, J. (2016) '"There's Intentionality Behind It…": A Genre Analysis of EAP Classroom Lessons', *Journal of English for Academic Purposes* 23: 99–112.
Liimatta, A. (2019) 'Exploring Register Variation on Reddit: A Multi-Dimensional Study of Language Use on a Social Media Website', *Register Studies* 1(2): 269–95.
Lindley, J. (2020) 'Discourse Functions of *Always* Progressives: Beyond Complaining', *Corpus Linguistics and Linguistic Theory* 16(2): 333–61.
Liu, C.-Y. and Chen, H.-J. (2019) 'Functional Variation of Lexical Bundles in Academic Lectures and TED Talks', *Register Studies* 2(2): 176–208.
Mahlberg, M., Wiegand, V., Stockwell, P. and Hennessey, A. (2019) 'Speech-Bundles in the 19th-Century English Novel', *Language and Literature* 28(4): 326–53.
Miller, D. (2011) 'ESL Reading Textbooks vs. University Textbooks: Are we Giving our Students the Input they May Need?', *Journal of English for Academic Purposes* 10: 32–46.
Nekrasova-Beker, T. (2019) 'Discipline-Specific Use of Language Patterns in Engineering: A Comparison of Published Pedagogical Materials', *Journal of English for Academic Purposes* 41: 1–12.
Nesi, H. and Basturkmen, H. (2006) 'Lexical Bundles and Discourse Signaling in Academic Lecturers', *International Journal of Corpus Linguistics*, 11(3): 283–304.
Nesselhauf, N. and Römer, U. (2007) 'Lexical-Grammatical Patterns in Spoken English: The Case of the Progressive with Future Time Reference', *International Journal of Corpus Linguistics* 12(3): 297–333.
Noguera-Diaz, Y. and Perez-Paredes, P. (2019) 'Register Analysis and ESP Pedagogy: Noun-Phrase Modification in a Corpus of English for Military Navy Submariners', *English for Specific Purposes* 53: 118–30.
Omidian, T., Shahriari, H. and Siyanova-Chanturia, A. (2018) 'A Cross-Disciplinary Investigation of Multi-Word Expressions in the Moves of Research Article Abstracts', *Journal of English for Academic Purposes* 36: 1–14.
Padula, M., Panza, C. and Munoz, V. (2020) 'The Pronoun *This* as a Cohesive Encapsulator in Engineering Semi-Popularization Articles Written in English', *Journal of English for Academic Purposes* 44: 100828.
Quaglio, P. (2009) *Television Dialogue: The Sitcom of Friends vs. Natural Conversation*, Amsterdam: John Benjamins.
Römer, U. (2010) 'Establishing the Phraseological Profile of a Text Type: The Construction of Meaning in Academic Book Reviews', *English Text Construction* 3(1): 95–119.

Samar, R. G., Talebzadeh, H., Kiany, G. R. and Akbari, R. (2014) 'Moves and Steps to Sell a Paper: A Cross-Cultural Genre Analysis of Applied Linguistics Conference Abstracts', *Text and Talk* 34(6): 759–85.

Smith, J. (2019) 'A Comparison of Prescriptive Usage Problems in Formal and Informal Written English', unpublished PhD thesis, Ames, IA: Iowa State University.

Staples, S., Egbert, J., Biber, D. and Gray, B. (2016) 'Academic Writing Development at the University Level: Phrasal and Clausal Complexity across Level of Study, Discipline, and Genre', *Written Communication* 33(2): 149–83.

Staples, S. and Reppen, R. (2016) 'Understanding First-year L2 Writing: A Lexico-Grammatical Analysis across L1s, Genres, and Language Ratings', *Journal of Second Language Writing* 32: 17–35.

Staples, S., Venetis, M. K. and Robinson, R. (2020) 'Understanding the Multi-Dimensional Nature of Informational Language in Health Care Interactions', *Register Studies* 2(2): 241–74.

Swales, J. (2004) *Research Genres*, Cambridge: Cambridge University Press.

Tankó, G. (2017) 'Literary Research Article Abstracts: An Analysis of Rhetorical Moves and their Linguistic Realizations', *Journal of English for Academic Purposes* 27: 42–55.

Thomspon, P., Hunston, S., Murakami, A. and Vajn, D. (2017) 'Multi-Dimensional Analysis, Text Constellations, and Interdisciplinary Discourse', *International Journal of Corpus Linguistics* 22(2): 153–86.

Tseng, M.-Y. (2018) 'Creating a Theoretical Framework: On the Move Structure of Theoretical Framework Sections in Research Articles Related to Language and Linguistics', *Journal of English for Academic Purposes* 33: 82–99.

Upton, T. (2002) 'Understanding Direct Mail Letters as a Genre', *International Journal of Corpus Linguistics* 7(1): 65–85.

Vásquez, C. (2012) 'Narrative and Involvement in Online Consumer Reviews: The Case of *TripAdvisor*', *Narrative Inquiry* 22(1): 105–21.

Wingrove, P. (2017) 'How Suitable Are TED Talks for Academic Listening?', *Journal of English for Academic Purposes* 30: 79–95.

Ye, Y. (2019) 'Macrostructures and Rhetorical Moves in Energy Engineering Research Articles Written by Chinese Expert Writers', *Journal of English for Academic Purposes* 38: 48–61.

Yoon, J. and Casal, J. E. (2020) 'P-Frames and Rhetorical Moves in Applied Linguistics Conference Abstracts', in U. Römer, V. Cortes and E. Friginal (eds) *Advances in Corpus-Based Research on Academic Writing: Effects of Discipline, Register, and Writer Expertise*, Amsterdam: John Benjamins, pp. 282–305.

Zhang, G. (2015) '*It is Suggested That*.... or *It is Better to*...? Forms and Meanings of Subject *it*-Extraposition in Academic and Popular Writing', *Journal of English for Academic Purposes* 20: 1–13.

Zhang, Y. and Vásquez, C. (2014) 'Hotels' Responses to Online Reviews: Managing Consumer Dissatisfaction', *Discourse, Context and Media* 6: 54–64.

Zou, H. and Hyland, K. (2019) 'Reworking Research: Interactions in Academic Articles and Blogs', *Discourse Studies* 21(6): 713–33.

18

What can a corpus tell us about discourse?

Gerlinde Mautner

1 Corpora and discourse: mapping the terrain

Corpus linguistics (CL) and discourse studies (DS) evolved roughly at the same time, in the 1980s and 1990s, in what was originally a parallel development. There were few, if any, connections between them. Most corpus linguists were involved in lexicography and grammar, aiming to discover and quantify patterns in ever-larger corpora. Most discourse analysts, by contrast, focused on small samples of text which were suitable for close reading, "thick" description, and qualitative analysis sensitive to social context. 'For some considerable time,' Partington (2004a: 11) points out, 'the dichotomy was virtually complete: corpus linguists were generally unaware that their quantitative techniques could have much to say about discourse, while discourse analysts rarely saw reason to venture forth very far from their qualitative ivory tower'. In those early days, then, the question posed in the chapter title would rarely have been asked, let alone answered.

Now, in the third decade of the twenty-first century, the situation looks very different. The boundaries between the two approaches to language have become more porous, and their 'synergic use' (Partington and Marchi 2015: 219) is now quite common. In fact, a new, combined field has emerged, generally referred to as *corpus-assisted discourse studies*, or *CADS*. The field has consolidated (Mautner 2019), and there is a growing community of linguists who specifically identify as practising this strand of research.

The development sketched earlier needs to be put into perspective, however. The narrative of CL and DS initially leading separate lives never entirely reflected reality, at least not as starkly as Partington's (2004a) original quote may lead us to believe. To a present-day researcher using corpora for DS, it is both interesting and humbling to see how many decades before CADS, as such, was conceived, linguists were very much aware of the social component of corpus-based work. One of the earliest and probably best-known statements to this effect was Firth's plea, as early as the mid-1930s, for 'research into the detailed contextual distribution of sociologically important words, what one might call *focal* or *pivotal* words' (Firth 1935 [1957]: 10; original italics). In this

DOI: 10.4324/9780367076399-18

quotation alone, the cornerstones of what was to become CADS are all there: *distribution* and *words* point to CL's strength in identifying lexical patterns, while *sociologically important* hints at the readiness of DS to be driven by relevance in the "real" world. And, of course, Firth's *focal or pivotal words* foreshadow keyword analysis, now a staple of CADS work.

Yet it was not until the 1990s that these ideas resurfaced and were developed further. Arguably the first paper to demonstrate how corpora could be studied from a social perspective was Leech and Fallon (1992). Tellingly, the title of their paper – echoed by the title of the present chapter – was "Computer corpora – What do they tell us about culture?" The idea of applying CL in this way gradually gained momentum. Stubbs and Gerbig (1993) investigated the use of verbs in geography textbooks; Caldas-Coulthard (1993) explored gender representation; and Hardt-Mautner (1995) used a study of European discourse in the British press to make a case for combining CL and discourse analysis, specifically its critical variety. It became apparent even then that the combination was not simply useful and interesting but had profound implications for all stages of the research process, and indeed for the nature of linguistic inquiry itself. Reflections in this vein are included, among others, in Stubbs (1996), Hunston (2002: 109–23), O'Halloran and Coffin (2004) and Mautner (2009, 2016).

Discourse: an elusive foundational concept

It speaks volumes that a term as central and widely used as *discourse* should still require clarification at all. As Thornbury (2010: 270) observed in the first edition of this handbook, '[t]he term *discourse* is both slippery and baggy: slippery because it eludes neat definition, and baggy because it embraces a wide range of linguistic and social phenomena'. There is general agreement that language plays a key role in it, but not everyone wishes to stop there. For Blommaert, for example (2005: 3), discourse 'comprises all forms of meaningful semiotic human activity seen in connection with social, cultural, and historical patterns and development of use'.

The picture becomes even more complex if we look across to the social sciences in general and individual disciplines, such as organisation studies. The so-called "linguistic turn" (Rorty 1992) has made *discourse* a term that is both *en vogue* and vague. It has such a wide range of meanings that Alvesson and Kärreman (2000: 1127) conclude: 'we cannot help sometimes feeling that the word discourse is used to cover up muddled thinking or postponed decisions on vital analytical matter'. And they continue: 'Discourse sometimes comes close to standing for everything, and thus nothing'.

In linguistics, however, the situation seems to be more straightforward. There, too, *discourse* can have fuzzy conceptual boundaries, but it is generally taken as read that at its core the term has two interconnected meanings: (i) stretches of language larger than single sentences and (ii) language embedded in social contexts and used to perform social functions. And whatever specific "brand" of discourse analysis a researcher subscribes to, they are unlikely to identify as working on "discourse" unless their research designs include both of these elements, "larger units" and "social context", in some form or other. Identifying specifically as a *critical* discourse analyst generally involves an interest in 'the semiotic dimensions of power, identity politics and political-economic or cultural change in society' (Wodak 2011: 38). With a brief as broad and complex as this, it is actually hard to see how we could do without "discourse". After all, as long as its meaning is not stretched too much, the concept has substantial explanatory power.

Whether explicitly of a critical persuasion or not, researchers investigating discourse typically ask research questions such as: In the texts that I am analysing, who are the main social actors, how are they described and what activities are they shown to be engaged in? How do the speakers/writers of these texts signal their own stance as well as social and professional identities? Can the patterns that emerge from the corpus be mapped on to and explained by the political, organisational and legal constraints under which the texts were produced? The actual questions asked will differ from project to project, but what unites all such undertakings is that the research journey begins and ends with text in context. Ideally, from the initial framing of the research design to the final interpretation of the data, the driving force is curiosity about how language and social reality are related. And at all stages of the journey, corpus analytic procedures can make a significant contribution.

Another attraction of CL is that it can be paired with any "brand" of discourse analysis, thus supporting a wide range of perspectives and methodologies. Some approaches may be a better fit than others, but it is hard to envisage a discourse analytical research design that cannot benefit at all from CL input. CL is flexible and adaptable. The only theoretical assumption the discourse analyst has to "buy into" to be comfortable with CL is that micro-linguistic choices and the macro-phenomenon of discourse are in a mutual relationship.

The intensity with which synergies are exploited may vary, of course. A study may be conceived as corpus assisted from the very outset, or it may merely dip into CL methods in order to confirm or refute a diagnosis reached by other means. Whatever the approach, there is a strong rationale for integrating corpus linguistics and discourse analysis, and this will be addressed in the next section.

2 The rationale for using corpus linguistic methods in discourse analysis

The two main methodological questions that first led to the emergence of corpus-assisted discourse studies are still the point of departure for most projects in this area today. How can we analyse discourse without relying too much on the researcher's intuition? And given that the traditional toolkit of discourse analysis is qualitative, how can we get a handle on our data when the corpus is too large to permit qualitative analysis? The answer to the first question is by working with a large and representative corpus of texts, by employing discovery procedures that are transparent and replicable and by relating one's findings to other corpora and thus putting them into perspective. The answer to the second is by employing CL techniques. It is not the only possible answer – with computer-based content analysis being a strong contender – but CL is the one that concerns us here. It has been widely shown to produce robust and insightful research exploring a range of questions at the discourse and society interface.

From the outset, the guiding principle of this partnership was to combine 'the quantitative rigour of corpus linguistics with the social perspective of qualitative approaches to discourse analysis' (Marchi and Taylor 2018: 4). The idea is not to replace qualitative approaches, but to put them on a sounder empirical footing. This, of course, addresses criticism of DS generally, and of critical discourse analysis in particular, that it is impressionistic and subjective and "cherry-picks" texts that are convenient rather than typical (cf. Widdowson 1995, 2004).

At the same time, there are heuristic benefits (i.e. related to how we arrive at new knowledge). 'A main aim of CADS', Subtirelu and Baker explain (2018: 108), 'is to discover non-obvious meaning and identify questions and puzzles that would otherwise have not been considered' (Subtirelu and Baker 2018: 108). A corpus-based perspective on discourse thus not only enriches existing qualitative methods but also encourages us to put different questions to our data.

3 Using corpus linguistic tools to explore themes, genres and perspectives

There is a large and growing body of research that studies discourse with the help of corpus linguistic tools. The social domains and issues covered include politics (e.g. Partington 2011; Jeffries and Walker 2012; and Chapter 42, this volume), the law (e.g. Fanego and Rodríguez-Puente 2019; Chapter 41, this volume), business (e.g. Lischinsky 2011; Mullany 2013; Mautner and Learmonth 2020), gender and sexuality (Baker 2013; Zottola 2018), health communication (Hunt and Harvey 2015; Chapter 43, this volume) and online communication and social media (e.g. Lutzky and Kehoe 2016; Collins 2019; Chapter 46, this volume). All of these domains and issues could be (and are) also studied without recourse to CL. Yet CL tools provide added value in the sense described in the previous section: making larger datasets manageable, strengthening empirical claims and preventing the biased selection of texts for analysis.

So, what exactly are these tools and what can they contribute to the study of discourse? The most commonly used ones are frequency lists of both individual lexical items and n-grams (i.e. recurring word clusters of two words or more); keywords (i.e. words which occur statistically more or less frequently in one corpus than another); collocations (i.e. the words that commonly co-occur with a particular item); and concordances, which show search words in their surrounding co-text (see Chapters 9, 10 and 14, this volume). Concordances enable the analyst to examine the social domains that lexical items refer to, as well their "semantic prosody", that is, whether their evaluative orientation is positive or negative (Louw 1993; Hunston 2004: 157; Partington 2004b).

In what follows, I will explain how using each of these tools can tell us something about discourse. By way of examples, I will refer to two ongoing projects of mine, a study of UK Supreme Court judgements, on the one hand, and of articles in a management journal, on the other. The *UK Supreme Court* (UKSC) *Corpus* comprises all the judgements between 2009 and 2018 that have at least one dissenting opinion in them (129 in total, amounting to 2.87 million words). The corpus of management writing consists of 3,547 articles and book reviews from the *Administrative Science Quarterly* (ASQ), amounting to 15,885,378 million words. To enable diachronic comparisons across this latter corpus, it is divided into six subcorpora of roughly equal size, with material from the 1950s and 1960s put together in one subcorpus, and the other six decades each forming their own. For this illustrative analysis, both the UKSC and ASQ corpora were uploaded to Sketch Engine, a fee-based, internet-based concordancing programme (www.sketchengine.eu). The two corpora represent very different genres, produced in different institutional settings and enacting different social functions. What unites them, however, is that they both contain highly specialised, argumentative prose written and read mainly by professionals. The two projects were not conceived with a comparison between them in mind, nor is the purpose of this section to describe them in full. Even so, looking at selected features in two different corpora will help illustrate and highlight the potential of CL to enrich discourse analytic research.

Frequency

At first glance, simple wordlists may seem too pedestrian to be of much analytical value to the discourse analyst. However, they can be useful in several ways, especially if we focus on lexical rather than grammatical items (i.e. on nouns, verbs, adjectives, etc. rather than articles and prepositions). Even the raw frequencies of lexical items give us a rough idea of what the salient themes in our corpus are and how they are framed. In some respects the quantitative evidence may only confirm what we already know, but in others the results will be less obvious. It will hardly come as a surprise, for example, that the ten most frequent content words in the UKSC corpus are all legal terms: *court, case, section, para* (short for *paragraph*), *act, Lord, law, right, state,* and *appeal.* What would have been harder to predict, however, is that half of these legal terms describe other texts (*case, section, para, act, article*). In the ASQ corpus, three meta-discursive nouns make it to the top ten most frequent content words, namely *study*, *research* and *model* (the status of *work*, also in the top ten, is ambiguous, as it may refer both to research and to paid employment). Thus, even before we have done any in-depth analysis at all, even a small portion of the frequency list tells us something about legal and academic discourse that could be worth following up, namely that the former is heavily intertextual and the latter frequently uses meta-discursive elements. Frequency alone cannot tell us how these elements are used, whether they are self-referential (talking about the texts themselves) or intertextual (talking about other texts). But at the very least, we have made a first step towards profiling our corpus.

N-grams can also be a good starting point (see Chapter 15, this volume). Sketch Engine offers users the choice to view 2- to 6-grams, all of which are potentially interesting in their own right. Generally speaking, the shorter the n-gram, the less distinctive of a particular corpus it is likely to be. For example, a typical 2-gram frequently found across any corpus is *of the*. The longer the n-gram, on the other hand, the more likely it is to be corpus-specific. Two of the high-frequency 6-grams from the ASQ and UKSC corpora are, respectively, *from the point of view of,* a stock phrase from academic discourse, and *the European Convention on Human Rights,* a key document around which many Supreme Court cases revolve. Depending on the specific research question, then, both very generic and very distinctive n-grams may be useful. For illustrative purposes, it seemed best to go for the middle ground. Hence I computed 4-grams for both the UKSC and ASQ corpora. As always, some of the results are underwhelming – predictable and effectively dead-ends because one cannot really take them any further. For example, in the USKC corpus, the most frequent 4-grams are all names of institutions which are bound to occur in legal proceedings taken to the level of the highest court, such as *the Court of Appeal* and *the Secretary of State.* Yet on both lists, many n-grams appear to be much more general. Phrases such as *in the course of* or *are more likely to* sound like prefabricated chunks that could occur anywhere. Except that many of them do not, in fact, occur anywhere, but are characteristic of one corpus but not another. To take our example, with the 4-grams in the ASQ and UKSC corpora, it seemed reasonable to expect a fair amount of overlap because both corpora represent formal, argumentative prose. Yet among the 40 most frequent 4-grams (to take a random cut-off point), only 8 occur in both corpora. Thus, the use of n-grams can be shown to reflect genre conventions – which, in turn, are shaped by speech communities and their discursive practices.

One of these genre conventions is that the court judgements – also referred to, tellingly, as *opinions* – are framed discursively as the judges' personal views and as links in an argumentative chain that includes lower-instance courts as well as other Supreme Court judges. That much we could also have ascertained by qualitative means through a close reading of individual judgements. We would probably also have noticed the following features: hedging devices and politeness markers (e.g. *I regret that I am unable to agree with his conclusion; I respectfully disagree; I respectfully agree but would add that …*); passages where judges engage directly with other judges' views (e.g. *I do not share his confidence about this*); meta-linguistic markers guiding the reader through the argument (e.g. *before considering these issues I should mention some other matters by way of background*); and rhetorical questions that give the texts an almost dialogic feel (e.g. *Can it be said that his decision would be immune from challenge? Surely not.*).

The added value of CL techniques is that they can help us substantiate such impressions and turn them into generalisable statements – and do both of these things very efficiently. Frequencies never give us the whole story, but they often provide interesting clues. To follow up on our impression that Supreme Court judgements sound personal, let us return to our n-grams. Among the 4-grams which occur in the top 40 of the UKSC corpus (but not the ASQ), two stand out in particular: *it seems to me* and *I agree with Lord.* Given the highly formal nature of judgements, the first person pronouns come as a surprise (at least to the analyst with a Continental-European background, where judgements give the opinion of the court and not of individual judges). The normalised, or relative, frequency of *it seems to me* is 131.5 occurrences per million words. As the next step, we may want to cast our net wider and search for *it seems to me* and *I agree with* in the *British National Corpus* (BNC), a large corpus suitable as a so-called "reference corpus", which reflects general usage (see Chapters 4, 10 and 39, this volume). In the BNC, it turns out, the two phrases are both considerably more frequent in the spoken subcorpus of the BNC than in the written one. (*It seems to me* occurs 28 times per million words in the BNC's spoken component, but only 5 times per million words in the written one; for *I agree with* the figures are 17 per million and 4 per million, respectively.) If we concluded from this evidence alone that the judgements use "spoken language", that would obviously be misguided and a case of rather simplistic "overinterpretation" (O'Halloran and Coffin 2004). Yet these frequencies do add a piece to the jigsaw puzzle, so that we can gradually build up the bigger picture and explain in more precise terms how the style, or "tone", that is typical of a genre actually comes about.

Thus, information about frequency is not only an interesting entry point into the data but can also yield substantive results that are relevant in their own right. To give another example, in Mautner and Learmonth (2020) we focus on lexical items that represent social actors in the ASQ. Comparing the normalised frequencies of selected social actor labels decade by decade, we found that across the time span covered, between 1956 and 2018, some social actor labels became more frequent (e.g. *CEO, entrepreneur* and *team member*), while others became less frequent or disappeared altogether (e.g. *administrator, bureaucrat, foreman, subordinate* and *supervisor*). These frequencies match what we know about more general socio-political and institutional trends in the last few decades (Learmonth and Morrell 2019). Broadly speaking, in management writing, bureaucratic elites and hierarchical relationships appear to have fallen out of favour, whereas labels that reflect managerialism, equality and neo-liberal rhetoric are now more popular. It ought to be stressed, however, that this narrative cannot be "read off" the corpus directly, but results from linking quantitative evidence with qualitative background knowledge. For the necessary interpretative act, the quality criterion is not "truth", but plausibility.

Keywords

Although normalised frequencies are a very useful measure, the comparison between a corpus and a reference corpus is best served by the computation of keywords (see Chapters 9 and 10, this volume). The software will flag up lexical items as "key" if the difference in frequency is statistically significant. Keywords are a robust measure that tells us what is distinctive, in lexical terms, about one corpus as opposed to another. Word choice is central to discursive construction, which, in turn, is central to social life. Thus, keyword analysis also allows us a glimpse of the similarities and differences between the socio-cultural contexts in which the texts in the corpus were produced.

Using a diachronic corpus, divided into subcorpora according to time periods, we can apply keyword analysis to explore how lexical choices have changed over time. To take an example from the *ASQ* study (Mautner and Learmonth 2020), we may want to compare the latest subcorpus, comprising articles published between 2010 and 2018, with the oldest subcorpus, dating from the 1950s and 1960s. The latter would serve as the so-called "reference corpus". Some of the words that appear as keywords are entirely predictable because their referents simply did not exist 60 years ago, such as *software* and *online*. Others refer to social roles and phenomena that certainly existed back then but were not conceptualised and written about in the way that they are now. Three items in that category are among the 50 items with the highest "keyness" scores: *CEO, gender* and *lesbian*. We can also "flip" the comparison, using the 2010s subcorpus as the reference corpus. The items that emerge as keywords for the older subcorpus include *foreman, bureaucracy* and *morale*, which ties in with our earlier diagnosis that the older subcorpus includes more terms associated with traditional business administration.

Like all other CL tools (and indeed empirical tests of any kind), keyword and frequency analysis can produce both interesting and boring results. Telling which is which, however, is not always entirely straightforward. "Interesting" is often associated with unexpected findings, and "boring" with predictable, "so what" kind of results (Baker and McEnery 2015: 9). Yet the latter, too, can be of value. On the one hand, they can substantiate what we may have suspected all along but were not able to back up empirically, and on the other they may lead to new observations that are not in fact that obvious.

There is no question that some disappointing results remain just that. But it is not uncommon for data to yield up their secrets much later, after a great deal more thinking and digging. The thinking part is about trying to work out why the corpus does not appear to be "behaving itself". The answer may be linguistic, connected to the lexico-grammatical properties of the items in question. Or it may lie outside the corpus itself, at the interface of discourse and institutional settings. The "digging" part typically involves studying collocations and concordances, which we will address now.

Collocations

The concept of collocation takes us back to Firth (1957: 11), who defined collocations as 'the mere word accompaniment, the other word-material in which [words] are most commonly or most characteristically embedded'. That "word-material" provides us with a wealth of information about discourse. Perhaps most significantly, it allows us to pinpoint how a speaker or writer expresses their stance towards certain people and events, how the roles of social actors are framed discursively and how they construct their own identities.

Studying collocations can also help us make sense of quantitative findings that appear not to add up – either because they are counterintuitive or at odds with information gleaned from other sources. In the ASQ study, we found that the frequencies for *manager* and *leader* had remained more or less constant during the period investigated, even though all our background reading around the subject suggested very strongly that *leader* should have become more common over time. If the difference did not lie in their frequency of occurrence, then it had to lie in *how* they were used. We therefore examined the collocates of the lemmata *manager* and *leader* in each of the subcorpora and within a span of three words to the left and right. (*Lemma* refers to 'a base form of a word together with its inflected forms' [Collins 2019: 197].) We noticed that, overall, *manager* and *leader* share few collocates (Mautner and Learmonth 2020: 284). The ten most frequent collocates for *manager* in the earliest subcorpus are labels indicating areas of responsibility (e.g. *departmental, district* and *sales*), as well as positions in a hierarchy (e.g. *assistant*). From the 1970s onwards, further hierarchical labels come in, including *top*, *middle* and *senior*. The collocates of *leader*, on the other hand, are originally terms associated with the public domain (e.g. *community, political* and *legislative*). From the 1980s onwards, *team* appears as a frequent collocate, and in the most recent corpus, leading up to 2018, *leaders* are typically labelled as *corporate*. Thus, while the frequencies of *manager* and *leader* have not changed significantly over time, their collocational profiles have, reflecting different and changing perspectives of these roles.

Concordances

Up to this point in the research process, the analytical output has been quantitative and focused on individual words or short phrases. We have seen that such information can help us identify dominant discursive constructions in large corpora. However, if we want to see language come to life, we need to go beyond individual words and examine propositions, that is, descriptions and evaluations of situations, people and activities. This is where concordances come in. By showing us search words surrounded by their co-text, they take us much closer to the original texts than do computational procedures. Naturally, in using concordances, we are still at some distance from the originals, but we are as close as we can get if we want to work with a corpus too large for manual analysis. In our *leader* and *manager* example, concordancing these two focal terms in the most recent subcorpus opens a window on contemporary organisational life (as seen through the lens of management scholarship, given the nature of the corpus). We learn from the concordances that: ***leaders*** *are expected to set moral examples for their followers; employed men in traditional marriages tend to (…) perceive organizations with female* ***leaders*** *as relatively unattractive; the prevalence of narcissistic* ***leaders*** *in American corporations may be a direct product of the society's prevalent individualistic culture;* ***managers*** *are typically cut off from the process of generating novel ideas;* ***managers*** *are likely to develop feelings of resentment toward the CEO; and once* ***managers*** *become desperate, they may act aggressively to remedy their problem quickly.*

Often the concordance lines contain words that catch our interest specifically in light of what we know about the socio-political background of our corpus. In our example, these could be *society*, *culture*, *female*, *effectiveness*, *resentment* and *frustrated*, to name just a few. For these expressions we could produce separate concordances, examine their frequency in the same or other subcorpora or search for them in reference corpora such as the *Corpus of Contemporary American English* (*COCA*, https://www.english-corpora.org/coca/).

Quite literally, one thing will lead to another in a process that should be equally focused and playful.

At the stage in the research process where concordances are analysed, CL edges towards the qualitative end of the methodological spectrum, while also maintaining its link with a quantitative view, which one can easily go back to if required. What Thornbury (2010: 282) calls 'cyclical alternation between counting and interpreting' is indeed at the heart of corpus-based discourse research. Whichever metaphor one uses to describe this process – whether it is "oscillating" (Mautner 2007: 66) or "shunting" (Partington and Marchi 2015: 231) – the idea is the same, describing a back-and-forth movement between quantitative and qualitative views of the data and triangulating one with the other. Ultimately, this approach is meant to bridge the divide between these two modes of analysis, or perhaps even dissolve it.

4 Epistemological issues

Epistemology boils down to a question that sounds deceptively simple: How do we know what we know? Earlier in the chapter, we argued that bringing in CL puts DS on a sounder empirical footing because it enables us to work with large datasets and delays the point at which interpretation sets in. Yet like all methods – including purely quantitative ones – the application of CL in discourse research raises a range of epistemological issues. I believe that these do not undermine the approach, but unless they are confronted, they may compromise the quality of the research.

The main challenges are these (Mautner 2016: 174–6). First, although quantitative corpus evidence can be seductive, it is never self-explanatory. As soon as you start explaining the evidence, which research is meant to do, subjectivity is inevitably back on the scene. The software lists frequencies for us and computes the strength of collocational attraction (see Chapters 9, 10, 15 and 13, this volume, on statistical measures of collocational strength), but it tells us nothing about what any of this means in a wider social context and why these linguistic choices were made in the first place.

Second, in interpreting findings, the temptation to jump to conclusions can prove almost irresistible. Yet it is not enough for the researchers themselves to claim connections between linguistic evidence and social meaning; they need to succeed in making others see these connections as well. Hence my appeal earlier in this chapter to keep a watchful eye on plausibility.

Third, even if the results are entirely convincing, we should always be careful not to overgeneralise from them. Every corpus, no matter how large and representative, is selective and an artefact in its own right. In making claims about the discourse concerned, or even language in general, it is always best to err on the side of caution.

Fourth, amid frequency tables and concordances, it is easy to lose sight of the complete texts that went into the corpus and the social context they were lifted from. Egbert and Schnur (2018: 172) are right to warn that 'discourse analysts must be wise in their use of corpus data and methods to ensure that the text retains its rightful status as the fundamental discourse unit'.

Fifth, statements about frequency must be comparative (frequent in relation to what?). Care must also be taken not to describe results in pseudo-quantitative terms (using vague descriptors such as *most*, *many* or *few* without backing them up with actual figures). In the qualitative phase of the analysis, involving concordances or complete texts, the attempt to quantify findings is often misplaced.

Sixth, when assessing the utility of the method, a degree of scepticism and humility is always a useful corrective. Discourse analyses that use CL are certainly different from those that do not, but they are not inherently superior. Nor are they necessarily the best fit for all research questions.

Seventh and finally, CL methods are not a "wonder drug" that will cure every ill that a research design may be suffering from, such as bias built into the corpus, through skewed sampling, for instance.

Overall, we have to be aware that, in spite of its benefits, 'the corpus approach in itself does not remove bias' (Baker 2018: 270). Even its "number-crunching" elements invariably involve decisions on the part of the analyst, such as which items to focus on, which corpora to compare and which cut-off points to use when it comes to deciding what is an important result. These concerns should not dampen our enthusiasm for employing CL tools, but should encourage critical reflexivity and healthy scepticism. Most importantly, we should not allow ourselves to be lured into thinking that employing corpus methods makes research completely "objective". Rather, it ought to be viewed as 'a means of achieving greater precision, richness as well as awareness' (Marchi and Taylor 2018: 6).

5 What a corpus cannot tell us about discourse

Methodological reflection and critique is as much about what a method cannot do as about what it can do. The potential of computer assistance in discourse studies is considerable, but it should not be oversold. For example, some "dusty corners" and "blind spots" remain (Marchi and Taylor 2018: 9). While CL has traditionally focused on differences between corpora and the presence of items, a strong case has been made to concentrate more on similarity (Taylor 2018) and absence (Partington 2014; Duguid and Partington 2018). Likewise, a preoccupation with high frequencies may not be suitable when the discourses to be explored are marginalised – those of or about minorities, for example – and for that reason leave few traces in texts (Motschenbacher 2018: 167).

Another area that is notoriously under-researched is multimodality (see Chapter 7, this volume). In building purely text-based corpora, we strip texts of pictures, sound and the haptic dimension, all of which may be essential for how texts are understood. Similarly, if spoken language is reduced to transcripts of what was said, important clues conveyed by facial expression and gesture will be lost, as will be information on how meaning unfolds in interaction and how it is co-constructed dynamically by the participants. The same applies to the study of metaphor. It has been shown to be amenable to corpus approaches (e.g. Deignan 2005; Deignan and Semino 2010), but there are bound to be areas that these cannot reach, such as the role that metaphors play in establishing cohesion across distant parts of texts.

In fact, quite generally, corpus techniques are not the "go-to" method when we are interested in what happens below the surface of the text (Thornbury 2010: 275). At least for standard CL procedures, we need lexical items that we can search for in the first place. It is only natural that this simple and incontrovertible fact should privilege some perspectives on discourse but hamper or even prevent others. Thus, to return to the question posed in the chapter's title, a corpus can tell us a lot about discourse, but not everything. But then, which method can? To unpack the intricate connections between text and context, we will always need a variety of methods as well as creative, joined-up thinking to integrate them.

Further reading

Baker, P. (2006) *Using Corpora in Discourse Analysis*, London: Continuum. (This book remains a classic and a good starting point for those embarking on their first corpus-assisted discourse analysis. It combines hands-on tips with theoretical reflection and methodological critique.)

Collins, L. C. (2019) *Corpus Linguistics for Online Communication: A Guide for Research*, London: Routledge. (Although the book's focus is on online communication, it is also instructive for those doing corpus-assisted research on discourse in other areas. It also contains a glossary and tasks, with commentaries in an appendix.)

Taylor, C. and Marchi, A. (eds) (2018) *Corpus Approaches to Discourse: A Critical Review*, London: Routledge. (This edited volume is a thought-provoking account that experienced researchers are likely to find particularly useful. In three parts, it examines hitherto overlooked areas, triangulation and questions of research design.)

References

Alvesson, M. and Kärreman, D. (2000) 'Varieties of Discourse: On the Study of Organizations Through Discourse Analysis', *Human Relations* 53(9): 1125–49.

Baker, P. (2006) *Using Corpora in Discourse Analysis*, London: Continuum.

Baker, P. (2013) 'From Gay Language to Normative Discourse: A Diachronic Corpus Analysis of Lavender Linguistics Conference Abstracts 1994-2012', *Journal of Language and Sexuality* 2(2): 179–205.

Baker, P. (2018) 'Language, Sexuality and Corpus Linguistics. Concerns and Future Directions', *Journal of Language and Sexuality* 7(2): 263–79.

Baker, P. and McEnery, T. (2015) 'Introduction', in P. Baker and T. McEnery (eds) *Corpora and Discourse Studies. Integrating Discourse and Corpora*, Basingstoke: Palgrave MacMillan, pp. 1–19.

Blommaert, J. (2005) *Discourse. A Critical Introduction*, Cambridge: Cambridge University Press.

Caldas-Coulthard, C. R. (1993) 'From Discourse Analysis to Critical Discourse Analysis: The Differential Re-Presentation of Women and Men Speaking in Written News', in J. M. Sinclair, M. Hoey and G. Fox (eds) *Techniques of Description: Spoken and Written Discourse*, London: Routledge, pp. 196–208.

Collins, L. C. (2019) *Corpus Linguistics for Online Communication: A Guide for Research*, London: Routledge.

Deignan, A. (2005) *Metaphor and Corpus Linguistics*, Amsterdam and Philadelphia: Benjamins.

Deignan, A. and Semino, E. (2010) 'Corpus Techniques for Metaphor Analysis', in L. Cameron and R. Maslen (eds) *Metaphor Analysis: Research Practice in Applied Linguistics, Social Sciences and the Humanities*, London: Equinox, pp. 161–79.

Duguid, A. and Partington, A. (2018) 'Absence: You Don't Know What You're Missing. Or Do You?' in C. Taylor and A. Marchi (eds) *Corpus Approaches to Discourse. A Critical Review*, London: Routledge, pp. 38–59.

Egbert, J. and Schnur, E. (2018) 'The Text in Corpus and Discourse Analysis. Missing the Trees for the Forest', in C. Taylor and A. Marchi (eds) *Corpus Approaches to Discourse: A Critical Review*, London: Routledge, pp. 159–73.

Fanego, T. and Rodríguez-Puente, P. (eds) (2019) *Corpus-Based Research on Variation in English Legal Discourse*, Amsterdam: Benjamins.

Firth, J. R. (1935 [1957]) 'A Synopsis of Linguistic Theory, 1930-1955', in *Studies in Linguistic Analysis*, Oxford: Blackwell, pp. 1–32.

Firth, J. R. (1957) 'A Synopsis of Linguistic Theory 1930-55', in *Studies in Linguistic Analysis, Philosophical Society*, Oxford, reprinted in Palmer, F. (ed) (1968) Selected Papers of J.R. Firth, London: Longman, pp. 168–205.

Hardt-Mautner, G. (1995) '"Only Connect": Critical Discourse Analysis and Corpus Linguistics', UCREL Technical Paper 6, Lancaster: University of Lancaster. Available at http://ucrel.lancs.ac.uk/papers/techpaper/vol6.pdf.

Hunston, S. (2002) *Corpora in Applied Linguistics*, Cambridge: Cambridge University Press.

Hunston, S. (2004) 'Counting the Uncountable: Problems of Identifying Evaluation in a Text and in a Corpus', in A. Partington, J. Morley and L. Haarman (eds) *Corpora and Discourse*, Bern: Peter Lang, pp. 157–88.

Hunt, D. and Harvey, K. (2015) 'Health Communication and Corpus Linguistics: Using Corpus Tools to Analyse Eating Disorder Discourse Online', in P. Baker and T. McEnery (eds) *Corpora and Discourse Studies. Integrating Discourse and Corpora*, Basingstoke: Palgrave Macmillan, pp. 134–54.

Jeffries, L. and Walker, B. (2012) 'Key Words in the Press: A Critical Corpus-Driven Analysis of Ideology in the Blair Years (1998-2007)', *English Text Construction* 5(2): 208–29.

Learmonth, M. and Morrell, K. (2019) *Critical Perspectives on Leadership: The Language of Corporate Power*, London: Routledge.

Leech, G. and Fallon, R. (1992) 'Computer Corpora - What Do They Tell Us About Culture?', *ICAME Journal* 16: 29–50.

Lischinsky, A. (2011) 'In Times of Crisis: A Corpus Approach to the Construction of the Global Financial Crisis in Annual Reports', *Critical Discourse Studies* 8(3): 153–68.

Louw, B. (1993) 'Irony in the Text or Insincerity in the Writer? The Diagnostic Potential of Semantic Prosodies', in M. Baker, G. Francis and E. Tognini-Bonelli (eds) *Text and Technology. In Honour of John Sinclair*. Amsterdam: Benjamins, pp. 157–76.

Lutzky, U. and Kehoe, A. (2016) 'Your Blog is (the) Shit: A Corpus Linguistic Approach to the Identification of Swearing in Computer Mediated Communication', *International Journal of Corpus Linguistics* 21(2): 165–91.

Marchi, A. and Taylor, C. (2018) 'Introduction: Partiality and Reflexivity', in C. Taylor and A. Marchi (eds) *Corpus Approaches to Discourse. A Critical Review*, London: Routledge, pp. 1–15.

Mautner, G. (2007) 'Mining Large Corpora for Social Information: The Case of *Elderly*', *Language in Society* 36(1): 51–72.

Mautner, G. (2009) 'Corpora and Critical Discourse Analysis', in P. Baker (ed.) *Contemporary Corpus Linguistics*, London: Continuum, pp. 32–46.

Mautner, G. (2016) 'Checks and Balances: How Corpus Linguistics can Contribute to CDA', in R. Wodak and M. Meyer (eds) *Methods of Critical Discourse Analysis*, London: Sage, pp. 154–79.

Mautner, G. (2019) 'A Research Note on Corpora and Discourse: Points to Ponder in Research Design', *Journal of Corpora and Discourse Studies* 2: 1–13.

Mautner, G. and Learmonth, M. (2020) 'From *Administrator* to *CEO*: Exploring Changing Representations of Hierarchy and Prestige in a Diachronic Corpus of Academic Management Writing', *Discourse and Communication* 14(3): 273–93.

Motschenbacher, H. (2018) 'Corpus Linguistics in Language and Sexuality Studies. Taking Stock and Looking Ahead', *Journal of Language and Sexuality* 7(2): 145–74.

Mullany, L. (2013) 'Corpus Analysis of Language in the Workplace', in C. Chapelle (ed.) *The Encyclopedia of Applied Linguistics*, Chichester: Wiley-Blackwell, pp. 1–9.

O'Halloran and Coffin, C. (2004) 'Checking Overinterpreation and Underinterpretation: Help from Corpora in Critical Linguistics' in A. Hewings, C. Coffin and K. O'Halloran (eds) *Applying English Grammar*, London: Arnold, pp. 275–97.

Partington A. (2004a) 'Corpora and Discourse, a Most Congruous Beast', in A. Partington, J. Morley and L. Haarman (eds) *Corpora and Discourse*, Bern: Peter Lang, pp. 9–18.

Partington (2004b) 'Utterly Content in Each Other's Company: Semantic Prosody and Semantic Preference', *International Journal of Corpus Linguistics* 9(1): 131–56.

Partington, A. (2011) '"Double-speak" at the White House: A Corpus-Assisted Study of Bisociation in Conversational Laughter-Talk', *Humor: International Journal of Humor Research* 24(4): 371–98.

Partington, A. (2014) 'Mind the Gaps. The Role of Corpus Linguistics in Researching Absences', *International Journal of Corpus Linguistics* 19(1): 118–46.

Partington, A. and Marchi, A. (2015) 'Using Corpora in Discourse Analysis', in D. Biber and R. Reppen (eds) *The Cambridge Handbook of English Corpus Linguistics*, Cambridge: Cambridge University Press, pp. 216–34.

Rorty, R. (ed.) (1992) *The Linguistic Turn. Essays in Philosophical Method*, Chicago: Chicago University Press.

Stubbs, M. and Gerbig, A. (1993) 'Human and Inhuman Geography: On the Computer-Assisted Analysis of Long Texts', in M. Hoey (ed.) *Data, Description, Discourse. Papers on the English Language in Honour of John McH Sinclair on his Sixtieth Birthday*, London: Harper Collins, pp. 64–85.

Stubbs, M. (1996) *Text and Corpus Analysis: Computer-Assisted Studies of Language and Culture*, Oxford: Blackwell.

Subtirelu, N. C. and Baker, P. (2018) 'Corpus-Based Approaches', in J. Flowerdew and J. E. Richardson (eds) *The Routledge Handbook of Critical Discourse Studies*, London: Routledge, pp. 106–19.

Taylor, C. (2018) 'Similarity', in C. Taylor and A. Marchi (eds) *Corpus Approaches to Discourse: A Critical Review*, London: Routledge, pp. 19–37.

Taylor, C. and Marchi, A. (eds) (2018) *Corpus Approaches to Discourse: A Critical Review*, London: Routledge.

Thornbury, S. (2010) 'What Can a Corpus Tell Us About Discourse?', in A. O'Keeffe and M. J. McCarthy (eds) *The Routledge Handbook of Corpus Linguistics*, London: Routledge, pp. 270–87.

Widdowson, H. (1995) 'Discourse Analysis: A Critical View', *Language and Literature* 4(3): 157–72.

Widdowson, H. (2004) *Text, Context, Pretext: Critical Issues in Critical Discourse Analysis*, Oxford: Blackwell.

Wodak, R. (2011) 'Critical Discourse Analysis', in K. Hyland and B. Paltridge (eds) *Continuum Companion to Discourse Analysis*, London and New York: Continuum, pp. 38–53.

Zottola, A. (2018) 'Transgender Identity Labels in the British Press: A Corpus-Based Discourse Analysis', *Journal of Language and Sexuality* 7(2): 237–62.

19

What can a corpus tell us about pragmatics?

Christoph Rühlemann

1 What is pragmatics?

Pragmatics is a relatively young discipline. While its beginnings reach back as far as the early twentieth century, it has established itself as a subfield of linguistics since the 1970s. Pragmatics has been called 'the art of the analysis of the unsaid' (Mey 1991: 245). What this means becomes clear if we look carefully enough at almost any utterance we make. Consider, for instance, utterance (1) taken from the conversational subcorpus of the British National Corpus, referred to as BNC-C throughout the chapter, from which all examples in this chapter are taken unless otherwise indicated:

(1)
See you tomorrow.

The seeming simplicity of the utterance is treacherous. We begin to see why once we try to describe what "tomorrow" means. It turns out the adverb has a rather abstract and convoluted meaning, something like "the day after the day at which 'tomorrow' is used", which is "today". In other words: to understand what "tomorrow" means we must have an understanding of what "today" means – and we must be able to connect the two! That is, "tomorrow" said on a Monday means "Tuesday", but while "tomorrow" is *said*, neither "Monday" nor "Tuesday" is said – and still they are meant by the speaker *and* understood by the recipient.

This shows that to understand everyday utterances, we do not rely only on the verbally said – the text, we also need to co-process what is unsaid – the context. Context brings with it a bewildering kaleidoscope of variables. An arguably non-exhaustive list includes:

- The spatio-temporal context (coding-time and coding-place as well as receiving-time and receiving-place of the utterance, as in example [1]);
- The sequential context (the utterances that were made before an utterance and that

DOI: 10.4324/9780367076399-19

the utterance is a response to and also the utterances that are conditionally relevant to follow);

- The activity context (the recognisable activity the speaker and the hearer are engaged in, such as storytelling, debating, teasing, informing, etc.);
- The multimodal context (the speaker's bodily conduct into which the utterance is integrated, including their gestures, tone of voice, facial expressions, etc.);
- The emotive context (the speaker's affective involvement or disinvolvement with what the utterance is about);
- The epistemic context (the almost infinite range of what the speakers know about each other, the entities talked about and the world at large); and
- The social context (the relationship that holds between speaker and hearer, be it one between familiars or peers or between a superior and an inferior, etc.).

So pragmatic meaning results from *inference* – a co-computation of what is said and what is not said but contextually relevant. But context is boundless – anything really is context, but surely not everything is *relevant* context (Cook 1990). For example, bodily movements such as iconic gestures used to depict size or position of objects contribute decisively to meaning (e.g. Holler *et al.* 2009), but how do we segregate them from 'incidental or accidental motions (e.g. flicking one's hair, scratching the lower arm, or grasping a drink while talking)' (Holler and Levinson 2019: 640)? That is, the inferential processes required to process pragmatic meaning are complex: two such processes are filtering relevant from irrelevant context and connecting relevant context with text.

Inference-making would be utterly challenging were it not guided by principles. One such principle is Grice's (1975) 'cooperative principle' (CP).[1] It holds that speakers observe a set of four "maxims": the maxims of quantity (informativeness), quality (truthfulness), relation (relevance) and manner (clarity). Where talk fails to conform to the maxims, hearers will assume that the talk conforms to the maxims at some deeper level – the level of "implicature". Consider extract (2):

(2)

((children playing and speaking in the background))

1	Dorothy:	Hav' seen an'thing of Sarah this weekend, (.)
2		She alright¿=
3	B:	=°No: (.) no
4		(1.8)
5		Saw her on Friday and said (.)
6		force fed her a hot cross bun°
7	Dorothy:	**↑Oh well done**
8		(0.5)
9		.hh huh

[BNC: KBW 7686–7688; corrected transcription]

Dorothy is enquiring about Sarah, a friend of hers and speaker B's, in line 1. Speaker B reports that Sarah has been 'force fed a hot cross bun' in line 6, to which Dorothy responds '↑Oh well done' followed by a slight pause and laughter.[2] It is implausible that Dorothy actually approves of her friend Sarah being force-fed, as force-feeding constitutes a serious imposition on free will and is legally practised only under exceptional circumstances. In Gricean terms, then, the utterance violates the maxim of quality. The utter incongruence of praising a friend's being force-fed blocks a literal interpretation and instead suggests an implicature as *irony*, that is, as a reversal of evaluation, 'from favourable evaluation in the dictum [the said] to unfavourable evaluation in the implicatum' (Partington 2007: 1565).

Tracing the lines from what is said to what is not said but meant nonetheless is, then, what pragmatics does – indeed, an artful enterprise.

2 What is corpus pragmatics?

Given that pragmatic meaning requires recourse to the unsaid, pragmatic analysis is inherently qualitative analysis, relying on small numbers of texts, which are carefully read "horizontally" by paying attention to minute details *in situ*. This provides a sharp contrast with corpus linguistics, where the primary methodology is "vertical": Large quantities of data are ploughed through using corpus tools such as concordancers or collocation analysis, and attention to co-textual detail is drastically reduced, as the overarching goal is to discern *patterns*. A pattern requires that an occurrence be *recurrent*, that is, that it occur with sufficient frequency. Therefore, 'strictly speaking at least, the only thing corpora can provide is information on frequencies' (Gries 2009: 11), making corpus linguistics an essentially quantitative discipline.

Corpus pragmatics, as a relatively new field in linguistics, seeks to reconcile the two contrary methodologies of pragmatics and corpus linguistics by integrating vertical and horizontal analyses. The integration can be achieved essentially in three ways.

One way is the form-to-function approach. First, you vertically read a corpus for word forms, lemmas or constructions that previous research has shown to be associated with certain pragmatic functions. An example is Vaughan *et al.*'s (2017) study into vague category markers such as 'or something', 'that kind of thing', etc. The authors start from a list of such markers elaborated in earlier corpus research, including Carter and McCarthy (2006: 202–3) and O'Keeffe (2004). Based on this *a priori* list they conduct finely detailed qualitative analyses of the markers in their sequential context, with particular attention paid to what responses the markers trigger and how they contribute to conversational "confluence".

The inverse approach – function-to-form – starts from a pragmatic function, seeking to find the range of forms implementing the function. This approach presupposes careful horizontal reading of data to identify functions as they emerge from the corpus data. For example, working on the TOEFL 2000 *Spoken and Written Academic Language Corpus* (T2K-SWAL) and adopting a Searlian framework, Garcia McAllister (2015) deploys the function-to-form approach to identify speech acts such as directives, commissives, etc., in academic settings. Once the data are analysed and coded in this way, subcorpora – for example, for specific speech acts – can be defined, which, in turn, can be read vertically for recurring patterns in them. While this approach is undoubtedly time-consuming and labour-intensive, it has great merit, as the human-implemented functional categories will be highly reliable.

The third approach is a spin-off off the function-to-form approach – using a pragmatically annotated corpus. For example, the Narrative Corpus (Rühlemann and O'Donnell 2012) features exhaustive annotation of constructed dialog (more commonly known as "direct speech"). That is, the corpus is built on the back of the horizontal-reading stage the corpus constructors went through to identify constructed dialog in the transcripts, allowing corpus users to "skip" that stage and proceed directly to vertical analysis. The number of such pragmatically annotated corpora is still small. They include, for example, (a subcorpus of) the Michigan Corpus of Academic Spoken English

(MICASE), which is tagged for some speech acts (cf. Maynard and Leicher 2007); the Corpus of Verbal Response Mode (VRM) Annotated Utterances, in which all utterances are coded twice: once for their literal meaning and once for their pragmatic meaning, using a principled taxonomy of speech acts (cf. Stiles 1992); and SPICE Ireland (Kallen and Kirk 2012), which features, *inter alia*, annotation for speech acts and pragmatic markers. Another rather new branch of pragmatically annotated corpora comprises multimodal corpora, recording not only speech but also non-verbal conduct (see Section 5).

Finally, mention should be made of attempts to *automate* pragmatic corpus annotation. For example, Weisser's (2014) Dialogue Annotation and Research Tool (DART) detects and classifies speech acts semi-automatically. The tool, however, has so far only been tested on small and "orderly" speech data (Weisser 2014). How much further successful automation of pragmatic phenomena can be taken despite the massive "outsourcing" of meaning into the contextually unsaid remains to be seen in future research.

3 What pragmatic phenomena have been studied in corpora?

This section reviews corpus-pragmatic research in two core pragmatic areas: pragmatic markers and speech acts.[3] A new strand of corpus-pragmatic research, on turn-taking, is presented in Section 4.

Pragmatic markers

Pragmatic markers are small words, including "okay", "well", "you know", "I mean", "right", "actually", "like", "I (would) think", "so" and "cos", to name the ten most frequent in English (Carter *et al.* 2000: 179). They occur every four to five seconds (Jucker and Smith 1998: 176). Their high rate is due to their basic function: They invoke a frame of interpretation for (parts of) utterances (cf. Gumperz 1996: 379). On the one hand, they can flag how discourse *relates* to other discourse, as continuation (e.g. "cos"), elaboration (e.g. "I mean"), digression (e.g. "anyway"), transition (e.g. "so"), segmentation (e.g. "okay"), etc.; in this case the term "discourse markers" is appropriate. On the other hand, they can alert the hearer that the most relevant interpretation of discourse requires contextual support (that is, the co-computation of the said and the unsaid) (cf. Brinton 2010: 286). The appropriate term here is "pragmatic markers".

A much-researched *discourse* marker is the marker "like", which can serve multiple subfunctions (e.g. Andersen 2001). Extracts (3) and (4) illustrate two of them: In (3), "like" functions as an approximator, indicating that the numerical information preceding it may be imprecise; in (4), 'like' introduces constructed dialog indicating that 'don't be ridiculous' is not addressed to the co-present hearer but an utterance made by a non-present speaker:

(3)
I mean I've been in two shops now there's fifty pound difference **like**, you know
(4)
Yeah that's what I, why, that's what I said to Susanna and she was **like** don't be ridiculous!

To appreciate how *pragmatic* markers tap into not the text (discourse) but the (unsaid) context, consider the role of 'you know' in line 8 in extract (5). Ena is telling Alan about her parents' Welsh speaking skills. In lines 7 and 8, she expresses her regret that her father never taught her Welsh, to which she adds 'you know', phonetically realised as a separate unit by the rise-fall on it (expressed in ^):

(5)

1	Ena:	my father, well he couldn't spea:k Welsh=
2	Alan:	=mhm=
3	Ena:	and my mother could understand it
4	Alan:	I see
5	Ena:	but she couldn't speak it
6	Alan:	mm
7	Ena:	and I'd always been sorry that my dad
8		>my dad< never <<taught us ^**you know**>>
		(0.5)
9	Alan:	I've been trying to learn it, but I haven't got very far

[BNC KB0: 218–223; corrected transcription]

Alan has no prior knowledge of Ena's lifelong regret of not having learned Welsh. Rather than alluding to shared knowledge, then, Ena's 'you know' issues an invitation for Alan to "participate" in her experience (cf. Schiffrin 1987: Chapter 9). Witness how Alan does, in line 9: He relates his experience of trying to learn the language.

Unlike "like" and "you know", which can occur in various positions in turns, discourse/pragmatic markers generally tend to occur at the beginning of turns (Brinton 2010; see also Section 4). In turn-first position, they provide early indications as to what speech act, or action, the speaker of the incipient turn is going to perform.

Because pragmatic markers are relatively fixed lexically and thus retrievable from a corpus, corpus linguistic research on them has been extremely productive and is likely to yield more insights into how speakers flag discourse and tap into context to facilitate comprehension and interaction.

Speech act expressions

Speech act research deals with the 'things we do with words' (Austin 1962), referred to as speech acts, or, in conversation analysis, actions. Several speech act taxonomies have been proposed. The most influential has been Searle's (1975). Its five speech act categories (with various subcategories) include (i) representatives (which commit the speaker to the truth of a proposition, as in statements and conclusions); (ii) directives (by which the speaker aims to get the hearer to do something, as in orders and suggestions); (iii) commissives (which commit the speaker to some future kind of action, as in promises and threats); (iv) expressives (which express a psychological state, as in apologies or assessments); and (v) declarations (which effect immediate changes in the institutional state of affairs, as in christening and marrying).

Most speech acts are indirect, that is, an utterance performs a speech act 'indirectly by way of performing another' (Searle 1975: 60). Research on indirect speech acts has seen valuable input from corpus research. This subsection will highlight one such study, namely Adolphs (2008), based on the *Cambridge and Nottingham Corpus of Discourse in English* (CANCODE). The focus is on "speech act expressions" introducing suggestions; the expressions investigated in Adolphs include, among others, *why don't you.*

Why don't you can be used both for direct and indirect speech acts: When used to introduce a request for information, a direct speech act is performed; when used to make a suggestion, a question format is used to put forward a proposal for consideration by the addressee.[4] Consider extract (6): The participants are talking about how to address Melanie. Brian teases Melanie by calling her with her full name (lines 1–3). In line 6, Jess, who is Melanie's friend and Brian's daughter, asks her father to call her "Mel", apparently as this is Mel's preferred way of being addressed. In line 11, Brian, curious about Mel's dislike of being called by her full name, enquires about the reason for it by asking 'Why don't you like bein' called <u>tha:(</u>t)¿', to which request for information Mel provides the answer in line 15: 'cos th' only time (they call) me Melanie is when I'm in trouble':

(6)

1	Brian:	[( )] Melanie
2		(0.7)
3		I'll call you <u>Me</u>lanie <u>agai:n</u> (.) <u>Me</u>lanie
4	UNK:	( ) yeah
5	Brian:	>°heh heh heh heh°<
6	Jess:	Dad call her Me:l
7	Brian:	°E:rm yeah°
8		(1.7)
9	UNK:	( )
10		(0.8)
11	Brian:	**Why don't you like bein' called <u>tha:(</u>t)¿**
12		(0.6)
13	Mel:	↑Oh
14		(0.3)
15		cos th' only time (they call) me Melanie is when I'm in trouble eh [heh heh]
16	Brian:	[Ah ri:ght]

[BNC: KBL 1798–1807; corrected transcription]

Conversely, in extract (7), Gordon is offering Kevin a lift, in line 2. The offer is weighed by Kevin in lines 3 to 7 but not (yet) accepted as he is not sure which day it will be possible for him to go. In line 8, Gordon suggests to Kevin '[Why don't you go] on Fri::day' as he is going on that day (line 9). At this point, the suggestion is taken up by Kevin, who politely asks 'Are you su::re?' twice (lines 10 and 12).

(7)

1	Gordon:	Er d'ya wanna ta-
2		do you want us to **take** you¿
3	Kevin:	↑Well it depends (.)
4		(whe/well) er (.) it depends on what what day
5		you'll be going
6		and what day
7		Elaine °will want the° (.) [sort of date from]
8	Gordon:	**[Why don't you go] on Fri::day**
9		We're going [on Friday]
10	Kevin:	[Are you] su::re?=
11	Gordon:	=Take you with us=
12	Kevin:	=Are you su::re?

[BNC: KBC 1610-1616; corrected transcription]

A much-debated question in pragmatics is how listeners resolve the ambiguity between, in the case of *why don't you*, request and suggestion. As noted earlier, it is often assumed that indirect speech acts require complex cognitive processes by which a recipient first decodes the literal force – that is, the direct speech act – then realises that the direct speech act is not contextually plausible, to finally infer the intended implicature. Corpus evidence, by contrast, suggests that at least as critical as inference-making is the way a speech act is patterned in discourse.

To demonstrate that direct and indirect *Why don't you* speech acts pattern in different ways in discourse, Adolphs chooses a context-rich approach by elaborating functional profiles 'based on the distributional and collocational patterns in use' (2008: 10).

She observes that suggestion-*why don't you,* henceforth S-WDY, is often preceded by a form of SAY to introduce constructed dialog. Where this is the case, S-WDY is used as part of a *reported speech act*, as in (8), whereas no such association with constructed dialog is found for request-*why don't you*, henceforth R-WDY.

(8)
oh I think it's because I was *saying* **why don't you** come up like this week

Further, S-WDY is regularly followed by transitive verbs such as *ask*, *get*, *tell* and *use,* whereas R-WDY collocates with volitional and modal verbs such as *like*, *want* and *have to*. Another key collocate is the pragmatic marker *just*, which tones down the imposition implied in suggestions. Consider (9):

(9)
Why **don't you just** sit down somewhere?

Moreover, S-WDY and R-WDY are distinguished by the type of response they trigger: While the responses to S-WDY 'range from minimal acknowledgment tokens to agreement, or evaluations of the suggestion' (Adolphs 2008: 62), R-WDY requires a more detailed answer. Finally, Adolphs found that S-WDY was most frequent in the "intimate" speaker relationship category, that is, in interactions between people whose social closeness is maximal (partners, family, very close friends). In this context type, speakers are most "off-guard" and the imposition implied in S-WDY as a directive is felt as less threatening.

The uses of R-WDY and S-WDY are, then, "idiomatic", that is, they are embedded in distinctly different patternings in discourse, and conversationalists are likely to capitalise on them to disambiguate the two speech acts.

Adolphs's functional speech act profiles, which draw on multiple contextual layers, present a distinct methodological advance over traditional methods in speech act research, which have relied heavily on utterances in isolation from context (cf. Schegloff 1988: 61). They thus enable a more realistic view of how conversationalists go about ascribing speech acts.

4 Focus on corpora and turn-taking

Another pragmatics-related area that has benefitted from corpus research is turn-taking. In the following, three corpus studies on turn-taking will be presented: Tao (2003) on turn-initiators, Rühlemann (2020) on turn structure and inserts and O'Keeffe and Adolphs (2008) on backchannels.

Turn-openers and turn-initiators

Tao (2003) examines spoken data from the Switchboard corpus, which features US telephone conversations, and the *Cambridge University Press/Cornell University Corpus*, which records face-to-face conversations. The study distinguishes "turn openers" and "turn initiators". In (10) all highlighted items are "turn openers", the very first word in their respective turn:

(10)

1	Stefan:	°**mm**° artists never give satisfac[tory] answer
2	Katherine:	[↑**why**].
3	Stefan:	**because** they're art(hh)ists(hh)
4	Katherine:	**really**?

[BNC: KCV 3093–3100; corrected transcription]

"Turn openers" are an inclusive class hosting any word form used in turn-first position. Tao shows that despite this inclusivity, turn openers are in fact a small class, with the top 20 most frequent types alone accounting for 60 per cent (Tao 2003: 190) of the total number of turn openers. In other words, the set of words speakers choose from to start a turn is limited – in fact much more limited than the sets of words available for other turn positions, as shown in Figure 19.1.

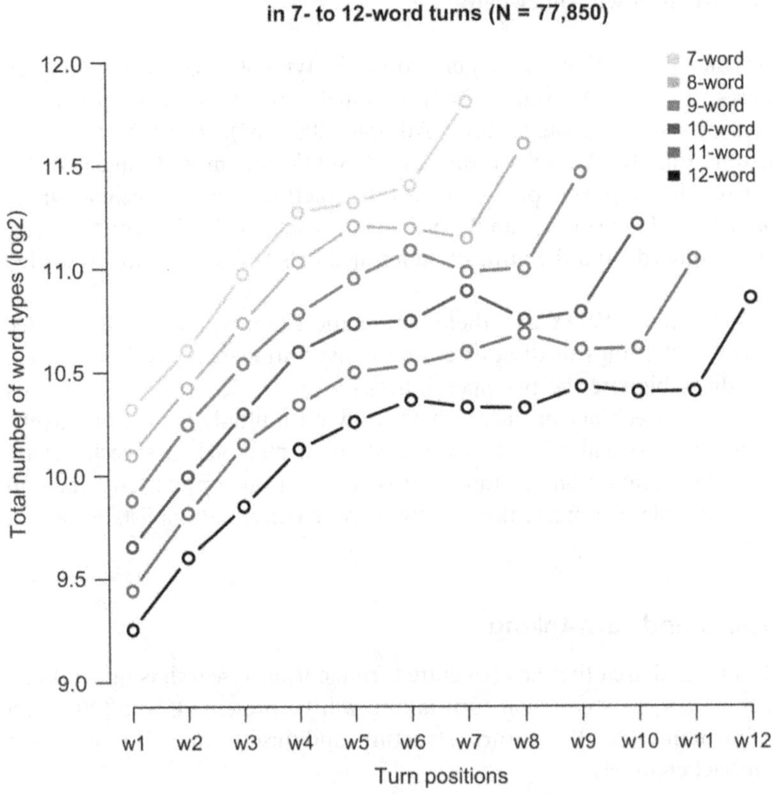

Figure 19.1 Number of distinct word types in 7- to 12-word turns in BNC-C

"Turn initiators", by contrast, are a much more exclusive class, defined as 'those elements, if any, that show some degree of *exclusivity*' (Tao 2003: 192; my emphasis) in turn-initial position. The degree of exclusivity is calculated by dividing the opener's frequency in the turn-first position by its frequency overall (i.e. in any position in the turn).

The resulting list of turn-initiators most prominently includes interjections, that is, '"syntactically" independent lexical forms or vocalisations which can be used without co-occurrence of any other forms' (Tao 2003: 190); (cf. also Heritage 2013). In Tao's study, the top ten turn-initiators are (in that order): 'mhm' (100 per cent use as turn initiator), 'uh-huh' (88 per cent), 'oh' (75 per cent), 'yeah' (74 per cent), 'okay' (52 per cent), 'well' (45 per cent), 'no' (44 per cent), laughter (43 per cent), 'right' (35 per cent) and 'so' (21 per cent). Note that Tao's turn-initiators are by and large *pragmatic markers*, thus underscoring the positional preference of markers for the turn-initial slot noted in Section 3.

So, Tao's (2003) study suggests that the turn-first "slot" is special in lexical terms: The range of distinct words occupying it is smaller than for other turn positions, and those words that almost only occur in the first position are syntactically independent interjections.

Turn structure and inserts

Rühlemann (2020) builds on Tao's study by asking how not only interjections but also other types of syntactic isolates classified as *inserts* (Biber *et al.* 1999) are distributed across positions in turns and also by probing into what functions they perform in the turn. Inserts are a newly recognised class of words alongside the traditional classes of lexical words and function words; inserts 'do not form an integral part of syntactic structure (…) often marked off by intonation, pauses (…) characteristically carry emotional and interactional meaning and are especially frequent in spoken texts' (Biber *et al.* 1999: 56). Inserts are a functionally diverse class, including backchannel forms ("mm"), pragmatic markers ("like"), response items ("yeah"), hesitation markers ("erm"), greetings ("hi"), farewells ("bye") and more (cf. Biber *et al.* 1999).

Working on large sets of turns extracted from BNC-C, the author finds a very clear distributional skew: Inserts thrive in the turn-first position, as visualised in Figure 19.2.

Moreover, the study investigates the association of inserts with the *structure* of turns. Sacks *et al.* (1974) observed that turns have a systematically potential three-part structure, likely reflecting the fact that any turn is a turn in a series (Sacks *et al.* 1974: 722): Turns may have 'one [part] which addresses the relation of a turn to a prior, one involved with what is occupying the turn, and one which addresses the relation of the turn to a succeeding one' (Sacks *et al.* 1974: 722). Sacks *et al.* (1974) refer to the three parts as (i) pre-start, (ii) turn-constructional unit (TCU) and (iii) post-completer.

Based on manual analysis of a subsample of 1,000 ten-word turns from the BNC-C, items satisfying the condition of 'addressing the relation of the turn to the prior' were identified.[5] A handful of the 347 inserts identified in the subsample were not at the same time (part of) a pre-start.

This suggests the following: If a speaker uses an insert as the first word in a turn (which they do in 40 per cent of the turns in the subsample), the insert will perform the function of a pre-start, creating a link between the thus-begun turn and the prior. This

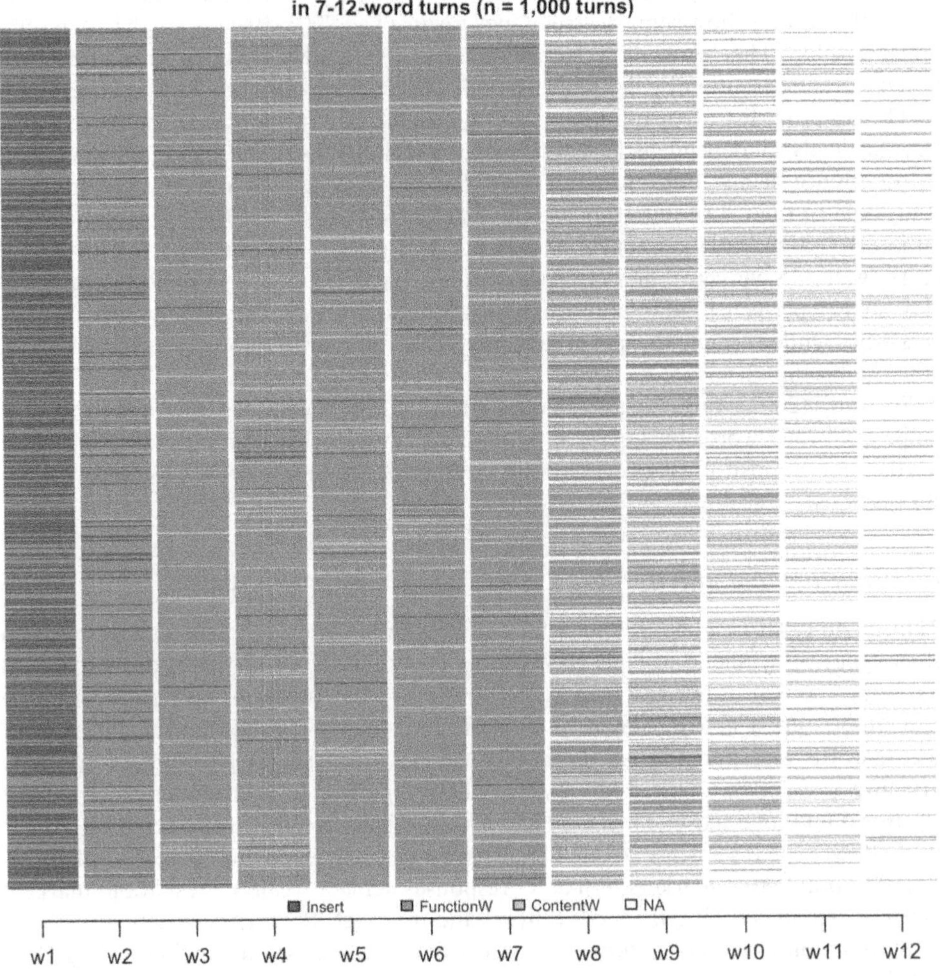

Figure 19.2 Distribution of inserts, function words and content words in a sample of 1,000 turns from 7- to 12-word turns in the BNC-C

indicates that a whole class of words *exists* because it has a distinct job to do – building a bridge between turns.

The ways in which inserts/pre-starts build that bridge are virtually infinite, depending on which item is used, on how fully it is articulated, on where in the *sequence* the turn occurs, etc. Given this complexity and space limitations, only a glimpse will be possible (but see Heritage and Sorjonen's 2018 research volume dedicated to turn-initial particles in various languages). The following extract illustrates how "well" creates a linkage from one turn to the next:

(11)

1 Alb: Is that June's boyfriend then.
2 J: **we:ll** (0.601) that Phil, (.) he's a (0.454) screw I think.

[BNC: KB1 5128–5129; corrected transcription]

Albert asks a simple yes/no question about Phil: 'Is that June's boyfriend then.' (line 1). Its statement intonation suggests he is expecting a positive answer. The response by J, however, could hardly be less unexpected: 'he's a (0.454) screw' (line 2). This turn clashes with the prior turn in two ways: First it does not answer the question straightforwardly and second it proffers an explicit assessment that diverges dramatically from Albert's implicit assessment of Phil as someone who might qualify as June's boyfriend. Conversation analysts call such a turn "dispreferred" as it departs from the understandings, expectations and projections established in the prior turn—the pre-start "well" acts as a "warning particle" (Levinson 2013) that such a departure is underway (Heritage 2015: 89). It thus satisfies the front-loading bias, a universal bias toward inserting cues to action type early in the turn to facilitate the interlocutor's action recognition/action ascription (cf. Levinson 2013: 112).

Turn-taking and backchannels

Not every utterance in conversation is a turn. For example, so-called backchannel utterances are generally 'not construed as full turns, but rather pass up the opportunity to take a turn' (Levinson and Torreira 2015: 8). Backchannels are small, unobtrusive signals (of any modality – verbal, vocal, or bodily) by which current non-speakers register listenership, illustrated in (12):

(12)

Ena:	but they got jobs, quite good jobs
	and the ↑fella (0.32) [that 'as]
Alan:	[**hm**]
Ena:	employed 'em
Alan:	**hm**
Ena:	he' (0.43) (s) one himself
(0.58)	
Alan:	**I [see]**
Ena:	[so] he employs (0.50) that sort of people you [see]
Alan:	[**m]mm**

[BNC: KBG 303–334; corrected transcription]

Backchannels are positionally closely associated with the completion of a TCU (e.g. Goodwin 1986: 208; Stivers 2013: 201), that is, 'a coherent and self-contained utterance, recognizable in context as "possibly complete"' (Clayman 2013: 151). In extract (12), for example, "hm" (line 5), "I see" (8) and "mmm" (10) all occur at TCU end points.[6] (Only "hm" [3] occurs in the "interjacent position" [Jefferson 1986: 158] far ahead of the TCU completion, arguably as a sign of Alan's continued listenership during Ena's word search.)

The most common sequential environment for backchannels is in "tellings" (cf. Schegloff 2007), that is, multi-turn sequences that systematically offer 'places in it for others' talk' (Sacks 1992: 526). For example, the backchannels in extract (12) are all part of a *storytelling*, a key type of telling sequence, where backchannels represent by far the most common response type produced by story recipients (Rühlemann 2013).

Extract (12) highlights yet another defining feature of backchannels: As shown by the square brackets around (parts of) the backchannels in lines 3, 8 and 10, backchannels have a marked tendency to occur in overlap. Indeed, backchannels account for more than 70 per cent of *all* overlap (Levinson and Torreira 2015: 8). Taking advantage of this association, corpus linguists have investigated backchannels using corpus mark-up as the means of identification (e.g. Wong and Peters 2007).

Backchannels occur massively in natural conversation: Estimates backed up by experimental research suggest that backchannels 'occur more than a thousand times in a single hour of talk' (Gardner 1998: 205; see also Bavelas *et al.* 2000).

Consistent with this high frequency, backchannels serve a wide range of functions. While the foundational function is to signal understanding (Gardner 1998), O'Keeffe and Adolphs (2008) identify four additional broad functions:

- Continuers (cf. Schegloff 1982), which index the recipient's alignment with the structural asymmetry of the telling sequence (cf. Stivers 2008: 34); all backchannels in extract (12) seem to serve this function;
- Convergence tokens, associated with (i) topic boundaries or closures and (ii) points 'where there is a need to converge on an understanding of what is common ground or shared knowledge between participants' (O'Keeffe and Adolphs 2008: 84);
- Engagement tokens, which 'express genuine emotional responses such as surprise, shock, horror, sympathy, empathy, and so on' (O'Keeffe and Adolphs 2008: 84); cf. Goodwin (1986) who refers to them as assessments (and assigns them turn status);
- Information receipt tokens, which simply ratify receipt of information, often at topic boundaries and thus, unlike continuers, not as part of a continued telling sequence.

Convergence tokens are illustrated in extract (13): Merielle's 'mm' ratifies recognition of the location described by Martine, thus confirming that she now shares with her a mental "map" where the near-accident happened:

(13)
Martine: Go::', I was nearly in an accident last night, °that reminds me.°
Coming- I'd just turned off the (0.4) Wrexham road, (1.3)
er going along the Paisword one (.)
Merielle: **mm**

[BNC KD8: 7592–7593; corrected transcription]

Extract (14), taken from the Limerick Corpus of Irish English (LCIE), illustrates engaged response tokens; witness how speaker A's 'Aaahhhh' signals strong affective engagement upon learning that speaker B had made up with her boyfriend after a row with him a few days earlier:

(14)
A: Were you out last night?
B: I was.
A: Where were you?
B: Am you see we had to reconcile last night and get it all back on.
A: ***Aaahhhh***

(O'Keeffe and Adolphs 2008: 87)

Information receipt tokens, finally, form a small group of backchannels. An illustrative example is given in extract (15), again from the LCIE:

(15)
A: He's been in Wexford for years right. I told you he's separated didn't I? And that he has a child.
B: Yeah.
A: ***Right.***
((story continues))

(O'Keeffe and Adolphs 2008: 87)

Speaker A is relating background information to an incipient story by providing numerous details on the male story character. As suggested by the use of 'right' and 'didn't I?' she seeks confirmation by speaker B that these details have been received. Once the confirmation has come forward in B's 'Yeah.', she receipts this receipt with 'Right.' to finally start with the 'meat' of the story.

To conclude this section, backchannels, as a subtype of inserts, and other conversational features that have in common that they are small and often border on the non-verbal have long been among the most marginalised items in linguistic research but are in fact part of the core DNA of talk-in-interaction. Corpus research has just begun to uncover the ways these small words do their magic of structuring talk and facilitating smooth interaction.

5 Multimodal corpora: the way forward in corpus linguistics?

The vast majority of present-day spoken corpora are speech-only corpora: They record non-speech conduct such as intonation, gaze or gesture only crudely and highly selectively – the BNC, for example, has rudimentary paralinguistic annotation – or not at all. This is a serious shortcoming, given the trivial fact that '[l]anguage as it is used in its central ecological niche – that is, in face-to-face interaction – is embedded in multimodal displays by both speaker and addressee' (Holler and Levinson 2019: 639). These displays involve not only verbal but also vocal and kinesic choices (Arndt and Janney 1987). Moreover, non-verbal choices are highly relevant to what participants communicate and orient to in face-to-face interaction: In some contexts, gestures provide between 50 per cent and 70 per cent of the overall information in turns (Holler *et al.* 2018).

A particular challenge for current corpus-pragmatic research is therefore the construction, annotation and analysis of multimodal corpora recording speech in its integration with the non-verbal modalities (see Chapter 3, this volume). The challenges are considerable. The non-verbal semiotic systems may be as highly differentiated as the verbal system. For example, Rimé and Schiaratura (1991: 248) present a taxonomy of speech-related hand gestures which includes six broad variables: speech markers, ideographs, iconic gestures, pantomimic gestures, deictic gestures and symbolic gestures; Lücking *et al.* (2013) distinguish eight kinds of gestures. Ekman and O'Sullivan (1991: 176) discuss evidence for the cross-cultural recognition of at least six emotions expressed via facial actions: happiness, anger, fear, sadness, surprise and disgust. Variables of the vocal modality include rhythm, tempo, pitch, intensity, voice quality and intonation with its manifold subvariables (e.g. Wennerstrom 2001). To add to this wealth of variables there is also the 'binding problem' (Holler and Levinson 2019: 639) – multimodal signals are inherently asynchronous: Although semantically or pragmatically related, two or more signals from different modalities may play out on completely different time scales. This is perhaps best researched for referential gestures, where the preparatory phase (the phase during which the hand is brought from a neutral position to the "stroke" position

– the gesture proper) tends to temporally precede the articulation of the lexical affiliate by roughly one second on average (Morrel-Samuels and Krauss 1992; cf. Kok 2017).

Given these challenges, the number of multimodal corpora is at present still small, and the corpora themselves are small too; for example, the *Nottingham Multimodal Corpus* (NMMC) contains just 250,000 words (Adolphs and Carter 2013). Probably the largest multimodal corpus to date is the *Corpus of Academic Spoken English* (CASE) with 2 million words (Diemer *et al.* 2016). Also, multimodal corpus analyses focus on narrow multimodal phenomena. For example, Carter and Adolphs's (2008) "Headtalk" project, based on the NMMC, explores head nods as a type of nonverbal backchannel in co-occurrence with verbal backchannels.

A fascinating study pointing the way for future multimodal-corpus investigations is Kok (2017). Working on the Bielefeld Speech and Gesture Alignment Corpus (SaGA; Lücking *et al.* 2013), which, with 40,000 words, is quite small but boasts fine-grained annotation of thousands of gesture tokens, he explores the integration of gesture and speech by discovering gesture-attracting and gesture-repelling lemmas and parts of speech. The analyses suggest, that, for example, verbs of cognition such as "know" and "believe", as well as the class of interjections, *repel* gestures (i.e. occur without them), whereas proximal locatives such as "here" or "this", as well as spatial prepositions and noun phrases, attract gestures (i.e. co-occur with them).

To illustrate, consider Figure 19.3, where the speaker's finger-bunch gesture (cf. Kendon 2004: 229) is fully synchronised with the noun "location": The gesture starts at shoulder height on the unstressed syllable "loc" and is pushed down with the accented syllable in "ation". The synchrony is not by chance, as there is a close *semantic* relation between the iconic gesture and the affiliate "location": The bunched-together fingers depict the bunched-together entities (e.g. houses) that define a location (cf. Holler and Beattie 2003). Importantly, the speech-gesture alignment exemplified in this utterance is not just an artifact of communicative exuberance or signal redundance but communicatively relevant, as combinations of speech and iconic gestures are responded to and, by extension, understood faster than speech-only, and co-speech gestures thus have the effect of enhancing comprehension (e.g. Holler *et al.* 2018; Holler and Levinson 2019).

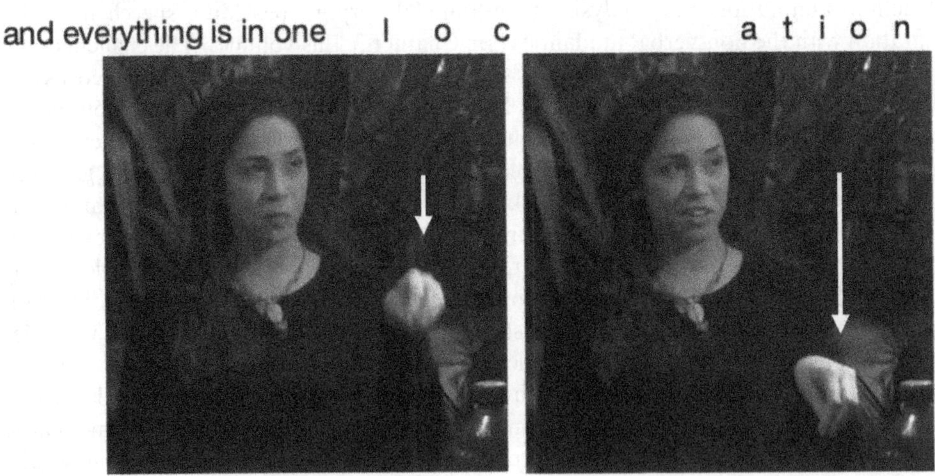

Figure 19.3 Finger-bunch gesture depicting the word "location"

To conclude, Kok's study is a welcome trail-blazer drawing on the best of two worlds by integrating multimodal data and concepts, on the one hand, and corpus-linguistic methodologies, on the other. The study illuminates the promise that lies ahead for corpus pragmatic multimodal research: to unravel the rich ways in which we orchestrate multiple modalities into the multilayered messages that we use in face-to-face interaction.

Notes

1 Another principle is Sperber and Wilson's (1986) cognitive principle of relevance, which holds that speakers and hearers search for relevance less because of an intrinsic willingness to co-operate but because human cognition is geared toward optimal relevance in the first place.
2 Irony closely co-occurs with laughter (Norrick 2003). Thus, it can be analyzed corpus-linguistically by computing concordances of laughter episodes, a method used by Partington (2007).
3 Other core-pragmatic areas notably not covered include evaluative prosody (e.g., Partington 2007), vagueness (e.g., O'Keeffe 2004) and deixis (e.g., Rühlemann and O'Donnell 2015).
4 In Searle's (1975) taxonomy of speech acts, both requests for information and suggestions count as subcategories of 'directives'.
5 Another condition was that the item be appositional, that is, syntactically separated, as is the case with inserts, or separable from the utterance without compromising its grammaticality, as is the case with conjunctions.
6 By contrast, visual backchannels, including, for example, head nods, blinks and gestures, are far more versatile in their positioning.

Further reading

Adolphs, S. (2008) *Corpus and Context. Investigating Pragmatic Functions in Spoken Discourse*, Amsterdam: John Benjamins. (This path-breaking study makes important contributions to the theory of speech acts.)

Grice, H. P. (1975) 'Logic and Conversation', in P. Cole and J. L. Morgan (eds) *Syntax and Semantics III*, New York: Academic Press, pp. 43–58. (This paper is perhaps one of the most fundamental works in pragmatics.)

Sacks, H., Schegloff E. A. and Jefferson, G. (1974) 'A Simplest Systematics for the Organisation of Turn-Taking for Conversation', *Language* 50(4): 696–735. (This work is most widely cited in studies on turn-taking.)

References

Adolphs, A. (2008) *Corpus and Context: Investigating Pragmatic Functions in Spoken Discourse*, Amsterdam: Benjamins.

Adolphs, S. and Carter, R. A. (2013) *Spoken Corpus Linguistics. From Monomodal to Multimodal*, London: Routledge.

Andersen, G. (2001) *Pragmatic Markers and Sociolinguistic Variation. A Relevance-Theoretic Approach to the Language of Adolescents*, Amsterdam/Philadelphia: John Benjamins.

Arndt, H. and Janney, R. W. (1987) *InterGrammar. Towards an Integrative Model of Verbal, Prosodic and Kinesic Choices in Speech*, Berlin: Mouton de Gruyter.

Austin, J. L. (1962) *How to Do Things with Words*, Oxford: Oxford University Press.

Bavelas, J. B., Coates, L. and Johnson, T. (2000) 'Listeners as Co-Narrators', *Journal of Personality and Social Psychology* 79: 941–52.

Biber, D., Johansson, S., Leech, G., Conrad, S. and Finegan, E. (1999) *Longman Grammar of Spoken and Written English*, Harlow: Pearson Education Limited.

Brinton, L. J. (2010) 'Discourse Markers', in A. H. Jucker and I. Taavitsainen (eds) *Historical Pragmatics* (Handbooks of Pragmatics 8), Berlin: De Gruyter Mouton, pp. 285–314.

Carter, R. A. and Adolphs, S. (2008) 'Linking the Verbal and the Visual: New Directions for Corpus Linguistic', *Language and Computers* 64: 275–91.

Carter, R. A. and McCarthy, M. J. (2006) *Cambridge Grammar of English*, Cambridge: Cambridge University Press.

Carter, R. A. , Hughes, R. and McCarthy, M. J. (2000) *Exploring Grammar in Context*, Cambridge: Cambridge University Press.

Clayman, S. E. (2013) 'Turn-Constructional Units and the Transition-Relevance Place', in J. Sidnell and T. Stivers (eds) *The Handbook of Conversation Analysis*, Oxford: Wiley Blackwell, pp. 150–66.

Cook, G. (1990) 'Transcribing Infinity: Problems of Context Presentation', *Journal of Pragmatics* 14: 1–24.

Diemer, S., Brunner, M.-L. and Schmidt, S. (2016) 'Compiling Computer-Mediated Spoken Language Corpora: Key Issues and Recommendations', *International Journal of Corpus Linguistics* 21(3): 349–71.

Ekman, P. and O'Sullivan, M. (1991) 'Facial Expression: Methods, Means, and Moues', in R. S. Feldman and B. Rimé (eds) *Fundamentals of Nonverbal Behaviour*, Cambridge: Cambridge University Press, pp. 163–99.

Garcia McAllister, P. (2015) 'Speech Acts: A Synchronic Perspective', in K. Aijmer and C. Rühlemann (eds) *Corpus Pragmatics: A Handbook*, Cambridge: Cambridge University Press, pp. 29–51.

Gardner, R. (1998) 'Between Speaking and Listening: The Vocalisation of Understandings', *Applied Linguistics* 19(2): 204–24.

Goodwin, C. (1986) 'Between and within Alternative Sequential Treatments of Continuers and Assessments', *Human Studies* 9: 205–17.

Grice, H. P. (1975) 'Logic and Conversation', in P. Cole and J. L. Morgan (eds) *Syntax and Semantics III*, New York: Academic Press, pp. 43–58.

Gries, St. Th. (2009) *Quantitative Corpus Linguistics with R. A Practical Introduction*, New York/ London: Routledge.

Gumperz, J. J. (1996) 'The Linguistic and Cultural Relativity of Conversational Inference', in J. J. Gumperz and S. C. Levinson (eds) *Rethinking Linguistic Relativity*, Cambridge: University Press, pp. 374–406.

Heritage, J. (2013) 'Turn-Initial Position and Some of Its Occupants', *Journal of Pragmatics* 57: 331–7.

Heritage, J. (2015) '*Well*-Prefaced Turns in English Conversation: A Conversation Analytic Perspective', *Journal of Pragmatics* 88: 88–104.

Heritage, J. and Sorjonen, M.-L. (2018) 'Analyzing Turn-Initial Particles', in J. Heritage and M.-L. Sorjonen (eds) *Between Turn and Sequence. Turn-Initial Particles Across Languages*, Amsterdam: Benjamins, pp. 1–22.

Holler, J. and Beattie, G. (2003) 'How Iconic Gestures and Speech Interact in the Representation of Meaning: Are Both Aspects Really Integral to the Process?', *Semiotica* 146: 81–116.

Holler, J., Shovelton, H. and Beattie, G. (2009) 'Do Iconic Gestures Really Contribute to the Semantic Information Communicated in Face-to-Face Interaction?', *Journal of Nonverbal Behavior*, 33:73–88.

Holler, J., Kendrick, K. H. and Levinson, S. C. (2018) 'Processing Language in Face-to-Face Conversation: Questions with Gestures Get Faster Responses', *Psychonometric Bulletin Review* 25(5): 1900–8.

Holler, J. and Levinson, S. C. (2019) 'Multimodal Language Processing in Human Communication', *Trends in Cognitive Sciences* 23(8) 639–52.

Jucker, A. H. and Smith, S. W. (1998) 'And People Just You Know Like "Wow". Discourse Markers as Negotiating Strategies', in A. H. Jucker and Y. Ziv (eds) *Discourse Markers. Descriptions and Theory*, Amsterdam: John Benjamins, pp. 171–201.

Jefferson. G. (1986) 'Notes on "Latency" in Overlap Onset', *Human Studies* 9: 153–83.

Kallen, J. and Kirk, J. (2012) *SPICE-Ireland: A User's Guide*, Belfast: Cló Ollscoil na Banríona.

Kendon, A. (2004) *Gesture: Visible Action as Utterance*, Cambridge: Cambridge University Press.

Kok, K. (2017) 'Functional and Temporal Relations between Spoken and Gestured Components of Language: A Corpus-Based Inquiry', *International Journal of Corpus* 22(1): 1–26.

Levinson, S. C. (2013). 'Action Formation and Ascription', in J. Sidnell and T. Stivers (eds) *The Handbook of Conversation Analysis*, Malden/MA and Oxford: Wiley Blackwell, pp. 103–30.

Levinson, S. C. and Torreira, F. (2015) 'Timing in Turn-taking and its Implications for Processing Models of Language', *Frontiers in Psychology* 6:731. https://doi.org/10.3389/fpsyg.2015.00731.

Lücking, A., Bergmann, K., Hahn, F., Kopp, S. and Rieser, H. (2013) 'Data-Based Analysis of Speech and Gesture: The Bielefeld Speech and Gesture Alignment Corpus (Saga) and Its Applications', *Journal on Multimodal User Interfaces* 7(1–2): 5–18.

Maynard, C. and Leicher, S. (2007) 'Pragmatic Annotation of an Academic Spoken Corpus for Pedagogical Purposes', in E. Fitzpatrick (ed) *Corpus Linguistics Beyond the Word: Corpus Research from Phrase to Discourse*, Amsterdam: Rodopi, pp. 107–16.

Mey, J. L. (1991) 'Pragmatic Gardens and Their Magic', *Poetics* 20: 233–45.

Morrel-Samuels, P. and Krauss, R.M. (1992) 'Word Familiarity Predicts Temporal Asynchrony of Hand Gestures and Speech', *Journal of Experimental Psychology of Learning, Memory and Cognition* 18: 615–22.

Norrick, N. (2003) 'Issues in Conversational Joking', *Journal of Pragmatics* 35: 1333–59.

O'Keeffe, A. (2004) '"Like the Wise Virgin and all that Jazz": Using a Corpus to Examine Vague Categorisation and Shared Knowledge', in U. Connor and T. A. Upton (eds) *Applied Corpus Linguistics. A Multidimensional Perspective*, Amsterdam/New York/NY: Rodopi, pp. 1–20.

O'Keeffe, A. and Adolphs, S. (2008) 'Response Tokens in British and Irish Discourse: Corpus, Context and Variational Pragmatics', in K. P. Schneider and A. Barron (eds) *Variational Pragmatics*, Amsterdam: John Benjamins, pp. 69–98.

Partington, A. (2007) 'Irony and Reversal of Evaluation', *Journal of Pragmatics* 39: 1547–69

Rimé, B. and Schiaratura, L. (1991) 'Gesture and Speech', in R. S. Feldman and B. Rimé (eds) *Fundamentals of Nonverbal Behaviour*, Cambridge/New York: Cambridge University Press, pp. 239–81.

Rühlemann, C. (2020) 'Turn Structure and Inserts', *International Journal of Corpus Linguistics* 25(2): 185–214.

Rühlemann, C. and O'Donnell, M. B. (2012) 'Introducing a Corpus of Conversational Narratives. Construction and Annotation of the Narrative Corpus', *Corpus Linguistics and Linguistic Theory* 8(2): 313–50.

Rühlemann, C. and O'Donnell, M. B. (2015) 'Deixis', in Aijmer, K. and C. Rühlemann (eds) *Corpus Pragmatics. A Handbook.* Cambridge: Cambridge University Press, pp. 331–59.

Sacks, H. (1992) *Lectures on Conversation. Vols. I and II*, Oxford: Blackwell.

Sacks, H., Schegloff, E. and Jefferson, G. (1974) 'A Simplest Systematics for the Organization of Turn-Taking for Conversation', *Language* 50(4): 696–735.

Schegloff, E. A. (1982) 'Discourse as an Interactional Achievement: Some Uses of "uh huh" and Other Things that Come between Sentences', in D. Tannen (ed.) *Georgetown University Round Table on Languages and Linguistics Analyzing Discourse: Text and Talk*, Washington DC: Georgetown University Press, pp. 71–93.

Schegloff, E. A. (1988) 'Presequences and Indirection', *Journal of Pragmatics* 12: 55–62.

Schegloff, E. A. (2007) *Sequence Organization in Interaction: A Primer in Conversation Analysis*, Cambridge: Cambridge University Press.

Schiffrin, D. (1987) *Discourse Markers*, Cambridge: Cambridge University Press.

Searle, J. R. (1975) 'Indirect Speech Acts', in P. Cole and J. L. Morgan (eds) *Syntax and Semantics III*, New York: Academic Press, pp. 59–82.

Sperber, D. and Wilson, D. (1986) *Relevance: Communication and Cognition*, Oxford: Blackwell.

Stiles, W. B. (1992) *Describing Talk. A Taxonomy of Verbal Response Modes*, Newbury Park/CA: Sage Publications.

Stivers, T. (2008) 'Stance, Alignment, and Affiliation During Storytelling: When Nodding Is a Token of Affiliation', *Research on Language and Social Interaction* 41(1): 31–57.

Stivers, T. (2013) 'Sequence Organization', in J. Sidnell and T. Stivers (eds) *The Handbook of Conversation Analysis*, Malden/MA and Oxford: Wiley Blackwell, pp. 191–209.

Tao, H. (2003) 'Turn Initiators in Spoken English: A Corpus-Based Approach to Interaction and Grammar', in C. Meyer and P. Leistyna (eds) *Corpus Analysis: Language Structure and Language Use*, Amsterdam: Rodopi, pp. 187–207.

Vaughan, E., McCarthy, M. J. and Clancy, B. (2017) 'Vague Category Markers as Turn-Final Items in Irish English', *World Englishes* 36(2): 208–23.
Wennerstrom, A. (2001) *The Music of Everyday Speech. Prosody and Discourse Analysis*, Oxford: Oxford University Press.
Weisser, M. (2014) *The Dialogue Annotation and Research Tool* (DART) Version 1.0 (Computer software), Available from: martinweisser.org/ling_soft.html.
Wong, D. and Peters, P. (2007) 'A Study of Backchannels in Regional Varieties of English, Using Corpus Mark-up as Means of Identification', *International Journal of Corpus Linguistics* 12 (4): 479–509.

20

What can a corpus tell us about phonetic and phonological variation?

Alexandra Vella and Sarah Grech

1 The speech community and variation in speech

Studies in phonetic and phonological variation oriented in CL often encounter significant challenges right from the outset. The advantages of utilising the large datasets which CL promises are frequently offset by the often tedious processes involved in readying such large datasets for effective phonetic and/or phonological analysis. Lieberman (2019) predicts that the trend towards increased use of corpora in phonetic research is set to continue to grow, whilst Durand (2017) claims that as long as a range of criteria are met when spoken corpora are constructed and developed, their utility in accounting for both intra- and inter-speaker variation will be inestimable. The growing subfields of corpus phonetics and corpus phonology also hold the key to ensuring that researchers working on different languages – and particularly under-resourced ones – increasingly get access to data which do more than simply tick the "spoken component" box. The complexity of the decisions needing to be taken is much more onerous in the case of speech given the much greater amount of pre-processing work necessary to ensure usability of the data (Ernestus and Warner 2011; Cole and Hasegawa-Johnson 2012). Additionally, it is easy to forget that the digital age favours well-resourced languages such as English, French, German or Spanish, while less resourced languages are often still faced with having to invest heavily in manual processing of data, which inevitably results in a limited digital presence and a bit of a vicious cycle (Besacier *et al.* 2014; Mena *et al.* 2020).

In this chapter, phonetic and phonological research is understood as encompassing the investigation of patterning in the spoken interaction humans undertake with each other. Such patterns can involve anything from acoustic analysis of different realisations of a given phoneme in different contexts to the study of the different intonational choices made by speakers when providing feedback in talk-in-interaction situations (Giles *et al.* 1991).

Understanding the myriad ways in which speech patterns vary is at the heart of much phonetic and phonological analysis. Whether the focus is on variability within one speaker (intra-speaker), or across different speakers (inter-speaker), on variation as a function of different speaking contexts or for other reasons, variation studies in this area

DOI: 10.4324/9780367076399-20

yield discussions on anything from the identification of speakers belonging to a particular speech community to how a listener's perception of an accent can be influenced by different factors, non-linguistic as well as linguistic. Examining variation at these levels often means having to deal with data which may be less discrete and more continuous, for example, vowel duration as opposed to lexical frequency information. This can pose challenges for phoneticians and phonologists working within CL.

Variationists are often concerned with the shifts and changes in language that can be observed within localised speech communities, rather than, say, within larger language groups. It is often within these more contained speech communities that change is likely to be noticed first. It is also within such speech communities that variation can be seen to be taking place in real time, as it were.

A speech community can be defined as 'a group of people who share the same language, speech characteristics and ways of interpreting communication' (Nordquist 2019, para. 1). These characteristics 'help people define themselves as individuals and community members and identify (or misidentify) others' (ibid). Definitions of this sort suggest some degree of "homogeneity" in the speech of members of such a community, to the extent that listeners are often instinctively very good at placing other speakers with precision in relation to their own speech community. Basically, people have always been interested in accents, and comments about how (other) people speak are as common as are comments about how people dress. Differences, or even similarities, at the level of the phonology, or even in phonetic detail, of the spoken output often lead to a judgement of the other either as a member of the same speech community or not. And yet, the factors which lead to such judgements, given that no accent can actually claim to be completely homogeneous or static, are poorly understood.

An understanding of variation as much more than a simple one-way indexical process where linguistic features act as a pointer to social group membership is starting to emerge. Variation is coming to be viewed as the result of a lively and ongoing dynamic interaction between a speech community and its language. In this view, individuals are actively engaged – whether consciously or subliminally so – in negotiating the ongoing shaping of language in ways which are meaningful to them (Eckert 2012).

Take, for example, the case of the unassuming postvocalic "r" in English. This has historically always been – and still remains – a litmus test for sociolinguistic variation. Romaine, writing in 1978, had already indicated that change in postvocalic "r" in Scottish English was in evidence. Picking up from this work, Stuart-Smith *et al.* (2007), report on variant use of this postvocalic "r" in Glaswegian English. The evidence indicates a trajectory of change noted first in younger working-class Glaswegian Scottish males: The well-recorded rhotic Scottish English is gradually becoming derhoticised, with contiguous vowel length also being affected. Further investigation shows a correlation between tongue position and sociolinguistic factors, with weaker rhotic variants noted in working-class speakers and strong rhoticity in middle-class females (Lawson *et al.* 2011). Stuart-Smith *et al.* (2007) note that their young participants were 'exploiting "non-local" variation in such a way that it is used, and seems to them to be, thoroughly local', providing further evidence for the notion that 'constructing identity through linguistic variation is crucially connected to the local context' (p. 222).

As humans interacting with each other, we have perhaps come to take such richness in speech for granted. We can tune in to important information carried in language whenever we need to, and we can also ignore the extra noise in order to focus more on the content of a message being conveyed, if necessary. However, the era we are navigating is one dictated by technological advances, where human–computer interaction is ever more present and evident in our daily lives requiring computational linguists to match the advances of smart technology which is increasingly offering ever more seamless interfaces between human and machine. As the drive for "hands-free" technology progresses, speech is likely to feature prominently in future advancements. Any number of entertaining memes serve to illustrate that we are not quite there yet, and this is in large part down to precisely the types of richness in human–human interaction described earlier. Nevertheless, the desire for such an interface is keenly felt (Olmstead 2017), with a 2018 survey conducted by Price Waterhouse Cooper in the United States reminding us in its preamble that 'voice is the future'. More bluntly, 'human machine interactions increasingly mimic human-human communication, and in some cases aim to substitute human socialization altogether' (Plaisance and Cruz 2019: 1).

The examples of variation referred to in this chapter are often based on the analysis of relatively small amounts of data involving small cohorts of speakers. However, the advantages of working with larger data samples, such as corpus-based studies would allow, are equally important in the drive towards better representation of speech communities and the range of variation that can be found there.

2 The spoken component in a sample of current corpora

The world of CL has already made efforts to recognise speech as a central part of any databank seeking to represent languages and language varieties. Here we consider some key corpora, starting with general corpora (Rühlemann 2019), which often include *a spoken component*, and moving on to dedicated spoken or speech corpora.

The term "speech corpus" is sometimes used 'to refer to multimedia corpora [which contain the actual speech signal and not just text transcripts] to distinguish them from others that are available in transcript form only or that contain sound recordings that are unsuitable for phonetic studies' (Lee 2010: 110). Nevertheless, the distinction is not clear-cut. Tognini Bonelli (2010: 25) suggests that speech corpora 'are built for the detailed study of individual sounds and phonetic features, and [therefore] do not need to be collected in natural situations', whilst Wichmann (2008: 187) cites the 'broad division between those researchers who focus on technological applications of speech research, and those whose focus is on the study of human language and communication for its own sake'. Clearly, the differences in intended use of a corpus are likely to impact on its ultimate shape.

A few words about the *British National Corpus* (BNC), a 100+-million-word corpus often still thought of as the gold standard in so far as general corpora of English go (see Chapter 4, this volume). The BNC continues to be the model often followed by those developing corpora for other languages or language varieties where considerations of balance and representativeness are concerned (see Chapters 3, 4 and 8, this volume). The spoken component of the BNC, estimated at around 10 per cent of the overall corpus, comprises demographically sampled (*spontaneous conversation*) and context-governed (*other text-types*) data (see Figure 20.1). The recently released spoken BNC, *Spoken BNC2014* (see Love *et al.* 2017: 334) comprises 11.5 million words. At the time of writing, the audio files are not yet available (for more on the BNC2014, see Chapter 39, this volume). When eventually made available, these files will be a great resource for the study of phonetic and phonological variation. In the meantime, as O'Keeffe and McCarthy (2010: 555) say, 'lack of accessibility of spoken data' continues to be an issue in corpus studies.

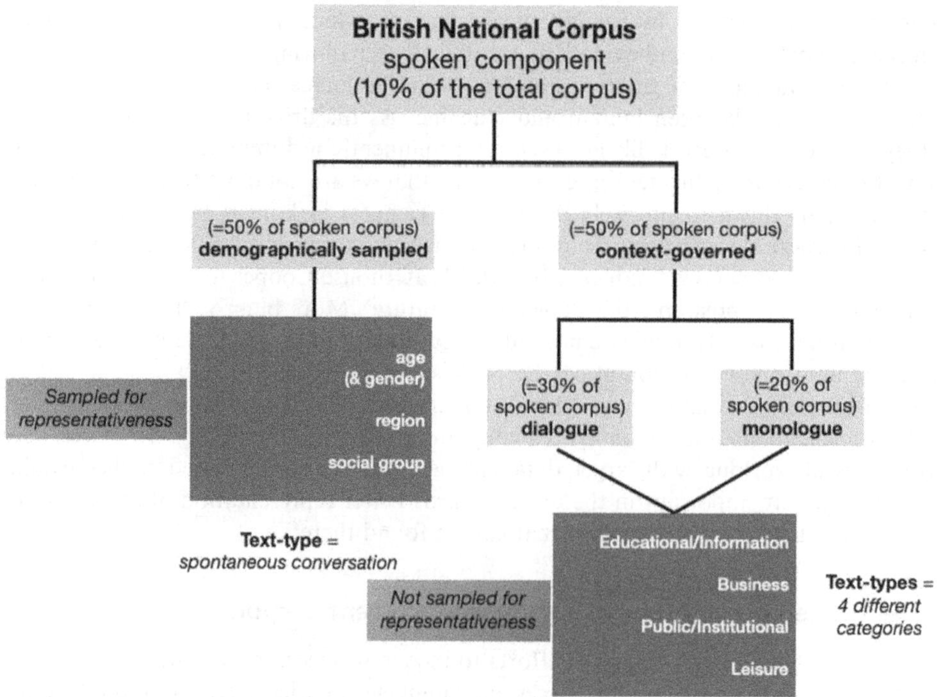

Figure 20.1 The composition of the spoken component of the BNC

A number of corpora designated as "national" follow, to some extent, the design of the BNC. We focus on a number of corpora for languages other than (different varieties of) English, using summary information provided in Chapter 8, this volume, as well as on the websites of the corpora described.

Like the BNC, many, although not all, "national" corpora start out with the intention of ensuring balance and representativeness, either through demographic sampling or by including different text-types in the corpus, or both. Consequently many, although not all, also include a spoken component, since speech is acknowledged to be an important element in linguistic behaviour.

A number of national corpora unapologetically accept from the start the necessity of relying on written data in order to be able to move forward on the important matter of building the corpus. These include the *Bulgarian National Corpus*, the *Hungarian National Corpus* and the *Thai National Corpus* see Table 20.1.

A number of national corpora contrast with this in that they do include a (small) spoken component. Three examples are the *National Corpus of Polish*, the *Turkish National Corpus* and the *Russian National Corpus*, listed in Table 20.2. Integrating a spoken component into a corpus requires that the spoken data be transcribed, at least orthographically, to create a text. Unfortunately, once a transcript to accompany the audio has been produced, it is often this text which gets included in the searchable part of the database. Of the corpora in this group, the *Corpus of Spoken Russian* is the only one which makes reference to inclusion, in the corpus, of the actual recordings. Transcripts included in the other corpora are treated in the same way as ordinary text, the goal being to search for 'the typical use of a single word or a phrase, as well as their

Table 20.1 General corpora and their spoken component

Name of corpus and when started/ developed	*Size (including by sub-corpora where relevant) and aims*	*Participants and/or text-types*	*Provenance and method of data collection*	*Types of transcription*
Bulgarian National Corpus- 2001–2009	1,200,000,000 words	Unspecified	Appears opportunistic	No mention of spoken component
Hungarian National Corpus- 1998–2002	187,600,000 words (original goal 100 m)	Different dialects, including dialects represented in text	Appears opportunistic	No mention of spoken component
Thai National Corpus	Unspecified size	Loosely follows BNC design	Opportunistic, mainly from available material in print	No spoken component

meaning and grammatical function' (http://nkjp.pl/index.php?page=0andlang=1). The spoken component in transcript form is then only different from other text-types in terms of structural differences, including the use of lexis.

Whilst a transcript to accompany the permanent record of samples of spoken language is important, the former is useless without the latter if the purpose is to examine phonetic and phonological variation in speech. Increasingly, the spoken component is not simply included in the corpus in the form of the transcripts which are searchable on the same basis as written texts. In many cases, the actual audio recordings too are being made available. Already with the Russian National Corpus, we see a nod to the importance of including recordings alongside transcripts in the corpus. Like this corpus, the *Slovak National Corpus* has a structure involving a collection of eight corpora (see Table 20.3). Of the two corpora which involve speech, those of relevance here are the spoken corpora which involve 'speech utterances and their transcriptions into standardized Slovak covering the whole territory of Slovakia' (https://korpus.sk/shk_en.html). Whilst still a meagre 5.5 million words compared to the 280 million words of written text, the latest version is nevertheless clearly intended to address the prevalent imbalance.

A "national" corpus which, like the Slovak National Corpus, includes a number of dedicated spoken corpora rather than one monolithic spoken component is the *Czech National Corpus*. Initially, this excellent example of a corpus of corpora was released mainly as written data; slowly, more and more spoken data also came to be released. Beginning with the *Prague Spoken Corpus* (*PSC*), recordings were initially restricted to the Prague area (Komrsková *et al.* 2017). A series of collections called *ORAL* (ORAL2006, 2008, 2013) followed. These consist of spontaneous conversations between family members and friends across the Czech Republic. Two further projects were carried out, *ORTOFON* and *DIALEKT* (Komrsková *et al.* 2017). Whereas only the

Table 20.2 Corpora with a spoken component and transcripts

Name of corpus and when started/ developed	*Size (including by sub-corpora where relevant) and aims*	*Participants and/or text-types*	*Provenance and method of data collection*	*Types of transcription*
National Corpus of Polish 2008–2012	Aim was to create a "reference corpus" of over 1500 m words	Variety of text-types	Appears opportunistic	Corpus includes transcripts - no audio
Turkish National Corpus 1990–2013	50 m words	Variety of text-types produced in different domains, on various topics	Appears opportunistic, but dedicated spoken data also collected	2 % of database is "transcriptions from spoken data", no audio
Russian National Corpus mid-eighteenth century 1930–2007	Over 300 m words	Mainly original prose, poetry including texts in non-standard modern Russian; spoken texts,	Opportunistic, from available material in print	N/A
	Corpus of Spoken Russian	speech, spontaneous and public, different genres/ and of different geographic origins; recordings of dialectal speech	Unspecified: includes transcripts of Russian movies	Transcripts of spoken material, including movies; some recordings

transcripts of the spoken data from the PSC, ORAL2006 and ORAL2008 collections made it into the corpus proper, an important change from the ORAL2013 collection onwards was inclusion of time-aligned transcripts alongside the recordings. This is a significant step forward. The time-aligned element is particularly useful, as it allows a researcher to start working with the spoken data using available speech analysis software without first needing to trawl through the transcript.

Let us look more closely at the onerous task of designing and building spoken corpora through a few examples. Take the *Australian National Database Of Spoken Language, ANDOSL*. Data were collected from carefully balanced phonologically defined speaker groups. The material consisted of highly controlled, phonetically rich, read material, and spontaneous, though task-oriented (Map Task), speech. High-quality studio recordings were made. Manual annotation at both word and phonemic levels was carried out by trained transcribers. Acoustic-phonetic level annotations reduced to the phonemic complexity level were used to train segmentation models, which were subsequently used to carry out automatic annotation.

Although ANDOSL appeared to satisfy the requirements of balance and representativeness at different levels (speakers and text-types), as well as quality of

Table 20.3 Corpora with a spoken component, transcripts and audio (in some cases time-aligned)

Name of corpus and when started/ developed	*Size (including by sub-corpora where relevant) and aims*	*Participants and/ or text-types*	*Provenance and method of data collection*	*Types of transcription*
Slovak National Corpus from 1955 onwards	280 m words in the *prim-9.0* version; contains various subcorpora, e.g.	Texts covering a range of language styles, genres, areas, regions	Unspecified	N/A
	Corpus of Spoken Slovak 5.5 m words in *s-hovor-6.0* version	760 recordings, c. 714 h of recorded utterances	Unspecified	Transcripts AND audio files which appear to be time-aligned
Czech National Corpus started in 1994	Currently over 3b words, corpus of corpora including a number of spoken corpora, e.g. • *Prague Spoken Corpus* • *ORAL2006* • *ORAL2008* • *ORAL2013* • *ORTOFON* • *DIALEKT*	Synchronic and diachronic corpora, both spoken and written	Unspecified, but see metadata at: https://wiki.korpus.cz/doku.php/en:cnk:uvod	N/A From ORAL2013, time-aligned transcripts included together with recordings

recording and accompanying annotations, it is, according to Estival (2015: 547), 'now outmoded'. The perception is that the number of speakers is small (108) and non-representative, with limited coverage of Australian English variation and limited tasks, recorded during one single session. The audio is viewed as 'low-fidelity by current standards'. The response of the Australian speech research community to these perceived gaps is the *AusTalk* audio-visual corpus, part of the *Big Australian Speech Corpus, Big ASC* project intended to establish the infrastructure, including recording equipment, for the collection of large quantities of spoken data 'from many locations across multiple sessions per speaker', as well as protocols for meta-data collection and storage in addition to annotation (Wagner *et al.* 2010: 166).

Size and participants

The written component of many general corpora is often sizable. Spoken corpora, by comparison, tend to be relatively small irrespective of whether they were designed to be stand-alone or part of a general corpus. The *Spoken English Corpus (SEC)* is an early spoken corpus consisting of '52,000 words of mostly prepared (and mostly monologic) southern British English speech' (http://martinweisser.org/corpora_site/spoken_corpora.html). Whilst still comparatively small at around 150,000 words, the *HCRC Map Task*

Corpus (Anderson *et al.* 1991) represents a much bigger effort. The unprepared speech in this case had to be transcribed. More recent examples of spoken corpora, though much larger, are still small in comparison to their written corpora counterparts (see the Slovak example earlier). Participants' background also continues to be important, if not to control for, at least to get information on. Many smaller corpora bypass the issue of representativeness by restricting participation to one type of profile. For example, SEC included data from speakers 'whose accent was as close to RP as possible' (http://korpus.uib.no/icame/manuals/SEC/COMP.HTM#2). Similarly, the specialised *Intonational Variation in English* (*IViE* corpus) includes adolescent speakers of nine urban varieties of English, balanced for gender. More recently, crowdsourcing is increasingly being seen as a viable method to address the issue of the size of the corpus, whilst also facilitating the collection of metadata or information on participant profiles. This avenue is a hopeful one, as demonstrated in the *Corpws Cenedlaethol Cymraeg Cyfoes – the National Corpus of Contemporary Welsh*, *CorCenCC* project, or the BNC2014, or the Big ASC.

Text-types

The spoken component of some of the earlier corpora ambitiously tried to ensure coverage of as wide as possible a range of different text-types (on similar lines to the context-governed part of the BNC). Conversely, some recent collections of spoken language (e.g. the Spoken BNC2014 and the various Czech spoken corpora) prioritise spontaneous conversation despite the obvious need, in the case of this text-type, for time and effort to be invested in creating an accompanying text. One way to bypass this hurdle is to use "read speech", which is essentially material written to be read aloud (Mena *et al.* 2020). Read speech comes with a ready text and although validation is sometimes needed, a substantial part of the usual pre-processing work can be avoided. Read speech also allows for direct comparability across speakers. It is, however, not at all useful for many linguistic analysis tasks, not least investigations into phonetic and phonological variation. Some collections, such as the HCRC Map Task Corpus, consist of quasi-spontaneous, task-oriented material which includes some possibilities for direct comparability across speakers. The compromise often resorted to by corpus developers is to collect data consisting of different text-types, including read speech data, which allows for direct comparability across speakers, on the one hand, and spontaneous conversation which needs to be transcribed, on the other.

Provenance and methods of data collection

Including as much opportunistic-type data as comes one's way is often seen as a relatively quick way to populate a corpus. It is easy to see how this works for corpora of written language. Good-quality recordings are, however, a crucial consideration in the case of corpora of spoken language, especially for the purposes of investigating different aspects of the phonetics and phonology of the language or language variety in question. Traditionally, this meant studio recordings, with all the restrictions involved. In more recent projects (e.g. the Spoken BNC2014, AusTalk and CorCenCC), a public participation in scientific research (PPSR) methodology, which exploits the improved audio recording capability of most smart phones, is being used. This methodology aims to 'strike a balance between high quality studio recording and field data collection' (Estival

2015: 547). Love (2020) compared data collected by volunteers using a dictaphone he provided, to data collected using volunteers' own smart phones. He concludes that 'there was no difference in the quality of the resulting audio recordings for the purpose of orthographic transcription'. He does, however, add that: 'One area of linguistic research which is likely to be excluded by this approach is phonetics. It is likely that only some, but not many, of the recordings produced by smartphones will be of sufficient quality for accurate phonetic analysis'. Whilst this "exclusion" is an important consideration, technology is advancing at speed, and therefore limitations of the past may become increasingly irrelevant as time goes by.

Levels of transcription

It is a fact that spoken data in audio (or video) format, without an accompanying written text, are not much use to anyone likely to use a spoken corpus. As a preliminary to preparing an orthographic transcript of a spoken text, a transcription scheme aimed at capturing in writing elements of speech for which no standard orthographic rendering is available also has to be developed (see Weisser 2016 and Chapters 2 and 3, this volume). In some cases, ad hoc systems of transcription may also need to be developed. Ernestus (2000: 554) refers to 'a dialectal, orthophonic transcription which is as close to the pronunciation as possible', which she used in the context of studies on dialectal variation. Furthermore, although a written version of a recording is also the prerequisite for any further transcription or annotation to be carried out, for the phonetician/phonologist, such a transcript is in fact only the beginning. Additional levels of transcription are often needed for different purposes. These could include the phonemic, broad and/or narrow phonetic, prosodic amongst others. Transcribing data at the level of prosody is particularly time consuming. Efforts in this direction such as the *Hong Kong Spoken Corpus* (Cheng *et al.* 2005) already exist, whilst similar endeavours, albeit usually on smaller corpora, continue.

More importantly, in order to be able to return to the data for continuing analysis, time-aligned segmentations to go with the transcriptions are a must. Using a programme such as PRAAT (Boersma and Weenick 2020) to segment and annotate spoken data is highly time-consuming. Systems can be trained to do forced alignment, but for this, training data consisting of spoken data, manually segmented to phone level, are needed. Therefore, especially in the case of less resourced languages, a fair amount of manual transcription at different levels is usually unavoidable.

In summary, spoken corpora minimally require reasonably good-quality audio (or video) data, including unscripted speech, together with an accompanying transcript. These requirements make spoken corpora time-consuming and costly to produce, thus resulting in corpora which tend to be relatively small.

3 Building a spoken corpus: the challenges of phonetic and phonological variation

Variation within the domains of phonetics and phonology infuses every aspect of language and speech with layer upon layer of meaning. It is so intimately interwoven into everything we say that in ordinary conversation we mostly ignore it until an unexpected element, like a new accent, comes up, at which point, we may tune in to work out what is going on (Grech 2015). The advantage of working within domains which have such widespread effects is that it is possible to work with any corpus at any level and discover something interesting. Tapping into existing corpora can prove to be a wonderful opportunity, no less for highlighting elements of potential interest in data which were not expressly conceived for the purposes of studying particular aspects of variation. Sometimes, the sheer scope of a large corpus, established on the basis of the criteria of balance and representativeness, is therefore a real opportunity. Identifying elements of variation at the levels of phonetics and/or phonology level can be a bit of a needle-in-a-haystack situation, however, in that it can be difficult to separate elements in data which are worthy of study from those which can be relegated to the status of mere 'noise'. When tapping into existing corpora "opportunistically", not only is there the reassurance that valuable resources are not being squandered on potential wild goose chases but the need to do the laborious data collection is also dispensed with.

As Cole and Hasegawa-Johnson (2012) suggest, being able to tap into readily available corpora undoubtedly saves both time and money, compared to what would be involved in building a dedicated corpus from scratch. Take, for example, a language internal problem such as phoneme mergers. One angle from which to approach such variation would involve trying to make sense of patterns in the speech community exhibiting evidence of such potential mergers. New Zealand English has been well documented, and Holmes and Bell (1992)) note an apparent reversal in the trend towards merging of the EAR and AIR diphthongs documented over the preceding half-century. The reversal seems to have been led chiefly by younger working-class women. One way to go about trying to account for such an observation would be to survey a wider array of data in search for a better understanding of the patterns at play, whilst also attempting to theorise about their development. Of course, the possibility of being able to tap into an already existing corpus or corpora would be an advantage.

In another study on phoneme mergers, Wedel *et al.* (2013) test the rather evasive hypothesis of functional load (Hockett 1967) as a theory to account for which phonemes might or might not merge in a language. This hypothesis posits that pairs or groups of phonemes which contrast in a given language are less likely to merge compared to those phonemes which are non-contrastive in that language. Phonemes which contribute significantly to the information content of a language are therefore unlikely to be modified or lost over time. The authors note that the hypothesis has been difficult to confirm because, prior to the availability of (phonemically transcribed) corpora, collecting and transcribing data from multiple languages for the purposes of comparison would have been an impossible task. Access to corpora of seven languages changed this, allowing for the testing of the functional load hypothesis as a predictor of phoneme merger across these languages, each of which 'is represented by a phonemically-transcribed word list from a published corpus' (Wedel *et al.* 2013: 180). A corpus-based study in this case was effective given that it dispensed with the necessity for the researchers to carry out their own data collection and related pre-processing work.

In contrast to this, O'Sullivan recalls (2019) that the idea of variation does not always sit comfortably with a large body of data which, by definition, risks being somewhat static (although see, e.g. Wagner *et al.* 2010, on the crowdsourcing infrastructure put in place in the case of the Big ASC). Cole and Hasegawa-Johnson (2012) note:

> In order to explore the variable phonetic substance of phonological elements, and the influence of phonetics in shaping sound patterns, the phonologist must go beyond the analysis of citation forms of words produced in isolation…The challenge

> arises from the inherent variability in the phonetic realization of a word, which can make it difficult to identify a unique description of its core phonetic properties.
>
> *(Cole and Hasegawa-Johnson 2012: 433)*

For example, imagine we wanted to investigate whether Maltese speakers of English (who may not have an /æ/ phoneme in their repertoire) are more likely to opt for a more /a/-like vowel rather than a more /e/-like one. Such variation is likely to be continuous rather than discrete, and occurrences of the target sound may not be that straightforward to retrieve; the requirements that a corpus is likely to need to fulfil at the design and the mark-up stages are, accordingly, not insignificant. Fricke *et al.* (2016) highlight some of these complexities in a multi-faceted study designed to investigate some of the phonetic cues which bilingual speakers and listeners may negotiate while codeswitching. On the one hand, a large representative corpus allows the researcher room to sift through a large volume of data in order to identify elements of relevance. The Fricke *et al.* (2016) study seeks to uncover some of the ways in which 'phonetic variation in the speech of habitual codeswitchers reveals multiple ways in which bilingual language regulation impacts the surface form of spoken language' (p. 120). Speech rate and voice onset time (VOT) are two cues to an upcoming switch between English and Spanish which were examined. The speech rate analysis required retrieval of utterances with evidence of codeswitching which were then time measured against non-codeswitched counterparts. No fine-grained phonetic analysis was required here. Speech rate was shown to slow down in codeswitched utterances and often leading up to nouns, suggesting that difficulties with lexical retrieval may be an important motivator for codeswitching. The VOT analysis was a little more difficult to set up. At the initial stages 60 per cent of the eligible data were discarded due to problems with the data, which included overlapped speech and poor sound quality. With the remaining tokens being too small for any statistically relevant analysis, the corpus was then processed manually by a research assistant, who hand-labelled all the available tokens for VOT. These two aspects of a corpus-based study indicate some of the different challenges presented by phonetic and phonological analysis, particularly when working with already existing corpora.

4 Building a spoken corpus: the technical challenges

Let us assume, then, that while in some cases, it is useful to tap into already existing corpora working within the parameters of CL, namely, driving towards ecologically valid and representative bodies of data, investigations of phonetic and phonological variation may sometimes need to draw on much more specialised and purposely designed corpora. One of the main concerns often hovers around whether to collect speech samples which are clean, noise-free and recorded under lab conditions, or more naturally occurring speech which will be noisy, cluttered and therefore more challenging to transcribe, annotate and analyse. The last 20 years have seen the publication of numerous robust and principled studies which have all first grappled with the choice of data before going on to the actual study. Using CL methodology, a corpus which has not been designed with phonetic analysis in mind is likely to require a considerable amount of the data to be discarded (Schuppler *et al.* 2008; Fricke *et al.* 2016). More categorically, Love *et al.* (2017: 334):

> explicitly exclude the study of phonetics (segmental or prosodic) from the list of areas that the [Spoken BNC2014] corpus caters for...[since] most phonetic research typically requires both (i) access to high-quality audio recordings and (ii) full phonetic transcription, neither of which was a possibility within the constraints of this project.

Even in cases where a corpus is expressly designed for phonetic and phonological variation analysis, the process required to arrive at machine-ready data is likely to be lengthy. We are currently undertaking this process in order to establish a repository for Maltese English (MaltE) which we will take as an example here.

Maltese is a language spoken by roughly half a million people, and MaltE has gradually become established as a distinct variety of English following extended contact between Maltese and English during colonial and ensuing expat settlement since 1800 (Vella 2012). Maltese, a language with a limited digital presence, and MaltE, a lesser known variety of English, both count as under-resourced. Researchers in both have been working to keep up with a technology revolution which, along with promising to democratise knowledge, still has a way to go in ensuring that native speakers can access information in their own languages.

Automatic speech recognition (ASR) can be an important support in preparing a corpus for machine-ready searchability and analysis. ASR programs are useful in converting speech to text, even if some manual correction may still be necessary. The first ASR system for Maltese is currently being developed (https://www.um.edu.mt/projects/masri/). There is a bit of a chicken-and-egg situation here, since annotated spoken data to train the system is still lacking (although see Vella and Farrugia 2006). A corpus specifically designed to address this need has been collected, where spoken data are based on highly controlled read speech samples, with a methodology for data collection which involves crowdsourcing (Mena *et al.* 2020). The situation is somewhat rosier in the case of MaltE, since, in this case, free tools for dictation to text designed for use with other varieties of English often work reasonably well also for MaltE.

In the case of both Maltese and MaltE, there is still a long way to go before any packages can be considered useful to facilitate the first stage of transcription at various levels, although a number of promising avenues to explore present themselves. Starting from an orthographic transcription, forced alignment programmes such as MAUS (Kisler *et al.* 2017), trained on a number of different varieties of English, work reasonably well for MaltE, Some manual correction is necessary, but not too much. A Maltese model has been incorporated into MAUS, although this has not been trained on Maltese data. Also promising at the level of creation of a preliminary orthographic transcription from naturally occurring speech, at least for MaltE, is the possibility of using subtitling features currently being trialled on platforms like YouTube as well for this variety. No such possibility is yet available for Maltese.

While inroads have been made and the future is exciting, none of the approaches outlined here as yet match the level of detail needed for working fully with phonetic and phonological variation given that it is at these levels that much of the indexical, dialect-specific or even speech community–relevant information is found. We nevertheless share Wagner *et al.*'s (2010) optimism on the opening up of possibilities to use big data corpora to examine variation at the levels of regional, ethnocultural and social speech style differences, as well as change over time. The good news is that a CL approach also enables the development of the technologies which, whilst much needed to accompany us into the future, will also feed into enhancing speech research of the kind we have been discussing.

5 Using spoken corpora to investigate variation in speech: ways forward

There is no shying away from the inescapable fact that CL was conceived within a heavily written text orientation. CL has grown in tandem with the awareness that the brand-new information age means lots of data, language and text. Linguists developing the first (electronic) corpora, however, inevitably remained true to their roots in a discipline which constantly reminds us of the primacy of speech and set about determining how best to incorporate spoken language at least into those corpora aiming to be more broadly representative of speech communities or languages. Nevertheless, the fact remains that corpora did not originally set out to deal with speech. It has not been an easy journey to work our way back to speech from writing, but we are starting to make some serious progress now. It is one of those cases where the knowledge built upon the journey is as valuable as the destination.

Further reading

Durand, J., Gut, U. and Kristoffersen, G. (eds) (2019) *The Oxford Handbook of Corpus Phonology*, Oxford: Oxford University Press. (A good place to go for an in-depth understanding of phonological analysis with a basis in CL. Delais-Roussarie and Post [Chapter 4] discuss issues also raised in this chapter. Also dealt with are applied studies in CL and phonology, methodology and key corpora designed for doing phonology.)

Ide, N. and Pustejovsky, J. (eds) (2017) *The Handbook of Linguistic Annotation*, Dordrecht: Springer. (A detailed description of the annotation of AusTalk by Cassidy, Estival and Cox. pp. 1287–302. The Handbook itself is an excellent resource for everything about annotation, its development, tools and techniques and current state-of-the-art.)

Walker, J. A. (2012) *Variation in Linguistic Systems*, London: Routledge. (An interesting perspective on variationist studies, discussing fieldwork and data analysis issues of relevance to the CL approach. Chapter 5 in particular discusses variation as a language-internal phenomenon, situating it within the speech community, whilst also dealing with sound change.)

References

Anderson, A. H., Bader, M., Bard, E. G., Boyle, E. H., Doherty, G. M., Garrod, S. C., Isard, S. D., Kowtko, J. C., McAllister, J. M., Miller, J., Sotillo, C. F., Thompson, H. S. and Weinert, R. (1991) 'The HCRC Map Task Corpus', *Language and Speech* 34(4): 351–66.

Boersma, P. and Weenick, D. (2020) *Praat: Doing Phonetics by Computer* Version 6.1.22, (Computer software), retrieved 24 September 2020 from: http://www.praat.org.

Besacier, L., Barnard, E., Karpov, A. and Schultz, T. (2014) 'Automatic Speech Recognition for Under-Resourced Languages: A Survey', *Speech Communication* 56: 85–100.

Cheng, W., Greaves, C. and Warren, M. (2005) 'The Creation of a Prosodically Transcribed Intercultural Corpus: The Hong Kong Corpus of Spoken English (Prosodic)', *ICAME Journal* 29: 47–68.

Cole, J. and Hasegawa-Johnson, M. (2012) 'Corpus Phonology with Speech Resources', in A. Cohn, C. Fougeron and M. Huffman (eds) *Handbook of Laboratory Phonology*, Oxford: Oxford University Press, pp. 431–40.

Durand, J. (2017) 'Corpus Phonology', in M. Aronoff (ed.), *Oxford Research Encyclopedia of Linguistics*, Oxford: Oxford University Press, pp. 1–20.

Eckert, P. (2012) 'Three Waves of Variation Study: The Emergence of Meaning in the Study of Linguistic Variation', *Annual Review of Anthropology* 41(1): 87–100.

Ernestus, M. (2000) *Voice Assimilation and Segment Reduction in Casual Dutch: A Corpus-Based Study of the Phonology-Phonetics Interface*, unpublished PhD thesis, University of Amsterdam.

Ernestus, M. and Warner, N. (2011) 'An Introduction to Reduced Pronunciation Variants', *Journal of Phonetics* 39 (3): 253–60.

Estival, D. (2015) 'AusTalk and Alveo: An Australian Corpus and Human Communication Science Collaboration Down Under', in N. Gala, R. Rapp and G. Bel-Enguix (eds) *Language Production, Cognition and The Lexicon*, London: Springer, pp. 545–60.

Fricke, M., Kroll, J. F. and Dussias, P. E. (2016) 'Phonetic Variation in Bilingual Speech: A Lens For Studying the Production-Comprehension Link', *Journal of Memory and Language* 89: 110–37.

Giles, H., Coupland, N. and Coupland, J. (1991) 'Accommodation Theory: Communication, Context, and Consequence', in H. Giles, N. Coupland and J. Coupland (eds) *Contexts of Accommodation: Developments in Applied Sociolinguistics*, Cambridge: Cambridge University Press, pp. 1–68.

Grech, S. (2015) *Variation in English: Perception and Patterns in the Identification of Maltese English*, unpublished PhD thesis, University of Malta, Institute of Linguistics.

Hockett, C. F. (1967) 'The Quantification of Functional Load', *Word* 23(1–3): 300–20.

Holmes, J. and Bell, A. (1992) 'On Shear Markets and Sharing Sheep: The Merger of EAR and AIR Diphthongs in New Zealand English', *Language Variation and Change* 4(3): 251–73.

Kisler, T., Reichel, U. D. and Shiel, F. (2017) 'Multilingual Processing of Speech Via Web Services', *Computer Speech and Language* 45: 326–47.

Komrsková, Z., Kopřivová, M., Lukeš, D., Poukarová, P. and Goláňova, H. (2017) 'New Spoken Corpora of Czech: Ortofon and Dialekt', *Journal of Linguistics* 68(2): 219–28.

Lawson, E., Scobbie, J. M. and Stuart-Smith, J. (2011) 'The Social Stratification of Tongue Shape for Postvocalic /r/ in Scottish English', *Journal of Sociolinguistics* 15(2): 256–68.

Lee, D. Y. W. (2010) 'What Corpora are Available?' in A. O'Keeffe and M. J. McCarthy (eds) *The Routledge Handbook of Corpus Linguistics*, London: Routledge, pp. 107–21.

Lieberman, M. (2019) 'Corpus Phonetics', *Annual Review of Linguistics* 5(1): 91–107.

Love, R. (2020) *Overcoming Challenges in Corpus Construction: The Spoken British National Corpus 2014*, London: Routledge.

Love, R., Dembry, C., Hardie, A., Brezina, V. and McEnery, T. (2017) 'The Spoken BNC2014: Designing and Building a Spoken Corpus of Everyday Conversations', *International Journal of Corpus Linguistics* 22(3): 319–44.

Mena, C. D., Gatt, A., DeMarco, A., Borg, C., van der Plas, L., Muscat, A. and Padovani, I. (2020) 'MASRI-HEADSET: A Maltese Corpus for Speech Recognition', Proceedings of the *12th Conference on Language Resources and Evaluation* (LREC 2020), Marseille, 11–16th May 2020, pp. 6381–8.

Nordquist, R. (2019) 'A Definition of Speech Community in Sociolinguistics', Retrieved from https://www.thoughtco.com/speech-community-sociolinguistics-1692120, 11 June 2020.

O'Keeffe, A. and McCarthy, M. J. (eds) (2010) *The Routledge Handbook of Corpus Linguistics*, London: Routledge.

Olmstead, K. (2017) 'Nearly Half of Americans Use Digital Voice Assistants, Mostly on their Smartphones', Pew Research Center, PwC, United States. Retrieved from https://www.pwc.com/us/en/services/consulting/library/consumer-intelligence-series/voice-assistants.html, 28 June 2020.

O'Sullivan, J. (2019) *Corpus Linguistics and the Analysis of Sociolinguistic Change: Language Variety and Ideology in Advertising*, London: Routledge.

Plaisance, P. L. and Cruz, J. (2019) 'The Incorporation of Moral-Development Language for Machine-Learning Companion Robots', in D. Wittkower (ed.), *2019 Computer Ethics - Philosophical Enquiry (CEPE) Proceedings*, https://digitalcommons.odu.edu/cepe_proceedings/vol2019/iss1/18.

Romaine, S. (1978) 'Postvocalic /r/ in Scottish English: Sound Change in Progress?', in P. Trudgill (ed.) *Sociolinguistic Patterns in British English*, London: Edward Arnold, pp. 144–58.

Rühlemann, C. (2019) *Corpus Linguistics for Pragmatics: A Guide for Research*, London: Routledge.

Schuppler, B., Ernestus, M., Scharenborg, O. and Boves, L. (2008) 'Preparing a Corpus of Dutch Spontaneous Dialogues for Automatic Phonetic Analysis', Proceedings of the 9th *Annual Conference of the International Speech Communication Association, INTERSPEECH 2008*, Brisbane, Australia, 1638–41.

Stuart-Smith, J., Timmins, C. and Tweedie, F. (2007) '"Talking Jockney"? Variation and Change in Glaswegian Accent', *Journal of Sociolinguistics* 11(2): 221–60.

Tognini Bonelli, E. (2010) 'The Evolution of Corpus Linguistics', in A. O'Keeffe and M. J. McCarthy (eds) *The Routledge Handbook of Corpus Linguistics*, London: Routledge, pp. 14–27.

Vella, A. (2012) 'Languages and Language Varieties in Malta' *International Journal of Bilingual Education and Bilingualism* 16(5): 532–52.

Vella, A. and Farrugia, P.-J. (2006) 'MalToBI - Building an Annotated Corpus of Spoken Maltese', *Proceedings of Speech Prosody 2006*, Dresden: Germany.

Wagner, M., Tran, D., Togneri, R., Rose, P., Powers, D., Onslow, M., Loakes, D., Lewis, T., Kuratate, T., Kinoshita, Y., Kemp, N., Ishihara, S., Ingram, J. Hajek, J. Grayden, D., Goecke, R., Fletcher, J., Estival, D., Epps, J., Dale, R., Cutler, A., Cox, F., Chetty, G., Cassidy, S., Butcher, A., Burnham, D., Bird, S., Best, C., Bennamoun, M., Arciuli, J. and Ambikairajah, E. (2010) 'The Big Australian Speech Corpus (The Big ASC)', Proceedings of the *13th Australasian International Conference on Speech Science and Technology*, Melbourne, Australia, pp. 166–70.

Wedel, A., Kaplan, A. and Jackson, S. (2013) 'High Functional Load Inhibits Phonological Contrast Loss: A Corpus Study', *Cognition* 128(2): 179–86.

Weisser, M. (2016) *Practical Corpus Linguistics: An Introduction to Corpus-Based Language Analysis*, West Sussex, UK: Wiley-Blackwell.

Wichmann, A. (2008) 'Speech Corpora and Spoken Corpora' in A. Lüdeling and M. Kytö (eds) *Corpus Linguistics: An International Handbook*, Vol. 1. Berlin/New York: Mouton de Gruyter, pp. 187–207.

Part III

Corpora, language pedagogy and language acquisition

21

What can a corpus tell us about language teaching?

Winnie Cheng and Phoenix Lam

1 Corpora and language teaching

Corpora and language teaching can best be introduced by Fligelstone's (1993) three-tiered model of teaching about corpora, teaching to exploit corpora and exploiting corpora to teach. Teaching about corpora refers to teaching corpus linguistics as an academic subject, teaching to exploit corpora introduces students to different methods and tasks to exploit corpora for learning purposes and exploiting corpora to teach involves using 'a corpora-approach to inform teaching' (Huang 2018: 383). Renouf (1997) adds a fourth tier, which is teaching to establish resources, and this involves learner participation in corpus data collection, corpus design and corpus compilation.

Another way of looking at the relation between corpora and language learning is Leech's (1997) distinction between indirect and direct corpus applications in pedagogy. While indirect corpus applications mostly involve corpus-based studies informing syllabus design, material writing and creation of reference tools, such as wordlists, dictionaries and grammars, direct corpus applications involve teachers and learners working with corpora in the classroom; direct access to corpora by learners spreads along a deductive-inductive cline, and at times the inductive and deductive approaches are combined in practice.

A form of direct corpus application is "data-driven learning" (DDL), proposed by Johns (1991), in which language learners can be simultaneously active learners and language researchers accessing corpus data directly. DDL is 'a learner-focused approach which promotes learners' discovery of linguistic patterns of use and meaning by examining extensive samples of attested uses of language' (Pérez-Paredes *et al.* 2019: 145). It involves 'using the tools and techniques of corpus linguistics for pedagogical purposes' (Gilquin and Granger 2010: 359). Gilquin and Granger (2010) summarise a few advantages of the DDL approach. These include bringing authenticity to the classroom, serving a major corrective function when learners compare their own writing with a corpus of expert writing or an error-annotated learner corpus and offering discovery learning which is potentially motivating and fun. O'Sullivan (2007: 277) proposes the potential acquisition or refining of a range of micro-cognitive skills through the DDL

DOI: 10.4324/9780367076399-21

approach, including 'predicting, observing, noticing, thinking, reasoning, analysing, interpreting, reflecting, exploring, making inferences (inductively or deductively), focusing, guessing, comparing, differentiating, theorising, hypothesising, and verifying'.

Recent research using DDL in language teaching and learning finds that it is generally effective and efficient (Boulton and Cobb 2017; Lee *et al.* 2019; Pérez-Paredes 2019) and receives positive feedback from learners (Chambers 2019). The use of corpora in DDL in English for academic purposes (EAP) has increased significantly in the past ten years (see Chapters 24, 28, 29 and 30, this volume), but few studies have examined the use of corpora by doctoral students during their thesis writing process (Charles 2018) and by secondary school students (Boulton and Pérez-Paredes 2014).

Still another way of looking at corpora and language teaching is the different ways in which teachers and learners, acting as corpus researchers, exploit corpora. Meunier and Reppen (2015), citing Tognini-Bonelli (2001), compare a corpus-driven and a corpus-based approach. The corpus in a corpus-driven approach 'serves as an empirical basis from which researchers extract their data and detect linguistic phenomena without [too many] [*our addition*] prior assumptions and expectations (Tognini-Bonelli 2001)', with the conclusions being 'drawn exclusively on the basis of corpus observations'; in contrast, in a corpus-based approach, 'linguistic information (frequencies, collocations, etc.) is extracted from a corpus to check expectations or confirm linguistic theories' (Meunier and Reppen 2015: 499).

In addition, Meunier and Reppen (2015) describe a "corpus-informed" approach, which comprises the following features:

- The inclusion of results, conclusions and discoveries from research carried out on a variety of corpora (e.g. native or learner corpora, spoken or written, from different genres, produced by expert or novice writers/ speakers);
- The selection of what exactly should be included (e.g. structures, vocabulary, contexts of use, collocational and colligational patterns, frequency);
- The decisions linked to the presentation of the corpus information (e.g. text, graphs, concordances, data-driven approach, other);
- When the materials focus on skills, the selection of suitable texts (oral or written) as a prompt for instruction.

(Meunier and Reppen 2015: 499)

In Poole's (2016) study conducted in a university in the United States, L2 writing was taught to develop 'rhetorical awareness and the understanding of the interrelation between language, rhetorical purpose, and context' (p. 101). A 'corpus-aided approach' was adopted, where it was the teacher who prepared the corpus data and materials, and students did not 'use a corpus program, perform a corpus query, or generate a single concordance line' (p. 103). Instead, the teacher mediated between the corpus materials and the students and assisted in the contextualisation of findings.

As noted by Chambers (2019), in the past decade, a number of studies have reviewed the development of the field of corpora and language learning, in particular DDL. Examples are narrative reviews of different topics and methods and the history of development (e.g. Boulton 2017); two meta-analyses of empirical, quantitative studies of DDL (Cobb and Boulton 2015; Boulton and Cobb 2017); one meta-study of corpora and vocabulary acquisition (Lee *et al.* 2019); one review of the uses and spread of corpora and DDL in CALL research (Pérez-Paredes 2019); and special issues on the role of corpora in two main journals in CALL, namely *The Journal of the European Association for Computer Assisted Language Learning* (ReCALL) (2014) and *Language Learning & Technology* (LLT) (2017). Callies and Götz (2015) point out that the use of corpora and corpus linguistics tools and methods has proven to be beneficial, especially for assessing L2 proficiency; however, such use is relatively new in the area of language testing and assessment.

The remainder of this chapter reviews the literature in three areas related to corpora and language teaching. First, corpus methods in language teaching are concerned with what corpus linguistics concepts, tools and techniques are involved in or applied to language teaching. Second, corpus evidence as teaching materials focuses on indirect applications or use of corpora in producing teaching and research resources such as dictionaries, grammars, course books and vocabulary lists. Third, corpus tasks for language teaching focus on direct applications or use of corpora by teachers, as well as learners, for a range of pedagogical purposes. The chapter ends with a discussion about future directions and areas for further research and practice.

2 Corpus methods in language teaching

Corpus methods in language teaching are related to basic corpus linguistics concepts and corpus tools and techniques that are involved in, or applied to, language teaching. They also beg the question of some key issues that teachers should consider when applying corpus methods to language teaching.

A review of recent research shows that the main corpus methods applied in language teaching are concordancing and word frequency counting. Hyland (2003) describes two uses of concordancing, namely a research tool for L2 writers to systematically investigate a specific linguistic item or phenomenon and infer underlying rules and a reference tool for L2 writers to consult to find immediate solutions to linguistic problems encountered when they are writing. Concordancing is performed by a concordancer, which is a typical tool for language learners to get access to a corpus and provide learners with a variety of language learning affordances (Flowerdew 2015) (see Chapters 9, 10 and 14, this volume).

Research in corpora and language teaching has examined different uses and purposes of concordancing. Huang (2014) discusses the use of concordancing for Chinese university students majoring in English to learn about the collocational and colligational patterns of abstract nouns. In Boulton and Cobb's (2017) meta-analysis of 64 experimental and quasi-experimental quantitative studies which examine the effectiveness of using corpus linguistics tools and techniques for second language learning or use, DDL is found to be most effective with a hands-on concordancer, with some key advantages including exposure to authentic language, identification of common patterns of language and promotion of learner autonomy. By contrast, Lee *et al.* (2019) find that purposefully curated concordance lines, rather than a hands-on concordancer, are more effective for learners and when learning materials and hands-on corpus practice are arranged concurrently. It should be noted, however, that Lee *et al.* (2019) only focus on vocabulary and measure the effect size through a quantitative approach different from that adopted in Boulton and Cobb (2017).

Learner concordance use, according to Charles (2018), is the focus of most DDL work, although most corpus software also offers other tools such as clusters, collocates, n-grams, concordance plots, wordlists and keyword lists, which tend to be under-used in

DDL. Charles (2018) highlights that different tools in *AntConc* allow learners to address different learning issues. Wordlists, n-grams and keyword lists, for example, require no user input and thus can identify potentially problematic issues which are unknown to the learners. For concordances, clusters, collocates and concordance plots, issues or problems which are already known to the learners can be addressed. Charles (2018) also explains the ways in which these tools can be used for editing purposes at the levels of content and organisation. Of all the *AntConc* tools introduced to the doctoral students, concordance was rated most highly, followed by clusters, collocates and keyword lists. It is argued that 'attention to the affordances of all available corpus tools is needed if corpus pedagogy is to realise its full potential as a valuable approach for language learning' (Charles 2018: 24).

Sha (2010) describes the characteristics of a search engine to be used in DDL, as follows:

- Should be capable of providing as many authentic usages and expressions as needed;
- Should be simple to use; the user does not have to learn complicated query syntax;
- Should guarantee a high search speed;
- Can be simultaneously used by thousands of students;
- Should require no registration or client installation;
- Should be cost-effective in the long run.

(Sha 2010: 382)

The student teachers in Ebrahimi and Faghih's (2016) study found that some corpus tools are more useful for language teachers and researchers than for learners. For *Lextutor*, the text-based concordances and n-gram phrase extractor tools are considered too technical for learners, whereas the Vocabprofile tool is considered useful for teachers for analysing learners' writing. For *AntConc*, while respondents felt that it could assist teachers in correcting learners' writing, they found it suitable only for adult learners with a high level of English proficiency.

In Yoon's (2016) study of concordancers and dictionaries as problem-solving tools for English as a second language (ESL) academic writing, a reference suite (RS) was developed. The RS is a mini web browser that allows free access to five concordancers and three types of dictionaries. The concordancers are *Corpus of Contemporary American English*, *Google* search engines, *Google Scholar* (GS), *Custom Search Engine* (CSE) and *JustTheWord* (JTW). The dictionaries are *Naver* (an online bilingual Korean-English/English-Korean dictionary), LDOCE (an online version of the *Longman Dictionary of Contemporary English*) and Thesaurus (Roget's 21st Century Thesaurus). The purpose of Yoon's (2016: 212) study was to examine 'the potential of the reference suite as a cognitive tool that extends the cognitive powers of L2 writers and mediates their problem solving while writing'. Research data were collected by getting students to record 'their writing processes using screen capture software' (p. 215) while working on the assignment, followed by 'a stimulated recall session' (p. 216). Results from the study showed that the reference suite was indeed effective as a cognitive tool, especially for helping learners with lexical and grammatical problems, though different learning goals and needs had to be taken into account to capitalise on its use.

Research has also examined the use of multimodal corpora and multimodal resources and tools for DDL. Meunier (2020) presents useful examples of tools to be used for DDL, including some multimodal resources (e.g. *PlayPhrase.me, LyricsTraining*). A new development has taken place combining 'mobile-assisted language learning (MALL)' and DDL (Pérez-Paredes *et al.* 2019: 145). As observed by Pérez-Paredes *et al.* (2019), despite the affordances of individualisation and personalisation of MALL, an integration of MALL and DDL has not yet been widely explored. The researchers conducted an evaluation study involving the creation and use of a self-created mobile language learning app, with the objective of exploring 'the opportunities and challenges of mobile DDL for language learners, teachers, and developers' (p. 148). Participants were learners of English, German and Spanish aiming to achieve an A2 or a B2 proficiency level, with reference to the Common European Framework of Reference (CEFR or CEF). The app was designed to improve the learners' writing skills by 'offering context-driven information through word frequency and vocabulary analysis' and to further help improve writing by 'providing lexical alternatives' (p. 148). The app used freely accessible natural language processing (NLP) tools, namely *Lextutor* for English (Cobb 2003), with 'a text analyser, a vocabulary profiler, and a part-of-speech tagger' (p. 148). After a learner's text had been analysed, improvement could be made by exploring corpus-based reference tools, namely the *Collins Dictionary*, *Netspeak* and *Stands4*, in the areas of 'definitions, synonyms, and example sentences' (p. 148).

While Ballance (2016) observes a long history of using computer-generated concordances for language learning, Ballance (2017) notes that concordancing has not been widely used in mainstream language learning contexts, possibly due to difficulty in interpreting the short, truncated keyword in context (KWIC) format, insufficient teacher training in this area, limited access to technological resources and conflict between the cognitive demands of concordance use and language learning. Chen and Flowerdew (2018) describe criticisms of corpus applications in language classrooms, including the decontextualisation of truncated concordance lines and the amount of time investment.

With regard to collocations (see Chapters 9, 14 and 15, this volume), they can be a challenging area for L2 learners because they contain 'some element of grammatical or lexical unpredictability or inflexibility' (Nation 2001: 324). Ackerman and Chen's (2013) study shows that the productive use of collocations is particularly challenging, and learners make mistakes concerning collocation in translation, rely on only a small number of collocations and use inappropriate synonyms. These issues may arise from L1 influence and require a high level of collocational competence for them to be addressed (Ackerman and Chen 2013).

3 Corpus evidence as teaching materials

The indirect applications of corpora in pedagogy are most common in the creation of dictionaries and grammars, and to a lesser extent in the design of course books and other supplementary materials. It has been remarked that the use of corpora in these teaching resources is so normalised that users may not actually know what a corpus is (Frankenberg-Garcia 2012) or may be unconscious of the role of corpora as a technology in motivating the paradigm change from a rule-based to an evidence-based approach to language teaching (Chambers 2019). In comparison, the influence of corpora in syllabus design and language assessment has not been well-documented thus far, though a small number of examples have suggested promising potential in these areas, such as McCarten and McCarthy (2010) (for more on the influence of corpora in syllabus design, see Chapters 25 and 26, this volume).

In dictionary making, the incorporation of corpus evidence has become mainstream since the first corpus-based dictionary, the *Collins Cobuild English Dictionary* (Sinclair 1995), was produced. Today, corpora are an indispensable item in a dictionary compiler's toolkit, and many major publishers have their own in-house corpora for this purpose. The use of corpora in dictionary-making provides important contents for entries such as frequency information, real-world examples and patterns of use (see Chapter 27, this volume). As such, corpora used in dictionary compilations are often very large in size. The *Macmillan English Dictionary*, for example, makes use of a general corpus now containing almost 1.6 billion words of written and spoken English as a basis for language description (Rundell 2020). Its online counterpart, MacmillanDictionary.com, is based on the World English Corpus, which is composed of 220 million words of written and spoken text from a variety of social and geographical contexts (Macmillan 2020).

In addition to general corpora, specialised corpora have increasingly been built and used to provide more specific empirical analyses, as well as to identify areas of interest for target audiences. The *Longman Language Activator*, produced in 1993, was the first dictionary to draw on the analysis of learner corpus data for its design. More recently, the *Cambridge Learner Corpus*, as part of the *Cambridge International Corpus*, is a 50-million-word collection of anonymised exam scripts produced by learners of English worldwide, which has been used for describing common problems in learner dictionaries compiled by the publisher (Cambridge University Press 2020). Another teaching-oriented corpus applied to dictionary making is the *Macmillan Curriculum Corpus*, which consists of 20 million words collected from school textbooks and examination syllabuses and has been used in the production of the *Macmillan School Dictionary* and *Macmillan Study Dictionary* (Rundell 2020). Corpus evidence has also been applied to the making of bilingual dictionaries and dictionaries of other languages, including the *Oxford-Hachette French-English Dictionary* and the *Frequency Dictionary of Czech* (Frekvencnı Slovnık Cestiny).

Like dictionaries, almost all grammars are to some extent corpus-based (Boulton and Pérez-Paredes 2014). Examples of major reference grammars are the *Longman Grammar of Spoken and Written English (LGSWE)* (Biber *et al.* 1999) and the *Cambridge Grammar of English* (Carter and McCarthy 2006), both of which provide descriptions of the use of English in both its written and spoken forms instead of simply focusing on the written language, as was customary in traditional grammar (see Chapters 16 and 25, this volume). Studies have shown that grammar books not based on corpus findings do not reflect authentic language use. Meunier and Reppen (2015), for example, demonstrate that crucial information on the passive voice is missing in non-corpus-informed ELT grammar materials. They argue that the description of some language features would particularly benefit from the incorporation of corpus findings, including the passive, the conditionals, relative clauses and aspect.

In language course book production, the role of corpora seems more contentious (see Chapter 26, this volume). While McCarten and McCarthy (2010: 13) remark that an ELT course book without corpus evidence is 'conspicuous' and cite a number of examples influenced by the use of corpora, including *face2face* and *Objective First Certificate*, Boulton (2010: 537) comments that corpora are often made 'invisible' in the presentation of course book content, even when the most well-known corpus-based English language course book example, the *Touchstone* series (McCarthy *et al.* 2005), is concerned. While its use of corpora may not be readily visible, the *Touchstone* series, together with the *English Vocabulary in Use* series (McCarthy and O'Dell 2008), has made the crucial move to incorporate common error warnings into the course book and to design tasks/activities based on error information identified from error-tagged learner corpora. A large degree of inconsistency, however, exists regarding the views and experiences of corpus use in course books. Although a number of empirical studies have reported that course books designed based on intuition do not mirror real-world language use, especially in relation to spoken language (e.g. Cheng and Warren 2006; Römer 2006), it remains unclear in the case of many language textbooks the extent to which and the ways in which they are corpus-informed, with only a minority of teaching materials thus far incorporating direct corpus evidence such as concordances into their design on a small scale (Boulton 2010) (see also Chapters 25 and 26, this volume). There is, however, a more promising development in this area in recent years, with the influence of two key corpus-based open resources on course book design. Both derived from the English Profile project, the English Vocabulary Profile (Capel 2010) and the English Grammar Profile (O'Keeffe and Mark 2017) are free online reference sources based on the *Cambridge Learner Corpus.* Importantly, the two resources offer valuable information concerning the typical lexical and grammatical profiles of learners at each level of the Common European Framework of Reference (CEFR or CEF), making it possible for course book writers to design evidence-based materials for language learners at different stages.

Finally, corpora have also found their way into the development of study lists, including the Academic Word List (Coxhead 2000); the Academic Keyword List (Paquot 2010); the Phrasal Expressions List (Martinez and Schmitt 2012); the Academic Collocation List (Ackerman and Chen 2013); the Academic Vocabulary List (Gardner and Davies 2014); and, most recently, the Oxford Phrasal Academic Lexicon (Oxford University Press 2020) (see Chapters 24 and 28, this volume). All of these lists have been produced with pedagogic purposes in mind and constitute examples of corpus-based teaching resources for testing and syllabus design. The Academic Collocation List, for example, was compiled based on the *Pearson International Corpus of Academic English* (PICAE) and designed for advanced learners of English. As advised by the authors, however, the list still requires teacher intervention for pedagogical use (Ackerman and Chen 2013). From the perspective of English as an international language (EIL), Flowerdew (2012) argues that teachers should be mindful of the variety of English on which teaching materials are based, as the so-called "modernisation" model of curriculum development has been criticised for the reason that 'Western models are applied by Western experts to Outer- and Expanding-Circle contexts' (Flowerdew 2012: 235). More information about the composition of corpora used in teaching materials will therefore allow teachers to make more informed decisions in this regard.

4 Corpus tasks for language teaching

The direct applications of corpora in language teaching involve the use of corpus tools and techniques in tasks for pedagogical purposes. In comparison with the indirect uses of corpora in pedagogy, the direct uses of corpora are regarded as being given a marginal treatment in the relevant literature (Leńko-Szymańska and Boulton 2015), with a slow development of the direct access to corpora by teachers and learners and of the use of corpus data in the classroom (Chambers *et al.* 2011). Outside the classroom, it has also been noted that learners' use of corpora is quite rare (Chen and Flowerdew 2018), though a number of studies have demonstrated positive responses from both trainee and in-service teachers regarding their perceptions of DDL and corpus-based instruction in language teacher education (Chen *et al.* 2019) (see Chapter 32, this volume).

Indeed, a large body of research has shown how corpus tasks can be designed to teach a variety of aspects of language, often with detailed illustrations of the tasks. The special issue of *Language Learning & Technology* devoted to corpora in language learning and teaching comprises articles which investigate the effect of DDL on different aspects of language teaching and learning, including phraseology, genre, collocation, lexico-grammatical knowledge and reading speed (Vyatkina and Boulton 2017). The most well-known corpus task is perhaps the classic DDL tasks, which involve the presentation of a concordance, either in paper or computer format, with a set of guiding questions for learners to identify patterns and make generalisations based on the patterns identified (Ballance 2016). Cotos (2014), for example, illustrates how such a discovery-oriented task based on teacher-selected examples can help in the teaching of the semantic roles, forms and syntactic distribution of linking adverbials. Another common task type is awareness-raising activities, which can be used for introducing a particular form or function. Chambers *et al.* (2011), for example, describe a task achieving this aim which focuses on the discourse functions of *right* through concordance lines to improve EFL students' conversation interactional strategies. Gablasova and Brezina (2018) also illustrate with an exercise how to heighten students' awareness of thc linguistic realisations of disagreement with a transcript from corpus data rather than with concordances. Crosthwaite *et al.* (2019) provide examples of corpus pedagogic tasks, most of which involve concordance use, including gap-filling, sentence completion and frequency observation, as supplementary materials for their study, which provide useful examples for teachers of postgraduate thesis writing.

To facilitate the direct use of corpora in language teaching, a number of corpus tools and interfaces have been made available. Of the resources which are publicly accessible, *Lextutor* is one which has been used in many studies reporting the direct use of corpora by learners in EAP writing classrooms (Chen and Flowerdew 2018). As a contemporary pedagogic resource, *Lextutor* consists of a collection of corpora with a built-in concordancer accompanied by language learning activities. It is, however, not only used for teaching academic writing to more advanced learners, as two corpora on *Lextutor*, the 1K and 2K graded corpora, are considered particularly useful by student teachers, but its "multi concordance" program is also found to be valuable for teaching near synonyms (Ebrahimi and Faghih 2016). Another interface which provides access to data from a number of corpora as well as corpus-based resources is corpus.byu.edu (Davies 2020). Other corpus-based teaching resources include the Academic word highlighter and Check My Words, which have been recommended for teachers specifically targeting the four skills (Timmis 2015). For the enhancement of language awareness, the *Scottish Corpus of Texts & Speech* (SCOT) allows the study of interactional features by native speakers in non-standard varieties of English. Anderson and Corbett (2009) give two specific examples of how material from the corpus can be used in a classroom setting to teach aspects of evaluative language and linguistic forms used for particular pragmatic functions in standard and local English as a lingua franca (ELF) varieties. Examples of pedagogic corpora in other languages include the SACODEYL corpus and the BACKBONE corpora, both of which contain interview data of native speakers of a number of European languages and transcripts, coupled by learning resources in the form of exercises.

For more advanced learners, especially in the fields of EAP and ESP, the creation of corpora either by teachers or learners based on one's own data has been advocated. Smith (2020) describes how the online corpus tool Sketch Engine can be used to generate corpora from teaching materials such as lecture notes, PowerPoint slides and test papers to create personal vocabulary portfolios for students. Chen *et al.* (2019) point to the availability of existing software tools for teachers and learners to automatically build large-scale, discipline-specific corpora. With the development of big data, an increasing number of studies also explore the use of search engines as a corpus tool, particularly concerning the use of Google searches (Sha 2010; Yoon 2016).

When corpus tasks are designed for pedagogical purposes, a number of issues need to be taken into account. Chambers *et al.* (2011), for example, suggest that teachers should consider which type of corpus to use and what information to add or remove from corpus texts to enhance readability. Clearly these decisions have to be made in relation to the level of learners. Boulton (2010), for instance, argues for the elimination of technical issues concerning DDL tasks by using paper-based corpus materials with less advanced language learners, as such materials are generally more teacher-led and may provide more guidance and support that these learners need. Flowerdew (2015), by contrast, shows that postgraduate students preparing for their thesis writing prefer a "high-tech" search engine interface and hands-on tasks to printed concordance output. Response to corpus-based tasks may also vary according to learning style. As suggested by Bridle (2019), inductive learners are more likely to rate corpus-based activities more positively, while reflective learners are not receptive to corpus consultation and consider it time-consuming and overwhelming. Pérez-Paredes (2010) also proposes that corpora should be pedagogically annotated and corpus texts should be carefully chosen based on the learners' learning context and proficiency level. For do-it-yourself (DIY) corpora, teachers may need to seek further support in the forms of 'refresher sessions, drop-in clinics, and online on-demand courses' (Charles 2014: 39). With thoughtful decisions and appropriate strategies, direct corpus use in pedagogy can be successfully implemented so that it is motivational and effective to language teaching.

5 Bridging corpus linguistics and language teaching

Bridging corpus linguistics and language teaching involves describing future directions and areas for further research and practice. The literature review clearly demonstrates that different approaches to the use of corpora in language teaching have been advocated and applied in various educational contexts. It also shows a range of corpus methods; that is, corpus linguistics concepts, tools and techniques, applied in language teaching, involving a variety of disciplines in different classroom settings. The review also presents a variety of corpus evidence as teaching materials involving primarily indirect applications or use of corpora in producing teaching and research resources, such as dictionaries, grammars, course books, and vocabulary lists, as well as a range of corpus tasks for language teaching involving primarily direct applications or use of corpora by teachers and learners for a range of pedagogical purposes.

Despite the fact that corpus linguistics and DDL have a relatively long history in the field, with many of the publications deriving from the COBUILD project in the late 1980s and 1990s specifically aimed at learners, as Römer (2006) notes, corpus linguistics and its applications have yet to become mainstream in language teacher education programmes or in language teaching. Römer (2006: 122) concludes that there is 'strong resistance towards corpora from students, teachers and materials writers'. Similarly, more recently, Boulton (2017) comments that DDL is still 'a marginal practice' (p. 1).

To date, a range of issues related to corpora and language teaching have been observed, and recommendations for future directions and areas for further research and practice have been made by corpus linguistics researchers and educational practitioners. According to Burton (2012), non-native speaker corpora may play a role in future course book production. Leńko-Szymańska and Boulton (2015) note that future directions in the field may include treating the internet as a corpus and using search engines such as Google as a concordancer. They compare the indirect and direct uses of corpora, remarking that 'the direct uses of corpora in language teaching are treated rather marginally in the literature in the field' (p. 3). Götz and Mukherjee (2019) note that to date, there is still little contribution of learner corpora to second language acquistion (SLA) and foreign language teaching. Crosthwaite (2020) observes that the use of DDL with pre-tertiary learners is rare, with a small number of studies found in the high school setting and none in a primary school context.

Chen and Flowerdew (2018) report on a critical review of research and practice in DDL in the EAP/academic writing classroom since 2000, based on 37 empirical studies. They conclude that the field of DDL in EAP/academic writing is 'still in its infancy' (p. 356) and make five recommendations for future research and practice, as follows:

i. More descriptions of different approaches in different geographical and classroom contexts;
ii. More such studies need to be carried out describing how corpora and more traditional teaching approaches could be combined in overall writing instruction;
iii. Researchers and practitioners need to come up with ways of helping students to become more autonomous in their use of corpora;
iv. [More resources][*our addition*] to show writers how to use corpus tools to identify problems in their writing without the aid of the teacher;
v. More research into specialist training in DDL for EAP practitioners.

(Chen and Flowerdew 2018: 356–7)

Based on the conclusion of the mobile DDL evaluation study, Pérez-Paredes *et al.* (2019) make suggestions in the areas of task design, such as 'the addition of further built-in tools and adaptation to hardware constraints'; specialised learner training; the creation of 'more fleshed-out tools'; and future studies to investigate 'the potential of combining DDL and MALL' (p. 145).

The concrete recommendations and suggestions presented here show the significant benefits corpus use can offer to language teaching. With continuous technological advancement and pedagogical development through the concerted effort of corpus linguists and language teachers, the research-practice gap between corpus linguistics and language teaching will be narrowed, enabling the two areas to be fruitfully bridged.

Acknowledgements

The authors are members of the English Department's Research Centre for Professional Communication in English (RCPCE), the mission of which is to pursue applied research and consultancy so as to deepen the understanding of professional communication and to better serve the communicative needs of professional communities. The work described in this chapter is intended to fulfil part of this mission.

The authors are very grateful for the reviewers' insightful and helpful suggestions.

Further reading

Cheng, W. (2012) *Exploring Corpus Linguistics. Language in Action*, London: New York: Routledge. (This book provides a practice guide to core theories and concepts in corpus linguistics with classroom examples, corpus-based analyses and tasks for learners and teachers.)

Reppen, R. (2010) *Using Corpora in the Language Classroom*, Cambridge: Cambridge University Press. (This book describes corpus-based materials, online corpus resources and example activities for use in the classroom.)

Timmis, I. (2015) *Corpus Linguistics for ELT: Research and Practice*, London: New York: Routledge. (This book introduces corpus linguistics to English language teachers and helps make it a regular part of a teacher's toolkit. It is designed to help ELT teachers be familiar with basic concepts in corpus linguistics and using corpora through three kinds of activities: corpus search, corpus question and discussion.)

References

Anderson, W. and Corbett, J. (2009) 'Teaching English as a Friendly Language: Lessons from the SCOTS Corpus', *ELT Journal* 64(4): 414–23.

Ackerman, K. and Chen, Y.-H. (2013) 'Developing the Academic Collocation List (ACL) – A Corpus-Driven and Expert-Judged Approach', *Journal of English for Academic Purposes* 12(4): 235–47.

Ballance, O. (2016) 'Analysing Concordancing: A Simple or Multifaceted Construct?', *Computer Assisted Language Learning* 29(7): 1205–19.

Ballance, O. (2017) 'Pedagogical Models of Concordance Use: Correlations between Concordance User Preferences', *Computer Assisted Language Learning* 30(3–4): 259–83.

Biber, D., Johansson, S., Leech, G., Conrad, S. and Finegan, E. (1999) *Longman Grammar of Spoken and Written English*, Harlow: Longman.

Boulton, A. (2010) 'Data-Driven Learning: Taking the Computer out of the Equation', *Language Learning* 60(3): 534–72.

Boulton, A. (2017) 'Research Timeline: Corpora in Language Teaching and Learning', *Language Teaching* 50(4): 483–506.

Boulton, A. and Cobb, T. (2017) 'Corpus Use in Language Learning: A Meta-Analysis', *Language Learning* 67(2): 348–93.

Boulton, A. and Pérez-Paredes, P. (eds) (2014) 'Researching Uses of Corpora for Language Teaching and Learning', *ReCALL* 26(2): 121–7.

Bridle, M. (2019) 'Learner Use of a Corpus as a Reference Tool in Error Correction: Factors Influencing Consultation and Success', *Journal of English for Academic Purposes* 37: 52–69.

Burton, G. (2012) 'Corpora and Coursebooks: Destined to Be Strangers Forever?', *Corpora* 7(1): 91–108.

Callies, M. and Götz, S. (eds) (2015) *Learner Corpora in Language Testing and Assessment*, Amsterdam: John Benjamins.

Cambridge University Press (2020) *Cambridge Learner Corpus*. Available at: https://www.cambridge.org/elt/corpus/learner_corpus2.htm.

Capel, A. (2010) 'Insights and Issues Arising from the English Profile Wordlists Project', *Research Notes* 41: 2–7. Cambridge: Cambridge ESOL.

Carter, R. A. and McCarthy, M. J. (2006) *Cambridge Grammar of English: A Comprehensive Guide: Spoken and Written English: Grammar and Usage*, Cambridge: Cambridge University Press.

Chambers, A. (2019) 'Towards the Corpus Revolution: Bridging the Research-Practice Gap', *Language Teaching* 52(4): 460–75.
Chambers, A., Farr, F. and O'Riordan, S. (2011) 'Language Teachers with Corpora in Mind: From Starting Steps to Walking Tall', *Language Learning Journal* 39(1): 85–104.
Charles, M. (2014) 'Getting the Corpus Habit: EAP Students' Long-Term Use of Personal Corpora', *English for Specific Purposes* 35(1): 30–40.
Charles, M. (2018) '*Corpus*-Assisted Editing: More than Just Concordancing', *Journal of English for Academic Purposes* 36: 15–25.
Chen, M. and Flowerdew, J. (2018) 'A Critical Review of Research and Practice in Data-Driven Learning (DDL) in the Academic Writing Classroom', *International Journal of Corpus Linguistics* 23(3): 335–69.
Chen, M., Flowerdew, J. and Anthony, L. (2019) 'Introducing In-Service English Language Teachers to Data-Driven Learning for Academic Writing', *System* 87: 102–48.
Cheng, W. and Warren, M. (2006) 'I Would Say Be Very Careful of…: Opine Markers in an Intercultural Business Corpus of Spoken English', in J. Bamford and M. Bondi (eds) *Managing Interaction in Professional Discourse. Intercultural and Interdiscoursal Perspectives*, Rome: Officina Edizioni, pp. 46–58.
Cobb, T. (2003) 'Analyzing Late Interlanguage with Learner Corpora: Québec Replications of Three European Studies', *The Canadian Modern Language Review* 59(3): 393–423.
Cobb, T. and Boulton, A. (2015) 'Classroom Applications of Corpus Analysis', in D. Biber and R. Reppen (eds) *Cambridge Handbook of English Corpus Linguistics*, Cambridge: Cambridge University Press, pp. 478–97.
Cotos, E. (2014) 'Enhancing Writing Pedagogy with Learner Corpus Data', *ReCALL* 26(2): 202–24.
Coxhead, A. (2000) 'A New Academic Word List', *TESOL Quarterly* 34(2): 213–38.
Crosthwaite, P. (2020) 'Data-Driven Learning and Younger Learners: Introduction to the Volume', in P. Crosthwaite (ed.) *Data-Driven Learning for the Next Generation: Corpora and DDL for Pre-Tertiary Learners*, London: Routledge, pp. 1–10.
Crosthwaite, P., Wong, L. and Cheung, J. (2019) 'Characterising Postgraduate Students' Corpus Query and Usage Patterns for Disciplinary Data-Driven Learning', *ReCALL* 31(3): 255–75.
Davies, M. (2020) *corpus.byu.edu*, Available at: https://corpus.byu.edu/overview.asp.
Ebrahimi, A. and Faghih, E. (2016) 'Integrating Corpus Linguistics into Online Language Teacher Education Programs', *ReCALL* 29(1): 120–35.
Fligelstone, S. (1993) 'Some Reflections on the Question of Teaching, from a Corpus Linguistics Perspective', *ICAME Journal* 17: 97–110.
Flowerdew, J. (2012) 'Corpora in Language Teaching from the Perspective of English as an International Language', in L. Alsagoff, S. L. McKay, G. Hu and W. R. Renandya (eds) *Principles and Practices for Teaching English as an International Language*, London; New York: Routledge, pp. 226–43.
Flowerdew, L. (2015) 'Using Corpus-Based Research and Online Academic Corpora to Inform Writing of the Discussion Section of a Thesis', *Journal of English for Academic Purposes* 20: 58–68.
Frankenberg-Garcia, A. (2012) 'Raising Teachers' Awareness of Corpora', *Language Teaching* 45(4): 475–89.
Gablasova, D. and Brezina, V. (2018) 'Disagreement in L2 Spoken English: From Learner Corpus Research to Corpus-Based Teaching Materials', in V. Brezina and L. Flowerdew (eds) *Learner Corpus Research: New Perspectives and Applications*, London: Bloomsbury Academic, pp. 69–89.
Gardner, D. and Davies, M. (2014) 'A New Academic Vocabulary List', *Applied Linguistics* 35(3): 305–27.
Gilquin, G. and Granger, S. (2010) 'How Can Data-Driven Learning Be Used in Language Teaching?', in A. O'Keeffe and M. McCarthy (eds) *The Routledge Handbook of Corpus Linguistics*, London: Routledge, pp. 359–70.
Götz, S. and Mukherjee, J. (eds) (2019) *Learner Corpora and Language Teaching*, Amsterdam: John Benjamins Publishing Company.
Huang, L.-S. (2018) 'Taking Stock of Corpus-Based Instruction in Teaching English as an International Language', *RELC Journal* 49(3): 381–401.

Huang, Z. (2014). 'The Effects of Paper-Based DDL on the Acquisition of Lexico-Grammatical Patterns in L2 Writing,' *ReCALL* 26(2): 163–83.

Hyland, K. (2003) *Second Language Writing*, Cambridge: Cambridge University Press.

Johns, T. (1991) 'From Printout to Handout: Grammar and Vocabulary Teaching in the Context of Data-Driven Learning', *English Language Research Journal* 4: 27–45.

Lee, H., Warschauer M. and Lee J. H. (2019) 'The Effects of Corpus Use on Second Language Vocabulary Learning: A Multilevel Meta-Analysis', *Applied Linguistics* 40(5): 721–53.

Leech, G. (1997) 'Teaching and Language Corpora: A Convergence', in A. Wichmann, S. Fligelstone, T. McEnery and G. Knowles (eds) *Teaching and Language Corpora*, Harlow: Addison Wesley Longman, pp. 11–23.

Leńko-Szymańska, A. and Boulton, A. (eds) (2015) *Multiple Affordances of Language Corpora for Data-Driven Learning*, Amsterdam: John Benjamins.

Macmillan (2020) *Corpus*, Available at: https://www.macmillandictionary.com/corpus.html.

Martinez, R. and Schmitt, N. (2012) 'A Phrasal Expressions List', *Applied Linguistics* 33(3): 299–320.

McCarten, J. and McCarthy, M. J. (2010) 'Bridging the Gap between Corpus and Course Book: The Case of Conversation Strategies', in A. Chambers and F. Mishan (eds) *Perspectives on Language Learning Materials Development*, Bern: Peter Lang, pp. 11–32.

McCarthy, M. J., McCarten, J. and Sandiford, H. (2005) *Touchstone 2a: Student's Book*, Cambridge: Cambridge University Press.

McCarthy, M. J. and O'Dell, F. (2008) *English Vocabulary in Use*, Cambridge: Cambridge University Press.

Meunier, F. (2020) 'A Case for Constructive Alignment in DDL: Rethinking Outcomes, Practices and Assessment in (Data-Driven) Language Learning', in P. Crosthwaite (ed.) *Data-Driven Learning for the Next Generation. Corpora and DDL for Pre-Tertiary Learners*, London: Routledge, pp. 1–18.

Meunier, F. and Reppen, R. (2015) 'Corpus versus Non-Corpus-Informed Pedagogical Materials: Grammar as the Focus', in D. Biber (ed.) *The Cambridge Handbook of English Corpus Linguistics*, Cambridge: Cambridge University Press, pp. 498–514.

Nation, I. S. P. (2001) *Learning Vocabulary in Another Language*. Cambridge: Cambridge University Press.

O'Keeffe, A. and Mark, G. (2017) 'The English Grammar Profile of Learner Competence: Methodology and Key Findings', *International Journal of Corpus Linguistics* 22(4): 457–89.

O'Sullivan, I. (2007) 'Enhancing a Process-Oriented Approach to Literacy and Language Learning: The Role of Corpus Consultation Literacy', *ReCALL* 19(3): 269–86.

Oxford University Press (2020) *OPAL (Oxford Phrasal Academic Lexicon)*, Available at: https://www.oxfordlearnersdictionaries.com/wordlists/opal.

Paquot, M. (2010) *Academic Vocabulary in Learner Writing: From Extraction to Analysis*, London and New-York: Continuum, pp. 56–8.

Pérez-Paredes, P. (2010) 'Corpus Linguistics and Language Education in Perspective: Appropriation and the Possibilities Scenario', in T. Harris and M. M., Jaén (eds) *Corpus Linguistics in Language Teaching*, Bern: Peter Lang, pp. 53–73.

Pérez-Paredes, P. (2019) 'A Systematic Review of the Uses and Spread of Corpora and Data-Driven Learning in CALL Research during 2011–2015', *Computer Assisted Language Learning*, doi: 10.1080/09588221.2019.1667832

Pérez-Paredes, P., Ordoñana Guillamón, C., Van de Vyver, J., Meurice, A., Aguado, P., Conole, G. and Hernández, P. (2019) 'Mobile Data-Driven Language Learning: Affordances and Learners' Perception', *System* 84: 145–59.

Poole, R. (2016) 'A Corpus-Aided Approach for the Teaching and Learning of Rhetoric in an Undergraduate Composition Course for L2 Writers', *Journal of English for Academic Purposes* 21: 99–109.

Renouf, A. (1997) 'Teaching Corpus Linguistics to Teachers of English', in A. Wichmann, S. Fligelstone, T. McEnery and G. Knowles (eds) *Teaching and Language Corpora*, London: Longman, pp. 255–66.

Römer, U. (2006) 'Pedagogical Applications of Corpora: Some Reflections on the Current Scope and a Wish List for Future Developments', *Zeitschrift für Anglistik und Amerikanistik* 54(2): 121–34.

Rundell, M. (2020) *From Corpus to Dictionary*, Available at: http://www.macmillandictionaries.com/features/from-corpus-to-dictionary/.

Sha, G. (2010) 'Using Google as a Super Corpus to Drive Written Language Learning: A Comparison with the British National Corpus', *Computer Assisted Language Learning* 23(5): 377–93.

Sinclair, J. (ed) (1995) *Collins COBUILD English Language Dictionary*, 2nd edn, London: Collins.

Smith, S. (2020) 'DIY Corpora for Accounting and Finance Vocabulary Learning', *English for Specific Purposes* 57: 1–12.

Timmis, I. (2015) *Corpus Linguistics for ELT: Research and Practice*, London; New York: Routledge.

Tognini-Bonelli, E. (2001) *Corpus Linguistics at Work*, Amsterdam: John Benjamins.

Vyatkina, N. and Boulton, A. (ed) (2017) Special Issue on Corpora in Language Learning and Teaching, *Language Learning & Technology* 21(3).

Yoon, C. (2016) 'Concordancers and Dictionaries as Problem-Solving Tools for ESL Academic Writing', *Language Learning & Technology* 20(1): 209–29.

22

What can corpora tell us about language learning?

Pascual Pérez-Paredes and Geraldine Mark

1 What is language learning?

In this chapter we take a two-pronged approach to considering what corpora can tell us about language learning: (1) the "can of affordability/facility" of corpora – what they represent and what they enable/allow us to look at and (2) the "can of possibility" – the potential for a broader understanding and representation of language learning.

What distinguishes a corpus linguistics perspective from other approaches to language learning research is its emphasis on the study of language as a product. Language, as a semiotic resource, is situated at the micro level of social activity where L2 users engage in the completion of tasks in instructed learning contexts or in real life, both face-to-face and virtual, interactions with other speakers and increasingly more so, with automated agents through voice and text interaction. In learner language research, corpora are used as proxies of usage, that is, as providers of evidence of communication, spoken or written. The question is, once evidence of this usage has been gathered, what do researchers do with it and what does it tell us about learning?

As Tyler and Ortega have put it, learning a language 'is one of the most complex accomplishments humans achieve. This is true for the first language learner and perhaps even more so for the second language learner' (2018: 3). Amid this complexity, expert views both on the nature of language and the nature of learning differ, and here we note the existence of at least two approaches to how the term has been conceptualised by researchers in the broader field of applied linguistics.

Inclusive conceptualisations are mindful of the heterogeneity in the language learning endeavour, encompassing different languages across space, social contexts, lifespan, language status and roles of instruction. Mitchell, Myles and Marsden advocate a broad understanding of the term that includes 'the learning of any language, to any level, provided only that the learning of the "second" language takes place sometime later than the acquisition of the first language' (2013: 1). The Douglas Fir Group (a transdisciplinary group led by the belief that language acquisition is too complex to be explained by one or two theoretical approaches) (2016: 19) claim that the broader language learning field is interested in 'school-aged children, adolescents, and adults [and how

DOI: 10.4324/9780367076399-22

they] learn and use, at any point in life, an additional language', including second, foreign, indigenous, minority or heritage languages. Inclusive conceptualisations accept, therefore, that different language learning theories co-exist and compete with each other to explain specific areas that are considered relevant when accounting for how language learning occurs: 'language inextricably involves cognition, emotions, consciousness, experience, embodiment, brain, self, human interaction, society, culture, mediation, instruction, and history in rich, complex, and dynamic ways' (Douglas Fir Group 2016: 39).

When specific approaches are concerned with a limited set of learner types, contexts of learning and scope of theorisation, we are dealing with what we may label as *narrow conceptualisations* about language learning. These may range from, for example, young learners' language learning in classroom contexts through explicit instruction to language learning in immersive instructional or naturalistic contexts.

Narrow conceptualisations tend to prioritise one aspect of learning over others and as a result can expose a fragmentation of the phenomenon into cognitive, social and emotional elements. We note a tendency in learner corpus research (LCR) to conceptualise language learning as a cognitive phenomenon where language is primarily observed as a bounded system of formal rules. We argue, following Mitchell *et al.* (2013), that language learning needs to account for quite a long list of evidence and theorisation around the nature of language and language use; the learning process itself; the role of variability in L2 learning, as well as the target language models pursued; the role of the L1(s) and L2(s); and, among others, the role of the language learner and learner differences.

When it comes to analysing the contribution of corpora to language learning, it is necessary, therefore, to try to understand what language learning is being contributed: Are there specific views of language learning that have been embraced by CL researchers? If so, how have they bridged that gap between theory and empirical research? To address these questions, we will look at how learner language has been represented in corpora, how these corpora have evolved and what methods and approaches we use to investigate them. We note here that while both L1 and L2 corpora have been used in language learning to teach languages (see Chapter 30, this volume) as part of a research resource in second language acquisition (SLA) (see Chapter 23, this volume) to build teaching materials, coursebooks, dictionaries, etc., and in data-driven learning (see Chapters 24–31, this volume), the main focus of this chapter is on corpora that contain learner language.

2 Learner language in corpora

History and focus

In corpus linguistics-inspired research, the term "learner language" is used to denote the body of language produced by L2 users. Within SLA studies, Ellis and Barkhuizen have defined the scope of learner language as 'the primary data for the study of L2 acquisition' (2005: 4) and situate their discussion in the context of the *limitations* that the collection of natural use imposes. While they cite a wide range of data collection and analysis methods, the study of language, as conceptualised from the corpus linguistics camp, with its well-defined set of methods and data collection procedures, has not necessarily been conceived as mainstream in traditional SLA research (Dornyei 2007).

The emergence of learner corpora claimed a new turn in providing 'systematic collections of authentic continuous and contextualised language use by foreign/second (L2) learners' (Callies 2015: 35). Pre-corpus work on learner language is often associated first with learner error, with errors as a window into the learning process, as evidence of learner strategies and processes, departing from the view of error as "bad habits" (Corder 1967), and then with "interlanguage" (Selinker 1972), and the idea of learner language as an independent system worthy of analysis in itself. The Louvain-born *International Corpus of Learner English* (ICLE) project marked a major landmark in the collection and study of learner language with the emergence of the Contrastive Interlanguage Analysis (CIA) tradition (Granger 1994) and the gathering and analysis of large-scale learner data from a variety of L1 backgrounds. The ICLE project (see Table 22.1) was built within the design matrix for the L1 *International Corpus of English* (ICE) (Greenbaum 1990) and brought with it the wealth of methodological approaches already afforded by corpus linguistics. Many new learner corpora were built following the ICLE design (Tono 2003; Tono and Díez-Bedmar 2014), and new error-coding and tagging systems were developed. A perceived strength of this design at the time was that it allowed researchers to identify those learner "errors" that were universal to all learners from all L1 backgrounds as well as those that were L1-specific. The CIA approach has had such a lasting impact on the field of learner corpus research that most corpus-based studies have adopted a comparative design, either contrasting learner language with an L1 benchmark corpus or to another L2 dataset. LCR, following in the coat-tails of L1 corpus research, brought with it a broadening of the topic of analysis in learner language, with a shift from the traditional SLA focus on morphology to attention on lexis and phraseology and register and the wide range of variables afforded by metadata and tagging systems.

Learner corpora continue to gather for a myriad of research purposes (see https://uclouvain.be/en/research-institutes/ilc/cecl/learner-corpora-around-the-world.html). Much of the pioneering work in corpus development originated as a result of commercial and academic partnerships (e.g. the seminal work of the BNC and the COBUILD project), with commercial interests leading the way. A similar impetus can be seen in learner corpus development, e.g. the *Cambridge Learner Corpus* (CLC), the *Longman Learners' Corpus* and, most recently, the *Trinity Lancaster Corpus* (TLC), which have all been developed as commercial resources, for example, by publishers and exam boards for the production of published materials and related academic research.

From description to understanding, from error to competence

Methodological issues of comparative studies, control of variables, subjectivity in the assignment and categorisation of both learner-related features (e.g. proficiency level, variation) and annotation (e.g. error tagging) have been widely debated (Tono 2003; Ädel 2015; Granger 2015; Gablasova *et al.* 2017; McEnery *et al.* 2019) and are issues which endure in corpus design to the present day. While acknowledging the impact made by LCR in mobilising the creation of learner corpora and *describing* learner language, there has long been a desire 'to test some of the current hypotheses [in SLA] on larger and better constructed datasets, as has happened in L1 acquisition' (Myles 2005: 376) and still more recently a call for LCR to engage beyond the contrastive descriptive paradigm and to realise the promise for its usefulness in *understanding* language learning (McEnery *et al.* 2019).

Frequency and comparability have persisted as a central focus of LCR. Descriptions of learner language use are often still provided in deficit terms of overuse, underuse and misuse or error in relation to a target L1 or comparable L2 dataset. Recent developments in the field are nudging the focus away from error-based to competency-based analysis, describing the data in terms of what learners can do rather than what they are getting "wrong", with a view to understanding development and the "learning" process. Emergence of aspects of this pursuit is seen *inter alia* in the developmental studies of "criterial features" – the linguistic properties characteristic of a given level of competence (Hawkins and Buttery 2010), patterns of L2 accuracy (Thewissen 2013), L2 morphemes (Murakami 2014) and, more recently, formative usage-based studies (Ellis *et al.* 2016; Römer and Garner 2019; Pérez-Paredes *et al.* 2020; see also Chapter 23, this volume). These studies represent to varying degrees the coming together of SLA and LCR research, all motivated by the study of language learning though with diverse goals and methodologies. Increasingly, both fields are seeing the relevance of the data and methods of the other, particularly when creating triangulated research designs. They represent some effort to shift the focus in both the design and analysis of learner corpora from description to interpretation, but the movement is slow (Myles 2015).

Design, data and focus

A declared aim of corpus designers is to contribute to our understanding of language learning, and Table 22.1 outlines three areas that define how research designs are approached. These areas relate to tasks, language collection considerations and the learners participating. Although learner corpora vary in scope, most consider all three elements, while often prioritising them differently.

Learner corpora in general, as represented by a sample in Table 22.2, are intended to shed some light on learner language usage in essays or other types of written tasks and spoken tasks, either monologic or dialogic, at different points in time and across different groups of L1 speakers.

Table 22.1 Corpus design elements and considerations

Research design element	*Considerations*
Mode/Tasks	Task types: the degree of semi-experimental control during the collection of these tasks varies across corpora. Tasks dictate written/spoken mode, degree of interaction, time allowed for task, etc.
Collection	Cross-sectional: data collected at one time point from multiple groups (see Chapter 23, this volume). Dynamic, longitudinal: data collected from the same group at multiple time points. Pseudolongitudinal or quasilongitudinal: a mix of data collected from the same learners at different points in time and from learners at different proficiency levels at the same point in time.
Learners	Learners are usually grouped according to their L1 and, depending on the corpus, their proficiency level or year of study. The number of learners involved and the sampling strategies vary.

Table 22.2 A sample of learner corpora and their research purposes and content

International Corpus of Learner English (ICLE)
https://uclouvain.be/en/research-institutes/ilc/cecl/icle.html

Argumentative essays written by upper intermediate to advanced learners of English from several L1 backgrounds. Allows for the regular inclusion of new subcorpora, highlighting the fundamentally dynamic nature of the ICLE project.

Key elements: L2 English, 25 L1 backgrounds, written, cross-sectional, 5.5 million words, high-level proficiency.

Louvain International Database of Spoken English Interlanguage (LINDSEI)
https://uclouvain.be/en/research-institutes/ilc/cecl/lindsei.html

Spoken counterpart to ICLE, produced by advanced learners of English from different L1 backgrounds.

Key elements: L2 English, 11 different L1 backgrounds, spoken, cross-sectional, 1 million+ words.

Trinity Lancaster Corpus (TLC)
https://www.trinitycollege.com/about-us/research/Trinity-corpus

A large corpus of learner (and examiner) speech which can be used in a wide range of research contexts, including SLA, language testing, L2 pedagogy and materials development, etc.

Key elements: L2 English, nine different linguistic and cultural backgrounds, spoken, pseudolongitudinal, proficiency levels B1 to C2.

Corpus Escrito del Español como L2 (CEDEL2)
http://cedel2.learnercorpora.com/#section6

Investigating how people learn Spanish grammar (morphology and syntax). A comparative corpus of L1 Spanish – L2 English, called WriCLE (Written Corpus of Learner English) was also created.

Key elements: L2 Spanish, L1 English, written, average age 20 years; 512,873 words, cross-sectional.

Longitudinal Corpus of Chinese Learners of Italian (LOCCLI)
https://www.unistrapg.it/cqpweb/doc_corpora/LOCCLI_documentation.pdf

350 essays written by 175 Chinese learners of Italian, who attended Italian language courses in Perugia for 6–8 months, and it was collected in 2016. Data was collected in two different points in time, from the same learners.

Key elements: L2 Chinese, L1 Italian, 175 learners; longitudinal

Guangwai-Lancaster Chinese Learner Corpus (GLCLC)
http://cass.lancs.ac.uk/wp-content/uploads/2016/05/Poster_GLC-small.pdf

A balanced sample that covers three proficiency levels: beginner, intermediate and advanced, providing a unique insight into L2 Chinese lexical and grammatical development.

Key elements: L2 Chinese; written and spoken, different proficiency levels, longitudinal, 80 countries represented, over 1 million.

The design and collection of learner corpora are subject to the same gamut of considerations, processes, affordances and pitfalls as any other corpus; they are representative only of what they contain, whatever efforts are made for balance and representativeness. There are more learners of English than any other language globally, and therefore there are strikingly more corpora of L2 English than of any other language. Ease of collection may tend inevitably towards the written over spoken and cross-sectional over longitudinal and also to a disproportionate number of corpora of high-proficiency-level L2 users studying a target language at university over lower-level and young L2 learners (see Chapter 23, this volume). There is a host of variables specific to learner corpora (e.g. L1 background, L1 context, proficiency level, learning history, task effect, type of language instruction/input) to consider and accommodate. Added to this, Buttery and Caines (2010) point out that for fair accounts of learner language to be made, "opportunity of use" must also be controlled for. Learners may be using their linguistic resources strategically, not necessarily displaying what they know, constrained by the limitations of the context.

A detailed list of individual studies (c.2000 references at the time of writing) can be found in the learner corpus bibliography (https://uclouvain.be/en/research-institutes/ilc/cecl/learner-corpus-bibliography.html). The objects of focus of these studies can be categorised as follows:

> *Discrete features*: e.g. individual parts of speech; adverbials; articles; cohesion; discourse markers; formulaic language; lexical bundles; tenses; verbs, etc.;
> *Composite features*: e.g. measures of phraseological sophistication; measures of clausal and phrasal complexity, etc.;
> *Constructs*: e.g. metadiscourse features; involvement; information packaging; grammar and language learning, etc.

We note that not all areas of potential study receive equal attention. Using the learner corpus bibliography, Paquot and Plonsky (2017) have shown that lexis (including single words and multi-word units) is, by a long way, the main focus of study, accounting for 65 per cent of all studies, in contrast with discourse and pragmatics, accounting for 30 per cent and 10 per cent, respectively. Given the range of targets chosen for analysis, currently available learner corpora offer a window on a narrow conceptualisation of language learning, which may explain some of the challenges to making corpora more relevant in the broader field of language learning research and practice.

3 Learner corpus research in practice

Here we zone in on three case studies, representing different types of data, approaches and findings, and consider how they have contributed to our understanding of language learning.

The first study looks at exploratory longitudinal corpora, encouraging the building and analysis of small-scale data with a focus on discrete and composite features of language, including syntactic complexity. It demonstrates the potential for a triangulated approach, complementing corpus tools and statistical analysis with natural language processing tools. The second is a study of adverb use in spoken English in cross-sectional data across a variety of tasks. The third study investigates grammatical development across proficiency levels, in a pseudolongitudinal corpus of written exams.

Case study 1: examining the evolution of language learning

Here we examine two robust approaches to corpus longitudinal designs. The first approach uses a longitudinal corpus to track the development. Vyatkina (2013) looked at the development of syntactic complexity in two beginning L2 German learners over four semesters in a US college. She collected data every three or five weeks and gathered 19 pieces of both timed and untimed essays from each student. She looked at syntactic structures such as coordinate and complex nominal structures per clause, using developmental profiling techniques (Figure 22.1) – a combination of POS tagging with manual checking and annotation, using concordance software.

This approach can reveal the point when L2 target features emerge in the writing after focused instruction. Vyatkina suggests that language teachers compile their own small learner corpora and develop learner developmental profiles for learning, feedback and assessment purposes.

The second approach (Siyanova-Chanturia and Spina 2019) uses the *Longitudinal Corpus of Chinese Learners of Italian* (LOCCLI) (see Table 22.1) to understand the effects of a six-month instructional period on the acquisition of noun + adjective word combinations by L1 Chinese learners of Italian (n = 175) at three CEFR levels (A1, A2 and B1). The learners wrote two essays at the beginning and end of the teaching period. The researchers used a variety of measures to analyse 1,401 observations of [N + Adjective] combinations and mixed-effects modelling to examine changes between the two collection points. They did not find a correlation between time effects and the frequency of the aforementioned measures; that is, after six months the learners did not produce more word combinations. The authors argue that L2 collocational knowledge is slow and uneven, though they found that the decrease in use of word combinations was more significant in the A1 level. The authors conclude that the learning of collocations is a process 'fraught with difficulties… in which more exposure and higher proficiency may not necessarily lead

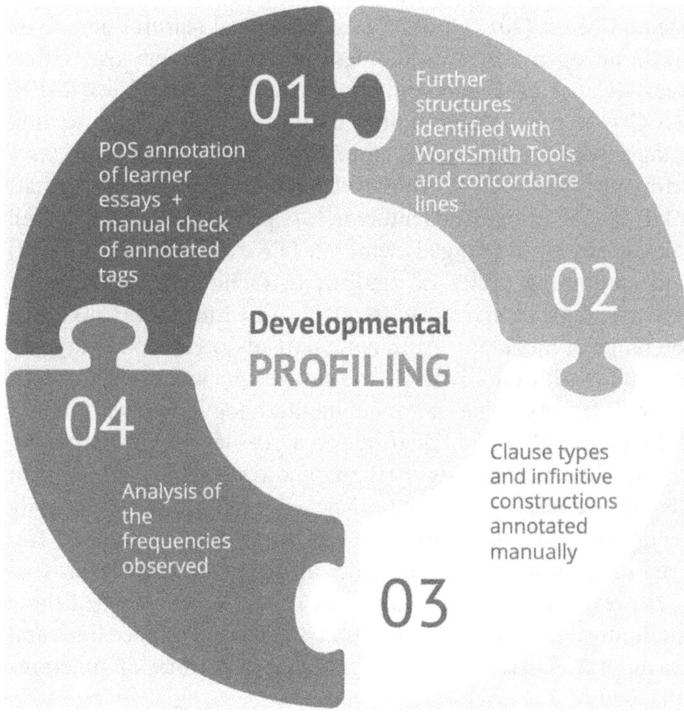

Figure 22.1 Developmental profiling techniques used in Vyatkina (2013)

to a more idiomatic and target-like output and may, indeed, result in lower levels of idiomaticity and greater reliance on lower frequency combinations' (2019: 452).

Case study 2: researching the use of stance adverbs in a spoken corpus

Pérez-Paredes and Díez-Bedmar (2019) provide evidence to suggest that task selection and design needs further attention in LCR. They examined the use of *really*, *actually* and *obviously* in two populations of Spanish L1 speakers of English in the TLC (see Table 22.2). Frequency differences were found at B1 and B2 levels in discussion tasks. L1 Mexican and European Spanish speakers used these stance adverbs in significantly different ways. At B2 level, this difference was also significant in both conversation and discussion tasks. The use of *really* and *actually* as device-making devices in dialogic discourse is more frequent as language learners' communicative competence increases. These uses are, additionally, less epistemic. Usage differences in the learner groups who share the same L1 but have a different cultural and geographical background (Mexico and Spain) also point to the influence that different varieties of L1 English may have on learners. This research lends further evidence (Mark and Pérez-Paredes 2018; Pérez-Paredes and Bueno 2019) to the way in which tasks influence the elicitation of language.

Case study 3: using a large-scale corpus of written exam data to examine competence and development

A large-scale corpus project, *The English Profile* (www.englishprofile.org), used the CLC to develop detailed profiles of learner language use at each of the CEFR levels (Harrison and Barker 2015). O'Keeffe and Mark (2017) looked at grammatical features across six proficiency levels, resulting in an open access online description of learner use. Other strands focused on vocabulary (Capel 2012) and communicative functions (Green 2012).

The 55-million word CLC is a pseudolongitudinal corpus compiled from written exams. Each document is tagged for L1 (143 L1s), nationality, level of education, age, gender, exam taken, performance achieved, CEFR level, task type, style and format, allowing for a developmental view of a linguistic feature across proficiency levels, as well as a cross-sectional view across any of the tagged elements. O'Keeffe and Mark (2017) devised an iterative design, combining cycles of analysis to facilitate an aggregated picture of usage, moving from a single element (e.g. frequency of form) to a breakdown of detail of usage across the range of metadata. Automatic part-of-speech (POS) tagging (in the *Sketch Engine* toolkit) allowed for analysis of structural sequences using a corpus query language (CQL) search facility. The iterative methodology involved first a quantitative view based on frequency of use and distribution across levels, L1s and tasks, complemented with a close qualitative analysis of the concordance lines. By way of example, past simple relative frequencies across the proficiency levels are retrieved using a CQL search on a past simple tag. A quantitative view of forms and normalised frequencies shows a fairly even distribution of usage across all six proficiency levels (between 24,391 and 28,601). However this hides a complexity of use, revealed when these frequencies are explored qualitatively through detailed analysis of concordance lines and collocational patterns at each level. What emerges is a growing repertoire of functions and associated lexis, summarised in Table 22.3.

Table 22.3 Development of past simple form and functions across proficiency levels

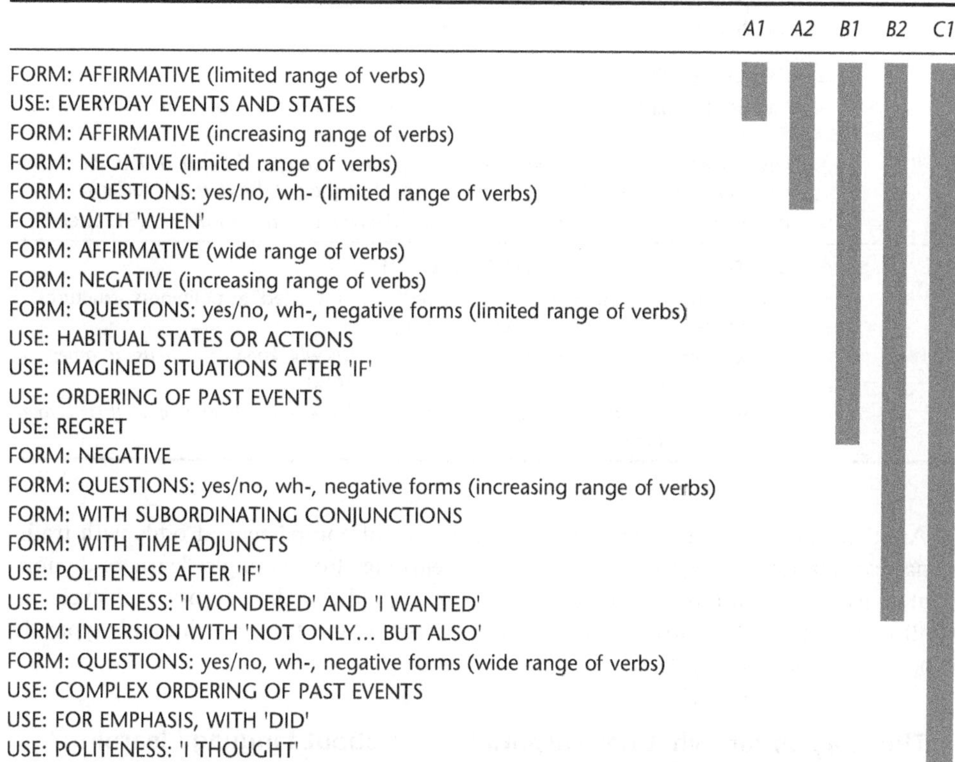

	A1	*A2*	*B1*	*B2*	*C1*
FORM: AFFIRMATIVE (limited range of verbs)					
USE: EVERYDAY EVENTS AND STATES					
FORM: AFFIRMATIVE (increasing range of verbs)					
FORM: NEGATIVE (limited range of verbs)					
FORM: QUESTIONS: yes/no, wh- (limited range of verbs)					
FORM: WITH 'WHEN'					
FORM: AFFIRMATIVE (wide range of verbs)					
FORM: NEGATIVE (increasing range of verbs)					
FORM: QUESTIONS: yes/no, wh-, negative forms (limited range of verbs)					
USE: HABITUAL STATES OR ACTIONS					
USE: IMAGINED SITUATIONS AFTER 'IF'					
USE: ORDERING OF PAST EVENTS					
USE: REGRET					
FORM: NEGATIVE					
FORM: QUESTIONS: yes/no, wh-, negative forms (increasing range of verbs)					
FORM: WITH SUBORDINATING CONJUNCTIONS					
FORM: WITH TIME ADJUNCTS					
USE: POLITENESS AFTER 'IF'					
USE: POLITENESS: 'I WONDERED' AND 'I WANTED'					
FORM: INVERSION WITH 'NOT ONLY... BUT ALSO'					
FORM: QUESTIONS: yes/no, wh-, negative forms (wide range of verbs)					
USE: COMPLEX ORDERING OF PAST EVENTS					
USE: FOR EMPHASIS, WITH 'DID'					
USE: POLITENESS: 'I THOUGHT'					

This illustrates a developmental pathway, one of the key findings of the study, that learners know a syntactic pattern or structure early on in their learning, and their competence increases as a developing repertoire of lexis and functions and lexis, including pragmatic meaning. Table 22.4 shows an illustration of this development from http://www.englishprofile.org/english-grammar-profile/egp-online at levels A1, A2, B1 and B2.

Table 22.4 Extracts from the *English Grammar Profile* of past simple development

Level	*Guideword, Can-do statement and Examples*
A1	USE: EVERYDAY EVENT AND STATES Can use the past simple to talk about everyday events or states. *The people were very polite* (A1, French). *Every time I went to Hendon Park, I saw so many people there* (A1, Polish).
A2	FORM: AFFIRMATIVE Can use the affirmative form with an increasing range of verbs. *I forgot to tell you some details about tomorrow evening* (A2, Turkish). *I spent £35 on all those clothes* (A2, Spanish - European).

(*Continued*)

Table 22.4 (Continued)

Level	*Guideword, Can-do statement and Examples*
B1	USE: ORDERING OF PAST EVENTS Can use the past simple to order sequences of events in the past, in the context of narratives. *I remember her as a shy girl but I read she became a manager, she went on lots of trips, she met a lot of new friends, she got married and then she got divorced* (B1, Italian). *We waited for the suitcase for two days and then we bought new dresses* (B1, Czech).
B2	USE: POLITENESS: 'I WONDERED', 'I WANTED' Can use the past simple with 'I wondered' and 'I wanted' as politeness structures, when making polite requests and thanking. *So, I wondered if you could introduce me to somebody who knows how to use a camera, so that I will be able to record my trip for you* (B2, Greek). *I wanted to know if the rooms are single or double, if they have showers and if there is room service?* (B2, Spanish - European).

Another key insight from the study was evidence of competence at odds with traditional expectations of grammar teaching and learning. For example, learners demonstrated use of 27 different structures to express conditionality across the levels, in contrast with the prescriptive paradigm of first, second and third conditionals typically expected and taught in grammar teaching syllabi.

4 The story so far: what has corpora told us about language learning?

Corpora so far have managed to offer researchers and teachers powerful insights into usage that has widened our understanding of constructs such as interlanguage. As Granger (2015) has observed, CIA and learner corpora have advanced several new dimensions of study, particularly in the areas of lexis and discourse. Language learning professionals now have access to studies that give them a comprehensive picture of L1 and L2 varieties through the analysis of discrete language features, collocations, lexical bundles, colligations and collostructions, which have considerably enhanced our knowledge of the L2 phrasicon. Corpus linguistics research methods offer important analytical affordances to those interested in the analysis of lexicogrammatical features with an emphasis on frequency and distribution of language items. The main contribution of corpora to language learning, therefore, is an increased understanding of the linguistic outputs produced by learners when engaged in a wide range of tasks and interactions across different media of delivery. We can use these outputs as evidence of a variety of learning factors such as the effect of L1 input, frequency of certain items in L2 input, saliency of discrete linguistic features in both L1 and L2 language and L1 influence. The evidence found in the corpora can inform language learning pedagogy and practice in many different ways (as demonstrated by other chapters in this section) and thus promote reflexivity in learners and teacher education and practice.

The three case studies in this chapter exemplify some important insights with implications for learning. The two longitudinal approaches showcased in the first case study display some of the most interesting contributions of corpora to language learning: tracking development. Whether development is located at the grammatical, the lexical or the lexicogrammatical level is for the language teachers and researchers to decide. In any case, they represent the need for a solid understanding of the methods used and show how small-scale approaches are useful in combining automatic analysis with manual tagging. A common thread through these representative studies is that they provide a glimpse of learning; they reveal a tip of the iceberg and raise many more questions not just about language learning theories, e.g. order of acquisition theory (Murakami 2014), explicit vs. implicit knowledge, teaching and learning (Ellis 2015), but also language learning contexts, e.g. classroom instruction, data-driven learning (see Chapter 29, this volume), the importance of input and its dynamic nature and availability in the digital age. Murakami (2014), which challenges the long-held belief of fixed L2 order of acquisition, is one such example demonstrating the central role that LCR is now playing in our understanding of learning. The second case study illustrates that the use of well-designed corpora allows researchers to understand monologic and dialogic communication as they reveal aspects of frequency, collocation, colligation, function and speaker variation that would otherwise remain hidden. The range of roles played by adverbs and their wider linguistic contexts reveal speakers' codification of meaning that goes from boosting to hedging, from disagreement to topic shift, from minimising to the expression of solidarity. Lack of exposure and awareness of the colligational frames where adverbs occur in conversation (Carter and McCarthy 2017; Hunston 2019) expressing stance-related meanings may contribute to L2 speakers' lack of understanding of the meanings construed and the most common lexical items integrating them. These studies both exemplify and emphasise the importance of the form–function relationship in language learning and challenge long-held beliefs of what to teach when. McCarthy (2020) describes the wider pedagogical impact of this kind of research, highlighting evidence of "grammaring" (Larsen-Freeman 2003) and the acquisition of grammar as a constant creative process.

We have seen the affordances offered by learner corpora and now turn to future possibilities. Does the nature of the data, the predominance of cross-sectional over longitudinal corpora, and the methodologies applied, the contexts of collection, inevitably result in studies offering narrow, static descriptions of language use, heavily reliant on quantitative approaches? What are we missing? Are there specific views of learner corpus research that have led us down the path of description but fallen short of what this means for learning, and how we might apply this to pedagogical settings?

5 Ways ahead: harnessing the potential

One of the main criticisms of existing corpora is that they fail to provide fine-grained data that can account for how the *learning* of the attested language actually happened, for example, in terms of the implicit vs. explicit nature of language learning, the presence of prototypical features in the L2 input or cognitive-related features associated with the processing of the L2. This criticism was echoed by McEnery *et al.* (2019), who voiced the aspiration to compile learner corpora that can resonate with a wider range of researchers and theoretical positionings.

LCR is relatively young; it is and should be a work in progress. The design elements in Table 22.2 may paint a picture of language learning that is biased towards a narrow conceptualisation. Speech and its unfolding development are the primary focus of L1 acquisition studies. Most L2 corpora are of written language. In the minority of spoken learner corpora available, there is little attempt to align spoken forms with anything other than written norms of the target language. Most learner corpora assume monolingual realities by grouping learners attending to one native tongue and by identifying one L2 target. This may point to a monolingual bias in the way the data are collected. Alternatively, we may think that the multilingual turn (Douglas Fir Group 2016) will take some time to be visible in how learner language is collected and how it is factored into corpus design. Also, having groups of L1 speakers learning an L2 immediately visualises the native language of the learners as the independent variable in most research designs, leaving aside other considerations that are crucial in language learning, as we have seen in the previous paragraphs. For example, if we decided to embrace the view that language learning is a complex adaptive system (Beckner *et al.* 2009), which explains the nonlinearity nature of language learning and the existence of so-called phase transitions, existing corpora may only be capable of providing some of the data that are required to understand these changes. It is expected that future developments in artificial intelligence (AI), machine learning and data processing will bring together new ways of looking at learner language development, offering more opportunities to analyse learner language using larger datasets and adaptive systems (e.g. Ballier *et al.* 2020). Expected outcomes will include more attention to adaptive learning, self-directed language learning and automatic assessment.

The emphasis on the comparison with "native-speaker" data has probably driven most of the findings in CIA and LCR to a narrow conceptualisation of language learning that is not currently massively endorsed by SLA researchers or L2 teaching professionals.

Perhaps this is the main challenge ahead for learner corpora: to imagine a method (a discipline perhaps?) that builds on Granger's (2015) reconceptualisation of CIA, but at the same time can successfully relate to current language learning characterised by the overlapping of material and digital social contexts in a multilingual world (Douglas Fir Group 2016; Ortega 2013) across language learning theories. For example, O'Keeffe (2021) points out how learner corpora are increasingly being explored so as to identify the process of construction development across levels of competence in usage-based accounts of language learning (see Chapter 23, this volume). Complementarity with other research methods and theories presents a good opportunity to increase the spread and the relevance of corpora in language learning. And this must be done in a context where learning goals are re-assessed in order to capture the multilingual nature of both learning and communication, both spoken and written, including attention to the learner as a person, the formation and transformation of identities (Leung and Scarino 2016) and the recognition of the situatedness of the learning and use beyond the analysis of errors.

Our current and future challenges are discovering ways of capturing, representing and understanding this in its broadest, deepest and most inclusive conceptualisations. Even when it is possible to measure general tendencies and find recurrent patterns in large-scale data and look at general frequency, distribution, collocational and colligational pattering, variation is always below the surface. McEnery *et al.* (2019: 84) call for a move beyond the 'immediately discoverable'. We suggest embracing this position as the starting point to look ahead.

Further reading

Carter, R. A. and McCarthy, M. J. (2017) 'Spoken Grammar: Where Are We and Where Are We Going?', *Applied linguistics* 38 (1): 1–20. (This review argues for a re-thinking of grammatical description based on spoken corpus evidence and considers development in digital communication and implications for description and pedagogy.)

Díez-Bedmar, M. B. (2018) 'Fine-Tuning Descriptors for CEFR B1 Level: Insights from Learner Corpora', *ELT Journal* 72(2): 199–209. (A conceptualisation of CEFR performance levels using learner data and a reformulation of the grammatical accuracy descriptor at the B1 level to raise learner awareness of frequent errors.)

Kyle, K. and Crossley, S. (2018) 'Measuring Syntactic Complexity in L2 Writing Using Fine-Grained Clausal and Phrasal Indices' *The Modern Language Journal* 102(2): 333–49. (A study of the predictive validity of three types of syntactic complexity indices related to clausal and phrasal complexity in the TOEFL exam, which suggests that more attention should be paid to phrases, in particular noun phrases, in language education.)

References

Ädel, A. (2015) 'Variability in Learner Corpora', in S. Granger, G. Gilquin and F. Meunier (eds) *The Cambridge Handbook of Learner Corpus Research*, Cambridge University Press, pp. 379–400.

Ballier, N., Canu, S., Petitjean, C., Gasso, G., Balhana, C., Alexopoulou, T. and Gaillat, T. (2020) 'Machine Learning for Learner English: A Plea for Creating Learner Data Challenges', *International Journal of Learner Corpus Research* 6(1): 72–103.

Beckner, C., Ellis, N. C., Blythe, R., Holland, J., Bybee, J., Ke, J., Christiansen, M. H., Larsen-Freeman, D., Croft, W., Schoenemann, T. and Five Graces Group (2009) 'Language is a Complex Adaptive System: Position Paper' *Language Learning* 59: 1–26.

Bley-Vroman, R. (1983) 'The Comparative Fallacy in Interlanguage Studies: The Case of Systematicity', *Language learning* 33(1): 1–17.

Buttery, P. and Caines, A. (2010) 'Normalising Frequency Counts to Account for "Opportunity of Use" in Learner Corpora', in Y. Tono, Y. Kawaguchi and M. Minegishi (eds) *Developmental and Crosslinguistic Perspectives in Learner Corpus Research*, Amsterdam: John Benjamins, 187–204.

Callies, M. (2015) 'Learner Corpus Methodology', in S. Granger, G. Gilquin and F. Meunier (eds) *The Cambridge Handbook of Learner Corpus Research*, Cambridge University Press, pp. 35–55.

Capel, A. (2012) 'Completing the English Vocabulary Profile: C1 and C2 Vocabulary', *English Profile Journal* 3(1): 1–14.

Carter, R. A. and McCarthy, M. J. (2017) 'Spoken Grammar: Where Are We and Where Are We Going?', *Applied linguistics* 38(1): 1–20.

Cook, V. (1991) 'The Poverty-of-the-Stimulus Argument and Multicompetence', *Second Language Research* 7: 103–17.

Corder, S. P. (1967) 'The Significance of Learners' Errors', *International Review of Applied Linguistics* 5: 161–70.

Dornyei, Z. (2007) *Research Methods in Applied Linguistics*, Oxford: Oxford University Press.

Douglas Fir Group (2016) 'A Transdisciplinary Framework For SLA in a Multilingual World', *Modern Language Journal* 100: 19–47.

Ellis, N. C. (2015) 'Implicit and Explicit Language Learning: Their Dynamic Interface and Complexity', in P. Rebuschat (ed.) *Implicit and Explicit Learning of Languages*, Amsterdam: John Benjamins, pp. 1–24.

Ellis, N. C., Römer, U. and O'Donnell, M. B. (2016) *Usage-Based Approaches to Language Acquisition and Processing: Cognitive and Corpus Investigations of Construction Grammar*, Malden, MA: Wiley.

Ellis, R. and Barkhuizen, G. P. (2005) *Analysing Learner Language*, Oxford: Oxford University Press.

Gablasova, D., Brezina, V. and McEnery, T. (2017) 'Collocations in Corpus-Based Language Learning Research: Identifying, Comparing, and Interpreting the Evidence', *Language Learning* 67(S1): 155–79.

Granger, S. (1994) 'The Learner Corpus: A Revolution in Applied Linguistics', *English Today* 10(3): 25–33.

Granger, S. (2009) 'The Contribution of Learner Corpora to Second Language Acquisition and Foreign Language Teaching', in K. Aijmer (ed.) *Corpora and Language Teaching*, Amsterdam: John Benjamins Publishing, pp. 13–32.

Granger, S. (2015) 'Contrastive Interlanguage Analysis: A Reappraisal', *International Journal of Learner Corpus Research* 1(1): 7–24.

Green A. (2012) *Language Functions Revisited: Theoretical and Empirical Bases for Language Construct Definition Across the Ability Range. English Profile Studies 2*, Cambridge: Cambridge University Press.

Greenbaum, S. (1990) 'Standard English and the International Corpus of English', *World Englishes*, 9(1): 79–83.

Harrison, J. and Barker, F. (eds) (2015) *English Profile in Practice. English Profile Studies 5*, Cambridge: Cambridge University Press.

Hawkins, J. A. and Buttery, P. (2010) 'Criterial Features In Learner Corpora: Theory And Illustrations', *English Profile Journal* 1(1): 1–23.

Hunston, S. (2019) 'Patterns, Constructions, and Applied Linguistics', *International Journal of Corpus Linguistics* 24(3): 324–53.

Larsen-Freeman, D. (2003) *Teaching Language: From Grammar to Grammaring*, Boston, MA: Heinle.

Leung, C. and Scarino, A. (2016) 'Reconceptualizing the Nature of Goals and Outcomes in Language/s Education', *The Modern Language Journal* 100(S1): 81–95.

Mark, G. and Pérez-Paredes, P. (2018) 'Examining High Frequency Adverbs in Learner and Native Speaker Language: Some Implications for Spoken EFL Learning and Teaching', *13th Teaching and Language Corpora conference (TaLC 2018)*, Faculty of Education, University of Cambridge, July 2018.

McCarthy, M. J. (2020) *Innovations and Challenges in Grammar*, London: Routledge.

McEnery, T., Brezina, V., Gablasova, D. and Banerjee, J. (2019) 'Corpus Linguistics, Learner Corpora, and SLA: Employing Technology to Analyze Language Use', *Annual Review of Applied Linguistics* 39: 74–92.

Mitchell, R., Myles, F. and Marsden, E. (2013) *Second Language Learning Theories*, London: Routledge.

Murakami, A. (2014) *Individual Variation and the Role of L1 in the L2 Development of English Grammatical Morphemes: Insights from Learner Corpora*, unpublished PhD thesis, University of Cambridge.

Myles, F. (2005) 'Interlanguage Corpora and Second Language Acquisition Research', *Second Language Research* 21(4): 373–31.

Myles, F. (2015) 'Second Language Acquisition Theory and Learner Corpus Research', in S. Granger, G. Gilquin and F. Meunier (eds) *The Cambridge Handbook of Learner Corpus Research*, Cambridge: Cambridge University Press, pp. 309–31.

O'Keeffe, A. (2021) 'Data-Driven Learning - A Call for a Broader Research Gaze', *Language Teaching* 54(2): 259–72

O'Keeffe, A. and Mark, G. (2017) 'The English Grammar Profile of Learner Competence. Methodology and Key Findings', *International Journal of Corpus Linguistics* 22(4): 457–89.

Ortega, L. (2013) 'SLA for the 21st Century: Disciplinary Progress, Transdisciplinary Relevance, and the Bi/Multilingual Turn', *Language Learning* 63: 1–24.

Paquot, M. and Plonsky, L. (2017) 'Quantitative Research Methods and Study Quality in Learner Corpus Research', *International Journal of Learner Corpus Research* 3(1): 61–94.

Pérez-Paredes, P. (2019) 'English Language Teacher Education and Second Language Acquisition', in S. Walsh and S. Mann (eds) *Routledge Handbook of English Language Teacher Education*, London: Routledge, pp. 253–67.

Pérez-Paredes, P. and Díez-Bedmar, B. (2019) 'Certainty Adverbs in Spoken Learner Language: The Role of Tasks and Proficiency', *International Journal of Learner Corpus Research* 5(2): 253–79.

Pérez-Paredes, P. and Bueno, C. (2019) 'A Corpus-Driven Analysis of Certainty Stance Adverbs: *Obviously, Really* and *Actually* in Spoken Native and Learner English', *Journal of Pragmatics*, 140, 22–32.

Pérez-Paredes, P., Mark, G. and O'Keeffe, A. (2020) *The Impact of Usage-Based Approaches on Second Language Learning And Teaching*, Cambridge: Cambridge University Press, retrieved from: https://www.cambridge.org/us/educationreform/insights.

Römer, U. and Garner, J. R. (2019) 'The Development of Verb Constructions in Spoken Learner English: Tracing Effects Of Usage and Proficiency', *International Journal of Learner Corpus Research* 5(2): 206–29.

Selinker, L. (1972) 'Interlanguage', *International Review of Applied Linguistics* 10(3): 209–31.

Siyanova-Chanturia, A. and Spina, S. (2019) 'Multi-Word Expressions in Second Language Writing: A Large-Scale Longitudinal Learner Corpus Study', *Language Learning*, 70(2): 420–63.

Thewissen, J. (2013) 'Capturing L2 Accuracy Developmental Patterns: Insights from An Error Tagged Learner Corpus', *The Modern Language Journal* 97: 77–101.

Tono, Y. (2003) 'Learner Corpora: Design, Development and Applications', in D. Archer, P. Rayson, A. Wilson and T. McEnery (eds) *Proceedings of the Corpus Linguistics 2003 Conference, UCREL Technical Paper 16*, Lancaster: Lancaster University, pp. 800–9.

Tono, Y. and Díez-Bedmar, M. B. (2014) 'Focus on Learner Writing at the Beginning and Intermediate Stages: The ICCI Corpus', *International Journal of Corpus Linguistics* 19(2): 163–77.

Tyler, A. and Ortega, L. (2018) 'Usage-Inspired L2 Instruction an Emergent, Researched Pedagogy', in A. Tyler, L. Ortega, M. Uno and H. I. Park (eds) *Usage-Inspired L2 Instruction: Researched Pedagogy*, Amsterdam: John Benjamins, pp. 3–26.

Vyatkina, N. (2013) 'Specific Syntactic Complexity: Developmental Profiling of Individuals Based on an Annotated Learner Corpus', *The Modern Language Journal* 97(S1): 11–30.

23

What can corpus linguistics tell us about second language acquisition?

Ute Römer and Jamie Garner

1 Corpus research for second language acquisition

Our chapter starts from the assumption that CL has a lot to offer to researchers in the field of SLA. We consider CL a particularly powerful set of tools and methods for language analysis that allows us to pursue usage-based approaches to linguistics and language acquisition that highlight the importance of language input and focus on how language structure emerges from use (Tomasello 2003). It does so by helping us uncover patterns in the linguistic input and output of language learners. SLA research has as its central aim to better understand how a second language develops in learners over time (e.g. Kramsch 2000; Ortega 2012) but is broad in its scope, encompassing 'basic and applied work on the acquisition and loss of second (third, etc.) languages and dialects by children and adults, learning naturalistically and/or with the aid of formal instruction, as individuals or in groups, in foreign, second language, or lingua franca settings' (Doughty and Long 2003: 3). Among the core things that SLA researchers aim to better understand are (i) the process of SLA; (ii) developmental stages in SLA; (iii) the input learners receive and the effect it has on them; (iv) the linguistic choices learners make and how they differ from those made by first language (L1) speakers; (v) patterns in learner production data; and (vi) potential effects of learner L1, age, motivation, etc., on the acquisition process. We argue that (and will illustrate how) CL can provide useful insights into all of these topics.

We consider corpora of L1 and L2 production data an ideal data source for SLA researchers. As Lozano and Mendikoetxea (2013: 66) point out, '[m]uch of SLA research has traditionally relied on elicited experimental data while disfavouring natural language data'. Corpora consist of such natural language data (both spoken and written), collected in a variety of settings from usually hundreds, sometimes thousands, of speakers of a wide range of linguistic backgrounds. In a recent conceptual review article on data sharing in SLA, MacWhinney (2017) also stresses the importance of combining data collected in experiments with 'corpus data documenting the course of SLA' (p. 254). We would argue, in agreement with Granger (2009: 16), that research based on corpora can 'lay claim to greater representativeness than previous SLA studies', studies that

DOI: 10.4324/9780367076399-23

attempted to measure language acquisition based on data from grammaticality judgment tasks, fill-in-the-blank exercises or acceptability tasks. The good news for SLA researchers is that, thanks to corpus linguists who have compiled learner corpora, the availability and accessibility of data produced by language learners have increased dramatically over the last two decades (Mackey 2014). We now have access to searchable databases of hundreds or thousands of learner texts or speech events, consisting of several hundred thousand to several million words (see Chapter 22, this volume). In the following sections, we will illustrate how some of these databases have been used to contribute to a better understanding of SLA. Our focus will be on research that, by describing learner performance data at various stages of acquiring an L2, highlights the *process* rather than the product of SLA. This research is essentially based on three types of corpora (as Sections 2, 3 and 4 will detail):

- Cross-sectional learner corpora, containing language from different groups of learners of different proficiency levels collected at one point in time;
- Longitudinal learner corpora, containing language from the same learner or group of learners collected at multiple points in time;
- Pseudolongitudinal learner corpora, containing language from different but overlapping groups of learners collected at multiple points in time.

We believe that SLA researchers would particularly benefit from using these corpora types to complement their methodological toolbox, as they provide a rich amount of empirical data which allow the researcher to study language development.

2 Research on cross-sectional learner corpora

A corpus type that is commonly used to describe the process of language acquisition is the cross-sectional learner corpus. Cross-sectional learner corpora contain spoken and/or written data collected at one point in time from groups of learners at different levels of proficiency (Jarvis and Pavlenko 2008; Granger 2013). They allow the researcher to compare, for instance, language produced by a group of L1 Chinese learners of English at one proficiency level with the linguistic output of a group of L1 Chinese learners at a lower or higher proficiency level. Examples of cross-sectional learner corpora that have been used in recent research on L2 development include the *Trinity Lancaster Corpus* (TLC; Gablasova *et al.* 2019), the *International Corpus Network of Asian Learners of English* (ICNALE; Ishikawa 2013) and the *International Corpus of Crosslinguistic Interlanguage* (ICCI; Hong 2012; Tono and Díez-Bedmar 2014). Researchers have used these and other cross-sectional collections of learner data to investigate a wide range of language phenomena, including lexicogrammatical features, tense and aspect, complexity and accuracy and pragmatic features.

Cross-sectional learner corpus studies that provide insights into the development of L2 learners' lexicogrammatical or phraseological knowledge include Chen (2019) on fixed multiword sequences, Xu (2016) on ditransitive constructions, Gilquin (2019) on light verb constructions and Römer and Garner (2019) on verb–argument constructions. Chen (2019) used 5,200 L2 essays written by learners from various countries in Asia included in ICNALE to describe how learners' formulaicity of recurrent, fixed, multiword combinations of different lengths (2-grams to 5-grams) develops with growing proficiency (see Chapter 15, this volume). Using the directional association strength measure ΔP and with the help of mixed-effect modeling, the author was able to show that formulaicity (both directed forward, e.g. predicting the word *for* when given *apply*, and backward, e.g. predicting the word *at* when given *home*) increased with proficiency (see Chapters 13 and 14, this volume). Xu (2016) compared *give*-ditransitives in the written cross-sectional *Chinese Learner English Corpus* (CLEC) and in the *Louvain Corpus of Native English Essays* (LOCNESS) to highlight differences in learner use of the construction across proficiency levels. Results from this study indicate developments from short and simple to more complex and semantically varied structures, as well as a decrease in the occurrence of erroneous *give*-ditransitives as learners move from lower to higher proficiency levels. Focusing on light-verb constructions (LVCs; consisting of a high-frequency, semantically bleached verb and an eventive noun phrase) involving verbs such as GIVE, MAKE or TAKE and using spoken learner data from a TLC sample, Gilquin (2019) compares construction use across proficiency levels and L1 groups, distinguishing between English as a foreign language (EFL) (Italy, Mexico, Spain) and English as a second language (ESL) acquisitional settings (India). Her results point towards a 'tendency towards an increased frequency of LVCs, as well as more complex and abstract uses' from intermediate to advanced levels and from EFL to ESL contexts (Gilquin 2019: 181). Using data from the same corpus (TLC), Römer and Garner (2019) provide insights into how L2 learners' productive knowledge of English verb–argument constructions (VACs; i.e. combinations of verbs and their arguments; e.g, "V *about* n" as in "talk about the weather") develops with increasing proficiency and in what ways this knowledge is affected by L1 English usage. The authors found that verb distributions for advanced learners were generally more productive, more predictable and more similar to L1 English usage than for low-intermediate learners. They also observed that verb-VAC frequency (i.e. the frequency of a verb in a specific VAC) in native English usage is predictive of verb-VAC frequencies in the L2 learner data across proficiency levels.

Worth highlighting among the TAM (tense, aspect, and modality) studies that draw upon cross-sectional corpora are Zhao and Shirai (2018) on past tense, Fuchs and Werner (2018) on stative progressives and Elturki and Salsbury (2016) on modal expressions. Zhao and Shirai (2018) use a corpus of oral narratives produced by L1 Arabic EFL learners of two broad proficiency groups (beginner vs. intermediate/advanced) to study what effects phonological saliency and lexical aspect play in the L2 acquisition of past tense morphology. Zhao and Shirai's findings confirm the aspect hypothesis (AH) which predicts that learners' use of tense-aspect markers in the L2 is influenced by semantic aspectual verb classes (e.g. activity verbs are associated with progressive aspect; Andersen and Shirai 1994). The results presented by Zhao and Shirai indicate that the learners who participated in their study were indeed strongly influenced by the lexical aspect classes of verbs as they acquired past tense marking. Using written data from learners of typologically different L1s from the ICCI, Fuchs and Werner (2018) assess whether low and intermediate EFL learners commonly extend the progressive to stative verbs (which would contradict the AH). They observe that across L1s and across levels, learners very rarely use stative progressives – a finding which confirms this specific claim of the AH. Another TAM acquisition study by Elturki and Salsbury (2016) uses a corpus of 1,200 essays written by high school students in Dubai (UAE) to investigate the development of English modality in L1 Arabic learners across six proficiency levels. They find that at the lowest levels, learners heavily rely on the high-frequency modal *can*, but other modals become more frequent, and new forms (including periphrastic expressions of modality, such as *BE able to* or *HAVE to*) emerge as learners advance in their L2 proficiency. Access to data from a cross-sectional learner corpus enabled the authors to trace learners' abilities to distinguish modal meanings and to describe how these abilities differ across proficiency levels.

Researchers interested in learner development of syntactic complexity and accuracy have demonstrated the usefulness of cross-sectional learner corpora as well. Thewissen (2013) uses an error-tagged and CEFR-scored subset of the *International Corpus of Learner English* (223 essays written by L1 French, German and Spanish learners at CEFR levels B1 to C2) to uncover developmental patterns in L2 learner accuracy. The author found that different error types follow distinct developmental trajectories and that progress towards fewer errors 'is often located between B1 and B2' (p. 77) at the intermediate learner level. De Clercq and Housen (2017) examine syntactic complexity development in beginner to advanced L1 Dutch learners of English and French (divided into four proficiency levels) based on 200 oral narratives produced by these learners (half of them in English, half in French). A range of measures of syntactic diversity and syntactic elaboration applied to this learner production data indicate gradual increases in these measures and trends towards 'overall diversification with increased proficiency' (p. 327). Using a different corpus, the Spanish component of the cross-sectional ICCI, Pérez-Paredes and Díez-Bedmar (2019a) also explore the syntactic complexity of learner writing at different secondary school grade levels with a goal to identify 'development milestones in language acquisition' (p. 101). They list especially the presence of 'countable nouns, prepositional phrases, verbs and general adverbs' (p. 101) as indicative of the transition from lower to higher levels.

Finally, cross-sectional learner corpora have also been used to study how pragmatic features develop in L2 learners. Inspired by studies that described links between adverb use and communicative competence, Pérez-Paredes and Sánchez-Tornel (2014) and Pérez-Paredes and Díez-Bedmar (2019b) examine adverbs in learner language at different proficiency levels. While the former study focuses on L1 Chinese, Polish and Spanish learners' use of general adverbs in written texts produced from grades 3 to 12 retrieved from the ICCI, the latter zooms in on three certainty adverbs (*actually*, *really*, *obviously*) used in the spoken language of L1 Spanish learners at intermediate to advanced proficiency levels (CEFR levels B1 to C1) culled from the TLC. Both studies describe a more frequent and varied use of adverbs in L2 learner language as the learner's age and level of proficiency increase, as well as a development towards adverb frequencies observed in native English usage. Another study on a pragmatic feature in a cross-sectional corpus is Götz (2019) which focuses on L2 learner use of filled pauses (*er*, *ehm*, etc.). With the help of spoken intermediate and advanced learner production data from the TLC, the author shows that the frequency and distribution of filled pauses are significantly influenced by learner proficiency level (decrease at C1/C2 levels), but even more so by other variables like the learner's country of origin and age of acquisition. Götz's findings hence have implications not only for SLA theory but also for learner corpus design and compilation. Taken together, these studies provide insights into how learners' communicative language competence develops as they move towards advanced levels of proficiency.

As Doughty and Long (2003: 3) have pointed out, 'the vast majority of SLA studies are cross-sectional, with serious resulting limitations on the conclusions that can be drawn on some important issues'. This criticism also applies to learner corpus studies. We could argue that in order to fully understand the process of language acquisition, we need to study data collected from the same learners at different points in time as they move from one proficiency level to the next, rather than from different learners at different levels of proficiency at one point in time. The next section will showcase studies that use such data collections: longitudinal learner corpora.

3 Research on longitudinal learner corpora

Given the need to investigate language development for learners over an extended period of time, there has recently been an increase in research that uses longitudinal learner corpora. In contrast to their cross-sectional counterparts, longitudinal learner corpora consist of learner speech or writing collected from the same group of learners at multiple time points. These corpora can vary in terms of the number of learners included and the number of texts collected per learner, usually with a trade-off existing between the two. That is, longitudinal learner corpora that include a large number of learners (i.e. more than 20) typically only collect a few texts from each learner. In contrast, learner corpora with fewer learners tend to contain more texts produced by each learner at different points in time. Longitudinal learner corpora also vary in the length of time covered, with most of them covering between one semester of study and two years. In terms of linguistic features examined in research using longitudinal learner corpora, these studies are similar to their cross-sectional counterparts in that they tend to examine the development of lexicogrammatical features (especially constructions), productive vocabulary knowledge and grammatical complexity and accuracy.

Most learner corpus studies investigating the development of constructions in learner language have tended to be longitudinal in nature. These studies have investigated the development of a range of different constructions in both naturalistic and instructed settings. Using the European Science Foundation corpus, a corpus of spoken interactions between L1 speakers and naturalistic L2 English learners from multiple L1 backgrounds over a period of five years, Ellis and Ferreira-Junior (2009a, 2009b), investigate the development of three verb–argument constructions (verb-locative, verb-object-locative and verb-object-object) in learner language. The findings from both studies indicate that the learners first produced verbs in each construction that were semantically general, prototypical and most frequent in their partners' speech. Over time these learners expanded their repetoire to produce other frequently occuring and strongly associated verbs in the selected constructions.

Using the *Multimedia Adult English Learner Corpus* (MAELC; Reder *et al.* 2003), a longitudinal corpus of spoken classroom interactions over multiple years, Eskildsen and colleagues examine the development of a wide range of constructions, including *can*-patterns (Eskildsen 2009), negation constructions (Eskildsen 2012), questions (Eskildsen 2015) and motion constructions (Li *et al.* 2014; Eskildsen *et al.* 2015). Overall, the results from these studies indicate that learners move from a reliance on fixed constructions to more target-like, varied and productive schematic templates that are based on those fixed exemplars. For example, the two subjects in Eskildsen (2012) move from a reliance on fixed expressions such as *I don't know* to a more schematic "subj *don't* Verb" construction, with an increasing variety of subjects and verbs occupying the variable slots. Additionally, given their use of corpus data compiled from classroom interactions, these studies are able to show how local affordances in the communicative context can lead to construction development. In each of the studies, the learners' use of the target constructions become more variable and schematic as the interactive needs of their communicative context change and demand the use of more variable constructions.

In addition to research on construction development, multiple studies have investigated the longitudinal development of other types of lexicogrammatical features, such as bigrams (two-word sequences) and trigrams (three-word sequences). Overall, these studies demonstrate mixed patterns of development. For example, Li and Schmitt (2010), in their analysis of adjective–noun bigrams in a corpus of course papers produced by highly advanced L1 Chinese ESL writers, find that these writers used a less diverse range of adjective–noun bigrams and used them less frequently over the course of one year. Bestgen and Granger (2014) used the Michigan State University (MSU) corpus (Connor-Linton and Polio 2014), a corpus of essays written by university-aged learners enrolled in a semester of intensive English writing courses, to analyse the development of bigram use (e.g. *at the*, *for example*) in L2 writing. Their results indicate that intermediate and advanced L2 writers produced slightly less strongly associated bigrams consisting of high-frequency words (as measured by t-score) over time.

Learner corpus studies investigating the longitudinal development of bigram and trigram production in speech have produced slightly different results from writing studies such as Li and Schmitt (2010) or Bestgen and Granger (2014). Crossley and Salsbury (2011), utilising a corpus of spoken interviews between native speakers and six ESL learners collected over the course of one year, find that learners become more accurate in their bigram use over time. Similarly, results from Garner and Crossley (2018) indicated that L2 speakers produce a greater proportion of target-like bigrams and trigrams over the course of four months. Their corpus consisted of conversations between L1 speakers and L2 speakers at multiple proficiency levels, as well as more proficient and less proficient L2 speakers. Additionally, their results show differences in development across both proficiency levels and L1 status of the learner's conversation partners. Specifically, the results show that less proficient speakers had the greatest amount of growth in bigram proportions, while learners' whose conversation partners were L2 speakers experience greater growth in their use of frequent bigrams.

Studies focusing on longitudinal development of single-word knowledge and use have also revealed how different measures of productive L2 lexical knowledge, such as lexical sophistication and diversity, develop over time. Tracy-Ventura (2017) uses data from the Language and Social Networks Abroad Project (LANGSNAP; Mitchell *et al.* 2017), a corpus of oral and written tasks, to examine the development of lexical sophistication in L2 Spanish over a nine-month study abroad period. Her findings indicate that, after nine months of study in Spanish-speaking contexts, the learners produced more low-frequency words and fewer very frequent words. Zheng (2016) finds similar results in her study of productive L2 vocabulary knowledge over the course of one year for L1 Chinese writers. The learners represented in her corpus produce more low-frequency words as well as a greater diversity of words in their compositions over time. However, results of the study show little development in the areas of lexical density and academic trigram and 4-gram (four-word sequences) use over the same amount of time.

Longitudinal learner corpus research has also focused on the development of syntactic complexity and accuracy in L2 English as well as other languages. Crossley and McNamara (2014) and Bulté and Housen (2014) analyse the development of syntactic complexity in L2 writing development over the span of one semester of intensive English study using the MSU corpus. Crossley and McNamara use indices in Coh-Metrix (Graesser *et al.* 2004) that measure complexity at the clausal and phrasal levels, while Bulté and Housen (2014) manually annotate the texts for clausal, phrasal and sentence-level complexity measures. Results from Crossley and McNamara (2014) show that the learners produced fewer verb phrases, more words before the main verb, more negation and fewer similarly constructed sentences from their first essay to the last. Results from Bulté and Housen (2014) show that from their first essay to their last, the L2 writers increase the length of their sentences, t-units (i.e. main clauses with all their modifiers) and finite clauses; use fewer simple sentences; and produce more complex and compound sentences. Both studies also find significant increases in the length of noun phrases produced by the L2 writers. Vyatkina (2013) examines syntactic complexity development for two L2 German learners using a corpus of essays produced over four semesters of coursework. Her results indicate that while both learners experienced development in some indices of syntactic complexity, one learner showed stronger and more linear developmental trends than the other. Lastly, Meunier and Littré (2013) combine learner corpus and experimental techniques to examine the development of accuracy in the use of the tense and aspect system by advanced L1 French learners of English. They use the *Longitudinal Database of Learner English* (LONGDALE; Meunier 2015b), a corpus consisting of three essays per learner written over the span of three years. The results of their analysis indicate that the number of tense and aspect errors decreased over the course of three years, both at the group and individual levels.

4 Research on pseudolongitudinal learner corpora

A third and final type of learner corpus that has been successfully used to study L2 learner language development is the pseudolongitudinal (also sometimes referred to as "quasi-longitudinal") learner corpus. Pseudolongitudinal learner corpora contain a mix of data from the same learners as they move through different stages in the language acquisition process, capturing their evolving linguistic knowledge (i.e. longitudinal data) and from learners at different proficiency levels collected at the same point in time (i.e. cross-sectional data). So while some learners move through all levels in a course from which production samples are collected, others may enter at the non-beginner level or drop out before they reach the most advanced level of proficiency. Two examples of pseudolongitudinal learner corpora that are frequently accessed by usage-based SLA researchers are the *Education First-Cambridge Open Language Database* (EFCAMDAT; Alexopoulou *et al.* 2015)[1] and the *Cambridge Learner Corpus* (CLC; Nicholls 2003).[2] Both are large collections of texts produced by thousands of L2 learners from a variety of L1 backgrounds. The CLC currently consists of over 56 million words produced by more than 250,000 learners taking *Cambridge English* exams (Barker *et al.* 2015), while the second release of EFCAMDAT contains over 83 million words from assignments written by more 174,000 learners (Huang *et al.* 2018).

In an early EFCAMDAT-based publication, Alexopoulou *et al.* (2015) demonstrate that this corpus can support what they call a 'key empirical task of SLA research', namely 'to document the developmental trajectories of individual structures' (p. 126). The structures that their study focuses on are different types of relative clauses (RCs), which they track in learner nationality-specific subsets of the corpus across proficiency levels. The authors are able to trace increases in the use of some RC types with increasing proficiency and document L1 effects on RC production (e.g. a strong preference of Mexicans, Italians and Brazilians for *that*-RCs). Alexopoulou *et al.* (2017) use EFCAMDAT to study how learner language develops over time in terms of linguistic complexity and accuracy of language use and to uncover potential effects of the writing task type on complexity and accuracy phenomena. The rich dataset combined with a multifactorial study design allowed the authors to demonstrate that 'linguistic complexity and accuracy can characterize both development from early to advanced proficiency and tasks' (p. 202). Three other recent studies have used subsets of EFCAMDAT to investigate the development of L2 learner phraseological knowledge. The focus in Garner (2016) is on so-called "phrase-frames" in collections of texts produced by beginner to advanced L1 German learners (levels A1 to C1). Phrase-frames are repeatedly used word sequences of specific lengths (in Garner's case, four words) that have at least one variable slot (e.g. *on the * hand*, capturing *on the one hand* and *on the other hand*). Garner finds that as learners' proficiency increased, their most frequently used phrase-frames became 'more variable, less predictable, and more functionally complex' (p. 31). Similar trends in expansions of L2 learners' phraseological repertoires were also observed by Römer and Berger (2019) and Römer (2019). Both studies use data from EFCAMDAT to trace the development of VACs in L1 German and L1 Spanish learners of English. While Römer and Berger (2019) focus on a set of 19 VACs of the verb-preposition-noun phrase type (e.g. "V *with* n", "V *for* n"), Römer (2019) takes a more comprehensive approach in systematically extracting all constructions of over 700,000 verb tokens from EFCAMDAT subsets with the help of NLP technology. Both studies confirm expansions of the learners' VAC repertoires in terms of VAC types, productivity and complexity from lowest to highest proficiency levels. With increasing proficiency, learners also show a 'development from pre-dominantly fixed sequences to more flexible and productive ones' (Römer 2019: 270) and a 'move in verb-VAC associations toward a native usage norm' (Römer and Berger 2019: 1107).

With the goal of generating an 'English Grammar Profile of learner competence' (p. 457), O'Keeffe and Mark (2017) access the CLC to shed light on multiple aspects of learner grammar across CEFR proficiency levels A1 through C2. Level by level they observe 'an expanding repertoire of grammatical uses' of forms (p. 477) and a development of learner pragmatic competence that goes with it. For example, while learners acquire the simple past at level A1, they only start to use the form with the verbs *wonder* and *want* to express politeness at the B2 level. In another comprehensive study of learner lexicogrammatical development, Hawkins and Filipovic (2012) use the CLC to identify for each proficiency level sets of so-called grammatical "criterial features", which they define as 'properties of learner English that are characteristic and indicative of L2 proficiency at each of the levels and that distinguish higher levels from lower levels' (Hawkins and Filipovic 2012: 11; see also Hawkins and Buttery 2010). Another outcome of this research (in addition to sets of criterial features) are lists of error types that improve from one level to the next. The authors observe a particularly significant decrease in error type numbers between upper-intermediate (B2) and advanced levels (C1), indicating significant developmental progress as learners move from the B2 to C1 level.

5 Bringing corpus linguistics and second language acquisition closer together

As the various studies summarized in our chapter have hopefully managed to illustrate, learner corpora are a valuable resource for SLA research and have allowed us to gain a better understanding of trajectories in the process of language acquisition. Learner corpora are powerful tools that have enhanced our understanding of SLA theory and challenged existing assumptions of SLA, for example, assumptions about characteristics of learner interlanguage or learners' morpheme acquisition order (Murakami 2016;

Murakami and Alexopoulou 2016). However, despite the progress that has already been made in learner corpus-based research on L2 development, we still see several avenues for improvement in learner corpus creation that could increase the use and usefulness of this data source in SLA research.

The first way in which learner corpora could be improved for use in SLA research would be to create additional truly longitudinal learner corpora. At present, most publicly available learner corpora that capture learner data produced at multiple proficiency levels are cross-sectional. While these learner corpora are useful for describing generalised stages of L2 development, they cannot provide the evidence needed to examine individual developmental processes. This is important because, as Lowie and Verspoor (2015: 78) note, '[a]ll of the most relevant questions about SLA [...], are implicitly or explicitly about change over time'. To really examine the process of SLA at both the individual and group level, longitudinal learner corpora are needed. If it can make more of these corpora available to researchers, corpus linguistics as a tool for studying language development will likely become more attractive to scholars in SLA.

Secondly, we not only need more longitudinal learner corpora but also corpora that are better designed. Improvements in learner corpus design could include the collection of more, and more varied, texts from individual learners. Regarding the former, it would be beneficial for future longitudinal learner corpora to be denser in terms of the number of texts collected from each learner, similar to resources available in English L1 acquisition research (e.g. MacWhinney 2000). With denser collections of learner production, researchers working with these corpora can perform more detailed analyses of individual developmental trajectories (Meunier 2015a). This means collecting data from learners at regular intervals and more often than at the beginning, middle and end of the study period. In terms of types of tasks, future learner corpora ought to include spoken and written texts produced in response to a wider variety of tasks and prompts and belonging to genres other than the argumentative essay. By including a wider variety of spoken and written tasks and text types, CL can provide SLA researchers with better access to evidence of the ways in which learner language develops.

Lastly, future learner corpora would benefit from including more learner and contextual metadata (see also Hasko 2013). Most current learner corpora only contain basic facts about learners such as L1 background, proficiency, gender and age. Other potentially influential learner and contextual variables, such as motivation and time spent studying English, are often left unaccounted for. We also rarely know enough about the instructional setting in which data were collected (What teaching methods were dominant? What textbooks and assessment tools were used?). By including such metadata, learner corpora can provide SLA researchers with stronger datasets from which more detailed explanations of L2 developmental trajectories can be derived. In the case of longitudinal learner corpora, these metadata would ideally be collected at multiple time points, providing even more information about the relationships between these factors and L2 development.

An example of a newly developed learner corpus that incorporates some of these suggestions is the *Kansas Developmental Learner Corpus* (KANDEL; Vyatkina 2016). KANDEL is a pseudolongitudinal corpus of L2 German by L1 English speakers, consisting of data from five cohorts of students over four semesters of study. Texts were written every three weeks, varied in terms of topic and were related to the course work students were completing. The corpus includes metadata related to learner (e.g. age, gender, languages spoken), context (e.g. course level, track of study) and task (e.g. genre, topic, associated learning materials). The wide range of metadata included in KANDEL allows for detailed analyses of learner and contextual differences and their dynamic interaction with language development.

We would argue that successful developments of more relevant and robust longitudinal learner corpora for SLA (as outlined here) require greater collaboration between corpus linguists (especially corpus compilers) and SLA researchers. We would like to echo Mackey (2014: 89) who suggests that 'partnerships need to be developed between experts on current theories and data in SLA and experts in the processes of automatic annotation and analysis of large learner corpora'. Such partnerships will be crucial to ensure that newly designed longitudinal learner corpora are fully beneficial to SLA researchers and meet their needs. In the meantime, we encourage the SLA community to explore some of the longitudinal, cross-sectional and pseudolongitudinal learner corpora that are currently available and to see in what ways access to such resources may help them accomplish their research goals.

Notes

1 https://corpus.mml.cam.ac.uk/efcamdat2/public_html/
2 https://www.cambridge.org/elt/corpus/learner_corpus2.htm

Further reading

De Knop, S. and Meunier, F. (2015) 'The "Learner Corpus Research, Cognitive Linguistics, and Second Language Acquisition" Nexus: A SWOT Analysis', *Corpus Linguistics and Linguistic Theory* 11(1): 1–18. (This introduction to the journal's special issue presents an analysis of the potential strengths, weaknesses, opportunities and threats (SWOT) of combining learner corpora and cognitive linguistic theory in the study of SLA.)

Hasko, V. (2013) 'Capturing the Dynamics of Second Language Development via Learner Corpus Research: A Very Long Engagement', *The Modern Language Journal* 97(S1): 1–10. (This introduction to the journal's special issue discusses the potential of learner corpora for SLA and some of the challenges that need to be overcome if we want to bring the fields of learner corpus research and SLA closer together.)

McEnery, T., Brezina, V., Gablasova, D. and Banerjee, J. (2019) 'Corpus Linguistics, Learner Corpora, and SLA: Employing Technology to Analyse Language Use', *Annual Review of Applied Linguistics* 39: 74–92. (This position paper discusses the brief history of learner corpus research, its (so far limited) engagement with SLA and opportunities and challenges for future collaboration between the two fields.)

Meunier, F. (2015) 'Developmental Patterns in Learner Corpora', in S. Granger, G. Gilquin and F. Meunier (eds) *The Cambridge Handbook of Learner Corpus Research*, Cambridge: Cambridge University Press, pp. 379–400. (This handbook chapter reviews some of the core issues regarding the use of learner corpora to investigate developmental patterns in SLA, including study design and methods for analysing group and individual trajectories. It also describes future avenues for learner corpus design that allow for better analysis of developmental trajectories.)

References

Alexopoulou, T., Geertzen, J., Korhonen, A. and Meurers, D. (2015) 'Exploring Big Educational Learner Corpora for SLA Research: Perspectives on Relative Clauses', *International Journal of Learner Corpus Research* 1(1): 96–129.

Alexopoulou, T., Michel, M., Murakami, A. and Meurers, D. (2017) 'Task Effects on Linguistic Complexity and Accuracy: A Large-Scale Learner Corpus Analysis Employing Natural Language Processing Techniques', *Language Learning* 67(S1): 180–208.

Andersen, R. W. and Shirai, Y. (1994) 'Discourse Motivations for Some Cognitive Acquisition Principles', *Studies in Second Language Acquisition* 16: 133–56.

Barker, F., Salamoura, A. and Saville, N. (2015) 'Learner Corpora and Language Testing', in G. Granger, G. Gilquin and F. Meunier (eds) *The Cambridge Handbook of Learner Corpus Research*, Cambridge: Cambridge University Press, pp. 511–33.

Bestgen, Y. and Granger, S. (2014) 'Quantifying the Development of Phraseological Competence in L2 English Writing: An Automated Approach', *Journal of Second Language Writing* 26: 28–41.

Bulté, B. and Housen, A. (2014) 'Conceptualizing and Measuring Short-Term Changes in L2 Writing Complexity', *Journal of Second Language Writing* 26: 42–65.

Chen, A. C.-H. (2019) 'Assessing Phraseological Development in Word Sequences of Variable Lengths in Second Language Texts Using Directional Association Measures', *Language Learning* 69(2): 440–77.

Connor-Linton, J. and Polio, C. (2014) 'Comparing Perspectives on L2 writing: Multiple Analyses of a Common Corpus', *Journal of Second Language Writing* 26: 1–9.

Crossley, S. A. and McNamara, D. S. (2014) 'Does Writing Development Equal Writing Quality? A Computational Investigation of Syntactic Complexity in L2 Learners', *Journal of Second Language Writing* 26(4): 66–79.

Crossley, S. A. and Salsbury, T. (2011) 'The Development of Lexical Bundle Accuracy and Production in English Second Language Speakers', *International Review of Applied Linguistics* 49: 1–26.

De Clercq, B. and Housen, A. (2017) 'A Cross-Linguistic Perspective on Syntactic Complexity In L2 Development. Syntactic Elaboration and Diversity', *The Modern Language Journal* 101: 315–34.

Doughty, C. J. and Long, M. H. (2003) 'The Scope of Inquiry and Goals of SLA', in C. J. Doughty and M. H. Long (eds) *Handbook of Second Language Acquisition*, Malden, MA: Blackwell, pp. 3–16.

Ellis, N. C. and Ferreira-Junior, F. (2009a) 'Construction Learning as a Function of Frequency, Frequency Distribution, and Function', *The Modern Language Journal* 93(3): 370–85.

Ellis, N. C. and Ferreira-Junior, F. (2009b) 'Constructions and their Acquisition: Islands and The Distinctiveness of their Occupancy', *Annual Review of Cognitive Linguistics* 7: 188–221.

Elturki, E. and Salsbury, T. (2016) 'A Cross-Sectional Investigation of the Development of Modality in English Language Learners' Writing: A Corpus-Driven Study', *Issues in Applied Linguistics* 20(1): 51–72. https://escholarship.org/uc/item/19z4h5h0.

Eskildsen, S. W. (2009) 'Constructing Another Language. Usage-Based Linguistics in Second Language Acquisition', *Applied Linguistics* 30(3): 335–57.

Eskildsen, S. W. (2012) 'L2 Negation Constructions at Work', *Language Learning* 62(2): 335–72.

Eskildsen, S. W. (2015) 'What Counts as a Developmental Sequence? Exemplar-Based L2 Learning of English Questions', *Language Learning* 65(1): 33–62.

Eskildsen, S. W., Cadierno, T. and Li, P. (2015) 'On the Development of Motion Constructions in Four Learners of L2 English', in T. Cadierno and S. W. Eskildsen (eds) *Usage-Based Perspectives on Second Language Learning*, Berlin: Walter de Gruyter, pp. 207–32.

Fuchs, R. and Werner, V. (2018) 'The Use of Stative Progressives by School-Age Learners of English and the Importance of the Variable Context', *International Journal of Learner Corpus Research* 4(2): 195–224.

Gablasova, D., Brezina, V. and McEnery, T. (2019) 'The Trinity Lancaster Corpus. Development, Description, and Application', *International Journal of Learner Corpus Research 5*(2): 126–58.

Garner, J. (2016) 'A Phrase-Frame Approach to Investigating Phraseology in Learner Writing across Proficiency Levels', *International Journal of Learner Corpus Research 2*(1): 31–67.

Garner, J. and Crossley, S. A. (2018) 'A Latent Curve Model Approach to Studying L2 N-Gram Development', *The Modern Language Journal* 102(3): 494–511.

Gilquin, G. (2019) 'Light Verb Constructions in Spoken L2 English. An Exploratory Cross-Sectional Study', *International Journal of Learner Corpus Research* 5(2): 181–206.

Götz, S. (2019) 'Filled Pauses across Proficiency Levels, L1s and Learning Context Variables. A Multivariate Exploration of The Trinity Lancaster Corpus Sample', *International Journal of Learner Corpus Research* 5(2): 159–79.

Graesser, A. C., McNamara, D. S., Louwerse, M. M. and Cai, Z. (2004) 'Coh-Metrix: Analysis of Text on Cohesion and Language', *Behavior Research Methods, Instruments, and Computers* 36: 193–202.

Granger, S. (2009) 'The Contribution of Learner Corpora to Second Language Acquisition and Foreign Language Teaching: A Critical Evaluation', in K. Aijmer (ed.) *Corpora and Language Teaching*, Amsterdam: John Benjamins, pp. 13–32.

Granger, S. (2013) 'Learner Corpora', in C. A. Chapelle (ed.) *The Encyclopedia of Applied Linguistics*, London: Blackwell Publishing, pp. 3235–42.

Hasko, V. (2013) 'Capturing the Dynamics of Second Language Development via Learner Corpus Research: A very Long Engagement', *The Modern Language Journal* 97(S1): 1–10.

Hawkins, J. A. and Buttery, P. (2010) Criterial Features in Learner Corpora: Theory and Illustrations', *English Profile Journal* 1: 1–23.

Hawkins, J. A. and Filipovic, L. (2012) *Criterial Features in L2 English. Specifying the Reference Levels of the Common European Framework*, Cambridge: Cambridge University Press.

Hong, H. (2012) 'Compilation and Exploration of ICCI Corpus for Learner Language Research', in Y. Tono, Y. Kawagushi and M. Minegishi (eds) *Developmental and Crosslinguistic Perspectives in Learner Corpus Research*, Amsterdam: John Benjamins, pp. 47–62.

Huang, Y., Murakami, A., Alexopoulou, T. and Korhonen, A. (2018) 'Dependency Parsing of Learner English', *International Journal of Corpus Linguistics* 23(1): 28–54.

Ishikawa, S. (2013) 'The ICNALE and Sophisticated Contrastive Interlanguage Analysis of Asian learners of English', in S. Ishikawa (ed.) *Learner Corpus Studies in Asia and the World*, Kobe, Japan: Kobe University, pp. 91–118.

Jarvis, S. and Pavlenko, A. (2008) *Crosslinguistic Influence in Language and Cognition*, New York: Routledge.

Kramsch, C. (2000) 'Second Language Acquisition, Applied Linguistics, and the Teaching of Foreign Languages', *The Modern Language Journal* 84: 311–26.

Li, J. and Schmitt, N. (2010) 'The Development of Collocation Use in Academic Texts by Advanced L2 Learners: A Multiple Case Study Perspective', in D. Wood (ed.) *Perspectives on Formulaic Language: Acquisition and Communication*, London: Continuum, pp. 23–45.

Li, P., Eskildsen, S. W. and Cadierno, T. (2014) 'Tracing an L2 Learner's Motion Constructions Over Time: A Usage-Based Classroom Investigation', *The Modern Language Journal* 98: 612–28.

Lowie, V. and Verspoor, M. (2015) 'Variability and Variation in Second Language Acquisition Orders: A Dynamic Reevaluation', *Language Learning* 65: 63–88.

Lozano, C. and Mendikoetxea, A. (2013) Learner Corpora and Second Language Acquisition. The Design and Collection of CEDEL2', in A. Díaz-Negrillo, N. Ballier and P. Thompson (eds) *Automatic Treatment and Analysis of Learner Corpus Data*, Amsterdam: John Benjamins, pp. 65–100.

Mackey, A. (2014) Practice and Progression in Second Language Research methods', *AILA Review* 27: 80–97.

MacWhinney, B. (2000) *The Childes Project: Tools for Analyzing Talk*, 3rd edn, New York, NY: Psychology Press.

MacWhinney, B. (2017) 'A Shared Platform for Studying Second Language Acquisition', *Language Learning* 67(S1): 254–75.

Meunier, F. (2015a) 'Developmental Patterns in Learner Corpora', in S. Granger, G. Gilquin and F. Meunier (eds) *The Cambridge Handbook of Learner Corpus Research*, Cambridge: Cambridge University Press, pp. 379–400.

Meunier, F. (2015b) 'Introduction to the LONGDALE Project' in E. Castello, K. Ackerley and F. Coccetta (eds) *Studies in Learner Corpus Linguistics: Research and Applications for Foreign Language Teaching and Assessment*, Bern: Peter Lang, pp. 124–6.

Meunier, F. and Littré, D. (2013) 'Tracking learners' progress: Adopting a Dual "Corpus Cum Experimental Data" Approach', *The Modern Language Journal* 97(S1): 61–76.

Mitchell, R., Tracy-Ventura, N. and McManus, K. (2017) *Anglophone Students Abroad: Identity, Social Relationships and Language Learning*, New York: Routledge.

Murakami, A. (2016) 'Modeling Systematicity and Individuality in Nonlinear Second Language Development: The Case of English Grammatical Morphemes', *Language Learning* 66(4): 834–71.

Murakami, A. and Alexopoulou, T. (2016) 'L1 Influence on the Acquisition Order of English Grammatical Morphemes: A Learner Corpus Study', *Studies in Second Language Acquisition* 38(3): 365–401.

Nicholls, D. (2003) 'The Cambridge Learner Corpus – Error Coding and Analysis for Lexicography and ELT', in D. Archer, P. Rayson, A. Wilson and T. McEnery (eds) *Proceedings of the Corpus Linguistics 2003 Conference. UCREL Technical Paper 16,* Lancaster, UK: UCREL, pp. 572–81.

O'Keeffe, A. and Mark, G. (2017) The English Grammar Profile of Learner Competence: Methodology and Key Findings', *International Journal of Corpus Linguistics* 22(4): 457–89.

Ortega, L. (2012) 'Interlanguage Complexity: A Construct in Search of Theoretical Renewal', in B. Szmrecsanyi and B. Kortmann (eds) *Linguistic Complexity in Interlanguage Varieties, L2 Varieties, and Contact Languages*, Berlin: Walter de Gruyter, pp. 127–55.

Pérez-Paredes, P. and Díez-Bedmar, M. B. (2019a) 'Researching Learner Language through POS Keyword and Syntactic Complexity Analyses', in S. Götz and J. Mukherjee (eds) *Learner Corpora and Language Teaching*, Amsterdam: John Benjamins, pp. 101–27.

Pérez-Paredes, P. and Díez-Bedmar, M. B. (2019b) 'Certainty Adverbs in Spoken Learner Language. The Role of Tasks and Proficiency', *International Journal of Learner Corpus Research* 5(2): 252–78.

Pérez-Paredes, P. and Sánchez-Tornel, M. (2014) 'Adverb Use and Language Proficiency in Young Learners' Writing', *International Journal of Corpus Linguistics* 19(2): 178–200.

Reder, S., Harris, K. A. and Setzler, K. (2003) 'A Multimedia Adult Learner Corpus', *TESOL Quarterly* 37: 546–57.

Römer, U. (2019) 'A Corpus Perspective on the Development of Verb Constructions in Second Language Learners', *International Journal of Corpus Linguistics* 24(3): 268–90.

Römer, U. and Berger, C. M. (2019) 'Observing the Emergence of Constructional Knowledge: Verb Patterns in German and Spanish learners of English at Different Proficiency Levels', *Studies in Second Language Acquisition*, Advance online publication. 10.1017/S0272263119000202

Römer, U. and Garner, J. R. (2019) 'The Development of Verb Constructions in Spoken Learner English: Tracing Effects of Usage and Proficiency' *International Journal of Learner Corpus Research* 5(2): 206–29.

Thewissen, J. (2013) 'Capturing L2 Accuracy Developmental Patterns: Insights from an Error-Tagged EFL Learner Corpus', *The Modern Language Journal* 97: 77–101.

Tomasello, M. (2003) *Constructing a Language: A Usage-Based Theory of Language Acquisition*, Cambridge, MA: Harvard University Press.

Tono, Y. and Díez-Bedmar, M. B. (2014) 'Focus on Learner Writing at the Beginning and Intermediate Stages: The ICCI Corpus', *International Journal of Corpus Linguistics* 19(2): 163–77.

Tracy-Ventura, N. (2017) 'Combining Corpora and Experimental Data to Investigate Language Learning During Residence Abroad: A Study of Lexical Sophistication', *System* 71, 35–45.

Vyatkina, N. (2013) 'Specific Syntactic Complexity: Developmental Profiling of Individuals Based on an Annotated Learner Corpus', *The Modern Language Journal* 97(S1): 11–30.

Vyatkina, N. (2016) 'The Kansas Developmental Learner Corpus (KANDEL): A Developmental Corpus of Learner German', *International Journal of Learner Corpus Research* 2(1): 102–20.

Xu, Q. (2016) 'Item-Based Foreign Language Learning of *Give* Ditransitive Constructions: Evidence from Corpus Research', *System* 63: 65–76.

Zhao, H. and Shirai, Y. (2018) 'Arabic Learners' Acquisition of English Past Tense Morphology', *International Journal of Learner Corpus Research* 4(2): 253–76.

Zheng, Y. (2016) 'The Complex, Dynamic Development of L2 Lexical Use: A Longitudinal Study on Chinese Learners of English', *System* 56: 40–53.

24

What can a corpus tell us about vocabulary teaching materials?

Martha Jones and Philip Durrant

1 What vocabulary is important for my learner?

Language teachers have long used lists of important vocabulary to guide course design and materials preparation, and corpus data have played a major part in developing these lists since at least the early twentieth century (Howatt and Widdowson 2004). This work is motivated by the fact that it is not practical for most learners to acquire the huge repertoire of words known to educated native speakers and that they therefore need to focus their learning on a limited subset of the language. Wordlists are based on the assumption that some words are more useful than others and that we can identify in advance what those words are (Durrant 2016).

Central to this endeavour is the principle that words can be prioritised based on their frequency in a corpus: The more frequent a word is, the more important it is to learn. Proponents of a frequency-based approach point to the fact that a relatively small number of very common items accounts for a large majority of language we use. Nation (2013: 11) reports that just 2,000 high-frequency words account for around 80 per cent of written English. This suggests that a focus on such items will pay substantial dividends for novice learners (Nation and Waring 1997).

The development of computerised corpus analysis has made the job of compiling word-frequency statistics far easier than it once was and has given impetus to a new wave of pedagogically oriented wordlist research (e.g. Brezina and Gablasova 2013; Gardner and Davies 2014). Importantly, the widespread availability of corpora and the ease of carrying out automated word counts also offer individual teachers the possibility of creating specialised vocabulary lists tailored to their learners' own needs (Ward 2009; Lu and Durrant 2017) or of customising existing lists to fit their own contexts (Burkett 2015, 2017). However, teachers wishing to create or adapt lists need to make a number of important methodological decisions.

The first of these concerns is the choice or construction of a suitable corpus. With the large number of corpora available and the relative ease of constructing a tailor-made corpus, it should be possible to ensure a good match between corpus and target

DOI: 10.4324/9780367076399-24

language. However, it remains essential that this be based on careful needs analysis. Section 3 of the present chapter describes these issues in more detail.

A second, less well-researched, decision is that of defining what sorts of items constitute individual "words". At one level, we need to decide if polysemous words (e.g. *run* [a race]/run [a company]) should be counted as one word or two. At another, we need to decide if morphologically related forms (e.g. *run* and *running*) should be combined – that is, if words should be grouped into *lemmas*. At a still broader level, we need to decide whether to combine derivationally related words (e.g. *run* as a verb/a noun) into what are referred to as *word families* (Gardner 2008).

A list which conflates different forms, meanings and phrases under a single *word* will achieve excellent economy of description. However, this is bought only with the loss of potentially important information. Some forms, senses and collocations of a high-frequency headword like *run* are more important to learn than others, and many are probably less important than lower-frequency words. Unless separate frequency counts are given, a list will give no grounds for prioritising such learning.

Some researchers have justified combining multiple forms and senses on the grounds that once one form of a word is learned, learning the related forms requires little extra effort and that abstract semantic representations can cover a range of senses (Nation 2013). However, others have argued that the learning of morphologically related items may not be as automatic as has sometimes been thought (Gardner 2008), and it is not clear that abstract meaning representations will give learners the information they need to use words effectively. It also seems likely that learners will need to have multi-word expressions brought explicitly to their attention (see also Chapters 15 and 28, this volume).

Any decision on this issue should depend on what the list will be used for. If it is intended primarily as an inventory of important vocabulary for comprehension, for example, distinctions between forms and senses of a word become less important, since related forms and meanings may be deducible by learners in context. However, if the intention is to specify items which learners need to use accurately in writing, a more fine-grained approach will be needed. Another important factor is the time allowed for carrying out the research: Automated tools are not yet able to adequately distinguish between different word senses. Extensive manual analysis is therefore needed to provide a listing which takes sense variation into account.

A further consideration is that frequency is not the only factor which might make a word worthy of attention. In compiling the influential *General Service List* (West 1953) a range of criteria were considered: Less frequent words were included if they could be used to convey a range of important concepts, words were excluded if a synonym was available and "intensive emotional" words (i.e. items 'whose only function is to be the equivalent of underlining, or an exclamation mark') were excluded (West 1953: 9–10). Other factors which may be important include the likely difficulty of a word for the learners in question (Ghadessy 1979), something that may differ based on the learners' first language – words which are challenging for Chinese- or Arabic-speaking learners may not be challenging for Spanish-speaking learners, whose Latinate vocabulary overlaps with that of English. Teachers may also need to consider which words belong together as natural "sets". O'Keeffe *et al.* (2007: 40), for example, point out that there are wide differences in the frequencies of the names of different days of the week, with Friday, Saturday and Sunday being the most common and Tuesday and Wednesday being less frequent. As these authors remark, however, we would not suggest teaching only the most frequent of these names as basic vocabulary and leaving the others for later. In short, a careful consideration of a range of factors other than frequency is likely to improve the value of any pedagogical list.

2 Vocabulary materials and formulaic language

One of the central insights to come from corpus linguistics is the extent to which competent language users draw not only on a lexicon of individual words but also on combinations of words which have come to be known as "formulaic sequences" (Wray 2002). Exactly what should count as a formulaic sequence remains disputed, but a list might include:

- Collocations and colligations: *hard luck, tectonic plates, black coffee, by the way;*
- Pragmatically specialised expressions: *happy birthday, pleased to meet you;*
- Idioms: *the last straw, fall on your sword, part and parcel;*
- Lexicalised sentence stems: X BE *sorry to keep* TENSE *you waiting* (as in *Mr Jones is sorry to have kept you waiting.*

What these items have in common is that they appear to be, in Wray's words, 'pre-fabricated: that is, stored and retrieved whole from memory at the time of use, rather than being subject to generation or analysis by the language grammar' (2002: 9). So defined, formulaic sequences are arguably part of the vocabulary of the language which learners need to acquire. Constructing utterances from formulas, rather than stringing together individual words according to the rules of grammar, is held both to be cognitively efficient (Ellis 2003) and to give speakers a better chance of expressing themselves in a way that strikes listeners as *natural* (Hoey 2005). For these reasons, a good knowledge of formulas is thought to be important for achieving both fluency and native-like production (Pawley and Syder 1983). Some researchers have further claimed that the acquisition of grammar is based on a process of abstracting from an inventory of initially rote-learned formulas (Wulff 2019 gives a good recent overview of this model).

Recognising the importance of formulas in language learning, many researchers have created lists of pedagogically useful formulaic language. Prominent examples include Shin and Nation's (2008) list of common collocations, Martinez and Schmitt's (2012) list of non-transparent multiword expressions and Simpson-Vlach and Ellis's (2010) list of academic formulas.

As with the wordlists described earlier, lists of formulaic language usually start from corpus-derived frequency information. Alongside simple frequency counts, such lists often draw on a number of other types of corpus-derived statistics. In particular:

- *Dispersion*: how evenly a word combination is distributed throughout a corpus. Dispersion gives a measure of whether formulas are frequent because they are widely used or because they happen to be frequently repeated within a small number of texts. This measure has been especially relevant in lists of academic formulas (e.g. Simpson-Vlach and Ellis 2010; Ackermann and Chen 2013), where they are used to ensure that formulas are not exclusive to particular disciplines.
- *Keyness*: how distinctive a formula is of a particular area of discourse. Researchers interested in identifying the formulaic language characteristic of a particular area of discourse (e.g. spoken formulas, academic formulas) have sometimes included only

those formulas which are found significantly more frequently in that area than in general English (e.g. Durrant 2009; Simpson-Vlach and Ellis 2010). Another use of this statistic has been to identify formulas which are more frequent in published writing than in student writing, the logic being that these are formulas which students need but do not yet use (Eriksson 2012).

- *Association measures*: quantify either:
    a. How confident we can be that a combination of words occurs more frequently than chance would predict, so that we have reliable evidence that it is a genuine formula. This type of measure (e.g. *t-score, z-score, log-likelihood*) tends to emphasise high-frequency combinations like *other hand* or *long time*.
    b. How strongly the words in a combination are associated with each other. This type of measure (e.g. *MI; MI3*) tends to emphasise words which are relatively exclusive to each other, such as *pop music* or *vicious circle*.

As we saw earlier, frequency by itself is not usually a sufficient criterion for inclusion in a wordlist. Similarly, researchers who construct lists of formulaic language usually combine corpus-derived statistics with other types of information. These include ratings of the meaningfulness of a combination as a unit, teachers' perceptions of the value of a combination to their learners and the semantic opacity of a combination (e.g. Simpson-Vlach and Ellis 2010; Martinez and Schmitt 2012; Hsu 2014).

Though the rationale for pedagogical lists of formulaic language parallels that for wordlists, this rationale can only be transferred with a strong caveat. While a key part of the justification for wordlists was that most texts comprise a relatively small number of high-frequency word types, it is not true that the majority of texts comprise a small number of high-frequency formulas. Reviewing work on academic word and formula lists, Durrant (2019) shows that whereas the Academic Word List (Coxhead 2000) achieves 10 per cent coverage of academic texts with 570 word families (i.e. 10 per cent of words used in academic writing are from this list), and the Academic Vocabulary List (Gardner and Davies 2014) covers 25 per cent of lexical words in academic texts with 587 lemmas, academic formula lists tend to be much less efficient. Ackermann and Chen's (2013) list of 2,468 lemmatised lexical collocations (i.e. collocations composed of nouns, verbs, adjectives and adverbs), for example, covered only 1.4 per cent of academic texts. This should not surprise us: Combinations of words are, by definition, less frequent than the words that comprise them.

Where formula lists include combinations with function words (e.g. *such as; at least*), frequencies are higher. Martinez and Schmitt (2012), for example, identify 32 such items with frequencies that put them on a par with the 1,000 most frequent words in English. For this type of collocation, therefore, the logic of wordlists may transfer more effectively. Durrant's (2009) list of 1,000 frequent academic collocations, which was dominated by collocations including at least one function word, achieves coverage of between 3.5 and 7.1 per cent, depending on the academic discipline, while Hsu's (2014) list of 475 two- to five-word semantically opaque sequences achieves 2.1 per cent. These figures remain modest, of course, in comparison with those achieved by wordlists.

A problem for creators of formula lists is that formulas tend to be highly contextually specific. Indeed, this is one of the reasons they are of interest: For researchers, they provide an excellent means of identifying and describing differences between text types; for learners, their effective use shows a detailed command of the specificities of a particular context of use. This context specificity, however, also partly undermines the logic of listing, since it becomes difficult to identify a set of formulas that will be widely useful.

One response to this issue has been to move away from lists and instead help learners use corpus resources to identify formulaic language within the texts that happen to be important to them (Vincent 2013). Given the limitations of formula lists, an approach along these lines seems to offer great promise for the future.

3 What type of corpus is suitable for academic vocabulary learning in EAP/ESAP contexts?

As mentioned in Section 1, a corpus used for vocabulary learning purposes should aim to meet the needs of students in terms of the target language they will encounter in texts they will need on their academic programmes. EAP courses may be the best place for students to acquire the academic and disciplinary vocabulary which they will be expected to use in their writing in their academic departments. A number of corpora focusing on EAP have recently been developed which aim to meet the needs of international students studying in higher education. This section provides information on existing corpora of academic English, which could be used to teach academic and disciplinary vocabulary. It also reports on a recently compiled list of academic vocabulary, which could be accessed in order to develop vocabulary teaching materials.

The *British Academic Written English Corpus* (BAWE) (Nesi *et al.* 2005) includes 6.5 million words of proficient student writing focusing on four levels of study on undergraduate and taught postgraduate programmes and four broad disciplinary areas. The corpus is available to researchers for research purposes, provided that certain conditions are met.

The *Michigan Corpus of Upper-Level Student Papers* (MICUSP) is a corpus consisting of 2.6 million words which includes student writing covering argumentative essays, creative writing, critique/evaluation, proposals, reports, research papers and response papers at four levels. O'Keeffe *et al.* (2020) used this corpus extensively to create an e-resource with tasks which draw users' attention to important aspects of lexico-grammatical patterns and pragmatics for study and research purposes. This e-resource has proved to be very user-friendly.

The *New Academic Vocabulary List* (AVL) (Gardner and Davies 2014) is based on the 120-million-word academic component of the *Corpus of Contemporary American English*. This component consists of journal articles from nine disciplines.

The AVL is considered to be a core academic list, as it is based on a large and representative corpus of academic English. Frequency and dispersion statistics were criteria to select the words for this list. According to Gardner and Davies (ibid), beginning learners in academic settings should focus on the top 500 words, as these high-frequency words come from academic texts.

Practitioners and researchers have developed short EAP courses which encourage students to compile their own corpora. Lee and Swales (2006), for example, report on a course aimed at non-native speaker doctoral students which focused on the investigation of language using specialised corpora of academic writing and speaking through hands-on concordancing. Charles (2012) conducted a study which included the development of a six-week, open-access and unassessed EAP academic writing course at a UK university. Master's and doctoral students analysed two theses corpora developed by the tutor in order to familiarise themselves with the software programme and subsequently compiled their own corpora. A more recent study, conducted by Chen and Flowerdew (2018), reports on a project which focused on the implementation of a data-driven approach to research writing involving PhD students in Hong Kong universities. At the beginning of the course, the students had access to the BNCweb and AntConc (Anthony 2016) for problem solving purposes related to the use of lexico-grammatical patterns during the process of writing research. The students were subsequently asked to compile their own corpus in order to meet their own needs.

In order to build a corpus which meets the specific needs of EAP students, a number of important considerations should be taken into account:

- Type of language, e.g. general and academic language or discipline-specific language;
- Corpus size, e.g. a large corpus covering a wide range of soft and hard disciplines or a smaller specialised corpus;
- Whether to compile a grammatically or semantically tagged or untagged corpus;
- Availability of analytical tools, e.g. concordancing programmes for teachers to produce sample output in the form of frequency lists and concordance texts around which tasks could be developed to help students notice how specific words or phrases are used in context.

This section has provided an overview of possible corpora appropriate for vocabulary learning for EAP use. It has also described the AVL, which could be the basis for the development of vocabulary teaching materials. In Section 5 we describe the rationale behind the compilation of a specialised corpus of science and engineering research articles, examine approaches to the design of vocabulary teaching materials and provide samples of teaching materials based on this corpus.

4 What vocabulary input do teaching materials on EAP/ESAP programmes provide?

This section aims to illustrate how corpus analysis can help us investigate how vocabulary input included in EAP lesson materials is exploited on some writing courses. It provides an overview of the content of writing courses on EAP in-session programmes at six UK universities, which is more likely to be relevant to specific student needs in terms of tasks and materials for vocabulary learning. These programmes offer courses and workshops aimed at postgraduate students who are already in their academic departments in order to provide support for these students to cope with the demands of academic study and research. The development of in-house materials, which are often adapted from authentic academic texts, is common in this teaching context. As Samuda (2005: 235) points out, 'teachers engage in re-design, tweaking, adjusting and adapting materials to suit particular needs'.

A cursory glance at the information on writing courses available to postgraduate master's and research students at the six UK universities reveals that the focus is often on the language and structure of main chapters in dissertations and theses, e.g. abstract, introduction, literature review methods, materials and discussion of results. Some attention is devoted to aspects of accuracy in writing at the micro-level, e.g. grammatical structures and aspects of cohesion. It is interesting to see that at three universities there were courses devoted to the development of vocabulary, and one university focuses specifically on the development of vocabulary for science, technology, engineering and mathematics writing.

An examination of existing in-house materials for the development of research writing skills aimed at PhD students on an in-session programme at a UK university revealed that a small corpus consisting of 24 review articles had been compiled covering disciplines such as medicine, engineering software, pharmacy, nursing, marketing, human relations, public policy, social policy, archaeology, economics, political science and law. This corpus was used to produce frequency lists and concordances of keywords such as *aim* and *goal* and of reporting verbs. The lists and concordances were used in class to illustrate patterns, but the tutor who compiled the corpus concluded that the small size of the corpus yielded results that could not be generalised to characterise a discipline The results were specific to either the individual topic or the individual writer. In this case, the tutor decided that the students would benefit more from compiling individual small corpora within their discipline, as described in Chen and Flowerdew's (2018) study.

5 What approaches should be used for designing teaching materials focusing on phraseology in ESAP learning contexts?

This section describes a corpus of science and engineering journal articles compiled by the authors and possible corpus-based approaches to the teaching of vocabulary and formulaic sequences by using keyword lists and concordance lines, as well as awareness-raising tasks based on this corpus.

Section 3 discussed the usefulness of corpora which include academic vocabulary across different disciplines and provided three examples of corpora which can be used for teaching and research purposes. It also reported on studies involving the compilation of corpora by students and the examination of grammatical and lexical items using concordancing programmes. After the series of workshops focusing on data-driven approaches to the learning of specialised vocabulary, the students in Chen and Flowerdew's (2018) study requested more exercises, materials and examples of the type of language they had to focus on in order to write for publication purposes.

As mentioned in Section 4, it is encouraging to see that with some EAP in-session programmes there are courses focusing on the development of academic and disciplinary vocabulary, where data from small corpora have been integrated within in-house EAP materials.

A number of science and engineering corpora have been developed in the last 30 years, which have been analysed in order to generate wordlists. Some examples are the *Jiaotong Daxue Computer corpus of Texts in English for Science and Technology* (JDEST) (Yang 1985) and the *Student Engineering English Corpus* (SEEC) (Moudraia 2004). Wordlists have also been compiled based on science and engineering sources, for example, Kuo's (2007) *Scientific Research Word List* (SRWL) and *The Basic Engineering List* (BEL) developed by Ward (2009). However, the corpora the wordlists are based on include mainly data from textbooks. Whilst this type of raw data can be considered useful to generate wordlists in the areas of science and engineering, the target student audience often consists of students at pre-tertiary or undergraduate levels who need to develop basic disciplinary knowledge of vocabulary use. There is therefore a call for the development of corpora of journal articles which provide the true picture of up-to-date empirical research in different science and engineering branches. This kind of resource can be used to generate wordlists which can be examined by PhD students so that they are able to use the type of language used by the members of their disciplinary community.

Academic journal articles in specific disciplines, which can be accessed electronically, are considered to be a useful resource for PhD students. Analysing the content, the style of writing and the macro structure of the articles is important so that the students are aware of conventions used by the members of their disciplinary community to construct and disseminate knowledge. Journal articles can also be used for the teaching of academic and disciplinary vocabulary and phrases. A corpus aimed at first-year PhD science and engineering students at a UK university was compiled in order to create keyword lists, concordances and concgrams which were the basis to create vocabulary teaching materials. The corpus consists of 11,709,243 words (accessed online) and includes a wide range of disciplines in the faculties of science and engineering. Table 24.1 includes a list of the top 50 keywords generated by using *Wordsmith 7.0* (Scott 2019), arranged according to log likelihood values in descending order. Log likelihood is considered a reliable statistic when two corpora of a different size are compared (Dunning 1993; Rayson 2002).

This list was based on the comparison of the *Written British National Corpus* as the reference corpus and the science and engineering corpus.

As mentioned in Section 1, frequency is only one of the criteria used for the selection of particular lexical items to be taught. Other important factors to consider are range of word meanings, availability, level of difficulty and usefulness. The list of keywords was subsequently examined by one of the authors and by a subject specialist, a chemical engineer with a background in science, at a UK university in order to select words which are likely to be useful for research writing in the areas of science and engineering. Table 24.2 shows this list.

After a suitable list of keywords was created, the next stage in materials development involved the production of concordance lines for students to examine. Awareness-raising tasks included clear instructions regarding data analysis methods and questions guiding the students' exploratory data analysis.

It is important for students to learn how to structure research articles at the macro level, but it is also necessary to help them use accurate language at the sentence level. Wolfe *et al.* (2011: 122) claim that focusing 'on production helps writers to develop language chunks or multiword phrases which many linguists believe is an important step in lexis and language learning'. They go on to add that writers may be able to recall language chunks through repeated sentence combinations and pattern practice when they produce texts.

Studies which report on the use of concordances to develop EAP/ESP teaching materials include Thurstun and Candlin (1998). They produced problem-solving tasks around concordances for independent study of vocabulary and claim that this type of material offers students exposure to numerous examples of the same vocabulary item in context and raises awareness of collocational relationships. Section 3 provides examples of more up-to-date studies which involved data-driven approaches to the learning of grammar and vocabulary using corpora and concordance texts (Lee and Swales 2006; Charles 2012, 2014; Chen and Flowerdew 2018; Lee *et al.* 2019).

A list of keywords can be further analysed in terms of their potential to be included in phrases which students can learn to use as lexical chunks, rather than single words alone.

Table 24.1 List of the most frequent keywords in the science and engineering corpus according to log likelihood (LL) values

Rank	*Word*	*Log likelihood*	*Rank*	*Word*	*Log Likelihood*
1	data	35363.89	26	effects	14939.59
2	using	34099.23	27	equation	14756.92
3	results	31550.35	28	cell	14556.41
4	observed	25591.09	29	linear	14469.59
5	values	24422.00	30	parameter	14383.37
6	parameters	23303.98	31	phase	13970.15
7	temperature	22872.36	32	figure	13858.58
8	function	21343.29	33	measured	13481.05
9	respectively	21320.62	34	algorithm	13179.92
10	flow	21104.42	35	matrix	13055.82
11	obtained	21060.90	36	protein	12991.31
12	models	19425.16	37	concentrations	12807.90
13	cells	19194.11	38	corresponding	12675.84
14	method	18157.68	39	ratio	12285.30
15	surface	17831.32	40	characteristics	12026.92
16	shown	17459.12	41	table	11312.33
17	analysis	17432.65	42	calculated	10992.35
18	study	17102.19	43	distribution	10881.26
19	samples	17010.63	44	studies	10860.05
20	concentration	16713.71	45	variables	10676.45
21	behaviour	16032.08	46	effect	10561.39
22	solution	15758.92	47	experiments	10501.56
23	sample	15439.41	48	based	10492.93
24	density	15409.15	49	reaction	10448.08
25	experimental.	15064.95	50	particles	9896.31

One of the advantages of focusing on formulaic language, according to Wray (1999: 213), is that it 'offers processing benefits to speakers and hearers, by providing a short cut to production and comprehension'. As pointed out in Section 2, despite the various labels used to refer to formulaic sequences, what they have in common is the fact that they can be stored and retrieved in their entirety from memory when needed. We have also claimed that formula lists are highly context specific and offer the opportunity to analyse their use in a particular context of use. Hyland (2012: 161) claims that the distribution of bundles is 'a strong disciplinary marker'. He conducted a study which focused on the analysis of lexical bundles in academic texts from electrical engineering, business studies, applied linguistics and biology. A closer examination of bundles used by engineers revealed that in this discipline:

> …there is considerably greater reliance on prefabricated structures than in other fields, possibly reflecting the dependence of engineering rhetoric on visual representation where formulas and graphs are linked in routinely patterned, almost formulaic ways.
>
> *(Hyland 2012: 162)*

Table 24.2 List of 50 keywords selected from the science and engineering corpus considered to be useful or very useful

Rank	*Word*	*Useful/very useful*	*Rank*	*Word*	*Useful/very useful*
1	data	U	26	significant	U
2	parameters	VU	27	equations	VU
3	temperature	U	28	properties	U
4	flow	VU	29	coefficients	U
5	method	U	30	conditions	VU
6	analysis	U	31	probability	VU
7	samples	VU	32	constant	U
8	concentration	VU	33	adsorption	U
9	experimental	U	34	coefficient	U
10	effects	U	35	correlation	VU
11	equation	VU	36	spectra	U
12	phase	U	37	oxidation	U
13	measured	U	38	energy	VU
14	algorithm	U	39	analyses	U
15	matrix	U	40	numerical	VU
16	concentrations	VU	41	estimation	VU
17	characteristics	U	42	variance	VU
18	distribution	VU	43	modeling	U
19	variables	VU	44	regression	VU
20	experiments	U	45	error	VU
21	reaction	VU	46	boundary	VU
22	particles	U	47	distributions	VU
23	measurements	VU	48	catalyst	U
24	velocity	U	49	differences	U
25	structure	VU	50	components	U

Concgram 1.0 (Greaves 2009) is a phraseological search engine which can handle constituency variation and positional variation. Cheng *et al.* (2006: 414) define a "concgram" as 'all of the permutations of constituency variation and positional variation generated by the association of two or more words'. The term "origin" is used when referring to words on which the automated concgram search is based. Greaves and Warren (2007) point out that concgrams are key to determining the level of phraseology in a text or corpus, thus establishing its phraseological profile.

The ten words that were used to generate concgrams were *parameters*, *flow*, *samples*, *concentration*, *equation*, *concentrations*, *distribution*, *variables*, *reaction* and *measurements*. A two-word concgram search was conducted using each of these words as a single origin, and a list of configurations showing constituency and positional variation was produced. As shown in Figure 24.1, associated words are listed for each single origin with information on the raw frequency of positional and compositional variation.

If we take *flow* as an example, it can be seen that *flow rate* is a contiguous form which occurs very frequently (AB occurs 714 times, where A = *flow* and B = *rate*).

This could be considered a *canonical form*, 'the benchmark against which all of the other concgram configurations are compared' based on frequency (Cheng *et al.* 2008: 236).

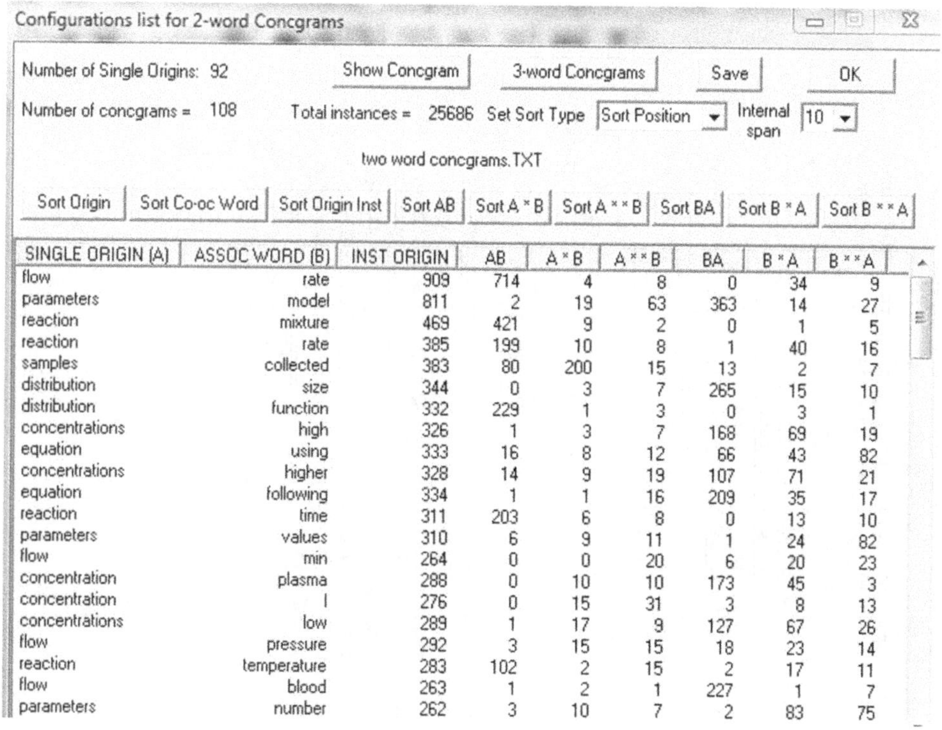

Configurations list for 2-word Concgrams

Number of Single Origins: 92 | Show Concgram | 3-word Concgrams | Save | OK

Number of concgrams = 108 | Total instances = 25686 | Set Sort Type: Sort Position | Internal span: 10

two word concgrams.TXT

Sort Origin | Sort Co-oc Word | Sort Origin Inst | Sort AB | Sort A * B | Sort A * * B | Sort BA | Sort B * A | Sort B * * A

SINGLE ORIGIN (A)	ASSOC WORD (B)	INST ORIGIN	AB	A * B	A * * B	BA	B * A	B * * A
flow	rate	909	714	4	8	0	34	9
parameters	model	811	2	19	63	363	14	27
reaction	mixture	469	421	9	2	0	1	5
reaction	rate	385	199	10	8	1	40	16
samples	collected	383	80	200	15	13	2	7
distribution	size	344	0	3	7	265	15	10
distribution	function	332	229	1	3	0	3	1
concentrations	high	326	1	3	7	168	69	19
equation	using	333	16	8	12	66	43	82
concentrations	higher	328	14	9	19	107	71	21
equation	following	334	1	1	16	209	35	17
reaction	time	311	203	6	8	0	13	10
parameters	values	310	6	9	11	1	24	82
flow	min	264	0	0	20	6	20	23
concentration	plasma	288	0	10	10	173	45	3
concentration	l	276	0	15	31	3	8	13
concentrations	low	289	1	17	9	127	67	26
flow	pressure	292	3	15	15	18	23	14
reaction	temperature	283	102	2	15	2	17	11
flow	blood	263	1	2	1	227	1	7
parameters	number	262	3	10	7	2	83	75

Figure 24.1 Configurations list of two-word *concgrams*

Examples of the *canonical form*, as well as the other configurations of non-contiguous forms showing positional and constituency variations, are listed next:

AB	A similar trend between feed *flow rate* and enrichment ratio was also observed
A*B	The *flow* rising *rate*
A***B	*flow* at a constant *rate*
B*A	... for a slow change in the total *rate* of *flow*
B**A	Overall, the heat removal *rate* in two-phase *flow* is higher than in single phase

This type of analysis can inform the development of teaching materials for science and engineering PhD students to raise awareness of phrases which can be found in the science and engineering journal articles they read as part of their research programme.

Sample task based on concordances of "flow rate" and "rate flow"

The following questions will help you *notice* a range of phrases which include the words *flow* and *rate*. Discuss the answers with the members of your group.

1. In your discipline in what contexts would the words *flow* and *rate* be used?;
2. In what section of a research article would these words be found?;

2-word concgram: flow / rate

742	fluid viscosity, µ, the square of the volumetric	flow rate, and inversely proportional to the fourth
743	a given buoyancy forcing, the highly asymmetric	flow has a rate of overturning close to a maximum and
744	temperature. The sample was then heated in He	flow, at a rate of 10 °C min-1. The desorbed NOx
745	seven times of dry season, respectively. The	flow rising rate is 3.22 (dry season) and 22.48 (wet
746	3 shows the effect of area available for air	flow on the rate of entrainment. The areas available
747	multiple-reaction systems. For the segregated	flow model, rate equations such as those previously
748	peristaltic pump that permitted the infusate to	flow at the rate of 60 ml h for 8 h. The MRD was left
749	multiple-reaction systems. For the segregated	flow model, rate equations such as those previously
750	and elongation as a function of type of	flow, strain rate, and chain length. At equilibrium,
751	(?v=1.3, ?=1.6). At the beginning of the shear	flow with shear rate , the fibres deviate from their
752	radial flow impeller (see Fig. 7). For two-loop	flow pattern the rate of exchange between the two
753	to a steady, long-lived, pressure-driven inward	flow of gas at a rate of up to 1000 M year1 (Fabian
754	system at about 0.01 Torr, an entraining Ar gas	flow at a constant rate of 100 SCCM was introduced and
755	The measurements were carried out in nitrogen	flow with a heating rate of 10 °C min. 2.2.4. Chemical
756	(2003) show that the drop size as a function of	flow rates and flow rate ratios of the two liquids
757	whereas in the slug flow (and the slug-bubbly	flow) the mass flow rate is even lower but the shear
758	rabbit IgG (12.5-100 nM) was injected into the	flow cell at a flow rate of 20 µl min for 2 min at 25
759	3b in their paper for fibre suspension in shear	flow with unit shear rate for different values of nL3
760	microstructure properties of the foam metal,	flow properties (flow rate, velocity, Reynolds number,
761	(1993) and is briefly summarized here. In linear	flow, the extensional rate is greater than the rate of
762	of the simulated liquid. It expands in the	flow direction at the rate , and contracts at the rate
763	in the bubble column, and air was allowed to	flow at a desired flow rate. An amount 1 mL of the
764	shear rate of 0.8, and steady-state elongational	flow at a reduced strain rate of 0.2 are displayed in
765	v known, constant value of time for travelers hp	flow on path p (departure rate from the origin node of
766	indeed in a very subtle way: in the bubbly	flow regime the mass flow rate is lower, but the
767	U.S.) that was connected to the TEOM bypass	flow and operated at a flow rate of 2.0 1 min-1. As in
768	the distribution narrows and orients toward the	flow direction as the shear rate is increased. Notice

Figure 24.2 Phrases including *flow* and *rate*

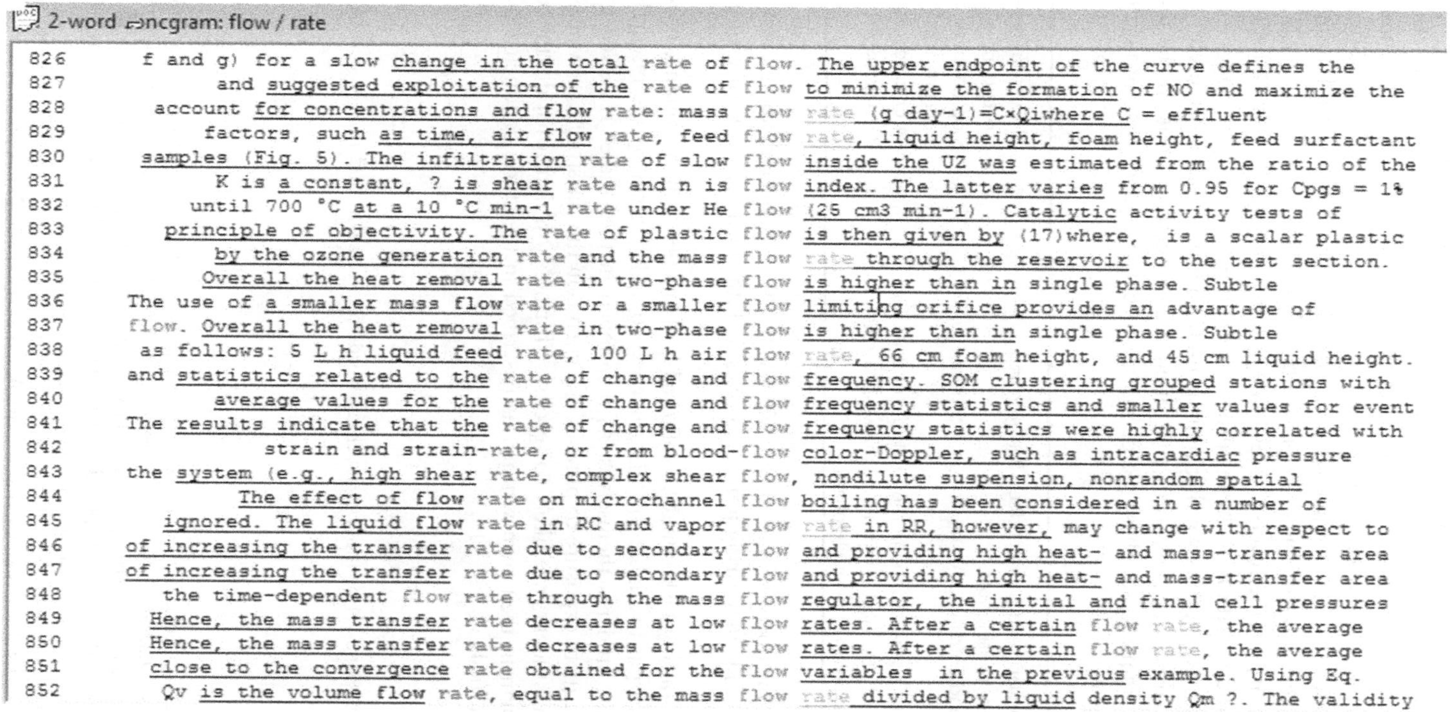

2-word concgram: flow / rate

826	f and g) for a slow change in the total rate of flow. The upper endpoint of the curve defines the
827	and suggested exploitation of the rate of flow to minimize the formation of NO and maximize the
828	account for concentrations and flow rate: mass flow rate (g day-1)=C×Qiwhere C = effluent
829	factors, such as time, air flow rate, feed flow rate, liquid height, foam height, feed surfactant
830	samples (Fig. 5). The infiltration rate of slow flow inside the UZ was estimated from the ratio of the
831	K is a constant, ? is shear rate and n is flow index. The latter varies from 0.95 for Cpgs = 1%
832	until 700 °C at a 10 °C min-1 rate under He flow (25 cm3 min-1). Catalytic activity tests of
833	principle of objectivity. The rate of plastic flow is then given by (17)where, is a scalar plastic
834	by the ozone generation rate and the mass flow rate through the reservoir to the test section.
835	Overall the heat removal rate in two-phase flow is higher than in single phase. Subtle
836	The use of a smaller mass flow rate or a smaller flow limiting orifice provides an advantage of
837	flow. Overall the heat removal rate in two-phase flow is higher than in single phase. Subtle
838	as follows: 5 L h liquid feed rate, 100 L h air flow rate, 66 cm foam height, and 45 cm liquid height.
839	and statistics related to the rate of change and flow frequency. SOM clustering grouped stations with
840	average values for the rate of change and flow frequency statistics and smaller values for event
841	The results indicate that the rate of change and flow frequency statistics were highly correlated with
842	strain and strain-rate, or from blood-flow color-Doppler, such as intracardiac pressure
843	the system (e.g., high shear rate, complex shear flow, nondilute suspension, nonrandom spatial
844	The effect of flow rate on microchannel flow boiling has been considered in a number of
845	ignored. The liquid flow rate in RC and vapor flow rate in RR, however, may change with respect to
846	of increasing the transfer rate due to secondary flow and providing high heat- and mass-transfer area
847	of increasing the transfer rate due to secondary flow and providing high heat- and mass-transfer area
848	the time-dependent flow rate through the mass flow regulator, the initial and final cell pressures
849	Hence, the mass transfer rate decreases at low flow rates. After a certain flow rate, the average
850	Hence, the mass transfer rate decreases at low flow rates. After a certain flow rate, the average
851	close to the convergence rate obtained for the flow variables in the previous example. Using Eq.
852	Qv is the volume flow rate, equal to the mass flow rate divided by liquid density Qm ?. The validity

Figure 24.3 Phrases including *rate* and *flow*

3. Think of a sentence where these words would be used in your discipline and share this information with the members of your group;
4. In your small group examine the phrases in Figure 24.2, which include the words *flow* and *rate*. Look at the left context of the word and make a list of variation in the composition and position of these words in the phrases. For example, sometimes these words will be included in a noun phrase or in a long noun phrase followed by a prepositional phrase, e.g. 'the volumetric *flow rate*' (line 742) and 'a steady long-lived, pressure-driven, inward *flow* of gas at a *rate* of' (line 753);
5. Now look at the words in the reverse order *rate / flow* in Figure 24.3. Make a list of the composition and variation of these words in the phrases;
6. Learning single words in your own discipline is useful but it is even more useful if you are able to learn groups of words that often occur together. Look at the information on the frequency of these words in a science and engineering corpus of journal articles below:

AB	A similar trend between feed *flow rate* and ...	714 occurrences
A*[1]B	The *flow* rising *rate*	4 occurrences
A***B	... and entraining Ar gas *flow* at a constant *rate* of ...	8 occurrences
BA		0 occurrences
B*A	... for a slow change in the total *rate* of *flow*	34 occurrences
B**A	Overall, the heat removal *rate* in two-phase *flow* is higher than in single phase	9 occurrences

7. Discuss with the members of the group what you have discovered about phraseology in science and engineering journal articles with the members of your group.

This initial awareness-raising task could be followed by hands-on concgramming, provided that there is a corpus available to PhD students, compiled either by the research writing tutor or by the students themselves, as mentioned in the studies reviewed in Section 3. Through frequent exposure to phrases in a corpus in the classroom, as well as outside the classroom, students are likely to recognise formulas in their own discipline and eventually use them in their own writing, as described in the study conducted by Jones and Haywood (2004).

Note

1 The asterisk represents one (*) or more intervening words between *flow* and *rate* or between *rate* and *flow*.

Further reading

Cortes, V. (2006) 'Teaching Lexical Bundles in the Disciplines: An Example from a Writing Intensive History Class', *Linguistics and Education* 17: 391–406. (This study describes a teaching approach to lexical bundles in a writing history class which involved pre- and post-instruction of lexical bundles. The students were exposed to the data in a corpus of history journal articles where four-word lexical bundles were identified.)

Hassan, L. and Wood, D. (2015) 'The Effectiveness of Focused Instruction of Formulaic Sequences in Augmenting L2 Learners' Academic Writing Skills: A Quantitative Research

Study', *Journal of English for Academic Purposes* 17: 51–62. (This study highlights the effectiveness of focused instruction of formulaic sequences on an L2 writing skills course.)

Nekrasova-Beker, T., Beker, T. and Sharpe, A. (2019) 'Identifying and teaching Target Vocabulary in an ESP Course', *TESOL Quarterly* 10(1): 1–27. (Based on a case study from an introductory engineering course, this study describes the procedure to develop teaching materials for L2 vocabulary instruction using corpus-based techniques.)

References

Ackermann, K. and Chen, Y.-H. (2013) 'Developing the Academic Collocation List (ACL) – A Corpus-Driven and Expert-Judged Approach', *Journal of English for Academic Purposes* 12(4): 235–47.

Anthony, L. (2016) *AntConc (Version 3.44) [Computer Software]*, Tokyo, Japan: Waseda University, Available from http:// www.lawrenceanthony.net/.

Brezina, V. and Gablasova, D. (2013) 'Is There a Core General Vocabulary? Introducing the New General Service List', *Applied Linguistic* 36(1): 1–22.

Burkett, T. (2015) 'An Investigation into the Use of Frequency Vocabulary Lists in University Intensive English Programs', *International Journal of Bilingual and Multilingual Teachers of English* 3(2): 71–83.

Burkett, T. (2017) *An Investigation into the Use of Word Lists in University Foundation Programs in the United Arab Emirates*, unpublished Doctoral dissertation, University of Exeter.

Charles, M. (2012) 'Proper Vocabulary and Juicy Collocations': EAP Students Evaluate Do-It-Yourself Corpus-Building', *English for Specific Purposes* 31: 93–102.

Charles, M. (2014), 'Getting the Corpus Habit: EAP Students' Long-Term Use of Personal Corpora', *English for Specific Purposes*, 35: 30–40.

Chen, M. and Flowerdew, J. (2018) 'Introducing Data-Driven Learning to PhD Students for Research Writing Purposes: A Territory-Wide Project in Hong Kong', *English for Specific Purposes* 50: 97–112.

Cheng, W., Greaves, C., Sinclair, J. M. and Warren, M. (2008) 'Uncovering the Extent of the Phraseological Tendency: Towards a Systematic Analysis of Concgrams', *Applied Linguistics* 30(2): 236–52.

Cheng, W., Greaves, C. and Warren, M. (2006) 'From N-Gram to Skipgram to Concgram', *International Journal of Corpus Linguistics* 11(4): 411–33.

Coxhead, A. (2000) 'A New Academic Wordlist', *TESOL Quarterly* 34(2): 213–38.

Dunning, T. (1993) 'Accurate Methods for the Statistics of Surprise and Coincidence', *Computational Linguistics* 19: 61–74.

Durrant, P. (2019) 'Formulaic Language in English for Academic Purposes', in A. Siyanova-Chanturia and A. Pellicer-Sánchez (eds) *Understanding Formulaic Language: A Second Language Acquisition Perspective*, London: Routledge, pp. 211–27.

Durrant, P. (2016) 'To What Extent Is the Academic Vocabulary List Relevant to University Student Writing?', *English for Specific Purposes* 43(1): 49–61.

Durrant, P. (2009) 'Investigating the Viability of a Collocation List for Students of English for Academic Purposes', *Journal of English for Specific Purpose*, 28(3): 157–79.

Ellis, N. C. (2003) 'Constructions, Chunking, and Connectionism: The Emergence of Second Language Structure', in C. J. Doughty, and M. H. Long (eds) *The Handbook of Second Language Acquisition*, Oxford: Blackwell, pp. 63–103.

Eriksson, A. (2012) 'Pedagogical Perspectives on Bundles: Teaching Bundles to Doctoral Students in Biochemistry', in J. Thomas, and A. Boulton (eds) *Input, Process and Product: Developments in Teaching and Language Corpora*, Brno: Masaryk University Press, pp. 195–211.

Gardner, D. and Davies, M. (2014) 'A New Academic Vocabulary List', *Applied Linguistics* 35(3): 305–27.

Gardner, D. (2008) 'Validating the Construct of *Word* in Applied Corpus-Based Vocabulary Research: A Critical Survey', *Applied Linguistics* 28(2): 241–65.

Ghadessy, M. (1979) 'Frequency Counts, Word Lists and Materials Preparation', *English Teaching Forum*, 17: 24–27.
Greaves, C. (2009) *ConcGram 1.0: A Phraseological Search Engine*, Amsterdam: John Benjamins.
Greaves, C. and Warren, M. (2007) 'Concgramming: A Computer-Driven Approach to Learning the Phraseology of English', *ReCALL Journal* 17(3): 287–306.
Hoey, M. (2005) *Lexical Priming: A New Theory of Words and Language*, London: Routledge.
Howatt, A. P. R. and Widdowson, H. G. (2004) *A History of English Language Teaching*, Oxford: Oxford University Press.
Hsu, W. (2014) 'The Most Frequent Opaque Formulaic Sequences in English-Medium College Textbooks', *System* 47: 146–61.
Hyland, K. (2012) 'Bundles in Academic Discourse', *Annual Review of Applied Linguistics* 32: 150–69.
Jones, M. and Haywood, S. (2004) 'Facilitating the Acquisition of Formulaic Sequences', in N. Schmitt (ed.) *Formulaic Sequences*, Amsterdam: John Benjamins, pp. 269–300.
Kuo, C.-H. (2007) 'Constructing a Scientific Research Word List', *JALT CALL Presentation Abstracts*, Waseda University, Japan, p. 25.
Lee, D. and Swales, J. (2006) 'A Corpus-Based EAP Course for NNS Doctoral Students: Moving from Available Specialized Corpora to Self-Compiled Corpora', *English for Specific Purposes* 25: 56–75.
Lee, H., Warschauer, M. and Lee, J. H. (2019) 'The Effect of Corpus Use on Second Language Vocabulary Learning: A Multi-Level Meta-Analysis', *Applied Linguistics* 40(5): 721–53.
Lu, C. and Durrant, P. (2017) 'A Corpus-Based Lexical Analysis of Chinese Medicine Research Articles', *Asian Journal of Applied Linguistics* 4(1): 3–15.
Martinez, R. and Schmitt, N. (2012) 'A Phrasal Expressions List', *Applied Linguistics* 33(3): 299–320.
Moudraia, O. (2004) 'The Student Engineering English corpus', *ICAME Journal* 28: 139–43.
Nation, P. (2013) *Learning Vocabulary in Another Language*, Cambridge: Cambridge University Press.
Nation, P. and Waring, R. (1997) 'Vocabulary Size, Text Coverage and Word Lists', in N. Schmitt and M. J. McCarthy (eds) *Vocabulary: Description, Acquisition and Pedagogy*, Cambridge: Cambridge University Press, pp. 6–19.
Nesi, H., Gardner, S., Forsyth, R., Hindle, D., Wickens, P., Ebeling, S. Leedham, M., Thompson, P. and Heuboeck, A. (2005) 'Towards the Compilation of a Corpus of Assessed Student Writing: An Account of Work in Progress', paper presented at Corpus Linguistics University of Birmingham, published in the *Proceedings from the Corpus Linguistics Conference Series*, 1, Available from www.corpus.bham.ac.uk/PCLC.
O'Keeffe, A., Clancy, B. and Adolphs, A. (2020) *Introducing Pragmatics in Use*, 2nd edn, London: Routledge.
O'Keeffe, A., McCarthy, M. J. and Carter, R. A. (2007) *From Corpus to Classroom: Language Use and Language Teaching*, Cambridge: Cambridge University Press.
Pawley, A. and Syder, F. H. (1983) 'Two Puzzles for Linguistic Theory: Nativelike Selection and Nativelike Fluency', in J. C. Richards and R. W. Schmidt (eds) *Language and Communication*, New York: Longman, pp. 191–226.
Rayson, P. (2002) *Matrix: A Statistical Method and Software Tool for Linguistic Analysis through Corpus Comparison*, unpublished PhD thesis, Lancaster University.
Samuda, V. (2005) 'Expertise in Pedagogic Task Design', in K. Johnson (ed.) *Expertise in Second Language Learning and Teaching*, Basingstoke: Palgrave, Macmillan, pp. 230–54.
Scott, M. (2019) *WordSmith Tools Version 7*, Stroud: Lexical Analysis Software.
Shin, D. and Nation, P. (2008) 'Beyond Single Words: The Most Frequent Collocations in Spoken English', *ELT Journal* 62(4): 339–48.
Simpson-Vlach, R. and Ellis, N. C. (2010) 'An Academic Formulas List: New Methods in Phraseology Research', *Applied Linguistics* 31(4): 487–512.
Thurstun, J. and Candlin, C. N. (1998) 'Concordancing and the Teaching of Vocabulary of Academic English', *English for Specific Purposes* 17: 267–80.
Vincent, B. (2013) 'Investigating Academic Phraseology through Combinations of Very Frequent Words: A Methodological Exploration', *Journal of English for Academic Purposes* 12(1): 44–57.

Ward, J. (2009) 'A Basic Engineering English Word List for Less Proficient Foundation Engineering Undergraduates', *English for Specific Purposes* 28(3): 170–82.
West, M. (1953) *A General Service List of English Words*, London: Longman.
Wolfe, J., Britt, C. and Alexander, K. P. (2011) 'Teaching the IMRaD Genre: Sentence Combining and Pattern Practice Revisited', *Journal of Business and Technical Communication* 25(2): 119–58.
Wray, A. (1999) 'Formulaic Language in Learners and Native Speakers', *Language Teaching* 32: 213–31.
Wray, A. (2002) *Formulaic Language and the Lexicon*, Cambridge: Cambridge University Press.
Wulff, S. (2019) 'Acquisition of Formulaic Language from a Usage-Based Perspective', in A. Siyanova-Chanturia and A. Pellicer-Sánchez (eds) *Understanding Formulaic Language: A Second Language Acquisition Perspective*, London: Routledge, pp. 19–37.
Yang, H. (1985) 'The JDEST Computer Corpus of Texts in English for Science and Technology', *ICAME News* 9: 24–5.

25

What can a corpus tell us about grammar teaching materials?

Graham Burton

1 Historical contexts

This chapter will consider the case of the grammatical content typically taught to learners of English as a foreign language (EFL), that is to say, the "pedagogical grammar" of EFL. The discussion starts with historical contexts because this will help us to understand where the grammatical rules and traditions that make up this consensus come from and if, when and how they have been influenced by corpora, or corpus-linguistic type methods, over the years.

The earliest account of English grammar is said to be Bullokar's 1586 *Pamphlet for Grammar* (Linn 2006). The grammatical accounts of English that emerged in the centuries following – collectively termed "traditional grammar" – were highly opinionated, generally attempting to improve the language and resolve doubts in marginal cases of use rather than provide a full account of grammar. For example, Lindley Murray, in his highly influential *English Grammar*, stated that grammarians may 'reason and remonstrate' in '[c]ases which custom has left dubious' (Murray 1795: 145). Grammarians in this period often made use of written evidence in compiling their grammars, but not in the way we would expect today: Rather, they mined written texts to find *counter-examples* of their own prescriptions in order to give examples of the usage "errors" of which they disapproved (Meyer 2009).

Modern, "scientific" descriptions of English grammar emerged around the turn of the twentieth century; written by grammarians such as Henry Sweet, Otto Jespersen, Etsko Kruisinga, John Nesfield and Reinard Zandvoort, to name only a small selection, these were descriptive accounts based on observation of real language use. Like the older grammarians, many illustrated their explanations with examples from written texts, including personal correspondence (McCarthy 2020) but this was now to *illustrate* usage rather than criticise it. Jespersen, for instance, used examples taken from his personal "corpus" of hundreds of sources in his *A Modern English Grammar on Historical Principles*, stating that these were 'in many ways more satisfactory than even the best made-up examples' (Jespersen 1909: vi).

 DOI: 10.4324/9780367076399-25

Some decades later, Charles Fries produced, in his *The Structure of English*, perhaps the earliest near equivalent to a modern, corpus-informed grammar (Fries uses the word "body" rather than "corpus"). Fries' grammar was informed by a 250,000-word "proto-corpus" (a term I will use to refer to collections compiled for analysis before the advent of modern, computer-assisted corpus analysis) of spoken English, making it the first grammar to be based on live, spoken data (Linn 2006). Fries chose spoken data ('actual English speech observed and recorded in a university community in the North-Central part of United States' (Fries 1952: 30) because of his desire to describe not 'great literature', but the 'language of the people as used in practical affairs of life' (ibid: 5).

When, in the first decades of the twentieth century, ELT as a practice and profession became distinct from the teaching of other European languages (Howatt and Smith 2014), there was no particular tradition of *pedagogical* grammar for EFL. As late as 1947, W. Stannard Allen, in the introduction to his trail-blazing practice grammar *Living English Structure* (1947), states that 'a large number of [grammar books] that are intended for foreigners have not managed to free themselves entirely from the purely analytical point of view' of traditional school grammars (1947: vii). While they are brief, the references included in titles such as Allen's, as well as in titles written by two other key ELT figures in this period, Harold Palmer and A. S. Hornby, showed that they had access to the new wave of descriptive, scientific grammars that had recently appeared. Allen, for example, offers a list of 'useful books for further reference', including works by Jespersen and Zandvoort; Palmer makes reference to other grammars, most frequently to Sweet's *New English Grammar*; and Hornby shows great familiarity with the new generation of grammarians in numerous articles in the *ELT Journal*, including effusive praise for Fries's *The Structure of English* in a book review (Hornby 1954a). There therefore seems to have been a flow of insights from the turn-of-the-century descriptive grammars to ELT pedagogy and teaching materials.

Palmer and Hornby are also largely responsible for the development of a strand of grammatical analysis which emerged in parallel to the application of the descriptive accounts to ELT, now typically known as "pattern grammar". To adequately explain Palmer and Hornby's contribution to this strand, we must briefly consider their research on vocabulary. At the beginning of the twentieth century, vocabulary control was the principal area of enquiry among a group of researchers, including Palmer and Hornby, because of the predominance of graded readers as a key element of instruction materials. One well-known output of this research was the *Interim Report on Vocabulary Selection for English as a Foreign Language* (Faucett *et al.* 1936), published again, more famously and in slightly modified form, as the *General Service List of English Words* (West 1953). This 2,000-word list was intended to be used to assist in teaching and the production of teaching materials and was compiled by Palmer and three other researchers: Laurence Faucett and Michael West, both EFL teachers and researchers, and the American "statistical lexicographer", Edward L. Thorndike (see also Chapter 28, this volume). The list considered i) existing, frequency- and dispersion-based wordlists, which themselves had been compiled from proto-corpora of millions of words, and ii) the more subjective criteria of structural value, universality, subject range, definition words, word-building capability and style (Gilner 2011). The exact meaning of these "subjective" criteria need not detain us here; the important point is that even in this period, long before computerised corpora, before Fries constructed his spoken corpus and before the start (in 1959) of Quirk's *Survey of English Usage*, empirically based descriptions were being created to inform ELT materials.

The wordlist in the *Interim Report on Vocabulary Selection* did not contain syntactic information. However, Palmer and Hornby's work had started to move in this direction, with two minor publications on "collocations" (a term they used with a broader meaning than today, which included syntactic patterns) and "construction patterns" appearing in the mid 1930s. Following this, Palmer published his *A Grammar of English Words* (Palmer 1938), focussing on the syntactic structures associated with 1,000 words, followed by Hornby's (1954b) *A Guide to Patterns and Use in English*, which became a standard reference work for materials writers (Richards and Rodgers 2001).

It is not entirely clear whether Palmer and Hornby made use of frequency and/or proto-corpus data in choosing structures to include in these and other titles. Cowie (1999) – a later colleague of Hornby – argues that the fact that the two strands of research (on wordlists and patterns) proceeded in parallel made cross-fertilisation likely and points out that the work on wordlists had brought structural words – 'the essential building blocks of sentence construction' (1999: 7) – into special prominence. At the very least, it appears safe to say that the idea of considering frequency data, based on empirical observation of language, was in the air in the first half of the twentieth century; this can also be seen, for example, in the introduction to *Living English Structure* (Allen 1947), where Allen states that many of his exercises 'are based on the results of personal "structure-counts" [...] carried out while listening to the speech of educated English people over considerable periods' (1947: vii–viii).

By the second half of the twentieth century, a 'standard model' (Howatt and Widdowson 2011: 299) had started to emerge in ELT, as part of what Smith describes as the 'standardization of English as a foreign language' (Smith 2004: 71). Just as the work of the EFL teacher-scholars in the first half of the twentieth century had been influenced by the accounts created by the turn-of-the-century grammarians, materials writers in the second half of the century, and up to the present, have "inherited" a sizeable body of work on EFL grammar, including a new kind of analysis based on patterns, which simply was not in existence 50 years previously. As we have seen, some of what made up this body of work was often either directly or indirectly empirically based. Nonetheless, there have been a number of attempts to audit, assess and critique many aspects of the standard model. We will now turn to these and begin to answer the question of what corpora can tell us about this current consensus.

2 Corpora and existing pedagogical grammar descriptions

Writing pedagogical grammar explanations requires the juggling of different, and sometimes competing, considerations (see, for example, Swan's discussion of six 'design criteria' for language rules, some of which 'necessarily conflict' (1994: 46)). It is therefore perhaps unsurprising that the pedagogical accounts born as a consequence of these conflicting criteria, and out of the historical processes described above, have often been criticised.

One frequently discussed area of grammar coverage in ELT materials is conditional forms. Maule's (1988) study compares the typical categorisation system used in ELT accounts to 'a collection of 100 conditionals from television', finding that the "bulk" of authentic examples did not fit the ELT account. Gabrielatos (2003, 2006) and Jones and Waller (2011) come to similar conclusions, in both cases using a much larger data set: the *British National Corpus*. Frazier's (2003) study focuses on just one possible element of conditional forms – *would*-clauses – in intermediate and advanced-level coursebooks. He reports corpus evidence that shows it is common for a *would*-clause to appear without an *if*-clause or overt conditional form, and that when an *if*-clause does appear, it is often non-adjacent to the related *would*-clause; this differs from ELT accounts, which invariably present both *if*-clauses and *would* clauses together.

A similar misrepresentation in coursebooks of actual usage is described in Shortall's (2007) study, which compares coursebook coverage of present perfect aspect forms with spoken data in the Bank of English. Shortall finds that coursebooks over-represent the active forms of the present perfect simple and continuous, at the expense of present perfect passive forms and modal perfect forms, as well as over-representing certain time adverbials, such as *since* and *for*, and under-representing others such as *now*. In a similar vein, Barbieri and Eckhardt (2007) compare reported speech in coursebooks to data from the *Longman Spoken and Written English Corpus* and the *TOEFL 2000 Spoken and Written Academic Language Corpus*, finding that ELT grammar accounts do not present an accurate picture of usage, neglecting features of authentic direct and indirect reported speech, including the choice of reporting verbs taught, and some frequent verb combinations found in reported speech (see also McCarthy 1998 for a detailed analysis of reported speech, based on data from the CANCODE corpus).

A further three studies of this type are Conrad (2004), Römer (2005) and Vandenhoek (2018). Conrad presents a corpus investigation of the adverb *though*, in its "useful function" as an adverbial of contrast and concession. A comparison of this data to coverage in four ELT textbooks of the same word shows a mismatch: only one of the four textbooks taught *though* as a linking adverbial, and, even in that case, only as an adverb of contrast, not concession. None of the books showed *though* being used to "soften disagreement between speakers" – a key use identified in the corpus analysis. Römer's (2005) study focuses on progressive forms, comparing spoken data from the BNC and *Bank of English* to a small corpus of coursebooks. The coursebook accounts were found to simplify and misrepresent many aspects of actual usage, often neglecting, for example, the function of "repeatedness", despite its frequency in the corpus data. Finally, Vandenhoek's (2018) study focuses on the past perfect, again comparing coverage in coursebooks to corpus data, and discussing a number of inaccuracies in coursebook descriptions, including over-representing the co-occurrence of time expressions with the past perfect, failing to focus on stylistic/discursive uses (see also Hughes and McCarthy 1998) over the preferred (in coursebooks) function of establishing chronological order, failing to teach the link between the past perfect and the present perfect, and failing to reflect corpus data showing that the past perfect is "overwhelming associated" with written fiction.

Biber and Reppen (2002) focus on three areas of grammar to put forward a more general argument: that the content and organisational principles of grammar materials should be informed by frequency data from corpora. Contrasting the coverage in six ELT grammar books of noun premodifiers, the progressive aspect, and the lexis chosen to illustrate grammatical features to EFL grammar book treatments, they show that the published materials under-represent the use of noun premodifiers compared to adjectives and *-ing* / *-ed* forms, over-represent the use of the progressive over the simple aspect, and often make use of relatively infrequent lexical verbs to illustrate examples of grammar. They argue that these discrepancies are due to authors 'mak[ing] pedagogical decisions based on their beliefs about language use, in many cases without even acknowledging that decisions are being made' (2002: 200), and stating that '[b]y using information based on actual frequency and context of use (e.g. register differences), materials developers and teachers should be able to increase the meaningful input that is provided to learners' (ibid: 207).

Biber and Reppen's comments are not unusual. The authors of studies of the kind described in this section generally recommend, often in relatively strong terms, that materials designers take into account the findings reported, or at least suggest that teaching materials might be improved were they to do so. Frazier's conclusion is typical, stating that the study's findings 'would seem to *dictate*' a change in pedagogical descriptions, and that authors '*should* develop a new, comprehensive categorization of conditional structures based on corpora of authentic language (2003: 464, all emphasis added). Despite such entreaties, however, pedagogical grammar descriptions in ELT publications appear to have changed little, if at all, as a result of such studies, despite the fact that corpus linguistics has been influential in other fields, such as automatic translation, speech recognition, and human-computer interaction (Hughes 2012).

Shortall (2007) offers an explanation for this, with a somewhat different perspective on possible reasons for the gap between corpus data and descriptions in ELT materials. He argues that while there should be a role for the 'consultation and exploration of corpora' in developing teaching materials, it should also be accepted that frequency information 'is not the only consideration in providing input for learners' and that 'pedagogic considerations may sometimes override considerations of frequency'. His conclusion is that there is a role for both frequency data and 'pedagogic necessity' when designing teaching materials. Timmis (2015) makes similar arguments, asking, for example, whether a teacher might choose to spend more time on the present continuous than the present simple – regardless of which is more frequent – because it is problematic for a particular of learners and/or easy to illustrate in class (c.f. Römer 2005), and querying whether pre-modification of a noun is actually likely to cause problems for learners (c.f. Biber and Reppen 2002). From this point of view, corpora can tell us not only about grammar teaching materials themselves, but perhaps also about the particular requirements that teachers have of grammar teaching materials.

To such arguments we might also add Burton's (2012) findings, based on a survey completed by thirteen ELT coursebook authors, that many materials writers do not have the time during the writing process or the necessary expertise to carry out their own corpus research, are not encouraged to do so by publishers, and, in many cases, do not perceive that it is necessary to do so (one notable exception is the *Touchstone* series (Cambridge University Press), which, in its explanations of grammar, makes extensive use of corpus data (McCarthy 2004)). In any case, there exists a strong tradition and consensus on the content of grammar syllabuses in ELT (Biber and Reppen 2002; Ellis 2006; Burton 2019), and innovations away from this appear to be neither requested nor desired by the end users of teaching materials: teachers and learners. It may therefore be the case that some of the attempted explanations for why ELT grammar accounts are the way they are perhaps overlook more practical, "real world" considerations.

3 Using corpora to build pedagogical grammar accounts

Another frequent area of research in corpus linguistics has been to identify areas of language that have not previously featured in standard descriptions of grammar, and discuss how the latter could be extended to include them. This is therefore more an application of corpus research to build new or complement existing grammatical descriptions, rather than simply to critique them.

One example of this kind of research is the work, initiated in the 1990s, by Ronald Carter and Michael McCarthy on "spoken grammar", using the *Cambridge and Nottingham Corpus of Discourse English* (CANCODE) spoken corpus. Carter and McCarthy's seminal (1995) article presents a number of aspects of spoken grammar which appear to have the potential to be applied to pedagogical accounts; for example, ellipsis, fronted topics and tail slots are all argued to be pedagogically relevant, but rarely feature in traditional ELT descriptions of language. Carter and McCarthy argue that the latter two features should be considered as part of "interpersonal grammar", in that they are tools that allow a speaker to identify elements he or she wants to highlight and reinforce for the listener. More recently (Carter and McCarthy 2017), the same authors argued that many such "spoken" language features are also found in e-communication (i.e. text messages, emails, online "chats" etc.); this context is likely to be equally, or perhaps even more, interesting to many learners of EFL.

Fuller lists of features of spoken language can be found in McCarthy and Carter (2002) and Cullen and Kuo (2007). The latter identify nine features of spoken grammar and examine their coverage in 24 coursebooks at 5 levels. While many of the coursebooks examined did include coverage of some of the features identified, there was a marked preference for fixed, lexicogrammatical units (for example *sort of*, *and things like that*, *a bit*, *you know*, *I mean*), but far more limited coverage of grammatical features such as the use of the past continuous to introduce reported speech, fronted topics and tails, and also grammatical features associated with informal, spoken contexts (e.g. *less* + plural noun).

Cullen and Kuo make an explicit call for pedagogical grammar treatments to include more coverage of spoken grammar. One of the arguments is by now familiar: such language is highly frequent, often more so than well-established, in pedagogical accounts, features of language (for example, heads and tails are said to be twice as frequent as *get* passives and *ought to*). Cullen and Kuo point out that there appears to be nothing "bad" or inappropriate about features of spoken grammar, and therefore no reason why they should not be treated in grammar materials and learners should not have the opportunity to learn about and practise using them.

One response to this position is also familiar: pedagogic considerations might be argued to outweigh considerations over accuracy. Widdowson (1991: 20) puts this position starkly: 'language teaching cannot simply be based on descriptive facts [...] Their relevance is not self-evident. It has to be established by reference to pedagogic material'. This argument is echoed in Seidlhofer, who states that 'it is obvious that new findings cannot go directly into syllabuses and teaching materials without any pedagogical treatment: the very existence of classrooms, syllabuses and teaching materials makes some pedagogic agency a logical necessity' (2011: 79).

The question of whether the features of spoken language discussed in this section constitute suitable content for the language classroom was the subject of a well-known exchange in the *ELT Journal* between Carter and McCarthy and the coursebook author Luke Prodromou (Carter and McCarthy 1996; Prodromou 1996a, 1996b). One particularly relevant aspect of the debate relates to authenticity, with Prodromou asking, 'What happens when I take this natural discourse out of its original context and transplant into another context [...], for example, by putting it into a textbook for the consumption of learners of English as a Foreign Language?' (1996b: 371). In other words, does authentic language lose its authenticity when removed from its original context and reproduced elsewhere? Widdowson (1998) suggests that it does, as 'learners are outsiders, by definition, not members of user communities [s]o the language that is authentic for native speaker users cannot possibly be authentic for learners' (1998: 711). Widdowson goes on to argue that it is learners who must "authenticate" the language in their teaching materials; whether or not they do so depends not on where the language comes from, but on whether it 'can be made real by the community of learners' (ibid.: 715). McCarthy and McCarten (2019) argue that learners will authenticate the language in their teaching materials if it is 'representative of the discourse type in question' and if they 'perceive how they might use or adapt [it] for their own utterances and successful participation in exchanges'. The original source, in this view, is not particularly important; what is important is what learners make of the language and how they perceive they might use it.

A somewhat different take on the use of corpora to build pedagogical accounts is offered by McCarthy (2015), who uses corpus evidence not to assess coverage of a specific grammatical structure, but to suggest how the grammatical content of particular competency levels (specifically, the "upper-intermediate" and "advanced" levels of coursebook series) might be decided on. McCarthy argues that at these levels, there is the least amount of agreement across coursebook series on grammatical content, and that corpora can be usefully mined to identify relevant, but comparatively less frequent structures which may be of interest to more advanced learners. Some structures suggested are *such* + uncountable noun, *what* + noun, the past continuous passive, sentence-initial non-finite passive clauses, and subjunctive verb forms following a noun (e.g. *Dr. Reed's insistence that he* ***go*** *to work*). McCarthy argues that this kind of content can be differentiated according to learners' specific needs, stating that if these are 'mainly oriented towards academic, professional or vocational writing in formal contexts', then 'some forms that may be low frequency or rare may yet be appropriate [...] and enrich the writers' style and enhance the reception of their texts.' (2015: 94). The question of the specific needs of learners is of course not limited to advanced levels. Corpus based studies have contributed to a greater understanding of features of language associated with specific purpose language use (see Flowerdew (2011) for a review of corpus-based studies in the field of English for Specific Purposes). The outcome of such research can be teaching materials focussing – partly or wholly – on the grammar associated with the language used in specific fields, contexts etc. (for example, McCarthy *et al.* 2009; Brieger 2011; Swales and Feak 2012).

This chapter has already discussed the emergence of the analysis of the 'patterned' nature of language. While the insights developed by Palmer and Hornby were initially intended to inform grammar teaching materials (c.f. Palmer's (1938) *A Grammar of English Words*), they were eventually incorporated not into classroom materials but learner dictionaries, becoming part of the distinctive "productive" character (Cowie 2002) that distinguishes them from "standard" dictionaries. However, the development of the COBUILD project in the 1980s brought new life to the analysis of patterns. Hanks (2008) makes explicit the link between Hornby's work and COBUILD, arguing that corpus linguistics has brought things "full circle" to Hornby's "original vision", with a focus on patterns now allowing new theories of language to be developed (2008: 89).

Interestingly, the COBUILD project in a sense reversed the situation with Palmer and Hornby's work: the former was originally intended as a resource for lexicography (Conrad 2012), and lead to the publication of the COBUILD dictionaries, but this was then followed by the publication of a series of grammar practice titles dealing with "pattern grammar" (for example, COBUILD 1998). Hunston *et al.* (1997) have made the case for the explicit teaching of patterns in ELT, arguing that understanding, accuracy, fluency, and flexibility can all benefit from their explicit study. However, most coursebooks and pedagogical grammars do not go beyond covering basic verb combinations, for example verb + *-ing* form, verb + infinitive and verb + *to* + infinitive, and this may be a remnant of Palmer and Hornby's work early in first half of the twentieth century rather than a response to such calls.

The discussion thus far has focussed exclusively on corpora of native-speaker English. Should there also be a role for learner corpora in the design of grammar teaching materials? Up until the present, the primary role for non-native speaker corpora in grammar teaching materials has been to inform focuses within explanations on common learner errors. This in many ways is nothing new, as it takes us back to the Contrastive Analysis Hypothesis (Lado 1957); modern corpora, however, allow such analyses to be carried out with more precision, with the language in a learner corpus compared to that in a native speaker corpus, identifying differences, particularly in either what is termed over-, under- or misuse (Granger 2003) of certain language features.

Others, however, have made the case for the use of non-native speaker corpora as a more realistic model for language learners to aspire to, and for teaching materials to be based on. Prodromou (2003), for example, suggests that corpora of "successful users" of English may be more useful for language teaching, a thought echoed by O'Keeffe *et al.* (2007), who argue that there is a need to 'move away from the native versus non-native speaker dichotomy' and focus on 'a continuum of successful or expert users of a language' (2007: 248). Such a move does not seem to have occurred yet in grammar teaching materials; however, the recent development of learner corpora tagged for competency level may represent an opportunity for change, and it is to this which we will shall now turn.

4 Corpora and grammar syllabuses

One particular characteristic of pedagogical grammar accounts is that in many cases the grammatical material is sequenced. This is particularly, and perhaps most obviously, the case with coursebooks, which are typically published across competency levels, with different grammatical content selected for inclusion at each level (and, possibly, also sequenced *within* each level). Once materials are organised in this way, the question naturally arises of how level assignment and sequencing can be done in a logical and systematic way.

Richards (2001) offers five criteria for sequencing content: simplicity and centrality, frequency, learnability, intrinsic difficulty and communicative needs. However, making judgements on how "simple" or "central" a particular grammatical structure is, or how "intrinsically difficult" it is likely to be for learners, is not straightforward, and may in many cases may require a series of largely subjective decisions to be made. Others have made the claim for the existence of an "internal, learner syllabus", which is impervious to teaching (see, for example, Long 2015), arguing that pre-determined grammar syllabuses are essentially doomed to failure. In the case of the grammar syllabuses typically used in ELT materials, however, the key deciding factor appears, once again, to be consensus: there is not only strong agreement within the profession on overall grammatical content, but also on how this this content should be split across levels (Burton 2019).

What, then, can a corpus tell us about sequencing decisions? While native-speaker corpora are unlikely to reveal much about L2 developmental sequences, learner corpora may be of more use. A number of learner corpora have been created using data from learners at different competency levels (for example, the Cambridge Learner Corpus, the EF-Cambridge Open Language Database, and the Trinity Lancaster Corpus), meaning that analyses can be carried out of learner output both at any single level, and also *across* levels, potentially shedding light on developmental sequences. One significant outcome of such research is the English Grammar Profile (EGP), a searchable database (available online from englishprofile.org) containing over 1,000 grammar competency statements across competence levels. These are based on an analysis of the *Cambridge Learner Corpus*, a 55.5 million word corpus of exam scripts from Cambridge English exams, calibrated to the six CEFR levels (see O'Keeffe and Mark 2017 for further details).

A full comparison of the EGP competency statements to the typical sequencing of grammar points in ELT coursebooks has not been carried out. However, some limited comparisons have been made (Mark and O'Keeffe 2016; Burton 2019), with results showing that learners are able to use many grammatically structures before they are typically taught in coursebooks and that they display a wider grammatical repertoire than is typically presented to them in teaching materials. Burton (2019), for example, reports that learners at A2 level are able to produce both defining and non-defining relative clauses, a range of future forms (including *going to* to make predictions, *will* to show willingness, and present simple to talk about timetabled events), and a number of conditional forms (including the so-called "zero conditional" and the non-canonical combinations of *if* + present simple, *can* and *if* + present simple, imperative) at least a level earlier than these are typically taught.

What are we to make of the differences found between coursebook syllabuses and empirical evidence on learner output? In the previous sections we said that at times, pedagogical exigencies may be behind such inaccuracies; at other times, materials designers may simply not be aware of any inaccuracies and, in any case, the weight of tradition may itself be more influential than the need for accuracy. In the case of the ordering of elements of a grammatical elements, the same arguments may well apply: teachers are used to teaching particular grammatical structures at certain levels, so much so that level (or perceived level) has, in ELT, become a characteristic of grammatical structures. Learner corpora calibrated by level of proficiency may therefore be able to tell us that the typical ordering of grammar points in ELT materials is not a reflection of the development sequence learners actually follow, but of what the end users of teaching materials perceive to be "best practice".

5 Future directions

The picture this chapter has painted has been somewhat mixed. Accounts of grammar in ELT were first developed at the beginning of the twentieth century, and while obviously not corpus-informed, were certainly influenced by the increasingly empirical descriptions of English grammar that had started to be published. Research within the emerging ELT profession on word lists and patterns in the first half of the century suggested that empirical evidence was at the heart of the development of language descriptions for ELT at the time, but as the century progressed, trusted, standardised accounts emerged, which may contain inaccuracies.

What can we expect in the future? ELT publishing is often said to be inherently conservative, favouring tried and trusted approaches over innovation, due mainly to the commercial imperatives that publishers must always consider (Littlejohn 1992; Burton

2012). While a corpus can tell us that a pedagogical grammatical description is inaccurate, little appears to have changed since Hughes' prediction that 'it is unlikely that published materials, in the traditional sense, will take a lead in this field' (2012: 408). Any changes that do occur are likely to be "minimally evolutionary" (Littlejohn 1992) rather than revolutionary. One compromise approach is suggested by Chambers (2019), who argues that publishers could make available parts of their own corpora to teachers as a teaching resource, 'accompanied by guidance in the exploration of the corpus in the teaching and learning context' (2019: 471). It may also be the case that increasing interest – from teachers and learners – in English for Specific Purposes may be an impetus for publishers to produce more corpus-based materials.

A further potential cause for optimism relates to learner corpora. As we have seen, learner corpora compiled at multiple competency levels have the potential to provide exciting insights into how grammatical competency develops as learners advance through competency levels. The fact that resources such as the EGP have been made publicly available is certainly positive, as this gives teachers "on the ground" immediate access to the data. A related, freely accessible resource is the spoken *Trinity Lancaster Corpus* (corpora.lancs.ac.uk/trinity), which users can use to search for, and create concordances of, real spoken language produced by learners at CEFR levels B1-C2. Like the CLC, this corpus is based on language produced in exams (in this case, from Trinity's Graded Examinations in Spoken English). A potential criticism of such corpora is that language exams represent a rather limited, unnatural data source; however, McCarthy (personal communication) argues that a distinction can be made between "natural" and "authentic" language sources, meaning that 'if the learner perceives something as an authentic learning (or testing) task, then it may be effective in its own right'. A learner preparing for a language exam might therefore find it far easier to "authenticate" language produced by a learner sitting the same exam they are planning to sit, than language produced by a native speaker or simply invented by a materials writer.

Further reading

Biber, D. and Reppen, R. (2002) 'What Does Frequency Have to Do with Grammar Teaching?' *Studies in Second Language Acquisition* 24(2): 199–208. (This provides clear and persuasive arguments for using frequency as a driver of decisions on grammar descriptions and content.)

Gablasova, D., Brezina, V. and McEnery, T. (2019) 'The Trinity Lancaster Corpus: Applications in Language Teaching and Materials Development', in S. Götz and J. Mukherjee (eds) *Learner Corpora and Language Teaching*, Amsterdam: John Benjamins, pp. 8–28. (This chapter discusses how the TLC can be applied to language teaching and the development of teaching materials to develop speaking skills, focussing particularly on expression of disagreement, ability to adjust language choice according to linguistic setting, and engaged listenership.)

O'Keeffe, A. and Mark, G. (2017) 'The English Grammar Profile of Learner Competence: Methodology and Key Findings', *International Journal of Corpus Linguistics*, 22(4): 457–89. (This paper explains how the EGP was created. This is interesting in that it shows how it is possible to move from raw, learner corpus data to a pedagogical resource for materials designers and teachers.)

Timmis, I. (2015) *Corpus Linguistics for ELT: Research and Practice*, London: Routledge. (Timmis' book offers a comprehensive account of how corpora can be applied to ELT. There is an entire chapter on corpus research and grammar, and the discussion at times offers an interesting counterpoint to Biber and Reppen (2002) above, explaining how pedagogical arguments might sometimes be more relevant than frequency-based arguments.)

References

Allen, W. S. (1947) *Living English Structure*, London: Longman.

Barbieri, F. and Eckhardt, S. E. B. (2007) 'Applying Corpus-Based Findings to Form-Focused Instruction: The Case of Reported Speech', *Language Teaching Research* 11(3): 319–46.

Biber, D. and Reppen, R. (2002) 'What Does Frequency Have to Do with Grammar Teaching?' *Studies in Second Language Acquisition* 24(2): 199–208.

Brieger, N. (2011) *Collins Business Grammar and Practice Intermediate*, London: HarperCollins.

Burton, G. (2012) 'Corpora and Coursebooks: Destined to Be Strangers Forever?' *Corpora* 7(1): 91–108.

Burton, G. (2019) *The Canon of Pedagogical Grammar for ELT: A Mixed Methods Study of Its Evolution, Development and Comparison with Evidence on Learner Output*, unpublished PhD thesis, University of Limerick.

Carter, R. A. and McCarthy, M. J. (1995) 'Grammar and the Spoken Language', *Applied Linguistics* 16(2): 141–58.

Carter, R. A. and McCarthy, M. J. (1996) 'Correspondence', *ELT Journal* 50(4): 369–71.

Carter, R. A. and McCarthy, M. J. (2017) 'Spoken Grammar: Where Are We and Where Are We Going?', *Applied Linguistics* 38(1): 1–20.

Chambers, A. (2019) 'Towards the Corpus Revolution? Bridging the Research-Practice Gap', *Language Teaching* 52(4): 460–75.

COBUILD (1998) *Verbs: Patterns and Practice. Classroom Edition*, London: HarperCollins.

Conrad, S. (2004) 'Corpus Linguistics, Language Variation, and Language Teaching', in J. McH Sinclair (ed.) *How to Use Corpora in Language Teaching*, Amsterdam: John Benjamins, pp. 67–85.

Conrad, S. (2012) 'What Can a Corpus Tell us about Grammar?', in A. O'Keeffe and M. J. McCarthy (eds) *The Routledge Handbook of Corpus Linguistics*, London: Routledge, pp. 227–40.

Cowie, A. P. (1999) 'Learners' Dictionaries in a Historical and a Theoretical Perspective', in T. Herbst and K. Popp (eds) *The Perfect Learners' Dictionary (?)* Tübingen: Niemeyer, pp. 3–14.

Cowie, A. (2002) *English Dictionaries for Foreign Learners: A History*, Oxford: Oxford University Press.

Cullen, R. and Kuo, I.-C. V. (2007) 'Spoken Grammar and ELT Course Materials: A Missing Link?' *TESOL Quarterly* 41(2): 361–86.

Ellis, R. (2006) 'Current Issues in the Teaching of Grammar: An SLA Perspective', *TESOL Quarterly* 40(1): 83–107.

Faucett, L., Palmer, H., Thorndike, E. and West, M. (1936) *Interim Report on Vocabulary Selection*, London: P.S. King and Son, Ltd.

Flowerdew, L. (2011) 'ESP and Corpus Studies', in D. Belcher, A. Johns and B. Paltridge (eds.) *New Directions in English for Specific Purposes Research*, Ann Arbor: University of Michigan Press.

Frazier, S. (2003) 'A Corpus Analysis of Would-Clauses without Adjacent If-Clauses', *TESOL Quarterly* 37(3): 443–66.

Fries, C. (1952) *The Structure of English*, New York and Burlingame: Harcourt, Brace & World, Inc.

Gabrielatos, C. (2003) 'Conditional Sentences: ELT Typology and Corpus Evidence', *36th Annual BAAL Meeting*, 4 September, 2003, 140, Available at: http://eprints.lancs.ac.uk/140.

Gabrielatos, C. (2006) 'Corpus-Based Evaluation of Pedagogical Materials: If - Conditionals in ELT Coursebooks and the BNC', *7th Teaching and Language Corpora Conference*, 1 July, 2006, Available at: http://eprints.lancs.ac.uk/882/1/TALC_2006-CG.pdf [Accessed 23 May 2019].

Gilner, L. (2011) 'A Primer on the General Service List', *Reading in a Foreign Language* 23(1): 65–83.

Granger, S. (2003) 'The International Corpus of Learner English: A New Resource for Foreign Language Learning and Teaching and Second Language Acquisition Research', *TESOL Quarterly* 37(3): 538–46.

Hanks, P. (2008) 'Lexical Patterns: from Hornby to Hunston and Beyond', *Proceedings of the XIII Euralex International Congress*, Universitat Pompeu Fabra, Barcelona, pp. 89–129.

Hornby, A. S. (1954a) 'The Structure of English', *ELT Journal* 9(1): 18–24.

Hornby, A. S. (1954b) *A Guide to Patterns and Use in English*, Oxford: Oxford University Press.

Howatt, A. and Smith, R. (2014) 'The History of Teaching English as a Foreign Language, from a British and European Perspective', *Language & History* 57(1): 75–95.

Howatt, A. and Widdowson, H. G. (2011) *A History of English Language Teaching*, 2nd edn, Oxford: Oxford University Press.

Hughes, R. (2012) 'What a Corpus Tells Us about Grammar Teaching Materials', in A. O'Keeffe and M. J. McCarthy (eds) *The Routledge Handbook of Corpus Linguistics*, London: Routledge, pp. 401–12.

Hughes, R. and McCarthy, M. J. (1998) 'From Sentence to Discourse: Discourse Grammar and English Language Teaching', *TESOL Quarterly* 32(2): 263–87

Hunston, S., Francis, G. and Manning, E. (1997) 'Grammar and Vocabulary: Showing the Connections', *ELT Journal* 51(3): 208–16.

Jespersen, O. (1909) *A Modern English Grammar on Historical Principles*, London: George Allen and Unwin Ltd.

Jones, C. and Waller, D. (2011) 'If Only It Were True: The Problem with the Four Conditionals', *ELT Journal* 65(1): 24–32.

Lado, R. (1957) *Linguistics across Cultures: Applied Linguistics for Language Teachers*, Ann Arbor: University of Michigan Press.

Linn, A. (2006) 'English Grammar Writing', in B. Aarts and A. McMahon (eds) *The Handbook of English Linguistics*, Oxford: Blackwell, pp. 72–92.

Littlejohn, A. (1992) *Why Are English Language Teaching Materials the Way They Are?*, unpublished PhD thesis, University of Lancaster.

Long, M. H. (2015) *Second Language Acquisition and Task-Based Language Teaching*, Chichester: Wiley-Blackwell.

Mark, G. and O'Keeffe, A. (2016) 'Using the English Grammar Profile to Improve Curriculum Design', paper read at *50th Annual IATEFL Conference*, Birmingham, UK, 14th April, 2016.

Maule, D. (1988) 'Sorry, But If He Comes, I Go': Teaching Conditionals', *ELT Journal* 42(2): 117–23.

McCarthy, M. J. (1998) *Spoken Language and Applied Linguistics*, Cambridge: Cambridge University Press.

McCarthy, M. J. (2004) *Touchstone: From Corpus to Course Book*, Cambridge: Cambridge University Press.

McCarthy, M. J. (2015) 'The Role of Corpus Research in the Design of Advanced-Level Grammar Instruction', in M.-A. Christison, D. Christian, P. A. Duff and N. Spada (eds) *Teaching and Learning English Grammar: Research Findings and Future Directions*, London: Routledge, pp. 87–102.

McCarthy, M. J. (2020) *Innovations and Challenges in Grammar*, London: Routledge.

McCarthy, M. J. and Carter, R. A. (2002) 'Ten Criteria for a Spoken Grammar', in E. Hinkel and S. Fotos (eds) *New Perspectives on Grammar Teaching in Second Language Classrooms*, Mahwah, N.J: L. Erlbaum Associates, pp. 51–75.

McCarthy, M. J. and McCarten, J. (2019) 'Interaction Management in Academic Speaking', *Linx* 79. doi: 10.4000/linx.3611

McCarthy, M. J., McCarten, J., Clark, D. and Clark, R. (2009) *Grammar for Business*, Cambridge: Cambridge University Press.

Meyer, C. (2009) 'Pre-Electronic Corpora', in A. Lüdeling and M. Kytö (eds) *Corpus Linguistics: An International Handbook*, Berlin: Walter de Gruyter, pp. 1–14.

Murray, L. (1795) *English Grammar: Adapted to the Different Classes of Learners*, Hallowell, Maine: Goodale, Glazier and Co.

O'Keeffe, A. and Mark, G. (2017) 'The English Grammar Profile of Learner Competence: Methodology and Key Findings', *International Journal of Corpus Linguistics* 22(4): 457–89.

O'Keeffe, A., McCarthy, M. J. and Carter, R. A. (2007) *From Corpus to Classroom: Language Use and Language Teaching*, Cambridge: Cambridge University Press.

Palmer, H. (1938) *A Grammar of English Words*, London: Longman, Greens and Co.

Prodromou, L. (1996a) 'Correspondence', *ELT Journal* 50(1): 88–9.

Prodromou, L. (1996b) 'Correspondence', *ELT Journal* 50(4): 371–3.

Prodromou, L. (2003) 'In Search of the Successful User of English', *Modern English Teacher* 12(2): 5–14.

Richards, J. C. (2001) *Curriculum Development in Language Teaching*, Cambridge: Cambridge University Press.
Richards, J. C. and Rodgers, T. S. (2001) *Approaches and Methods in Language Teaching*, 2nd edn, Cambridge: Cambridge University Press.
Römer, U. (2005) *Progressives, Patterns. Pedagogy: A Corpus-Driven Approach to English Progressive Forms, Functions, Contexts, and Didactics*, Amsterdam: John Benjamins.
Seidlhofer, B. (ed.) (2011) *Controversies in Applied Linguistics*, Oxford: Oxford University Press.
Shortall, T. (2007) 'The L2 Syllabus: Corpus or Contrivance?', *Corpora* 2(2): 157–85.
Smith, R. (2004) *An Investigation into the Roots of ELT, with a Particular Focus on the Career and Legacy of Harold E. Palmer* (1877–1949), unpublished PhD thesis, University of Edinburgh.
Swales, J. and Feak, C. (2012) *Academic Writing for Graduate Students. Essential Tasks and Skills*, 3rd edn, Ann Arbor: University of Michigan Press.
Swan, M. (1994) 'Design Criteria for Pedagogic Language Rules', in M. Bygate, A. Tonkyn and E. Williams (eds) *Grammar and the Language Teacher*, New York: Prentice Hall, pp. 45–55.
Timmis, I. (2015) *Corpus Linguistics for ELT: Research and Practice*, London: Routledge.
Vandenhoek, T. (2018) 'The Past Perfect in Corpora and EFL/ESL Materials', *Research in Language* 16(1): 113–33.
West, M. (1953) *A General Service List of English Words*, London: Longman, Green & Co.
Widdowson, H. G. (1991) 'The Description and Prescription of Language', in J. E. Alatis (ed.) *Georgetown University Round Table on Languages and Linguistics (GURT) 1991*, Washington D.C.: Georgetown University Press, pp. 11–24.
Widdowson, H. G. (1998) 'Context, Community, and Authentic Language', *TESOL Quarterly* 32(4): 705–16.

26

Corpus-informed course design

Jeanne McCarten

1 English language teaching courses and corpora

An ELT course is a carefully sequenced, graded set of teaching materials whose aim is to improve the language knowledge and performance of learners, taking them from one level to another. Typically, courses include presentation and practice of language systems: grammar, vocabulary, communicative functions, pronunciation and the so-called 'four skills': reading, writing, listening and speaking, often together with culture, examination or life skills modules, within thematic units. General courses with multi-stranded syllabuses usually aim to give equal weight to the various language areas and skills and provide integrated and balanced attention to accuracy and fluency. Courses may teach "general" language, stratified by age or geographical region, or specialised business or academic language. They may include print, audio and online elements, either as discrete components or in a "blended" formula where print and online media deliver the same learning outcomes (McCarten and Sandiford 2016). A course is a complex, lengthy and expensive undertaking, and there is great pressure for it to be successful to return the investment required. Therefore courses must strike a balance between offering something new while remaining user-friendly, familiar, even "safe". Corpora have informed English dictionaries and grammar reference books since the publication of the *Collins COBUILD English Language Dictionary* in 1987 (COBUILD 1987) and the *Collins COBUILD English Grammar* in 1990 (COBUILD 1990). Curiously, apart from *The COBUILD English Course* (Willis and Willis 1987–88), courses were slow to exploit corpora until McCarthy *et al.* (2005–6). Many studies, including Biber *et al.* (1998), Gilmore (2004), Römer (2004), Cheng and Warren (2007), Cullen and Kuo (2007) and Shortall (2007), point to disparities between language descriptions and models in ELT courses and naturally occurring language as evidenced in corpora. Even so, few courses seemed to take advantage of corpora, which Burton (2012) attributes partly to publishers' lack of incentive to innovate and writing schedule time pressures. The benefits of using corpora to inform materials cannot be overstated, especially for the spoken language. The analysis tools give objective information about frequency, collocation, lexico-grammatical patterns and the data allow the writers access

DOI: 10.4324/9780367076399-26

to a wealth of language that has occurred outside of ELT classrooms. This is an invaluable resource for developing a knowledge of language and helping learners acquire it.

2 What kind of corpus is needed to write an ELT course?

ELT courses differ in terms of their intended geographic markets, institution type (primary, secondary, adult; public and private sectors) and the type of language they teach (general, academic, etc.). It therefore makes sense to use corpora whose content is broadly similar in nature to the language variety and genre that the end users aspire to learn. In choosing a corpus, the following considerations may be useful.

Variety

Most internationally marketed ELT courses are "American English" or "British English". Writers therefore need access to a corpus of the chosen variety to ensure that their syllabus and language models accurately reflect usage. While some differences between North American and British English are well known (e.g. *elevator* vs. *lift* and *gotten* vs. *got* and certain spellings), a corpus can reveal more subtle differences in frequency and use. For example, in the *Cambridge Spoken Corpus* (not publicly available, but made available to the present author in the creation of co-authored courses), the question form *have you got …?* is approximately 24 times more frequent in British English than in American English and so merits an earlier inclusion in an elementary British English course than in a North American one.

Genre

Some courses are described as "general", "four skills" courses and others are more specialised, such as business or academic English courses. Corpora of different genres may give different results in terms of their most frequent items of vocabulary, grammar or patterns of use. If the course aims to teach conversation skills, a corpus of written texts will not give the writer accurate information about the interactive language of conversation. Equally, a spoken corpus is unlikely to help the writer of an academic writing course identify the common vocabulary and structures which learners need to master. For example, the word *nice* is in the top 120 words in the *Spoken British National Corpus 2014* (*Spoken BNC 2014*), occurring 1,166 times per million words, and is a useful word in a general or conversation course. In contrast, in the *British Academic Written English* (BASE) *corpus nice* occurs just under nine times per million words and so may not be as useful for the academic writer.

Some words may have different meanings or uses in different genres. Figure 26.1 shows the top 12 collocates of the word form *see* in BAWE and *Spoken BNC 2014*. In academic written English *see* is often used to refer readers to other parts of the text (appendices, figures, tables, above, below, etc.) or to other publications, as in *see for example Bloggs 2007* as well as meaning of "observe" (*we can see that the sales in Asia increased*). In spoken English, *see* has various uses, including *let's see, let me see,* leave-taking (*see you later*), showing understanding (*I see*) and in *you see* to impart what the speaker feels is new information for the listener (*You see, he travels first class*). See Carter and McCarthy (2006: 109b).

(a)

		Word	Cooccurrences ?	Candidates ?	T-score	MI	LogDice ↓
1	☐	Appendix	288	1,474	16.92	8.50	10.63
2	☐	we	680	10,807	25.85	6.87	10.51
3	☐	appendix	179	692	13.35	8.91	10.15
4	☐	figure	166	1,584	12.82	7.61	9.81
5	☐	We	169	2,413	12.90	7.02	9.65
6	☐	can	567	25,202	23.24	5.39	9.29
7	☐	how	200	6,219	13.91	5.90	9.26
8	☐	1	208	9,132	14.08	5.40	8.97
9	☐	if	176	7,993	12.94	5.35	8.85
10	☐	Figure	110	3,829	10.29	5.74	8.76
11	☐	you	94	2,990	9.53	5.87	8.69
12	☐	(	1,134	90,538	32.23	4.54	8.61

Collocates of *see* in BAWE

(b)

		Word	Cooccurrences ?	Candidates ?	T-score	MI	LogDice ↓
1	☐	can	2,340	37,724	47.03	5.17	10.37
2	☐	you	7,553	310,650	80.77	3.82	9.55
3	☐	if	1,462	47,165	36.12	4.17	9.47
4	☐	'll	1,128	32,253	31.94	4.35	9.46
5	☐	could	860	22,267	28.02	4.49	9.37
6	☐	let	513	6,170	22.18	5.60	9.31
7	☐	ca	757	19,446	26.30	4.50	9.28
8	☐	see	717	20,302	25.47	4.36	9.18
9	☐	what	1,649	73,762	37.49	3.70	9.17
10	☐	did	1,253	51,317	32.91	3.83	9.16
11	☐	how	750	22,949	25.95	4.25	9.15
12	☐	to	3,763	200,208	55.74	3.45	9.13

Collocates of *see* in BNC Spoken (2014)

Figure 26.1 Collocates of *see* in BAWE and *Spoken BNC* (2014)

A useful tool in distinguishing differences between genres is keyword analysis (see Chapters 9 and 10, this volume). This identifies words or phrases which occur statistically significantly more (or less) frequently in one corpus than another benchmark corpus. In research for the *Oxford Phrasal Academic Lexicon* (OPAL)[1] comparing academic written English with a benchmark corpus of fiction, the modal verbs *can, may, might* and *should* were shown to be key modal verbs in academic written English, and the chunks *in the case of* and *as a result of* emerged as frequent key four-word items, indicating their importance in academic writing.

Age

While corpora of children's and teenage writing and speaking do exist (see *The Growth in Grammar Corpus*[2] of writing data up to age 11 in the UK, as well as sections of the BNC), it is perhaps fair to say that the majority of data collected (and researched) has been that of adults. The *Bergen Corpus of London Teenager Language* (COLT) (see Andersen and Stenström 1996) collected in 1993 is an exception. Courses for adults and young adults can span a wide age group, potentially from age 14 upwards. The course writer therefore often needs to be mindful of attributing to mature speakers usages typically associated with younger people and vice versa. A comparison of COLT with *Cambridge and Nottingham Corpus of Discourse in English* (CANCODE) (see McCarthy 1998) reveals that certain stance markers (*to be honest, in fact, I suppose*) and discourse markers, especially the more idiomatic types (*on the other hand, at the end of the day*) occur with greater frequency in the adult corpus. Such comparisons can identify what is typical of and appropriate to a target age group. More recent comparisons of usage between age groups (as well as other categories) can be obtained at http://corpora.lancs.ac.uk/bnclab.

Learner and non-native-speaker data

Corpora of learner data, especially corpora that can be searched by level or first language background, are useful for authors writing for specific levels and markets. Error coded corpora also enable the writer to identify and address common problems learners have with specific language items, for example, uncountable and countable nouns, verb complementation and spelling (see Chapters 22 and 23, this volume). Courses might address such errors through information panels and/or activities which focus (implicitly or explicitly) on areas where errors are often made (see McCarthy *et al.* 2012: 18, 107 and 117 for examples).

Taking a different approach to learner corpora, the *English Profile* project focused on learner competence. Its aim was to establish empirically validated reference-level descriptions for English according to the six levels of the *Common European Framework of Reference for Languages* (CEFR). Based on the *Cambridge Learner Corpus* collected by Cambridge Assessment, the *English Vocabulary Profile* and *English Grammar Profile* are publicly available online resources which show at which CEFR levels learners use (the meanings and functions of) lexical and grammatical items (see Capel 2015; O'Keeffe and Mark 2017). Although the *English Profile* project is a *description* of learner competence at different levels, the *English Profile* website might suggest that it sees itself rather as setting a *prescription* for course syllabuses.

> This tells teachers, curriculum developers, course-book authors and test writers what is suitable for learning at each level.
>
> *(www.englishprofile.orgl)*

In the case of English, a major debate surrounds the status of the native speaker. Cook (1999), Widdowson (2000), Jenkins (2006), Seidlhofer (2004, 2005) and others question whether learners should be judged against the models and norms evidenced in native speaker corpora and advocate instead corpora of English as a lingua franca (ELF), or world Englishes (Kirkpatrick 2007). They argue that realistic models for learners are to be found in non-native-speaker corpora, such as the *Vienna-Oxford International Corpus of English* (VOICE) corpus at (Seidlhofer 2004). Prodromou (2003) proposes the notion of the 'successful user of English' as a focus, rather than the native speaker. Others argue that learners may prefer to approximate native-speaker norms without losing what Timmis (2005) calls their 'cultural integrity' (see also Carter and McCarthy 1996; Timmis 2002).

Size of corpus

McCarthy and Carter (2001) assert that 'size isn't everything', arguing that small, carefully constructed corpora can yield fruitful research results for writers, particularly so in the case of specialised courses (see Chapter 31, this volume). While any corpus is usually better than no corpus, the bigger the corpus, the better, not just for information on frequency but also for coverage of a wider range of topics and situations from which to draw examples.

3 What areas of the course can a corpus inform?

A corpus can assist a course writer in several ways, including constructing a graded lexico-grammatical syllabus and finding appropriate texts and realistic settings for the presentation and practice of language.

Information about the language syllabus

First, a corpus provides information about different aspects of the language, which is normally the basis of the syllabus. Tognini-Bonelli (2001) advocates the "corpus-driven" approach, where the corpus provides the basis of the description of language usage without recourse to previously held beliefs, above the "corpus-based" approach, where the corpus provides examples for pre-existing rules. McCarthy (1998) proposes a third, "corpus-informed" approach, which borrows from the other two approaches.

Vocabulary syllabus

Corpus software can generate lists of the most frequent words (lemmatised or as individual word-forms) (see Chapters 9 and 10, this volume). These enable the writer to establish the common core vocabulary that learners are likely to need as a priority as opposed to a more advanced vocabulary, which can be taught later (see O'Keeffe *et al.* 2007). Frequency lists which "band" vocabulary into the most frequent 1,000 words, 2,000 words, etc., can be the basis for organising vocabulary for different levels of a course. The syllabus of the *COBUILD English Course* (Willis and Willis 1987–8) with its lexical approach was determined by word frequency. The most frequent 700 words with their common patterns were taught in Level 1, the next 800 in Level 2 and so on (see Willis 1990). Frequency also helps the writer to prioritise which members of large lexical sets to teach first or see which of two or three synonyms is more frequent (e.g. *sofa* or *couch*; *eat breakfast* or *have breakfast*) and identify the most frequent collocates of delexical verbs such as *make* and *do*. For English for academic purposes courses, the *Academic Wordlist* created by Averil Coxhead (Coxhead 2000) from a corpus of 3,500,000 academic texts provides an invaluable resource of lists of 570 word families (excluding the top 2,000 most frequent words in English) from which to devise a vocabulary syllabus (see Chapters 27 and 28, this volume). A further corpus-based resource is the *Oxford Phrasal Academic Lexicon* (OPAL), which comprises four discrete lists of key words and chunks in spoken and written academic English. Authors may also produce their own lists, depending on their software resources, from their chosen corpus.

While frequency is a useful guide, it may not always be the only criterion in building a syllabus. Members of some vocabulary sets, such as colours, have different frequencies (*red* being six times more frequent than *orange* in the spoken North American English sections of the *Cambridge International Corpus*) and so may occur in different frequency "bands". Days of the week, for example, have very different frequencies (see Figure 26.2), but it would be perverse not to teach the seven days together.

Word	Frequency ↓
Friday	1,631
Sunday	1,403
Saturday	1,400
Monday	1,179
Wednesday	947
Thursday	892
Tuesday	720

Figure 26.2 Frequency of days of the week in the *Spoken BNC* (2014)

Many corpora are collected in native-speaker environments: homes, work places, social gatherings and service encounters; they contain the everyday interactions of native speakers' professional and social settings (see Chapters 2, 3 and 4, this volume). Learners may operate in different settings, interacting either as host or visitor in their own or a different language environment. Their communication needs are not necessarily always the same as in native-speaker interactions. Furthermore, classrooms have their own particular vocabulary, for example, classroom objects (*board, highlighter pen*), processes and instructions, (*underline, fill in the gaps*) and linguistic metalanguage (*noun, verb* etc.), which might not occur as frequently in general corpora (see Walsh 2006). Finally, some of the most frequent words in a native-speaker corpus may present a major learning challenge to elementary learners because of their associated patterns. For example, *supposed* and *already* are both in the first 500 words in conversation, but in order to use these, learners may need to learn grammatical structures or meanings which are not usually taught or which are difficult to explain at an elementary level. Therefore the writer must make judgments about which items to include and in what order, balancing what is frequent with what is useful, easily taught and learned. However, as mentioned earlier, the English Vocabulary Profile has become the *de facto* vocabulary syllabus for mainstream published courses, which to some extent removes the responsibility of vocabulary choice from individual authors, a prescription which some might see as restrictive (see also Timmis 2015 for more on corpora and lexis).

Grammar syllabus

Corpora have much to offer the grammar syllabus (see Timmis 2015). In general, generating lists of the most common grammatical structures has not been as straightforward as listing the most frequent vocabulary. Although part-of-speech (PoS) tagged corpora can assist, they are not always 100 per cent accurate, especially for spoken language. For example in the *Spoken BNC* (2014), the tag for adjective [JJ] includes the response token *Okay,* the verb *repent*, the determiner *other* and the hesitation markers *er* and *erm.* Further, although the frequency of some grammatical items is retrievable, there is often still a need to disambiguate the results in terms of their meaning and use so that the more frequent one(s) may be taught first. For example, the authors of *Touchstone* (McCarthy et al. 2014a–d) manually counted hundreds of occurrences of the modal verb *must* in North American conversation to determine the percentage of uses for speculation (*You must be tired*), obligation (*You must go to the doctor tomorrow*) and in fixed phrases (*I must admit*), information which guided them in the ordering of the uses taught and which was shared with students in a "corpus factoid" in the material (see McCarthy *et al.* 2014d: 45).

Research into corpora of conversation has brought to light frequent structures in spoken language previously ignored by courses (McCarthy and Carter 1995, 1997). Past continuous verbs for speech reporting (McCarthy 1998) is just one example of a structure which is easy to accommodate in materials (see McCarthy *et al.* 2014d: 90–1).

As with vocabulary, frequency may not be the only criterion for deciding what to teach. There are often strong expectations as to which grammatical structures should be taught and in what order – in other words an ELT canon (see Burton 2012; McCarthy 2020) – especially at lower levels, with far less consensus at advanced levels (McCarthy 2013). For example, some teachers may prefer to teach present continuous forms before the simple past, even though the present continuous is far less frequent in a general spoken corpus. This may be because it builds on the present of *be* – traditionally the first grammatical structure taught – or because it is useful in class in describing pictures and actions. Examinations and the syllabuses of available courses also influence what grammar is required or expected. As a result some items may be given undue prominence while more common structures are neglected (see Chapter 25, this volume). A course which ignores teacher expectation may not succeed commercially (or even be accepted by the publisher). Again, it remains to be seen what effect the English Grammar Profile may have course syllabuses in the future.

Lexico-grammatical patterns

Corpus software can yield information not just about vocabulary patterns, i.e. collocations, but also patterns that grammar and vocabulary form together. With POS-tagged corpora, it is possible, for example, to find the vocabulary used in a particular structure, such as the most frequent verbs in the gap: *have you ever* ____. Another example is verb complementation, which is often tested in examinations at intermediate levels, especially of verbs such as *mind, suggest* and *recommend.* For example, in requests and permission-seeking speech acts with *do you mind* and *would you mind,* four basic patterns seem possible:

Requests

1. Do you mind + …ing: e.g. Do you mind helping me for a second?
2. Would you mind + …ing: e.g. Would you mind helping me for a second?

Asking for permission

3. Do you mind + if: e.g. Do you mind if I leave early today?
4. Would you mind + if: e.g. Would you mind if I leave (or left) early today?

The *North American Conversation* section of the *Cambridge International Corpus* shows a far less complex use of these verbs than is suggested by the amount of testing these verbs have been subjected to over the years in examinations. Two patterns emerge as overwhelmingly more frequent: *Do you mind **if I*** … to ask permission to do something and *Would you mind …**ing*** to ask others to do something. Sometimes *do you mind* and *would you mind* are used with no complement. More complex patterns with an object (*Would you mind **me** asking* …) or possessive (*Would you mind **my** asking* …) are possible but infrequent. This kind of information can help the writer determine what is "core" and what is more advanced, though occasionally institutional or testing syllabuses may overrule their choice.

Discourse management

In addition to the staple vocabulary and grammar syllabuses, a conversation corpus can inform the creation of a discourse management syllabus, i.e. the language speakers use to organise and manage their discourse (see McCarthy *et al.* 2005, 2006, 2012, 2014a, 2014b, 2014c, 2014d, 2014e for examples). As well as providing lists of single words and sets of collocations, corpus software can generate lists of items of more than one word, normally between two and seven words, referred to variously as "multi-word units", "n-grams", "chunks" and "lexical bundles", among others (see O'Keeffe *et al.* 2007 and Chapters 10 and 15, this volume). Some of these chunks are "fragments", or sequences of words that do not have a meaning as integrated expressions in their own right, such as *in the, and I* and *of the.* These are frames for extended structures, for example, ***in the** beginning,* etc. However, a large number of items can be considered as expressions with a unitary meaning, as in Table 26.1.

Many of these items are much more frequent than the everyday, single words that are taught at an elementary level. Chunks such as *I mean, I don't know* and *or something* are more frequent than the single words *six*, *black* and *woman,* which are undeniably part of an elementary syllabus. With such frequency, these multi-word items are worthy of inclusion in the syllabus, whether as vocabulary or as part of conversation skills (see O'Keeffe *et al.* 2007). It could be argued that teaching expressions such as *I mean* to

Table 26.1 Examples of chunks as expressions with unitary meaning from the *Spoken BNC* (2014)

No. of words in phrase	*Examples*
two	*you know, I mean, or something*
three	*a little bit, and all that*
four	*or something like that, and things like that, I don't know if*
five	*as a matter of fact*
six	*and all that kind of stuff, do you know what I mean*

introduce reiteration or repetition or *Well* to take thinking time can be seen as enabling, especially for elementary learners, who often need time and more than one attempt to assemble their turn or answer questions. At the very least, their inclusion would make listening scripts more natural.

Such multi-word items can be classified into broad functional categories. For example, in the small selection of items provided earlier, there are vague category markers (*or something like that, and things like that*) and hedging and stance expressions (*a little bit, as a matter of fact)*, which are characteristic of casual conversation. Many of the four-word chunks in conversation include the phrase *I don't know* (+ *if, what, how,...* etc.), which often functions as an softened question or as an "involving phrase" to acknowledge that the listener may have experience or knowledge of a topic before the speaker gives information or an opinion as in *I don't know if you've seen that movie, been to that city,* etc. (See Carter and McCarthy 2006: Sections 109 and 505c.) O'Keeffe *et al.* (2007) refer to such language as "relational" as opposed to "transactional", as it is concerned with establishing and managing relationships with interlocutors rather than conveying information. Together with single-word discourse markers (*well, anyway, so, now*), this vocabulary may be said to constitute a vocabulary *of* conversation, i.e. a vocabulary which characterises conversation, as distinct from more general vocabulary found *in* conversation (McCarten 2007). In McCarthy *et al.* (2012, 2014a, 2014b, 2014c, 2014d, 2014e), this relational language and associated discourse management strategies are classified into four broad macro functions, which form the basis of a conversation management syllabus:

- Managing your own talk – discourse markers, which enable speakers to manage their own turns in a conversation (*I mean, the thing is, on the other hand*);
- Taking account of the listener – for example, vague category markers, hedging and stance expressions (*and stuff, kind of, to be honest with you*);
- "Listenership" (see McCarthy 2002) – response tokens and expressions used to acknowledge the contribution of another speaker (*That's great, I know what you mean*);
- Managing the conversation as a whole – for example, changing topics (*going back to*) or ending a conversation (*well anyway*).

While writing shares some of the relational language of conversation, such as formal vague language (*and so on, etc.*) and discourse marking (*in conclusion, on the other hand*), chunks in writing are more frequently associated with orienting the reader in space and time (*at the end of the, for the first time,*) and expressing connections (*in terms of, as a result of*) (see O'Keeffe *et al.* 2007). These chunks perform important strategies and thus merit inclusion in academic writing courses, a subject which is beyond the scope of this chapter (see Chapters 10 and 15, this volume).

Contexts of use

A corpus can also confirm the frequency of structures in certain contexts. One example is the use of the past tense, especially of the verbs *have, need* and *want* in requests or offers, as in the exchange here:

(1) (In a restaurant)

SERVER: How was everything?
DINER: Brilliant. As you can see by the empty plates it was good [...]
SERVER: **Did you want** to see a dessert menu?

[Spoken BNC Corpus (2014)]

Another example is the common use of the historic present in spoken narratives about the past to highlight key events, people or things (Schiffrin 1981), as in Example 2, where the speaker switches from the past tense to the present once the context is set:

(2) (Informal narrative)

SPEAKER 1: We went into the shop and this bloke said we never have snow here never and then **he says**
SPEAKER 2: Yeah
SPEAKER 1: We had four inches of snow

[Spoken BNC Corpus (2014)]

The decision to include such arguably controversial relational uses of grammar may be influenced by space and time factors, teacher or publisher acceptance and whether students could be penalised in examinations for not using the anticipated "correct" tense forms.

Representative examples for presentation and practice

By observing in a corpus how people use language according to their situation and interlocutors, the writer can select appropriate, realistic and typical contexts in which to present and practise grammatical structures or vocabulary. An example from grammar is the aforementioned use of *must* in conversation, which is used overwhelmingly to express a high degree of certainty in speculation rather than obligation and is often found in responses and reactions.

(3) (Conversation about making homemade pasta)

SPEAKER 1: Do you make your own?
SPEAKER 2: Yes.
SPEAKER 1: Ooh that **must be** interesting

[Open American National Corpus Spoken]

This use can be practised in listenership activities which offer a choice of responses to prompts using simple and familiar exercise formats. (e.g. *A I only had four hours' sleep last night. B You must be happy / exhausted / annoying*). This can be developed by asking students for their own ideas for responses and followed by freer personalised speaking practice based on the listening activity. See McCarthy *et al.* 2014c: 112 for examples.

4 How can corpus data be directly used in an ELT course?

Information about the language

Published ELT courses have generally borrowed little from the explicit use of corpus data in data-driven learning (DDL) (see Chapters 24, 28, 29 and 30, this volume). Indeed, it is possible to exploit corpus research in materials completely "invisibly" by including the most frequent structures, vocabulary, collocations and patterns without comment. Corpus data (with relevant permission from the copyright holder) can be used 'to provide authentic examples of how the language is used' (Sowton and Hewings 2012: 5) or as the basis for practice items. However, it can be useful to give users corpus-derived information such as the relative frequency of similar items (*everybody* vs. *everyone*) or patterns (*like to do* vs. *like doing*) and differences in levels of formality (*and stuff* vs. *and so on)* or between speaking and academic writing (distribution of *it*-clefts and *wh*-clefts). For some high-frequency spoken discourse markers and chunks, such as *well, I mean, and things,* etc., such information can legitimise their inclusion and provide a motivation for learning. McCarthy *et al.* (2012, 2014a, 2014b, 2014c, 2014d, 2014e) provide "corpus factoids" about different aspects of frequency and use of such items in conversation, or in conversation as opposed to writing or more formal speaking. See, for example, McCarthy *et al.* (2014a: 39) for information on the frequency of *well* and McCarthy *et al.* (2012: 130) for a comparison of the frequency of vague expressions in conversation and more formal spoken genres.

Using corpus texts for presentation

Authentic written texts from real-world sources such as published fiction, non-fiction, newspapers, news websites, advertising and everyday written "realia" have long been used in courses for language presentation, more so than spoken texts, which are often used for listening comprehension rather than language study. Swan and Walter (1984) were among the first to include "untidy natural language" as listening practice. Real conversations can provide excellent raw material for presentations, exposing learners to features of language usage that are often lacking in textbooks and which they will encounter outside the classroom. Printed in materials they enable learners to see what conversation "looks like" and that repetition, reiteration, false starts, hesitation, pausing, etc., are an integral part of native speakers' and expert users' repertoire. Real conversations also potentially offer other benefits, as discussed by Gilmore (2004), including easier comprehension by virtue of their lower lexical density and the development of the listening skill of identifying a main message among the redundancy of real language. However, judicious choice and, arguably, editing of real conversations are often required, as simply using unedited transcripts of conversations in materials can be problematic.

- Conversations can be of limited interest with little "content" to build on in activities. The external "reader" may have difficulty understanding the context and purpose of the conversation (see Mishan 2004) with references to people or things known only to the original speakers and topics veering in seemingly confusing ways, with no discernible start or end;
- Conversations can be long (word limits are often imposed by publishers), dominated by one speaker or contain considerable rephrasing, repetition, hesitation, false starts, digression or overlapping turns, which can pose problems for comprehension, reading aloud and practice in class. See also Timmis (2012) on learners' and teachers' reactions to the sight of real spoken language;
- Real conversations may include language that distracts from the main teaching goal, being too advanced or arcane, or even taboo words or topics;
- Spoken, dialectal or informal usage (e.g. *would have went, less* or *there's* + plural countable noun) may not be considered appropriate by some teachers (or even allowed by publishers' editors);
- Some teachers may feel unprepared to teach features of spoken usage.

One issue in representing conversation in written form is punctuation, for example, of pauses, incomplete words, ellipsis, false starts, overlapping or latched turns. Similarly, there is no accepted orthographic form for common articulations of some structures (e.g. *wouldn't've* for *wouldn't have; what's he do* for *what* ***does*** *he do?*).

As noted previously, there are many ways in which real conversations differ from those in traditional courses. However, it is possible to incorporate features of actual language use and replicate natural-sounding conversations by applying some general principles:

- Keep turns generally short, unless someone is telling a story. Even then, backchannelling and non-minimal responses can be included (McCarthy 2002, 2003);
- Ensure that speakers interact, for example, by reacting to the previous speaker before adding a new contribution to the conversation (see Tao 2003);
- Create conversations with low lexical density, where information is not tightly packed, with a balance of transactional and relational language (Ure 1971; Stubbs 1986), and include "smallwords" (*you know, well, right*), which Hasselgreen (2004) found contributes to the perceived fluency of learners;
- Build in some repetition, rephrasing, fragmented sentences and features of real speech in ways that do not interfere with comprehension;
- Adhere to politeness norms in the sense described by Brown and Levinson (1987), avoiding unrealistically confrontational discussions. It is worth noting here that native speakers of English are more likely to prefer indirect strategies in discussion, for example, *I disagree with* ***that*** rather than *I disagree with* ***you***. See also Tao (2007). This is not to deny learners 'the right to be impolite' (Mugford 2008).

In order to teach features of conversation management, we need a non-threatening, classroom-friendly meta-language and familiar methodologies. Concepts such as "hedging", "sentence frames", "reciprocation" and "pre-closing" can be translated into more transparent terms for students, for example, "softening what you say", "introducing what you say", "keeping the conversation going" and "ending the conversation". Such features may be taught using techniques that ask learners to notice (see Schmidt 1990) and try them out in personalised conversational contexts. See McCarthy and McCarten (2018) for more on teaching social conversation.

5 A more corpus-informed present or future?

In the earlier edition of this chapter, several hopes were expressed: that in the future more courses would be corpus-informed, including courses for younger learners and specialised courses (e.g. business); that language descriptions from corpus research, including multi-modal corpora (Adolphs and Carter 2007; Carter and Adolphs 2008), might enhance materials; and that the online medium might present new opportunities for teachers to experiment with corpus software.

Of these aspirations, it is true that more courses carry a "corpus-informed" logo, often in relation to the authors' use of a resource such as the English Profile. It may well turn out to be the case that projects such as the English Profile and OPAL funded by examinations and publishing institutions will redefine the term "corpus-informed". This is understandable. Corpus research is a highly specialised task that requires training and experience; it also takes time – a rare commodity in writing schedules. And although authors now have greater access to online corpora, commercial rights to exploit them may be limited.

Courses may now be delivered not only in printed book form but also in online learning environments, which users can access individually in addition to, or independently of, the classroom. Potentially the online medium could allow DDL approaches to become more widespread as part of blended learning packages, though there is little evidence to date that this has happened in mainstream publications.

We continue to hope corpus-informed courses will have a bright future in the sense that sustained corpus research will feed into materials more insights into how naturally occurring language is used in face-to face and in electronic communications (see Carter and McCarthy 2017 on possible directions for spoken grammar, for example). Bringing into the classroom the language of the world outside it, with clearer, more accurate descriptions, will hopefully give learners greater opportunities to increase their understanding of natural language and the choices they have in using it. This is surely the ultimate aim of all of us who are engaged in language teaching.

Notes

1 https://www.oxfordlearnersdictionaries.com/wordlists/opal/
2 http://socialsciences.exeter.ac.uk/education/research/centres/writing/projects/growthingrammar/

Further reading

Burton, G. (2012) 'Corpora and Coursebooks: Destined to be Strangers Forever?' *Corpora* 7(1): 91–108. (An interesting article containing findings of a survey of authors about the benefits and challenges of exploiting corpus data in published materials.)

Cullen, R. and Kuo, I-C. (2007) 'Spoken Grammar and ELT Course Materials: A Missing Link?' *TESOL Quarterly* 41(2): 361–86. (An interesting analysis of how spoken grammar is represented in ELT courses.)

Gilmore, A. (2004) 'A Comparison of Textbook and Authentic Interactions', *ELT Journal* 58(4): 363–71. (A good overview of differences between real conversations and those in ELT courses.)
O'Keeffe, A., McCarthy, M. J. and Carter, R. A. (2007) *From Corpus to Classroom, Language Use and Language Teaching*, Cambridge: Cambridge University Press. (An excellent introduction to corpus research and its practical pedagogical applications.)
Timmis, I. (2015) *Corpus Linguistics for ELT*, London: Routledge. (A practical guide to corpus research and how it can inform various aspects of English language teaching.)

References

Adolphs, S. and Carter, R. A. (2007) 'Beyond the Word: New Challenges in Analysing Corpora of Spoken English', *European Journal of English Studies* 11(2): 133–46.

Andersen, G. and Stenström A.-B. (1996) 'COLT: A Progress Report', *ICAME Journal* 20: 133–6.

Biber, D., Conrad, S. and Reppen, R. (1998) *Corpus Linguistics: Investigating Language Structure and Use*, Cambridge: Cambridge University Press.

Brown, P. and Levinson, S. (1987) *Politeness: Some Universals in Language Usage*, Cambridge: Cambridge University Press.

Burton, G. (2012) 'Corpora and Coursebooks: Destined to be Strangers Forever?', *Corpora* 7(1): 91–108.

Capel, A. (2015) 'The English Vocabulary Profile', in J. Harrison and F. Barker (eds) *English Profile in Practice*, Vol. 5, Cambridge: Cambridge University Press, pp. 9–27.

Carter, R. A. and Adolphs, S. (2008) 'Linking the Verbal and Visual: New Directions for Corpus Linguistics', *Language and Computers* 64: 275–91.

Carter, R. A. and McCarthy, M. J. (1996) 'Correspondence', *ELT Journal* 50: 369–71, Oxford: Oxford University Press.

Carter, R. A. and McCarthy, M. J. (2006) *Cambridge Grammar of English*, Cambridge: Cambridge University Press.

Carter, R. A. and McCarthy, M. J. (2017) 'Spoken Grammar: Where Are We and Where Are We Going?', *Applied Linguistics* 38(1): 1–20.

Cheng, W. and Warren, M. (2007) 'Checking Understandings: Comparing Textbooks and a Corpus of Spoken English in Hong Kong', *Language Awareness* 16(3): 190–207.

COBUILD (1987) *Collins COBUILD English Language Dictionary*, London: Collins.

COBUILD (1990) *Collins COBUILD English Grammar*, London: Collins.

Cook, V. (1999) 'Going Beyond the Native Speaker in Language Teaching', *TESOL Quarterly* 33(2): 185–209.

Coxhead, A. (2000) 'A New Academic Word List', *TESOL Quarterly* 34(2): 213–38.

Cullen, R. and Kuo, I.-C. (2007) 'Spoken Grammar and ELT Course Materials: A Missing Link?', *TESOL Quarterly* 41(2): 361–86.

Gilmore, A. (2004) 'A Comparison of Textbook and Authentic Interactions', *ELT Journal* 58(4): 363–71.

Hasselgreen, A. (2004) *Testing the Spoken English of Young Norwegians: A Study of Test Validity and the Role of 'Smallwords' in Contributing to Pupils' Fluency*, Cambridge: Cambridge University Press.

Jenkins, J. (2006) 'Current Perspectives on Teaching World Englishes and English as a Lingua Franca', *TESOL Quarterly* 40(1): 157–81.

Kirkpatrick, A. (2007) *World Englishes*, Cambridge: Cambridge University Press.

McCarten, J. (2007) *Teaching Vocabulary - Lessons from the Corpus, Lessons for the Classroom*, New York: Cambridge University Press.

McCarthy, M. J. (1998) *Spoken Language and Applied Linguistics*, Cambridge: Cambridge University Press.

McCarthy, M.J. (2002) 'Good Listenership Made Plain: British and American Non-minimal Response Tokens in Everyday Conversation', in R. Reppen, S. Fitzmaurice and D. Biber (eds) *Using Corpora to Explore Linguistic Variation*, Amsterdam: John Benjamins, pp. 49–71.

McCarthy, M. J. (2003) 'Talking Back: 'Small' Interactional Response Tokens in Everyday Conversation', *Research on Language and Social Interaction* 36(1): 33–63.

McCarthy, M. J. (2013) 'Corpora and the Advanced Level: Problems and Prospects', *English Australia Journal* 29(1): 39–49.
McCarthy, M. J. (2020) *Innovations and Challenges in Grammar*, London: Routledge.
McCarthy, M. J. and Carter, R. A. (1995) 'Spoken grammar: What Is It and How Should We Teach It?', *ELT Journal* 49(3): 207–17.
McCarthy, M. J. and Carter, R. A. (1997) 'Grammar, Tails and Affect: Constructing Expressive Choices in Discourse', *Text* 17(3): 405–29.
McCarthy, M. J. and Carter, R. A. (2001) 'Size Isn't Everything: Spoken English, Corpus, and the Classroom', *TESOL* Quarterly 35(2): 337–40.
McCarthy, M. J. and McCarten, J. (2018) 'Practising Conversation in Second Language Learning', in C. Jones (ed.) *Practice in Second Language Learning*, Cambridge: Cambridge University Press, pp. 7–29.
McCarthy, M. J., McCarten, J. and Sandiford, H. (2005, 2006) *Touchstone Student's Books 1 – 4*, Cambridge: Cambridge University Press.
McCarthy, M. J., McCarten, J. and Sandiford, H. (2012) *Viewpoint Student's Book 1*, Cambridge: Cambridge University Press.
McCarthy, M. J., McCarten, J. and Sandiford, H. (2014a) *Touchstone Student's Book 1, Second Edition*, Cambridge: Cambridge University Press.
McCarthy, M. J., McCarten, J. and Sandiford, H. (2014b) *Touchstone Student's Book 2, Second Edition*, Cambridge: Cambridge University Press.
McCarthy, M. J., McCarten, J. and Sandiford, H. (2014c) *Touchstone Student's Book 3, Second Edition*, Cambridge: Cambridge University Press.
McCarthy, M. J., McCarten, J. and Sandiford, H. (2014d) *Touchstone Student's Book 4, Second Edition*, Cambridge: Cambridge University Press.
McCarthy, M. J., McCarten, J. and Sandiford, H. (2014e) *Viewpoint Student's Book 2*, Cambridge: Cambridge University Press.
McCarten, J. and Sandiford, H. (2016) 'A Case Study in Blended Learning Course Design', in M. J. McCarthy (ed.) *The Cambridge Guide to Blended Learning for Language Teaching*, Cambridge: Cambridge University Press, pp. 200–15.
Mishan, F. (2004) 'Authenticating Corpora for Language Learning: A Problem and Its Resolution', *ELT Journal* 58(3): 219–27.
Mugford, G. (2008) 'How Rude! Teaching Impoliteness in the Second-language Classroom', *ELT Journal* 62(4): 375–84.
O'Keeffe, A. and Mark, G. (2017) 'The English Grammar Profile of Learner Competence Methodology and Key Findings', *International Journal of Corpus Linguistics* 22(4): 457–89.
O'Keeffe, A., McCarthy, M. J. and Carter, R. A. (2007) *From Corpus to Classroom, Language Use and Language Teaching*, Cambridge: Cambridge University Press.
Prodromou, L. (2003) 'In search of the Successful User of English', *Modern English Teacher* 12(2): 5–14.
Römer, U. (2004) 'Comparing Real and Ideal Language Learner Input: The Use of an EFL Textbook Corpus in Corpus Linguistics and Language Teaching', in G. Aston, S. Bernardini and D. Stewart (eds) *Corpora and Language Learners*, Amsterdam: John Benjamins, pp. 151–68.
Schiffrin, D. (1981) 'Tense Variation in Narrative', *Language* 57(1): 45–62.
Schmidt, R. (1990) 'The Role of Consciousness in Second Language Learning', *Applied Linguistics* 11:129–58.
Seidlhofer, B. (2004) 'Research Perspectives on Teaching English as a Lingua Franca', *Annual Review of Applied Linguistics* 24: 209–39.
Seidlhofer, B. (2005) 'English as a Lingua Franca', *ELT Journal* 59(4): 339–41.
Shortall, T. (2007) 'The L2 Syllabus: Corpus or Contrivance?', *Corpora* 2(2): 157–85.
Sowton, C. and Hewings, M. (2012) *Cambridge Academic English B2 Upper Intermediate Student's Book: An Integrated Skills Course for EAP Teacher's Book*, Cambridge: Cambridge University Press.
Stubbs, M. (1986) 'Lexical Density: A Computational Technique and Some Findings', in R. M. Coulthard (ed.) *Talking About Text*, Birmingham: English Language Research, pp. 27–42.
Swan, M. and Walter, C. (1984) *The Cambridge English Course Teacher's Book 1*, Cambridge: Cambridge University Press.

Tao, H. (2003) 'Turn Initiators in Spoken English: A Corpus-Based Approach to Interaction and Grammar' in P. Leistyna, and C. F. Meyer (eds) *Language and Computers, Corpus Analysis: Language Structure and Language Use*, Amsterdam: Rodopi, pp. 187–207.
Tao, H. (2007) 'A Corpus-Based Investigation of Absolutely and Related Phenomena in Spoken American English', *Journal of English Linguistics* 35(1): 5–29.
Timmis, I. (2002) 'Native-speaker Norms and International English: A Classroom View', *ELT Journal* 56(3): 240–9.
Timmis, I. (2005) 'Towards a Framework for Teaching Spoken Grammar', *ELT Journal* 59(2): 117–125.
Timmis, I. (2012) 'Spoken Language Research: The Applied Linguistic Challenge', in B. Tomlinson (ed.) *Applied linguistics and Materials Development*, London: Bloomsbury, pp. 79–94.
Timmis, I. (2015) *Corpus Linguistics for ELT*, London: Routledge.
Tognini-Bonelli, E. (2001) *Corpus Linguistics at Work*, Amsterdam: John Benjamins.
Ure, J. (1971) 'Lexical Density and Register Differentiation', in G. E. Perren and J. L. M. Trim (eds) *Applications of Linguistics: Selected Papers of the Second International Congress of Applied Linguistics, Cambridge, 1969*, Cambridge University Press, pp. 443–52.
Walsh, S. (2006) *Investigating Classroom Discourse*, London: Routledge.
Widdowson, H. G. (2000) 'On the Limitations of Linguistics Applied', *Applied Linguistics* 21(1): 3–25.
Willis, D. (1990) *The Lexical Syllabus, A New Approach to Language Teaching*, Glasgow: Collins.
Willis, D. and Willis, J. (1987–88) *The COBUILD English Course*, Glasgow: Collins.

27

Using corpora to write dictionaries

Geraint Rees

1 Why use corpora to write dictionaries?

Lexicographers are often characterised as pioneer corpus linguists. This argument is valid to a degree. In the past, lexicographers were supported in their work by "corpora" comprising millions of slips of paper recording examples of words in use. However, taking a more pedantic stance, as lexicographers are apt to do, the extent to which these collections of citations constitute what is currently understood as a corpus in corpus linguistics is questionable. Citation slips are not complete texts, but rather extracts recorded by citation readers. The decision on what to record is subject to readers' intuitions and prejudices. Corpus evidence has shown that intuitions are an unreliable basis on which to build an accurate picture of language use, since we tend to notice utterances which are unusual in some way rather than those that are typical or mundane. Prejudice comes into play, since we tend to have preconceived, frequently inaccurate, ideas about what constitutes normal language use.

The implied criticism of pre-corpus lexicographers here is hardly fair. Scholarly dictionaries, for example, Samuel Johnson's *Dictionary of the English Language* (1755) or *A New English Dictionary on Historical Principles* (Murray 1884) (NEDHP), were not primarily focused on recording language as it was used at the time. Like those working on historical dictionaries today, for example, NEDHP's descendent, the *Oxford English Dictionary* (Proffitt 2020), they were more concerned with documenting the roots of words or expressions. This was often accompanied by the assumption that the original meaning was somehow more valid. The subtitle of Johnson's dictionary boasts '*IN WHICH The WORDS are deduced from their ORIGINALS…*' (original capitalisation maintained). These lexicographers were not unique in assuming original meaning was more valid. "Etymology" was a major organisational division in many grammars ranging from the ancient Greek and Roman grammars of antiquity to those of the nineteenth century. In the anglophone world, it was not until the late twentieth century that dictionaries attempting to describe current rather than historical word meaning were widely available. In addition to achieving commercial success, pre-corpus monolingual learners' dictionaries (MLDs) succeeded in codifying many intuitions about the

DOI: 10.4324/9780367076399-27

importance of phraseology in language learning that have subsequently been borne out by research in language acquisition and corpus linguistics. Pre-corpus bilingual dictionaries are also impressive. That compilers were able to produce highly practical resources with little more than pen, ink, index cards and time is testament to their skill and dedication.

There are, however, examples of pre-corpus lexicographers' intuitions not accurately reflecting language as it is used. These include intuitions about the relative importance of a word's senses, definitions and the typicality of dictionary examples. These failings can be explained by the absence of a means of examining instances of word use in context on a massive scale that is offered by corpus analysis. *The Collins Birmingham University International Language Database*, a project led by John Sinclair, who is regarded as a lodestar of corpus linguistics, led to the creation of the *Collins COBUILD English Language Dictionary* (COBUILD) (Sinclair 1987). It was not the first dictionary to be developed using corpora. The creators of early corpus dictionaries, such as the first editions of *The American Heritage Dictionary of the English Language* (Morris 1969) and the *Longman Dictionary of Contemporary English* (Proctor 1979) (LDOCE1), consulted the 1-million-word *Brown* (Francis and Kucera 1964) and *Lancaster-Oslo/Bergan* (Johansson *et al.* 1978) corpora, respectively. However, relying on a 20-million-word corpus, COBUILD had evidence on the scale necessary to gain insight beyond the use of a few frequent words. Comparing the corpus-driven COBUILD with pre-corpus and early corpus dictionaries illustrates the deficiency of lexicographer intuition in judging the importance of senses and providing appropriate definitions and examples.

Sense selection

Comparing the word senses listed for a given headword – the word in the alphabetical index of a print dictionary – in pre-corpus and corpus-driven dictionaries reveals much about the unreliability of our intuitions about the relative importance of word senses. This is not just a matter of disagreement about where one sense ends and another begins. Such disagreements are commonplace in both pre-corpus and corpus dictionaries. A distinction is commonly drawn between "lumpers" – who tend to group closely related senses together – and "splitters" – who tend to emphasise differences between senses. More telling of the limits of intuition are those senses that are prominent in pre-corpus dictionaries yet not found in corpus-driven works or vice versa.

The first verbal sense of *fire* given in the third, pre-corpus, edition of the *Oxford Advanced Learner's Dictionary of Current English* (Hornby 1974) (OALDCE) is defined: 'set fire to with the intention of destroying; cause to being burning'. The example given is 'fire a haystack'. A cursory look at evidence from the *British National Corpus* (BNC) reveals that common object collocates of *fire* (*shot, bullet, gun, missile, rocket* [see the Word Sketch in Figure 27.3]) denote the act of discharging a weapon. In OALDCE this is the sixth of seven senses provided. Presumably this is of lesser importance for the user in the eyes of the dictionary creators than the *burn* sense. In the post-corpus COBUILD the *weapon* sense is the first verbal sense listed; the *burn* sense is not present.

Definition

Definitions in post-corpus dictionaries often give subtle generalisations about meaning that are missing from pre-corpus dictionaries. For example, *primitive* in COBUILD is defined: 'Something that is primitive... is very simple in style or old fashioned; *often used showing disapproval*' (my emphasis). The examples provided are 'Conditions were often primitive... The sleeping accommodation is somewhat primitive when judged by normal standards'. The sense of disapproval in these typical examples is not conveyed by the definitions given in the pre-corpus OALDCE.

Exemplification

The tendency to focus on interesting rather than typical uses explains examples such as 'It was the managing director who *perpetrated* that frightful statue' (Nesi 2000: 112) in early corpus and pre-corpus MLDs (in this case LDOCE1). The concordances in Figure 27.1 are typical of those found for *perpetrate* in the BNC 1994. In these concordances, typical object collocates of *perpetrate* do not denote inanimate objects such as *statue*, but rather acts, usually undesirable ones (e.g. *crime, treachery, bluff)*. They show that the word *perpetuate* has a negative sematic prosody. In the example provided earlier, this negative connotation has been exploited for rhetorical effect to denote a statue that is so objectionable for the writer or speaker that it is akin to an act of violence. This effective rhetorical device grabbed the attention of the lexicographer. Unfortunately, a user could feasibly be misled by this example into thinking that a sentence such as 'I perpetrated the painting' constitutes normal use.

The inadequacy of intuition is not limited to monolingual lexicography. This is evident from a comparison of the treatment of phraseology in post-corpus bilingual dictionaries with their pre-corpus counterparts. The entry for *day* in the post-corpus *Oxford Hachette French Dictionary* (Corréard and Grundy 1994) is more focused than that found in the pre-corpus *Collins-Robert French Dictionary* (Atkins and Duval 1978). The post-corpus dictionary focuses on phraseology which emphasises the semantic distinction between *jour* and *journée* and phrases where there is no French word that can be literally translated as *day* such as "la vielle" (the day before) and "à cette époque" (in those days) (Hanks 2012).

How dictionary makers use corpora also reflects an ongoing debate about what precisely dictionaries are for. There is a utilitarian view of dictionaries as tools designed to satisfy punctual information needs (c.f. manuals, telephone directories). There is also a symbolic view of dictionaries as embodiments of the political or cultural identity of a group of speakers. In this case, dictionaries are often created to revendicate the political or cultural identity of a group. These views are by no means mutually exclusive and frequently intersect. For example, dictionaries often provide a synchronic record of language usage for the purposes of historical research. Occasionally, these records are used to make claims about political or cultural identities.

Today almost all dictionary makers have recourse to corpora in some way. One might think that this recourse to large banks of data would cement the utilitarian view of dictionaries as information tools. Overall, this is not the case. A key consideration here is the way that corpora are used in dictionary making. In corpus lexicography, as in corpus linguistics, a distinction can be made between corpus-based and corpus-driven approaches. In corpus-driven approaches to lexicography, the facts of the language – the relative salience of different senses of a headword, usage information, etc. – are inducted bottom-up from the corpus. In contrast, a corpus-based methodology allows lexicographers to work top-down at times, choosing corpus data to fit received wisdom about language, public expectations about dictionary contents and socio-political

	Details	Left context	KWIC	Right context
1	Written books and …	broke, and from this Sherlock Holmes infers that he	perpetrated	the crime: although the information may have been ir
2	Written books and …	appalling thought of the treachery she had so nearly	perpetrated	on herself. </s><s> If, back there in the dining-room,
3	Written books and …	<s> She realised that finally. </s><s> A bluff she had	perpetrated	mainly on herself to give herself the strength to go or
4	Written books and …	d be tearing their hair out trying to work out who was	perpetrating	such deeds, but you know who's doing it!' </s><s> 'R
5	Written books and …	3431 0 (pb) </s><s> In Derridian thinking violence is	perpetrated	by the dominant partner in a hierarchy: the" Original"
6	Written books and …	e" on what he termed" the foulest piece of journalism	perpetrated	in this country in many a long year," indicating a parti
7	Spoken context-go…	s><s> . </s><s> Conservatives, this government has	perpetrated	some dastardly things </s><s> . </s><s> in recent ye
8	Spoken context-go…	he time because of the squalid frauds that are being	perpetrated	there a and the government is lagging behind er in ca
9	Written books and …	there.' </s><s> 'Lord, I hope not. </s><s> They were	perpetrated	by my great-aunt Olwen, an eccentric lady with more
10	Written books and …	e enemy's morale and, second, in retaliation for acts	perpetrated	by the other side. </s><s> Iraq's attacks on shipping

Figure 27.1 Concordance lines for "perpetrate" in the BNC 1994 shown in *Sketch Engine*

circumstances, for example, by excluding borrowings from the languages of neighbouring regions or other social groups.

Received wisdom about what constitutes correct and incorrect use of language is widespread. An oft-cited example involves the so-called misuse of the adverb *literally* as a marker of exaggeration (e.g. 'The ball has literally given him a haircut' – said by a football commentator on seeing the ball fly close over the head of a player). It is common to hear people mock this use. Even for dictionaries created with a utilitarian role in mind, there is the expectation that they should play a symbolic role by ensuring the purity of language. In other words, there is the expectation that a dictionary – often regarded as a repository of "correct" language use – should not contain this supposedly incorrect use of *literally* or somehow condemn it. The first sense, and presumably the most important in the mind of the compilers, given in the entry for *literally* in the corpus-based Merriam-Webster.com Dictionary (2020) reads: 'In a literal sense or manner: such as a: in a way that uses the ordinary or primary meaning of a term or expression…' The second and final sense given reads: ': in effect: VIRTUALLY – used in an exaggerated way to emphasize a statement or description that is not literally true or possible'. This is followed by the warning: 'Sense 2 is common and not at all new but has been frequently criticized as an illogical misuse'. In contrast, in the corpus-driven COBUILD, this exaggeratory sense is listed as the first, and presumably most typical, sense of the three. No prescriptive warnings about misuse are given.

A corpus-based rather than corpus-driven approach is often adopted for socio-political reasons. In the creation of a bilingual English-Aranese dictionary (Aranese is spoken in the Catalonian Aran Valley region close to the border with France), Furness (2004) argues for analysis of spoken corpora to ensure that widely used words borrowed from neighbouring languages Catalan, French and Spanish are excluded. Purism is not the only factor involved in the relation between dictionaries and identity assertion. Lexicographers working on lesser documented languages are often motivated by a desire to document a language and assert the identity of its users. For several lesser or undocumented languages (e.g. Lusoga spoken in Eastern Uganda; see de Schryver and Nabirye 2018), corpus methods have made dictionary making feasible with limited resources.

2 What do lexicographic corpora look like?

There is no neat answer to this question. Ultimately, the form a corpus takes varies as a function of the dictionary or lexicographic resource being created. However, it is possible to outline several general characteristics common to most lexicographically useful corpora.

General characteristics

Metadata

Lexicographic corpora are typically accompanied by metadata describing the corpora themselves and the texts they contain (see Chapters 3 and 4, this volume). These include data about the diatopic variety (i.e. the dialect spoken in different regions), domain, genre, register and medium of texts, which is useful in lexical analysis. In addition, information about authorship and date of publication is useful for commercial reasons such as ensuring compliance with copyright guidelines. Information about diatopic variety is useful; a lexicographer analysing the word *server* needs to know that the sense 'a person who serves food at a restaurant' is typically used in US English. Information about the domain of the text is valuable for specialised dictionaries. For example, to discover the prototypical senses of *server* in hospitality and computer science. Knowing the publication date is also crucial for lexicographers working on historical or etymological dictionaries. In academic lexicography, there is a push to standardise the format of metadata. Somewhat paradoxically, several standards are used to encode metadata on lexicographical corpora. The Text Encoding Initiative (TEI 2020) has received particular attention in lexicography circles lately.

Representativity

Corpora should be representative of the language the lexicographer wants to document. To achieve this, a carefully balanced variety of language from different modes and sources should be included in the corpus (see Chapters 2, 3 and 4, this volume, for more on representativeness). This is not a straightforward task. In general-purpose dictionaries there is a view that gathering texts on a massive scale holds the key to this problem. This view has gained strength since the large-scale scraping of texts from the Web became feasible. Dissenting voices point to the problems of noise, for example, text that is reproduced in more than one place on the internet (newswires, press releases, advertisements, etc.) and the tendency of web-crawled corpora to underrepresent spoken language. The problem of how to achieve representativity is more acute still in corpora of specialised language where there is necessarily a limited quantity of text available. Yet overall, lexicographers are pragmatic and do the best they can with the data they have available. This is particularly true of those working on special-purpose dictionaries or dictionaries of lesser documented languages.

Tokenisation, lemmatisation and part-of-speech tagging

Tokenisation – including segmentation in languages which do not use whitespace to separate words (e.g. Chinese, Korean and Thai) – lemmatisation and part-of-speech tagging are important ante-steps to many forms of analysis in corpus linguistics (see Chapter 2, this volume).

Deciding where a word ends is a perennial problem in corpus linguistic analysis. However, it is worth pointing out that the seemingly trivial tokenisation problem of distinguishing between '.' as a sentence boundary and a sign of abbreviation is of special importance in lexicographic analysis, where a sentence view is often necessary to tease out distinctions between different senses and uses.

Lemmatisation allows lexicographers to search for various inflected forms of the same headword so that a search for *look* would give results for *looks*, *looking* and *looked*. This allows lexicographers to determine the typical forms of words used in a given context. For example, to show the dictionary user that it is more typical to end a business letter with *look forward to hearing from you* than *looking forward to hearing from you*.

Part-of-speech tagging allows lexicographers to analyse words in terms of their grammatical role. For example, to quickly distinguish between homographic forms (c.f. *undertake research* (noun) and *research* (verb) *the problem of*). It is also a necessary ante-step to many advanced corpus analysis techniques (see Section 4). The standardisation of tagging to link words and part-of-speech labels in a consistent way is particularly important for those working on multi-lingual resources or comparing diatopic varieties.

Types of corpora

It is beyond the scope of this chapter to provide a complete typology of dictionaries and the corpora used to make them. However, it is worth discussing the types of corpora most frequently used in lexicography and the types of resources they are used to make.

Monolingual

In general-monolingual lexicography there is a clear trend towards larger corpora (*Birmingham Collection of English Text*, 1980s = 10 million words; BNC 1990s = 100 million words; *Corpus of Contemporary American English* [COCA], 2020 = 1.1 billion words; *Oxford English Corpus* [OEC], 2019 = almost 2 billion words). The technical reasons for this trend include a vast increase in available computational power and the explosion in the quantity of text in digital formats on the internet. One practical reason is that the bigger a corpus is, the more likely it is to be representative of language as a whole. An important caveat here is that true representativity is impossible since language is constantly evolving.

However, in lexicographic corpus construction, size is not everything, there are other factors to consider:

- Mode – this is more than a question of including written and/or spoken texts. Speech is recorded in many real-world situations; it is also a key component of many works of fiction;
- Medium – the language found in novels typically differs from that found in journalistic texts. In the case of reporting verbs, journalistic texts are characterised by a higher frequency of structuring reporting verbs (e.g. *said, stated*), while novels are characterised by descriptive reporting verbs which mark the attitude of the speaker in relation to what is being said (e.g. *exclaimed, whispered*). The form of reporting verbs typically used also varies by medium. For example, the *-ing* form occurs more frequently in everyday informal speech (e.g. *They were saying that…)* than in journalistic texts (e.g. *They stated that*…) or novels (e.g. *They boasted that*…) (McCarthy 1998);
- Domain or topic – everyday conversation is rarely confined to one topic, even academic texts are frequently interdisciplinary.

In addition to these broad categories, texts have other characteristics which it is useful to take note of. These include the intended audience, the authorship (i.e. number of authors, their gender) and the degree of technicality – was the text written by experts for other experts or by experts for novices? In the case of spoken language (see Chapter 3, this volume), it is useful to note whether the text was spontaneous, based on notes, entirely scripted and/or post edited.

The appropriate proportion of each text type to include in a corpus is a vexing question. Figure 27.2 shows the broad categories and approximate proportions used in the BNC 1994.

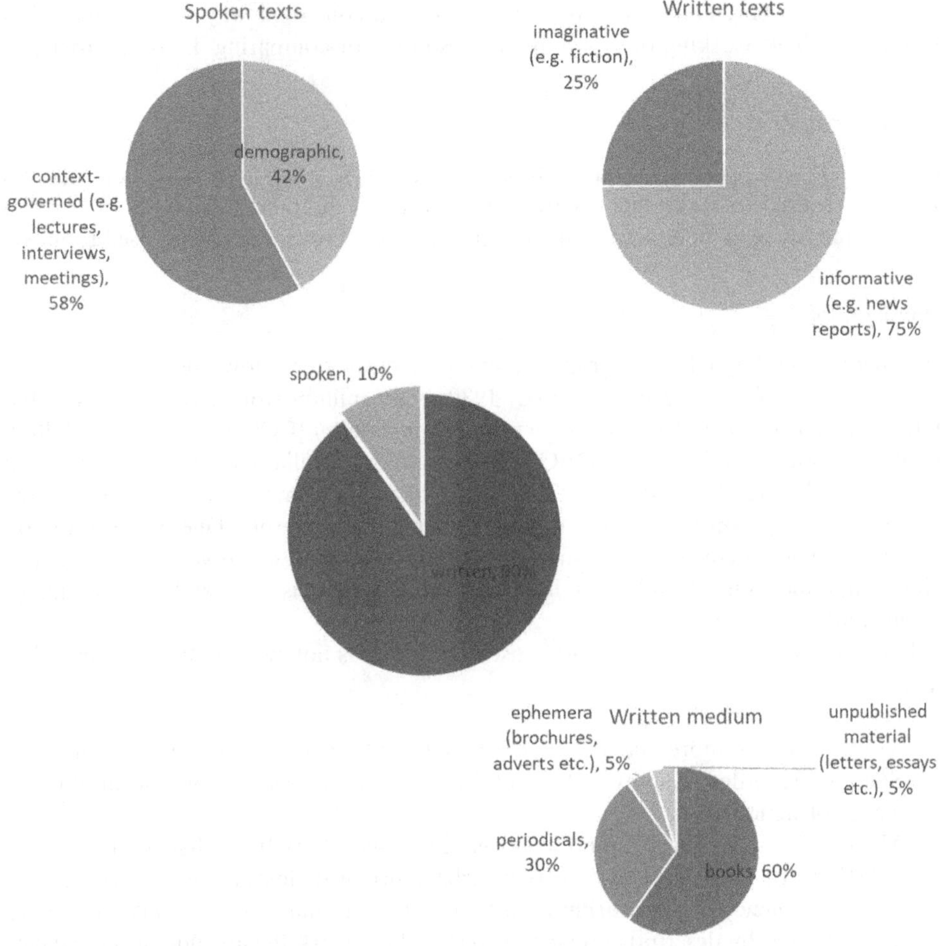

Figure 27.2 Approximate text proportions in the BNC 1994

Despite the diversity of text types available on the Web, the need to reflect a full range of language in general-purpose dictionaries means that even large, predominantly web-sourced lexicographic corpora such as the OEC complement web-sourced texts with printed sources.

Specialised corpora

In corpora intended for the creation of specialist lexical resources for certain fields, representativeness by size is not an option since a limited amount of text is available. In such cases a carefully constructed sampling frame is needed.

The *Oxford Corpus of Academic English*, an 85-million-word corpus used in the creation of the *Oxford Learner's Dictionary of Academic English* (Lea 2014), is an example of a corpus constructed to inform a specialist dictionary. To represent the language that users of academic English encounter and strive to produce, its creators sampled undergraduate textbooks and academic journals from the physical sciences, life sciences, social sciences and humanities. Researchers working on more specialist resources employ narrower frames. The EcoLexicon English corpus (León-Araúz *et al.* 2018) is a 23-million-word corpus of texts about the environment. It was used to inform *EcoLexicon* (EcoLexicon n.d.EcoLexicon: Terminological Knowledge Base on the Environment), a terminological knowledge base on the environment.

In bilingual lexicography

Bilingual lexicography trailed its monolingual counterpart in adopting corpus techniques. The first major commercial bilingual dictionary compiled using corpus methods was the *Oxford Hachette French Dictionary* (Corréard and Grundy 1994). In most commercial bilingual dictionaries, monolingual corpora are used to compile a candidate list of headwords and senses in the source language (i.e. the list of English words in an English-French dictionary); these are then translated to the target language (i.e. from English into French). Typically, a target language monolingual corpus is then used to check these translations.

In theory, there are obvious applications for bilingual corpora in this translation process. It is helpful to make a distinction between two types of bilingual corpora: parallel and comparable (see Chapter 34, this volume). Parallel corpora contain texts in a source language aligned (matched up) with corresponding translated texts in target languages. Comparable corpora contain texts in two or more languages which are comparable in terms of genre or function. They are sometimes aligned. In practice, the use of bilingual corpora in dictionary making is not widespread. This is chiefly due to the difficulty in sourcing parallel and comparable texts. There are academic studies which advocate the use of parallel corpora in dictionary making (Hartmann 1994; Héja 2010). There are also practical worked examples of how this might proceed. Atkins and Rundell (2008) describe how an abundance of French translation equivalents of English headwords can be derived from the *Europarl corpus* before concluding that, in practice, this abundance could prove unwieldly in editing and printing dictionaries. A further argument against using parallel corpora in the dictionary making process is the status of translated texts as representing a third code or translationese. In short, translated texts perfectly reflect neither the content of the original source texts nor that of texts originally written in the target language.

Although comparable corpora have been posited as an excellent source of original text in context in lexicographic research and training, in the secretive world of commercial lexicography, it is difficult to ascertain exactly how and how widely they are used. Atkins and Rundell (2008) claim that their use is not economic 'in a serious dictionary project'. However, in the creation of the *Oxford Portuguese Dictionary* (López Fuentes *et al.* 2015), a comparable corpus was used to revise the translation work (Frankenberg-Garcia personal communication).

Diachronic corpora

Until relatively recently, historical corpora available to lexicographers were too small to facilitate thoroughgoing lexicographic investigation (Svensén 2009). When constructing or selecting corpora to make historical dictionaries, lexicographers, by dint of the scarcity of data available, sometimes have to relax requirements for balance and representativeness. They find themselves faced with a choice between using corpus data that is narrow in terms of the domain and genre of texts covered yet deep in terms of the period covered, or corpora containing a broader range of texts covering a shorter period. The extent to which this dilemma applies depends on the language and period under study. Lexicographers working on English, Finish, German and Hungarian resources covering c. 1800 to c. 2000 are among the best served by existing historical corpora. For example, the 400-million-word Corpus of Historical American English (Davies 2012) (COHA) covers the period 1810–2009. It was used in the creation of the *Dictionary of Canadianisms on Historical Principles* (Dollinger and Fee 2017), providing negative evidence to confirm the Canadianness of words (Brinton 2016).

Focusing on the near past, monitor corpora, regularly updated with new texts, can be used to collect neologisms. The extent to which this approach is adopted in the creation of commercial dictionaries is unclear. In practical terms, there is necessarily a lag between a word first being used and appearing with enough frequency in a monitor corpus to be noticeable.

Learner corpora

Learner corpora, comprising texts written by language learners, are also useful to lexicographers. The *Cambridge Learner Corpus* (CLC) comprises English exam scripts from students studying English at a variety of levels and from many first-language backgrounds (see Chapter 22, this volume). The language errors it contains are labelled using a special schema. Data from the CLC was used to inform the "Common Mistake" feature in the *Cambridge Advanced Learners Dictionary* (McIntosh 2013). Similarly, usage notes tailored to the first language of the user provided in the *Louvain EAP Dictionary* (Granger and Paquot 2015) are informed by the *International Corpus of Learner English* (Granger *et al.* 2009).

Spoken corpora

Spoken language, with its frequent false starts and repetitions, is not an ideal source from which to extract candidate headwords based on frequency. However, the conventions followed in transcribing the spoken components of the large reference corpora used by lexicographers elide these characteristics of spoken language. Traditionally the use of corpora of spoken language in lexicography has been limited to a means of comparison with the written portion of corpora to highlight words typically used in speech. Even with the benefit of data from spoken corpora, explaining the numerous pragmatic functions of spoken words and expressions poses a significant challenge. For example, with variations in tone and intonation, *alright* can serve several functions, ranging from a friendly greeting (*alright?*) to a harsh interjection (*alright!*) with a similar function to *enough! Den Danske Ordbog* (Lorentzen 2019) "*The Danish Dictionary*" is particularly well supported by spoken data. Around 8 million words of the 40-million-word corpus used to create it represent speech. The resulting dictionary contains over 7,000 examples from spoken sources and 300 explicit usage notes about spoken Danish.

Several studies have highlighted the potential benefits of phonetically transcribed corpora for lexicography, particularly in the creation of learners' dictionaries (Verdonik and Maučec 2017). For example, the *College Learners' Spoken English Corpus* (Yang and Wei 2005), consisting of phonetic transcripts of the Chinese National Spoken English Test, has been mooted as a source of pronunciation information on words which

Chinese English as a foreign language (EFL) learners find challenging (Xia 2015). The use of phonetically transcribed corpora is not yet widespread in the creation of commercial dictionaries. From the perspective of the dictionary user, the availability of audio recordings of pronunciation – including dialect variants (e.g. British English vs. North American English) – in many online dictionaries has lessened the need for phonetic transcription.

3 Corpus tools and dictionary making

The most carefully designed corpus is of no use if there is no means of accessing and analysing the data it contains (see Chapter 9, this volume). Lexicography has been a driving force in the development of corpus tools. Key features of these tools were originally developed with lexicographic tasks in mind. Lexicographers were among the first to put pre-corpus intuitions of neo-Firthian linguists (Halliday 1966; Sinclair 1966) about the relevance of co-occurrence statistics to lexical analysis into practice (Church and Hanks 1990). Those working on early corpus-driven dictionaries appreciated the value of concordances, although at this early stage, they had to give advance notice of the concordances they required and wait while these were prepared and printed (Clear 1987). Given the centrality of lexicography to the development of corpus linguistics tools and techniques, it is hardly surprising that four of the five most widely used corpus tools reported by Tribble (2012) (the COCA interface [latterly, English-Corpora.org] [Davies 2020]; *AntConc* [Anthony 2020]; *WordSmith Tools* [Scott 2020]; *Sketch Engine* [Kilgarriff *et al.* 2014; *Sketch Engine* n.d.]; and Xaira [Burnard 2010]) have been used in dictionary projects.

It is possible to place corpus tools used in lexicography into broad categories:

Corpus-bound tools

These tools were specifically developed to analyse a given corpus or set of corpora. They usually have web-based interfaces. At their most basic, they include functionalities for generating concordances. Many national language institutions provide such tools and use them in the creation of their dictionaries. For example, *Corpus de Referencia del Español Actual* (CREA) has been used in the creation of several dictionaries published by the Real Academia Española (RAE n.d.).

Stand-alone offline tools

These tools can be used with any corpora to which the user has access. The tool and the corpora must be downloaded to the user's computer. Typically, these tools offer more advanced features than corpus-bound tools. *Antconc* and Wordsmith tools have been used in the development of a *Frequency Dictionary of German* (Tschirner and Möhring 2020).

Stand-alone online tools

These tools allow access to several corpora in an online environment. The COCA interface has been used in the creation of frequency dictionaries of Portuguese (Davies and Preto-Bay 2007) and Spanish (Davies and Davies 2017). *Sketch Engine* (Kilgarriff *et al.*

2014) is the leader in terms of use in dictionary projects. This is hardly surprising, since it has been developed with lexicographic tasks in mind. It generates statistical measures designed specifically for use in lexicography (Rychlý 2008). *Sketch Engine* allows users to upload their own corpora and quickly create corpora from the Web (Baroni *et al.* 2006). As a commercial enterprise, it is better-resourced than other tools available. This is reflected in its relatively high degree of user-friendliness and user support. By and large, lexicographers are not computer scientists – user-friendly design and comprehensive support allow them to maximise the time they spend on lexicographic tasks.

In addition to allowing the processing of giant datasets which would be technologically challenging with stand-alone tools, a web-based architecture is valuable to large-scale dictionary projects employing many lexicographers. It facilitates teamwork, avoids duplication of data and allows publishers to control who accesses data. Several major dictionary publishers use customised versions of *Sketch Engine*. The following section sets out how corpus tools are applied in dictionary making.

4 Analysing corpora to make dictionaries

As discussed in Section 2, before lexicographical analysis of a corpus can take place, several pre-processing steps must be carried out. These include noting relevant metadata, tokenisation (or segmentation), lemmatisation and part-of-speech tagging. In bilingual lexicography using comparable or parallel corpora, alignment – lining up texts to show how words have been translated in context – is also necessary. Alignment is not straightforward, since translators do not always translate linearly. They chop and change sentences, adding some elements and leaving others out (see Chapter 34, this volume). Since pre-existing corpora may have already undergone some pre-processing, it is not always necessary to carry out all these steps.

At its core, analysing corpora to make dictionaries takes advantage of two activities at which computers excel: counting and sorting. There are several ways of counting and sorting lexical data which are useful in lexicography.

Wordlists

Generating lists of words sorted by their frequency of occurrence in a corpus allows the creation of lists of potential headwords. These automatically generated wordlists are revised throughout the dictionary-making process. Since contextual factors are not usually considered when generating wordlists, they lack information about different word senses. For example, *the doctor treats the patient* and *this article treats the issue of reform* would both be subsumed under *treat* in a wordlist.

Lists of repeated strings of text

Sometimes called n-grams or lexical bundles (see Chapter 15, this volume), strings of a given length which occur above a given frequency threshold are used to isolate multi-word units such as connectors (e.g. *on the one hand…*), phrases and idioms. Setting appropriate thresholds can be difficult. The challenge lies in filtering out phrases that will be useful to the user from noise (e.g. *one of the, it is a, to be a*).

Lists of keywords

Keyness statistics are generated by comparing a specialised corpus with a general corpus. Words that appear significantly more frequently in the specialised corpus are considered key to that corpus. This approach is used to generate potential headword lists for specific-purpose dictionaries. The Academic Keyword List (Paquot 2010) was used in the creation of the *Louvain EAP Dictionary* (Granger and Paquot 2015). While it is undoubtedly useful, words which have distinct general and specialised senses (e.g. *table* = item of furniture; *table* = means of presenting data) can be overlooked using this approach. Frankenberg-Garcia *et al.* (2021) discuss the pitfalls of uncritical use of keyness statistics (and several other corpus lexicography techniques).

Concordances

Lexicographers use concordances to analyse a word's meaning and use both in terms of its lexico-grammar and its place in wider discourse. The notion of collocation is central to lexico-grammatical analysis. Examining collocates to the left and right of *treat* reveals two distinct senses: a discourse organising sense (e.g. *this article treats the issue of reform*) and a medical sense (e.g. *the doctor treats the patient*). Many corpus query tools have sorting functions which enable concordances to be sorted by the word to the left and right of the keyword (see Chapter 9, this volume). The enormous corpora available to lexicographers can be overwhelming. Features which take a random sample of concordance lines help alleviate this problem. The illustrative examples in many corpus dictionaries are taken from concordances (edited for length and clarity). GDEX (Kilgarriff *et al.* 2008) is a tool designed to help lexicographers find good dictionary examples from concordances. It takes factors such as length and anaphora into account. Such tools have not yet replaced lexicographers, but can save them time by effectively reducing the pool of potential examples they need to consider.

Statistical measures of collocation

Statistical measures of word association give useful information about the strength of combinations of words (see Chapters 9, 13, 14 and 15, this volume). They help lexicographers find typical collocations and assess the appropriateness of context in potential dictionary examples. Different measures of collocation give insights into different aspects of linguistic behaviour. T-score gives useful insight into grammatical behaviour, MI score tends to highlight restricted lexical collocations and logDice has been characterised as a "lexicographer friendly association score" insomuch as it is not influenced by corpus size and gives an indication of the relative difference in collocation strength (Rychlý 2008).

Word sketches

Word sketches are one-page summaries of a word's collocational behaviour. They use part-of-speech tags and statistical measures of collocation to list the collocates for a given headword sorted by grammatical relation and association score. This saves a great deal of time for lexicographers by giving them an overview of a word's meaning at a glance. Previously this would have involved painstaking analysis of hundreds, if not

modifiers of "fire"		
indiscriminately	4	7.92
twice (fired twice)	10	6.78
again (fired again)	40	5.85
deliberately	4	5.29
successfully	5	5.28
indeed	4	4.57
back (fired back)	25	4.07
first	6	3.75
once	5	3.7
then (then fired)	23	3.68
actually	8	3.35
even	9	3.08

objects of "fire"		
shot	219	10.87
bullet	56	9.89
gun	93	9.75
imagination	39	9.06
missile	34	9.04
rocket	23	8.74
heating (gas fired central heating)	21	8.46
rifle	19	8.35
burst	18	8.3
pistol	17	8.22
cannon	15	8.16
squad (executed by firing squad)	17	8

subjects of "fire"		
gas (gas fired central heating)	34	9.24
gun (guns firing)	27	9.15
cannon	9	8.38
gunman	9	8.07
oil	11	7.78
coal	8	7.56
soldier (soldiers fired)	15	7.52
troop	11	7.22
engine (the engine fired)	10	7.12
guerrilla	4	6.98
shot	6	6.97
police (police fired)	25	6.33

Figure 27.3 Partial word sketch for the verb "fire" in the BNC 1994 using Sketch Engine

thousands, of concordances. Figure 27.3 shows a partial word sketch for the verb *fire* in the BNC 1994. The object collocates of *fire* reveal the prototypical *weapon* sense discussed in Section 1.

Word sketch differences

Word sketch differences give a summary comparison of the collocational behaviour of two lemmas and word forms in a single corpus or two lemmas across sub-corpora. Sub-corpora comparisons are used in lexicography to illustrate differences in word senses in different domains. Figure 27.4 shows a word sketch difference for *table* in the Academic Written and Written Domain Imaginative sub-corpora of the BNC 1994. It elucidates two senses of the lemma *table* (*a piece of furniture* and *a means of presenting data*).

Diachronic analysis

Diachronic analysis is necessary for the creation of historical and etymological dictionaries and the study of neologisms. Tools such as Trends in *Sketch Engine* exploit metadata on corpus texts and statistical techniques to help lexicographers identify changes in word use over time.

Making thesauri

Corpus tools can be helpful in the making of thesauri. *Sketch Engine*'s Thesaurus tool suggests synonyms for a given keyword by calculating the number of collocates that

table (Written Academic) 4,298× (Written Domain Imaginative) 6,982×

"table" and/or ...			
fig	8	0	...
1989a	7	0	...
treasury	11	0	...
graph	6	0	...
des	5	0	...
desk	6	5	...
chair	11	119	...
bookcase	0	4	...
sofa	0	6	...
stool	0	8	...
armchair	0	9	...
bench	0	13	...

verbs with "table" as object			
construct	8	0	...
negotiate	4	0	...
analyse	4	0	...
publish	8	0	...
see	226	12	...
operate	4	6	...
round	4	65	...
lay	0	61	...
clear	0	46	...
litter	0	17	...
scrub	0	23	...
dress	0	50	...

verbs with "table" as subject			
summarise	4	0	...
show	63	0	...
illustrate	6	0	...
consist	4	0	...
contain	5	0	...
give	12	0	...
lay	0	4	...
stand	0	22	...
bear	0	9	...
eat	0	10	...
groan	0	4	...
overlook	0	7	...

Figure 27.4 Word sketch difference for "table" across two BNC 1994 sub-corpora using Sketch Engine

words in the corpus have in common with the keyword. With very large corpora, the use of word embeddings has been posited as a means of producing thesauri. Crudely put, word embedding can be thought of as representing words as points on a graph and calculating distances between these points to quantify similarity in meaning between words.

5 Future directions

Corpus techniques have already transformed how dictionaries are made, changed dictionary contents and provoked debate about the purpose of dictionaries. This will undoubtedly continue.

A possible consequence of the use of increasingly sophisticated corpus tools in lexicography is a more limited role for lexicographers in dictionary making. Ostensibly, it is easy to envisage a future where headwords, definitions and examples are derived automatically from corpora, with little human intervention. However, although wordlists, word sketches and tools such as GDEX undoubtably save lexicographers time, occasions will remain when the only means of elucidating word meaning and use accurately involves the manual analysis of concordances.

Corpus lexicography is also changing the form dictionaries take. Corpus methods have spurred the migration from paper-based lexicography to electronic resources such as personal electronic dictionaries, apps and online dictionaries. In computer science the term "ubiquitous computing" is used to describe the seamless integration of computers which require little specialist knowledge or training to use with everyday objects such as microwaves and televisions. Lexicographical developments such as increasingly sophisticated and user-friendly writing assistants, spelling checkers and grammar checkers point to a future characterised by "ubiquitous lexicography" where dictionaries and corpus data are seamlessly integrated with other information tools. Eventually, this invisibility may lessen the extent to which dictionaries are considered symbols of culture and identity, instead fomenting the view of dictionaries as just another tool.

Further reading

Atkins, B. and Rundell, M. (2008) *The Oxford Guide to Practical Lexicography*, Oxford: Oxford University Press. (A practical guide to dictionary making with worked examples using corpora.)

Fuertes-Olivera, P. (2018) *The Routledge Handbook of Lexicography*, London: Routledge. (A resource with an emphasis on lexicography in the internet era.)

Granger, S. and Paquot, M. (2012) *Electronic Lexicography*, Oxford: Oxford University Press. (An edited volume which provides a guide to the why and how of dictionary making in the digital age.)

References

Anthony, L. (2020) *AntConc*, Tokyo: Waseda University, Available at http://www.antlab.sci.waseda.ac.jp/ [Accessed 16 April 2020].

Atkins, B. and Duval, A. (eds) (1978) *Collins-Robert French-English Dictionary*, 1st edn, London: William Collins & Sons.

Atkins, B. and Rundell, M. (2008) *The Oxford Guide to Practical Lexicography*, Oxford: Oxford University Press.

Baroni, M., Kilgarriff, A., Pomikálek, J. and Rychl, P. (2006) 'WebBootCaT: Instant Domain-Specific Corpora to Support Human Translators', in *Proceedings of EAMT 2006. 11th Annual Conference of the EAMT*, Oslo: European Association for Machine Translation, pp. 247–52.

Brinton, L. J. (2016) 'Using Historical Corpora and Historical Text Databases', in P. Durkin (ed.) *The Oxford Handbook of Lexicography*, Oxford: Oxford University Press, pp. 203–20.

Burnard, L. (2010) *Xaira 1.26*, Available at: https://sourceforge.net/projects/xaira/ [Accessed 16 April 2020].

Church, K. W. and Hanks, P. (1990) 'Word Association Norms, Mutual Information, and Lexicography', *Computational Linguistics* 16(1): 22–29.

Clear, J. (1987) 'Computing: Overview of the Role of Computing in Cobuild', in J. Sinclair (ed.) *Looking Up: An Account of the COBUILD Project in Lexical Computing*, London: Collins ELT, pp. 41–61.

Corréard, M.-H. and Grundy, V. (eds) (1994) *Oxford-Hachette French Dictionary*, Oxford: Oxford University Press.

Davies, M. and Preto-Bay, A. M. R. (2007) *A Frequency Dictionary of Portuguese*, London: Routledge.

Davies, M. (2020) *English-Corpora.org*, Available at https://www.english-corpora.org/ [Accessed 16 April 2020].

Davies, M. (2012) 'Expanding Horizons in Historical Linguistics with the 400-Million-Word Corpus of Historical American English', *Corpora* 7(2): 121–57.

Davies, M. and Davies, K. H. (2017) *A Frequency Dictionary of Spanish: Core Vocabulary for Learners*, London: Routledge.

de Schryver, G.-M. and Nabirye, M. (2018) 'Corpus-Driven Bantu Lexicography Part 1: Organic Corpus Building for Lusoga', *LEXIKOS* 28: 32–78.

Dollinger, S. and Fee, M. (eds) (2017) *DCHP-2: The Dictionary of Canadianisms on Historical Principles*, 2nd edn, Vancouver, BC: University of British Columbia, Available at www.dchp.ca/dchp2 [Accessed 16 April 2020].

EcoLexicon: Terminological Knowledge Base on the Environment (n.d.), Available at http://ecolexicon.ugr.es/en/index.htm [Accessed 19 April 2020].

Frankenberg-Garcia, A., Rees, G. and Lew, R. (2021) 'Slipping through the Cracks in e-Lexicography', *International Journal of Lexicography* 34(2): 206–234.

Francis, N. and Kucera, H. (1964) *Brown Corpus Manual*, Providence, RI: Brown University.

Furness, R. (2004) 'Sociolinguistics and Dictionary-Making', in P. Battaner and J. DeCesaris (eds) *De lexicografia: actes del I Sympoium Internacional de Lexicografia. I Sympoium Internacional de Lexicografia*, Barcelona: Doumenta Universitaria, pp. 403–10.

Granger, S., Dagneaux, E., Meunier, F. and Paquot, M. (2009) *International Corpus of Learner English V2*, Louvain-la-Neuve: Presses Universitaires de Louvain.

Granger, S. and Paquot, M. (2015) 'Electronic Lexicography Goes Local: Design and Structures of a Needs-Driven Online Academic Writing Aid', *Lexicographica* 31(1): 118–41.

Halliday, M. A. K. (1966) 'Lexis as a Linguistic Level', in C. E. Bazell, J. C. Catford, M. A. K. Halliday and R. H. Robins (eds) *In Memory of J. R. Firth*, London: Longman, pp. 148–62.

Hanks, P. (2012) 'Corpus Evidence and Electronic Lexicography', in S. Granger and M. Paquot (eds) *Electronic Lexicography*, Oxford: Oxford University Press, pp. 57–82.

Hartmann, R. R. K. (1994) 'The Use of Parallel Text Corpora in the Generation of Translation Equivalents for Bilingual Lexicography', in W. Martin, W. Meijs, M. Moerland, E. ten Pas, P. van Sterkenburg and P. Vossen (eds) *Proceedings of the 6th EURALEX International Congress, EURALEX94*, Amsterdam: Euralex, pp. 291–7.

Héja, E. (2010) 'The Role of Parallel Corpora in Bilingual Lexicography', in N. Calzolari, K. Choukri, B. Maegaard, J. Mariani, J. Odijk, S. Piperidis, M. Rosner, D. Tapias (eds) *Proceedings of the Seventh International Conference on Language Resources and Evaluation*, Valletta: European Language Resources Association, pp. 2798–805

Hornby, A. S. (1974) *Oxford Advanced Learner's Dictionary of Current English*, 3rd edn, Oxford: Oxford University Press.

Johansson, S., Leech, G. and Goodluck, H. (1978) *Manual of Information to Accompany the Lancaster-Oslo/Bergen Corpus of British English, for Use with Digital Computers*, Oslo: University of Oslo.

Johnson, S. (ed.) (1755) *Dictionary of the English Language*, London: J. & P. Knapton.

Kilgarriff, A., Husák, M., McAdam, K., Rundell, M. and Rychlý, P. (2008) 'GDEX: Automatically Finding Good Dictionary Examples in a Corpus', in E. Bernal and J. DeCesaris (eds) *Proceedings of the XIII EURALEX International Congress*, Barcelona: Universitat Pompeu Fabra, pp. 425–32.

Kilgarriff, A., Baisa, V., Bušta, J., Jakubíček, M., Kovář, V., Michelfeit, J., Rychlý, P. and Suchomel, V. (2014) 'The Sketch Engine: Ten Years on', *Lexicography* 1(1): 7–36.

Lea, D. (2014) *Oxford Learner's Dictionary of Academic English*, Oxford: Oxford University Press.

León-Araúz, P., Martin, A. S. and Reimerink, A. (2018) 'The EcoLexicon English Corpus as an Open Corpus in Sketch Engine', in J. Čibej, V. Gorjanc, I. Kosem and S. Krek (eds) *Proceedings of the 18th EURALEX International Congress, EURALEX 2018*, Ljubljana: Euralex, pp. 893–901.

López Fuentes, S., Frankenberg-Garcia, A. and Newstead, H. (eds) (2015) *Oxford Portuguese Dictionary*, Oxford: Oxford University Press.

Lorentzen, H. (ed.) (2019) *Den Danske Ordbog*, Copenhagen: Det Danske Sprog- og Litteraturselskab, Available at https://ordnet.dk/ddo [Accessed 19 April 2020].

McCarthy, M. J. (1998) *Spoken Language and Applied Linguistics*, Cambridge: Cambridge University Press.

McIntosh, C. (ed.) (2013) *Cambridge Advanced Learner's Dictionary*, 4th edn, Cambridge: Cambridge University Press.

Merriam-Webster.com Dictionary (2020) Springfield, MA: Merriam-Webster, Available at https://www.merriam-webster.com/ [Accessed 19 April 2020].

Morris, W. (1969) *The American Heritage Dictionary of the English Language*, Boston: Houghton Mifflin.

Murray, J. (ed.) (1884) *A New English Dictionary on Historical Principles*, Oxford: Clarendon Press.

Nesi, H. (2000) *The Use and Abuse of EFL Dictionaries: How Learners of English as a Foreign Language Read and Interpret Dictionary Entries*, Tübingen: Max Niemeyer Verlag.

Paquot, M. (2010) *Academic Vocabulary in Learner Writing: From Extraction to Analysis*, London: Continuum.

Proctor, P. (ed.) (1979) *Longman Dictionary of Contemporary English*, Harlow: Longman.

Proffitt, M. (ed.) (2020) *The Oxford English Dictionary (online)*, 3rd edn, Oxford: Oxford University Press, Available at https://www.oed.com/ [Accessed 16 April 2020].

RAE (no date) *Banco de datos, RAE*, Available at https://www.rae.es/recursos/banco-de-datos [Accessed 16 April 2020].

Rychlý, P. (2008) 'A Lexicographer-Friendly Association Score', in P. Sojka and A. Horák (eds) *Proceedings of Recent Advances in Slavonic Natural Language Processing, RASLAN 2008*, Brno: Masaryk University, pp. 6–9.

Scott, M. (2020) *WordSmith Tools Version 8*. Stroud: Lexical Analysis Software, Available at https://lexically.net/wordsmith/ [Accessed 16 April 2020].

Sinclair, J. (1966) 'Beginning the Study of Lexis', in C. E. Bazell, J. C. Catford, M. A. K. Halliday and R. H. Robins (eds) *In Memory of J. R. Firth*, London: Longman, pp. 410–30.

Sinclair, J. (ed.) (1987) *Collins COBUILD English Language Dictionary*, London: Collins.

Sketch Engine (n.d.) http://www.sketchengine.eu/ [Accessed 16 April 2020].

Svensén, B. (2009) *A Handbook of Lexicography: The Theory and Practice of Dictionary Making*, Cambridge: Cambridge University Press.

TEI - Language Corpora Guidelines (2020) *Text Encoding Initiative*, Available at https://tei-c.org/release/doc/tei-p5-doc/en/html/CC.html#CCREC [Accessed 14 April 2020].

Tribble, C. (2012) 'Teaching and Language Corpora: Quo Vadis?', paper read at the *10th Teaching and Language Corpora Conference (TALC)*, Warsaw, 12th–14th July 2012.

Tschirner, E. and Möhring, J. (2020) *A Frequency Dictionary of German*, London: Routledge.

Verdonik, D. and Maučec, M. S. (2017) 'A Speech Corpus as a Source of Lexical Information', *International Journal of Lexicography* 30(2): 143–66.

Xia, L. (2015) *A Study of a Multi-Dimensional Definition Model of the Chinese-English Dictionary for Chinese EFL Learners*, Beijing: The Commercial Press.

Yang, H. and Wei, N. (2005) *Construction and Data Analysis of a Chinese Learner Spoken English Corpus*, Shanghai: Shanghai Foreign Language Education Press.

28

What can corpora tell us about English for Academic Purposes?

Oliver Ballance and Averil Coxhead

1 What is EAP?

EAP is a subfield of English for specific purposes. EAP is not concerned with learning English in a general, unspecified, abstract sense, but in facilitating specific, purposeful use of language within academic contexts (Hyland 2016). This definition leads to two important questions for the field of EAP: What constitutes an academic context – the boundary of the field's purview – and how can we facilitate specific, purposeful language learning within this domain? These are important questions because English is seen as 'a near-universal academic lingua franca' (Hyland and Shaw 2016: 5). English is being used for a wide range of academic purposes in a wide range of contexts by a wide range of people.

The key pedagogical issues in EAP result from the diverse ways in which English is used within academia. We imagine most readers will have a stereotype of academic language in their mind; we imagine it will consist of big, difficult words, interminably long sentences, and high-status speakers using high-status varieties of the language: perhaps the "old white men" we hear so much about. But we do not need to go very far to see evidence contrary to our stereotypes. Universities are (quite?) diverse places. Many students and many academics are non-native users of English – sometimes even the majority, even when English is the institutionally endorsed language. Governments around the world are tying academic funding streams to demonstrable "impact", and with this comes a drive to make research accessible – for it to be articulated not only in English but also in layman's terms. As enrolments in the tertiary sector have increased internationally, student populations have diversified, and so universities have responded by diversifying both teaching and assessment practices. We all have some notion of what academic language "is like" in our minds, but how accurate are these notions? If the EAP practitioner's job is to prepare learners for academic work, study and/or life, surely it is necessary to find out.

Little wonder then that needs analysis is often identified as the defining characteristic of EAP just as it is for English for specific purposes more generally (Upton 2012). The appropriate terminology and theoretical underpinnings for needs analysis have been the

DOI: 10.4324/9780367076399-28

subjects of extensive debate in EAP, but the debates are centred around who and what should be included in such an analysis, rather than a wholesale rejection of the enterprise (see Bocanegra-Valle 2016 for an overview). If we are to effectively prepare our learners for specific, purposeful language use within the English-speaking academy, we will need to know something about what people do there and how they use English to do it. This is not an *a priori* matter, but rather an empirical question. Corpora and corpus tools allow us to analyse EAP needs in ways that would not be possible without them.

2 What have corpora told us about EAP?

Corpora can provide a window on the language needed for academic purposes because they can facilitate management of large datasets and analysis of lexis, register, genre and discourse (see Chapters 14–20, this volume). In so doing, corpora of language from academic contexts have shown us that academic language is not monolithic.

Corpora of academic language have been central to Douglas Biber's body of research on how language is used in academic contexts. Drawing on more than a decade of corpus linguistic studies, Biber (2006) provides a detailed analysis of a corpus of 2.7 million words of speech and writing from an American university setting. Using factor analysis to group texts by the presence or absence of various linguistic features, he concludes that 'the distinction between speech and writing is by far the most important factor in determining the overall patterns of linguistic variation across university registers' (Biber 2006: 213). That is, university speech is different from university writing. It is not possible to summarise the analysis in full, but by way of illustration, Biber finds that *referential bundles* (e.g. *at the same time*, *in the middle* of) are highly prevalent in written university registers, but rare in spoken university registers, while the opposite is true of *certainty verb + that clauses*. Biber's work highlights the very different linguistic demands that using university speech places on learners as compared with university writing. He also draws attention to the importance of advising/management language in university contexts (as opposed to the more obvious instructional language that one might expect), along with the importance of language for expressing stance and the complexity of linguistic variation that correlates with academic discipline.

Taken together, Biber's findings highlight the importance of conducting needs analysis for EAP. By shedding light on the linguistic demands of one academic context, Biber's work has shown that many of our assumptions about academic language can be incomplete, inaccurate or even misleading. EAP teachers need to be aware of such analyses of academic language so that they can ask the right questions: Will their learners need to use English as both a spoken and written medium of communication (as opposed to only one or the other)? Will they need to engage in advisory/managerial discourse alongside more instructionally focused discourse? Will they need to learn how to express stance in the ways expected by the discourse community they are joining? Corpora can inform EAP by helping EAP practitioners identify the real linguistic demands academic contexts place on learners.

Another important line of corpus-based research focuses on academic text types. Nesi and Gardner (2012) present a large-scale, genre-based corpus study of student academic writing at a university. They identified 13 types of academic writing tasks and used discourse analysis to identify the functions and purposes of those tasks. Each task type has different genre features that present quite different writing demands. These task types and features can be very different from those that are commonly used for university entrance exams, such as argumentative, opinion-based essays; data-transfer-focused descriptions of data; or personal statements. Other research in this vein includes the genre features of academic laboratory reports (Parkinson 2017), the types and quantities of lexical bundles that are used in lectures (Nesi and Basturkmen 2006) and the lexical bundles that occur in university teaching and textbooks (Biber *et al.* 2004). Corpus analyses such as these are important because they help us realise the extent of linguistic variation in the wide range of written and spoken text types that EAP students may need to be prepared for.

Ken Hyland's corpus-based work has also been very important for creating a more accurate picture of the complexity of EAP needs. For instance, Hyland (2005) uses corpus data to demonstrate that the use of metadiscoursal language (for example, *self-mentions*, *hedging*, *evidentials* and so forth) are unusually common in academic discourse. Indeed, it is interesting to note that the frequent occurrence of self-mentions in academic texts may be at odds with many traditional ideas about academic style in which the use of personal pronouns is discouraged. Hyland also uses corpus analysis to explore differences in academic discourse on the basis of academic discipline, finding that language is used in diverse ways within different academic fields and, hence, that an accurate description of what constitutes EAP needs will depend in part upon the academic area concerned.

Corpora have been important in identifying the lexical demands of academic texts via corpus-derived wordlists. The tension between a sense of academic language in general and the specific needs of particular people in particular academic contexts is seen very clearly in the generation of such wordlists, because wordlists are typically presented as pertaining to either English for general academic purposes (EGAP) or English for specific academic purposes (ESAP). EGAP wordlists focus on words that occur across a wide range of academic disciplines. The most well-known is the Academic Word List (AWL; Coxhead 2000, 2016). It identifies words that occur unusually frequently across a range of academic fields and are not part of a core, basic vocabulary. Another influential wordlist is the Academic Vocabulary List (AVL; Gardner and Davies 2014). The AVL also identifies words that are unusually common in academic texts, but it does not exclude very basic words. Durrant (2016) looked into the use of lexical items from the AVL and found high use of the lexical items in the list overall, but also found variability depending on the type of text and discipline. The Academic Keyword List (AKL) (Paquot 2010) is also an EGAP wordlist, but it is based on keyness, which means the relative frequency of academic lexical items are taken into account, rather than raw frequency (see Chapter 10, this volume). ESAP wordlists identify words that are frequent in a particular subject or discipline such as chemistry (Valipouri and Nassaji 2013), medicine (Lei and Liu 2016), engineering (Ward 2009; Watson-Todd 2017), computer science in China (Bi 2020) and science (Coxhead and Hirsh 2007).

While the majority of EAP wordlists have been developed with a specific focus on written language, more recent work has focused on spoken academic English. Hence there is now an Academic Spoken Word List (ASWL) (Dang *et al.* 2017) with a general EGAP focus and Dang's (2018) more specialised exploration of vocabulary in hard and soft sciences. The ASWL holds great potential for learners because it accounts for around 90 per cent of a spoken academic text such as lectures (Dang *et al.* 2017), tutorials and laboratory sessions (Coxhead and Dang 2019).

Moving beyond lists of single words, corpus research has also identified common collocations and multiword units in EAP. Several lists of academic collocations (two-word units, such as *brief overview* and *combined effect*) are available for general EAP, such as Ackermann and Chen's (2013) *Academic Collocation List* of 2,469 items and the *Academic English Collocation List* by Lei and Liu (2018). Simpson-Vlach and Ellis (2010) combined corpus-based research and consultation with language teachers and testers in the development of the Academic Formulas List, which is divided into written, spoken and shared formulas. In a study that looked into multiword lists in university tutorials and laboratory sessions, Coxhead *et al.* (2017) combined a corpus and textbook analysis to explore multiword expressions for preparing EAP learners for speaking in small groups in a university context. They found that the multiword units in the academic spoken corpora were predominantly made up of high-frequency words and suggest that fluency with high-frequency items is particularly important in university settings. They also provide a list of multiword units commonly used in tutorials and laboratory sessions. For more on making and evaluating wordlists, see Nation (2016).

Corpora studies have also brought insight into the size of the task of learning enough vocabulary to understand spoken texts for academic purposes. Dang and Webb (2014) found that 4,000-word families plus proper nouns and marginal words (such as *um*) are needed to reach 95 per cent coverage of lectures and seminars, and 8,000 for 98 per cent. These results can be compared to figures for laboratory sessions and tutorials: 3,000 for 95 per cent coverage of both laboratory sessions and tutorials, but 4,000 for 98 per cent coverage of tutorials and 7,000 for 98 per cent coverage of laboratory sessions (Coxhead *et al.* 2017).

Finally, a new line of research has emerged in which corpora are used in combination with discourse analysis to explore EAP teachers' classroom discourse (see Chapter 18, this volume). For instance, Li *et al.* (2018) present a case study of an experienced EAP teacher. If a corpus could be built to represent EAP classroom discourse in general (EAP's heterogeneity notwithstanding), the same kind of analyses could be generalised to provide a window onto EAP classroom discourse in general.

3 What influence have corpora had on EAP materials?

In Section 2, we focused on how corpora have revealed the diversity of academic language. This awareness has led to the development of a wide variety of corpus-based EAP resources. This section provides an overview of such resources.

The rapid rise of the online environment has seen a growth in websites that draw on corpus-based research in EAP. For example, the EAP Foundation website (Smith n.d.) draws extensively 'the': ...draws extensively on the vocabulary research... research highlighted earlier, such as the Academic Formulas List, allowing users to investigate the occurrences and frequency of these formulas in their own texts. The exceptional Academic Word and Phrase website (Davies n.d.) provides searchable and downloadable copies of the AVL (Gardner and Davies 2014), allows users to analyse their own academic texts for the items in the AVL and links to an interactive website for searching the Corpus of Contemporary American English (COCA). Tom Cobb's *Compleat Lexical Tutor* website (Cobb n.d.) (commonly referred to as *Lextutor*) contains a wealth of tools built on research, including analysis of texts using Coxhead's (2000) AWL, as well as a concordancer that has built in access to the *British Academic Written English* (BAWE), its sister corpus containing spoken academic texts (*British Academic Spoken English*, BASE) and several specific corpora focused on disciplines such as medicine, law, commerce and social sciences.

Early adoption of corpus-based research in EAP in terms of materials can be seen in dictionaries for language learners. Various dictionary publishers have focused on academic vocabulary and collocations in entries. They may also include short explanations of academic language use which can assist EAP learners. An example of this connection between corpus-based research and dictionaries is the collaboration between the learner corpora experts in the Centre for English Corpus Linguistics (Université Catholique de Louvain) and Macmillan Education (see Gilquin *et al.* 2007). The particular difficulties for second-language academic writers which were identified in a corpus-based analysis, such as a lack of awareness of register and problems with academic phrasing, led to an advice section in the second edition of the Macmillan English Dictionary for Advanced Learners.

Other evidence of the impact of corpus-based research in EAP can be found in textbooks which have been developed on the basis of academic wordlists: for example, by ensuring that items from academic wordlists appear in reading texts and are part of the focus of activities and strategy development. Such use of research findings is not as widespread as might be expected, given the potential for pedagogy and learning that EAP corpus-based research has. Coxhead *et al.* (2017), for example, examined 16 EAP/ESP textbooks and found only 3 that were focused on phrases and vocabulary that might be considered helpful for academic speaking skill development. However, there was little evidence of those phrases being used in corpora of university tutorials and laboratories. Similarly, Miller (2011) investigated textbooks for English as a second language learners and university textbooks, finding that the ESL textbooks contained a great deal of narrative and fairly low amounts of academic vocabulary compared to the university textbooks.

There is also some evidence of corpus-based analysis informing EAP testing. Coxhead's (2000) AWL was the basis for the academic section of the Vocabulary Levels Test (Schmitt *et al.* 2001), and a more recent example is Pecorari *et al.*'s (2019) academic vocabulary test based on Gardner and Davies's (2014) AVL.

Another way in which corpora are being used for EAP materials is the development of corpus-informed writing aids. This kind of software provides real-time suggestions for collocations, something that could be very useful for EAP writers. Such suggestions are offered on the basis of algorithmic corpus analysis (see, for example, Frankenberg-Garcia *et al.* 2019).

4 How can teachers use corpora to do EAP needs analysis?

As well as informing descriptions of academic discourse and materials developed for EAP, corpus tools can be used directly by EAP teachers. There are two main uses of corpora by EAP teachers: description and analysis of learner language and description and analysis of target language. They correspond with the two ends of needs analysis: the learners' starting point and the learners' target context or goal. In both cases, key considerations for the EAP teacher are the type of corpora available and how the affordances of available tools relate to pedagogical goals.

In terms of affordances, corpus tools can help EAP teachers take a data-driven approach to needs analysis. Corpus tools can automatise indexing and counting of linguistic features in text, allowing an EAP professional to quickly find and analyse far more than they ever could manually (see Chapters 9 and 10, this volume).

Frequency counts and keyness measures can provide the basis for judging whether a particular feature is typical of a domain of academic discourse or not. As well as producing descriptions of common linguistic features in particular domains, analyses of two domains can be produced to determine whether they are similar or not: for instance, whether TED talks and academic lectures contain similar linguistic features. An individual text can also be analysed and compared to a corpus (either directly or to the data reported in relevant literature), and this can help a teacher decide such things as whether a potential input text is really representative of the target domain or the extent to which a learner's output conforms to or diverges from a target domain.

An important consideration in this kind of corpus analysis for EAP purposes is how to define one's unit of counting (see Chapters 10 and 14, this volume). From an EAP perspective, this issue is important once we try to relate the unit of counting (word form, lemma, word family and so forth) to what learners know. For example, Hyland and Tse (2007) show how a word type can have a markedly different prototypical meaning in different academic fields. For instance, *attribute* typically means *a feature of something* in academic business, sociology and computer science discourse, but it typically means *credit to something* in applied linguistics, biology and physics. These kinds of issues are further complicated when units of counting include inflections and derivations of words. Research from Japan has shown that very low-proficiency learners can struggle to interpret a known word form used in a different word class (Stoeckel *et al.* 2020) or to relate derived forms to each other (McLean 2018). It is perhaps important to note that while neither study mentions EAP, the participants in Stoeckel *et al.* (2020) and McLean (2018) were all studying English as part of their university studies. Hence, when attempting to relate corpus analyses to learners' needs, EAP teachers need to carefully consider the extent of their leaners' morphological knowledge (see Nation 2016, for a general discussion of this issue).

An analysis of collocates, n-grams, skipgrams (strongly collocating words with other statistically insignificant collocates between them) or concgrams (see Chapter 15, this volume) can be useful in EAP for several reasons. First, the sense of individual word forms can be disambiguated via observation of their collocates. Second, metadiscourse and discourse markers typically consist of cooccurring word forms and not individual word forms: i.e. *we find that* or *in relation to the above point*. Third, technical academic lexis often consists of collocating word forms: for instance, *adjusted gross income* or *vocabulary coverage level*.

Analysing an EAP corpus more qualitatively through a concordance (see Chapters 9 and 10, this volume) provides a convenient means of locating and exemplifying a specific feature in use. This is particularly useful to EAP practitioners in exemplifying, in undertaking register or genre analysis (see Chapter 17, this volume) or in training advanced EAP students in how to conduct such an analysis for themselves (see for instance, Charles 2011).

However, as noted earlier, while corpus tools can offer EAP practitioners a wide range of tools, taking advantage of these affordances is predicated on being able to obtain (see Chapter 8, this volume) or else build an appropriate corpus (see Chapters 1–7, this volume). In terms of the learner, corpora could be built to represent the language they are able to produce before a course begins or during a course itself, either as an assessment or as part of a portfolio of work. These types of texts can provide information about the learners' current abilities. In terms of the target context of use, this could be published material, course notes or work by previous EAP learners who have completed a programme successfully. In conjunction with information about what learners can currently do, these kinds of corpora can provide information about the language the learners need to develop. Importantly, the type of text chosen as a target should reflect the future context appropriately. Published academic materials illustrate how academics use language, but in many EAP contexts, the target performance level and the types of text that will be produced will differ from that of published work. Therefore, in many situations, it is useful to collect texts that illustrate good student performance at the target level. For instance, while some EAP students are PhD students and may be expected to write research articles for publication, many EAP students are working at an undergraduate level. How suitable is a needs analysis based on corpora of research publications for the former, and how suitable is it for the latter?

Once the affordances of corpus-based analysis have been considered and the practicalities of developing a corpus have been scoped, it is worth considering the qualities of the resource that can be made and its implications for interpretation. In a technical sense, a corpus is a scientific sample of a language domain. But this is not a realistic goal for many EAP projects due to the typical constraints that EAP practitioners work under, including limited personpower, financial resources, technical expertise and time frames. However, that does not mean that corpus tools cannot be used to produce useful descriptions and analyses. Adolphs (2006) makes an insightful distinction between true corpus linguistics and electronic text analysis (ETA). While a corpus requires careful sampling of a well-defined target domain and thereby provides a basis for robust generalisation, ETA uses the same technology to address the more modest goal of providing localised descriptions of particular texts. Indeed, in the context of language for specific purposes (LSP) (e.g. Japanese for tourism or English for nursing), Gavioli (2005) has argued for interpreting ETA for local relevance. In most EAP contexts, ETA is the most realistic type of "corpus" project to undertake – and in fact, much reference to corpora in EAP research would better described as this kind of ETA. Using corpus tools to analyse even a single text can still be a useful exercise, as long as we are judicious in our attempts to generalise!

Once a text or collection of texts has been selected and processed, EAP teachers can use analyses of these texts to adapt or create EAP tests or materials or to assess learner outputs. This is very useful in EAP contexts where the future domain of language use can be specified in some detail, because commercially produced materials are unlikely to be available for that specific site of EAP. One approach is to write new materials or to select or edit existing materials, using insights gained from corpus analysis as a guide. Another approach is to use the texts themselves as resources in an approach known as data-driven learning.

5 How can learners use corpora in EAP?

Of course, as well as teachers using corpora and corpus tools to guide EAP work, it is possible for learners to make use of corpora and corpus tools directly (see Chapters 29 and 30, this volume). There are two primary motivations for encouraging learners to do this. One is the potential for corpora to provide learners with resources at a very high level of specificity (i.e. that most closely match their needs). The second is to promote an autonomous, inductive, data-driven approach to language study. This last section discusses these affordances, potential challenges to effective use of corpora by learners and potential solutions to these challenges.

As discussed earlier, a perennial issue in EAP work is the level of specificity that can be achieved. In many EAP contexts, the learners will be orientated to a wide range of academic contexts, thereby problematising the task of describing the target domain of language use. Academic discourse as represented in publicly available corpora is unlikely to be an ideal fit with any given group of learners, either being quite general or specific to a different context. Even if teachers develop corpora (or text banks) for their classes to use, the extent to which these resources reflect the needs of learners will be affected by the relative homogeneity or heterogeneity of the class. Hence, a number of researchers have experimented and advocated for learners making their own corpora (e.g. Lee and Swales 2006; Charles 2012), which allows each learner to tailor the resource to their own specific needs. These studies have reported very favourably on such projects. However, it is important to note that these learner-directed corpus projects were undertaken with advanced learners who had clearly definable language goals, such as producing a thesis within their specialist field. In many other contexts, whether such an approach is feasible is questionable.

The other major affordance of language learners using corpora is the potential to orientate learners towards an inductive, data-driven approach to language study. The language teaching industry is still dominated by a rules-based view of language use, and there is often a considerable gap between the rules as pronounced and attested usage (e.g. Sinclair 1991). Hence, scholars working within the field of data-driven learning have advocated for learners learning how to interrogate corpus data so as to answer their own questions about how language works. Johns, who coined the term *data-driven learning* (DDL), illustrates possible models for his work in a series of papers (e.g. Johns 2002). Indeed, several recent meta-analyses report favourably on the effectiveness of such DDL (Boulton and Cobb 2017; Lee *et al.* 2018). But it should be acknowledged that learner use of corpora is far from commonplace in the majority of EAP contexts, and this would appear to be due to problems around accessibility, time and expertise.

A number of EAP-focused corpora are available publicly (see Chapter 8, this volume), and tools and guides are available for constructing one's own corpora (see Chapters 2–6, this volume). However, to a large extent, the value in accessing or building such resources depends on having sufficient expertise to make effective use of these resources (see Chapters 29 and 30, this volume). As many people working within the field of DDL have noted, a major barrier to more widespread use of corpora with language learners is the absence of training in corpus techniques from most teacher training courses (see Chambers 2019). It is argued that this creates a negative feedback loop within which teachers are unable to introduce their learners to corpus creation and consultation techniques because they themselves are not familiar with them. That is, until more teacher education programmes upskill teachers, learners are unlikely to be taught the skills they need to start using or creating corpora (Pérez-Paredes 2019).

At a deeper level, there are also questions about the cognitive demands of corpus consultation. Interrogating raw corpus data can be a cognitively demanding task that requires scientific reasoning skill straining and time. Sinclair's excellent *Reading Concordances* (Sinclair 2003) is a book-length, step-by-step treatment of how corpus data can be analysed. But it is aimed in the first instance at master's-level linguists, not the broader language learning constituency. Reports vary on the appropriateness of using corpora with language learners at various different proficiency levels and in various different contexts (Boulton and Cobb 2017). When assessing the potential benefits and challenges of teaching learners how to use corpora for themselves, a very significant factor within this equation is the type of corpus use being envisioned. In a systematic review of DDL, Pérez-Paredes

(2019) calls for more research exploring learner use of corpora in relation to language learning theory. Corpora (or text banks) vary greatly in terms of their size, make-up and possibly also mark-up (i.e. whether they have been tagged or not). The corpus tools used to interrogate corpora can also differ greatly in terms of the functionality they offer and the interfaces they provide. Furthermore, the way that the learner interacts with the corpus data – that is, how they make use of the corpus analyses they generate – can also vary considerably. Each of these factors can have an effect on the overall complexity and efficacy of corpus consultation, and this has led to recurrent calls for the development of more pedagogical models of corpus consultation (Pérez-Paredes 2010).

Ballance (2016, 2017) demonstrates that different types of corpus users are marked by different corpus consultation preferences. On the basis of his analysis, he suggests that we can think of two primary models of corpus consultation: analysis and reference. Analysis type use refers to *keyword in context* (KWIC)–formatted citations from large general corpora being used to identify patterns of co-occurrence across multiple citations. This model of concordance use corresponds to Sinclair's *Reading Concordances* (2003). For example, learners might identify patterns in how reporting verbs are being used in a set of concordance lines. Reference type use refers to using sentence- or paragraph-formatted citations, extracted from small, narrow corpora, which are then compared with a site of external use, such as a sentence in an article that the user is writing. For instance, a learner might search a relevant corpus for an example of how other writers have used "claims that". Ballance (2017) found that analysis type use was the preferred model of corpus consultation for corpus linguistic researchers and also the preferred model of use for teachers who were presenting corpus data to learners. However, the learners in the study preferred the reference-type use of corpora, and this preference was shared by people using corpora for translation or as a reference resource. On this basis, Ballance argues that, by default, learners should be introduced to the reference-type use of corpora. It is likely that this type of use is most relevant to their goals and potentially less cognitively demanding than analysis type use. Corpora can tell us a great deal about what constitutes EAP and how we can support specific and purposeful learning and teaching within this domain.

Further reading

Anthony, L. (2019) 'Tools and Strategies for Data-Driven Learning (DDL)', in K. Hyland and L. Wong (ed.) *Specialised English: New directions in ESP and EAP Research and Practice*, London: Routledge, pp. 162–80. (This chapter provides a useful and readable discussion of DDL and a range of tools and strategies. While the focus of the chapter is English for specific purposes (ESP), much of this chapter is just as relevant to EAP.)

Biber, D. (2006) *University Language: A Corpus-Based Study of Spoken and Written Registers*, Amsterdam: John Benjamins. (This book is fundamental reading for EAP researchers and teachers, as it provides an in-depth and thoughtful analysis of what corpora can show us about EAP.)

Hyland, K. and Shaw, P. (eds) (2016) *The Routledge Handbook of English for Academic Purposes*, London/New York: Routledge. (This book contains highly readable chapters on all aspects of EAP, as well as useful references.)

References

Ackermann, K. and Chen, Y.-H. (2013) 'Developing the Academic Collocation List (ACL) – A Corpus-Driven and Expert-Judged Approach', *Journal of English for Academic Purposes* 12(4): 235–47.

Adolphs, S. (2006) *Introducing Electronic Text Analysis*, London: Routledge.

Ballance, O. J. (2016). 'Analysing Concordancing: A Simple or Multifaceted Construct?' *Computer Assisted Language Learning* 29(7): 1205–19.

Ballance, O. J. (2017) 'Pedagogical Models of Concordance Use: Correlations Between Concordance User Preferences', *Computer Assisted Language Learning* 30(3-4): 259–83.

Bi, J. (2020) 'How Large A Vocabulary Do Chinese Computer Science Undergraduates Need to Read English-Medium Specialist?', *English for Specific Purposes* 58: 77–89.

Biber, D., Conrad, S. and Cortes, V. (2004) ' "If You Look At…": Lexical Bundles In University Teaching And Textbooks', *Applied Linguistics* 25(3): 371–405.

Biber, D. (2006) *University Language: A Corpus-Based Study of Spoken And Written Registers*, Amsterdam: John Benjamins.

Bocanegra-Valle, A. (2016) 'Needs Analysis for Curriculum Design', in K. Hyland and P. Shaw (eds) *The Routledge Handbook of English for Academic Purposes*, London/New York: Routledge, pp. 560–76.

Boulton, A. and Cobb, T. (2017) 'Corpus Use in Language Learning: A Meta-Analysis', *Language Learning* 67(2): 348–93.

Chambers, A. (2019) 'Towards The Corpus Revolution? Bridging the Research-Practice Gap', *Language Teaching* 52(4): 460–75.

Charles, M. (2011) 'Using Hands-on Concordancing To Teach Rhetorical Functions: Evaluation and implications for EAP writing classes', in A. Frankenberg-Garcia, L. Flowerdew and G. Aston (eds) *New Trends In Corpora And Language Learning*, London: Continuum, pp. 26–43.

Charles, M. (2012) 'Proper Vocabulary and Juicy Collocations': EAP Students Evaluate Do-It-Yourself Corpus-Building', *English for Specific Purposes*, 31: 93–102.

Cobb, T. (n.d.). *Compleat Lexical Tutor*, Retrieved from https://www.lextutor.ca.

Coxhead, A. (2000) 'A New Academic Word List', *TESOL Quarterly* 34(2): 213–38.

Coxhead, A. (2016) 'Reflecting on Coxhead (2000) A New Academic Word List', *TESOL Quarterly* 50(1): 181–5.

Coxhead, A., Dang, T. N. Y. and Mukai, S. (2017) 'University Tutorials and Laboratories: Corpora, Textbooks and Vocabulary', *English for Academic Purposes* 30: 66–78.

Coxhead, A. and Hirsh, D. (2007) 'A Pilot Science Word List for EAP', *Revue Française de Linguistique Appliqueé XII* (2): 65–78.

Coxhead, A. and Dang, T. N. Y. (2019) 'Vocabulary in University Tutorials and Laboratories: Corpora and Word Lists', in K. Hyland and K. Wong (eds) *Specialised English: New directions in ESP and EAP Research*, London: Routledge, pp. 120–34.

Dang, T. N. Y. (2018) 'The Nature of Vocabulary in Academic Speech of Hard and Soft-Sciences', *English for Specific Purposes* 51: 69–83.

Dang, T. N. Y., Coxhead, A. and Webb, S. (2017) 'The Academic Spoken Word List' *Language Learning* 67(3): 959–97.

Dang, T. N. Y. and Webb, S. (2014) 'The Lexical Profile of Academic Spoken English', *English for Specific Purposes* 33: 66–76.

Davies, M. (n.d.). Word and Phrase Academic, Retrieved from https://www.wordandphrase.info/academic/.

Durrant, P. (2016) 'To What Extent is The Academic Vocabulary List Relevant to University Student Writing?' *English for Specific Purposes*, 43: 49–61.

Frankenberg-Garcia, A., Lew, R., Roberts, J., Rees, G. P. and Sharma, N. (2019) 'Developing a Writing Assistant to Help EAP Writers with Collocations in Real Time', ReCALL 31(1): 23–39.

Gardner, D. and Davies, M. (2014) 'A New Academic Vocabulary List', *Applied Linguistics* 35(3): 305–27.

Gavioli, L. (2005) *Exploring Corpora for ESP Learning*, Amsterdam: John Benjamins.

Gilquin, G., Granger, S., and Paquot, M. (2007) 'Learner Corpora: The Missing Link in EAP Pedagogy', *Journal of English for Academic Purposes* 6: 319–35.

Hyland, K. (2005) *Metadiscourse*. London: Continuum.

Hyland, K. (2016) 'General and Specific EAP', in K. Hyland and P. Shaw (eds) *The Routledge Handbook of English for Academic Purposes*, London/New York: Routledge, pp. 17–29.

Hyland, K. and Shaw, P. (2016) 'Introduction', in K. Hyland and P. Shaw (eds) *The Routledge Handbook of English for Academic Purposes*, London/New York: Routledge, pp. 1–14.

Hyland, K. and Tse, P. (2007) 'Is There an "Academic Vocabulary"?', *TESOL Quarterly* 41(2): 235–53.
Johns, T. (2002) 'Data-Driven Learning: The Perpetual Challenge', in B. Kettemann and G. Marko (eds) *Teaching and Learning by Doing Corpus Analysis*, Amsterdam: Rodopi, pp. 107–17.
Lee, D. and Swales, J. (2006) 'A Corpus-Based EAP Course for NNS Doctoral Students: Moving from Available Specialized Corpora to Self-Compiled Corpora', *English for Specific Purposes 25*(1): 56–75.
Lee, H., Warschauer, M. and Lee, J. H. (2018) 'The Effects of Corpus Use on Second Language Vocabulary Learning: A Multilevel Meta-Analysis', *Applied Linguistics* 40(5): 721–53.
Lei, L. and Liu, D. (2016) 'A New Medical Academic Word List: A Corpus-Based Study with Enhanced Methodology', *Journal of English for Academic Purposes* 22: 42–53.
Lei, L. and Liu, D. (2018) 'The Academic English Collocation List', *International Journal of Corpus Linguistics 23*(2): 216–43.
Li, Y., Flowerdew, J. and Cargill, M. (2018) 'Teaching English for Research Publication Purposes to Science Students in China: A Case Study of an Experienced Teacher in the Classroom', *Journal of English for Academic Purposes* 35: 116–29.
McLean, S. (2018) 'Evidence for the Adoption of the Flemma as an Appropriate Word Counting Unit', *Applied Linguistics* 39(6): 823–45.
Miller, D. (2011) 'ESL Reading Textbooks vs. University Textbooks: Are We Giving Our Students the Input They May Need?', *English for Academic Purposes* 10: 32–46.
Nation, I. S. P. (2016) *Making and Using Word Lists for Language Learning and Testing*, Amsterdam: John Benjamins.
Nesi, H. and Basturkmen, H. (2006) 'Lexical Bundles and Discourse Signalling in Academic Lectures', *International Journal of Corpus Linguistics* 11(3): 147–68.
Nesi, H. and Gardner, S. (2012) *Genres across the Disciplines: Student Writing in Higher Education*, Cambridge: Cambridge University Press.
Paquot, M. (2010) *Academic Vocabulary in Learner Writing: From Extraction to Analysis*, London and New-York: Continuum.
Parkinson, J. (2017) 'The Student Laboratory Report Genre: A Genre Analysis', *Journal of English for Specific Purposes* 45: 1–13.
Pecorari, D., Shaw, P. and Malmström, H. (2019) 'Developing A New Academic Vocabulary Test', *English for Academic Purposes* 39: 59–71.
Pérez-Paredes, P. (2010) 'Corpus Linguistics and Language Education in Perspective: Appropriation and the Possibilities Scenario', in T. Harris and M. Moreno Jaén (eds) *Corpus Linguistics in Language Teaching*, Bern: Peter Lang, pp. 53–73.
Pérez-Paredes, P. (2019) 'A Systematic Review of the Uses and Spread of Corpora and Data-Driven Learning in CALL Research During 2011-2015', *Computer Assisted Language Learning*. 10.1080/09588221.2019.1667832
Schmitt, N., Schmitt, D. and Clapham, C. (2001) 'Developing and Exploring the Behaviour of Two New Versions of the Vocabulary Levels Test', *Language Testing* 18(1): 55–88.
Simpson-Vlach, R. and Ellis, N. C. (2010) 'An Academic Formulas List: New Methods in Phraseology Research', *Applied Linguistics* 31(4): 487–512.
Sinclair, J. (1991) *Corpus, Concordance, Collocation*, Oxford: Oxford University Press.
Sinclair, J. (2003) *Reading Concordances: An Introduction*, London, UK: Pearson.
Smith, S. (n.d.) Academic Vocabulary, Retrieved from https://www.eapfoundation.com/vocab/academic/.
Stoeckel, T., Ishii, T. and Bennett, P. (2020) 'Is the Lemma More Appropriate than the Flemma as a Word Counting Unit?', *Applied Linguistics* 41(4): 601–06. 10.1093/applin/amy059
Upton, T. A. (2012) 'LSP at 50: Looking Back, Looking Forward', *Ibérica* 23: 9–28.
Valipouri, L. and Nassaji, H. (2013) 'A Corpus-Based Study of Academic Vocabulary in Chemistry Research Articles', *Journal of English for Academic Purposes* 12: 248–63.
Ward, J. (2009) 'A Basic Engineering English Word List for Less Proficient Foundation Engineering Undergraduates', *English for Specific Purposes* 28(3): 170–82.
Watson-Todd, R. (2017) 'An Opaque Engineering Word List: Which Words Should a Teacher Focus on?', *English for Specific Purposes* 45: 31–9.

29

What is data-driven learning?

Angela Chambers

1 The context of data-driven learning

As the developments described in the previous chapters have shown, the analysis of large collections of naturally occurring discourse, both written and spoken, came to play a central role in linguistic research in the twentieth century. The application of this research in language learning and teaching, however, was a slow process, which has been referred to by metaphors such as percolation (McEnery and Wilson 1997) or trickle down (Leech 1997). The fact that developments did take place is easy to explain when one considers the context of research and practice, both in language learning and teaching and in applied linguistics. Firstly, the communicative approach emphasised the use of authentic texts, although for several decades accompanying exercises tended to be based on invented examples, and such examples can still be found. Secondly, research by McCarthy (1998) and others revealed that the language of course books continued to differ significantly from actual language use, particularly in relation to the spoken language (see also Chapter 26, this volume). The production of corpus-based dictionaries and grammars as well as course books now gives learners access to actual language use. It is nonetheless important to note that a DDL approach implies a level of active participation in the learning process, which such resources cannot provide in the same way as learner (and teacher) interaction with the corpus itself.

DDL takes the developments listed earlier a step further, in that it not only uses corpus data in the preparation of language-learning materials, but gives learners access to more substantial amounts of corpus data than can be found in a dictionary, grammar or course book. This can involve either indirect access, where they learn about language use by studying concordances prepared in advance by the teacher, or direct access, where they use concordancing software to carry out their own searches of corpora. The increasing availability of computers from the 1980s onwards, and also of concordancers, either commercially or available freely via the Web, has made developments in DDL possible. Teachers can have access to – and even create – corpora, allowing learners to study the patterns of language use, mostly through observing concordances, and work out for themselves how a word or a phrase is used. This process of inductive learning, in

DOI: 10.4324/9780367076399-29

which the learner plays an active part in the learning process, is the essence of DDL. It also corresponds closely to current thinking in educational research in general, and in language-learning pedagogy in particular, in a constructivist paradigm where the active role of the learner is of crucial importance. Researchers who were also language teachers in higher education with an interest in the use of corpus data with language learners experimented with different ways of using the data with their learners and with using different types of corpora (for example, large reference corpora or small genre-specific corpora). This has given rise to a substantial body of research publications reporting on the success of this new approach and the obstacles which the learners noted in their explorations of the corpus data.

Although there has been considerable progress in research and practice in DDL since the 1980s, certain limitations which have persisted throughout all the developments must be noted here. Firstly, it has tended to focus mostly on the English language, although we shall see some examples involving French, as the author has experience of using corpus data in teaching that language, and also references to the use of corpora in the teaching of other languages, for example, Kennedy and Miceli's (2001, 2017) work involving learners of Italian (see also Chapters 22, 23 and 34, this volume, for multilingual and learner corpora). However, only monolingual corpora of L2 or expert speakers or writers will be considered here. There is also a dearth of publications involving the use of DDL in the teaching of lesser-used languages, although there are some current developments. For example, the creators of the *National Corpus of Contemporary Welsh/ Corpws Cenedlaethol Cymraeg Cyfoes* (Knight *et al.* 2021) have included a pedagogical toolkit in the design and construction of the corpus. Inspired by *Lextutor*, a corpus-based, pedagogic website (more details are provided later in this chapter), the toolkit aims to provide learners with the ability to access relevant corpus data in a directed way, obviating the need for explicit training.

The second limitation involves the educational sector in which DDL research is generally situated. As the researchers who report on their use of corpora in their teaching tend to work in higher education, publications on DDL almost exclusively report on experimentation in that context, with very few researchers focusing on secondary education. Notable exceptions include Braun (2005, 2007), Breyer (2009), Lee (2011) and Crosthwaite (2020). Even less research relates to primary education (see, for example, Sealey and Thompson 2007). Boulton (2020) notes that of 378 empirical studies of DDL which he has discovered, only 19 relate to secondary education and none to the primary level. According to Crosthwaite (2020), however, a focus on young learners is finally emerging in DDL research. The fact remains, however, as a number of researchers have noted (Granger 2015; Chambers 2019; Pérez-Paredes 2020), that there is little evidence that DDL has successfully crossed the research–practice gap. In other words, it has not yet become widely used and integrated in language learning and teaching at all levels of education in the same way as other major developments, such as the communicative approach, have done.

2 A brief history of data-driven learning

The first publications disseminating information internationally on the use of corpus data with language learners appeared in the 1980s, notably those by Tim Johns, who coined the term DDL. Johns initially used the concordancing software *MicroConcord* as a tool for learners to use, although he also recognised its usefulness for the teacher

(1986). He introduced concordancing in his work teaching English for specific purposes to nonnative speakers of English, and also situated it in the context of similar developments by a number of researchers, citing experimentation by his then colleague in Birmingham, Antoinette Renouf, and also by Ahmad *et al.* (1985) in Surrey (Johns 1986). McEnery and Wilson (1997) situate the first attested use of concordances in language teaching as early as 1969, by Peter Roe in Aston University, Birmingham. Interestingly, librarians and social scientists were also using keyword in context (KWIC) concordances at around this time (Kent and Lancour 1968; Matsuda and Matsui 1975). It was not until the late 1980s and the early 1990s, however, that it was brought to public attention in the discourse community of researchers in applied linguistics by the work of Johns, and also to language teachers by Tribble and Jones (1990). Johns used the simile of the language learner as researcher (1986) and the Sherlock Holmes metaphor (1997) to highlight the more active role of the learner in this approach and described the computer and the concordancer as a research tool for both learner and teacher (1986). His learners considered working with a concordance printout to be a much more effective way of studying the use of common prepositions, finding that an exercise such as underlining the headword colligating with the preposition *on* ("depending on", "on demand") was more helpful than a gap-filling exercise involving filling in the prepositions (1986: 160). The concordancer also served as a research tool for Johns himself in his role as teacher.

> It is important that teachers themselves should have experience in using concordance output if they expect their students to make use of it. In my own case, examining output has often proved chastening: for example a concordance of "if" showed how often in scientific and technical texts it is followed by the bare adjective or past participle e.g. "if available", "if known" – a usage I found I had neglected in my materials on conditional constructions in English.
>
> *(Johns 1986: 159)*

As we shall see, this early experimentation by Johns and others was to develop into a substantial research area from the 1990s onwards, particularly in the context of language learning in higher education.

This research was accompanied by, and to a large extent dependent on, technological developments. More sophisticated concordancers, such as *Wordsmith Tools* (Scott 2020), became available commercially at a modest cost, with some versions now freely available. Freely available concordancers, such as *AntConc* (Anthony 2019), soon followed (see Chapter 9, this volume). In addition to these concordancers, which allow users to load and consult the corpus of their choice, huge corpora became available, such as the *British National Corpus (BNC)*, and later collections of corpora such as the BYU corpora. While these were primarily intended for linguistic researchers, the needs of learners and teachers were not neglected, and easily usable resources are now available. A noteworthy multilingual descendent of the work of Johns and his fellow researchers is to be found in *Lextutor*, a resource which allows corpus consultation without the training necessary to use the more sophisticated concordancers. The *Lextutor* website includes a variety of corpora in English, French, German and Spanish, providing teachers and learners with easy access to multiple examples of actual language use.

The potential of using the Web as a source of data for corpus creation has given rise to a number of developments in the twenty-first century. To give just one example here,

Sketch Engine, which includes a collection of vast corpora in more than 90 languages, also provides a simple tool for language learners, SKELL, in 6 languages. A very simple interface allows the user to enter a word or phrase and provides 40 examples of complete sentences. In a study of the use of SKELL by Japanese university students of English, Hirata and Hirata (2019) found that this limited number of good examples provides a solution to two problems which they identified in the use of concordancers such as those named earlier. They identified the incomplete sentences and the large numbers of results as problematic for learners. The results of their study were generally very positive, although one learner commented that they would have preferred to have had access to the wider context, something which a more sophisticated concordancer would provide.

Of particular interest in the context of higher education is the BAWE corpus (Nesi and Gardner 2012), which contains over 6.5 million words of proficient student writing in several genres and disciplines (BAWE is available on *Lextutor* and *Sketch Engine*). A feature of the BAWE project relevant to a DDL approach is *Quicklinks* (Vincent and Nesi 2018), a resource for both teachers and university students who are not native speakers of English writing in that language. *Quicklinks* makes available to teachers and learners of English for academic purposes (EAP) a database of hyperlinks to concordances of words and expressions which are problematic for them (Vincent and Nesi 2018). Thus a teacher marking an essay as an e-document or via Turnitin could add in the margin a hyperlink with concordance lines to illustrate correct or more appropriate usage. The examples which the authors provide include concordance lines for 'beyond the scope of' where a student had written 'there isn't room' (Vincent and Nesi 2018: 10) or the concordance lines below where a student had written 'bring a negative impact on' (Vincent and Nesi 2018: 6). Four of the 45 examples of 'negative impact' are given next.

(1)

Reduced purchasing power of the masses has **a negative impact** on the growth of the domestic market and on the

Surprisingly, the level of urbanization has **a negative impact** on child mortality at the ten percent level of

Divisions in the union movement can have **a negative impact** on trade union membership (Bean 1994: 41;

Capacity leakage. Again, this could have **a negative impact** on staff motivation, as it could remove a great....

[BAWE on Sketch Engine]

As the hyperlink is linked to *Sketch Engine*, the learner has the opportunity to further investigate – in this case by finding occurrences of "effect" as well as "impact", for example. Interestingly, this project corresponds perfectly with a comment made by Johns more than three decades earlier (1986) to the effect that he had considered placing a capital C in the margin of student essays to indicate that the use of English could be improved by consulting a corpus.

While these easily available and, more important, easy-to-use resources may well have the greatest potential for popularising the use of corpus data by language learners and teachers, the substantial number of publications reporting on the use of corpora by learners tend to concentrate on the use of commercial concordancers by either the teacher or the learners themselves. Two types of corpora are chosen: either large publicly available corpora or small custom-made corpora. These are used to investigate a variety of aspects of language learning, particularly the acquisition of vocabulary, grammar and specialised language use. Li (2017), for example, uses both the *BNC* and COCA (Davies 2008). Many publications, however, involve small corpora created by the researchers for their own learners, what some researchers call pedagogic corpora (Willis 1998; Pérez-Paredes 2020). Stevens (1991), for example, created a small corpus based on the physics textbook of his students to investigate whether concordance-based exercises were better than gap-fill exercises for learning vocabulary and concluded that they were. Small corpora also have their limits, however, in that they may contain no or very few occurrences of certain items. While Cobb (1997) used a corpus of just 10,000 words assembled from his students' reading materials to investigate the use of corpus data for vocabulary learning, he co-authored a later publication using a larger corpus. Gaskell and Cobb (2004), who investigated the use of concordances to correct writing errors, concluded that a corpus of more than 1 million words would be more likely to produce a substantial number of occurrences of the words and expressions which the learners wished to study. Another important limitation of these small corpora created specifically to meet learners' needs is that they are often not publicly available. The impact of the research is thus weakened, as the activity carried out by the researcher is not directly replicable.

At the time of writing all these trends coexist, with large and small corpora increasingly available to learners and teachers, and an increasing number of researchers experimenting with ways to make DDL a reality for the majority of language learners. The large body of research on corpus consultation by learners has produced largely positive results, suggesting that they benefit from corpus consultation in learning vocabulary, grammar and phraseology and in improving writing skills (Stevens 1991; Cobb 1997; Gaskell and Cobb 2004; Ackerley 2017). The learners appreciate having access to a large number of genuine examples of the aspect of language use which they are studying (Chambers 2005; Hirata and Hirata 2019). They also enjoy the exploratory nature of the activity, what Johns had in mind in the well-known phrase 'Every learner [is] a Sherlock Holmes' (1997: 101).

Negative reactions to corpus consultation by learners come from two sources: from the learners themselves and from academia. Firstly, many learners in the empirical studies, even those whose reactions were generally very positive, found the activity of analysing the corpus data time-consuming, laborious and tedious (Chambers 2005; Smith 2011; Hadley and Charles 2017). Even the limited number of 40 examples provided by SKELL was considered too many by some learners (Hirata and Hirata 2019). The second source of negative reactions involves the issue of context. For Widdowson (2000: 7) corpora contain 'decontextualised language'. Charles (2007) comments, however, that it is arguable that a corpus contains more context than much classroom material which consists of extracts, as the learner consulting a corpus of complete texts may have access to the full text corresponding to each concordance line. In other publications reporting on the use of corpora with learners, the authors also underline that teachers preparing materials using concordances should ensure that the context is meaningful, that it contains 'somewhere in it some clue, however small, to assist students in placing the target word in that context' (Stevens 1991: 51).

As the research on corpus consultation by teachers and learners continued to increase in the twenty-first century, an important development was the publication of meta-analyses (Cobb and Boulton 2015; Boulton and Cobb 2017; Lee *et al.* 2019; Pérez-Paredes 2019). In addition, analyses of the substantial number of empirical studies from pedagogical and theoretical perspectives were published, such as learning objectives (Boulton 2010) and language-learning theories (Flowerdew 2015). Boulton's (2017) timeline provides a useful overview. Alongside this research activity, following on from Tribble and Jones's (1990) early guide for teachers on how to put DDL into practice, works by Friginal (2018) and Poole (2018) also concentrate on advising teachers and learners on the practice of DDL. The question remains, however, as to whether DDL has effectively crossed the research–practice gap and become an aspect of everyday practice for teachers who are not research-active in DDL (see Chambers 2019; Pérez-Paredes 2020).

3 DDL and actual language use

In this section we shall see some examples of how easily and freely available written and spoken corpora can provide data which can be used by the teacher or learner in a DDL approach. As written corpora can be created more easily than their spoken counterparts, it is not surprising that they are more readily available. Using a concordancer or simply by accessing *Lextutor*, a teacher or learner can consult a number of freely available corpora (see Chapter 10, this volume). The examples that follow are taken from the *Chambers-Le Baron Corpus of Research Articles in French* (Chambers and Le Baron 2007), a pedagogic corpus of approximately 1 million words created to be of use to learners when writing essays in French and available via the *Oxford Text Archive*. The corpus contains 159 articles taken from 20 journals which are available online. The articles, published between 1998 and 2006, belong to one of ten categories: media/culture, literature, linguistics and language learning, social anthropology, law, economics, sociology and social sciences, philosophy, history and communication.

The use of the first person plural in research articles in French has given rise to a substantial amount of phraseology related to the meta-language of the article, the language used by the author to signal to the reader how the article is organised. The equivalent phrases for "as we have seen" and "as we shall see", for example, include a redundant definite article and may refer to the article in spatial rather than temporal terms: "plus haut" and "plus loin" rather than "earlier" and "later". I had corrected inappropriate phrases in learner essays, writing in the phrases, "*comme nous l'avons vu plus haut*" and "*comme nous le verrons plus loin*". I discovered from studying the 74 occurrences of "*comme nous*" in the corpus, however, that there is a much wider variety of phrases than this, with only 15 occurrences of the verb "to see" and verbs such as "underline", "describe", "indicate", "mention", "observe", "show", "explain", "note" and "remind" commonly occurring.

(2)
Comme nous l'avons souligné précédemment
comme nous venons de le décrire.
Comme nous l'avons déjà indiqué,
Comme nous l'avons mentionné plus haut
comme nous avons pu le constater à plusieurs reprises lors de l'analyse
D'autre part, **comme nous** l'observerons en seconde partie de cet article,
Comme nous allons tenter de le montrer dans la suite de ce texte,
comme nous le montrerons dans les pages qui suivent.
Comme nous l'avons expliqué dans le paragraphe précédent,

comme nous l'avons rappelé,
Comme nous en avons fait état plus haut,
comme nous allons maintenant le noter,

(Chambers and Le Baron 2007)

A variety of adverbial expressions occur as well as "plus haut" and "plus loin". In addition, inversion of the subject and verb is sometimes found in these phrases.

(3)
Comme nous l'a suggéré un rapporteur anonyme.
Comme nous l'apprend son dossier de faillite,
Comme nous le dit cet interviewé, "la communauté ne nous appartient pas".
comme nous l'a précédemment montré la scène de leur premier face à face
comme nous le laisse entendre la section Religion de sa Phénoménologie

(Chambers and Le Baron 2007)

Like Tim Johns in the references to the use of "if" earlier, I found the consultation of the corpus a useful way of getting immediate information on the practices of a substantial number of expert writers, prompting me to include in my teaching features which I had hitherto neglected.

At very advanced levels, a small number of publications report on projects in which doctoral researchers who are not native speakers of English create their own specialised corpus and use it to investigate language use in English by expert writers in their published research. The small number of participants in Lee and Swales's study (2006) stated that they found the use of corpora confidence-building and empowering, in that they could check aspects of language use without consulting native speakers. They reported that the examples which they found were 'closer to their contextual and textual circumstances' than those found in reference books or grammars (2006: 71). They also stated that they would consider using corpora in the future. In a rare example of a longitudinal study, Charles (2014) examined 40 graduate students' perceptions of the usefulness of having a personally created corpus of discipline-specific academic writing. The survey took place one year after they had created the corpus as part of a course in academic writing in English. Of the 40 participants, 35 (86 per cent) either had used or intended to use the corpus. Asked to evaluate on a five-point scale if they thought the corpus consultation had improved their writing, the majority responded "yes, definitely" (50 per cent) or "yes, probably" (43 per cent) (p. 35). In a less advanced context, Smith (2011) offered his learners the possibility of creating a corpus in areas of interest to them in their studies and reported that they considered corpus creation to be an empowering experience.

Although freely available spoken corpora are less common than their written counterparts, they are slowly becoming more accessible (see Chapter 8, this volume). SACODEYL, for example, is a collection of spoken pedagogic corpora which learners and teachers in secondary education can easily access via the Web. This resource focuses on teen talk, including video-recorded interviews and transcripts of approximately ten minutes with 20 to 25 teenagers in secondary schools in each of the following languages: English, French, German, Italian, Lithuanian, Romanian and Spanish. (For a study of the use of the English corpus, see Pérez-Paredes 2020.) The interview transcripts are available as online corpora. The interviews cover the following topics: personal information, home and family, present and past living routines, hobbies and interests, holidays, school and education, job experiences, plans for the future and open discussion topics. The SACODEYL site illustrates how the problem of decontextualised concordances can be overcome relatively easily, as the context will be very familiar to teenagers. With its combination of videos, transcripts and concordances, SACODEYL provides a rich learning environment for teenagers, integrating the concordances with more traditional language-learning resources such as text and video (see Chapter 7, this volume).

4 DDL, language acquisition and meaning

As empirical studies have revealed generally positive reactions by learners to the consultation of concordances, the question arises as to how this new approach relates to research on second language acquisition. It could be said to constitute a form of comprehensible input (Krashen 1988), particularly when the content of the corpus is carefully chosen to be familiar to the learners (Allan 2009). Corpora such as SACODEYL do, however, differ from Krashen's scenario in one important way. The simplified language or caretaker talk which he describes as helpful to the learner) is absent here, as the language in a native speaker monolingual corpus can be challenging for learners. The speed of the speech and other factors such as repetitions and unfinished sentences may make comprehension difficult without careful scaffolding by the teacher. It does have the great advantage, however, of providing learners with a rich variety of examples and helping them to notice – in the sense in which Schmidt (1990) uses the term – the salient features of the type of language use in the target language which they wish to master.

The examples provided so far, while of interest to the learner and teacher, do not fully convey one of the essential characteristics of DDL. While traditional language-learning resources and methods, and even research, tend to separate the learning of grammar and lexis, in DDL they are seen as fully integrated. Distinguishing between the open-choice principle, according to which the language user has freedom to slot different parts of speech together to form utterances, and the "idiom principle", Sinclair (1991: 110) defines the latter as follows: 'The principle of idiom is that a user has available to him or her a large number of semi-preconstructed phrases that constitute single choices, even though they might appear to be analysable into segments'. For proponents of this approach, concordances facilitate the application of the idiom principle, giving teachers and learners easy access to large numbers of attested examples of use so that the patterns can become clear and the learners can creatively integrate them in their own language use (see Chapter 11, this volume). We have seen how patterns can be illustrated in the highly formulaic context of academic writing. If generally applied in a way which is easily accessible to the learner and teacher, access to multiple examples from appropriate corpus data could thus have a profound effect on language learning and teaching.

The concept of semantic prosody (Louw 1993: 157) takes this patterning a step further, showing how certain forms can be imbued with 'a consistent aura of meaning' by their collocates. Xiao and McEnery (2006: 106) provide a useful table of semantic prosodies in English which have been observed by various researchers, showing how "happen", "cause", "end up", "a recipe for" and "signs of" have negative connotations. They also point out that 'semantic prosodies are typically negative, with relatively few of them bearing an affectively positive meaning'. However, as Louw (1993: 173) noted, a speaker/writer can violate a semantic prosody to achieve some effect in the hearer, such as irony, insincerity or humour.

In French, for example, the verb *"se jouer"* normally has connotations of major events with genuinely or potentially disastrous connotations. In the following concordance lines from a million-word corpus of journalistic writing in French (Chambers and Rostand 2005), the potentially negative connotations are clear. (The corpus contains 54 occurrences of this pronomial verb, of which 16 are literal: 11 referring to sporting events and 5 to theatrical performances. The remaining 38 are used in the figurative sense as discussed here.)

(4)

les chaises renversées, les traces de sang sur les murs disent le drame qui **s'est joué** ici, où trois kamikaze ont opéré. « J'ai entendu deux explosions

Dans le box des accusés, celui-ci est tendu. Il sait que son sort **se joue** peut-être dans cette audience.

est devenue politique, au point que l'on peut supposer que tout, en réalité, va **se jouer**, maintenant, entre l'Elysée et la Maison Blanche.

avec Clemenceau et de Gaulle, parmi ces grands irréguliers dont la destinée **s'est jouée** sur un moment crucial où leur singularité l'a emporté

« Notre avenir **se jouera** demain matin, au tribunal de commerce de Béthunes.

(Chambers and Rostand 2005)

This strong semantic prosody is, however, violated in the reference to "L'acteur principal du petit drame qui s'est joué à l'arrivée, au télésiège", which describes the journalist's ironic account of the minor drama of the cancellation of a skiing competition. Consulting a concordance is thus a useful way for a learner at an advanced level not only to discover instances of semantic prosody but also the contexts in which it can be violated, thus providing examples of language creativity.

Ellis 2002 The examples of semantic prosody illustrate another aspect of second language acquisition theory which is of particular relevance to the use of corpora, namely the importance of frequency. The term is used in different ways by corpus linguists and by those researching the language-learning process. For the corpus linguist, frequency refers to the fact that by analysing a corpus, one can discover what words, expressions and collocations occur very frequently. This information is important both for researchers in linguistics and for language-learning professionals so that they can ensure that they are emphasising the most frequently occurring aspects of language use in their classes, course books or grammars, or at the very least not omitting them. In the language-learning context, frequency refers rather to the number of times a learner has to encounter an aspect of language use to be aware of it and to be able to use it. DDL brings these two uses of the term together by allowing the learners to have access to corpora so that they can discover frequent patterns and, perhaps more importantly, observe a large variety of examples of their use. Thus DDL, while encouraging learners to take an active part in their learning, is also contributing to a revival of interest in frequency, not the mindless repetition of behaviourism, but rather what Ellis (2002: 177) calls 'mindful repetition in an engaging communicative context by motivated learners' (see also Chapter 23, this volume).

5 DDL: changing language pedagogy?

We have already seen how the role of the learner is more active in DDL. This can take the form of analysing a concordance prepared by the teacher, following up on feedback on a piece of written work, consulting a corpus directly to find an answer to a specific problem or studying the language use of a particular group of native or expert speakers or writers, such as teenagers or academic writers. The role of teachers also changes fundamentally, as they are no longer the sole source of knowledge about the target language, but rather facilitators of the learning process, helping the learners to interpret the data and giving them advice on how best to search the corpus and analyse their search results. Kennedy and Miceli propose a four-stage search strategy for learners:

1. Formulate the question
2. Devise a search strategy
3. Observe the examples and select relevant ones
4. Draw conclusions.

(Kennedy and Miceli 2001: 82)

As they analyse the results of their students' exploration of a corpus, they develop a series of tips to help the learners to get the most benefit from the data. In a later publication, Kennedy and Miceli (2017) argue that the aim to give language learners at the intermediate level the corpus analysis skills of linguistic researchers is inappropriate. Their approach is rather 'to downplay the learner-as-researcher notion, and instead seek to cultivate in learners a propensity for open-ended searches, and an "observe and borrow chunks" mentality' (2017: 93).

This new learning environment thus demands new skills from teachers, including knowledge about what corpora are available, pedagogic approaches to corpus consultation and analysis skills and the capacity to decide how best to present the data to the learners, either as pre-prepared concordances, through resources such as *Quicklinks*, or as a resource to be directly explored by the learners. In addition, teachers and learners now engage in a new way of "reading" a text – not just left to right, but from the centre outwards, and vertically up and down, something which the majority of them will not have done before (Timmis 2015: 138). In an environment where web literacy is the norm, however, the innovative aspect of this practice may be less of a challenge, particularly for the learners.

In addition to the challenge of acquiring these new skills, consulting corpus data changes the relationship between the teacher and the target language. When faced with examples of variation in a corpus, a teacher is encouraged – or even obliged – to adopt a descriptive rather than a prescriptive approach to target language use. After studying the 236 occurrences of the singular noun "majorité" in *The Chambers-Rostand Corpus of Journalistic French* in relation to singular and plural verb forms, for example, a teacher would be forced to rethink the practice of correcting students' use of the plural. Singular and plural forms both commonly occur, including one use of the plural by a former French president: '*D'ailleurs Jacques Chirac lui-même l'a dit: "Je sais que la grande* ***majorité*** *des Corses veulent rester français*'. It is nonetheless tempting at times to edit a pre-prepared concordance, not with a desire to be prescriptive, but to avoid confusing the learners, particularly when looking for examples of an aspect of language use which is problematic for them. Other challenges are also presented to teachers, such as the presence of taboo language in corpora of spontaneous conversation for example, such as the *Corpus of London Teenagers* or the *Limerick Corpus of Irish English* (Farr *et al.* 2004).

The teacher wishing to include corpus data thus faces a number of challenges, particularly as this is an area for which the majority of language teacher education courses do not prepare them. As Leńko-Szymańska (2017: 217) notes, 'the development of a model of effective teacher training in data-driven learning is a challenge which has not been adequately tackled in the literature to date'. A number of researchers in corpora and language learning (Conrad 2000; Chambers 2019; Farr and O'Keeffe 2019) recommend the inclusion of corpus consultation in language teacher education as the way to overcome the barrier which currently exists to the addition of corpora to the resources commonly available to learners: the grammar, dictionary and course book. However, Leńko-Szymańska's (2017) study concludes that a one-off course or module focusing specifically on corpora is not the most effective way to provide student teachers with the necessary skills. She recommends rather that corpus consultation should be integrated in various parts of the teacher education programme.

In a review of DDL research within the broad area of computer-assisted language learning between 2011 and 2015, Pérez-Paredes (2019) notes that it concentrates mainly on writing skills in higher education and identifies two further factors which inhibit the expansion of DDL across the landscape of mainstream language education. These are the lack of syllabus integration and the lack of contribution from language teachers other than researchers. It is easy to understand the lack of syllabus integration, as teachers in higher education have much greater freedom in syllabus choices than their counterparts at other levels of language education. Some of the developments mentioned earlier in this chapter, such as customised corpora for learners (Allan 2009), multimodal corpora in relevant genres such as SACODEYL and integrated web-based resources such as *Quicklinks*, could make an important contribution to the expansion of DDL. In conclusion, despite the very substantial body of research which exists on DDL and the increasing availability of resources, it seems clear that there is still ample scope for developments if it is to cross the research–practice gap and become integrated in day-to-day practice across language education in a wide variety of languages.

Further reading

Friginal, E. (2018) *Corpus Linguistics for English Teachers*, New York and London: Routledge. (This book provides a lot of detail on available corpora, corpus query tools, research publications on corpora and language learning and practical ideas for using corpora in the classroom.)

Leńko-Szymańska, A. and Boulton, A. (eds) (2015) *Multiple Affordances of Language Corpora for Data-Driven Learning*, Amsterdam: Benjamins. (This volume includes introductory chapters relating corpora to language pedagogy and language-learning theories, followed by chapters reporting on projects involving corpora in both language learning and translator education.)

Poole, R. (2018) *A Guide to Using Corpora for English Language Learners*, Edinburgh: Edinburgh University Press. (This book is aimed at both teachers and learners. It is a practical guide which provides suggestions for learners and teachers who wish to incorporate consultation of corpus data in the language-learning process.)

References

Ackerley, K. (2017) 'Effects of Corpus-Based Instruction on Phraseology in Learner English', *Language Learning & Technology* 21(3): 195–216.

Ahmad, K., Corbett, G. and Rogers, M. (1985) 'Using Computers with Advanced Language Learners: An Example', *The Language Teacher* 9(3): 4–7.

Allan, R. (2009) 'Can a Graded Reader Corpus Provide "Authentic" Input?' *ELT Journal* 63(1): 23–32.

Anthony, L. (2019) *AntConc* (Version 3.5.8) (Computer Software), Tokyo, Japan: Waseda University.

Boulton, A. (2010) 'Learning Outcomes from Corpus Consultation', in M. Moreno Jaén, F. Serrano Valverde and M. Calzada Pérez (eds) *Exploring New Paths in Language Pedagogy: Lexis and Corpus-Based Language Teaching*, London: Equinox, pp. 129–44.

Boulton, A. (2017) 'Corpora in Language Teaching and Learning', *Language Teaching* 50(4): 483–506.

Boulton, A. (2020) 'Foreward: Data-Driven Learning for Younger Learners: Obstacles and Optimism', in P. Crosthwaite (ed.) *Data-Driven Learning for the Next Generation: Corpora and DDL for Pre-Tertiary Learners*, London: Routledge, pp. 14–20.

Boulton, A. and Cobb, T. (2017) 'Corpus Use in Language Learning: A Meta-Analysis', *Language Learning* 67(2): 348–93.

Braun, S. (2005) 'From Pedagogically Relevant Corpora to Authentic Language Learning Contents', *ReCALL* 17(1): 47–64.

Braun, S. (2007) 'Integrating Corpus Work into Secondary Education: From Data-Driven Learning to Needs-Driven Corpora', *ReCALL* 19(3): 307–28.

Breyer, Y. (2009) 'Learning and Teaching with Corpora: Reflections by Student Teachers', *Computer Assisted Language Learning* 22(2): 153–72.

Chambers, A. (2005) 'Integrating Corpus Consultation in Language Studies', *Language Learning & Technology* 9(2): 111–25.

Chambers, A. (2019) 'Towards the Corpus Revolution? Bridging the Research-Practice Gap', *Language Teaching* 52(4): 460–75.

Chambers, A. and Le Baron, F. (eds) (2007) *The Chambers-Le Baron Corpus of Research Articles in French/Le Corpus Chambers-Le Baron d'Srticles de Recherche en Français*, Oxford: Oxford Text Archive. http://ota.ox.ac.uk/desc/2527 [Accessed 31 May 2020].

Chambers, A. and Rostand, S. (eds) (2005) *The Chambers-Rostand Corpus of Journalistic French/ Le Corpus Chambers-Rostand de Français Journalistique*, Oxford, University of Oxford: Oxford Text Archive. http://ota.ox.ac.uk/desc/2491 [Accessed 31 May 2020].

Charles, M. (2007) 'Reconciling Top-Down and Bottom-Up Approaches to Graduate Writing: Using a Corpus to Teach Rhetorical Functions', *Journal of English for Academic Purposes* 6(4): 289–302.

Charles, M. (2014) 'Getting the Corpus Habit: EAP Students' Long-Term Use of Personal Corpora', *English for Specific Purposes* 35: 30–40.

Cobb, T. (1997) 'Is There Any Measurable Learning from Hands On Concordancing?', *System*, 25(3): 301–15.

Cobb, T. and Boulton, A. (2015) 'Classroom Applications of Corpus Analysis', in D. Biber and R. Reppen (eds) *The Cambridge Handbook of English Corpus Linguistics*, Cambridge: Cambridge University Press, pp. 478–97.

Conrad, S. (2000) 'Will Corpus Linguistics Revolutionize Grammar Teaching in the Twenty-First Century?', *TESOL Quarterly* 34(3): 548–60.

Crosthwaite P. (2020) 'DDL and Young Learners: Introduction to the Volume', in P. Crosthwaite (ed.) *Data-Driven Learning for the Next Generation: Corpora and DDL for Pre-Tertiary Learners*, London: Routledge, pp. 1–10.

Davies, M. (2008) *The Corpus of Contemporary American English: 450 Million Words, 1990-Present*, Retrieved from http://corpus.byu.edu/coca/ [Accessed 31 May 2020].

Ellis, N. (2002) 'Frequency Effects in Language Processing. A Review with Implications for Theories of Implicit and Explicit Language Acquisition', *Studies in Second Language Acquisition* 24: 143–88.

Farr, F., Murphy, B. and O'Keeffe, A. (2004) 'The Limerick Corpus of Irish English: Design, Description and Application', *Teanga* 21: 5–29.

Farr, F. and O'Keeffe, A. (2019) 'Using Corpus Approaches in English Language Teacher Education', in S. Walsh and S. Mann (eds) *The Routledge Handbook of English Language Teacher Education*, London: Routledge, pp. 268–82.

Flowerdew, L. (2015) 'Data-Driven Learning and Language Learning Theories: Whither the Twain Shall Meet', in A. Leńko-Szymańska and A. Boulton (eds) *Multiple Affordances of Language Corpora for Data-Driven Learning*, Amsterdam: Benjamins, pp. 15–36.

Friginal, E. (2018) *Corpus Linguistics for English Teachers*, New York and London: Routledge.

Gaskell, D. and Cobb, T. (2004) 'Can Learners Use Concordance Feedback for Writing Errors?', *System* 32(3): 301–19.

Granger, S. (2015) 'The Contribution of Learner Corpora to Reference and Instructional Materials Design', in S. Granger, G. Gilquin and F. Meunier (eds) *The Cambridge Handbook of Learner Corpus Research*, Cambridge: Cambridge University Press, pp. 486–510.

Hadley, G. and Charles, M. (2017) 'Enhancing Extensive Reading with Data-Driven Learning', *Language Learning & Technology* 21(3): 131–52.

Hirata, Y. and Hirata, Y. (2019) 'Applying "Sketch Engine for Language Learning" in the Japanese English classroom', *Journal of Computing in Higher Education* 31: 233–48.

Johns, T. (1986) 'Micro-Concord: A Language Learner's Research Tool', *System* 14(2): 151–62.

Johns, T. (1997) 'Contexts: The Background, Development, and Trialling of a Concordance-Based CALL Program', in A. Wichmann, S. Fligelstone, T. McEnery and G. Knowles (eds) *Teaching and Language Corpora*, London; New York: Longman, pp. 100–15.

Kennedy, C. and Miceli, T. (2001) 'An Evaluation of Intermediate Students' Approaches to Corpus Investigation', *Language Learning and Technology* 5(3): 77–90.

Kennedy, C. and Miceli, T. (2017) 'Cultivating Effective Corpus Use by Language Learners', *Computer Assisted Language Learning* 30(1–2): 91–114.

Kent, A. and Lancour, H. (eds) (1968) *Encyclopedia of Library and Information Science*, Vol. 1, New York: Basel: Marcel Dekker Inc.

Knight, D., Morris, S. and Fitzpatrick, T. (2021) *Corpus Design and Construction in Minoritised Language Contexts – Cynllunio a Chreu Corpws mewn Cyd-destunau Ieithoedd Lleiafrifoledig*, London: Palgrave MacMillan.

Krashen, S. (1988) *Second Language Acquisition and Second Language Learning*, London: Prentice-Hall International.

Lee, S. (2011) 'Challenges of Using Corpora in Language Teaching and Learning: Implications for Secondary Education', *Linguistic Research* 28(1): 159–78.

Lee, D. and Swales, J. (2006) 'A Corpus-Based EAP Course for NNS Doctoral Students: Moving from Available Specialized Corpora to Self-Compiled Corpora', *English for Specific Purposes* 25(1): 56–75.

Lee, H., Warschauer, M. and Lee, J. H. (2019) 'The Effects of Corpus Use on Second Language Vocabulary Learning: A Multilevel Meta-Analysis', *Applied Linguistics* 40(5): 721–53.

Leech, G. (1997) 'Teaching and Language Corpora: A Convergence', in A. Wichmann, S. Fligelstone, T. McEnery and G. Knowles (eds) *Teaching and Language Corpora*, London; New York: Longman, pp. 1–23.

Leńko-Szymańska, A. (2017) 'Training Teachers in Data-Driven Learning: Tackling the Challenge', *Language Learning & Technology* 21(3): 217–41.

Li, S. (2017) 'Using Corpora to Develop Learners' Collocational Competence', *Language Learning & Technology* 21(3): 153–71.

Louw, B. (1993) 'Irony in the Text or Insincerity in the Writer? The Diagnostic Potential of Semantic Prosodies', in M. Baker, G. Francis and E. Tognini-Bonelli (eds) *Text and Technology: In Honour of John Sinclair*, Amsterdam: John Benjamins, pp. 157–76.

Matsuda, Y. and Matsui, S. (1975) 'Effectiveness of KWIC Index as an Information Retrieval Technique for Social Sciences', *Hitot Subashi Journal of Economics* 15(2): 15–40.

McCarthy, M. J. (1998) *Spoken Language and Applied Linguistics*, Cambridge: Cambridge University Press.

McEnery, T. and Wilson, A. (1997) 'Teaching and Language Corpora', *ReCALL* 9(1): 5–14.

Nesi, H. and Gardner, S. (2012) *Genres across the Disciplines: Student Writing in Higher Education*, Cambridge: Cambridge University Press.

Pérez-Paredes, P. (2019) 'A Systematic Review of the Uses and Spread of Corpora and Data-Driven Learning in CALL Research during 2011-2015', *Computer Assisted Language Learning*. 10.1080/09588221.2019.1667832

Pérez-Paredes, P. (2020) 'The Pedagogic Advantage of Teenage Corpora for Secondary School Learners', in P. Crosthwaite (ed.) *Data Driven Learning for the Next Generation: Corpora and DDL for Pre-Tertiary Learners*, London: Routledge, pp. 67–87.
Poole, R. (2018) *A Guide to Using Corpora for English Language Learners*, Edinburgh: Edinburgh University Press.
SACODEYL. System Aided Compilation and Open Distribution of European Youth Language, Retrieved from http://webapps.ael.uni-tuebingen.de/backbone-search/ [Accessed 31 May 2020].
Schmidt, R. (1990) 'The Role of Consciousness in Second Language Learning', *Applied Linguistics* 11(2): 129–58.
Scott, M. (2020) *WordSmith Tools*, version 8, Stroud: Lexical Analysis Software.
Sealey, A. and Thompson, P. (2007) 'Corpus, Concordance, Classification: Young Learners in the L1 Classroom', *Language Awareness* 16(3): 208–23.
Sinclair, J. (1991) *Corpus, Concordance, Collocation*, London: Longman.
Smith, S. (2011) 'Learner Construction of Corpora for General English in Taiwan', *Computer Assisted Language Learning* 24(4): 291–316.
Stevens, V. (1991) 'Concordance-Based Vocabulary Exercises: A Viable Alternative to Gap-Fillers', in T. Johns and P. King (eds) *Classroom Concordancing: English Language Research Journal 4*, Centre for English Language Studies: University of Birmingham: 47–63.
Tribble, C. and Jones, G. (1990) *Concordances in the Classroom: A Resource Book for Teachers*, Harlow: Longman.
Timmis, I. (2015) *Corpus Linguistics for ELT: Research and Practice*, London and New York: Routledge.
Vincent, B. and Nesi, H. (2018) 'The BAWE Quicklinks Project: A New DDL Resource for University Students', *Lidil* [Online] 58.
Widdowson, H. G. (2000) 'On the Limitations of Linguistics Applied', *Applied Linguistics* 21(1): 3–25.
Willis, J. (1998) 'Concordances in the Classroom without a Computer: Assembling and Exploiting Concordances of Common Words', in B. Tomlinson (ed.) *Materials Development in Language Teaching*, Cambridge: Cambridge University Press, pp. 44–66.
Xiao, R. and McEnery, T. (2006) 'Collocation, Semantic Prosody and Near Synonymy: A Cross-Linguistic Perspective', *Applied Linguistics* 27(1): 103–29.

30

Using data-driven learning in language teaching

Gaëtanelle Gilquin and Sylviane Granger

1 The pedagogical functions of data-driven learning

Data-driven learning DDL consists of using the tools and techniques of corpus linguistics for pedagogical purposes (see Chapter 29, this volume). After a modest beginning in the 1980s, the approach started to attract more advocates, and the number of publications began to rise, especially after the turn of the millennium, which can presumably be related to the spread of technologies in language teaching. This rise in DDL publications goes hand in hand with diversification of DDL practices. For example, while DDL was for a long time confined to English, studies on other languages have begun to appear (e.g. Yao 2019); while it was initially more oriented towards university students, its use with young learners has become more widespread (e.g. Crosthwaite 2020); and while it was first almost exclusively limited to writing, activities involving spoken and multimodal corpora have now emerged (e.g. Hirata 2020; Meunier 2020). Recent meta-analyses have started to take stock of the body of research on DDL, either in general (e.g. Boulton and Cobb 2017; Pérez-Paredes 2019) or with a more specific focus (e.g. Lee *et al.* 2019 on DDL for vocabulary learning; Mizumoto and Chujo 2015 on DDL for English learning in Japan).

The use of DDL in language teaching presents several advantages. The first one is that it brings authenticity into the classroom. Not only do corpora make it possible to expose learners to authentic language, but they can actually present them with a large number of authentic instances of a particular linguistic item. This 'condensed exposure' (Gabrielatos 2005: 10) can, among other things, contribute to vocabulary expansion or heightened awareness of language patterns.

Secondly, DDL has an important corrective function. Learners, by comparing their own writing with data produced by (native) expert writers or by consulting a learner corpus where errors have been annotated, can find the help they need to correct their own interlanguage features (misuse, overuse, underuse) and thus improve their writing. As pointed out by Nesselhauf (2004: 140), this is particularly useful for fossilised errors.

The DDL approach also has the advantage of including an element of discovery which arguably makes learning more motivating and more fun. In the DDL literature,

DOI: 10.4324/9780367076399-30

learners are described, alternatively, as travellers (Bernardini 2001: 227), researchers (Johns 1997: 101) or detectives with Johns's (1997: 101) slogan 'Every student a Sherlock Holmes'. By means of various activities (see Section 3), learners are encouraged to observe corpus data, make hypotheses and formulate rules in order to gain insights into language (inductive approach) or to check the validity of rules from their grammars or textbooks (deductive approach). They thus become more involved, more active and, ultimately, more autonomous in the learning process.

More generally, learners are said to acquire (or at least refine) a number of crucial learning skills through the use of DDL. O'Sullivan (2007: 277) lists the following: 'predicting, observing, noticing, thinking, reasoning, analysing, interpreting, reflecting, exploring, making inferences (inductively or deductively), focusing, guessing, comparing, differentiating, theorising, hypothesising, and verifying'. These skills can be used to explore language, but since they are general cognitive skills, they may also be transferred to other fields of study.

2 Data-driven learning material

In order to adopt a DDL methodology, two main resources are needed: a corpus and a tool to exploit it. The choice of the corpus is crucial. It would probably not be wrong to say that any type of corpus may be used in DDL, and indeed, the literature on DDL mentions quite a large range of corpora: written, spoken or multimodal, monolingual or bilingual, general or specialised, native or non-native, raw or annotated, etc. As can be expected, however, particular corpora are best suited for certain purposes. English for specific purposes corpora, for example, allow teachers to 'equip students with the communicative skills they need to participate in particular disciplinary contexts' (Hyland 2019: xiii; see Chapters 24 and 28, this volume). Bilingual corpora, which show original texts and their translations side by side, may help translation trainees by 'drawing [their] attention to (un)typical solutions for typical problems found by *mature*, expert translators' (Bernardini 2004: 20, emphasis original; see also Chapter 34, this volume). Learner corpora, which are made up of data produced by non-native speakers of the language, can be extremely useful for form-focused instruction (see, e.g. Granger and Tribble 1998) by making students aware of typical interlanguage features, while also contributing to increased motivation.

Whatever the type of corpus chosen, one important issue is that of its authenticity. Of course, in a way, corpora are always authentic in the sense that they contain language produced in natural settings. However, scholars like Widdowson (2000) argue that corpora may lack authenticity at the receptive end. Thus, learners may find it hard to relate to texts that were produced in a different culture within a context that is not necessarily familiar to them. Sripicharn (2004), who compares how native speakers and learners deal with concordance-based tasks, shows that native speakers are better able than learners to contextualise the concordance lines (by identifying the setting of the concordances and the text type from which they are extracted). Several solutions have been proposed in the literature to help learners 'authenticate' (Widdowson 2003: 66) the materials they are working with, for example, using a corpus of recent news items (Chambers 2005) or asking the students to compile their own 'personal corpus' (Chen and Flowerdew 2018: 343), which could, for instance, include research articles in their discipline (see Chapters 24 and 29, this volume).

Two types of corpora that appear particularly helpful for the process of authentication are the pedagogic corpus (Willis 2003) and the local learner corpus (Seidlhofer 2002). The former is a corpus 'created not for linguistic research but specifically for language learning purposes' (Chambers 2019: 464), which could, for example, consist of the texts used in the classroom to support teaching. Such corpora are better contextualised and more directly relevant to learners.

The second type of corpus that seems promising in terms of authenticity is the local learner corpus, which contains data produced by the very same students who use the corpus. These students are thus 'both participants in and analysts of their own language use' (Seidlhofer 2002: 213), and the interlanguage features represented in the corpus are the features of their own interlanguage. This also means that the teacher can provide 'tailor-made feedback' (Mukherjee 2006: 19) to the learners, either as a group or individually. As shown by Cotos (2014: 218), the use of local learner corpora is a particularly effective practice that can be readily integrated into DDL instruction.

Another important issue when it comes to the choice of a corpus is annotation (see Chapter 2, this volume). Corpora can be used as raw text, i.e. with no annotation of any kind, or they can be annotated with additional information such as part-of-speech (POS tagging), syntactic structure (parsing) or, in the case of learner corpora, errors (error tagging). Raw corpora offer numerous possibilities for the exploration of language by learners. However, they also have their limitations. For example, a raw corpus may involve a lot of editing (by the teacher or learner) to get rid of unwanted concordance lines, whereas a POS-tagged or parsed corpus may help refine the search query (for example, selecting *to* as a preposition and not as an infinitive marker) and thus reduce the amount of necessary editing. As for error tagging, it makes it much easier to notice interlanguage features and often comes with possible corrections, which can help learners revise their own texts.

Corpora are of little help if they are not combined with a tool to exploit them (see Chapters 9 and 10, this volume). Corpus query tools used in DDL should be 'learner-friendly' (Lee *et al.* 2019: 747) and accessible to users who have limited experience with corpora. As rightly underlined by Crosthwaite and Cheung (2019: 171), '[c]omplicated or unappealing corpus query tools are (…) one of the biggest hurdles for the successful uptake of DDL'. Kilgarriff *et al.* (2015: 66), for instance, describe how they designed *SKELL* (*Sketch Engine for Language Learners*) as 'a stripped-down, non-scary version of Sketch Engine for use by learners'. *BNClab* (Brezina *et al.* 2018), a platform developed at Lancaster University, makes it easy to search a spoken sample of the *British National Corpus* and to compare the first edition of the corpus with the 2014 edition. The platform is particularly attractive through data visualisation, which arguably makes learners more receptive to the information they discover. *TLC Hub*, also developed at Lancaster University, offers the same facilities to query learner speech from the *Trinity Lancaster Corpus* (Gablasova *et al.* 2019; http://cass.lancs.ac.uk/trinity-lancaster-corpus). Other tools, like the MICASE and MICUSP interfaces or Mark Davies's English-Corpora.org website, can also be useful for learners, especially if they are combined with some guides explaining how to use the tools (see, e.g., Poole 2018 for English-Corpora.org). *WordSmith Tools* (Scott 2020) has an interesting option for DDL, namely the possibility of creating exercises by blanking out the search words in concordances.

3 The operationalisation of data-driven learning

The range of activities that are possible in DDL is wide and, as Breyer (2006: 162) puts it, 'limited only by the imagination of the user'. Space prevents the reviewing of all these possibilities, but in this section, we give a broad overview of the way DDL may be operationalised and we show how the choice of presentation and activity may depend on a variety of factors (see Chapters 28, 29 and 31, this volume).

The first major decision when doing DDL is whether to let learners query the corpus themselves (direct approach) or to provide them with materials prepared by the teacher on the basis of corpus analysis (indirect approach) (see Yoon and Jo 2014 on this distinction). This choice depends on the availability – or not – of the necessary hardware and software for learners, but it is also a function of the learners' level. Thus, Boulton (2008a: 38) suggests that 'DDL in early stages can eliminate the computer from the equation by using prepared materials on paper'. The effect of a direct vs. indirect approach to DDL is still relatively unclear. While it has often been claimed that the indirect approach, through the use of printed materials, is more effective, Boulton and Cobb's (2017) meta-analysis shows that the opposite seems to be true, and Vyatkina (2016) finds the two approaches equally effective.

In indirect DDL, teachers have the possibility of presenting the corpus data in various ways. Concordance lines may be truncated (keyword-in-context [KWIC] view) or take the shape of complete sentences, the whole concordance may be provided to the learner or just a selection of it and the concordance lines may be edited or presented in their original form. Each presentation has its pros and cons. The KWIC view may be confusing, especially for beginners. Johns (1986: 157) observes that learners' first reaction is often to complain about the 'unfinished sentences'. However, the KWIC view, with all the occurrences of the search word aligned under one another, makes patterns more visible than the sentence view, and Boulton (2009a) actually reports an experiment with lower-intermediate learners where KWICs provided better results than full sentence contexts. Next, the concordancer output may be used as is or be manipulated in some way. Manipulation may involve the selection of a subset of the concordance, often with the aim of reducing the data to manageable quantities. Several criteria have been proposed in the literature to perform this selection, including readability (the most difficult concordance lines are discarded, cf. Kuo *et al.* 2001), frequency (only the concordance lines illustrating the most frequent uses are kept, cf. Levy 1990) and usefulness (only those concordance lines that are judged useful are kept, cf. Tribble 1997). DDL has been claimed to be more effective when the concordance lines are carefully selected by the teacher (Lee *et al.* 2019). However, as rightly pointed out by Gabrielatos (2005: 18), '[t]his manipulation should be carried out with the understanding that the adapted samples are not good guides to the frequency of a language item'. Manipulation may also consist in editing the concordances, either superficially (e.g. through colour coding or highlighting, cf. Wicher 2020) or, more substantially, by simplifying them (cf. Gabrielatos 2005). While such simplification might be said to undermine the authenticity advantage of DDL and leave learners unprepared 'for the realities of the authentic language we are presumably preparing them for' (Boulton 2009b: 89), Nesselhauf's (2004) discussion of a concordance of the verb *suggest* in the LOCNESS corpus (a corpus of argumentative essays by British and American students) and the German subcorpus of the *International Corpus of Learner English* is a good example of why manipulation is sometimes necessary in DDL (especially with beginners):

> As the lines are now, they could be confusing for learners in many respects: there is at least one typographical error (*suggested than* instead of *that* in LOCNESS); one of the occurrences of *to* after *suggest* does not constitute wrong complementation (*could suggest to her two colleagues*); and, as *suggesting* only occurs in the learner but not in the native speaker corpus, learners might even come to the conclusion that this construction is not possible in English.
>
> *(Nesselhauf 2004: 143–4)*

DDL activities may be located along a cline ranging from teacher-led to learner-led (Mukherjee 2006; see also Gabrielatos 2005). At the teacher-led end, we find relatively controlled tasks such as cloze tests and fill-in exercises. At the learner-led end, we find what Bernardini (2004: 22) calls 'discovery learning', which involves 'brows[ing] large and varied text collections in open-ended, exploratory ways'. As we move from one end of the cline to the other, learners have more freedom and bear more responsibility for their own instruction, deciding, for example, what they are going to investigate and how they want to go about it. In between totally teacher-led DDL and totally learner-led DDL, there is a whole range of activities, with various types of 'filters' exercised by the teacher (Gavioli 2005: 30). By way of illustration, here are a few activities that could be undertaken in the classroom. Learners could be shown a concordance sorted alphabetically and be encouraged to notice the repetition of certain lexical chunks or be asked to group the patterns in a meaningful way. They could be given a series of blanked-out concordances illustrating different contexts of a word and be required to find the missing word. Alternatively, the concordances could come from a bilingual corpus, so that learners can use the translations to help them find the missing word. The potential of DDL for editing one's own work has already been mentioned earlier, and many studies in the literature show how students can use corpora to revise their work, either by correcting problems underlined by the teacher or by deciding themselves what they want to check with the help of the corpus (Kennedy and Miceli 2001; see also Crosthwaite and Stell 2020 on DDL for text revision in a first language context). One use that tends to be neglected in the DDL literature is the use of the corpus as a 'sleeping resource' (Johns 1988: 22) to help learners when the need arises, for example, to answer a question that has suddenly arisen during the lesson.

While concordances are probably the main component of DDL, other formats are possible. Frequency lists, which list all the words of the corpus in descending order of frequency, may prove to be a valuable resource as well, for example, as a means of learning more about the subject of a text and its meaning (Aston 2001). It is also possible to compare two frequency lists built on the basis of different corpora. The comparison could involve two varieties of English (e.g. British vs. American English) or two genres or text types (e.g. fiction vs. journalese, speech vs. writing), with the aim of making learners more sensitive to language variation. Learners could also compare a frequency list representing learner production (ideally, their own production) and one representing expert production, which would make them aware of the words that tend to be underused or overused by learners. The words from the frequency lists can then be used as a starting point for concordance analysis. Most corpus query tools nowadays also enable users to automatically extract collocates and lexical bundles. These, like frequency lists, may serve as a good starting point for the further analysis of language – in this case, language in its phraseological dimension. Another way to exploit corpora in the classroom is to read entire portions of the corpus. This is what Charles (2007: 295) recommends for the study of rhetorical functions: A particular search item is used as 'a probe to locate the part of a text in which a given rhetorical function may occur', and the context is then expanded to the whole paragraph or the whole text to see how the function is expressed. Finally, although DDL has mainly been used with written data, it can also be used with speech, provided spoken or multimodal corpora are available. Meunier (2020: 13) hence recommends 'adopting new ways of DDL-izing teaching practices by including more multimodality (sound, video, pictures)' and provides illustrations of how internet videos can be used for DDL.

The choice of presentation and activity depends on a number of factors, among them the learning context, learners' level and the phenomenon investigated. Thus, the direct approach to DDL and focus on the learner's individual needs may be easier in the context of a one-to-one consultation (such as described by Johns 2002) than in the context of a classroom activity. An activity meant to be carried out as part of a homework assignment or in distance education (cf. Collins 2000) may have to contain more explicit instructions and "signposts" than one which takes place in class, with the teacher as a guide and the fellow students as "travel companions". The learner's level (both in terms of language proficiency and familiarity with DDL) is also important when deciding on a particular presentation of the data and a specific activity. This probably explains why scholars do not seem to agree on the level of the learners for whom DDL is appropriate. Depending on the methods they have in mind, DDL may be suitable for a given audience or not. In fact, it has been argued that DDL is possible with all learners (even beginners), but that (i) the method has to be adapted to the learners' level (Hadley 2002) and (ii) results may vary, with beginners 'draw[ing] relatively low-level conclusions about the structuring of the language' and more advanced learners 'mak[ing] more subtle high-level inferences' on the basis of one and the same concordance (Johns 1986: 159). Meta-analyses like Boulton and Cobb (2017) and Lee *et al.* (2019), however, suggest that DDL works best from an intermediate level upwards. Another aspect that should be taken into account when choosing a way of approaching DDL is the phenomenon to be investigated. Many authors claim that DDL is most effective 'on the "collocational border" between syntax and lexis' (Johns 2002: 109; see also Levy 1990 or O'Sullivan and Chambers 2006). However, it can also work with other phenomena and with larger units than individual words, for example, syntactic constructions (e.g. Gilquin 2021) or aspects of discourse (e.g. Charles 2007), although, here again, some adaptation may be required.

A final note is that despite the attraction of some methods (like concordances) and some phenomena (Kennedy and Miceli 2001: 83 refer to the 'lure of prepositions'), a key word in DDL is variety. Not only does variety make it possible to prevent tediousness among learners (a problem often highlighted in the literature, cf. Chambers 2007), but it also caters to learners' different preferences. Similarly, since it is precisely one of the goals of DDL to foster more autonomous learning, the teacher should avoid conformity as far as possible and agree to let the students approach corpora in the way they feel most comfortable with (Hunston 2002).

4 Evaluating data-driven learning

Like any pedagogical method, it is important that DDL be properly evaluated. As pointed out by Boulton (2008b), three types of evaluation can be carried out: evaluation of the attitudes (what do participants think about DDL?), practices (how well are learners doing with DDL?) and efficiency (can learners gain benefit from DDL?). While attitudes and practices are important, the criterion that ultimately should be decisive in determining whether DDL is worth doing or not is efficiency. Learners may enjoy DDL and be good at it, but if they do not learn anything from it, there is no point in adding this to a curriculum that is already overloaded.

With regard to attitudes, a survey of the literature reveals generally positive feelings among learners (e.g. Mizumoto and Chujo 2015), but also some negative ones (e.g. Quan 2016). Certain authors even report both positive and negative attitudes among the same learners. The students in Kennedy and Miceli (2001), for example, found DDL helpful and confidence-boosting, but sometimes also discouraging, time-consuming and frustrating. What is often neglected in such evaluative studies and should be considered more closely is teachers' attitudes towards DDL. The evaluation of practices, i.e. learners' capacities to do DDL, also produces mixed results (cf. Kennedy and Miceli 2001; Hadley 2002). As for efficiency, which can be considered crucial for the future of DDL, recent meta-analyses like Boulton and Cobb (2017) reveal generally large effect sizes for comparisons of pre- and post-tests or control and experimental groups, which suggests that DDL does work. However, some caveats should be mentioned. First, effect sizes may display a great deal of variation according to the moderator variables that are taken into account in these meta-analyses (study design, language focus, etc.). Second, these meta-analyses only consider certain types of studies – in particular, experimental and quantitative studies. For approaches that are not (or not well) represented in the meta-analyses, the jury is still out. Thus, although Boulton and Cobb (2017: 378) mention rather positive results for the few studies that have evaluated the use of corpora as reference resources, Ackerley (2017) obtains mixed results in a free writing task, while observing that short-answer activities such as gap-filling tend to generate more positive results. Third, delayed post-testing is often lacking (Boulton and Cobb 2017), which means that the longer-term effects on the development of more general skills that is regularly presented as a strength of DDL have so far not really been evaluated. Given the difficulty of assessing such effects (see Cobb and Boulton 2015), however, this is unlikely to change anytime soon. As this brief survey shows, many results are still inconclusive and even contradictory. The effects of DDL are dependent on so many different variables that replication studies are particularly needed in this field and should be encouraged.

5 The problems and limitations of data-driven learning

While the evaluations of DDL seem to suggest that its future 'looks rather bright' (Boulton and Cobb 2017: 388), one must recognise along with Mizumoto and Chujo (2015: 12) that 'not so many researchers and practitioners make use of its potential in their teaching practice'. This may be because the implementation of DDL in the classroom presents a number of difficulties, some of which are examined here.

Logistics has often been cited as one of the biggest problems of DDL. Thanks to the increasingly widespread use of laptops among students, as well as the development of DDL on mobile devices (cf. Quan 2016), in most situations this is no longer seen as a major problem (although it may still be a real issue in less developed countries). In addition, many resources are now freely available: corpus query tools like *AntConc* (Anthony 2019) and a large number of texts or off-the-shelf corpora downloadable from the internet (see Chapter 9, this volume). What is still largely missing is ready-made

DDL materials for teachers in the form of worksheets, teaching plans or textbooks. For teachers who have no such materials available to them, the preparation of DDL activities is time-consuming. Equally time-consuming is the DDL task itself (Díez Bedmar 2006 describes an activity that took one hour and a half for just one word). And according to some, the results 'might not repay the time taken' (Willis, cited in Hunston 2002: 178).

If we consider the teacher's point of view, one reason for not doing DDL might simply be that the teacher does not know enough about corpora and the possibility of using corpora in the classroom. There is therefore a need for better integration of DDL into teacher training programmes (Hirata 2020; see also Chapter 32, this volume), as well as guides to using corpora that are specifically designed for teachers (e.g. Friginal 2018). As Mauranen (2004: 100) points out, '[b]efore learners can be introduced to good corpus skills, their teachers need to possess them in the first place'. In some cases, the teacher may be familiar with corpora and DDL but prefer, for some reason, not to adopt such a methodology with his or her students. A number of practical objections might be raised by the teacher, but these may actually be 'camouflage for more profound theoretical concerns about the nature of learning' (Boulton 2009b: 99), and more especially about the teacher's possible loss of control over what happens during the lesson, which may be experienced as a 'loss of expertise' by the teacher (Hunston 2002: 171).

For learners too, DDL may sometimes appear rather off-putting. Although most learners will be used to technologies, working with corpora may not be straightforward to them and may necessitate quite some training to acquire the basic skills (reading concordances, interpreting lists of collocates, etc.) – what Mukherjee (2002: 179) calls 'corpus literacy' (see also Sripicharn 2010 on the importance of preparing learners for using corpora). Students may have 'difficulty devising effective search strategies' (O'Sullivan and Chambers 2006: 60) because of faulty spelling, for example, or simply because of the complexity of the processes involved (see Sun 2003 for a good example of ineffective search strategy), and they may draw wrong inferences on the basis of the evidence – what O'Keeffe (2021) calls 'fake discovery' (see Sripicharn 2004 for an illustration). It must also be stressed that DDL (and, in particular, the inductive learning strategies that it often entails) may be more suitable for certain learners than for others (Gilquin 2021).

The final aspect that may explain some of the reluctance to apply DDL has to do with its content. We have already mentioned the problem of authentication (or lack thereof) of the corpus data. In addition, the output of the search query may contain too much or too little data, or no data at all – which, for learners, poses the question of the distinction between 'The phenomenon does not exist' and 'There is no evidence for it in this corpus' (Kennedy and Miceli 2001: 86). It may include too much noise, i.e. irrelevant hits, or it may be too difficult for learners to understand because of insufficient knowledge of the target language (Koosha and Jafarpour 2006: 206). It could also be that the corpus shows more details than the student is expected to learn or contains language which the teacher does not want the students to imitate, for example, non-standard forms, swear words or literary phrases. Another problem is that the DDL approach may not be effective for all aspects of language, with some questions more 'concordance-ready' than others (Johns 1988: 25). As pointed out by Ädel (2010: 48), DDL has tended to focus on 'surface forms', especially lexico-grammatical features, which lend themselves well to corpus analysis, while disregarding genre-related aspects which are less obviously tractable (but see Cotos *et al.* 2017; Crosthwaite and Cheung 2019). More generally,

Gabrielatos (2005: 21) warns against the dangers of 'corpus worship' and 'frequency worship', hence suggesting that corpora are no panacea and that other factors besides frequency have to be considered for teaching to be successful.

These problems should not deter us from doing DDL, which, as was shown earlier, is a promising technique bringing learners into contact with potentially large amounts of authentic language, motivating them through the element of discovery, developing important cognitive skills and, more generally, providing benefits which arguably go well beyond the knowledge of the phenomenon under study and could really empower students. However, it is important to use this technique in full awareness of its limitations to avoid the risk of "DDL worship". This should imply, among other things, adapting DDL to the specific learning situation in which it takes place, but also better integrating DDL into the national curriculum (Papaioannou *et al.* 2020) and combining it with more traditional teaching methods (Chen and Flowerdew 2018). If DDL is to become a viable technique, it is also crucial that it should move out of its favourite spheres of action: from English classes to classes in other languages and from universities to secondary and primary education (see Vyatkina 2020), but also from the classroom to everyday life (see Chen and Flowerdew 2018; Meunier 2020). Studies have shown that learners usually stop using corpora after the in-class DDL training/activities (see, e.g. Crosthwaite and Cheung 2019), although, as shown by Charles (2014), when learners build their personal corpus in their own field, they tend to continue using it after the course has finished. Capitalising on the young generation's technological habits (cf. the parallel drawn between corpus consultation and internet searches in Cobb and Boulton 2015), one needs to induce a transfer of corpus skills from a language learning situation to an everyday language use situation, thus turning "data-driven learning" into "data-driven use" and making language *learners* evolve into autonomous language *users*.

Further reading

Boulton, A. and Cobb, T. (2017) 'Corpus Use in Language Learning: A Meta-Analysis', *Language Learning* 67(2): 348–93. (This meta-analysis considers the learning outcomes of DDL in 64 quasi-experimental studies and attempts to identify relevant moderator variables.)

Chen, M. and Flowerdew, J. (2018) 'A Critical Review of Research and Practice in Data-Driven Learning (DDL) in the Academic Writing Classroom', *International Journal of Corpus Linguistics* 23(3): 335–69. (Focusing on the context of academic writing, this review paper discusses 37 empirical studies and offers recommendations for future DDL.)

Leńko-Szymańska, A. and Boulton, A. (eds) (2015) *Multiple Affordances of Language Corpora for Data-Driven Learning*, Amsterdam: John Benjamins. (This volume presents advances in DDL, based on corpora for language learning, skills development and translation training and using a variety of research methodologies.)

O'Keeffe, A. (2021) 'Data-Driven Learning – A Call for a Broader Research Gaze', *Language Teaching* 54(2): 259–72. (This paper provides an innovative perspective by showing how DDL can be positioned theoretically. It also identifies avenues for further research in DDL.)

Poole, R. (2018) *A Guide to Using Corpora for English Language Learners*, Edinburgh: Edinburgh University Press. (Designed for both language learners and language teachers, this book provides illustrated examples of how to search corpora, interpret findings and build one's own corpus; it includes many screenshots and hands-on exercises.)

References

Ackerley, K. (2017) 'Effects of Corpus-Based Instruction on Phraseology in Learner English', *Language Learning and Technology* 21(3): 195–216.

Ädel, A. (2010) 'Using Corpora to Teach Academic Writing: Challenges for the Direct Approach', in M. C. Campoy-Cubillo, B. Bellés-Fortuño and M. L. Gea-Valor (eds) *Corpus-Based Approaches to English Language Teaching*, London: Continuum, pp. 39–55.

Anthony, L. (2019) *AntConc (Version 3.5.8) [Computer Software]*, Tokyo: Waseda University, Available from https://www.laurenceanthony.net/software.

Aston, G. (2001) 'Learning with Corpora: An Overview', in G. Aston (ed.) *Learning with Corpora*, Houston: Athelstan, pp. 7–45.

Bernardini, S. (2001) '"Spoilt for Choice": A Learner Explores General Language Corpora', in G. Aston (ed.) *Learning with Corpora*, Houston: Athelstan, pp. 220–49.

Bernardini, S. (2004) 'Corpora in the Classroom. An Overview and some Reflections on Future Developments', in J. Sinclair (ed.) *How to Use Corpora in Language Teaching*, Amsterdam: John Benjamins, pp. 15–36.

Boulton, A. (2008a) 'DDL: Reaching the Parts Other Teaching Can't Reach?', in A. Frankenberg-Garcia (ed.) *Proceedings of the 8th Teaching and Language Corpora Conference*, Lisbon: Associação de Estudos e de Investigação Cientifica do ISLA-Lisboa, pp. 38–44.

Boulton, A. (2008b) 'Esprit de Corpus: Promouvoir l'Exploitation de Corpus en Apprentissage des Langues', *Texte et Corpus* 3: 37–46.

Boulton, A. (2009a) 'Testing the Limits of Data-Driven Learning: Language Proficiency and Training', *ReCALL* 21(1): 37–54.

Boulton, A. (2009b) 'Data-Driven Learning: Reasonable Fears and Rational Reassurance', *Indian Journal of Applied Linguistics* 35(1): 81–106.

Boulton, A. and Cobb, T. (2017) 'Corpus Use in Language Learning: A Meta-Analysis', *Language Learning* 67(2): 348–93.

Breyer, Y. (2006) '*My Concordancer*: Tailor-Made Software for Language Teachers and Learners', in S. Braun, K. Kohn and J. Mukherjee (eds) *Corpus Technology and Language Pedagogy*, Frankfurt: Peter Lang, pp. 157–176.

Brezina, V., Gablasova, D. and Reichelt, S. (2018) BNClab. [electronic resource], Lancaster University. http://corpora.lancs.ac.uk/bnclab.

Chambers, A. (2005) 'Integrating Corpus Consultation in Language Studies', *Language Learning and Technology* 9(2): 111–25.

Chambers, A. (2007) 'Popularising Corpus Consultation by Language Learners and Teachers', in E. Hidalgo, L. Quereda and J. Santana (eds) *Corpora in the Foreign Language Classroom*, Amsterdam: Rodopi, pp. 3–16.

Chambers, A. (2019) 'Towards the Corpus Revolution? Bridging the Research-Practice Gap', *Language Teaching* 52(4): 460–75.

Charles, M. (2007) 'Reconciling Top-Down and Bottom-Up Approaches to Graduate Writing: Using a Corpus to Teach Rhetorical Functions', *Journal of English for Academic Purposes* 6: 289–302.

Charles, M. (2014) 'Getting the Corpus Habit: EAP Students' Long-Term Use of Personal Corpora', *English for Specific Purposes* 35: 30–40.

Chen, M. and Flowerdew, J. (2018) 'A Critical Review of Research and Practice in Data-Driven Learning (DDL) in the Academic Writing Classroom', *International Journal of Corpus Linguistics* 23(3): 335–69.

Cobb, T. and Boulton, A. (2015) 'Classroom Applications of Corpus Analysis', in D. Biber and R. Reppen (eds) *Cambridge Handbook of English Corpus Linguistics*, Cambridge: Cambridge University Press, pp. 478–97.

Collins, H. (2000) 'Materials Design and Language Corpora: A Report in the Context of Distance Education', in L. Burnard and T. McEnery (eds) *Rethinking Language Pedagogy from a Corpus Perspective*, Frankfurt: Peter Lang, pp. 51–63.

Cotos, E. (2014) 'Enhancing Writing Pedagogy with Learner Corpus Data', *ReCALL* 26(2): 202–24.

Cotos, E., Link, S. and Huffman, S. (2017) 'Effects of DDL Technology on Genre Learning', *Language Learning and Technology* 21(3): 104–30.

Crosthwaite, P. (ed.) (2020) *Data-Driven Learning for the Next Generation: Corpora and DDL for Pre-Tertiary Learners*, London: Routledge.

Crosthwaite, P. and Cheung, L. (2019) *Learning the Language of Dentistry: Disciplinary Corpora in the Teaching of English for Specific Academic Purposes*, Amsterdam: John Benjamins.

Crosthwaite, P. and Stell, A. (2020) '"It Helps me Get Ideas on How to Use my Words": Primary School Students' Initial Reactions to Corpus Use in a Private Tutoring Setting', in P. Crosthwaite (ed.) *Data-Driven Learning for the Next Generation: Corpora and DDL for Pre-Tertiary Learners*, London: Routledge, pp. 150–70.

Díez Bedmar, M. B. (2006) 'Making Friends with DDL: Helping Students Enrich their Vocabulary', *Humanising Language Teaching* 8(3). http://old.hltmag.co.uk/may06/mart02.htm

Friginal, E. (2018) *Corpus Linguistics for English Teachers. New Tools, Online Resources, and Classroom Activities*, New York: Routledge.

Gablasova, D., Brezina, V. and McEnery, T. (2019) 'The Trinity Lancaster Corpus: Development, Description and Application', *International Journal of Learner Corpus Research* 5(2): 126–58.

Gabrielatos, C. (2005) 'Corpora and Language Teaching: Just a Fling or Wedding Bells?', *TESL-EJ* 8(4): 1–35.

Gavioli, L. (2005) *Exploring Corpora for ESP Learning*, Amsterdam: John Benjamins.

Gilquin, G. (2021) 'Using Corpora to Foster L2 Construction Learning: A Data-Driven Learning Experiment', *International Journal of Applied Linguistics*. 31(2): 229–47.

Granger, S. and Tribble, C. (1998) 'Learner Corpus Data in the Foreign Language Classroom: Form-Focused Instruction and Data-Driven Learning', in S. Granger (ed.) *Learner English on Computer*, London: Longman, pp. 199–209.

Hadley, G. (2002) 'An Introduction to Data-Driven Learning', *RELC Journal* 33(2): 99–124.

Hirata, E. (2020) 'The Development of a Multimodal Corpus Tool for Young EFL Learners: A Case Study on the Integration of DDL in Teacher Education', in P. Crosthwaite (ed.) *Data-Driven Learning for the Next Generation: Corpora and DDL for Pre-Tertiary Learners*, London: Routledge, pp. 88–105.

Hunston, S. (2002) *Corpora in Applied Linguistics*, Cambridge: Cambridge University Press.

Hyland, K. (2019) 'Foreword: Corpora and Specialised English in the University Curriculum', in P. Crosthwaite and L. Cheung (eds) *Learning the Language of Dentistry: Disciplinary Corpora in the Teaching of English for Specific Academic Purposes*, Amsterdam: John Benjamins, pp. 11–14.

Johns, T. (1986) 'Micro-Concord: A Language Learner's Research Tool', *System* 14(2): 151–62.

Johns, T. (1988) 'Whence and Whither Classroom Concordancing?', in T. Bongaerts, P. de Haan, S. Lobbe and H. Wekker (eds) *Computer Applications in Language Learning*, Dordrecht: Foris, pp. 9–33.

Johns, T. (1997) 'Contexts: The Background, Development and Trialling of a Concordance-Based CALL Program', in A. Wichmann, S. Fligelstone, T. McEnery and G. Knowles (eds) *Teaching and Language Corpora*, London: Longman, pp. 100–15.

Johns, T. (2002) 'Data-Driven Learning: The Perpetual Challenge', in B. Kettemann and G. Marko (eds) *Teaching and Learning by Doing Corpus Analysis*, Amsterdam: Rodopi, pp. 107–17.

Kennedy, C. and Miceli, T. (2001) 'An Evaluation of Intermediate Students' Approaches to Corpus Investigation', *Language Learning and Technology* 5(3): 77–90.

Kilgarriff, A., Marcowitz, F., Smith, S. and Thomas, J. (2015) 'Corpora and Language Learning with the Sketch Engine and SkELL', *Revue Française de Linguistique Appliquée* XX(1): 61–80.

Koosha, M. and Jafarpour, A. A. (2006) 'Data-Driven Learning and Teaching Collocation of Prepositions: The Case of Iranian EFL Adult Learners', *Asian EFL Journal* 8(4): 192–209.

Kuo, C.-H., Wible, D., Wang, C.-C. and Chien, F. (2001) 'The Design of a Lexical Difficulty Filter for Language Learning on the Internet', in *Proceedings of the IEEE International Conference on Advanced Learning Techniques (ICALT'01), Madison, WI, 6-8 August 2001*, pp. 53–4.

Lee, H., Warschauer, M. and Lee, J. H. (2019) 'The Effects of Corpus Use on Second Language Vocabulary Learning: A Multilevel Meta-Analysis', *Applied Linguistics* 40(5): 721–53.

Levy, M. (1990) 'Concordances and their Integration into a Word-Processing Environment for Language Learners', *System* 18(2): 177–88.

Mauranen, A. (2004) 'Spoken Corpus for an Ordinary Learner', in J. Sinclair (ed.) *How to Use Corpora in Language Teaching*, Amsterdam: John Benjamins, pp. 89–105.

Meunier, F. (2020) 'A Case for Constructive Alignment in DDL: Rethinking Outcomes, Practices, and Assessment in (Data-Driven) Language Learning', in P. Crosthwaite (ed.) *Data-Driven Learning for the Next Generation: Corpora and DDL for Pre-Tertiary Learners*, London: Routledge, pp. 13–30.

Mizumoto, A. and Chujo, K. (2015) 'A Meta-Analysis of Data-Driven Learning Approach in the Japanese EFL Classroom', *English Corpus Studies* 22: 1–18.

Mukherjee, J. (2002) *Korpuslinguistik und Englischunterricht: Eine Einführung*, Frankfurt: Peter Lang.

Mukherjee, J. (2006) 'Corpus Linguistics and Language Pedagogy: The State of the Art - and Beyond', in S. Braun, K. Kohn and J. Mukherjee (eds) *Corpus Technology and Language Pedagogy*, Frankfurt: Peter Lang, pp. 5–24.

Nesselhauf, N. (2004) 'Learner Corpora and their Potential for Language Teaching', in J. Sinclair (ed.) *How to Use Corpora in Language Teaching*, Amsterdam: John Benjamins, pp. 125–52.

O'Keeffe, A. (2021) 'Data-Driven Learning – A Call for a Broader Research Gaze', *Language Teaching* 54(2): 259–72.

O'Sullivan, I. (2007) 'Enhancing a Process-Oriented Approach to Literacy and Language Learning: The Role of Corpus Consultation Literacy', *ReCALL* 19(3): 269–86.

O'Sullivan, I. and Chambers, A. (2006) 'Learners' Writing Skills in French: Corpus Consultation and Learner Evaluation', *Journal of Second Language Writing* 15: 49–68.

Papaioannou, V., Mattheoudakis, M. and Agathopoulou, E. (2020) 'Data-Driven Learning in a Greek Secondary Education Setting: The Implementation of a Blended Approach', in P. Crosthwaite (ed.) *Data-Driven Learning for the Next Generation: Corpora and DDL for Pre-Tertiary Learners*, London: Routledge, pp. 187–207.

Pérez-Paredes, P. (2019) 'A Systematic Review of the Uses and Spread of Corpora and Data-Driven Learning in CALL Research during 2011–2015', *Computer Assisted Language Learning*. 10.1080/09588221.2019.1667832

Poole, R. (2018) *A Guide to Using Corpora for English Language Learners*, Edinburgh: Edinburgh University Press.

Quan, Z. (2016) 'Introducing "Mobile DDL (Data-Driven Learning)" for Vocabulary Learning: An Experiment for Academic English', *Journal of Computers in Education* 3(3): 273–87.

Scott, M. (2020) *WordSmith Tools version 8*, Stroud: Lexical Analysis Software.

Seidlhofer, B. (2002) 'Pedagogy and Local Learner Corpora: Working with Learning-Driven Data', in S. Granger, J. Hung and S. Petch-Tyson (eds) *Computer Learner Corpora, Second Language Acquisition and Foreign Language Teaching*, Amsterdam: John Benjamins, pp. 213–34.

Sripicharn, P. (2004) 'Examining Native Speakers' and Learners' Investigation of the Same Concordance Data and its Implications for Classroom Concordancing with ELF Learners', in G. Aston, S. Bernardini and D. Stewart (eds) *Corpora and Language Learners*, Amsterdam: John Benjamins, pp. 233–45.

Sripicharn, P. (2010) 'How Can we Prepare Learners for Using Language Corpora?', in A. O'Keeffe and M. McCarthy (eds) *The Routledge Handbook of Corpus Linguistics*, London: Routledge, pp. 371–84.

Sun, Y.-C. (2003) 'Learning Process, Strategies and Web-Based Concordancers: A Case Study', *British Journal of Educational Technology* 34(5): 601–13.

Tribble, C. (1997) 'Improvising Corpora for ELT: Quick-and-Dirty Ways of Developing Corpora for Language Teaching', in B. Lewandowska-Tomaszczyk and P. J. Melia (eds) *PALC '97: Practical Applications in Language Corpora*, Lodz: Lodz University Press, pp. 106–17.

Vyatkina, N. (2016) 'Data-Driven Learning of Collocations: Learner Performance, Proficiency, and Perceptions', *Language Learning and Technology* 20(3): 159–79.

Vyatkina, N. (2020) 'Corpora as Open Educational Resources for Language Teaching', *Foreign Language Annals* 53(2): 359–70.

Wicher, O. (2020) 'Data-Driven Learning in the Secondary Classroom: A Critical Evaluation from the Perspective of Foreign Language Didactics', in P. Crosthwaite (ed.) *Data-Driven Learning for the Next Generation: Corpora and DDL for Pre-Tertiary Learners*, London: Routledge, pp. 31–46.

Widdowson, H. G. (2000) 'On the Limitations of Linguistics Applied', *Applied Linguistics* 21(1): 3–25.
Widdowson, H. G. (2003) *Defining Issues in English Language Teaching*, Oxford: Oxford University Press.
Willis, D. (2003) *Rules, Patterns and Words. Grammar and Lexis in English Language Teaching*, Cambridge: Cambridge University Press.
Yao, G. (2019) 'Vocabulary Learning through Data-Driven Learning in the Context of Spanish as a Foreign Language', *Research in Corpus Linguistics* 7: 18–46.
Yoon, H. and Jo, H. (2014) 'Direct and Indirect Access to Corpora: An Exploratory Case Study Comparing Students' Error Correction and Learning Strategy Use in L2 Writing', *Language Learning and Technology* 18(1): 96–117.

31

Using corpora for writing instruction

Lynne Flowerdew

1 Why use corpora for writing instruction?

In a 1997 article examining the link between language corpora and teaching, Leech remarks on the "trickle down" effect from corpus research to teaching, which only really took off in the early nineties. The main instigator of the exploitation of corpora in language teaching, specifically on the application to writing, was Johns, whose seminal work in the field of data-driven learning (DDL) is reported in Johns (1984). Another landmark publication in the field is the volume by Tribble and Jones (1990), which also acted as a catalyst for the pedagogic application of corpora. Since then, as Leech (1997: 2) humorously observed: 'The original "trickle down" from research to teaching is now becoming a torrent'! The purpose of this chapter is to review the veritable cascade of corpus applications to various aspects of writing over the past three decades. But first a brief overview is in order of the affordances of corpora for enhancing different features of writing, the types of corpora and software used and the main ways in which corpora have been used.

The multiple lines of concordance output can reveal grammatical features, such as the different use of tenses and aspect with *for* and *since* in time expressions in English. Likewise, concordance data can shed light on vocabulary items, e.g. the most common senses of a word or its meaning (see Coxhead 2018). However, aside from individual grammatical or lexical features, one of the main affordances of corpora in writing is in their uniqueness of showing what can loosely be termed as phraseological patterning, involving collocations, colligations and lexical bundles, i.e. '…sequences of words that commonly go together in natural discourse' and which are the building blocks of academic writing (Biber *et al.* 1999: 990). Corpora are ideally suited to helping learners master such patterning in writing classes, as these phraseological features tend not to be easily accessible in either dictionaries or grammars. Another advantage of using a corpus is that it can shed light on common phrases presented in textbooks on writing. Corpus evidence shows that "on the other hand" is not always preceded by "on the one hand", which contravenes what is often presented in textbooks.

DOI: 10.4324/9780367076399-31

This focus on the usage patterns of words and variations thereof has been accompanied by greater attention with regard to their occurrences in specific genres. This has led to more initiatives to build small, specialised corpora, especially for the area of disciplinary writing; see Flowerdew (2004) for a discussion on the advantages of using small corpora, as well as Chapter 6, this volume. These are no longer confined to expert writing, but also encompass learner writing (see Gilquin *et al.* 2007). It is to be noted that many of the writing modules described in the two main sections of this chapter involve the construction of small, specialised corpora by the class teacher, either of expert or learner writing, with a few reporting self-compilation by students of their own work or of expert writing from their own discipline. Hyland (2006) has noted that such corpora are ideally suited for genre-based writing instruction, as they reveal the prototypical and frequently occurring phraseologies associated with rhetorical move structures (Swales 1990).

In addition to the small, specialised corpora constructed either by the class tutor or self-compiled by learners in a localised setting, a wide variety of publicly available larger-scale corpora have been used in writing instruction. Such corpora include the written academic sub-sections of the *British National Corpus* (BNC) and the *Corpus of Contemporary American English* (COCA), as well as learner corpora (see Chapter 8, this volume). One category of learner corpus, such as the *International Corpus of Learner English* (ICLE) and *Varieties of English for Specific Purposes dAtabase* (VESPA), reflects novice learner writing, which is often compared with expert writing The other type of learner corpus is seen as proficient student writing. Two corpora comprising tertiary-level student merit/distinction written assignments: the *Michigan Corpus of Upper-level Student Papers* (MICUSP) (Römer 2012) and the *British Academic Written English* (BAWE) corpus (Nesi 2011), fall into this category. These corpora have been used in research studies as a control corpus to compare proficient with less proficient student writing and have also been used to prepare classroom activities. The *Corpus of Repository of Writing* (CROW) (Staples and Dilger 2018) straddles both types of learner corpora, as it contains a range of assignments in terms of proficiency level, which can be filtered according to TOEFL scores (see https://crow.corporaproject.org/). As for software tools, *AntConc* is the most widely used, one of the main reasons being that it was created specifically for classroom use by learners (see Anthony 2018, 2019 for an overview and Chapter 9, this volume). Other tools such as Tom Cobb's *Lextutor* incorporate a suite of corpora, while resources such as COCA come with their own tools.

Corpora have principally been used in two main ways to inform writing instruction, either through a *corpus-based* approach where worksheet materials (e.g. gap-filling exercises) are derived from concordance output, or through a "hands-on" *corpus-driven* approach, commonly referred to as (DDL, which requires the student to interact directly with the corpus. One advantage of the corpus-based approach in having students work with worksheet output of concordance data is that it is a valuable means of providing them with "corpus competence", thereby gently familiarising them with corpus methodologies such as the inductive approach, the mainstay of DDL, interpretation of frequency data, etc. Another advantage is that it allows teachers to sift through what may be a vast number of concordance lines to reduce and select data on the basis of utility value. Of note is that in Boulton and Cobb's (2017) meta-study of 64 empirical studies of DDL, hands-on tasks were found to be more effective than paper-based activities, and, as will be seen, the corpus-driven approach is far more prevalent. Also, many writing instruction programmes commence with initial consciousness-raising pen-and-paper tasks, often involving analysis of whole texts, before embarking on concordancing activities. Importantly, many of the accounts incorporate strategy training into the module, moving through a carefully graded sequence of teacher-centred activities to more student-centred ones.

Another consideration is the kind of writing instruction being delivered. As the traditional distinction between English for general academic purposes (EGAP) and English for specific academic purposes (ESAP) is by no means clear-cut (see Flowerdew 2015b), I have opted to classify academic writing instruction according to its main communicative purpose, depending on whether the writing tasks are assigned by the class tutor, e.g. argumentative essay writing or project reports constituting general academic writing; or they address authentic disciplinary written genres, such as dissertations, forming the basis of writing instruction in ESP classes. Moreover, disciplinary writing can best be viewed on a continuum ranging from quite general meta-disciplinary writing, e.g. thesis writing for doctoral students, to more subject-specific disciplinary writing, e.g. thesis writing for biochemistry students, commonly referred to as "wide angle" vs. "narrow angle" perspectives on course design (Basturkmen 2006). The following sections review the increasingly important role that corpora, especially corpora of a specialist nature, are now playing in academic writing and discuss how various types of corpora have been exploited at different stages of the writing process from initial drafting through to the final proofreading and editing stages.

2 Using corpora for general EAP writing

In the accounts that follow I make a distinction between those corpus initiatives which focus on aspects of academic writing but which, in a sense, are standalone, as they are not integrated into a particular writing programme, and those where the corpora are integrated.

Using corpora to teach the language and rhetoric of EAP writing

The focus of the kind of preparatory argumentative essay/composition writing generally taught in undergraduate EAP classes is to raise students' awareness of key academic vocabulary and lexico-grammar for specific rhetorical functions. In this respect, a prime example of the corpus-based approach is Thurstun and Candlin's (1998) textbook *Exploring Academic English: A Workbook for Student Essay Writing*, based on the 1-million-word *MicroConcord Corpus of Academic Texts*. In this workbook the lexico-grammar is introduced according to its specific rhetorical function, e.g. referring to the literature, reporting the research of others. Within each broad function, each keyword (e.g. *claim*, *identify*) is examined within a chain of activities, which progress from controlled to more open-ended writing activities. Karpenko-Seccombe (2018), making use of the online corpus resource interface *Lextutor*, also advocates the progression of corpus tasks; in this instance, a sequencing based on a revised version of Bloom's taxonomy of the cognitive processes involved in learning.

Other pedagogic initiatives focus on just one important rhetorical function, namely citation practices for reporting the research of others (see Bloch 2009). Bloch makes the important point that with lower-level students, it is necessary to control for the types of language and text that the teacher wants to focus on. To this end, he designed a programme with a user-friendly interface that presented users with only a limited number of hits for each query and a limited number of criteria for querying the database, e.g.

attitude towards claim, strength of claim, etc. (cf. Thompson and Tribble's 2001 suite of activities designed for postgraduate students).

Integrating corpora into general EAP writing programmes

Apart from a focus on rhetorical functions and citation practices, other accounts in the literature report DDL initiatives where the corpus has been used by students as a self-correction tool, which invariably involves some kind of 'pedagogic mediation' on the part of the teacher using a guided inductive approach (see Flowerdew 2009). For example, Flowerdew (2008) reports on an initiative targeted at lexical and grammatical errors in undergraduate student project reports mediated through discussion activities using an in-house suite of corpora and other resources. The corpus instruction progressed through the following three stages: teacher-identified errors, student-identified errors and student-generated queries for writing up the final project report. Students were divided into groups and in their process of enquiry asked to discuss various questions such as which corpus or sub-corpus would be most appropriate for their enquiry and which search word they would use, facilitated by the tutor who circulated amongst the groups to guide discussion (see Quinn 2015 for a similar instructional approach to error correction). Besides the use of corpora as a self-correction tool at different stages of the writing process, corpora have been used for other purposes.

Xiao and Chen (2018) illustrate how COCA has been variously used in a college English writing instruction in China; for example, at the pre-writing stage, COCA is applied for vocabulary ideas and preparation, while during the writing stage, COCA is used for improving language quality in terms of lexical and grammatical accuracy and complexity. Xiao and Chen's instruction is one of the few to use corpus consultation at the drafting stage (see Liou and Yang 2020 for a study on students' reuse of vocabulary items for drafting essays).

Yet a different pedagogic orientation from those noted earlier is taken by Poole (2016), whose focus is on the teaching and learning of rhetoric in an undergraduate writing course. This was grounded in a controversial topic of local relevance: the proposal to build a large copper mine near the campus. Students first read and discussed a company brochure and interest group blog posts and viewed an opposition group's video. Poole made use of extracts of corpus data, selected from two self-compiled, specialised, localised pedagogic corpora (the first included blog posts from an opposition group website and the second consisted of press releases from the mine company) for follow-up corpus-aided activities, using data selected from the two corpora. This involved discussion work around, for example, the use of *will* in sentences such as the following: 'the mine will produce over 400 direct jobs and around 1600' (Poole 2016: 104). Poole also devised activities incorporating keyword lists (words of unusually high frequency when compared with a reference corpus) to alert students to rhetorically important words, with the aim of developing in students a critical capacity to see how rhetorical choices reflect the ideologies and values embodied in various interest groups.

3 Using corpora for disciplinary writing

Starting from a top-down genre perspective

The DDL initiatives described in this section combine Swalesian top-down genre analysis with more bottom-up lexico-grammatical analysis (see Flowerdew 2005) and range

Table 31.1 Concordance lines for "delimiting the case under consideration" (adapted from Weber 2001: 17)

Received Brian's letter.	Assuming	The offer does remain open, Brian's Thursda
proceeding on the latter	assumption	In order to discuss the law related to
to discuss. I now have to	consider	whether B's message, left on the answerphone
third party. Bata v. Bata.	Considering	first the story about The BCDs, can the ba
With	regard to	contracts *ex facie* illegal it is necessary to
second part of the story.	Regarding	the potential claim of Evangeline, it is subm

from quite "narrow-angle" to more "wide angle" accounts. The starting point tends to be with initial pen-and-paper awareness-raising activities with follow-up direct corpus consultation. Moreover, the corpora used are as close as possible in terms of genre, discipline, etc., to the student disciplinary assignment.

Not surprisingly, instruction on various legal genres occupy the "narrow angle" end of the spectrum. An early corpus initiative, specifically formal legal essays written by undergraduates, is reported in Weber (2001). First, Weber's students were inducted into the genre of legal essays by reading through whole essays taken from the University of London LLB Examinations written by native speakers and identifying some of the prototypical rhetorical features, e.g. identifying and/or delimiting the legal principle involved in the case. They were then asked to identify any lexical expressions which seemed to correlate with the genre features. This was followed up by consulting the corpus of the legal essays to verify and pinpoint regularities in lexico-grammatical expressions. For example, items such as *assume, consider* and *regard* in various constructions were all found to act as signals in an opening-type move, delimiting the case under consideration before the principle involved in it was defined, as exemplified by the extract shown (Table 31.1).

In an interesting departure from the normal type of ESAP work, Weber's students were also exposed to corpora of different, non-legal genres in order to sensitise them to the highly specific use and patterning of certain lexical items, such as *held* and *submit*, in legal texts. However, Bhatia *et al.* (2004: 224) caution that as legal genres are highly complex and 'dynamically embedded in one another', one has to go beyond the immediate textual concordance lines and look at discursive and institutional concerns and constraints to fully interpret and, by extension, become a skilled writer (see also Hafner and Candlin 2007 on this point).

Turning to another ESP area, that of psychology, Bianchi and Pazzaglia (2007) adopted a genre perspective in a cycle of activities for helping Italian students write psychology research articles in English using a self-compiled 500,000-word corpus 'representative of the language of the psychology community, which includes authors from different nationalities using English as a *lingua franca*' (Bianchi and Pazzaglia 2007: 265). An innovative feature of this writing instruction cycle is that students were asked to subdivide their choice of written article into moves and annotate it themselves using a functional and meta-communicative coding system devised by the authors, before embarking on data-driven guided writing tasks on key the lexico-grammatical patterning for different moves. Diani (2012) adopts a similar approach in her EAP module aimed at developing students' awareness and understanding of the pragmatic functions of a research paper, in this case, using a sub-corpus of linguistics papers from MICUSP. In order to sensitise students to how rhetorical and lexical choices are used to express particular values, students were encouraged to expand the concordance lines for the verb *argue* and extrapolate from this 'extended unit of meaning' that the verb *argue* tends to be used for creating a negative evaluation of the reported claim, e.g. *Cortazzi argues that* narratives are introduced into turn-by-turn talk… *While very insightful, Cortazzi's model seems somewhat narrow…* (Diani 2012: 57). These two accounts could be seen as occupying the mid-point of the "wide angle"/"narrow angle" spectrum, as they address writing in broad disciplinary fields, i.e. psychology and linguistics, rather than sub-fields.

A few initiatives reside more towards the "wide angle" end of the spectrum, as the students were not a homogeneous group from the same discipline. A case in point is the workshop for postgraduate science and engineering students reported in Flowerdew (2015a) for writing up the discussion section of a thesis. Flowerdew made use of a freely available corpus of research articles and also MICUSP to hone students' mastery of lexico-grammatical patterns for core move structures. For example, the following key phrase for 'commenting on the data' was found: '*This is not surprising given that…* signalling the relation of logical reasoning' (Flowerdew 2015a: 63) (see also Flowerdew 2016). However, it is still possible to accommodate a discipline-specific perspective within a mixed-discipline class, as reported by Cortes (2007), who compiled ten sub-corpora of research articles reflecting the disciplines of her students. Other initiatives focus on aspects of stance and voice, e.g. Charles's (2007) students investigated the two-part structure of "defending your work against criticism", and Chang's (2012) students examined devices for projecting an effective authorial stance.

Starting from a bottom-up lexico-grammatical perspective

In contast to the earlier accounts, those discussed in this section take as their starting point either lexico-grammatical devices, lexical bundles or vocabulary. One of the first such courses is that reported in Lee and Swales (2006), in which participants compiled corpora of their own writing (term papers, dissertation drafts, etc.) in addition to using a variety of expert corpora. In the first part of the course students used context to disambiguate similar lexical pairs (e.g. *effective* v. *efficient*) and in the final part presented their corpus findings on self-selected queries to their peers. Other early corpus-based materials are those by Hewings and Hewings (2002) on the use of metadiscoursal anticipatory "it" and extraposed subject in business writing (e.g. "It is interesting to note that no solution is offered").

Of interest is that there are only a few accounts in the literature where lexical bundles are the focus of attention. Eriksson (2012) describes a module on teaching lexical bundles to doctoral students of biochemistry based on his comparison of three-word lexical bundles (e.g. *the absence of*) from his self-compiled corpora of articles from biochemistry, his corpus of student writing and Hyland's list of bundles. Eriksson's pre-instruction lexical bundle analysis is noteworthy, as it acts as a needs analysis to determine which bundles to teach and also provides corpus evidence for disciplinary specificity and, by extension, the value of using specialised corpora, as more than half of the top 50 bundles in his two self-compiled biochemistry corpora did not appear on Hyland's academic list. In contrast, a somewhat different orientation to pedagogic treatment of lexical bundles is reported in Tribble and Wingate (2013). Bundles were extracted from an Apprentice Writing Corpus of two assessed disciplinary genres (critical assignments in applied linguistics and laboratory reports in pharmacy), but were not introduced until the second phase of the course for the development of linguistic knowledge at the level of wording. For the first phase of the course not only texts but also grading and feedback information from academic departments and input from disciplinary specialists were collected. Together, these provided the basis of the first phase, which was designed to help students understand the overall structure of the text, with attention paid to those moves considered by disciplinary specialists to be strategically important and challenging for students.

A number of vocabulary lists of both general academic and disciplinary items have been compiled (see Coxhead 2018 and Chapters 24 and 28, this volume). The most useful for writing purposes are those which examine vocabulary within its wider context of meaning, such as Sing's (2016) research using a 1-million-word student corpus of *Academic Business English* (ABE). Her initial wordlist was used as a starting point to investigate how students define, exemplify and explain and revealed students' inability to "technicalise" with an overreliance on superordinate expressions.

As witnessed by these accounts, over the past few years there has been a steady stream of articles reporting on the manifold applications of corpora to general EAP and disciplinary writing, mainly at the individual or institutional level. Learner corpora also now play a more prominent role, which was not the case a few years ago (see Chambers 2015; Flowerdew 2015b). Corpora have also been used for general EFL/ESL writing, in the main to produce corpus-informed writing materials integrated with grammar or with other skills. For example, McCarthy *et al.*'s (2012) skills-based series *Viewpoint 1 and 2*, informed by findings from the 1-billion-word *Cambridge English Corpus* (CEC), contain a writing section in each unit (e.g. Write an email enquiry about volunteering). Reppen's (2012) EFL/ESL *Grammar and Beyond* series, used in community colleges in the United States, is also informed by research data from CEC. While corpus initiatives are far more common in tertiary settings than in secondary school and workplace settings, expansion is underway (see Section 5).

4 How effective is the use of corpora for writing instruction?

Various challenges and issues have been raised in using corpora for writing instruction (see Ädel 2010; Yoon 2011; Anthony 2019 for a review of these). A decade ago, one of the most pressing issues concerned the effectiveness of corpus consultation. However, there is now a substantial body of experimental studies supplemented by questionnaire and interview data on learners' performance, validating the efficacy of corpus consultation in writing programmes. Here, I focus on selected studies published post-2010 for want of space (key pre-2010 studies are referenced in these). Several studies have examined the effects of using corpora for error correction in second drafts of various types of writing (see Tono *et al.* 2014; Crosthwaite 2017; Dolgova and Mueller 2019). The use of pre- and post-tests supplemented with questionnaires has been used by Cotos (2014) to examine the use of linking adverbials, using one activity which relied on a native speaker corpus only and the second combining native speaker and learner data. Other studies, using experimental and control groups, focus on improvement in students' writing instruction in a particular area (see Friginal 2013 for a study on key linguistic features in forestry reports of L1 writers and Shin *et al.* 2018 for reporting verbs in first-year composition writing). Phraseology has also been the focus of investigation, as reported in the studies by Huang (2014) and Ackerley (2017).

Of note is that qualitative studies are far less common. Yoon's (2008) study examined the L2 writing process of six students over a two-semester period. Her aims were not only to investigate how students use corpus technology but also to gauge how this affected their language learning and approaches to L2 writing, as well as exploring individual student experiences (see Bridle 2019 for a qualitative study on error correction). Another case study is reported in Chang (2014), who examined students' experiences of using general and specialized corpora for academic writing over a 22-week period. The advantage of these case studies is that corpus use is embedded in the writing programme and investigated over an extended period of time; this tends not to be the case with experimental studies (but see the experimental study by Li 2017). Chang (2014) also makes the important point that the ultimate aim is to foster independent scholars and writers, as called for by Chambers (2007: 13), who signalled that the next important step in the use of corpora was 'out of the classroom'. However, while these studies offer generally positive evidence that corpus pedagogy is effective, it remains yet to be seen to what extent this promotes autonomous learning with the gains carrying over into long-term benefits (see Charles 2014 for one of the few studies in the area).

5 Ongoing and future developments

Expansion of corpora into other languages

One omission in the field is that very little has been done to address writing instruction in other languages. More projects, such as those reported in Chambers and O'Sullivan (2004) and O'Sullivan and Chambers (2006) on writing in French, Vyatkina (2020) on writing in German and Kennedy and Miceli (2010) on writing in Italian, would certainly provide a welcome expansion to the field. Of note is that these initiatives have a strong strategy component built into the instruction. For example, Kennedy and Miceli's (2010) apprenticeship model consists of a "pattern-hunting" (initially browsing through whole texts or scrutinising frequency lists) followed by a "pattern-defining" (checking the corpus for a particular phrase in mind) phase. A related issue is the question of cross-cultural/cross-linguistic features, which Moreno and Swales (2018) have flagged, and the need to create pedagogic resources from a cross-cultural perspective to help, in their case, Spanish speakers compose more efficiently. Apart from other languages and cross-cultural perspectives, the EFL phenomenon, alluded to by Bianchi and Pazzaglia (2007), merits more consideration as web sources and research articles reflect the writing of authors from different nationalities.

Expansion of corpora into other genres and settings

Not only is there room for writing instruction to pay attention to other languages but also other settings besides tertiary-level education. One secondary school initiative at the International School of Prague is the construction of the *Corpus of High School Academic Texts* (COHAT), containing academic writing from four disciplines (see Bohát *et al.* 2015). The texts in COHAT, like those in the BAWE corpus, represent successful writing by both native and non-native peers. One activity using COHAT, similar to the one reported in Lee and Swales (2006), required students to present their semantic and grammatical discoveries to their peers, thereby fostering classroom interaction and discussion. Vocabulary lists from textbooks used in secondary schools in a variety of countries have recently been compiled (see Coxhead 2018), with suggestions given in Green (2019) for writing tasks focusing on the grammar patterns of vocabulary lists derived from school textbooks.

It is envisaged that workplace/professional written genres will receive more attention. Such work, mostly addressed at present in university settings, includes Conrad's (2017) materials on civil engineering reports, Miller and Pessoa's (2018) investigation on information system project reports and Crosthwaite and Cheung's (2019) analysis of, and materials for, dentistry genres. It is less common to find corpus-informed writing materials designed to be used primarily in vocational settings, such as the writing components in McCarthy *et al.*'s (2009) *Grammar for Business* textbook based on the 200-million-word *Cambridge English Corpus* (see also Coxhead *et al.* 2020 on language use for occupational purposes in trades education). In an oft-quoted phrase Johansson (1991) remarked "Times change, and so do corpora"; it is instructive to bear in mind that so do genres and disciplines, requiring writing programmes to adjust accordingly. In this respect, the area of English for research publication purposes (ERPP) is gaining increasing traction, as many science and engineering postgraduate students no longer write a traditional thesis, but rather produce a series of publications on their research (see Chen and Flowerdew 2018).

Development of user-friendly tools for different writing levels

A number of technological advances over the last decade have served to facilitate corpus pedagogy for writing. Several online tools and programmes have applied Swalesian genre analysis to advanced academic writing using corpora tagged for move structures (see Chang and Kuo 2011; Cotos *et al.* 2015; Wong 2019). However, one thorny question has often surfaced: How can students search a corpus for something they don't know? The ongoing *BAWE quicklinks* project seeks to meet this important need. For instance, if a student wrote *Shulman (1989) quoted that*… a link is provided to corpus lines extracted from the BAWE corpus showing more appropriate examples, e.g. *proposed that…; claimed that…; suggested that…*. Another writing aid tool under development to assist students in real time with uncertainties on collocations is *ColloCaid* (https://www.collocaid.uk/), which integrates information on collocations extracted from academic corpora with text editors (see Frankenberg-Garcia *et al.* 2019). Importantly, *ColloCaid* makes use of data visualisation techniques to present collocational information at different levels of incrementation to suit students' needs. Another visualisation tool for collocations is *GraphColl* in the *LancsBox* suite of programmes (Brezina *et al.* 2018). *GraphColl*, which generates collocation networks providing insights into meaning relationships, has also been used for teaching collocations in academic writing (Liu in press/2021). However, it must be emphasised that a great deal can be achieved using existing user-friendly tools; Charles (2018) describes how students have used some hitherto under-exploited functionalities in *AntConc* (clusters, keywords, concordance plot, etc.) for editing their theses.

To conclude, this chapter has revealed the many innovative ways in which corpora have been used to produce materials and the myriad ways corpus-driven learning has been integrated into the different stages of writing programmes. However, such initiatives are still to be adopted at a more national level or be implemented outside the classroom for autonomous lifelong learning. Recent innovations in corpora and tools and the greater emphasis put on strategy training for both learners and teachers hold promise of a trickle-down effect.

Further reading

Charles, M. and Frankenberg-Garcia, A. (eds) (2021) *Corpora in ESP/EAP Writing Instruction*, London: Routledge. (This edited volume deals with the following areas: corpus use for preparing DDL instruction, corpus use by students and corpus use for analysing student writing.)

Chen, M. and Flowerdew, J. (2018) 'A Critical Review of Research and Practice in Data-Driven Learning (DDL) in the Academic Writing Classroom', *International Journal of Corpus Linguistics* 23(3): 335–69. (This survey article covers both research and practice in DDL.)

Karpenko-Seccombe, T. (2020) *Academic Writing with Corpora*, London: Routledge. (This book provides a practical introduction to DDL, using *Lextutor* as well as other resources such as *SkELL* and MICUSP.)

References

Ackerley, K. (2017) 'Effects of Corpus-Based Instruction on Phraseology in Learner English', *Language Learning and Technology* 21(3): 153–71.

Ädel, A. (2010) 'Using Corpora to Teach Academic Writing: Challenges for the Direct Approach', in M. Campoy-Cubillo, B. Bélles-Fortuño and M. Gea-Valor (eds) *Corpus-Based Approaches to English Language Teaching*, London: Continuum, pp. 41–55.

Anthony, L. (2018) 'Introducing Corpora and Corpus Tools into the Technical Writing Classroom through Data-Driven Learning', in J. Flowerdew and T. Costley (eds) *Discipline-Specific Writing*, London: Routledge, pp. 162–80.

Anthony, L. (2019) 'Tools and Strategies for Data-Driven Learning in the EAP Writing Classroom', in K. Hyland and L. Wong (eds) *Specialised English. New Directions in ESP and EAP Research and Practice*, London: Routledge, pp. 179–94.

Basturkmen, H. (2006) *Ideas and Options in English for Specific Purposes*, London: Routledge.

BAWE Quicklinks (n.d.), Available at: https://bawequicklinks.coventry.domains/ [Accessed 21 September 2020].

Bhatia, V. K., Langton, N. and Lung, J. (2004) 'Legal Discourse: Opportunities and Threats for Corpus Linguistics', in U. Connor and T. Upton (eds) *Discourse in the Professions*, Amsterdam: John Benjamins, pp. 203–31.

Bianchi, F. and Pazzaglia, R. (2007) 'Student Writing of Research Articles in a Foreign Language: Metacognition and Corpora', in R. Facchinetti (ed.) *Corpus Linguistics 25 Years On*, Amsterdam: Rodopi, pp. 259–87.

Biber, D., Johannson, S., Leech, G., Conrad, S. and Finnegan, E. (1999) *Longman Grammar of Spoken and Written English*, Harlow: Pearson Education.

Bloch, J. (2009) 'The Design of an Online Concordancing Program for Teaching about Reporting Verbs', *Language Learning & Technology* 13(1): 59–78.

Bohát, R., Rödlingová, B. and Horák, N. (2015) 'Corpus of High School Academic Texts (COHAT): Data-Driven, Computer Assisted Discovery in Learning Academic English', in F. Helm, L. Bradley, M. Guarda and S. Thouësny (eds) *Critical CALL: Proceedings of the 2015 EUROCALL Conference, 22nd, Padova, Italy, August 26–29, 2015*, Dublin: Research-publishing.net, pp. 71–76.

Boulton, A. and Cobb, T. (2017) 'Corpus Use in Language Learning: A Meta-Analysis', *Language Learning* 67(2): 348–93.

Brezina, V., Timperley, M. and McEnery, T. (2018) #LancsBox v. 4.x [software], Available at: http://corpora.lancs.ac.uk/lancsbox [Accessed 21 September 2020].

Bridle, M. (2019) 'Learner Use of a Corpus as a Reference Tool in Error Correction: Factors Influencing Consultation and Success', *Journal of English for Academic Purposes* 37: 52–69.

Chambers, A. (2007) 'Popularising Corpus Consultation by Language Learners and Teachers', in E. Hidalgo, L. Quereda and J. Santana (eds) *Corpora in the Foreign Language Classroom*, Amsterdam: Rodopi, pp. 3–16.

Chambers, A. (2015) 'The Learner Corpus as a Pedagogic Corpus', in S. Granger, G. Gilquin and F. Meunier (eds) *The Cambridge Handbook of Learner Corpus Research*, Cambridge: Cambridge University Press, pp. 445–64.

Chambers, A. and O'Sullivan, I. (2004) 'Corpus Consultation and Advanced Learners' Writing Skills', *ReCALL* 16(1): 158–72.
Chang, C.-F. and Kuo, C.-H. (2011) 'A Corpus-Based Approach to Online Materials Development for Writing Research Articles', *English for Specific Purposes* 30: 222–34.
Chang, J.-Y. (2014) 'The Use of General and Specialized Corpora as Reference Sources for Academic English Writing: A Case Study', *ReCALL* 26(2): 243–59.
Chang, P. (2012) Using a Stance Corpus to Learn about Effective Authorial Stance-Taking. A Textlinguistic Approach', *ReCALL* 24(2): 209–36.
Charles, M. (2007) 'Reconciling Top-Down and Bottom-Up Approaches to Graduate Writing: Using a Corpus to Teach Rhetorical Functions', *Journal of English for Academic Purposes* 6(4): 289–302.
Charles, M. (2014) 'Getting the Corpus Habit: EAP Students' Long-Term Use of Personal Corpora', *English for Specific Purposes* 35: 30–40.
Charles, M. (2018) 'Corpus-Assisted Editing: More than Just Concordancing', *Journal of English for Academic Purposes* 36: 15–25.
Chen, M. and Flowerdew, J. (2018) 'Introducing Data-Driven Learning to PhD Students for Research Writing Purposes: A Territory Wide Project', *English for Specific Purposes* 50: 97–112.
Cobb, T. (n.d.) *Online Concordancer*, Available at: http://lextutor.ca/conc/eng [Accessed 21 September 2020].
Conrad, S. (2017) 'A Comparison of Practitioner and Student Writing in Civil Engineering', *Journal of Engineering Education* 106(2): 191–217.
Cortes, V. (2007) 'Exploring Genre and Corpora in the English for Academic Writing Class', *The ORTESOL Journal* 25: 8–14.
Cotos, E. (2014) 'Enhancing Writing Pedagogy with Learner Corpus Data', *ReCALL* 26(2): 202–24.
Cotos, E., Huffman, S. and Link, S. (2015) 'Furthering and Applying Move/Step Constructs: Technology-Driven Marshalling of Swalesian Genre Theory for EAP Pedagogy', *Journal of English for Academic Purposes* 19: 52–72.
Coxhead, A. (2018) *Vocabulary and English for Specific Purposes Research*, London: Routledge.
Coxhead, A., Parkinson, J., Mackay, J. and McLaughlin, E. (2020) *English for Vocational Purposes. Language Use in Trades Education*, London: Routledge.
Crosthwaite, P. (2017) 'Retesting the Limits of Data-Driven Learning: Feedback And Error Correction', *Computer Assisted Language Learning* 30: 447–73.
Crosthwaite, P. and Cheung, L. (2019) *Learning the Language of Dentistry. Disciplinary corpora in the teaching of English for Specific Academic Purposes*, Amsterdam: John Benjamins.
Diani, G. (2012) 'Text and Corpus Work, EAP Writing and Language Learners', in R. Tang (ed.) *Academic Writing in a Second or Foreign Language*, London: Continuum, pp. 45–66.
Dolgova, N. and Mueller, C. (2019) 'How Useful are Corpus Tools for Error Correction? Insights from Learner Data', *Journal of English for Academic Purposes* 39: 97–108.
Eriksson, A. (2012) 'Pedagogical Perspectives on Bundles: Teaching Bundles to Doctoral Students of Biochemistry', in J. Thomas and A. Boulton (eds) *Input, Process and Product. Developments in Teaching and Language Corpora*, Brno, Czech Republic: Masaryk University Press, pp. 195–211.
Flowerdew, L. (2004) 'The Argument for Using English Specialized Corpora to Understand Academic and Professional Language,' in U. Connor and T. Upton (eds) *Discourse in the Professions: Perspectives from Corpus Linguistics*, Amsterdam: John Benjamins, pp. 11–33.
Flowerdew, L. (2005) 'An Integration of Corpus-Based and Genre-Based Approaches to Text Analysis in EAP/ESP: Countering Criticisms against Corpus-Based Methodologies', *English for Specific Purposes* 24(3): 321–32.
Flowerdew, L. (2008) 'Corpus Linguistics for Academic Literacies Mediated through Discussion Activities', in D. Belcher and A. Hirvela (eds) *The Oral-Literate Connection: Perspectives on L2 Speaking, Writing and Other Media Interactions*, Ann Arbor, MI: University of Michigan Press, pp. 268–87.
Flowerdew, L. (2009) 'Applying Corpus Linguistics to Pedagogy: A Critical Evaluation', *International Journal of Corpus Linguistics* 14(3): 393–417.

Flowerdew, L. (2015a) 'Using Corpus-Based Research and Online Academic Corpora to Inform Writing of the Discussion Section of a Thesis', *Journal of English for Academic Purposes* 20: 58–68.

Flowerdew, L. (2015b) 'Learner Corpora and Language for Academic and Specific Purposes', in S. Granger, G. Gilquin and F. Meunier (eds) *The Cambridge Handbook of Learner Corpus Research*, Cambridge: Cambridge University Press, pp. 465–84.

Flowerdew, L. (2016) 'A Genre-Inspired and Lexico-Grammatical Approach for Helping Postgraduate Students Craft Research Grant Proposals', *English for Specific Purposes* 42: 1–12.

Frankenberg-Garcia, A., Lew, R., Roberts, J., Rees, G. and Sharma, N. (2019) 'Developing a Writing Assistant to Help EAP Writers with Collocations in Real Time', *ReCALL* 31(1): 23–39.

Friginal, E. (2013) 'Developing Report Writing Skills Using Corpora', *English for Specific Purposes* 32(4): 208–20.

Gilquin, G., Granger, S. and Paquot, M. (2007) 'Learner Corpora: The Missing Link in EAP Pedagogy', *Journal of English for Academic Purposes* 6(4): 319–35.

Green, C. (2019) 'Enriching the Academic Wordlist and Secondary Vocabulary Lists with Lexicogrammar: Toward a Pattern Grammar of Academic Vocabulary', *System* 87: 102–12.

Hafner, C. and Candlin, C. (2007) 'Corpus Tools as an Affordance to Learning in Professional Legal Education', *Journal of English for Academic Purposes* 6(4): 303–18.

Hewings, M. and Hewings, A. (2002) '"It is Interesting to Note that…": A Comparative Study of Anticipatory 'It' in Student and Published Writing', *English for Specific Purposes* 21(4): 367–83.

Huang, Z. (2014) 'The Effects of Paper-Based DDL on the Acquisition of Lexico-Grammatical Patterns in L2 Writing', *ReCALL* 26(2): 163–83.

Hyland, K. (2006) *English for Academic Purposes*, London: Routledge.

Johansson, S. (1991) 'Times Change, and So Do Corpora', in K. Aijmer and B. Altenberg (eds) *English Corpus Linguistics*, London: Longman, pp. 305–14.

Johns, T. (1984) 'From Printout to Handout: Grammar and Vocabulary Teaching in the Context of Data-Driven Learning', in T. Odlin (ed.) *Perspectives on Pedagogical Grammar*, Cambridge: Cambridge University Press, pp. 293–313.

Karpenko-Seccombe, T. (2018) 'Practical Concordancing for Upper-Intermediate and Advanced Academic Writing: Ready-to-Use Teaching and Learning Materials', *Journal of English for Academic Purposes* 36: 135–41.

Kennedy, C. and Miceli, T. (2010) 'Corpus-Assisted Creative Writing: Introducing Intermediate Italian learners to a Corpus as a Reference Resource', *Language Learning & Technology* 14(1): 28–44.

Lee, D. and Swales, J. (2006) 'A Corpus-Based EAP Course for NNS Doctoral Students: Moving from Available Specialized Corpora to Self-Compiled Corpora', *English for Specific Purposes* 25(1): 56–75.

Leech, G. (1997) 'Teaching and Language Corpora: A Convergence', in A. Wichmann, S. Fligelstone, T. McEnery and G. Knowles (eds) *Teaching and Language Corpora*, London: Longman, pp. 1–23.

Li, S. (2017) 'Using Corpora to Develop Learners' Collocational Competence', *Language Learning & Technology* 21(3): 153–71.

Liou, H.-C. and Yang, T.-W. (2020) 'Data-Driven Learning at the English Drafting Stage', in M. Kruk ad M. Peterson (eds) *New Technological Applications for Foreign and Second Language Learning and Teaching*, pp. 282–304.

Liu, T. (In press/2021) 'Data-Driven Learning: Using #LancsBox in Academic Collocation Learning', in P. Pérez-Paredes and G. Mark (eds) *Beyond Concordance Lines: Corpora in Language Education*, Amsterdam: John Benjamins.

McCarthy, M. J., McCarten, J., Clark, D. and Clark, R. (2009) *Grammar for Business*, Cambridge: Cambridge University Press.

McCarthy, M. J., McCarten, J. and Sandiford, H. (2012) *Viewpoint 1 and 2*, Cambridge: Cambridge University Press.

Miller, R. and Pessoa, S. (2018) 'Corpus-Driven Study of information System Project Reports', in V. Brezina and L. Flowerdew (eds) *Learner Corpus Research. New Perspectives and Applications*, London: Bloomsbury, pp. 112–33.

Moreno, A. and Swales, J. M. (2018) 'Strengthening Move Analysis Methodology towards Bridging the Form-Function Gap', *English for Specific Purposes* 50: 40–63.

Nesi, H. (2011) 'BAWE: An Introduction to a New Resource', in A. Frankenberg-Garcia, L. Flowerdew and G. Aston (eds) *New Trends in Corpora and Language Learning*, London: Bloomsbury, pp. 213–28.

O'Sullivan, I. and Chambers, A. (2006) 'Learners' Writing Skills in French: Corpus Consultation and Learner Evaluation', *Journal of Second Language Writing* 15(1): 49–68.

Poole, R. (2016) 'A Corpus-Aided Approach for the Teaching and Learning of Rhetoric in an Undergraduate Composition Course for L2 Writers', *Journal of English for Academic Purposes* 21: 99–109.

Quinn, C. (2015) 'Training L2 Writers to Reference Corpora as a Self-Correction Tool', *ELT Journal* 69(2): 165–77.

Reppen, R. (2012) *Grammar and Beyond*, Cambridge: Cambridge University Press.

Römer, U. (2012) 'Corpora and Teaching Academic Writing: Exploring the Pedagogic Potential of MICUSP', in J. Thomas and A. Boulton (eds) *Input, Process and Product. Developments in Teaching and Language Corpora*, Brno, Czech Republic: Masaryk University Press, pp. 70–82.

Shin, J.-Y., Velázquez, A. J., Swatek, A., Staples, S. and Partridge, R. S. (2018) 'Examining the Effectiveness of Corpus-Informed Instruction of Reporting Verbs in L2 First-Year College Writing', *L2 Journal* 10(3): 31–46.

Sing, C. (2016) 'Writing for Specific Purposes: Developing Business Students' Ability to "Technicalise"', in S. Göpferich and I. Neumann (eds) *Developing and Assessing Academic and Professional Writing Skills*, Bern: Peter Lang, pp. 15–45.

Staples, S. and Dilger, B. (2018-) *Corpus and Repository of Writing*, Available at: https://crow.corporaproject.org [Accessed 21 September 2020].

Swales, J. M. (1990) *Genre Analysis: English in Academic and Research Settings*, Cambridge: Cambridge University Press.

Thompson, P. and Tribble, C. (2001) 'Looking at Citations: Using Corpora in English for Academic Purposes', *Language Learning and Technology* 5(3): 91–105.

Thurstun, J. and Candlin, C. (1998) *Exploring Academic English: A Workbook for Student Essay Writing*, Macquarie University: NCELTR.

Tono, Y., Satake, Y. and Miura, A. (2014) 'The Effects of Using Corpora on Revision Tasks in L2 Writing with Coded Error Feedback', *ReCALL* 26(2): 147–62.

Tribble, C. and Jones, C. (1990) *Concordances in the Classroom*, London: Longman.

Tribble, C. and Wingate, U. (2013) 'From Text to Corpus: A Genre-Based Approach to Academic Literacy Instruction', *System* 41: 307–21.

VESPA (n.d.) https://uclouvain.be/en/research-institutes/ilc/cecl/vespa-research.html [Accessed 21 September 2020].

Vyatkina, N. (2020) 'Corpus-Informed Pedagogy in a Language Course: Design, Implementation and Evaluation', in M. Kruk and M. Peterson (eds) *New Technological Applications for Foreign and Second Language Learning and Teaching*, pp. 306–35.

Weber, J.-J. (2001) 'A Concordance- and Genre-Informed Approach to ESP Essay Writing', *ELT Journal* 55(1): 14–20.

Wong, L. (2019) 'Implementing Disciplinary Data-Driven Learning for Postgraduate Thesis Writing', in K. Hyland and L. Wong (eds) *Specialised English. New Directions in ESP and EAP Research and Practice*, London: Routledge, pp. 195–213.

Xiao, G. and Chen, X. (2018) 'Application of COCA in EFL Writing Instruction at the Tertiary Level in China', *International Journal of Emerging Technologies in Learning* 13(9): 160–73.

Yoon, C. (2011) 'Concordancing in L2 Writing Class: An Overview of Research and Issues', *Journal of English for Academic Purposes* 10(3): 130–9.

Yoon, H. (2008) 'More than a Linguistic Reference: The Influence of Corpus Technology on L2 Academic Writing', *Language Learning and Technology* 12(2): 31–48.

32

How can corpora be used in teacher education?

Fiona Farr

1 The language teacher education landscape

As I write an update of this chapter for the second edition of this Handbook, I am sitting at home during the great "lockdown" of the 2020 COVID-19 pandemic. Never has the face of teacher education changed as much globally as in the last six to eight weeks as we have scurried and rallied to move all of our teacher education programmes into some sort of acceptable technology-mediated distance format, with little time to check adherence to the kind of principles detailed by those more expert in the use of information and communication technologies (ICT) for programme delivery (for example, McCarthy 2016; Kiddle and Prince 2019). Face-to-face tutorials have become uploaded voiced-over presentations; classroom interactions with student teachers have become Skype, Zoom or MS Teams online gatherings; teaching practice has been abandoned and replaced with observations of videos followed by shared reflective blogs; and chat rooms and discussion fora have become part of everyday professional life. And with all of that, never have I been so convinced of the value of corpus linguistics (CL), nor so thankful for the free availability of such a vast range of corpora, which has meant that my student teachers have been able to continue to work quite independently with very little requirement for further support from me (more on that later).

Having moved beyond the important but limited use of corpora for language research and the development of reference materials, many in the language teaching profession have been busy investigating, discussing, designing and evaluating ways in which corpus techniques may be used with learners in both direct and mediated ways. All of these very worthy endeavours have placed applied linguists and language teachers in a very privileged position, with an array of corpus-based teaching and reference materials, online resources and an extended repertoire of approaches that can be employed in the classroom. In fact, 'there has been a transition from the days when corpora were considered to be an obscure pursuit with few practical applications outside of the creation of dictionaries to the present when insights from corpus linguistics are having an ever-increasing influence on the design of teaching materials, from grammar- and vocabulary-learning materials to whole courses, and where learner corpora are more and more being

 DOI: 10.4324/9780367076399-32

seen as valuable sources of evidence for language development' (McCarthy 2016: 8). It is possible, and relatively easy, to prepare an English language class exclusively based on findings from corpus research, using corpus-based dictionary, grammar and course book material; prepare some frequency, keyword or concordance lists in advance; and even get students to do some independent exploring (for a meta-analysis of CL in language learning see Boulton and Cobb 2017). While such developments have been enhancing language teaching, I think I can now say with some confidence that the same can be said to be true of the integration of CL in ELTE. This is not what I said in the first edition of this Handbook. I acknowledge that some challenges remain (Leńko-Szymanska 2017; Callies 2019), but these are diminishing with time.

As a piece of light-touch survey research for the first edition, an online investigation of the curriculum contents of some MA programmes in ELT/TESOL/TEFL revealed that few of the programmes made any direct reference to CL in their syllabus descriptions. I undertook a similar search in preparation for writing this update, and it revealed that many such programmes now include CL. What is interesting this time is how it is framed within the programme. In cases where it occurs as a standalone module, it tends to be an optional choice for students. Otherwise, as part of a core module, it can generally be found to be integrated in any one (or more) of four ways. Firstly, as part of some sort of technology-enhanced learning module where the emphasis is typically on the use and integration of CL as a pedagogic tool. Secondly, it can be found included as part of a discourse or language analysis module with a focus on its potential for language research. Related to this is the place of CL in research methods courses as one of a range of technological tools, often alongside text analysis software such as NVivo. And fourthly, I have found examples of its presence in general pedagogy and materials development courses.

Although these are far from empirical findings, they do suggest that teachers may now more commonly be exposed to these concepts and techniques during their education. And, of course, it is no coincidence that this growth in integration has coincided with the more widespread and open availability of large-scale corpora and powerful analysis software, for example, the BYU billion-word multi-language collections, or the Sketch Engine resources (freely available to EU universities for at least the next couple of years) (see also Murphy and Riordan 2016). The issue which existed when I first started to use corpora in the mid-1990s was trying to get your hands on them. At the time they were rare, clunky to use and cost a lot of money. In addition, they rarely came with integrated software, which added another technological hurdle. Now students run a couple of Google searches and "there's a corpus for that". This easy access and growth in integration, however, bring another challenge. Corpora of the magnitude now available are generally compelling to the linguistics student. The temptation is to begin interacting with the corpus technology without any real understanding of the principles of corpus compilation, corpus searching or corpus interpretation. In other words, the technology becomes the pedagogy, and this, along with the distraction potential of the collections, can seriously undermine the value of this approach. To counteract this in instructional contexts I now begin with fairly extensive critical coverage of the theories behind CL, as well as providing lots of examples of corpus-based studies, before the student teachers get to experience using a corpus first-hand. This can be for a number of weeks in many cases so that by the time they search a corpus, they have a comprehensive understanding of what they are doing and why they are doing it. In very recent years my efforts in this respect have been greatly facilitated by online resources such as academic talks and even entire corpus MOOCs, such as the one offered at the time of writing by Tony McEnery and his Lancaster colleagues on the FutureLearn platform (and although the concept of a MOOC itself could become dated or obsolete at some point in the future, the COVID-induced learning trends have triggered a significant increase in registration for these courses, which is likely to enhance their sustainability for some time to come). While the student teachers do still sometimes ask the "wrong" questions of the corpus or feel overwhelmed by the number of hits they get, the chances of this happening are greatly reduced.

Based on the examination of the MA programmes mentioned earlier, as well as reports in the published literature on the inclusion of CL in ELTE (Hunston 1995; Coniam 1997; O'Keeffe and Farr 2003; McCarthy 2008; Callies 2019; Farr and O'Keeffe 2019), two broad themes emerge. Firstly, a number of accounts relay how corpora can support the development and critical evaluation of pedagogic skills. These will be explored in Section 3. Secondly, CL is being used in the promotion of critical language awareness skills to provide new dimensions to language description. This will be elaborated on in Section 4. Both of these discussions will answer the question: How can CL be used to develop pedagogic and linguistic awareness on ELTE programmes? But there is a further question which might push the boundaries in terms of what we currently do with CL in the field of ELTE, and that is: What can corpus explorations tell us about the ways in which social interaction occurs in ELTE contexts and how these understandings can help us to develop as a profession of teacher educators? This essentially converts CL into a tool for the reflective practice, professional understanding and enhancement of not just student teachers but one which can be utilised by teacher educators to examine and improve their practices (in a context where there still doesn't exist a formal and internationally recognised "train the trainer" qualification), as well as providing evidence-based accounts for those at the initial stages of embarking on such a career. These discussions will be given due attention towards the end of this chapter, as it is a field which is still at the relatively early stages of development.

2 Current philosophies of teacher education and the place of corpus linguistics

Where are we in terms of what we believe about good teacher education? It is probably safe to say that we are in a cocoon of post-transmissive and post-directive approaches, and we now find ourselves influenced strongly by notions of independent and self-directed learning and critical and reflective engagement (Walsh and Mann 2019). Certainly, in European and North American contexts, many teacher educators would claim close alliances with these approaches and their theoretical underpinnings. Social constructivism and the work of Vygotsky (1978) have had an important impact in how teacher education pedagogy is materialised (Golombek and Johnson 2019). An evolution from retrospective to prospective education has taken place and has come to a conclusion (Kozulin 1998; Kinginger 2002). In this move, the acquisition and reproduction of a body of information does not retain its former elevated status. The focus in current educational theory is on the continuing development of students' cognitions. Consequently, their role becomes much more involved, stemming from two theoretical perspectives (Kozulin 1998: 157): Piaget's thoughts on the need for a stimulating, problem-solving context so that innate discovery predispositions are best utilised (Farrell 2012), and Vygotskian views that an independent learner is the culmination of education and not an assumed given at the initial stages of learning. Consequently, there has been much discussion of the development of the teacher as reflective practitioner and action researcher (Edge and Richards 1998; Wallace 1998; Burns 2010; Mann and Walsh 2017; T.S. Farrell 2019; Dragas 2019) in attempts to appropriate theory, practice and research and to allow for the integration of individual and contextual variables. Such developments are also a concerted attempt to close "the gap" (Baguley 2019) as student teachers move from ELTE programmes towards their professional careers. We continue to question the nature of knowledge, including practical knowledge (Thornbury 2019), and content (Morton 2019) in ELTE. More importantly, we have moved from transmission to a more holistic knowledge construction approach (Malderez and Bodóczky 1999: 10; Freeman 2001: 73–4).

In a rare and relatively recent volume focussing exclusively on this field, Freeman (2016) discusses the predominant theoretical frameworks and introduces a "Design Theory" for second language teacher education as an alternative to 'second language teacher education [...] largely defined by prescriptive ideas about what the content should be and how it should be taught' (2016: 227). He suggests that this theory, although highly descriptive, can function to proactively influence what happens in the future. This theory describes the six major components of contemporary ELTE as he sees them:

1. ***Tools and opportunities*** to use them, is the central purpose of teacher education;
2. ***Social facts*** – recognising and using the tools appropriately in practice in ways which are normative and accepted in the teaching community;
3. ***Local and professional languages*** – appropriate social knowledge and use of language in the profession and the local context;
4. ***Communities***, with their theoretical origin in situated learning theory;
5. ***Articulation***, defined as 'the process of negotiating entry to a community of activity and explanation' (Freeman 2016: 243). This takes place in the period when a newcomer is working to be recognised as part of the community and acting as if they were;
6. When articulation becomes full ***explanation*** in socially appropriate ways, it marks individuals as full members of the community. So articulation is "participating with", as a peripheral member, whereas explanation is "participating in", as a full member.

I suggest that a corpus-based approach is one way to support, promote and critically examine these philosophies in practice. It is not the only way, but in my experience over the last 25 years I have found many easy fits between the integration of CL approaches and current philosophies and practices in ELTE. There are different types of "knowledge" that student teachers acquire during an education programme. Farr and O'Keeffe (2019) summarise these as linguistic, pedagogic and technological content, couched in teacher research and wisdom of practice. Considering this content base, along with current practices (informed by theoretical and philosophical approaches), key alignments with CL are summarised here:

1. The construction of knowledge through scaffolded self-direction
   A clear principle of Vygotsky's approach is that learning is most effective within the Zone of Proximal Development (Golombek and Johnson 2019), which requires an individual to be supported so that they can attain a level of acquisition that could

not otherwise have been achieved. The pedagogic implementation of CL fits well here. Essentially there are two approaches to the use of CL in any educational context. One, and usually the first, is to prepare, edit and mediate corpus-based materials for use with the student teachers. The second is to allow the student teachers to experience the corpora first-hand in an unmediated way directly on the computer. Many use the first approach as a stepping-stone to the second (O'Keeffe and Farr 2003), and this fits perfectly with scaffolded learning. Another advantage here is that it allows for individual learner preferences, as some students like to engage immediately and directly with the technology, while others do not (Farr 2008), although I would suggest that this has become much more normalised in the last decade.

The idea that individuals take responsibility for their own learning fits perfectly with notions of discovery-based data-driven learning (Johns 1991; Warren 2016). Student teachers can explore corpora at their own pace and with their own hypotheses for investigation, and on the journey to discovering some of the answers they may also serendipitously uncover further interesting examples of language use. While acknowledging that knowledge transfer may be useful in specific contexts, it is now accepted that noticing, language awareness and inductive investigatory learning are preferred approaches. Corpora are artefacts in this respect, as the manipulation of the data through the use of computer software can help to highlight frequent and repeated patterns of language use which might not otherwise be visible in one-off examples of discourse.

2. The centrality of context, social facts and communities

   A key aspect of ELTE is context-based learning, present in all dimensions of Freeman's Design Theory summarised earlier. An understanding of the social context can be enhanced in two ways through CL. Firstly, the fact that language varies considerably in different contexts, varieties and genres is, thanks to corpus evidence, now beyond dispute (Reppen *et al.* 2002; Carter and McCarthy 2006). The judicious examination of a range of language varieties exposes student teachers to the influence of linguistic context. Secondly, in terms of pedagogic development, examples of practice from local and relevant situations, for example, EFL classroom data (A. Farrell 2019) or teacher education data (Riordan 2018), are of much greater benefit in the development of students' own pedagogic repertoires (Bax 1997). In this way CL provides a very suitable framework for the collection, analysis and application of appropriate materials in and for the local teaching context.

3 Corpora and pedagogy

This section is about pedagogy, which has a range of complementary dimensions in teacher education. I will discuss three in the following subsections.

Learning how to use CL in the English language classroom

This aspect of CL often finds a home in pedagogy modules in ELTE. It relates to helping student teachers understand the affordances of CL as a pedagogic tool. Since writing this chapter for the first edition of this Handbook, two excellent resources have become available. The first relates to the integration of CL in schools (Braun 2007; Pérez-Paredes

2019; Karlsen and Monsen 2020). There is an online resource centre hosted by Lancaster University as part of a project called *Corpus for Schools* led by Dana Gablasova. Of current relevance are the worksheets and activities that are being developed by the team for use in ESL classrooms and separately for A-level classrooms, for example, language and age, and spoken communication. Student handouts, supporting texts and very useful teacher notes are available for each of the topics. The second is an applied book series edited by McCarthy and O'Keeffe called *Routledge Corpus Linguistics Guides*. Although the series espouses to be research and practice oriented, I have found several of the volumes extremely useful when teaching student teachers about the potential pedagogic uses of corpora. Some obvious examples include *Corpus Linguistics for ELT* (Timmis 2015), *Corpus Linguistics for Vocabulary* (Szudarski 2017) and *Corpus Linguistics for Grammar* (Jones and Waller 2015). These two resources coupled with pedagogic corpora, or corpora which have been specifically designed for language teaching purposes (for example, the Backbone corpus and accompanying resources), rather than linguistic analysis per se now provide a wide-ranging repertoire for the student teacher.

In relation to pedagogic applications of corpora the task for ELTE programmes is simply one of making the student teachers aware of which are available and the possibilities for exploitation of corpus resources in the classroom, a topic on which many have now published (see, for example, O'Keeffe *et al.* 2007). And of course, we must remember that the largest corpus of all, albeit uncensored and unedited, is available to our student teachers in the form of the World Wide Web. *Sketch Engine* provides sophisticated tools to build corpora from the Web using combinations of search words and other criteria almost instantaneously (see Reppen 2016, and Chapter 2, this volume, for guidelines on how to design and build a corpus). Such resources and appropriate techniques provide a relatively easy route to the creation of relevant and interesting materials for classroom use. There is a related issue of using what are claimed to be corpus-based or corpus-informed publications (course books, etc.) by the publishers. It is important in teacher education programmes to alert student teachers to the type of criteria to use when evaluating the extent to which these claims hold true. This works well in a materials' evaluation component of the programme by encouraging the student teachers to ask critical questions such as: Which corpus resources were used? How are they integrated into the coursebook? Have they been edited or modified in any way? Are corpus statistics integrated or were they used in arbitrating the content in any way? Is their inclusion appropriate for the targeted level and learners? And others. This will go some way towards engendering a critical disposition among student teachers, although these questions may not be immediately answerable.

Using specialised corpora of classroom contexts to explore pedagogic practices

Moving to the second dimension of corpora and pedagogy, I would like to discuss the potentials of CL to help student teachers understand and develop their own general classroom pedagogy and interactions (Sert 2019). This requires the examination of more specialised corpora collected from appropriate contexts. The first, and most obviously relevant, is a corpus of classroom language, which can give a much better insider's perspective and can complement more traditional ELTE practices of classroom and peer observations. This type of work began in the 1970s with the publication of Sinclair and Coulthard's (1975) volume, reporting on data collected in the British primary school context and which identified the typical IRF classroom interaction pattern formally. More recently, research by Walsh (2006) investigates the EFL context. Consideration has also been given to the ways in which CL and conversation analysis can be merged for the exploitation of this type of discourse (Walsh and O'Keeffe 2007), and this combines well with other debates on appropriate and triangulated methodologies for the analysis of corpus data (Egbert and Baker 2019).

An excellent recent example is Farrell (2019), who researches a 60,000-word corpus of EFL classrooms to provide a rare corpus-based account of the issues and challenges that arise from the use of "non-standard" varieties of spoken English by teachers, alongside the use of Standard British English. The quantitative results and qualitative analysis using a wide range of classroom language extracts provide rich material for student teachers to explore classroom discourse, pedagogic practices and relevant sociolinguistic issues. This type of highly relevant applied research is expanding, and a forthcoming volume likely to be of interest is Nicaise's *Native and Non-Native Teacher Talk in the EFL Classroom: A Corpus-Informed Study* (2021). Baumgart's research (2012) highlights a second strand to data collected from such educational contexts, which has not normally been married with corpus linguistics, but which, arguably, should. Reference is being made here to the type of data used to uncover social and linguistic issues of specific communities, usually in mainstream education. More general sociolinguistic dimensions have also been explored through the lens of CL in volumes such as Murphy (2010) and Friginal (2017).

Using learner corpora for pedagogic purposes

A more direct route to learners' linguistic difficulties is often found in the examination of learner corpora (Meunier 2016; Friginal *et al.* 2017, and Chapters 22, 23and 30, this volume). It is extremely useful for student teachers to have access directly to learner language in order to identify differences and possible errors and the frequency with which these occur. The *International Corpus of Learner English* project was one of the first large-scale endeavours of this type. Now at Version 3, it is a corpus of writing by higher intermediate to advanced learners of English. It contains 3.7 million words of EFL writing from learners representing 16 mother tongue backgrounds. Although a very useful resource, it could be suggested that the greatest benefit can be derived from student teachers engaging in action research projects where they actually collect, create and analyse their own learner corpora. Student teachers always gain enormous insights into methodological issues (Egbert and Baker 2019) and experience a real sense of achievement from being in the role of teacher researcher. Corpora are also being used to profile learner competencies, especially in relation to vocabulary and grammar across the levels of proficiency in the *Common European Framework of Reference for Languages* (CEFR) (see Chapter 22, this volume).

4 Corpora and language awareness

However it is labelled, a knowledge and awareness of the way in which a language operates in formal, functional, discoursal and pragmatic ways, is inevitably a core component in ELTE. In the achievement of this goal, language teacher educators are very much indebted to CL in two very significant ways. Firstly, we are in the enviable position of having an array of reference materials available commercially, which are completely corpus-based, and this includes two comprehensive grammars based on authentic examples, frequency information and context-differentiated comparative accounts (Biber *et al.* 1999; Carter and McCarthy 2006). Secondly, much has been written on how to use corpora both in teaching and ELTE contexts for raising language awareness. Corpus-based language awareness now extends far beyond word- and sentence-level descriptions to more discourse-oriented perspectives (Cutting 2014; Clancy and McCarthy 2019), many with an important pragmatic focus (Rühlemann 2019; O'Keeffe *et al.* 2020). In this section, we discuss two associated issues of language awareness that relate specifically to language varieties.

At the time of the first edition of this book, many language genres had not yet been the subject of corpus-based examination. This has changed radically over the last ten years, and we now see very specific language contexts appearing in the research literature (see, for example, the Routledge series *Applying Corpus Linguistics*). These are all potentially extremely rich sources to use in ELTE programmes for the purposes of developing language awareness skills, and it may encourage student teachers to collect their own corpora and interpret them in an emic way. One of the primary motivations behind the creation of the Limerick Corpus of Irish English (LCIE) (Farr *et al.* 2004) was to capture the variety of English spoken in Ireland, which had not been done in any systematic way when the project began. This has proved a very worthwhile investment. Not only is it a significant source of spoken casual conversation, it is localised and therefore more relevant for learners in the Irish-English context in helping them to appreciate language variety issues but also in heightening awareness of their own personal language use before entering the world of ELT. Over the last ten years there has been a small explosion of corpus-based research into Irish English using L-CIE and complementary corpora (for example, Vaughan and Clancy 2016; Amador-Moreno and O'Keeffe 2018). In general, there is much overlap between the ways in which corpora are useful for raising language awareness in both ELT and ELTE contexts, the former of which receives much attention in this volume and therefore has received briefer attention in this chapter.

5 The discourses of ELTE: using specialised corpora for the reflective practices and professional development of educators and student teachers

In the final substantive section of this chapter, I return to the important issue raised in the introduction, and which has the potential to further discussions on ways in which we can extend the potential uses of CL in ELTE contexts. For me, this is the most exciting and innovative aspect. The key question here is what can corpus explorations tell us about the ways in which we conduct ELTE and how can we develop as a profession of teacher educators? The basic idea is to add to the techniques and tools used by teacher educators for the purposes of reflective practice and continued professional development by providing evidence-based accounts, as called for by many (Mann and Walsh 2017). We are all familiar with activities such as attending courses and conferences, keeping diaries, peer observations and personal development activities, among others, as part of our professional development (Farr 2015). The suggestion I make here is to record everyday professional activities and have them available for our own and others' reflection, critique and ultimate improvement. This can be done through audio-recordings and transcriptions and the collection of written artefacts from teacher education contexts, but in the move towards multi-modal corpora (see Chapter 3, this volume), it would probably be even more beneficial if at least some of those corpora were to exist in visual format also.

The present author's work in this area began some years ago, at first focusing on the teaching practice (TP) arena. A number of one-to-one TP feedback sessions were recorded, transcribed and analysed. The big departure from previous work is the fact that the examination was corpus-based. Some of the early examinations of the data (Farr 2005a) focused on the corpus as a piece of discourse and identified the relational strategies used by both parties in the interactions, as well as types of authoritative interventions (including prescriptive, informative and confrontational) and facilitative interventions (including supportive, catalytic and cathartic) (Farr 2005b). Both of these established this type of interaction as being generally within the area of support and advice type discourse used in ELTE contexts and in therapeutic contexts, which is really important given the focus on emotional aspects of teaching (Gkonou *et al.* 2020). The corpus analysis produced, for example, statistics on levels of participation for the student teachers and the tutors (a ratio of approximately 30:70 per cent) and identified the language which is relatively more significant in corpus data (metadiscourse, cognitive and cathartic words, personal and impersonal referencing techniques, words indicating interactivity and hedges) (for a full account, see Farr 2010).

In addition to my own endeavours investigating the social interactions in ELTE Riordan (2018) has expanded the range of contexts under scrutiny. In this highly relevant work, she collected a corpus of online and face-to-face interactions between student teachers and mentors. Her analysis shows different patterns of interaction depending on a range of speaker variables. Even more recently, Farr *et al.* (2019) created the *Teacher Education Corpus* (TEC). Using results from the analysis of this expanded corpus (consisting of the TP feedback and online interactions just mentioned, plus data in the form of spoken, written and online discourse from more experienced teachers), we examine three overlapping thematic areas in detail, all of which have high relevance in ELTE. The first of these is teacher socialisation and communities of practice (see Vaughan 2007 and Chapter 33, this volume); the second is identity and how it is articulated; the third is how teachers reflect and develop professionally during their ELTE programmes. This research has strongly influenced how we engage with our student teachers but also, perhaps more valuably, provide us with an excellent range of authentic data from the very context in which these teachers are studying. As well as being a rich source for action research, the data can be used as an awareness-raising tool for the induction of new tutors into teaching practice and for new student teachers who can now get a preview of what the various contexts will entail before being fully immersed. In other words, it allows for another mode of legitimate peripheral participation in the social contexts of ELTE and provides support for evidencing transformations in practice (for example, Vásquez and Reppen 2007).

This chapter has illustrated the ways in which CL can support current models and approaches in teacher education and how its adaptation into many of the subject contents can aid in the development of student teachers' awareness and understanding of pedagogic issues and practices, as well as their appreciation of formal, discoursal and pragmatic aspects of language used in a variety of contexts. All of this can be done in exploratory and investigatory ways through both mediated and direct access to corpora, which have the potential to enhance the educational experience and complement other effective, existing approaches. However, to reiterate what I said earlier, I see CL as one approach in ELTE, among others. I fully agree with McCarthy's position (2020: 10) that 'as a profession, we have been at our best when not hamstrung by ideology, whether it be exclusive slot-and-filler structuralism, blinkered CLT, narrow-minded SLA, dogmatic ELF or a heedless juggernaut of corpus-driven zeal'. For publishers, corpora are a given; for researchers, corpora are a given; and now our future teachers have become actively and critically engaged with corpus linguistics in their ELTE. For this to continue to happen, teacher educators need to take an active role in affording corpus integration the required space in education programmes, not as a segregated specialisation, but as a thread woven through many components of the course delivery. In my own practice over the past 20 years, this seems to have worked well.

Further reading

Farr, F., Farrell, A. and Riordan, E. (2019) *Social Interaction in Language Teacher Education. A Corpus and Discourse Perspective*, Edinburgh: Edinburgh University Press. (This volume examines a corpus of teacher education discourse around three main themes: socialisation and communities, identity, and reflective and developmental talk.)

Farr, F. and O'Keeffe, A. (2019) 'Using Corpus Approaches in English Language Teacher Education', in S. Walsh and S. Mann (eds) *The Routledge Handbook of English Language Teacher Education*, London: Routledge, pp. 268–82. (This outlines a number of ways in which localised and specialised corpora in particular can be included to enhance the ways in which teacher education is conducted.)

McCarthy, M. J. (2008) 'Accessing and Interpreting Corpus Information in the Teacher Education Context', *Language Teaching* 41(4): 563–74. (This raises issues in relation to the lack of inclusion of corpus-based approaches and materials in teacher education and outlines the ways in which they could and should be included to give future teachers more critical adaptation skills and influential lobbying power with researchers and publishers of corpus-based teaching materials.)

Vásquez, C. and Reppen, R. (2007) 'Transforming Practice: Changing Patterns of Participation in Post-Observation Meetings', *Language Awareness* 16(3): 153–72. (This illustrates how the collection of a corpus of teaching practice feedback meetings was used to identify what was considered to be an unsatisfactory participation balance between students teachers and tutors, the remedial action taken by the tutors and the resulting improvement in the second part of the teaching practice cycle.)

References

Amador-Moreno, C. P. and O'Keeffe, A. (2018) '"He's After Getting Up a Load of Wind": A Corpus-Based Exploration of *be+ after+ V-ing* Constructions in Spoken and Written Corpora', in D. Villanueva-Romero, C. P. Amador-Moreno and M. Sánchez García (eds) *Voice and Discourse in the Irish Context*, Palgrave Macmillan, pp. 47–73.

Baguley, N. (2019) '"Mind the Gap": Supporting Newly Qualified Teachers on their Journey from Pre-Service Training to Full-Time Employment', in S. Walsh and S. Mann (eds) *The Routledge Handbook of English Language Teacher Education*, London: Routledge, pp. 125–37.

Baumgart, J. (2012) 'Looking at the Multicultural Classrooms in Ireland: Teacher Educators' Perspectives', in F. Farr and M. Moriarty (eds) *Language, Learning and Teaching: Irish Research Perspectives*, Berlin: Peter Lang, pp. 113–40.

Bax, S. (1997) 'Roles for a Teacher Educator in Context-Sensitive Teacher Education', *English Language Teaching Journal* 51(3): 232–41.

Biber, D., Johansson, S., Leech, J., Conrad, S. and Finegan, E. (1999) *Longman Grammar of Spoken and Written English*, London and New York: Longman.

Boulton, A. and Cobb, T. (2017) 'Corpus Use in Language Learning: A Meta-Analysis', *Language Learning* 67(2): 348–93.
Braun, S. (2007) 'Integrating Corpus Work into Secondary Education: From Data-Driven Learning to Needs-Driven Corpora', *ReCALL* 19(3): 307–32.
Burns, A. (2010) *Doing Action Research in English Language Teaching. A Guide for Practitioners*, New York: Routledge.
Callies, M. (2019) 'Integrating Corpus Literacy into Language Teacher Education: The Case of Learner Corpora', in S. Götz and J. Mukherjee (eds) *Learner Corpora and Language Teaching*, Amsterdam; Philadelphia: John Benjamins, pp. 245–63.
Carter, R. A. and McCarthy, M. J. (2006) *Cambridge Grammar of English*, Cambridge: Cambridge University Press.
Clancy, B. and McCarthy, M. J. (2019) 'From Language as System to Language as Discourse', in S. Walsh and S. Mann (eds) *The Routledge Handbook of English Language Teacher Education*, London: Routledge, pp. 201–15.
Coniam, D. (1997) 'A Practical Introduction to Corpora in a Teacher Training Language Awareness Programme', *Language Awareness* 6(4): 199–207.
Cutting, J. (2014) *Language in Context in TESOL*, Edinburgh: Edinburgh University Press.
Dragas, T. (2019) 'Embedding Reflective Practice in an INSET Course', in S. Walsh and S. Mann (eds) *The Routledge Handbook of English Language Teacher Education*, London: Routledge, pp. 138–54.
Edge, J. and Richards, K. (1998) 'Why *Best Practice* is not Good Enough', *TESOL Quarterly* 32(3): 569–76.
Egbert, J. and Baker, P. (eds) (2019) *Using Corpus Methods to Triangulate Linguistic Analysis*, London: Routledge.
Farr, F. (2005a) 'Relational Strategies in the Discourse of Professional Performance Review in an Irish Academic Environment: The Case of Language Teacher Education', in K. Schneider and A. Barron (eds) *The Pragmatics of Irish English*, Berlin: Mouton de Gruyter, pp. 203–34.
Farr, F. (2005b) 'Reflecting on Reflections: The Spoken Word as a Professional Development Tool in Language Teacher Education', in R. Hughes (ed.) *Spoken English, Applied Linguistics and TESOL: Challenges for Theory and Practice*, Hampshire: Palgrave Macmillan, pp. 182–215.
Farr, F. (2010) *The Discourse of Teaching Practice Feedback. An Analysis of Spoken and Written Modes*, London: Routledge.
Farr, F. (2015) *Practice in TESOL*, Edinburgh: Edinburgh University Press.
Farr, F. (2008) 'Evaluating the Use of Corpus-Based Instruction in a Language Teacher Education Context: Perspectives from the Users', *Language Awareness* 17(1): 25–43.
Farr, F., Farrell, A. and Riordan, E. (2019) *Social Interaction in Language Teacher Education. A Corpus and Discourse Perspective*, Edinburgh: Edinburgh University Press.
Farr, F., Murphy, B. and O'Keeffe, A. (2004) 'The Limerick Corpus of Irish English: Design, Description and Application', *Teanga (Yearbook of the Irish Association for Applied Linguistics)* 21: 5–29
Farr, F. and O'Keeffe, A. (2019) 'Using Corpus Approaches in English Language Teacher Education', in S. Walsh and S. Mann (eds) *The Routledge Handbook of English Language Teacher Education*, London: Routledge, pp. 268–82.
Farrell, A. (2019) *Corpus Perspectives on the Spoken Mode*practitioner and action researcher*ls Used by EFL Teachers*, London: Routledge.
Farrell, T. S. (2012) 'Reflecting on Reflective Practice: (Re)Visiting Dewey and Schon', TESOL *Journal 3*(1): 7–16.
Farrell, T. S. (2019) 'Reflective Practice in L2 Teacher Education', in S. Walsh and S. Mann (eds) The Routledge Handbook of English Language Teacher Education, London: Routledge, pp. 38–51.
Freeman, D. (2001) 'Second Language Teacher Education', in R. A. Carter, and D. Nunan (eds) *The Cambridge Guide to Teaching English to Speakers of Other Languages*, Cambridge: Cambridge University Press, pp. 72–9.
Freeman, D. (2016) *Educating Second Language Teachers*, Oxford: Oxford University Press.
Friginal, E. (ed.) (2017) *Studies in Corpus-Based Sociolinguistics*. New York: Routledge.
Friginal, E., Lee, J., Polat, B. and Roberson, A. (2017) *Exploring Spoken English Learner Language from Corpora: Learner Talk*, London: Palgrave McMillan.

Gkonou, C., Dewaele, J. M. and King, J. (eds) (2020) *The Emotional Rollercoaster of Language Teaching*, London: Multilingual Matters.

Golombek, P. R. and Johnson, K. E. (2019) 'Materialising a Vygotskian-Inspired Language Teacher Education Pedagogy', in S. Walsh and S. Mann (eds) *The Routledge Handbook of English Language Teacher Education*, London: Routledge, pp. 25–37.

Hunston, S. (1995) 'Grammar in Teacher Education: The Role of a Corpus', *Language Awareness* 4(1): 15–31.

Johns, T. (1991) 'Should You Be Persuaded – Two Samples of Data-Driven Learning Materials', *English Language Research Journal* 4: 1–16.

Jones, C. and Waller, D. (2015) Corpus Linguistics for Grammar, London: Routledge.

Karlsen, P. H. and Monsen, M. (2020) 'Corpus Literacy and Applications in Norwegian Upper Secondary Schools: Teacher and Learner Perspectives', *The Nordic Journal of English Studies* 19(1): 118–48.

Kiddle, T. and Prince, T. (2019) 'Digital and Online Approaches to Language Teacher Education', in S. Walsh and S. Mann (eds) *The Routledge Handbook of English Language Teacher Education*, London: Routledge, pp. 111–24.

Kinginger, C. (2002) 'Defining the Zone of Proximal Development in US Foreign Language Education', *Applied Linguistics* 23(2): 240–61.

Kozulin, A. (1998) Psychological Tools. *A Sociocultural Approach to Education*, Cambridge, Massachusetts: Harvard University Press.

Leńko-Szymanska, A. (2017) 'Training Teachers in Data-Driven Learning: Tackling the Challenge', *Language Learning and Technology* 21(3): 217–14.

Malderez, A. and C. Bodóczky (1999) Mentor Courses. *A Resource Book for Trainer-Trainers*, Cambridge: Cambridge University Press.

Mann, S. and Walsh, S. (2017) *Reflective Practice in English Language Teaching. Research-Based Principles and Practices*, New York and London: Routledge.

McCarthy, M. J. (2020) 'Fifty-Five Years and Counting: A Half-Century of Getting it Half-Right?' *Language Teaching* 54(3): 1–12. 10.1017/S0261444820000075

McCarthy, M. J. (2016) 'Issues in Second Language Acquisition in Relation to Blended Learning', in M. J. McCarthy (ed.) *The Cambridge Guide to Blended Learning for Language Teaching*, Cambridge: Cambridge University Press, pp. 7–24.

McCarthy, M. J. (2008) 'Accessing and Interpreting Corpus Information in the Teacher Education Context', *Language Teaching* 41(4): 563–74.

Meunier, F. (2016) 'Learner Corpora and Pedagogic Applications' in F. Farr and L. Murray (eds) *The Routledge Handbook of Language Learning and Technology*, London: Routledge, pp. 376–86.

Morton, T. (2019) 'Teacher Education in Content-Based Language Education', in S. Walsh and S. Mann (eds) *The Routledge Handbook of English Language Teacher Education*, London: Routledge, pp. 169–83.

Murphy, B. (2010) *Corpus and Sociolinguistics: Investigating Age and Gender in Female Talk*, Amsterdam: John Benjamins.

Murphy, B. and Riordan, E. (2016) 'Corpus Types and Uses', in F. Farr and L. Murray (eds) *The Routledge Handbook of Language Learning and Technology*, London: Routledge, pp. 388–403.

Nicaise, E. (2021) *Native and Non-Native Teacher Talk in the EFL Classroom: A Corpus-Informed Study*, London: Routledge.

O'Keeffe, A., Clancy, B. and Adolphs, S. (2020) *Introducing Pragmatics in Use*, 2nd edn, London: Routledge.

O'Keeffe, A. and Farr, F. (2003) 'Using Language Corpora in Language Teacher Education: Pedagogic, Linguistic and Cultural Insights', *TESOL Quarterly* 37(3): 389–418.

O'Keeffe, A., McCarthy, M. J. and Carter, R. A. (2007) *From Corpus to Classroom: Language Use and Language Teaching*, Cambridge: Cambridge University Press.

Pérez-Paredes, P. (2019) 'The Pedagogical Advantage of Teenage Corpora for Secondary School Learners', in P. Crosthwaite (ed.) *Data-Driven Learning for the Next Generation: Corpora and DDL for Pre-tertiary Learners*, London: Routledge, pp. 67–87.

Reppen, R. (2016) 'Designing and Building a Corpus for Language Learning', in F. Farr and L. Murray (eds) *The Routledge Handbook of Language Learning and Technology*, London: Routledge, pp. 404–12.

Reppen, R., Fitzmaurice, S. and Biber, D. (eds) (2002) *Using Corpora to Explore Linguistic Variation*, Amsterdam: John Benjamins.
Riordan, E. (2018) TESOL Student Teacher Discourse. *A Corpus-Based Analysis of On-line and Face-to-Face Interactions*, London: Routledge.
Rühlemann, C. (2019) *Corpus Linguistics for Pragmatics. A Guide for Research*, London: Routledge.
Sert, O. (2019) 'Classroom Interaction and Language Teacher Education', in S. Walsh and S. Mann (eds) *The Routledge Handbook of English Language Teacher Education*, London: Routledge, pp. 216–38.
Sinclair, J. M. and Coulthard, M. (1975) *Towards an Analysis of Discourse. The English used by Teachers and Pupils*, Oxford: Oxford University Press.
Szudarski, P. (2017) *Corpus Linguistics for Vocabulary*, London: Routledge.
Thornbury, S. (2019) 'Methodology Texts and the Construction of Teachers' Practical Knowledge', in S. Walsh and S. Mann (eds) *The Routledge Handbook of English Language Teacher Education*, London: Routledge, pp. 509–21.
Timmis, I. (2015) *Corpus Linguistics for ELT*, London: Routledge.
Vásquez, C. and Reppen, R. (2007) 'Transforming Practice: Changing Patterns of Participation in Post-Observation Meetings', *Language Awareness* 16(3): 153–72.
Vaughan, E. (2007) "I think we should just accept … our horrible lowly status': Analysing Teacher-Teacher Talk within the Context of Community of Practice', *Language Awareness* 16(3): 173–88.
Vaughan, E. and Clancy, B. (2016) 'Sociolinguistic Information and Irish English Corpora', in R. Hickey (ed) *Sociolinguistics in Ireland*, London: Palgrave Macmillan, pp. 365–88.
Vygotsky, L. S. (1978). *Mind in Society: The Development of Higher Psychological Processes*, Cambridge, MA: Harvard University Press.
Wallace, M. (1998) *Action Research for Language Teachers*, Cambridge: Cambridge University Press.
Walsh, S. (2006) *Investigating Classroom Discourse*, London: Routledge.
Walsh, S. and Mann, S. (eds) (2019) *The Routledge Handbook of English Language Teacher Education*, London: Routledge.
Walsh, S. and O'Keeffe, A. (2007) 'Applying CA to a Modes Analysis of Third-Level Spoken Academic Discourse', in H. Bowles and P. Seedhouse (eds) *Conversation Analysis in Languages for Specific Purposes*, Berlin: Peter Lang, pp. 101–39.
Warren, M. (2016) 'Introduction to Data-Driven Learning', in F. Farr and L. Murray (eds) *The Routledge Handbook of Language Learning and Technology*, London: Routledge, pp. 337–47.

33

How can teachers use a corpus for their own research?

Elaine Vaughan

1 Using a corpus for your own research: being professionally curious

This chapter is aimed at teachers who are interested in conducting their own professional and/or pedagogical research and want to explore the possibilities of using a corpus approach in this regard. Practising language teachers engage in and/or with research (cf. Borg 2013), including corpus research, for a wide variety of reasons. Motivation for this engagement may arise from challenges or opportunities in the immediate teaching and learning environment, personal or academic interests, interaction with colleagues or as response to research findings which have been released into the public domain. However, a unifying feature of such research – and one which is crucial to the profession of teaching as a whole – is professional curiosity. The potential range of research that curiosity might generate is hard to predict, given that there is much to be done, and not all of what is being done finds its way into the public domain. However, professional engagement in research (of whatever type) is critical to quality research of benefit to the practice and profession of second language teaching and learning. The nexus of teaching and research has at different times been problematised as imbalanced and top-down, unsustainable or bearing little practical value for the language classroom (see Medgyes 2017; Paran 2017), although the classroom is not necessarily, nor should it be, the sole end of any "teaching-related" research. Discussion of the relationship between teaching and research does often pivot around a perceived nexus of roles, hierarchies and priorities (e.g. Xerri 2017). There are deeper issues of access to research (Sato and Loewen 2019), its intrinsic usefulness and whether or not it actually reflects or informs the profession or practice (McKinley 2019). Early advocates of corpus linguistics in second language pedagogy emphasised integration of corpus-based research into teachers' professional repertoires and practices (e.g. Fligelstone 1993; Coniam 1997; Leech 1997). In tandem with this, *corpus literacy*, the ability to access, exploit and interpret corpus output, has been advocated (Mukherjee 2006; Frankenberg-Garcia 2012; Callies 2019). The importance of novice teachers' and experienced practitioners' participation in corpus-based research is also a consistent refrain over time (e.g. O'Keeffe and Farr 2003; Tsui 2005; McCarthy 2008; Breyer 2009; Römer 2009, 2011; Farr 2011; Timmis 2015).

DOI: 10.4324/9780367076399-33

However, this has not necessarily translated into widespread provision of corpus linguistics in language teacher education and training programmes (O'Keeffe and Farr 2003; McCarthy 2008; Granath 2009; O'Keeffe and Farr 2019; and Chapter 32, this volume). Nor, indeed, has it translated into global awareness of corpus research and methods within language teaching as a profession. Clearly, despite regular discussion of the "potential" of corpus linguistics vis-à-vis language teaching and learning (see Timmis 2015: 7–8), language teaching professionals' ownership of and engagement in corpus research is still a relatively elusive factor. The selection of work surveyed later in this chapter focuses broadly on corpus research that intersects with key areas of second language teaching and learning and then zones in on professional interaction on the spoken to written spectrum, including work which focuses on language use *inside* the classroom, the context that most pervades the published literature. *Outside* the classroom, the lion's share of work takes place in developmental contexts such as language teacher education (LTE). This chapter advocates work that considers professional language in the workplace, a site of research that language teaching professionals are uniquely positioned to conduct as individuals and teams. This can be achieved through a combination of professional engagement and a desire to stand back and survey the evidence objectively – or professional curiosity allied with a research perspective.

There is no scarcity of published work which deals specifically with the relationship between corpora, corpus linguistics, language research, pedagogy and education (see McEnery and Xiao 2011 or Vaughan and McCarthy 2017). This work defines and describes types of corpora, demonstrating the direct and indirect applications corpora may have for the classroom and language-based research in the sphere of second language teaching and learning (see Flowerdew 2012 for a book-length treatment). The present chapter offers in its contribution to this plethora an outline of the various contexts of corpus research in second language teaching and learning and contributes a perspective on how teachers, researchers and teacher-researchers can and have been using corpora for their own research. One of the major benefits of corpus-based based research for language teachers lies in its potential as a teacher development tool (e.g. O'Keeffe and Farr 2003; O'Keeffe *et al.* 2007; Farr 2011). To conceptualise how, Waters's (2005) characterisation of the tripartite elements within his preferred superordinate term "teacher education" is useful: teacher *training*, teacher *education* and teacher *development*. Teacher training, or perhaps more appropriately "preparation" (see Mann 2005), concerns itself with the practical, for example, classroom-based skills. Teacher education is more connected to research and background knowledge, while teacher development has a focus on raising awareness of practices and fostering reflection and change (Waters 2005: 211). He characterises these three interconnected aspects as *doing* (teacher training), *knowing* (teacher education) and *being* (teacher development). While the first two tend to be a mediated experience for teachers, the latter is different in that it is most often self-directed. Corpus-based research can be a means of investigating the *doing*, *knowing* and *being* of teaching and learning. In this regard, what the practitioner-researcher needs is genuine professional curiosity, a sense of how corpora are built and work and what sort of questions they have the potential to provide whole or partial answers for. This chapter also suggests that those of us engaged in researching professional contexts and practices reconsider the limits of our purview and what teaching-related research might logically encompass. It suggests one instance of where we might extend these boundaries, presenting an excerpt from a case study of teacher professional life, not within the classroom or language education context, but within the professional workplace. This is a context that is relatively unexplored by comparison, but can yield rich insights on one of the (many) 'occluded genres' (Swales 1996: 46) of the profession of English language teaching.

2 Issues in using corpora for educational research

The provenance of corpus linguistics as a research field is mapped out more comprehensively by McCarthy and O'Keeffe (2010 and Chapter 1, this volume), but anywhere an initial definition is presented, the preliminary step is usually to define what a corpus is (and, of course, indicate the clunky plural form, *corpora*). This is because corpus linguistics is 'ultimately about *finding out about the nature and usage of language*' (McEnery and Hardie 2012: 228; italics in original), via the construction/investigation of language corpora using a range of corpus analysis techniques (see Vaughan and O'Keeffe 2015 and Chapter 9, this volume). All corpora are collections of texts of various types, but are characterised by purpose and design; the use of corpus software to explore features and patterning; and, critically, comparison with other corpora. Most descriptions of defining characteristics of a corpus make mention of corpus size. Indeed, the issue of how large a corpus should be, or even how small a corpus *can* be, has been a recurrent theme (see Vaughan and Clancy 2013). There has never been an upper limit on corpora, particularly those designed to inform grammar reference works or for use in lexicography. The *Cambridge International Corpus* (CIC), contains over a billion words of spoken and written texts and has been used to inform Cambridge dictionaries, but also English language course books, vocabulary builders and grammar reference works, such as *The Cambridge Grammar of English* (Carter and McCarthy 2006). Many of the corpora available via the online corpus management platform *Sketch Engine* run to billions of words. Clearly, to inform reference works, a corpus should be as large as possible, and the same holds true for corpora that are designed to represent national varieties. However, capturing the totality of any language variety, of whatever specific type (see Chapter 6, this volume), is a virtual impossibility: that would mean capturing all of language use, all the time, everywhere. The challenge, then, is to sample from an impossible-to-define population, an appropriate, *representative* amount.

Representativeness within a corpus, 'or the extent to which a sample includes the full range of variability in a population' (Biber 1993: 243), is probably a more salient issue than corpus size where corpora are designed to produce generalisable findings (see Chapters 2–6, this volume). Language data have proven resistant to standard approaches to statistical sampling (Clear 1992: 21) and sampling frames, and so Biber proposes strata and sampling frames suitable for language based on *register*, or situationally defined text categories such as "fiction", "news article", etc., and linguistically defined *text types*, such as various written or spoken modes (see Chapters 2–6, this volume). With regard to sample size, Biber's previous research on 1,000-word samples from the *London-Lund and Lancaster/Oslo/Bergen* corpus had concluded that these relatively small samples yielded similar functional and grammatical findings (Biber 1990). These connected points raise questions that are important for teachers planning to actually build corpora for their own research, though it should be emphasised that it is not necessarily essential to build a corpus. Whether or not that happens is entirely dependent on the nature of the research being planned. For many, it may be possible to do independent research on particular language features using existing corpora, some of which are accessible via user-friendly online search platforms, such as the *Corpus of*

Contemporary American English (COCA) (see Davies 2010), and produce more generalisable results. For most *small corpus studies*, the best way to describe many of those discussed later, results are not strictly generalisable, and while that should always be acknowledged, in many ways they actually do not need to be, given the equal value placed on generating context-dependent knowledge in the broader fields of language description. It is more important to be able to establish whether or not a broad or specific finding that emerges from a small corpus study might be particular to the very specific context it describes or hold across other examples of that context type via comparison with published results, for example.

In terms of consulting existing corpora, one obvious obstacle is corpus literacy (discussed later). Other obstacles may be access to resources such as basic corpus training, online corpus platforms, free-standing corpus software and computer labs for use with students, amongst others. These are rarely emphasised across a literature that, on the whole, assumes its audience is the university-based language teacher/pre-service trainee (Frankenberg-Garcia 2016). While some of these resources are a prerequisite for any form of research and hands-on activities with language learners, the lack of some of these types of facilities in the immediate environment does not preclude engagement with corpus-based research for pedagogical/professional activity. These concerns aside, there are a number of essential skills practitioners new to using corpora need to develop. These include having a broad overview of the range and types of corpora that exist and are freely and commercially accessible (see Chapter 8, this volume) in order to develop awareness of what these corpora can, and cannot, offer. The vast majority of accessible, large, general-purpose corpora will be useful for generating examples of particular structures and features that may be the language focus in a class. This is a common reason for corpus consultation, which might not be considered as formal research per se but is a good way of becoming familiar with corpora.

Being able to critically evaluate and make an informed choice in relation to whether an existing corpus is appropriate for the investigation of a research question or whether a new, more specialised corpus is required is the first step for the early-stage practitioner-researcher. Corpus literacy, or the ability to generate and frame corpus queries, as well as interpret results is essential. From a research perspective, understanding how corpora are compiled, formulating appropriate corpus queries and being aware of the impact of corpus size and composition on output related to these queries are skills as critical as mastering the mechanics of using specific software to explore corpora. For the mechanics and beyond, the Lancaster University MOOC *Corpus Linguistics: Method, Analysis, Interpretation*, hosted by *Future Learn* at the time of writing, is an excellent resource. Investigating language use questions, for example, establishing the lexical characteristics of written academic texts like journal articles, or queries around most frequent phrasal verbs in informal conversation, is likely to be possible using existing corpora. However, teachers about to embark upon corpus research – the readers of this chapter – are likely to have framed research questions linked to their professional practices or domains, for which there may not be an existing corpus that will answer these questions adequately. Therefore, the next section deals specifically with research that is predicated on gathering naturally occurring samples of professional language use and focuses on aspects of building a bespoke corpus of language data for this purpose that this entails.

3 Building your own corpus based on your practice

Among the many advantages that practising teachers have when it comes to investigating professional and pedagogical questions is that their position in teaching institutions means that the relevant participants and data are within immediate proximity. Adopting a corpus approach is, naturally, only one of the many methodological approaches that might be appropriate to the investigation of questions immediate to the profession and practice of language teaching. It is particularly useful if the research is based on the investigation of spoken or written interaction, which can be captured and contained electronically. Corpus methods can coexist harmoniously with many paradigms of research and can be used in tandem with complementary discourse analytic methods, such as conversation analysis (e.g. Walsh *et al.* 2011). This means that the contents of a small corpus can be explored in a more detailed way once corpus analytical procedures have yielded an overview of patterns in the data (see Chapters 2–4, this volume). There are some specific points to consider, related to the macro- and micro-ethics of doing research in the second language teaching and learning environment (cf. Kubanyiova 2008), especially one's own, which should be mentioned here. The macro-ethics are procedural, usually codified by institutions and organisations. These generally outline professional conduct around approaching access to sites of research, ensuring informed consent is gained, and provide guidelines around using and protecting data. Micro-ethics are of particular concern for situated research of the type that we move towards here. These are closer, context-specific issues, such as our own position vis-à-vis the research, our research values and other aspects of working ethically with the participants involved, where the participants are typically our colleagues and/or students.

Once access has been negotiated, the next step is securing consent to record/collect, use and safely store data. This means that students' or colleagues' permission to record (in the case of spoken data) or compile (in the case of written data) language material that 'belongs' to them. Most learners and colleagues are more likely to engage if teacher-researchers are up-front about why the interaction or language materials are necessary for the research and are clear about the purpose of the research itself. This is even more the case if it is going to address a practical problem or highlight good practices (see Healy and Onderdonk 2013). Informed consent should be obtained at the beginning of the research, and the learners or colleagues who cooperate in the research should be confident that their data will be treated ethically, understand how the data will be used and disseminated, for example, in presentations publications or as a contribution to a larger project (a thorough consent form will cover all these possibilities). Where the research community at large is concerned, the corpus design should be carefully considered, fully described and its contextual information preserved in order to ensure that it is replicable (information about the data is commonly referred to as "metadata"; see Chapters 2–4, this volume). As a rule of thumb, another researcher should be able to add to the corpus or build a companion corpus by adhering to the design principles. This creates the possibility for what is originally a context-specific corpus research project to become an organic, community endeavour.

If the corpus is to contain spoken texts, then sensitive enough recording devices, a consistent system of transcription and secure storage of sound files will be important (see Chapter 3, this volume). Transcription is a slow process; McCarthy (2008: 571) estimates that 1 hour of talk can take 12 to 15 hours to transcribe, and that process becomes more complex depending on the number of speakers (see Chapter 3, this volume). Despite its labour-intensive nature, the transcription of spoken data by the researcher conducting the study brings serious advantages. For one thing, it augments familiarity with the data the corpus contains, and, as transcription proceeds, particular language features which will be interesting to look into in greater detail can be identified for preliminary analysis. While written text sources, especially those derived via web scraping, may not require the same type of processing, the same type of attention is required. If, for example, a corpus of student essays or other written work is not submitted electronically, these will also need to be transliterated, and the same sort of familiarity and insight proceeds as with spoken transcription. Transcription itself should be sensitive, consistent and principled (see Jenks 2011).

Two final points should be made on the building of corpora which are implicated in the third of the issues outlined earlier, the position of the researcher and the broader micro-ethics of this type of research. When teachers create their own spoken corpora, they are often amongst the participants in the interaction they are recording; for example, a corpus of students performing interactive classroom tasks may include the instructions given by the class teacher, who is also the corpus compiler. Being involved in an authentic situation as a participant-analyst can be extraordinarily positive, but it is also important to acknowledge the potential biases this dual role may bring. In setting out to record authentic, spoken interaction, an oft-mentioned Catch-22–like situation occurs; inevitably, a degree of artificiality is introduced into a previously authentic situation, which is physically present as the recording device (no matter how discreet it is). Any negative impact that recording has on the comfort and behaviour of participants can be mitigated in the early stages of the study by ensuring that participants are clear about the purpose of the study and why it is useful to do. As previously mentioned, informed consent is a fundamental consideration, and participants should be confident that their contributions will be treated ethically, for example, by protecting the anonymity of participants thoroughly, changing names, place names and any other features in the transcript that could identify the precise location or participants. A short time into recording, most participants forget that the microphone is there and so the "microphone effect" is by and large mitigated. It would be responsible practice to ensure that the participants have access to the corpus, or at least the transcribed texts, for review, approval, use in instruction or their own research. This should be discussed and agreed in advance and is not without its own caveats. While institutions and organisations have their own ethical guidelines, for teachers doing research with corpora outside of research institutions, the British Association for Applied Linguistics (BAAL) *Recommendations on Good Practice in Applied Linguistics Research* (2016) is a good resource. De Costa (2015) is an insightful guide on the micro-ethical issues that arise in conducting educational research as a professional insider/institutional outsider doing research.

4 What can be done with corpora inside and outside the classroom?

Ultimately, the only possible answer to the question "how can teachers use a corpus for their own research?" is "it depends on the question". We might ask instead how corpora have been deployed in investigating the *doing*, *knowing* and *being* of language teaching and considering what sort of insights a corpus approach have already been disseminated. Discussions of the relevance of corpus studies for educational domains tend to distinguish between different points of impact, both indirect and direct (Leech 1997; Johansson 2009; Römer 2009, 2011; Flowerdew 2012; Timmis 2015). Indirect applications are seen as reference works, materials and the design and validation of language tests, for example; applications construed as direct include students using corpora in the classroom, by directly accessing corpora guided by teachers conversant in their pedagogical application. Some areas, such as compiling dictionaries or the production of grammar reference books (e.g. Biber *et al.* 1999; Carter and McCarthy 2006), are more firmly established, while others, particularly the use of corpora in the classroom, as products of teacher choice and discretion, are arguably less widespread (see Timmis 2015). Where testing and assessment are concerned, corpora have informed major reviews and evaluation of language tests as well as informing current practices in developing and validating tests (Barker 2014; Park 2014 and Chapter 45, this volume). A major project, English Profile, which has a core aim of developing and substantiating the reference level descriptions of L2 users of English based on the Common European Framework of Reference (CEFR), uses a subset of the *Cambridge Learner Corpus* containing learner language produced under examination conditions (see Saville and Hawkey 2010 for an overview) (see Chapter 22, this volume).

Early work by Mindt (1996) identified a mismatch between corpus evidence based on natural contexts of language use and the content of English language textbooks; Meunier and Gouverneur (2009) provide an overview of studies of this type, and Chapter 26, this volume, looks at the applications of contemporary corpus research in designing and developing coursebooks. Researchers are interested in investigating learner language and compiling large learner corpora to do so in the consideration of the relationship between materials used to teach and what could be prioritised in language teaching (Meunier and Reppen 2015; Paquot 2018). Learner corpora are used to investigate the practical and theoretical bases of foreign language teaching, and learner corpus research has been one of the more rapidly developing independent fields of research at the intersection of corpus linguistics and language education (see Granger *et al.* 2015; Brzezina and Flowerdew 2017). From a language education perspective, edited volumes such as Sinclair (2004) and Aijmer (2009) present case studies of how corpora can be used directly and indirectly in the classroom by informing pedagogical practices and priorities, but also, as with language testing, to add to theory development in, for example, second language acquisition research (see also Seedhouse 2019 and Chapter 23, this volume). Chambers (2019) focuses on closing the research–practice gap between studies that report on the direct or mediated use of corpora in the classroom, studies that use corpora to interrogate the content, theoretical bases and practices of language teaching and the criticality of language educators who are not corpus linguists actively engaging with corpora data in the classroom (O'Keeffe and Mark 2017; O'Keeffe 2020; see also Chapter 29, this volume).

Where teacher professional language is concerned, the aspects of teacher language that have been prioritised in the existing (not exclusively corpus-based) research is generally centred on understanding teacher language in connection to how classrooms work and how the profession considers its practices within them reflexively. Walsh (2006, 2011, 2013) shows that teacher language in the L2 context is typified by 1) teachers controlling patterns of communication, 2) question and answer routines, 3) "repair" or correction of learner errors being the prerogative of the teacher and 4) modification of teacher speech to accommodate learners. He posits a framework (*Self-Evaluation of Teacher Talk*, or *SETT*) to facilitate the description of language in the classroom and as a conduit for understanding the complex interactional processes that occur within it (*ibid*: 62–92; see also Sert 2019). While SETT developed as an applied conversation analytic framework, it provides an excellent discourse-level structure for teachers using a corpus to research classroom discourse. Elements of the framework and the potential linguistic proxies associated with them can be validated and explored. For example, Yang (2014) blends SETT and corpus linguistics to investigate teacher's use of discourse markers in the classroom.

Findings from the field of LTE have illuminated the concerns of language teachers in training. For example, (corpus) analyses of post-observation interaction in the LTE context have led to unique insights into its characteristics, the discursive construction of supervisory interventions and how they are responded to, and this has enhanced pedagogical practices developed around them (Vásquez 2004; Vásquez and Reppen 2007; Copland 2008; Farr 2011; Farr *et al.* 2019). This specific language event in the life of the trainee – feedback meetings on trainee's observed classes – is inherently face-threatening and necessitates deft interpersonal and linguistic negotiation. Corpus-based work on discourse produced in contexts of initial teacher education, such as teaching practice, post-observation feedback and reflective blogs produced during third-level courses also provide important insights into specific elements of the trajectories of professional development with participants that are in the process of *becoming* teachers (see Farr *et al.* 2019 for a comprehensive overview of these LTE contexts and Chapter 32, this volume). The final aspect of how teachers have been using corpora to carry out research such as in the broad categories outlined earlier, the investigation of language teaching practices and professional research is one that is ripe for expansion: namely, the investigation of teachers' professional language, particularly that which occurs outside the classroom.

5 What can a corpus tell us about a professional language teaching context? The case of C-MELT

This study we discuss here aimed to investigate teacher talk in the workplace and required recourse to a corpus which contains samples of that language in use. As this very specific corpus did not exist, it was necessary to build one. The *Corpus of Meetings of English Language Teachers* (C-MELT) consists of six meetings in two language teaching institutions in two different countries, México and Ireland. In all approximately 3.5 hours of interaction were recorded (c. 40,000 words). It therefore represents a sample of the situated language use and practices of two local communities of teachers who form part of a hypothesised larger, global community (Vaughan 2007). Its underlying purpose was to put practising teachers in the frame, the rationale being that practices outside the classroom are at least as interesting and just as deserving of research attention as those that occur within it. In C-MELT, teachers talk about the day-to-day business of teaching: placing students according to ability, examinations/assessment, student attendance and motivation, administrative issues, workplace frustrations, etc. To place C-MELT in the larger context of teacher professional interaction, some of the contexts of language use *inside* and *outside* the classroom are outlined in Figure 33.1. This should come with the caveat that, in the first instance, professional language use happens in multiple modes and within each will be overlaps and blurred boundaries; in addition, encompassing all of the suggested contexts could be digital environments, as well as within each element of the schematic. Another way of characterising the contexts is to consider whether they occur in the professional *frontstage* (classroom) or *backstage* (outside the classroom) (Goffman 1971; this is a blunt division, and the practical rationale for making it in this way can be found in Vaughan 2007). Most research on teacher language is conducted with an eye to the classroom, but this research is about what happens unrehearsed in the staffroom when the "gloves are off". This was the crux of the larger study which emerged from close analysis of C-MELT.

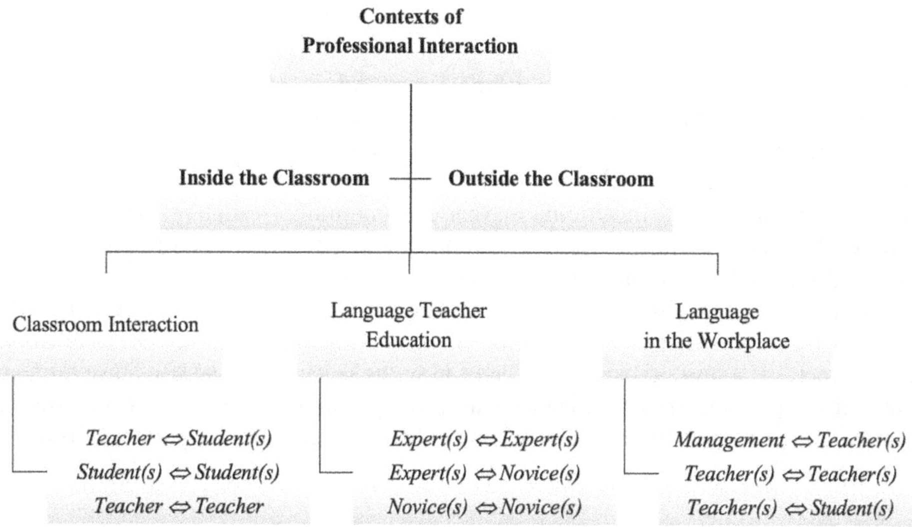

Figure 33.1 Some contexts of professional interaction

The output of corpus analysis tools such as wordlists, clusters, keywords and concordancing (see Chapters 9, 10 and 14, this volume) were allied with the aim of investigating what linguistic markers of community and identity could be extrapolated from them. Lists of words and clusters on their own compared with larger corpora meant that sometimes "small" items carrying multiple meanings were working in specialised ways in the interaction, such as highly contextualised referential aspects of pronouns such as *you*, *we* and *they* (see Vaughan and Clancy 2013). As the corpus was small, it was possible to explore specific aspects of the teachers' shared linguistic and professional repertoire (see Vaughan 2007: 179) and go in-depth where particular practices associated with language teaching came to the fore. Particular shorthand for talking about student ability and negotiating which classes students enrolling in the school should be placed in is one example of the types of practices that were particularly salient; extract 1 next, taken from a meeting in an Irish language school, shows an example of how this practice is negotiated in the interaction.

(1)
SIOBHÁN: He's not strong.
SALLY: Now he's he's weak in it you know.
SIOBHÁN: Hm.
SALLY: The others would be all stronger than him.
NIALL: Ali? I had him on Friday.
SALLY: Yeah did how did you find him he'd be weak now in that class.
NIALL: Yeah I would then I'd suggest maybe.
AOIFE: Switch.
NIALL: Swapping the two of them.

[C-MELT04: Sub-corpus 2: Ireland]

One of the most interesting features of the terms that have become part of the community's shared repertoire is the fact that the language itself is neither highly esoteric in form nor complex in basic linguistic meaning, but rather encodes highly detailed and entailed professional knowledge. Information such as laughter, sighing or any other marked extralinguistic behaviour was included in the transcription, and the wordlist revealed an unexpected frequency in *laughs*, *laughing* and *laughter*. Humour turned out to be a highly salient, multifunctional marker of community (Vaughan 2008). It is used to invoke shared knowledge, create and maintain solidarity, resist authority in a socially sanctioned way and downtone potentially face-threatening acts. When the teachers wish to vent frustrations, resist institutional strictures or criticise (or mock) students, the humorous frame provides a way of doing so that will not contravene the professional code. Extract 2 is a quite typical example of how the teachers in C-MELT use humour (note that *ye* is used in Irish English to denote *you* plural and <$E>…<\$E> is used to mark extralinguistic information, such as laughter, or laughing as part of a turn, in this case).

(2)

CIARÁN: So anyone to go down?

MICHAELA: No but it would cheer us up a lot if you could tell us when Juan is leaving. <$E> laughter </$E>

SIOBHÁN: That's exactly what I wanted to know.

CIARÁN: <$E> laughing </$E> I'll check that out for ye.

SIOBHÁN: Please do <$E> laughs </$E>.

MICHAELA: It would make it worth the time.

SIOBHÁN: Oh he's unbearable. He's unbearable.

[C-MELT05: Sub-corpus 2: Ireland]

These are just two aspects of community that corpus-based analysis prompted and revealed. It would be interesting to see corpus research that focuses on, for example, more informal staffroom talk, or any context which pertains to the backstage practices of being a teacher (for a conversation analytic perspective, see Richards 2006). The interaction taking place on public fora online is a rich resource for the sorts of stances new and experienced teachers take up with relation to their profession, some of which is undeniably gloves off (e.g. a 2013 post on one forum stating 'work in a language school and it's death by a 1000 cuts to your soul'). This would, to some extent, extend our understanding of language teaching beyond the classroom and provide some life and colour for the picture of the liminal spaces in the language teaching professionals' life. These are the places where the professional mask that is presented to students is put to one side and a new one, used to do the hidden work of teaching, assumed; the backstage spaces where professional successes and failures are discussed, critiqued and laughed about and bonds of community and professional identity forged. More corpus-based research that pushes the boundaries of what linguistic genres are taken to represent the profession of English language teaching would be most welcome. O'Keeffe *et al.* (2007: 246) have underlined the need for reciprocity in the relationship between language researchers and language teachers and have claimed that for the future '…research questions need to be driven by teachers, and indeed a more critical response to the findings of corpus linguistics needs to come from teachers'. Teachers defining the scope of the agenda for research based on their profession and, above all, using corpora for their own research will be the decisive factor for this in the future.

Further reading

O'Keeffe, A., McCarthy, M. J. and Carter, R. A. (2007) *From Corpus to Classroom: Language Use and Language Teaching*, Cambridge: Cambridge University Press. (This practical introduction to the discipline of corpus linguistics remains one of the most popular for good reason. It provides an extensive overview of the relationship between corpus-based research and language teaching, using numerous practical examples of the types of linguistic information a corpus can provide.)

Timmis, I. (2015) *Corpus Linguistics for ELT*, London: Routledge. (This book surveys the relationship between research in corpus linguistics and practice in ELT critically and in depth. It advocates for greater practitioner awareness and engagement vis-a-vis corpus research and asserts this a a critical factor for the reflective professional.)

Vaughan, E. and McCarthy, M. J. (2017) 'Research in Corpora in Second Language Teaching and Learning', in E. Hinkel (ed.) *Handbook of Research in Second Language Teaching and Learning*, Vol.*III*. New York: Routledge, pp. 173–85 (Provides a broad-ranging, critical survey of the impact corpora and corpus research have had on second language teaching and learning, including corpora and reference/pedgagogical materials for language learners, corpora and L2 pragmatics, SLA and learner corpora and the importance of questions of classroom models and world Englishes.)

References

Aijmer, K. (ed.) (2009) *Corpora and Language Teaching*, Amsterdam: John Benjamins.

Barker, F. (2014) 'Using Corpora to Design Assessment', in A. J. Kunnan (ed.) *The Companion to Language Assessment*, NJ: Wiley-Blackwell, pp. 1013–28.

Biber, D. (1990) 'Methodological Issues Regarding Corpus-Based Analyses of Linguistic Variation', *Literary and Linguistic Computing* 5(4): 257–69.

Biber, D. (1993) 'Representativeness in Corpus Design', *Literary and Linguistic Computing* 8(4): 243–57.

Biber, D., Johansson, S., Leech, G., Conrad, S. and E. Finegan (1999) *Longman Grammar of Spoken and Written English*, Harlow: Pearson.

Borg, S. (2013) *Teacher Research in Language Teaching*, Cambridge: Cambridge University Press.

Breyer, Y. (2009) 'Learning and Teaching with Corpora: Reflections by Student Teachers', *Computer Assisted Language Learning* 22(2): 153–72.

British Association for Applied Linguistics (BAAL) (2016) *Recommendations on Good Practice in Applied Linguistics*, Available https://baalweb.files.wordpress.com/2016/10/goodpractice_full_2016.pdf.

Brzezina, V. and Flowerdew, L. (eds) (2017) *Learner Corpus Research*, London: Bloomsbury.

Callies, M. (2019) 'Integrating Corpus Literacy into Language Teacher Education,' in S. Götz and J. Mukherjee (eds) *Learner Corpora and Language Teaching*, Amsterdam: John Benjamins, pp. 245–63.

Carter, R. A. and McCarthy, M. J. (2006) *Cambridge Grammar of English*, Cambridge: Cambridge University Press.

Chambers, A. (2019) 'Towards the Corpus Revolution? Bridging the Research–Practice Gap. *Language Teaching* 52(4): 460–75.

Clear, J. (1992) 'Corpus Sampling', in G. Leitner (ed.) *New Directions in English Language Corpus Methodology*, Berlin: Mouton de Gruyter, pp. 21–31.

Coniam, D. (1997) 'A Practical Introduction to Corpora in a Teacher Training Language Awareness Programme', *Language Awareness* 6(4): 199–207.

Copland, F. (2008) 'Deconstructing the Discourse: Understanding the Feedback Event', in S. Garton and K. Richards (eds) *Professional Encounters in TESOL: Discourses of Teachers in Training*, Basingstoke: Palgrave, pp. 5–23.

Davies, M. (2010) 'The Corpus of Contemporary American English as the First Reliable Monitor Corpus of English', *Literary and Linguistic Computing* 25(4): 447–64.

De Costa, P. (2015) 'Ethics and Applied Linguistics Research', in B. Paltridge and A. Phatiki (eds) *Research Methods in Applied Linguistics: A Practical Resource*, London: Bloomsbury, pp. 245–57.

Farr, F. (2011) *The Discourse of Teaching Practice Feedback: An Investigation of Spoken and Written Modes*, London: Routledge.

Farr, F., Farrell, A. and Riordan, E. (2019) *Social Interaction in Language Teacher Education: A Corpus and Discourse Perspective*, Edinburgh: Edinburgh University Press.

Fligelstone, S. (1993) 'Some Reflections on the Question of Teaching, from a Corpus Perspective', *ICAME Journal* 17: 97–109.

Flowerdew, L. (2012) *Corpora and Language Education*, London: Routledge.

Frankenberg-Garcia, A. (2012) 'Raising Teachers' Awareness of Corpora', *Language Teaching* 45(4): 475–89.

Frankenberg-Garcia, A. (2016) 'Corpora in ELT', in G. Hall (ed.) *The Routledge Handbook of English Language Teaching*, London: Routledge, pp. 383–98.

Goffman, E. (1971) *The Presentation of Self in Everyday Life*, Harmondsworth: Penguin.

Granath, S. (2009) 'Who Benefits from Learning How to Use Corpora?', in K. Aijmer (ed.) *Corpora and Language Teaching*, Amsterdam: John Benjamins, pp. 47–65.

Granger, S., Gilquin, G. and Meunier, F. (eds) (2015) *The Cambridge Handbook of Learner Corpus Research*, Cambridge: Cambridge University Press.

Healy, M. and Onderdonk, K. (2013) 'Looking at Language in Hotel Management Education', in F. Farr and M. Moriarty (eds) *Language, Learning and Teaching: Irish Research Perspectives*, Bern: Peter Lang, pp. 141–65.

Jenks, C. (2011) *Transcribing Talk and Interaction*, Amsterdam: John Benjamins.

Johansson, S. (2009) 'Some Thoughts on Corpora and Second Language Acquisition', in K. Aijmer (ed.) *Corpora and Language Teaching*, Amsterdam: John Benjamins, pp. 33–44.

Kubanyiova, M. (2008) 'Rethinking Research Ethics in Contemporary Applied Linguistics: The Tension between Macroethical and Microethical Perspectives in Situated Research', *The Modern Language Journal* 92(4): 503–18.

Leech, G. (1997) 'Teaching and Language Corpora: A Convergence', in A. Wichmann, S. Fligelstone, T. McEnery and G. Knowles (eds) *Teaching and Language Corpora*, London: Longman, pp. 1–23.

McCarthy, M. J. (2008) 'Accessing and Interpreting Corpus Information in the Teacher Education Context', *Language Teaching* 41(4): 563–74.

McCarthy, M. J. and O'Keeffe, A. (2010) 'Historical Perspective: What Are Corpora and How Have They Evolved?', in A. O'Keeffe and M. J. McCarthy (eds) *The Routledge Handbook of Corpus Linguistics*, London: Routledge, pp. 3–13.

McEnery, T. and Hardie, A. (2012) *Corpus Linguistics: Method, Theory and Practice*, Cambridge: Cambridge University Press.

McEnery, T. and Xiao, R. (2011) 'What Can Corpora Offer in Language Teaching and Learning', in E. Hinkel (ed.) *Handbook of Research in Second Language Teaching and Learning*, VolII, New York: Routledge, pp. 364–80.

McKinley, J. (2019) 'Evolving the TESOL Teaching-Research Nexus', *TESOL Quarterly* 53(3): 875–84.

Mann, S. (2005) 'The Language Teacher's Development', *Language Teaching* 38(3): 103–18.

Medgyes, P. (2017) 'The (Ir)relevance of Academic Research for the Language Teacher', *ELT Journal* 71(4): 491–8.

Meunier, F. and Gouverneur, C. (2009). 'New Types of Corpora for New Educational Challenges: Collecting, Annotating and Exploiting a Corpus of Textbook Material', in K. Aijmer (ed.) *Corpora and Language Teaching*, Amsterdam: Benjamins, pp. 179–01.

Meunier, F. and Reppen, R. (2015) 'Corpus versus Non-Corpus-Informed Pedagogical Materials: Grammar as the Focus', in D. Biber and R. Reppen (eds) *The Cambridge Handbook of English Corpus Linguistics*, Cambridge: Cambridge University Press, pp. 498–514.

Mindt, D. (1996) 'English Corpus Linguistics and the Foreign Language Teaching Syllabus', in J. Thomas and M. Short (eds) *Using Corpora for Language Research*, London: Longman, pp. 232–47.

Mukherjee, J. (2006) 'Corpus Linguistics and Language Pedagogy: The State of the Art of and Beyond', in S. Braun, K. Kohn and J. Mukherjee (eds) *Corpus Technology and Language Pedagogy: New Resources, New Tools, New Methods*, Frankfurt am Main: Peter Lang, pp. 5–23.

O'Keeffe, A. (2020) 'Data-Driven Learning – A Call for a Broader Research Gaze', *Language Teaching* 1–14. 10.1017/S0261444820000245

O'Keeffe, A. and Farr, F. (2003) 'Using Language Corpora in Initial Teacher Education: Pedagogic Issues and Practical Applications', *TESOL Quarterly* 37(3): 389–418.

O'Keeffe, A. and Mark, G. (2017) 'The English Grammar Profile of Learner Competence: Methodology and Key Findings', *International Journal of Corpus Linguistics* 22(4): 457–89.

O'Keeffe, A. and Farr, F. (2019) 'Using Corpus Approaches in English Language Teacher Education', in S. Walsh and S. Mann (eds) *The Routledge Handbook of English Language Teacher Education*, London: Routledge, pp. 268–82.

O'Keeffe, A., McCarthy, M. J. and Carter, R. A. (2007) *From Corpus to Classroom: Language Use and Language Teaching*, Cambridge: Cambridge University Press.

Paquot, M. (2018) 'Corpus Research for Language Learning and Teaching', in A. Phakiti, P. de Costa, L. Plonsky and S. Starfield (eds) *The Palgrave Handbook of Applied Linguistics Research Methodology*, London: Palgrave Macmillan, pp. 359–74.

Paran, A. (2017) '"Only Connect": Researchers and Teachers in Dialogue', *ELT Journal* 71(4): 499–508.

Park, K. (2014) 'Corpora and Language Assessment: The State of the Art', *Language Assessment Quarterly* 11(1): 27–44.

Richards, K. (2006) *Language and Professional Identity. Aspects of Collaborative Interaction*, Basingstoke: Palgrave Macmillan.

Römer, U. (2009) 'Corpus Research and Practice', in K. Aijmer (ed.) *Corpora and Language Teaching*, Amsterdam: John Benjamins, pp. 83–98.

Römer, U. (2011) 'Corpus Research Applications in Second Language Teaching', *Annual Review of Applied Linguistics*, 31: 205–25.

Sato, M. and Loewen, S. (2019) 'Do Teachers Care about Research? The Research-Pedagogy Dialogue', *ELT Journal* 71(4): 1–10.

Saville, N. and Hawkey, R. (2010) 'The English Profile Programme – The First Three Years', *English Profile Journal* 1(1). 10.1017/S2041536210000061

Seedhouse P. (2019) 'The Dual Personality of 'Topic' in the IELTS Speaking Test', *English Language Teaching Journal* 73(3): 247–56.

Sert, O. (2019) 'Classroom Interaction and Language Teacher Education', in S. Walsh and S. Mann (eds) *The Routledge Handbook of English Language Teacher Education*, London: Routledge, pp. 216–38.

Sinclair, J. M. (ed.) (2004) *How to Use Corpora in Language Teaching*, Amsterdam: John Benjamins.

Swales, J. M. (1996) 'Occluded Genres in the Academy: The Case of the Submission Letter', in E. Ventola and A. Mauranen (eds) *Academic Writing: Intercultural and Textual Issues*, Amsterdam: John Benjamins, pp. 45–58.

Timmis, I. (2015) *Corpus Linguistics for ELT*, London: Routledge.

Tsui, A. B. M. (2005) 'ESL Teachers' Questions and Corpus Evidence'. *International Journal of Corpus Linguistics* 10(3): 335–56.

Vásquez, C. (2004) '"Very carefully managed": Advice and Suggestions in Post-Observation Meetings', *Linguistics and Education* 15(1–2): 33–58.

Vásquez, C. and Reppen, R. (2007) 'Transforming Practice: Changing Patterns of Interaction in Post-Observation Meetings', *Language Awareness* 16(3): 153–72.

Vaughan, E. (2007) '"I think we should just accept our horrible lowly status": Analysing Teacher-Teacher Talk in the Context of Community of Practice', *Language Awareness* 16(3): 173–89.

Vaughan, E. (2008) '"Got a date or something?": An Analysis of the Role of Humour and Laughter in the Workplace', in A. Ädel and R. Reppen (eds) *Corpora and Discourse*, Amsterdam: John Benjamins, pp. 95–115.
Vaughan, E. and Clancy, B. (2013) 'Small Corpora and Pragmatics' in J. Romero-Trillo (ed.) *Yearbook of Corpus Linguistics and Pragmatics*, Vol. I, Dordrecht: Springer, pp. 53–73.
Vaughan, E. and O'Keeffe, A. (2015) 'Corpus Analysis', in K. Tracey (ed.), *The International Encyclopedia of Language and Social Interaction*, Hoboken, NJ: John Wiley and Sons, pp. 252–68.
Vaughan, E. and McCarthy, M. J. (2017) 'Research in Corpora in Language Teaching and Learning', in E. Hinkel (ed.) *Handbook of Research in Second Language Teaching and Learning*, Vol. III, New York: Routledge, pp. 173–85.
Walsh, S. (2006) *Investigating Classroom Discourse*, London: Routledge.
Walsh, S. (2011) *Exploring Classroom Discourse: Language in Action*, London: Routledge.
Walsh, S. (2013) *Classroom Discourse and Teacher Development*, Edinburgh: Edinburgh University Press.
Walsh, S., Morton, T. and O'Keeffe, A. (2011) 'Analysing University Spoken Interaction', *International Journal of Corpus Linguistics* 16(3): 326–45.
Waters, A. (2005) 'Expertise in Teacher Education: Helping Teachers to Learn', in K. Johnson (ed.) *Expertise in Second Language Learning and Teaching*, Basingstoke: Palgrave Macmillan, pp. 210–29.
Xerri, D. (2017) 'Split Personality/Unified Identity,' *ELT Journal* 71(1): 96–8.
Yang, S. (2014) 'Interaction and Codability: A Multi-Layered Approach to Discourse Markers in Teachers' Spoken Discourse', in J. Roméro-Trillo (ed.) *Yearbook of Corpus Lingustics and Pragmatics 2014*, New York: Springer International Publishing, pp. 291–313.

Part IV

Corpora and applied research

34

How to use corpora for translation

Silvia Bernardini

1 Translation and technology: corpora, computer-assisted translation and machine translation

Translation is an operation that concerns texts: Through interlinguistic translation, texts in one language are re-created for delivery in another language. In this chapter we will not be concerned with what this means exactly: Issues of equivalence, accuracy, faithfulness and adequacy have occupied philosophers, sociologists, literary scholars and linguists for millennia. Here it is important to point out that whatever the *skopos*, or purpose, of a translation task (Nord 1997), the *habitus*, or set of dispositions, of a translator (Bourdieu 1977) the socio-cultural *norms* operating at a specific point in time (Toury 1995) and any other constraint operating on this complex process and affecting its success conditions, translation at its most basic entails text understanding and text production. It is no surprise therefore that corpora, namely *text* collections, should be especially relevant to translation, both from the point of view of those who *translate* and from the point of view of those who *study translation*. Certain types of corpora are more useful for the former, and others for the latter, although substantial overlap exists. The bulk of this chapter will describe translation-relevant types of corpora and the main ways in which they can be used to (learn to) translate and to study translation. Before we concern ourselves with the foreground, however, it is important to position corpora and corpus use for translation against the wider background of related translation technology.

Virtually all professional translators nowadays, and also most non-professional translators and students of translation, are familiar with translation memories (TMs). These resources, that lie at the core of computer-assisted translation (CAT) tools, consist of databases of aligned source text (ST) and target text (TT) segment pairs – where a segment is usually the size of a sentence. CAT tools provide automatic look-up facilities during translation, offering translators partial and complete matches retrieved from the TM whenever (a portion of) a segment they are translating is found in the database of previously translated segments. A related resource is that of *bitexts* (Melby *et al.* 2015): complete ST-TT pairs aligned at the segment level. Some CAT tools are able to query bitexts, offering users the added value of accessing whole-text contexts for the retrieved

DOI: 10.4324/9780367076399-34

matches. Thanks to translation memories and bitexts, 'human knowledge and translation competence [are] captured in machine-processible format' (Melby *et al.* 2015: 668; see also Section 2 on bitexts and parallel corpora).

The same recycling principle and the same textual resources also underlie current approaches to machine translation (MT) systems. *Statistical* machine translation and the more recent and highly successful *neural* machine translation differ substantially from the point of view of the computational techniques they use to process textual data. Yet they are similar in taking advantage of extremely large TMs or bitexts to produce their output. In this sense, both technologies are data- or corpus-driven (Forcada 2017), differently from previous standards that relied on grammar rules (so called *rule-based* approaches).

Corpora can thus be said to be the engine that has propelled the two major transformations we have witnessed since the 1990s in the translation world: CAT and, more recently, MT. However, this role has remained somewhat hidden, since the main emphasis has been on the efficient retrieval of translation matches by more or less sophisticated algorithms. While responsibility for reviewing and approving suggestions by CAT tools and for post-editing machine-translated output is bound to remain with the translator, in CAT and MT it is the software that does most of the corpus-related work, and translators may be only vaguely aware of the inner workings of the technology they use daily. In the type of corpus work described in the remainder of this chapter, corpora and corpus users instead take centre stage; efficient retrieval is not a priority, and responsibility for querying corpora and for interpreting results remains with the user. A much wider variety of corpus types than the mere collection of ST-TT pairs thus becomes available. We review these in the next section.

2 Translation-relevant corpus types

Users and their needs

Translation-relevant, or translation-*driven* corpora, using Zanettin's (2012) term, are corpora 'which are created and/or used for some translation-related purpose' (Zanettin 2012: 8). Adopting this broad definition, arguably any corpus can become translation-relevant, depending on one's purpose – the practical translation task or research questions one is addressing. In this section we sketch a corpus typology adopting first the viewpoint of the translation practitioner and student and then that of the translation scholar, laying the bases for the explanation of applied and descriptive/theoretical translation-related purposes that concern us in Sections 3 and 4.

Applied needs: corpora for translators and translation students

From the viewpoint of the translator and translation student, the most relevant corpora are bilingual comparable corpora and parallel corpora. Bilingual comparable corpora are collections of texts in two languages – the source and target languages of one's translation task – that have been assembled adopting similar selection criteria. The relevant selection criteria should at least include similarity in topic and similarity in text type (or genre), both with respect to the source text at hand and with respect to one another. Similarity in topic is essential if one needs terminology and subject matter information, e.g. What is the term for *bone regeneration* in language x? What is the difference between *bone regeneration* and *bone remodeling*? Similarity of text type is to be prioritised when familiarisation with genre conventions is a priority (e.g. What verbs are used to present results in an academic paper? Is *bone [re]growth* a better solution than *bone regeneration* when translating a cosmetic dentistry website into English?). Of course, texts that tick both boxes would be ideal candidates for inclusion, but may not be easy to find when one is dealing with a very specialised subject matter: Clarifying in a simple *readme* file how the corpus will be used and what criteria are therefore applied to text collection will save time when collecting texts, lead to a more useful resource when consulting it and act as a memo for future use when related reference needs emerge.

Bilingual comparable corpora of this kind do not need to be very large: Corpora of about 100,000 words and about 20 to 40 texts per component may prove useful as a starting point and can be further refined and enlarged while carrying out the translation. They can be collected by searching the web and saving documents to separate text files with informative names, within separate folders for the two languages, and can be searched using stand-alone applications such as *AntConc* (Anthony 2019) (see Chapter 9, this volume). An application like *BootCaT* (Zanchetta 2020) can speed up the collection of web texts, though some compromises on quality or control over contents may have to be made. A similar corpus building tool is available from within the commercial corpus manager and query application Sketch Engine (Kilgarriff *et al.* 2014), which also allows upload of local corpora, provides part-of-speech tagging and lemmatisation for many languages and offers sophisticated search and display options. Depending on the time available and the characteristics of the translation task, the monolingual source language component of a comparable corpus may be dispensed with, while a specialised target language corpus remains, in most cases, indispensable.

A final note is needed on large/general monolingual corpora of the source and/or target language. These corpora are often available in the public domain and easily accessible through dedicated interfaces (such as the *KonText* corpus query interface, Machálek 2020). While they are unlikely to be of help with terminology and genre conventions, they do offer precious support, particularly when interpreting or rendering the creative ironic or evaluative force of an expression (Partington 2017). Some publicly available general corpora were even constructed according to similar criteria for different languages and may thus be considered comparable at a rather high level – this is the case, for instance, of the *Aranea* corpora (Benko 2014) or the *WaCky* corpora (Baroni *et al.* 2009).

Moving on to *parallel* corpora, these are collections of bitexts: in other words, source texts aligned segment-by-segment to their translations or translations aligned to each other. We have already mentioned the role of bitexts and translation memories for automatic retrieval of equivalents in CAT tools and MT engines. But parallel corpora can also be queried through parallel concordancers to observe strategies and retrieve equivalents in context, thus tapping into the translation competence of fellow translators. For instance, the Italian-English Cambridge dictionary online (https://dictionary.cambridge.org/dictionary/italian-english/) lists *apparatus*, *device*, *system*, *mechanism*, *contrivance* and *gear* as equivalents of the Italian word *dispositivo*. A search of the Intercorp parallel corpus (Čermák 2019) returns *mechanism* but also *arrangement* as equivalents of *dispositivo* from administrative/legal texts and shows how the different equivalents collocate with different adjectives and nouns (*dispositivo giuridico / legal mechanism*, *dispositivo di valutazione / evaluation arrangement*).

There is no doubt that equivalents can be more easily retrieved from parallel than comparable corpora. It is no coincidence that students of translation are keen on using platforms like *Reverso Context* (https://context.reverso.net/) and *Linguee* (https://www.linguee.com), which provide results from TMs. Yet this ease of retrieval comes at a price. First of all, building a parallel corpus takes a long time for locating adequate text pairs and for aligning them. While automatic aligners exist that facilitate the process, painstaking manual correction is almost always needed to obtain a usable resource; a user-friendly application that can be used both for alignment and for correction is *Intertext Editor* (Vondřička 2016). Second, some expertise is needed to make sure that the alignment output format complies with the requirements of the parallel concordancer of choice (such as *ParaConc*Barlow (2002), *AntPConc*Anthony (2017) and the parallel concordancing facility of the *Sketch Engine*). In practice, building a parallel corpus for reference purposes in translation practice is hardly ever worth the effort. It makes more sense to familiarise oneself, on the one hand, with parallel concordancers and sources of aligned parallel texts (such as the *Opus corpus*, Tiedemann 2012) and, on the other, with self-contained platforms providing access to parallel corpora, such as the *KonText* corpus query platform.

A final note of caution concerns directionality of translation and the reliability of equivalents found in parallel corpora. Many sources of parallel corpora do not state explicitly the direction of translation (this is the case, for instance, with multilingual text production at the European Union), and even when we know what language is the source and what is the target in a bitext or TM, we cannot rule out that translations differ from related texts originating in the target context due to cultural reasons. To fully exploit the potential of parallel and comparable corpora, these should be used together: Parallel corpora (from the public domain) may provide suggestions about translator strategies and translation equivalents, while (self-made) specialised comparable corpora of non-translated target language texts may be used to (dis)confirm the general currency of the choices made by translators (Bernardini and Zanettin 2004; Kenning 2010).

Descriptive/theoretical needs: corpora for translation scholars

The corpus types of greatest relevance to translation scholars are, unsurprisingly, those that include one or more translated components. We have already discussed one such corpus type, the parallel one, in which translations are set alongside their STs or other translations of the same ST. In general, a prototypical parallel corpus such as the ones described in the previous section, and made of ST-TT pairs, is especially apt at investigating the (hypothesised) decisions made while translating, variously conceptualised as translation shifts (Catford 1965: 73), translation procedures (Vinay and Darbelnet 1995 [1958]) or transfer operations (Klaudy and Károly 2005). However, depending on one's research questions, this design can be extended in several ways. Rather than text pairs, corpora may contain several target texts to each source: this is the case, for instance, with corpora of learner translations (Castagnoli *et al.* 2011) and corpora of literary classics for which several published translations exist (Malmkjær 2004). Another popular corpus design is the bilingual bidirectional one, exemplified by the ENPC for Norwegian/English (Johansson 2007), or COMPARA for Portuguese/English (Frankenberg-Garcia and Santos 2003). These corpora are made of two parallel subcorpora: STs in language A and their translations into language B, comparable STs in language B and their translations into A. As suggested by Johansson (2007: 38), analysing a corpus of this type is 'a kind of navigation, where new perspectives may be revealed depending upon the direction of exploration': Comparing STs (or "originals") in two languages (as in traditional contrastive studies), STs and TTs in two directions (as in parallel corpora), and originals and translations in the same language(s).

The latter corpus type, known as *monolingual comparable*, has been central to corpus-based translation studies from the very beginning. These corpora are often a combination of an existing non-translated corpus and a translation corpus designed to be comparable to the former. Examples are the *English Comparable Corpus* (Laviosa 1997), made of a subset of the *British National Corpus* and the purpose-built *Translational English Corpus* (TEC) for English, and the *XJU Corpus of Translational Chinese* (XCTC) plus the *Lancaster Corpus of Mandarin Chinese* (LCMC) for Chinese (Xiao and Hu 2015). Even though it might seem counterintuitive to exclude source texts from a corpus meant to study translation, Mona Baker (1993) in fact suggested that translations are, first and foremost, communicative events of relevance to the *target* language context. Shedding the 'longstanding obsession' (Baker 1993: 237) with source texts and with the myth of equivalence, translation studies, with the support of corpora, could concentrate on the linguistic patterns that are specific to translated texts with respect to comparable non-translated texts in the target language and arrive at generalisations about more or less universal features of translated texts (a thorough description of which can be found in Laviosa 2002). For instance, several studies have hypothesised that translated texts are more explicit than non-translated texts (Baumgarten *et al.* 2008). One way to confirm this hypothesis is to compare the frequency of more or less explicit words and structures, such as connectives or premodified/postmodified noun phrases, in translated and non-translated texts.

A monolingual comparable corpus is thus no different from corpora used to study sociolinguistic or register variation, where components representing different language varieties are paired. As in comparative studies in general, the two subcorpora should ideally be comparable to each other along all dimensions but the one under study, in this case the translated/non-translated one. In reality, comparability across cultures is particularly tricky, and researchers adopting this corpus design should use extra care when interpreting their findings as being due to translation rather than any other variable. Aware of the complexity of their object of study, translation scholars have called for triangulation of different data sources and methods (Serbina *et al.* 2015; Malamatidou 2018; Wang and Li 2020).

Monolingual comparable corpora provide a bird's-eye view of the general quantitative differences across translated and non-translated texts in the same language, but parallel corpora allow one to zoom in on choices made in distinct acts of translation. Triangulation of these two types of corpora thus fruitfully links the general and the particular, allowing one to argue, for instance, that *explicitness* in translated texts is the result of *explicitation* in the translation process.

3 In practice: how to use corpora to (learn to) translate

In this section we concentrate on the different ways in which corpora of the kinds described in Section 2 can be of use to translators and provide one example, among the innumerable ones one could make. Many more examples can be found in the references provided in this section. These come mainly from classroom research and practice, since, as suggested in Section 1, corpora are to this day less widely used by professionals than other technological aids (Frankenberg-Garcia 2015; Frérot 2016), despite some signals that the situation may be changing (Gallego-Hernández 2015).

Kübler and Aston (2010) subdivide an act of translation into three phases: documentation, in which translators familiarise themselves with the source text, the domain and the terminology; drafting, in which, chunk after chunk, the ST is comprehended and re-created; and revision, in which all aspects of the TT are evaluated: Its internal consistency and flow, its adequacy with respect to the ST, its acceptability for the target linguaculture and so on. Specialised source language corpora, including the ST used as a mini-corpus, can be used for understanding the ST domain: wordlists (lists of the most frequent words in the text/corpus) or keyword lists (lists of the most typical words in the text/corpus when compared to another corpus) are particularly useful for this purpose. Concordances from parallel corpora and bilingual comparable corpora can be used to generate and subsequently check hypotheses about target language equivalents in context. In particular, purpose-built corpora are required to check denotational correctness and register appropriateness of specialised terms and phrases (López-Rodríguez and Tercedor-Sánchez 2008), while large general corpora can assist with finding out about more subtle aspects of language use such as evaluation (Stewart 2009; Munday 2011), conventionality (Hoey 2011) and creativity (Philip 2009). Finally, to evaluate the internal and external consistency of the choices made in the TT, we can resort to target language corpora, including the TT used as a mini-corpus.

Experts recommending the use of corpora in the translation classroom stress the beneficial side effects of using corpora for reference purposes: 'corpora, because they can provide data which is not pre-digested […], allow translators to acquire and apply skills which are after all central to their trade – ones of text interpretation and evaluation' (Kübler and Aston 2010: 503). They also stress their potential for the development of autonomy in the learning and translation processes and of capacity for self-assessment (see also Frérot 2016; Giampieri 2020). For these purposes, learner corpora, particularly if annotated for errors and translation strategies, can offer a further promising resource, both for teaching and for classroom research (Castagnoli *et al.* 2011).

Given the impossibility to illustrate all the different ways in which the corpora described in this chapter can help in the translation process, I will briefly describe a case study that brings together reference use and autonomous learning (a fuller account can be found in Frank *et al.* 2020). The starting point for this case study is the Italian word *contaminazione* (which the Cambridge English/Italian dictionary translates as *contamination* or *pollution*) and its French dictionary equivalent *contamination*. The definitions provided by Italian and French monolingual dictionaries for the two words are virtually identical: The two words may refer to pollution and corruption or to a mixture of literary or artistic forms. A translation student may thus conclude that the phrase *contaminazione di stili* (*mixture of styles*), common in Italian texts about fashion and design, can be appropriately translated as *contamination de styles*.

To check if these two phrases are in fact good translation equivalents of each other, we need to first establish if the semantic preferences and prosodies of *contaminazione* and *contamination* are similar (Sinclair 2004). To this aim we look up the two lemmas in two large corpora of Italian and French, the *Araneum Italicum Maius* and the *Araneum Francogallicum Maius* (Benko 2014), that were built approximately at the same time using similar procedures and can be consulted through the KonText corpus platform (among others). First of all, we observe that the frequencies of the two lemmas are very similar (8.81 and 8.86 per million words respectively). After browsing a few screenfuls of randomly sorted concordance lines to get an informal impression, we obtain lists of collocates of the two words using the platform default parameters (a span of five words to the left and right, with minimum frequency in the corpus of five, and minimum frequency in the span of three). We then group collocates into semantic sets (semantic preferences) and assess whether the evaluation conveyed is positive or negative. Notice that there is no corpus tool for this: The grouping is done manually in a word processor or spreadsheet application (Table 34.1).

French *contamination* has semantic preferences for words denoting dangers (*risque*, *prévenir*), contamination agents (*OGM*, *VIH*), contaminated substances (*eaux*, *sols*) and types of contamination (*croisées*, *chimique*). The semantic prosody is therefore consistently negative, at least when judged from a non-technical point of view. Among the

Table 34.1 The top 20 collocates of *contamination* and *contaminazione* in two web corpora of French and Italian [with English glosses in square brackets]

French			*Italian*		
Collocate	*Frequency*	*logDice*	*Collocate*	*Frequency*	*logDice*
radioactive *[radioactive.fem.sing]*	185	9.006	linguaggi*[languages]*	16	4.399
croisée *[cross.fem.sing.]*	180	8.462	sotterranee *[underground.fem.sing]*	7	4.104
virus	290	7.912	falde*[acquifers]*	7	3.979
bactérienne *[bacterial.fem.sing.]*	84	7.794	contaminazione *[contamination]*	8	3.892
VIH*[HIV]*	177	7.779	jazz	13	3.830
microbienne *[microbial.fem.sing]*	61	7.448	generi*[genres]*	11	3.746
prévenir *[prevent]*	193	7.332	falda*[acquifer]*	5	3.588
risque *[risk]*	821	7.248	artistiche*[artistic.fem.plur]*	10	3.588
risques *[risks]*	499	7.216	potabili*[drinkable.plur]*	4	3.572
sols *[soils]*	135	7.213	laicità*[secularism]*	5	3.501
microbiologique *[microbiological]*	47	7.114	Chernobyl	4	3.470
contamination *[contamination]*	83	7.097	acque*[waters]*	21	3.470
fécale *[faecal]*	44	7.045	microrganismi *[microorganisms]*	4	3.278
chimique *[chemical]*	101	7.036	manipolazione*[manipulation]*	5	3.238
souterraines *[underground.fem.plur]*	59	7.021	espressive*[expressive]*	4	3.131
accidentelle *[accidental.fem.sing]*	49	6.990	minzione*[urination]*	3	3.127
croisées *[cross.fem.plur.]*	52	6.928	IPA*[PAH]*	3	3.059
éviter *[avoid.inf]*	478	6.928	sedimenti*[sediments]*	3	3.031
eaux *[waters]*	227	6.904	arti*[arts]*	9	3.012
OGM *[MGO]*	79	6.892	colte*[learned.fem.plur.]*	3	3.010

top 20 collocates of Italian *contaminazione*, some refer to contaminated substances (*acque*, *sedimenti*) and agents (*microrganismi*), but types of contamination and dangers are absent, and the only potentially negative collocate is *manipolazione*. Instead, several words are related to creativity and artistic expression (*linguaggi*, *jazz*, *artistiche*, *espressive*, *arti*), which express positive evaluation. Through a much more extensive analysis, Frank *et al.* are able to confirm that *contaminazione* as a mixture of artistic expressions cannot be translated as *contamination*, despite the dictionary definitions. They then search the French corpus for collocates of words related to arts, literature and culture (the French equivalents of words that collocate with *contaminazione* in Italian) and obtain a list of potentially more appropriate equivalents, such as *mélange*, *échange*, *rencontre* and *carrefour*. While such a list could be more easily obtained from a parallel corpus (if available), its reliability might be called into question, given that translators themselves might not be aware of the differences highlighted by the earlier corpus analysis. Indeed, the starting point for this study was Mélanie Frank's doubts about the appropriateness of the phrase *contamination de styles*. Mélanie, a French student of specialised translation and professional translator, then went on to investigate this hunch with a corpus-assisted study that finally grew into the cited paper, thus transforming an instance of reference use into an autonomous learning experience.

4 In practice: how to use corpora to study translation

In Section 2 we have mentioned several corpus types used to study translation and, in passing, some of the research objectives that can be pursued thanks to these corpora. Adopting the monolingual comparable corpus design, one of the major undertakings in corpus-based translation study has been the attempt to find empirical proof for the existence of typical (or universal) features of translated language. Translated texts have been suggested to be simpler, more explicit, more proper (or conventional), more similar to each other and richer in target-language–specific linguistic structures than comparable non-translated texts (Laviosa 2002). While not always conclusive, this evidence has been used to support generalisations about underlying socio-cognitive mechanisms at work in the translation process, as well as in other kinds of bilingual processing (Lanstyák and Heltai 2012; Halverson 2017).

Singling out one hypothesised typical feature of translation, namely explicitness, in this section we show how to carry out a simple comparison aiming to confirm whether translated texts are more explicit than corresponding non-translated (or original) texts in the same language. For reasons of space, the comparison will be limited to two equivalent part-of-speech (POS) patterns: noun phrases premodified by another noun (noun–noun sequences) and noun phrases post-modified by a prepositional phrase (noun–preposition–noun sequences). According to Biber *et al.* (1999: 588), 'premodifiers are consistently more condensed than postmodifiers, [and] are much less explicit in identifying the meaning relationship that exists between the modifier and head noun'. This is especially true of nominal premodification, since the meaning relations holding between the two nouns cannot easily be reconstructed if one is not already familiar with the meaning of the phrase as a whole. Consider the phrase "food fight", which out of context could easily be understood to mean "fight over/for food", rather than "fight using food (as a weapon)".

If translators make meanings that are implicit in the source text explicit more often than they make explicit meanings implicit (Klaudy and Károly 2005), then translated

Table 34.2 Statistical significance and effect size values for the comparison of the frequencies of the two patterns in original and translated English

	Original English	*English translated from Italian*	*Log-likelihood*	*Bayes factor (BIC)*
Number of tokens	152,228	184,465	---	---
Noun–noun sequences	2,692	2,599	68.23 ($p < 0.0001$)	55.5
Noun–preposition–noun sequences	1,558	2,088	9.09 ($p < 0.01$)	-3.63

texts will contain more noun phrases with nominal post-modification than comparable non-translated texts and fewer noun phrases with nominal pre-modification. Notice that this is a very simplified comparison that only takes into account two basic noun phrase structures, ignoring alternative structures or structural variation. Furthermore, it is misleading to speak of "structures" in the first place, since the corpus used for this study is lemmatised and POS-tagged, but not syntactically parsed. We in fact compare the frequencies of POS sequences *approximating* the two structures of interest, on the assumption that false positives (sequences matching the query but not the target structure, such as "way bankers" in the phrase "the irresponsible way bankers acted") are similarly frequent in translated and untranslated texts. Keeping these limitations in mind, we can proceed with our analysis.

To limit the variables at play, we restrict our study to a single register (journalistic commentaries from the Intercorp v.12 corpus) and a single source language (Italian). Table 34.2 shows corpus size in tokens (words, numbers, punctuation marks, etc.) and number of occurrences of the two patterns in the two subcorpora. The log-likelihood significance values and effect size values in Table 34.2 are calculated using Rayson's LL wizard available from http://ucrel.lancs.ac.uk/llwizard.html.

Using the original English data as a point of comparison, our results suggest that the compact noun–noun sequences are under-represented in English commentaries translated from Italian, while the more explicit noun–preposition–noun sequences are over-represented. Indeed, log-likelihood results are statistically significant for both comparisons. Yet effect size results confirm the under-representation of noun–noun sequences only, while the negative value obtained for noun–preposition–noun sequences is to be interpreted as confirming the null hypothesis: There is no evidence that the frequencies of this pattern in original and translated English differ. One would tentatively conclude that translators avoid the condensed, implicit noun–noun sequence, while they use the more explicit noun–preposition–noun alternative to a similar extent as authors of original English texts.

It should not be forgotten, however, that the translated texts have Italian as a source language. The observed lower frequency of the condensed premodified structure could be due to the fact that a corresponding Italian structure does not exist; therefore there is no prompt for the English one. This explanation would be coherent with Tirkkonen-Condit's (2004) *unique items hypothesis*, as well as with Halverson's (2017) *gravitational pull hypothesis*, but would be unrelated to the explicitness/explicitation hypothesis (Blum-Kulka 1986). In order to investigate our hypothesis further, we could therefore vary the source language of the translated texts used in the comparison, for instance, substituting Italian with German, a language where a corresponding structure exists and in which therefore the unique items and gravitational pull hypotheses would not predict lower frequencies of the target structure in translated than original English.

5 Summing up and looking ahead: the future of corpora for translation

The focus in this chapter has been on corpus use for translation practice, teaching and research. I have argued that corpora are a central component of the main technological innovations that have boosted change in translation practice in the last three decades: first CAT and then MT. Yet general uptake by professional translators has been slower, probably due to the perceived complexity of corpus querying and analysis. The bulk of the chapter has focused on types of corpus resources and ways of exploiting them for translation-related purposes. With regard to the former, I have provided a typology distinguishing bilingual comparable corpora (of use mainly in translation practice), monolingual comparable corpora (of use main in translation research) and bilingual parallel corpora that are relevant for both practice and description/theory. Moving on to corpus use for translation, the subject of the practice-oriented case study has been the use of bilingual comparable corpora for reference purposes in translation from Italian into French (based on Frank *et al.* 2020). Here I showed how a rather straightforward reference use (checking if two look-alike words in different languages are good translation equivalents in context) can turn into a more structured learning experience thanks to the rich evidence offered by corpora. My research-oriented example focused on the frequency of nominal pre-modification and post-modification in a monolingual comparable corpus of translated and original English texts. The main aim in this case was methodological: I pointed out that alternative explanations are often possible for observed differences, and that data triangulation may be needed to arrive at sounder generalisations.

Looking ahead, there are various ways in which corpora and corpus methods are likely to further contribute to translation teaching, practice and research in the near future. As advances in technology make certain routine translation tasks amenable to MT treatment, human translation is likely to become more and more specialised and to require even higher levels of expertise than was previously the case. At the same time, translators may lose access to translation memories if post-editing of machine-translated text is carried out outside of computer-assisted translation environments. Faced with such a fast-changing, highly technologized and specialised professional environment, the need for carefully constructed, documented and curated reference materials is likely to increase, as is the need to learn how to efficiently obtain information from such materials while translating, post-editing or doing terminology work.

Research-wise, the field is moving in several interesting directions and a number of fascinating hypotheses are being explored. I have already mentioned, albeit in passing, triangulation of data and methods. A related development concerns the creation of corpora of simultaneous and consecutive interpreting and the corpus-based comparison of interpreted and translated language (Shlesinger and Ordan 2012, Bernardini *et al.* 2016; Pan 2019). Finally, the relevance of translation to other kinds of discourses is actively being explored. Researchers conceptualising translation as a type of bilingual language production are trying to single out similarities and differences with respect to contact language varieties and second language use (Kolehmainen *et al.* 2014; Kruger and van Rooy 2016); at the same time, use of translation data in corpus-assisted critical discourse analysis is proposed to 'escape the contagious nature of dominant discourses' in the search for 'an alternative language with which to argue against established institutional rhetoric' (Baker 2019: 1).

After almost three decades of work in corpus-based translation studies, the centrality of corpus methods to translation is undisputable. Corpora and corpus analysis have improved our understanding of translational behaviour and made translation ever more relevant to linguistic research. At the same time, corpus-based technological innovation in the form of MT has progressed at such a pace that it is already replacing human translation, at least for specific purposes and in specific settings. As fast and inexpensive – but not necessarily reliable or creative – translation is provided by machines, the ability to use the different kinds of corpora discussed in this contribution for translation learning, practice and research will become even more important than in the past, to endow human translators with the knowledge they need to outperform machines in that most human task of building bridges between cultures.

Further reading

Beeby, A., Rodríguez Inés, P. and Sánchez-Gijón, P. (eds) (2009) *Corpus Use and Translating. Corpus Use for Learning to Translate and Learning Corpus Use to Translate*, Amsterdam: Benjamins. (This volume is a collection of papers on different aspects of corpus use in the classroom, including reports on corpus use by learners, corpus construction, use of specialised and general corpora and their use for evaluation purposes. It will be of interest to translator trainers and trainees and researchers in applied linguistics, corpus linguistics and translation studies.)

Hu, K. and Kim K. H. (eds) (2020) *Corpus-based Translation and Interpreting Studies in Chinese Contexts. Present and Future*, London: Palgrave Macmillan. (This edited collection makes corpus-based translation studies involving the Chinese language and culture accessible also to non-Chinese-speaking researchers. Its four parts cover central themes in descriptive translation studies (translation norms and universals, interpreting, equivalence and style), as well as touching on the neighbouring fields of critical discourse analysis and cognitive research.)

Ji, M., Oakes, M., Li, D. and Hareide, L. (2016) *Corpus Methodologies Explained. An Empirical Approach to Translation Studies*, Oxford and New York: Routledge. (The five chapters that, together with the introduction, make up this volume, investigate some of the central topics in descriptive corpus-based translation studies – machine translation, linguistic variation, style and universals – providing thorough descriptions of relevant theoretical background and methods.)

Zanettin, F. (2012) *Translation-Driven Corpora. Corpus Resources for Descriptive and Applied Translation Studies*, Oxford: Routledge. (This handbook covers corpus design, encoding and analysis, with a special focus on multilingual corpora and translation-oriented research questions, providing extensive exemplification and activities.)

References

Anthony, L. (2017) *AntPConc* (Version 1.2.1) [Computer Software], Tokyo: Waseda University, Available from https://www.laurenceanthony.net/software.

Anthony, L. (2019) *AntConc* (Version 3.5.8) [Computer Software], Tokyo: Waseda University, Available from https://www.laurenceanthony.net/software.

Baker, M. (1993) 'Corpus Linguistics and Translation Studies: Implications and Applications', in M. Baker, G. Francis and E. Tognini-Bonelli (eds) *Text and Technology: in Honour of John Sinclair*, Amsterdam: Benjamins, pp. 233–50.

Baker, M. (2019) 'Rehumanizing the Migrant: The Translated Past as a Resource for Refashioning the Contemporary Discourse of the (Radical) Left', *Palgrave Communications* 6(12): 1–16.

Barlow, M. (2002) 'ParaConc: Concordance Software for Multilingual Parallel Corpora', in *Proceedings of LREC-2002: Third International Conference on Language Resources and Evaluation*, Las Palmas: ELRA, pp. 20–4.

Baroni, M., Bernardini, S., Ferraresi, A. and Zanchetta, E. (2009) 'The WaCky Wide Web: A Collection of Very Large Linguistically Processed Web-Crawled Corpora', *Language Resources and Evaluation* 43(3): 209–26.

Baumgarten, N., Meyer, B. and Özçetin, D. (2008) 'Explicitness in Translation and Interpreting. A Review and some Empirical Evidence (of an Elusive Concept)', *Across Languages and Cultures* 9(2): 177–203.

Benko, V. (2014) 'Compatible Sketch Grammars for Comparable Corpora', in A. Abel, C. Vettori and N. Ralli (eds), *Proceedings of the XVI EURALEX International Congress: The User in Focus*, Bolzano/Bozen: Eurac Research, pp. 417–30.

Bernardini, S., Ferraresi, A. and Miličević, M. (2016) 'From EPIC to EPTIC — Exploring Simplification in Interpreting and Translation from an Intermodal Perspective', *Meta* 28(1): 61–86.

Bernardini, S. and Zanettin F. (2004) 'When is a Universal not a Universal? Some Limits of Current Corpus-based Methodologies for the Investigation of Translation Universals', in A. Mauranen and P. Kujamäki (eds) *Translation Universals: Do they exist?* Amsterdam: Benjamins, pp. 51–62.

Biber, D., Johansson, S., Leech, G., Conrad, S. and Finegan, E. (1999) *Longman Grammar of Spoken and Written English*, London and New York: Longman.

Blum-Kulka, S. (1986) 'Shifts of Cohesion and Coherence in Translation', in J. House and S. Blum-Kulka (eds) *Interlingual and Intercultural Communication*, Tübingen: Narr, pp. 17–35.

Bourdieu, P. (1977) *Outline of a Theory of Practice* (Translated by Richard Nice), Cambridge: Cambridge University Press.

Castagnoli, S., Ciobanu, D., Kunz, K. and Kübler, N. (2011) 'Designing a Learner Translator Corpus for Training Purposes' in N. Kübler (ed.) *Corpora, Language, Teaching and Resources: From Theory to Practice*, Bern: Peter Lang, pp 221–48.

Catford, J. C. (1965) *A Linguistic Theory of Translation*, Oxford: Oxford University Press.

Čermák, P. (2019) *InterCorp: A Parallel Corpus of 40 Languages*, Amsterdam: Benjamins.

Forcada, M. (2017) 'Making Sense of Neural Machine Translation', *Translation Spaces* 6(2): 291–309.

Frank, N., Bartolesi, F., Bernardini, S. and Partington, A. (2020) 'Is *Contamination* Good or Bad? A Corpus-assisted Case Study in Translating Evaluative Prosody', in A. Ferraresi, R. Pederzoli, R. Scansani and S. Cavalcanti (eds) *Mediazioni Special Issue on Research Methods and Themes in Translation, Interpreting and Intercultural Studies 29*, online: http://www.mediazioni.sitlec.unibo.it/index.php/no-29-special-issue-2020.html.

Frankenberg-Garcia, A. (2015) 'Training Translators to Use Corpora Hands-On: Challenges and Reactions by a Group of 13 Students at a UK University', *Corpora* 10(2), online: https://www.euppublishing.com/doi/full/10.3366/cor.2015.0081.

Frankenberg-Garcia, A. and D. Santos (2003) 'Introducing COMPARA: The Portuguese-English Parallel Corpus', in D. Stewart, F. Zanettin and S. Bernardini (eds) *Corpora in Translator Education*, Manchester: St Jerome, pp. 71–87.

Frérot, C. (2016) 'Corpora and Corpus Technology for Translation Purposes and Academic Environments. Major Achievements and New Perspectives', *Cadernos de Tradução* 36(1): 36–61.

Gallego-Hernández, D. (2015) 'The Use of Corpora as Translation Resources: A Study Based on a Survey of Spanish Professional Translators', *Perspectives* 23(3): 375–91.

Giampieri, P. (2020) 'Volcanic Experiences: Comparing Non-corpus-based Translations with Corpus-based Translations in Translation Training', *Perspectives*, online: https://www.tandfonline.com/doi/full/10.1080/0907676X.2019.1705361.

Halverson, S. (2017) 'Gravitational Pull in Translation. Testing a Revised Model', in G. De Sutter, M.-A. Lefer and I. Delaere (eds) *Empirical Translation Studies New Methodological and Theoretical Traditions*, Berlin: De Gruyter Mouton, pp. 9–46.

Hoey, M. (2011) 'Lexical Priming and Translation' in A. Kruger, K. Wallmach and J. Munday (eds) *Corpus-Based Translation Studies. Research and Applications*, London: Continuum, pp. 153–68.

Johansson, S. (2007) *Seeing through Multilingual Corpora. On the Use of Corpora in Contrastive Studies*, Amsterdam: Benjamins.

Kenning, M.-M. (2010) 'What are Parallel and Comparable Corpora and How Can We use Them?' in A. O'Keeffe and M. J. McCarthy (eds) *The Routledge Handbook of Corpus Linguistics*, London: Routledge, pp. 487–500.

Kilgarriff, A., Baisa, V., Bušta, J., Jakubíček, M., Kovář, V., Michelfeit, J., Rychlý, P. and Suchomel, V. (2014) 'The Sketch Engine: Ten Years On', *Lexicography* 1: 7–36.

Klaudy, K. and Károly, K. (2005) 'Implicitation in Translation: Empirical Evidence for Operational Asymmetry in Translation', *Across Languages and Cultures* 6(1): 13–29.

Kolehmainen, L., Meriläinen, L. and Riionheimo, H. (2014) 'Interlingual Reduction: Evidence from Language Contacts, Translation and Second Language Acquisition', in H. Paulasto, L. Meriläinen, H. Riionheimo and M. Kok (eds) *Language Contacts at the Crossroads of Disciplines*, Newcastle: Cambridge Scholars Publishing, pp. 3–32.

Kruger, H. and van Rooy, B. (2016) 'Constrained Language: A Multidimensional Analysis of Translated English and a Non-native Indigenised Variety of English', *English World-Wide* 37(1): 26–57.

Kübler, N. and Aston, G. (2010) 'Using Corpora in Translation', in A. O'Keeffe and M. McCarthy (eds) *The Routledge Handbook of Corpus Linguistics*, London: Routledge, pp. 501–15.

Lanstyák, I. and Heltai, P. (2012) 'Universals in Language Contact and Translation', *Across Languages and Cultures* 13(1): 99–121.

Laviosa, S. (1997) 'How Comparable Can "Comparable Corpora" Be?', *Target* 9(2): 287–317

Laviosa, S. (2002) *Corpus-Based Translation Studies: Theory, Findings, Applications*, Amsterdam: Rodopi.

López-Rodríguez, C. I. and Tercedor-Sánchez, M. I. (2008) 'Corpora and Students' Autonomy in Scientific and Technical Translation training', *JoSTrans. The Journal of Specialised Translation* 9, online: https://www.jostrans.org/issue09/art_lopez_tercedor.php.

Machálek, T. (2020) 'KonText: Advanced and Flexible Corpus Query Interface', *Proceedings of the 12th Language Resources and Evaluation Conference*, Marseille: ELRA, pp. 7003–8.

Malamatidou, S. (2018) *Corpus Triangulation. Combining Data and Methods in Corpus-Based Translation Studies*, London: Routledge.

Malmkjær, K. (2004) 'Translational Stylistics: Dulcken's Translations of Hans Christian Andersen', *Language and Literature: International Journal of Stylistics* 13(1): 13–24.

Melby, A. K., Lommel, A. and Morado Vázquez, L. (2015) 'Bitext', in S. Chan (ed.) *Routledge Encyclopedia of Translation Technology*, London: Routledge, pp. 409–24.

Munday, J. (2011) 'Looming Large: A Cross-Linguistic Analysis of Semantic Prosodies in Comparable Reference Corpora', in A. Kruger, K. Wallmach and J. Munday (eds) *Corpus-Based Translation Studies. Research and Applications*. London: Continuum, pp. 169–86.

Nord, C. (1997) *Translating as Purposeful Activity*, Manchester: St Jerome.

Pan, J. (2019) 'The Chinese/English Political Interpreting Corpus (CEPIC): A New Electronic Resource for Translators and Interpreters', in I. Temnikova, C. Orasan, G. Corpas Pastor and R. Mitkov (eds) *Proceedings of the 2nd Workshop on Human-Informed Translation and Interpreting Technology (HiT-IT 2019)*, Varna, Bulgaria, pp. 82–8.

Partington, A. (2017) 'Evaluative Clash, Evaluative Cohesion and How we Actually Read Evaluation in Texts', *Journal of Pragmatics* 117: 190–203.

Philip, G. (2009) 'Arriving at Equivalence. Making a Case for Comparable General Reference Corpora in Translation Studies', in A. Beeby, P. Rodríguez Inés and P. Sánchez-Gijón (eds) *Corpus Use and Translating. Corpus Use for Learning to Translate and Learning Corpus Use to Translate*, Amsterdam: Benjamins, pp. 59–73.

Serbina, T., Niemietz, P. and Neumann, S. (2015) 'Development of a Keystroke Logged Translation Corpus', in C. Fantinuoli and F. Zanettin (eds) *New Directions in Corpus-Based Translation Studies*, Berlin: Language Science Press, pp. 11–33.

Shlesinger, M. and Ordan, N. (2012) 'More Spoken or More Translated? Exploring a Known Unknown of Simultaneous Interpreting', *Target* 24(1): 43–60.

Sinclair, J. McH. (2004) *Trust the Text*, London: Routledge.
Stewart, D. (2009) 'Safeguarding the Lexicogrammatical Environment: Translating Semantic Prosody', in A. Beeby, P. Rodríguez Inés and P. Sánchez-Gijón (eds) *Corpus Use and Translating. Corpus Use for Learning to Translate and Learning Corpus Use to Translate*. Amsterdam: Benjamins, pp. 29–46.
Tiedemann, J. (2012) 'Parallel Data, Tools and Interfaces in OPUS', *Proceedings of the 8th International Conference on Language Resources and Evaluation (LREC'2012)*, Istanbul: ELRA, pp. 2214–8.
Tirkkonen-Condit, S. (2004) 'Unique Items — Over- or Under-represented in Translated Language?' in A. Mauranen and P. Kujamäki (eds) *Translation Universals: Do they Exist?* Amsterdam: Benjamins, pp. 177–84.
Toury, G. (1995) *Descriptive Translation Studies and Beyond*, Amsterdam: John Benjamins.
Vinay, J.-P. and Darbelnet, J. (1995) *Comparative Stylistics of French and English* (Translated by J. C. Sager), Amsterdam: Benjamins.
Vondřička, P. (2016) *Intertext Editor* (Version 1.5), Prague: Charles University, Available from https://wanthalf.saga.cz/.
Wang, Q. and Li, D. (2020) 'Looking for Translator's Fingerprints: A Corpus-Based Study on Chinese Translations of Ulysses', in K. Hu (ed.) *Corpus-Based Translation and Interpreting Studies in the Chinese Context: Present and Future*, London: Palgrave Macmillan, pp. 155–79.
Xiao, R. and Hu, X. (2015) *Corpus-Based Studies of Translational Chinese in English-Chinese Translation*, Berlin and Heidelberg: Springer-Verlag.
Zanchetta, E. (2020) *BootCaT. Simple Utilities to Bootstrap Corpora And Terms from the Web (version 1.3)*. Forlì: University of Bologna, Available from https://bootcat.dipintra.it/?section=download.
Zanettin, F. (2012) *Translation Driven Corpora*, Manchester: St Jerome.

35

Using corpus linguistics to explore the language of poetry: a stylometric approach to Yeats' poems

Dan McIntyre and Brian Walker

1 Poetry as the object of corpus linguistic analysis

Over the last 15 or so years, methods from corpus linguistics have become ever more common in the analysis of literary texts (see, for example, Semino and Short 2004; O'Halloran 2007; Mahlberg 2012; Mastropierro 2018; McIntyre and Walker 2019; O'Halloran 2007; Semino 2004). Much of this work has been largely stylistic in nature and has focused on the propensity of textual elements to function as triggers for literary effects. As a result, such work has come to be known generally as corpus stylistics. More recently, corpus stylistics has begun to turn its attention back to some of the earliest concerns of stylisticians, namely the characteristics of genre style (e.g. Montoro and McIntyre 2019) and authorial style (e.g. Evans 2018). In this endeavour, stylistics has started to draw on the methods of the closely related discipline of stylometry and its techniques of authorship attribution (e.g. Hoover and Hess 2009).

Our aim in this chapter is to demonstrate the value of combining corpus stylistic techniques with stylometric methods of analysis in order to generate stylistic insights into the language of poetry. We analyse a specially constructed corpus of William Butler Yeats' poetry containing 307 of his published poems to determine whether there is textual evidence of a change on Yeats' style over time. The poems in our corpus match those presented in *The Collected Works of W. B. Yeats* (Finneran 1997) and are available in electronic form at webpages hosted by California State University, Northridge (CSUN). We use our Yeats corpus of poems to answer a series of research questions which aim to show how combining corpus stylistics and stylometry can shed light on both authorial style and text style.

2 W. B. Yeats: literary critical responses to his poetry

W. B. Yeats was a prolific poet and dramatist who continued to write until his death in 1939. There is some agreement among literary critics that Yeats' style changed and

DOI: 10.4324/9780367076399-35

developed over his long writing career and that these changes fall into distinct writing phases. There is less agreement, however, about the number, timing and duration of these phases. Carter and McRae (2017), for instance, suggest that there are three: early (approximately 1889–99), middle (approximately 1904–28) and late (approximately 1930–39). Sarker (2002), on the other hand, says that it is "fashionable" to divide Yeats' style development into four phases: Celtic twilight (1889–99), middle (1904–14), transitional (1919–35) and last (1938–9). There is a consensus that Yeats' first writing phase comprises poems published during the late nineteenth century and was influenced by the pre-Raphaelites, romanticism and Irish mythology. His subsequent writing moved away from these influences and became shaped by modernism. Luebering (2011), for example, notes that Yeats' poems of the late 1800s have a "dreamlike atmosphere" and are heavily reliant on Irish folklore and legend, whilst, in the first of his twentieth-century volumes: *In the Seven Woods* (1904) and *The Green Helmet* (1910), Yeats 'discarded the Pre-Raphaelite colours and rhythms of his early verse and purged it of certain Celtic and esoteric influences' (Luebering 2011: 168; see also Davis 2015). For Jeffares (1968: 100), the poems of *The Green Helmet* (1910) are 'transitional' in the sense that Yeats was 'still forming a new style' and 'stripping off the decoration of the old' (see also Carpenter 1969: 51–9). Matthews (2014) and Sarker (2002) suggest that 1914 saw a notable change in Yeats' style, with Matthews (2014: 335) arguing that *Responsibilities* (1914) 'marked a radical shift in his style toward the techniques and values of Pound and the younger generation'. Our analysis in Section 4 aims to determine whether there is textual evidence for some of these literary critical claims concerning Yeats' changes in style over time.

3 Stylometry and corpus stylistics

Our aim in this chapter is to explore some of the claims regarding Yeats' changing style using a combination of two computational approaches to stylistics: stylometry and corpus stylistics. From stylometry we use cluster analysis and principal components analysis (PCA), and from corpus stylistics we use keyword analysis. Our stylometric analysis is aimed at establishing groupings of Yeats' volumes of poetry to determine whether there is any linguistic evidence for literary critical views concerning the constituent periods of Yeats' career as a poet. Our corpus stylistic analysis of keywords is aimed at investigating Yeats' style more closely to determine whether there are any language features that are common to particular periods of his writing life.

Stylometric analysis (sometimes referred to as computational stylistics) draws on a range of techniques, including cluster analysis and principal components analysis, which we use for our analysis. Both are data reduction methods that can be used to look for underlying patterns in the data. For example, while we might intuitively assume that Yeats' early poems share more lexical characteristics with each other than they do with his later work, stylometric analysis reveals whether this is actually the case. In effect, stylometry offers a data-driven approach to identifying similarities between texts. So, instead of asserting, say, three distinct periods to Yeats' poetry and then looking for textual evidence of this, stylometric methods group the target texts based on lexical frequencies in the texts. It is then up to the analyst to decide whether the outcome of the statistical analysis supports non-statistically derived claims.

Cluster analysis is a statistical procedure by which texts are grouped together into clusters based on similarities of word frequencies within the texts. One famous and ground-breaking method is that developed by the linguist John Burrows, known as the

Burrows method (see Burrows 1987, 2002, 2003). The basic principle is to establish the most frequent words (MFWs) and their frequencies across a group of texts and then assess how the frequencies of those words within individual texts measure up against the group frequencies. The number of MFW (written *n*MFW) can vary, but for the purposes of this explanation, we will assume 100 MFW (written *n*MFW = 100). To ensure comparability, normalised frequencies are used (for more on normalisation, see Chapters 10 and 39, this volume) and these are compared against the group frequencies using a distance measure (i.e. measuring "distance" between frequencies; Burrows (2002) uses a measure called Delta). The texts under analysis are thus grouped based on the 100 most frequent words and their distances from the frequencies established for the group. The process also involves applying a method of linkage, which is a mathematical technique for organising the results into groups based on the distance calculations (see Hoover 2003). The closest two texts in terms of similarity of MFW are grouped together into what is known as a cluster. The process then continues, with the next most similar texts being grouped together and so on. The process results in all the texts under analysis being grouped together into one cluster of multiple strands (see Hoover 2013 for further explanation). The visual output from a cluster analysis is called a dendrogram (see Figures 35.1 and 35.2). We discuss how to interpret dendrograms in the next section.

Like cluster analysis, principal components analysis is a data reduction method. However, rather than grouping texts based on the 100 MFW, PCA aims to simplify the dataset in order to reveal the cause of most of the variation in the data. A non-linguistic example may make this easier to follow. Imagine you are collecting statistics on motorbikes, particularly speed, colour, number of cylinders and manufacturer. As you look at your data, you realise that the relationship between speed and number of cylinders is so close that it is simpler to conflate these two variables into one new variable: power. By so doing, you have reduced the complexity of the dataset and made it easier to see what distinguishes certain motorbikes from others. When applied to language, PCA works on the same principle. The procedure aims to conflate information about the 100 MFWs into a smaller number of variables known as components. The visual output of PCA is a graph on which the values of the two most significant components are plotted (see Figures 35.3 and 35.4). These two components – principal component 1 (PC1) and principal component 2 (PC2) – are deemed to be the most significant because they account for most of the variation in the data (again, see Hoover 2013 for more details). PC1 is plotted on the horizontal axis, while PC2 is plotted on the vertical axis. At this stage, the analyst's task is to interpret what non-linguistic variable (e.g. author, genre, time period) the grouping of the texts on the PCA graph reflects.

To carry out our cluster analysis and principal components analysis, we used the *Stylo* package for *R* (Eder *et al.* 2016), developed by the Computational Stylistics Group at the Institute of Polish Language in Kraków. *Stylo* provides a convenient and well-documented way to perform Burrows-style analyses using *R*.

Turning now to our corpus stylistic methods, in addition to our stylometric analyses, we carried out keyword analysis of Yeats' poems. Keyword analysis is based on the notion of keyness, which refers to unusually high or unusually low frequencies of particular words within a source text or corpus when compared, using statistical tests to a reference corpus or text (see Chapter 9, this volume). Keyness analysis offers a principled way to discover avenues for further investigation in a text or corpus. Keyness, however, is not necessarily an indication that a word is interpretively significant. This needs to be established by qualitative analysis of each keyword in context.

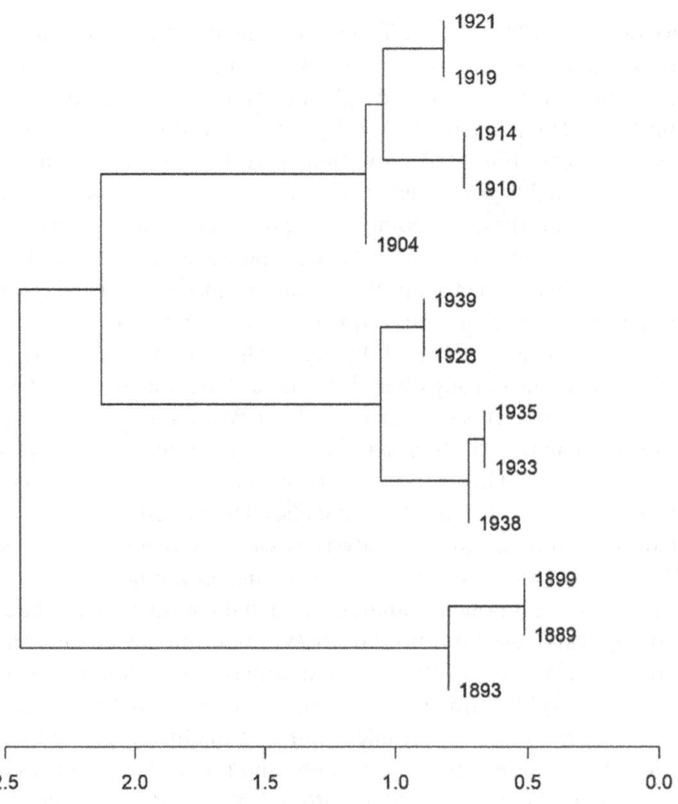

Figure 35.1 Cluster analysis of Yeats' poetry in 13 volumes based on *n*MFW = 100

In our study we made comparisons between the words and their associated frequencies in different volumes of Yeats' poetry using the keyword facility in *AntConc* (Anthony 2019), which is freely available corpus analysis software. Current thinking on the calculation of keywords (see Gabrielatos 2018) is that two statistical measures are required: statistical significance and effect size. The use of effect size as part of statistical testing has been argued for within social sciences more generally (see Levin and Robinson 1999; Thompson 1999). The current version of *AntConc* (Anthony 2019) offers several different statistics for this purpose. We used log likelihood for keyness and log ratio for effect size.

Log likelihood (LL) is an inferential statistic used to measure statistical significance (see Chapter 13, this volume). It indicates the confidence with which we can infer that any keywords are a result of the datasets being different in some way. Such statistical significance testing depends on the notion of a null hypothesis (usually denoted by H_0), which states that there is no difference between the two datasets or, more precisely, no difference in the populations from which the datasets were drawn (see McIntyre and Walker 2019: 154–8 for further explanation). Log likelihood provides an indication of the probability of getting the results if H_0 were true (i.e. no difference). The higher the log likelihood value, the lower the probability that the results would be obtained if H_0 is true. The probability is usually presented as a *p*-value, where the lower the number, the lower the probability. A *p*-value of less than 0.05 ($p < 0.05$) indicates that there is a 5 per

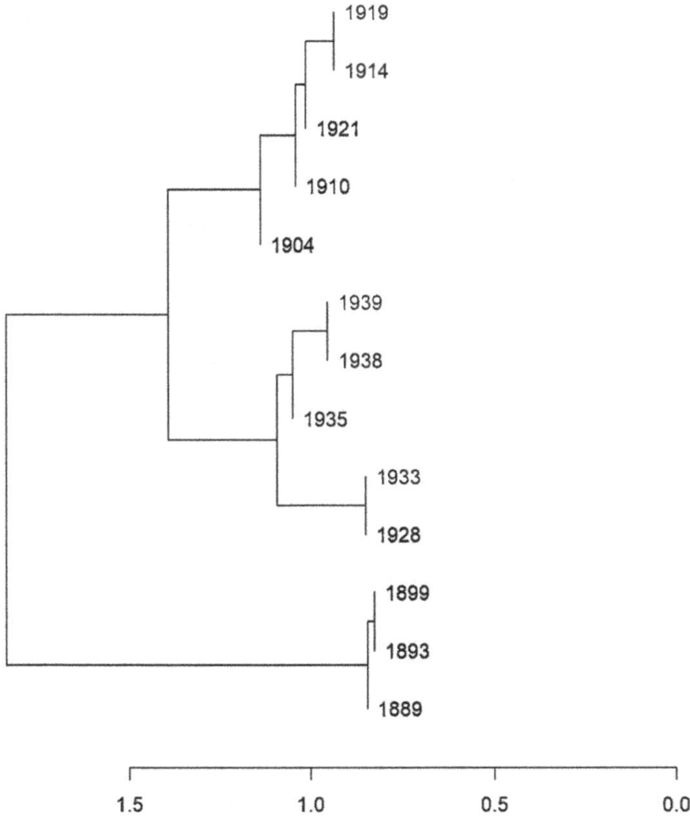

Figure 35.2 Cluster analysis of Yeats' poetry in 13 volumes based on *n*MFW = 1,000

cent chance that the results would be obtained if the null hypothesis were true; $p < 0.01$ indicates a 1 per cent chance, and $p < 0.001$ indicates a 0.01 per cent chance. The usual practice is to set a level of significance below which results are ignored. This means setting the level of confidence at which you are happy to reject the null hypothesis (i.e. that there is no difference between datasets). With LL the higher the score, the more confidently we can reject H_0. Using the settings in AntConc, we used a statistical cut-off of 10.83 (which equates to $p < 0.001$), so words with LL scores below 10.83 were ignored. This threshold is arbitrary but is a recognised cut-off in linguistics and social sciences more generally.

Log ratio (LR) is a descriptive statistic developed by Hardie (2014) for keyword research. It indicates the scale of the difference between word frequencies, which is known as effect size. A log ratio of 1 means that the frequency in the target corpus is twice as much as the frequency in the reference corpus; an LR of 2 means that the difference is four times as much, an LR of 3 means an eightfold difference and so on. We applied an (arbitrary) log ratio cut-off of 1 in order to eliminate keywords where the difference in frequencies was small (for further explanation of LR, see McIntyre and Walker 2019: 158–64).

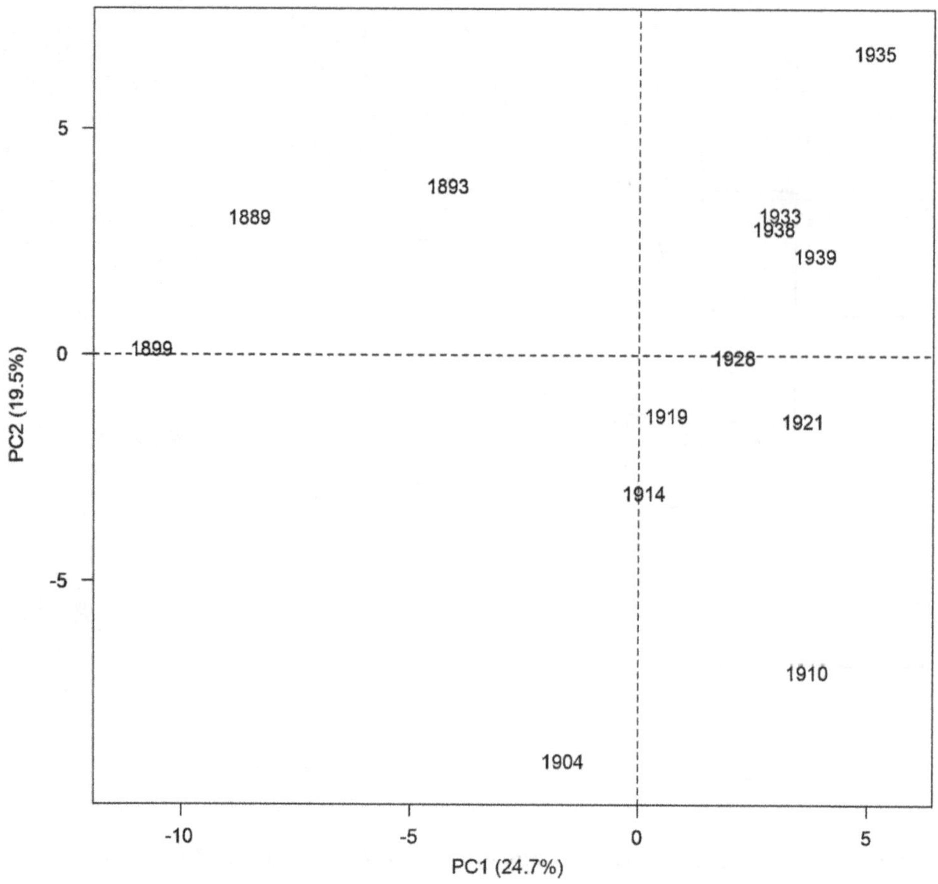

Figure 35.3 PCA of 13 volumes of Yeats' poetry *n*MFW = 100

4 A multivariate analysis of the style of W. B. Yeats

Cluster analysis and principal components analysis are methods of multivariate analysis, hence the title of this section. The research questions that we set out to answer in our multivariate analysis are:

1. Does multivariate analysis reveal lexical differences and/or similarities that support the literary critical claim that Yeats' style changes over time?
2. Does PCA group the collections of Yeats' poetry by style phase similar to those suggested by literary scholars?

To carry out our multivariate analysis of Yeats' style, we began by downloading the poems from the CSUN website in plain text format, one poem per file, using a web-scraper extension to *Google Chrome*. This gave us a total of 307 files spread across 13 volumes (see Table 35.1). To carry out the computational analysis, we merged the poems associated with each volume into one file so that there was just one file per volume, giving 13 files in total.

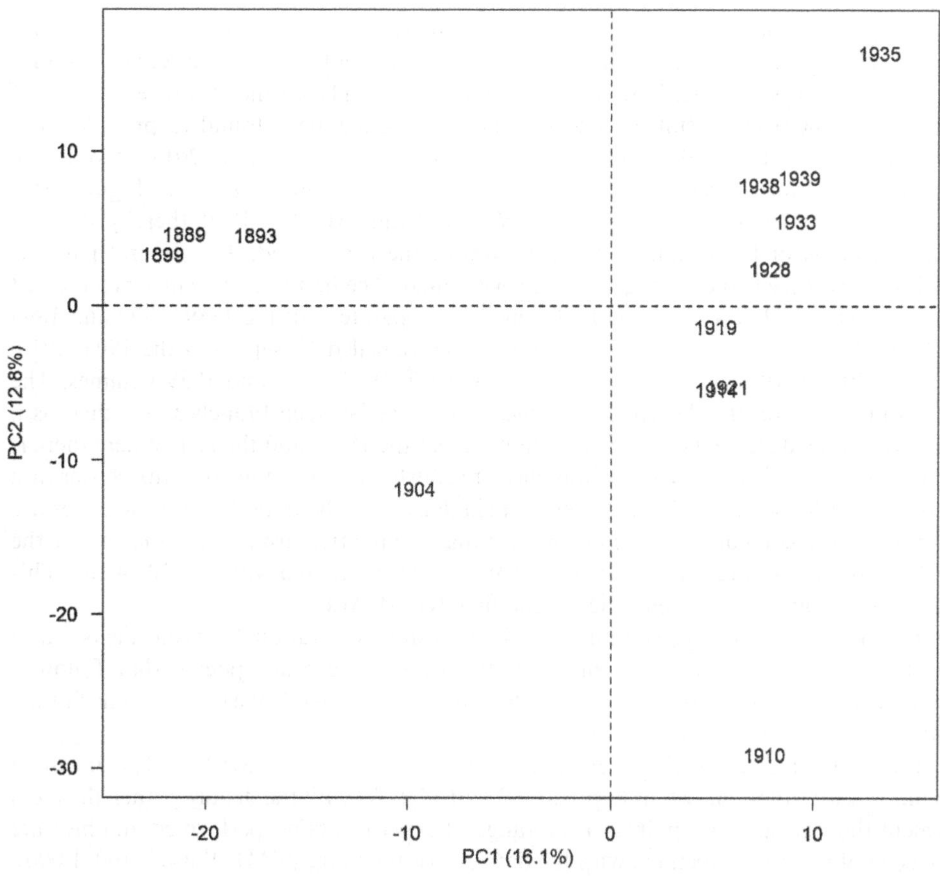

Figure 35.4 PCA of 13 volumes of Yeats' poetry *n*MFW = 1000

Table 35.1 The *Yeats Corpus of Poetry*

Volume no.	*Year of publication*	*Volume title*	*No. of poems*	*Total words*
1	1889	*Crossways*	16	4193
2	1893	*The Rose*	23	4511
3	1899	*The Wind Among The Reeds*	37	4194
4	1904	*In The Seven Woods*	14	2231
5	1910	*The Green Helmet and Other Poems*	21	1925
6	1914	*Responsibilities*	31	5443
7	1919	*The Wild Swans at Coole*	40	9024
8	1921	*Michael Robartes and The Dancer*	15	3258
9	1928	*The Tower*	20	7644
10	1933	*The Winding Stair and Other Poems*	30	7664
11	1935	*Parnell's Funeral and Other Poems*	6	1951
12	1938	*New Poems*	35	5529
13	1939	*Last Poems*	19	4634
Totals			**307**	**62201**

Using *Stylo* for *R* we performed a cluster analysis and PCA based on the MFWs across the volumes, ranging from 100 to 1,000 in increments of 50. To calculate distance between volumes, we used Smith and Aldridge's (2011) cosine distance variant of Burrows's (2002) Delta statistic because this statistic has been found to provide more accurate and reliable results (see Smith and Aldridge 2011; Evert et al. 2017). Two of the results of the cluster analyses are shown in the form of dendrograms (see Figures 35.1 and 35.2). The dendrograms are for *n*MFW = 100 and *n*MFW = 1000, thereby showing two snapshots of the results at the extremes of the range used. The general patterns indicated by these two dendrograms are very similar. The first branch, which is indicated by a vertical line known as a clade (labelled X), separates out the 1889, 1899 and 1893 volumes from the rest. The second major branch (labelled Y) separates the 1904, 1910, 1914, 1919 and 1921 volumes from the 1928, 1933, 1935, 1938 and 1939 volumes. The horizontal lines on the dendrogram indicate distance between branches. So, there is a relatively large distance between the volumes from the 1800s and the rest. Where there is a large difference between cluster branches, it is fairly safe to assume that the clusters are showing a reliable view of differences and similarities in the data. Small differences are indicative of less reliable groupings. Notice that the relative distances (indicated by the scale on the x-axis) are smaller when *n*MFW = 1,000 compared with *n*MFW = 100. This suggests that greater difference lies in the first 100 MFWs.

The dendrograms suggest that there is a reliable separation between Yeats' early nineteenth-century romantic poems and the twentieth-century poems that followed them. They also suggest that the twentieth-century poems, while part of the same family, differ in style, forming two sub-groups.

Two of the results for the PCA analysis (*n*MFW = 100 and *n*MFW = 1,000) can be found in scatterplots shown in Figures 35.3 and 35.4. As with the dendrograms, the plots present the start and end points of the range of experiments we performed and indicate the general patterns associated with the data across the range of MFW used (100–1,000). The PCA scatterplots provide visualisations of the data from a different analytical perspective and help to clarify the patterns observed in the dendrograms.

The scatterplots plot the volumes of poetry based on their scores along principal component 1 (PC1), which is plotted on the x-axis, and principal component 2 (PC2), which is plotted on the y-axis. Distances based on *n*MFW 100 to 1,000 are therefore plotted in two dimensions (horizontal and vertical). The twentieth-century volumes are largely separated by PC2 (indicated by vertical distance). The noticeable exception is the 1904 volume, which differs from the nineteenth century and the rest of the twentieth century on both PC1 and PC2. Another noticeable outlier is 1910, which aligns with the rest of the twentieth-century volumes in relation to PC1 but differs in relation to PC2.

The graphs shown in Figures 35.3 and 35.4 are divided into quadrants. In both graphs, the 1889, 1893 and 1899 volumes occupy the top left quadrant, although this pattern is more definite and the volumes closer together in Figure 35.4 (where *n*MFW = 1,000). The 1928–39 volumes occupy the top right quadrant, although when *n*MFW = 100, 1928 sits on the dividing line between the top right and bottom right quadrants. The 1935 volume is distanced vertically from other volumes in that quadrant. The bottom right quadrant contains the 1910, 1914, 1919 and 1921 volumes. The 1910 volume is at some vertical distance from the other volumes in that quadrant, with the latter being closer to top right quadrant. The 1904 volume sits alone in the bottom left quadrant.

Figure 35.4, which is the scatterplot for *n*MFW = 1,000, shows that the distances between volumes are closer than when *n*MFW = 100 (Figure 35.3). The 1914 and 1921 volumes are the most similar, since they occupy the same space on the graph. Closely related is the 1919 volume. The 1933, 1938 and 1939 volumes form a reasonably close grouping, with the 1928 volume falling in between but being closer to the 1914, 1919 and 1921 volumes. These seven volumes differ mostly in relation to PC2 and are similar in relation to PC1, meaning that they are fairly well aligned horizontally, but less well aligned vertically.

The graph shows three outliers: 1904, 1910 and 1935. All three are shown to be a large distance from other volumes of poetry. All three volumes are drastically different from the rest in terms of PC2. The 1910 and 1935 volumes are similar to the other twentieth-century volumes in terms of PC1, while the 1904 volume falls in between the nineteenth and twentieth century.

Stylo for *R* can also create a scatterplot that includes the MFW used in the analysis. The position of the words on the plot indicates loadings, which is their ability or power to differentiate texts. Figure 35.5 shows a scatterplot with loadings for *n*MFW = 200 (any more words than this and the plot starts to become unreadable). It is still possible to

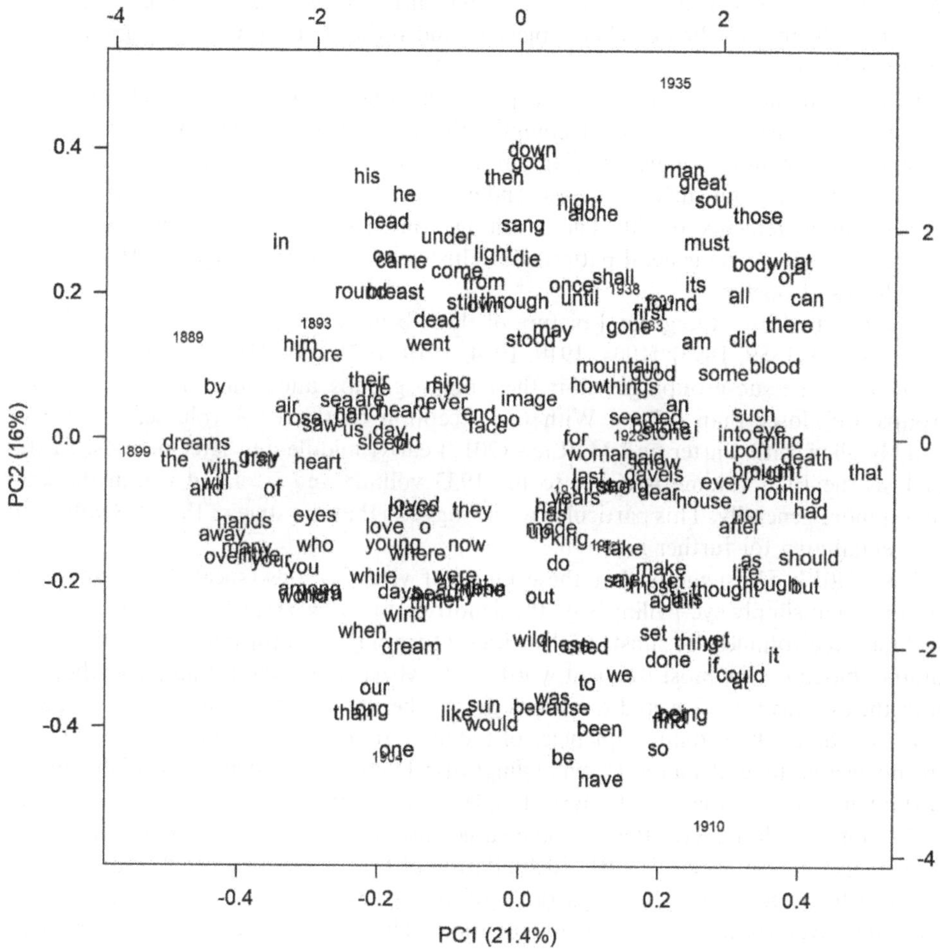

Figure 35.5 PCA of 13 volumes of Yeats' poetry *n*MFW = 200 with loadings

see in Figure 35.5 the general pattern of Yeats' volumes and to discern the words that exert a strong influence on the principal components. So, we can see that PC1 is influenced by *the* and *dreams* on the left-hand side of the chart and *that* on the right-hand side. (It is interesting to note that Meir 1974: 82 claims that 'Yeats' use of *that* and *what* most consistently marks his later style as distinctively Anglo-Irish'. It is indeed the case that Yeats on several occasions in his late works uses *that* instead of *who* and *what* instead of *which* and *whom*). PC2 is influenced by *down* at the top of the chart and *have* at the bottom.

As we mentioned at the start of this section, the cluster analysis and PCA experiments we carried out used a range of *n*MFW from 100 to 1,000 in increments of 50. Our results and discussion focussed on the start and end points of that range. However, as Eder (2017) points out, the choice of the number of MFW is completely arbitrary, so we could just as easily have looked at the results for *n*MFW = 101 and *n*MFW = 997. Eder also notes that small variances in the number of MFW can produce unpredictable and inexplicable differences in results (e.g. *n*MFW = 100 could produce different clusters from, say, *n*MFW = 103). This presents the researcher with the problem of working out which *n*MFW to use and which results to report, which might lead to the dendrograms that best fit the hypothesis being "cherry picked" and those that do not being ignored (see Rudman 2003).

In order to address some of these problems, Eder and his colleagues developed bootstrap consensus analysis which compiles the results of multiple PCA analyses across a range of MFW into a single tree diagram. Following the recommendations of Eder, we used *Stylo* to carry out such an analysis and generated a consensus tree for *n*MFW = 100 to 1000 in increments of 50. The resulting consensus tree, which can be seen in Figure 35.6, shows the general patterns for clustering across the range of MFW for the 13 volumes of poetry.

The tree reaffirms the general picture of there being three main groupings of Yeats' poetry: [1889, 1889, 1893]; [1904, 1910, 1914, 1919, 1921]; and [1928, 1933, 1935, 1938, 1939]. There are sub-groupings within these major groups, and some volumes within the groups are closer than others. With the exception of the 1928 volume, the groups roughly align with Carter and McRae's (2017) early, middle and later periods. In this analysis the 1928 volume is closer to the 1933 volume and is placed within the later period more generally. This particular result suggests that the style of the 1928 volume is a potential area for further research.

Eder (2017: 51) suggests that these kinds of visualisations 'speak for themselves', meaning that simply eye-balling, say, the dendrograms shows that Yeats' early poems in his first three volumes are substantially different from the rest (in some linguistic way or another based on the most frequent words). The visualisations, informative as they are, nevertheless leave unanswered questions about the nature and development of Yeats' style over time. Other than frequencies of the most frequent words in Yeats' poetry, we are no nearer to understanding what linguistic features and structures might be important in, for example, Yeats' lyrical style. The MFW analyses and subsequent visualisations do, however, offer us some sufficiently reliable groupings that allow us to confirm Carter and McRae's (2017) delimitation of the distinct periods of Yeats' writing life. Furthermore, these groupings (and, of course, the outliers) point to potentially profitable avenues of qualitative investigation. This is what we turn to in the next section.

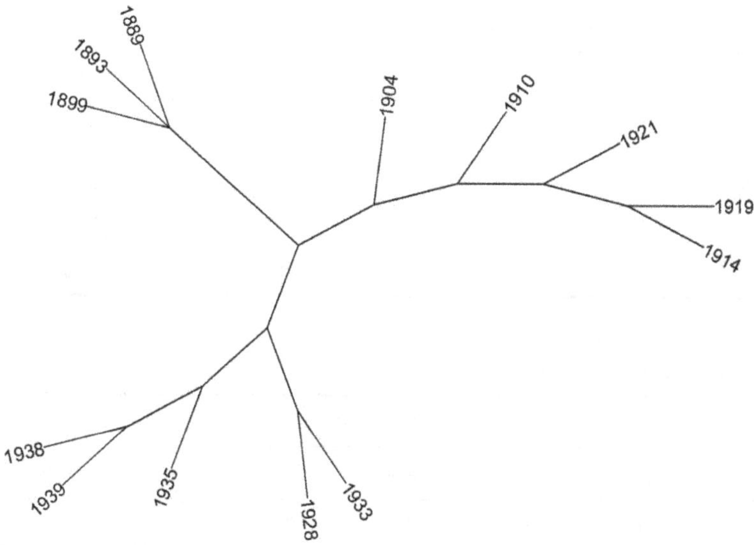

Figure 35.6 Bootstrap consensus tree of Yeats' poetry in 13 volumes based on *n*MFW = 100 to 1,000 in increments of 50

Table 35.2 The *Early Yeats Corpus*: volumes included and totals

Volumes included	*Year of publication*	*No. of poems*	*No. of words*
Crossways	1889	16	4193
The Rose	1893	23	4511
The Wind Among The Reeds	1899	37	4194
Totals		**76**	**12898**

5 Keywords and style

On the basis of the PCA results, we performed keyword comparisons on Yeats' poetry from the 1800s (early Yeats) and from 1928 to 1939 (late Yeats). We created two corpora containing the relevant collections, the details of which are shown in Tables 35.2 and 35.3.

We generated two sets of keywords by comparing the two corpora against each other using *AntConc* (Anthony 2019). We used a log likelihood cut-off 10.83 ($p < 0.001$) and a log ratio lower limit of 1. We also dismissed any keywords with a frequency less than 20 on the grounds that low-frequency keywords are less likely to reveal general style features across the period in question. The results are shown in Tables 35.4 and 35.5.

The keywords in both tables can be divided into different types based, to some extent, on grammatical class. There are those which carry meaning relating to content or theme (typically nouns, adjectives and lexical verbs) and those which relate to structuring of content and themes (typically grammatical words such as pronouns, prepositions, conjunctions and auxiliary verbs). Both can be said to be important for discerning style. That is, the style of Yeats' romantic poems is likely to concern a combination of themes and the manner in which those themes are presented.

Table 35.3 The *Late Yeats Corpus*: volumes included and totals

Volumes included	*Year of publication*	*No. of poems*	*No. of words*
The Tower	1928	20	7644
The Winding Stair and Other Poems	1933	30	7664
Parnell's Funeral and Other Poems	1935	6	1951
New Poems	1938	35	5529
Last Poems	1939	19	4634
Totals		**110**	**27422**

Table 35.4 Keywords in the *Early Yeats Corpus*

		Early Yeats		*Late Yeats*			
Rank	*Keyword*	*Freq.*	*%*	*Freq.*	*%*	*LL*	*LR*
1	sad	20	0.16	0	0.07	45.61	6.410
2	stars	33	0.26	1	0.12	67.03	6.133
3	sorrow	22	0.17	2	0.08	37.95	4.548
4	heavy	20	0.16	2	0.07	33.75	4.410
5	leaves	30	0.23	4	0.11	46.88	3.995
6	grey	22	0.17	4	0.08	30.93	3.548
7	little	27	0.21	8	0.10	30.12	2.843
8	rose	33	0.26	10	0.12	36.34	2.811
9	white	24	0.19	8	0.09	24.91	2.673
10	will	35	0.27	12	0.13	35.68	2.633
11	while	23	0.18	9	0.08	21.36	2.442
12	wandering	20	0.16	8	0.07	18.27	2.410
13	hair	34	0.26	14	0.12	30.39	2.368
14	dreams	22	0.17	11	0.08	16.64	2.088
15	you	104	0.81	56	0.38	73.39	1.981
16	go	22	0.17	12	0.08	15.27	1.963
17	dream	25	0.19	14	0.09	16.88	1.925
18	your	62	0.48	40	0.23	35.65	1.721
19	world	31	0.24	20	0.11	17.80	1.721
20	away	36	0.28	26	0.13	17.81	1.558
21	who	43	0.33	33	0.16	19.46	1.470
22	with	141	1.09	115	0.51	58.24	1.382
23	him	41	0.32	36	0.15	14.83	1.276
24	me	60	0.47	60	0.22	16.73	1.088

The keywords that carry semantic content (keywords 1–9, 12–14, 17, 19) potentially reflect thematic attention on particular emotions and flora. It is possible that the over-representation of the lexical items *dream* and *dreams* in the Early Yeats corpus is partly what motivated Luebering's (2011: 168) comment about the poems having a 'dreamlike atmosphere'. Here, for reasons of space, we will look more closely at just a small number of grammatical keywords. Focusing on grammatical keywords, highlighted in grey on the tables, is motivated by the fact these are more likely to suggest general language

Table 35.5 Keywords in the *Late Yeats Corpus*

	Late Yeats		*Early Yeats*			
Keyword	*Freq.*	*%*	*Freq.*	*%*	*LL*	*LR*
mountain	32	0.12	0	0.00	24.68	4.912
such	51	0.19	1	0.01	31.75	4.584
back	20	0.07	0	0.00	15.42	4.234
tomb	20	0.07	0	0.00	15.42	4.234
nothing	32	0.12	1	0.01	18.00	3.912
should	31	0.11	1	0.01	17.29	3.870
run	27	0.10	1	0.01	14.48	3.667
might	25	0.09	1	0.01	13.08	3.556
blood	47	0.17	2	0.02	24.11	3.466
keep	22	0.08	1	0.01	11.02	3.371
dear	38	0.14	2	0.02	17.99	3.160
soul	61	0.22	4	0.03	26.13	2.843
house	28	0.10	2	0.02	11.46	2.719
what	231	0.84	17	0.13	93.37	2.676
every	36	0.13	3	0.02	13.45	2.497
death	33	0.12	3	0.02	11.64	2.371
those	82	0.30	8	0.06	27.52	2.269
can	110	0.40	12	0.09	33.81	2.108
mind	51	0.19	6	0.05	14.66	1.999
did	42	0.15	5	0.04	11.94	1.982
thought	65	0.24	8	0.06	17.91	1.934
found	40	0.15	5	0.04	10.85	1.912
could	46	0.17	6	0.05	11.96	1.850
body	44	0.16	6	0.05	10.92	1.786
or	274	1.00	40	0.31	63.34	1.688
an	92	0.34	14	0.11	20.14	1.628
if	75	0.27	13	0.10	13.79	1.440
had	144	0.53	25	0.19	26.45	1.438
it	166	0.61	29	0.22	30.23	1.429
that	714	2.60	130	1.01	123.89	1.369
great	81	0.30	15	0.12	13.46	1.345
man	205	0.75	43	0.33	27.46	1.165
s	315	1.15	74	0.36	33.3	1.002

patterns across corpora that relate to style, since they do not of themselves indicate aboutness (that is, they are markers of style rather than of theme). In this respect they constitute what Enkvist (1973) terms style markers.

The keyword *you* is one of four personal pronouns in the keywords list. In order to assess whether the over-representation of *you* in the Early Yeats corpus was interpretatively significant in comparison to Late Yeats, we exported the concordance lines for *you* from both corpora into an Excel spreadsheet and analysed the context of use and referent of the pronoun. Forty-four per cent of the 104 occurrences of *you* in Early Yeats are part of interactions within poems (as in, for example, "Anashuya and Vijaya", "Fergus and the Druid"), as demonstrated by example 1. Most of the remaining occurrences (55 per cent) are of the poetic persona (or poet) addressing someone or something via the poem (see example 2). Just 1 per cent of occurrences are of *you* being used generically (example 3).

(1) The sick man's wife opened the door:
'Father! you come again!'
('The Ballad of Father Gilligan')

(2) Were you but lying cold and dead,
And lights were paling out of the West,
You would come hither, and bend your head,
('He Wishes His Beloved Were Dead')

(3) Gay bells or sad, they bring you memories
('The Dedication To A Book Of Stories Selected From The Irish Novelists')

By contrast, 21 per cent of the occurrences of *you* in the poems in the Late Yeats corpus are in interactions in the poems (for example "The Three Bushes" and "Colonel Martin"), with 75 per cent being used to address someone or something via the poem. The remaining 4 per cent are generic *you*.

A further difference in the use of *you* between the poems in the two corpora is that in the Early Yeats corpus there are more occurrences of *you* used when the poetic persona (or poet) apparently addresses directly non-sentient objects and supernatural beings (for example Ireland, a fish, a deer, the heart, a valley, an angel) and unnamed individuals (potential lovers) than in the Late Yeats corpus. By contrast, in the Late Yeats corpus the poetic persona apparently directly addresses named people (Anne Gregory, Dorothy Wellesley, Von Hugel) and groups of people (*you, that have grown old* "The New Faces"; *Parnellites* "Come gather Round Me Parnellites"; *you that would judge me* "The Municipal Gallery Revisited"; *You that Mitchel's prayer have heard* "Under Ben Bulben") and also the reader or people generally, as example 4 demonstrates:

(4) Swift has sailed into his rest;
Savage indignation there
Cannot lacerate his breast.
Imitate him if you dare,
World-besotted traveller; he
Served human liberty.
('Swift's Epitaph')

This quantitative analysis of the keyword *you* shows that as well as an over-representation of the pronoun in the Early Yeats corpus, there is a change in the poetic stance of the poet in relation to his addressees. This does not go unnoticed by Ellman (1964), who suggests that 'Yeats altered the position of the reader' from the reader being 'almost an intruder on the poet's contemplations' to one of over-hearer or direct addressee.

As for the keywords *while* and *who* and *with*, these can all be used to connect additional information in the form of modifying phrases or clauses to other parts of the sentence in which they occur. In both the Early and Late Yeats corpora all but one instance of *while* acts as a subordinating conjunction as demonstrated in example 5:

(5) come near me while I sing the ancient ways
('The Rose Upon The Rood Of Time')

The preposition *with* is used to provide additional information to verb phrases in the form of adverbials, as in (6):

(6) And blame you with many bitter words.
('The Fish')

Example 7 demonstrates that *with* is also used in the post-modification of noun phrases, as is *who*; both being used to post-modify 'a glimmering girl':

(7) It had become a glimmering girl
With apple blossom in her hair
Who called me by my name and ran
And faded through the brightening air.
('The Song Of Wandering Aengus')

Who is also used in questions, which is a topic we address in more detail later.

These sorts of uses also occur in the Late Yeats poems, but the frequency is less. This points to the more frequent use of adjuncts in poems in the Early Yeats corpus than in the Late Yeats corpus.

Turning now to the keywords in the Late Yeats corpus, Table 35.5 shows that the modal auxiliary verbs *should, might, can* and *could* are all key in the Late Yeats corpus and occur only a handful of times in the Early Yeats corpus. These keywords, along with *if* and *what*, relate to a comparative prevalence of evaluations and judgements of possibility, probability, beliefs and knowledge and present a view of how the poet sees the world. For example, the use of *can* in example 8 (emphatically) presents strong possibility. The choice of modal form (and indeed, the decision to use a modal form at all) nevertheless makes explicit the poetic persona's opinion and judgement.

(8) Nothing but stillness can remain when hearts are full
Of their own sweetness, bodies of their loveliness
('Meditations In Time Of Civil War')

The same is true of the modal auxiliary verb *should* which, even though prototypically associated with deontic modality, is used epistemically 18 times out of 31. Of the 13 deontic uses, 4 are in questions where the poetic persona asks 'why should [...]?', apparently questioning existing states of affairs, as examples 9 and 10 demonstrate:

(9) Why should the imagination of a man
Long past his prime remember things that are
Emblematical of love and war?
('A Dialogue Of Self And Soul')

(10) Why should he think me cruel
Or that he is betrayed?
('A Woman Young And Old')

If is used in the construction of hypothetical scenarios in poems and for expressing possibility (e.g. examples 11). It is used 16 times, in combination with *what*, in questions (e.g. example 12).

(11) If Folly link with Elegance
No man knows which is which,
('The Old Stone Cross')

(12) What if I bade you leave
The cavern of the mind?
('Those Images')

The keyword *what* is predominantly used in interrogatives (62 per cent) in the Late Yeats poems, with the other occurrences being pronouns (28 per cent) or determiners (10 per cent). Questions in general are more prevalent in the Late Yeats corpus than in Early Yeats. We determined this by counting the question marks in each corpus and found 179 in the former and 33 in the latter. Even when the difference in the size of the corpora is taken into account (the Late Yeats being just over twice the size of Early Yeats), this five-fold difference suggests a difference in rhetorical style in Yeats' late poetry.

While the keyword analysis is brief, it does begin to suggest indicative linguistic characteristics of early and late style in Yeats' poetry. For instance, the comparative over-representation of modality and mood in the Late Yeats corpus suggests a development in one aspect of Yeats' style, whereby the poet is expressing doubts, suggesting what is possible or probable and questioning. Further keyness analysis, combined with other standard corpus linguistic techniques such as collocation and n-gram analysis, could be carried out to further explore the claims we have made in this section.

This chapter has aimed to demonstrate the value of combining stylometric methods of analysis with corpus stylistics in order to shed light on the changing nature of Yeats' poetic style. We first carried out a multivariate analysis of Yeats' poems using cluster analysis and PCA. In so doing, we focused on answering two questions:

1. Does multivariate analysis reveal lexical differences and/or similarities that support the literary critical claim that Yeats' style changes over time?
2. Does PCA group the collections of Yeats' poetry by style phase similar to those suggested by literary scholars?

In answer to these questions, the multivariate analysis provided some support for Carter and McRae's (2017) division of Yeats' poetry into three distinct stylistic periods. The secondary value of the cluster analysis and PCA was to motivate our corpus stylistic comparison of Yeats' poetry from the 1800s and that of 1928–39. By so doing, we were able to make some inroads into identifying some of the potential lexical characteristics of early and late Yeats. Of course, the keyword analysis presented here is only the beginning of what would need to be a more detailed and involved study, but it begins to illustrate how corpus stylistic methods can be used in association with computational stylistic techniques to generate insights into style that would be impossible to uncover otherwise.

Further reading

Hoover, D., Culpeper, J. and O'Halloran, K. (2014) *Digital Literary Studies: Corpus Approaches to Poetry, Prose, and Drama*, London: Routledge. (This book covers both corpus and computational approaches to stylistics and includes numerous case studies exemplifying some of the techniques discussed in this chapter.)

McIntyre, D. and Walker, B. (2019) *Corpus Stylistics: Theory and Practice*, Edinburgh: Edinburgh University Press. (This book outlines a theoretically informed approach to corpus stylistic analysis; chapter 7 deals with the corpus stylistic analysis of poetry particularly.)

Murphy, S. (2015) 'I Will Proclaim Myself What I Am: Corpus Stylistics and the Language of Shakespeare's Soliloquies', *Language and Literature* 24(4): 338–54. (This article demonstrates the value of keyword analysis in differentiating texts according to genre.)

References

Anthony, L. (2019) *AntConc 3.5.8*, Tokyo, Japan: Waseda University, Available at: https://www.laurenceanthony.net/software.

Burrows, J. (1987) *Computation into Criticism: Study of Jane Austen's Novels and an Experiment in Method*, Oxford: Clarendon Press.

Burrows, J. (2002) '"Delta": A Measure of Stylistic Difference and a Guide to Likely Authorship', *Literary and Linguistic Computing* 17(3): 267–87.

Burrows, J. (2003) 'Questions of Authorship: Attribution and Beyond', *Computers and the Humanities* 37: 1–26.

Carpenter, W. M. (1969) 'The "Green Helmet" Poems and Yeats' Myth of the Renaissance', *Modern Philology* 67(1): 50–9.

Carter, R. A. and McRae, J. (2017) *The Routledge History of Literature in English: Britain and Ireland*, 3rd edn, London: Routledge.

Davis, A. (2015) 'Edwardian Yeats: *In the Seven Woods*', *Études Anglais* 68(4): 454–67.

Eder, M. (2017) 'Visualization in Stylometry: Cluster Analysis Using Networks', *Digital Scholarship in the Humanities* 32(1): 50–64.

Eder, M., Rybicki, J. and Kestemont, M. (2016) 'Stylometry with R: A Package for Computational Text Analysis', *R Journal* 8(1): 107–121.

Ellman, R. (1964) *The Identity of Yeats*, New York, NY: Oxford University Press.

Enkvist, N. E. (1973) *Linguistic Stylistics*, The Hague: Mouton.

Evans, M. (2018) 'Style and Chronology: A Stylometric Investigation of Aphra Behn's Dramatic Style and the Dating of *The Young King*', *Language and Literature* 27(2): 103–32.

Evert, S., Proisl, T., Jannidis, F., Reger, I., Pielström, S., Schöch, C., & Vitt, T. (2017). 'Understanding and Explaining Delta Measures for Authorship Attribution', *Digital Scholarship in the Humanities* 32(2): 4–16. https://doi.org/10.1093/llc/fqx023

Finneran, R. J. (1997) *The Collected Works of W. B. Yeats. Volume 1: The Poems*, 2nd edn, New York, NY: Scribner.

Gabrielatos, C. (2018) 'Keyness Analysis: Nature, Metrics and Techniques', in C. Taylor and A. Marchi (eds) *Corpus Approaches to Discourse: A Critical Review*, London: Routledge, pp. 225–58.

Hardie, A. (2014) 'Log Ratio: An Informal Introduction', (Blog post), *ESRC Centre for Corpus Approaches to Social Science (CASS)*, Available at: http://cass.lancs.ac.uk/log-ratio-an-informal-introduction.

Hoover D. (2003) 'Frequent Collocations and Authorial Style', *Literary and Linguistic Computing* 18(3): 261–86.

Hoover, D. (2013) 'Textual Analysis', in K. Price and R. Siemens (eds) *Literary Studies in the Digital Age: An Evolving Anthology*, New York, NY: MLA Commons, Available at: https://dlsanthology.mla.hcommons.org/textual-analysis/.
Hoover, D. and Hess, S. (2009) 'An Exercise in Non-Ideal Authorship Attribution: The Mysterious Maria Ward', *Literary and Linguistic Computing* 24(4): 467–89.
Jeffares, N. A. (1968) *A Commentary on the Collected Poems of W. B. Yeats*, London: Palgrave Macmillan.
Levin, J. R. and Robinson, D. H. (1999) 'Rejoinder: Statistical Hypothesis Testing, Effect-Size Estimation, and the Conclusion Coherence of Primary Research Studies', *Educational Researcher* 29(1): 34–6.
Luebering, J. E. (ed.) (2011) *English Literature from the 19th Century Through Today*, New York, NY: Britannica Educational Publishing.
Mahlberg, M. (2012) *Corpus Stylistics and Dickens's Fiction*, London: Routledge.
Mastropierro, L. (2018) *Corpus Stylistics in Heart of Darkness and its Italian Translations*, London: Bloomsbury.
Matthews, S. (2014) 'W. B. Yeats', in D. E. Chinitz and G. McDonald (eds) *A Companion to Modernist Poetry*, Oxford: Wiley Blackwell, pp. 335–47.
McIntyre, D. and Walker, B. (2019) *Corpus Stylistics: Theory and Practice*, Edinburgh: Edinburgh University Press.
Meir, C. (1974) *The Ballads and Songs of W. B. Yeats: The Anglo-Irish Heritage in Subject and Style*, London: Macmillan.
Montoro, R. and McIntyre, D. (2019) 'Subordination as a Potential Marker of Complexity in Serious and Popular Fiction: A Corpus Stylistic Approach to the Testing of Literary Critical Claims', *Corpora* 14(1): 275–99.
O'Halloran, K. (2007) 'The Subconscious in James Joyce's "Eveline": A Corpus Stylistic Analysis that Chews on the "Fish Hook"', *Language and Literature* 16(3): 227–44.
Rudman, J. (2003) 'Cherry Picking in Nontraditional Authorship Attribution Studies', *CHANCE* 16(2): 26–32.
Sarker, S. K. (2002) *W. B. Yeats: Poetry and Plays*, New Delhi: Atlantic Publishers and Distributors.
Semino, E. and Short, M. (2004) *Corpus Stylistics: Speech, Writing and Thought Presentation in a Corpus of English Writing*, London: Routledge.
Smith, W. H. and Aldridge, W. (2011) 'Improving Authorship Attribution: Optimizing Burrows' Delta Method', *Journal of Quantitative Linguistics* 18(1): 63–88.
Thompson, B. (1999) 'Improving Research Clarity and Usefulness with Effect Size Indices as Supplements to Statistical Significance Tests', *Exceptional Children* 65(3): 329–37.

36

Using corpus linguistics to explore literary speech representation: non-standard language in fiction

Carolina P. Amador-Moreno and Ana Maria Terrazas-Calero

1 Real and fictional speech: similarities and differences

Various studies in stylistics and other areas have discussed how fictional conversations differ from real-life conversations (see Bublitz 2017). Fictional dialogues often display traces of orality to a greater or lesser extent. However, verbal interaction in fiction can only be understood and interpreted in relation to the same rules of discourse that govern everyday interaction. As Fowler (1981: 21) points out, fictional dialogues are built upon models of language use which tend to occur in "non fictional" texts (conversation, meetings, political speeches, news reports, etc.). Although evidently lacking the spontaneity of spoken oral interaction, fictional dialogue is, nonetheless, rooted in ordinary discourse and everyday situations.

In that sense, the authorial mimesis of oral language and the significance of the selection of spoken features that an author makes in order to represent characters' voices are of interest to linguists and stylisticians. How a particular author imagines a speech community into existence is rather telling in terms of the degree of language awareness they display. Also, how a particular character is perceived by the reader is very much subject to the inclusion of certain linguistic features, which often also contribute to creating a literary and linguistic environment that renders a story believable and engaging. The representation of non-standard features is an important element in the construction of such environment. This will be discussed further in the following sections.

Speech representation in literature

Linguistic elements associated with language variation may be especially interesting when analysing a particular author's use of language (for a discussion of this see Planchenault 2017). The use of non-standard or regionally marked patterns of cohesion, forms of reference and address, strategies of politeness and discourse pragmatic markers (DPMs) is as much a characteristic of literary dialogue as conversation (Johnstone 1991). In general, non-standard forms are often found in fictional dialogues and are

DOI: 10.4324/9780367076399-36

employed as indicators of social or regional differences which depict a character (Taavitsainen *et al.* 1999).

The role and effectiveness of linguistic non-standardness in text are key aspects of what Kirk (1999) refers to as the stylistic approach to the study of dialect. However, the use of literary data as a valid source of linguistic evidence is controversial and has often been questioned on the grounds of realism and consistency. Although it is true that a certain degree of caution is essential when analysing literary dialect, it is important to bear in mind that, as pointed out by Labov (1972), as long as it is observed and evaluated in relation to the spoken language, the study of literary dialect can be a valuable complement to the evidence of real speech data (see discussion in Amador-Moreno 2010a).

One of the main problems the use of literary dialect data as linguistic evidence can present, however, is that of authenticity. Linguistic "realism" rests on the author's ability to strike a balance between the standard and non-standard forms they use so as not to alienate or distract the readers from the story. This also applies to cinematic and televisual dialogue, where accent or dialect are strategically used to enrich the characters with a fleshed-out sociocultural identity (Kozloff 2000). The representation of naturally occurring linguistic elements in televisual dialogue not only creates 'realistic scenarios' (Lambrou 2014: 144) but also makes the characters seem more 'believable for the audience' (Queen 2015: 105). Quaglio (2009), for example, examines a corpus of dialogues from the US sitcom *Friends*, finding that while sharing several items from natural conversations, the scripted dialogue tended to be more colloquial and real than unscripted interactions. Nevertheless, and as Hodson (2014: 200) argues, the level of authenticity of the fictional dialogue, be it literary or telecinematic, will also depend on the readers/viewers who, as the ultimate "judges" of realism, must be aware of and familiar with the dialect that is being mimicked in the fiction 'to be able to experience it as "real"'. From a stylistic perspective, however, an author's ability to represent the nuances and complexities of spoken language in an authentic way adds enormous value to their work.

Whether studying this point from a stylistic or a dialectological angle, most researchers working on the representation of dialect in fiction (using literary or telecinematic corpora) are conscious of the fact that consistency is not found in real spoken dialects. Therefore, if an author aims at achieving authenticity, they must 'incorporate variation in the speech of each individual character' (Tamasi 2001: 135). Walshe's (2011: 132) study of the dialogue in Irish TV show *Father Ted* finds a number of features which transmit a valid representation of Irish discourse, despite not being as regionally recognisable as other features. Contrastively, Bednarek (2017) proposes continuity as another function of televisual dialogue (adding it to Kozloff's 2000 functions of film dialogue) in the context of TV series. Thus, while inconsistency is expected, she states that fictional discourse has to adhere to what the audience (or readers, if we extrapolate it to literary dialogue and literary series) expects of the series and the character regarding their behaviour and speech (ibid: 142). She proposes catchphrases and 'signature interjections' (Bednarek 2010: 137) as linguistic tools through which continuity can be established in the fictional world. All of this lends itself to analysis through the lens of corpus linguistics, or more specifically, it may fall within the domain of corpus stylistics.

2 Using a corpus to compare real and represented speech

The use of computers for systematic analysis of fictional dialogue is still relatively new when compared to more established fields. However, in order to assess literary dialect, for example, we need to determine which are the features that are used artistically by an author or a group of authors belonging to the same literary movement and to compare them (if possible) with other contemporary evidence of local speech. In that regard, corpus stylistics offers the possibility to incorporate quantitative and qualitative corpus methodologies which 'link[s] in with the concerns in literary stylistics and criticism' (Mahlberg and McIntyre 2011: 216), allowing the researcher to investigate linguistic patterns that their own intuition may have overlooked. Since the publication of the first edition of this Handbook in 2010, this field appears to have flourished, as demonstrated by the exponential growth in the number of corpus stylistics studies, ranging from (initially) small sections which described this approach in contributions to other handbooks (see Semino 2011: 547–8; or Gibbons and Whiteley 2018), to a substantial number of publications dealing specifically with corpus stylistics (see Mahlberg this volume; or Bednarek [2011, 2017] for telecinematic discourse). Finally, there also seems to be a growing number of monographs devoted to demonstrating the approach and its practical application (see Fischer-Starcke 2010; Ho 2011; Montoro 2012; Mastropierro 2018; McIntyre and Walker 2019 and various contributions to Locher and Jucker 2017), which attest to the popularity of this approach in the last decade.

In order to conduct corpus stylistic analyses, researchers may use specialised software, like the widely known software suites used for text analysis, such as *WordSmith Tools*, (Scott 2020), *AntConc* (Anthony 2019), *Sketch Engine* (Kilgarriff *et al.* 2004) or *Wmatrix* (Rayson 2009). There are two more tools worth mentioning. For example, the *Corpus Linguistics in Context* (CLiC) web app, which is part of Dicken's Project at the University of Birmingham (Mahlberg *et al.* 2019). Dörk and Knight's (2015) *WordWanderer* web app provides both experts and novices of any age with a 'playful' (ibid: 84) visualisation of language patterns in any uploaded text(s), taking into consideration corpus tools such as concordances (or "context view"). The basic tasks that all these suites perform are similar: they generate statistics, wordlists, frequency charts, concordances, lists of collocations and keywords, etc., all of which may be revealing in the context of literary dialect, as will be shown later.

When investigating literary dialect, diachronic studies can shed light on the developments of dialectal features by looking at written sources, whereas the synchronic study of different varieties of English allows us to compare written and spoken corpora. Thus, corpora such as the *Helsinki Corpus*, which contains around 1.6 million words from the Old English, Middle English and Early Modern English periods, may be used for diachronic study; whereas others, like the *International Corpus of English* (ICE), contain both written and spoken data to allow for the synchronic study of different varieties of English (see Chapter 8, this volume). In both diachronic and synchronic studies literary dialect can lend itself to two basic types of approaches: intra-textual analyses, which tend to take a deeper look at one specific text, and inter-textual analyses, which compare different texts by the same or various authors. An example of an intra-textual approach is Culpeper (2002), who compares the speech of six of the characters in *Romeo and Juliet* with all of the other characters in the play. Other intra-textual studies include Mahlberg and McIntyre's (2011) analysis of *Casino Royale*, in which they propose a general classification of key words into "thematic" (i.e. concrete, world-building elements like objects or places in the fictional world) and "reader-centered" (i.e. often evaluative and open to interpretation), or Stockwell and Mahlberg's (2015) examination of mind modelling in Dicken's *David Copperfield.* An inter-textual approach, in contrast, is employed in Montoro's (2019) analysis of the alleged syntactic simplicity of popular fiction (as opposed to "highbrow" literature). Using the *Lancaster Speech, Writing and Thought Presentation Corpus* and her own corpora in contrast with the written section of the *British National Corpus*, she disproves the claim.

The inter-textual approach is particularly relevant in synchronic studies of literary dialect, given that, since the advent of recording devices, we can now compare literary dialogues with real spoken data. The use of a baseline corpus of contemporary spoken language makes comparisons between fictional and real spoken data possible. In the context of Irish literature, for example, O'Keeffe and Amador-Moreno (2009) use the *Limerick Corpus of Irish English* (henceforth LCIE, see Farr *et al.* 2002) as a baseline for comparison. LCIE is a 1-million-word spoken corpus of Irish English (hereafter IrE) discourse. The transcribed recordings that form the corpus range across age, gender, socio-economic background and geographical location, and they include conversations recorded in a wide variety of mostly informal settings throughout Ireland (excluding Northern Ireland). This makes it an invaluable source for the comparison of real and fictional contemporary IrE. It allows us to analyse, for instance, the distribution and use of the widely known structure *be* + *after* + *V-ing* (e.g. *I'm after breaking the pen*) as a way of expressing a recently completed action in IrE. By looking at software-generated word frequency lists, concordances, etc., it is also possible to compare the use of DPMs in the LCIE data with their occurrence in contemporary writing (Amador-Moreno 2010b), as well as to examine the appearance of more recent features such as "New Intensifying *So*" (NISo) (e.g. *I am so not going there*) in IrE, as will be illustrated in Section 4.

When setting out to study the (re-)creation of a variety of English, one has to consider whether the text(s) one is interested in is already part of a corpus. For the study of IrE, for instance, the test corpus supplied with *Corpus Presenter* (Hickey 2003) contains a small sample of literary IrE which, although consisting mostly of drama, is useful for researchers interested in stylistic and diachronic analyses of this variety. One could also consider the possibility of building their own corpus, especially for the study of contemporary Irish writing, as in the case of Terrazas-Calero's *Corpus of Contemporary Fictionalized Irish English* (2020), in which case copyright issues would also need to be taken into account (see Chapters 2 and 4, this volume for more on collecting, databasing and preserving written data).

3 What can a corpus tell us about speech representation in literature?

As we know, corpus methods complement stylistic analyses. One of the first questions the researcher must ask when considering speech representation in literature is whose speech they are interested in (i.e. is it the narrator's voice, a character or group of characters in particular we want to focus on?). One option would be to isolate all the dialogues in a novel in order to concentrate on the direct representation of the speaker(s) of interest. In analysing Irish novelist Roddy Doyle's fictionalisation of IrE, Hehir (2005), for example, focuses on the dialogues from the novel *The Snapper* only, while in his study of Northern Irish cinematic discourse, Walshe (2017) only transcribes sentences that contain recognisable items of IrE. Sometimes, however, one may also be interested in the author's voice, especially if we are dealing with autobiographical novels; or we might come across a narrative voice that contains dialogue. While other times deciphering when dialogues begin and end may be more problematic. In cases like these, one should include not just the dialogues but the whole novel.

Semino and Short (2004) propose a classification of speech representation that is relevant in this context, as it allows for a more exhaustive account of the (re-) presentation of speech in writing. Building on the work of Leech and Short (1981), they develop a manual annotation system for speech, writing and thought which is based on the following main categories:

N	Narration (e.g. She looked at her compassionately)
NRSA	Narrative Report of Speech Acts (e.g. She looked at her compassionately and told her about the death of her friend.)
IS	Indirect Speech (e.g. She looked at her compassionately and told her that her friend had died. She was shocked.)
FIS	Free Indirect Speech (e.g. She looked at her compassionately. Her friend had died!)
DS	Direct Speech (e.g. She looked at her compassionately and said 'Maureen has died')
FDS	Free Direct Speech (e.g. She looked at her compassionately. 'Maureen has died'. She was shocked)

The application of Leech and Short's model led them to extend and refine some of these categories. The refined categories can then be more easily located once a particular narrative has been tagged following this classification. This tagging system facilitates the study of spoken features, something that will be revisited in Section 5. Having discussed some of the key issues of fictional speech representation, this chapter will turn to a case study of a feature of contemporary IrE, which will illustrate how spoken features in general can be analysed through computer analysis.

4 Case study of corpus-based stylistic analysis

In order to demonstrate some possible uses of corpus-based stylistic analyses, this section uses the work of best-selling Dublin author Paul Howard, whose series, based on the character of *Ross O'Carroll-Kelly* (hereafter RO'CK), has been praised by critics for its accurate portrayal of the type of English spoken in some parts of Dublin. Corpus linguistics methods have been used to investigate this claim and show how this effect might be achieved by the author. An example of this was illustrated in Amador-Moreno's contribution to the first edition of this Handbook (2010b), where the DPM *like* and the IrE construction *be + after + V-ing* were used to show how quantitative data can complement qualitative stylistic analysis in terms of speech representation. Word frequency information allowed for the identification of *like* as a DPM, while comparing frequency lists of fictional and non-fictional discourse provided interesting results in relation to how *like* is fictionalised in the RO'CK series mentioned. A detailed analysis of the concordances of *like* led to the discussion of sociolinguistic and pragmatic issues that are revealing both from a stylistic and a dialectological perspective. Also revealing are the comparisons of real spoken discourse and various fictional sources where the construction *be + after + V-ing* (e.g. *She's after changing the code*) features prominently. By looking closely at the patterns of use in the corpora, the analyses of DPM *like* and of the *be + after + V-ing* construction in the chapter clearly showed how corpus analytic techniques can be a useful complement to the study of literary IrE.

As we will show now, corpus methodology can also be applied to the analysis of linguistic features which may not have been traditionally associated with this variety.

Table 36.1 The RO'CK corpus texts

Title	*Publication Year*	*Word Count*
The Curious Incident of the Dog in the Nightdress (CIDN) (O'Carroll-Kelly 2005)	2005	89,861
Downturn Abbey (DA) (O'Carroll-Kelly 2013)	2013	133,873
Keeping up with the Kalashnikovs (KUK) (O'Carroll-Kelly 2014)	2014	126,347
		Total word count: 350, 081

This is the case of "New Intensifying *So*" (henceforth NISo, as per Amador-Moreno and Terrazas-Calero's 2017 terminology). NISo is the label we apply to the use of intensifying SO in traditionally ungrammatical contexts, such as 'He is *so* not that person'.

For the present case study, we used a corpus of three RO'CK novels (Table 36.1) to investigate the form and pragmatic functions this "new" intensifier serves in IrE (as perceived and portrayed by Paul Howard).

In Amador-Moreno and Terrazas-Calero (2017) we found that a keyword analysis which contrasted DA and KUK against CIDN as a reference corpus (RC) highlighted SO (encompassing all its general uses, not only its intensifying value) as a negative keyword (i.e. a word that occurs less statistically frequently than expected) in KUK when compared to the RC.

The narrative value of SO in everyday interaction warranted further research into the way Dubliners use it (as perceived by Howard). Thus, a wordlist was generated, and this showed that while general SO fell within the top 100 most frequent words in the corpus, there was a progressive and marked decrease over time, going from position forty-seven (CIDN) to sixty (DA) and finally to sixty-six (KUK). Using qualitative analysis, we were able to discern that while appearing in a wide array of forms (including its use as a pragmatic marker, tag, set phrase and substitute *so*), its intensifying form was the most recurrent. The use of NISo in non-standard contexts like 'She's so not going' was particularly substantial within this category.

The representation of NISo in Howard's fiction

Our study begins with a quantitative analysis of the frequency of use of NISo in Howard's books (Table 36.2), which reveals a striking decrease over time, with the intensifier reaching its frequency pinnacle in CIDN but declining in DA and being substantially cut down in the last book.

If we take Howard's literary IrE as a representation of real-life linguistic use in Ireland, then this finding suggests a fall in the use of NISo, thus replicating the natural tendency of intensifiers to rapidly go in and out of fashion among speakers.

As with all intensifiers which are partly motivated by the speakers' wish for linguistic originality (Stoffel 1901; Quirk *et al.* 1985), the use of innovative NISo, which, as we show later, intensifies a wider range of words, clauses and phrases than traditional SO, highlights the delexicalisation of the original word (i.e intensifier SO). This is a progressive loss of the meaning (Partington 1993) whereby the word gradually becomes less

Table 36.2 Raw token count per book

Book Acronym and Publication Year	*NISo Tokens*
CIDN (2005)	36
DA (2013)	28[1]
KU (2014)	9

lexically and contextually restricted as it gains popularity among speakers (Lorenz 2002). A quantitative colligation analysis (see Chapters 11 and 15, this volume) of Howard's portrayal of NISo use in Dublin English (DubE) indicates that it can occur in the following traditionally non-standard contexts[2]:

(1)
Within (or preceding) a noun phrase: 'Oh my God, this is so lollers[3].'

[DA]

(2)
Within (or preceding) an adverbial phrase: 'I'm just telling you that patent leather is SO last year.'

[CIDN]

(3)
Within (or preceding) a prepositional phrase: '[...] they're so off their head'

[KUK]

(4)
Within (or preceding) whole predicate/whole predicate: 'I so love being a member of this family!'

[DA]

According to Howard's literary representation, therefore, the conventionally ungrammatical contexts in which NISo occurs in Dublin range from modifying (1) a noun or nominal phrase to (2) adverbial phrases (3) prepositional phrases or (4) verbs. Furthermore, NISo may also cluster with other collocations such as DPM *like* and intensifying "Oh my God" or "fucking" (e.g. 'I am SO focking out of here.').

Co-occurrence with negative verbal constructions such as ('She is SO not going to the gym anymore, that's for sure.') is also attested to in Howard's novels. Our collocation analysis using *Wordsmith Tools* highlighted not only their creativity but also the fact that *not* seems to lend an extra layer of intensification to NISo. This is better illustrated below, where occurrences of the NISo + NEGATIVE pattern are found to modify mostly the negative particle (5) but also full clauses (6) and ellipsis (7):

(5)
'Oh my God! That is SO not the case.

[CIDN]

(6)
'Ross, don't think that. Oh my God, so don't think it.'

[KUK]

(7)
'Ross,' she goes, 'you're not a loser. You're *so* not.'

[DA]

Quantitative and qualitative colligation-pattern analyses were subsequently conducted which revealed a significant shift in terms of colligate preference across the books. As illustrated in Figure 36.1, our findings indicate the fact that while the preferred construction in CIDN is NISo + V/VP, the most frequent pattern in DA and KUK is NISo + N/NP. We believe this shift regarding the grammatical contexts that NISo co-occurs with evidences the potential delexicalisation this particular intensifier may have undergone in the context of Dublin (as perceived by Howard).

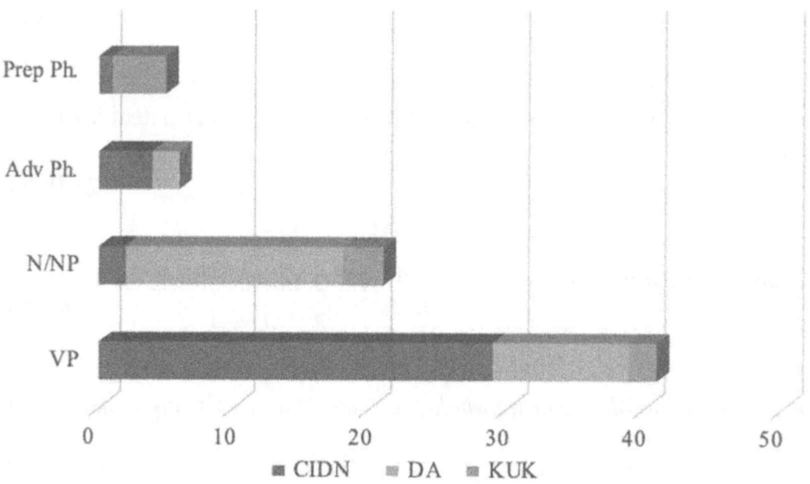

Figure 36.1 Colligation patterns across the books per 100 tokens

An examination of the pragmatic functions/emotion connotations (see Bednarek 2008) transmitted by each of those patterns was also undertaken at this stage. The results indicate that the majority of the verbs in the NISo + VPs in CIDN are verbs of action, although there are some cases where we find verbs of cognition (e.g. 'I'm SO not listening to that for another twenty minutes'). We then manually classified the emotions/connotations conveyed by this pattern into positive/neutral or negative and attributed an emotion to each. The quantitative analysis of the classification highlighted the more frequent conveyance of personal and interpersonally negative emotions (in CIDN and DA only), including dislike, sarcasm [see (8) next], insults, mockery, anger, self-deprecation or defensiveness. While considerably fewer in number, cases where this construction conveyed positive/neutral feelings (e.g. amplified determination, excitement, or eagerness) were also found [i.e. (9)].

(8)
'She is SO not going to the gym anymore, that's for sure. I heard she piled it on when she went on the pill.'

[CIDN]

(9)
'We are SO putting a Jacuzzi in the library'.

[CIDN]

As the second most recurrent pattern (and first in DA/KUK), we also investigated the pragmatic functions of the NISo + N/NP construction, following the same classification. Its quantitative analysis and qualitative classification highlighted the existence of a significantly frequent pattern within this construction in the novels: NISo + (Positive) Adjective + N/NP [see (10) and (11)]. Pragmatically, our investigation reveals that most occurrences of NISo + (Positive) Adjective + N/NP (i.e. 82, 35 per cent) transmit positive emotions or neutral ones in the form of emphasis (10–11), and there were also instances where negative feelings like self-deprecation [see (12)] or defensive statements [i.e. (13)] may be transmitted through adjectivised noun phrases.

(10)
'I just think that's, like, *so* an inspiring quote'

[KUK]

(11)
Well, if I know Charles, there'll be some—oh my God—so, so romantic story involved. I'm sure we'll hear it in time

[DA]

(12)
'That's what a lot of people say, including - I don't know if you've ever heard of her- but Felicity Fox, when my mum and dad were originally *selling* the place? And I am *so* a Lady Mary! Ross will even tell you that!'

[DA]

(13)
Sorcha's there, 'I am so a parent,' just defending herself.

[DA]

Upon inspection of its form, we hypothesise that the use of NISo in this particular pattern serves as a substitute for *such* [see (10)] or *very* [in (11)]. The study of the distribution of occurrence of this pattern per novel, however, indicates that while present in DA/KUK (ten and two occurrences respectively), this particular pattern was absent from CIDN. We believe this further substantiates the delexicalisation of NISo in DubE, where the intensifier gains unrestrainability with time, collocating in more unrestricted contexts as it becomes more established in this variety. This theory, however, needs validation via contrast with real spoken DubE. Another reason for the existence of this pattern in the books, nevertheless, might be its use as an authorial, stylistic device through which Howard mocks the more “linguistically trendy” Southern Dubliners, *who may not know how to use* NISo “correctly”.

The prosodic portrayal of NISo representation in the corpus also merits attention. While it is obvious that fictional dialogue lacks certain paralinguistic elements of real-life communication (e.g. intonation, stress, pitch, etc.), Howard manages to convey the phrasal stress that this construction requires in two ways: through emphatic capitalisation and italicisation of the intensifier.

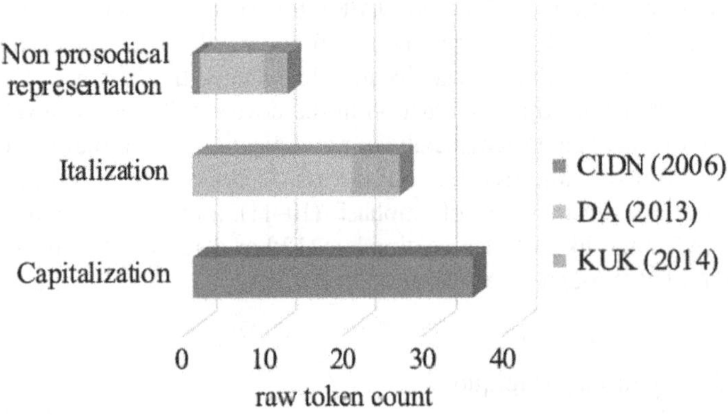

Figure 36.2 Raw token count illustrating prosodic representation of NISo

The quantitative analysis of these prosodic “reproductions” (see Figure 36.2) indicates that while capitalisation was the primary mode of emphasis representation in CIDN, it seems to have been abandoned in favour of italisation, which despite its non-occurrence in the first book, accounts for 20 of the 28 occurrences of NISo in DA and 6 out of the 9 in KUK. It is also interesting to notice the gradually rising number of unprosodically represented NISos. The increasing amount of italicised and non (extra) stressed NISos in the books could showcase the fact that by 2014 the speakers in Dublin (i.e. Southside Dubliners in particular), and the readers in general, were so familiar with this intensifier that there was no need for Howard to provide added layers of visual emphasis that rendered NISo’s necessary phrasal stress. Another possible explanation may be the fact that phrasal emphasis is no longer required in the production of NISo in Dublin. This claim, again, needs contrasting with real, spoken DubE.

In the next section we explore the sociolinguistic value of NISo as represented in our RO’CK corpus.

The sociolinguistic value of NISo in Ireland

NISo is by no means an exclusively Irish phenomenon. In fact, and while it is popularly perceived as having originated in the United States, its use has been registered in other varieties of English where it seems to be indexical of speaker identity. On the one hand, it appears to be age and gender-distinctive, with scholars like Tagliamonte and Roberts (2005), for example, documenting its increasing salience among young speakers, particularly females, in the United States (see also Zwicky 2011) or in Canada (Tagliamonte 2005, 2008).

In our case study, we find that NISo appears to mirror the indexical value it holds in other varieties for the great majority of (fictional) speakers that use it in the books are in their twenties to thirties. Furthermore, a quantitative analysis of the distribution of NISo per gender (see Table 36.3) is revealing. It illustrates a rather balanced distribution in CIDN, with males using it slightly more recurrently. However, there is a noticeable shift in the later books which establishes a clear link between NISo and the (fictional) female speakers in Howard's literary portrayal of DubE. We believe that while this shift could be due to a change in his linguistic perception, its pronounced salience may also indicate a potential linguistic development whereby this intensifier was associated with female speech in Dublin, mirroring its use in other varieties of English. That would certainly account for the distinct decrease in terms of male production over the span of nine years between the publication of CIDN (2005) and DA (2013).

Table 36.3 Raw distribution of tokens by gender and book

Gender distribution		
	Female	*Male*
CIDN	17	19
DA	28	0
KUK	7	2

The use of NISo also appears to be geographically bound to the South Dublin City, a part that has traditionally been associated with the accommodated class who use more globalised linguistic items. It is never produced by characters from North Dublin City, an area often linked with the working and middle classes who tend to use more locally bound linguistic features. Given the exclusive use of NISo by Southsiders, we believe this particular feature is a stylistic tool that functions as a sociolinguistic marker of a specific community of speakers (i.e. the Southsiders) who seek to detach themselves from the identity of the group of speakers (i.e. the North Dubliners) coming from a different socioeconomic background who use more regionally distinctive language (i.e. tag *so*, 'It's lucky Ross was there, *so it was*').

To conclude, utilising corpus linguistics and stylistics methods in the analysis of NISo in our RO'CK corpus has allowed us to discern its colligation pattern preference in IrE, as well as shifts in preference over time. It has also revealed the pragmatic functionality of this intensifier, as well as the types of emotions it may transmit. Finally, it has underlined the sociolinguistic value of NISo as an intensifier which, according to the corpus, indexes the voice of a (fictional) young, often female South Dubliner.

5 What a corpus cannot tell us about representation in literature

One of the limitations of using fictional corpora to study speech representation in general is the question of style in a broader sense. The appearance or absence of a particular feature in the work of an author may be due to their personal style, and this is something that researchers interested in corpus analysis of the kind discussed here need to take into account.

It is important to acknowledge that there may be other limitations in terms of the results obtained with this type of analysis as far as fictional dialogue is concerned. As argued earlier, prosodic information is almost impossible to track in a literary corpus unless there are audiovisual aids (i.e. public readings/audiobooks read by the author) which would allow us to measure the reaction of the audience to the fiction which is built upon the language, without which elements like humour would be lost.

Infrequent uses such as idiomatic expressions or metaphoric language might also not be found in fictional representations, and if they are, they will not appear as frequently used items when running word frequency counts. However, this does not mean that they are not used in real spoken language.

Another limitation has to do with the different spellings of words. Returning to our case study of the representation of IrE, it is worth considering that authors sometimes mark different dialects orthographically in order to render pronunciation. Thus, we often find *just* and *jist*, *sure* and *shure*, *think* and *tink*, *right* and *roysh*, *like* and *loike*, etc. Corpus annotation in that sense can help us find those words at a later stage so that all the variant spellings are included in the word count. The addition of tags or labels can certainly be of great benefit. Phonetic annotation in this case would be useful for the purpose expressed earlier. Stylistic annotation, as discussed in Section 3, would add information about speech (re-)presentation (direct speech, indirect speech, free indirect speech, etc.) so that the features one is looking for can be more easily identified and contextualised. A tagging system based on characters' names of the kind used by Culpeper (2002) or Terrazas-Calero (2020) can equally be of great benefit, as it can identify the speech of each character and/or exclude non-speech material, such as stage directions in drama, or dialogue by characters the researcher may not be interested in analysing. As Leech (2005) points out, 'what has been built into the corpus in the form of annotations can also be extracted from [it…] and used in various ways'. In that sense, different corpora will require different types of annotation, depending on the kind of analysis the researcher wants to undertake. In a larger literary corpus, for example, it would help if one were able to distinguish *so* (conjunction) from *so* (intensifier) and NISo without having to search through hundreds or thousands of concordance lines (see Reppen 2010). If this distinction is already signalled in the corpus by tags, the retrieval can be automatic. Equally, if one is interested in investigating the use of a feature such as cleft sentences, then having this structure labelled from the start will save a lot of painstaking searching.

Keeping a record of the annotation scheme is always recommended. Although different annotation systems are already available (see Leech 2005; McEnery and Xiao 2005), their usefulness depends on the type of analysis one is considering. In any case, good corpus design would help the researcher avoid at least some of the limitations highlighted here (see Reppen 2010).

Notes

1 There are three occurrences where NISo is duplicated in cases like 'It was so, so a pleasure to meet you'. In the current chapter, the duplicates were counted as an individual occurrence.
2 Emphasis placed on the NISos in the original texts. While only one example is selected to illustrate each category, categories encompass all the findings.
3 Nominalisation of the texting abbreviation 'LOL' (i.e. laughing out loud).

Further reading

Adolphs, S. (2006) *Introducing Electronic Text Analysis: A Practical Guide for Language and Literary Studies*, London: Routledge. (This is a good introduction to the topic of written corpora, and it provides very useful insights into the analysis of electronic texts in general.)

Culpeper, J. (2009). 'Keyness: Words, Parts-of-Speech and Semantic Categories in the Character-Talk of Shakespeare's Romeo and Juliet', *International Journal of Corpus Linguistics* 14(1): 29–59. (This paper analyses keywords in *Romeo and Juliet*. It is a good introduction to corpus analysis in the context of drama. Keyword analysis, as the author suggests, can be applied to other kinds of data, such as particular registers, dialects, media, documents or writings.)

McIntyre, D. and Walker, B. (2019) *Corpus Stylistics: Theory and Practice*, Edinburgh: Edinburgh University Press. (This is the most updated monograph explaining the theory and methodology of corpus stylistics with practical examples. It begins with an introduction to the theory of corpus linguistics and stylistics and how they intersect. It also offers an overview of the current state of the field and explores the application of corpus stylistics methods to pedagogy, historical linguistics and even its potential use in the real world.)

References

Amador-Moreno, C. P. (2010a) *An Introduction to Irish English*, London: Equinox.

Amador-Moreno, C. P. (2010b) 'How Can Corpora be Used to Explore Literary Speech Representation?', in A. O'Keeffe and M. J. McCarthy (eds) *The Routledge Handbook of Corpus Linguistics* London: Routledge, pp. 531–44.

Amador-Moreno, C. P. and Terrazas-Calero, A. M. (2017) 'Encapsulating Irish English in Literature', *World Englishes* 36 (2): 254–68.

Anthony, L. (2019) *AntConc* (Version 3.5.8) [Computer Software], Tokyo, Japan: Waseda University, Available from https://www.laurenceanthony.net/software.

Bednarek, M. (2008) *Emotion Talk Across Corpora*, Basingstoke: Palgrave Macmillan.

Bednarek, M. (2010) *The Language of Fictional Television: Drama and Identity*, London/New York: Continuum.

Bednarek, M. (2011) 'Expressivity and Televisual Characterization', *Language and Literature* 20(1): 3–21.

Bednarek, M. (2017) 'The Role of Dialogue in Fiction,' in M. A. Locher and A. H. Jucker (eds) *Pragmatics of Fiction*, Berlin/Boston: De Gruyter Mouto, pp. 129–58.

Bublitz, W. (2017) 'Oral Features in Fiction,' in M. Locher and A. H. Jucker (eds) *Pragmatics of Fiction*, Berlin/Boston: De Gruyter Mouton, pp. 235–63.

Culpeper, J. (2002) 'Computers, Language and Characterisation: An Analysis of Six Characters in Romeo and Juliet,' in U. Melander-Marttala, C. Östman, and M. Kytö (eds) *Conversation in Life and in Literature*, Uppsala: Universitetstryckeriet, pp. 11–30.

Dörk, M. and Knight, D. (2015) 'WordWanderer: A Navigational Approach to Text Visualisation', *Corpora* 10(1): 89–94.

Farr, F., Murphy, B. and O'Keeffe, A. (2002) 'The Limerick Corpus of Irish English: Design, Description and Application', *Teanga* 21: 5–29.

Fischer-Starcke, B. (2010) *Corpus Linguistics in Literary Analysis: Jane Austen and her Contemporaries*, London/New York: Continuum.

Fowler, R. (1981) *Literature as Social Discourse*, London: Batsford.

Gibbons, A. and Whiteley, S. (2018) *Contemporary Stylistics: Language, Cognition, Interpretation*, Edinburgh: Edinburgh University Press.

Hehir, G. (2005) 'Authentic or wha?: A Corpus-based Linguistic Analysis of the Conversational Language of Roddy Doyle's 'The Snapper'', unpublished MA dissertation, University of Limerick.

Hickey, R. (2003) *Corpus Presenter: Software for Language Analysis with a Manual and A Corpus of Irish English as Sample Data*, Amsterdam: John Benjamins.

Ho, Y. (2011) *Corpus Stylistics in Principles and Practice. A Stylistic Exploration of John Fowles' The Magus*, London/New York: Continuum.

Hodson, J. (2014) *Dialect in Film and Literature*, Basingstoke: Palgrave Macmillan.

Johnstone, B. (1991) 'Discourse-Level Aspects of Dialect in Diction: A Southern American Example', *Language and Style* 24(4): 461–471.

Kilgarriff, A., Rychly, P., Smrz, P. and Tugwell D. (2004) 'The Sketch Engine', *Proceedings from EURALEX*, Lorient, France, pp. 105–15.

Kirk, J. M. (1999) 'Contemporary Irish Writing and a Model of Speech Realism,' in I. Taavitsainen, G. Melchers and P. Pahta (eds) *Writing in Nonstandard English*, Amsterdam: John Benjamins, pp. 45–62.

Kozloff, S. (2000) *Overhearing Film Dialogue*, Berkeley, CA: University of California Press.

Labov, W. (1972) 'Some Principles of Linguistic Methodology', *Language in Society* 1: 97–120.

Lambrou, M. (2014) 'Stylistics, Conversation Analysis and the Cooperative Principle,' in M. Burke (ed.) *The Routledge Handbook of Stylistics*, London: Routledge, pp. 136–54.

Leech, G. (2005) 'Adding Linguistic Annotation', in M. Wynne (ed.) *Developing Linguistic Corpora: A Guide to Good Practice*, Oxford: Oxbow Books, pp. 17–29.

Leech, G. N. and Short, M. H. (1981) *Style in Fiction*, London: Longman.

Locher, M. A. and Jucker, A. H. (eds) (2017) *Pragmatics of Fiction*, Berlin/Boston: De Gruyter Mouton.

Lorenz, G. (2002) '*Really Worthwhile or Not Really Significant?* A Corpus-Based Approach to the Delexicalization and Grammaticalization of Intensifiers in Modern English,' in I. Wischer and G. Diewald (eds.) *New Reflections on Grammaticalization*, Amsterdam/Philadelphia: John Benjamins, pp. 143–162.

Mahlberg M. and McIntyre, D. (2011) 'A Case for Corpus Stylistics: Ian Fleming's Casino Royale', *English Text Construction* 4(2): 204–27.

Mahlberg, M., Wiegand, V., Stockwell, P. and Hennessey, A. (2019) 'Speech-Bundles in the 19th-Century English Novel', *Language and Literature* 28(4): 326–53.

Mastropierro, L. (2018) *Corpus Stylistics in Heart of Darkness and its Italian Translations*, London: Bloomsbury.

McEnery, A. and Xiao, R. (2005) 'Character Encoding in Corpus Construction,' in M. Wynne (ed.) *Developing Linguistic Corpora: A Guide to Good Practice*, Oxford: Oxbow Books, pp. 47–58.

McIntyre, D. and Walker B. (2019) *Corpus Stylistics Theory and Practice*, Edinburgh: Edinburgh University Press.

Montoro, R. (2012) *Chick Lit: The Stylistics of Cappuccino Fiction*, London: Bloomsbury Academic.

Montoro, R. (2019) 'Investigating Syntactic Simplicity in Popular Fiction A Corpus Stylistics Approach,' in R. Page, B. Busse and N. Nørgaard (eds) *Rethinking Language, Text and Context: Interdisciplinary Research in Stylistics in Honour of Michael Toolan*, London: Routledge, pp. 63–78.

O'Carroll-Kelly, R. [P. Howard] (2005) *The Curious Incident of the Dog in the Nightdress*, London: Penguin Books.

O'Carroll-Kelly, R. [P. Howard] (2013) *Downturn Abbey*, Dublin: Penguin Ireland.

O'Carroll-Kelly, R. [P. Howard] (2014) *Keeping up with the Kalashnikovs*, Dublin: Penguin Ireland.

O'Keeffe, A. and Amador-Moreno, C. P. (2009) 'The Pragmatics of the *Be + After + V-ing* Construction in Irish English', *Intercultural Pragmatics* 6 (4): 517–34.

Partington, A. (1993) 'Corpus Evidence of Language Change: The Case of Intensifiers,' in M. Baker, G. Francis and E. Tognini-Bonelli (eds) *Text and Technology: In Honour of John Sinclair*, Amsterdam: John Benjamins, pp. 177–92.

Planchenault, G. (2017) 'Doing Dialects in Dialogues: Regional, Social and Ethnic Variation in Fiction,' in M. Locher and A. H. Jucker (eds) *Pragmatics of Fiction*, Berlin: De Gruyter Mouton, pp. 265–96.

Quaglio, P. (2009) *Television Dialogue: The Sitcom Friends vs. Natural Conversation*, Amsterdam/Philadelphia: John Benjamins.

Queen, R. (2015) *Vox Popular: The Surprising Life of Language in the Media*, Chichester, UK: Wiley-Blackwell.

Quirk, R. Greenbaum, S. Leech, G. and Svartvik, J. (1985)*A Comprehensive Grammar of the English Language*, London: Longman.

Rayson, P. (2009) 'Wmatrix: A Web-Based Corpus Processing Environment', Computing Department, Lancaster University. http://ucrel.lancs.ac.uk/wmatrix/.

Reppen, R. (2010) 'Building a Corpus: What Are The Key Considerations?', in A. O'Keeffe and M. J. McCarthy (eds) *The Routledge Handbook of Corpus Linguistics*, London: Routledge, pp. 31–7.

Semino, E. and Short, M. (2004) *Corpus Stylistics. Speech, Writing and Thought Presentation in a Corpus of English Writing*, London: Routledge.

Semino, E. (2011) 'Stylistics', in J. Simpson (ed.) *The Routledge Handbook of Applied Linguistics*, London: Routledge, pp. 541–53.

Scott, M. (2020) *WordSmith Tools,* version 8, Stroud: Lexical Analysis Software.

Short, M., Semino, E. and Wynne, M. (2002) 'Revisiting the Notion of Faithfulness in Discourse Presentation Using a Corpus Approach', *Language and Literature*, 11(4): 325–55.

Stockwell, P. and Mahlberg, M. (2015) 'Mind-Modelling with Corpus Stylistics in David Copperfield', *Language and Literature* 24(2): 129–47.

Stoffel, C. (1901) *Intensives and Down-Toners: A Study of English Adverbs*, Heidelberg: Winter.

Taavitsainen, I., Melchers, G. and Pahta, P. (eds) (1999) *Writing in Nonstandard English*. Amsterdam: John Benjamins.

Tagliamonte, S. (2005) "*So* Who? *Like* How? *Just* What?': Discourse Markers in the Conversations of Young Canadians', *Journal of Pragmatics* 37(11): 1896–915.

Tagliamonte, S. (2008) 'So Different and Pretty Cool! Recycling Intensifiers in Toronto, Canada', *English Language and Linguistics, Intensifiers* 12(2): 361–94.

Tagliamonte, S. and Roberts, C. (2005) "So Weird; So Cool; So Innovative': The Use of Intensifiers in the Television Series *Friends', American Speech* 80(3): 280–300.

Tamasi, S. (2001) 'Huck Doesn't Sound Like Himself: Consistency in The Literary Dialect of Mark Twain', *Language and Literature* 10 (2): 129–44.

Terrazas-Calero, A. M. (2020) "These Kids Don't Even Sound … Irish Anymore': Representing 'New' Irishness in Contemporary Irish Fiction', in R. Hickey and C. P. Amador-Moreno (eds) *Irish Identities: Sociolinguistic Perspectives*, Berlin: De Gruyter Mouton, pp. 252–82.

Walshe, S. (2011) '"Normal People Like Us Don't Use That Type of Language. Remember This Is the Real World". The Language of Father Ted: Representations of Irish English in a Fictional World', *Sociolinguistic Studies* 5(1): 127–48.

Walshe, S. (2017) 'The Language of Irish films', *World Englishes*, 36: 283–99.

Wynne, M. (2005) 'Archiving, Distribution and Preservation,' in M. Wynne (ed.) *Developing Linguistic Corpora: A Guide to Good Practice*, Oxford: Oxbow Books, pp. 71–8.

Zwicky, A. (2011) 'GenX So', *Arnold Zwicky's Blog: A Blog Mostly about Language*, 14 November, Available at: https://arnoldzwicky.org/2011/11/14/genx-so/.

37

Exploring narrative fiction: corpora and digital humanities projects

Michaela Mahlberg and Viola Wiegand

1 How do corpora relate to other digital resources?

Narrative fiction can be studied as a register of the language, just like a corpus of business writing, academic prose or conversation. In this sense, corpus research contributes to identifying and describing the linguistic features that are found across a range of fictional texts and that define narrative fiction as a register. To describe a register, the context of situation is important. As Biber and Conrad (2009: 132) highlight, '[f]rom a situational perspective, fiction is one of the most complicated registers'. This is because of the complex relationship between the fictional worlds created in the texts and the context of the real world in which the texts are written and read. In this chapter, our focus is on novels as a type of narrative fiction. Our main interest is in how we can use corpus methods to study novels as fiction, i.e. with a focus on the fictional worlds rather than exclusively on the linguistic features that define a register compared to other registers. The study of fiction is ultimately a very broad topic, as every fictional text can be approached from a number of perspectives and a number of disciplines. It is beyond this chapter to fully capture this breadth. The way we tackle the variety of approaches to fiction is by relating corpora to other projects and resources in the wider digital humanities.

Narrative fiction in corpora and fiction corpora

A corpus is a collection of texts that is created for the purpose of linguistic analysis. So criteria for which texts to include, how to group texts into sections or subcorpora, how to balance the composition of the subcorpora, etc., are all driven by the aims and standards of linguistic analysis. Fiction can be included as a subcorpus in a general corpus, or corpora are created specifically for the study of fiction.

The *Brown* corpus, the first general corpus of modern English, contains a total of 1 million words. It is made up of 500 text samples, which each contains about 2,000 words. One hundred and twenty-six of these samples are classified as 'Imaginative Prose', which is subdivided into six types of fiction: 'General Fiction', 'Mystery and

DOI: 10.4324/9780367076399-37

Detective Fiction', 'Science Fiction', 'Adventure and Western Fiction', 'Romance and Love Story' and 'Humor' (Francis and Kučera 1964/1979). Over the decades, the *Brown* corpus design has been the basis for several corpora of British and American English from 1931, 1961, 1991 and 2006 (and sometimes from adjacent years), forming the Brown "family" of corpora (Baker 2009; Hinrichs *et al.* 2010; Potts and Baker 2012). All corpora in this family contain works of fiction in the categories noted and can therefore facilitate the comparison of fiction across British and American English and across time periods. Another well-known, but much larger general corpus, the original *British National Corpus* (BNC1994), also includes fiction. Lee's (2002) category of fictional prose ('W_fict_prose') contains 431 texts and just over 16 million words according to the version available via BNCweb (http://bncweb.lancs.ac.uk; Hoffmann *et al.* 2008). The fictional prose sections in general corpora have been used both as a primary source of data for corpus stylistic analysis (e.g. Kreyer 2010, who focuses on the role of syntactic constructions in spatial representation in fiction) and as a reference corpus (e.g. in the study of *Casino Royale* by Mahlberg and McIntyre 2011).

The Lancaster *Speech, Thought and Writing Presentation* corpus (STWP) is one of the first corpora that was compiled specifically for corpus stylistic analysis. It contains about 250,000 words, composed of text samples from fiction, (auto)biography and newspapers of approximately 2,000 words in length (Culpeper *et al.* 2008). The main purpose of this corpus is to facilitate the analysis of speech, thought and writing presentation in fiction based on the model developed by Leech and Short (2007) and Semino and Short (2004). Accordingly, all texts have been marked up manually for speech, thought and writing presentation categories. The corpus is publicly available from the *Oxford Text Archive* (Culpeper *et al.* 2008).

While the standardised length of the text extracts in these corpora facilitates comparisons across authors and genres, the use of text samples rather than full-length texts has implications for the meaningful analysis of individual texts. As Sinclair (2004: online) points out:

> Samples of language for a corpus should wherever possible consist of entire documents or transcriptions of complete speech events, or should get as close to this target as possible.

This is particularly true for novels. Novels create fictional worlds. So the full text is a unit of meaning, which contains, for instance, everything that is said about a particular character. Therefore, for certain types of analysis, it will be vital to have access to the entire text. In practice, the creation of fiction corpora can be restricted by copyright. A lot of effort in the compilation of fiction corpora has focused on historical texts that are out of copyright. An example of a resource that will be particularly useful for corpus stylisticians interested in contrastive work is the *European Literary Text Collection* (ELTeC). It is currently being developed by the *Distant Reading for European Literary History* project (Odebrecht *et al.* 2021; www.distant-reading.net/eltec/). ELTeC version 1.1.0 contains over 1200 novels in 14 European languages from the sampling period 1840–1920, with the largest components being the German (12.74 million words), English (12.23 million words), French (8.71 million words) and Polish (8.50 million words) corpora. The collection is still growing (see https://distantreading.github.io/ELTeC/index.html for updates). ELTeC is an example of a "corpus", but there is still room for corpus linguists to engage more directly with such projects in distant reading.

Discussing the Linguateca corpora with their literary subcorpus as an example for Portuguese, Santos (2019) also highlights links between corpus linguistics and digital humanities.

Digital texts and resources

In the same way that corpora are created for the purpose of linguistic analysis, other disciplines have benefited from digital developments, too. Digital projects can contribute to the preservation of literary texts, or they can create new types of textual editions, methods of analysis, academic collaboration and forms of engagement with literary works that are open to the wider public. As fiction can be approached from a range of angles, digital projects open up a variety of forms of exploration and engagement taking account of fictional texts as well as their cultural and historical contexts. A notable project is *Dickens Journals Online* (DJO). It provides scanned pages of Dickens's weekly magazines *Household Words* and *All the Year Round.* These magazines were very popular at the time of their publication. They contained instalments of novels, but also poetry, travel writing, investigative journalism, etc. Transcriptions of the scans are available for part of the issues created in a community effort (see e.g. Drew *et al.* 2012). DJO is a valuable resource for nineteenth-century scholars, making available the original instalments of novels like *Great Expectations* and *Hard Times*, as well as texts that are not widely accessible in print anymore.

Orford (2019) argues that the contemporary engagement with Victorian novels in instalments has more general implications for the modern reception of these works. He emphasises the importance of going beyond digitising simply for purposes of preservation: 'offering content is only the beginning of a digital project: the second stage is to encourage readers to use that content' (Orford 2019: 168). This encouragement can come in the form of digital reading projects that often instruct participants to read instalments following the original publication schedule (i.e. in the same week in which they were originally published). A recent example is the #HardTimes2020 readalong in which participants read and commented on Dickens's *Hard Times* via the project blog (http://hardtimes.wordpress.org) and on Twitter. By contrast, the 2014 "Our Mutual Friend Tweets" monthly serial reading project (https://dickensourmutualfriend.wordpress.com/; Curry 2015) took a social media role-play approach: volunteers performed the plot of Dickens's *Our Mutual Friend* via tweets from character-based accounts. In this collective interpretative effort, which Curry (2015: 3) terms 'crowd-sourced close reading', participants' creativity was particularly salient, as tweets blended Dickens's original wording with imagined dialogues to fill narrative gaps, and nineteenth-century expressions were combined with hashtags and memes.

Digital projects for narrative fiction can provide a perspective that was not possible (or only to a very limited degree) in analogue form. This is illustrated well by the growing number of digital "mapping" initiatives that visualise places in texts. An example of a large-scale undertaking of this kind is the "Mapping the Republic of Letters" project (http://republicofletters.stanford.edu/; also see Edelstein *et al.* 2017), which covers case studies from multiple countries and networks of scholarly correspondence in Europe and the Americas in the seventeenth and eighteenth century. The focus of this project has been historical rather than linguistic, and the analysis has been based on metadata (such as authors, source and destination of letters), not on the content of the letters. Nonetheless, this and other projects on networks of correspondence (e.g. "Six

Degrees of Francis Bacon" www.sixdegreesoffrancisbacon.com; and "Cultures of Knowledge" http://www.culturesofknowledge.org/) demonstrate the potential – and challenges – for integrating visualisation methods from areas such as social network analysis into humanities approaches (see e.g. Davison 2019, with a focus on early modern history). As the work by Murrieta-Flores *et al.* (2017) or Baker *et al.* (2019) shows, digital humanities and corpus linguistics specifically have a shared interest in exploring relationships between geographical location and texts.

Digital resources as described in this section tend to address mainly an academic research audience. There is scope, too, to engage wider audiences. The LitLong interactive map of Edinburgh (https://litlong.org/; Alex *et al.* 2019) is an example with potential impact in tourism. Using data from books that use Edinburgh as a setting, LitLong maps extracts that mention place names onto the city. Used on a mobile phone, LitLong can serve as a literary walking app to explore Edinburgh. A factor that contributes to how a digital resource is used is its curation. The *Corpus Linguistics in Context* (CLiC) web app, Mahlberg *et al.* (2020a), which we introduce in Section 3, has been designed for research as well as educational purposes. CLiC is a concordancer for corpus stylistic analysis and both distant and close reading. To share examples of research with CLiC, it is accompanied by a blog where users can publish short contributions illustrating their own work. Such blogs are an opportunity to open up dialogue around resources and developments in the field.

Digital humanities projects on fiction often include the digitisation of texts, and sometimes digitisation is a means of preserving printed fiction. At the same time, born-digital formats of fiction are on the increase, with digital narratology developing as a field in its own right (Page and Thomas 2011). Just like printed fiction, born-digital formats can pose challenges for preservation due to rapid technical developments and emerging as well as disappearing formats (Schiller and Grigar 2019; also see https://digitalfiction.co.uk/). Similarly, sustainability is an issue for the tools that are used in digital humanities (see Burdick *et al.* 2012; and for related points in corpus linguistics, e.g. Rehm *et al.* 2009; Kesäniemi *et al.* 2018). Often digitised materials are made accessible and searchable through online interfaces. While the front-end that provides the user experience tends to receive the most attention, the infrastructure behind it plays a crucial role, too. Drucker (2018) points out that the development of the "back-end" is not merely technical work – it is part of the intellectual process. The way a data infrastructure is set up, the metadata that is included, and the documentation that is provided involve assumptions about how a resource will be used, and so has direct implications for the research that can be carried out. This does not just apply to digital humanities. In corpus linguistics, the pitfalls of fitting research questions to the affordances of tools have also been highlighted (e.g. Mahlberg and Smith 2010; Anthony 2013).

2 Where to start your corpus study

Corpus linguistic methods are particularly useful for the quantification of linguistic phenomena and for the identification of patterns of linguistic features. Quantitative methods work well for the study of fiction as a register, but also for research that is interested in literary and cultural history at scale (Underwood 2019), or studies aimed at the identification of authorship (e.g. Evert *et al.* 2017). Not every question that you might want to investigate, however, will lend itself to a quantitative approach. Often, corpus methods are best combined with qualitative approaches. Such research is referred to as work in 'corpus stylistics' (Carter 2010; Mahlberg 2013; McIntyre and Walker 2019).

One of the most fundamental methods in corpus linguistics is the analysis of concordances, which are used to identify lexico-grammatical patterns around a node word (see Chapter 10, this volume). For the study of narrative fiction, concordances can be a useful tool to support the close reading of a text. Figure 37.1 shows 10 of the 28 concordance lines of the word *Daisy* in *David Copperfield.* The character Steerforth compares David to a daisy and calls him by that name. A concordance retrieves the occurrences of *Daisy* and so can support the analyst in tracing the relationship between David and Steerforth throughout the novel. Names used for David have particular significance in the novel. His wife, Dora, calls him *Doady*. In addition to listing occurrences of a word in contexts, concordances can visualise or "plot" where in a text the word occurs. Figure 37.2 contains distribution plots for *Daisy*, *Doady* and *Davy* throughout the novel, with the white vertical lines representing occurrences in relation to the location in the text. It shows how both Steerforth and Dora are relevant to very specific parts of David's story, whereas the Peggotty family is more of a constant for David, as illustrated by the distribution of the name *Davy.*

Simple observations based on concordances or the distribution of individual words will not constitute an analysis of a novel, but they can complement the close reading of a text and other methods of text analysis. A challenge for the analysis of fiction is that relevant features of the text might not straightforwardly relate to linguistic forms. In order to trace or quantify textual features, it can be necessary to first annotate the text for the features in question. The speech, thought and writing categories mentioned in Section 1 are one example of such annotation (see also Busse 2020 for a study of nineteenth-century speech, thought and writing). Another example is Ho *et al.*'s (2019) annotation according to the categories of text world theory, a cognitive model for discourse processing (Gavins 2007).

Even more challenging than dealing with the annotation of text can be to address significant absences, as Montoro (2018) demonstrates with her study of creative absences in the Henry Green novel *Living*. In this novel, determiners (particularly the definite article), are often left out where they would normally be expected, and Montoro shows how this feature contributes to the meaning of the novel. She initially creates a working definition of absences as a basis for a manual analysis of the novel and contextualises her manual counts of the absences through a key comparison of grammatical categories using parts-of-speech tags, combined with a multidimensional analysis (Biber 1988). This approach of complementary methods enables Montoro (2018) to achieve a more comprehensive account of the effects of absences in the Green novel in relation to its macro-structure.

Overall, a corpus stylistic study will work best when it begins with understanding how questions about the literary nature of a text relate to formal textual features that can be identified, traced and quantified (see also Mahlberg 2013; McIntyre and Walker 2019). Such textual features can be specific to individual texts, or they are typical of narrative fiction more generally, as we will discuss in the next section.

3 What is special about narrative fiction?

In this chapter, when we talk about narrative fiction, we specifically mean novels. Novels are interesting from a corpus stylistic point of view, because long texts generally present

1	clapping me on the shoulder again, 'you are a very	Daisy.	The daisy of the field, at sunrise, is not fresher	DC	
2	on the shoulder again, 'you are a very Daisy. The	daisy	of the field, at sunrise, is not fresher than you	DC	
3	I take a degree!' cried Steerforth. 'Not I! my dear	Daisy	- will you mind my calling you Daisy?' ¶ 'Not at all	DC	
4	I! my dear Daisy - will you mind my calling you	Daisy?'	¶ 'Not at all!' said I. ¶ 'That's a good fellow! My	DC	
5	at all!' said I. ¶ 'That's a good fellow! My dear	Daisy,'	said Steerforth, laughing. 'I have not the least desire	DC	
6	¶ 'But the fame -' I was beginning. ¶ 'You romantic	Daisy!'	said Steerforth, laughing still more heartily: 'why sho	DC	
7	not to mention the pleasure of a journey with you,	Daisy),	to see that sort of people together, and to make	DC	
8	While we were talking, he more than once called me	Daisy;	which brought Miss Dartle out again. ¶ 'But really, M	DC	
9	ge. ¶ 'When do you propose to introduce me there,	Daisy?'	he said. 'I am at your disposal. Make your own	DC	
10	give you joy, my boy. My hand upon that, too!	Daisy,	stir the fire, and make it a brisk one! and	DC	

Figure 37.1 10 Concordances lines of D*aisy* in *David Copperfield*

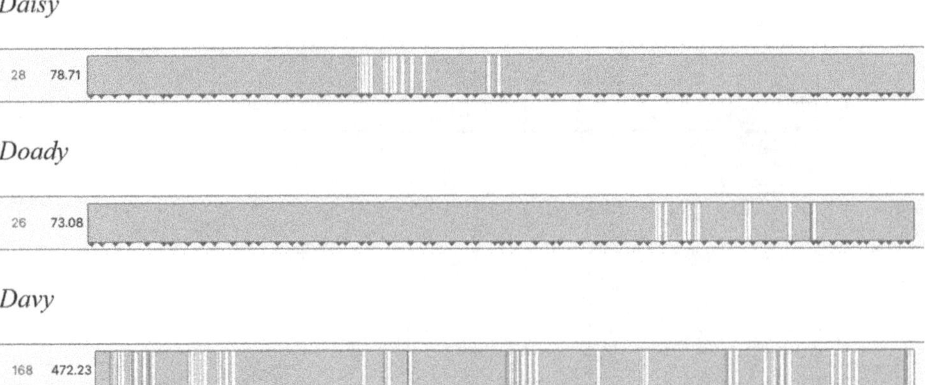

Figure 37.2 Distribution plots for *Daisy, Doady* and *Davy* in *David Copperfield* (retrieved with CLiC)

a challenge for detailed stylistic analyses, which necessarily focus on text extracts or selected examples taken from such longer forms of texts. As a literary text, a novel will display a degree of literariness, i.e. language use that is characterised through a certain amount of creativity as well as conformity with literary conventions. Each novel will create its own fictional world, with a narrator and the fictional characters who observe, experience and articulate the events of the story. In a novel, there are different discourse levels. The simplest distinction is between the direct speech of the fictional characters and the narration. There are also a range of more or less direct forms of character speech, thought and writing intertwined with the narration (as illustrated by corpora annotated for Speech, Thought and Writing categories, see Semino and Short 2004; Busse 2020).

Narrative fiction is different from plays and films in the way that fictional characters are presented. This has implications for how corpus methods can be used to study these different types of fiction. The text of plays mainly consists of the speech of the fictional characters, which can be relatively straightforwardly studied with corpus methods (see e.g. Culpeper 2009). Similarly for films, the scripts or transcripts of what characters say make for relatively neat corpora (see for example Quaglio 2009; Bednarek 2010, 2018, 2020; and Chapter 38, this volume). Corpus studies of narrative fiction that treat the text of novels as a whole, without any further annotation, will make for equally neat corpora, but they will also take a very specific perspective of analysis.

The example corpus analysis that we will introduce in the next section uses data from the CLiC corpora. CLiC is a web application (https://clic.bham.ac.uk) that has been designed for the analysis of corpora where direct speech and narration can be treated as separate subcorpora. For the CLiC corpora, direct speech is approximated through text within quotation marks and narration through text outside of quotation marks. As the focus of the current CLiC corpora has been on nineteenth-century fiction, this is a definition that works reasonably well. CLiC version 2.0.3 (corpora version 2a3a120) contains the *Corpus of Dickens's Novels* (DNov; 15 texts; 3.8 million words), the *19^{th}Century Reference Corpus* (19C; 29 texts; 4.5 million words), the *19^{th}Century Children's Literature Corpus* (ChiLit; 71 texts; 4.4 million words) and the *African American Writers 1892–1912* corpus (AAW; eight texts; approximately 520,000 words). It also holds the *Corpus of Additional Requested Texts* (ArTs), a collection of texts requested by CLiC users, covering nineteenth-century and early twentieth-century fiction as well as a limited number of non-fiction texts. As with the ELTeC collection (see Section 1), the CLiC texts are all in the public domain, so it was possible to include full texts rather than text samples.

Once speech and narration can be studied separately, questions around the creation of fictional characters can be approached from a range of angles. By comparing repeated sequences (or) of words in direct speech with such sequences in real spoken language, Mahlberg *et al.* (2019) were able to show similarities between real and fictional speech that relate to the interpersonal behaviour of fictional people (see also Chapter 36, this volume).

The ability to study speech and narration separately also makes it possible to gain insights into the body language of fictional people. As narrative fiction has to do without the visuals of plays and films, the narration fulfils an important function in creating effects of authenticity and naturalness. In the next section, we will discuss an example of eye language that illustrates the relevance of body language for the creation of fictional people.

4 Eye language and the example of *looking*

Eye language is an important component of narrative fiction. It significantly contributes to characterisation. The plural form *eyes* is among the most frequent bodily descriptors across nineteenth-century British fiction (Mahlberg *et al.* 2020b). In addition to direct references to the eyes, a range of language patterns is used to describe eye language in narrative fiction. An example is the verb form *looking*, which we discuss later in this section.

To study eye language in fiction, as well as body language more generally, a focus on particular textual locations is a good starting point. The proximity to fictional speech plays an especially important role here, because speech and body language often happen simultaneously. Since text, unlike film, can only express these modes sequentially, linguistic strategies are employed to create effects of simultaneity. One of these strategies is the narrator's interruption of fictional speech through 'suspensions'. Such narratorial interruptions tend to contain reporting verbs and often additional character information, such as body language. Especially *-ing* clauses (Mahlberg 2013; Mahlberg *et al.* 2013) are found to present a sense of simultaneity while providing the opportunity for foregrounding particular actions.

Figure 37.3 shows the top 20 *-ing* forms in the long suspensions of the DNov corpus ('long' suspensions contain five or more words, for brevity we will simply refer to them as suspensions in the following). These forms were retrieved with the CLiC web app by filtering a wordlist of DNov suspensions for the letters *ing*. The top ranks of the resulting list are all occupied by *-ing* forms of verbs. Other words that contain the sequence of letters *ing*, such as *forefinger*, occupy ranks farther down the list. As Figure 37.3 shows, *looking* is the most frequent verb form with a large gap between its frequency and the frequencies of the other verbs. Overall, the figure clearly confirms the link between *-ing* forms and body language or bodily actions. There are two exceptions, the speech verbs *speaking* and *addressing*. The form *raising* is an example that highlights how speech and body language are linked – characters can raise their eyes, hands, eyebrows, etc., as in (1), but also their voice, as in (2).

(1)
'You don't,' said the guest, **raising** his eyes to John's fat face, 'you don't mean-- [...]'
[Barnaby Rudge]

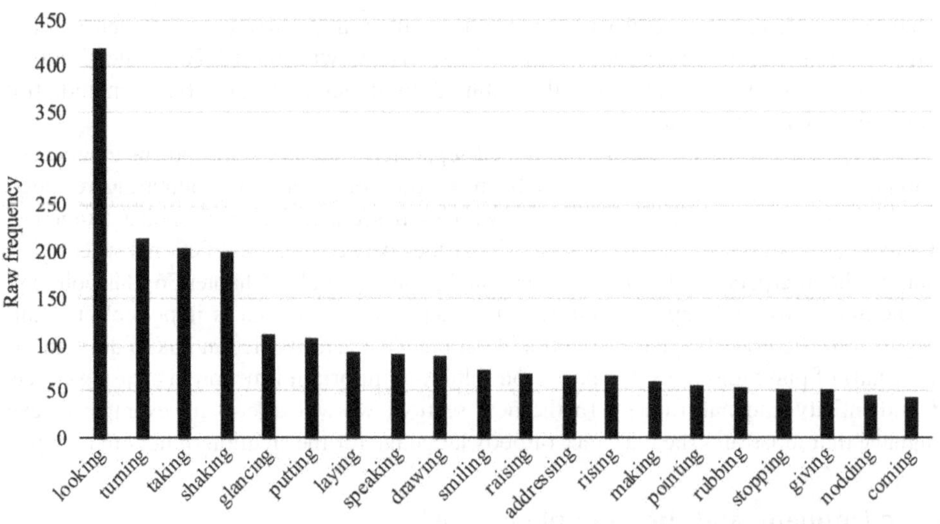

Figure 37.3 The top 20 *-ing* forms in DNov long suspensions (retrieved with CLiC)

(2)
'Now, I will be judged,' said Mr Lammle, **raising** his voice a little, 'by my friend Fledgeby.'

[Our Mutual Friend]

In systemic functional linguistic (SFL) terms, a first glance at Figure 37.3 suggests that the frequent *-ing* forms tend to be 'behavioural' processes. Behavioural processes are situated between 'material' processes (involving actions that have an effect on people or things) and 'mental' processes (such as thinking) (Halliday and Matthiessen 2004: 171). So, behavioural processes 'represent the outer manifestations of inner workings, the acting out of processes of consciousness (e.g. *people are laughing*) and physiological states (e.g. *they were sleeping*)' (Halliday and Matthiessen 2004: 171). This makes them a prime technique for what John (2001) refers to as the 'externalisation' of fictional characters. As John (2001) shows, Dickens was a master of depicting characters through descriptions of their external features. Figure 37.3 provides textual evidence for this point. Further support for our approach to behavioural processes as externalising devices comes from Halliday and Matthiessen (2004: 252), who observe how these processes often introduce fictional speech: 'while "behavioural" clauses do not "project" indirect speech or thought, they often appear in fictional narrative introducing direct speech, as a means of attaching a behavioural feature to the verbal process of "saying"'.

Table 37.1 compares the top 20 *-ing* forms in DNov with 19C, a reference corpus of novels by other British nineteenth-century authors, and ChiLit, a corpus of nineteenth-century British children's fiction. The word forms marked with an asterisk are statistically significantly more frequent in Dickens's suspensions compared to 19C and ChiLit combined (based on the CLiC Keywords tab, all with a log-likelihood value >15.13, $p < 0.0001$). These key *-ing* forms take us some way to finding "Dickensian" actions. The other italicised words only appear in the top 20 list for 19C and ChiLit, respectively. Conversely, the bold forms in Table 37.1 are shared across the top 20 ranks of all three corpora. So, *looking* and *turning* are particularly popular across authors.

Table 37.1 Top 20 forms ending with *ing* in long suspensions (bold – in top 20 of all three corpora; italics – only in top 20 of that corpus; * – keywords in DNov long suspensions vs. 19C and ChiLit combined)

Rank	*DNov*	*19C*	*ChiLit*
1	**looking**	**looking**	**looking**
2	**turning**	**turning**	**turning**
3	**taking***	**speaking**	**pointing**
4	**shaking***	**taking**	king
5	*glancing**	**rising**	*saying*
6	**putting**	**shaking**	**taking**
7	laying*	**pointing**	**speaking**
8	**speaking**	addressing	**putting**
9	drawing*	**smiling**	**shaking**
10	**smiling**	**putting**	going
11	*raising*	feeling	feeling
12	addressing	**coming**	**coming**
13	**rising**	drawing	*sitting*
14	making	*having*	*holding*
15	**pointing**	going	laying
16	*rubbing**	fingers	**smiling**
17	*stopping*	*starting*	*standing*
18	*giving*	*fixing*	**rising**
19	*nodding**	making	*trembling*
20	**coming**	*seeing*	*trying*

To study the most frequent *-ing* form, *looking*, in more detail, we examined concordance lines from DNov. Concordance analysis allows us to see patterns in the lexico-grammatical context of a verb form to understand the functions it fulfils and determine the SFL process type. Frequency lists alone give only a rough indication of process types in the dataset (Goatly 2004).

The most frequent pattern for *looking* is related to characters *looking at* something (the ground, the fire, their watch): *looking* (…) *at* makes up 41 per cent of the occurrences of *looking* in DNov suspensions (171 out of 418), where *at* occurs within a span of five words to the right. Examples may provide simple descriptions of eye behaviour, as in (3), or add extra detail and circumstantial information, as in (4) and (5).

(3)
"I play my Ace, Mr. Barsad," said Carton, taking the answer on himself, and **looking at** his watch, "without any scruple, in a very few minutes."

[A Tale of Two Cities]

(4)
'Mr Pinch, Mr Pinch!' said Pecksniff, wheeling his chair about, and **looking at** him *with an aspect of the deepest melancholy*, 'I did not expect this from you. I have not deserved this from you!'

[Martin Chuzzlewit]

(5)
'Well, that certainly is most capital cold punch,' said Mr. Pickwick, **looking** *earnestly* **at** the stone bottle; 'and the day is extremely warm, and-- Tupman, my dear friend, a glass of punch?'

[Pickwick Papers]

Examples (6) and (7) illustrate other spatial prepositions:

(6)
'This,' said Mr Pecksniff, rising and **looking round upon** them with folded hands, 'does me good. [...]'

[Martin Chuzzlewit]

(7)
'And I fear,' he added, with great energy, **looking towards** the bar, 'I really fear that he is ill.'

[Oliver Twist]

Nørgaard (2003: 82) describes a cline of '[p]aradigmatic options for the realization of processes of perception' from a 'static' end, realised by mental processes ('He saw the moon') to a 'dynamic' end realised by behavioural processes ('He gazed at the moon'), where the middle ground is realised by descriptions of mental states like 'His gaze was fixed on the moon'. In her analysis of Joyce's *Two Gallants* that draws on earlier work by Chris Kennedy, Nørgaard (2003) uses this cline to contrast the eye language of two characters, arguing that differences in the descriptions of their gaze present one of them (Corley) as more active and the other (Lenehan) as more passive. Nørgaard's (2003) example is based on the verb *gaze*, which functions similarly to *look*. Dickens's suspensions generally appear to describe characters' eye language actively. Compared to the frequent examples of *looking* emphasising active characters, *seeing* appears just ten times in DNov suspensions. There are also examples describing a middle ground with the verb *fixed*, as in (8).

(8)
'Shall I tell you,' she continued, with her eyes **fixed** on her mother, 'who already knows us [...]'

[Dombey and Son]

The verb form *looking* can also have another meaning, where it does not relate to eye language, but describes a character's appearance or condition (see Mahlberg 2013: 141–3), as in (9) and (10). These examples illustrate *looking* as a relational rather than a behavioural process, with the following adjective functioning as an attribute of the character.

(9)
'Dear me,' said the merry-faced gentleman, **looking merrier** still, 'I merely intended to inquire--'

[Nicholas Nickleby]

(10)
'Oh! my eye!' he said, **looking very low-spirited**, 'I am sorry for that.'
[David Copperfield]

The description can also become more ambiguous, as in (11).

(11)
'Why, Durdles!' exclaims Jasper, **looking on amused**, 'you are undermined with pockets!'
[The Mystery of Edwin Drood]

In sum, a corpus stylistic approach can help to identify textual patterns in narrative fiction that illustrate characterisation techniques. As we have shown with the example of eye language and *looking*, corpus methods help to identify formal textual features that can then be related to properties of fiction. So we were able to describe behavioural processes in suspensions in terms of their effects of externalised characterisation.

5 Where to go from here?

We have argued in this chapter that the corpus linguistic study of narrative fiction is not a simple application of existing corpus methods to just another set of texts. It requires consideration of the types of text under analysis, as well as the types of questions that we want to address. More work is needed to create corpora, tools and other resources that enable innovative types of analyses. The examples we included on treating fictional speech and narration separately are one step in this direction. Importantly, corpus linguistics needs to enter a constructive dialogue with research in the digital humanities more widely to be able to address a broader range of research questions. Ultimately, the study of narrative fiction is an interdisciplinary endeavour.

A crucial aspect of innovation will be how the creation of corpora is approached. Principles of corpus creation reflect theoretical approaches to literary texts. The approach we have presented views characterisation as a central topic for the study of narrative fiction (see also the discussion in Mahlberg, Wiegand *et al.* 2019). It also allows us to highlight similarities between real and fictional people. When we find patterns of body language descriptions that are shared across a number of corpora, these patterns reflect observations that are relevant to the real world. What is shared across large amounts of fiction connects to the real-world background knowledge that readers bring to a text. This is an important point for literary corpora in general. It relates to approaches that use corpora to study literary and cultural history (e.g. Underwood 2019). Similarly, Herrmann and Lauer (2018) make the point that corpus studies of literature shift the focus from significant examples in the canon to more general trends in fiction, which they illustrate with their KOLIMO project. Through large corpora of literature, there is an opportunity to take a fresh view on the relationship between fictional worlds and real worlds, which also has implications for studying the significance of fiction reading and reading for pleasure.

Finally, an aspect of corpus linguistics that comes into focus through the link with literary studies is the role of corpora within society, i.e. beyond the specific research projects they were created for. In digital humanities, the preservation of texts plays an important role. In corpus linguistics, this aspect has received little attention so far. It is connected with questions around sustainability as well as interoperability of tools. More needs to be done to address principles of open research that are crucial for the sharing of resources in corpus linguistics. We need to work towards even better standards of documentation that enable the replicability of research and support the sustainability of resources. Closely connected with practical aspects of preservation is the accessibility of resources for the wider academic and societal community. After all, part of the significance of fiction is how people engage with it.

Further reading

Mahlberg, M. (2013) *Corpus Stylistics and Dickens's Fiction*, London: Routledge. (This monograph introduces a lexically driven approach to the building blocks of fictional worlds. It combines quantitative and qualitative analyses of clusters, i.e. repeated sequences of words, and studies their textual functions for characterisation. Beyond its particular focus on Dickens, the book outlines fundamental principles of corpus stylistics.)

Mastropierro, L. (2017) *Corpus Stylistics in Heart of Darkness and its Italian Translations*, London: Bloomsbury. (Mastropierro explores the interaction between corpus stylistics and translation studies. The book combines qualitative and quantitative methods to show how changes in the style of translation can affect the interpretation of a translated literary work compared to the original text.)

McIntyre, D. and Walker, B. (2019) *Corpus Stylistics: Theory and Practice*, Edinburgh: Edinburgh University Press. (This textbook provides an up-to-date introduction to corpus stylistics, a field that has seen many developments over the past decade. McIntyre and Walker guide the reader through hands-on examples for a range of registers, including fiction and non-fiction.)

Simpson, P. (2014) *Stylistics: A Resource Book for Students*, 2nd edn, London: Routledge. (The second edition of Simpson's textbook includes new sections on recent trends in stylistics and has significantly expanded on corpus stylistics. This resource book contains units on foundational knowledge in the field, as well as 'extension' sections with reprints of publications by a range of scholars.)

Underwood, T. (2019) *Distant Horizons: Digital Evidence and Literary Change*, Chicago: University of Chicago Press. (Underwood's monograph represents an approach to digital methods for analysing fiction that is routed in literary culture and history. It introduces analyses of large amounts of data, larger than most corpus stylistic studies, and offers corpus linguists an opportunity to see connections between corpus research and distant reading.)

References

Alex, B., Grover, C., Tobin, R. and Oberlander, J. (2019) 'Geoparsing Historical and Contemporary Literary Text Set in the City of Edinburgh', *Language Resources and Evaluation* 53(4): 651–75.

Anthony, L. (2013) 'A Critical Look at Software Tools in Corpus Linguistics', *Linguistic Research* 30(2): 141–61.

Baker, H., Gregory, I. N., Hartmann, D. and McEnery, T. (2019) 'Applying Geographical Information Systems to Researching Historical Corpora: Seventeenth-Century Prostitution', in V. Wiegand and M. Mahlberg (eds) *Corpus Linguistics, Context and Culture*, Berlin: De Gruyter Mouton, pp. 109–36.

Baker, P. (2009) 'The BE06 Corpus of British English and Recent Language Change', *International Journal of Corpus Linguistics* 14(3): 312–37.

Bednarek, M. (2010) *The Language of Fictional Television: Drama and Identity*, New York: Continuum.

Bednarek, M. (2018) *Language and Television Series: A Linguistic Approach to TV Dialogue*, Cambridge: Cambridge University Press.

Bednarek, M. (2020) 'The Sydney Corpus of Television Dialogue: Designing and Building a Corpus of Dialogue from US TV Series', *Corpora* 15(1): 107–19.

Biber, D. (1988) *Variation Across Speech and Writing*, Cambridge: Cambridge University Press.

Biber, D. and Conrad, S. (2009) *Register, Genre, and Style*, Cambridge: Cambridge University Press.

Burdick, A., Drucker, J., Lunenfeld, P., Presner, T. and Schnapp, J. (2012) *Digital_Humanities*, Cambridge: MIT Press.

Busse, B. (2020) *Speech, Writing, and Thought Presentation in 19th-Century Narrative Fiction: A Corpus-Assisted Approach*, Oxford: Oxford University Press.

Carter, R. A. (2010) 'Methodologies for Stylistic Analysis: Practices and Pedagogies', in D. McIntyre and B. Busse (eds) *Language and Style: In Honour of Mick Short*, Basingstoke: Palgrave Macmillan, pp. 55–68.

Culpeper, J. (2009) 'Keyness: Words, Parts-of-Speech and Semantic Categories in the Character-Talk of Shakespeare's *Romeo and Juliet*', *International Journal of Corpus Linguistics* 14(1): 29–59.

Culpeper, J., Semino, E., Short, M. and Wynne, M. (2008) *Speech, Thought and Writing Presentation Corpus (STWP)*, Available at: https://ota.bodleian.ox.ac.uk/repository/xmlui/handle/20.500.12024/2540 [Accessed 23 March 2020].

Curry, E. (2015) 'Doing the Novel in Different Voices: Reflections on a Dickensian Twitter Experiment', *19: Interdisciplinary Studies in the Long Nineteenth Century* 2015(21), Available at: 10.16995/ntn.736 [Accessed 6 October 2021].

Davison, K. (2019) 'Early Modern Social Networks: Antecedents, Opportunities, and Challenges', *The American Historical Review* 124(2): 456–82.

Drew, J., Mackenzie, H. and Winyard, B. (2012) 'Household Words, Volume I March 30 – September 21, 1850', *Dickens Quarterly* 29(1): 50–67.

Drucker, J. (2018) 'The Back End: Infrastructure Design for Scholarly Research', *The Journal of Modern Periodical Studies* 8(2): 119–33.

Edelstein, D., Findlen, P., Ceserani, G., Winterer, C. and Coleman, N. (2017) 'Historical Research in a Digital Age: Reflections from the Mapping the Republic of Letters Project', *The American Historical Review* 122(2): 400–24.

Evert, S., Proisl, T., Jannidis, F., Reger, I., Pielström, S., Schöch, C. and Vitt, T. (2017) 'Understanding and Explaining Delta Measures for Authorship Attribution', *Digital Scholarship in the Humanities* 22(suppl_2): ii4–ii16.

Francis, W. N. and Kučera, H. (1964/1979) *Brown Corpus Manual: Manual of Information to Accompany A Standard Corpus of Present-Day Edited American English, for Use with Digital Computers*. Providence: Brown University, Department of Linguistics, Available at: http://icame.uib.no/brown/bcm.html [Accessed 6 October 2021].

Gavins, J. (2007) *Text World Theory: An Introduction*, Edinburgh: Edinburgh University Press.

Goatly, A. (2004) 'Corpus Linguistics, Systemic Functional Grammar and Literary Meaning: A Critical Analysis of *Harry Potter and the Philosopher's Stone*', *Ilha do Desterro. A Journal of English Language, Literatures in English and Cultural Studies* 46: 115–54.

Halliday, M. A. K. and Matthiessen, C. (2004) *Introduction to Functional Grammar*, 3rd edn, London: Edward Arnold.

Herrmann, J. B. and Lauer, G. (2018) 'Korpusliteraturwissenschaft. Zur Konzeption und Praxis am Beispiel eines Korpus zur literarischen Moderne [Corpus Literary Studies. On the Conceptualization and Practice with the Example of a Corpus on Modern Literature]', in *Osnabrücker Beiträge zur Sprachtheorie (OBST) 92*, Duisburg: Universitätsverlag Rhein-Ruhr OHG, pp. 127–55.

Hinrichs, L., Smith, N. and Waibel, B. (2010) 'Manual of Information for the Part-of-Speech-Tagged, Post-Edited "Brown" Corpora', *ICAME Journal* 34: 189–231.

Ho, Y.-F., Lugea, J., McIntyre, D., Xu, Z. and Wang, J. (2019) 'Text-World Annotation and Visualization for Crime Narrative Reconstruction', *Digital Scholarship in the Humanities* 34(2): 310–34.

Hoffmann, S., Evert, S., Smith, N., Lee, D. and Berglund Prytz, Y. (2008) *Corpus Linguistics with BNCweb: A Practical Guide*, Frankfurt am Main: Peter Lang.

John, J. (2001) *Dicken's Villains: Melodrama, Character, Popular Culture*, Oxford: Oxford University Press.

Kesäniemi, J., Vartiainen, T., Säily, T. and Nevalainen, T. (2018) 'Open Science for English Historical Corpus Linguistics: Introducing the Language Change Database', in E. Mäkelä, M. Tolonen and J. Tuominen (eds) *Proceedings of the Digital Humanities in the Nordic Countries 3rd Conference, Helsinki, Finland, March 7–9, 2018*, pp. 51–62, Available at: http://ceur-ws.org/Vol-2084/paper4.pdf [Accessed 18 March 2020].

Kreyer, R. (2010) 'Syntactic Constructions as a Means of Spatial Representation in Fictional Prose', in H. Dorgeloh and A. Wanner (eds) *Syntactic Variation and Genre*, Berlin: De Gruyter Mouton, pp. 277–303.

Lee, D. (2002) 'Genres, Registers, Text Types, Domains and Styles: Clarifying the Concepts and Navigating a Path through the BNC Jungle', *Language and Computers* 42(1): 247–92.

Leech, G. and Short, M. (2007) *Style in Fiction: A Linguistic Introduction to English Fictional Prose*, 2nd edn, Harlow: Pearson.

Mahlberg, M. (2013) *Corpus Stylistics and Dickens's Fiction*, London: Routledge.

Mahlberg, M. and McIntyre, D. (2011) 'A Case for Corpus Stylistics: Ian Fleming's *Casino Royale*', *English Text Construction* 4(2): 204–27.

Mahlberg, M. and Smith, C. (2010) 'Corpus Approaches to Prose Fiction: Civility and Body Language in Pride and Prejudice', in B. Busse and D. McIntyre (eds) *Language and Style: In Honour of Mick Short*, Basingstoke: Palgrave Macmillan, pp. 449–67.

Mahlberg, M., Smith, C. and Preston, S. (2013) 'Phrases in Literary Contexts: Patterns and Distributions of Suspensions in Dickens's Novels', *International Journal of Corpus Linguistics* 18(1): 35–56.

Mahlberg, M., Wiegand, V., Stockwell, P. and Hennessey, A. (2019) 'Speech-Bundles in the 19th-century English Novel', *Language and Literature* 28(4): 326–53.

Mahlberg, M., Stockwell, P., Wiegand, V. and Lentin, J. (2020a) *CLiC 2.1. Corpus Linguistics in Context*. Available at:: https://clic.bham.ac.uk/ [Accessed 7 October 2021].

Mahlberg, M., Wiegand, V. and Hennessey, A. (2020b) 'Eye Language - Body Part Collocations and Textual Contexts in the Nineteenth-Century Novel', in L. Fesenmeier and I. Novakova (eds) *Phraseology and Stylistics of Literary Language/Phraséologie et Stylistique de la Langue Littéraire*, Bern: Peter Lang, pp. 143–76.

McIntyre, D. and Walker, B. (2019) *Corpus Stylistics: Theory and Practice*, Edinburgh: Edinburgh University Press.

Montoro, R. (2018) 'The Creative Use of Absences', *International Journal of Corpus Linguistics* 23(3): 279–310.

Murrieta-Flores, P., Donaldson, C. and Gregory, I. N. (2017) 'GIS and Literary History: Advancing Digital Humanities Research through the Spatial Analysis of Historical Travel Writing and Topographical Literature', *Digital Humanities Quarterly* 11(1): 40.

Nørgaard, N. (2003) *Systemic Functional Linguistics and Literary Analysis: A Hallidayan Approach to Joyce – A Joycean Approach to Halliday*, University Press of Southern Denmark.

Odebrecht, C., Burnard, L. and Schöch, C. (eds) (2021) *ELTeC: European Literary Text Collection (ELTeC)*, version 1.1.0, April 2021. COST Action Distant Reading for European Literary History (CA16204), Available at: 10.5281/zenodo.4662444 [Accessed 8 October 2021].

Orford, P. (2019) 'Speculation and Silence', in L. Litvack and N. Vanfasse (eds) *Reading Dickens Differently*, Hoboken: John Wiley & Sons, pp. 165–84.

Page, R. and Thomas, B. (2011) 'Introduction', in R. Page and B. Thomas (eds) *New Narratives: Stories and Storytelling in the Digital Age*, Lincoln: University of Nebraska Press, pp. 1–16.

Potts, A. and Baker, P. (2012) 'Does Semantic Tagging Identify Cultural Change in British and American English?', *International Journal of Corpus Linguistics* 17(3): 295–324.

Quaglio, P. (2009) *Television Dialogue: The Sitcom Friends vs. Natural Conversation*, Amsterdam: John Benjamins.

Rehm, G., Schonefeld, O., Witt, A., Hinrichs, E. and Reis, M. (2009) 'Sustainability of Annotated Resources in Linguistics: A Web-Platform for Exploring, Querying, and Distributing Linguistic Corpora and Other Resources', *Literary and Linguistic Computing* 24(2): 193–210.

Santos, D. (2019) 'Literature Studies in Literateca: Between Digital Humanities and Corpus Linguistics', in M. Doerr Eide, O. Grønvik and B. Kjelsvik (eds) *Humanists and the Digital Toolbox (in Honour of Christian-Emil Smith Ore)*, Oslo: Novus, pp. 89–109.

Schiller, N. and Grigar, D. (2019) 'Born Digital Preservation of E-Lit: A Live Internet Traversal of Sarah Smith's King of Space', *International Journal of Digital Humanities* 1(1): 47–57.

Semino, E. and Short, M. (2004) *Corpus Stylistics: Speech, Writing and Thought Presentation in a Corpus of English Writing*, London: Routledge.

Sinclair, J. (2004) 'Corpus and Text: Basic Principles', in M. Wynne (ed.) *Developing Linguistic Corpora: A Guide to Good Practice*, Available at: http://users.ox.ac.uk/~martinw/dlc/chapter1.htm [Accessed 18 March 2020].

Underwood, T. (2019) *Distant Horizons: Digital Evidence and Literary Change*, Chicago: University of Chicago Press.

38

Corpora and the language of films: exploring dialogue in English and Italian

Maria Pavesi

1 What is film dialogue?

Film is a complex artefact in which several channels and codes act simultaneously to produce meaning for the viewing audience. Although film shows more than it tells, dialogue is an essential part of such a multimodal and multisemiotic complex. It simultaneously provides background knowledge, moves the plot forwards, defines characters, verbalises their beliefs, emotions and stances, and involves and entertains viewers. Most importantly, dialogue is paramount to film realism. It is an essential component of screen representation, 'given that fiction has a mimetic dimension in the broad sense of referring back somehow to our understanding of reality and commenting on it' (Delabastita 2019: 190). Hence, film dialogue stages face-to-face conversation, while carrying genre-specific meanings.

Film dialogue belongs to the wider family of audiovisual dialogue and telecinematic discourse (Piazza *et al.* 2011). These labels highlight the commonality between the language of films and television series, soap operas and sitcoms, all instances of language 'written to be spoken as if not written' (Gregory 1967: 191–92). Film and fictional television genres share both a mimetic and a narrative function, as they operate on the two layers of diegetic and extradiegetic communication. The diegetic layer pertains to the interaction between characters talking on screen 'oblivious of the audience' (Dynel 2011: 1644); conversely, the extradiegetic layer relates to the film team addressing the audience through the represented scene. Within film's complex architecture, viewers are thus the ultimate addressees of the production team's intended meaning. As a result, they can be regarded as ratified hearers in film discourse, while characters' interactions 'are based on, and can be described by, the same participation framework as real interactions' (Dynel 2011: 1643–4, see also Goffman 1981). More generally, through the simulation of spontaneous spoken language, film dialogue contributes to the audience's immersion and suspension of disbelief. Dialogue is here to be interpreted as a hypernym standing for any verbal exchange between two or more people, although film, by accentuating a trait of spontaneous conversation, has a bias towards duologues (Kozloff 2000: 72–3).

DOI: 10.4324/9780367076399-38

Film and television audiovisual dialogues overlap considerably in terms of functions, communicative setting and the roles of participants in fictional discourse – characters, production team and audience – (for an overview, see Messerli 2017). They differ, however, in narrative structure because of the essentially episode-driven nature of television series and soap operas (Veirano Pinto 2014) and due to the more salient artistic-symbolic intent of cinema (Alvarez-Pereyre 2011). One may also argue that in films the verbal component plays a lesser role than in television registers, a consequence of the different historical origins of the two media and the traditionally diverse modalities of screening and viewing.

Films travel easily across language borders and, thanks to audiovisual translation, they become available to large international audiences that access foreign products mainly through dubbing and subtitling. Wide availability makes translated film dialogue a socially as well as a linguistically significant object of investigation and brings to the fore a broad range of additional factors to consider in corpus linguistics studies. These include language contrastivity, cross-linguistic register comparability and, most obviously, translational dynamics.

2 How to study original and translated film dialogue with corpora

The study of film dialogue has relied on several theoretical and descriptive approaches, including conversation analysis, sociolinguistics, pragmatics and descriptive translation studies, all offering different perspectives on the object of research. Corpus linguistics in turn contributes a powerful methodological apparatus that provides unique means to look for film dialogue's recurring and distinctive patterns and typicalities empirically. With corpus linguistics, it is possible to surmount the limitations of subjective perception and individual case studies alongside validating insights from film studies (McIntyre 2012). Through corpora, researchers can draw linguistic profiles and study dimensions of variation of film dialogue, compare and contrast similar registers within and across languages, unveil evaluative and ideological meanings that prevail in different genres and address translational issues including translation shifts and strategies (Pavesi 2019). As researchers' interest in film dialogue has increased in the past few years, so have the corpora of film dialogue and the studies specifically employing a corpus-assisted methodology. Bednarek and Zago (2021) publish a periodically updated bibliography of the field of telecinematic linguistics, which, while distinguishing between research on films and television series, reports on the major corpora of original and translated film dialogue.

The largest corpus of original Anglophone film dialogue to date is Davies's (2019) online *Movie Corpus*, including more than 25,000 American films, released from the 1930s to 2018 and amounting to a total of 200 million words (Zago 2021: 170). One limitation of the *Movie Corpus*, however, lies in the fact that it contains subtitles instead of fully fledged transcriptions of screened spoken English (Zago 2021: 171). Although sharing many features with original filmic speech (Levshina 2017), subtitles are a register of their own, conceived and realised as written language. They are affected by simplification strategies and space constraints that typically result in a reduction of speech features and interpersonal markers. Internet scripts vis-à-vis transcriptions also raise concerns of reliability in the rendition of filmic conversation, since they, too, undergo reduction and normalising processes that tend to involve spoken language features (Forchini 2012: 31). Transcription is a major issue in the building of a corpus, in that the process is lengthy and costly, a fact that ultimately affects the size, range and type of investigations that the corpus will allow (see Chapters 2 and 3, this volume). As a result, corpora of transcribed soundtracks inevitably tend to be small collections that comprise fewer texts than those in corpora of subtitles, internet scripts or screenplays. Corpora of interlingual or intralingual subtitles, however, have a special status in the study of those target languages that mostly subtitle rather than dub foreign products, or in case of audiovisual media made accessible to deaf and hard-of-hearing audiences (Tirkkonen-Condit and Mäkisalo 2007).

We can distinguish three main types of translation-driven film corpora: parallel corpora, translational corpora and comparable corpora. Parallel corpora include a principled set of source language dialogues together with their translations into a given target language. Translational corpora only contain translated texts, as the corpus of audio descriptions created by Salway (2007) to identify the linguistic typicalities of audiovisual texts originating from the translation of visuals into spoken words. Comparable corpora of film language comprise two independent sets of audiovisual texts chosen using similar design criteria, either in different languages or in the same language (containing translations and non-translations). An example of a parallel and comparable spoken corpus of filmic speech is the Pavia Corpus of Film Dialogue (PCFD). The PCFD is made of Anglophone films, their dubbed versions and comparable original Italian films. The dialogues – which presently run to about 1,000,000 words – were orthographically transcribed and enriched with contextual and paralinguistic information (Pavesi 2019). In corpus-based research on film dialogue, researchers also employ reference corpora, i.e. representative corpora of the source or target language, functioning as baselines for comparison. At its best, corpus-based research on film language draws on a combination of multiple corpus resources to formulate more accurate and reliable hypotheses.

Tools of corpus analysis in the in the study of film dialogue

Corpus research of film dialogue has relied on several tools of analysis, including frequency counts, monolingual concordances and bilingual or aligned concordances. Bonsignori *et al.* (2012), for instance, compiled frequency lists of greeting and leave-taking formulas in a do-it-yourself (DIY) corpus of Anglophone films and their Italian dubbing translations to compare formality levels and naturalness in source and target texts and investigated the motivations that underlie recurrent translation choices. In several studies, the frequency of n-grams has been compared across corpora or sub-corpora to examine the differences between source and target texts or between comparable texts in the same target language and to study naturalness and the impact of translation on film language (Freddi 2011; Forchini 2012; Levshina 2017). As for bilingual concordances, in a study aimed at mapping out register shifts in racist discourse, Mouka *et al.* (2015) annotated for categories of appraisal a corpus of Anglophone films subtitled into Greek to assess the intensifying or mitigating effect of each register shift in translation. For example, the weakening in the target texts of the negative evaluation implicit in the American compound *border jumpers* was indexed by the omission in the Greek translation of taboo expressions co-occurring with the node in the original corpus. The shift in semantic prosody between the original and translated expressions was subsequently checked against monolingual concordance lines and collocates for the same compound and its translations in reference corpora of English and Greek.

The study of original Anglophone film dialogue has considerably benefitted from multi-dimensional analysis and other more advanced computational tools such as keyness (see Chapter 10, this volume). Multi-dimensional analysis is a corpus-based approach developed by Biber (1988) to investigate register variation by quantitatively detecting patterns of co-occurrence among lexico-grammatical features in texts (see Chapter 17, this volume). This approach relies on factor analysis to identify the clusters of linguistic features that tend to occur together in texts. Corpus files are tagged – usually with Biber's grammatical tagger – before factor analysis is implemented. The resulting factors are subsequently interpreted functionally to uncover the main dimensions of register-bound variation, originally in speech and writing. Multi-dimensional analysis in corpus research on film language has been employed to compare the register of spontaneous spoken English with film dialogue both sychronically and diachronically (Forchini 2012; Zago 2016). One major study has examined the verbal language of American film subtitles in a multi-genre corpus of 640 titles from the 1930s to 2010 (Veirano Pinto 2014). Seven dimensions of variation have emerged indicating that film genre, year of release, movie length and the origin of the script – original or adapted – partially explain the variation within the broader register.

Keyness – the tendency for a word or word phrase to occur in a text more often than expected by chance – has been instrumental to the study of characterisation and gender. McIntyre (2012) calculated keywords and key semantic domains via *Wmatrix* to find what was idiosyncratic about the speech of male versus female characters in a corpus of blockbuster movies. Among the idiosyncrasies in the two gendered discourses, the semantic domains of SAILING, SWIMMING and IN POWER were prevalent in men's speech, and PERSONAL NAMES and POLITE (mostly as THANKING) in women's. These domains validated previous assertions about physical activities and opposition to authority as characteristic of male parlance vis-à-vis the attention to the interpersonal sphere in female filmic speech. The patterns emerging from these research analyses are all relevant to the identification of systematic linguistic and translational behaviour in source, target and reference texts, as will be illustrated in the following sections.

3 From orality to register specificity in film dialogue

As film dialogue offers a representation of spokenness, for over 40 years orality and naturalness of speech have been central concerns of film language research, where they have been discussed in opposition to so called artificiality and anti-realism. Corpus linguistics has been paramount to the investigation of naturalness, orality and authenticity of film dialogue; at the same time, it has contributed to defining film language's specificity. Although a rich array of settings and communicative purposes are staged on screen, spontaneous conversation has been taken as the baseline for describing and assessing the degree of orality of fictional dialogue, while corpora of conversational English have provided the main ground for comparisons.

How close is film dialogue to spontaneous spoken language?

The attention to orality in films also arises out of the interest in spoken language that has acquired momentum starting from the last decades of the twentieth century (Carter and McCarthy 2017). Research on spoken language soon expanded to include spoken language in cinema and television (e.g. Quaglio 2009), as well as spoken language in audiovisual translation. In the investigation of spoken language, researchers see the lexico-grammar of conversation as rooted in its pragmatic and sociolinguistic components and study it in context, looking at the functions it performs and with reference to socio-geographic and genre-specific varieties. This functional and empirical perspective couples naturally with a corpus-based methodology and with a descriptive translation studies approach with its search for recurrent patterns and norms to address issues concerning the mimetic, face-to-face and interactional dimension of audiovisual dialogue. Other linguistic issues – e.g. verbal artistry and creativity – are more involved with the narrative, entertaining and aesthetic functions of film dialogue, which can in turn be addressed via corpus-based investigations (Pavesi 2019).

Much research has dealt with translated and non-translated film dialogue with reference to the continuum of speech and writing. By comparing the frequency lists from a corpus of Anglophone films with frequency lists derived from the conversational and written components of the British National Corpus (BNC), Rodríguez Martín (2010) has shown that the language of the Anglophone films is closer to face-to-face spoken English than to written English. The occurrence of spoken language features in film dialogue has broader implications than its similarity to spontaneous conversation. For instance, as in everyday conversation, the frequency of the personal pronouns *I* and *you* underlines the significance of shared context and interactivity in film. In turn, the extensive distribution of the response token *yes* points to the pervasive activation of turn taking and adjacency pairs, two basic organisational structures of spontaneous dialogicity and co-construction of meaning enacted in film dialogue. A more complex picture of colloquiality in films is offered by corpus studies that have applied a multi-dimensional analysis and have provided fleshed-out descriptions of film's fictional orality. These investigations have used transcriptions of spoken dialogues rather than dialogue lists or internet scripts and have accounted for large sets of co-occurring features. Consequently, the data can be more reliably employed when researchers study screen dialogue in relation to spontaneous conversation. By applying Biber's (1988) multi-dimensional model and its dimensions of register variation, Forchini (2012) compared the language of a corpus of 11 American films, the American Movie Corpus (AMC), with the Longman Spoken American Corpus (LSAC). She found that Biber's first and main dimension of *involved versus informational production* mostly accounts for the similarity between the films investigated and the language of face-to-face spontaneous interaction. On this dimension, film language globally exhibits an overall mean score – 35.3 – which closely matches that of spontaneous conversation – 35.0 (p. 67). Filmic speech displays many of the same features of involvement typifying conversation, such as personal pronouns, present tense markers, imperatives and private verbs, adverbs and qualifiers – empathics and discourse particles. The following extract from Forchini's (2012: 75) corpus highlights conversational features in film language (bold in the original).

(1)
<S> **Hey** Russ! Rusty. **What's up man**?
Let me ask you a question **now**. **Are you** incorporated?

Using a similar methodology, Zago (2016: 165) started from the assumption that films exhibit colloquial language, defined as 'the language of immediacy/closeness in non-binding contexts', to test the hypothesis of an increasing colloquialisation in film language in time. Multi-dimensional analysis was applied to a small diachronic corpus of eight American original films (from the 1950s and 1960s) and their remakes (from the 1990s and 2000s, respectively). Two main factors emerged from the analysis. These identify the language of immediacy and closeness (the positive poles) in film scenes that feature highly interpersonal dialogues versus the language of distance (the negative poles) in scenes that focus on facts and actions. Most remakes overall showed more positive factor scores than the originals, with a relevant rise in interactional features such as interjections, intensifiers and colloquial questions in all eight remakes. As a result, Zago's (2016) findings generally support the hypothesis that the language of American films has developed a more interpersonal tenor in time, although a good degree of colloquiality already characterised the original films.

Is film language register-specific?

The dual nature of film language as both a representation of conversational language and a register of its own was evidenced by the analyses of clusters and n-grams, i.e. recurrent clusters of words, also called lexical bundles. By drawing on film subtitles collected from the online repository OpenSubtitles.org compared to samples from the BNC, the Corpus of Contemporary American English and the Santa Barbara Corpus of Spoken American English, Levshina (2017) carried out correlation and cluster analyses based on n-grams. In both hierarchical models, film subtitles clustered more quickly with British and American conversation than with fiction and broadcast language in both geographical varieties. This clustering qualifies as empirical evidence of proximity between spontaneous conversation and on-screen conversation. At the same time, however, Levshina's analysis of subtitles' distinctive n-grams also highlights the specificity of the register, which relates to the specific functions subtitles perform in film contexts. The subtitles' most distinctive 1-grams *Mr* and *sir*, for example, index the dynamicity of the social situations and the relevance of formal encounters in films. The distinctive 3-grams *let's go* and *get out of* stand out, in turn, as they propel the action forward.

The analysis of n-grams in corpora of transcribed film dialogues similarly draws attention to the specificity of film dialogue, as deriving from film's double-layered communication between characters on-screen and between production team and audience. Moving from the assumption that 'different styles and registers are characterised by different distributions of clusters' (p.141), Freddi (2011) examined the ranking and dispersion of 4-grams in the PCFD. She processed the data with the concordance software *Wordsmith Tools v. 4.0* and found that the 11 top 4-grams found in the PCFD are distinctively more frequent in film dialogue that they are in the BNC conversational component. These clusters mark typical dimensions of filmic speech such as conveying formulaic politeness and emotionality. *Thank you very much* and *Nice to meet you* overrepresented the routines found in daily interactions. By contrast, *wh*-centred clusters, such as *What are you doing?* and *What do you mean?*, serve a plot-advancing, narrative function, while contributing to the representation of conflict as constitutive of screenwriting (Freddi 2011: 146). The sample bilingual concordances from the PCFD (Table 38.1) illustrate the adversarial function of the cluster *What are you doing?*, often made explicit by the Italian dubbing translation.

Carriers of orality

Orality is not given only by overall proximity to spontaneous spoken language, but can also derive from the profiling of a few selected features that evoke conversational language in viewers. The distinction made by Bublitz (2017) between spoken language and

Table 38.1 Bilingual concordances for a four-word cluster from the PCFD (Freddi 2011: 152–5; back translations in brackets)

Film	*Line No.*	*Language*	*Character*	*Text*	*Translator*
Ae Fond Kiss	105	English	TAHARA	What are you doing? You stupid bastard?	
Ae Fond Kiss	105	Italian	TAHARA	Ma guarda che hai combinato![But look at what (you) have done!]	Depaolis Federica
Ocean's Eleven	905	English	BARRY	I'm out what are you doing?	
Ocean's Eleven	905	Italian	BARRY	Ma che fai?[But what do you do?]	Mete Marco

orality is relevant here. Spoken language is the product of the act of speaking, which is a physical act of producing meaningful sounds accompanied by kinetic signs. Conversely, orality is a more encompassing notion that comprises a medial level with the concrete (phonic) realization of language, along with a conceptual level where speech is an abstract principle of construction. The latter conceptualisation has been especially productive in corpus research on audiovisual translation. Dealing with the language of dubbing, Pavesi (2009: 209) identifies a group of 'privileged carriers of orality', spoken language features that systematically occur in film translation and 'from which the impression of spontaneity can be derived'. The major studies on orality of dubbed languages share a corpus-based methodology through which they have investigated phonological, lexical, syntactic and pragmatic features of dialogue on screen (see the contributions in Baños *et al.* 2013). While they have quantitatively brought to light that dubbed language is further removed from spontaneous conversation than original filmic speech, these investigations also show that a few spoken features do stand out and are likely to trigger the experience of orality in target viewers. They have also highlighted the specificity of dubbed dialogue as well as film language in general. For example, second person pronouns have been found to be overrepresented in all corpora of audiovisual language, where they highlight interlocutors on screen while simultaneously involving viewers (see Pavesi 2019). Consider the concordances in Table 38.2.

Table 38.2 Bilingual concordances for second person pronouns from the PCFD

Original English	*Dubbed Italian*	*Film*
((overlap)) **You** won't be going anywhere. Everything is all right.	**Tu** non vai da nessuna parte.[You don't go anywhere]	(*Looking for Eric*, Ken Loach, 2009)
You ever seen him?	Ma **tu** l'hai mai visto?[But did you see him?]	(*Finding Forrester*, Gus Van Sant, 2001)
Mommy **you**'re not eating?	Mamma, **tu** non mangi?[Mommy, aren't you eating?]	(*Erin Brockovich*, Steven Soderberg, 2000)

4 Topics in corpus research: how to use a corpus to study orality and register specificity

This section looks at research carried out on the PCFD investigating features that characterise filmic language both as a representation of spontaneous spoken language and a self-standing register. The studies reviewed are concerned with three phenomena central to face-to-face communication, which were also posited to play a key role in film dialogue.

Demonstrative deixis

Deixis is 'the single most obvious way in which the relationship between language and context is reflected in the structures of languages themselves' (Levinson 1983: 54). Demonstratives in particular are prototypical deictics performing a focussing function. According to Diessel (2014: 125), they index 'joint focus of attention', a notion 'used to characterise triadic situations in which speaker and addressee share their attention on a particular referent'. This function is basic in both communication and social cognition, as it coordinates the speaker's and the addressee's attention on a specific, shared object of reference. Of the two English demonstratives, proximal *this* is more powerful, as it introduces information associated with the here and now, while it forcefully brings a new referent into discourse. Conversely, distal *that* is unmarked and less emphatic. *That* is hearer-oriented, often indicating that the speaker is assuming the addressee's point of view. The highlighting and interactional functions of demonstratives are highly relevant for filmic discourse. Here the pronouns *this* and *that* operate on the two diegetic and extra-diegetic levels by pointing to significant segments of the extra-linguistic reality or current discourse for the benefit of both on-screen characters and viewers. They refer to objects perceivable in the scene but can also symbolically evoke broader situations belonging to the narrative.

Moving from the hypothesis that demonstratives play a central role in film's multimodal context and double-layered communication, Pavesi (2013, 2020) investigated the frequency and functions of demonstrative pronouns in English film dialogue and its Italian dubbing. All demonstrative pronouns in the 12 films of the initial version of the PCFD were annotated for syntactic role, pragmatic function in the source texts and the strategy used in translation. A first analysis showed that overall demonstrative pronouns are as frequent in the PCFD as they are in corpora of conversational English. This finding provides further evidence of the similarity between fictional and spontaneous orality and substantiates the interactivity, involvement and casualness of film discourse. When dubbing English into Italian, however, the majority of the English demonstrative pronouns were *not* carried over into the Italian texts, as only 12.8 per cent were translated with formally equivalent pronouns. Various translation strategies accounted for the mismatch between source and target texts including omission (ex. 2), the replacements with weaker pronouns (ex. 3) and explicitation, that is, the full form of the referent (ex. 4).

(2)
That is a nice gun! → *Mh, pistola di lusso!* [Mh, luxury gun!]
(Crash, Paul Haggis 2004)

(3)
I figure **that**. → *Sì, **lo** avevo immaginato.* [Yes, I had imagined it.]
(Finding Forrester, Gus Van Sant 2001)

(4)
I promise… I'm gonna find out **who did this**, mom → *io ti prometto… che troverò **l'assassino**, mamma* [I promise you that I'll find the murderer, mum.]
(Crash, Paul Haggis 2004)

The corpus analysis suggested that the reduction of demonstratives was due to the syntactic and pragmatic contrasts between English and Italian. Ultimately, the language of the Italian dubbing appeared to rely more on the visual and acoustic components of the multi-modal product. 'By contrast, the original English dialogue appeare[d] to provide characters and viewers alike with more verbal directions to specific aspects of the unfolding dialogue and context of situation' (Pavesi 2013: 128). The following extract highlights the contrast:

(5)

(*Secrets and Lies*, Mike Leigh, 1996)

DOG-OWNER	Are you gonna see that flea collar? Are you gonna see that?	Si vede molto il collare antipulci? Si vede?[Does one see the flea collar much? Does one see it?]
MAURICE	Don't worry about that.	Non si preoccupi.[Don't worry.]

A closer analysis of *this* in the English component of the PCFD additionally revealed that the proximal pronoun is considerably more frequent in the film corpus than in corpora of spontaneous spoken English. Four hundred and forty-nine tokens per 100,000 words were recorded in the PCFD versus 150 reported for conversation in Biber *et al.* (1999: 349). As a result, it was argued that English film language displays greater intensity in highlighting contextual and textual entities (Pavesi 2020). These are drawn closer to viewers, thanks to the 'heightened emotivity and subjectivity [conveyed by *this*] in referring to object, propositions or situations in which the speaker is closely involved personally' (Cornish 2001: 305):

(6)
Really. I can only offer you what we've got right now. Just **this**.
(Autumn in New York, Joan Chen 2000)

(7)
What's that? - **This**? **This** is a Harley-Davidson. It's the best damn motorcycle ever made.
(Erin Brockovich, Steven Soderberg 2000)

More broadly, in the PCFD, not only does *this* contribute to the multimodality of film language, it also plays a distinct role in the narrative. Within the exophoric function it overwhelmingly performs (83.8 per cent of occurrences of *this* refer to the external context), the proximal pronoun often focusses on the film's wider situation and narrative. This means that exophoric *this* extends its reference beyond concrete objects to index facts, events and situations. In the following extract, two sisters, Pinky and Jess, are getting ready for Pinky's wedding. *This* variably refers to the specific day, what comes with it and the status of being married.

(8)
PINKY: Jess, don't you want all of **this**? **This** is the best day of your life, innit?
JESS: I want more than **this**. They've offered me and Jules a scholarship to go to America.

(Bend It Like Beckham, Gurinder Chandha 2002)

The question was subsequently asked whether *this* was neutral or carried an evaluative colouring when performing the function of isolating immaterial, narrative entities from the flow of narration. Exophoric *this* pronouns from a subset of the PCFD were further annotated distinguishing abstract and symbolic uses from concrete, gestural ones (Levinson 1983: 65–6). Collocations of the former in the PCFD were perused (Pavesi 2020: 32), for example:

(9)
You're right, Roisin. I *shouldn't* have let **this** *happen*. I should have foreseen the *hurt*. I'm on an emergency case. Yes, but could **this** be a *mistake*? I very much *doubt* it. Look,
I don't know. She's gone. I *can't fucking* believe **this**! *What's going on here?*

It was observed that abstract *this* collocates with negatively connoted verbs, adjectives and nouns, such as *spoil* and *destroyed, ridiculous* and *stupid, mistake* and *shock*. It co-occurs with swear words and comes with hedges and apologies: *I'm afraid this is your last day, I'm sorry, I know this must be a shock to you.* The pronoun is often embedded in negative clauses, *You can't do this*, and within face-threatening speech acts, *Is this why we got you educated?, So what is this*? The concordance analysis thus confirmed that when *this* focuses on a situation emerging from discourse, it prevalently exhibits a negative prosody and mostly occurs in conflictual and adversarial exchanges.

Interrogatives

Film dialogue mimics face-to-face conversation in relying on adjacency pairs as the basic mechanism for turn taking. In the construction of adjacency pairs, in turn, interrogatives are pivotal syntactic constructions, employed to obtain information and carry an array of pragmatic meanings. Ghia (2014, 2019) examined the roles of these constructions in both original English dialogue and its dubbing translation. Interrogatives were identified in a sample of the PCFD and annotated for form and function. Formally, interrogatives were tagged as *yes-no* questions, *wh*-questions, alternative questions and fragments. Functionally, information-seeking questions were separated from non-questioning or pragmatic interrogatives. These express interpersonal functions such as alignment and disalignment (e.g. *How many times have I asked you to put me on a litigation team?*). By comparing the frequencies in the PCFD and the conversational section of the LSWEC, it was found that interrogatives in English film dialogue are almost twice more frequent than they are in spontaneous conversation (3,192 vs. 1,762 occurrences per 100,000 words, respectively, in the PCFD and LSWE corpus). This initial result indexes a heightened interactivity in film dialogue, which is mostly realised through *yes-no* questions and *wh*-questions. The main function for both interrogative types is characterisation and storytelling, as 62 per cent of all questions seek to gather information from the interlocutor: *So, Harry, what do you do?*; *How else am I gonna get the money?*; *Hang on a minute! Where are you going?* This high frequency may also contribute to film dialogue's pragmatic economy as interrogative forms are loaded with pragmatic functions that are performed by a variety of forms in extended phatic communication.

Although not as frequent as information-seeking questions, pragmatic questions indeed represent a prominent means to construct and represent interpersonal relationships in film dialogue (Ghia 2019). In the PCFD, they account for about 30 per cent of the total direct questions and mostly express a disaffiliative stance, hence typically embodying the conflict-generating function of audiovisual dialogue. They come in a variety of patterns that closely parallel English spontaneous conversation, including conversational ellipses (10) and highly elliptical patterns (11) (Ghia 2019: 587–88):

(10)
- He's the kind of guy who's got this whole life, his family and shit. **You think he's gonna leave all that**?

(11)
- I'm gonna go to the ladies' room.
- **Again, baby?**

The investigation of interrogatives also compared the devices used in English affiliative and disaffiliative questions with those used in Italian dubbing (Ghia 2014, 2019). The Italian interrogatives in the PCFD sample were tagged applying the same functional categories employed for the English component with the addition of recurrent structural patterns in Italian interrogatives. Overall, there is evidence of hybridisation in this area of translated fictional orality. 'Dubbing safeguards the alignment and disalignment patterns present in the original dialogues, operating a balance between ST interference and TT needs and norms' (Ghia 2019: 595). Hence dubbed Italian preserves the prevalence of disaffiliative questions but tends to mark them by means of target language strategies, including initial weak connectors such as *e* "and" functioning as a question opener and the adversative *ma* "but". These relay a variety of English patterns, as shown by the following concordances (Table 38.3):

Table 38.3 Bilingual concordances for Italian adversative *ma* "but" from the PCFD

Original English	*Dubbed Italian*	*Film*
What are you talking about? I fell in the water.	**Ma** che stai dicendo? Sono caduto.[But what are you saying? I fell.]	(*Two Lovers*, James Gray, 2008)
What exactly has got into you?	**Ma** si può sapere che cosa ti è preso?[But can one know what has got into you?]	(*The Holiday*, Nancy Meyers, 2006)

Vocatives

The high interactivity of film dialogue is sustained by the high frequency of vocatives in the PCFD. In an analysis of the whole corpus compared to both the BNC (1994) and the LSWEC, Formentelli (2014) reported that vocatives in film dialogue are four times as frequent as in spoken interaction (1642.2 vs. 409.4 vocatives per 100,000 words). In films, vocatives not only highlight the interpersonal function of dialogue and qualify as strategic markers of orality, they also sustain dialogue's ability to anchor a narrative and disclose characters' identities while (re)stating the relationships that hold between them (Kozloff 2000: 36–7). Consider:

(12)

TONY BLAIR: Of course. **Your Majesty**, my party has won the election, so I come now to ask your permission to form ((overlap)) a government.

QUEEN: ((overlap)) No, **Mr Blair. Mr Blair**, I ask the question.

(The Queen, Stephen Frears, 2006)

The multifunctionality and register-specific nature of vocatives in film dialogue clearly emerges from the different categories of vocatives occurring in the corpus. If names are overwhelmingly the most frequent category, familiarisers also burgeon in the PCFD. They evoke the informality, closeness and emotionality of the register, where the majority of frequent familiarisers in English are at least five times more frequent than in spontaneous conversation. Interestingly, a divide clearly exists between the British and the American films in the corpus. The two components closely parallel conversation in the two national varieties as additional evidence of the 'realistic reproduction of sociolinguist variation on screen' (Formentelli 2014: 69). This is foregrounded by the recurrent and sociopragmatically diversified use of *mate* and *man* in the two screen varieties. Consider the following (Table 38.4):

Table 38.4 Concordances for *mate* and *man* from the PCFD

TRAVIS	Eric, what's going on, **mate**?	(*Looking for Eric*, Ken Loach, 2009)
ALASTAIR	"People's princess", **mate**. You owe me.	(*The Queen*, Stephen Frears, 2006)
FLY	You'll be okay, **man**, come on, come on, get up!	(*Finding Forrester*, Gus Van Sant, 2001)
MAN to BOB	Bob? Bob Harris? You're awesome, **man**.	(*Lost in Translation*, Sofia Coppola, 2003)

5 Applications and implications

Corpora of film dialogue can be of use beyond the study of film language. Research has shown that audiovisual dialogue exhibits register specific features and is characterised by few disfluency phenomena, increased discourse immediacy and reduced vagueness, as well as increased emotionality and conflictuality (e.g. Quaglio 2009; Bublitz 2017). Yet quantitative corpus investigations have confirmed that film closely matches spontaneous conversation. A good alignment also appears between spontaneous British and American conversation and the language of English subtitles. One can hence argue that corpora of film language can be used in the study of spoken language, especially for those features that are difficult to record in real-life interactions. Research has indeed drawn attention to the sociolinguistic and pragmatic relevance of film data, provided due attention is paid to the constraints set by the screen and the translation processes. Alvarez-Pereyre (2011) discusses fiction films as simultaneously language artefacts and language specimens, that is, validated language data that can contribute to our knowledge about language.

As for cross-linguistic analyses, features performing a major role both in spontaneous speech and in film language can be profitably inspected in original and translated dialogue to highlight possible correspondences across spontaneous spoken languages. Translated films and television series supply unique sources of parallel spoken texts. With spoken corpora of audiovisual translation, we can thus examine functionally equivalent expressions in the source and target texts through bilingual concordances. If such corpora are made multimodal as with FORLIXT (e.g. Valentini and Linardi 2009), they further allow for the investigation of verbal-nonverbal combinations in invariant, although culturally not equivalent, situations.

Corpus findings also support the use of film dialogue inside and outside the classroom as a form of spoken language input viable for second language acquisition. What appears to be most relevant for acquisitional purposes is the considerable occurrence in audiovisual dialogue of features of spontaneous spoken language and the proximity between the two registers. As a self-standing register, the language of screen dialogue, however, cannot be expected to overlap with natural conversation. For this reason, we cannot assess its appropriateness for second language acquisition purposes only with reference to its similarity to spontaneous spoken language. More corpus-based research is needed to identify which spoken features are overrepresented and underrepresented on-screen to find out how film dialogue can foster language learning beyond realism of input. Some of these features may have to do with reduced vagueness, discourse immediacy, formulaicity and emotionality. They are all features that corpus studies have shown to contribute to film language's register specificity and that may make the L2 easier to understand, process and memorise for learners.

Further reading

Berber Sardinha, T. and Veirano Pinto, M. (2019) 'Dimensions of Variation across American Television Registers', *International Journal of Corpus Linguistics* 24(1): 3–32. (Multi-dimensional analysis in this wide-ranging article is used to compare and group television programmes, including films, hence revealing the dimensions that appear to account for their variations.)

Pavesi, M. (2019) 'Corpus-based Audiovisual Translation Studies: Ample Room for Development', in L. Pérez-González (ed.) *The Routledge Handbook of Audiovisual Translation Studies*, London: Routledge, pp. 315–33. (This chapter offers an overview of corpus linguistics methodology and data analysis in research on the translation of audiovisual dialogue.)

Piazza, R., Bednarek, M. and Rossi, F. (eds) (2011) *Telecinematic Discourse: Approaches to the Language of Films and Television Series*, Amsterdam: John Benjamins. (This pioneering edited volume is most widely cited in studies on film and television dialogue.)

References

Alvarez-Pereyre, M. (2011) 'Using Film as Linguistic Specimen', in R. Piazza, M. Bednarek and F. Rossi (eds) *Telecinematic Discourse: Approaches to the Language of Films and Television Series*, Amsterdam: John Benjamins, pp. 47–67.

Baños R., Bruti S. and Zanotti, S. (eds) (2013) Corpus Linguistics and Audiovisual Translation: In Search of an Integrated Approach, *Special issue of Perspectives: Studies in Translatology* 21(4).

Bednarek, M. and Zago, R. (2021) *Bibliography of Linguistic Research on Fictional (narrative, scripted) Television Series and Films/Movies,* Version 4 (January 2021), https://unico.academia.edu/RaffaeleZago.

Biber, D., Johansson, S., Leech, G., Conrad S. and Finegan E. (1999) *Longman Grammar of Spoken and Written English*, London: Longman.

Biber, D. (1988) *Variation across Speech and Writing*, Cambridge: Cambridge University Press.

Bonsignori, V., Bruti, S. and Masi, S. (2012) 'Exploring Greetings and Leave-Takings in Original and Dubbed Language', in A. Remael, P. Orero and M. Carroll (eds) *Audiovisual Translation and Media Accessibility at the Crossroads: Media for All 3*, Amsterdam: Rodopi, 357–79.

Bublitz, W. (2017) 'Oral Features in Fiction', in M. A. Locher and A. H. Jucker (eds) *Pragmatics of Fiction*, Berlin: Mouton De Gruyter, pp. 235–63.

Carter R. and McCarthy, M. J. (2017) 'Spoken Grammar: Where Are We and Where Are We Going?', *Applied Linguistics* 38(1): 1–20.

Cornish, F. (2001) '"Modal" *That* as Determiner and Pronoun: The Primacy of the Cognitive-Interactive Dimension', *English Language and Linguistics* 5(2): 297–315.

Davies, M. (2019) The TV Corpus. Available online at: https://www.english-corpora.org/tv/

Delabastita, D. (2019) 'Fictional Representation', in M. Baker and G. Saldanha (eds) *Routledge Encyclopedia of Translation Studies*, 3rd edn, London: Routledge, pp. 189–95.

Diessel, H. (2014) 'Demonstratives, Frames of Reference, and Semantic Universals of Space', *Language and Linguistics Compass* 8(3): 116–32.

Dynel, M. (2011) '"You Talking to Me?' The Viewer as a Ratified Listener to Film Discourse', *Journal of Pragmatics* 43(6): 1628–44.

Forchini, P. (2012) *Movie Language Revisited: Evidence from Multi-Dimensional Analysis and Corpora*, Bern: Peter Lang.

Formentelli, M. (2014) 'Vocatives Galore in Audiovisual Dialogue: Evidence from a corpus of American and British films', *English Text Construction* 7(1): 53–83.

Freddi, M. (2011) 'A Phraseological Approach to Film Dialogue: Film Stylistics Revisited', *Yearbook of Phraseology* 2: 137–63.

Ghia, E. (2014) '"That is the Question": Direct Interrogatives in English Film Dialogue and Dubbed Italian', in M. Pavesi, M. Formentelli and E. Ghia (eds) *The Languages of Dubbing: Mainstream Audiovisual Translation in Italy*, Bern: Peter Lang, pp. 57–88.

Ghia, E. (2019) '(Dis)aligning across Different Linguacultures: Pragmatic Questions from Original to Dubbed Film Dialogue', *Multilingua* 38(5): 583–600.

Goffman, E. (1981) *Forms of Talk*, Philadelphia, PA: University of Pennsylvania Press.

Gregory, M. (1967) 'Aspects of Varieties Differentiation', *Journal of Linguistics* 3(2): 177–98.

Kozloff, S. (2000) *Overhearing Film Dialogue*, Berkeley: University of California Press.

Levinson, S. C. (1983) *Pragmatics*, Cambridge: Cambridge University Press.

Levshina, N. (2017) 'Online Film Subtitles as a Corpus: An N-Gram Approach', *Corpora*, 12(3): 311–38.

McIntyre, D. (2012) 'Prototypical Characteristics of Blockbuster Movie Dialogue: A Corpus Stylistic Analysis', *Texas Studies in Literature and Language*, 54(3): 402–25.

Messerli, T. C. (2017) 'Participation Structure in Fictional Discourse: Authors, Scriptwriters, Audiences and Characters', in M. A. Locher and A. H. Jucker (eds) *Pragmatics of Fiction*, Berlin: Mouton De Gruyter, pp. 25–54.

Mouka, E., Saridakis, I. E. and Fotopoulou, A. (2015) 'Racism Goes to the Movies: A Corpus-Driven Study of Cross-linguistic Racist Discourse Annotation and Translation Analysis', in C. Fantinuoli and F. Zanettin (eds) *New Directions in Corpus-based Translation Studies*, Berlin: Language Science Press, pp. 35–70.

Pavesi, M. (2009) 'Dubbing English into Italian: A Closer Look at the Translation of Spoken Language', in J. Díaz-Cintas (ed.) *New Trends in Audiovisual Translation*, Bristol: Multilingual Matters, pp. 197–209.

Pavesi, M. (2013) '*This* and *That* in the Language of Film Dubbing: A Corpus-based Analysis', *Meta* 58(1): 107–37.

Pavesi, M. (2019) 'Corpus-based Audiovisual Translation Studies: Ample Room for Development', in Luis Pérez-González (ed.) *The Routledge Handbook of Audiovisual Translation Studies*, London: Routledge, pp. 315–33.

Pavesi, M. (2020) '"I shouldn't have Let this Happen": Demonstratives in Film Dialogue and Film Representation', in C. Hoffmann and M. Kirner-Ludwig (eds) *Telecinematic Stylistics*, London: Bloomsbury, pp. 19–38.

Piazza, R., Bednarek, M. and Rossi, F. (eds) (2011) *Telecinematic Discourse: Approaches to the Language of Films and Television Series*, Amsterdam: John Benjamins.

Quaglio, P. (2009) *Television Dialogue: The Sitcom Friends vs. Natural Conversation*, Amsterdam: John Benjamins.

Rodríguez Martín, M. E. (2010) 'Comparing Conversational Processes in the BNC and a Micro-Corpus of Movies: Is Film Language the "Real Thing"?', in T. Harris and M. Moreno Jaén (eds) *Corpus Linguistics in Language Teaching*, Bern: Peter Lang, pp. 147–75.

Salway, A. (2007) 'A Corpus-Based Analysis of Audio Description', in J. Díaz Cintas, P. Orero and A. Remael (eds) *Media for All: Subtitling for the Deaf, Audio Description and Sign Language*, Amsterdam: Rodopi, pp. 151–74.

Tirkkonen-Condit, S. and Mäkisalo, J. (2007) 'Cohesion in Subtitles: A Corpus-Based Study', *Across Languages and Cultures* 8(2): 221–30.

Valentini, C. and Linardi, S. (2009) 'Forlixt 1: A Multimedia Database for AVT Research', *inTRAlinea*, http://www.intralinea.org/specials/article/1715.

Veirano Pinto, M. (2014) 'Dimensions of Variation in North American Movies', in T. Berber Sardinha and M. Veirano Pinto (eds) *Multi-Dimensional Analysis, 25 Years on: A Tribute to Douglas Biber*, Amsterdam: John Benjamins, pp. 109–47.

Zago, R. (2016) *From Originals to Remakes: Colloquiality in English Film Dialogue over Time*, Acireale/Roma: Bonanno Editore.

Zago, R. (2021) 'Corpus-Assisted Approaches to the Analysis of Film Discourse', in E. Friginal and J. A. Hardy (eds) *The Routledge Handbook of Corpus Approaches to Discourse Analysis*, London: Routledge, pp. 168–82.

39

How to use corpus linguistics in sociolinguistics: a case study of modal verb use, age and change over time

Paul Baker and Frazer Heritage

1 Framing sociolinguistics within corpus research

In this chapter we consider how corpora can be used in order to carry out research from a sociolinguistic perspective. Sociolinguistics is a somewhat broad term, with Labov (1972: 183) indicating that it can appear redundant, as all language is social. Despite this, sometimes language can be considered from less "social" perspectives e.g. in terms of a description of how it is structured or to the extent that it resembles other languages. Researchers like Wardhaugh (2005) and Bloome and Green (2002) have identified sociolinguistics as involving consideration of social context and the relationship between language and society. Sociolinguistics can thus involve analysing aspects of language use as they relate to a person's identity or the community they belong to. It can involve examination of variation between individuals or groups and change over time. In particular, it can concern interactive aspects of language, resulting in corpus-based sociolinguistic studies that have involved concepts like discourse features (Aijmer 2015), politeness (Culpeper and Gillings 2018) and representation of identity (Johnson and Partington 2017). Several studies also have examined where at least two of these concepts overlap (Taylor 2017).

For the purposes of this chapter, we are taking a somewhat narrower focus, considering sociolinguistics from the perspective of speaker identity. We begin by reflecting on why a corpus approach is worth taking in order to answer sociolingusitic questions, followed by a short review of corpus studies of sociolinguistics. We then move on to a case study which is situated as a continuation of research on diachronic change in modal verb usage (e.g. Leech 2002, 2011; Millar 2009). While these studies have used written corpora, we have employed two spoken corpora in order to examine use of the modal verb *may*. The first is the spoken section of the *British National Corpus* (Aston and Burnard 1998), a general corpus of speech and writing collected between 1991 and 1994 (henceforth referred to as the BNC1994), which we compare against the *Spoken British National Corpus* 2014, a second corpus of speech from 2014 (Love *et al.* 2017), referred

DOI: 10.4324/9780367076399-39

to as the BNC2014. Both corpora are relatively similar in terms of containing transcriptions of private conversations among friends and family, although the data collection methods differed slightly.

2 Great challenges bring great benefits

One consideration to be taken into account when using corpora to address sociolinguistic questions is that it tends to be easier to build or find corpora that consist of written texts, particularly if such texts are available in online contexts that already exist in electronic form (as opposed to, say, converting the contents of a handwritten diary). Written corpora *can* be used to examine sociolinguistic variation, particularly if records are kept regarding aspects of the identities of their authors. For example, Cermakova and Farova (2017) have examined variation between male and female authors in corpora of British and Czech fiction. However, many sociolinguistic studies tend to focus on naturally occurring speech, which has traditionally been more problematic for corpus linguists to examine. It can be complicated, expensive and time consuming to collect the large amounts of data required to carry out a meaningful spoken corpus analysis. While the means of recording a conversation has become easier, thanks to the ubiquity of smartphones that can record sound, the resulting audio files still have to be keyed in using a consistent transcription scheme for representing accents as well as para-linguistic and non-linguistic features. Additionally, issues involving ethics, including permission and anonymisation, are, if anything, more salient than they perhaps were 30 years ago. Corpus builders might also struggle to construct a well-balanced corpus that contains speech from a wide range of speaker identities. The BNC2014, for example, contains speech from 671 people and contains a wide range of identity categorisations, with some categories being better populated than others. If we start to combine categories (e.g. counting the possible permutations of age plus gender plus social class), some of the resulting demographic groups will contain very low numbers of speakers. Such studies can be easier if carried out on data collected online, however, e.g. see Subtirelu's (2017) examination of the intersection of gender and race in student evaluations of lecturers on a "rate my professor" website.

With those points considered, though, the benefits of using a corpus (spoken or not) to investigate sociolinguistic issues are great and thus worth engaging with. A large amount of transcribed speech, encoded for different speaker characteristics, presents a huge advantage for analysts, both in terms of claiming representativeness about a particular social group and in terms of allowing existing hypotheses to be explored. Furthermore, this method allows for the identification of linguistic features that may not have been noticed if the analyst had used manual means of identification or was limited to a much smaller dataset. For example, taking a keywords approach to compare different types of women's personal adverts, it was found that women who were seeking relationships with men tended to use the word *me* more often than those seeking relationships with women, resulting in the former group of women making higher use of statements where they positioned themselves as the recipient of actions of the desired other e.g. 'Looking for someone to show me around town' (Baker 2017).

Broadly speaking, corpora have been used in order to examine demographic variation, particularly utilising existing spoken corpora like the BNC1994 see, for example, Schmid's (2003) comparison of lexical items traditionally associated with male and female speech or Rayson *et al.*'s (1997) keyword comparisons of demographic differences. Some studies have used corpora as part of a larger multi-method study, such as McEnery's (2005) examination of swearing in the BNC1994 which complemented corpus analysis with historical analysis of texts about swearing in seventeenth- and twentieth-century written texts. While lexical and/or grammatical studies have generally been easier to carry out due to the lower requirements in terms of annotation, there have also been (smaller-scale) studies that have considered phonetic or prosodic variation such as Grabe and Post's (2002) examination of stress in different dialects, Maclagan and Hay's (2007) consideration of pronunciation in a corpus of New Zealand speech and Torgersen *et al.*'s (2006) focus on short monophthongs by younger and older speakers in southeast England.

Spoken corpus projects tend to involve data collection over a short period, and it can be difficult to replicate the conditions of an earlier spoken corpus study in order to examine change over time. Therefore, diachronic studies have again tended to involve written corpora, bringing us to a point which this chapter aims to address.

3 Changing frequencies of modal verbs over time

The case study we describe in the following section is based on comparing two spoken corpora to identify change in modal verb use over time. Modal verbs are verbs of necessity or possibility like *would, should* or *may* which are often used in conjunction with the base form of another verb (e.g. *might go*). In a diachronic study which compared four British and American reference corpora (known as the Brown Family) containing written texts taken from two time periods, Leech (2002) found that the collective frequencies of 11 modal verbs were lower in the 1990s corpora compared to the 1960s ones. This pattern was more pronounced for the American corpora, which also had lower frequencies of the modal verbs in both time periods when compared to the equivalent British corpora. In particular, verbs which expressed strong modality like *shall, need, must* and *ought* showed much lower differences in frequency between the two time periods compared to weaker modals like *might, will, would, can* and *could* (with the latter two modals being slightly more frequent in the 1990s American corpus compared to the 1960s one). On the other hand, a group Leech refers to as semi-modals, like *had better, want to* and *have (got) to,* had higher frequencies in both 1990s corpora and had higher use overall in the American corpora compared to the British ones. Leech suggests that the patterns reflect a wider trend towards colloquialisation of written language, shown by adoption of features more common to speech (contractions, progressive verbs, questions, genitives, zero relative use), appearing more often in writing. He cautiously discusses other social explanations like democratisation (a tendency to avoid unequal and face-threatening modes of interaction) and Americanisation (the influence of North American habits of expression and behaviour on other nations).

A related corpus study of modal verbs (Millar 2009) analysed the 100-million-word *TIME Magazine Corpus*, containing text from issues of the American *Time* magazine from 1923 onwards. The study found a 22 per cent increase in modals overall between the 1920s and 2000s, although some modals like *shall* had drastically decreased in frequency over time and some, like *would,* showed fluctuation while others like *may, can* and *could* had increased. Leech (2011) responded by arguing that the language of *Time* magazine is not representative of all language use, and by including the analysis of additional members of the Brown family of corpora, he shows that modal verb decline is most notable when comparing corpora from the 1960s, 1990s and 2000s. Similarly, his analysis of the *Corpus of Historical American English* (COHA) shows decline in modal use across the decades of the twentieth century which accelerates from the 1970s. His study notes that *may* is a bone of contention in that it is where his findings disagree most dramatically from Millar (2009). While *may* appears to have decreased over time in the COHA, during the same period, it has increased over time in the TIME corpus. Both Millar and Leech suggest that the rise in frequency of *may* in Time magazine could be due to change in content, style or editorial policy, with a shift towards speculation in reporting and less focus, particularly in magazines, on the past and present – with modal verbs being used to speculate on possible future events in this genre.

In British English, *may* has been associated with politely powerful ways of speaking. Stubbs (1996) describes how the word was used frequently in a court case by a judge during his summing up, in phrases like "you may think/feel/remember" that were addressed to the jury. In some cases, the judge used *may* to signify a course of action he intended to take e.g. "when I sum up I may very well make some comments upon the evidence", while in others the judge appeared to be politely instructing the jury e.g. "one of the questions you may want to ask yourselves is this". In the spoken section of the BNC1994, *may* is used more frequently by AB speakers (the highest-earning social class). However, the creation of a second *British National Corpus* (BNC2014) opens up numerous opportunities for the investigation of diachronic variation, as we will demonstrate in the following section.

4 Case study: spoken use of the modal verb *may*

In this chapter, we examine diachronic changes in how different age groups use the modal verb *may*. In order to do this, we use two comparable corpora of speech (the spoken section of the BNC1994 and the BNC2014). The BNC1994 contains 100 million words, although only 12 million of these are transcribed speech. Within the transcribed speech, 7 million words originate from "context-governed" speech – such as language produced in the workplace. The remaining 5 million words derive from private conversations. At present, the BNC2014 contains 11.4 million words of speech, all of which come from private conversations. For comparability, we have only used the 5-million-word sub-corpus of private conversations from the BNC1994 and the whole of the spoken BNC2014. The two corpora are highly comparable and use the same age categorisation system: 0- to 14-year-olds, 15- to 24-year-olds, 25- to 34-year-olds, 35- to 44-year-olds, 45- to 59-year-olds and 60-year-olds and up. Thus, we can study the diachronic change from several perspectives. First, we can compare how the same age groups use language across a single time period, e.g. by comparing all of the age groups in 1994 or all the age groups in 2014. If both time periods show similar patterns, then this would indicate evidence that people's use of language changes as they get older. But we can also compare speakers of similar age who were born in different time periods, for example, by comparing one set of people who were 0 to 14 years old in the BNC1994 with a second set of people who were 0 to 14 years old in the BNC2014. This kind of analysis allows us to consider possible cohort effects, whether the time period someone was born in will affect their language use. Additionally, we can examine how age cohorts have changed their use of language between the two points of measurement (1994 and 2014). If we assume that the demographically sampled speakers are representative of their cohorts at the time of recording, it would thus be possible to observe how four different cohorts' use of the modal verb *may* changes as they age. These cohorts are presented in Table 39.1.

Table 39.1 Age cohorts and how old members of those cohorts would have been in the BNC1994 and BNC2014

Cohort birth year	*Age range in BNC1994*	*Age range in BNC2014*
People born in the 1950s	35–44	60+
People born in the 1960s	25–34	45–59
People born in the 1970s	15–24	35–44
People born in the 1980s	0–14	25–34

Each of the age groups is representative of people born within decades, rather than across decades. That is to say that the cohorts will stretch from, for example, the birth years of 1950–59 as opposed to, for example, 1954–63. Throughout the rest of this case study, when we refer to age groups, we refer to set age categories (for example, 0- to 14-year-olds). When we refer to decade of birth cohorts, we refer to the groups noted in Table 39.1 (for example, people born in the 1980s).

Any diachronic differences in how members of a given decade of birth cohort use language could reflect two types of change. The first type of change relates to what is seen as socially appropriate uses for a modal verb, such as how the modal *ought* is now seen as archaic. The second change relates to how a birth cohort view their use of the modal verb as they age (or how they believe they should be talking for their age). In other words, diachronic changes could reflect both what is viewed as an appropriate way to use a modal verb in the time period being studied and how age groups apply this to their own language, bearing in mind their age at a given point in time. By taking into account the variables of age group and decade of birth cohort, we can obtain a better picture of variation in the use of *may* among British English speakers at a diachronic level, something which until the availability of the BNC2014 has not been easy to do.

Both corpora are hosted on CQPweb – a freely accessible website hosted at Lancaster University (Hardie 2012). CQPweb has numerous functions which are indispensable to sociolinguists. For example, CQPweb automatically applies the CLAWS tagger to uploaded corpora. The CLAWS tagger annotates the grammatical part of speech for each word and is accurate 96 to 97 per cent of the time (see Fligelstone *et al.* 1997). *May* is polysemous, meaning that if researchers do not specify the part of speech they are interested in, CQPweb will return all forms of *may* – including not only the modal form but also forenames, surnames and references to the month of May. The BNC1994 is tagged using the C5 tag set, and the BNC2014 is tagged using a modified version called the C6 tag set. There are minor differences between the two tag sets (for example, modal verbs are tagged as VM0 in the C5 tag set and as VM in the C6 tag set), but this does not impact on our results. To restrict the results of *may* to only show modal verb uses, we used the search terms “may_VM0” and “may_VM” with the BNC1994 and BNC2014, respectively.

In this study, we use the data disclosed by speakers to investigate how different social groups use language. All the speech in the corpora has been tagged with speaker attributes which include age, gender and social class. These attributes are included in the metadata assigned to each speaker, meaning that analysts can look at how members who hold identity “x” use feature “y”. We use the Distribution function in CQPweb, which allows a researcher to examine how frequently members of a particular social identity use a specified word. We have also examined concordance lines of occurrences of the features associated with different age groups, leading to a more qualitative analysis based on functional differences.

Our analysis therefore uses two different methods for interpreting the data: the first is to analyse the changes in frequencies at which the modal verb *may* occur. The second is a close reading of extended concordance lines in order to examine if the function of the modal verb has diachronically changed. Within this latter method we also explore the phraseological patterns to examine how speakers use language to achieve the functions associated with the modal verb (requesting permission, hedging and giving permission). These functions were selected because they emerged from a close reading of the concordance lines which contained the modal verb. For both methods, we explore differences by comparing age groups and cohorts. However, in the analysis derived from the second method, we focus on three groups in particular: those who were aged 0 to 14 in the BNC1994, those who were 0 to 14 in the BNC2014 and those who were 25 to 35 in the BNC2014 (members of this group would have been 0 to 14 in the BNC1994).

Before we examine how different age groups use *may*, it is first worth knowing how frequently it is used in the two corpora. Without imposing the restriction of age categories, within the BNC1994, *may*_VM0 occurs 637 times across 97 texts (127.03 occurrences per million words). In the BNC2014, *may*_VM occurs 1,365 times across 592 texts (119.50 instances per million words). Thus, the general usage of *may* appears to have slightly decreased across time at a rate of 7.53 occurrences per million words. Bearing this in mind, Figure 39.1 outlines the diachronic differences in the frequency at which *may* (as a modal) occurs across comparable age groups.

The data from Figure 39.1 paint a rather complex picture: Across all six comparable age groups, three (0- to 14-year-olds, 25- to 34-year-olds and 45- to 59-year-olds) appear to use the modal verb *may* more frequently in 2014 than in 1994. In contrast, the other three (15- to 24-year-olds, 35- to 44-year-olds and 60+-year-olds) appear to use *may* as a modal verb less often in 2014 than in 1994. While the frequency at which *may* occurs as a modal in the BNC2014 as a whole has decreased by 7.53 per million words, when we examine how often different groups use it, the amount of change ranges from 0- to 14-year-olds, who use *may* 63.36 times per million words more often in 2014 compared to 1994, to 35- to 44-year-olds who use *may* 38.99 occurrences per million words less in 2014 compared to 1994. These differences in usage compared to the general picture of diachronic changes to the modal form of *may* give weight to why sociolinguistic analyses of corpora are needed. Although examinations of diachronic change in the frequency at which a word is used can provide interesting findings, they do not necessarily reflect the behaviours of different social groups, which can deviate from the perceived diachronic change in a general sense.

Does Figure 39.1 show evidence of an age effect? Considering just the bars for 1994, there does appear to be a shift in frequency which is weakly related to age, with the younger three age groups (people aged under 35) using *may* less than the older three age groups (people aged 35 and over). However, the bars for 2014 show a different pattern, with no perceivable linear trend. Therefore, age differences in *may* do not appear to be consistent across the two points of measurement, indicating that the age effect cannot fully explain use of *may*.

What about the cohort effect? We can take the data from Figure 39.1 and arrange the bars differently to compare how the birth cohorts use *may* across the two time periods (Figure 39.2).

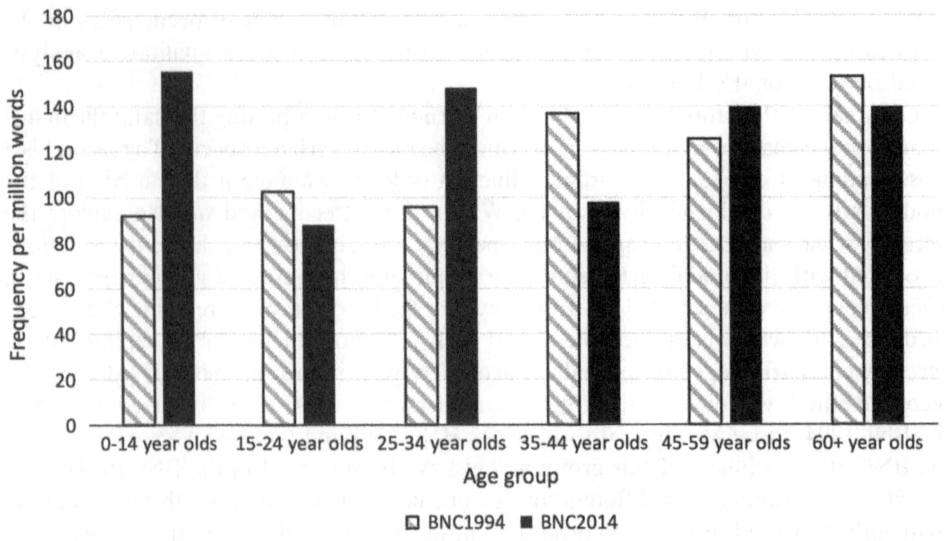

Figure 39.1 Diachronic change in *may* as a modal verb across comparable age groups

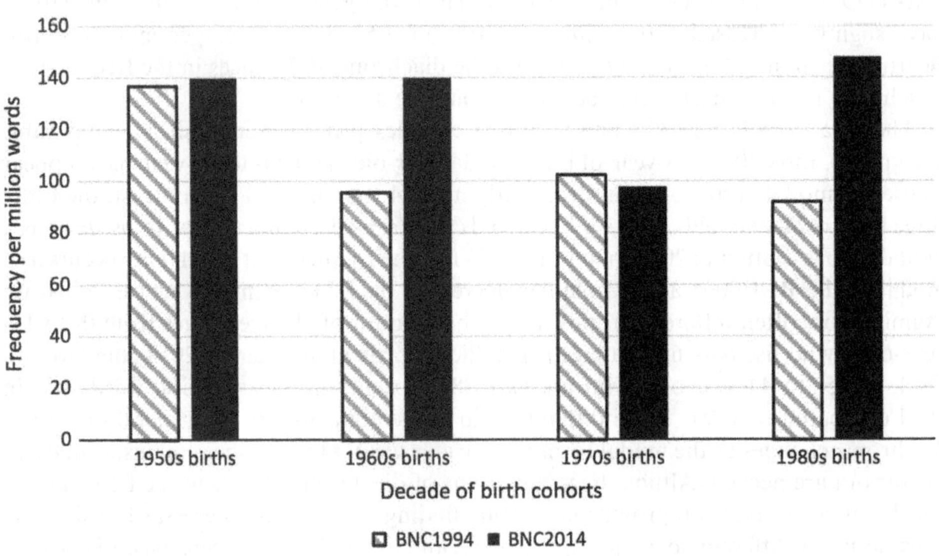

Figure 39.2 Diachronic changes in how frequently decade of birth cohorts used the modal verb *may*

Figure 39.2 indicates a different picture compared to the data presented in Figure 39.1. The 1950s and 1970s births show very little change in their use of *may* between the two time periods when they were recorded. Of course, this should not indicate their use of *may* has been constantly at the same level for all the years between 1994 and 2014, but we can at least say that when 1994 and 2014 are compared, there are only tiny differences in relative frequency for these two age cohorts. While the 1950s births have high use of *may* in both periods, the 1970s births have relatively low use of it.

However, the 1960s and 1980s births follow a different pattern: lower use of *may* in 1994 and higher use in 2014. Given that there are cohort differences which do not match the age group differences, it appears that both the time period a person is living in (whether it is the 1990s or 2010s) and their age at the time play a part in the frequency which they use *may*.

Quantitative findings such as these can provide a useful broad picture of diachronic changes in how a word is used. However, it is useful to combine them with an analysis of context, as this can reveal how a particular word is used in different time periods by different age groups and members of decade of birth cohorts.

In order to gain a clearer understanding of how *may* is used in both corpora, we conducted a close reading of concordance lines. When working with reasonably large frequencies, it can often be useful to examine collocates of a word (see for example Hunston, this volume; Jones, this volume), as a way of down-sampling concordance lines to a manageable amount. However, when we considered occurrences of *may* based on use within particular age groups, we found that its frequency was too low to produce collocates that met traditional significance thresholds (for a discussion of these thresholds see Brezina 2018). Given the limitations of space, we only focus on three groups: those who were 0 to 14 years old in the BNC1994, those who were 0 to 14 years old in the BNC2014 and those who were 25 to 34 years old in the BNC2014. These groups were selected for closer analysis because 0- to 14-year-olds in the BNC1994 and the BNC2014 had the greatest difference in normalised frequencies at which *may* occurs as a modal verb (see Figure 39.1). In other words, 0- to 14-year-olds in the BNC2014 used the modal verb *may* much more than their comparable group from the BNC1994. Furthermore, the group who were 0 to 14 years old in the BNC1994 (who are the same decade of birth cohort as the 25- to 34-year-old group in the BNC2014) had the largest increase in the normalised frequency of use of *may* as modal as they aged (see the 1980s births in Figure 39.2). We thus start by analysing how these age groups used the modal verbs in the BNC1994 compared to the BNC2014 in terms of whether they use it to request permission (e.g. *may I have some milk*), hedge propositions (e.g. *you may want to go*), give permission (e.g. *you may do that*) or other uses (e.g. cases that were unclear due to interruptions). We examined all concordance lines in which *may* was used (as a modal verb) by a speaker within these groups. These quantified frequencies (as a percentage of the raw total for each group) are presented in Figure 39.3.

The figure indicates notable changes – both diachronically across the comparable age group and within the 1980s decade of birth cohort. First, across the comparable age groups (consider the first two sets of columns), the 0- to 14-year-olds in the BNC1994 appear to use *may* as a modal to request permission much more than their 2014 counterparts, who instead use may more to hedge a proposition.

We can use Figure 39.3 to focus just on people born in the 1980s by comparing the first and third sets of bars together. In 1994, this age-cohort were children, and as noted earlier, they tended to use may to request permission. However, in 2014 they were in their late twenties/early thirties, and use of *may* was used much more often to hedge a proposition.

The middle set of bars in Figure 39.3 thus resembles the final set of bars more than it does the first set of bars, indicating that the children of 2014 are more similar in their use of *may* to older people in the same time period as them, compared to the children of 1994. The figure also indicates some evidence that the function of *may* might be changing over time – from being used to make polite requests to instead hedge propositions.

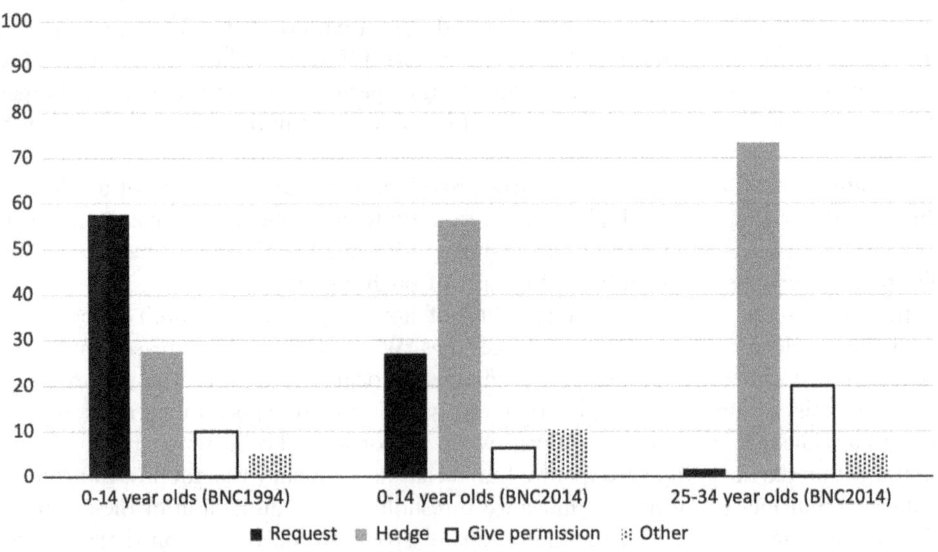

Figure 39.3 Percentages of the functions of *may* in three groups

However, we have only examined three age groups and would need to make a fully study of all the other age groups across both time periods in order to investigate this hypothesis further.

The analysis indicates that there are not only differences in how comparable age groups use language, but there are also differences in how members of the same decade of birth use language. However, while quantifying how frequently these different functions occur may be helpful in painting a picture of diachronic change on a quantitative level, it does not necessarily explain how the modal verb is used at a phraseological level. That is to say, it does not necessarily reveal how *may* is used to achieve these functions. In order to do this, we examined the phraseological patterns around *may* for these groups within the datasets.

Table 39.2 notes the different phraseological lexical units in which *may* was used. In order to ascertain these, we used the "sort" function in CQPweb. This function orders concordance lines by alphabetising co-occurring words in a pre-set slot to the left or right. Although analysts have control of which slot is set for the sort function, the results we present are based on sorting the concordance lines by the co-occurring word one place to the right. We only noted a phraseological pattern if it occurred in at least 10 per cent of the concordance lines for a particular group. This prevented low-frequency patterns being taken as representative usages.

One immediate difference between the language used by 0- to 14-year-olds in the BNC1994 and the BNC2014 is that those in the BNC1994 appear to use *may I* much more regularly than those in the BNC2014. In both datasets, the modal construction of *may I* is used in order to request permission to do something and to request physical items, which could explain the difference in the frequency at which *may* is used to request permission demonstrated in Figure 39.3. However, the 0- to 14-year-olds who were recorded for the BNC2014 use a greater variety of phraseological constructions which incorporate *may*, compared to children of a similar age who were recorded for the BNC1994. Additionally, the phraseological constructions appear to suggest that the

Table 39.2 Common phraseological units containing *may* for different age groups

Age group (Data set)	*Raw frequency*	*Notable phraseological lexical units(raw frequency of occurrence) example (filename)*
0- to 14-year-olds (BNC1994)	40	*may I* (21) *may I have my pudding please?* (KBW 9002)
0- to 14-year-olds (BNC2014)	48	*may be* (5) *it may be a chocolate goose it may be a giant Easter egg* (S8LG 404)
		may have (6) *she touched him and got it and er and she may have been electrocuted I can't remember* (SNZS 175)
		may I (12) *may I have some cake?* (SCG9 533)
		may not (8) *she thinks she's a witch but she may not be a witch* (S46J 244)
25- to 34-year-olds (BNC2014)	240	*may as well* (24) *if there's a little two you can make you may as well try and make it* (S968 1083)
		may be (43) *United States somewhere that's bigger where if we get where we may be able to afford property* (SVZB 1386)
		may have (33) *he may have been drunk when they were talking about this deal* (S4S5 631)

0- to 14-year-olds in the BNC2014 use constructions containing the modal form of *may* to talk about events they remember from the past, request items and hedge ideas (such as seeing if something is a goose or an egg in Table 39.2). This contrasts with the 0- to 14-year-olds from the BNC1994, who mostly only use it to request items. In turn, these phraseological patterns provide some qualitative explanation for the data presented in Figure 39.3.

In contrast to both 0- to 14-year-old groups, the 25- to 34-year-old group in the BNC2014 appears to use *may* in ways which suggest uncertainty about more abstract concepts, such as finances and biological phenomena. Furthermore, the 0- to 14-year-olds in the BNC2014 exclusively use *may have* to refer to past events. In the BNC1994, those who were 0 to 14 only used *may have* three times (so it was not considered a phraseological lexical unit): two of these occurrences were references to past events, and one was a request. Comparatively, the 25- to 34-year-olds in the BNC2014 appear to use *may have* to refer to both past events and potential future events, for example: *we may not need the twelfth month we may have finished all our work and done everything and therefore that would save us like seven hundred and fifty quid in rent* (SBTC 1149). Indeed, for this group there are 7 occurrences (out of 33) which use *may have* to refer to future possibilities, all of these refer to events in the distant future, rather than the immediate future.

When specifically examining the difference between how members of the decade of birth cohort born in the 1980s use language, it can be seen that they no longer retain the frequent use of *may I.* This politeness form, which appears to have been appropriate for 0- to 14-year-olds in 1994, appears to have been discarded later in life. Furthermore, the fact that *may I* is used much less by children born in later generations, indicates that perhaps it is not being taught to children as an appropriate way to make requests.

5 Reflecting and future directions

This case study has demonstrated how corpora can be used to explore not just social variation but also diachronic changes with regard to the use of modal verbs. It is now worth stepping back and considering some of the issues with using corpora in this way. In particular, the study raises issues regarding essentialist approaches to language. Throughout, we have tried to avoid the claim that "x" age group use "y" feature because they are part of the "x" age bracket. To exemplify this problem, one must ask "when someone has a birthday which pushes them into the next age bracket, do they suddenly stop using a linguistic feature?" The likely answer to this is no. In turn, this serves to demonstrate the issues of using statically categorised social groups. Although we have done our best to avoid essentialist claims, the practice of putting people into categories and then counting frequencies of linguistic features does face the risk of appearing essentialist, particularly as we cannot account for every intersection of a speaker's identity (age, social class, gender), and even when we are able to account for a number, these identities may not even play a role in the language used by that speaker (for a discussion of intersectionality, see Crenshaw 1990). Importantly, to avoid essentialist thinking, a sociolinguistic corpus analysis should first note that differences in frequency are usually not absolute, but more a matter of gradience, with one social group using a feature more than others, but often not having full ownership of that feature. To that end, the qualitative forms of analysis favoured by examining concordance lines allow us to consider differences within a particular social group as well as differences between them. Of course, it is often the case that a corpus search will yield too many concordance lines and in such cases the analyst might decide to analyse a random sample of, say, 100 lines, noting the main trends and deciding to look at further lines if the patterns appear inconclusive. Considering context of usage via an analysis of an expanded concordance line allows us to identify individual speaker variation that can indicate that people within a group can use a word for different purposes (and indeed, the same speaker can vary in the way they use a word). Such considerations will help us to provide a more sophisticated sociolinguistic analysis that goes beyond a table of numbers and claims that group "x" use feature "y".

Given the limitations of space and the limitations of the corpora (which would need to be even bigger to downscale sample sizes to account for more identities), it has not been fully possible to explore all intersections of identity in our exploration. While it would be interesting to compare these changes to how other social groups use the same feature and how adding other dimensions changes the variation, even larger corpora would be required to do so. However, we should return to a point made earlier in this chapter, regarding the fact that when we divide speakers into groups, the larger the number of groups, the smaller the frequencies. Particularly for speakers aged 0 to 14 in both spoken BNCs, the amount of data to work with is smaller compared to the older speakers. There are 435,286 words of 0- to 14-year-olds' speech in the BNC1994 and 309,177 words in the BNC2014. Particularly for the latter corpus, word counts for the older age groups are much higher (e.g. 2,777,761 words for people aged 15 to 24, while this was only 795,250 for the same age bracket in the BNC1994). As a result of the smaller amounts of children's speech, the raw frequencies of *may* are low in both corpora (40 and 48 occurrences), meaning that classification into functional categories results in even lower frequencies, giving less confidence that results are generalisable and would be replicated if carried out on an equivalent sample. Also, the age group 0 to 14 covers an extremely crucial period of language development, resulting in very marked changes, so care must be taken not to generalise use of *may* as being similar for children aged 2 compared to a teenager of 14. When using spoken corpora, we thus need to consider the extent to which identity categories contain a workable amount of data and are actually useful constructs for our purposes.

Future research that utilises corpus approaches to sociolinguistics may want to focus on using corpus methods on data generated from communities of practice (see Eckert and McConnell-Ginet 2007). By using language from communities that are known to organise around a particular identity, it might be possible to compare and contrast variation which is community specific, and avoid some of the essentialism that naturally occurs when using large reference corpora. Additionally, future research may want to examine both different modal verbs and how they are used within the social groups that are the focus of this chapter. It would be interesting, for example, to examine other modal verbs used to signal politeness and compare this across age groups. Elsewhere, other researchers may want to examine how the modal verb *may* changes across different identities and how and why these identities might play a role in the use of the modal verb *may*. Having noted that children no longer seem to use the *may I* form to make requests, we might want to consider alternative forms that they might use e.g. *give me* or *can I*.

Finally, this study has only been able to answer the question "how do these groups use language?" Future research might elect to attempt to answer the question "why do these groups use these features?" We might want to form hypotheses based on the patterns found e.g. younger children are taught formal, polite forms of language less than used to be the case, which anecdotally, might be worth exploring. Analysing the data itself might also provide clues (although we did not find any cases in either corpus of older people correcting children's language e.g. "No, if you want something, say *may I have…*"). Instead, a deeper and more nuanced study, which uses interviews, discourse completion tasks, focus groups or media texts to examine attitudes towards these kinds of modal verbs and how people recall their own experience of language use and ideologies as they were growing up, could complement this one, providing further insights into this kind of social variation.

Further reading

Baker, P. (2010) *Sociolinguistics and Corpus Linguistics*, Edinburgh: Edinburgh University Press. (This book acts as a general primer for a range of ways that corpora can aids sociolinguistics, having chapters on demographic variation, comparing language use across different cultures and examining language change over time, studying transcripts of spoken interactions and identifying attitudes or discourses.)

Friginal, E. (ed.) (2017) *Studies in Corpus-based Sociolinguistics*, London: Routledge. (This edited collection of 14 chapters from a range of authors is divided into three sections: languages and dialects, social demographics and register characteristics.)

Friginal, E. and Hardy, J. (2013) *Corpus-based Sociolinguistics: A Guide for Students*, London: Routledge. (This book functions as a practical guide for students who wish to carry out their own studies, containing case studies, discussion questions and activities.)

Murphy, B. (2010) *Corpus and Sociolinguistics: Investigating Age and Gender in Female Talk*, Amsterdam: John Benjamins. (This monograph involves a detailed analysis of age and gender in a 90,000-word spoken corpus of Irish English, considering features like hedges, vagueness, intensifiers and swearing.)

References

Aijmer, K. (2015) 'Analysing Discourse Markers in Spoken Corpora: *Actually* as a Case Study' in P. Baker and T. McEnery (eds) *Corpora and Discourse Studies*, London: Palgrave, pp. 88–109.

Aston, G. and Burnard, L. (1998) *The BNC Handbook: Exploring the British National Corpus with SARA*, Edinburgh: Edinburgh University Press.

Baker, P. (2017) 'Corpora and Social Demographics', in E. Friginal (ed.) *Studies in Corpus-Based Sociolinguistics*, London: Routledge, pp. 157–77.

Bloome, D. and Green, J. (2002) 'Directions in the Sociolinguistic Study of Reading', in P. D. Pearson, R. Barr, M. L. Kamil and P. Mosenthal (eds) *Handbook of Reading Research*, Mahwah, NJ: Lawrence Erlbaum, pp. 395–421.

Brezina, V. (2018) *Statistics in Corpus Linguistics: A Practical Guide*, Cambridge: Cambridge University Press.

Cermakova, A. and Farova, A. (2017) '*His Eyes Narrowed—Her Eyes Downcast:* Contrastive Corpus-Stylistic Analysis of Female and Male Writing', *Linguistica Pragensia* 28 (2): 7–34.

Crenshaw, K. (1990) 'Mapping the Margins: Intersectionality, Identity Politics, and Violence against Women of Color', *Stanford Law Review*, 43(6): 1241–99.

Culpeper, J. and Gillings, M. (2018) 'Politeness Variation in England. A North-South Divide?', in V. Brezina, R., Love and K. Aijmer (eds) *Corpus Approaches to Contemporary British Speech*, London: Routledge, pp. 33–59.

Eckert, P. and McConnell-Ginet, S. (2007) 'Putting Communities of Practice in their Place', *Gender & Language* 1(1): 27–37.

Fligelstone, S., Pacey, M. and Rayson, P. (1997) 'How to Generalize the Task of Annotation', in R. Garside, G. Leech, and A. McEnery (eds) *Corpus Annotation: Linguistic Information from Computer Text Corpora*, Longman, London, pp. 122–36.

Grabe, E. and Post, B. (2002) 'Intonational Variation in English', in B. Bel and I. Marlin (eds) *Proceedings of the Speech Prosody 2002 Conference*, 11-13 April 2002, Aix-en-Provence: Laboratoire Parole et Language: 343–46.

Hardie, A. (2012) 'CQPweb - Combining Power, Flexibility and Usability in a Corpus Analysis Tool', *International Journal of Corpus Linguistics* 17(3): 380–409.

Johnson, J. and Partington, A. (2017) 'Corpus-Assisted Discourse Study of Representations of the 'Under-Class' in the English-Language Press', in E. Friginal (ed) *Studies in Corpus-Based Sociolinguistics*, London: Routledge, pp. 293–318.

Labov, W. (1972) 'The Logic of Nonstandard English', in P. Giglioli (ed.) *Language and Social Context*, Harmondsworth: Penguin, pp. 179–215.

Leech, G. (2002) 'Recent Grammatical Change in English: Data, Description, Theory', in K. Aijmer and B. Altenberg (eds) *Proceedings of the 2002 ICAME Conference*, Gothenburg: 61–81.

Leech, G. (2011) 'The Modals ARE Declining. Reply to Neil Millar's 'Modal verbs in TIME: Frequency Changes 1923-2006'', *International Journal of Corpus Linguistics* 16(4): 547–64.

Love, R., Dembry, C., Hardie, A., Brezina, V. and McEnery, T. (2017) 'The Spoken BNC2014: Designing and Building a Spoken Corpus of Everyday Conversations', *International Journal of Corpus Linguistics* 22(3): 319–44.

Maclagan, M. A. and Hay, J. (2007) 'Getting Fed Up with Our Feet: Contrast Maintenance and the New Zealand English "Short" Front Vowel Shift', *Language Variation and Change* 19(1): 1–25.

McEnery, T. (2005) *Swearing in English: Bad Language, Purity and Power from 1586 to the Present*, London: Routledge.

Millar, N. (2009) 'Modal verbs in TIME', *International Journal of Corpus Linguistics* 14(2): 191–220.

Rayson, P., Leech, G., and Hodges, M. (1997) 'Social Differentiation in the Use of English Vocabulary: Some Analyses of the Conversational Component of the British National Corpus', *International Journal of Corpus Linguistics* 2(1): 133–52.

Schmid, H. J. (2003) 'Do Men and Women Really Live in Different Cultures? Evidence from the BNC', in A. Wilson, R. Rayson and T. McEnery (eds) *Corpus Linguistics by the Lune. Łódź Studies in Language 8*, Frankfurt: Peter Lang, pp. 185–221.

Stubbs, M. (1996) *Texts and Corpus Analysis*, London: Blackwell.

Subtirelu, N. (2017) 'Exploring the Intersection of Gender and Race in Evaluations of Mathematics Instructors on *Ratemyprofessors.com*', in E. Friginal (ed.) *Studies in Corpus-Based Sociolinguistics*, London: Routledge, pp. 219–35.

Taylor, C. (2017) 'Women are Bitchy but Men are Sarcastic? Investigating Gender and Sarcasm', *Gender and Language* 11(3): 415–45.

Torgersen, E., Kerswill, P. and Fox, S. (2006) 'Ethnicity as a Source of Changes in the London Vowel System', in F. Hinskens (ed.) *Language Variation – European Perspectives. Selected Papers from the Third International Conference on Language Variation in Europe (ICLaVE3)*, Amsterdam, June 2005, Amsterdam: Benjamins: 249–63.

Wardhaugh, R. (2005) *An Introduction to Sociolinguistics*, London: Blackwell.

40

Corpus linguistics in the study of news media

Anna Marchi

1 Why study news discourse using corpora?

The definition of "news discourse" can be rather broad and accommodate various forms of journalistic output. Bednarek and Caple describe it as 'the kind of discourse we encounter when we turn on the television, when we open the newspapers, when we go online or when we switch on the radio to get our dose of daily happenings' (Bednarek and Caple 2012: 1). The qualities which make news discourse an ideal territory for corpus linguistics are inbuilt in the definition: its relevance and its abundance.

The consumption of news discourse is a regular routine fulfilling a common need, as journalism represents 'one of the ways society tells itself about itself' (Dickinson 2008: 1); therefore, journalism is a powerful agency of symbolic control also because of its ubiquity. Everyday news outlets produce an enormous amount of text. The *New York Times* published online approximately 230 pieces of content daily in 2016 (Meyer 2016), a print edition of (the pre-tabloid, i.e. pre-January 15, 2018) *Guardian* contained, on average, 90,000 words on a weekday and more than twice as much on Sundays, the word count of a 55 minutes *BBC World News* programme is around 11,000 words. In the past two decades the emergence of news aggregator databases, such as *LexisNexis* or *Factiva*, has meant that newspaper content – and, to a lesser extent, broadcast transcribed content – is easy to access in a ready-to-search format, making it possible to compile comprehensive news corpora relatively quickly and with a reasonable level of accuracy.

Given the influence and the availability of news discourse, it not surprising that the majority of studies adopting various combinations of corpus and discourse approaches (see Marchi 2019Marchi and Taylor 2018: 5) are based on news corpora. Nartey and Mwinlaaru (2019) reviewed 121 studies combining corpus linguistics and critical discourse analysis between 1995 and 2016 and found that the distribution of "domains of engagement" was dominated by media 53 per cent (prominently newspapers), followed by politics (38 per cent) and social media (14 per cent).

The work presented in this chapter will mainly focus on print, or newspaper journalism, as it represents the target of the vast majority of corpus studies of news discourse to date. The term newspaper journalism might seem rather outdated in an age of fluid

DOI: 10.4324/9780367076399-40

formats and proliferation of platforms: Some of the journalism classified as such might have never even been published on paper. Selling copies represents a negligible source of revenue for most news outlets. The *Independent* discontinued its print edition in 2016. Since 2011 the *Guardian* has adopted a "digital first" (Jarvis 2011) strategy; the readers of the print version represent nowadays a tiny portion of the readership of a newspaper, and in some cases (for instance, with the *Daily Mail* compared to the *Mail Online*) a very different readership altogether. What can be problematic for a corpus linguist is that digital versions of news items often have different headlines and other variations, as well as including much more material, such as podcasts or live blogs. Under the simplified label "newspaper journalism" I include the static, text-only output of mainstream traditional press; while I am convinced that traditional journalism is still alive and very relevant, I am also well aware that the definition is reductive, and this will be discussed broadly both in the next section and in the final one.

Section 2 will be dedicated to methodological aspects, including corpus design, particularly with reference to corpus use. In Sections 3 and 4 I will review key studies using newspaper corpora to investigate news form (its structure and function) and content (representations and ideologies). Finally, Section 5 will reflect on the limitations of doing corpus work on news media texts and look into perspectives and potential developments.

2 News texts and news corpora

Newspapers are used as corpora, or in corpora, in different ways. They can be part of general corpora compiled to study language at large. For example newspapers and magazines constitute 30 per cent of the *British National Corpus* (1994) and the Brown family corpora include different types of press texts (44 reportage samples for each corpus: 1931, 1961, 1991 and 2006). There are then specialised corpora, either entirely composed of newspapers or where newspapers represent a main partition that can be compared with other types of text. One of the largest (non-topic-specific) newspaper-only corpora is the SiBol corpus (or the Siena-Bologna family of newspaper corpora). Accessible on *Sketch Engine*, SiBol is a 650-million-word collection of the whole output of British broadsheets (1.5 million articles) for the years 1993, 2005, 2010 and 2013 (the 2013 corpus was extended to include British tabloids and English language newspapers from different countries).

Studies of media corpora can be of two main kinds: studies of news structure and discourse function (reviewed in Section 3) and studies of media representation/construction of specific topics (reviewed in Section 4). Sometimes a research project will contain a mixture of the two types.

The corpus we use and what we want to do with it are the fundamental elements of any research: 'the corpus data we select to explore a research question must be well matched to that research question' (McEnery and Hardie 2012: 2). In other words, the question has to suit the corpus *or* the corpus has to suit the question. This may seem self-evident, but the issue is far from trivial and is perhaps worth some explicit reflection. The architecture of a corpus has enormous repercussions on what we can do with it. Clearly, if we are interrogating a pre-existing corpus, we have to be aware of the limitations that come with adapting a datset to purposes which are most likely different from those the corpus was originally built for. Let us take as an illustration a large, balanced, general corpus created for a broad range of linguistic research; one such example is the *Corpus of Contemporary American English* (COCA), which is freely accessible online and, at the time of writing, contains more than 1 billion words coming from a variety of sources, including newspapers, over the past 20 years. The newspapers partition contains about 123 million words (approximately 4 million per year), sampled from all sections of ten US newspapers of a very different nature in terms of readership or geographical distribution; this corpus is an extraordinary resource for synchronic and diachronic genre analysis of news discourse; however, because of its composition, it is not particularly suitable for topic-specific studies, say, for instance, an investigation of changing representations of the Muslim world in the US press. We *can* use general corpora to study specific social, cultural and political issues, but the generalisations we can make are constrained by external criteria (e.g. sampling balanced on the basis of source and news section), which may not match the scope of our research. This is why in order to study a specific topic, such as the one hypothesised, researchers prefer to create specialised corpora, compiled following criteria which attempt to strike the best balance between recall (i.e. including all relevant texts) and precision (i.e. including only texts that are relevant) – see Gabrielatos (2007: 6).

Obviously the definition of relevance depends not only on the specific topic at hand but also on how we intend to approach that topic, and this is reflected in the two main kinds of custom-built newspaper corpora: search term(s) based and whole output. Search term(s)–based corpora rely on the completeness and unambiguity of the query to achieve an accurate coverage of the topic. A well-formed query optimises precision and recall and, by reducing the overall volume of the data collection (compared to complete output), it also makes it easier to download and store data for a continuous stretch of time (as opposed to sampling points in time, e.g. years). On the other hand, with this type of design the re-usability of the corpus is rather limited; moreover, we lose relevant information, most notably about the weight and distribution of the topic under scrutiny with respect to the overall content of the source. The size of newspapers has changed considerably over time, and different publications differ substantially in the number and size of pieces they publish; therefore, it may be important to be able to observe coverage of topic/event relative to the volume of the whole newspaper coverage. I discuss this in detail in Marchi (2018), in particular reference to diachronic research, and reach the conclusion that the ideal solution in terms of corpus compilation would be 'collecting the complete output of a source of data for a continuous stretch of time' (Marchi 2018: 178).

A minimization *a priori* impact of corpus design still does not efface the fact that any corpus is *made* (no matter how "intelligent" the design) and the choices on which it is based not only will, but should, determine its use. Even if we are compiling custom corpora using the entire output of a source, compilation requirements depend on the purpose of the research and rest on reasoned choices which may be arranged on three levels: source (i.e. where do data come from?), substance (i.e. what data are included?) and structure (i.e. how are data structured?).

Source

An initial distinction on data collection procedures and platforms depends on whether we are compiling a corpus of contemporary news or of historical newspapers.

There are established historical newspaper corpora, such as the *Zurich English Newspapers corpus* (or ZEN, a 1.2-million-word collection of newspapers, covering 120 years of British press history between 1671 and 1791). Some corpora allow for long-term diachronic research, for example, the *Rostock Newspaper corpus*, comprising ten samples drawn from six British newspapers (10,000 words per newspaper) from 1700 to 2000 at 30- or 40-year intervals. However, for historical research as well, it has become relatively easy to compile custom corpora using newspaper archives (e.g. the *Times Digital Archive*) or commercial databases storing digitalised newspapers (such as *ProQuest*). The British Newspapers Archive stores almost 36 million pages dating from the 1700s; the Library of Congress has an online repository of newspapers printed in the United States between 1789 and 1963. The main challenge for some historical corpus research can be making the format suitable for corpus analysis, i.e. converting scanned images to full text, an issue which is widely discussed in digital humanities.

For contemporary datasets, that is corpora of newspapers published in the digital age, obviously there is not a problem converting from the analog format. There might, however, be an issue of variability of content depending on the point of access. Before *Nexis,* some newspapers sold editions on CD-ROM, which were used to extract data for large newspaper corpora from the late 1990s and early 2000s (for example, SiBol 1993 and SiBol 2005). News aggregators rapidly made disks obsolete, but reliance on aggregators still determined which sources would be used for research, depending on availability and level of accessibility. Not all newspapers are available on news aggregators, and the newspaper content directed to a database is never complete: Some may be omitted (Leetaru 2011) and the same newspaper may be available on different databases but the content may not coincide. Nevertheless the content stored from databases tends to be relatively stable over time. The alternative is harvesting online editions of the newspapers using web crawlers (such as BootCat) or web-scraping scripts (using programming languages such as Python); in this case, the content may be more complete, but it is subject to greater variability: Articles may be (and frequently are) removed, edited or updated over time.

Substance

Web-based corpora grant greater richness but at the cost of greater noise, such as ads; some of the noise is easy to detect and remove, for example, duplicates or near-duplicates, other "hybrid" material less so, for example, paid for (journalistic) content. As Baroni and Ueyama point out, though, 'it is not correct to refer to the problems above as "problems of Web corpora"; rather they are problems of large corpora built in short time and with little resources, and they emerge clearly with Web corpora since the Web makes it possible to build "quick and dirty" large corpora' (Baroni and Ueyama 2006).

Decisions need to be made concerning cleaning the corpus and how much cleaning to do. What to do, for example, with "boilerplate" information, that is repeated formulaic strings such as:

> It is the policy of the Guardian to correct significant errors as soon as possible. Please quote the date and page number. Readers may contact the office of the readers' editor.
>
> [repeated 317 times in the Guardian 2005]

Independently from the source used to collect the data, decisions must be made in terms of what to include in the collection and what to exclude from it. For example, registry articles (birth, marriages and deaths), legal and court announcements, church services or weather forecasts all present very repetitive language, which may skew the analysis.

Many issues may be solved by annotating the corpus. Mark-up allows us to include everything in the corpus and at the same time selectively isolate elements from the analysis. Exploiting the Hypertext Markup Language (HTML) code of web pages or the editorial and descriptive metadata in the database storage makes some level of mark-up relatively easy to encode (for example, encoding sections), but annotating a corpus remains a time-consuming task (see Chapter 2, this volume).

Structure

The substance of a corpus and its structure are strictly related, as they define the corpus architecture. Perhaps the single most important decision we make when designing a corpus is defining the organising principle of its structure: what will be the unit of analysis. The way data are stored determine the way they will be analysed. The level of aggregation of documents (e.g. 1 file = 1 daily edition or 1 file = 1 article) determines the granularity with which we can analyse the data (unless texts are marked up in a way that gives us access to multiple levels). This is particularly relevant in the case of online newspapers, as texts published online are increasingly a blend of locally produced texts and material from other sources, but it has always been a concern since, as Hundt points out, 'more variation within traditional text categories (such as "newspapers") exists than between different text categories' (Hundt 2008: 171), and – she continues – 'the question is whether one year's worth of The Guardian or The Times can be considered a single-register corpus or not' (*ibid.* 179).

As Egbert and Schnur (2018) elegantly explain: 'just as neither leaves nor forests can exist without trees, textual features and corpora cannot exist without texts' (2018: 161). According to the authors the fact that the text is the sampling unit in corpus design and construction ensures that the corpus 'represents the way naturally occurring discourse is produced' (*ibid.*: 165). Individual texts then may or may not be the observational unit. This depends on the research question at hand – and we may need to consider different units for different purposes. However, failing to carefully consider what should constitute the building bricks of our corpus will dramatically limit what we can do with it. Some corpora are often exploitable for a long time after their origin, and we cannot envisage future research needs. Because of the 'serendipitous nature' (Partington 2009: 282) of corpus-assisted research, we cannot even predict the ramifications of our ongoing analysis. Therefore, the corpus structure has to be deliberate and flexible (see Cirillo *et al.* 2009).

The discussion of corpus design is limited by space constraints, but I hope I have managed to convey its importance: 'Data collection is often regarded as the easiest step of the entire analytical process, yet it is actually one of the most complex, with the quality of the collection and the preparation process impacting on every other stage of the project' (Leetaru 2011: 7). It may be true that newspapers are the favoured source for corpus-assisted research because they are easy to collect, but apparent convenience quickly fades when we reflect on the implications of corpus compilation. I will come back to a reflection on methodological and practical issues at the end of the chapter. The next two sections will focus on applications of corpus research in the analysis of news discourse, with a brief review of crucial work in the area.

3 News form

Newspaper corpora are used in a variety of linguistic areas of interest, such as stylistics (Semino and Short 2004), pragmatics, historical linguistics (Studer 2008), sociolinguistics and, of course, discourse analysis (see Section 4). Studies of formal features of news discourse, such as broad-spectrum lexico-grammatical studies and studies of textual position, provide an understanding of the discourse type (or types), which is fundamental for any study of newspaper corpora.

Biber (1988) developed a typology of texts on the basis of a model of variation across registers, where each dimension of variation comprises a set of lexico-grammatical features that occur frequently in texts and reflect shared communicative functions (e.g. exposition or persuasion), establishing essential knowledge about the structure and function of news. Dimensional studies such as Biber's describe the characteristics of a specific register (e.g. newspaper reportage) by comparing it with other registers (e.g. academic prose, editorials, conversation) or comparing different variables with respect to frequent co-occurring lexical and syntactic features (e.g. modal verbs, stance adverbs). Exploring variation, Biber *et al.* (1998) observed, for example, the high frequency of temporal adverbs in news and that temporal references such as *yesterday*, *last night* and *tomorrow* are more frequent in British news than in American news, while the latter shows higher frequency of mentions of days of the week. This difference might not exist anymore, as there probably was (but it would be worth checking and it would make a neat little study) an overall move to days of the week or specific dates when content was made available online, where readers can access it at any time and potentially forever.

Following Biber, Morley (2004) analysed persuasion in British newspaper editorials by comparing them with news reports. Morley used comparison across text types, setting editorials against news reports, as well as comparison within texts, contrasting the last paragraph of editorials with the rest of the text. He found an increased frequency in the use of modal verbs, adverbs of epistemic stance and the construction *it is* followed by an evaluative adjective followed by *that/to* in the conclusive paragraph, thus demonstrating how text-final position ("the sting in the tail") accomplishes a specific persuasive goal and showing the correlation between the structure of editorial discourse and its function of telling the relevant authority what it must do.

Textual position in hard-news reports was the focus of a large-scale project developed at the University of Liverpool (see Hoey and O'Donnell 2015) aiming, among other things, at testing Hoey's theory of lexical priming (2005), which states that words can be textually primed and that an aspect of priming is the position within the text where a word tends to appear. The researchers investigated frequency and usage of lexical-items in text-initial or paragraph-initial position in a corpus of the Guardian Home news section between 1998 and 2004. The corpus was subdivided into sub-corpora on the basis of structural sub-divisions (e.g. a sub-corpus of text-initial sentences, one of non-initial sentences, etc.) and the sub-corpora were compared in order to access positional frequency of lexical items and to analyse words that are primed to appear in text-initial position. The analysis proved strong associations of words and phrases with textual positions and showed recurrent patterns of usage depending on position within a text in accordance with linguistic as well as extra-linguistic claims about the relationship between form and meaning. For example, the function of the *nucleus* (White 1997)/headline lead as the textual 'anchor point' (White 1997: 116) in newspaper discourse: i.e. the gravitational centre towards which subsequent text links back (see O'Donnell *et al.* 2012).

As mentioned earlier, broad studies such as these offer fundamental corpus-derived knowledge about the specificity of the texts under examination, for example, the fact that texts in a newspaper are not homogeneous and neither are different stretches of text within an article. This kind of evidence is relevant to all research done on newspapers, as it provides empirical anchoring for further investigations. For instance, starting from the set of register-defining categories (as identified by Biber *et al.* 1998), Duguid (2010) found a diachronic increment (between 1993 and 2005) in the frequency of lexico-grammatical items that are typical of spoken language, such as intensifiers and markers of vagueness, indicating an informalisation of newspaper discourse and a tendency to adopt common evaluative terms suggesting conversational style. This tendency has been progressing in the course of the eighteenth and nineteenth century and, according to Biber, 'over the past few decades, these changes towards more oral styles in newspaper language have accelerated' (Biber 2003: 170). This change over time is well documented in media studies and is known as "tabloidisation" (see, for example, Connell 1998 or McLachlan and Golding 2000), with reference to the classic distinction in the British press between popular newspapers or tabloids and quality newspapers or broadsheets. The comparison of broadsheet and tabloid corpora has been a fertile ground in stylistic research, see, for example, Takami (2004) on the morphological and semantic analysis "broadsheet adjectives" and "tabloid adjectives", or (Semino) 2006 on metaphorical uses of speech activity expressions. And this is just one example of convergent findings between corpus work (in particular, in the area of corpus stylistics) and non-linguistic approaches and shows how a linguistic analysis of news discourse can yield valuable corroboration as well as insights for a broader understanding of how journalism operates.

4 News content

CADS, as coined by Partington in 2004, and the constellation of variously labelled corpus and discourse approaches (see Marchi and Taylor 2018) interested in investigating language from a social as well as from a structural perspective find a natural habitat in journalistic discourse corpora.

The paper that iconically started CADS is a study of newspaper editorials. Hardt-Mautner (1995) investigates the discourse on the EU in the British press in a corpus of editorials from four British papers dealing with the European Union/Community from 1971 to 1994. The corpus she uses is very small (168,000 words), but each article included in the corpus is not only relevant to the research question but also has a high relevance in terms of journalistic status (since editorials encapsulate the official voice of a newspaper). This ensures homogeneity (comparability across articles) and generalisability (representativeness of the findings with respect to press attitudes at large). One of the aspects she investigates in her work is the representation of participants by comparing across newspapers positioned on the opposite sides of the political spectrum. Presumably aiming at optimal comparability (both for size and typology), she contrasted the views of two tabloids (shorter articles, personalised style and popular audience): the *Sun* (Conservative-leaning) and the *Daily Mirror* (Labour-leaning),and of two broadsheets (longer articles and more information-rich content covering a broader range of topics): the *Telegraph* and the *Guardian*. On top of being one of the earliest attempts to integrate corpus linguistics and corpus discourse analysis (CDA), which served as springboard for subsequent research and for reflection on the methodology, Mautner's paper is also an example of sound and interesting work with small-scale but carefully designed corpora.

Europe-related issues have been a rather popular topic in CADS (see, for example, Bayley and Williams 2012 on media representations of European identity, citizenship and institutions in a 23 million-word corpus of newspapers and broadcast news from four European countries) and recently found renewed interest with Brexit (see, for example, Islentyeva 2021). Lutzky and Kehoe 2019 investigate the discourse of Brexit in a corpus containing every article published on the *Guardian* website since 2000. Bednarek (2006a) examined patterns of evaluation surrounding the European constitution in British broadsheets and tabloids. From this study she constructed a parameter-based theory of evaluation (Bednarek 2006b) and described the composite manifestations of evaluative style in the British press and the pervasiveness of evaluation in news discourse.

Evaluation and evaluative prosody are a major focus and/or a major outcome of much CADS research done on media texts. Discourse studies (corpus-assisted or otherwise) are often concerned with issues of ideology (e.g. Taylor 2008 on metaphors of anti-Americanism in the British, Italian and American press), stereotyping (e.g. Jaworska and Krishnamurty 2012 on the representation of feminism in the British and German press) and the shaping of perceptions and attitudes through language (e.g. Bevitori 2014 on the social construction of "knowing and believing" in editorial opinion discourse about climate change). An influential set of studies on stereotyping and polarisation has been carried out at Lancaster University: Baker and McEnery (2005) looked at the discourses surrounding refugees and asylum seekers in two kinds of texts, newspaper articles and United Nations documents. They created a news corpus containing all articles mentioning the terms *refugee(s)* and/or *asylum seeker(s)* in 2003 and a corpus of the UNHCR documents on refugees for the same year. This piece of work is particularly interesting from a methodological point of view because, rather than comparing the corpora directly (e.g. using keywords analysis), the researchers analysed collocational patterns in the two sets of texts; they identified categories, such as "quantification", "movement", "tragedy", "aid" and "crime"; and they compared findings for the two corpora. This kind of analysis of collocates makes similarity visible as well as difference and allows for a comprehensive view on the representation of identities, which are often complex and intertwined, rather than being realised in clear-cut discourses. This research was followed up and expanded in the project *Discourses of Refugees and Asylum Seekers in the UK Press 1996–2006*, known as RASIM (Baker *et al.* 2008). The researchers compiled a 140-million-word corpus, spanning over a nine-year period, which included a large selection of British broadsheets and tabloids; all articles dealing with refugees, asylum seekers, immigrants and migrants (Gabrielatos 2007) were included in the corpus. RASIM (Gabrielatos and Baker 2008) is a key in modern-diachronic CADS for the richness of its approach, as it employs a variety of ways into the data (combining methods from corpus linguistics and CDA), a range of different perspectives onto the corpus (e.g. looking at diachronic change or stability of representations, at political stance differences and comparing styles between quality and popular newspapers) and a wide spectrum of tools. The researchers look at the distribution of RASIM stories identifying spikes of prominence; they do an extensive collocation analysis of the target terms and group collocates in semantic categories (giving access to discourse prosodies, stereotypes, analysis of metaphors, and so on); and they look at "consistent-collocates" (that is, collocates that remain stable over time) showing how some discourses are progressively confirmed and reinforced. A similar corpus and a similar approach are adopted in Baker *et al.* (2012) (see Further Reading section) to study the representation of Muslims and Islam in the British press between 1999 and 2005.

Another key set of studies in diachronic corpus-assisted analysis of newspapers (Partington *et al.* 2013) is the work done on the SiBol corpora (presented earlier in this chapter). Rather than tracking the evolution of discourses over a continuous period of time, with SiBol, researchers can compare corpora from different points in time in order to identify change or stability. Since the SiBol corpora contain the whole output of the newspapers for the years under investigation, a wide range of different topics can be researched. Additionally, since the particular newspapers were the left-leaning *Guardian*, the right-leaning *Telegraph* and the centrist *Times*, socio-political, issues can be viewed and contrasted from different perspectives. For example, Partington (2012) examined changing patterns in the discourses relating to antisemitism from 1993 to 2009. Partington (2010) identified which social concerns were labelled "moral panics" by the left and by the right in 1993 and then in 2005 to see which ones remained and which appeared and disappeared (see also the Further Reading section).

Mutation over time is a fundamental aspect of research on newspaper discourse. Another core aspect, which, however, has remained somewhat underexplored until recently is the imprint of journalistic practices on news discourse. As Cameron says:

> If we are interested in the way language is used in media texts, it is useful to bring our analysis to bear not only on the texts themselves, but also on the rules journalists, broadcasters and their editors follow in the production of those texts; and where possible, on the institutional processes whereby those rules are promulgated, amended and enforced.
>
> *(Cameron 1996: 332)*

One way to do this is to investigate self-reflexive language in the media. Spiros and Spitzmüller (2010), for example, analyse how *media language* is discussed in a corpus of Greek and German newspapers, focussing on the period from the mid-1990s to the early 2000s. Despite the small scale of the analysis (based on only 80 texts for each language, selected individually on the basis of relevance to the topic) and the consequent lack of a quantitative grasp, this study represents a rare example of analysis of metalanguage in journalistic texts. Journalistic self-reflexivity is at the core of my own work (see Marchi 2019 in the Further Reading section). The intersection between the study of journalistic products and journalistic practices is the new frontier of CADS research. Because of its intrinsic interdisciplinary vocation and "serendipitous" nature (Partington 2009: 286), CADS should foster an holistic approach that takes into account the complex interaction between production, message and reception. A recent corpus-based attempt to assess reception is Kehoe and Gee's (2019) analysis of the comment section on the *Guardian* website; their take is, howeve,r solely textual. Wright *et al.* (2020) look at the interaction between readers and producers combining a quantitative content analysis of comments with in-depth interviews with practitioners, but their study entirely disregards language. Most corpus work to date remains grounded on the message part and the discursive level. The most influential and innovative example of discursive approach to the analysis of production to date is Bednarek and Caple's (2017) discursive news values analysis (see Further Reading section). The authors analyse how the newsworthiness of events is mediated through language and image and how newsworthiness values are constructed discursively through the repetition of patterns, both verbal and visual. This brings us to the limitations and perspectives of corpus-assisted research on newspaper corpora.

5 Limitations and perspectives

I reserved a large portion of this short chapter to corpus compilation because we tend to think that our research begins once we have data, whereas it starts well before then. I believe it is important to emphasise this to make a more general point, that is, that we need to pay more attention to what is often overlooked, if not in the research process itself, then in its account: the "blind spots" and the "dusty corners" (see Marchi and Taylor 2018).

There are things we may miss when studying journalistic discourse using corpora (or, rather, using just corpora), and greater awareness about these limitations will help in overcoming them. When utilising large corpora, for example, we may fail to consider the diversity of text types a newspaper contains, as well as other textual aspects which would be available to a finer-grained investigation, such as intertextuality or attribution and averral. This kind of drawback is relatively easily solved; in fact corpus-assisted approaches encourage a constant shunting between the "big picture" and close reading. However a 'corpus can only reveal its own contents' (Baker 2006: 181), and text corpora solely contain text (and sometimes annotation for para-textual features). Because of the rapid evolution beyond the printed paper, the growing importance of multimodal texts and the overall impact of digital technologies on the news media industry, a mono-semiotic and mono-source analysis is reductive (i.e. limited) and forcedly reductionist (i.e. unduly oversimplified). We need a more comprehensive approach, one that takes into account multiple signs, but also one that goes beyond the message and takes into account aspects of production and reception. We need a holistic approach which is 'practice oriented' (Richardson 2008: 153) and contextualised. The linguistic analysis should be informed by extra-linguistic elements, incorporate an investigation of the broader context and, ideally, embed an interdisciplinary approach. Luckily an 'intrinsic interdisciplinary vocation' (Marchi *et al.* 2017: 174) and its 'omnivorous interests' (*ibid.*) are CADS's strong suits, and therefore we are well equipped to work in this direction.

The chapter you just read comes with its own baggage of flaws, perhaps the most obvious is that the work presented, as well as the considerations made about journalism, are self-evidently Anglo-centric. This is in part due to space constraints, but it is also a warning on the need to be aware of, and reflect on, our partial perspectives and our individual primings.

For further reading I chose three monographs, a collection of edited articles and a recent journal article, which, in my opinion, combine methodological soundness and innovation. All choices also share the characteristic of being at the same time inward looking (i.e. they encourage awareness of and reflection on the impact of research practices) and outward looking (i.e. they encourage attention towards the extra-linguistic context and journalistic practices).

Further reading

Baker, P., Gabrielatos, C. and McEnery, T. (2012) *Discourse Analysis and Media Attitudes: The British Press on Islam*, Cambridge: Cambridge University Press. (This book is a fundamental reference for diachronic corpus analysis and an achievement in terms of social relevance of the research and of its impact beyond linguistics and beyond academia. It tackles questions about the British media and society, looking at the representations of Islam and Muslims in the press and revealing how prejudice is discursively mediated.)

Bednarek, M. and Caple, H. (2017) *The Discourse of News Values. How Organizations Create Newsworthiness*, Oxford: Oxford University Press. (This volume overcomes many of the limitations associated with corpus approaches to discourse, as well as to text-only approaches in general. The authors propose a multisemiotic approach to the study of media discourse and show how the newsworthiness of events is constructed discursively through words and images.)

Hansen, K. R. (2016) 'News from the Future: A Corpus Linguistic Analysis of Future-Oriented, Unreal and Counterfactual News Discourse', *Discourse & Communication*, 10(2): 115–36. (This study is 'a grammatically founded approach to future-oriented journalism' [p. 116], i.e. of journalism reporting on planned events and discussing consequences, expectations and agendas. By analysing patterns of use of modal verbs, verb tenses and speech acts, this longitudinal study of four Danish newspapers describes the shift towards a less event-centred and more analytical kind of journalism.)

Marchi, A. (2019) *Self-Reflexive Journalism. A Corpus Study of Journalistic Culture and Community in the Guardian*, London: Routledge. (This is a book-length study of how journalists define the boundaries of their community and set the standards of good vs. bad journalism in constructing and negotiating representations of their profession. The study has a strong methodological focus, employing and encouraging eclecticism and flexibility in the use of tools and constant scrutiny of the impact of research practices.)

Partington, A. (2010) Special Issue on *'Modern Diachronic Corpus-Assisted Discourse Studies'*, Corpora 5(2), Edinburgh, Edinburgh University Press. (Another fundamental reference for diachronic analysis of newspaper corpora. The six articles in this edited collection cover different types of corpus analysis as well as a broad range of topics, using the same dataset: the *SiBol* corpora.)

References

Baker, P. (2006) *Using Corpora in Discourse Analysis*, London and New York: Continuum.

Baker, P. and McEnery, T. (2005) 'A Corpus-Based Approach to Discourses of Refugees and Asylum Seekers in UN and Newspaper Texts', *Journal of Language and Politics* 4(2): 197–226.

Baker, P., Gabrielatos, C., Khosravinik, M., Krzyzanowski, M., McEnery, T. and Wodak, R. (2008) 'A Useful Methodological Synergy? Combining Critical Discourse Analysis and Corpus Linguistics to Examine Discourses of Refugees and Asylum Seekers in the UK Press', *Discourse & Society* 19(3): 273–305.

Baker, P., Gabrielatos, C. and McEnery, T. (2012) *Discourse Analysis and Media Attitudes: The British Press on Islam*, Cambridge: Cambridge University Press.

Baroni, M. and Ueyama, M. (2006) 'Building General- and Special-Purpose Corpora by Web Crawling', *Proceedings of the 13th NIJL International Symposium*, 31–40.

Bayley, P. and Williams, G. (eds) (2012) *European Identity: What the Media Say*, Oxford: Oxford University Press.

Bednarek, M. (2006a) 'Evaluating Europe – Parameters of Evaluation in the British Press', in C. Leung and J. Jenkins (eds) *Reconfiguring Europe – the Contribution of Applied Linguistics (British Studies in Applied Linguistics 20)*, London: BAAL/Equinox, pp. 137–56.

Bednarek, M. (2006b) *Evaluation in Media Discourse*, London: Continuum.

Bednarek, M. and Caple, H. (2012) *News Discourse*, London: Continuum.

Bednarek, M. and Caple, H. (2017) *The Discourse of News Values. How Organizations Create Newsworthiness*, Oxford: Oxford University Press.

Bevitori, C. (2014) 'Values, Assumptions and Beliefs in British Newspaper Editorial Coverage of Climate Change', in C. Hart and P. Cap (eds) *Contemporary Critical Discourse Studies*, London: Bloomsbury Academic, pp. 603–25.

Biber, D. (1988) *Variation across Speech and Writing*, Cambridge: Cambridge University Press.

Biber, D. (2003) 'Compressed Noun Phrase Structures in Newspaper Discourse: The Competing Demands of Popularization Vs. Economy', in J. Atchison and D. Lewis (eds) *New Media Language*, London and New York: Routledge, pp. 169–81.

Biber, D., Conrad, S. and Reppen, R. (1998) *Corpus Linguistics. Investigating Language Structure and Use*, Cambridge: Cambridge University Press.

Cameron, D. (1996) 'Style Policy and Style Politics: A Neglected Aspect of Language of the News', *Media Culture Society* 18: 315–33.

Cirillo, L. Marchi, A. and Venuti, M. (2009) 'The Making of the Cordis Corpus. Compilation and in J. Morley and P. Bayley (eds) *Corpus-Assisted Discourse Studies on the Iraq Conflict: Wording the War*, London: Routledge, pp. 13–33.

Connell, I. (1998) 'Mistaken Identities: Tabloid and Broadsheet News Discourse', *The Public* 5(3): 11–31.

Dickinson, R. (2008) 'Studying the Sociology of Journalists: The Journalistic Field and the News World', *Sociology Compass* 2: 1–17.

Duguid, A. (2010) 'Newspaper Discourse Informalisation: A Diachronic Comparison from Keywords', *Corpora* 5(2): 109–38.

Egbert, J. and Schnur, E. (2018) 'The Role of the Text in Corpus and Discourse Analysis: Missing the Trees for the Forest', in C. Taylor and A. Marchi (eds) *Corpus Approaches to Discourse: A Critical Review*, pp. 159–73.

Gabrielatos, C. (2007) 'SELECTING QUERY TERMS to Build a Specialised Corpus from a Restricted-Access Database', *ICAME Journal* 31: 5–43.

Gabrielatos, C. and Baker, P. (2008) 'Fleeing, Sneaking, Flooding: A Corpus Analysis of Discursive Constructions of Refugees and Asylum Seekers in the UK Press, 1996-2005', *Journal of English Linguistics* 36(1): 5–38.

Hardt-Mautner, G. (1995) 'Only Connect: Critical Discourse Analysis and Corpus Linguistics', UCREL Technical Paper 6, Lancaster: Lancaster University. Available at: http://ucrel.lancs.ac.uk/papers/techpaper/vol6.pdf.

Hoey, M. (2005) *Lexical Priming: A New Theory of Words and Language*, London: Routledge.

Hoey, M. and O'Donnell, M. B. S. (2015) 'Examining Associations between Lexis and Textual Position in Hard News Stories, or According to a Study by…', in N. Groom, M. Charles and J. Suganthi (eds) *Corpora, Grammar and Discourse. In Honour of Susan Hunston*, Amsterdam: John Benjamins, pp. 117–44.

Hundt, M. (2008) 'Text Corpora', in A. Lüdeling and M. Kytö (eds) *Corpus Linguistics: An International Handbook*, vol. I, Berlin: de Gruyter, pp. 168–86.

Islentyeva, A. (2021) *Corpus-Based Analysis of Ideological Bias: Migration in the British Press*, London: Routledge.

Jarvis, J. (2011) 'Digital First: What it Means for Journalism', *The Guardian* 26th June 2011.

Jaworska, S. and Krishnamurty, R. (2012) 'On the F-Word: A Corpus-Based Analysis of the Media Representation of Feminism in British and German Press Discourse, 1990-2009', *Discourse and Society* 23(4): 401–31.

Kehoe, A. and Gee, M. (2019) '"Thanks for the Donds". A Corpus Linguistic Analysis of Topic-Based Communities in the Comment Section of The Guardian', in U. Lutzky and M. Nevala (eds) *Reference and Identity in Public Discourse*, Amsterdam: John Benjamins, pp. 127–58.

Leetaru, K. (2011) *Data Mining Methods for Content Analysis: An Introduction to the Computational Analysis of Content*, London: Routledge.

Lutzky, U. and Kehoe, A. (2019) 'Friends Don't Let Friends Go Brexiting without a Mandate,' in V. Koller, S. Kopf and M. Miglbauer (eds) *Discourses of Brexit*, London: Routledge.

Marchi, A. (2018) 'Dividing up the Data. Epistemological, Methodological and Practical Impact of Diachronic Segmentation', in C. Taylor and A. Marchi (eds) *Corpus Approaches to Discourse: A Critical Review*, London: Routledge, pp. 174–96.

Marchi, A. (2019) *Self-Reflexive Journalism. A Corpus Study of Journalistic Culture and Community in the Guardian*, London: Routledge.

Marchi, A., Lorenzo-Dus, N. and Marsh S. (2017) 'Churchill's Inter-Subjective Special Relationship: A Corpus-Assisted Discourse Approach', in S. Marsh and A. P. Dobson (eds) *Churchill's Special Relationship: Commemorating the 70th anniversary of the Fulton Iron Curtain Speech*, Oxford: Oxford University Press.

Marchi, A. and Taylor, C. (2018) 'Introduction', in C. Taylor and A. Marchi (eds) *Corpus Approaches to Discourse: A Critical Review*, London: Routledge, pp. 1–15.
McEnery, T. and Hardie, A. (2012) *Corpus Linguistics*, Cambridge: Cambridge University Press.
McLachlan, S. and Golding, P. (2000) 'Tabloidization in the British Press: A Quantitative Investigation into Changes in British Newspapers, 1952-1997', in C. Sparks and J. Tulloch (eds) *Tabloid Tales: Global Debates over Media Standards*, Maryland: Rowman & Littlefield Publishers, pp. 75–90.
Meyer, R. (2016) 'How Many Stories Do Newspapers Publish Per Day?', *The Atlantic*, 26th May 2016.
Morley, J. (2004) 'The Sting in the Tail: Persuasion in English Editorial Discourse', in A. Partington, J. Morley and L. Haarman (eds) *Corpora and Discourse*, Bern: Peter Lang, pp. 239–55.
Nartey, M. and Mwinlaaru, I. N. (2019) 'Towards a Decade of Synergising Corpus Linguistics and Critical Discourse Analysis: A Meta-Analysis', *Corpora* 14 (2): 203–35.
O'Donnell, M. B., Scott, M., Mahlberg, M. and Hoey, M. (2012) 'Exploring Text-Initial Words, Clusters and Concgrams in a Newspaper Corpus', *Corpus Linguistics and Linguistic Theory* 8(1): 73–101.
Partington, A. (2004) 'Corpora and Discourse, A Most Congruous Beast', in A. Partington, J. Morley and L. Haarman (eds) *Corpora and Discourse*, Bern: Peter Lang, pp. 11–20.
Partington, A. (2009) 'Evaluating Evaluation and Some Concluding Thoughts on CADS', in J. Morely and P. Bayley (eds) *Corpus-Assisted Discourse Studies on the Iraq Conflict*, London: Routledge, pp. 261–303.
Partington, A. (ed.) (2010) *Corpora Special Issue. Modern Diachronic Corpus-Assisted Studies*, Edinburgh: Edinburgh University Press.
Partington, A. (2012) 'The Changing Discourses on Antisemitism in the UK Press from 1993 to 2009: A Modern-Diachronic Corpus-Assisted Discourse Study', *Journal of Language and Politics* 11(1): 51–76.
Partington, A., Duguid, A. and Taylor, C. (2013) *Patterns and Meanings in Discourse: Theory and Practice in Corpus-Assisted Discourse Studies (CADS)*, Amsterdam: John Benjamins
Richardson, J. E. (2008) 'Language and Journalism. An Expanding Research Agenda', *Journalism Studies* 9(2): 152–60.
Semino, E. (2006) 'A Corpus-Based Study of Metaphors for Speech Activity in British English', in A. Stefanowitsch and St. Th. Gries (eds) *Corpus-Based Approaches to Metaphor and Metonymy*, Berlin: Mouton de Gruyter, pp. 36–62.
Semino, E. and Short, M. (2004) *Corpus Stylistics: Speech, Writing and Thought Presentation in a Corpus of English Writing*, London: Routledge.
Spiros, M. and Spitzmüller, J. (2010) 'Metalinguistic Discourse in and about the Media: Some Recent Trends in Greek and German Prescriptivism', in S. Johnson and T. M. Milani (eds) *Language Ideologies and Media Discourse: Texts, Practices, Politics*, London: Continuum, pp. 17–40.
Studer, P. (2008) *Historical Corpus Stylistics: Media, Technology and Change*, London: Continuum.
Takami, S. (2004) 'A Corpus-Driven Identification of Distinctive Words: "Tabloid Adjectives" and "Broadsheet Adjectives" in the Bank of English', in N. Inoue and T. Tabata (eds) *English Corpora under Japanese Eyes*, Amsterdam: Rodopi, pp. 93–113.
Taylor, C. (2008) 'Metaphors of Anti-Americanism in a Corpus of UK, US and Italian Newspapers', *ESP Across Cultures* 5: 137–52.
White, P. (1997) 'Death, Disruption and the Moral Order: The Narrative Impulse in Mass-Media "Hard News" Reporting,' in F. Christie and J. R. Martin (eds) *Genre and institutions. Social processes in the workplace and school*, London: Continuum, pp. 101–33.
Wright, S., Jackson, D. and Graham, T. (2020) 'When Journalists Go "Below the Line": Comment Spaces at The Guardian (2006-2017)', *Journalism Studies* 21(1): 107–26.

41

How to use corpus linguistics in forensic linguistics

Mathew Gillings

1 Forensic linguistics and the role of corpora

The fields of corpus linguistics and forensic linguistics have both come a long way since Malcolm Coulthard wrote in 1994 that the former was 'a major new resource for the forensic linguist' (Coulthard 1994: 27). Whilst Coulthard had the foresight to predict, quite accurately, that 'any improved methodology must depend, to a large extent, on the setting up and analysing of corpora' (1994: 40), it would have been difficult to predict the wide range of applications that corpus linguistics has had, both as a research area and as a practice-based endeavour. Since then, various linguistic frameworks and subdisciplines have been applied to, and shown an interest in, this application to the forensic setting. Researchers in pragmatics, critical discourse analysis, phonetics and stylistics have all contributed to the field of forensic linguistics, applying different forms of language analysis in unique ways.

But what is *forensic linguistics* exactly, and how can corpus analysis be useful? According to Johnson and Coulthard (2010: 7), the field of forensic linguistics can be split three ways:

1. The study of the written language of the law;
2. The study of interaction in the legal process, which in criminal cases includes everything from an initial call to the emergency services to the sentencing of someone who has been found guilty;
3. The description of the work of the forensic linguist when acting as an expert witness.

(Johnson and Coulthard 2010: 7)

Forensic linguistics is not restricted to any specific case, law or situation, but instead covers the interaction between language (both spoken and written), the law and the criminal justice system at large. Corpus linguistics, then, is a useful tool to interrogate that language use in context, using the techniques discussed in this handbook. By 2010, in the first edition of *The Routledge Handbook of Corpus Linguistics,* Janet Cotterill suggested that 'the use of corpora in many types of

DOI: 10.4324/9780367076399-41

forensic linguistic analysis is becoming increasingly commonplace' (Cotterill 2010: 578), identifying authorship attribution research in particular as one such area where corpus linguistics has the potential to offer a contribution. Whilst this chapter does not aim to provide a complete review of corpus-based forensic linguistic research (see Nini 2020 for an overview, and Larner 2015 for an annotated bibliography), it does aim to provide a guide to how corpus-based methods can be applied to a range of forensic settings – in both traditional, well-researched areas and emerging areas. It will offer a flavour of the types of analysis that both have been, and could be, achieved through combining corpus methods and forensic linguistics across both real-life casework and academic research. Whilst the application of corpus methods to authorship attribution in present-day scholarship is discussed (as Cotterill 2010 predicted), that is just one of many applications of the method. What we will find, therefore, is that rather than the use of corpora *becoming* increasingly commonplace, it *is* now commonplace.

The types of texts that might comprise a corpus within forensic linguistic casework or research can vary substantially, and it wholly depends on the individual case, availability of data and aims. Traditional avenues of enquiry, for example, include texts such as ransom demands, suicide notes, threats, courtroom transcripts and telephone conversations. However, as the field of forensic linguistics has grown, and as new methods of text production have been developed (namely via electronic means), researchers may now find themselves analysing SMS messages, instant messages (e.g. *WhatsApp* or *Facebook* conversations), tweets, social media status updates, (phishing) emails, forum posts or chat room logs. Some texts, such as those produced and disseminated by bots, may not have even been directly constructed by a human, adding an additional layer of enquiry to those working in this area.

The arsenal of methods available to the corpus linguist in order to interrogate those text types has been discussed at length within the corpus linguistic literature (see for example, Chapters 9, 10 and 18, this volume). In light of this, rather than this chapter being organised or led by technique, it has been divided into a series of discussions about how different types of corpora might be used to tackle a series of forensic issues. Within those discussions, the corpus-based methods we are now familiar with (frequency information, concordances, collocation and keyword analysis) are demonstrated through various case studies and examples.

One of the main benefits of corpus linguistics is that it combines both quantitative and qualitative analysis. Such an approach not only allows the researcher to take different theoretical points of view into account, but it also allows them to take both a coarse-grained and fine-grained view of a dataset, beginning with frequency information, before diving into the data to take a closer look at language use within context. This approach is even more useful for a *forensic* linguist, given the importance of the *Daubert* Standard which sets out criteria that must be met for expert testimony to be admissible in a US court. In *Daubert v. Dow Merrill Pharmaceuticals, Inc.* (509 U.S. 579 [1993]), the Supreme Court of the United States emphasised that 'federal judges must act as "gatekeepers" to ensure that expert testimony is allowed only when it is sufficiently grounded in valid and reliable scientific techniques' (Solan and Tiersma 2004: 451). To determine whether expert testimony is 'grounded in reliable scientific techniques,' the Court provided the following factors for judges to consider, before deeming it admissible:

1. Whether the theory offered has been tested;
2. Whether it has been subjected to peer review and publication;
3. The known rate of error;
4. Whether the theory is generally accepted in the scientific community.

(Solan and Tiersma 2004: 451)

It is clear to see here why Solan and Tiersma 'believe that expert testimony based on a corpus approach would be admissible in the USA' (2004: 462). Whilst the method may not meet all of the criteria, all of the time (especially criterion 3, although see both Johnson and Wright (2014) and Wright (2017) for work on this matter), it is 'almost certainly the best placed of all of the tools at the disposal of the forensic linguist to enable linguistic evidence to be admitted in court' (Cotterill 2010: 588). To name but one example, statistical significance measures are readily available to corpus linguists to substantiate their findings, whilst other subfields may struggle to stake a similar claim. This combination of quantitative and qualitative approaches was effective in Grant's (2013) work on the high-profile *Amanda Birks* case. Thus, applied to the British context, Grant writes:

> [...] admissibility [of evidence] is subject to review by the UK Law Commission. On the basis of the published Law Commission report, it seems that the UK courts are likely to require a showing of the scientific validity of techniques not dissimilar to the *Daubert* criteria currently applicable in the United States federal courts. Although scientific validity and reliability do not require quantification, and quantification is by no means sufficient to demonstrate appropriate scientific status, there appears to be a presupposition in some literature that an appropriate quantified method can make it easier to demonstrate that a method is both reliable and valid.
>
> *(Grant 2013: 469–70)*

As such, taking into account these views across US and UK contexts, corpus linguistics is perhaps one of the few methods with which forensic linguistic analysis can be admissible in court.

2 Using specialised corpora for authorship attribution

Broadly speaking, authorship attribution refers to the process whereby linguists attempt, as far as possible, to identify the author(s) of an anonymous or queried/questioned text. Given the range of different forensic situations in which a text may come to have a disputed authorship, there are a range of text types which may be under investigation. This could include a note left behind at the scene of a crime, a ransom demand, a potential terrorist manifesto or even a student essay under investigation for plagiarism. It could also include investigations that are non-forensic in nature, often concerning texts that are better known and highly popularised. For example, scholars (e.g., Hope 1994) have attempted to determine the extent to which Shakespeare collaborated with other playwrights, which scenes could be wholly or partially attributed to others and which plays may (or should) be included in the canon. Regardless of whether they are analysed for forensic or non-forensic purposes, these texts all have one thing in common: within the context of a corpus-based analysis, they would be considered *specialised corpora* in that they have been designed either for a particular project or to study a particular genre (Baker *et al.* 2006: 147).

Whilst the corpora used for an authorship analysis are indeed considered specialised, they are rarely *designed* as such. O'Keeffe *et al.* point out that 'any old collection of texts does not make a corpus' (2007: 1), but this is, unfortunately, often what is provided by the police to forensic linguists involved in casework. As Cotterill notes, the police are 'unaware of genre/register differences, variations in text size and temporal factors, all of which may influence the potential of texts to be analysed' (2010: 578). In most cases, corpora used for this type of analysis can only be as large as the amount of data that is available to the forensic linguist working on the case. For comparison, the Unabomber manifesto comes in at just under 35,000 words, whereas a ransom demand could be less than 100 words in length. These are all considered specialised corpora but weigh in at drastically different sizes. What is perhaps more important, then, is the affordances of these smaller datasets. Koester argues that 'they allow a much closer link between the corpus and the contexts in which the texts in the corpus were produced', and given that the 'corpus compiler is often also the analyst, [they] therefore usually [have] a high degree of familiarity with the context' (Koester 2010: 67). Where authorship attribution analyses are usually part of much larger cases, this familiarity is therefore highly useful.

Authorship attribution aims to answer one main question: *Did the person who wrote Text A also write Text B?* Of course, there are variations on that question, depending on the number of texts under analysis, and depending on which of those texts are known, disputed or anonymous. However, the general premise remains the same in that we are attempting to determine the similarity between texts. Naturally, as with most work carried out by corpus linguists and forensic linguists alike, it is difficult to claim anything with 100% certainty. Even a perfect matching of styles between texts may fall apart if more data come to light and speak to the contrary. Corpus linguistics offers a way to measure that certainty and similarity through various statistical measures, which is why the two fields come together so well for this type of casework. However, the fundamental basis is thus: linguists can only give their opinion – their *expert* opinion – on a particular case, backed up by whatever evidence they have available to them.

Historically, authorship attribution has been carried out without the aid of any corpus-based analysis, coming under the umbrella term of *stylometry*. Stylometry is defined as 'the analysis of style features that can be statistically quantified, such as sentence length, vocabulary density, and frequencies of words [or] word forms' (Gómez-Adorno *et al.* 2018: 50). Whilst there is not the space within this chapter to offer a complete overview of different style features that may be measured to determine authorship, Grieve (2007) evaluates a series of techniques, by using the same dataset, to determine which are the best indicators of authorship.

However, Coulthard *et al.* argue that these kinds of 'purely stylometric techniques are rarely applied in forensic casework' (2017: 154), often due to a lack of data making it difficult to 'use solely quantitative techniques' (2017: 160–1). Instead, a stylistic approach seems to be favoured. The *forensic stylistic* approach, pioneered by McMenamin (1993), starts with the premise that all speakers have an idiolect, and pinpointing style markers – linguistic features that appear to be distinctive to that speaker – may help the forensic linguist in determining authorship of a disputed text. When these style markers are identified and combined, they become representative of a speaker's idiolect, allowing comparisons to be made with other (disputed) texts. This *forensic stylistic* approach focuses on the *choices* that speakers make: for example, the analyst may note that a speaker tends to overuse one specific idiom more than any other, signs off their emails in a very specific way, or consistently misspells a particular word. These style markers are helpful because they are both *consistent* and *distinct*, with Grant (2013) distinguishing between *population-level distinctiveness* and *pairwise distinctiveness*. The former refers to 'stylometric markers of authorship' which requires 'there be significant differences in the occurrence of the marker between authors, regardless of other textual variables such as topic, register, or genre' (Grant 2013: 470–1). The latter refers to distinctiveness 'between potential authors, thus avoiding some of the population sampling issues which otherwise arise' (472–3). The former is, naturally, difficult to test. When these style markers are taken in combination with each other, they may help to provide further insight into the authorship attribution process.

Both methods – traditional quantitative stylometric techniques and the forensic stylistic approach – garner mixed responses from forensic linguists. Coulthard *et al.* (2017) note that whilst the statistical stylometric techniques are often difficult to use on such small datasets, they are considered by some forensic linguists to be more reliable and more useful within the courtroom, especially within the context of the *Daubert* standard as discussed earlier. Likewise, they also note that whilst the identification of style markers seems to be successful for authorship attribution, the method is often 'criticised for being too subjective, relying heavily on the intuition of the expert witness' (Coulthard *et al.* 2017: 160). It seems that a combination of the two methods may be beneficial, and corpus-based methods may have a large part to play within the further development of authorship attribution as a field.

Johnson and Wright's (2014) approach to identifying idiolect in forensic authorship attribution using n-grams is one way in which this combination of methods has been achieved. N-grams in linguistics, broadly speaking, refer to 'sequences of *n* elements (usually words) that occur directly one after another in a corpus, where *n* is two or more' (McEnery and Hardie 2012: 247). Depending on the discipline or theoretical approach, n-grams are also referred to as *clusters* or *lexical bundles* (see Chapters 10 and 15, this volume). However, the definition remains the same in that they are a way to 'operationalise the analysis of *collocation*'. (McEnery and Hardie 2012: 247). Using the *Enron Email Corpus* (a dataset consisting of 63,000 emails written by 176 employees of the now-disbanded Enron Corporation) as the basis for the experimental study, Johnson and Wright (2014) compared n-gram usage across a set of disputed and known emails in an attempt to determine whether authorship attribution was possible through this method. This was carried out using a procedure known as Jaccard's coefficient, which is a 'binary correlation analysis in that it hinges on the appearance or non-appearance of a particular word *n*-gram in the two samples compared, rather than how frequently this feature appears' (Johnson and Wright 2014: 45). The authors demonstrated that it was possible to identify idiolectal variation within the corpus. To give but one example, the analysis found that one employee in the dataset consistently used highly distinctive *please*-initial word strings that other employees did not use. These word strings, identified through quantitative means, therefore became style markers for the purposes of authorship attribution. Johnson and Wright conclude by suggesting that 'if sufficiently distinctive, these textbites are able to identify authors by reducing a mass of data to key segments that move us closer to the elusive concept of idiolect' (2014: 37).

Johnson and Wright's (2014) work therefore follows in the footsteps of other pioneering work (e.g. Coulthard 2000) which has combined both quantitative and qualitative analysis in authorship attribution. It uses quantitative and statistical methods to identify style markers and then uses that information in a judgement of authorship.

3 Using reference corpora to aid forensic linguistic analyses

In contrast to the use of *specialised* corpora, explored earlier within the context of authorship attribution studies, researchers also use *reference* corpora within forensic linguistic analyses. The term *reference corpus* is primarily used to describe any corpus that 'is not a sample of any particular language variety, domain or text type, but is instead an attempt to represent the general nature of the language through a wide-sampling corpus design' (Baker *et al.* 2006: 138) (see also Chapter 39, this volume). A reference corpus is therefore highly useful if the forensic linguist is called to advise on how natural language works within context. This could include, for example, questions of how specific words or phrases are used by different speakers or within different texts, how those words function in context, and what kinds of meaning they take on within those contexts.

The term *design* in Baker *et al.*'s (2006) definition is key here, as reference corpora, which attempt to represent a whole language, tend to be constructed according to a carefully thought-out process to ensure representativeness and balance (although achieving this is, in practice, often difficult). Whilst the design of a reference corpus changes depending on its intended use, decisions must be made, for example, with regard to 'type, content, structure, and size' (Baker *et al.* 2006: 55). These decisions all help to ensure that the corpus fulfils its purpose, allowing the analyst to answer the types of questions set out earlier with confidence.

Luckily, a number of reference corpora are already available to the forensic linguist, depending on individual research aims and interests. The *Spoken British National Corpus 2014* (hereafter *Spoken BNC2014*), for example, is a 11.5-million-word corpus containing samples of real-life, informal, spoken interactions between L1 speakers of British English from across the United Kingdom (Love *et al.* 2017). Its predecessor, the spoken component of the *British National Corpus* 1994 (BNC1994), has been widely regarded as the 'go-to dataset' (Love *et al.* 2017: 321) for spoken British English, and so this updated corpus aims to provide a more accurate snapshot of present-day language usage. One of the most useful affordances of the Spoken BNC2014 is not only its size but also the large amount of metadata that has been encoded within it. Using the CQPweb interface (Hardie 2012), users are able to restrict query searches according to speakers' age, gender, dialect, social status and highest qualification, amongst several other text-level restrictions such as the year of recording and the number of speakers in the interaction. To a forensic linguist, this level of detail is highly useful.

A second frequently used corpus is the *Corpus of Contemporary American English (COCA)* which contains more than 1 billion words in total (Davies 2008). It contains texts from across eight genres and is accessible via the *english-corpora.org* interface. Like the functions of CQPweb explored earlier, this interface allows the user to look at the distribution of search terms across genres, view suggested synonyms and view word clusters. Due to the size and text variation within the corpus, COCA is considered a representative sample of contemporary American English.

Determining meaning

One type of forensic linguistic casework for which reference corpora are particularly useful is for the determination of meaning. The following analysis, which demonstrates this, was carried out by Cunningham and Egbert (2020) in relation to a real court case. The case in question is CREW v. Trump (276F. Supp. 3d 174 (S.D.N.Y 2017)), one that was ongoing whilst Donald Trump remained president of the United States, but was later dismissed in January 2021 after Joe Biden succeeded to the presidency. In it, the plaintiffs alleged that whilst in office, Donald Trump, was in violation of the Foreign Emoluments Clause, a provision in the US Constitution which bars a 'public official from accepting "any present, Emolument, Office, or Title, of any kind whatever, from any King, Prince, or foreign state"' (Blake, 2019). The plaintiffs argued that because Trump-owned buildings and hotels received rent, room rentals and other associated fees from foreign governments, this is therefore in contravention of the aforementioned clause. However, there is disagreement as to exactly what the word *emolument* means and the extent to which the *meaning* of the word extends to all Trump-owned businesses, or only his work in an official capacity as the sitting president. The term is generally not in use today, and the clause has only rarely been tested in courts (Blake 2019).

Trump's legal team, in defence, cite definitions in some eighteenth-century dictionaries, written around the period in which the US Constitution was written. They argue that *emolument* has a narrow definition, suggesting it is a type of profit 'arising from an office or employ – i.e. something leveraged by a position of power'; this, therefore, would not include payments to his businesses (Blake 2019). However, an amicus brief submitted to the Fourth Circuit appeal, by Clark D. Cunningham and Jesse Egbert, uses corpus-based methods to investigate what the original meaning of *emolument* was in the US Constitution.

Cunningham and Egbert (2020) achieved this by consulting a reference corpus – the *Corpus of Founding Era American English (COFEA)* – which contains 'in digital form over 126,000 texts created between 1760 and 1799, totalling more than 136,800,000 words' (Cunningham and Egbert 2020: 474). According to the BYU Law interface (where the corpus can be accessed: https://lawcorpus.byu.edu/), it contains documents from 'the ordinary people of the day, the Founders, and legal sources, including letters, diaries, newspapers, non-fiction-books', suggesting it is a suitable dataset to be used as a reference corpus. Within this corpus, Cunningham and Egbert (2020) found over 2,800 examples of the word *emolument*. By investigating the types of words and grammatical features that occur alongside the word (collocation analysis) before investigating how the word acts within context (concordance analysis), Cunningham and Egbert (2020) identify, amongst others, the three key findings:

1. *Emolument* often appeared within a list of nouns, and it was often the last noun in that list, indicating it was being used as a "catch-all" term;
2. *Pay* was a kind of emolument, and there were other kinds of emolument than just *pay*;
3. The word *official* (in contrast to the word *personal*) was a frequent collocate of *emolument*, which would be inappropriate if that were its prototypical meaning.

These findings led Cunningham and Egbert to conclude that 'the research findings discussed above do provide evidence that Founding Era Americans could have used *emolument* to describe revenue derived from ownership of a hotel' (2020: 486) and 'using the word in such a way would have been consistent with what has been shown to be the broad meaning and wide usage of [the word]' (2020: 486). Tellingly, the authors identify 'actual examples where *emolument* was specifically used to refer to revenue from ownership interest in a business' (Cunningham and Egbert 2020: 486).

Cunningham and Egbert's (2020) analysis therefore highlights both the utility and usefulness of corpus-based methods within forensic linguistic casework. The data available to them (in the form of COFEA), combined with corpus-based methods (beginning with simple frequency counts and then progressing to both collocation and concordance analysis), means that they were able to build up a strong case arguing for how a specific word would have been interpreted – both by those writing the US Constitution in the eighteenth century and their contemporaries. At the time of writing, *CREW v. Trump* is one of three ongoing lawsuits alleging Donald Trump's violations of the *Foreign Emoluments Clause*. Other noteworthy examples of where corpus-based methods have been employed to help interpret these kinds of statutory texts include Solan and Gales (2016) and Strang (2017).

4 Other key applications of corpus-based methods to forensic issues

A large portion of this chapter thus far has been dedicated to discussing how corpus methods may be useful to inform forensic linguistic casework, but it is important to remember that this is only part of the picture. There is a large body of *academic* work taking place too, which may not be directly related to any kind of ongoing case, but still fits Johnson and Coulthard's (2010) tripartite definition of *forensic linguistics*. Whilst this work may not be presented in the courtroom as expert testimony, it often has highly important implications and applications outside of academia. Forensic linguists, for example, frequently collaborate with other agencies and organisations, therefore combining expertise and having real-world impact. This section aims to highlight some of those other avenues of research which combine corpus linguistics and forensic linguistics.

Courtroom and legal discourse

A large proportion of research within forensic linguistics which has utilised corpus-based methods is the analysis of courtroom discourse. This involves linguistic analysis of verbal and written proceedings within a courtroom, often between different parties and organisations. Acquiring courtroom transcripts can often be expensive and/or time-consuming, given that there are restrictions on where recordings and transcripts can take place. However, Heffer (2005) notes that this can also be construed as a benefit to the researcher due to the fact that there are only two available sources to gather this data: 'the researcher's presence in the public gallery and transcripts made from the official court reporter's recording' (Heffer 2005: 53). These court recordings only tend to be transcribed by an approved transcription service when they are required or requested, but the benefit is that they are transcribed "verbatim" (i.e. word for word), which is highly useful for a linguist interested in naturally occurring language, as they provide a real insight into how language is used in this highly specialised setting. With that said, ironically, Heffer notes that these verbatim transcripts can often undergo a form of 'narrative smoothing, in which the intricacy or noisiness of the spoken language has been smoothed out into the clear and coherent calm of the written text' (2005: 54).

To briefly highlight some work in this area, Heffer's (2005) book provides a comprehensive insight into courtroom discourse using corpus-based methods. It includes analyses of opening and closing remarks, various examinations, summing-up speeches, sentencing and counsel–witness interactions. Also contributing to this topic is Cotterill (2003), who investigates the interaction between language and power in the courtroom (exemplified in the trial of O. J. Simpson); Cotterill, who uses collocation analysis to investigate the role of lexis in creating 'nuances of meaning for the jury' (Cotterill 2004: 513); and Cavalieri (2009), who investigates the use of metadiscourse, repetition, and reformulation within witness cross-examinations. There is also work that utilises historical data, investigating the use of question-and-answer interactions between participants (Archer 2005). It is clear, then, that the corpus linguistic toolkit provides an excellent means to investigate not only courtroom discourse in general but a whole range of linguistic phenomena working across several levels too – lexis, semantics and pragmatics.

Deception detection

Deception detection is another area that has received considerable attention within the academic literature, with its results going on to inform police work at airport security scans and police interrogations. The field of deception detection has been steadily growing amongst psychology researchers for decades, and it primarily relies on identifying linguistic features that occur more frequently in speakers' deceptive language over their truthful language. For example, there is now a relatively well-supported body of evidence suggesting that deceptive statements tend to feature a higher occurrence of second-person pronoun *you,* more temporal words (e.g. *minutes, days*) and more instances of the word *just,* often being used as a stalling technique or form of hedge (McQuaid *et al.* 2015; Gillings 2020). Fitzpatrick and Bachenko (2010) first introduced corpus linguists to this field, with their chapter exploring the usefulness of a forensic corpus to test indicators of deception providing an insight into what may be possible. Some years later, Archer and Lansley (2015), along with McQuaid *et al.* (2015), further developed the field by using *Wmatrix* (Rayson 2008) to see how particular semantic tags differed across a dataset of genuine and deceptive pleaders (for the return of missing people) in televised press conferences. Work by Larner (2019) went on to investigate whether formulaic sequences have a part to play in the difference between truthful and deceptive language and, more recently, Gillings (2021) investigated those indicators of deception both within context (using collocation and concordance analysis) and across different sociolinguistic groups. This latter work not only warns against treating indicators of deception as a finite set of linguistic features that remains constant across all groups, it also emphasises the need to investigate them within the contexts in which they occur (Gillings 2021). Naturally, corpus-based methods provide a good way for this to be investigated further.

Disinformation

Whilst corpus-based research into courtroom discourse and deception detection has been around for a number of years, the field of *disinformation* research is a more recent example of how corpus methods can be useful to emerging areas of scholarship. Disinformation itself is by no means a new concept (there is evidence that the term "false news" dates back to 1534 (Dance 2019)), but it has recently gained considerable attention within academia as a result of ex-President Trump's use of the term "fake news" throughout his presidential bid and subsequent election. Dance (2019) explores how and why people share disinformation on social media by comparing a corpus of tweets which share some form of disinformation to a corpus of tweets made up simply of shared news links (i.e. disinformation vs. non-disinformation). Utilising *Wmatrix* (Rayson 2008), keyword analysis was used to identify semantic domains that were much more frequent within the disinformation corpus compared to the non-disinformation corpus of news links. Dance (2019) found that the tweets sharing disinformation contained words that belong to the semantic categories of both *Closed; Hiding/hidden* and *Open; Finding/showing*. It is suggested that this is because 'disinformation is the revelation of fabricated "facts" previously unknown to anyone but the author' (Dance 2019: 21), and this is therefore flagged as significant through such an analysis. It is also reported in the same analysis that there is a strong emotional element involved with the sharing of disinformation, with *anger* coming through as a particularly strong sentiment, evidenced by frequent terms relating to unpleasant appearance (Dance 2019). This highlights that corpus-based analyses are able to not only provide a coarse-grained overview of the many semantic fields at play within a corpus but also the more fine-grained usages by investigating individual concordance lines.

5 Looking ahead: pitfalls and opportunities

It is clear that work at the intersection of corpus linguistics and forensic linguistics is growing, as more researchers turn towards larger datasets to investigate language use in the forensic context. As has been demonstrated throughout this chapter, corpus-based methods have been useful to researchers in real-life casework, where forensic linguists have been called upon to act as expert witnesses. They have also been useful to further academic scholarship within forensic linguistics, which often occurs in partnership with other agencies and organisations and thereby has a tangible impact on real-world issues.

As with any method, there are a number of issues that this partnership between corpus and forensic linguistics suffers from too. As alluded to earlier, in instances where the forensic linguist acts as an expert witness, there is very little control over the data that they receive. Some of the most important factors to think about in corpus construction – size, representativeness and balance – are difficult, if not impossible, to give due consideration. The forensic linguist cannot simply request a longer ransom demand to increase the likelihood of finding style markers, and they cannot ask the police to somehow reduce the number of suspects or ask for higher-quality metadata. Likewise, casework may be dealing with highly sensitive topics, and accessing further data may be, at best, difficult or, at worst, unethical. The forensic linguist working in this capacity therefore has a significant lack of control in the data collection process, and the type of analysis they are doing is often at odds with the foundations of corpus design (as detailed in Chapter 2, this volume). As a result, forensic linguists utilising corpus methods must often work with what they have and attempt, as far as possible, to provide their informed opinion based on the evidence available.

With that said, corpus linguistics and forensic linguistics do share a common endeavour in that they both value quantitative evidence (evidenced by the *Daubert* criteria), underpinned with solid qualitative interpretation. Likewise, they both value real, naturally occurring language data. Regardless of whether the researcher is dealing with a large representative reference corpus or a smaller specialised corpus of a particular language variety, there is a common purpose in that real data is being interrogated, via qualitative and quantitative means, to investigate how people use language as they go about their lives. These are some of the main benefits of corpus linguistics as a method, and it is clear to see why they would be important for forensic analysis too.

It is difficult to say which direction the field will take next. Whilst there are researchers who would define themselves, first and foremost, as a *forensic linguist* utilising corpus methods, there are others who would define themselves as a *corpus linguist* with an interest in forensic datasets and issues (see also Clarke and Kredens 2018 for a wider discussion about how forensic linguists construct their identities). Forensic linguistics is therefore a field that is wide open to a whole range of scholars, datasets, methods and theoretical frameworks, and it seems likely that subfields will grow out of that. Corpus-based forensic linguistics is increasingly being referred to as a field within its own right, and it seems likely based on recent trends (in journals and conference proceedings alike) that this should grow.

It is also encouraging that dedicated forensic linguistics research centres are not only being established but also being backed by publicly funded research councils. The Aston Institute for Forensic Linguistics, for example, recently received significant investment from Research England, leading to the hiring of several new staff and allowing a number of different research projects to take place. Many of these, it seems, utilise the corpus method as its main tool of language interrogation. This, combined with the continued success of forensic linguistic consultancy, appears to suggest that this synergy will continue to rise.

With all of this in mind, it is therefore clear that the research possibilities afforded through the combination of corpus-based methods and forensic linguistics are wide-ranging. There is considerable evidence that corpus linguistics, which values quantitative and objective evidence, is a good fit for forensic linguistic analyses, and many examples now show that it has provided benefits not only within the courtroom but to outside organisations and agencies too. The two fields are by no means a perfect fit, but recent (often experimental) work suggests that corpus linguistics will continue to provide new insights on forensic issues – both in well-established areas and in those that are only just emerging.

Further reading

Coulthard, M., Johnson, A. and Wright, D. (2017) *An Introduction to Forensic Linguistics: Language in Evidence*, London: Routledge. (This book not only provides a comprehensive introduction to forensic linguistics in general, but it advocates for the use of corpus-based methods and gives a whole range of examples where it has been, and can be, applied.)

Cunningham, C. D. and Egbert, J. (2020) 'Using Empirical Data to Investigate the Original Meaning of "Emolument" in the Constitution', *Georgia State University Law Review*, 36(5): 465–89. (This paper provides an excellent overview of how corpus methods can be used to determine the meaning of a word and its implications for a real-life case.)

Heffer, C. (2005) *The Language of Jury Trial: A Corpus-Aided Analysis of Legal-Lay Discourse*, Basingstoke: Palgrave. (This book is perhaps the most comprehensive investigation into courtroom discourse that utilises corpus-based methods. Several different techniques are used to investigate how the various participants within a courtroom use language to their advantage.)

Larner, S. D. (2015) 'From Intellectual Challenges to Established Corpus Techniques: Introduction to the Special Issue on Forensic Linguistics', *Corpora* 10(2): 131–43. (This paper is an introduction to a special issue of *Corpora* on forensic linguistics. After a brief history of how the two fields came to work together, Larner presents an annotated bibliography of over 50 references, pointing towards work which meets at that intersection.)

References

Archer, D. (2005) *Questions and Answers in the English Courtroom (1640-1760): A Sociopragmatic Analysis*, Amsterdam: John Benjamins.

Archer, D. and Lansley, C. (2015) 'Public Appeals, News Interviews and Crocodile Tears: An Argument for Multi-Channel Analysis', *Corpora* 10(2): 231–58.

Baker, P., Hardie, A. and McEnery, T. (2006) *A Glossary of Corpus Linguistics*, Edinburgh: Edinburgh University Press.

Blake, A. (2019) 'A Big Trump Case Hinges on the Definition of "Emoluments". A New Study Has Bad News for Him', *The Washington Post*, https://www.washingtonpost.com/politics/2019/01/29/big-trump-case-hinges-definition-emoluments-new-study-has-bad-news-him/.

Cavalieri, S. (2009) 'Reformulation and Conflict in the Witness Examination: The Case of Public Inquiries', *International Journal for the Semiotics of Law* 22(2): 209–21.

Clarke, I. and Kredens, K. (2018) '"I Consider Myself to be a Service Provider": Discursive Identity Construction of the Forensic Linguistic Expert', *International Journal of Speech, Language and the Law* 25(1): 79–107.

Cotterill, J. (2003) *Language and Power in Court: A Linguistic Analysis of the O. J. Simpson Trial*, Basingstoke: Palgrave.

Cotterill, J. (2004) 'Collocation, Connotation, and Courtroom Semantics: Lawyers' Control of Witness Testimony Through Lexical Negotiation', *Applied Linguistics* 25(4): 513–37.

Cotterill, J. (2010) 'How to Use Corpus Linguistics in Forensic Linguistics', in A. O'Keeffe and M. J. McCarthy (eds) *The Routledge Handbook of Corpus Linguistics*, 1st edn, London: Routledge, pp. 578–90.

Coulthard, M. (1994) 'On the Use of Corpora in the Analysis of Forensic Texts', *Forensic Linguistics: International Journal of Speech, Language and the Law* 1(1): 27–43.

Coulthard, M. (2000) 'Whose Text is it? On the Linguistic Investigation of Authorship', in S. Sarangi and M. Coulthard (eds) *Discourse and Social Life*, London: Routledge, pp. 270–87.

Coulthard, M., Johnson, A. and Wright, D. (2017) *An Introduction to Forensic Linguistics: Language in Evidence*, London: Routledge.

Cunningham, C. D. and Egbert, J. (2020) 'Using Empirical Data to Investigate the Original Meaning of 'Emolument' in the Constitution', *Georgia State University Law Review* 36(5): 465–89.

Dance, W. (2019) 'Disinformation Online: Social Media User's Motivations for Sharing 'Fake News'', *Science in Parliament* 75(3): 20–2.

Davies, M. (2008-) *The Corpus of Contemporary American English (COCA): 560 Million Words, 1990-Present*, Available online at https://corpus.byu.edu/coca/.

Fitzpatrick, E. and Bachenko, J. (2010) 'Building a Forensic Corpus to Test Language-Based Indicators of Deception', in M. Davies, S. Wulff and S. Thomas (eds) *Corpus-Linguistic Applications: Current Studies, New Directions*, Amsterdam: Rodopi, pp. 183–96.

Gillings, M. (2020) 'A Corpus-Based Investigation into Verbal Cues to Deception and Their Sociolinguistic Distribution', unpublished PhD Thesis, Lancaster University, UK.

Gómez-Adorno, H., Posadas-Duran, J., Ríos-Toledo, G., Sidorov, G. and Sierra, G. (2018) 'Stylometry-Based Approach for Detecting Writing Style Changes in Literary Texts', *Computación y Sistemas* 22(1): 47–53.

Grant, T. (2013) 'Txt 4N6: Method, Consistency and Distinctiveness in the Analysis of SMS Text Messages', *Journal of Law and Policy* 21(2): 467–94.

Grieve, J. (2007) 'Quantitative Authorship Attribution: An Evaluation of Techniques', *Literary and Linguistic Computing* 22(3): 251–70.

Hardie, A. (2012) 'CQPweb – Combining Power, Flexibility and Usability in a Corpus Analysis Tool', *International Journal of Corpus Linguistics* 17(3): 380–409.

Heffer, C. (2005) *The Language of Jury Trial: A Corpus-Aided Analysis of Legal-Lay Discourse*, Basingstoke: Palgrave.

Hope, J. (1994) *The Authorship of Shakespeare's Plays: A Socio-Linguistic Study*, Cambridge: Cambridge University Press.

Johnson, A. and Coulthard, M. (2010) 'Introduction: Current Debates in Forensic Linguistics', in M. Coulthard and A. Johnson (eds) *The Routledge Handbook of Forensic Linguistics*, London: Routledge, pp. 1–15.

Johnson, A. and Wright, D. (2014) 'Identifying Idiolect in Forensic Authorship Attribution: An N-Gram Textbite Approach', *Language and Law / Linguagem e Direito* 1(1): 37–69.

Koester, A. (2010) 'Building Small Specialised Corpora', in A. O'Keeffe and M. J. McCarthy (eds) *The Routledge Handbook of Corpus Linguistics*, 1st edn, London: Routledge, pp. 14–27.

Larner, S. D. (2015) 'From Intellectual Challenges to Established Corpus Techniques: Introduction to the Special Issue on Forensic Linguistics', *Corpora* 10(2): 131–43.
Larner, S. D. (2019) 'Formulaic Sequences as a Potential Marker of Deception: A Preliminary Investigation', in T. Docan-Morgan (ed.) *The Palgrave Handbook of Deceptive Communication*, London: Palgrave Macmillan, pp. 327–46.
Love, R., Dembry, C., Hardie, A., Brezina, V. and McEnery, T. (2017) 'The Spoken BNC2014: Designing and Building a Spoken Corpus of Everyday Conversations', *International Journal of Corpus Linguistics* 22(3): 319–44.
McEnery, T. and Hardie, A. (2012) *Corpus Linguistics: Method, Theory and Practice*, Cambridge: Cambridge University Press.
McMenamin, G. (1993) *Forensic Stylistics*, Amsterdam: Elsevier.
McQuaid, S. M., Woodworth, M., Hutton, E. L., Porter, S. and Ten Brinke, L. (2015) 'Automated Insights: Verbal Cues to Deception in Real-Life High-Stakes Lies', *Psychology, Crime & Law* 21(7): 617–31.
Nini, A. (2020) 'Corpus Analysis in Forensic Linguistics' in C. Chapelle (ed.) *The Concise Encyclopedia of Applied Linguistics*, Hoboken: Wiley-Blackwell, pp. 313–20.
O'Keeffe, A., McCarthy, M. J. and Carter, R. A. (2007) *From Corpus to Classroom: Language Use and Language Teaching*, Cambridge: Cambridge University Press.
Rayson, P. (2008) 'From Key Words to Key Semantic Domains', *International Journal of Corpus Linguistics* 13(4): 519–49.
Strang, L. J. (2017) 'The Original Meaning of "Religion" in the First Amendment: A Test Case of Originalism's Utilization of Corpus Linguistics', *BYU Law Review* 6: 1683–750.
Solan, L. M. and Tiersma, P. M. (2004) 'Authorship Identification in American Courts', *Applied Linguistics* 25(4): 448–65.
Solan, L. M. and Gales, T. (2016) 'Finding Ordinary Meaning in Law: The Judge, the Dictionary, or the Corpus?', *International Journal of Legal Discourse* 1(2): 253–76.
Wright, D. (2017) 'Using Word N-Grams to Identify Authors and Idiolects: A Corpus Approach to a Forensic Linguistic Problem', *International Journal of Corpus Linguistics* 22(2): 212–41.

Cases cited

CREW v. Trump.276 F. Supp. 3d 174 (S.D.N.Y 2017)
Daubert v. Dow Merrill Pharmaceuticals, Inc. 509 U.S. 579 (1993)

42

Corpus linguistics in the study of political discourse: recent directions

Charlotte Taylor

1 What do we mean by political discourse?

The question of what counts as *political discourse* (and *political discourse analysis*) has been extensively discussed (e.g. Wodak and de Cillia 2006), with much debate centring on where to draw the lines around these concepts. At the core, we have language produced by 'political institutions, governments, political media, and political supporters operating in political environments to achieve political goals' (Wilson 2001: 398), while on the periphery we have the assertion that all discourse is political. As we see in the following sub-sections, even within a relatively narrow remit of discourses produced by and about political institutions, actions and actors, there is a wide range of potential topics. In preparing this chapter, I surveyed over 50 peer-reviewed articles published in key corpus and discourse journals over the last decade (2010–20) to get a sense of the current direction of travel. This is not to overlook the giants on whose shoulders we stand, but by grasping what is currently being done, I hope the reader can take away ideas for how they could work within the area and identify aspects which seem under-represented and therefore ripe for future study.

Discourses produced by political institutions and actors

The main focus of political discourse analysis is the language produced within the institutions of political power and by actors who speak with an institutional identity. Within this subset, there are a wide range of discourse types which vary considerably in the amount of public attention they get and the level of interaction between participants.

Parliamentary debates: This is perhaps the prototypical genre of political discourse, and it has proved one of the most frequently studied, with research covering both the adversarial style of interaction and representations of socially important issues. Recent examples include investigations of the representation of same-sex relationships (Bachmann 2011), British national identity (Riihimäki 2019) and the Windrush generation (Taylor 2020). These all examined British parliamentary discourse, but this discourse type has been studied extensively in other contexts such as Montenegro

DOI: 10.4324/9780367076399-42

(Vuković 2012), Ghana (Sarfo-Kantankah 2018) and Brazil (Rebechi 2019). In terms of accessibility of data, the debates are often made available in text format, which aids corpus construction. However, we should be aware that these transcriptions may not fully and accurately represent the spoken event they purport to record (see Hughes 1996; Mollin 2009). Other kinds of parliamentary interaction such as select committees have received less attention, and this is an area for future work.

Election debates: Political debates outside the parliamentary space have also received extensive attention. In part, because they, too, often involve *verbal aggression* and are public performances which become the subject of meta-debate. Recent examples include Parvaresh (2018), who examines vague language in the 2016 US presidential debates, and Cabrejas-Peñuelas and Díez-Prados (2014), who examine positive self-presentation and negative other-presentation in the Spain 2011 pre-electoral debates. Recordings of debates and meta-comment are often made available online.

Interviews: Interviews with politicians may offer an opportunity to analyse a more spontaneous set of interactions. There are many potential texts available for analysis given that politicians are interviewed every day; from the area of hard news to soft settings such as magazine-style TV and radio programmes. Romaniuk (2016) addresses the performative nature of these events by analysing both interviews with Hillary Clinton and comments on those interviews.

Press briefings/conferences: Partington's (2003) account of the US press briefings shows these interactions to be a fascinating discourse type as 'the two parties involved, the podium and the press, have very different interests and aims in life which are in conflict on several levels' (2003: vii), and this is reflected in the positions they are able to take and the language they use. Gu (2018) investigates the less combative instance of an annual interpreted political press conference in China and compares source and target texts to show how the image is shaped for the target audience. The availability of these varies considerably, with some being very accessible while others are conducted off-record.

Social media: This is one of the most important means of contemporary political communication, but, surprisingly, language produced by political actors in this sphere has not yet received substantial attention from a corpus linguistic perspective. This may be because of challenges in the corpus compilation or because the importance has not been fully recognised. An important exception is Alcántara-Pla and Ruiz-Sánchez (2018) who show how migration was a silenced topic on social media in the 2015 Spanish elections through their analysis of Twitter accounts of the main political parties and candidates.

Speeches: These written-to-be-spoken texts have been studied extensively, continuing the traditional focus of rhetoric. As monoglossic interactions, they are one of the forms of political discourse where the politician has most control over their self-presentation and making them important for understanding how the politician wishes to present themselves and their party. For instance, Wei and Duann (2019) conduct a diachronic analysis of the use of first-person plural pronouns in speeches produced by three presidents of Taiwan. The texts of major political speeches are often made available on the speaker's website, and those which were considered newsworthy are likely to be available to watch too. What is less likely to be captured is the kind of speech which is crafted for a specific audience without a secondary global audience being anticipated in the production, and these offer exciting potential for investigating persuasion. The short talks to camera by politicians for circulation on their social media have not yet received attention either but are readily available for data collection (as this is a new area, permissions for each national context may need checking).

Manifestos: The manifesto is the most overt statement of intent from a political party, and the documents are usually accessible. Given that each manifesto is likely to be quite short, corpus techniques tend to be used when the aim is to investigate multiple instances. For example, Yan Eureka Ho and Crosthwaite (2018) compare three candidates for the Hong Kong Chef Executive election, and Evans and Jeffries (2015) investigate the concept of *choice* over a century of British manifestos.

Political websites: Rather like the manifesto, the political party website constitutes a statement of intent and identity construction. In addition, they are often archives of material the party continues to endorse. Engström and Paradis (2015) constructed a 900,000-word corpus of articles and policy documents published between 2005 and 2012 from two (far)-right British party political websites.

Reports produced by political organisations: The kinds of reports produced by political organisations can vary significantly, from those self-reporting their progress to those covering internal investigations. They are usually accessible, but they may not be widely known about unless they become newsworthy. Li and Zhu (2020) use work reports of the National Congress of the Chinese Communist Party to investigate self and other appraisal.

Press releases: These constitute another controlled means of interaction, as they offer a monoglossic official view. Breeze (2019) compares the press releases of the British Labour party and United Kingdom Indepence Party (UKIP) in order to draw out the discursive uses of emotion-talk.

Policy documents: This is an important political discourse type but one that starts to have blurred edges (e.g. with legal discourse or education discourse in the case of education policy documents and so on). In this area, Fitzsimmons-Doolan (2014) examines language ideologies in policy documents from the Arizona Department of Education website, while MacDonald *et al.* (2013) investigate UK security discourse in policy documents. It is an area that has perhaps captured less attention than might be expected given the importance of these documents as the final stage of a political discourse cycle and the relative ease of accessing them.

Other: Another sub-category could be occasions where politicians interact in non-political discourse contexts. This might involve those where they are present because of actions undertaken in their political role, such as Duguid (2007) on the key members of the Blair government being examined during a major public inquiry, or it might involve those where the (ex-)politician's primary identity is relocated, for instance, as a defendant in a trial or a contestant in a reality show. We might also expect consideration of discourse types such as political party broadcasts, but these have been less frequently addressed using corpus linguistics – perhaps because they tend to be short and multimodal. Finally, we might note that much of the everyday business of politics that does not involve adversarial interactions or receive public attention is generally overlooked.

Discourse about political events, institutions and actors

A significant amount of the politics-oriented talk which we observe and in which we ourselves participate, from protest songs to water-cooler chat to political memes, will not involve institutional actors, and yet it is uncontroversial to label this as political talk (though the question of whether it is *political discourse* may not be resolved so easily).

Discourses about political institutions and actors

Discussion of and around political institutions and their actors is clearly highly relevant for studies of political discourse, as this is part of how they are construed. Representations of institutions have been somewhat understudied, although an important exception is the EU, particularly in recent years. Kopf (2020) analyses Wikipedia contributors' debates around the EU's history, revealing how a resource often treated as neutral engages in (de)legitimisation of political institutions.

Discourses around political actors has received rather more attention, often with a focus on individuals, such as Barnes and Larrivée's (2011) study of how French presidential nominee Arlette Laguiller was named in press reports. Taking a broader approach, Formato (2016) reports on media names for female ministers in the Italian context.

Discourses about political events

A broader category is that of discourse about political events, and here we have a spectrum from those that are more central to the endeavour of political discourse to those that are more peripheral. To start closer to the centre, we might consider public and media discussion of political acts. Kreisher's (2019) study of the Irish Abortion debate in the press is undoubtedly engaging with a political topic, as the news stories analysed played a part in changing public discourses on abortion, ultimately leading to political action. Simaki *et al.* (2019) make use of a corpus of blog posts about Brexit, a political act, and Brindle (2016) examines a media corpus reporting on the Sunflower protests in Taiwan which sought to create political change.

At the margins of political discourse

As noted earlier, discourses about political events may be more or less central to the idea of *political discourse,* and there is a substantial fuzzy border because no discourse type exists in isolation or within neat borders. The first fuzzy border concerns discourses produced by non-political actors about politically salient phenomena such as poverty (e.g. Tranchese 2019), Islamophobia (Baker *et al.* 2013), the reimagined role of universities (Fotiadou 2020) or our environment (e.g. Poole 2016). The second regards language produced by government organisations, such as Hunter and MacDonald (2017) on public-facing texts produced by US security organisations or Wang and Ma (2020) on China's official English-language media. Each of these types may be considered more or less political depending on the context. The third is extremist texts (Baker and Vessey 2018) which are highly political and yet remain at the borders because at the point of production they are not written by powerful institutionally sanctioned figures and, therefore, under some definitions of political discourse, are not part of the object of study. Ultimately, it seems unwise to arbitrarily exclude comment on political action, institutions and actors as outside the sphere of political discourse on the basis that it is produced by less powerful participants. However, it will always be up to the individual researcher to make the argument as to how their study is part of political discourse.

2 Studying the structures of political discourse

In the following sections, we examine two types of political discourse analysis: those in which the primary aim is to describe the linguistic structures of the discourse type and those in which the primary aim is to investigate the representation of particular groups, events or ideologies within the discourse. As linguists, we know that there will be overlap between the two because meaning and form are inextricable, but I hope it will help the reader see the range of studies in which they could engage. We start with studies that have focussed more on the structures of political discourse. However, it should be noted that the assumption is still that the questions being asked are of interest to those working on political discourse and are not using the corpus as a decontextualised body of language.

Linguistic features that characterise political discourses

Earlier work on political discourse, like much earlier work in discourse analysis, set out to identify the language that characterises its genres. More recently, attention has turned towards identifying communication strategies and rhetorical devices. As noted in the previous section, one of the appeals of political discourse for linguists is that it offers an opportunity to observe impoliteness which has historically been neglected compared to the counterpart of politeness (Culpeper 2011). Furthermore, political discourse is characterised by the importance of competitive persuasion and contrasting evaluation (Chilton 2008) and therefore enables investigation of these aspects of communication. In the papers from the last decade, this was the aspect that dominated, with particular attention being paid to the interrelated notions of appraisal, evaluation and stance.

The challenge for the corpus linguist is operationalising these linguistic concepts. This may be addressed by working with a small set of lexicalisations. For instance, Arguedas (2020) investigates the use of evidentials (items that give information about the source of information and fulfil various pragmatic functions relating the speaker to the truth values and credibility of a statement) in Spanish parliamentary proceedings. They suggest that the analysis of evidentials can reveal defining features of the genre in which they are used and also enable identification of sequences of talk where criticism occurs or where argumentative positions are reinforced (2020: 79), thus making them a resource for analysis of non-obvious meanings in political discourse. In other cases, the analyst may not know yet how a concept may be lexicalised in the corpus and therefore may begin with a higher-level category. For instance, Breeze (2019) starts her analysis of emotional language in press releases by using the *Wmatrix* semantic tagger (Rayson 2008). The tagger has a pre-set list of categories which it applies to the words in the corpus, and so the researcher can start with an overview of semantic fields. As Breeze (2019) notes, this would not allow the researcher to capture all uses of emotion because 'politicians use many statements that would normally be regarded as simply factual in order to elicit emotions in their audiences' (2019: 29). However, it does provide a replicable starting point for a more qualitative investigation. Alternatively, researchers may take a more theory-driven approach to the challenge of identifying language structures. In these cases, the researcher starts with a set of categories and identifies the lexical/grammatical items that instantiate them. For instance, Simaki *et al.* (2019) annotated their corpus for different categories of stance. In these cases, a large proportion of the analysis is undertaken before the texts are treated as a corpus. Thus, we can see the importance of an approach which combines both discourse methods and models with corpus linguistics.

One of the most significant topics in this area is that of self/other and in-group/out-group-presentation, key concepts arising from critical discourse studies and discursive psychology. Researchers applying corpus methods have identified a range of tools for this area. One which has proved popular is Martin and White's (2003) model of appraisal which provides a detailed resource for annotating texts to identify what is appraised and how. For instance, Li and Zhu (2020) investigate self and other presentation in the Chinese government and find 'the negative evaluation of Self is more often related to things (*appreciation*) in China such as pollution while the negative evaluation of Others is often related to behaviours (*judgement*), for example, invasion, eavesdropping' (2020: 167, my italics). Gu (2018), who also addresses self and other representation in official Chinese government discourses, takes pronouns as the lexical entry point to the corpus and identifies the evaluations embedded around them. Knoblock (2020) also takes a lexical starting point in the analysis of self and other-presentation in pro- and anti-Trump comments on immigration by focusing on the use of the (semi) modals *must* and *have* (*got*) *to*. In their analyses of British far-right political parties, both Engström and Paradis (2015) and Edwards (2012) take as a starting point the manual identification of references to the self and those constructed as other by drawing on contextual knowledge.

Linguistic features that characterise specific political actors

Studies examining the linguistic structures of political discourse may also aim to isolate those which characterise a single group or speaker, with objects of study including UK Prime Ministers Blair (Mollin 2009) and Thatcher (Ponton 2010) and US Presidents Clinton and Trump (Parvaresh 2018). As this list indicates, the focus to date has tended to be high-profile politicians. The range of aspects studied is quite diverse, and just those mentioned here include idiolectal collocations, stylistic variation over time, vague language and gender identity construction. What these studies can tell us about political discourse is how key figures construct their identities and deploy linguistic resources for strategic aims. In this regard, studies here often have the notion of *politics as persuasion* at their centre.

3 Studying the content of political discourse

This section considers research which looks at how actors, actions and ideologies are represented in political discourse. The range of topics studied is wide and, for the most part, reflects the interests of (critical) discourse analysis and societal preoccupations.

LGBTQ+: In this area Bachmann (2011) investigates the framing of civil partnerships in the UK parliament and Wang and Ma (2020) report on the construal of LGBTQ+ issues in the Chinese media.

Gender: Recent work here includes how women are portrayed in political discussion forums (Karimullah 2020) and how female politicians are represented (Barnes and Larrivée 2011 on Arlette Laguiller; Romaniuk 2016 on Clinton).

Extremism: The attention given to this topic has increased substantially in recent times. Studies in this area have included the far right in the United States (Lorenzo-Dus and Nouri 2020 on the Traditionalist Worker Party) and the UK (Brindle 2016 on the

English Defence League), the language of Islamic extremism and radicalisation (Baker and Vessey 2018; Abdelzaher and Essam 2019). There has also been a smaller body of work looking at political discourse that responds to, or positions itself as responding to, extremist discourse (e.g. MacDonald *et al.* 2013 on UK security discourse).

National identity: This topic becomes especially salient in political discourse around elections, as the candidates need to show leadership and synchrony with the national identity. Riihimäki (2019) examines construction of British national identity in relation to the EU as a way of exploring the trajectory of Brexit. Wei and Duann (2019) approach identity in Taiwan's national leaders by tracing who "we" refers to over six decades.

Migration: In recent political discourse, this topic often intersects with framings of national identity. Pérez-Paredes *et al.* (2017) analyse UK legislation and UK administration informative texts to show how migrants were represented in official communications. Taylor (2020) compares the representation of one particular group of migrants, the Windrush Generation, in two different time periods in the UK parliament to investigate the role of nostalgia.

Language ideology: This topic often ties in with the previous two. For instance, Freake *et al.* (2011) explicitly link the construction of nationhood with language ideologies.

4 Applying corpus linguistics to political discourse

Added value

Fundamentally, the added value of applying corpus linguistics to the study of political discourse is the same as for all areas of discourse analysis. We can consider the combination of qualitative and quantitative approaches an opportunity to triangulate the methodological approach and so to approach the data in different ways, thus leading to different perspectives. We can also combine the corpus and discourse findings to allow one to shape the other, so the corpus investigation may be informed by the discourse analytic theories and categories. In this way, meaning and motivation are added at the beginning. Alternatively, the data may first be approached in a more exploratory, inductive way, with the corpus tools being used to allow the researcher to find unexpected results; the opportunity to be surprised by findings is one of the great contributions of corpus methods. With reference specifically to political discourse, Partington (2012) notes the power to trace political discourses across different discourse types, a concept that is developed *as transdiscursive political messaging* in Duguid and Partington (2017).

We should, of course, also flip the relationship and ask what added value is presented to the corpus linguist who starts to analyse political discourse. In this case, intertextuality is again important. In examining political discourse, we have the opportunity to track and observe discourses as they develop and consolidate; from the individual politician's or protest group's social media account, through to discussion in parliamentary debates or select committees and into policy. This trajectory is rarely studied, which is a missed opportunity to examine the life cycle of a discourse. Other elements of added value for the corpus linguist are those that characterise political discourse more broadly, from the opportunity to observe power relationships and the ability to investigate topics which impact on our society.

Corpora

The first step in any corpus study of political discourse is identifying suitable texts for analysis. In some cases, there are pre-existing corpora which are made publicly available (e.g. the *British Hansard* corpus or the HKBU *Corpus of Political Speeches*) but in most cases the researcher will need to construct their own corpora, especially if they want to up-to-date texts. As noted in Section 1, many official communications will be made available online. The researcher who is new to the area may need to spend time researching both what texts exist (reflecting what political processes exist) and which are available.

When building corpora from spoken interactions, the researcher is required to make a series of detailed decisions about what to include (e.g. gesture, intonation and so on) (see Chapter 3, this volume). Corpora built from social media also entail complex planning (e.g. how to handle interaction patterns, retweets, likes and so on) (see Chapter 46, this volume), and there are some dedicated tools such as *FireAnt* (Anthony and Hardaker 2017) which may facilitate this process. In many cases, corpora will require annotation prior to analysis to encompass non-verbal elements of communication. One type of annotation is mark-up which includes information about the speakers (for instance political affiliation) and the texts (for instance, whether a tweet is a retweet). A second involves adding linguistic annotation, which may include automated and manual tagging (see Chapters 2–4, this volume).

Good practice follows that which applies to corpus and discourse studies more generally (see Taylor and Marchi 2018). The researcher needs to know the context and recognise that the ability to gather large amounts of data does not exclude the need to read a sample of the texts and to acquaint oneself with the discourse type. For instance, the researcher would need to know the conventions of parliamentary discourse and what is unmarked behaviour in that context before interpreting language behaviours. A second aspect that is particularly relevant for political discourse when investigating extremist discourses or highly sensitive topics is how to protect the researcher from the effects of working with that kind of data, and from potential repercussions, as well as how to communicate findings in ways that are considerate of the effects on the audience.

Tools and approaches

As outlined earlier, studies vary in how they bring together discourse analysis and corpus linguistics. The most frequently used corpus tools are the central pillars of the concordance line, collocation analysis and keyness comparisons (see Chapter 9 and 10, this volume). In terms of the models from discourse analysis that are used, the discourse-historical approach (Wodak 2001), as used in Engström and Paradis (2015), is employed frequently, as is van Leuwen's (1996) model of social actors, as used in Salama (2012). The latter often goes hand-in-hand with use of collocational tools for analysis. However, there is a wide range of theoretical foundations being used from discourse theory and pragmatics. One of the most interesting concepts for its ability to really bring corpus and discourse work together is the operationalisation of *discourse keywords* which draws on the concepts of cultural keywords and conceptual history and operationalises this in tandem with the corpus linguistics concept of keyness (as explained in Schröter *et al.* 2019). In studies that fall within this kind of approach, the analysis of political discourse often centres around a single, highly salient term (for instance, *choice* in Evans and

Jeffries 2015), and collocation is likely to be the core tool. We may also note that certain discourse-pragmatic tools are employed repeatedly. Perhaps one of the most studied in recent years is deixis, particularly as used for self-reference (e.g. Mulderrig 2012 on inclusion in education policy). Another is metaphor, which can give the researcher a way to access *non-obvious* meanings (those that 'might not be readily available to naked eye perusal' [Partington 2007: 97]) which underpin the framing of a given topic (e.g. L'Hôte 2010 on metaphors of globalisation in New Labour discourse).

5 Future directions

We can assume that many of the topics covered here will continue to be of interest and relevance to studies of political discourse using corpus methods. Other developments will reflect changes in the feeder areas of discourse studies, corpus linguistics and political science. Regarding the first, we may say that discourse analysis has moved away from describing topic areas (e.g. what does political discourse look like) to nuanced analyses of interaction patterns or content-focussed investigations. This reflects the social shift in discourse studies more generally, occasioned perhaps by the (European) funding imperative for research projects to have impact outside academia.

Since the last edition of this chapter (Ädel 2010) was published, some changing trends can be noted, and these may indicate the direction of travel. First, the increase in corpus and discourse studies investigating extremist and terrorist texts (as discussed earlier). Here we may be seeing the push for impact being realised in research projects or perhaps an increase in recognition outside the academic context of the value of collaborating with scholars who can bring the ability to analyse very large datasets in a meaningful way that recognises context.[1] A second area of development is the rise of social media studies. Although Facebook and Twitter were launched in the mid-2000s, it is probably true to say that the 2008 presidential elections in the United States really brought them to the attention of political discourse analysts. Now, it would be unthinkable to look at any election campaign without considering social media texts. However, the interconnected nature of the texts raises many issues for a corpus approach which are still being addressed. A third area of increased attention is diachronic studies. These have covered longitudinal studies of the same topic, such as Sealey and Bates (2016) on the prime minister's self-reported actions in parliamentary debates, and contrastive studies of topics at different points in time, such as Love and Baker's (2015) comparison of the language of opposition to the equalisation of the age of consent for anal sex with the oppositional language in debates on same-sex marriage. To date, these largely fall under the heading of modern-diachronic corpus assisted discourse studies (MD-CADS, Partington 2010), and many investigate parliamentary discourse – perhaps because it is the political discourse type with the longest history of recording and making available interactions.

The survey of current work can also indicate under-represented areas. First among these is the lack of uptake of corpus linguistics methods among non-linguists who work on political discourse. To take a recent example, the 2020 conference of the European Consortium for Political Research had no papers with *corpus/corpora* in the 1,000+ paper titles. In a mirror image of this, it appears that in existing corpus work there is relatively low engagement with significant theoretical concepts developed in political sciences. Van Dijk (1997) argues that political discourse analysis 'should not merely be a contribution to discourse studies, but also to political science and the social sciences more generally' (1997:11), and at present it is not clear this is the case for corpus and discourse work on political contexts. Second, and this is a broader trend in corpus linguistics, there is still a relative absence of work on multimodal corpora that makes full use of corpus linguistic tools. This means some genres within political discourse are only partially addressed and other genres, such as protest music, signs or memes, are overlooked. The continued development of frameworks for corpus-assisted multimodal discourse analysis (Bednarek and Caple 2014) and tools to facilitate this (e.g. Kaleidographic, presented in Caple *et al.* 2019) may lead to more research. Third, most research on interactive texts focusses on powerful participants in political-political or political-media interfaces. There is less research on politicians' talk in different footings or in interactions between lay and institutional participants. This indicates there is space for significant impact-related research which looks at participation in politics and political frameworks. Fourth, as noted earlier, there are surprisingly few intertextual studies tracing the development of discourses through the various political discourse types.

Note

1 The importance of the Lancaster University-based ESRC Centre for Corpus Approaches to Social Science has undoubtedly had a role in the UK context.

Further reading

The items chosen here are short article-length publications which the reader can use as case studies to explore methods (for book-length reports of projects, see Partington (2003) and Koteyko (2014)).

Baker, P. and McEnery, T. (2015) 'Who Benefits When Discourse Gets Democratised? Analysing a Twitter Corpus around the British Benefits Street Debate', in A. McEnery and P. Baker (eds) *Corpora and Discourse Studies*, London: Palgrave Macmillan, pp. 244–265. (This is an example of analysis which focusses on representation of a political issue in social media. The corpus is built from Twitter data, and the study uses keyness as the starting point for analysis.)

Clarke I. and Grieve J (2019) 'Stylistic Variation on the Donald Trump Twitter Account: A Linguistic Analysis of Tweets Posted between 2009 and 2018', *PLoS ONE* 14(9): e0222062 (This is an example of research which focusses on style in political discourse. The paper uses multidimensional analysis to track variation over time in Trump's tweets.)

Gabrielatos, C. (2020, July 28) *Bibliography of Discourse-Oriented Corpus Studies*, Retrieved from http://ehu.ac.uk/docsbiblio. (This useful online resource is continuously updated.)

Riihimäki, J. (2019) 'At the Heart and in the Margins: Discursive Construction of British National Identity in Relation to the EU in British Parliamentary Debates from 1973 to 2015', *Discourse & Society* 30(4), 412–31. (This is an example of diachronic research into parliamentary discourse. The starting point for the analysis is co-occurrence of lexical items.)

References

Abdelzaher, E. M. and Essam, B. A. (2019) 'Weaponizing Words: Rhetorical Tactics of Radicalization in Western and Arabic Countries', *Journal of Language and Politics* 18(6): 893–914.

Ädel, A. (2010) 'How to Use Corpus Linguistics in the Study of Political Discourse', in A. O'Keeffe and M. McCarthy (eds) *The Routledge Handbook of Corpus Linguistics*, London: Routledge, pp. 619–32.

Alcántara-Pla, M. and Ruiz-Sánchez, A. (2018) 'Not for Twitter: Migration as a Silenced Topic in the 2015 Spanish General Election', in M. Schröter and C. Taylor (eds) *Exploring Silence and Absence in Discourse: Empirical Approaches*, Basingstoke: Palgrave Macmillan, pp. 25–64.

Anthony, L. and Hardaker, C. (2017) *FireAnt* (Version 1.1.4) [Computer Software], Tokyo, Japan: Waseda University, Available from https://www.laurenceanthony.net/software.

Arguedas, M. E. (2020) 'The Evolution of Parliamentary Debates in Light of the Evolution of Evidentials: Al Parecer and Por lo Visto in 40 Years of Parliamentary Proceedings from Spain', *Corpus Pragmatics* 4(1): 59–82.

Bachmann, I. (2011) 'Civil Partnership–"Gay Marriage in All but Name": A Corpus-Driven Analysis of Discourses of Same-Sex Relationships in the UK Parliament', *Corpora* 6(1): 77–105.

Baker, P., Gabrielatos, C. and McEnery, T. (2013) *Discourse Analysis and Media Attitudes: The Representation of Islam in the British Press*, Cambridge: Cambridge University Press.

Baker, P. and Vessey, R. (2018) 'A Corpus-Driven Comparison of English and French Islamist Extremist Texts', *International Journal of Corpus Linguistics* 23(3): 255–78.

Barnes, J. and Larrivée, P. (2011) 'Arlette Laguiller: Does the Mainstay of the French Political Far-Left Enjoy Linguistic Parity with her Male Counterparts?', *Journal of Pragmatics* 43(10): 2501–8.

Bednarek, M. and Caple, H. (2014) 'Why Do News Values Matter? Towards a New Methodological Framework for Analyzing News Discourse in Critical Discourse Analysis and Beyond', *Discourse & Society* 25(2): 135–58.

Breeze, R. (2019) 'Emotion in Politics: Affective-Discursive Practices in UKIP and Labour', *Discourse & Society* 30(1): 24–43.

Brindle, A. (2016) 'A Corpus Analysis of Discursive Constructions of the Sunflower Student Movement in the English-language Taiwanese Press', *Discourse & Society* 27(1): 3–19.

Cabrejas-Peñuelas, A. B. and Díez-Prados, M. (2014) 'Positive Self-Evaluation Versus Negative Other-Evaluation in the Political Genre of Pre-Election Debates', *Discourse & Society* 25(2): 159–85.

Caple, H., Anthony, L. and Bednarek, M. (2019) 'Kaleidographic: A Data Visualization Tool', *International Journal of Corpus Linguistics* 24(2): 245–61.

Chilton, P. (2008) 'Political Terminology', in R. Wodak and V. Koller (eds) *Handbook of Communication in the Public Sphere*, Berlin: Mouton de Gruyter, pp. 223–42.

Culpeper, J. (2011) *Impoliteness: Using Language to Cause Offence*, Cambridge: Cambridge University Press.

Duguid, A. (2007) 'Soundbiters Bit. Contracted Dialogistic Space and the Textual Relations of the No. 10 Team Analysed through Corpus Assisted Discourse Studies', in N. Fairclough, G. Cortese, and P. Ardizzone (eds) *Discourse and Contemporary Social Change*, Frankfurt: Peter Lang, pp. 73–94.

Duguid, A. and Partington, A. (2017) 'Lexical Primings in Transdiscoursive Political Messaging: How They Are Produced and How They Are Received', in M. Pace-Sigge and K. J. Patterson (eds) *Lexical Priming: Applications and Advances*, Amsterdam: John Benjamins, pp. 67–92.

Edwards, G. O. (2012) 'A Comparative Discourse Analysis of the Construction of 'In-Groups' in the 2005 and 2010 Manifestos of the British National Party', *Discourse & Society* 23(3): 245–58.

Engström, R. and Paradis, C. (2015). 'The In-group and Out-groups of the British National Party and the UK Independence Party: A Corpus-Based Discourse-Historical Analysis'. *Journal of Language and Politics* 14(4): 501–27. 10.1075/jlp.14.4.02eng

Evans, M. and Jeffries, L. (2015) 'The Rise of Choice as an Absolute 'Good': A Study of British Manifestos (1900–2010)', *Journal of Language and Politics* 14(6): 751–77.

Fitzsimmons-Doolan, S. (2014) 'Using Lexical Variables to Identify Language Ideologies in a Policy Corpus', *Corpora* 9(1): 57–82

Formato, F. (2016) 'Linguistic Markers of Sexism in the Italian Media: A Case Study of Ministra and Ministro', *Corpora* 3(11): 371–99.

Fotiadou, M. (2020) 'Denaturalising the Discourse of Competition in the Graduate Job Market and the Notion of Employability: A Corpus-Based Study of UK University Websites', *Critical Discourse Studies* 17(3): 260–91.

Freake, R., Gentil, G. and Sheyholislami, J. (2011) 'A Bilingual Corpus-Assisted Discourse Study of the Construction of Nationhood and Belonging in Quebec', *Discourse & Society* 22(1): 21–47.

Gu, C. (2018) 'Forging a Glorious Past via the 'Present Perfect': A Corpus-Based CDA Analysis of China's Past Accomplishments Discourse Mediat(is)ed at China's Interpreted Political Press Conferences', *Discourse, Context & Media* 24: 137–49.

Hughes, R. (1996) *English in Speech and Writing: Investigating Language and Literature*, London: Routledge.

Hunter, D. and M. N. MacDonald. (2017) 'The Emergence of a Security Discipline in the Post 9-11 Discourse of U.S. Security Organisations', *Critical Discourse Studies* 14(2): 206–22.

Karimullah, K. (2020) 'Sketching Women: A Corpus-Based Approach to Representations of Women's Agency in Political Internet Corpora in Arabic and English', *Corpora* 15(1): 21–53.

Koteyko, N. (2014) *Language and Politics in Post-Soviet Russia: A Corpus Assisted Approach*, Basingstoke: Springer.

Knoblock, N. (2020) 'Negotiating Dominance on Facebook: Positioning of Self and Others in Pro- and Anti-Trump Comments on Immigration', *Discourse & Society* 31(5): 520–39.

Kopf, S. (2020) '"This is Exactly How the Nazis Ran it": (De)legitimising the EU on Wikipedia', *Discourse & Society* 31(4): 411–27.

L'Hôte, E. (2010) 'New Labour and Globalization: Globalist Discourse with a Twist?', *Discourse & Society* 21(4): 355–76.

Li, T. and Zhu, Y. (2020) 'How Does China Appraise Self and Others? A Corpus-Based Analysis of Chinese Political Discourse', *Discourse & Society* 31(2): 153–71.

Lorenzo-Dus, N. and Nouri, L. (2020) 'The Discourse of the US Alt-Right Online – A Case Study of the Traditionalist Worker Party Blog', *Critical Discourse Studies*, 10.1080/17405904.2019.1708763 [online first].

Love, R. and Baker, P. (2015) 'The Hate that Dare not Speak its Name?', *Journal of Language Aggression and Conflict* 3(1): 57–86.

MacDonald, M. N., Hunter, D. and O'Regan, J. P. (2013) 'Citizenship, Community, and Counter-Terrorism: UK Security Discourse, 2001–2011', *Journal of Language and Politics* 12(3): 445–73.

Martin, J. R. and White, P. R. (2003) *The Language of Evaluation*, London: Palgrave Macmillan.

Mollin, S. (2009) '"I entirely understand" is a Blairism: The Methodology of Identifying Idiolectal Collocations', *International Journal of Corpus Linguistics* 14(3): 367–92.

Mulderrig, J. (2012) 'The Hegemony of Inclusion: A Corpus-Based Critical Discourse Analysis of Deixis in Education Policy', *Discourse & Society* 23(6): 701–28.

Partington, A. (2003) *The Linguistics of Political Argument: The Spin-Doctor and the Wolf-Pack at the White House*, London: Routledge.

Partington, A. (2007) 'The Armchair and the Machine', in C. Taylor Torsello, K. Ackerley and E. Castello (eds) *Corpora for University Language Teachers*, Bern: Peter Lang, pp. 189–213.

Partington, A. (2012) 'Corpus Analysis of Political Language', in C. Chappelle (ed.) *The Encyclopedia of Applied Linguistics*, Oxford: Blackwell. [online].

Partington, A. (2010) 'Modern Diachronic Corpus-Assisted Discourse Studies (MD-CADS) on UK Newspapers: An Overview of the Project', *Corpora 5*(2): 83–108.

Parvaresh, V. (2018) '"We Are Going to Do a Lot of Things for College Tuition": Vague Language in the 2016 U.S. Presidential Debates', *Corpus Pragmatics* 2 (3): 167–92.

Pérez-Paredes, P., Jiménez, P. A. and Hernández, P. S. (2017) 'Constructing Immigrants in UK Legislation and Administration Informative Texts: A Corpus-Driven Study (2007–2011)', *Discourse & Society* 28(1): 81–103.

Ponton, D. M. (2010) 'The Female Political Leader: A Study of Gender-Identity in the Case of Margaret Thatcher', *Journal of Language and Politics* 9(2): 195–18.

Poole, R. (2016) 'A Corpus-Aided Ecological Discourse Analysis of the Rosemont Copper Mine Debate of Arizona, USA', *Discourse & Communication* 10(6): 576–95.

Rayson, P. (2008) 'From Key Words to Key Semantic Domains', *International Journal of Corpus Linguistics* 13(4): 519–49

Rebechi, R. R. (2019) 'God, Nation and Family in the Impeachment Votes of Brazil's Former President Dilma Rousseff: A Corpus-Based Approach to Discourse', *Journal of Corpora and Discourse Studies* 2: 144–74.

Riihimäki, J. (2019) 'At the Heart and in the Margins: Discursive Construction of British National Identity in Relation to the EU in British Parliamentary Debates from 1973 to 2015', *Discourse & Society* 30(4): 412–31.

Romaniuk, T. (2016) 'On the Relevance of Gender in the Analysis of Discourse: A Case Study from Hillary Rodham Clinton's Presidential Bid in 2007–2008', *Discourse & Society* 27(5): 533–53.

Salama, A. H. Y. (2012) 'The Rhetoric of Collocational, Intertextual and Institutional Pluralization in Obama's Cairo Speech: A Discourse-Analytical Approach', *Critical Discourse Studies* 9(3): 211–229.

Sarfo-Kantankah, K. S. (2018) 'It's about People: Identifying the Focus of Parliamentary Debates through a Corpus-Driven Approach', *Corpora* 13 (3): 393–430.

Schröter, M., Veniard, M., Taylor, C. and Blätte, A. (2019) 'A Comparative Analysis of the Keyword Multicultural (ism) in French, British, German and Italian Migration Discourse', in L. Viola and A. Musolff (eds) *Migration and Media Discourses about Identities in Crisis*, Amsterdam: John Benjamins, pp. 13–44.

Sealey, A. and Bates, S. (2016) 'Prime Ministerial Self-Reported Actions in Prime Minister's Questions 1979–2010: A Corpus-Assisted Analysis', *Journal of Pragmatics* 104: 18–31.

Simaki, V., Paradis, C. and Kerren, A. (2019) 'A Two-Step Procedure to Identify Lexical Elements of Stance Constructions in Discourse from Political Blogs', *Corpora* 14(3): 379–405.

Taylor, C. (2020) 'Representing the Windrush Generation: Metaphor in Discourses Then and Now', *Critical Discourse Studies* 17(1): 1–21.

Taylor, C. and Marchi, A. (eds) (2018) *Corpus Approaches to Discourse: A Critical Review*, London: Routledge.

Tranchese, A. (2019) 'Getting off Benefits or Escaping Poverty? Using Corpora to Investigate the Representation of Poverty in the 2015 UK General Election Campaign', *Journal of Corpora and Discourse Studies* 2: 65–93.

Van Dijk, T. A. (1997) 'What is Political Discourse Analysis', *Belgian Journal of Linguistics* 11(1): 11–52.

Van Leeuwen, T. (1996) 'The Representation of Social Actors', in C. R. Caldas-Coulthard and M. Coulthard (eds) *Texts and Practices: Readings in Critical Discourse Analysis*, London: Routledge, pp. 32–70.

Vuković, M. (2012) 'Positioning in Pre-Prepared and Spontaneous Parliamentary Discourse: Choice of Person in the Parliament of Montenegro', *Discourse & Society* 23(2): 184–202.

Wang, G., and X. Ma. (2020) 'Representations of LGBTQ+Issues in China in its Official English-Language Media: A Corpus-Assisted Critical Discourse Study', *Critical Discourse Studies,* [online first].

Wei, J. M. and Duann, R. F. (2019) 'Who Are We?: Contesting Meanings in the Speeches of National Leaders in Taiwan During the Authoritarian Period', *Journal of Language and Politics* 18(5): 760–81.

Wilson, J. (2001) 'Political Discourse', in D. Schiffrin, D. Tannen and H. Hamilton (eds) *Handbook of Discourse Analysis*, Oxford: Blackwell, pp. 398–415.

Wodak R. (2001) 'The Discourse-Historical Approach', in R. Wodak and M. Meyer (eds) *Methods of Critical Discourse Analysis*, London: Sage, pp. 63–95.

Wodak, R. and de Cillia, R. (2006) 'Politics and Language: An Overview', in K. Brown (ed.) *Encyclopaedia of Language and Linguistics*, Amsterdam: Elsevier, pp. 707–19.

Yan Eureka Ho, S. and Crosthwaite, P. (2018) 'Exploring Stance in the Manifestos of 3 Candidates for the Hong Kong Chief Executive Election 2017: Combining CDA and Corpus-Like Insights', *Discourse & Society* 29(6): 629–54.

43

Corpus linguistics and health communication: using corpora to examine the representation of health and illness

Gavin Brookes, Sarah Atkins and Kevin Harvey

1 Introduction

Language is central to how we constitute our experiences of health and illness, as well as being of clear practical importance to health (care) professionals, who must communicate medical ideas on a regular basis. Experiences of health and illness are not simply based in the biological "realities" of our bodies but, crucially, in the language we use to talk about them:

> illness cannot be just illness, for the simple reason that human culture is constituted in language ... and that health and illness, being things which fundamentally concern humans, and hence need to be "explained", enter into language and are constituted in language, regardless of whether or not they have some independent reality in nature.
>
> *(Fox 1993: 6)*

The field of health (care) communication addresses an impressive breadth of topics and genres, including (but not limited to) patient–practitioner interactions, communication between practitioners, illness narratives, government health education material, media representations of health and advertisements that project particular ideas about health and our bodies. Linguistic studies of health (care) language were initially (largely) preoccupied with the discourse of spoken interactions between patients and a range of health care practitioners, such as doctors (Candlin 2000), nurses (Crawford *et al.* 1998), physiotherapists (Parry 2004) and pharmacists (Pilnick 1999). However, by the late 1990s, greater attention was paid to written medical discourse in various communicative contexts, such as medical note-taking (Hobbs 2003) and case histories (Francis and Kramer-Dahl 2004), and then more recently on online texts such as online support groups (Hunt and Brookes 2020) and health care provider websites (Brookes and Harvey 2016).

As a result of the long-standing focus on spoken interaction, studies of health (care) communication have tended to rely on relatively small datasets, such as samples of

DOI: 10.4324/9780367076399-43

clinical exchanges, which were most amenable to fine-grained, qualitative analysis. As such, methodologically, much health (care) communication research has taken a sociolinguistic and discourse analytic perspective, utilising approaches like conversation analysis, text/genre analysis and (critical) discourse analysis. Many health (care) language studies have combined perspectives, for example, the tendency for conversation analysis and interactional sociolinguistic methodologies to be supplemented by a strain of critical discourse analysis, with the research impetus being as much to criticise and change practices in institutional health (care) settings as to describe and understand them (e.g. McHoul and Rapley 2001).

Although small-scale datasets – and the qualitative approaches used to analyse them – have produced rich insights into the linguistic dynamics of health (care), research employing such approaches has been criticised for basing findings on limited datasets that are not necessarily representative of wider communication within the particular domains under study. Thus, since the late 1990s health (care) communication scholars have increasingly harnessed the opportunities afforded by corpus linguistic approaches to obtain a more widely representative, and so generalisable, picture of how language is used in various clinical contexts.

This chapter demonstrates how some of the corpus linguistic techniques introduced so far in this book can be usefully applied to study health (care) communication. To do this, we provide two case studies, which each explore a different health-related topic, are based on corpora representing distinct textual genres and modes and utilise a different corpus technique as their point of entry. The first case study utilises keywords to examine characteristic themes in a corpus of adolescents' health advice–seeking emails. The second uses collocation to identify metaphors used to represent dementia in a corpus of newspaper articles. In each of these case studies we supplement each of the quantitative approaches with qualitative, theory-informed analysis of patterns of interest. Before addressing these case studies, we first provide a brief overview of existing applications of corpus linguistic methods to the study of health (care) communication.

2 Health (care) communication and corpus linguistics

Initial corpus studies of health (care) communication focused primarily on spoken interactions between patients and clinical staff. For example, Thomas and Wilson (1996) utilised a 1.25-million-word corpus of practitioner–patient exchanges and set out to demonstrate that computer content analysis can overcome the 'shortcomings of straight quantitative analysis' and has 'the potential to provide results which are in some respects comparable to manual discourse analysis' (1996: 92). Although corpus techniques enabled the researchers to quickly and accurately identify significant aspects of the health practitioners' language use, this study gave little emphasis to extended stretches of language in use and to how linguistic components actually functioned in the dialogic context of the practitioner–patient exchanges under investigation.

Later research by Skelton and colleagues (e.g. Skelton and Hobbs 1999) demonstrated the methodological advantages of integrating quantitative with qualitative approaches. As a starting point, they used frequency counts of words and phrases, complementing such quantitative insights with qualitative assessments of how such phrases operate in context through the analysis of concordance outputs. Rather than providing a broad linguistic characterisation of the particular communicative practices in question, the authors confine their analyses to investigating specific linguistic phenomena (e.g. metaphor and imprecision). For this reason, their studies did not harness comparative data, contrasting, for example, their datasets with general reference corpora.

Such a comparative approach was adopted by Adolphs *et al.* (2004) to analyse NHS Direct exchanges between professionals and patient callers. Adolphs *et al.* compared a corpus of health professionals' language with a corpus of general spoken English, identifying keywords that appeared with greater frequency in the NHS Direct consultations. The researchers examined these key items in their original discourse environments using concordance lines and techniques from conversation analysis to provide close descriptions of interactional processes. These methodological stages afforded the authors a means of understanding the uniqueness of the professional–patient exchanges, enabling them to characterise the nature of NHS Direct consultations where they identified an overarching tendency for professionals to use politeness strategies and the language of convergence in their interactions with callers.

Following the early studies of spoken health (care) interactions, corpus methods then began to be applied to the study of written health (care)–related texts, for example, Crawford *et al.*'s (1998) study of nurses' written reports. An increasingly popular area of focus for corpus studies of written communication is the print media, with researchers examining press representations of (usually contemporary) health topics, for example, Brookes and Baker's (2021) corpus study of representations of obesity in the British press. More recently, corpus techniques have also been employed in conjunction with stylistic approaches to analyse literary representations of illness and health, such as Demjén's (2015) investigation of the language of affective states in Sylvia Plath's writing.

In recent years, corpus studies of health (care) communication have focused increasingly on language in digital contexts, with research exploring online platforms for advice seeking and giving being particularly prominent. For example, Harvey and colleagues examined variations of a corpus containing emails sent by young people to a health website aimed at adolescents (e.g. Harvey 2012). Another popular area of focus in corpus studies of online health (care) interaction is online, peer-to-peer support groups. A recent example includes Hunt and Brookes's (2020) study of the language around mental health in online support groups for people with anorexia, depression and diabulimia. An emerging, but less studied, area of focus for corpus studies of digital health (care) communication is patient feedback. For example, Baker *et al.* (2019) analysed the language of patient feedback in a 29-million-word corpus of online comments, along with an 11-million-word corpus of providers' responses. The recent and growing focus on digital discourse in corpus studies of health (care) communication partly reflects the growing influence of digital (communicative) technologies over the ways that people communicate – and indeed act – in relation to their health (Lupton 2017). Meanwhile, on a practical level, this penchant might also reflect the relative ease with which ready-digitised texts can be collected and prepared for corpus analysis (compared to written and spoken language).

The number of corpus studies of health (care) communication, while still relatively small, continues to grow. A notable feature of this work is its tendency towards methodological plurality – particularly the combination of quantitative corpus techniques with more qualitative approaches to linguistic analysis. Like other approaches to the study of health (care) language, the corpus approach also tends towards interdisciplinarity – incorporating perspectives from fields as diverse as medicine, psychology and sociology into linguistic analyses. This methodological and theoretical diversity also mirrors the diversity of corpus linguistic approaches, whose flexibility provides fertile ground for such multiplicity of methods and theoretical approaches.

In the sections that follow, we provide two case studies which showcase the ways in which corpus linguistic methods can be used to interrogate health (care) language. Each case study utilises a different, established corpus technique as its starting point to investigate discourse produced in two different contexts with relevance to health. The first, which addresses the context of e-health, makes use of keywords to explore the thematic make-up of a corpus of emails submitted to an adolescent health website and gives a more in-depth analysis of the language used to disclose concerns relating to sexual health. The second, which focuses on the media, utilises collocation as a means of identifying the metaphors used by sections of the British press in their coverage of the topic of dementia. Although their respective approaches are based primarily on different corpus techniques (keywords and collocation), both of these case studies supplement their initial use of these techniques with more qualitative, context-sensitive analyses facilitated by concordance output, as well as recourse to the wider contexts of the original texts themselves.

3 Keywords: adolescent emails and sexual health

The first case study utilises the corpus technique of keywords to analyse online health communication. As a reminder, the keywords approach compares the frequency information for one corpus against another (i.e. the reference corpus) to indicate which words occur with a markedly high frequency in a target corpus, with such words constituting characteristic lexis in that data and so providing useful entry points for analysis (see Chapters 9 and 10, this volume). This case study focuses on the *Adolescent Health Email Corpus* (AHEC), a corpus of health advice-seeking emails sent to the *Teenage Health Freak* (www.teenagehealthfreak.org), a UK-based adolescent health advice website. These online requests for advice do not constitute emails in the traditional sense; they are not sent via the contributors' individual, personal email accounts, but communicated anonymously via a universal posting platform on the website. Our corpus analysis is based on the adolescent communiqués rather than the professionals' comparatively infrequent returns. Permission was given to collect and analyse emails sent to the *Teenage Health Freak* website between January 2004 and December 2005. The total dataset comprises 62,794 messages (approximately 1 million words).

In order to ascertain salient themes in the AHEC, *WordSmith Tools* (Scott 2016) was used to generate keywords by comparing this corpus against the original *British National Corpus* (BNC1994). Keywords were generated using the log-likelihood test (Dunning 1993) and then grouped thematically based on analysis of each keyword in its original contexts of use. The resultant keyword categories reflect the range of health themes raised in the adolescents' emails and includes (example keywords in brackets): mental health (e.g. *depression*, *depressed*, *suicide*), body weight and image (e.g. *anorexia*, *anorexic*, *weight*), drugs and alcohol (e.g. *drugs*, *cannabis*, *cocaine*), serious conditions (e.g. *cancer*, *epilepsy*, *diabetes*), minor conditions (*acne*, *zits*, *blackhead*) and medication (e.g. *medicine*, *medication*, *prescribed*). In this chapter, we focus on the theme of sexual health, which exhibited not only the largest number of keywords but also comprised some of the strongest keywords in the corpus. The keywords assigned to this theme are displayed in Table 43.1.

A full analysis of this theme would attend to most, if not all, of the keywords shown in this table. However, for the purpose of this case study, we focus on the topic of

Table 43.1 Sexual health keywords in AHEC, ranked by log-likelihood score

sex, sexual, penis, pregnant, period, orgasm, AIDS, infertile, STD, STI, sperm, contraception, HIV, clitoris, vagina, vulva, PMS, erection, condom, masturbate, gay, abortion, foreplay, intercourse, virgin, unprotected, lesbian, oral, pill, ovulation, herpes, thrush, chlamydia, pregnancy, tampon, testicles, genitalia, viagra, scrotum, labia, glans, ovaries, foreskin, balls, fanny, bisexual, miscarriage

sexually transmitted infections (STIs), specifically the keywords *AIDS* (n = 209) and *HIV* (114), and the adolescents' knowledge and representation of these concepts. Our choice of this topic for closer scrutiny is motivated not only by its prevalence in this corpus but also by its significance to the teenage population more generally.

Examining emails mentioning the keywords *HIV* and *AIDS* (314 in total) through the prism of concordance, we observed that these texts covered a range of themes, central among which are questions relating to HIV/AIDS terminology and conceptual definitions of the terms (of which there are 78 occurrences: 24 per cent), concerns regarding transmission and causation (72: 23 per cent) and questions about symptoms and the likelihood of having HIV/AIDS (60: 19 per cent). The lexical item *AIDS* appears nearly twice as often (209) as *HIV* (114). Of the 209 occurrences of *AIDS*, 17 co-occur with *HIV* (L5 to R5), which suggests a relationship between the two. These emails ask such questions as: "*how does **HIV/AIDS** get passed on*" and "*what happens when a man or women is **hiv** and has **aids***" (note: these and other extracts are presented with their original spelling, punctuation and capitalisation). In these instances, the adolescents clearly, and crucially, distinguish the concepts of HIV and AIDS, conceiving of them as separate entities, while also being connected in some way, given the oblique (/) or conjuncts ("and", "or") that coordinate them.

However, most of the occurrences of *AIDS* in the corpus (192: 92 per cent) appear without mention of HIV, the virus that can cause AIDS (UNESCO 2006). The following examples are typical of the range of contexts in which AIDS in isolation is used:

1. How do i know if iv got **aids**
2. Can you get **AIDS** by being fingered?
3. I had sex without using a condom and i am really scared i might be pregnant or might have **aids**
4. I have had sex with my boyfriend for the first time and the condom kept snapping so we decided to not use one what are the chances of me bein pregnant or having **aids**? please answer this im really really wottied

The absence of any reference to HIV and the foregrounding of AIDS indicate a terminological conflation of the two concepts, a misconception that is liable to have profound consequences in terms of how the adolescents conceive of and understand HIV and AIDS. For instance, in a number of the examples, there is the underlying belief that AIDS is a communicable infection, not a syndrome or range of conditions (UNESCO 2006), with its being constructed as, and confused with, a virus or disease, something that can be readily transmitted via sexual activity.

Collapsing the distinction between HIV and AIDS in this way inevitably results in confusion and reinforces 'unrealistic and unfounded fears' (Watney 1989: 184) on the part of the adolescents who might mistakenly believe themselves to be at risk of AIDS but not HIV. Such extreme worst-case scenarios conceive of AIDS as something that sets in immediately after infection, a unitary phenomenon rather than a collection of different medical conditions – beliefs which obscure, if not efface altogether, the existence of HIV, the virus, which is indeed infectious. Such erroneous conflation of HIV infection with AIDS (by definition, the stage of HIV infection 'when a person's immune system can no longer cope'; Terrence Higgins Trust 2007: 1) repeats some of the early and fundamental misconceptions and negative attitudes about AIDS that were widespread during the 1980s and 1990s (Sikand *et al.* 1996; Helman 2007). For example, Warwick *et al.*'s (1988) in-depth study into youth beliefs about AIDS revealed that a significant number of young people, as with many adults, were unable to distinguish between HIV infection and AIDS, a finding which they attributed to the media's consistent failure to provide the public with accurate information. This fundamental misunderstanding (identifying AIDS as a transmissible disease) was related to the 'public terror about "catching" AIDS from people in public places or during casual contact' (Grover 1990: 145). Such beliefs (and the emotive linguistic choices encoding them) prevalent during that period are still apparent in the adolescent health emails communicated over 20 years later. For instance, one of the central ways in which adolescents describe becoming infected with HIV or developing AIDS is through use of the lemma CATCH, the second most common verb (13 times) used to signify Contraction after GET (n = 52). The use of CATCH as a verb encoding transmission of HIV/AIDS is telling, implying a more active role for subjects:

5. how do you prevent **catching** h. i. v
6. is the aids virus difficult to **catch**?
7. if i have sex with someone with aids without protection can i **cath** it
8. can you **catch** aids if someone masterbates you.

Biber *et al.* (1999) describe 'catch' as an 'activity verb', a verb denoting actions and events 'that could be associated with choice' (1999: 361). As these emails illustrate, 'catch' implies notions of agency on the part of subjects in the sense that it is within their power to prevent infection, with responsibility framed in terms of both general or universal agency, encoded via the second person: "Can *you* catch …?", or individual control via the first-person singular pronoun: "Can *I* catch …?". As Johnson and Murray (1985: 152) put it, "catching" an ailment (as in catching a cold) semantically implies a degree of co-operation: 'We catch things … in ways which are our own fault; we blame ourselves – we should have worn galoshes, and should not have sat in a draught'. This notion of personal agency and responsibility, communicated through the verbal concept of "catching", is also apparent in questions referring explicitly to prevention and avoidance strategies (e.g. "how do you prevent catching h. i. v?", "is the aids virus difficult to catch?"). Similarly, it is evident in messages in which the adolescents seek clarification as to whether specific activities are liable to result in contracting HIV/AIDS and which should therefore be avoided (e.g. "can you catch aids if someone masterbates you?", "if I have sex with someone with aids without protection can i cath it?"). Here, then, both HIV and AIDS are constructed as preventable through individual agency and requisite care. Infection with HIV is not an inevitable outcome, as, alarmingly, some young people have perceived it to be (Warwick *et al.* 1988).

However, commentators and public health bodies stress that neither HIV nor AIDS can be "caught" (Watney 1989: 184). Contemporary health promotion literature produced by organisations such as UNESCO continually warns against the use of this verb to signify the way that people might become HIV positive, since it only helps to reproduce myths about HIV and AIDS (UNESCO 2006). In the health emails noted earlier, for example, the various realisations of the lemma CATCH unavoidably and infelicitously conjure notions of the common cold and influenza, as evidence from the general language *British National Corpus* (BNC) attests. Consulting the 100-million-word BNC1994 reveals that, as a transitive verb, "catch" co-occurs with the direct objects "cold" (113), "chill" (21), "bug" (20) and "colds" (7). As these collocates indicate, one typical use of the verb "catch" in general English is to describe the acquisition of relatively minor infections, in the sense of their being widespread and generally innocuous (though "bug", of course, potentially relates to more serious infections such as methicillin-resistant *Staphylococcus aureus* [MRSA], the so-called "super bug"; Knifton 2005). With regard to more serious viruses and illnesses, other less euphemistic constructions are used in the BNC1994 to describe the process of becoming infected and the onset of morbidity: for example, HIV is typically "contracted", "got", "acquired", while AIDS is "got", "developed", "contracted". Given this association, a corollary of using "catch" to describe infection with HIV/ AIDS is to encode the assumption that the virus can be acquired via casual contact, possessing a transmission efficacy similar to both colds and influenza. As such, talk of "catching" HIV/AIDS figuratively transforms the virus from something which is, in reality, difficult to transmit and is only communicable via specific routes (Terrence Higgins Trust 2007: 2) to something highly contagious, and liable to spread rapidly and extensively.

From this short case study, it is evident that the adolescents contributing to the AHEC possessed a range of misconceptions about HIV and AIDS, among which perhaps the most alarming was the tendency for some to conflate the two, reinforcing the idea that HIV and AIDS are identical. Such a conflation is liable to obscure awareness of the ways the virus is transmitted, potentially impeding assessments of risk in relation to sexual behaviour. The corpus analysis further highlighted some of the folk conceptualisations of sexual health that the adolescents operated with, beliefs that may need to be addressed by educators. Responding to lay beliefs like these is crucial, since people are liable to filter official health education messages through popular beliefs about health (Helman 2007), reinterpreting them to suit their own needs (Aggleton and Homans 1987: 25). However, not all of the adolescents' emails, in the shape of distorting metaphorical transformations and alarmist folk beliefs, display irrational responses to HIV and AIDS. The most commonly occurring emails about HIV and AIDS in the adolescent health corpus are fundamental questions concerning definitions and terminology, specifically: "What is HIV/AIDS?" and "What does HIV/AIDS stand for?" One way of interpreting these open and elementary types of enquiry is, of course, to regard them as emblematic of knowledge deficits about sexual health. Yet equally, such questions might be considered vital responses to a contemporary and potentially life-threatening condition that is still commonly misunderstood (Helman 2007).

4 Collocation: dementia metaphors in the press[1]

Our second case study uses collocation analysis to explore the metaphors used to represent dementia in articles published by the British tabloid, the *Daily Mail*. *Dementia* is an umbrella term used to refer to a range of diseases which cause a series of cognitive impairment symptoms, such as problems with memory, reasoning, perception and communication (World Health Organization [WHO] 2017). The most prevalent type of dementia is Alzheimer's disease, but other types include vascular dementia, dementia with Lewy bodies and frontotemporal dementia. Dementia is a progressive syndrome, meaning that its symptoms worsen over time. It is widely claimed that dementia represents a major global public health challenge, as it is currently understood to affect as many as 47.5 million people worldwide, with an estimated 7.7 million new cases each year (WHO 2017). The number of people living with dementia is projected to rise to 75.6 million by 2030, trebling to 135.5 million by 2050.

At present, there is no pharmacological cure for dementia, meaning that people living with the syndrome today will also die with it. However, it is important to note that while people living with dementia will also die with it, they will not die *of* it, for dementia itself does not cause death. Indeed, although dementia is associated with reduced life expectancy, when people with dementia die, their death is more likely to be caused by co-occurring conditions such as pneumonia, rather than by dementia directly.

With no cure in immediate sight, there is a need for research focusing on people's lived experiences and understandings of dementia in the here and now. This includes how experiences and perceptions of the syndrome might be shaped by cultural constructions of it, for instance in the media, which constitutes a primary source through which people routinely access information about, and form their impressions of, health concerns (Seale 2003). As mentioned, this case study focuses on the metaphors used to represent dementia in the *Daily Mail*. Put simply, *metaphor* refers to 'the phenomenon whereby we talk and, potentially, think about something in terms of something else', where the two things involved are different but are perceived by the speaker to share some similarity (Semino 2008: 1). Because they are often used to express abstract, subjective, sensitive and taboo subjects, it stands to reason that talk about health and illness is often rife with metaphorical language (ibid: 175–6).

For this case study, we draw upon a purpose-built, specialised corpus containing articles from the *Daily Mail* mentioning *dementia* either once in their headline or three or more times throughout the rest of the article, published between 2007 and 2017. The resulting corpus contains a total of 1,674 articles and 1,155,675 words. We decided to focus on just this newspaper, as it published more articles about dementia (i.e. mentioning *dementia* once in the headline or three or more times in the article body) during this period than any other UK national newspaper.

To identify the metaphors used to represent dementia, we utilised collocation analysis. Collocation is a linguistic device whereby words, in associating strongly with one another, become bearers of meaning by virtue of co-occurrence (see Chapters 9, 14 and 15, this volume). Collocation is typically judged to exist using a word-association measure that tells us how often two or more words occur alongside one another and whether this association is notable as a sizeable effect in our data (i.e. the words have a measurably strong preference to occur together as opposed to being randomly associated). For this analysis, we used *WordSmith Tools* to generate a list of collocates of the word *dementia* (n = 12,095) (L5 to R5, frequency ≥5). We then ranked our list of collocates using the Mutual Information (MI) statistic and removed collocates which were not assigned an MI score of at least 3 (Hunston 2002). The resulting collocates were then analysed in context to ascertain whether or not they tended to be used metaphorically. This analysis indicated the use of numerous source domains (Lakoff and Johnson 1980). However, for this case study we will focus on the source domain which exhibited not only the most but also the most frequent collocates, namely VIOLENCE. Table 43.2 shows the collocates assigned to this domain.

Table 43.2 VIOLENCE metaphorical collocates of *dementia* (MI ≥ 3), ranked by collocation frequency (in brackets)

against (121), *battle* (81), *fight* (65), *ward* (62), *victims* (48), *stricken* (40), *battling* (36), *hit* (35), *beat* (30), *killed* (20), *losing* (20), *victim* (20), *cruel* (17), *killer* (16), *struck* (15), *struggle* (15), *killing* (14), *struggling* (13), *tackle* (13), *wards* (13), *kill* (12), *robbed* (11), *tackling* (11), *war* (9), *beating* (8), *toll* (8), *hits* (7), *succumbed* (7), *weapon* (7), *enemies* (6), *combat* (5), *cosh* (5), *fighting* (5), *onslaught* (5), *striking* (5), *struggled* (5)

Although the metaphorical collocates in Table 43.2 all relate to dementia, more specifically these violence tropes target dementia itself, the person living with dementia (and their experience of the syndrome) and responses to the condition, including by individuals but also larger institutions like the government and medico-scientific researchers. Beginning with the representation of dementia itself, several of the collocates in the table contribute to the anthropomorphisation of the syndrome. This agent is described as *cruel* and is framed as inflicting acts of violence on people, foremost the act of murder. For example, dementia is construed as a killer (*killed*, *killer*, *killing*, *kill*) (collocates underlined):

9. Cancer accounts for almost a third of cases while heart disease is the biggest killer of men and **dementia** in women. Dementia now claims the lives of more than 51,000 women and men a year. **Dementia** and Alzheimer's kill three times more women than breast cancer. It's now the second biggest killer of men, with most dying of heart disease.Giana Hennigan,

   (2018)

Similarly, it is also described as inflicting a *toll* and *onslaught* on those affected by it:

10. But now scientists claim the hot drink is more than just an enjoyable treat, it can actually help to prevent the onslaught of **dementia**.

    (2016)

It is worth remembering at this point, as noted earlier, that although people with dementia have a reduced life expectancy and will die *with* the condition, they do not die *of* it. Thus, we can question the logic and accuracy of these fatalistic tropes. Yet in addition to murder, dementia commits other acts of violence, such as *hit*[ting] and *striking*. Another form of violence that dementia is presented as inflicting upon those diagnosed with it is theft. Specifically, the lexical verb collocate *robbed* is used to characterise dementia as stealing individuals' ability to perform certain actions such as walking and speaking:

11. Poor old Terry Jones, as he calls him, has since been revealed to be suffering from a form of **dementia** that has robbed him of the power of speech. There will definitely be no more reunions now. Palin's eyes fill with tears as we talk about him.

    (2017)

Consistent with the types of metaphorical framings seen so far, the experience of dementia could equally be framed as a violent conflict, with life with dementia characterised as an ongoing battle (*battle*, *battling*), struggle (*struggle*, *struggling*, *struggled*) or fight *(fighting)*:

12. Her heartbreaking story of a woman struggling with **dementia** was inspired by her grandmother's battle with the cruel disease.

(2016)

Other metaphors used to represent the lived experience of dementia did so in ways that were similarly violent but implied a more limited prospect for agency on the part of the person living with the syndrome. This could manifest in words implying a fatalistic outcome of life with dementia, such as characterising people with dementia as victims (*victims*, *victim*), *stricken* and as having lost (*losing*) or succumbed to the syndrome.

13. Frail WWII veteran, 89, faces five years in jail after admitting keeping loaded revolver by his bed 'so he could kill himself if he succumbed to **dementia**'

(2015)

This reduced agency was also evident in lexical verb collocates denoting violent processes (*hit*, *struck*) of which people with dementia are the passive objects:

14. TINY MEMORY LAPSES? **DEMENTIA** COULD HIT YOU IN JUST 12 YEARS

(2014)

The final aspect of the dementia experience that was framed metaphorically in violent terms was responses to the syndrome. This includes advising readers on measures they as individuals can take to reduce their risk of developing the syndrome. These actions could be lexicalised as helping to "ward off" dementia, with the implication being that the condition is an unwanted invader that individuals need to defend themselves against. More commonly, violence metaphors were used to characterise the actions and responses of larger institutions, such as the government and medico-scientific researchers. In these scenarios, dementia is cast as an enemy (*enemies*), with whom these actors are engaged in a violent conflict (*against*, *fight*, *beat*, *tackle*, *tackling*, *war*, *beating*). As the use of the term *weapon* (also a collocate of *dementia*) in this example attests, in this scenario the (prospective) pharmacological solutions to obesity were also lexicalised as violent weapons (*weapon*, *cosh*):

15. NEW WEAPON IN THE WAR ON **DEMENTIA**: THE TWO RONNIES!

(2016)

Violence metaphors are often considered problematic when used in relation to health and illness. For example, Sontag (1978) famously cautioned against the use of war [sic] metaphors to talk about illness, arguing that they can be stigmatising for those affected by the illness in question, who could be rendered as the enemy in such scenarios, and their bodies the metaphorical "battlefields". Moreover, it is argued that if the disease prevails and the person fails to recover from it, they could be viewed as having "lost" the battle.

While these criticisms can likewise be directed at the use of violence metaphors in relation to dementia, such arguments have been countered by more recent claims that people can find such violence metaphors empowering, as they grant them a greater sense of agency in their illness experience, helping them to feel like they have greater influence over their prognosis. However, given that there is not currently a cure for or prospect of recovery from dementia, this is a battle that is inevitably lost in this case. Indeed, the focus on pharmacological interventions in metaphors describing responses to dementia not only places emphasis on prospective treatments that are not currently available but also serves to simultaneously shift focus *away from* other, non-pharmacological measures which help people with dementia to live with and manage the syndrome in the here-and-now. Moreover, such emphasis could also influence public thinking and policy decisions relating to appropriate ways of responding to dementia in the future – a relevant argument when we consider the current disparity between funding for medico-scientific research and social care.

In conclusion, then, we can question the extent to which such tropes are likely to produce contented attitudes for people with dementia and their relatives and carers and actually raise genuine awareness of the syndrome. The effect of recycling such fear-inducing tropes, which seem just as much calculated to sensationalise as they do to inform, cannot be underestimated, for as Chivers (2011: 60) observes, the public are liable to associate 'dementia with the most horrifying possible loss of self', an assumption that is deeply embedded and continues to persist in western culture. Of course, readers' responses to dementia are not always uniform, and readers can resist dominant media narratives about topics like dementia. Most analyses of corpora of media texts, such as the one presented here, do not (and cannot) provide empirical insight into the ways in which audiences respond to media representations of health topics. Recent corpus studies of media texts have begun to address this limitation by engaging with readers' comments on online articles (so-called "below-the-line" comments), in which readers offer their own views and perspectives on stories and in the process offer their own representations which can be consistent with but also challenge those offered in the corresponding articles. An example relevant to media representations of health is Brookes and Baker's (2021) corpus study of British press representations of obesity, in which they compare discourses in a sample of reader comments against the articles on which they are based. Yet it remains a fact that many people have a poor understanding of and continue to fear dementia more than they do other serious diseases, such as cancer, a view shared not only by older adults but also young people (Alzheimer's Research Trust 2011).

Although we have focused on the *Daily Mail* in this study, the metaphorical patterns we have identified are certainly not particular to this newspaper but reflect wider trends in UK press discourse. In defence of the press, we could argue that metaphor provides a useful set of linguistic and conceptual apparatus with which to communicate about complex conditions like dementia, conferring a sense of symbolic order over them for the purposes of communicating about them with the general public. However, for this purpose we would prefer to see the press utilising other metaphors that are not only less stigmatising for people living with dementia but which also help to raise more accurate and useful public awareness of it. Possible alternatives include metaphors of JOURNEY and COMPANIONSHIP, which, respectively, articulate the progressive and chronic nature of the syndrome. Although there is some evidence of such tropes in our *Daily Mail* corpus, they are comparatively infrequent relative to the VIOLENCE metaphors explored here. It is perhaps the case, then, that the pressure on (particularly tabloid) newspapers to print negative and sensationalistic headlines in order to sell more copies (Conboy 2006), or to generate more clicks, outweighs their sense of duty to combat stigma and raise accurate and genuinely useful awareness of health concerns like dementia.

5 Conclusion

The case studies reported in this chapter demonstrate the capacity of corpus linguistic methods to provide both quantitative *and* qualitative perspectives on data that represents a wider range of communicative styles, routines, lived experiences and understandings of health (care) and illness than would be feasible using purely qualitative approaches, producing – by and large – more generalisable findings in the process. Although this chapter has focused on language in two specific health (care) contexts, the analytical techniques afforded by corpus linguistics are flexible and can, in theory, be applied to the analysis of language produced in relation to any health issue or within any health (care) context. Whatever the topic under study, by affording the opportunity to examine large quantities of authentic language data, corpus linguistic methods could be said to go some way towards appeasing the commitment to more objective approaches to large datasets that is commonplace in the domain of empirical health research (Brown *et al.* 2006), potentially helping researchers to bridge the gap between social scientific and biomedical perspectives on health and illness.

In terms of future applications, with increasing emphasis on evidence-based practice in health care training (Brown *et al.* 2006), corpus linguistic methods could provide practitioners and instructors with substantial evidence bases on which to both teach and learn about the communicative routines of particular (clinical) groups. Indeed, given the significant contribution that corpus linguistics has already made to practices in language teaching, including increasingly in the teaching of languages for health care purposes, it is not difficult to envisage a role for corpora – as vast repositories of authentic health (care) language – in more general clinical communication training. The main challenge, as we see it, resides in convincing health practitioners and policymakers, who are familiar with and committed to their own already established research methods and standards of data representativeness, of the virtues and values of corpus linguistic approaches in the long-term.

Note

1 This research is supported by a UKRI Future Leaders Fellowship, grant reference MR/V022954/1.

Further reading

Gwyn, R. (2002) *Communicating Health and Illness*, London: Sage. (This is an accessible discourse-based survey to health communication.)

Harvey, K. and Koteyko, N. (2012) *Exploring Health Communication*, London: Routledge. (This text provides an accessible overview of key concepts in language and health but also has more focus on corpus linguistic applications in this domain.)

Jones, R. (2013) *Health and Risk Communication: An Applied Linguistic Perspective*, London: Routledge. (This book introduces key concepts in linguistic studies of health discourse.)

References

Adolphs, S., Brown, B., Carter, R., Crawford, P. and Sahota, O. (2004) 'Applied Clinical Linguistics: Corpus Linguistics in Health Care Settings', *Journal of Applied Linguistics* 1: 9–28.

Aggleton, P. and Homans, H. (1987) 'Teaching about AIDS', *Social Science Teacher* 17: 24–8.

Alzheimer's Research Trust (2011) *Alzheimer's Research UK Launches as Public Dementia Fears Spiral*, Retrieved from: http://www.alzheimersresearchuk.org/AlzheimersResearchUKlaunch/.

Baker, P., Brookes, G. and Evans, C. (2019) *The Language of Patient Feedback: A Corpus Linguistic Study of Online Health Communication*, London: Routledge.

Biber, D., Johansson, S., Leech, G., Conrad, S. and Finegan, E. (1999) *Longman Grammar of Spoken and Written English*, London: Longman.

Brookes, G. and Baker, P. (2021) *Obesity in the News: Language and Representation in the Press*, Cambridge: Cambridge University Press.

Brookes, G. and Harvey, K. (2016) 'Opening up the NHS to Market: Using Multimodal Critical Discourse Analysis to Examine the Ongoing Corporatisation of Health Care Communication', *Journal of Language and Politics* 15: 288–302.

Brown, B., Crawford, P. and Carter, R. (2006) *Evidence-Based Health Communication*, Maidenhead: Open University Press.

Candlin, S. (2000) 'New Dynamics in the Nurse–Patient Relationship?', in S. Sarangi and M. Coulthard (eds) *Discourse and Social Life*, London: Longman, pp. 230–45.

Chivers, S. (2011) *The Silvering Screen: Old Age and Disability in Cinema*, Toronto: University of Toronto Press.

Conboy, M. (2006) *Tabloid Britain*, London: Routledge.

Crawford, P., Brown, B. and Nolan, P. (1998) *Communicating Care: The Language of Nursing*, Gloucester: Stanley Thornes.

Demjén, Z. (2015) *Sylvia Plath and the Language of Affective States Written Discourse and the Experience of Depression*, London: Bloomsbury.

Dunning, T. (1993). 'Accurate Methods for the Statistics of Surprise and Coincidence'. *Computational Linguistics* 19(1): 61–74.

Fox, N. (1993) *Postmodernism, Sociology and Health*, Buckingham: Open University Press.

Francis, G. and Kramer-Dahl, A. (2004) 'Grammar in the Construction of Medical Case Histories', in C. Coffin, A. Hewings and K. O'Halloran (eds) *Applying English Grammar: Functional and Corpus Approaches*, London: Arnold, pp. 172–90.

Grover, J. (1990) 'AIDS: Keywords', in C. Ricks and L. Michaels (eds) *The State of the Language*, 1990s edition, London: Faber & Faber, pp. 142–62.

Harvey, K. (2012) 'Disclosures of Depression: Using Corpus Linguistics Methods to Interrogate Young People's Online Health Concerns', *International Journal of Corpus Linguistics* 17: 349–79.

Helman, C. (2007) *Culture, Health and Illness*, 5th edn, London: Hodder Arnold.

Hobbs, P. (2003) 'The Use of Evidentiality in Physician's Progress Notes', *Discourse Studies* 5: 451–78.

Hunston, S. (2002) *Corpora in Applied Linguistics*, Cambridge: Cambridge University Press.

Hunt, D. and Brookes, G. (2020) *Corpus, Discourse and Mental Health*, London: Bloomsbury.

Johnson, D. and Murray, J. (1985) 'Do Doctors Mean What They Say?', in D. Enright (ed.) *Fair of Speech: The Uses of Euphemism*, Oxford: Oxford University Press, pp. 151–58.

Knifton, C. (2005) 'Social Work and the Rise of the MRSA "Super Bug"', *Practice* 17: 39–42.

Lakoff, G. and Johnson, M. (1980) *Metaphors We Live By*, Chicago: University of Chicago Press.

Lupton, D. (2017) *Digital Health: Critical and Cross-Disciplinary Perspectives*, London: Routledge.

McHoul, A. and Rapley, M. (2001) 'Preface: With a Little Help from Our Friends', in A. McHoul and M. Rapley (eds) *How to Analyse Talk in Institutional Settings*, London: Continuum, pp. 25–38.

Parry, R. (2004) 'Communication During Goal-Setting in Physiotherapy Treatment Settings', *Clinical Rehabilitation* 18: 668–82.

Pilnick, A. (1999) '"Patient Counselling" by Pharmacists: Advice, Information or Instruction?', *Sociological Quarterly* 40: 613–22.

Scott, M. (2016) *WordSmith Tools, version 7*, Stroud: Lexical Analysis Software.

Seale, C. (2003) *Media and Health*, London: Sage.
Semino, E. (2008) *Metaphor and Discourse*, Cambridge: Cambridge University Press.
Sikand, A., Fisher, M. and Friedman, S. (1996) 'AIDS Knowledge, Concerns, and Behavioural Changes among Inner-City High School Students', *Journal of Adolescent Health* 18: 325–28.
Skelton, J. and Hobbs, F. (1999) 'Concordancing: Use of Language-Based Research in Medical Communication', *Lancet* 353: 108–11.
Sontag, S. (1978) *Illness as Metaphor*, New York: Farrar, Straus and Giroux.
Terrence Higgins Trust (2007) *Understanding HIV Infection: HIV? AIDS?*, 5th edn, London: Terrence Higgins Trust.
Thomas, J. and Wilson, A. (1996) 'Methodologies for Studying a Corpus of Doctor-Patient Interaction', in J. Thomas and M. Short (eds) *Using Corpora for Language Research*, London: Longman, pp. 92–109.
UNESCO (United Nations Educational, Scientific and Cultural Organisation) (2006) UNESCO Guidelines on Language and Content in HIV- and AIDS-Related Materials, Paris: UNESCO.
Warwick, I., Aggleton, P. and Homans, H. (1988) 'Young People's Health Beliefs and AIDS', in P. Aggleton and H. Homans (eds) *Social Aspects of AIDS*, Sussex: Falmer Press, pp. 106–25.
Watney, S. (1989) 'AIDS, Language and the Third World', in E. Carter and S. Watney (eds.) *Taking Liberties: AIDS and Cultural Politics*, London: Serpent's Tail, pp. 183–92.
World Health Organization (2017) *Dementia: Fact Sheet*, Retrieved from http://www.who.int/mediacentre/factsheets/fs362/en/.

44

Corpus linguistics and intercultural communication: avoiding the essentialist trap

Michael Handford

1 Bringing together intercultural communication and corpus linguistics

There is considerable debate and disagreement about how intercultural communication should be defined and what it should cover. As there are several excellent introductions to and surveys of the field (e.g. Piller 2011; Martin *et al.* 2014; Jackson 2014), these debates will only be briefly addressed here. Nevertheless, this chapter takes an inclusive approach and interprets "intercultural communication" (hereafter IC) as an umbrella term: here, any research that examines topics such as culture, conceptions of culture, cultural differences, (socio)cultural identities, cultural competencies, cross-cultural comparisons, attitudes to culture or interactions where culture or cultural difference may be relevant, is included.

As a field, IC draws on and has informed many disciplines, including social psychology, anthropology, communication studies, gender studies, organisational communication, (critical) discourse analysis, conversation analysis and pragmatics (Zhu 2016). While IC has grown out of these various disciplines and subdisciplines, it does not have a fixed or inherent methodology and employs a variety of methods from the earlier disciplines such as surveys and questionnaires, interviews and ethnographic observations (Zhu 2016: xv). Furthermore, it has tended to analyse people's perceptions of intercultural encounters and related issues and has received criticism for not sufficiently engaging with authentic practices of interaction (Carbaugh 2007). In other words, it largely analyses communication about intercultural contexts, rather than analysing people doing IC. Analysis of intercultural interactions that has occurred often features the close analysis of single interactions, rather than 'analysis of systematicities across large collections of interactional phenomena' (Brandt and Mortensen 2016: 307).

In a survey of corpus-informed IC research (Handford 2016), I argue that corpus methods have been rarely used to examine issues central to IC, such as cultural identity, intercultural interactions, intercultural competencies and conceptions of culture. This is surprising, because many of the advantages gained by combining corpus linguistics (CL) with discourse analysis or genre analysis (Stubbs 1996; Baker 2006; Baker *et al.* 2008; Handford 2010), such as improved rigour and scope of analysis through methodological

DOI: 10.4324/9780367076399-44

triangulation, could also be achieved in the combination of corpus linguistics and intercultural communication (hereafter CLIC). Such a combination would enable the analysis of "systematicities" across corpora that Brandt and Mortensen (2016) exhort, in the area of interactional practices that Carbaugh (2007) notes as an under-researched and in several other relevant areas. As such, corpus methods have much to offer intercultural research, and the fruitful synergies achieved elsewhere are achievable through such a combination. While there have been some studies classifiable as CLIC, they involve differing and arguably conflicting conceptualisations of culture and cultural identity. This is to be expected, because within the broad field of IC, there are long-standing, ongoing and heated debates about what culture is, what can be classified as intercultural communication and what role the researcher should play in approaching, analysing and responding to (or indeed with) subjects involved in intercultural contexts. An important issue in the analysis of IC is therefore the researcher's orientation to essentialism.

2 Intercultural communication: essentialist and anti-essentialist orientations

While the approach here to defining studies as intercultural is inclusive, the discussion of such studies is critical in stance: I argue that IC studies involve a set of assumptions concerning how they implicitly or explicitly define culture, along with the meanings attributed to cultural difference and/or cultural identity. Such assumptions then dictate the questions that are asked and the methods that are used.

Comparing essentialism and anti-essentialism

Bucholtz (2003: 400) defines essentialism as 'the position that attributes and behaviour of socially defined groups can be determined and explained by reference to cultural and/or biological characteristics believed to be inherent to the group'. Behaviour here includes communication, hence the relevance of essentialism for IC studies. Evidently, essentialism is concerned with the way we define and understand groups, and the two key assumptions on which essentialism is based are, firstly, that such groups can be clearly demarcated, and secondly that all members of each group share, to varying degrees, its inherent characteristics (Bucholtz 2003). While many studies in IC have assumed an essentialist stance, increasingly researchers in certain disciplines and approaches (such as sociology, anthropology, discourse analysis and ethnography) have overtly rejected this orientation in favour of one that engages with culture and cultural identities as socially constructed, emergent, fluid and performative (Piller 2011). In other words, culture is something that you do, rather than have: Culture is a practice.

To recap, the difference between essentialism and anti-essentialism is discussed at some length here because it helps clarify different IC research orientations, with some studies clearly or implicitly essentialist and others avowedly not. The difference itself can be the explicit focus of both theoretical (e.g. Holliday 2011; Piller 2011) and empirical research (e.g. Zhu *et al.* 2017; Handford *et al.* 2019). Moreover, we can regard essentialism as both a theoretical position, as outlined by the Bucholtz quote, or as an 'ethnographic fact' (2003: 375). The latter forms the basis of mainstream or folk understandings of identity in society.

It is therefore possible to categorise IC research into that which implicitly or explicitly assumes an essentialist stance and that which rejects such a stance in favour of one which recognises the fluid and socially constructed nature of identity (Bucholtz 2003; Holliday 2011). In the former, essentialist paradigm, cultural difference is seen as a given, and problems in IC are attributed to cultural differences. Cultural categories, usually nationality, are seen as relevant prior to analysis; "British" or "Chinese" are ascribed as cultural identities that explain and can predict behaviour. In contrast, the anti-essentialist position rejects such a paradigm, arguing that cultural identities are emergent and are constructed through discourse, as indeed is culture itself. Researchers in the latter camp also argue that essentialism can and does lead to stereotyping, the Othering of people positioned as different from ourselves, increased levels of ethnocentrism and a blindness towards the way power and discrimination operate in the service of certain cultural groups and to the detriment of others (Holliday 1999; Piller 2011; Handford *et al.* 2019).

Intercultural versus cross-cultural communication

A related debate concerns intercultural communication versus cross-cultural communication. They are sometimes seen as interchangeable terms, although research that compares communication of different cultures is typically defined as cross-cultural, whereas interaction involving participants from different cultural backgrounds is defined as intercultural (Jackson 2014: 3). Much work in "contrastive rhetoric" (Connor 2002) is cross-cultural in motivation, in that it compares texts (often written) produced or used by members of different cultures and then seeks to explain how any differences can be understood from a cultural perspective. CL has played a key role in many such studies (e.g. Connor *et al.* 2008; Moreno 2008) through the use of parallel corpora. Parallel corpora are defined in contrastive rhetoric as collections of comparable original texts in two or more languages that are written independently (see Moreno 2008), although there is debate in CL about definitions of parallel corpora and related terms such as bilingual corpora and comparable corpora (see McEnery and Hardie 2012: 18–21) (see Chapter 34, this volume).

Because such cross-cultural studies assume that cultures can be classified as independent variables (Moreno 2008), meaning cultures are seen as static and at least partly determining the language that is produced, they have been criticised as being essentialist or neo-essentialist in orientation (Holliday 2011; Handford 2016). The same charge is made about non-corpus-informed intercultural studies. For instance, Clyne (1994) analyses intercultural workplace interactions, and while he initially eschews essentialist assumptions, he then goes on to frame the interactions in terms of national differences. Such a pattern is evident in much intercultural research and has been termed "neo-essentialist" (Holliday 2011).

Avoiding the essentialist trap in analysis

We may well ask, 'Is it actually possible to conduct research into intercultural communication that does not assume the relevance of cultural difference prior to analysis?' This question is important for the analysis of IC in general, and therefore for CLIC. It is certainly a straightforward process to assume the relevance of social categories like nationality before doing any kind of sociolinguistic study, intercultural or otherwise, but such an approach can lead to circular reasoning (Sealey and Carter 2001; Piller 2011), what Sarangi terms the 'essentialist trap' (Sarangi 1994: 413); an example would be 'These Japanese people behave like this; they behave like this because they are Japanese'. By framing our analysis in such a way, we ignore the variables or identities or ideologies that may be more relevant than nationality. As Holliday and MacDonald (2019: 8) argue:

> Straight nationality comparisons are virtually impossible to isolate from other small culture factors such as profession or family background, political or religious affiliation, or from how these variables are constructed by both participants and researchers at any given time.

In contrast, an alternative question is, 'What cultural identities or conceptions of culture are made relevant in this discourse?' (e.g. Scollon and Scollon 2001; Piller 2011; Zhu *et al.* 2017; Handford *et al.* 2019; Holliday and MacDonald 2019). As such, this approach treats culture as something that needs explaining, rather than something that explains behaviour. It is a potentially more critical perspective (Piller 2011) and is less likely to lead into the quagmire of essentialism. This approach does not reject essentialism as an "ethnographic fact" (Bucholtz 2003: 375); indeed, the focus of such research can be essentialism, as it is used in authentic contexts.

Furthermore, by freeing up the concept of culture, and by extension cultural identity, from the traditional large categories like nationality, we can consider the question in relation to the "small" cultural categories referred to in the Holliday and MacDonald quote earlier, such as professional culture. Holliday's theory of "small cultures" (1999) has been very influential in IC research, as it allows for culture to be discussed and analysed without recourse to essentialist assumptions. Other related concepts include Wenger's (1998) Community of Practice or Gee's (2005) Discourse with a big "D": They all eschew a simplistic, static, homogenous view of culture and cultural identities in favour of seeing them as dynamic, socially constructed and constituted (at least partly) through discursive practices.

In the next section, several corpus studies that partially or fully address the question, 'What cultural identities or conceptions of culture are made relevant in this discourse?' are discussed. I have used Carbaugh's model of "cultural discourse analysis" as way of categorising relevant CL studies and of suggesting how future studies may be conducted.

3 Types of inquiry in IC

Carbaugh (2007) proposes five modes of inquiry in his study of cultural discourse analysis. Although Carbaugh's five modes of inquiry (2007) focus on spoken interactions, it is argued here that the modes are also relevant to studies of written, multimodal and online data. He defines a mode as 'a particular stance an analyst takes in order to accomplish an integral part of a research project' (2007: 171). I use this model to categorise various corpus studies that relate in some way to IC analysis as defined in the introduction section, although the studies themselves may not use the term "intercultural". An example is Baker *et al.*'s (2008) influential study of discourses of refugees and asylum seekers in the UK media. Although the paper does not mention "intercultural", it examines the discursive construction and representation of cultural identities, Otherisation and stereotyping.

Theoretical

This mode refers to new ways of understanding key concepts, such as power, identity, nation, culture and so on, as a discursive process; it conceptualises IC as communicative practice, a central concept in much anti-essentialist research. As the critical intercultural researchers Martin, Nakayama and Carbaugh argue, 'This relocates the site of the theoretical concern from individuals' or aggregate minds or abstract structures into social practices' (Martin et al. 2014: 25). Concordance lines can provide evidence of social practices, a point made in passing by Tognini-Bonelli (2001), but which deserves careful consideration. Indeed, much of the important work in corpus-assisted discourse studies (CADS) and CL-informed corpus discourse analysis (CDA) (some of which is outlined later) demonstrates this (see also Chapter 18, this volume). Two such studies, discussed at some length in Sections 4 and 5, analyse how "culture" is conceptualised in different educational contexts: Zhu *et al.* (2017) analyse a corpus of promotional websites of Master of Arts in IC programmes, and Handford *et al.* (2019) analyse a corpus of engineering education articles.

Descriptive

This category encourages a focus on the actual details of IC interactions. Carbaugh encourages the creation of 'a descriptive corpus of multiple instances of study' (2007: 172) from data that is naturally occurring, thus aligning well with CL. Nevertheless, depending on how we define "IC interactions", there is a temptation to fall into Sarangi's (1994: 413) 'essentialist trap' of assuming that cultural categories (like nationality) are relevant prior to analysis. This is a danger for discourse analysis generally and particularly for CL: particular because CL methods lend themselves to studies of difference and comparison, therefore encouraging and enabling an essentialist approach. One example is a study of computer-mediated communication between British and Taiwanese teenagers (Lin 2016). The corpus developed is called *The British and Taiwanese Teenage Intercultural Communication Corpus*: It is assumed to be intercultural because the participants are of different nationalities. The research in corpus-informed contrastive rhetoric discussed earlier similarly falls into this trap. A solution is to examine interactions that are *potentially* – in other words, interactions where the participants may make differing cultural identities relevant in the interaction – and to analyse to what extent, when, how and why they do. In Handford (2014), I conduct a CLIC analysis of international, inter-organisational and inter-professional meetings to see which identities are made relevant through the versatile keyword *we*. There is no assumption that a particular identity is relevant; instead, the analysis sheds light on which are made relevant and which are not. Such a stance sees culture as something dynamic and emergent that we do, a practice, rather than something we inherently have.

Interpretive

According to Carbaugh, this mode is concerned with understanding the significance or meaning of the particular phenomenon in the communicative practice in question. While we may assume this can be unearthed through follow-up questions with the participants, he stresses that this is a question for the analyst and is not necessarily an interviewer's question. The analyst can analyse the enactment of the practice in question and through this offer plausible interpretations of the inferred practices, whereas an interview elicits a report about it; while the two may complement each other, they may in fact diverge, and this potential range of meanings can form part of the interpretation. The relevance of this point goes beyond CLIC, of course.

In Tsuchiya and Handford (2014), we conduct a mixed-methods corpus analysis of the quantifiable lengths and qualitative content of speaker turns in a three-hour English as a lingua franca (ELF) business meeting involving participants from different professions, organisations and nationalities. In other words, the meeting was a mix of potentially relevant different large and small cultural identities (Holliday 1999). Two recurrent practices become apparent in the analysis of turns: those of repair and reformulation. Most interestingly, "other-initiated other-repair", for instance, one speaker correcting another without any encouragement from the latter, was found to be common. This goes against claims in pragmatics (e.g. Levinson 1983) and the consensus in ELF research (see Koester 2010) that such face-threatening language is unusual. In seeking to understand why these particular practices are so common, we conducted interviews with key participants, such as the chairperson. He told us that such practices are imperative in ELF meetings in an industry like construction, where safety is so important, given the range of linguistic competences in the room and the differences in knowledge and expectations of the various professions (interpreted as cultural differences). We also interpreted the practices as markers of power, although this was not raised by the participants. It is also possible to see these two interpretations as conflicting, with apparent desire for clarity perhaps masking the desire for control over the direction of the meeting and hence the project it was discussing.

Comparative

The focus of this mode is to compare communication in different cultural discourses or speech communities in order to shed light on what is shared and what is different. It should be evident that CL lends itself to a comparative mode, either from a top-down or a bottom-up perspective: Some studies unearth evidence of different discourses using bottom-up methods, whereas others assume a top-down stance through deciding what will be compared prior to analysis.

An example of a top-down study is Taylor's (2014) cross-linguistic analysis of the representation of migrants in the UK and the Italian press. The first stage of the analysis examines the collocates of salient items, such as "refugee" and "asylum seekers" (and the equivalent terms in Italian). The second stage involves the interpretation of the selected items through a framework of "moral panic", thus examining to what extent the negative representation of migrants in the two national presses exists. The study is of interest here because, like Baker *et al.*'s (2008) study on refugees, asylum seekers, immigrants and migrants (RASIMs), it employs a top-down but non-essentialist approach: Both studies are concerned with the way certain groups are represented in the media. They do not seek to explain the behaviour of RASIMs in terms of the assumed characteristics of their particular national or ethnic backgrounds. By examining the representation of marginalised groups in society and the extent of the negative coverage about them, these studies are clearly critical in orientation and demonstrate the power of corpus linguistics to provide empirical, quantified evidence for negative coverage in the media (see also Chapters 39 and 42, this volume).

Critical

This mode involves assuming an evaluative stance towards the practice in question, asking whether it advantages or disadvantages some groups rather than others. It is therefore an ethical orientation and may involve critiquing the positions or practices of the researched group in question. The mode clearly relates to much work involving the combination of CL and CDA (e.g. Stubbs 1996; Baker 2006; Baker *et al.* 2008), as well as that exploring language ideology (e.g. Vessey 2015), and examines topics such as power, injustice and inequalities. The comparative studies on RASIMs are also critical, given that they investigate the way marginalised groups are negatively portrayed in the influential media. Similarly, Zhu *et al.* (2017) argue that the predominance of simplistic essentialist orientations and the relative lack of critical orientations in master's degree IC programme websites may be explained through a practice of obfuscation of social inequalities in marketing practices and wider society.

According to Carbaugh (2007), the first three modes are obligatory for any IC study. If we accept this, it is clear that CL can straightforwardly be used in the descriptive mode, as well as the interpretative as defined here, and in terms of the remaining optional modes, CL can be used to great effect in comparative studies. CL can also be employed in theoretical and critical inquiries, but not as simply. While these points seem plausible at the time of writing, it also seems plausible that in the future, CLIC may alter the theoretical assumptions and therefore modes of theoretical inquiry in IC. Indeed, the work of CL has already led to such changes in other fields, including lexicography, translation studies and (critical) discourse analysis (McEnery and Hardie 2012). At present, in IC there is a frequent divide between quantitative analysis in the form of surveys, and which often assume an essentialist epistemology and ontology, and qualitative analysis of interactional data, which is often anti-essentialist in orientation. Given that CL employs quantitative methods which do not necessitate the adoption of a positivist (or essentialist) ontology (Stubbs 2007) and employs both quantitative and qualitative methods to unearth hitherto unexpected findings, we can be optimistic about the benefits CLIC may bring.

4 Using corpus methods in IC

Here, some issues and suggestions related to the practicalities of doing CLIC are outlined. An initial question we might ask is, 'Do we need to build an original corpus to do CLIC?' This depends on the research question we are asking and the pre-existing and accessible corpora. Some available corpora may lend themselves to IC analysis; for instance, if we accept that ELF communication is inherently intercultural (Holliday 2011), a relevant corpus is the VOICE corpus (https://www.univie.ac.at/voice/). For many IC studies, however, constructing a specialised corpus may be needed. For instance, Zhu *et al.* (2017) examine online promotional discourse for master's courses in IC to understand whether the notion of culture employed therein is typically essentialist or more anti-essentialist. Because there was no pre-existing corpus of such data, it was necessary to construct one first (see Chapters 2, 3 and 4, this volume).

In the Zhu *et al.* (2017) paper, a series of quantitative and qualitative steps for conducting CLIC analysis are proposed, which can be applied consecutively, and if needed, iteratively. The steps are a combination of two methodologies, we argue. The first is Sinclair's 'extended units of meaning' (2004), which move from the analysis of lexical items, their collocations and concordance lines, to inferences about semantic prosody. The second draws on Gee's approach to discourse analysis, specifically his "situated meaning" tool (2005), which proposes that to understand a linguistic feature (such as a lexical item), we need to understand the meaning it has in its specific context. Gee gives the example of spilling some coffee on the floor and how the situated meaning of coffee in that particular context will dictate whether a brush or mop is needed to clean it up. At first sight, this methodological combination might appear contradictory: The former set of steps might be seen as pulling us away from specific contexts, whereas the latter does the opposite. It is argued here that this is a necessary tension when doing not only IC analysis but also CADS more generally because an appreciation of context is what distinguishes CADS and corpus-informed IC analysis from decontextualised CL studies (e.g. Hunston 2002). As Baker *et al.* (2008: 293) argue: 'Corpus analysis does not normally take into account the social, political, historical and cultural context of the data', but for CLIC studies, such contextual factors are paramount.

The seven steps employed by Zhu *et al.* (2017) are listed in Table 44.1; the corpus software used are a combination of *Antconc* (Anthony 2015) (steps 1–4) and *Wmatrix* (Rayson 2008) (step 5). The steps listed are therefore a version of CADS and address the theoretical, descriptive and interpretative modes of inquiry (Carbaugh 2007): the theoretical through the engagement with the concept of essentialism, description through the linguistic analysis and interpretative through a discussion of the reasons for the patterns and their possible implications. It is also partly comparative as differences in certain types of universities are found and then examined. As mentioned earlier, the paper also raises points that are critical in orientation.

Table 44.1 Example CLIC steps

1. Create corpus, produce frequency lists of single words and multi-word units and keyword lists.
2. Select salient specific items from produced frequency and keyword lists. In other words, items that might potentially shed light on the research questions.
3. Pinpoint collocations of the selected items.
4. Examine concordance lines of selected items.
5. Produce semantic categories of the selected keywords and frequent items.
6. Infer "situated meaning" (Gee 2005) and "discourse prosody" (Stubbs 1996).
7. Longer stretches of discourse are examined "manually", i.e. without corpus software, to see whether the corpus insights are supported by the situated meaning analysis of relevant items in the extracts.

In Section 5, a CLIC analysis of engineering education articles will be outlined as a case study. Before that, it is worth briefly explaining the typical corpus steps for intercultural analysis (see Handford 2016 for an extended discussion of these points). It will be immediately apparent that the methods used here are not different from many typical corpus-based studies; this is an important point as it shows that CLIC, at least in terms of certain methods, can be relatively straightforward for the corpus analyst.

Frequency lists of multi-word units, and collocation more generally, have shown that English, like other natural languages, is more phraseological than traditional "slot and filler" conceptions would suggest (Sinclair 2004); this insight has implications for language learning and intercultural encounters in English. Keywords, items that occur far more frequently in one text type compared to another (see Kilgarriff *et al.* 2014), can shed light on the context-specific aspects of the discourse in question (Stubbs 1996; Baker 2006). As Stubbs (2007: 154) argues, 'Frequency in the corpus is evidence of a social norm'. So for us to understand particular norms in communicative contexts, and therefore understand the relationship between language and culture, frequency and keyness are very useful tools. When conducting some kind of cultural comparison, discourse prosody (following Stubbs 1996, used here in preference to "semantic prosody") is another very useful tool. Discourse prosody allows for the inferential analysis of an item's connotative meaning: For instance, does the linguistic item, when used in a particular context, reflect a more positive, negative or neutral stance? Discourse prosody allows us to understand what the underlying discourses in a text may be (Baker, 2006) through uncovering the evaluative stance the text producers have taken. For translation studies or for language learners, for instance, understanding how seemingly similar items may differ in different cultural contexts is crucial, and discourse prosody is a way of unearthing such pragmatic differences. The example later of *must/müssen* demonstrates the potential risks of conflating semantic meaning with pragmatic force.

It is worth noting that the Zhu *et al.* (2017) steps involve a bottom-up approach, with the lexical findings driving the analysis. A more top-down approach would also be possible; Biber *et al.* (2007), for instance, argue that CADS-type studies typically start with the communicative or functional analysis of a text or texts, and then move on to the lexical analysis. A combination of both approaches is also possible in IC studies, for instance, O'Connor *et al.* (2008). In this study, the move structure in comparable corpora of US and Spanish medicine labelling (top down) are analysed first, with the move differences being attributed to the relatively litigious nature of US society. A bottom-up analysis starting with the lexicogrammatical features is also conducted, highlighting differences in this area.

A top-down approach can also be used with other forms of interaction, including spoken discourse, for instance, comparing different groups of speakers (as members of social categories) and examining their use of certain linguistic features. For instance, in Handford (2010) I examined different ELF groups according to first language and found that German speakers of business English use the potentially face-threatening deontic modal verb 'must' six times more frequently than other groups in the CANBEC corpus. This finding has been used in anti-essentialist intercultural consultancy work in corporations (Handford 2020), where trainees are presented with the finding and asked to speculate why this may be so. This usually leads to a certain amount of Otherisation by non-German speakers and the invocation of some well-trodden stereotypes. The argument over the semantic similarity but pragmatic difference between the English *must* and the German verb *müssen* is then presented highlighting that the issue is one of pragmalinguistic transfer rather than essentialised national character (see also Gumperz 1982). This can lead to a range of reactions, many emotional, which may be necessary for change in attitudes to have much chance of occurring (Jackson 2014).

In summary, a list of issues to consider for those intending to conduct CLIC is suggested in Table 44.2.

This section has discussed some of the issues around conducting CLIC in terms of corpus creation and methods. In the next section a case study of an interdisciplinary CLIC study is explored.

Table 44.2 Checklist for conducting CLIC 5

i.Can a corpus approach help me answer my research question?
  1. If so, why: what is the rationale?
  2. If so, how: what CL methods might I use (see iv.1)?

ii.Do I need to build a new corpus or use an existing one?
  1. What is the population/discourse community I'm aiming to analyse, and is an existing corpus representative of the population I'm aiming to analyse?
  2. Does an existing corpus contain the appropriate texts I'm aiming to analyse?

iii.What other types of data (and methods to analyse them) do I need?
  1. Considering Carbaugh's 2007 exhortation about obligatory modes, would interviews or insights from expert informants, for example, allow for interpretation (see iv.)?

iv.What methods/tools should I use?
  1. Should I use top-down or bottom-up corpus approaches, and how would the specific methods (e.g. keyness) relate to specific research questions?
  2. What non-corpus methods are most appropriate for the type of analysis I'm intending to do? How will I triangulate the methods, and findings?

v.Do I need co-authors with expertise in other areas/disciplines? Or can I glean sufficient knowledge from extant literature? Can I find an expert critical friend to read a draft?

Case study

This study into the way culture is conceptualised in engineering education was conducted by an interdisciplinary team with specialties in IC for engineers (Jan van Maele), civil engineering (Petr Matous and Yu Maemura) and engineering communication/CLIC (me). Such a team was deemed necessary because a single individual would not have sufficient theoretical, methodological and discipline-specific knowledge to examine the issue alone. The research was motivated partly by shared unease concerning perceived essentialist educational practices relating to IC in engineering education and partly by calls from within and beyond engineering education for the topic of intercultural education for engineers to be given more attention (e.g. Global Engineering Excellence Initiative 2006). We therefore set out to use CLIC to test our hypothesis that approaches to IC in engineering education were predominantly essentialist. This involved categorising relevant academic articles as employing an essentialist "culture as given" or a "culture as construct" stance, with the former essentialist and the latter not.

We developed a three-stage methodology, with the first stage using similar steps to those outlined earlier from the Zhu *et al.* (2017) paper (Table 44.1). This involved initially creating the *Journal Articles of Intercultural Communication Engineering Education* (JAICEE) *Corpus*. It is composed of all articles published between the period 2000 and 2015, in either engineering or applied linguistics/intercultural communication journals, that dealt with the areas of IC for engineers, "global engineers" or related topics. Only 31 relevant articles were found, totalling 205, 544 words, which we argue reflects the lack of attention in engineering education on this important area. Using *Sketch Engine* (Kilgarriff *et al.* 2014) with the *Open American National Corpus* as the reference corpus, we then produced and selected salient keywords (*cultural*, *culture*, *cultures* and *diversity*) and analysed their collocates and colligates in Word Sketches, concordance lines or, where necessary, extended extracts (see Chapters 9 and 10, this volume). This allowed for an indicative response to the research question, 'How is culture conceptualised in engineering education? For the item *culture*, we found that *different* and *other* accounted for 19 per

Table 44.3 JAICEE "different cultural" concordances

needs and expectations of students from	*different cultural*	backgrounds
in a world that is composed of people of	*different cultural*	backgrounds
Pursuing active engagement with students from	*different cultural*	backgrounds
intercultural skills as the ability to understand	*different cultural*	contexts and viewpoints
Students from	*different cultural*	backgrounds had diverse conventions
interaction with peers, TAs, and faculty from	*different cultural*	and linguistic backgrounds
differences that exist among people from	*different cultural*	backgrounds

cent of all its collocates. Furthermore, several of the remaining most frequent collocates are concerned with the national level, such as *nationality*, *country*, *foreign* or specific nationalities such as *American*. Similar patterns were found with the cognates *cultural* and *cultures,* and the concordance analysis of bigrams (see Chapters 10 and 15, this volume), like *different cultural,* demonstrates how the prevailing "culture as given" stance uncritically constructs cultural identities in terms of essentialised difference. It is possible, for instance, to imagine "different cultural" to be framed in a more critical way, for instance, "the assumption that nationalities have inherently different cultural backgrounds was discussed", but such examples were not apparent in the corpus (Table 44.3).

The keyword *diversity* was also examined to see whether it reflected a "culture as construct" tendency in some of the articles, but this was not the case. An investigation of its colligates and collocates revealed a negative or neutral discourse prosody. For instance, the most frequent noun or verb modified by *diversity* was *issues*. We argue that framing diversity in this way is symptomatic of much essentialist literature that sees cultural difference as an obstacle and fails to engage with the evidence that engaging with diversity can bring considerable benefits when effectively managed (Rock and Grant 2016).s

The next step involved manually reading each of the 31 articles that comprised the corpus, categorising them in terms of their stance towards essentialism: On a continuum, we categorised papers as explicitly or implicitly operationalising a "culture as given" approach or a "culture as construct" approach, or somewhere in between. This second stage confirmed the corpus findings that the bulk of the papers were indeed either implicitly or explicitly essentialist. However, five articles were found that at least implicitly operationalised a "culture as construct" approach, a finding which we argue cautions against a wholesale reliance on corpus methods: 'by prioritizing frequency, a corpus approach does not draw attention to marginal phenomena in the corpus' (Handford *et al.* 2019: 169).

The final stage of the analysis involved a close reading of two papers, one from each end of the continuum. The "culture as given" paper (Downey *et al.* 2006) also happened to be by far the most cited paper in the corpus, and therefore arguably the most influential. It framed culture in uncritically national, essentialist terms and encouraged students to predict behaviour based on nationality. For instance, an example examination question asks students 'to imagine themselves as Japanese engineers working with Americans on a given project, describing likely conflicts among Mexican engineers' (2006: 8). We provide a strong critique of this paper and its underlying assumptions, arguing that 'students with a high degree of cultural sensitivity would be more likely to fail this course than those with rigid stereotypes… [the approach would] encourage the type of behavior that can lead to unsuccessful communication' (2019: 170). The same evaluation can arguably be made of other research that is essentialist in orientation. We conclude by proposing an alternative approach to IC in engineering contexts, one that embraces concepts like Holliday's "small cultures", eschews prediction based on nationality and other "large culture" categories and embraces practices that reduce ethnocentrism and stereotyping.

To conclude, this chapter has explored how corpus methods can be employed in the analysis of IC and has argued that despite there having been relatively few corpus-informed studies of IC to date, a potential synergy for combining CL and IC is apparent. On the one hand, research into IC can benefit from the rigour, reduction of research bias and opportunities for systematic study of collections of texts provided by a corpus methodology. Conversely, CL could benefit from building on existing work in CADS, for instance, through engaging with context at the level of culture, further appreciating the importance of context in understanding intercultural interactions, or through analysing concepts that underpin the way we engage with others we may perceive as different from ourselves. As a field with real-world relevance, IC can benefit from improved validity through engaging with corpus methods. Such an engagement can make the emancipatory and critical intent of much IC research (Scollon and Scollon 2001; Piller 2011; *inter alia*) more persuasive. Nevertheless, as discussed at length in this chapter, the danger for CL researchers is of falling into the essentialist trap when conducting IC studies. Certain corpus studies of IC that claim to embrace complexity and dynamism may in fact limit the scope of interpretation to the essentialised nationality of the study participants. While this is a danger for all methodologies used in IC, it is argued here that the bias in much CL research towards finding difference means an essentialist orientation is seductive. Sometimes the most straightforward analysis is not the most worthwhile.

Further reading

Jackson, J. (ed.) (2014) *The Routledge Handbook of Language and Intercultural Communication*, London: Routledge. (This collection provides a comprehensive coverage of the foundations, methods and theories in IC.)

Piller, I. (2011) *Intercultural Communication: A Critical Introduction*, Edinburgh: Edinburgh University Press. (This is an engaging and accessible introduction to many of the themes discussed in this chapter.)

Zhu, H. (2016) (ed.) *Research Methods in Intercultural Communication*, Oxford: Wiley-Blackwell. (This book provides an excellent explanation of various methodologies used in IC.)

References

Anthony, L. (2015) *AntConc* (Version 3.4.3) [Computer Software], Tokyo, Japan: Waseda University, Available from http://www.laurenceanthony.net.

Baker, P. (2006) *Using Corpora in Discourse Analysis*, London: Continuum.

Baker, P., Gabrielatos, C., Khosravinik, M. , Krzyżanowski, M., McEnery, T. and Wodak, R. (2008) 'A Useful Methodological Synergy? Combining Critical Discourse Analysis and Corpus Linguistics to Examine Discourses of Refugees and Asylum Seekers in the UK Press', *Discourse and Society* 19(3): 273–306.

Biber, D., Connor, U. and Upton, T. (2007) *Discourse on the Move: Using Corpus Analysis to Describe Discourse Structure*, Amsterdam: John Benjamins.

Brandt, A. and Mortensen, K. (2016) 'Conversation Analysis', in H. Zhu (ed.), *Research Methods in Intercultural Communication: A Practical Guide*, Oxford: Wiley-Blackwell, pp. 297–310.

Bucholtz, M. (2003) 'Sociolinguistic Nostalgia and the Authentication of Identity', *Journal of Sociolinguistics* 7(3): 398–416.

Carbaugh, D. (2007) 'Cultural Discourse Analysis: Communication Practices and Intercultural Encounters', *Journal of Intercultural Communication Research* 36(3): 167–82.

Clyne, M. (1994) *Inter-Cultural Communication at Work: Cultural Values in Discourse*, Cambridge: Cambridge University Press.

Connor, U. (2002) 'New Directions in Contrastive Rhetoric', *TESOL Quarterly* 36: 493–510.

Connor, U., Ruiz-Garrido, M., Rozycki, W., Goering, E., Kinney, E. and Koehler, J. (2008) 'Patient-Directed Medicine Labeling: Text Differences between the United States and Spain', *Communication and Medicine* 5(2): 117–32.

Downey, G. L., Lucena, J. C., Moskal, B. M., Parkhurst, R., Bigley, T., Hays, C., Jesiek, B. K., Kelly, L., Miller, J., Ruff, S., Lehr, J. L. and Nichols-Belo, A. (2006) 'The Globally Competent Engineer: Working Effectively with People Who Define Problems Differently', *Journal of Engineering Education* 95(2): 101–22.

Gee, J. P. (2005) *An Introduction to Discourse Analysis*, London: Routledge.

Global Engineering Excellence Initiative (2006) *In Search of Global Engineering Excellence: Educating the Next Generation of Engineers for the Global Workplace, Final Report*, Hanover, Germany: Continental AG. www.cont-online.com.

Gumperz, J. (1982) *Discourse Strategies*, Cambridge: Cambridge University Press.

Handford, M. (2010) *The Language of Business Meetings*, Cambridge: Cambridge University Press.

Handford, M. (2014) 'Cultural Identities in International, Inter-Organisational Meetings: A Corpus-Informed Discourse Analysis of Indexical "we"', *Language and Intercultural Communication* 14(1): 41–58.

Handford, M. (2016) 'Corpus Linguistics, in H. Zhu (ed.) *Research Methods in Intercultural Communication*, Oxford: Wiley-Blackwell, pp. 311–26.

Handford, M. (2020) 'Training "International Engineers" in Japan: Discourse, Discourse and Stereotypes', in L. Mullany (ed.) *Language in the Professions: Consultancy, Advocacy, Activism*, London: Palgrave, pp. 29–46.

Handford, M., van Maele, J., Matous, P. and Maemura, Y. (2019) 'Which Culture? A Critical Analysis of Intercultural Communication in Engineering Education', *Journal of Engineering Education* 108: 161–77.

Holliday, A. (1999) 'Small Cultures', *Applied Linguistics* 20(2): 237–64.

Holliday, A. (2011) *Intercultural Communication and Ideology*, London: Sage.

Holliday, A. and MacDonald, M. (2019) 'Researching the Intercultural: Intersubjectivity and the Problem with Postpositivism', *Applied Linguistics* 0/0: 1–20.

Hunston, S. (2002) *Corpora in Applied Linguistics*, Cambridge: Cambridge University Press.

Jackson, J. (2014) *Introducing Language and Intercultural Communication*, London: Routledge.

Kilgarriff, A., Baisa, V., Bušta, J., Jakubíček, M., Kovvář, V., Michelfeit, J., Rychlý, P. and Suchomel, V. (2014) 'The Sketch Engine: Ten Years On', *Lexicography* 1: 7–36.

Koester, A. (2010) *Workplace Discourse*, London: Continuum.

Levinson, S. (1983) *Pragmatics*, Cambridge: Cambridge University Press.

Lin, Y.-L. (2016) 'Non-Standard Capitalisation and Vocal Spelling in intercultural Computer-Mediated Communication', *Corpora* 11(1): 63–82.

Martin, J., Nakayama, T. and Carbaugh, D. (2014) 'The History and Development of the Study of Intercultural Communication and Applied Linguistics', in J. Jackson (ed.) *The Routledge Handbook of Language and Intercultural Communication*, London: Routledge, pp. 17–36

McEnery, T. and Hardie, A. (2012) *Corpus Linguistics*, Cambridge: Cambridge University Press.

Moreno, A. (2008) 'The Importance of Comparable Corpora in Cross-Cultural Studies' in U. Connor, E. Nagelhout and W. Rozycki (eds) *Contrastive Rhetoric: Reaching to Intercultural Rhetoric*, Amsterdam: John Benjamin, pp. 25–41.

Piller, I. (2011) *Intercultural Communication: A Critical Introduction*, Edinburgh: Edinburgh University Press.

Rock, D. and Grant, H. (2016) 'Why Diverse Teams are Smarter?', *Harvard Business Review*, https://hbr.org/2016/11/why-diverse-teams-are-smarter.

Rayson, P. (2008) 'From Key Words to Key Semantic Domains', *International Journal of Corpus Linguistics* 13(4): 519–49.

Sarangi, S. (1994) 'Intercultural or not? Beyond celebration of cultural differences in miscommunication analysis', *Pragmatics* 4(3): 409–27.

Scollon, R. and Scollon, W. (2001) *Intercultural Communication: A Discourse Approach*, Oxford: Blackwell.

Sealey, A. and Carter, B. (2001) 'Social Categories and Sociolinguistics: Applying a Realist Approach', *International Journal of the Sociology of Language* 152: 1–19.

Sinclair, J. (2004) *Trust the Text*, London: Routledge.

Stubbs, M. (1996) *Text and Corpus Analysis*, Oxford: Blackwell.

Stubbs, M. (2007) 'On Texts, Corpora and Models of Language', in M. Hoey, M. Mahlberg, M. Stubbs and W. Teubert (eds) *Text, Discourse and Corpora*, London: Continuum, pp. 163–90.

Taylor, C. (2014) 'Investigating the Representation of Migrants in the UK and Italian Press: A Cross-Linguistic Corpus-Assisted Discourse Analysis' *International Journal of Corpus Linguistics* 19(3): 368–400.

Tognini-Bonelli, E. (2001) *Corpus Linguistics at Work*, Amsterdam: John Benjamins.

Tsuchiya, K. and Handford, M. (2014) 'A Corpus-Driven Analysis of Repair in a Professional ELF Meeting: Not "Letting it Pass"', *Journal of Pragmatics* 64: 117–31.

Vessey, R. (2015) 'Corpus Approaches to Language Ideology', *Applied Linguistics* 38(3): 277–96.

Wenger, E. (1998) *Communities of Practice: Learning, Meaning, Identity,* Cambridge: Cambridge University Press.

Zhu, H. (ed.) (2016) *Research Methods in Intercultural Communication*, Oxford: Wiley-Blackwell.

Zhu, H., Handford, M. and Young, T. (2017) 'Framing Interculturality: A Corpus-Based Analysis of On-Line Promotional Discourse of Higher Education Intercultural Communication Courses', *Journal of Multilingual and Multicultural Development* 38(3): 283–300.

45

Corpora in language testing: developments, challenges and opportunities

Sara T. Cushing

1 What is language testing?

This chapter provides an overview of how corpus linguistics tools and techniques can be used in language testing and assessment (LTA). The terms testing and assessment are often used interchangeably, although testing is more often associated with large-scale, high-stakes examinations, while assessment is associated with evaluation in the classroom. For the purposes of this chapter, I will use both terms to mean the same thing, though for the most part I will be discussing large-scale testing.

LTA has been defined as 'the systematic gathering of language-related behavior in order to make inferences about language ability and capacity for language use on other occasions' (Chapelle and Plakans 2012: 241). Given this definition, it is not surprising that there are numerous applications of corpus linguistics to the enterprise of language testing, since the systematic collection and analysis of language data are at the very heart of corpus linguistics. What makes LTA distinct from other applications of corpus linguistics is the second half of the definition: 'to make inferences about language ability and capacity for language use on other occasions'. That is, while corpus linguists strive to collect representative existing examples of language in a particular context, language tests are intended to elicit novel instances of language performance or other observable language-related behaviour, from which inferences about underlying ability or predictions of future behaviour are made (Xi 2017).

More importantly, the inferences made from language test scores typically serve as the basis, alone or in combination with other data, for making decisions about people or programmes. These decisions may have high or low stakes for an individual test taker. Low-stakes decisions based on test scores include such things as whether a student decides to put more effort into learning or a teacher decides that their class is ready to move on to a new lesson. High-stakes decisions are much more consequential, such as whether a student will be admitted to a university, an airline pilot will be allowed to fly on international routes or a family will be allowed to immigrate to a new country. Thus, high-stakes tests frequently serve as gatekeeping devices in education, immigration and employment contexts (McNamara *et al.* 2019). For this reason, language testing scholars

DOI: 10.4324/9780367076399-45

are concerned with the fairness of these decisions and with ensuring that the information provided by a test is sufficient and appropriate to the decision being made. In other words, validity in language testing is a central concern, as a test claims to provide evidence of the communicative ability of a person that is sufficient for making decisions, and the nature of this evidence must be scrutinised to ensure the fairness of decisions based on the test.

Before considering how corpora can be used in language testing, it may be useful to define the scope of LTA and outline the steps involved in creating a language test for a given purpose. Useful introductions to LTA can be found in numerous sources, such as Bachman and Palmer (1996), Green (2013) and Fulcher (2013), to name a few.

The process of test development is iterative and recursive, in that the phases of test development are not always distinct and may be completed concurrently or revisited at a later time, but for the sake of simplicity they are presented here in a linear fashion. Once the purpose for the test has been established, test development first involves defining the construct, or ability, to be measured. The construct typically includes both the nature of language to be elicited and the context in which the language will be used: e.g. reading and writing English for academic purposes or spoken Japanese for tour guides. The next step is to conduct an analysis of what is often called the Target Language Use (TLU) domain (Bachman and Palmer 1996), which involves systematically collecting and analysing authentic examples of the language used in the setting for which the test takers will need to use the language in terms of lexis, grammatical structures and typical language functions. Test developers next need to make decisions about what task types will be included and write specifications, or blueprints, for individual test items or task types and for the test as a whole. Once these preliminary decisions are made, items are written, reviewed and revised as necessary and answer keys, rubrics or scoring guides are written. Items are pilot tested so that their statistical characteristics are known (i.e. item difficulty and discrimination, or the degree to which an item can distinguish between lower- and higher-ability test takers) and to make sure that items and directions are clear. Pilot testing may result in additional modifications to test tasks, rubrics or individual items. Decisions also need to be made about how scores will be used (i.e. cut-off scores for particular decisions) and reported to test takers and other test users. Once the test development team is satisfied with the results of the pilot testing, the finalised test is assembled, administered and scored and the results disseminated, with ongoing monitoring for quality control.

Traditionally, tests have been evaluated based on at least four essential qualities: *reliability*, or consistency across test items, forms, and raters; *validity*, or evidence that the test is measuring what it claims to measure; *practicality*, the capability of administering and scoring a test given limited resources of time, money, and person hours; and *washback*, or beneficial consequences of the test (see, for example, Green 2013, for more information). As noted earlier, validity is often seen as the central concern of testing, so a more in-depth discussion of validity may be useful here.

A traditional view of validity involves what is sometimes called the "three Cs" of validity: content, criterion and construct validity. Evidence for content validity – the match of the test content to the skills or abilities being tested—typically comes from expert review of the test items to make sure that they test the intended skills and knowledge and that they do so as comprehensively as possible within the constraints of the test. Criterion-related validity has to do with the relationship between performance on the test and performance on another measure of the same ability, either administered at the same time (concurrent validity) or at some future date (predictive validity). For example, if I wanted to demonstrate that my 15-minute test of English was useful for university admissions, I could administer it along with TOEFL or IELTS and calculate the correlation between these two tests (concurrent validity), or I could calculate the correlation between my test and students' grade point averages at the end of their first semester of study (predictive validity). Construct validity has to do with the relationship between test performance and a theoretical construct. Models such as Bachman and Palmer's model of communicative language ability (Bachman and Palmer 1996) have been developed to provide the theoretical underpinnings for language tests. Since Messick's (1989) seminal paper on validity, LTA scholars have come to see construct validity as all-encompassing; that is, the evidence that a test is measuring what it claims to be measuring can include both content and criterion-related evidence, as well as evidence that relates the test more directly to a theoretical construct, often through sophisticated statistical means.

More recently, scholars in LTA have been using argument-based frameworks for test validation based on the writing of Michael Kane (e.g. 1992, 2013). Kane expands upon Messick (1989), agreeing with Messick that it is not the test itself that is valid, but the 'adequacy and appropriateness of inferences and actions based on test scores or other modes of assessment' (1989: 13). Kane's contribution to the field is to lay out in greater detail the assumption and warrants that link test performance to these inferences and actions in what he calls an interpretive argument. The evidence supporting these warrants, or claims, comprises a validity argument.

Other scholars in language testing have expanded upon Kane's notion of an interpretive argument; Bachman and Palmer (2010), for example, lay out what they call an Assessment Use Argument for an assessment that involves several claims. Similarly, Chapelle *et al.* (2008) present an interpretive argument for the TOEFL iBT comprising six key inferences. While a complete discussion of these inferences is beyond the scope of this chapter, I will return to them later in discussing the ones that are most relevant to corpus linguistics.

To summarise, research in LTA comprises efforts not only to develop useful assessments that are fit for a specific purpose but to provide evidence supporting a chain of inferences that lead from test performance (observed behaviour) to decisions that are made on the basis of that performance and the consequences of those decisions. In the next section I provide some historical background on the application of corpus linguistics to these endeavours.

2 Milestones in the use of corpora in language testing

Prior to the 1990s, while corpus linguistics was beginning to make inroads in the related fields of second language studies and language teaching, most large-scale testing programmes did not rely on corpus data to inform test development or validation (Barker 2006). It was not until 1996 that a prominent LTA scholar, Charles Alderson, laid out a case for the usefulness of corpus data for test development (Alderson 1996: 254). One of the first authors to publish an article describing the use of corpus data in test development was Coniam (1997), who proposed a method for using corpus-based word frequency data for the automatic generation of cloze tests. Meanwhile, corpus linguists within applied linguistics were beginning to point out the usefulness of corpus data to LTA specialists around the same time; see, for example, Biber *et al.* (1998).

Since 2000, more attention has been paid to the use of corpus data in LTA, with review articles written by Barker (2006, 2010, 2013), Taylor and Barker (2008), Park (2014), Weigle and Goodwin (2016) and Cushing (forthcoming). A symposium on corpora in language testing was organised at the Language Testing Research Colloquium, the major international LTA conference, in 2003 (Taylor and Barker 2008), and in 2017, a special issue of *Language Testing* was devoted to applications of corpus linguistics to LTA (Cushing 2017). A recent review of ten years of language testing research (Plakans 2018: 6) notes that the topic of technology in testing journals had become a "deluge", with corpus linguistics and automated scoring (which relies heavily on corpus data) as the two most important areas within technology discussed.

The increased interest in corpus linguistics within LTA comes from both the increased availability of appropriate corpora and the development of new tools for analysing corpus data that are accessible to researchers with limited programming knowledge. Another driver for the need to use corpus data in assessment is the proliferation of automated scoring engines for writing, and increasingly for speaking as well. In the rest of the section I outline these considerations.

LTA researchers and test developers draw on both learner corpora, as a basis for examining the features of language used by learners at different levels of proficiency, and specialised reference corpora, so that test content can be reflective of authentic language use in the TLU domain. An excellent survey of early corpora of interest to language testing is found in Taylor and Barker (2008). In the early 1990s, researchers under the direction of Sylviane Granger began to compile the *International Corpus of Learner English* (ICLE), which consists of the writing of advanced learners of English, along with background information of the writers such as age, first language and so on (see Granger *et al.* 2002) (see Chapters 22 and 23, this volume). Another important learner corpus, the *Cambridge Learner Corpus* (CLC), developed by the EFL Division of the University of Cambridge Local Examinations Syndicate (UCLES) in association with Cambridge University Press, consists of exam scripts (i.e. written responses) from Cambridge examinations at different levels of proficiency, along with demographic information about the candidates. A proportion of the CLC is error-coded, allowing for searches of specific errors alongside more traditional lexical and collocational searches (Taylor and Barker 2008)

Around the same time, test developers began compiling or commissioning specialised corpora specifically to inform test development. An important example is the *TOEFL 2000 Spoken and Written Academic Language Corpus* (T2K-SWAL), a large corpus of spoken and written academic language commissioned by the Educational Testing Service (ETS), to inform the transformation of the paper-based TOEFL to what is now the TOEFL internet-based test (TOEFL iBT; Biber *et al.* 2004). Similarly, the *Pearson International Corpus of Academic English* (PICAE; Ackermann *et al.* 2011) was compiled to inform the development of the Pearson Test of English Academic, comprising written and spoken curricular and extracurricular materials.

A milestone event that has had a major impact on LTA was the publication of the Common European Framework of Reference (CEFR, Council of Europe 2001), originally intended to provide a common vocabulary for referring to proficiency levels across European languages. The six CEFR levels range from A1 (beginner) to C2 (mastery), with descriptions of what learners can do at each level of proficiency. Since its publication, many test developers, particularly in the UK and Europe, have aligned their tests to the CEFR, so that a passing score on a particular test is evidence that a candidate has reached a given level, such as B2 or C1. The CEFR can-do statements are functional rather than linguistic in nature, so scholars have long been interested in exploring the characteristics of the language used at different levels of proficiency. For example, one of the can-do statements at Level A2 is that learners 'can communicate in simple and routine tasks'; researchers are interested in knowing what vocabulary and language structures (e.g. verb tenses, clause structure and so on) learners have control over to successfully communicate in routine situations. Test developers and curriculum designers also became interested in specifying the characteristics of texts that would serve as appropriate input for each level. The English Profile programme (Hawkins and Buttery 2010; Hawkins and Filipović 2012) is an example of a large project intended to identify "criterial features" for each CEFR level using texts from the CLC; i.e. features that will distinguish learners at one level from those at adjacent levels (Salamoura and Saville 2010) (see also Chapter 22, this volume).

As corpora began to be used more for assessment, corpus analysis tools along with natural language processing tools were improving as well, lending themselves to applications to LTA. Before the late 1990s, corpus tools tended to be limited in their functionality, including only being able to process ASCII characters (Anthony 2013). Tools such as *AntConc* and *Wordsmith* made corpus data more widely available, as they could be used on larger corpora, were not limited to ASCII characters, included commonly used statistics and, importantly, had user-friendly interfaces (see Chapter 9, this volume). In recent years, computational linguists have begun developing free online tools that can provide sophisticated analyses of such phenomena as cohesion, lexical sophistication and syntactic complexity, which are of particular relevance to language testing scholars seeking to understand the linguistic characteristics of texts at various levels of proficiency. Coh-Metrix (Graesser *et al.* 2004) and Lu's Syntactic Complexity Analyzer (Lu 2010) are examples.

An important development in language assessment has been the increased use of computer-delivered tests, which allow for the possibility of automated scoring and feedback on language production, particularly for writing. These systems rely heavily on corpus data, i.e. large collections of essays that have been scored by trained raters. Automated scoring systems typically predict human scores by measuring a set of features in the texts to be scored that are considered relevant to the construct, even if they may not be identical to the features human raters attend to in scoring (Williamson *et al.* 2012). Even though automated scoring was originally developed in the 1960s, it has only been applied to large-scale language tests in the past two decades or so (see Dikli 2006, for a review). One of the first automated scoring systems to be used on high-stakes tests was e-rater, developed by ETS and first used on the GMAT in 1999 (Williamson *et al.* 2012). E-rater is currently used in conjunction with human scorers on the TOEFL iBT Independent and Integrated writing tasks. The Pearson Test of Academic English was the first large-scale test to feature completely automated scoring, using the Intelligent Essay Assessor (IEA) scoring engine by Knowledge Analysis Technologies (Landauer *et al.* 2003). A relatively new addition to the landscape is the Duolingo Test of English (LaFlair and Settles 2019), which is administered online and is automatically scored. In any of these systems, natural language processing techniques allow for the extraction of numerous linguistic features from a corpus of texts and then determining the combination of features that best predict human scores.

Similarly, automated feedback systems such as Cambridge English's *Write and Improve* (https://writeandimprove.com/) rely on large learner corpora as a basis for provide instant feedback on writing, including highlighting possible sentence-level errors; see Stevenson and Phakiti (2019) for a recent review of the potential and current limitations of automated feedback systems. Automated scoring of speaking is less advanced than scoring of writing but similarly relies on large corpora of learner data. As anyone who uses a smart phone knows, current voice-to-text software relying on automated speech recognition (ASR) is not completely reliable, and is even less so for learners of a language, due to such things as deviations from the norm in grammar, vocabulary and pronunciation, along with an increase in disfluencies and hesitations (Litman *et al.* 2018). In assessment, such systems are currently only reliable for highly constrained tasks such as reading aloud or providing highly predictable responses to questions. Improvements in ASR for language learners will only improve with better corpora of learner data for training these systems.

3 Using corpora for test development

Corpus linguistics can inform both test development and test validation. For test development, corpus data are useful both for targeting test items at particular proficiency levels and for ensuring that test language is both appropriate for the test audience and authentic to a particular language use situation (see discussion of content validity earlier). In testing, a distinction can be made between selected response items (sometimes called objective items), such as multiple-choice or matching items, and constructed response items (or subjective items), such as prompts for speaking or writing. Selected response items are typically, though not exclusively, used for assessing the receptive skills of reading and listening and for assessing discrete enabling skills such as grammar and vocabulary. Both reference corpora and learner corpora are useful for developing these items. As Barker (2010, 2013) notes, corpus data can help item writers base their work on authentic language and target specific aspects of language that are relevant to a population of test takers. For example, learner corpus data can provide insights into collocational patterns typical of learners at different proficiency levels, which can help test developers identify collocations to include in a test targeted at a particular level (see Voss 2012, as an example) and also identify collocational errors that may be useful as distractors.

Corpus data can confirm or disconfirm intuitive judgments about language use patterns, which were the basis for much test design in the mid-to-late twentieth century. Word frequency is often thought to be a useful proxy for difficulty, for example. However, Alderson (2007: 402) found that correlations between expert judgments and objective frequency of words in the *British National Corpus* were 'only moderate'.

Corpus data are particularly relevant to specific purpose testing; that is, tests that are used to certify language proficiency for specific occupations, which may have their own specialised lexicon or other structures. An example of a corpus designed for a specific purpose is discussed in Moder and Halleck (2012), who compiled a corpus of authentic communications between pilots and air traffic controllers, which served as the basis for the Versant Aviation English Test (Van Moere *et al.* 2009)

Constructed responses tend to be lengthier instances of language production in speaking or writing based on a prompt. In independent production tasks, the prompt is generally simple (no more than a sentence or two). In integrated tasks, test-takers must first read and/or listen to one or more input texts and then respond to a prompt that requires incorporating content from the input. While it is more common for test developers to rely on corpus data for developing listening and reading items, Xi (2017) suggests that corpus analysis can be useful in developing language tasks for speaking and writing as well, based on the analysis of a reference corpus, which might suggest that certain linguistic features are salient in a given language use context that is relevant to an assessment. Aspects of the task, such as specification of the purpose or audience for the language production in the prompt, might be manipulated to elicit those salient features more naturally. Another application of corpus data is ensuring comparable 'opportunity of use' (Caines and Buttery 2018: 6) that is, test takers need to have equal opportunities to display their language competence. In a study of responses to a variety of writing prompts in the CLC, they found that different task-topic types tend to elicit different lexico-syntactic constructions, suggesting that test developers should control for these factors in task development.

Extended speaking or writing tasks are typically evaluated by human raters using a rubric or rating scale that defines several levels of performance in terms of their communicative effectiveness and/or the characteristics of the language used; computers are increasingly being called upon to automate scoring, to be discussed later. Corpus data can be useful for developing or improving these scales. For example, Hawkey and Barker (2004) developed a common set of writing descriptors that could be applied across tests at different proficiency levels using corpus analysis techniques. Römer (2017) uses corpus linguistics tools to argue against the traditional separation of lexis and grammar in rating scales in favor of multi-word expressions that cross the boundaries between grammar and vocabulary, suggesting that rating scales for spoken language might benefit from considering lexico-grammatical ability as a single construct.

4 Using corpora for test validation

As noted earlier, many LTA scholars have promoted an argument-based approach to test validity in which the inferences leading from the test performance to the consequences of decisions based on test scores are outlined and then evidence gathered to either support or refute these inferences. At least three of these inferences can be supported using corpus data: domain description, explanation and extrapolation. The inference of domain description in a test states that test performance reveals skills, knowledge and abilities that are representative of the target domain (Chapelle *et al.* 2011) – that is, where the language will ultimately be used, such as academic settings, employment, etc. Corpus evidence for this inference comes from an analysis of the situational characteristics of the target domain along with the lexico-grammatical characteristics of language used in the domain. Examples of corpus linguistics methods being used to support domain description include several studies using the T2KSWAL corpus to analyse college-level academic spoken and written language (e.g. Biber *et al.* 2004; Biber and Gray 2013) and the use of corpus-based techniques using a systemic functional linguistics perspective to compare the knowledge structures and language functions of international teaching assistants (ITAs) with those found in a corpus of TOEFL iBT speaking test responses (Cotos and Chung 2018).

The explanation inference connects test scores to a theoretical construct or latent ability being measured by the test. Corpus-based studies of test-taker language production in constructed responses and their relationships to scores support the explanation inference. In terms of validating scoring rubrics, Knoch and Chapelle (2018: 489) present the following warrant supporting the explanation inference: 'the descriptors in the rating scale...are identifiable in the candidates' discourse in the response'. Evidence for this warrant can come from a corpus-based analysis of candidate discourse in reference to the scale descriptors and the features of discourse that differentiate between adjacent scoring levels. Examples of corpus-based studies that address this inference include Banerjee *et al.* (2007), Cumming *et al.* (2005) and Friginal and Weigle (2014).

Finally, the extrapolation argument states that performance on a test is related to performance in the target domain. One study explicitly using corpus data to investigate the extrapolation inference is LaFlair and Staples (2017), who conducted a corpus-based register analysis to compare the linguistic features elicited by an oral proficiency interview with the language features of several registers in the TLU domains for the test, including both academic and nursing contexts. Evidence that the language elicited by test tasks approximates language expected in the target domain provides support for the extrapolation inference.

In summary, corpus analyses are useful for test validation in three principal ways: First, comparing test features with appropriate reference corpora provides evidence that the test content adequately represents the domain of interest; second, corpus analysis of test-taker responses with respect to both the descriptors in the rating scale and investigations of the features of test-taker language that are related to test scores provides evidence that test performance is related to the construct of interest; and finally, comparisons of test-taker language with language produced in authentic real-life situations provide evidence that test performance is related to performance in relevant non-test situations.

5 Caveats and future developments

It is clear from this discussion that corpus linguistics has much to offer LTA. Before moving on to possibilities for the future, however, I will briefly discuss cautions and caveats that have been raised with regard to the use of corpus data to inform language test development and validation. The first caveat has to do with the choice of corpora to represent the target domain, input to learners or learner production. Egbert (2017) cautions against conflating learner corpora with corpora of test responses, since test responses tend to fall near the unnatural end of a continuum of naturally occurring language. The degree to which test responses produced under timed conditions for the purpose of displaying language ability are comparable to L2 language produced outside of a testing situation for authentic communication is an empirical question, relating to the extrapolation inference referenced earlier. Another issue that scholars need to contend with is the appropriateness of using L1 corpora to represent the target language domain. Egbert suggests that it is particularly problematic to use L1 corpora as a proxy for input or the exposure of L2 learners to the language. For example, he critiques the use of COCA as a proxy for L2 learner experience in Kyle and Crossley's (2017) study of verb–argument constructions, since the registers in COCA are unlikely to be identical to the registers that learners will encounter, nor does the balance of texts among different registers in COCA replicate the experience of learners.

Both Egbert (2017) and Xi (2017) caution against too much reliance on computer programs that extract, count and analyse linguistic features from corpora in test validation or in the development of automated scoring engines, since the linguistic features that can be extracted automatically are not always relevant to the construct being assessed. For such analysis to be useful in language testing, the extracted features must be related to a construct with a clear operational definition. Similarly, both authors express caution over the direct application of findings from corpus analysis to scoring rubrics. As Egbert (2017: 563) notes, a corpus analysis can reveal patterns of language use that may not be salient to human raters, and it is necessary to establish whether raters can be trained to notice and reliably assess these patterns.

Furthermore, Xi (2017:571) notes that the corpus linguist's goal of providing rich description of authentic language used in naturalistic environments does not completely overlap with the goal of test developers, which is to 'provide an adequate representation of the target language use domain and to elicit a performance that is indicative of a potential performance in corresponding real-world contexts', rather than 'to mimic faithfully real-world tasks or elicit exactly the same language as in the target domain'. Language testers have developed frameworks and tools to select a subset of relevant linguistic features and test tasks that are feasible and practical in a given context, and it is unrealistic to expect a test to replicate the conditions of authentic language use.

Despite these caveats, there are numerous ways in which new developments in corpus linguistics can inform LTA and developments in LTA can benefit from corpus data. In this section, drawing primarily on recommendations by Park (2014), Xi (2017) and Weigle and Goodwin (2016), I discuss some of these developments. First, there is a need for large longitudinal learner corpora, preferably with error annotations and parallel corpora of corrections. Such corpora would be useful to trace language development over time and across proficiency levels, assist in accurately identifying criterial features that are reliably associated with different proficiency levels and mitigate the serious challenge of establishing comparability between learner and expert corpora. These corpora could also be useful in formative and dynamic assessment, where learners could have access immediately to exemplars of authentic language appropriate for their current stage of learning (see also Chapters 22 and 23, this volume).

In addition, corpora of regional varieties of English, such as English used in Singapore or Malaysia, would also be valuable in establishing the legitimacy of these varieties in the local context. Speakers of these varieties are often assessed against criteria representing a more prestigious variety of English (e.g. British or American English), which may be less relevant in the local contexts (Park 2014).

In terms of corpus analysis tools, as natural language processing (NLP) tools and knowledge become more sophisticated, it would be helpful for language testers to have more user-friendly corpus-based tools at their disposal. A suite of freely available text analysis tools by Kris Kyle and Scott Crossley is available at https://www.linguisticanalysistools.org/. These are welcome additions to the language tester's toolkit, with the caveats mentioned earlier. Tools for the automated analysis of features beyond syntax and vocabulary, such as textual cohesion and organisation, are critically important, as are tools that can extract a wider range of phenomena found in spoken language (Xi 2017).

One area where corpus linguistics is providing new insights is in assessing interactional competence, defined both as a psychological (individual) construct and as a social construct, in that interaction is co-constructed between participants (McNamara and Roever 2006). Galaczi and Taylor (2018) identify several contributions of corpus linguistics to understanding the features of interaction, such as the role of turn-opening tokens (e.g. Tao 2003) or the use of stance markers by L2 speakers (Gablasova *et al.* 2015) (see also Chapters 22 and 23, this volume). This is an area that is ripe for future development.

Another area where work is beginning to appear is in adapting spoken dialog systems (SDSs) for assessment use to simulate the one-on-one interaction of an oral interview in proficiency tests (Litman *et al.* 2018). While such systems are in common use in applications such as call centers and intelligent personal assistants such as Apple's *Siri* or Amazon's *Alexa*, the corpus data needed for such an effort would have to go beyond what is currently available for SDS, such as dialogs including data from non-native speakers that have been assessed for proficiency (see Litman *et al.* 2016, for an example).

For more progress in these areas, I concur with Xi's (2017) call for broader co-operation between corpus linguists, computational linguists and assessment scholars. As Xi points out, such collaboration can lead to advances in the following areas: (1) improving automated scoring systems by incorporating more construct-relevant features of language, (2) enhancing automated feedback systems by making feedback more meaningful to teaching and learning and (3) using automated linguistic analysis tools to develop learning progressions.

Further reading

Barker, F. (2013) 'Using Corpora to Design Assessment', *The Companion to Language Assessment* 2: 1013–28. (This article provides information on the use of corpora in large-scale test design.)

Cushing, S. T. (ed.) (2017) 'Corpus Linguistics in Language Testing Research' [Special issue], *Language Testing* 34(4). (This special issue presents five articles that use corpus linguistics tools and techniques to explore LTA issues, along with an introduction by the editor and commentaries by a corpus linguist and an LTA specialist.)

Park, K. (2014) 'Corpora and Language Assessment: The State of the Art', *Language Assessment Quarterly* 11(1): 27–44. (This article provides an overview of computational approaches to language assessment and advances in the use of corpora for LTA.)

References

Ackermann, K., De Jong, J. H. A. L., Kilgarriff, A. and Tugwell, D. (2011) 'The Pearson International Corpus of Academic English (PICAE)', *Proceedings of Corpus Linguistics*, Available at: https://www.birmingham.ac.uk/documents/college-artslaw/corpus/conference-archives/2011/Paper-47.pdf.

Alderson, J. C. (1996) 'Do Corpora Have a Role in Language Assessment?' in J. Thomas and M. Short (eds), *Using Corpora for Language Research: Studies in the Honour of Geoffrey Leech*, London: Longman, pp. 248–59.

Alderson, J. C. (2007) 'Judging the Frequency of English Words', *Applied Linguistics* 28(3): 383–409.

Anthony, L. (2013) 'A Critical Look at Software Tools in Corpus Linguistics', *Linguistic Research* 30(2): 141–61.

Bachman, L. F. and Palmer, A. S., (1996) *Language Testing in Practice: Designing and Developing Useful Language Tests*, Oxford: Oxford University Press.

Bachman, L. F. and Palmer, A. S. (2010) *Language Assessment in Practice: Developing Language Assessments and Justifying their Use in the Real World*, Oxford: Oxford University Press.

Banerjee, J., Franceschina, F. and Smith, A. M. (2007) 'Documenting Features of Written Language Production Typical at Different IELTS Band Score Levels', *International English Language Testing System (IELTS) Research Reports 2007* 7(1). Canberra: IELTS Australia and British Council.

Barker, F. (2006) 'Corpora and Language Assessment: Trends and Prospects', *Research Notes* 26: 2–4.

Barker, F. (2010) 'How can Corpora be Used in Language Testing?' in A. O'Keeffe and M. J. McCarthy (eds) *The Routledge Handbook of Corpus Linguistics*, 1st edn, London: Routledge, pp. 661–74.

Barker, F. (2013) 'Using Corpora to Design Assessment', in A. Kunnan (ed.) *The Companion to Language Assessment*, Vol. 2, Oxford: John Wiley and Sons, pp. 1013–28.

Biber, D., Conrad, S. and Reppen, R. (1998) *Corpus Linguistics: Investigating Language Structure and Use*, Cambridge: Cambridge University Press.

Biber, D., Conrad, S., Reppen, R., Byrd, P., Helt, M., Clark, V., Cortes, V., Csomay, E. and Urzua, A. (2004) *Representing Language Use in the University: Analysis of the TOEFL 2000 Spoken and Written Academic Language Corpus (TOEFL Monograph Series MS-25)*. Princeton, NJ: Educational Testing Service.

Biber, D. and Gray, B. (2013) *Discourse Characteristics of Writing and Speaking Task Types on the TOEFL ibt® Test: A Lexico-Grammatical Analysis (ETS Research Report Series, 2013(1)*. Princeton, NJ: Educational Testing Service.

Caines, A. and Buttery, P. (2018) 'The Effect of Task and Topic on Opportunity of Use in Learner Corpora', in V. Brezina and L. Flowerdew (eds) *Learner Corpus Research: New Perspectives and Applications*, London: Bloomsbury, pp. 5–27.

Chapelle, C. A., Enright, M. K. and Jamieson, J. M. (eds) (2008) *Building a validity argument for the Test of English as a Foreign Language™*, London: Routledge.

Chapelle, C. A. and Plakans, L. (2012) 'Assessment and Testing: Overview', in C. A. Chapelle (ed.) *The Encyclopedia of Applied Linguistics*, Hoboken, NJ: John Wiley and Sons, Inc, pp. 241–44.

Coniam, D. (1997) 'A Preliminary Inquiry into Using Corpus Word Frequency Data in the Automatic Generation of English Language Cloze Tests', *Calico Journal* 14: 15–33.

Cotos, E. and Chung, Y. R. (2018) *Domain Description: Validating the Interpretation of the TOEFL iBT® Speaking Scores for International Teaching Assistant Screening and Certification Purposes (ETS Research Report Series RR-18-45)*, Princeton, NJ: Educational Testing Service.

Council of Europe (2001) *Common European Framework of Reference for Languages: Learning, Teaching, Assessment*, Cambridge: Cambridge University Press.

Cumming, A., Kantor, R., Baba, K., Eouanzoui, K., Erdosy, U. and James, M. (2005) *Analysis of Discourse Features and Verification of Scoring Levels for Independent And Integrated Prototype Writing Tasks for New TOEFL (TOEFL Monograph No. MS-30)*, Princeton, NJ: Educational Testing Service.

Cushing, S. T. (2017) 'Corpus Linguistics in Language Testing Research', *Language Testing* 34(4): 441–9.

Cushing, S. T. (forthcoming) 'Corpus Linguistics and Language Testing', in G. Fulcher and L. Harding (eds) *The Routledge Handbook of Language Testing*, 2nd edn, London: Routledge.

Dikli, S. (2006) 'An Overview of Automated Scoring of Essays', *The Journal of Technology, Learning and Assessment* 5(1): 1–36

Egbert, J. (2017) 'Corpus Linguistics and Language Testing: Navigating Uncharted Waters', *Language Testing* 34(4): 555–64.

Fulcher, G. (2013) *Practical Language Testing*, London: Routledge.

Friginal, E. and Weigle, S. C. (2014) 'Exploring Multiple Profiles of L2 Writing Using Multidimensional Analysis', *Journal of Second Language Writing* 26: 80–95.

Gablasova, D., Brezina, V., McEnery, T. and Boyd, E. (2015) 'Epistemic Stance in Spoken L2 English: The Effect of Task and Speaker Style', *Applied Linguistics* 38(5): 613–37.

Galaczi, E. and Taylor, L. (2018) 'Interactional Competence: Conceptualisations, Operationalisations, and Outstanding Questions', *Language Assessment Quarterly* 15(3): 219–36.

Graesser, A. C., McNamara, D. S., Louwerse, M. M. and Cai, Z. (2004) 'Coh-Metrix: Analysis of Text on Cohesion and Language', *Behavior Research Methods, Instruments, and Computers* 36(2): 193–202.

Granger, S., Dagneaux, E. and Meunier, F. (eds) (2002) *The International Corpus of Learner English. Handbook and CD-ROM*, Louvain-la-Neuve: Presses Universitaires de Louvain.

Green, A. (2013) *Exploring Language Assessment and Testing: Language in Action*, London: Routledge.

Hawkey, R. and Barker, F. (2004) 'Developing a Common Scale for the Assessment of Writing', *Assessing Writing* 9(2):122–59.

Hawkins, J. and Buttery, P. (2010) 'Criterial Features in Learner Corpora: Theory and Illustrations', *English Profile Journal* 1: E5. doi: 10.1017/S2041536210000103

Hawkins, J. A. and Filipović, L. (2012) *Criterial Features in L2 English: Specifying the Reference Levels of the Common European Framework*, Vol. 1, Cambridge: Cambridge University Press.

Kane, M. T. (1992) 'An Argument-Based Approach to Validity', *Psychological Bulletin* 112: 527–35.

Kane, M. T. (2013) 'Validating the Interpretations and Uses of Test Scores', *Journal of Educational Measurement* 50: 1–73.

Knoch, U. and Chapelle, C. A. (2018) 'Validation of Rating Processes within an Argument-Based Framework', *Language Testing* 35(4): 477–99.

Kyle, K. and Crossley, S. (2017) 'Assessing Syntactic Sophistication in L2 Writing: A Usage-Based Approach', *Language Testing* 34(4): 513–35.

LaFlair, G. T. and Staples, S. (2017) 'Using Corpus Linguistics to Examine the Extrapolation Inference in the Validity Argument for a High-Stakes Speaking Assessment', *Language Testing* 34(4): 451–75.

LaFlair, G. T. and Settles, B. (2019) *Duolingo English Test: Technical Manual*, Pittsburgh, PA: Duolingo, Retrieved 6/9/2020 from https://s3.amazonaws.com/duolingo-papers/other/Duolingo%20English%20Test%20-%20Technical%20Manual%202019.pdf.

Landauer, T. K., Laham, D. and Foltz, P. W. (2003) 'Automated Scoring and Annotation of Essays with the Intelligent Essay Assessor', in M. D. Shermis and J. C. Burstein (eds) *Automated Essay Scoring: A Cross-Disciplinary Perspective*, Hillsdale, NJ: Lawrence Erlbaum Associates, pp. 87–112.

Litman, D., Strik, H. and Lim, G. S. (2018) 'Speech Technologies and the Assessment of Second Language Speaking: Approaches, Challenges, and Opportunities', *Language Assessment Quarterly* 15(3): 294–309.

Litman, D., Young, S., Gales, M., Knill, K., Ottewell, K., van Dalen, R. and Vandyke, D. (2016) 'Towards Using Conversations with Spoken Dialogue Systems in the Automated Assessment of Non-Native Speakers of English', in *Proceedings of the 17th Annual Meeting of the Special Interest Group on Discourse and Dialogue*, pp. 270–75.

Lu, X. (2010) 'Automatic Analysis of Syntactic Complexity in Second Language Writing', *International Journal of Corpus Linguistics* 15(4): 474–96.

McNamara, T., Knoch, U. and Fan, J. (2019) *Fairness, Justice and Language Assessment*, Oxford: Oxford University Press.

McNamara, T. and Roever, C. (2006) *Language Testing: The Social Dimension*, Malden, MA/Oxford, UK: Blackwell.

Messick, S. (1989) ' Validity', in R. L. Linn (ed.) *Educational Measurement*, 3rd edn, Washington, DC: American Council on Education and National Council on Measurement in Education, pp. 13–103.

Moder, C. L. and Halleck, G. B. (2012) 'Designing Language Tests for Specific Social Uses', in G. Fulcher and F. Davidson (eds) *The Routledge Handbook of Language Testing*, London: Routledge, pp. 137–49.

Park, K. (2014) 'Corpora and Language Assessment: The State of the Art', *Language Assessment Quarterly* 11(1): 27–44.

Plakans, L. (2018) 'Then and Now: Themes in Language Assessment Research', *Language Education and Assessment* 1(1): 3–8.

Römer, U. (2017) 'Language Assessment and the Inseparability of Lexis and Grammar: Focus on the Construct of Speaking', *Language Testing* 34(4): 477–92.

Salamoura, A. and Saville, N. (2010) 'Exemplifying the CEFR: Criterial Features of Written Learner English from the English Profile Programme', *Communicative Proficiency and Linguistic Development: Intersections between SLA and Language Testing Research. EuroSLA Monographs Series* (1): 101–32.

Stevenson, M. and Phakiti, A. (2019) 'Automated Feedback and Second Language Writing', in K. Hyland and F. Hyland (eds) *Feedback in Second Language Writing: Contexts and Issues*, Cambridge: Cambridge University Press, pp. 125–42.

Tao, H. (2003) 'Turn Initiators in Spoken English: A Corpus-Based Approach to Interaction and Grammar', in P. Leistyna and C. F. Meyer (eds) *Corpus Analysis: Language Structure and Language Use*, Amsterdam: Rodopi, pp. 187–207.

Taylor, L. and Barker, F. (2008) 'Using Corpora in Language Assessment', in E. Shohamy and N. Hornberger (eds) *Language Testing and Assessment, Encyclopedia of Language and Education*, Vol. 7, New York: Springer, pp. 241–54.

Van Moere, A., Suzuki, M., Downey, R. and Cheng, J. (2009) 'Implementing ICAO Language Proficiency Requirements in the Versant Aviation English Test', *Australian Review of Applied Linguistics*, 32(3): 1–17.

Voss, E. (2012) 'A Validity Argument for Score Meaning of a Computer-Based ESL Academic Collocational Ability Test Based on a Corpus-Driven Approach to Test Design', unpublished PhD dissertation, Lowa State University.

Weigle, S. C. and Goodwin, S. (2016) 'Applications of Corpus Linguistics in Language Assessment', in J. V. Banerjee and D. Tsagari (eds) *Contemporary Second Language Assessment: Contemporary Applied Linguistics*, Vol. 4, New York, NY: Bloomsbury, pp. 209–24.

Williamson, D. M., Xi, X. and Breyer, F. J. (2012) 'A Framework for Evaluation and Use of Automated Scoring', *Educational Measurement: Issues and Practice* 31(1): 2–13.

Xi, X. (2017) 'What Does Corpus Linguistics Have to Offer to Language Assessment?' *Language Testing* 34(4): 565–77.

46

Corpus linguistics and the study of social media: a case study using multi-dimensional analysis

Tony Berber Sardinha

1 What is social media?

Social media refers to the communication generated on platforms that enable users to send text messages and multimedia content to a group of other users. Many different social media outlets exist today, like *Facebook, Twitter, Instagram, YouTube, Tumblr, Snapchat* and *TikTok*, among others. Each was introduced to serve a particular purpose for a particular audience. When it was created in 2003, *Facebook's* predecessor *Facemash* allowed Harvard University to rate the appearance of fellow students. YouTube, which was registered in 2005, was originally meant for people to share home videos on the Web. Two years later, Tumblr was introduced as a blogging site that provided a "tumblelog" – that is, a space where they could post "tumblin" (one-paragraph) messages, photos and videos.

Unlike *Facebook, YouTube* and *Tumblr*, which were devised as websites, *Twitter* was designed to run on cell phones as an SMS service. *Twitter* came about in 2006, conceived as a tool for users to update each other on their whereabouts and activities (Weller *et al.* 2014: x). Other social media outlets were developed first and foremost as mobile technology applications. *Instagram* was released in 2010 as a mobile phone application for photo sharing. Snapchat was introduced a year later as a photo app in which the post would quickly vanish, so users would not feel pressured to post "Kodak-perfect moments". The mobile app *TikTok* came to the scene more recently, when it absorbed the short video-sharing app Music.ly in 2017. Like its predecessor, *TikTok* allows users to share short video content such as lip-sync and dance routines.

When these social media applications were first introduced, many catered to a particular audience and sought to meet or create a particular demand. However, over time many converged to offer some form of text and multimedia content sharing. The current leading social media platforms all provide the means for users to post texts, pictures and audio and video files. In addition, all offer mobile technology applications, which have become the predominant environment in which users engage with the social networks.

Mobile technology has helped social media platforms gain enormous popularity because smart phones and wireless broadband have become more affordable worldwide, thereby helping these social networks penetrate markets in the developing world, adding

DOI: 10.4324/9780367076399-46

billions of users to the networks in addition to enabling more users to shoot, edit and post video footage. Such expansion has caused a major shift in the social networks: They have become less a space for sharing content and more a tool to influence human behavior. Nowadays, engaging with social media is increasingly a way of life rather than a distraction, where millions of digital influencers dictate social, cultural and political norms. *Twitter*, for instance, has repositioned itself as a leading news source – so much so that its posts are widely quoted in mainstream news reports. Major public figures use *Twitter* as an official channel of communication. *Instagram* has been adopted as a prime outlet for major fashion brands to advertise their products and build their corporate image. *YouTube* and *TikTok* have become major players in the music business, with more artists using these platforms as their primary source of income.

The widespread use and influence of social media have led scholars to argue that the social networks are a real world rather than a made-up world:

> When the study of the internet began people commonly talked about two worlds: the virtual and the real. By now it is increasingly evident that the online is just as real as the offline. In the same way no one today would regard a telephone conversation as taking place in a separate world from "real life".
>
> *(Miller et al. 2016: 7)*

This shift suggests that investigating social media enables us to understand both virtual and "real" life, as "real" life is increasingly influenced by social media. Corpus-based research on social media can seek answers to key questions such as what kind of language is used in these social media communities, how language use varies across groups and individuals, what text varieties exist and how they compare with non-digital varieties and how widespread non-standard forms such as contractions, hashtags, emoticons and emojis are.

Despite its growing importance, social media has received scant attention in our field due in part to the kinds of text used in social media posing challenges for corpus methods and techniques. Social media texts are generally "messy" – that is, they make extensive use of non-standard spelling, punctuation, abbreviations, emoticons, emojis and hashtags, which can cause serious problems for part-of-speech taggers and lemmatisers. In addition, social media texts are typically very short, which raises questions about the reliability of relative frequency counts of lexical and grammatical features. For such operations to be successful, the corpus generally needs to undergo several rounds of adaptation, as discussed next.

2 Collecting and handling a corpus of social media

A corpus of social media usually consists of many thousands of texts because social media posts are abundant (although some platforms impose restrictions on downloading). As manually collecting large numbers of individual texts is a tedious and error-prone process, many analysts resort to "scraping," which is automated collection using computer software. A range of scraping tools exist in the natural language processing community, but since these generally require programming skills (e.g. *Python*) to install and run, many corpus linguists do not make use of them. Researchers can find the currently available scraping tools by searching the Web (e.g. "scraping *Twitter* data"). Some scraping tools have the added benefit of downloading metadata for the posts, such as the username of the poster, their geographical location (geodata) and a count of likes for the post.

Social media posts are notorious for their use of non-conventional and innovative word forms. Consequently, once a corpus of social media has been collected, researchers need to decide whether the orthography and punctuation in the texts will be adapted ("normalised") and, if so, to what extent. This process of converting the orthographic features to a standard is generally referred to as "normalisation" in natural language processing. However, in order to avoid confusion with the term normalisation used in corpus studies to refer to the computation of relative frequencies (see Chapters 10 and 39, this volume), it will be referred to as "lexical normalisation".

Lexical normalisation refers to a set of procedures whose goal it is to adapt the texts to orthographic convention. For example, the fully normalised version of "john gave ALL HIS LOVE 2u" would be "John gave all his love to you". During lexical normalisation, many of the natural features of social media texts are stripped away, like emphasis by uppercase and character repetition, shortened forms and non-standard capitalisation. The downside of lexical normalisation is that by removing these features, layers of meaning are also removed. But a benefit is that corpus tools can retrieve all the instances of a token that were spelled differently, like "for," previously spelled "4," "just" ("jus") and "great" ("GREAAATTT"). A lack of normalisation can significantly affect part-of-speech tagging and lemmatisation, as unconventional spelling and non-standard capitalisation can cause tagging errors with taggers not trained with social media data. Lexical normalisation involves several individual processes, covering a range of textual and graphic aspects, such as:

1. Automatic spell-checking. This refers to detecting non-canonical spellings and converting these to conventionally spelled forms. For instance, the spell-corrected version of "I jus cant see u" would be "I just can't see you";
2. Truecasing. This is a special case of spell-checking that refers to determining the standard capitalisation of words and changing the capitalisation if needed. For instance, "i think new york is AWESOME" could be truecased as "I think New York is awesome";
3. Acronyms and abbreviations. Many posts normally include strings like "xoxo", "imho" and "afaik". If these strings were normalised, they would be replaced with "hugs and kisses", "in my humble opinion" and "as far as I know", respectively;
4. Emoticons. These are strings of keyboard characters that express such features as emotions, attitudes and feelings. For instance, normalising :-) and :-] would convert these strings to "smile" or "smiling face"; :-D to "smile", "smiling face", "grin" or "grinning face"; and :-O to "surprise", "shock" or "yawn". A definitive dictionary of emoticons does not exist; therefore, a single emoticon may be normalised in different ways;
5. Emojis. These are in-text graphic characters depicting all sorts of objects, body parts and animals as well as human emotions, attitudes and feelings (like their predecessors, the emoticons). There is no consensus on how to translate emojis to text, so a single emoji can be described in a variety of ways. For instance, the emoji 😀 can be rendered as "laughing", "laughing face", "happy", etc. Additional shades of meaning can be added to emojis, like skin color; for instance, 🤚🏿 is referred to in emoji indexes as "Raised Back of Hand: Dark Skin Tone". In addition to denotative meaning, emojis embody pragmatic meaning; a raised hand emoji can mean "me", "I want to talk", "I'm here", etc., depending on the context, and skin colour can add further instances of meaning;

6. Hashtag segmentation. Hashtags are strings of characters that signal the contents of the post and make it possible to link different posts that refer to a similar topic. They are initiated by the hash or pound sign (#) and generally comprise a sequence of words with no spaces between them. Hashtag segmentation is the process whereby the boundaries between the constituent word forms in a hashtag are detected and blanks are inserted between the word forms. For instance, the hashtag #ILOVENYC would be segmented as "I LOVE NYC".

Part-of-speech tagging can be carried out using general-purpose or specialised taggers. General-purpose taggers include such tools as the *Biber Tagger, TreeTagger* and CLAWS. General-purpose taggers will be affected by a lack of normalisation if they were not trained on social media texts, but if run on normalised posts, they can provide high-accuracy tagging for hundreds of linguistic features. Specialised taggers include CMU's *Twitter* tagger (aka "Gimpel tagger," http://www.cs.cmu.edu/~ark/TweetNLP). These provide better performance on non-normalised corpora, but their feature sets are usually more restricted than general-purpose taggers.

3 Using multi-dimensional analysis to investigate social media

MD analysis is a framework for corpus analysis that uses multivariate statistical analysis to identify correlations among linguistic features across the texts in a corpus (Berber Sardinha and Veirano Pinto 2014, 2019). MD analysis was introduced by Douglas Biber in the 1980s (Biber 1988), and since then it has been widely applied in corpus linguistics, primarily in register variation research. Two major MD analysis types exist: a grammatical variant, which focuses mostly on the structural characteristics of the texts, and a lexical variant, which focuses on the lexical units in the texts (single words, n-grams, collocations) (Berber Sardinha 2021). In the study reported in this chapter, a grammatical MD analysis was carried out to detect the major dimensions underlying the variation across platforms, user groups and individual users in social media.

A dimension of variation is the parameter underlying the variation across the texts. In a grammatical MD analysis, the dimensions correspond to the major communicative functions in the texts. For example, Biber (1988) identified five major dimensions of register variation for spoken and written English:

1. Involved versus Informational Production;
2. Narrative versus Non-Narrative Concerns;
3. Explicit versus Situation-Dependent Reference;
4. Overt Expression of Persuasion;
5. Abstract versus Non-Abstract Information.

Each dimension comprises a set of linguistic features identified statistically through factor analysis. The factors are interpreted qualitatively based on the overall function performed by the features. For example, the involved end of dimension 1 is a result of the cooccurrence of such features as first- and second-person pronouns, contracted forms, *that* deletions, private verbs, hedges and amplifiers, among many others. These features enable the production of interactive, oral forms of communication in both speech and writing. In speech, this can take the form of various registers, like face-to-face and telephone conversations, spontaneous speeches and interviews, whereas in writing it materialises as personal letters, stage plays and romantic fiction, among many other such registers.

The major steps involved in a typical MD analysis are as follows:

1. Corpus design and compilation. The corpus should be designed as a representative sample of the registers of interest. The text is the central unit for corpus construction in MD analysis. The boundaries between the texts must be preserved (i.e. the individual texts should not be lumped into single files), and the counts of linguistic features must be taken for each individual text rather than for whole sections or the corpus as a whole. In the MD analysis framework, the total word count of the corpus is less important than the total number of texts (in each of the different sections of the corpus);
2. Selection of linguistic features. The analyst should select the linguistic features of relevance based on the previous literature;
3. Tagging. The corpus must be tagged for the relevant linguistic features, with a reliable automatic tagger;
4. Frequency counts. After tagging, the features are counted for each text, and the counts are normed to a fixed rate (e.g. 1,000 words) to enable frequency comparisons across texts of different lengths;
5. Factor analysis. The normed counts are submitted to factor analysis, a statistical technique that enables the identification of factors and sets of correlated linguistic features that correspond to latent (unobserved) variables in the corpus;
6. Scoring. For each factor, a score is computed for each individual text, based on the counts of the linguistic features loading on the factor. Mean scores are calculated for the relevant sections of the corpus;
7. Interpretation of the factors. The factors are interpreted qualitatively so as to determine the underlying dimensions of variation. Each dimension receives an interpretive label that captures its essential communicative properties.

These major steps were followed for the analysis reported in this chapter. However, because social media has particular typographical and linguistic characteristics that set them apart from other registers, extra steps were needed to prepare the corpus for tagging, which are detailed next.

A corpus was collected consisting of texts posted in English on *Twitter, Instagram* and *Facebook* between 2018 and 2019 (see Tables 46.1 and 46.2). Researchers should consider the role of images and audio features in social media and gauge the impact of retaining or removing such features from their corpus. Removing the non-textual materials from a corpus of social media can lead to the criticism that posts are often direct responses to images or audio, and therefore, the text is impoverished by separating them. Spoken conversational corpora have also been criticised for de-contextualising the language. To prevent such criticism, one solution is to code the extra-linguistic features in the corpus files; however, manual coding is time-consuming, so researchers first need to evaluate its cost-effectiveness. In the current study, metadata for the visual and audio content would have no added benefit because the focus is on the grammatical characteristics of the texts. Therefore, the corpus was restricted to the actual posts only – namely, the written messages posted by the account owners on the platforms (the text plus any in-text graphic content; i.e. emojis), while photographs, sound and video content were not included, nor were the comments to the posts. The texts were obtained

Table 46.1 Corpus used in the study: breakdown by platform

Platform	*Texts*	*Tokens*	*Mean tokens*	*Min.*	*Max.*	*SD*
Facebook	14,468	498,222	34.44	1	1089	38.03
Instagram	13,904	592,884	42.64	1	429	47.79
Twitter	14,288	322,382	22.56	1	83	13.68
Overall	42,660	1,413,488	33.13	1	1089	36.95

Table 46.2 Corpus used in the study: breakdown by user group

Platform	*User group*	*Texts*	*Tokens*	*Mean tokens*	*Min.*	*Max.*	*SD*
Facebook	Celebrities	4706	106,441	22.61	1	410	23.36
	Corporations	4974	149,407	30.03	1	367	25.84
	Politics	4788	242,374	50.62	1	1089	52.16
Instagram	Celebrities	4388	124,276	28.32	1	416	38.00
	Corporations	4759	250,243	52.58	1	373	49.87
	Politics	4757	218,365	45.90	1	429	50.57
Twitter	Celebrities	4430	72,890	16.45	1	78	12.12
	Corporations	4915	102,979	20.95	1	72	12.14
	Politics	4943	146,513	29.64	1	83	13.29

using a variety of methods, including manually copying the posts, scraping the posts in bulk and downloading ready-made datasets from the Web. The corpus was designed around three major components: platform, user group and user. "Platform" is one of the three social media outlets where the text was posted, "user group" refers to a class of users (e.g. celebrities, corporations or political figures/groups) and "user" identifies the account where the posts originated. The user group "celebrities" includes pop artists, movie actors/actresses, athletes and TV personalities; "politics" comprises world leaders, political parties and political organisations; and "corporations" consists of international brands. The users were selected based on lists of the most followed personalities, companies and organisations available on the Web. With the exception of corporations, most users were based in the United States or Europe.

The corpus was normalised using the following tools:

1. Emojificate, for converting emojis to text, https://pypi.org/project/emojificate;
2. Truecase, for fixing the capitalisation, https://pypi.org/project/truecase;
3. Ekphrasis, for tokenisation and hashtag segmentation, https://github.com/cbaziotis/ekphrasis;
4. MoNoise: for spell correction and acronym conversion, https://bitbucket.org/robvanderg/monoise/src/master.

The abbreviations were expanded using a shell script developed especially for this project. Other scripts were further used to clean up and format the posts prior to tagging.

After lexical normalisation, the corpus was tagged for part of speech using the Biber Tagger, which is widely used in MD research (Gray 2019). It tags texts for hundreds of linguistic characteristics, including word class, clause types, discourse features, semantic categories and stance markers. Once the corpus was fully tagged up, it was run through the Biber Tag Count, a programme that counts the features in the tagged texts, normalises the counts to a rate per thousand words and returns a data file with counts for more than 100 different features.

Frequency normalisation is needed because raw frequency counts are sensitive to text length. Longer texts will naturally have a higher count of particular features simply because they are longer. To enable comparisons of the same feature across texts of different lengths, in MD studies, counts are normed to a fixed rate:

Normed count = (Count of feature in the text /Length of the text in words) × 1,000

The relative rate of incidence of a feature in a long text may be less than in a short text. For instance, a two-word-long post containing a single verb would have a relative frequency of verbs per 1,000 words of 500 ((1/2) * 1000), but a ten-word-long post having two verbs would have a relative frequency of verbs equal to 200 ((2/10) * 1000). Therefore, text 1 has relatively more verbs than texts 2. But does it make sense to say that in relative terms text 1 has 2.5 times as many verbs as text 2, or is it sufficient to say that text 1 has more verbs per 1,000 words than text 2?

According to Biber (1993: 252), 'with regard to the issue of text length, [...] text samples should be long enough to reliably represent the distributions of linguistic features'. Very short texts fail to reliably represent the distribution of the features because the features that are present will be overrepresented, while the majority of the features will be underrepresented as missing. To avoid these problems, researchers can impose a minimum word count for texts; for instance, Biber and Egbert (2018: 13) set a minimum length of 75 words for texts to be included in their corpus of web documents. However, in social media, short texts are the norm; therefore, texts cannot be excluded based on their short length (in our corpus, the average post is 33 tokens long).

As short text length is a register feature in social media, the resulting feature counts will be skewed. To avoid this problem, one option is to convert the actual counts from an interval to an ordinal scale, thereby reducing the drastic differences among the texts with respect to the frequency counts. Table 46.3 illustrates the use of an ordinal scale to rank the texts in terms of the incidence of a feature. As can be seen, the ordinal scale reduced the distance among the texts to one rank, whereas the interval scale increased the distance up to tenfold.

In their study of Donald Trump's tweets, Clarke and Grieve (2019) used a binary scale to represent the data, whereby the features were coded as either present or absent. If a

Table 46.3 Interval and ordinal scale example

Text	*Text length*	*Feature count*	*Relative frequency per 1,000 words (interval scale)*	*Rank (ordinal scale)*
1	10	3	300	3
2	20	3	150	2
3	100	3	30	1

binary scale were applied to the data in Table 46.3, all texts would be coded as "present" for this feature, which would erase the distinction among the texts. No consensus exists in the literature as to whether an interval or ordinal or binary scale is more appropriate for representing the feature counts in short text corpora. In this study, we used an ordinal scale, which enabled us to preserve the distinctions among the texts and reduce the effect of text size on the frequency counts. Since ordinal variables were used, polychoric correlations were computed for the factor analysis.

To date, social media has not received much attention in corpus linguistics in general or in MD studies in particular. One MD study is Berber Sardinha (2014), which reported an additive MD analysis that compared five online registers (email messages, webpages, blog posts and two social media varieties, namely Facebook posts and tweets) to the dimensions of register variation identified by Biber (1988). The results showed social media to be involved (dim. 1), non-narrative (dim. 2), situation-dependent (dim. 3), non-persuasive (dim. 4) and not marked for abstraction (dim. 5).

In a later study, Berber Sardinha (2018) carried out a full MD analysis of the same online registers, which identified three dimensions of variation: involved, interactive discourse versus informational focus (dim. 1); expression of stance: interactional evidentiality (dim.2); and stance: interactional affect (dim. 3). The two social media registers scored similarly on dimension 1 as very involved and interactive, but were distinguished on the stance dimensions: *Twitter* was more marked for evidentiality, whereas Facebook was more marked for affect. Emails scored more similarly to social media than the web registers on all dimensions. In summary, the study showed that social media outlets are interactive registers in which users routinely position themselves.

Clarke and Grieve (2019) examined a corpus of tweets by former US president Donald Trump, posted from 2004 to 2009 and identified five major dimensions: tweet length (dim. 1), conversational style (dim. 2), campaigning style (dim. 3), engaged style (dim. 4) and advisory style (dim. 5). The tweets were marked for the dimensions at different rates over time. For example, the conversational style was more prominent from the end of 2012 to mid-2013, whereas the campaigning style was dominant between 2016 and 2017.

4 Major dimensions of variation for social media

In the case study reported here, two dimensions were identified based on the factor analysis:

1. Formal, informational, argumentative discourse;
2. Informal, interactive, speaker-oriented discourse.

The first dimension is packed with features that enable a formal type of posting that generally conveys planned, edited, highly informational and argumentative content. With a total of 31 different linguistic features (Table 46.4), it includes specialised nouns (cognition, process, abstract, group), adverbial features (likelihood, certainty, attitudinal), conjunctions (coordinating as clausal connector, causative, subordinating), discourse features (downtoners, hedges, amplifiers), adjectives (topical, relational), modals (necessity/obligation, prediction/volition, possibility, permission, ability), clause types (*to* complement clauses controlled by nouns, wh-relative clauses) and pronouns (third person, *it*, demonstrative, nominal/indefinite). In addition, posts marked on this dimension are longer and display more lexical variety type-token ratio (TTR). The three

Table 46.4 Factor pattern for dimension 1

Feature	*Loading*
Type-token ratio	.790
Word count	.787
Likelihood adverbs	.538
Adverb within auxiliary	.522
Linking adverbials	.505
Coordinating conjunction as clausal connector	.489
Hedges	.480
Causative subordinating conjunction	.470
Certainty adverbials	.455
All wh-relative clauses	.446
Other subordinating conjunction	.425
Downtoner	.418
Third-person pronoun (except *it*)	.417
Adverb (excluding other types)	.392
Cognition nouns	.388
Attitudinal adverbs	.386
Amplifiers	.375
Modals of necessity or obligation	.374
Process nouns	.367
Pronoun *it*	.366
Topical adjectives	.364
Demonstrative pronouns	.351
Nominal / indefinite pronoun	.347
All passives	.346
Emphatics	.345
Modals of prediction or volition	.342
Modals of possibility, permission, and ability	.327
to complement clause controlled by stance nouns	.326
Abstract nouns	.318
Group/institution nouns	.300
Relational adjectives	.300

platforms are statistically identical with respect to this dimension, as the platform explains a mere 0.2 per cent of the variation (Figure 46.1). At the same time, the user groups explain 13 per cent of the variation (Figure 46.2), ranked as follows: politics, corporations and celebrities. The actual users, however, capture twice as much variation (26 per cent); Figure 46.3 shows the top ten highest- and lowest-scoring users.

Politicians use dimension 1 features to promote their political agenda, as in the following example, which shows the dense use of features for this dimension in a long Facebook post (128 words, 23.3 TTR) by a US Senator (in the examples, parentheses were added to indicate the features loading on the factor):

> Now (adverb), more (adverb) than (subordinating conjunction) ever (adverb), it (it) is abundantly (adverb) clear that high quality (abstract noun), affordable child care (abstract noun) is absolutely (amplifier) essential for families, as well (adverb) as for employers and the economy (abstract noun) as a whole (abstract noun). Fortunately

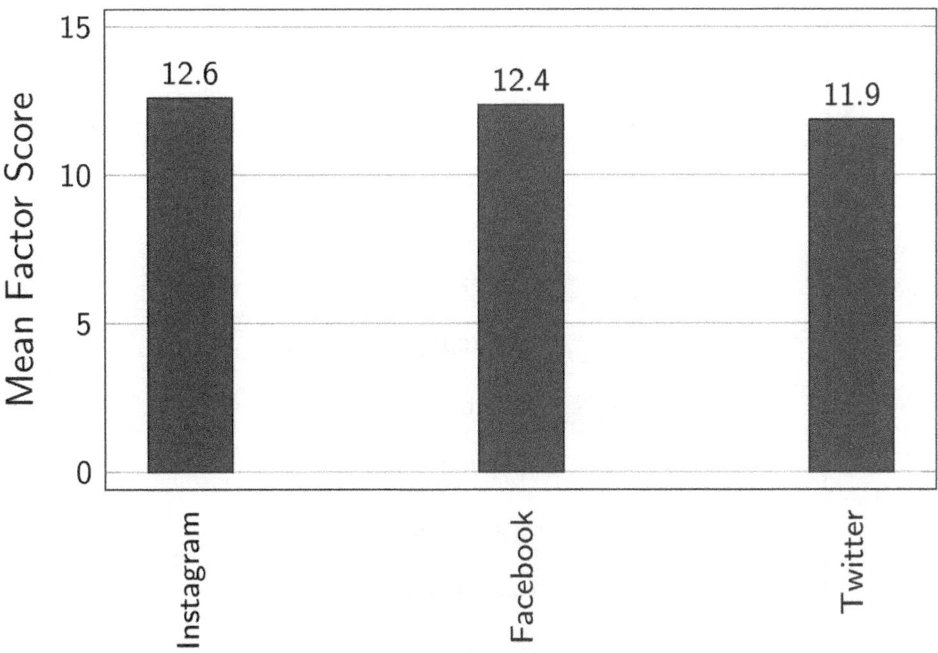

Figure 46.1 Means for platform dim. 1 (R^2 = .2%; F = 36.4; p < .0001)

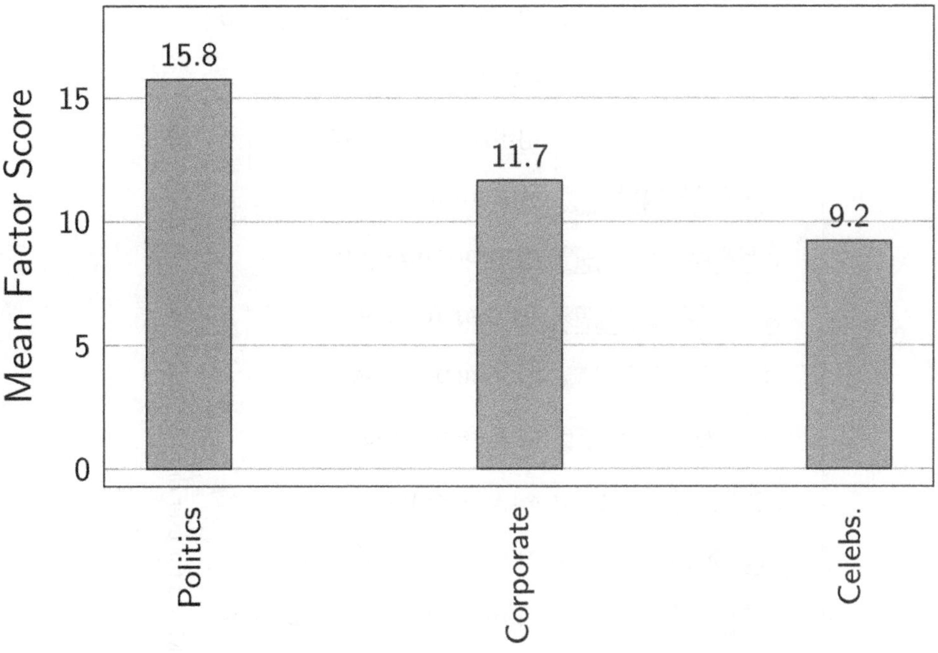

Figure 46.2 Means for user group dim. 1 (R^2 = 13.04%; F = 3198.53; p < .0001)

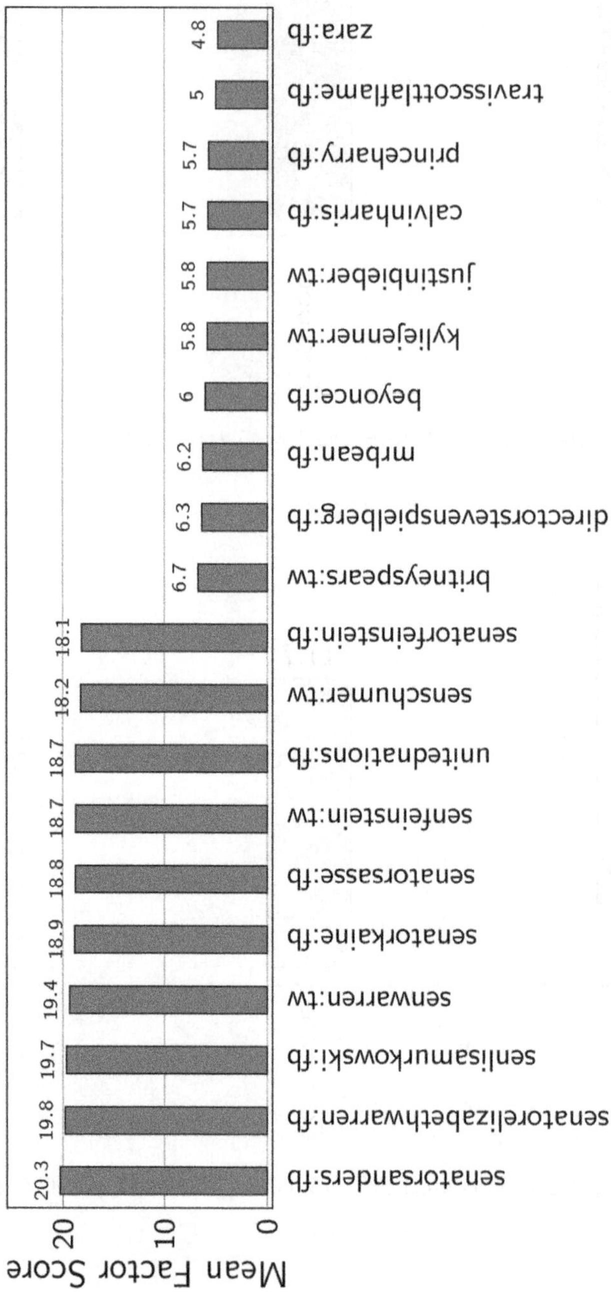

Figure 46.3 Means for user dim. 1 (R^2=26.4%; F=70.03; $p<.0001$)

> (linking adverbial), state and federal funding (abstract noun) is available to help families with the cost of child care (abstract noun) through Vermont's Child Care (abstract noun) Financial Assistance (abstract noun) Program. While (subordinating conjunction) we still (adverb) have a long way (abstract noun) to go to provide universal child care (abstract noun) to all and ensure our child care (abstract noun) providers are paid (passive voice) a fair wage for their (third-person pronoun) invaluable work (process noun), this program is an important tool for so many struggling families, including those (demonstrative pronoun) who (wh-relative clause) have experienced financial hardship (abstract noun) [...]

The following example, a United Nations post on Facebook, shows how abstract and process nouns can occur within hashtags, which the tagger was able to detect because the hashtags had been segmented:

> Not one country has achieved gender (abstract noun) equality (abstract noun) yet (adverb). At the current rate (abstract noun) of progress, it will (prediction modal) take 99.5 years to close the global gender (abstract noun) gap. But (coordinating conjunction as clausal connector), it (*it*) doesn't have to (necessity modal) be this way (abstract noun). Join #GenerationEquality <generation>(process noun) <equality>(abstract noun) by supporting women and girls, defying gender (abstract noun) roles (abstract noun), fighting gender (abstract noun)-based violence, and (coordinating conjunction as clausal connector) standing up for equality (abstract noun). <url>

The next example (a tweet by a US Senator) shows how shorter posts can make intensive use of the dimension features. Note how linguistic features were detected by the tagger after abbreviations were expanded:

> ICYMI<In><case><you><missed><it>(pronoun *it*) on @<handle> with @ <user>: @<handle> is a monopoly and they (third-person pronoun) are abusing their (third-person pronoun) power (abstract noun) to (*to* complement clause controlled by noun) unfairly (adverb) target and censor conservatives. They (third-person pronoun) must (modal of necessity or obligation) be stopped (passive voice).

In contrast to politicians and political groups, corporations rely on this dimension for customer relations and brand management. The following example shows how the dimension is used to provide technical support:

> @<handle> Hmm. An account can (possibility modal) be recovered (passive voice) for a limited time (abstract noun): https://<url>. You can (possibility modal) definitely (certainty adverbial; split auxiliary) create a new one here (adverb): https://<url>

Unlike the previous examples, posts with low scores on this dimension make scant use of these features, as shown in the following tweet by a singer:

> I love u <you> guys. This (demonstrative pronoun) is funny as hell

Table 46.5 Factor pattern for dimension 2

Feature	*Loading*
to complement clauses controlled by adjectives	.723
that complement clauses controlled by adjective	.578
Adjectives in predicative position	.537
that deletion	.535
that complement clauses controlled by verb	.518
Verb (not including auxiliary verbs)	.515
First-person pronoun / possessive	.404
Contraction	.399
to complement clauses controlled by verbs	.360
Conditional subordinating conjunction	.338

The set of features loading on dimension 2 indicate informality, speaker orientation, engagement, and interaction (Table 46.5). It comprises many verb-based constructions, such as a high number of verbs, *that* complement clauses controlled by either adjectives or verbs (which are often used as stance devices), contractions, and *that* deletions. It also includes adjectives in predicative position, first-person pronouns, and subordinating conjunctions, which enable elaboration in clausal structures and a focus on the speaker.

As with the first dimension, the effect of the platform is negligible, as this accounts for less than 1 per cent of the variation (Figure 46.4). Similarly, the majority of the variation is accounted for by user groups and by the individual users, albeit to a lesser extent (Figures 46.5 and 46.6).

The next example (a tweet by a US congressman) shows how politicians make use of this dimension to rally support for a cause:

> RT<retweet> if (conditional subordinating conjunction) you agree (verb) that (*that* complement clause controlled by verb) everyone risking their lives on the frontlines of this crisis deserves (verb) hazard pay. <man><raising><hand> https:<url>

The following is an example of a corporate tweet from a US car maker intended to provide customer support, which makes intensive use of the features loading on the dimension:

> @<handle> Sorry to hear (verb) that, <name>. Please let (verb) your friend, Jo, know (verb) that (*that* complement clause controlled by verb) if (conditional subordinating conjunction) they ever have (verb) vehicle concerns, we (first-person pronoun) are (verb) only an email away. He would only need (verb) to (*to* complement clause controlled by verb) send (verb) an email to socialmedia@gm.com. We (first-person pronoun) are (verb) always happy (adjective in predicative position) to (*to* complement clause controlled by adjective) provide (verb) support.

The dimension features are often used by corporations to promote products and services, as in this tweet from an American fast-food chain:

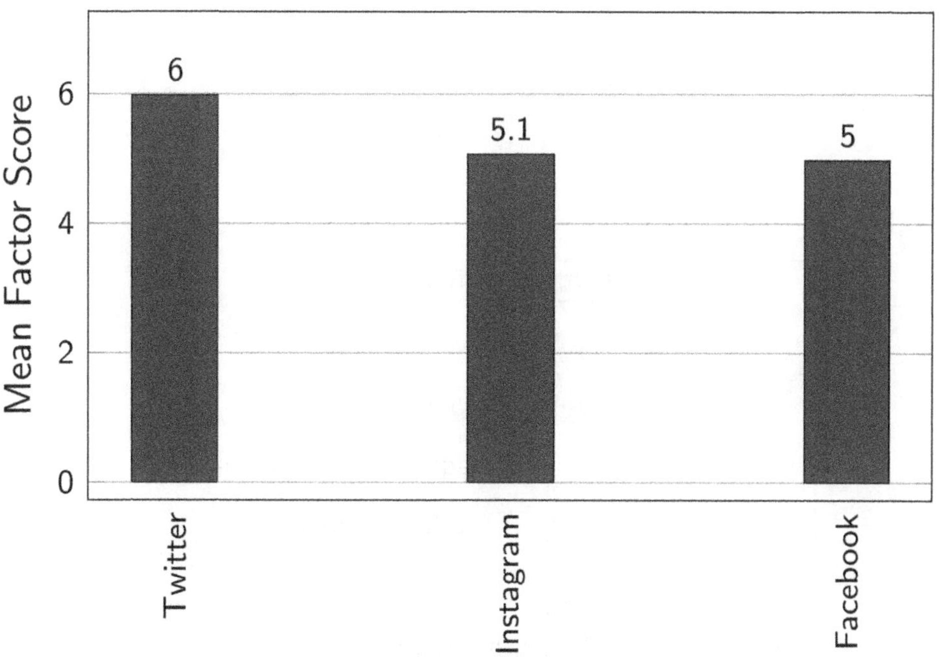

Figure 46.4 Means for platform dim. 2 (R^2 = .98%; F = 211.84; $p < .0001$)

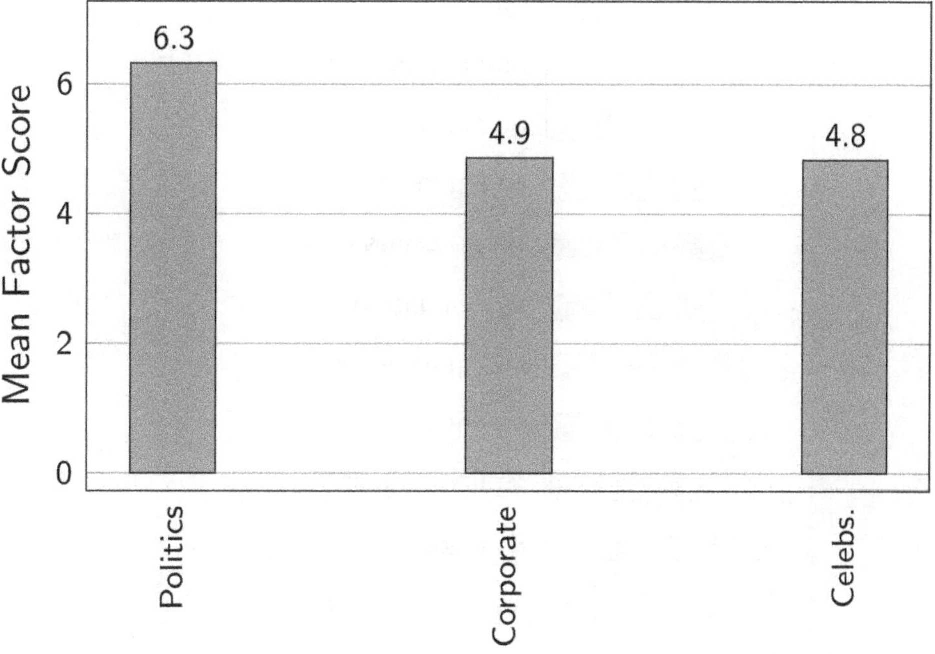

Figure 46.5 Means for user group dim. 2 (R^2 = 2.35%; F = 514.873; $p < .0001$)

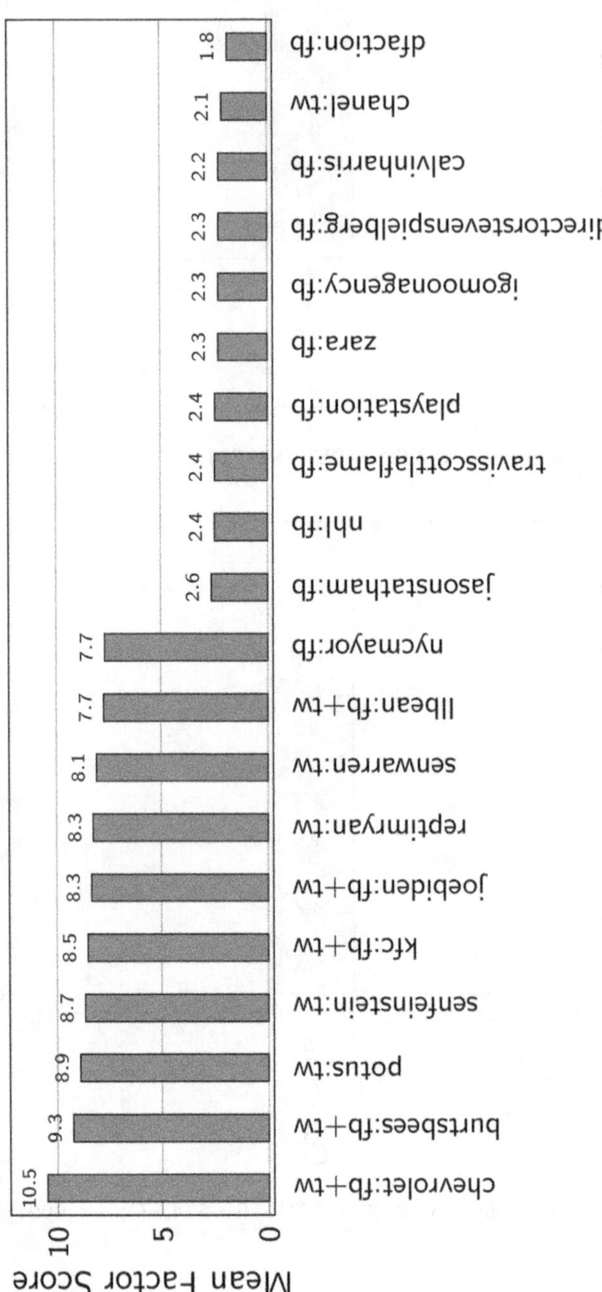

Figure 46.6 Means for user dim. 2 (R^2 = 14.36%; F = 32.8; p <.0001)

> They look (verb) similar (adjective in predicative position), but you'll (contraction) be surprised to learn (verb) that (*that* complement clause controlled by verb) one is (verb) full (adjective in predicative position) of helium, and one is full (adjective in predicative position) of 100 per cent white-meat chicken. #ColonelsRoadTrip <Coronel's><road><trip>#MacysParade <Macy's><parade>

Promotional posts can exploit the dimension features to create the illusion that companies are speaking with users, as in the following tweet from the same company:

> Does anybody know (verb) how to (*to* complement clause controlled by verb) take (verb) care of a gold goldfish? I (first-person pronoun) have (verb) no clue what I (first-person pronoun) 'm (contraction) doing (verb). All I (first-person pronoun) 've (contraction) learned (verb) so far is (verb) that (*that* complement clause controlled by verb) it doesn't (contraction) eat (verb) fried chicken.

Celebrities can also take advantage of emulating a conversation, for example, to announce events that promote their careers, as in this tweet by an American TV personality:

> I (first-person pronoun) 'm (contraction) so ready (adjective in predicative position) to (*to* complement clause controlled by adjective) see (verb) my fellow entrepreneurs at @<handle>#QBConnect <QB><connect> in San Jose next week! I (first-person pronoun) better C<see>(verb) U<you> there <face><throwing><a><kiss> http://<url>

As mentioned, the individual users play an important role in determining the variation across the posts: Some users choose a style more closely associated with dimension 1, while others choose a style more in line with dimension 2. However, some users choose a style consistent with both dimensions at the same time. To identify the individual preferences across the two dimensions, Pearson product correlations were computed for the dimension scores. The results showed that a minority of users (63 users, 21.5 per cent of the 293) scored a positive moderate correlation (r >=0.5) or higher between dimensions 1 and 2. Of these, only four had a high positive coefficient (r >=0.7). These users combine the formal, planned and information-based characteristics of dimension 1 with the informal, speaker-oriented, dialog-emulating characteristics of dimension 2. An example appears next, a post by an American performer which includes several dimension 1 and dimension 2 features:

> =< <folded><hands><medium><skin><tone>(dim. 1: abstract noun) THANK (dim. 2: verb) YOU @<handle> for BRINGING LIFE (dim. 1: abstract noun) BACK TO OUR (dim. 2: first-person pronoun) HOME (dim. 1: group noun)!!! THIS (dim. 1: demonstrative pronoun) WAS (dim. 2: verb) AN HONOR (dim. 1: abstract noun) FOR ME (dim. 2: first-person pronoun) AND (dim. 1: coordinating conjunction as clausal connector) IM (dim. 2: first-person pronoun) (dim. 2: contraction) THANKFUL (dim. 2: adjective in predicative position) TO (dim. 2: *to* complement clause controlled by adjective) BE (verb) FROM VIRGINIA!!! ; <heart> TIL (dim. 1: adverb) the wheels fall (verb) off

However, this style of post is rare, as the vast majority of users will write posts that are consistent with a single dimension at a time. In fact, the correlations show that, overall, the messages posted by an individual user will comprise a mixture of both dimension 1 marked posts and dimension 2 marked posts. For instance, a US apparel company (correlation r = 0.27) will often select a style that is consistent with dimension 1 for its posts, as in the first example shown, whereas at other times, it will prefer a style consistent with dimension 2, as in the second example:

> The Sk8-Hi MTE infuses (dim. 2: verb) style (dim. 1: abstract noun) and function (dim. 1: process noun) to (dim. 1: *to* complement clause controlled by noun) get (dim. 2: verb) you through the winter ahead (dim. 1: adverb). Shop (dim. 2: verb) the All Weather MTE collection (dim. 1: abstract noun) at <url> or your nearest store (dim. 1: group noun).

> We (dim. 2: first-person pronoun) had (dim. 2: verb) the best time (dim. 1: abstract noun) at the Stoke-O-Rama yesterday (dim. 1: adverb) down in Huntington Beach at the #VANSUSOPEN<Vans><US><Open>. Be (dim. 2: verb) sure (dim. 2: adjective in predicative position) to (dim. 2: *to* complement clause controlled by adjective) follow (dim. 2: verb) @<handle> to see (dim. 2: verb) more (dim. 1: adverb)! 📷 <camera>: @<handle>

5 Summary and future prospects

Social media provides a vast space for human interaction, where millions of posts are exchanged every day by billions of individuals and private and government institutions. Society is increasingly dependent on social media for information, entertainment, governance and work. This is a quickly changing mode of communication, shaped by human and societal demands as well as technological developments.

In this chapter, we showed how corpus linguistics can be used to model the variation in the verbal language encountered in the social networks. The results showed that despite the enormous opportunity for variation in social media language that the abundance of texts and users afford, the social media posts in the corpus follow two basic styles: a formal, information-based, often argumentative style and an informal, interactive, engaging, speaker-oriented style. Each one of these dimensions represents a continuum of variation: Posts can be either more or less formal, information-based and argumentative while at the same time be more or less informal and person-oriented. The results showed that although few users will post messages highly marked for both dimensions at the same time, users do rely on both dimensions.

These findings paint a complex picture of social media texts in which the variation seems to be driven primarily by the individual users, rather than by the platform or the types of user. Two major conclusions can be drawn. First, it seems possible to generalise from one platform to the others (at least across those examined here). Second, it seems prudent to acknowledge the importance of the variation across individual users in the corpus. For corpus-based studies, an implication is that corpora of social media should be designed around samples of individual users and the texts should be identified by the account where the post originated. This will ensure that researchers are able to track down the source of the posts and determine the extent of the variation explained by the users. Beyond users, future studies should be aware of confounding variables, like topic (Friginal *et al.* 2018) and time period (Clarke and Grieve 2019), which are often disregarded but can have a significant effect on the results.

The results reported here differ from those reported by Berber Sardinha (2014, 2018) to the extent that the current study found both a "literate" and a "persuasive" component (fused into dim. 1). The difference may be attributed to sampling, as the current study sampled heavily from "institutional" accounts, unlike Berber Sardinha (2014). The decision to sample from institutional accounts reflects the current social media environment, as social media has become an official communication channel for organised sectors of society. At the same time, our results support Clarke and Grieve's (2019) dimension 2, which comprises literate and interactive poles.

Social media researchers should strive to preserve the multimodal content found in social media, such as pictures (including memes), video and sound, as these are part and parcel of the social media environment and are likely to become more pivotal as multimedia technology improves. However, few tools for automatically annotating auditory and visual features exist today (see for instance Google Cloud Vision), and the features that are annotated by such tools may be restricted; as a result, a great deal of manual work may be required for annotating a whole corpus of social media.

Social media represents an increasingly influential form of communication. Corpus linguistics can offer key insights into how social media language is patterned, develops, varies and changes. Yet the medium remains under-researched in our field due to the challenges involved in building, preparing and analysing social media corpora, especially from a multimodal perspective. More user-friendly methods and tools need to be developed so that researching social media becomes more appealing and accessible to more corpus linguists.

Acknowledgement

I want to thank CNPq (Brasília, DF, Brazil; Processo # 306994/2017-8 and Processo # 407788/2018-2) and PiPEq (PUCSP) for funding this research. In addition, I want to thank Joe Collentine and Rob van der Goot for their invaluable support with the lexical normalisation tools used in this project.

Further reading

Baker, P. and McEnery, T. (2015) 'Who Benefits When Discourse Gets Democratised? Analysing a Twitter Corpus around the British Benefits Street Debate', in P. Baker and T. McEnery (eds) *Corpora and Discourse Studies: Integrating Discourse and Corpora*, Basingstoke: Palgrave Macmillan, pp. 244–65. (The authors analysed a corpus of tweets referring to the British TV show *Benefits Street* and to a televised debate about the programme. The show centred on people receiving government support ["benefits"] who lived in a poor area of Birmingham. The analysis detected some of the major discourses in the tweets, including "the idle poor", which framed people in need as idle and undeserving. Overall, the study shows that social media corpora are valuable sources of data for corpus-based discourse studies.)

Clarke, I. and Grieve, J. (2017) 'Dimensions of Abusive Language on Twitter', *Proceedings of the First Workshop on Abusive Language Online*, Vancouver, Canada, July 30 - August 4, 2017, pp. 1–10. (This paper presents an MD study of a corpus of 1,486 tweets coded for hate speech, such as racial, religious and sexist slurs. Through the MD analysis, the study shows that hate speech in social media is patterned for grammar. In general, tweets displaying sexism are more interactive and attitudinal than tweets displaying racism.)

Rüdiger, S. and Dayter, D. (eds) (2020) *Corpus Approaches to Social Media* (Studies in Corpus Linguistics, Vol. 98), Amsterdam: John Benjamins. (This edited collection comprises papers dealing with several important aspects of social media language, both verbal and visual. The volume includes case studies of different platforms such as Reddit, Twitter, WhatsApp and Facebook. The chapter by Christiansen, Dance and Wild tackles the challenges involved in analysing images, proposing the use of Google Artificial Intelligence tools to carry out visual constituent analysis.)

References

Berber Sardinha, T. (2014) 'Comparing Internet and Pre-Internet Registers', in T. Berber Sardinha and M. Veirano Pinto (eds) *Multi-Dimensional Analysis, 25 years on: A Tribute to Douglas Biber*, Amsterdam/Philadelphia, PA: John Benjamins, pp. 81–107.

Berber Sardinha, T. (2018) 'Dimensions of Variation across Internet Registers', *International Journal of Corpus Linguistics* 23(2): 125–57.

Berber Sardinha, T. (2021) 'Discourse of Academia from a Multi-Dimensional Perspective', in E. Friginal and J. Hardy (eds) *The Routledge Handbook of Corpus Approaches to Discourse Analysis*, London: Routledge, pp. 298–318.

Berber Sardinha, T. and Veirano Pinto, M. (eds) (2014) *Multi-Dimensional Analysis, 25 years on: A Tribute to Douglas Biber*, Amsterdam/Philadelphia, PA: John Benjamins.

Berber Sardinha, T. and Veirano Pinto, M. (eds) (2019) *Multi-Dimensional Analysis: Research Methods and Current Issues*, London: Bloomsbury Academic.

Biber, D. (1988) *Variation across Speech and Writing*, Cambridge: Cambridge University Press.

Biber, D. (1993) 'Representativeness in Corpus Design', *Literary and Linguistic Computing* 8(4): 243–57.

Biber, D. and Egbert, J. (2018) *Register Variation Online*, Cambridge: Cambridge University Press.

Clarke, I. and Grieve, J. (2019) 'Stylistic Variation on the Donald Trump Twitter Account: A Linguistic Analysis of Tweets Posted between 2009 and 2018', *PLOS ONE* 14(9): e0222062. 10.1371/journal.pone.0222062.

Friginal, E., Waugh, O. and Titak, A. (2018) 'Linguistic Variation in Facebook and Twitter Posts', in E. Friginal and J. A. Hardy (eds) *Studies in Corpus-Based Sociolinguistics*, London: Routledge, pp. 342–62.

Gray, B. (2019) 'Tagging and Counting Linguistic Features for Multi-Dimensional Analysis', in T. Berber Sardinha and M. Veirano Pinto (eds) *Multi-Dimensional Analysis: Research Methods and Current Issues*, London / New York: Bloomsbury / Continuum, pp. 43–66.

Miller, D., Costa, E., Haynes, N., McDonald, T., Nicolescu, R., Sinanan, J., Spyer, J., Venkatraman, S. and Wang, X. (2016) *How the World Changed Social Media*, London: UCL Press.

Weller, K., Bruns, A., Burgess, J., Mahrt, M. and Puschmann, C. (eds) (2014) *Twitter and Society*, New York: Peter Lang.

47

Posthumanism and corpus linguistics

Kieran O'Halloran

1. Introduction

Apps, chatbots, virtual reality, digital assistants, facial recognition, ubiquitous computing, augmented reality, the internet of things, fourth industrial revolution, online multi-player video games, etc. We are entangled with the digital, and our thinking and behaviour are affected by this entanglement. The more entangled we are, the more we operate as a different kind of human – "a posthuman". Scholarly reflection on the posthuman condition is "posthumanism". Scholars who reflect on the posthuman condition are "posthumanists".

This chapter situates corpus linguistics within posthumanism. Section 2 outlines some key posthumanist perspectives. Section 3 highlights salient ways in which corpus linguistics has been *implicitly* posthuman for some time. Section 4 demonstrates an *explicitly* posthuman use of corpus linguistics. Section 5 encourages a more explicit engagement with posthumanism to allow new possibilities for corpus linguistics.

2. Posthumanism

Orientation

Posthumanism implies *after* humanism. Humanism assumes that we are the most important species, that we are autonomously separate from our environments and distinct both from other animals and from machines, with a unique experience of consciousness. Posthumanists are critical of these anthropocentric assumptions (e.g. Braidotti 2013; Herbrechter 2013) because:

- Genes are shared across species; thus all life is interconnected;
- Many non-human animals display intelligent and emotional behaviours previously believed to be uniquely human, e.g. empathy in chimpanzees;
- In the new epoch of the "Anthropocene", human activity detrimentally affects the climate, reduces biodiversity and threatens the survival of all species;

DOI: 10.4324/9780367076399-47

- The entanglement of intelligent technologies with humans shapes new thoughts and actions.

This last point is my main focus here.

Human–machine assemblages and intra-action

This ever-increasing entanglement is reflected in "intra-action", a term coined by post-humanist philosopher Karen Barad. The everyday notion of "*inter*action" assumes that when we connect with non-human entities, we are in control, for example, when we decide to switch on a computer. In contrast, *intra*-action signals the agency that *emerges* once humans and non-humans are entangled. Intra-active agencies – somewhere between intention and non-intention – do not lie exclusively in humans, but in the dynamic *in-betweenness* of human and non-human (Barad 2007; Hollett and Ehret 2017). Our daily engagement with intelligent technologies involves intra-actions. Consider map apps and satellite navigation. Pedestrians and drivers consent to these intelligent technologies prompting their decision-making about routes. Other times, consent may not be black and white. A common downtime behaviour is flitting between web links on video sharing sites, whose contents reflect behind-the-scenes machine learning of our search/play behaviours. After a while, we may forget that we are within a human-digital entanglement where algorithms prompt "decisions" which involve us consuming ad after ad. In both examples, our behaviour depends on intra-actions within a *human–machine assemblage* (Savat 2013).

"Lively" data visualisations

Key phenomena of digitally-based research are visualisations which reconstruct quantitative findings into "lively" data (Savage 2013). The aesthetic liveliness of these visualisations is more absorbing than traditional 2D tables, pie charts and graphs.[1] It can also cue new intra-active engagements with data. That is to say, when prompted into fresh engagements by visualisations, the researcher *intra*-acts, rather than *inter*-acts, with the data and so is not always completely "in charge". Intra-active engagement is intensified by the accelerating usage of immersive augmented and virtual reality technologies as well as digital assistants.

Figure 47.1 is a screenshot from a video spotlighting "IBM immersive insights". Here the user intra-acts with data findings using augmented reality goggles and speaking with the IBM digital assistant. The use of such visualisations in tandem with digital assistants pushes quantitative research away from a purely (or naively) positivist perspective, where research data are seen as representing the truth about the world, towards a more complex postpositivist perspective. As posthumanist educationalist Siân Bayne holds (bracketed insertions are mine):

> ...we may choose to see a visualisation, for example, as a direct representation of an essential social "truth" [positivist]; or we may choose to see it as an aesthetic emergence of machinic agency, resulting from a rich and co-constitutive relation between social world, human coder, algorithm, designer, infrastructure and database [post-positivist].
>
> *(Bayne 2016: 92)*

From a postpositivist perspective, aesthetic digitised visualisations lead researchers into fresh viewpoints on relations between data and the world. In other words, such

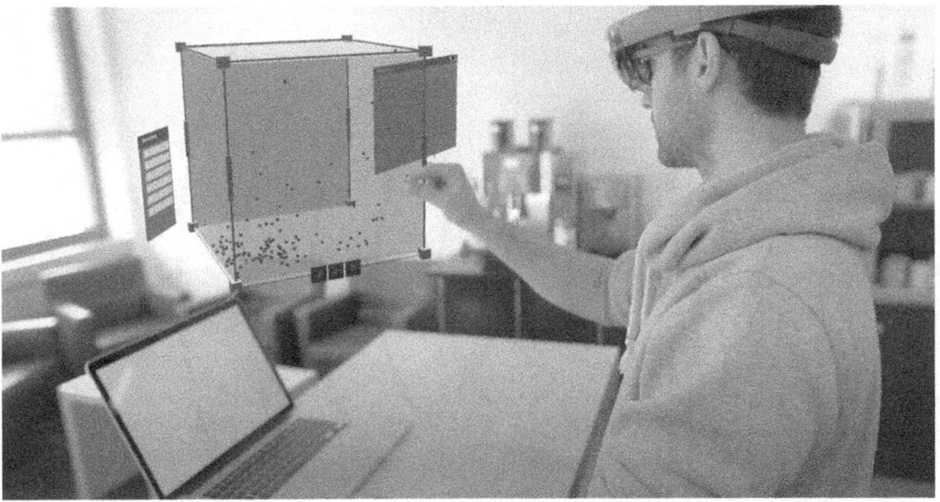

Figure 47.1 Augmented reality for analysing data with IBM immersive insights[2]

visualisations create new "subjectivities" as much as providing rigorous reporting on the world (with the usual postpositivist caveats that knowledge generated via the researcher's categories only approximates to actuality). Since these researcher subjectivities are intra-actively made via machine-generated visualisations, they can be described as *posthuman subjectivities*.

Transformation and surprise: posthuman reading

Diffraction

A mode of reading associated with posthumanism is "diffraction", originated by Donna Haraway and developed by Karen Barad. In physics, diffraction refers to the bending and spreading of waves on encountering an opening in a barrier (Figure 47.2). By analogy, diffractive reading involves reading one text through another to provoke "ripples" of thinking that move outwards in new and surprising directions (Barad 2007: 30). Thus, the focus is less on what the researcher does with the data and more on being open to what *the data does to the researcher*. The researcher should experience surprise, some resulting productive change. This entanglement of humans and data, rather than separation of humans from data, explains why diffraction is seen as a posthuman form of reading.

Sociologist Deborah Lupton views use of fitness apps as diffractive reading. The user examines their current fitness through the app's continual reports on number of steps taken, etc. (Lupton 2018). This diffractive reading, in turn, leads to further transformation of fitness. The app user responds intra-actively to the data, going on to review their fitness programme. The popularity of fitness apps suggests digitally-diffractive reading – and thus posthuman reading – is already a norm in the twenty-first century. This co-constitutive intra-active becoming of humans via digital data is a key feature of the posthuman condition, which Rosi Braidotti (2013) calls *becoming-machine*.

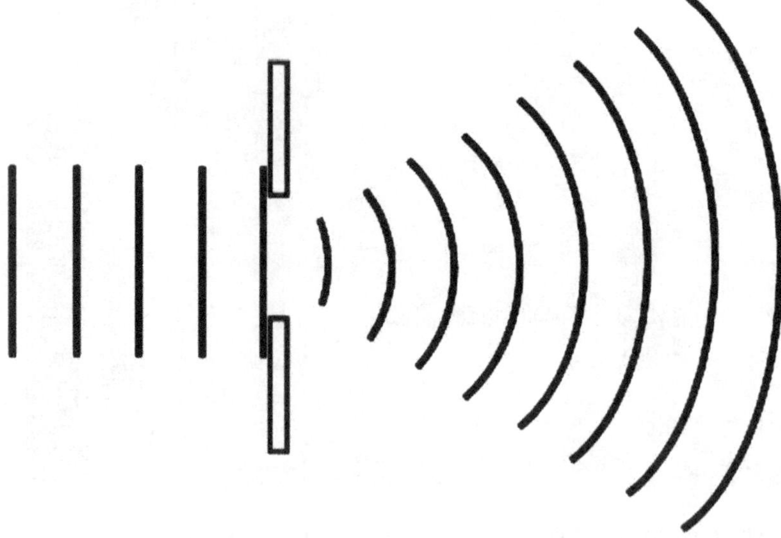

Figure 47.2 Diffraction pattern

Diffraction as ethical reading

For Barad (2012), diffractive reading can be ethical. This happens where we open out to an unfamiliar Other, human or non-human, who is marginalised, relatively powerless, disadvantaged, nonflourishing. This Other is neither at the centre of society nor adequately represented in democratic politics. Instead of reading from our pre-existing viewpoint, an ethical diffractive reading happens when we read:

i. A text, image, video, etc., which represents the centre of a culture (political, artistic, academic etc.)
   via
ii. Data illustrating the experiences of Others who are invisible, marginal, disadvantaged or nonflourishing in some way, or data from supporters of these Others.

We entangle with ii) and attend to its differences from i). This helps us spot relevant exclusions – whether deliberate or not – at the centre. In turn, greater ethical awareness of exclusion at the centre can ensue. (Naturally, any unfamiliar Other we open out to should espouse the principle of democratic politics.) In Section 4, I will model a posthuman critical reading strategy using corpus linguistic method which is based on Barad's ethical approach to diffraction.

Big data and disclosing relations

A salient characteristic of the posthuman condition is co-constitution of actual and virtual life via social media. This has led to a gargantuan volume of data on the internet. In exploring this *big social data* and other forms of *big data* from internet harvesting, a new science has emerged – *New Empiricism* (Kitchin 2014). This approach to data investigation differs from traditional, experimental deductive design in generating insights 'born from the data' rather than starting from hypotheses (Kelling *et al.* 2009: 614). A key aspect of New Empiricism is revelation of *relations* within and between big data. For example, Kosinski *et al.* (2013), from an analysis of big social data, posit a strong relationship between social media "Likes" and personal attributes, including sexual orientation and political views. Disclosure of relations can occur more prosaically as in social media networks where we discover that separate acquaintances know each other. As the posthumanist political scientist David Chandler writes: 'Data enables our embedded relationalities to become knowable' (Chandler 2015: 845). Big social data analysis enables researchers to see the recurrent relations of actual and virtual life – our posthuman lives.

Humanities scholarship using computational techniques, the so-called "digital humanities" (e.g. Adolphs and Knight 2020), is also commonly interested in ascertaining recurrent patterns across capacious data, e.g. usage of idioms across Shakespeare's comedies. Such data may not be equivalent in size to "big social data", but it is still big data in being too large for a human to notice many patterns across it. This relatively recent form of reading in the digital humanities, what Franco Moretti (2013) calls *distant reading*, also illuminates, at scale, relations between different variables (i.e., "embedded relationalities"). For example, working on a corpus of 5,000 novels from 1700 to 1900, Heuser *et al.* (2016) reveals relations between emotion, class and place across multiple narrative representations of London. Illumination by digital humanists of patterns and relations in single texts (novels, plays, etc), or collections of texts, produces vantages not so readily available to human reading alone, distant vantages dependent on entanglement of humans with software analytics. These vantages are not then human subjectivities but posthuman subjectivities which, in turn, can be used to prompt non-arbitrary diffractive close reading, resulting in fresh insight into individual texts (see Sections 3/4). Where such vantages and readings are dependent on human–digital assemblages – humans operating posthumanly – is this "digital *human*ities"? (see Section 5).

Having set out some key concepts and outlooks within posthumanism, I now highlight salient ways in which corpus linguistics is implicitly posthuman.

3. Situating corpus linguistics within posthumanism

Corpus linguists as primarily posthuman researchers

Distrusting human intuition about regular language usage

It is very difficult, if not impossible, to have accurate intuitions about regular usage across millions or billions of words in general language corpora. Self-evidently, we do not register or store information about recurrent language use with quantitative accuracy. In contrast, software analysis of a large general language corpus instantly yields its most common words and word patterns with quantitative precision. Corpus linguists quite rightly defer to software over their human intuitions about language use at scale. How posthuman! Corpus linguists use word frequency lists, keywords, concordances, etc., to guide their understanding of habitual language use. In other words, understanding of regular language use by human corpus linguists depends on them intra-acting with non-human representations of the same. The behaviour of humans acting posthumanly.

Ontology of digital data relations

Recurrent linguistic relations in a large general corpus, such as collocations (e.g. "world music") and phraseologies (e.g. "the greatest footballer in the world"), await discovery by the corpus linguist. Corpus linguistic research is no different, in principle, from artificial intelligence (AI) crunching of big datasets to discover "embedded relations" or, more mundanely, how the virtual world of social media can reveal separate acquaintances who know each other – "human collocations". Moreover, by crowdsourcing language data via apps, corpus linguists can link recurrent language production with both standard variables such as place and, more innovatively, language users' categories describing *their own* discourse, e.g. the topic. See, for example, the *National Corpus of Contemporary Welsh.*[3] Corpus linguistics rests on an ontology of digital data relations – increasingly involving entanglements of actual and virtual realms – made viable by advances in digital technology. The same ontology is encapsulated within the posthuman condition.

As further evidence of this ontology, corpus linguists regularly employ the technique of "keyness" analysis whose basis is the relationality between two datasets – a study text/corpus and a reference corpus. "Keyness" communicates where words, parts of speech and semantic domains are relatively more frequent in a text or study corpus than a "reference corpus", often a much larger corpus regarded as a norm of usage.

Corpus-driven linguistics

In *corpus-driven* linguistics, the corpus is the basis for generating insights into language rather than beginning from pre-figured hypotheses (Tognini-Bonelli 2001: 84–100). Corpus-driven linguistics can thus be seen as a form of "New Empiricism" (Kitchin 2014) where insights are born from digital data. A well-known corpus-driven concept is *semantic prosody*. John Sinclair noticed in machine-generated concordances that "naked eye" is commonly associated with restraint – "it can't be seen with the naked eye", "it is too far away to be visible with the naked eye". Semantic prosody, another way of seeing linguistic relations, was born (Sinclair 2004: 30–5). Put in a posthumanist fashion, Sinclair's creative thinking resulted from intra-active manipulations of and taking prompts from machine-generated concordance visualisations. The concept of semantic prosody derives from a "Sinclair–machine assemblage".

"Corpus-driven" is a deceptive description of this empirically based creative process. The researcher's focus is the software-generated *data* from the corpus, not the entire corpus. It is misleading to say that a collection of texts drives anything. Yet "data-driven (digital) linguistics" is not perfect either. Corpus-driven insights come via intra-active agency *between* machine-generated data and human researchers. Data do not drive autonomously from outside the human researcher in the cause-and-effect manner implied by "corpus-driven" or "data-driven". Thus, "*human-digital intra-active* linguistics" is preferable to "corpus-driven". But the expression is long and clunky. "Data-driven linguistics" can be retained if human digital intra-active agency is implicitly understood.

Corpus linguists as primarily human researchers

I have highlighted that, for large general language corpora, accurate intuitions about word patterns are not so likely. Linguists examining big general corpora act posthumanly in deferring to the representations of machines which then prompt intra-actively their understandings of language usage at scale. Yet with specialised corpora, especially for texts that linguists regularly consume, linguists are more likely to have worthwhile intuitions/hypotheses which they test with software.

Critical discourse studies (CDS) criticises texts sustaining an inequitable status quo (e.g., Flowerdew and Richardson 2018). Critical discourse analysts using corpus linguistic method (many do not) will often already have intuitions and hypotheses about whether particular media, such as tabloid national newspapers, negatively represent relatively powerless groups such as asylum seekers and refugees. After all, popular national newspapers are culturally salient and are repetitive in their representations. Critical discourse analysts generate intuitions and hypotheses about their datasets (human orientation). They then seek assistance from software to confirm, falsify or illuminate these intuitions and hypotheses by ascertaining word patterns beyond intuition in relevant corpora (posthuman orientation). See Baker *et al.* (2008), for example. A similar procedure happens commonly in corpus-assisted discourse studies (CaDS), unlike CDS, a non-politically aligned approach to discourse investigation which, by definition, non-optionally employs corpus linguistic method to find non-obvious meanings and word patterns (e.g. Partington 2008). The posthuman dimension *assists* the researcher with their human intuitions and hypotheses about specialist corpora and so is secondary to the human dimension.

Posthuman distant-diffractive reading

Posthuman diffractive reading already occurs implicitly in some corpus stylistics (e.g. O'Halloran 2007; Tribble 2006). Let me illustrate a posthuman diffractive reading using the final chapter of James Joyce's *Ulysses*, chapter 18. This chapter of over 24,000 words is the stream of consciousness of a main character, Molly Bloom. It has very little punctuation and paragraphing. A Joyce scholar who has read *Ulysses* umpteen times will have multiple intuitions. A student coming to *Ulysses* for the first time will have far fewer intuitions about this taxing chapter. They could, of course, read it over and over, as is the norm in humanist scholarship. Or they could approach the chapter, at least initially, as a human–machine assemblage, guided by software processing of its regularities. This way the student discovers, far sooner, salient features of the chapter and, indeed, stylistic features they are less likely to ascertain manually. I give a brief demonstration using the semantic domain function of the software tool, *WMatrix* (Rayson 2009).

WMatrix automatically labels ("tags") semantically related words in a text or corpus using a larger semantic category. So, for example, *WMatrix* tags the words, *eye, hand, heart* with the larger category, or "semantic domain", ANATOMY_and_PHYSIOLOGY. *WMatrix* can do this because it has been programmed to group lexical words under larger semantic categories following an in-built lexicon. The value is that the researcher can achieve a rigorous bird's-eye view of the "semantic content" of a text or corpus of texts. Figure 47.3 is a key semantic domain analysis of chapter 18 of *Ulysses*. "Key" means that these semantic domains are statistically significant as compared with a 1-million-word English reference corpus.[4] The larger the typeface in Figure 47.3, the larger the "keyness" of the domain. The reader can see, for example, that CLOTHES_and_PERSONAL_ BELONGINGS has a relatively large typeface in Figure 47.3, meaning that this is among the chapter's most statistically frequent semantic domains.

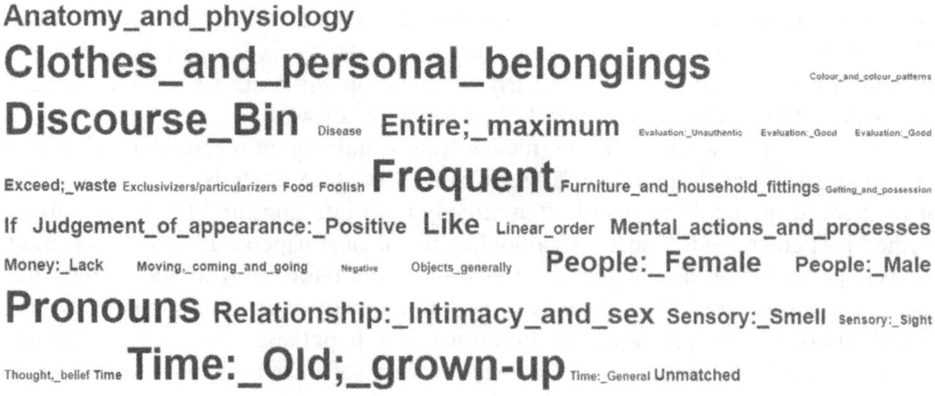

Figure 47.3 Key semantic domains for chapter 18 *Ulysses* – generated by *WMatrix*[5]

I put "semantic content" in quote marks because there is nothing *absolute* about the results in Figure 47.3; the results are *relative* to:

- The human design of semantic domain categories and decisions about the lexis they include;
- The particular reference corpus chosen;
- Statistical metrics chosen for calculating keyness.

One cannot treat Figure 47.3, then, as an objective representation of the semantic truth of the chapter. This does not mean Figure 47.3 lacks value. Analysis of chapter 18 by literary critics can lead to divergence of opinions, especially given its length and complexity. The consistency of the algorithmically generated Figure 47.3, however, advantageously furnishes literary critics with a *stable* semantic map – even if they later depart from it.

Figure 47.3, being an alternative and lively representation of chapter 18, usefully estranges reader from text. The estrangement works as a *distant reading*. As before, CLOTHES_and_PERSONAL_BELONGINGS is a key semantic domain in the bird's-eye view of Figure 47.3. That apparel is important to chapter 18 may not have been so apparent on a "worm's-eye view" or close reading of 24,000 words with little paragraphing and punctuation. Crucially, since all the semantic domains in Figure 47.3 are statistically significant, the researcher can rigorously use this information as *non-arbitrary* launch pads back into the chapter, going on to perform a close reading of Joyce's references to apparel. Since this involves the reader entangling with quantitative data, chapter 18 is read *diffractively* through Figure 47.3. And since cues are taken from these quantitative data, reading is intra-active. Diffractive reading via Figure 47.3 could be done via selecting single key semantic domains. Or, it could involve exploiting Figure 47.3 as *a new set of relations*, i.e., because all the domains are related by being statistically frequent. The researcher could experiment with possible connections between these key domains. For example, they could investigate criss-crossings of the key semantic domains CLOTHES_and_PERSONAL_BELONGINGS and "TIME:_OLD;_GROWN-UP" to see whether Joyce has linked clothing to time in some way.

Two general points from this posthuman reading:

- Examining software-generated visualisation of frequencies for a text (including word frequencies, part of speech frequencies, etc.) is a *distant* reading of that text. Using those frequencies to prompt close reading of the text is a *diffractive* reading of that text. In other words, this diffractive reading depends on the digitally enabled distant reading;
- This distant-diffractive reading takes place *intra-actively*, conducted by a *human–machine assemblage* rather than a human being (cf Adams and Thompson 2016; Tsao 2018).

Human/posthuman relations and tensions

Alan Partington, an important progenitor of CaDS, elegantly describes how corpus linguistics can be used productively in discourse analysis:

> …the frequency lists, semantic clouds, scattergrams, concordances, and so on are performed by an entity, the machine, which is not the eventual interpreter and has no intuitive, primed expectations (Hoey, 2005) and no ideological vested interest. It is these processes of recontextualisation and the deliberate "temporary alienation" of the analyst-observer-researcher from the object of research, their voluntary relinquishing of control over the research process, that act as a catalyst for the serendipitous discovery of non-obvious unforeseen information, the so-called "unknown unknowns"…
>
> *(Partington 2018: 4)*

There are posthuman resonances across this extract, such as in "voluntary relinquishing of control over the research process" to the machine. "Act[ing] as a catalyst for the serendipitous discovery of non-obvious unforeseen information" can be re-described as intra-actions between the human and machine, leading to fresh insight into language use. Here then is the CaDS researcher acting as posthuman to assist their primarily human-directed "object of research", an orientation which the name "corpus-assisted discourse studies" implies. Human and posthuman in relation with one another.

Partington's paragraph immediately continues as follows:

> …which can lead to entirely new avenues of research, sometimes so many it becomes a (learned) intuitive skill in itself choosing which to most profitably follow up.
>
> *(Partington 2018: 4)*

This way of operating is, to my mind, not captured by the expression "corpus-assisted discourse studies". Digital data are not being used to "assist" the human researcher with their "object of research" in this second chunk of text. Rather, the researcher is acting wholly as a posthuman, a human–machine assemblage, in intra-acting with software-produced data, allowing themselves to be driven into new research avenues. This is echoed by Partington in his description of human–machine adaptation as a learned skill. I am hardly criticising Partington's scholarship (which I value) or CaDS generally. But I am pointing out a tension in CaDS from a posthumanist perspective.

Partington seems to suggest that what we call discourse analysis using corpus linguistics is not so important:

> …corpus-based, corpus-driven, corpus-assisted discourse analysis, corpus approaches to discourse, however we wish to name it, definable as 'that set of studies into the form and/or function of language as communicative discourse which incorporate the use of corpora' (Partington Taylor Torsello 2008; Partington, Duguid and Taylor, 2013, p. 10).
>
> *(Partington 2018: 2)*

For posthumanist reasons, the distinction between "data-assisted" and "data-driven" *is* worth retaining, since it helps the digital linguist reflect on the degree to which they are *intra-acting* with a machine. And if names matter, so do their definitions:

- *Data-assisted* ("corpus-assisted") linguistics: indicates a primarily *human* orientation where the researcher generates intuitions/hypotheses about language (the human component) and then intra-acts with machine-produced data to assist their investigation (the posthuman component);
- *Data-driven* ("corpus-driven") linguistics (*human-digital intra-active* linguistics): indicates a primarily *posthuman* orientation where the researcher allows themselves to be wholly cued intra-actively into analyses and fresh research directions from within a human-machine assemblage.

"Data-driven" and "data-assisted" perspectives are not normally articulated *posthumanly* in CaDS, nor indeed corpus linguistics more generally. So, it seems reasonable to hold that there are i) covert human/posthuman *relations* within data-assisted corpus linguistics and ii) covert human/posthuman *tensions* between data-assisted and data-driven corpus linguistics. Such relations and tensions are not unique to corpus linguistics. They cut across numerous phenomena that began by default with a humanist orientation and now increasingly encounter posthuman vantages, not necessarily related to technology nor necessarily covert. For instance, a great humanist innovation after the Second World War – the Universal Declaration of Human Rights – is in relation and tension with the increasing need to protect the biosphere from humans, for example, by conferring rights on rivers[6] – i.e., posthuman rights (Baxi 2007).

Having situated corpus linguistics within posthumanism, I now outline a posthuman critical reading strategy I have developed that employs corpus linguistic method, with the analyst operating explicitly as a human–machine assemblage. Though a posthuman way of reading, I refer to it as "posthumanist" since it is explicitly embedded within posthumanist philosophy.

4. A critical posthumanist reading strategy

Procedure and rationale

This critical posthumanist reading strategy takes its bearings from Karen Barad's ethical diffractive reading (Section 2). Its purpose is to use the internet to extend horizons and to open out to unfamiliar problems, sufferings, disadvantages and nonflourishings, viewing the world empathetically from new perspectives. The user of this strategy learns systematically about a relatively unfamiliar campaign for a sustainable, equitable planet.

They gather data comprehensively from the campaign website into a corpus and use text analysis software to ascertain predominant concerns in the corpus – thus both a distant and *wide* reading. (As with chapter 18 of *Ulysses*, digital text analysis of a *single* text leads to a distant reading. However, where a *corpus* of texts is analysed using text analysis software, then a word frequency list, key semantic domain list, etc., furnishes both a distant reading and a wide reading. Where Franco Moretti (2013) gathers many literary texts into a corpus to afford a "distant reading" – as he terms it – it is, actually, both a distant *and* a wide reading.)

The next stage is critically contrastive. The reader selects a text (or texts) reproducing the status quo which the campaign opposes. They then read this status quo text diffractively via the key concerns mined from the campaign corpus. That is to say, they conduct a *distant/wide-diffractive* reading. The reader looks for illuminating differences, things which the status quo text does not address but which are highly significant in the campaign corpus. They ascertain whether any such absences affect the credibility of the status quo text. Since the reader identifies with machine-generated data – rather as a gamer identifies with an avatar – they create a posthuman subjectivity. In taking the campaign's perspective, the students' distant/wide-diffractive examination is ethical. And, because the corpus has been comprehensively compiled, students can claim their posthuman subjectivity has representativeness. Lastly, since creating a posthuman subjectivity introduces a fresh vantage point for contemplation, it can develop independent thinking too. After their analysis, the reader should reflect on where *they* stand on the previously unfamiliar campaign.

Illustration

To illustrate this critical posthumanist reading strategy, I choose a status quo text on animal testing. This comes from the website of the US Food and Drug Administration (FDA), the body responsible for protecting US public health.[7] At time of writing, explanation of the FDA's pro-animal testing policy is a 278-word text, henceforth "FDA text" (Figure 47.4). I read the FDA text diffractively and ethically through the People for the Ethical Treatment of Animals (PETA) campaign, which opposes animal testing and is the largest US campaign group against animal testing. As a UK citizen unfamiliar with PETA's perspectives on non-human animal testing, especially in the United States, I conjured extension of my horizons (even if, in the end, I might disagree with PETA).

To understand clearly how the FDA text frames animal testing, I highlight its most common words and phrases. Repetition of "medical product(s)"/devices(s)" provides a major conceptual framing of the text in relation to "animal testing" (highlighted in Figure 47.5).

Using WMatrix for distant/wide reading of the PETA corpus

The PETA website organizes its text content under "issues". One key issue is 'animals used for experimentation'.[8] In April 2019, I aggregated all texts located under this subcategory into a corpus.[9] In total, there were 56 texts which amount to 35,275 words. Figure 47.6 is a visualisation generated by *WMatrix* of key semantic domains for the PETA "animal testing" corpus, i.e., semantic domains which are more statistically frequent than those in a reference corpus.[10] A distant/wide reading of the PETA corpus is facilitated.

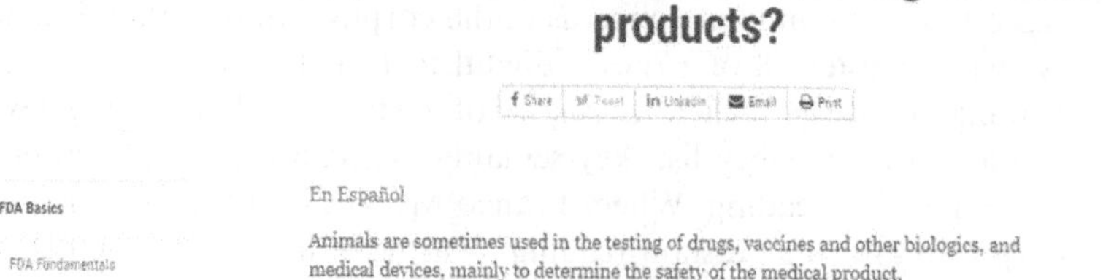

Why are animals used for testing medical products?

f Share | Tweet | in LinkedIn | Email | Print

FDA Basics

FDA Fundamentals

Preguntas generales sobre la Administración de Medicamentos y Alimentos (FDA, por sus siglas en inglés)

En Español

Animals are sometimes used in the testing of drugs, vaccines and other biologics, and medical devices, mainly to determine the safety of the medical product.

For drugs and biologics, the focus of animal testing is on the drug's nature, chemistry, and effects (pharmacology) and on its potential damage to the body (toxicology). Animal testing is used to measure

- how much of a drug or biologic is absorbed into the blood
- how a medical product is broken down chemically in the body
- the toxicity of the product and its breakdown components (metabolites)
- how quickly the product and its metabolites are excreted from the body

For medical devices, the focus of animal testing is on the device's ability to function with living tissue without harming the tissue (biocompatibility). Most devices use materials, such as stainless steel or ceramic, that we know are biocompatible with human tissues. In these cases, no animal testing is required. However, some devices with new materials require biocompatibility testing in animals.

There are still many areas where animal testing is necessary and non-animal testing is not yet a scientifically valid and available option. However, FDA has supported efforts to reduce animal testing. In addition, FDA has research and development efforts underway to reduce the need for animal testing and to work toward replacement of animal testing.

When animal testing is done to support applications for medical products regulated by FDA, manufacturers or sponsors are required to follow FDA's regulation, Good Laboratory Practice for Nonclinical Laboratory Studies (21 CFR Part 58). FDA also supports the use of independent animal care and use committees (IACUC) for laboratory studies involving animals.

Content current as of:
06/18/2019

Figure 47.4 Screenshot of FDA text on FDA website

Critical posthumanist analysis

Experimenting in the construction of posthuman subjectivities

By contrasting the much shorter FDA text with a corpus of 35,275 words, self-evidently there will be key semantic domains in the PETA corpus absent from the FDA text. I need then to *experiment* with different key semantic domains to discover, where possible, the following: novel (for me) compelling insights about what is absent or marginal from the FDA text relative to the PETA corpus which, in turn, unpredictably (for me) and legitimately problematise the conceptual framing of the FDA text.

Testing tobacco products on nonhuman animals

A salient key semantic domain *present* in the PETA corpus (Figure 47.6), but which subsumes lexis *absent* from the FDA text (Figure 47.5), is SMOKING_and_NON-MEDICAL_DRUGS. Clicking on this key semantic domain in the Figure 47.6 visualisation takes me to the 89 words grouped under this semantic domain (Table 47.1). Clicking on these words brings up their recurrent linguistic contexts. I encounter PETA's repeated questioning of why the FDA allows animal testing of new tobacco brands in the United States when it is common knowledge that smoking harms human health, e.g.:

FDA text

Why are **animals** used for testing medical products?

Animals are sometimes used in the testing of drugs, vaccines and other biologics, and medical devices, mainly to determine the safety of the medical product.

For drugs and biologics, the focus of **animal** testing is on the drug's nature, chemistry, and effects (pharmacology) and on its potential damage to the body (toxicology). **Animal** testing is used to measure:

- how much of a drug or biologic is absorbed into the blood
- how a medical product is broken down chemically in the body
- the toxicity of the product and its breakdown components (metabolites)
- how quickly the product and its metabolites are excreted from the body

For medical devices, the focus of **animal** testing is on the device's ability to function with living tissue without harming the tissue (biocompatibility). Most devices use materials, such as stainless steel or ceramic, that we know are biocompatible with human tissues. In these cases, no **animal** testing is required. However, some devices with new materials require biocompatibility testing in **animals.**

There are still many areas where **animal** testing is necessary and non-**animal** testing is not yet a scientifically valid and available option. However, FDA has supported efforts to reduce **animal** testing. In addition, FDA has research and development efforts underway to reduce the need for **animal** testing and to work toward replacement of **animal** testing.

When **animal** testing is done to support applications for medical products regulated by FDA, manufacturers or sponsors are required to follow FDA's regulation: 'Good Laboratory Practice for Nonclinical Laboratory Studies (21 CFR Part 58)'.

FDA also supports the use of independent **animal** care and use committees (IACUC) for laboratory studies involving **animals**.

Figure 47.5 Dominant conceptual framings across FDA text

To quote the National Cancer Institute, "There is no safe **tobacco** product." We already know from clinical research—and from basic common sense—that smoking is bad for us.

[…]

If the [US] **tobacco** industry wants to continue developing and marketing products that cause addiction and kill people, it should do so without the help of the [US] government and without harming animals. You can write to the FDA and request that it follow the lead of agencies in progressive countries by banning **tobacco** product and ingredient tests on animals.

Anatomy_and_physiology Danger Disease Education_in_general Health_and_disease Helping Investigate,_examine,_test,_search
Living_creatures:_animals,_birds,_etc
Medicines_and_medical_treatment Mental_object:_Means,_method People
Science_and_technology_in_general
Smoking_and_non-medical_drugs
Substances_and_materials_generally Unmatched Using

Figure 47.6 Key semantic domains for PETA "animal testing" corpus

Table 47.1 Frequencies for words under the key semantic domain SMOKING_and_NON-MEDICAL_DRUGS

Word	*Frequency*
tobacco	38
cigarette	17
smoking	9
cigarettes	8
nicotine	4
tobacco_companies	4
addicted	3
smokers	3
drug_addiction	1
cigars	1
drugged	1

That animals are still used in the United States for what would, indeed, seem to be superfluous tobacco-product testing was new information for me. Yet one cannot just automatically assume that campaign information is accurate. American tobacco company websites (at time of writing) confirm tobacco products are tested on animals in the United States.[11]

Critiquing the FDA text via distant/wide-diffractive reading

With this information from the PETA corpus corroborated, I can now move to critically distant/wide-diffractive reading of the FDA text via a posthuman subjectivity, i.e., by identifying with the machine-generated key semantic domain SMOKING_and_NON-MEDICAL_DRUGS from the campaign corpus. The information about using animals to test tobacco products illuminates misleading narrowness in the recurrent framing of "*medical* product" testing in the FDA text (Figure 47.5) since i) tobacco products patently are *non-medical* and ii) their testing on nonhuman animals is redundant. The medical product framing of the FDA text is deconstructed.

Reflection

In one sense, I controlled the reading: I chose the FDA text and PETA website. I loaded the PETA corpus onto *WMatrix* and activated the software, enabling a distant/wide reading of this corpus. These were all *inter*-actions. Yet the posthuman subjectivity that I used to read the FDA text in a diffractive manner was not exclusively under my control. This is because my critical exploration of the FDA text took its cues from what *WMatrix* revealed as statistically significant semantic domains, which I did not know in advance. In this *intra-active* entanglement with software-generated data from an unfamiliar corpus, the agency of the posthuman subjectivity *emerged* from within a *human–machine assemblage.*

Links to critical discourse studies

CDS criticises texts from a *political subjectivity* seeking to reduce inequality. So, in CDS, a text is a problem when it misrepresents the relatively powerless, as this helps to reproduce existing inequality. The critical posthumanist reading strategy outlined earlier is also critical of texts supporting inequitable conditions, employing a related political subjectivity to guide *selection* of a status quo text(s). I say "related" because CDS has predominantly focused on human concerns in contrast to the posthumanist focus on "transversal" intersections of humans, nonhumans and the environment (Braidotti 2019).

Yet while traditional CDS critiques status quo texts using the previously mentioned political subjectivity, in this posthumanist reading strategy, *critique* of status quo texts is instead performed using an *ethical subjectivity*. Reading is done diffractively by identifying empathetically with machine-generated data, taking on the viewpoint of relatively powerless/suffering Others. Alternatively, this diffractive reading adopts the viewpoint of those campaigning either for such human and/or non-human Others, or for sustainable environments where human and posthuman rights are harmonised. In this critical posthumanist reading strategy, a text is a problem not only as it would be in CDS, but also because it overlooks legitimate concerns of a relevant Other or campaign for a sustainable, equitable planet.

5. Conclusion

Human/posthuman relations and tensions

In the argument I have made, there is corpus linguistics research where the researcher's subjectivity is primarily human (with a secondary posthuman facet) and corpus linguistics research where the researcher's subjectivity has primarily a posthuman orientation because they are researching as a human–machine assemblage. I have suggested that "data-assisted" ("corpus-assisted") linguistic research suits the primarily human researcher orientation, and that "data-driven" suits the primarily posthuman researcher orientation (though "*human-digital intra-active linguistics*" is more accurate). I have also contended that there are i) covert human/posthuman *relations* within data-assisted corpus linguistics and ii) covert human/posthuman *tensions* between data-assisted and data-driven corpus linguistics. In addition, I have demonstrated a critical posthumanist reading strategy dependent on user intra-action with software-based results in a human–machine assemblage.

From corpus linguistics to digital linguistics and posthumanities

Once we appreciate that the key contribution of corpus linguistics is the discovery of linguistic relations and that text analysis software can reveal linguistic relations in a single text such as chapter 18 of *Ulysses*, "corpus" linguistics becomes something of a misnomer. It makes more sense to refer simply to corpus linguistics as *digital linguistics*: a type of "digital humanities" which specialises in the revelation of linguistic relations, looking at a single digitised text or a corpus of digitised texts.

Yet given the wider human/posthuman relations and tensions of our times, the so-called "digital humanities" likely have covert human/posthuman relations and tensions also, problematising the expression's appositeness. Indeed, digital technology, through enabling assemblages of human–machine researchers and, in turn, posthuman diffractive readings of canonical humanities texts, is transforming the humanities into the *posthumanities* (Mahon 2017). Better to say that all digital linguistics research, in fact all digital humanities research, falls within the single category of posthumanities. This category captures a range of human–machine entanglements with human agency predominating at one end of a continuum, machine agency (ideally with human consent) predominating at the other end and equally entangled human and machine agency in the middle.

Theorising digital linguistics

Digital linguists have developed software, analytical techniques and methods which have revolutionised linguistics and also been successfully applied in a variety of other disciplines. But aside from a few notable exceptions (e.g. Michael Stubbs and Wolfgang Teubert), there has been relatively little theoretical reflection on digital linguistics. As the posthuman condition intensifies through the increasing entanglement of AI with humanity, the lack of balance in digital linguistics between analytical techniques, methods, software development *and theory* is even more conspicuous. Sustained connection of digital linguistics with posthumanism and the philosophy of technology more generally, as well as with socio-cultural theorising of AI developments and effects on humans, should help engender a broader and more profound understanding of what it means to be a digital linguist in the twenty-first century, as well as excite generative challenges and possibilities for the field.

Acknowledgments

Sincere thanks to Guy Cook, Michael Handford and the editors for very useful comments on earlier drafts.

Notes

1 https://www.viar360.com/vr-transforming-data-visualization/ [Accessed November 2020].
2 https://www.youtube.com/watch?v=rj-m2SItDl4 [Accessed November 2020].
3 http://www.corcencc.org/ [Accessed November 2020].
4 The reference corpus, accessed by *WMatrix*, is the 1-million-word *British English 2006* corpus (BE06).

5 Following Gabrielatos (2018), key semantic domains were calculated using two metrics:
a) *effect size* (%DIFF) indicating salient semantic domains in *Ulysses* chapter 18 relative to the BE06 reference corpus; b) *statistical significance* (Log Likelihood 'LL') indicating effect size reliability.
LL ≥ 7 indicates statistical significance where $p < 0.01$.* Figure 47.3 shows key semantic domains with the highest %DIFF values carrying statistical significance. To manage results, Figure 47.3 displays key semantic domains which have LL ≥ 10 and include 20 or more lexical items.
*$p < 0.01$ indicates that there is a 1 per cent chance we would obtain the same or a larger frequency difference when, in reality, no such difference exists.
6 e.g. New Zealand's Whanganui River https://www.earthlawcenter.org/river-rights [Accessed November 2020].
7 https://www.fda.gov/about-fda/fda-basics/why-are-animals-used-testing-medical-products [accessed November 2020].
8 https://www.peta.org/issues/animals-used-for-experimentation/ [Accessed November 2020].
9 For ease, I used a webscraper, *Import.io* https://www.import.io/ [Accessed November 2020].
10 Since the FDA text uses American English, I chose the 1-million-word *American English 2006 corpus* (AmE06), which *WMatrix* accesses, as reference corpus. (See endnote 5 for how key semantic domains were generated). To manage results, Figure 47.6 displays key semantic domains which have LL ≥ 100 and include 10 or more lexical items.
11 https://www.pmi.com/resources/docs/default-source/our_company/product-assessment_v2.pdf?sfvrsn=164e8bb5_2 [November 2020]
https://www.altria.com/moving-beyond-smoking/conducting-the-science/animal-care-and-use-statement [Accessed November 2020]
https://www.bat.com/group/sites/UK__9D9KCY.nsf/vwPagesWebLive/DO52ANF5 [Accessed November 2020].

Further reading

Mahon, P. (2017) *Posthumanism*, London: Bloomsbury. (A clear guide to posthumanism, especially on its links with recent scientific/technological developments. Mahon's book is uncompromisingly pro-science and pro-digital.)

O'Halloran, K. A. (2017) *Posthumanism and Deconstructing Arguments: Corpora and Digitally-Driven Critical Analysis*, London: Routledge. (Provides an expanded account of the critical posthumanist reading strategy illustrated in Section 4, as well as of the strategy's relationship with critical discourse studies.)

O'Halloran, K. A. (2020) 'A Posthumanist Pedagogy Using Digital Text Analysis to Enhance Critical Thinking in Higher Education', *Digital Scholarship in the Humanities* 35(4): 845–80. (Develops the approach in O'Halloran [2017] and the analysis in this chapter's Section 4.)

References

Adams, C. and Thompson, T. (2016) *Researching a Posthuman World*, London: Palgrave Macmillan.

Adolphs, S. and Knight, D. (eds) (2020) *The Routledge Handbook of English Language and Digital Humanities*, London: Routledge.

Baker, P., Gabrielatos, P., Khosravinik, M., Krzyżanowski, M., McEnery, T. and Wodak, R. (2008) 'A Useful Methodological Synergy? Combining Critical Discourse Analysis and Corpus Linguistics to Examine Discourses of Refugees and Asylum Seekers in the UK Press', *Discourse and Society* 19(3): 273–306.

Barad, K. (2007) *Meeting the Universe Halfway*, Durham, NC: Duke University Press.

Barad, K. (2012) 'Interview with Karen Barad', in R. Dolphijn and I. van der Tuin (eds) *New Materialism: Interviews and Cartographies*, University of Michigan, Ann Arbor: Open Humanities Press, pp. 48–70.

Baxi, U. (2007) *Human Rights in a Posthuman World*, Oxford: Oxford University Press.
Bayne, S. (2016) 'Posthumanism and Research in Digital Education', in C. Haythornthwaite, R. Andrews, J. Fransman, E. Meyers (eds) *The SAGE Handbook of E-Learning Research*, 2nd edn, London: Sage, pp. 82–99.
Braidotti, R. (2013) *The Posthuman*, Cambridge: Polity.
Braidotti, R. (2019) *Posthuman Knowledge*, Cambridge: Polity.
Chandler, D. (2015) 'A World without Causation: Big Data and the Coming of Age of Posthumanism', *Millennium: Journal of International Studies* 43(3): 833–51.
Flowerdew, J. and Richardson, J. (eds) (2018) *The Routledge Handbook of Critical Discourse Studies*, London: Routledge.
Gabrielatos, C. (2018) 'Keyness Analysis: Nature, Metrics and Techniques', in C. Taylor and A. Marchi (eds) (2018) *Corpus Approaches to Discourse*, London: Routledge, pp. 225–58.
Herbrechter, S. (2013) *Posthumanism*, London: Bloomsbury.
Heuser, R., Moretti, F., Steiner, E. (2016) *The Emotions of London*, Literary Lab Pamphlet 13: Stanford University. https://litlab.stanford.edu/LiteraryLabPamphlet13.pdf [Accessed November 2020].
Hoey, M. (2005) *Lexical Priming: A New Theory of Words and Language*, London: Routledge.
Hollett, T. and Ehret, C. (2017) 'Relational Methodologies for Mobile Literacies: Intra-Action, Rhythm, and Atmosphere', in (eds) *The Case of the iPad*, New York: Springer, pp. 227–44.
Kelling, S., Hochachka, W., Fink, D., Riedewald, M., Caruana, R., Ballard, G. and Hooker, G. (2009) 'Data-Intensive Science: A New Paradigm for Biodiversity Studies', *BioScience* 59(7): 613–20.
Kitchin, R. (2014) 'Big Data, New Epistemologies and Paradigm Shifts', *Big Data & Society* 1(1): 1–12.
Kosinski, M., Stillwell, D. and Graepel, T. (2013) 'Private Traits and Attributes are Predictable from Digital Records of Human Behavior', *Proceedings of the National Academy of Sciences of the USA* 110(15): 5802–5.
Lupton, D. (2018) 'How do Data Come to Matter? Living and Becoming with Personal Data', *Big Data & Society* 5(2): 1–11.
Mahon, P. (2017) *Posthumanism*, London: Bloomsbury.
Moretti, F. (2013) *Distant Reading*, London: Verso.
O'Halloran, K. A. (2007) 'The Subconscious in James Joyce's "Eveline": A Corpus Stylistic Analysis which Chews on the "Fish Hook"', *Language and Literature* 16(3): 227–44.
Partington A. (2008) 'The Armchair and the Machine: Corpus-Assisted Discourse Studies', in C. Taylor Torsello, K. Ackerley and E. Castello (eds) *Corpora for University Language Teachers*, Bern: Peter Lang, pp. 189–213.
Partington, A. (2018) 'Welcome to the First Issue of the Journal of Corpora and Discourse Studies', *Journal of Corpora and Discourse Studies* 1(1): 1–7.
Rayson, P. (2009) 'Wmatrix: A Web-Based Corpus Processing Environment', Lancaster: Computing Department, Lancaster University. http://ucrel.lancs.ac.uk/wmatrix/ [Accessed November 2020].
Savage, M. (2013) 'The "Social Life of Methods": A Critical Introduction', *Theory, Culture & Society* 30(4): 3–21.
Savat D. (2013) *Uncoding the Digital*, London: Palgrave Macmillan.
Sinclair, J. McH. (2004) *Trust the Text*, London: Routledge.
Tognini-Bonelli, E. (2001) *Corpus Linguistics at Work*, Amsterdam: John Benjamins.
Tribble, C. (2006) 'Counting Things in Texts you Can't Count On: A Study of Samuel Beckett's *Texts for Nothing, 1*', in M. Scott and C. Tribble *Textual Patterns*, Amsterdam: John Benjamins, pp. 179–93.
Tsao, C.-R. (2018) 'A Posthumanist Reflection on the Digital Humanities and Social Sciences', in S. H. Chen (ed.) *Big Data in Computational Social Science and Humanities*, Cham, Switzerland: Springer, pp. 365–77.

Index